Honoring America

For Americans, the flag has always had a special meaning.
It is a symbol of our nation's freedom and democracy.

Flag Etiquette

Over the years, Americans have developed rules and customs concerning the use and display of the flag. One of the most important things every American should remember is to treat the flag with respect.

- The flag should be raised and lowered by hand and displayed only from sunrise to sunset. On special occasions, the flag may be displayed at night, but it should be illuminated.

- The flag may be displayed on all days, weather permitting, particularly on national and state holidays and on historic and special occasions.

- No flag may be flown above the American flag or to the right of it at the same height.

- The flag should never touch the ground or floor beneath it.

- The flag may be flown at half-staff by order of the president, usually to mourn the death of a public official.

- The flag may be flown upside down only to signal distress.

- The flag should never be carried flat or horizontally, but always carried aloft and free.

- When the flag becomes old and tattered, it should be destroyed by burning. According to an approved custom, the Union (stars on blue field) is first cut from the flag; then the two pieces, which no longer form a flag, are burned.

The American's Creed

I believe in the United States of America as a Government of the people, by the people, for the people, whose just powers are derived from the consent of the governed; a democracy in a republic; a sovereign Nation of many sovereign States; a perfect union, one and inseparable; established upon those principles of freedom, equality, justice, and humanity for which American patriots sacrificed their lives and fortunes.

I therefore believe it is my duty to my Country to love it; to support its Constitution; to obey its laws; to respect its flag, and to defend it against all enemies.

The Pledge of Allegiance

I pledge allegiance to the Flag of the United States of America and to the Republic for which it stands, one Nation under God, indivisible, with liberty and justice for all.

The Star-Spangled Banner

O! say, can you see, by the dawn's early light,
What so proudly we hail'd at the twilight's last gleaming?
Whose broad stripes and bright stars, thro' the perilous fight,
O'er the ramparts we watched were so gallantly streaming?
And the rockets' red glare, the bombs bursting in air,
Gave proof thro' the night, that our flag was still there.
O! say, does that Star-Spangled Banner yet wave
O'er the land of the free and the home of the brave?

On the shore, dimly seen thro' the mist of the deep,
Where the foe's haughty host in dread silence reposes,
What is that which the breeze, o'er the towering steep,
As it fitfully blows, half conceals, half discloses?
Now it catches the gleam of the morning's first beam,
In full glory reflected now shines on the stream.
'Tis the Star-Spangled Banner. O long may it wave
O'er the land of the free and the home of the brave.

And where is that band who so vauntingly swore,
That the havoc of war and the battle's confusion
A home and a country should leave us no more?
Their blood has wash'd out their foul footstep's pollution.
No refuge could save the hireling and slave
From the terror of flight or the gloom of the grave,
And the Star-Spangled Banner in triumph doth wave
O'er the land of the free and the home of the brave.

O thus be it e'er when free men shall stand
Between their lov'd home and war's desolation,
Blest with vict'ry and peace, may the Heav'n-rescued land
Praise the pow'r that hath made and preserv'd us a nation.
Then conquer we must, when our cause it is just,
And this be our motto, "In God is our Trust."
And the Star-Spangled Banner in triumph shall wave
O'er the land of the free and the home of the brave.

TEXAS EDITION

Glencoe
WORLD HISTORY

JACKSON J. SPIELVOGEL, Ph.D.

NATIONAL GEOGRAPHIC

Mc Graw Hill **Glencoe**
McGraw-Hill

New York, New York
Columbus, Ohio
Chicago, Illinois
Peoria, Illinois
Woodland Hills, California

Authors

Jackson J. Spielvogel

Jackson J. Spielvogel is associate professor emeritus of history at The Pennsylvania State University. He received his Ph.D. from The Ohio State University, where he specialized in Reformation history under Harold J. Grimm. His articles and reviews have appeared in such journals as *Moreana, Journal of General Education, Archiv für Reformationsgeschichte,* and *American Historical Review.* He has also contributed chapters or articles to *The Social History of the Reformation, The Holy Roman Empire: A Dictionary Handbook, Simon Wiesenthal Center Annual of Holocaust Studies,* and *Utopian Studies.* His book *Hitler and Nazi Germany* was published in 1987 (fourth edition, 2001). His book *Western Civilization* was published in 1991 (fourth edition, 2000). He is the co-author (with William Duiker) of *World History,* published in 1994 (third edition, 2001). Professor Spielvogel has won five major university-wide teaching awards, and in 1997, he became the first winner of the Schreyer Institute's Student Choice Award for innovative and inspiring teaching.

The National Geographic Society, founded in 1888 for the increase and diffusion of geographic knowledge, is the world's largest nonprofit scientific and educational organization. Since its earliest days, the Society has used sophisticated communication technologies, from color photography to holography, to convey geographic knowledge to a worldwide membership. The School Publishing Division supports the Society's mission by developing innovative educational programs—ranging from traditional print materials to multimedia programs including CD-ROMs, videos, and software.

About the Cover

Tutankhamen was 9 years old when he became pharaoh in 1333 B.C. and was only 18 when he died. Three thousand years later Tutankhamen's solid gold coffin was discovered by an English archaeologist named Howard Carter.

The lid of the coffin is a likeness of the young king. The gold rays of the headdress identify him with the sun, while the crook and the flail in his arms symbolize Osiris, the god of the afterlife. Today you can see this coffin and many other Egyptian artifacts in the Cairo Museum, Cairo, Egypt.

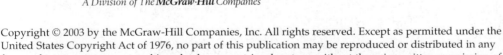

Glencoe/McGraw-Hill

A Division of The **McGraw·Hill** *Companies*

Printed in the United States of America.
Send all inquiries to:
Glencoe/McGraw-Hill
8787 Orion Place
Columbus, Ohio 43240-4027

ISBN 0-07-828557-7 (Student Edition)
ISBN 0-07-828555-0 (Teacher Wraparound Edition)

5 6 7 8 9   071/055   05 04 03

Contents

UNIT 2

New Patterns of Civilization, *400–1500*   **184**

Contents

UNIT 4

An Era of European Imperialism, *1800–1914* 574

CHAPTER 19
Industrialization and Nationalism, 1800–1870 . . . . **578**
  1 The Industrial Revolution 581
  2 Reaction and Revolution 589
  3 National Unification and the National State . . . 596
  4 Culture: Romanticism and Realism 605

CHAPTER 20
Mass Society and Democracy, 1870–1914 . . . . **612**
  1 The Growth of Industrial Prosperity 615
  2 The Emergence of Mass Society 621
  3 The National State and Democracy 629
  4 Toward the Modern Consciousness 636

CHAPTER 21
The Height of Imperialism, 1800–1914 . . . . **644**
  1 Colonial Rule in Southeast Asia 647
  2 Empire Building in Africa 654
  3 British Rule in India 666
  4 Nation Building in Latin America 671

CHAPTER 22
East Asia Under Challenge, 1800–1914 . . . . **680**
  1 The Decline of the Qing Dynasty 683
  2 Revolution in China 691
  3 Rise of Modern Japan 697

UNIT 5

The Twentieth-Century Crisis, *1914–1945* 710

CHAPTER 23
War and Revolution, 1914–1919 . . . . . . **714**
  1 The Road to World War I 717
  2 The War 721
  3 The Russian Revolution 732
  4 End of the War 739

CHAPTER 24
The West Between the Wars, 1919–1939 . . . . **748**
  1 The Futile Search for Stability 751
  2 The Rise of Dictatorial Regimes 758
  3 Hitler and Nazi Germany 766
  4 Cultural and Intellectual Trends 772

CHAPTER 25
Nationalism Around the World, 1919–1939 . . . . **778**
  1 Nationalism in the Middle East 781
  2 Nationalism in Africa and Asia 786
  3 Revolutionary Chaos in China 793
  4 Nationalism in Latin America 799

CHAPTER 26
World War II, 1939–1945 . . . . **806**
  1 Paths to War 809
  2 The Course of World War II 814
  3 The New Order and the Holocaust 824
  4 The Home Front and the Aftermath of the War 830

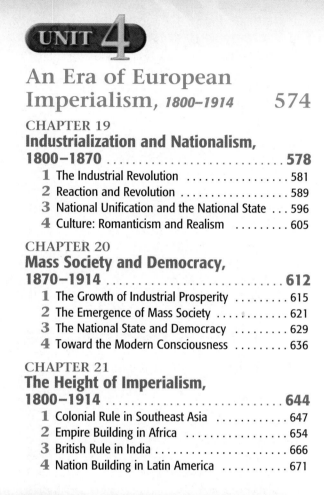

Contents

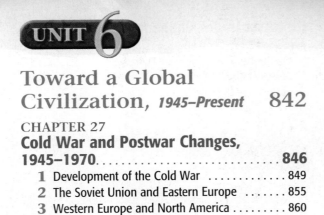

Appendix

Features

Features

CONNECTIONS

Around the World

Past to Present

What If...

EYEWITNESS TO HISTORY

WORLD LITERATURE

NATIONAL GEOGRAPHIC Special Report

A Story That Matters

People In History

Features

Primary Source Quotes

Primary Source Quotes

Unit 5

The Twentieth-Century Crisis

CHAPTER 24 • The West Between the Wars

Unit 4

An Era of European Imperialism

Primary Source Quotes

Charts, Graphs, & Tables

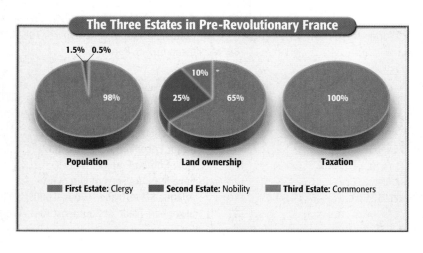

The Three Estates in Pre-Revolutionary France

Population — First Estate: Clergy 1.5%, Second Estate: Nobility 0.5%, Third Estate: Commoners 98%
Land ownership — 10%, 25%, 65%
Taxation — 100%

First Estate: Clergy   Second Estate: Nobility   Third Estate: Commoners

NATIONAL GEOGRAPHIC Maps

NATIONAL GEOGRAPHIC Reference Atlas

Unit 1

Unit 2

Unit 3

What Is History?

World history is more than just a series of dramatic events. It is the story of the human community—how people lived on a daily basis, how they shared ideas, how they ruled and were ruled, and how they fought. World history includes big subjects like economics, politics, and social change, but it is also the story of dreams fulfilled or unfulfilled, personal creativity, and philosophical and religious inspiration.

You may think of history as a boring list of names and dates, an irrelevant record of revolutions and battles, or the meaningless stories of kings, queens, and other rulers. History is not, however, just what happens to famous and infamous people. History includes everything that happens to everyone, including you.

A Record of the Past

The most common definition of history is "a record of the past." To create this record, historians use documents (what has been recorded or written); artifacts, such as pottery, tools, and weapons; and even artworks. History in this sense really began five thousand to six thousand years ago, when people first began to write and keep records. The period before written records we call *prehistory*.

Herodotus, a Greek who lived in the fifth century B.C., was one of the first historians. In his history of the Greek and Persian wars, he used evidence, tried to tell a good story, and showed concern for the causes and effects of events. Today's historians still try to discover what happened (the factual evidence), but

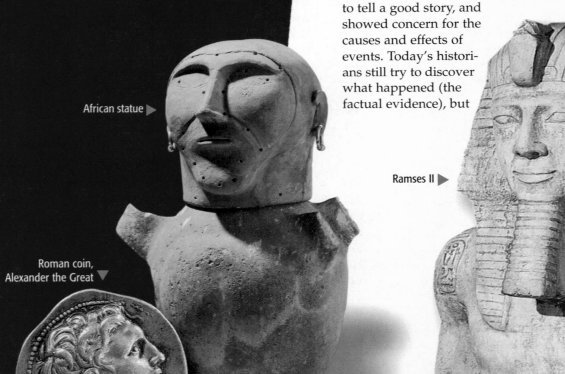

African statue ▶

Roman coin,
Alexander the Great ▼

Ramses II ▶

they also want to know why it happened. They use critical thinking and detailed investigation to explain the cause-and-effect relationships that exist among facts, and they look for new discoveries that might change our view of the past.

All of us are involved in the making of history. Alex Haley, the editor of *The Autobiography of Malcolm X*, grew up in Tennessee listening to his grandmother tell stories of Kunta Kinte, a family ancestor kidnapped in Africa during the 1700s and taken to America as a slave. Haley's search for his family's history led to his famous book, *Roots: The Saga of an American Family*. The book was turned into one of the most watched television miniseries of all time. Although Haley's family was a small part of larger historical events, the personal family history had universal appeal.

You will find, with some investigation, that history has been made by your own family and by the families of your friends. You are who you are because of the choices and experiences of your ancestors. Their experiences guide your choices and actions, just as

yours will guide your children's and grand-children's. You are an important link in a chain that stretches back into your ancestors' history and forward into your descendants' future.

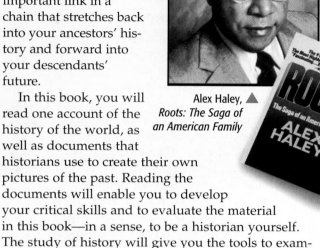

Alex Haley, ▲
Roots: The Saga of an American Family

In this book, you will read one account of the history of the world, as well as documents that historians use to create their own pictures of the past. Reading the documents will enable you to develop your critical skills and to evaluate the material in this book—in a sense, to be a historian yourself. The study of history will give you the tools to examine not only the lives of others, but also your own life. As Socrates, an ancient Greek philosopher, said, "The unexamined life is not worth living."

Themes for Understanding World History

To examine the past, historians often organize their material according to themes. This enables them to ask and then try to answer basic questions about the past. The following nine themes are especially important, and you will find them again and again in our story.

1 Politics and History

Historians study politics to answer certain basic questions about the structure of a society. How were people governed? What was the relationship between the ruler and the ruled? What people or groups of people held political power? What rights and liberties did the people have? What actions did people take to change their forms of government?

The study of politics also includes the role of conflict. Historians examine the causes and results of wars in order to understand the impact of war on human development.

2 The Role of Ideas

Ideas have great power to move people to action. For example, the idea of nationalism, which is based on a belief in loyalty to one's nation, has led to numerous wars and the deaths of millions of people. At the same time, nationalism has also motivated people to work together to benefit the lives of a nation's citizens. The spread of ideas from one society to another has also played an important role in world history.

3 Economics and History

A society's existence depends on meeting certain basic needs. How did the society grow its food? How did it make its goods? How did it provide the services people needed? How did individual people and governments use their limited resources? Did they spend more money on hospitals or military forces? By answering these questions, historians examine the different economic systems that have played a role in history.

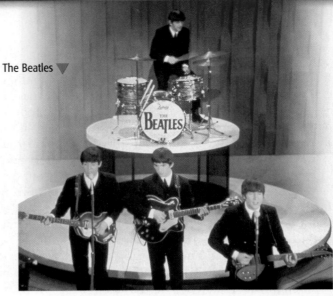

The Beatles ▼

④ The Importance of Cultural Development

We cannot understand a society without looking at its culture, or the common ideas, beliefs, and patterns of behavior that are passed on from one generation to another. Culture includes both high culture and popular culture. High culture consists of the writings of a society's thinkers and the works of its artists. Many of these people were illiterate and so passed on their culture orally. Today the term *popular culture* describes current trends and fashions such as popular television programs, movies, and music.

⑤ Religion in History

Throughout history, people have sought to find a deeper meaning to human life. How have the world's great religions—such as Hinduism, Buddhism, Judaism, Christianity, and Islam—influenced people's lives? How have those religions spread to create new patterns of culture?

⑥ The Role of Individuals

Julius Caesar, Queen Elizabeth I, Mohandas Gandhi, and Hitler remind us of the role of individuals in history. Decisive actions by powerful individuals have played a crucial role in the course of history. So, too, have the decisions of ordinary men and women who must figure out every day how to survive, protect their families, and carry on their ways of life.

⑦ The Impact of Science and Technology

For thousands of years, people around the world have made scientific discoveries and technological innovations that have changed our world. From the creation of stone tools that made farming easier to the advanced computers that guide our airplanes, science and technology have altered how humans have related to their world.

8 The Environment and History

Throughout history, peoples and societies have been affected by the physical world in which they live. In turn, human activities have had a profound impact on the world. From slash-and-burn farming to industrial pollution, people have affected the environment and even endangered the existence of entire societies.

9 Social Life

From a study of social life and customs, we learn about the different social classes that make up a society, the nature of family life, and how knowledge is passed on from one generation to the next. We also examine how people in history dressed, where they lived, how and what they ate, and what they did for fun.

These nine themes should be looked at in connection to each other, rather than individually. They help us to understand the forces that create civilizations and cause them to fall. At the same time, world history consists of more than just the study of individual civilizations. It should be seen in a broad comparative and global framework, as people and countries come into contact—and often into conflict—with one another.

In our time, the concept of contact between societies has changed. Computers, television, and multinational corporations have, to a certain extent, turned the world into a single community or global village.

Historians and the Dating of Time

In recording the past, historians try to determine the exact time when events occurred. World War II in Europe, for example, began on September 1, 1939, when Adolf Hitler sent German troops into Poland. The war in Europe ended on May 7, 1945, when Germany surrendered. By using dates, historians can place events in the order they occurred and try to determine the development of patterns over periods of time.

The dating system most commonly used in the Western world (Europe and the Western Hemisphere) is based on the assumed date of the birth of Jesus Christ (the year 1). An event that took place 400 years before the birth of Jesus would be dated 400 B.C. ("before Christ"). Dates after the birth of Jesus are labeled A.D. These letters stand for the Latin words *anno Domini*, which mean "in the year of the Lord." An event that took place 250 years after the birth of Jesus is written A.D. 250. It can also be written as 250.

Because B.C. and A.D. are so Western and Christian-oriented, some historians now prefer to use the abbreviations B.C.E. ("before the common era") and C.E. ("common era"). Thus, 1850 B.C. could be written as 1850 B.C.E.

Historians use other terms to refer to time. A decade is 10 years, a century is 100 years, and a millennium is 1,000 years. The fourth century B.C. is the fourth period of 100 counting backward from 1, the assumed date of the birth of Jesus. The first century B.C. is the years 100 to 1 B.C. Therefore, the fourth century B.C. refers to the years 400 to 301 B.C. We say, then, that an event in 650 B.C. took place in the seventh century B.C.

The fourth century A.D. is the fourth period of 100 years after the birth of Jesus. The first period of 100 years includes the years 1 to 100, so the fourth hundred-year period, or the fourth century, is the years 301 to 400. For example, we say that an event in 750 took place in the eighth century. Just as the first millennium B.C. is the years 1000 to 1 B.C., the first millennium A.D. is the years 1 to 1000.

General Dwight D. Eisenhower ▶ speaks to his troops just before the invasion of France in June 1944.

Reading for Information

When you read this textbook, you are reading for information, but you are also gaining insights into the world around you, the how and why of events that have happened. History is non-fiction writing—it describes real-life events, people, ideas, and places. Here is a menu of reading strategies that will help you become a better textbook reader. As you come to passages in your textbook that you do not understand, refer to these reading strategies for help.

✓ Before You Read

Set a Purpose
- Why are you reading the textbook?
- How does the subject relate to your life?
- How might you be able to use what you learn in your own life?

Preview
- Read the chapter title to find what the topic will be.
- Read the chapter key events and section titles to see what you will learn about the topic.
- Skim the photos, charts, graphs, or maps. How do they support the topic?
- Look for key terms that are in color and boldfaced. How are they defined?

Draw from Your Own Background
- What have you read or heard about concerning new information on the topic?
- How is the new information different from what you already know?
- How will the information that you already know help you understand the new information?

Question

- What is the main idea?
- How do the photos, charts, graphs, and maps support the main idea?

Connect

- Think about people, places, and events in your own life. Are there any similarities with those in your textbook?
- Can you relate the textbook information to other areas of your life?

Predict

- Predict events or outcomes by using clues and information that you already know.
- Change your predictions as you read and gather new information.

Visualize

- Pay careful attention to details.
- Create graphic organizers to show relationships in the reading. Use the graphic organizer in the Guide to Reading to help organize the information in each section.

Look For Clues

Compare and Contrast Sentences

- Look for clue words and phrases that signal comparison, such as *similarity, just as, both, in common, also,* and *too.*
- Look for clue words and phrases that signal contrast, such as *on the other hand, in contrast to, however, different, instead of, rather than, but,* and *unlike.*

Cause-and-Effect Sentences

- Look for clue words and phrases such as *because, as a result, therefore, that is why, since, so, for this reason,* and *consequently.*

Chronological Sentences

- Look for clue words and phrases such as *after, before, first, next, last, during, finally, earlier, later, since,* and *then.*

✓ After You Read

Summarize

- Describe the main idea and how the details support it.
- Use your own words to explain what you have read.

Assess

- What was the main idea?
- Did you learn anything new from the material?
- Can you use this new information in other school subjects or at home?
- What other sources could you use to find more information about the topic?

Geography's Impact On History

Throughout this text, you will discover how geography has shaped the course of events in world history. Landforms, waterways, climate, and natural resources all have helped or hindered human activities. Usually people have learned either to adapt to their environment or to transform it to meet their needs. Here are some examples of the role that geographic factors have played in the story of humanity.

Great Sphinx,
Giza, Egypt

Unit 1:
The First Civilizations and Empires

Rivers contributed to the rise of many of the world's early civilizations. By 3000 B.C. the Sumerians of Southwest Asia had set up 12 prosperous city-states in the Tigris-Euphrates River valley. The area is often called the Fertile Crescent because of its relatively rich topsoil and its curved shape.

Landforms and waterways also affected the political relationship of the world's ancient peoples. For example, the rugged landscape of Greece divided the ancient Greeks into separate city-states instead of uniting them into a single nation. Furthermore, closeness to the sea allowed the Greeks to expand their trade, culture, and sense of civic pride to other parts of the Mediterranean world.

Unit 2:
New Patterns of Civilization

The desire to control or to obtain scarce natural resources has encouraged trade and stimulated contact among the world's peoples. Civilizations developed at trade crossroads. From about A.D.

Singapore skyline ▶

400 to A.D. 1500, the city of Makkah (Mecca) in the Arabian Peninsula was a crossroads for caravans from North Africa, Palestine, and the Persian Gulf. The religion of Islam was based in Makkah and spread to Europe and Asia.

At the dawn of the modern era, Asians and Europeans came into contact with one another partly because Europeans wanted Asia's spices and silks.

When trade on overland routes was endangered, Europeans sought new water routes to Asia. This began a new global age that brought the peoples of Europe, Asia, Africa, and the Americas into closer contact with each other. In time, rivalries over land, trade, and transportation "choke points" or strategic locations, created shatterbelts, regions torn by internal and external conflicts, or buffer zones, areas separating rival powers.

Unit 3:
The Early Modern World

Climate often affects the way a country interacts with its neighbors. For example, many of Russia's harbors stay frozen during the long winter months. In the past, Russia has gone to war with other countries to capture land for warmer ports.

Climate was one reason why the Russians were able to stop the invasions of the French ruler Napoleon Bonaparte in 1812 and the German dictator Adolf Hitler in 1941. The Russians were used to the bitter cold and snow of their country's winter. The invaders were not equipped for months of battle in frigid conditions.

Unit 4:
An Era of European Imperialism

Utilizing natural resources, such as coal and iron, was an important factor in the growth of the Industrial Revolution. Modern industry started in Great Britain, which had large amounts of coal and iron ore for making steel. Throughout Europe and North America, the rise of factories that turned raw materials into finished goods prompted people eager for employment to move from rural areas to urban centers.

Also, the availability of land and the discovery of minerals in the Americas, Australia, and South Africa caused hundreds of thousands of Europeans to move to these areas in hopes of improving their lives. These mass migrations were possible because of improvements in industrial technology and transportation that enabled people to overcome geographic barriers.

Unit 5:
The Twentieth-Century Crisis

Environmental disasters during the first part of the 1900s affected national economies in various parts of the world. For example, during the 1930s, winds blew away so much of the soil in the Great Plains of central North America that the area became known as the Dust Bowl. Ruined by drought, many farmers packed up their belongings and headed west. It took many years of normal rainfall and improved farming techniques to transform the Great Plains from a Dust Bowl into productive land once again.

Unit 6:
Toward A Global Civilization

The world's peoples have become more aware of the growing scarcity of nonrenewable resources. Oil takes millions of years to form and the earth's supply is limited. Industrialized countries like the United States consume far more oil than they produce and must import large amounts. Many experts agree that consumption must be limited and alternative energy sources found.

Environmental problems are no longer limited to a single nation or region. For example, deforestation in one area and pollution in another area may be responsible for climate changes that cause floods and droughts all over the world. Global problems require global solutions, and nations are beginning to work together to ensure solutions that will work for all.

TEKS & TAKS Preview

A GUIDE FOR STUDENTS AND PARENTS

Succeeding in World History Studies

Welcome to World History Studies and *Glencoe World History.* This course provides an overview of human history from the earliest times to the present, with an emphasis on the study of significant people, events, and issues. You will trace the development of Western civilization as well as other civilizations around the world. You will be viewing and interpreting history from various perspectives, including historical, geographic, political, economic, and cultural. Together, these perspectives can help you come to understand how the past has led to our present and to appreciate your role in shaping our future.

On the following pages you will find:

- **The Texas Essential Knowledge and Skills (TEKS) for World History Studies.** The TEKS are the things you should learn and be able to do as you take the course. As a preview, you may want to read over the TEKS with your parents or caregivers. Many of the names and terms may not be familiar to you at first, but together

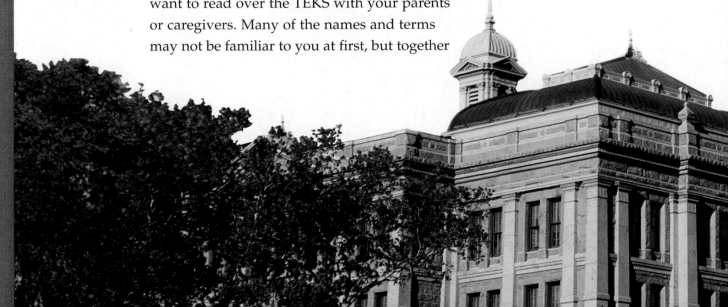

with your family you can outline some steps you can take to achieve proficiency. You may also plan to review these TEKS from time to time to help you organize the things you are learning.

- **Information about TAKS.** High school students take the TAKS tests for Social Studies at Grades 10 and 11. The Grade 11 TAKS is an Exit Level exam that students must pass to graduate. (For an overview of the TAKS program, see pages TEKS 14–15.) Use the **TAKS Preparation Handbook** following page 982 of this textbook to help you prepare for the test. Also, you can review the complete TAKS objectives by visiting the *Glencoe World History* Web site at <u>tx.wh.glencoe.com</u>.

  - **World History content tested on TAKS.** Both the Grade 10 and Grade 11 TAKS tests include student expectations drawn from the TEKS for World History Studies. On the following pages, we have indicated the TEKS statements that will be tested on TAKS. Furthermore, we have indicated TEKS that are correlated to World Geography TEKS that are tested on the Grade 10 and Grade 11 TAKS.

    The importance of the knowledge and skills you gain this year extends well beyond your classroom. As Americans we study history not only to learn names and dates but also to be prepared to live and prosper in a complex, interdependent world. Learning about the intellectual heritage of our civilization and other civilizations also helps us to become better citizens. It sheds new light on our American values and institutions, such as patriotism, free enterprise, and democracy. We hope that this textbook will help you succeed as a student and an informed citizen.

◀ *State Capitol, Austin*

The TAKS **symbol indicates TEKS that are tested on TAKS.**

History

1 The student understands traditional historical points of reference in world history. The student is expected to:

(A) identify the major eras in world history and describe their defining characteristics;

(B) identify changes that resulted from important turning points in world history such as the development of farming; the Mongol invasions; the development of cities; the European age of exploration and colonization; the scientific and industrial revolutions; the political revolutions of the 18th, 19th, and 20th centuries; and the world wars of the 20th century; TAKS

(C) apply absolute and relative chronology through the sequencing of significant individuals, events, and time periods; and

(D) explain the significance of the following dates: 1066, 1215, 1492, 1789, 1914-1918, and 1939-1945.

2 The student understands how the present relates to the past. The student is expected to:

(A) identify elements in a contemporary situation that parallel a historical situation; and

(B) describe variables in a contemporary situation that could result in different outcomes.

3 The student understands how, as a result of the collapse of the Western Roman Empire, new political, economic, and social systems evolved, creating a new civilization in Western Europe. The student is expected to:

(A) compare medieval Europe with previous civilizations;

(B) describe the major characteristics of the political system of feudalism, the economic system of manorialism, and the authority exerted by the Roman Catholic Church; and

(C) identify the political, economic, and social impact of the Crusades.

4 The student understands the influence of the European Renaissance and the Reformation eras. The student is expected to:

(A) identify the causes and characteristics of the European Renaissance and the Reformation eras; and

(B) identify the effects of the European Renaissance and the Reformation eras.

5 The student understands causes and effects of European expansion beginning in the 16th century. The student is expected to:

(A) identify causes of European expansion beginning in the 16th century; and

▼ *The Alamo and surrounding buildings, San Antonio*

TEKS & TAKS

(B) explain the political, economic, cultural, and technological influences of European expansion on both Europeans and non-Europeans, beginning in the 16th century.

6 The student understands the major developments of civilizations of sub-Saharan Africa, Mesoamerica, Andean South America, and Asia. The student is expected to:

(A) summarize the major political and cultural developments of the civilizations of sub-Saharan Africa;

(B) summarize the major political, economic, and cultural developments of civilizations in Mesoamerica and Andean South America; and

(C) summarize the major political, economic, and cultural developments of civilizations in China, India, and Japan.

7 The student understands the impact of political and economic imperialism throughout history. The student is expected to:

(A) analyze examples of major empires of the world such as the Aztec, British, Chinese, French, Japanese, Mongol, and Ottoman empires; and

(B) summarize effects of imperialism on selected societies.

8 The student understands causes and effects of major political revolutions since the 17th century. The student is expected to:

(A) identify causes and evaluate effects of major political revolutions since the 17th century, including the English, American, French, and Russian revolutions;

(B) summarize the ideas from the English, American, French, and Russian revolutions concerning separation of powers, liberty, equality, democracy, popular sovereignty, human rights, constitutionalism, and nationalism;

(C) evaluate how the American Revolution differed from the French and Russian revolutions, including its long-term impact on political developments around the world; and

(D) summarize the significant events related to the spread and fall of communism, including worldwide political and economic effects.

9 The student understands the impact of totalitarianism in the 20th century. The student is expected to:

(A) identify and explain causes and effects of World Wars I and II, including the rise of nazism/fascism in Germany, Italy, and Japan; the rise of communism in the Soviet Union; and the Cold War; and

(B) analyze the nature of totalitarian regimes in China, Nazi Germany, and the Soviet Union.

10 The student understands the influence of significant individuals of the 20th century. The student is expected to:

(A) analyze the influence of significant individuals such as Winston Churchill, Adolf Hitler, Vladimir Lenin, Mao Zedong, and Woodrow Wilson on political events of the 20th century; and

(B) analyze the influence of significant social and/or religious leaders such as Mohandas Gandhi, Pope John Paul II, Mother Teresa, and Desmond Tutu on events of the 20th century.

▼ *Guadalupe Mountains National Park*

The TAKS *symbol indicates TEKS that are tested on TAKS.*

Geography

11 The student uses geographic skills and tools to collect, analyze, and interpret data. The student is expected to:

(A) create thematic maps, graphs, charts, models, and databases representing various aspects of world history; and

(B) pose and answer questions about geographic distributions and patterns in world history shown on maps, graphs, charts, models, and databases. TAKS

12 The student understands the impact of geographic factors on major historic events. The student is expected to:

(A) locate places and regions of historical significance such as the Indus, Nile, Tigris and Euphrates, and Yellow (Huang He) river valleys and describe their physical and human characteristics;

(B) analyze the effects of physical and human geographic factors on major events in world history such as the effects of the opening of the Suez Canal on world trade patterns; and TAKS

(C) interpret historical and contemporary maps to identify and explain geographic factors such as control of the Straits of Hormuz that have influenced people and events in the past. TAKS

Economics

13 The student understands the impact of the Neolithic agricultural revolution on humanity and the development of the first civilizations. The student is expected to:

(A) identify important changes in human life caused by the Neolithic agricultural revolution; and

(B) explain economic, social, and geographic factors that led to the development of the first civilizations.

14 The student understands the historic origins of contemporary economic systems. The student is expected to:

(A) identify the historic origins of the economic systems of capitalism and socialism;

(B) identify the historic origins of the political and economic system of communism; and

(C) compare the relationships between and among contemporary countries with differing economic systems. **TAKS**

▼ *Cattle amongst bluebonnets, Texas Hill Country*

The **TAKS** *symbol indicates TEKS that are tested on TAKS.*

Government

15 The student understands the historical antecedents of contemporary political systems. The student is expected to:

(A) explain the impact of parliamentary and constitutional systems of government on significant world political developments;

(B) define and give examples of different political systems, past and present;

(C) explain the impact of American political ideas on significant world political developments; and

(D) apply knowledge of political systems to make decisions about contemporary issues and events.

(B) identify the impact of political and legal ideas contained in significant historic documents, including Hammurabi's Code, Justinian's Code of Laws, Magna Carta, John Locke's *Two Treatises of Government*, and the Declaration of Independence.

Citizenship

16 The student understands the process by which democratic-republican government evolved. The student is expected to:

(A) trace the process by which democratic-republican government evolved from its beginnings in classical Greece and Rome, through developments in England, and continuing with the Enlightenment; and

17 The student understands the significance of political choices and decisions made by individuals, groups, and nations throughout history. The student is expected to:

(A) evaluate political choices and decisions that individuals, groups, and nations have made in the past, taking into account historical context, and apply this knowledge to the analysis of choices and decisions faced by contemporary societies; and

(B) describe the different roles of citizens and noncitizens in historical cultures, especially as the roles pertain to civic participation.

18 **The student understands the historical development of significant legal and political concepts, including ideas about rights, republicanism, constitutionalism, and democracy. The student is expected to:**

(A) trace the historical development of the rule of law and rights and responsibilities, beginning in the ancient world and continuing to the beginning of the first modern constitutional republics;

(B) summarize the worldwide influence of ideas concerning rights and responsibilities that originated from Greco-Roman and Judeo-Christian ideals in Western civilization such as equality before the law;

(C) identify examples of political, economic, and social oppression and violations of human rights throughout history, including slavery, the Holocaust, other examples of genocide, and politically-motivated mass murders in Cambodia, China, and the Soviet Union; and

(D) assess the degree to which human rights and democratic ideals and practices have been advanced throughout the world during the 20th century.

Culture

19 **The student understands the history and relevance of major religious and philosophical traditions. The student is expected to:**

(A) compare the historical origins, central ideas, and the spread of major religious and philosophical traditions including Buddhism, Christianity, Confucianism, Hinduism, Islam, and Judaism; and

(B) identify examples of religious influence in historic and contemporary world events.

▼ *Padre Island National Seashore*

TEKS & TAKS Preview

The TAKS symbol indicates TEKS that are tested on TAKS.

20 The student understands the relationship between the arts and the times during which they were created. The student is expected to:

(A) identify significant examples of art and architecture that demonstrate an artistic ideal or visual principle from selected cultures;

(B) analyze examples of how art, architecture, literature, music, and drama reflect the history of cultures in which they are produced; and

(C) identify examples of art, music, and literature that transcend the cultures in which they were created and convey universal themes.

21 The student understands the roles of women, children, and families in different historical cultures. The student is expected to:

(A) analyze the specific roles of women, children, and families in different historical cultures; and

(B) describe the political, economic, and cultural influence of women in different historical cultures.

22 The student understands how the development of ideas has influenced institutions and societies. The student is expected to:

(A) summarize the fundamental ideas and institutions of Eastern civilizations that originated in China and India;

(B) summarize the fundamental ideas and institutions of Western civilization that originated in Greece and Rome; and

(C) analyze how ideas such as Judeo-Christian ethics and the rise of secularism and individualism in Western civilization, beginning with the Enlightenment, have influenced institutions and societies.

Science, Technology, and Society

23 **The student understands how major scientific and mathematical discoveries and technological innovations have affected societies throughout history. The student is expected to:**

(A) give examples of major mathematical and scientific discoveries and technological innovations that occurred at different periods in history and describe the changes produced by these discoveries and innovations; `TAKS`

(B) identify new ideas in mathematics, science, and technology that occurred during the Greco-Roman, Indian, Islamic, and Chinese civilizations and trace the spread of these ideas to other civilizations;

(C) summarize the ideas in astronomy, mathematics, and architectural engineering that developed in Mesoamerica and Andean South America;

(D) describe the origins of the scientific revolution in 16th-century Europe and explain its impact on scientific thinking worldwide; and

(E) identify the contributions of significant scientists such as Archimedes, Copernicus, Eratosthenes, Galileo, and Pythagoras.

◄*Lighthouse Rock at Palo Duro Canyon State Park*

The **TAKS** *symbol indicates TEKS that are tested on TAKS.*

24 The student understands connections between major developments in science and technology and the growth of industrial economies and societies in the 18th, 19th, and 20th centuries. The student is expected to:

(A) explain the causes of industrialization and evaluate both short-term and long-term impact on societies;

(B) describe the connection between scientific discoveries and technological innovations and new patterns of social and cultural life in the 20th century, such as developments in transportation and communication that affected social mobility; and

(C) identify the contributions of significant scientists and inventors such as Robert Boyle, Marie Curie, Thomas Edison, Albert Einstein, Robert Fulton, Sir Isaac Newton, Louis Pasteur, and James Watt.

Social Studies Skills

25 The student applies critical-thinking skills to organize and use information acquired from a variety of sources including electronic technology. The student is expected to:

(A) identify ways archaeologists, anthropologists, historians, and geographers analyze limited evidence;

(B) locate and use primary and secondary sources such as computer software, databases, media and news services, biographies, interviews, and artifacts to acquire information; **TAKS**

(C) analyze information by sequencing, categorizing, identifying cause-and-effect relationships, comparing, contrasting, finding the main idea, summarizing, making generalizations and predictions, and drawing inferences and conclusions; **TAKS**

(D) explain and apply different methods that historians use to interpret the past, including the use of primary and secondary sources, points of view, frames of reference, and historical context; **TAKS**

(E) use the process of historical inquiry to research, interpret, and use multiple sources of evidence;

(F) evaluate the validity of a source based on language, corroboration with other sources, and information about the author;

(G) identify bias in written, oral, and visual material; TAKS

(H) support a point of view on a social studies issue or event; and

(I) use appropriate mathematical skills to interpret social studies information such as maps and graphs.

26 The student communicates in written, oral, and visual forms. The student is expected to:

(A) use social studies terminology correctly;

(B) use standard grammar, spelling, sentence structure, and punctuation;

(C) interpret and create databases, research outlines, bibliographies, and visuals including graphs, charts, time lines, and maps; and TAKS

(D) transfer information from one medium to another, including written to visual and statistical to written or visual, using computer software as appropriate.

27 The student uses problem-solving and decision-making skills, working independently and with others, in a variety of settings. The student is expected to:

(A) use a problem-solving process to identify a problem, gather information, list and consider options, consider advantages and disadvantages, choose and implement a solution, and evaluate the effectiveness of the solution; and

(B) use a decision-making process to identify a situation that requires a decision, gather information, identify options, predict consequences, and take action to implement a decision.

▼ *Johnson Space Center, Houston*

A Guide to TAKS

Overview

In June 1999, Senate Bill 103 was signed into law establishing a new statewide testing program in Texas. The new program, called TAKS, has been designed to follow the state-required curriculum, the Texas Essential Knowledge and Skills (or TEKS). TAKS includes several changes from the previous testing program:

- It expands both the grades that are tested and the subject areas that are covered. The chart on page TEKS 15 shows the full TAKS testing program for Grades 3–11.
- Students are required to pass a new Exit Level exam given at the 11th grade in order to graduate from high school. (Students in the 11th grade in the 2003–2004 school year are the first to take the required exam.)
- The new Exit Level exam includes four subject areas: mathematics, English language arts, science, and social studies.
- By law, the Social Studies Grade 11 Exit Level exam includes some content from early American history (which is taught at the 8th grade).
- Because the TAKS tests are based on the TEKS, and because of the new exit-level testing requirement for graduation, TAKS is more comprehensive and rigorous than the previous assessment program.

The Exit Level TAKS are designed, according to the law, to "assess a student's mastery of the minimum skills necessary for high school graduation and readiness to enroll in an institution of higher education." (Students do not have to demonstrate a readiness for higher education, however, in order to graduate.) Students who do not perform satisfactorily on any part of the assessment when first tested will be given multiple opportunities to retake it.

Social Studies TAKS

Students take TAKS Social Studies tests at Grades 8, 10, and 11. While the specific knowledge and skills tested at each level vary, all the tests cover these broad content areas:

1. Issues and events in U.S. history.
2. Geographic influences on historical issues and events.
3. Economic and social influences on historical issues and events.
4. Political influences on historical issues and events.
5. Use of critical-thinking skills.

The following are general descriptions of the Social Studies TAKS tests:

- **Grade 8.** This test includes only TEKS from Social Studies Grade 8, the history of the United States from the early colonial period through Reconstruction.
- **Grade 10.** The Grade 10 TAKS test is meant to provide information on how students are progressing in social studies, but it is not a graduation requirement. The test includes content taught in Social Studies Grade 8, World History Studies, and World Geography Studies. Because students have the option of taking either World History or World Geography as part of the minimum high school requirements, the test planners incorporated only World History or Geography TEKS that are very similar or identical in both courses.
- **Grade 11 Exit Level.** The Grade 11 exam includes the content areas covered in the Grade 10 test (early American history, world history, and world geography), but the majority of TEKS are drawn from United States History Since Reconstruction, the required high school American history course. Passing this test is required for graduation.

TAKS Testing
(Implementation 2003-2005)

Grade 3	Grade 4	Grade 5	Grade 6	Grade 7	Grade 8	Grade 9	Grade 10	Grade 11	Grade 12
ENGLISH-VERSION ASSESSMENT									
Reading	Reading	Reading	Reading	Reading	Reading	Reading			
	Writing			Writing			English Language Arts	English Language Arts	
Math	Math	Math	Math	Math	Math	Math	Math	Math	
		Science					Science	Science	
					Social Studies		Social Studies	Social Studies	
SPANISH-VERSION ASSESSMENT									
Reading	Reading	Reading	Reading						
	Writing								
Math	Math	Math	Math						
		Science							
READING PROFICIENCY TESTS IN ENGLISH FOR LEP STUDENTS									
RPTE	RPTE		RPTE			RPTE			
ALTERNATIVE ASSESSMENT FOR SPECIAL EDUCATION STUDENTS									
Reading	Reading	Reading	Reading	Reading	Reading	Reading			
	Writing			Writing			English Language Arts		
Math	Math	Math	Math	Math	Math	Math	Math		

Source: Department of Curriculum, Assessment & Technology

REFERENCE ATLAS

NATIONAL GEOGRAPHIC

ATLAS KEY

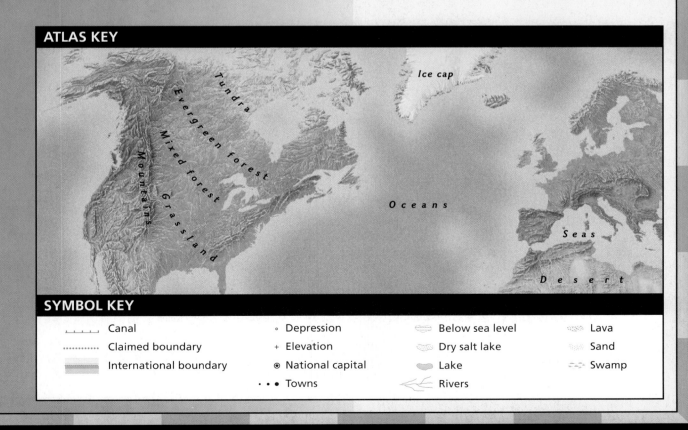

SYMBOL KEY

⊥⊥⊥⊥ Canal	∘ Depression	⬦ Below sea level	∿ Lava
·········· Claimed boundary	+ Elevation	⬦ Dry salt lake	∿ Sand
▨▨▨▨ International boundary	⊛ National capital	⬬ Lake	⋍⋍ Swamp
	• • ● Towns	⪡ Rivers	

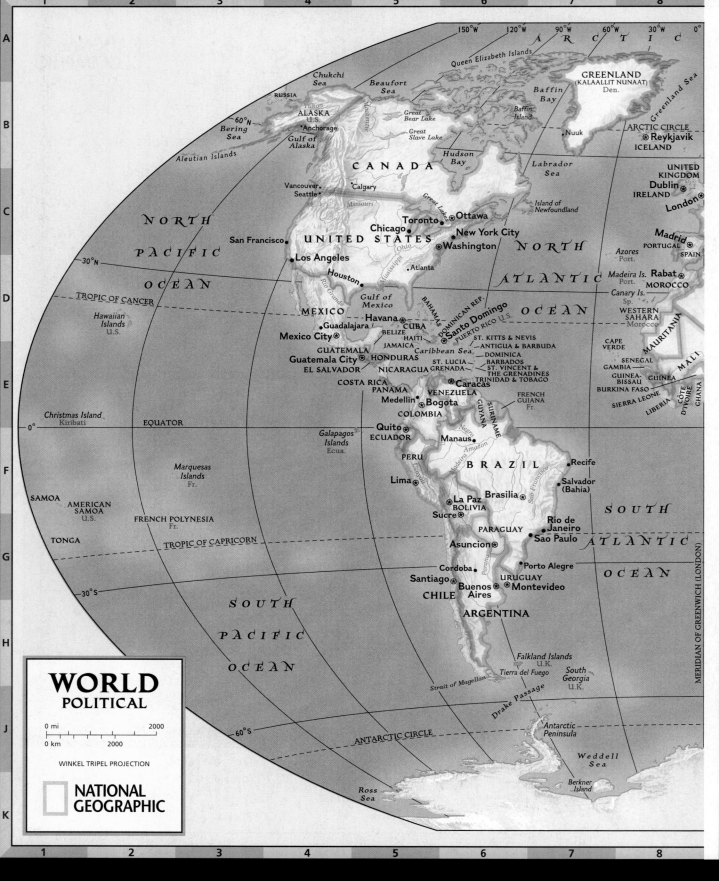

WORLD
POLITICAL

0 mi — 2000
0 km — 2000

WINKEL TRIPEL PROJECTION

NATIONAL GEOGRAPHIC

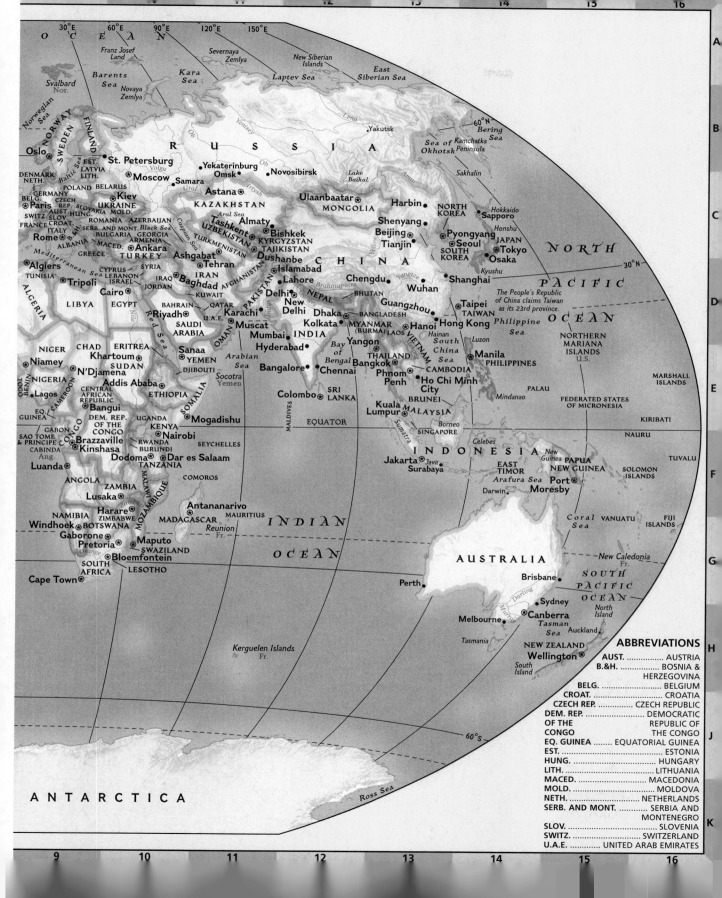

A B C D E F G H J K

9 10 11 12 13 14 15 16

OCEAN

30°E 60°E 90°E 120°E 150°E

Svalbard *Nor.*
Franz Josef Land
Norwegian Sea
Barents Sea
Novaya Zemlya
Kara Sea
Severnaya Zemlya
Laptev Sea
New Siberian Islands
East Siberian Sea

60°N
Bering Sea
Kamchatka Peninsula
Sea of Okhotsk
Sakhalin

R U S S I A

Yakutsk
Lena
Yenisey
Ob

NORWAY SWEDEN FINLAND
Oslo
St. Petersburg
DENMARK NETH.
Moscow
Yekaterinburg
Omsk
Novosibirsk
Lake Baikal
Amur
Samara
Ural

EST. LATVIA LITH.
Baltic Sea
BELG. GERMANY POLAND BELARUS
Paris CZECH REP.
SWITZ. AUST. HUNG. SLOVAKIA MOLD.
FRANCE SLOV. CROAT. ROMANIA UKRAINE
Rome ITALY SERB. AND MONT. BULGARIA
ALBANIA MACED. GREECE
Kiev AZERBAIJAN
Astana
KAZAKHSTAN
Aral Sea
Tashkent UZBEKISTAN
Almaty
Bishkek KYRGYZSTAN
TURKMENISTAN TAJIKISTAN
Dushanbe

Harbin
Shenyang
NORTH KOREA
Hokkaido
Sapporo
Honshu JAPAN
Ulaanbaatar
MONGOLIA
Beijing
Tianjin
Pyongyang
Seoul SOUTH KOREA
Tokyo
Osaka
Kyushu

Algiers
TUNISIA
Tripoli
Mediterranean Sea
GREECE
TURKEY
Ankara
CYPRUS LEBANON SYRIA
ISRAEL IRAQ
JORDAN
Cairo
Baghdad
Tehran IRAN
Ashgabat
Islamabad
Lahore
AFGHANISTAN
PAKISTAN
Delhi
New Delhi
NEPAL
BHUTAN
Brahmaputra

Chengdu
Yangtze
Wuhan
Guangzhou
Yellow
Taipei TAIWAN
Hong Kong

C H I N A

Shanghai

30°N

The People's Republic of China claims Taiwan as its 23rd province.

N O R T H   P A C I F I C   O C E A N

ALGERIA
LIBYA
EGYPT
Nile
Red Sea
SAUDI ARABIA
BAHRAIN QATAR
U.A.E.
Riyadh
KUWAIT
OMAN
Muscat
Karachi
Mumbai
INDIA
Hyderabad
Kolkata
BANGLADESH
Dhaka
MYANMAR (BURMA)
LAOS
Hanoi
Hainan
South China Sea
Manila
PHILIPPINES
Luzon
NORTHERN MARIANA ISLANDS U.S.
Philippine Sea

NIGER CHAD
ERITREA
SUDAN
Khartoum
N'Djamena
YEMEN
Sanaa
DJIBOUTI
Socotra Yemen
Arabian Sea
Bay of Bengal
Bangalore
Chennai
THAILAND
Bangkok
VIETNAM
Phnom Penh
CAMBODIA
Ho Chi Minh City
Mindanao
PALAU
FEDERATED STATES OF MICRONESIA
MARSHALL ISLANDS
KIRIBATI

NIGERIA
Niamey
BENIN TOGO
Lagos
CAMEROON
EQ. GUINEA
CENTRAL AFRICAN REPUBLIC
Bangui
Addis Ababa
ETHIOPIA
SOMALIA
Colombo
SRI LANKA
MALDIVES
EQUATOR
Kuala Lumpur
MALAYSIA
BRUNEI
SINGAPORE
Borneo
Sumatra
NAURU
TUVALU

SAO TOME & PRINCIPE
GABON
CONGO
Brazzaville
Kinshasa
DEM. REP. OF THE CONGO
CABINDA Ang.
UGANDA
KENYA
Nairobi
RWANDA BURUNDI
Dodoma
Dar es Salaam
TANZANIA
Mogadishu
SEYCHELLES
Celebes
Jakarta Java
Surabaya

I N D O N E S I A

New Guinea
PAPUA NEW GUINEA
EAST TIMOR
Arafura Sea
Port Moresby
SOLOMON ISLANDS
TUVALU

Luanda
ANGOLA
ZAMBIA
Lusaka
MALAWI
COMOROS
MOZAMBIQUE
Darwin
Coral Sea
VANUATU
FIJI ISLANDS

NAMIBIA
ZIMBABWE
Harare
Antananarivo
MADAGASCAR
MAURITIUS
Reunion Fr.

I N D I A N

O C E A N

Windhoek
BOTSWANA
Gaborone
Pretoria
Maputo
SWAZILAND
Bloemfontein
SOUTH AFRICA
LESOTHO
Orange
Cape Town

A U S T R A L I A

Brisbane
New Caledonia Fr.
Perth
Darling
Sydney
Canberra
Melbourne
Murray
Tasman Sea
Tasmania
North Island

S O U T H   P A C I F I C   O C E A N

Auckland
NEW ZEALAND
Wellington
South Island

Kerguelen Islands Fr.

60°S

A N T A R C T I C A

Ross Sea

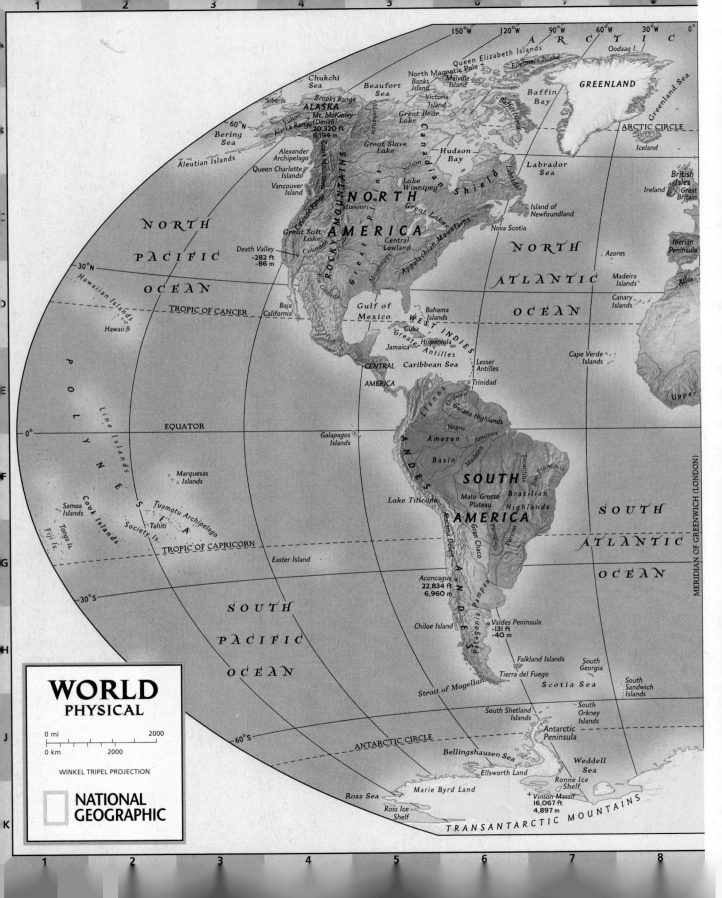

WORLD
PHYSICAL

0 mi   2000

0 km   2000

WINKEL TRIPEL PROJECTION

NATIONAL GEOGRAPHIC

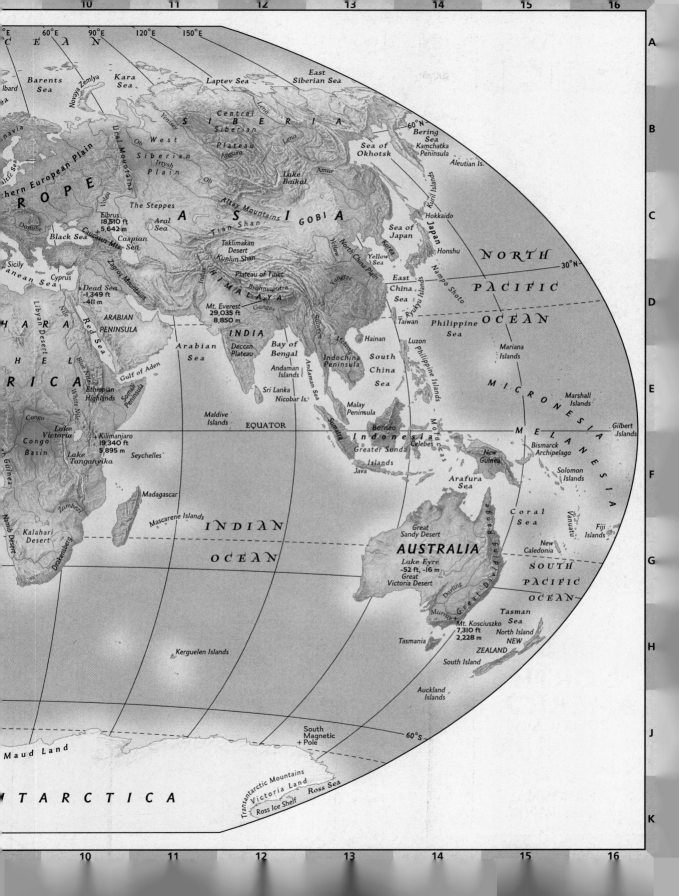

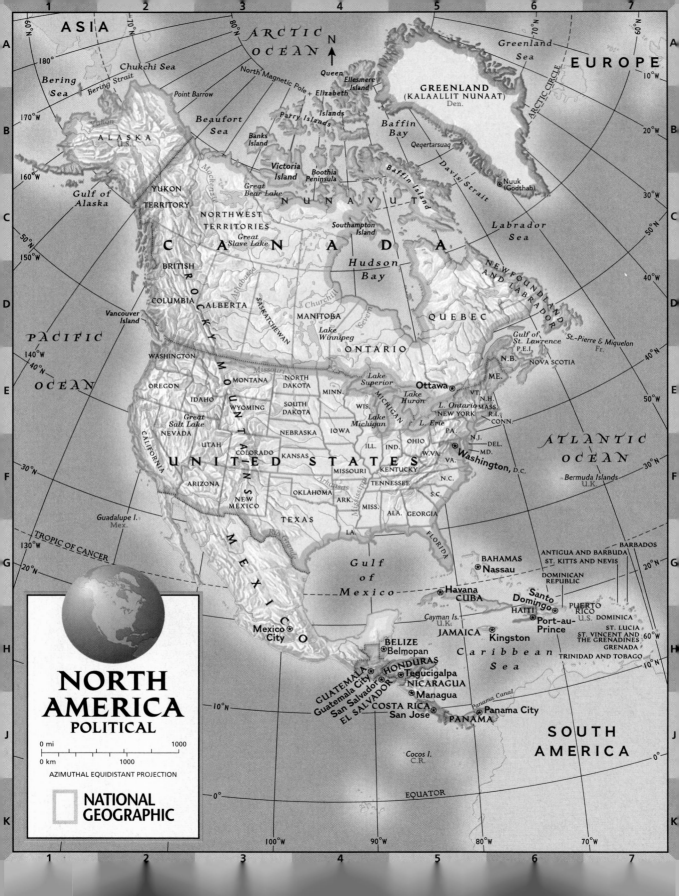

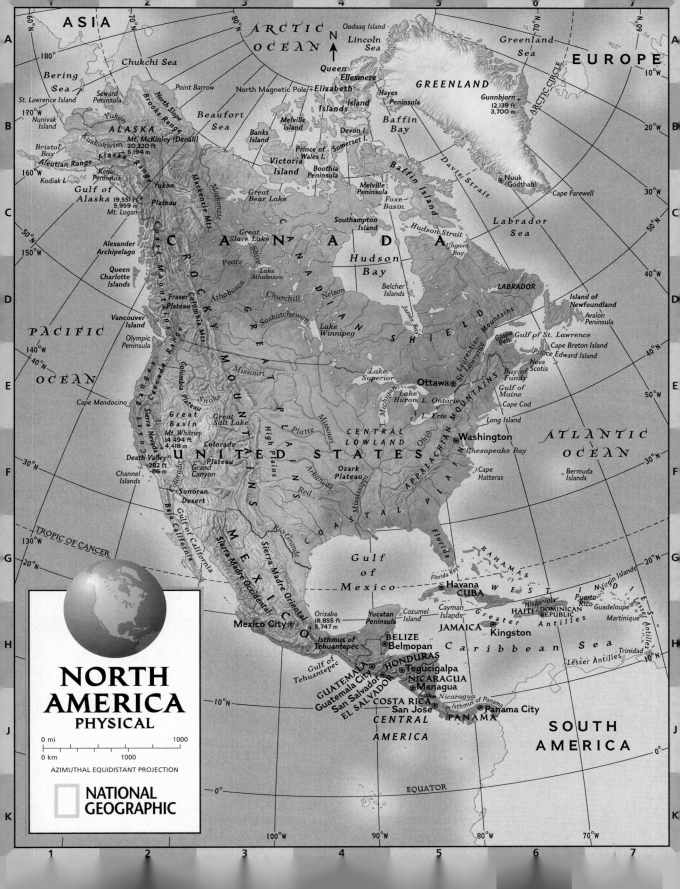

NORTH AMERICA
PHYSICAL

0 mi   1000
0 km   1000

AZIMUTHAL EQUIDISTANT PROJECTION

NATIONAL GEOGRAPHIC

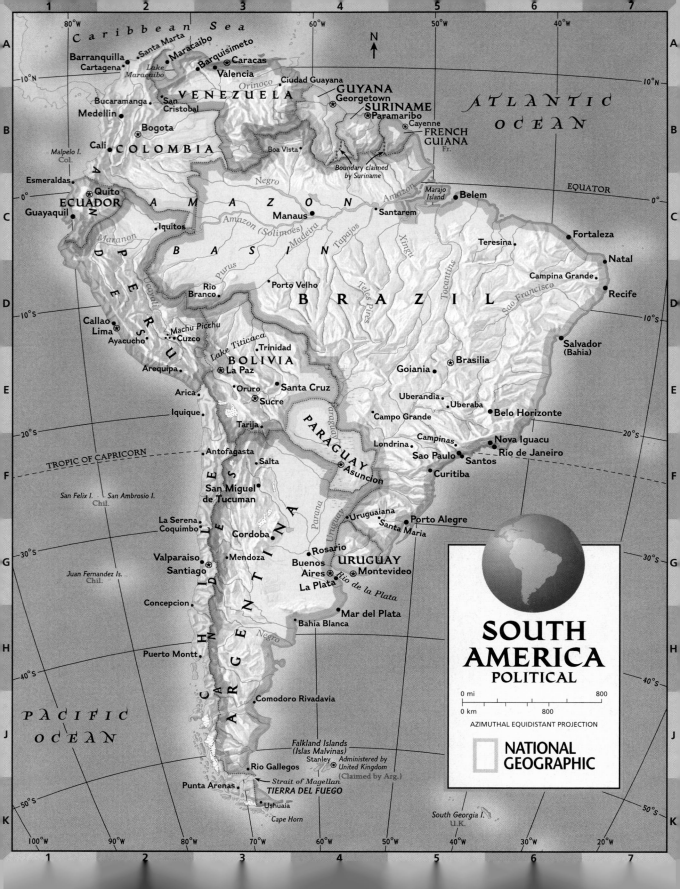

SOUTH AMERICA
POLITICAL

0 mi 800
0 km 800

AZIMUTHAL EQUIDISTANT PROJECTION

NATIONAL GEOGRAPHIC

SOUTH AMERICA
PHYSICAL

0 mi   800
0 km   800

AZIMUTHAL EQUIDISTANT PROJECTION

NATIONAL GEOGRAPHIC

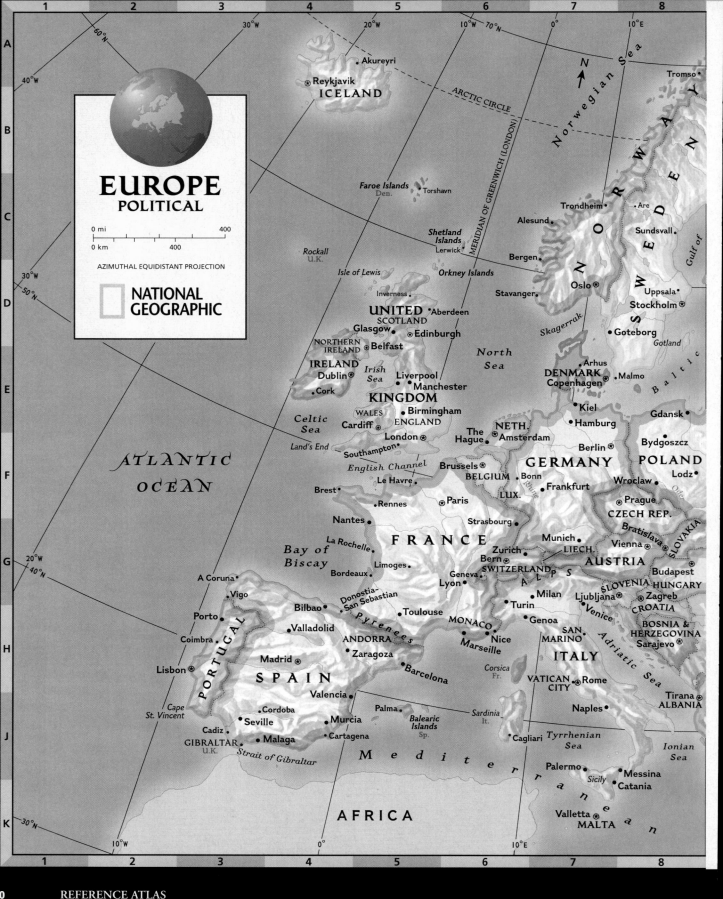

EUROPE
POLITICAL

0 mi ———————————— 400
0 km ———————————— 400

AZIMUTHAL EQUIDISTANT PROJECTION

NATIONAL GEOGRAPHIC

Akureyri
◉ Reykjavik
ICELAND

ARCTIC CIRCLE

Norwegian Sea

N

Tromso •

Faroe Islands
Den.   • Torshavn

Trondheim •   • Are

Alesund •   Sundsvall •

Shetland Islands
Lerwick •

Bergen •

MERIDIAN OF GREENWICH (LONDON)

Rockall
U.K.

Isle of Lewis

Orkney Islands

Stavanger •   Oslo ◉   Uppsala •

Inverness •

UNITED
SCOTLAND   • Aberdeen
Glasgow •   ◉ Edinburgh
NORTHERN
IRELAND   ◉ Belfast
IRELAND   *Irish Sea*   Liverpool •
Dublin ◉   • Manchester
• Cork   **KINGDOM**
WALES   • Birmingham
Celtic Sea   Cardiff •   ENGLAND
Land's End   London ◉
Southampton •
English Channel
Brussels ◉
Brest •   Le Havre •   **BELGIUM**   Bonn •
Rennes •   ◉ Paris   **LUX.**
Nantes •
Strasbourg •

Skagerrak   • Goteborg
Gotland
Arhus •
DENMARK   • Malmo
Copenhagen ◉
• Kiel   Gdansk •
• Hamburg
Berlin ◉   Bydgoszcz •
GERMANY   **POLAND**
Lodz •
Frankfurt •   Wroclaw •
CZECH REP.   ◉ Prague
Bratislava   **SLOVAKIA**
Munich •   Vienna ◉   Budapest •
LIECH.   **AUSTRIA**   **SLOVENIA HUNGARY**
Ljubljana ◉   ◉ Zagreb
CROATIA

North Sea
The ◉   **NETH.**
Hague   ◉ Amsterdam

Baltic   *Sea*

SWEDEN

Stockholm ◉

Gulf of

N O R W A Y

ATLANTIC
OCEAN

La Rochelle •

Bay of
Biscay

A Coruna •
• Vigo

Porto •

Coimbra •

Lisbon ◉

Cape
St. Vincent

Cadiz •

GIBRALTAR
U.K.

Bordeaux •   Limoges •

F R A N C E

Zurich •
Bern ◉
Geneva •   **SWITZERLAND**
Lyon •

Bilbao •   Donostia-
San Sebastian •

Valladolid •

Madrid ◉

P O R T U G A L

S P A I N

• Cordoba
Seville •   • Malaga

Strait of Gibraltar

Murcia •
• Cartagena

Toulouse •

ANDORRA
• Zaragoza

MONACO
Marseille •

• Barcelona

Valencia •

Palma •

Balearic
Islands
Sp.

Milan •
Turin •

A L P S

Nice •

Genoa •

Corsica
Fr.

ITALY

Venice •

SAN
MARINO

VATICAN
CITY   ◉ Rome

Naples •

Sardinia
It.

Cagliari •

M e d i t e r r

A F R I C A

Palermo •

Sicily   • Catania

Valletta ◉
MALTA

Vienna ◉

Adriatic   *Sea*

BOSNIA &
HERZEGOVINA
Sarajevo ◉

Tirana •
ALBANIA

Tyrrhenian
Sea

Ionian
Sea

a n e a n

• Messina

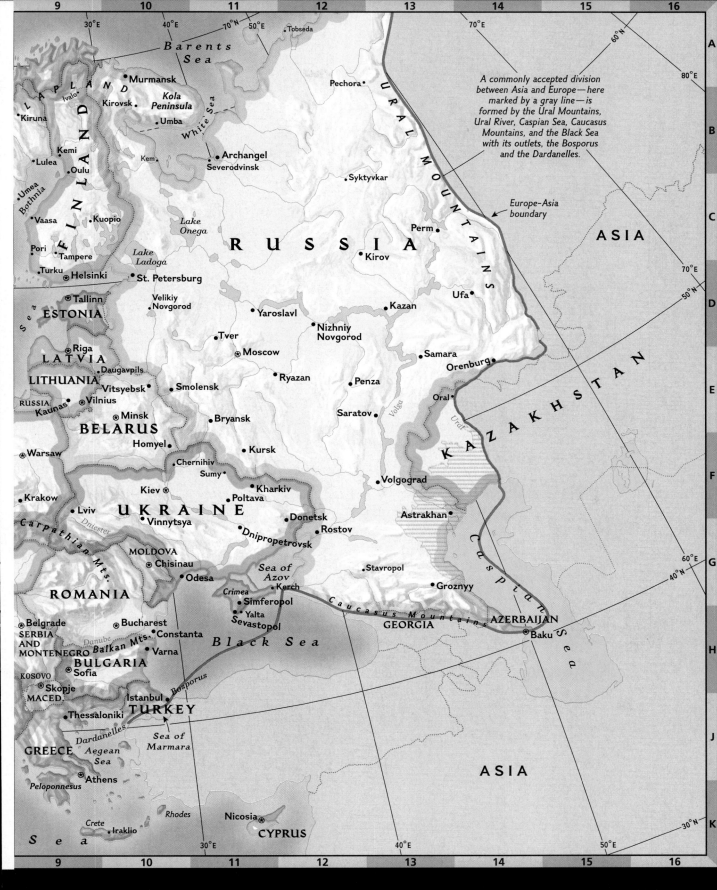

A commonly accepted division between Asia and Europe—here marked by a gray line—is formed by the Ural Mountains, Ural River, Caspian Sea, Caucasus Mountains, and the Black Sea with its outlets, the Bosporus and the Dardanelles.

Europe-Asia boundary

ASIA

RUSSIA

KAZAKHSTAN

Barents Sea

Tobseda
Pechora
Syktyvkar

Murmansk
Kirovsk
Kola Peninsula
Ivalo
Kiruna
Umba
White Sea

LAPLAND

Kemi
Kem
Lulea
Oulu

Bothnia
Umea
Vaasa
Kuopio

FINLAND

Archangel
Severodvinsk

Perm
Kirov

Pori
Tampere
Lake Onega
Ufa

Turku
Helsinki
St. Petersburg
Lake Ladoga

Tallinn
ESTONIA
Velikiy Novgorod
Yaroslavl
Kazan

LATVIA
Riga
Tver
Nizhniy Novgorod

Samara
Orenburg

LITHUANIA
Daugavpils
Moscow
Vitsyebsk
Smolensk
Ryazan

Oral

RUSSIA
Kaunas
Vilnius
Minsk
Penza

BELARUS
Bryansk
Saratov

Volga

Ural

Warsaw
Homyel
Kursk
Volgograd

Krakow
Chernihiv
Sumy

Lviv
UKRAINE
Kharkiv
Astrakhan

Vinnytsya
Poltava

Kiev
Donetsk

MOLDOVA
Dnipropetrovsk
Rostov

Chisinau

Stavropol

Carpathian Mts.
Odesa
Sea of Azov

Dniester
Crimea
Kerch
Groznyy

ROMANIA
Simferopol
Yalta
Sevastopol
Caucasus Mountains

Belgrade
Bucharest
Constanta
AZERBAIJAN

SERBIA AND MONTENEGRO
Danube
GEORGIA

Balkan Mts.
Varna
Baku

BULGARIA
Black Sea
Caspian Sea

KOSOVO
Sofia

Skopje
Bosporus

MACED
Istanbul

Thessaloniki
TURKEY

Dardanelles

GREECE
Aegean Sea
Sea of Marmara

Peloponnesus
Athens

ASIA

Crete
Rhodes
Nicosia

Sea
Iraklio
CYPRUS

EUROPE
PHYSICAL

0 mi   400
0 km   400

AZIMUTHAL EQUIDISTANT PROJECTION

NATIONAL GEOGRAPHIC

Map labels:

ICELAND — Reykjavik

ARCTIC CIRCLE

Faroe Islands

Shetland Islands

Orkney Islands

Outer Hebrides

Highlands

British Isles

NORWAY — Oslo

SCANDINAVIA

SWEDEN — Stockholm

Gulf of Bothnia

North Sea

Jutland

DENMARK — Copenhagen

Zealand

Baltic Sea

Edinburgh

Belfast

UNITED KINGDOM

IRELAND — Dublin

Irish Sea

Great Britain

Cardiff

London

Amsterdam

NETH.

Berlin

POLAND

Oder

BELGIUM — Brussels

LUX.

GERMANY

Elbe

Prague

CZECH REP.

Bratislava

SLOVAKIA

Vienna

AUSTRIA

Budapest

HUNGARY

LIECH.

Bern

SWITZ.

ALPS

SLOVENIA — Ljubljana

Zagreb

CROATIA

Drava

Danube

Sava

Po

BOSNIA & HERZEGOVINA — Sarajevo

Adriatic Sea

MONACO

Riviera

SAN MARINO

Apennines

ITALY

VATICAN CITY — Rome

Tirana

ALBANIA

ATLANTIC OCEAN

English Channel

Seine

Paris

Brittany

Loire

FRANCE

Bay of Biscay

Mont Blanc 15,771 ft 4,807 m

Rhône

Rhine

Danube

Massif Central

ANDORRA

Cantabrian Mountains

Pyrenees

Douro

PORTUGAL

Lisbon

Tagus

Madrid

SPAIN

IBERIAN PENINSULA

Ebro

Baetic Mountains

GIBRALTAR

Strait of Gibraltar

Corsica

Sardinia

Balearic Islands

Tyrrhenian Sea

Ionian Sea

Sicily — Etna 10,902 ft 3,323 m

Valletta

MALTA

Mediterranean Sea

AFRICA

Norwegian Sea

MERIDIAN OF GREENWICH (LONDON)

60°N   40°W   30°W   20°W   10°W   70°N   0°   10°E

50°N   30°W

20°W   40°N

30°N   10°W   0°   10°E

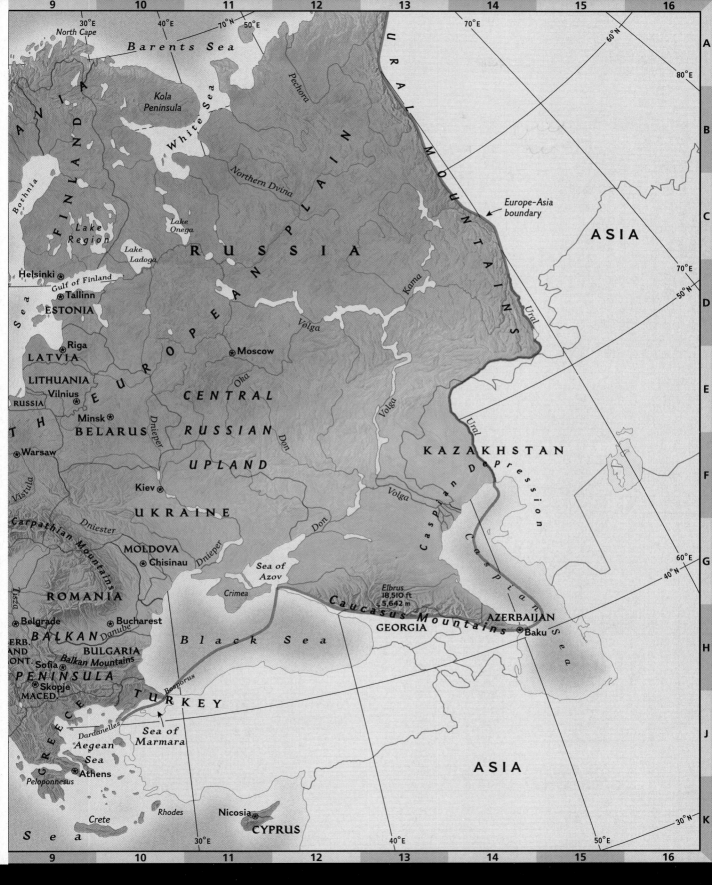

9 · 10 · 11 · 12 · 13 · 14 · 15 · 16

A · B · C · D · E · F · G · H · J · K

30°E
North Cape

Barents Sea

40°E · 70°N · 50°E · 70°E · 60°N · 80°N

Pechora

Kola
Peninsula

White Sea

Northern Dvina

*Europe-Asia
boundary*

ASIA

70°E
50°N

Bothnia

FINLAND

Lake
Region

Lake
Onega

Lake
Ladoga

RUSSIA

Ural Mountains

Kama

Ural

Helsinki

Gulf of Finland
Tallinn

ESTONIA

Volga

Moscow

C E N T R A L

Oka

Volga

Ural

K A Z A K H S T A N

Sea

Riga

LATVIA

LITHUANIA

Vilnius

RUSSIA

Minsk

BELARUS

Dnieper

R U S S I A N

Don

Volga

Caspian Depression

Warsaw

U P L A N D

Kiev

UKRAINE

Don

Caspian Sea

Vistula

Dniester

MOLDOVA

Chisinau

Dnieper

*Sea of
Azov*

Volga

Elbrus
18,510 ft
5,642 m

AZERBAIJAN

Carpathian Mountains

Crimea

GEORGIA

Baku

ROMANIA

Caucasus Mountains

Tisza

Belgrade

Bucharest

Danube

Black Sea

BALKAN

**SERB
LAND
ONT.**

BULGARIA

Sofia

Balkan Mountains

PENINSULA

Skopje

MACED.

Bosporus

T U R K E Y

Dardanelles

*Sea of
Marmara*

*Aegean
Sea*

Athens

ASIA

Peloponnesus

Crete

Rhodes

Nicosia

CYPRUS

Sea

60°E
40°N

40°E
30°N

30°E · 40°E · 50°E

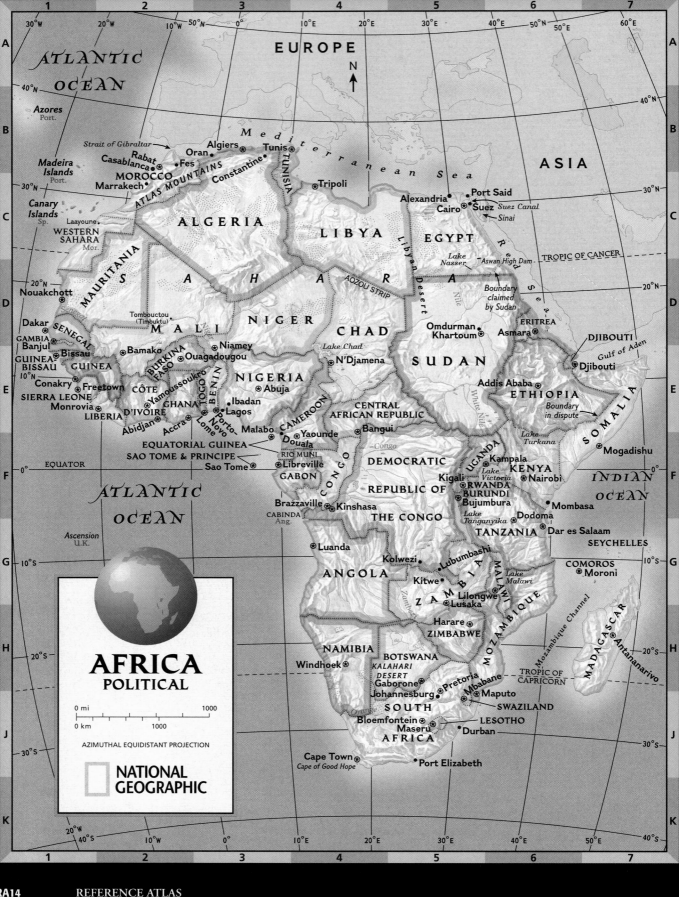

AFRICA
POLITICAL

0 mi 1000

0 km 1000

AZIMUTHAL EQUIDISTANT PROJECTION

NATIONAL GEOGRAPHIC

EUROPE

N

ASIA

ATLANTIC OCEAN

Azores
Port.

Madeira Islands
Port.

Canary Islands
Sp.

Strait of Gibraltar

Mediterranean Sea

Algiers
Tunis
Oran
Rabat
Casablanca
Fes
MOROCCO
Constantine
Marrakech
TUNISIA
Tripoli

Alexandria
Port Said
Cairo
Suez
Suez Canal
Sinai

ATLAS MOUNTAINS

ALGERIA

LIBYA

EGYPT

Libyan Desert

Lake Nasser
Aswan High Dam
TROPIC OF CANCER

Laayoune

WESTERN SAHARA
Mor.

S A H A R A

MAURITANIA

Nouakchott

20°N

AOZOU STRIP

NIGER

CHAD

Boundary claimed by Sudan

Red Sea

Omdurman
Khartoum

ERITREA
Asmara

DJIBOUTI
Gulf of Aden
Djibouti

Tombouctou
(Timbuktu)

M A L I

Dakar
SENEGAL
GAMBIA
Banjul
GUINEA-BISSAU
Bissau
Conakry
GUINEA
Freetown
SIERRA LEONE
Monrovia
LIBERIA

Bamako
BURKINA FASO
Niamey
Ouagadougou
Yamoussoukro
CÔTE D'IVOIRE
GHANA
Abidjan
Accra
TOGO
BENIN
Lome
Porto Novo

NIGERIA
Abuja
Ibadan
Lagos
Malabo
CAMEROON
Yaounde
Douala

N'Djamena

Lake Chad

S U D A N

White Nile
Nile

Addis Ababa
ETHIOPIA

Boundary in dispute

SOMALIA

Mogadishu

EQUATORIAL GUINEA
SAO TOME & PRINCIPE
Sao Tome
RIO MUNI
Libreville
GABON

CENTRAL AFRICAN REPUBLIC

Bangui

CONGO

DEMOCRATIC

REPUBLIC OF

THE CONGO

Congo

UGANDA
Kampala
Lake Victoria
RWANDA
Kigali
BURUNDI
Bujumbura

KENYA
Nairobi

Lake Turkana

INDIAN OCEAN

ATLANTIC OCEAN

EQUATOR

Ascension
U.K.

Brazzaville
Kinshasa
CABINDA
Ang.

Lake Tanganyika

Dodoma
TANZANIA

Mombasa

Dar es Salaam

SEYCHELLES

Luanda

ANGOLA

Kolwezi
Kitwe
Lubumbashi

Z A M B I A
Lusaka
Lilongwe

MALAWI
Lake Malawi

COMOROS
Moroni

Harare
ZIMBABWE

MOZAMBIQUE

Mozambique Channel

MADAGASCAR
Antananarivo

NAMIBIA
Windhoek

KALAHARI DESERT

BOTSWANA
Gaborone

TROPIC OF CAPRICORN

Johannesburg
Pretoria
Mbabane
Maputo
SWAZILAND

Bloemfontein
Maseru
LESOTHO
Durban

Orange

SOUTH AFRICA

Cape Town
Cape of Good Hope
Port Elizabeth

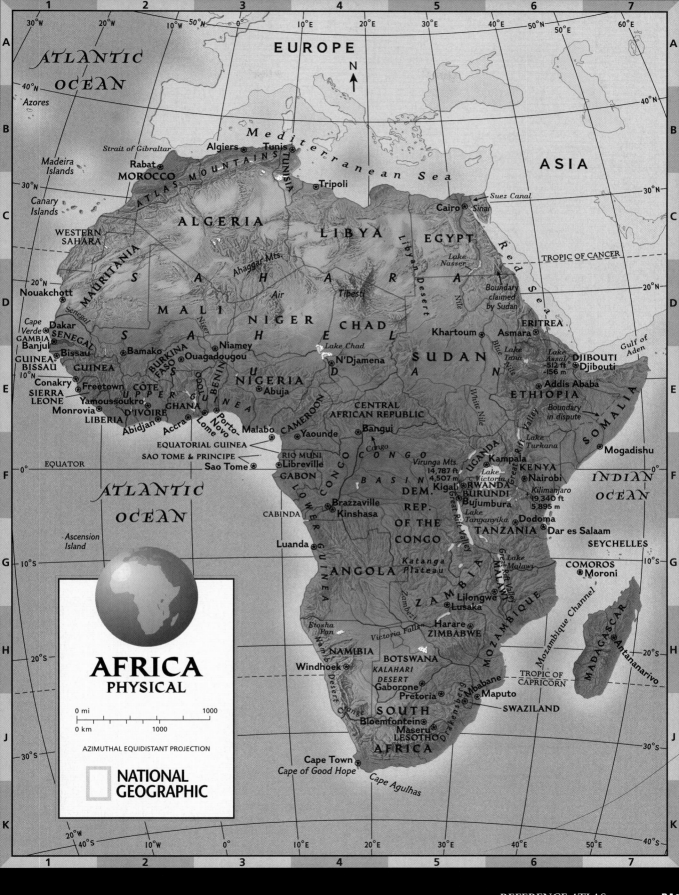

AFRICA
PHYSICAL

0 mi 1000
0 km 1000

AZIMUTHAL EQUIDISTANT PROJECTION

NATIONAL GEOGRAPHIC

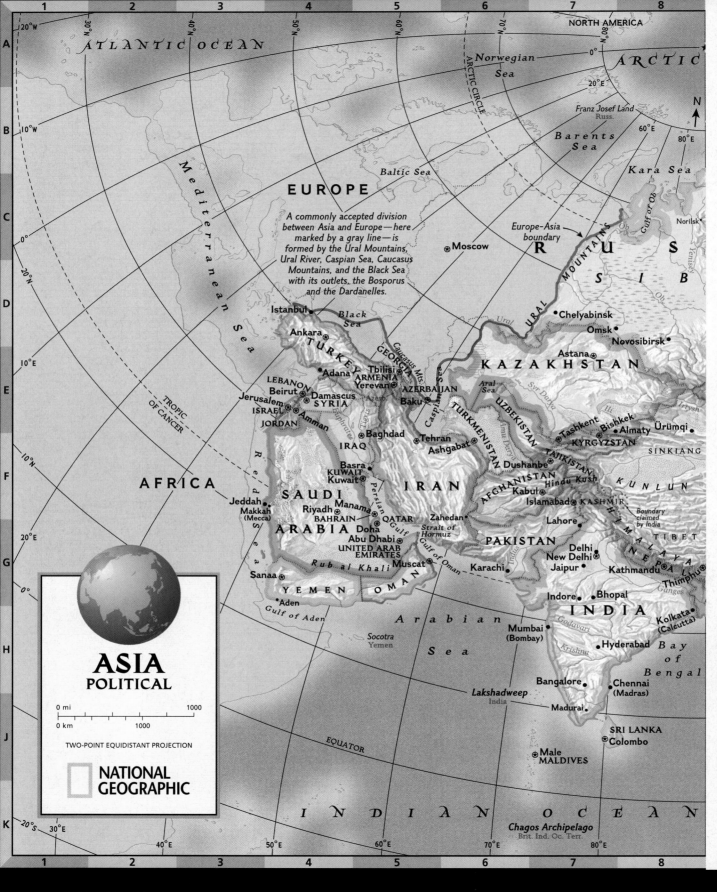

ASIA
POLITICAL

0 mi   1000
0 km   1000

TWO-POINT EQUIDISTANT PROJECTION

NATIONAL
GEOGRAPHIC

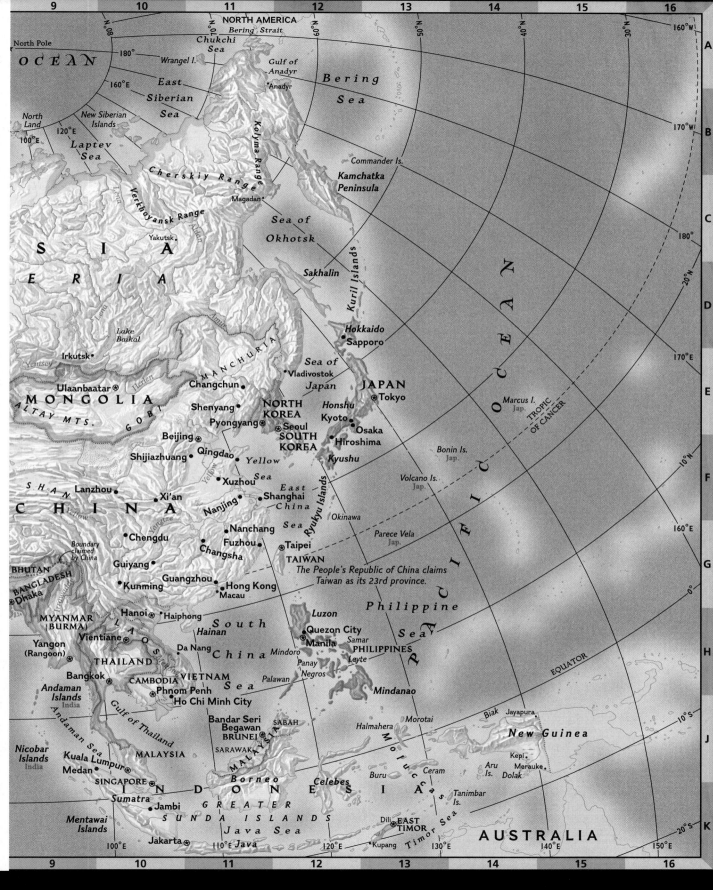

The People's Republic of China claims
Taiwan as its 23rd province.

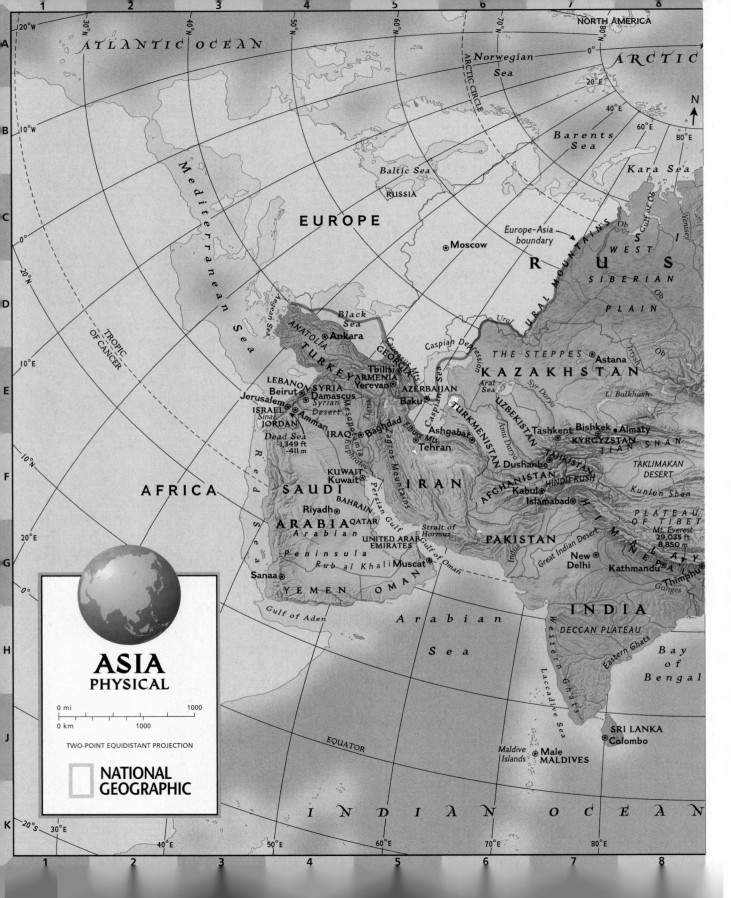

ASIA
PHYSICAL

0 mi   1000

0 km   1000

TWO-POINT EQUIDISTANT PROJECTION

NATIONAL
GEOGRAPHIC

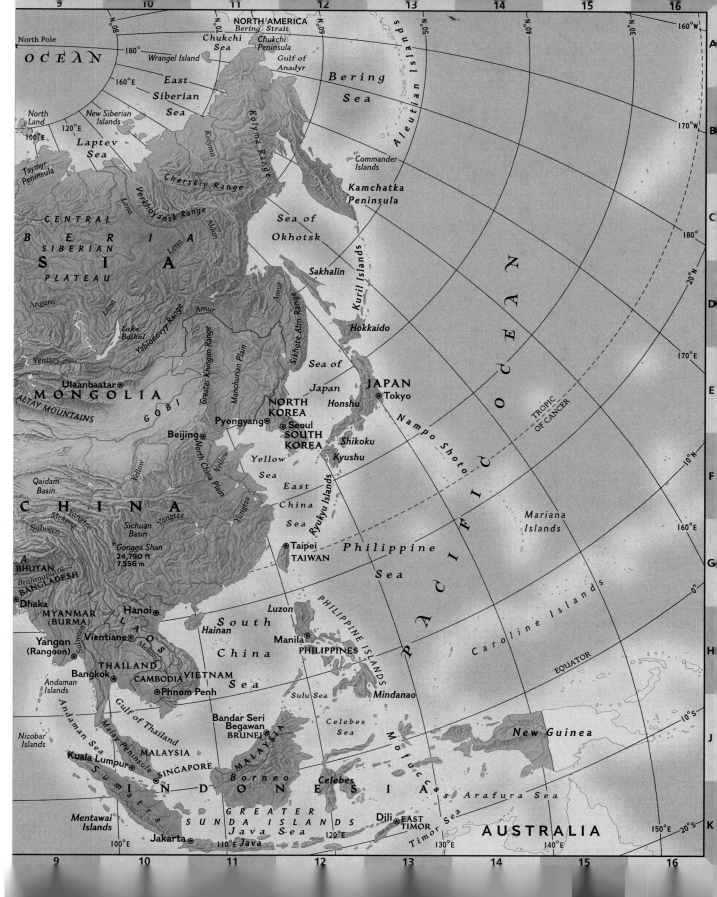

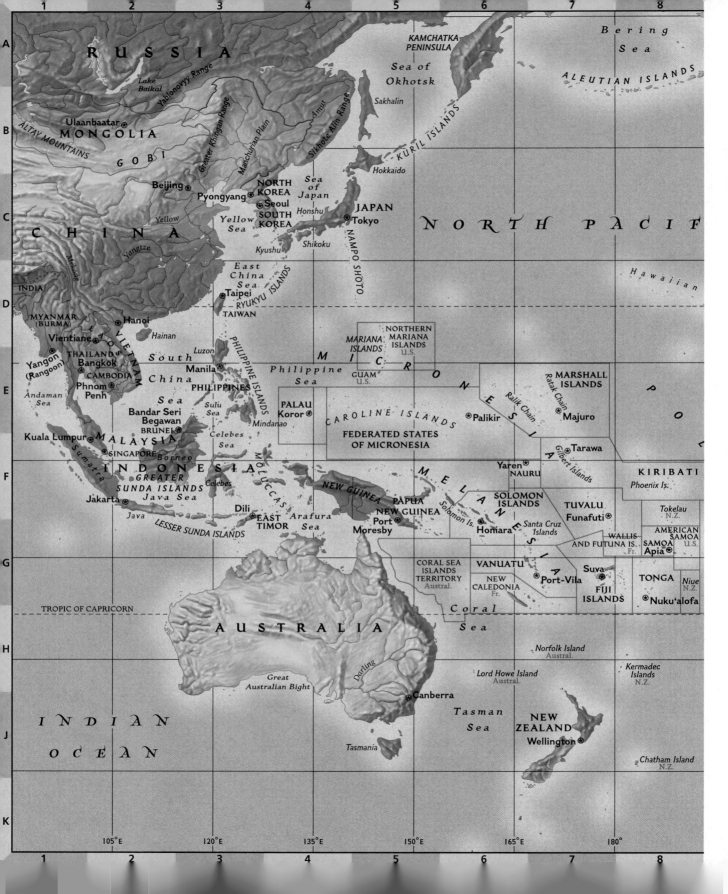

PACIFIC RIM
PHYSICAL/POLITICAL

0 mi   1500

0 km   1500

MILLER CYLINDRICAL PROJECTION

NATIONAL GEOGRAPHIC

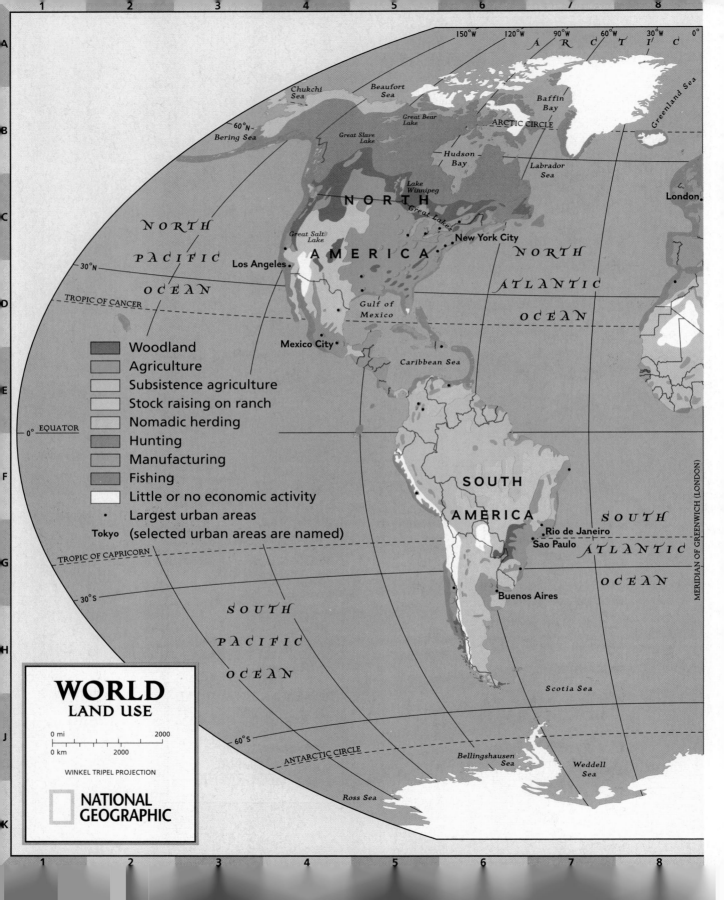

WORLD
LAND USE

Woodland
Agriculture
Subsistence agriculture
Stock raising on ranch
Nomadic herding
Hunting
Manufacturing
Fishing
Little or no economic activity
• Largest urban areas
Tokyo (selected urban areas are named)

0 mi   2000
0 km   2000

WINKEL TRIPEL PROJECTION

NATIONAL GEOGRAPHIC

A R C T I C

150°W   120°W   90°W   60°W   30°W   0°

Chukchi
Sea

Beaufort
Sea

Baffin
Bay

Greenland Sea

60°N
Bering Sea

Great Bear
Lake

ARCTIC CIRCLE

Great Slave
Lake

Hudson
Bay

Labrador
Sea

Lake
Winnipeg

N O R T H

Great Lakes

London

Great Salt
Lake

A M E R I C A

New York City

N O R T H

N O R T H

30°N

Los Angeles

P A C I F I C

A T L A N T I C

TROPIC OF CANCER

O C E A N

O C E A N

Gulf of
Mexico

Mexico City

Caribbean Sea

0° EQUATOR

S O U T H

A M E R I C A

S O U T H

F

Rio de Janeiro

Sao Paulo

A T L A N T I C

TROPIC OF CAPRICORN

MERIDIAN OF GREENWICH (LONDON)

G

O C E A N

30°S

S O U T H

Buenos Aires

P A C I F I C

H

O C E A N

Scotia Sea

J

60°S

ANTARCTIC CIRCLE

Bellingshausen
Sea

Weddell
Sea

K

Ross Sea

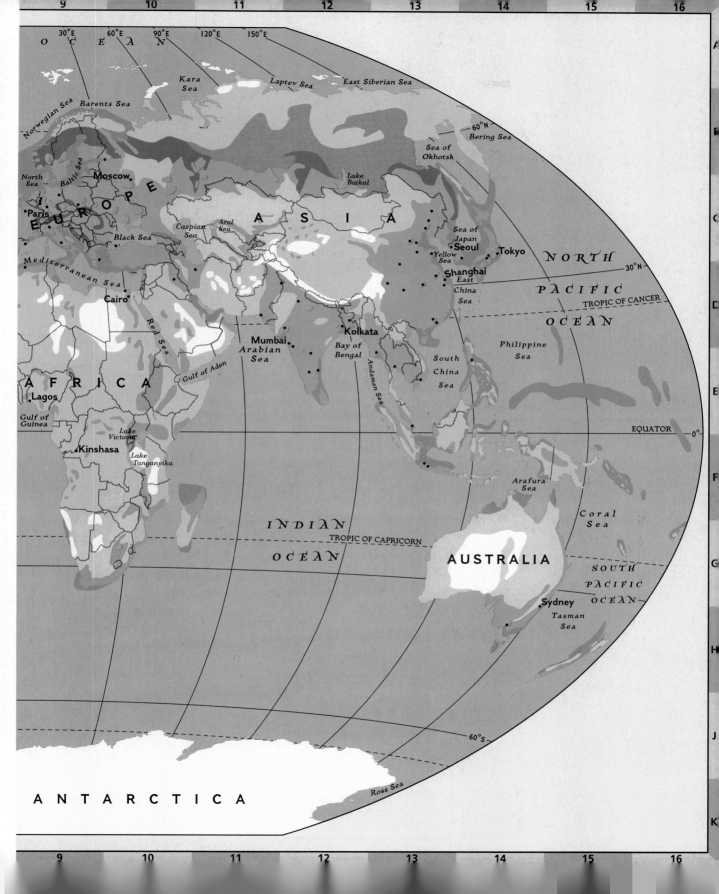

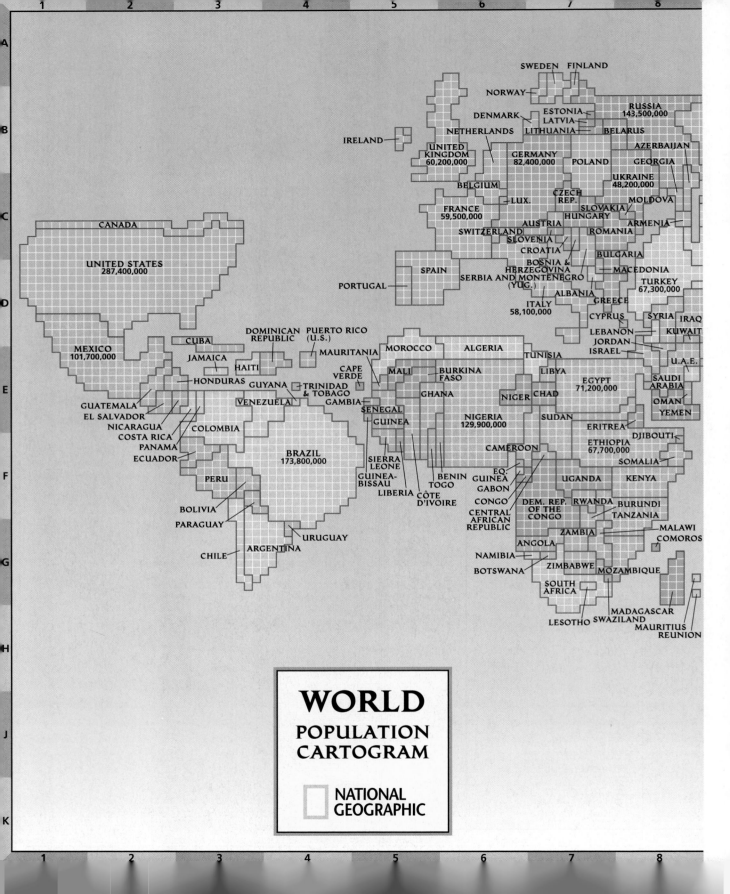

WORLD
POPULATION
CARTOGRAM

NATIONAL
GEOGRAPHIC

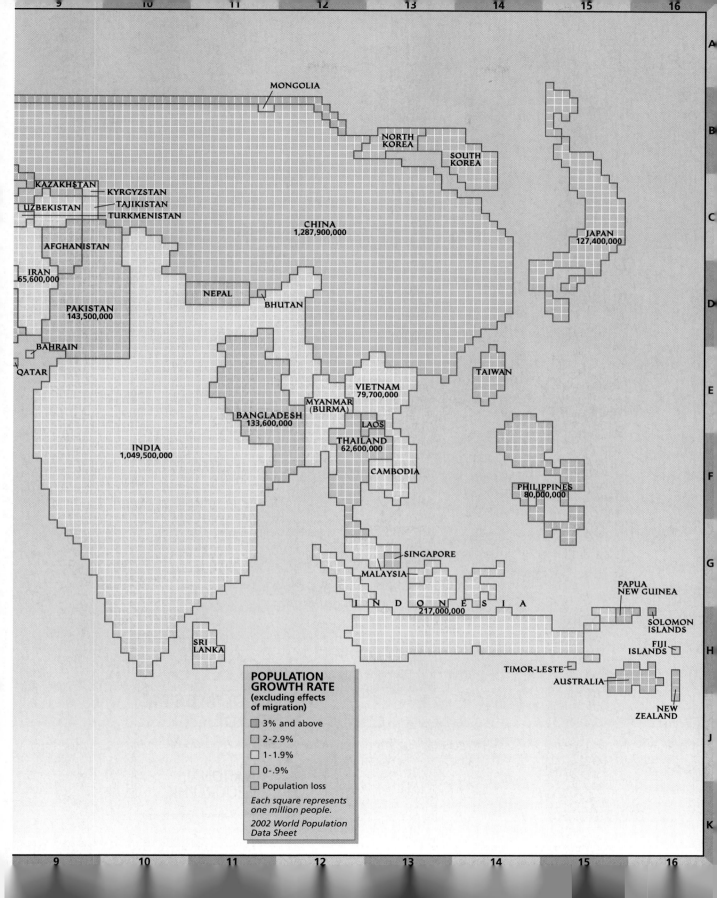

MONGOLIA

NORTH
KOREA

SOUTH
KOREA

JAPAN
127,400,000

KAZAKHSTAN
KYRGYZSTAN
UZBEKISTAN
TAJIKISTAN
TURKMENISTAN

CHINA
1,287,900,000

AFGHANISTAN

IRAN
65,600,000

NEPAL

BHUTAN

PAKISTAN
143,500,000

BAHRAIN

QATAR

VIETNAM
79,700,000

TAIWAN

MYANMAR
(BURMA)

BANGLADESH
133,600,000

LAOS

THAILAND
62,600,000

INDIA
1,049,500,000

CAMBODIA

PHILIPPINES
80,000,000

SINGAPORE

MALAYSIA

INDONESIA
217,000,000

PAPUA
NEW GUINEA

SOLOMON
ISLANDS

FIJI
ISLANDS

SRI
LANKA

TIMOR-LESTE

AUSTRALIA

NEW
ZEALAND

**POPULATION
GROWTH RATE**
(excluding effects
of migration)

☐ 3% and above

☐ 2-2.9%

☐ 1-1.9%

☐ 0-.9%

☐ Population loss

*Each square represents
one million people.*

*2002 World Population
Data Sheet*

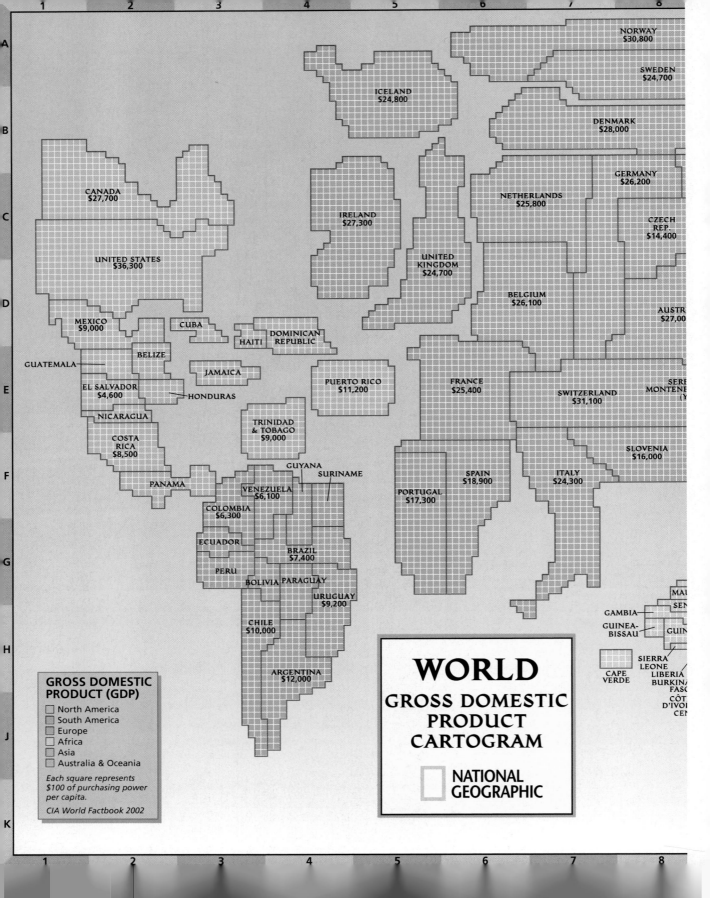

WORLD
GROSS DOMESTIC PRODUCT CARTOGRAM

NATIONAL GEOGRAPHIC

GROSS DOMESTIC PRODUCT (GDP)

- North America
- South America
- Europe
- Africa
- Asia
- Australia & Oceania

Each square represents $100 of purchasing power per capita.

CIA World Factbook 2002

NORWAY $30,800

SWEDEN $24,700

DENMARK $28,000

ICELAND $24,800

GERMANY $26,200

NETHERLANDS $25,800

CZECH REP. $14,400

IRELAND $27,300

CANADA $27,700

UNITED STATES $36,300

UNITED KINGDOM $24,700

BELGIUM $26,100

AUSTR $27,00

MEXICO $9,000

CUBA

DOMINICAN REPUBLIC

HAITI

GUATEMALA

BELIZE

JAMAICA

PUERTO RICO $11,200

FRANCE $25,400

SWITZERLAND $31,100

SERB MONTENE (Y)

EL SALVADOR $4,600

HONDURAS

NICARAGUA

COSTA RICA $8,500

TRINIDAD & TOBAGO $9,000

SLOVENIA $16,000

PANAMA

GUYANA

SURINAME

VENEZUELA $6,100

PORTUGAL $17,300

SPAIN $18,900

ITALY $24,300

COLOMBIA $6,300

ECUADOR

BRAZIL $7,400

PERU

BOLIVIA PARAGUAY

URUGUAY $9,200

MAU

SEN

GAMBIA

GUINEA-BISSAU

GUIN

CHILE $10,000

CAPE VERDE

SIERRA LEONE

LIBERIA

BURKINA FASO

CÔTE D'IVOI CEN

ARGENTINA $12,000

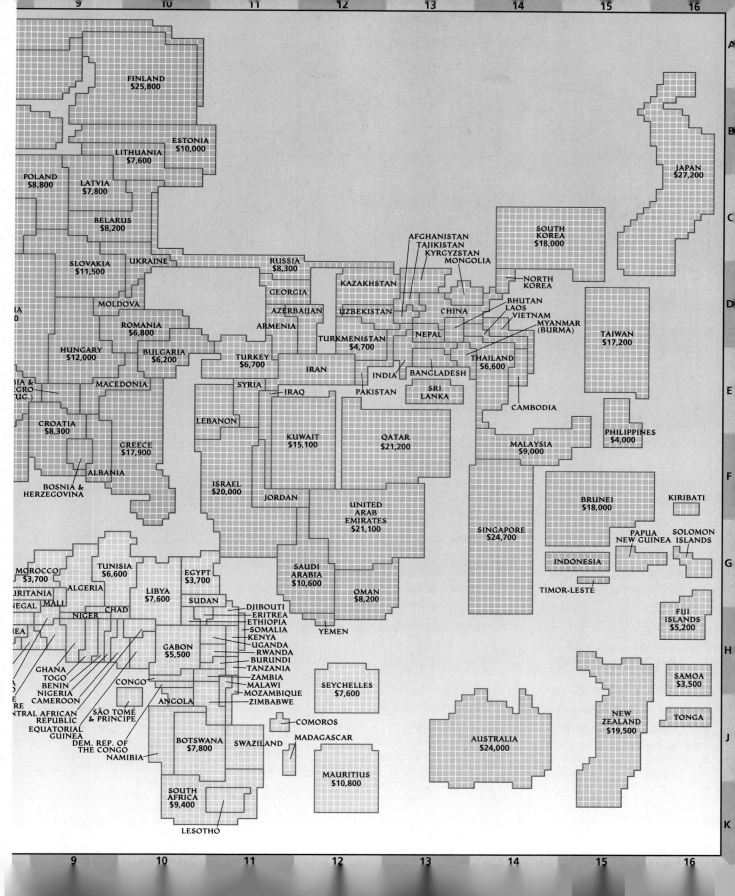

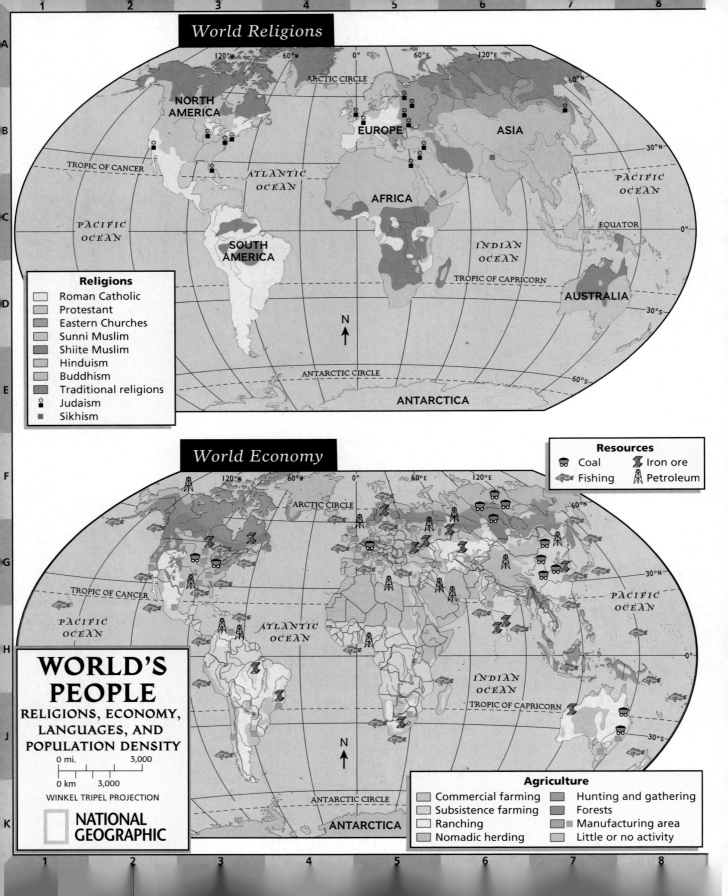

World Religions

Religions
- Roman Catholic
- Protestant
- Eastern Churches
- Sunni Muslim
- Shiite Muslim
- Hinduism
- Buddhism
- Traditional religions
- ☆ Judaism
- ▪ Sikhism

NORTH AMERICA
SOUTH AMERICA
EUROPE
ASIA
AFRICA
AUSTRALIA
ANTARCTICA

ARCTIC CIRCLE
TROPIC OF CANCER
ATLANTIC OCEAN
PACIFIC OCEAN
PACIFIC OCEAN
INDIAN OCEAN
EQUATOR
TROPIC OF CAPRICORN
ANTARCTIC CIRCLE

120°W 60°W 0° 60°E 120°E 60°N 30°N 0° 30°S 60°S

N

World Economy

Resources
- Coal
- Iron ore
- Fishing
- Petroleum

Agriculture
- Commercial farming
- Subsistence farming
- Ranching
- Nomadic herding
- Hunting and gathering
- Forests
- ▪ Manufacturing area
- Little or no activity

NORTH AMERICA
ARCTIC CIRCLE
TROPIC OF CANCER
ATLANTIC OCEAN
PACIFIC OCEAN
PACIFIC OCEAN
INDIAN OCEAN
TROPIC OF CAPRICORN
ANTARCTIC CIRCLE
ANTARCTICA

120°W 60°W 0° 60°E 120°E 60°N 30°N 0° 30°S

N

WORLD'S PEOPLE

RELIGIONS, ECONOMY, LANGUAGES, AND POPULATION DENSITY

0 mi. — 3,000
0 km — 3,000

WINKEL TRIPEL PROJECTION

NATIONAL GEOGRAPHIC

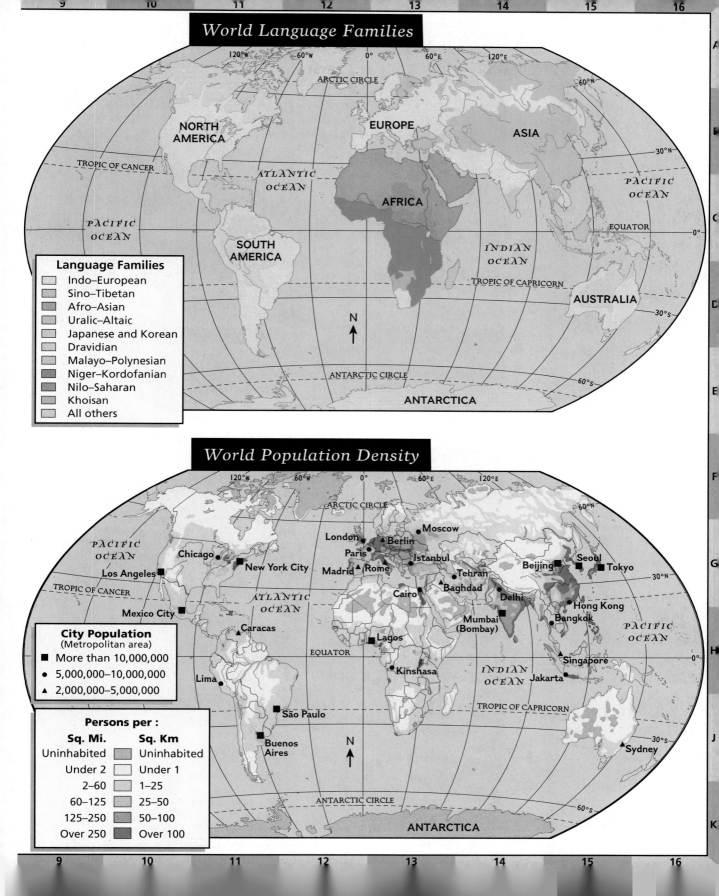

World Language Families

Language Families
- Indo–European
- Sino–Tibetan
- Afro–Asian
- Uralic–Altaic
- Japanese and Korean
- Dravidian
- Malayo–Polynesian
- Niger–Kordofanian
- Nilo–Saharan
- Khoisan
- All others

NORTH AMERICA
EUROPE
ASIA
AFRICA
SOUTH AMERICA
AUSTRALIA
ANTARCTICA

ATLANTIC OCEAN
PACIFIC OCEAN
PACIFIC OCEAN
INDIAN OCEAN

ARCTIC CIRCLE
TROPIC OF CANCER
EQUATOR
TROPIC OF CAPRICORN
ANTARCTIC CIRCLE

N

World Population Density

City Population
(Metropolitan area)
- ■ More than 10,000,000
- ● 5,000,000–10,000,000
- ▲ 2,000,000–5,000,000

Persons per :

Sq. Mi.	Sq. Km
Uninhabited	Uninhabited
Under 2	Under 1
2–60	1–25
60–125	25–50
125–250	50–100
Over 250	Over 100

Chicago
Los Angeles
New York City
Mexico City
Caracas
Lima
São Paulo
Buenos Aires
London
Paris
Madrid
Berlin
Rome
Moscow
Istanbul
Cairo
Baghdad
Tehran
Lagos
Kinshasa
Beijing
Seoul
Tokyo
Delhi
Mumbai (Bombay)
Hong Kong
Bangkok
Singapore
Jakarta
Sydney

PACIFIC OCEAN
ATLANTIC OCEAN
PACIFIC OCEAN
INDIAN OCEAN

ARCTIC CIRCLE
TROPIC OF CANCER
EQUATOR
TROPIC OF CAPRICORN
ANTARCTIC CIRCLE
ANTARCTICA

N

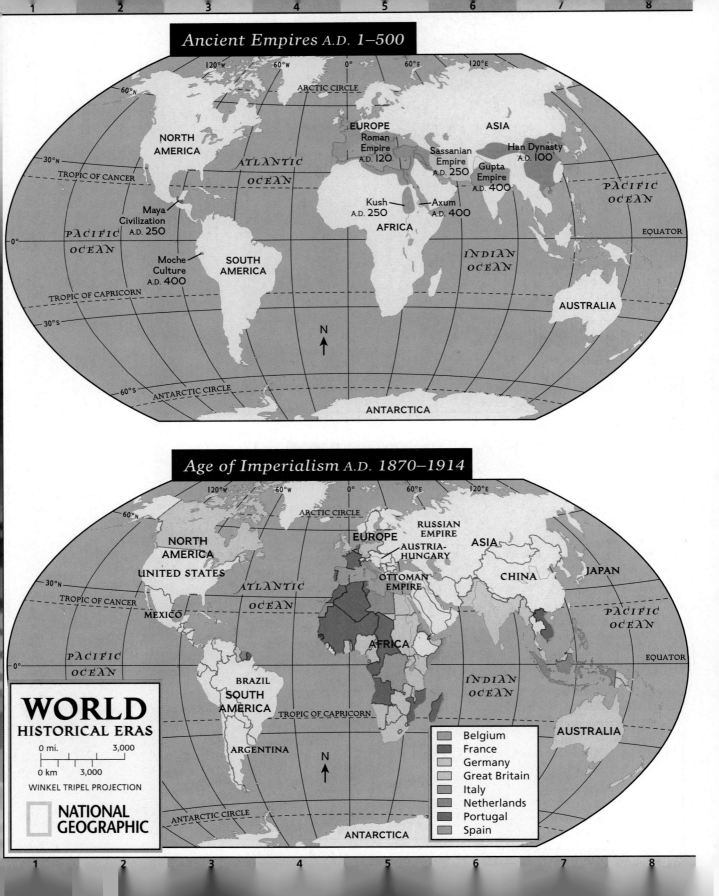

Ancient Empires A.D. 1–500

EUROPE
Roman Empire A.D. 120
Sassanian Empire A.D. 250
Gupta Empire A.D. 400
ASIA
Han Dynasty A.D. 100
NORTH AMERICA
ATLANTIC OCEAN
PACIFIC OCEAN
Maya Civilization A.D. 250
Moche Culture A.D. 400
Kush A.D. 250
Axum A.D. 400
AFRICA
SOUTH AMERICA
INDIAN OCEAN
PACIFIC OCEAN
AUSTRALIA
N
ANTARCTICA

ARCTIC CIRCLE
TROPIC OF CANCER
EQUATOR
TROPIC OF CAPRICORN
ANTARCTIC CIRCLE

Age of Imperialism A.D. 1870–1914

NORTH AMERICA
UNITED STATES
EUROPE
RUSSIAN EMPIRE
AUSTRIA-HUNGARY
OTTOMAN EMPIRE
ASIA
CHINA
JAPAN
MEXICO
ATLANTIC OCEAN
PACIFIC OCEAN
AFRICA
BRAZIL
SOUTH AMERICA
ARGENTINA
INDIAN OCEAN
PACIFIC OCEAN
AUSTRALIA
N
ANTARCTICA

ARCTIC CIRCLE
TROPIC OF CANCER
EQUATOR
TROPIC OF CAPRICORN
ANTARCTIC CIRCLE

WORLD
HISTORICAL ERAS

0 mi.   3,000
0 km   3,000
WINKEL TRIPEL PROJECTION

NATIONAL GEOGRAPHIC

■	Belgium
■	France
■	Germany
■	Great Britain
■	Italy
■	Netherlands
■	Portugal
■	Spain

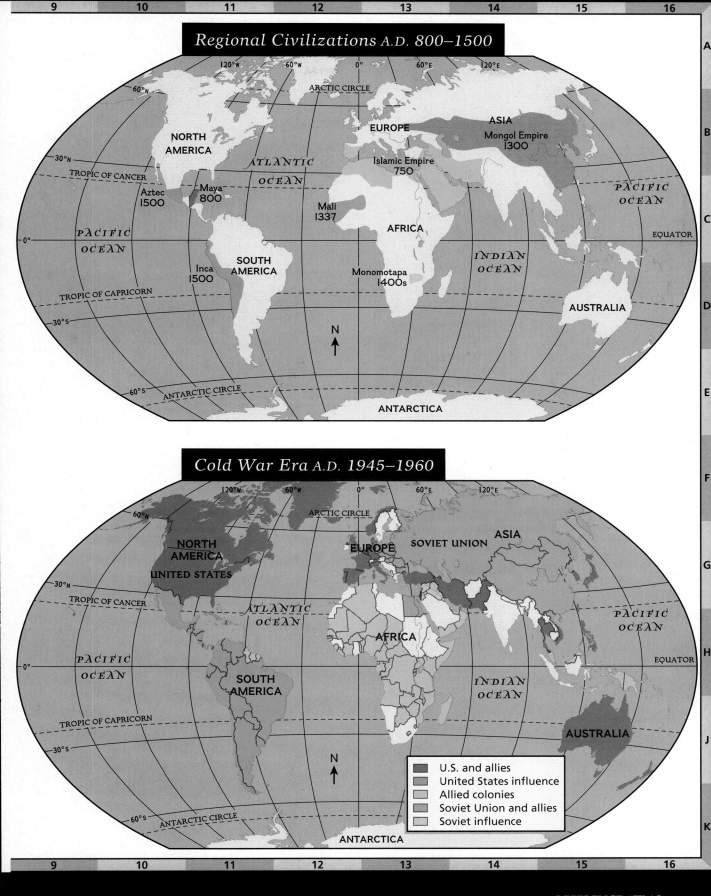

Regional Civilizations A.D. 800–1500

NORTH AMERICA

EUROPE

ASIA
Mongol Empire
1300

Islamic Empire
750

ATLANTIC OCEAN

Aztec
1500

Maya
800

Mali
1337

AFRICA

PACIFIC OCEAN

PACIFIC OCEAN

Inca
1500

SOUTH AMERICA

Monomotapa
1400s

INDIAN OCEAN

AUSTRALIA

ANTARCTICA

ARCTIC CIRCLE
TROPIC OF CANCER
EQUATOR
TROPIC OF CAPRICORN
ANTARCTIC CIRCLE

Cold War Era A.D. 1945–1960

NORTH AMERICA
UNITED STATES

EUROPE

SOVIET UNION

ASIA

ATLANTIC OCEAN

AFRICA

PACIFIC OCEAN

PACIFIC OCEAN

SOUTH AMERICA

INDIAN OCEAN

AUSTRALIA

ANTARCTICA

ARCTIC CIRCLE
TROPIC OF CANCER
EQUATOR
TROPIC OF CAPRICORN
ANTARCTIC CIRCLE

- U.S. and allies
- United States influence
- Allied colonies
- Soviet Union and allies
- Soviet influence

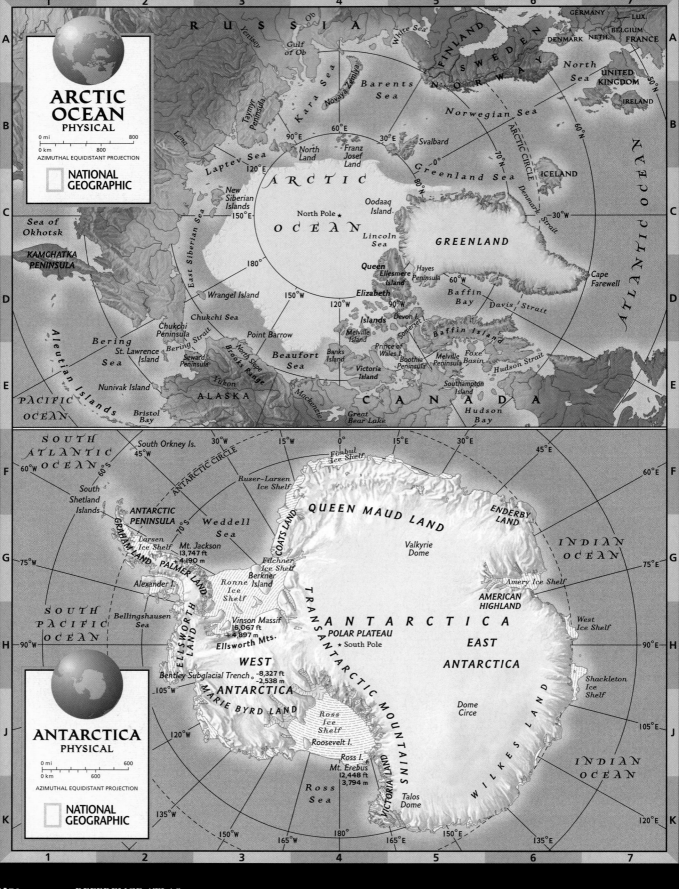

ARCTIC OCEAN
PHYSICAL

0 mi — 800
0 km — 800
AZIMUTHAL EQUIDISTANT PROJECTION

NATIONAL GEOGRAPHIC

R U S S I A

GERMANY · LUX.
DENMARK · NETH. · BELGIUM · FRANCE

Ob
Gulf of Ob
Yenisey
White Sea
FINLAND
SWEDEN
NORWAY
DENMARK
NORTH Sea
UNITED KINGDOM
IRELAND

Taymyr Peninsula
Kara Sea
Novaya Zemlya
Barents Sea
Norwegian Sea
ARCTIC CIRCLE
ICELAND

Lena
Laptev Sea
North Land
Franz Josef Land
Svalbard
Greenland Sea
ARCTIC OCEAN
ATLANTIC OCEAN

New Siberian Islands
A R C T I C   O C E A N
Oodaaq Island
Lincoln Sea
GREENLAND

North Pole ★

Sea of Okhotsk
East Siberian Sea
Wrangel Island
Queen Ellesmere Island
Hayes Peninsula
Cape Farewell

KAMCHATKA PENINSULA
Chukchi Sea
Elizabeth
Baffin Bay
Davis Strait

Chukchi Peninsula
Point Barrow
Islands
Devon I.
Somerset I.
Baffin Island

Bering Strait
North Slope
Beaufort Sea
Banks Island
Melville Island
Prince of Wales I.
Boothia Peninsula
Melville Peninsula
Foxe Basin

Bering Sea
St. Lawrence Island
Seward Peninsula
Brooks Range
Victoria Island
Southampton Island
Hudson Strait

Aleutian Islands
Nunivak Island
Yukon
A L A S K A
Mackenzie
C A N A D A
Hudson Bay

PACIFIC OCEAN
Bristol Bay
Great Bear Lake

90°E · 60°E · 30°E · 0° · 30°W · 60°N · 50°N
120°E · 150°E · 180° · 150°W · 120°W · 90°W · 60°W · 70°N · 80°N

ANTARCTICA
PHYSICAL

0 mi — 600
0 km — 600
AZIMUTHAL EQUIDISTANT PROJECTION

NATIONAL GEOGRAPHIC

SOUTH ATLANTIC OCEAN
South Orkney Is.
ANTARCTIC CIRCLE

South Shetland Islands
ANTARCTIC PENINSULA
GRAHAM LAND
Larsen Ice Shelf
Mt. Jackson 13,747 ft 4,190 m
Weddell Sea
Ruser-Larsen Ice Shelf
Fimbul Ice Shelf
QUEEN MAUD LAND
COATS LAND
ENDERBY LAND
INDIAN OCEAN

Alexander I.
PALMER LAND
Filchner Ice Shelf
Berkner Island
Ronne Ice Shelf
Valkyrie Dome
Amery Ice Shelf

SOUTH PACIFIC OCEAN
Bellingshausen Sea
ELLSWORTH LAND
Vinson Massif 16,067 ft 4,897 m
Ellsworth Mts.
A N T A R C T I C A
TRANSANTARCTIC MOUNTAINS
POLAR PLATEAU
★ South Pole
EAST ANTARCTICA
AMERICAN HIGHLAND
West Ice Shelf

WEST ANTARCTICA
Bentley Subglacial Trench -8,327 ft -2,538 m
Shackleton Ice Shelf

MARIE BYRD LAND
Ross Ice Shelf
Roosevelt I.
Ross I.
Dome Circe
WILKES LAND

Ross Sea
Mt. Erebus 12,448 ft 3,794 m
VICTORIA LAND
Talos Dome
INDIAN OCEAN

60°W · 30°W · 45°W · 15°W · 0° · 15°E · 30°E · 45°E · 60°E · 75°E
75°W · 90°W · 105°W · 120°W · 135°W · 150°W · 165°W · 180° · 165°E · 150°E · 135°E · 120°E · 105°E · 90°E
60°S · 70°S

NATIONAL GEOGRAPHIC

Geography Handbook

The story of the world begins with geography—the study of the earth in all of its variety. Geography describes the earth's land, water, and plant and animal life. It is the study of places and the complex relationships between people and their environment.

The resources in this handbook will help you get the most out of your textbook—and provide you with skills you will use for the rest of your life.

The Gui River, Guilin, China ▼

▲ Saharan sand dunes, Morocco

The Amazon, Brazil ▶

I Study Geography?

To understand how our world is connected, some geographers have divided the study of geography into five themes. **The Five Themes of Geography are** (1) location, (2) place, (3) human/environmental interaction, (4) movement, and (5) regions.

Six Essential Elements

Recently geographers have broken down the study of geography into **Six Essential Elements.** Being aware of these elements will help you better understand and organize what you are learning about geography.

Element 2

Places and Regions
Place has a special meaning in geography. It means more than where a place is. It also describes what a place is like. Physical characteristics such as landforms, climate, and plant or animal life help geographers distinguish different kinds of places. Human characteristics, including language and way of life, also describe places.

Geographers often group places or areas into regions. **Regions** are united by one or more common characteristics.

Element 1

The World in Spatial Terms
Geographers first take a look at where a place is located. **Location** serves as a starting point by defining where a place is. Knowing the location of places helps you develop an awareness of the world around you.

Element 3

Physical Systems
When studying places and regions, geographers analyze how **physical systems**—such as hurricanes, volcanoes, and glaciers—shape the earth's surface. As part of their study of physical systems, geographers look at communities of plants and animals that depend upon one another and their surroundings for survival.

Element 4

Human Systems

Geographers also examine **human systems,** or how people have shaped our world. Geographers look at how boundary lines are determined and analyze why people settle in certain places and not in others. A key theme in geography is the continual **movement** of people, ideas, and goods.

Element 5

Environment and Society

How does the relationship between people and their natural surroundings influence the way people live? Geographers study how people use the **environment** and how their actions affect the environment.

Element 6

The Uses of Geography

How does a war in the Middle East affect the economy of the United States? Knowing **how to use geography** helps people understand the relationships between people, places, and environments over time. Learning how to study geography also prepares you for life in our modern society.

Photographs from space show Earth in its true form—a great ball spinning around the Sun. The most accurate way to depict the earth is as a **globe,** a spherical scale model of the earth. A globe gives a true picture of the continents' relative sizes and the shapes of landmasses and bodies of water. Globes are proportionately correct, accurately representing distance and direction.

A **map** is a flat drawing of all or part of the earth's surface. Unlike globes, maps can show small areas in great detail. People use maps to locate places, plot routes, and judge distances. Maps can also display useful information, such as political boundaries, population densities, or even voting returns.

From Globes to Maps

Maps, however, do have their limitations. As you can imagine, drawing a round object on a flat surface is very difficult. Think about the surface of the earth as the peel of an orange. To flatten the peel, you might have to cut it like the globe shown here. **Cartographers,** or mapmakers, use mathematical formulas to transfer information from the three-dimensional globe to a two-dimensional map. However, when the curves of a globe become straight lines on a map, distortion of size, shape, distance, or area occurs.

How Map Projections Work

To create maps, cartographers *project* the round earth onto a flat surface—making a **map projection.** There are more than a hundred kinds of map projections, each with some advantages and some degrees of accuracy. The purpose of the map usually dictates which projection is used. Three of the basic categories of projections used are shown here: **planar, cylindrical,** and **conic.**

Planar Projection

Planar projections show the earth centered in such a way that a straight line going from the center to any other point on the map represents the shortest distance. Since they are most accurate at the center, they are often used for maps of the Poles.

Great Circle Routes

A *great circle* is an imaginary line that follows the curve of the earth. A line drawn along the Equator is an example of a great circle. Traveling along a great circle is called following a **great circle route.** Airplane pilots use great circle routes because they represent the shortest distances from one city to the next.

The idea of a great circle shows one important difference between a globe and a map. Because a globe is round, it accurately shows great circles. On a flat map, however, the great circle route between two points may not appear to be the shortest distance. For example, on map A the great circle distance (dotted line) between Tokyo and Los Angeles appears to be far longer than the true direction distance (solid line). In fact, the great circle distance is 345 miles (555 km) shorter, which is evident on map B.

Geographic Information Systems

Technology has changed the way maps are made. Most cartographers use software programs called **geographic information systems (GIS).** A GIS uses data from maps, satellite images, printed text, and statistics. Cartographers can program the GIS to produce the maps they need, and it allows them to make changes quickly and easily.

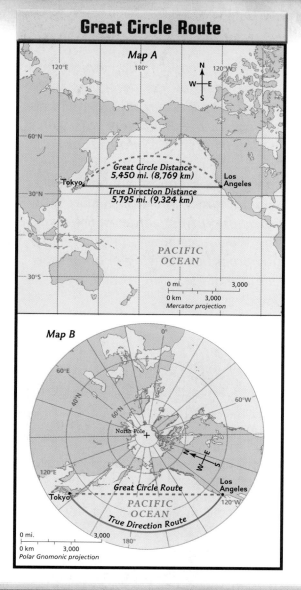

Great Circle Route

Map A

Great Circle Distance
5,450 mi. (8,769 km)

True Direction Distance
5,795 mi. (9,324 km)

Tokyo — Los Angeles

PACIFIC OCEAN

0 mi. — 3,000
0 km — 3,000
Mercator projection

Map B

North Pole

Great Circle Route

Tokyo — Los Angeles

PACIFIC OCEAN

True Direction Route

0 mi. — 3,000
0 km — 3,000
Polar Gnomonic projection

Cylindrical Projection

Cylindrical projections are based on the projection of the globe onto a cylinder. They are most accurate near the Equator, but shapes and distances are distorted near the Poles.

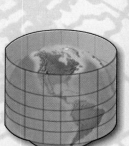

EQUATOR

Conic Projection

Conic projections are made by placing a cone over part of the globe. They are best suited for showing east-west areas that are not too far from the Equator. For these uses, a conic projection can indicate distances and directions fairly accurately.

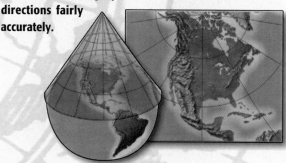

Map Projections

Four of the most popular map projections are named for the cartographers who developed them. These are the **Winkel Tripel** projection, the **Robinson** projection, **Goode's Interrupted Equal-Area** projection, and the **Mercator** projection. Remember, all map projections have some degree of inaccuracy in distance, shape, or size because the curved surface of the earth cannot be shown accurately on a flat map. Every map projection stretches or breaks the curved surface of the earth in some way.

Winkel Tripel Projection

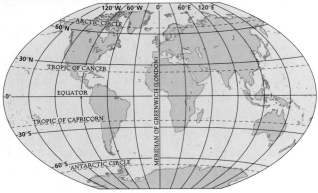

▲ Most reference world maps use the Winkel Tripel projection. Adopted by the National Geographic Society in 1998 for use in most maps, this projection provides a good balance between the size and shape of land areas as they are shown on the map. Even the polar areas are depicted with little distortion of size and shape.

Reading a Map

Maps include several important tools to help you interpret the information contained on a particular map. Learning to use these map tools will help you read the symbolic language of maps more easily.

Compass Rose A compass rose is a marker that indicates directions. The four cardinal directions—north, south, east, and west—are usually indicated with arrows or points of a star. Sometimes a compass rose may point in only one direction because the other directions can be determined in relation to the given direction. The compass rose on this map indicates all four cardinal directions.

Key Cartographers use a variety of symbols to represent map information. Because these symbols are graphic and commonly used, most maps can be read and understood by people around the world. To be sure that the symbols are clear, however, every map contains a key—a list that explains what the symbols stand for. This key shows symbols used for a battle map. It indicates troop movements, supply lines, and U.S. bases.

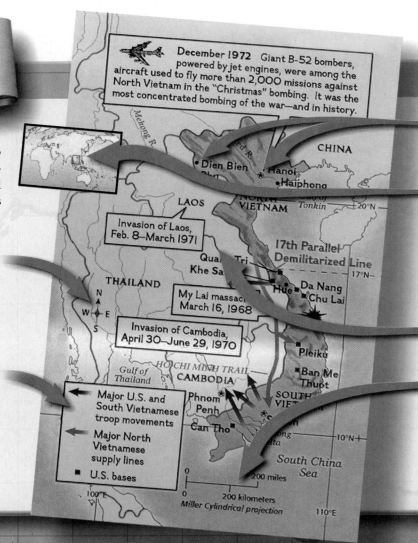

Robinson Projection

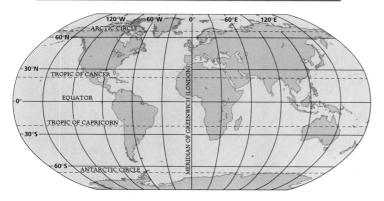

▲ The Robinson projection has minor distortions. The sizes and shapes near the eastern and western edges of the map are accurate, and the outlines of the continents appear much as they do on the globe. However, the shapes of the polar areas appear somewhat flat.

Goode's Interrupted Equal-Area Projection

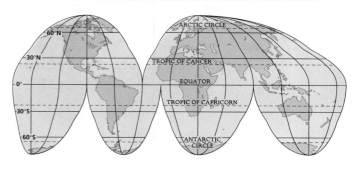

▲ An interrupted projection looks something like a globe that has been cut apart and laid flat. Goode's Interrupted Equal-Area projection shows the true size and shape of the earth's landmasses, but distances are distorted.

Cities and Capitals Cities are symbolized by a solid circle. Sometimes the relative sizes of cities are shown with circles of different sizes. Capitals are represented by a star within a circle.

Relative Location People use relative direction to indicate location. You may be told, for example, to look for a street that is "two blocks north" of another street. Relative location is the location of one place in relation to another place, while absolute location indicates the exact position of a place on the earth's surface. On this map, the relative position of where the Vietnam War took place is given in relation to the rest of the world.

Boundary Lines On political maps of large areas, boundary lines highlight the borders between different countries, states, provinces, or counties.

Scale Bar Every map is a representation of a part of the earth. The scale bar shows the relationship between map measurements and actual distance. Scale can be measured with a ruler to calculate actual distances in standard or metric measurements. On this map, three-fourths inch represents 200 miles (322 km).

Mercator Projection

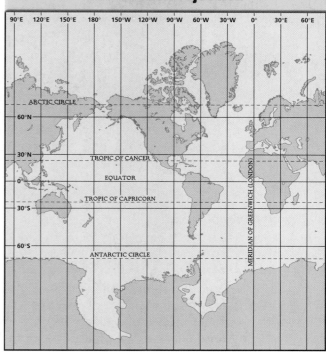

▲ The Mercator projection, once the most commonly used projection, increasingly distorts size and distance as it moves away from the Equator. This makes areas such as Greenland and Antarctica look much larger than they would appear on a globe. However, Mercator projections do accurately show true directions and the shapes of landmasses, making these maps useful for sea travel.

Latitude and Longitude

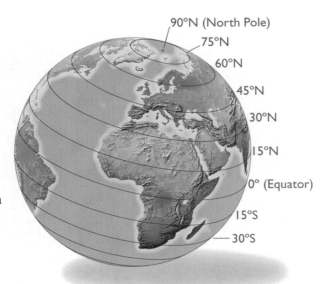

Lines on globes and maps provide information that can help you easily locate places on the earth. These lines—called *latitude* and *longitude*—cross one another, forming a pattern called a grid system.

Latitude

Lines of latitude, or **parallels,** circle the earth parallel to the **Equator** and measure the distance north or south of the Equator in degrees. The Equator is at 0° latitude, while the Poles lie at latitudes 90°N (north) and 90°S (south).

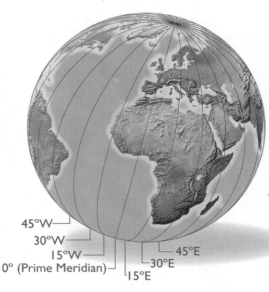

Longitude

Lines of longitude, or **meridians,** circle the earth from Pole to Pole. These lines measure distances east or west of the starting line, which is at 0° longitude and is called the **Prime Meridian.** The Prime Meridian runs through the Royal Observatory in Greenwich, England.

Absolute Location

The grid system formed by lines of latitude and longitude makes it possible to find the absolute location of a place. Many places can be found along a line of latitude, but only one place can be found at the point where a certain line of latitude crosses a certain line of longitude. By using degrees and minutes (points between degrees), people can pinpoint the precise spot where one line of latitude crosses one line of longitude—an absolute location.

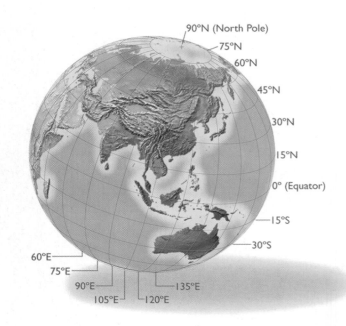

Types of Maps

Maps are prepared for many uses. The information depicted in the map depends on how the map will be used. Learning to recognize a map's purpose will help you make the best use of its content.

General-Purpose Maps

Maps that show a wide range of general information about an area are called **general-purpose** maps. Two of the most common general-purpose maps are physical maps and political maps.

Physical maps show the location and the topography, or shape, of the earth's physical features. They use colors or patterns to indicate relief—the differences in elevation, or height, of landforms.

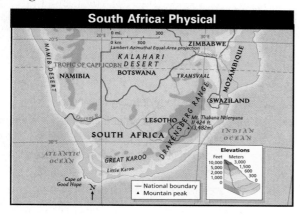

Political maps show the boundaries between countries. Smaller internal divisions, such as states or counties, may also be indicated by different symbols. Political maps usually feature capitals and other cities.

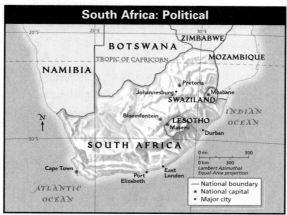

Special-Purpose Maps

Special-purpose maps show information on specific topics, such as climate, land use, or vegetation. Human activities, such as exploration routes, territorial expansion, or battle sites, also appear on special-purpose maps. Colors and map key symbols are especially important on this type of map.

LANDSAT Maps

LANDSAT maps are made from photographs by camera-carrying LANDSAT satellites in space. The cameras record millions of energy waves invisible to the human eye. Computers then change this information into pictures of the earth's surface. With LANDSAT images, scientists can study whole mountain ranges, oceans, and geographic regions. Changes to the earth's environment can also be tracked using the satellite information.

LANDSAT image, Mt. St. Helens, Washington ▼

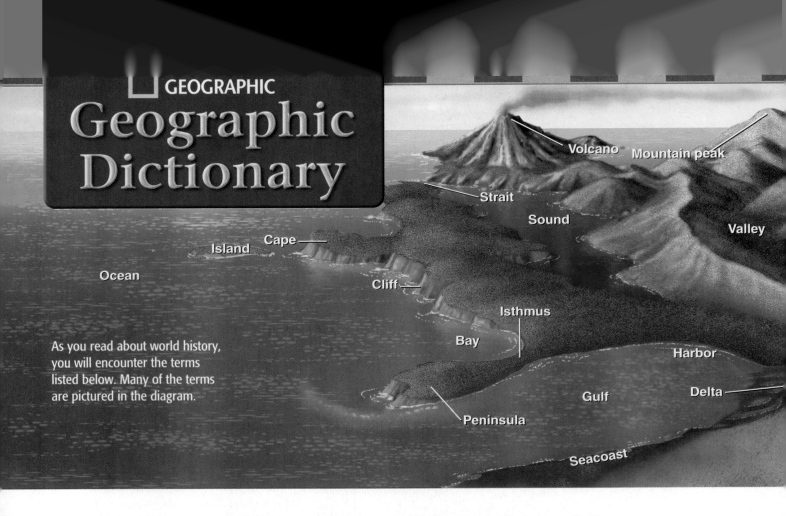

GEOGRAPHIC
Geographic Dictionary

As you read about world history, you will encounter the terms listed below. Many of the terms are pictured in the diagram.

absolute location exact location of a place on the earth described by global coordinates

basin area of land drained by a given river and its branches; area of land surrounded by lands of higher elevation

bay part of a large body of water that extends into a shoreline, generally smaller than a gulf

canyon deep and narrow valley with steep walls

cape point of land that extends into a river, lake, or ocean

channel wide strait or waterway between two landmasses that lie close to each other; deep part of a river or other waterway

cliff steep, high wall of rock, earth, or ice

continent one of the seven large landmasses on the earth

cultural feature characteristic that humans have created in a place, such as language, religion, housing, and settlement pattern

delta flat, low-lying land built up from soil carried downstream by a river and deposited at its mouth

divide stretch of high land that separates river systems

downstream direction in which a river or stream flows from its source to its mouth

elevation height of land above sea level

Equator imaginary line that runs around the earth halfway between the North and South Poles; used as the starting point to measure degrees of north and south latitude

glacier large, thick body of slowly moving ice

gulf part of a large body of water that extends into a shoreline, generally larger and more deeply indented than a bay

harbor a sheltered place along a shoreline where ships can anchor safely

highland elevated land area such as a hill, mountain, or plateau

hill elevated land with sloping sides and rounded summit; generally smaller than a mountain

island land area, smaller than a continent, completely surrounded by water

isthmus narrow stretch of land connecting two larger land areas

lake a sizable inland body of water

latitude distance north or south of the Equator, measured in degrees

longitude distance east or west of the Prime Meridian, measured in degrees

lowland land, usually level, at a low elevation

map drawing of the earth shown on a flat surface

meridian one of many lines on the global grid running from the North Pole to the South Pole; used to measure degrees of longitude

mesa broad, flat-topped landform with steep sides; smaller than a plateau

mountain land with steep sides that rises sharply (1,000 feet

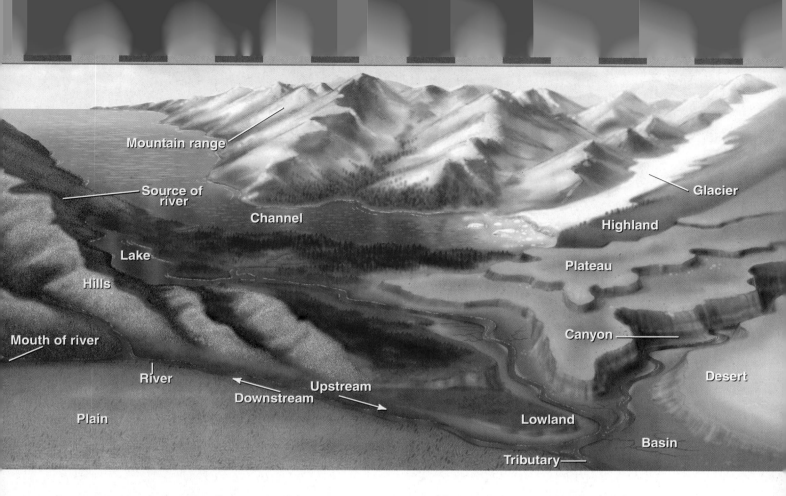

Mountain range

Source of river

Channel

Glacier

Highland

Lake

Plateau

Hills

Mouth of river

Canyon

River

Upstream

Desert

Downstream

Plain

Lowland

Basin

Tributary

[305 m] or more) from surrounding land; generally larger and more rugged than a hill

mountain peak pointed top of a mountain

mountain range a series of connected mountains

mouth (of a river) place where a stream or river flows into a larger body of water

ocean one of the four major bodies of salt water that surround the continents

ocean current stream of either cold or warm water that moves in a definite direction through an ocean

parallel one of many lines on the global grid that circle the earth north or south of the Equator; used to measure degrees of latitude

peninsula body of land jutting into a lake or ocean, surrounded on three sides by water

physical feature characteristic of a place occurring naturally, such as a landform, body of water, climate pattern, or resource

plain area of level land, usually at a low elevation and often covered with grasses

plateau area of flat or rolling land at a high elevation, about 300–3,000 feet (91–914 m) high

Prime Meridian line of the global grid running from the North Pole to the South Pole at Greenwich, England; starting point for measuring degrees of east and west longitude

relief changes in elevation over a given area of land

river large natural stream of water that runs through the land

sea large body of water completely or partly surrounded by land

seacoast land lying next to a sea or ocean

sea level position on land level with surface of nearby ocean or sea

sound body of water between a coastline and one or more islands off the coast

source (of a river) place where a river or stream begins, often in highlands

strait narrow stretch of water joining two larger bodies of water

tributary small river or stream that flows into a larger river or stream; a branch of the river

upstream direction opposite the flow of a river; toward the source of a river or stream

valley area of low land between hills or mountains

volcano mountain created as liquid rock or ash erupts from inside the earth

1 The First Civilizations and Empires

Prehistory–A.D. 500

The **P**eriod in Perspective

For hundreds of thousands of years, human beings lived in small communities, seeking to survive by hunting, fishing, and gathering food and supplies in an often hostile environment. Then, in the space of a few thousand years, there was an abrupt change of direction. Human beings in a few widely scattered areas of the globe began to master the art of growing food crops. As more food was produced, the population in these areas grew, and people began to live in cities, form governments, and develop writing and art. Historians call this process the beginnings of civilization. It occurred at about the same time in the river valleys of Western Asia, Egypt, India, and China.

Primary Sources Library

See pages 990–991 for primary source readings to accompany Unit 1.

*Use The World History **Primary Source Document Library CD-ROM** to find additional primary sources about The First Civilizations and Empires.*

▲ Grecian urns and pottery were often used to portray mythological scenes.

▶ The temple at Delphi was built to honor the Greek god Apollo.

"*...let no day pass without discussing goodness...*"

—Socrates, *The Apology*

Systems of Law

Law is a code of conduct and rights recognized by a society. It provides social control, order, and justice, and it enables people to know their rights and responsibilities. Law is also the cornerstone of a constitutional government, helping to ensure justice and fair treatment of all citizens. "Where law ends, tyranny begins," said William Pitt, an English leader in 1770.

451–450 B.C.
Twelve Tables posted
in Rome

A.D. 120
Roman law governs
the Mediterranean world

A.D. 533–534
Justinian Code
established

❶ *Roman Republic*

Laying the Foundation

Around 451–450 B.C., a group of judges posted 12 tablets in Rome's main forum, or marketplace. According to legend, the common people of Rome had demanded that the laws be written down for all to see, so that they would then know their rights.

The Twelve Tables, as they were called, remained in effect for almost 1,000 years. When Roman armies conquered other nations, they brought their laws with them. By A.D. 120, the entire Mediterranean world was governed by Roman law.

The Romans developed important legal principles: the law applied to all people regardless of wealth or power, and people should be ruled by law rather than the whims of their leaders. In A.D. 533–534, the Byzantine emperor Justinian consolidated all Roman law into a single written code. The Justinian Code, *The Body of Civil Law* as it is properly named, became the foundation of today's civil law system.

Justinian Code

Preamble to the United States Constitution

❷ *The United States*

A Model for Constitutional Government

The founders of the United States knew about and admired the Romans and their belief in limiting the power of government. When it came time to draw up a plan of government, the Framers wrote a constitution that balanced the powers of government among three branches.

To ensure that elected leaders did not place themselves above the law, the Framers included a provision that made the Constitution "the supreme law of the land." The Constitution was adopted on September 17, 1787.

A.D. 1787
United States
Constitution adopted

A.D. 1804
Napoleonic Code
established in France

❸ *France*

Unifying the Law

In 1799, a French general named Napoleon Bonaparte set out to build an empire even larger than Rome's. To rule this empire, Napoleon followed the Roman example. He appointed a commission to write a uniform code of laws. This code, known as the Napoleonic Code, was completed in 1804.

Although Napoleon ruled as emperor, he drew upon many of the legal precedents first introduced by the Romans. This included the principle that the same laws should be used to govern all people. Under Napoleon, this code was adopted in areas across the globe, such as present-day Belgium, Spain, and Latin America.

Napoleon Bonaparte

Why It Matters

The Romans developed the principle that people should be ruled by law rather than by the whims of leaders. How did the United States ensure that leaders would not place themselves above the law?

The First Humans

Prehistory–3500 B.C.

Key Events

As you read, look for the key events in the history of early humans and the beginnings of civilization.
- *Paleolithic peoples learned how to adapt to their nomadic lifestyle, improve on their primitive tools, and use fire to their advantage, thus enabling them to create a more sophisticated human culture.*
- *The agricultural revolution of the Neolithic Age gave rise to more complex human societies that became known as the first civilizations.*

The Impact Today

The events that occurred during this time period still impact our lives today.
- *Scientists continue to search for the remains of early humans, and their discoveries are changing the way we view the first humans.*
- *Paleolithic peoples used technological inventions to change their physical environment, just as humans do today.*

 World History Video *The Chapter 1 video, "Before History," chronicles the spread of humans and the emergence of the first cities and civilizations.*

Archaeologists reconstructing a human skeleton

3,000,000 B.C.
Australopithecines
flourish in Africa

1,500,000 B.C.
Homo erectus
appears

3,600,000 B.C.	2,000,000 B.C.	200,000 B.C.

2,500,000 B.C.
Paleolithic Age
begins

250,000 B.C.
Homo sapiens
species emerges

Paleolithic Era stone tools

Archaeologists excavate a cave used by Neanderthals more than 60,000 years ago.

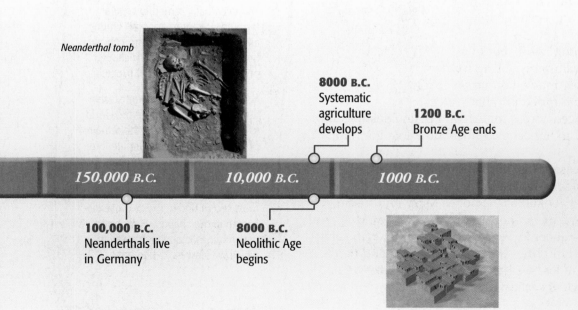

Neanderthal tomb

8000 B.C.
Systematic agriculture develops

1200 B.C.
Bronze Age ends

150,000 B.C.   *10,000 B.C.*   *1000 B.C.*

100,000 B.C.
Neanderthals live in Germany

8000 B.C.
Neolithic Age begins

Reconstruction of Çatal Hüyük

HISTORY
Online

Chapter Overview
Visit the *Glencoe World History* Web site at tx.wh.glencoe.com and click on **Chapter 1–Chapter Overview** to preview chapter information.

A Story That Matters

Mary Leakey

Louis Leakey

A Remarkable Discovery

*L*ouis B. Leakey and his wife, **Mary Nicol Leakey,** spent most of their lives searching for clues about early human life. Much of their time was spent at **Olduvai Gorge** in East Africa, where they dug up many stone tools and a variety of fossils. However, their ultimate goal—finding the skeleton of an early human being—had eluded them for many years.

Then, one morning, while her husband was back at camp recovering from the flu, Mary Leakey made a remarkable discovery. She jumped into her Land Rover and raced across the African plain back to camp, where she shouted to her startled husband, "I've got him! I've got him!"

Despite his illness, Louis jumped into the car, and the Leakeys headed back to where Mary had made her discovery. At the site, they looked at the bones Mary had found. Louis later described the scene: "I turned to look at Mary and we almost cried for sheer joy, each seized by the terrific emotion that comes early in life. After all our hoping and hardship and sacrifice, at last we had reached our goal—we had discovered the world's earliest known human."

AFRICA

ATLANTIC OCEAN

Olduvai Gorge

Why It Matters

The Leakeys and many other scientists have labored to form a picture of early human development. Thanks to their efforts, we know that early humans struggled to survive by hunting, fishing, and gathering, and eventually turned to regular farming. This dramatic step gradually led to larger and more complex human communities. This chapter presents the story of that process.

History and You Scientists continue to work throughout the world to discover and analyze the remains of humans. Find, read, and analyze four primary source documents that discuss the work of anthropologists or archaeologists. Compare the most recent findings with those discussed in the chapter. Have any new findings changed the way in which we view early humans?

Early Humans

Main Ideas
- By 10,000 B.C., *Homo sapiens sapiens* had spread throughout the world.
- Paleolithic peoples used technology.

Key Terms
prehistory, archaeology, artifact, anthropology, fossil, australopithecine, hominid, *Homo erectus, Homo sapiens,* Neanderthal, *Homo sapiens sapiens,* Paleolithic Age, nomad

People to Identify
Louis B. Leakey, Mary Nicol Leakey, Donald Johanson

Places to Locate
Olduvai Gorge, Lascaux

Preview Questions
1. What methods do scientists use to uncover the story of early humans?
2. What important and dramatic developments took place during the Paleolithic Age?

Reading Strategy
Categorizing Information As you read this section, complete a chart like the one below showing the effects of three tools on the lifestyle of early humankind.

Tool	Effect

Preview of Events

♦3,000,000 B.C.	♦1,500,000 B.C.	♦250,000 B.C.	♦100,000 B.C.	♦30,000 B.C.
3,000,000 B.C. Australopithecines make simple stone tools	**1,500,000 B.C.** *Homo erectus* uses larger, more varied tools	**250,000 B.C.** Species *Homo sapiens* emerges	**100,000 B.C.** *Homo sapiens sapiens* and Neanderthals appear	**30,000 B.C.** Neanderthals are extinct

Voices from the Past

In 1879, a Spanish landowner, who was an amateur archaeologist, took his 12-year-old daughter Maria with him to examine a cave on their farm in northern Spain. While her father busied himself digging for artifacts at the entrance to the cave, Maria wandered inside, holding a lantern. She was startled by what she discovered:

❝Ahead was a big dark hole like a doorway. Beyond it was a huge long room. I held my lantern high for a better look. Then, suddenly, I saw big red-and-black animals all over the ceiling. I stood amazed, looking at them.❞
— *Secrets from the Past,* **Gene S. Stuart, 1979**

Ten thousand years before, Stone Age artists had painted an entire herd of animals—horses, boars, bison, and deer—on the ceiling of the cave. Today, these simple paintings provide historians with clues to the lives of early humans.

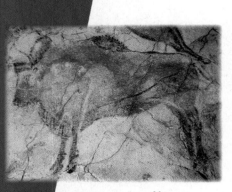

Cave painting of bison in Altamira, Spain

Before History

Historians rely mostly on documents, or written records, to create their pictures of the past. However, no written records exist for the prehistory of humankind. In fact, **prehistory** means the period before writing was developed.

The story of early humans depends on archaeological and, more recently, biological information. Archaeologists and anthropologists use this information to create theories about our early past. What are archaeologists and anthropologists, and what kinds of information do they provide?

Archaeology and Anthropology Archaeology is the study of past societies through an analysis of what people have left behind. Archaeologists dig up and examine artifacts—tools, pottery, paintings, weapons, buildings, and household items—of early peoples. Anthropology is the study of human life and culture. Anthropologists use artifacts and the remains of humans—human fossils—to determine how people lived their lives.

Archaeologists and anthropologists have developed scientific methods to carry out their work. Excavations of sites around the globe have uncovered fossil remains of early humans, ancient cities, burial grounds, and other objects. The examination and analysis of these remains give archaeologists a better understanding of ancient societies. By examining artifacts such as pottery, tools, and weapons, for example, these scientists learn about the social and military structures of a society. By analyzing bones, skins, and plant seeds, they are able to piece together the diet and activities of early people.

Dating Artifacts and Fossils One of the most important and difficult jobs of both archaeologists and anthropologists is dating their finds. Determining the age of human fossils makes it possible to

understand when and where the first humans emerged. Likewise, the dating of artifacts left by humans helps scientists understand the growth of early societies.

How, then, do archaeologists and anthropologists determine the ages of the artifacts and fossils they find? One valuable method is radiocarbon dating. All living things absorb a small amount of radioactive carbon (C-14) from the atmosphere. After a living thing dies, it slowly loses C-14. Using radiocarbon dating, a scientist can calculate the age of an object by measuring the amount of C-14 left in it.

Radiocarbon dating, however, is only accurate for dating objects that are no more than about 50,000 years old. Another method—thermoluminescence dating—enables scientists to make relatively precise measurements back to 200,000 years. This method of analysis dates an object by measuring the light given off by electrons trapped in the soil surrounding fossils and artifacts.

Microscopic and biological analyses of organic remains—such as blood, hairs, and plant tissues left on rocks, tools, and weapons—give scientists still

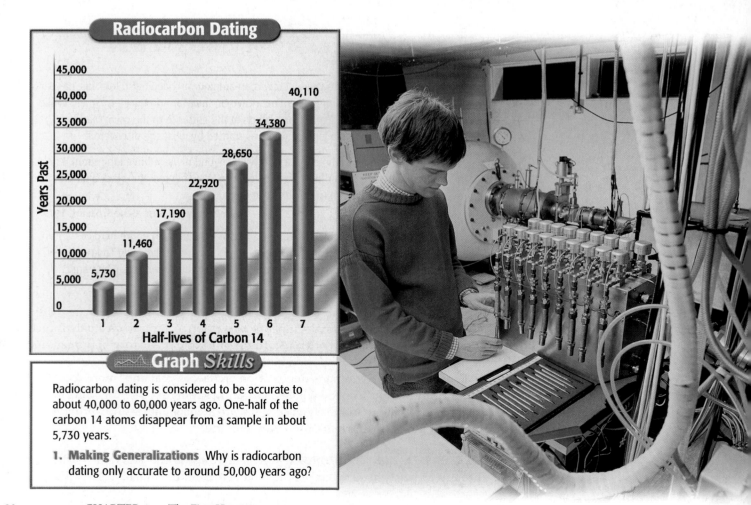

Radiocarbon Dating

Years Past vs **Half-lives of Carbon 14**

Half-life	Years Past
1	5,730
2	11,460
3	17,190
4	22,920
5	28,650
6	34,380
7	40,110

Graph *Skills*

Radiocarbon dating is considered to be accurate to about 40,000 to 60,000 years ago. One-half of the carbon 14 atoms disappear from a sample in about 5,730 years.

1. Making Generalizations Why is radiocarbon dating only accurate to around 50,000 years ago?

Heinrich Schliemann
1822–1890
German archaeologist

Heinrich Schliemann was an archaeologist from Germany. Schliemann had always been fascinated by the story of the Greek siege of Troy, a city in Asia Minor. Most people, including Schliemann's father, believed that the writer of the story, an ancient Greek poet named Homer, had made up his account. Schliemann, though, believed Homer's story was true. He told his father: "If such walls once existed, they cannot possibly have been completely destroyed: vast ruins of them must still remain." Schliemann became a wealthy businessman, learned Greek, and went to Asia Minor. After years of digging, he found his beloved Troy and proved that Homer's account was true.

more information. Such analysis has shown that blood molecules may survive millions of years. This recent scientific discovery is especially useful in telling us more about humans, their use of tools, and the animals they killed. Ancient deoxyribonucleic acid (DNA) is providing new information on human evolution. The analysis of plant remains on stone tools yields evidence on the history of farming. All of these techniques give us insight into the lives of early peoples.

✓ **Reading Check** **Describing** How do archaeologists and anthropologists determine the ages of fossils and artifacts?

Early Stages of Development

Although modern science has given us more precise methods for examining the prehistory of humankind than we have ever had before, much of our understanding of early humans still depends on guesswork. Given the rate of new discoveries, the current theory of early human life might well be changed in a few years.

From Hominids to *Homo Sapiens* The earliest humanlike creatures lived in Africa as long as three to four million years ago. Called **australopithecines** (aw•STRAY•loh•PIH•thuh•SYNS), or "southern apes," by their discoverer, **Donald Johanson,** they flourished in eastern and southern Africa. They were the first **hominids** (humans and other creatures that walk upright) to make simple stone tools.

Recently, however, archaeologists in Kenya have discovered a skull that they believe is from yet another form of hominid. They have called it *Kenyanthropus platyops*—the flat-faced man of Kenya—and think that it is about 3.5 million years old.

A second stage in early human development occurred with the appearance of *Homo erectus* ("upright human being"), a species that emerged around 1.5 million years ago. *Homo erectus* made use of larger and more varied tools. These hominids were the first to leave Africa and move into both Europe and Asia. They were able to do so in part because they learned to use fire to keep warm in colder areas.

Around 250,000 years ago, a third—and crucial—stage in human development began with the emergence of a new species, *Homo sapiens* ("wise human being"). Two distinct subgroups, Neanderthals and *Homo sapiens sapiens*, both developed from *Homo sapiens.*

Neanderthals were first found in the Neander Valley in Germany. Their remains have been dated between 100,000 and 30,000 B.C. and have been found in Europe and Southwest Asia. Neanderthals relied on a variety of stone tools and seem to be the first early people to bury their dead. Some scientists maintain that burial of the dead indicates a belief in an afterlife. Neanderthals in Europe made clothes from the skins of animals that they had killed for food.

History and Science
Human Origins: Different Points of View

People have different interpretations of the available data on human origins. Two sources of such data are the fossil record and fossil dating.

Fossil record Fossils provide insight into human origins but do not give a complete or conclusive history of human development. Fossils showing changes from one life-form to another are sometimes absent, producing gaps in the record.

Fossil dating Scientists analyze many different samples, using as many different methods as possible, because individual results may vary. Dating methods are constantly being refined to provide more accurate data.

Various ideas exist about the source of life. Many religions claim that a supreme being or a supernatural force created humans and other life-forms. Meanwhile, current scientific theories focus on chemical reactions in which organic materials have come together to form complex life-forms.

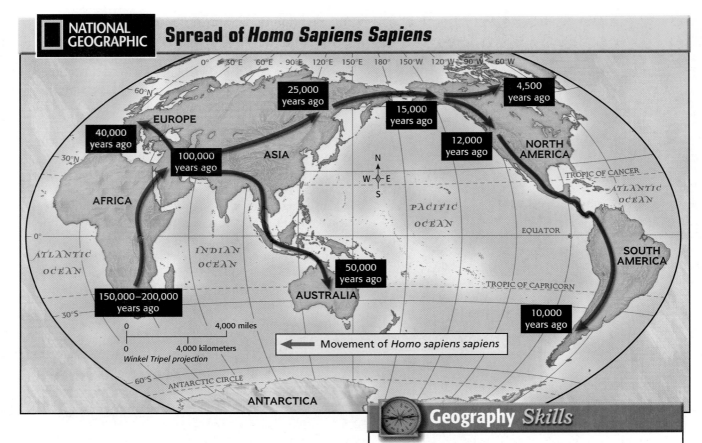

NATIONAL GEOGRAPHIC — Spread of *Homo Sapiens Sapiens*

25,000 years ago

15,000 years ago

4,500 years ago

40,000 years ago

12,000 years ago

100,000 years ago

EUROPE

ASIA

NORTH AMERICA

AFRICA

50,000 years ago

150,000–200,000 years ago

AUSTRALIA

SOUTH AMERICA

0   4,000 miles
0   4,000 kilometers
Winkel Tripel projection

← Movement of *Homo sapiens sapiens*

10,000 years ago

ANTARCTICA

The first anatomically modern humans (people who looked like us), known as *Homo sapiens sapiens* ("wise, wise human being"), appeared in Africa between 150,000 and 200,000 years ago. Recent evidence indicates that they began to spread outside Africa around 100,000 years ago.

The Spread of *Homo Sapiens Sapiens* By 30,000 B.C., *Homo sapiens sapiens* had replaced the Neanderthals, who had largely died out, possibly as a result of conflict between the two groups.

The spread of these first modern humans was a slow process. Groups of people, probably in search of food, moved beyond their old hunting grounds at a rate of only two to three miles per generation. This was enough, however, to populate the world over tens of thousands of years.

By 10,000 B.C., members of the *Homo sapiens sapiens* subgroup of the species *Homo sapiens* could be found throughout the world. All humans today, whether they are Europeans, Australian Aborigines (A•buh•RIJ•NEES), or Africans, belong to the same subgroups of human beings.

✔ **Reading Check** **Summarizing** Identify and describe the three stages of early human development.

Geography Skills

The search for food eventually took members of the *Homo sapiens sapiens* species to every habitable continent.

1. **Interpreting Maps** Across which two continents did *Homo sapiens sapiens* spread the most quickly?
2. **Applying Geography Skills** Into which area did *Homo sapiens sapiens* arrive most recently?

The Hunter-Gatherers of the Old Stone Age

►TURNING POINT◄ **Just as people do today, Paleolithic peoples used technological innovations, including stone tools, to change their physical environment.**

One of the basic distinguishing features of the human species is the ability to make tools. The earliest tools were made of stone. The term *Paleolithic Age* is used to designate the early period of human history (approximately 2,500,000 to 10,000 B.C.) in which humans used simple stone tools. Paleolithic is Greek for "old stone," and the Paleolithic Age is sometimes called the Old Stone Age.

The Paleolithic Way of Life For hundreds of thousands of years, humans relied on hunting and gathering for their daily food. Paleolithic peoples had a close relationship with the world around them. They came to know what animals to hunt and what plants to eat. They gathered wild nuts, berries, fruits, wild grains, and green plants. Around the world, they hunted and ate various animals, including buffalo, horses, bison, and reindeer. In coastal areas, fish provided a rich source of food.

Over the years, Paleolithic hunters developed better tools. The invention of the spear, and later the bow and arrow, made hunting much easier. Harpoons and fishhooks made of bone increased the catch of fish.

The hunting of animals and the gathering of wild food no doubt led to certain patterns of living. Paleolithic people were nomads (people who moved from place to place), because they had no choice but to follow animal migrations and vegetation cycles. Archaeologists and anthropologists have speculated that nomads lived in small groups of twenty or thirty. Hunting depended on careful observation of animal behavior patterns and demanded group effort for any real chance of success.

The Roles of Men and Women It is probable that both men and women were responsible for finding food—the chief work of Paleolithic peoples. Because women bore and raised the children, they were likely to have stayed close to their camps. There, they played an important role in acquiring food by gathering berries, nuts, and grains. Men did most of the hunting of large animals, which might take place far from camp. Still, both the men and the women were responsible for finding and acquiring the food needed

SCIENCE, TECHNOLOGY & SOCIETY

Tools

The word *technology* refers to the ability of human beings to make things that sustain them and give them some control over their environment. The technology available at the beginning of human history was quite simple. It consisted primarily of the ability to make stone tools.

To make such tools, early people used very hard stones, such as flint. They used one stone to chip away parts of another, creating an edge. Hand axes of various kinds—pointed tools with one or more cutting edges—were the most common. Eventually, axes were set into wooden handles, making them easier to use. By attaching wooden poles to spear points and hardening the tips in fire, humans created spears to kill large animals.

Over time, tool technology evolved and ever-smaller stone points and blades were made. Near the end of the Paleolithic period, there is evidence of such refined tools as bone needles. Needles formed from animal bones could be used for making nets and baskets and even sewing hides together for clothing.

The first tools served a variety of purposes. Humans used stone weapons to kill animals and butcher their meat. Other sharp-edged tools were used for cutting up plants, digging up roots, and cutting branches to build simple shelters. Scraping tools were used to clean animal hides for clothing and shelter.

Analyzing *How did the ability to make simple tools change human life?*

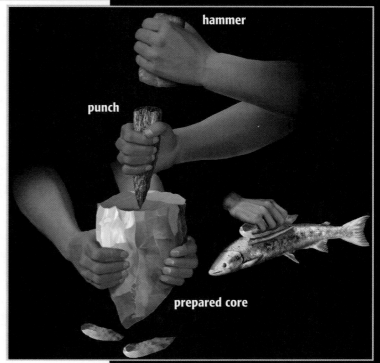

hammer

punch

prepared core

Making stone tools was laborious, but the tools were effective and durable.

to sustain life. By passing on their practices, skills, and tools to their children, Paleolithic peoples helped to ensure that later generations could survive.

Because both men and women played important roles in providing for the group's survival, some scientists have argued that a rough equality existed between men and women. It is likely that both men and women made decisions that affected the activities of the Paleolithic group.

Adapting to Survive Paleolithic peoples, especially those who lived in cold climates, found shelter in caves. Over time, they created new types of shelter. Perhaps most common was a simple structure of wood poles or sticks covered with animal hides. Where wood was scarce, they might use the bones of large animals to build frames, which were then covered by hides.

The Use of Fire As early hominids moved from the tropics into colder regions, they needed to adjust to new, often harsh, conditions. Perhaps most important to their ability to adapt was the use of fire. It was *Homo erectus* who first learned to make fires deliberately. Archaeologists have discovered the piled remains of ashes in caves that prove that Paleolithic people used fire systematically as long ago as five hundred thousand years. At a *Homo erectus* site in northern China, archaeologists have discovered hearths, ashes, charcoal, and charred bones. All of these were about four hundred thousand years old.

Fire gave warmth and undoubtedly fostered a sense of community for the groups of people gathered around it. Fire also protected early humans by enabling them to scare away wild animals. Fire might also have enabled early humans to flush animals out of wooded areas or caves and then kill them. In addition, food could be cooked with fire, making it better tasting, longer lasting, and easier to chew and digest (in the case of some plants, such as wild grains).

Scholars believe that different groups of early people discovered ways to start fires independently throughout the world. After examining methods used by traditional peoples, even into the twentieth century, archaeologists assume that the earliest methods for starting fires were probably based on friction, such as rubbing two pieces of wood together. Dry grass and leaves could be added as the wood began to smoke. Eventually, Paleolithic peoples devised sturdy, drill-like wooden devices to start fires. Other early humans discovered that a certain stone (iron pyrites), when struck against a hard rock, gave off a spark that could be used to ignite dry grass or leaves.

The Ice Ages Having fire to create a source of heat was especially important when Ice Age conditions descended on the Paleolithic world. The most recent Ice Age began about 100,000 B.C. and ended in about 8000 B.C. During this time, sheets of thick ice covered large parts of Europe, Asia, and North America.

Ice Age conditions posed a serious threat to human life, and the ability to adapt was crucial to human survival. The use of fire, for example, reminds us that early humans sometimes adapted not by changing themselves to better fit their environment but by changing the environment.

Creating Art The importance of art to human life is evident in one basic fact: art existed even in prehistory among the hunters and gatherers of the Paleolithic Age. The cave paintings of large animals found at **Lascaux** (la•SKOH) in southwestern France and at Altamira in northern Spain are evidence of this

cultural activity. One cave discovered in southern France in 1994 contained more than three hundred paintings of lions, oxen, owls, panthers, and other animals. Recent discoveries in other areas of the world have added yet more examples of the artistic achievements of early human beings. According to archaeologists, these cave paintings were done between 25,000 and 12,000 B.C.

All of the caves were underground and in complete darkness, but Paleolithic artists used stone lamps filled with animal fat to light their surroundings. By crushing mineral ores and combining them with animal fat, they could paint in red, yellow, and black. Apparently they used their fingertips, crushed twigs, and even brushes made with animal hairs to apply these paints to the walls. They also used hollow reeds to blow thin lines of paint on the walls.

Cave painting, Lascaux, France

Many of these cave paintings show animals in remarkably realistic forms. Few humans appear in these paintings, and when they do appear, they are not realistic but rather crude, sticklike figures. The precise rendering of the animal forms has led many historians to believe that they were painted as part of a magical or religious ritual intended to ensure success in hunting. Some believe, however, that the paintings may have been made for their own sake. They beautified caves and must have been pleasing to the eyes of early humans.

✓ Reading Check **Identifying** What are the two most important technological innovations of Paleolithic peoples?

🔶 TAKS Practice

SECTION 1 ASSESSMENT

Checking for Understanding

1. **Define** prehistory, archaeology, artifact, anthropology, fossil, australopithecine, hominid, *Homo erectus, Homo sapiens,* Neanderthal, *Homo sapiens sapiens,* Paleolithic Age, nomad.

2. **Identify** Louis B. Leakey, Mary Nicol Leakey, Donald Johanson.

3. **Locate** Olduvai Gorge, Lascaux.

4. **Explain** why obtaining food by hunting and gathering is characteristic of a nomadic lifestyle.

5. **List** the types of evidence archaeologists and anthropologists rely on to reconstruct prehistory.

Critical Thinking

6. **Compare and Contrast** Distinguish between the roles of Paleolithic men and women in finding food. Explain why finding food was the principal work of Paleolithic peoples.

7. **Compare and Contrast** Create a Venn diagram like the one shown below to compare and contrast the lifestyles of australopithecines and Neanderthals.

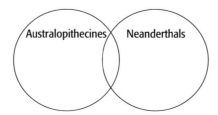

Australopithecines   Neanderthals

Analyzing Visuals

8. **Examine** the photographs of the Iceman on page 24 and the stone tools shown on page 23. How do archaeologists and anthropologists analyze limited evidence such as this skeleton and the stone tools to draw conclusions about the past?

Writing About History

9. **Descriptive Writing** Pretend you are part of an archaeological team uncovering artifacts and fossils at a recently dicovered site. Describe the conditions of the site, the sorts of artifacts and fossils you have been working with, and what you hope to find. Read articles or books in your school library to increase your understanding.

SKILLBUILDER

Understanding Map Projections

Why Learn This Skill?

On some maps, Greenland appears to be larger than Australia. Australia, however, actually has a larger landmass than Greenland. Have you ever wondered how this happens? Why do flat maps distort the size of landmasses and bodies of water? The answer lies in understanding the ways that flat maps are constructed.

Learning the Skill

To make flat maps, mapmakers project the curved surface of Earth onto a piece of paper. This is called a map projection. Unfortunately, the process is not exact. Different kinds of projections can accurately show either area, shape, distance, or direction. No one map, however, can show all four of these qualities with equal accuracy at the same time.

Mapmakers try to limit the amount of distortion by using different kinds of map projections. A *conformal map* shows land areas in their true shapes, but their actual size is distorted. An *equal-area map* shows land areas in correct proportion to one another but distorts the shapes of the landmasses.

The map on this page is a *Cylindrical Projection (Mercator)*. Imagine wrapping a paper cylinder around the globe. A light from within the globe projects its surface onto the paper. The resulting conformal projection makes Alaska appear larger than Mexico. Distortion is greatest near the North and South Poles.

A *Conic Projection* is formed by placing a cone of paper over a lighted globe. This produces a cross between a conformal and an equal-area map. This projection is best for showing the middle latitudes of Earth.

To understand map projections:
• Compare the map to a globe.
• Determine the type of projection used.
• Identify the purpose of the projection.

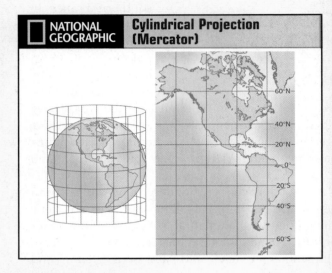

NATIONAL GEOGRAPHIC

Cylindrical Projection (Mercator)

Practicing the Skill

Turn to the map of the world in the Atlas in your textbook. Compare the sizes and shapes of the features on the map to those on a globe. Based on this comparison, answer the following questions:

❶ What is the map's projection?
❷ How does the map distort Earth's features?
❸ In what way does the map accurately present Earth's features?
❹ Why do you think the mapmaker used this projection?

Applying the Skill

Compare the size of Antarctica as it appears on a map with Antarctica on a globe. Determine the type of projection used on the map and then predict why that projection was chosen for the map. Share your findings in class.

 GO TO

Glencoe's **Skillbuilder Interactive Workbook, Level 2,** provides instruction and practice in key social studies skills.

The Neolithic Revolution and the Rise of Civilization

Guide to Reading

Main Idea
- Systematic agriculture brought about major economic, political, and social changes for early humans.

Key Terms
Neolithic Revolution, systematic agriculture, domestication, artisan, Bronze Age, culture, civilization, monarch

People to Identify
Mesoamericans, priest

Places to Locate
Jericho, Çatal Hüyük

Preview Questions
1. What changes occurred during the Neolithic Revolution that made the development of cities possible?
2. How did systematic agriculture spread in different areas of the world?

Reading Strategy
Summarizing Information As you read this section, fill in a chart like the one below listing the six major characteristics of a civilization.

1.	4.
2.	5.
3.	6.

Preview of Events

◆11,000 B.C.	◆9000 B.C.	◆7000 B.C.	◆5000 B.C.	◆3000 B.C.	◆1000 B.C.

8000 B.C.
Neolithic Age begins

8000 B.C.
Systematic agriculture develops

6700 B.C.
Regular farming gives rise to Neolithic villages such as Çatal Hüyük

5000 B.C.
Rice is grown in Southeast Asia

1200 B.C.
Bronze Age ends

Voices from the Past

Utnapishtim, from
The Epic of Gilgamesh

Around 3000 B.C., cities began to emerge around what had been only farming villages. The first city dwellers were amazed by their new environment. *The Epic of Gilgamesh,* the most famous piece of literature from the ancient Near East, reveals this amazement:

❝Look at the walls of Uruk: the outer wall shines with the brilliance of copper; and the inner wall, it has no equal! Climb upon the wall of Uruk; walk along it, I say; regard the foundation terrace and examine the masonry: is it not burned brick and good? The seven sages laid the foundations.❞

— *The Epic of Gilgamesh,* N.K. Sandars, ed., 1972

The cities that emerged in the river valleys of Mesopotamia, Egypt, India, and China gave rise to the first civilizations. However, it was the agricultural revolution of the Neolithic Age that made these cities possible.

The Neolithic Revolution

⌐TURNING POINT⌐ **Despite all of our technological progress, human survival still depends on the systematic growing and storing of food, an accomplishment of people in the Neolithic Age.**

The end of the last Ice Age, around 8000 B.C., was followed by what is called the Neolithic Revolution—that is, the revolution that occurred in the Neolithic Age, the period of human history from 8000 to 4000 B.C. The word *neolithic* is Greek for

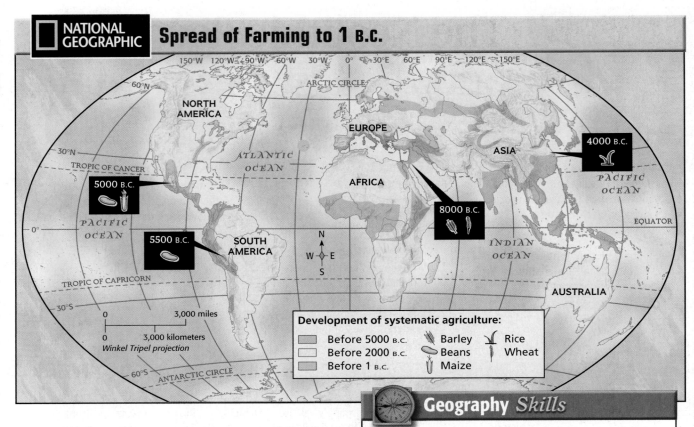

Development of systematic agriculture:

Before 5000 B.C.	Barley	Rice
Before 2000 B.C.	Beans	Wheat
Before 1 B.C.	Maize	

0 — 3,000 miles
0 — 3,000 kilometers
Winkel Tripel projection

Geography *Skills*

Agriculture developed independently in different regions of the world.

1. **Interpreting Maps** Between what latitudes did the earliest farming develop?
2. **Applying Geography Skills** What geologic, geographic, and climatic factors influenced the development of farming?

"new stone." The name *New Stone Age,* however, is somewhat misleading. The real change in the Neolithic Revolution was the shift from the hunting of animals and the gathering of food to the keeping of animals and the growing of food on a regular basis—what we call systematic agriculture.

The planting of grains and vegetables provided a regular supply of food. The domestication (adaptation for human use) of animals added a steady source of meat, milk, and wool. Animals could also be used to do work. The growing of crops and the taming of food-producing animals created what historians call an agricultural revolution. Some believe this revolution was the single most important development in human history.

Change is revolutionary when it is dramatic and requires great effort. The Neolithic Revolution marked a revolutionary change. The ability to acquire food on a regular basis gave humans greater control over their environment. It also meant they could give up their nomadic ways of life and begin to live in settled communities.

The Growing of Crops Between 8000 and 5000 B.C., systematic agriculture developed in different areas of the world. People in Southwest Asia had begun growing wheat and barley and domesticating pigs, cows, goats, and sheep by 8000 B.C. From Southwest Asia, farming spread into southeastern Europe. By 4000 B.C., farming was well established in central Europe and the coastal regions of the Mediterranean Sea.

The cultivation of wheat and barley had spread from southwestern Asia into the Nile Valley of Egypt by 6000 B.C. These crops soon spread up the Nile to other areas of Africa, especially the Sudan and Ethiopia. In the woodlands and tropical forests of central Africa, a separate farming system emerged with the growing of tubers (root crops), such as yams, and tree crops, such as bananas. The farming of wheat and barley also moved eastward into the highlands of northwestern and central India between 7000 and 5000 B.C.

By 5000 B.C., rice was being grown in Southeast Asia. From there, it spread into southern China. In northern China, the farming of millet and the domesticating of pigs and dogs seem to have been well established by 6000 B.C. In the Western Hemisphere, **Mesoamericans** (inhabitants of present-day Mexico and Central America) grew beans, squash, and maize (corn) between 7000 and 5000 B.C. They also domesticated dogs and fowl during this period.

Neolithic Farming Villages

The growing of crops on a regular basis gave rise to more permanent settlements. Historians refer to these settlements as Neolithic farming villages. Neolithic villages appeared in Europe, India, Egypt, China, and Mesoamerica. The oldest and biggest ones, however, were located in Southwest Asia. For example, **Jericho**, in Palestine near the Dead Sea, was in existence by 8000 B.C.

Çatal Hüyük (CHAH•tuhl hoo•YOOK), located in modern-day Turkey, was an even larger community. Its walls enclosed 32 acres, and its population probably reached six thousand inhabitants during its high point from 6700 to 5700 B.C. People in Çatal Hüyük lived in

simple mud brick houses built so close to one another that there were few streets. To get to their homes, people had to walk along the rooftops and then enter through holes in the roofs.

Archaeologists have found 12 products that were grown in this community, including fruits, nuts, and three kinds of wheat. People grew their own food and kept it in storerooms within their homes. Domesticated animals, especially cattle, yielded meat, milk, and hides. Hunting scenes on the walls of the ruins of Çatal Hüyük indicate that the people also hunted.

As a result of this food production, people often had more food than they needed right away. In turn, food surpluses made it possible for people to do things other than farming. Some people became artisans. These skilled workers made products such as weapons and jewelry that were traded with neighboring peoples. Trade exposed the people of Çatal Hüyük to the wider world around them.

Special buildings in Çatal Hüyük were shrines containing figures of gods and goddesses. Female statues have also been found there, often of women giving birth or nursing a child. These "earth mothers" may well have been connected with goddess figures. Both the shrines and the statues point to the growing role of religion in the lives of Neolithic peoples.

Consequences of the Neolithic Revolution

The Neolithic agricultural revolution had far-reaching consequences. The dramatic changes that took place during this period led to further changes, affecting the way that people would live for thousands of years. For example, once people began settling in villages or towns, they saw the need to build houses for protection and other structures for the storage of goods. The organized communities stored food and other material goods, which encouraged the development of trade. The trading of goods caused people to begin specializing in certain crafts, and a division of labor developed. Stone tools became more refined as flint blades were used to make sickles and hoes for use in the fields. Eventually, many of the food plants still in use today began to be cultivated. In addition, fibers from such plants as flax and cotton were used to spin yarn that was woven into cloth.

The change to systematic agriculture in the Neolithic Age also had consequences for the relationship between men and women. Men became more active in farming and herding animals, jobs that took them away from the home settlement. Women remained behind, caring for children and taking responsibility for weaving cloth, turning milk into cheese, and performing other tasks that required much labor in one place. As men took on more and more of the responsibility for obtaining food and protecting the settlement, they came to play a more dominant role, a basic pattern that would remain until our own times.

Ruins of the Great Bath, Mohenjo-Daro, Pakistan

Picturing History

The walled city of Skara Brae in Scotland was built about 5,000 years ago. Why did people start putting walls around their cities?

The End of the Neolithic Age Between 4000 and 3000 B.C., new developments began to affect Neolithic towns in some areas. The use of metals marked a new level of human control over the environment and its resources.

Even before 4000 B.C., craftspeople had discovered that by heating metal-bearing rocks, they could turn the metal to liquid. The liquid metal could then be cast in molds to make tools and weapons.

Copper was the first metal to be used in making tools. After 4000 B.C., craftspeople in western Asia discovered that a combination of copper and tin created bronze, a metal far harder and more durable than copper. Even after the introduction of bronze, people continued to use stone tools and weapons. Nevertheless, the widespread use of bronze has led historians to speak of a Bronze Age from around 3000 to 1200 B.C.

The Neolithic Age was drawing to a close, but it had set the stage for major changes to come. At first, Neolithic settlements had been hardly more than villages. As the inhabitants mastered the art of farming, they gradually began to develop more complex societies. As their wealth increased, these societies began to create armies and to build walled cities. By the beginning of the Bronze Age, large numbers of people were concentrated in the river valleys of Mesopotamia, Egypt, India, and China. This would lead to a whole new pattern for human life.

✓ **Reading Check** **Identifying** What changes resulted from the development of systematic agriculture?

The Emergence of Civilization

In general terms, the culture of a people is the way of life that they follow. As we have seen, early human beings formed small groups that developed a simple culture that enabled them to survive. As human societies grew and became more complex, a new form of human existence—called civilization—came into being.

A civilization is a complex culture in which large numbers of human beings share a number of common elements. Historians have identified the basic characteristics of civilizations. Six of the most important characteristics are cities, government, religion, social structure, writing, and art.

The Rise of Cities Cities are one of the chief features of civilizations. The first civilizations developed in river valleys, where people could carry on the large-scale farming that was needed to feed large populations. Although farming practices varied from civilization to civilization, in each civilization a significant part of the population lived in cities. New patterns of living soon emerged.

The Growth of Governments Growing numbers of people, the need to maintain the food supply, and the need to build walls for defense soon led to the growth of governments. Governments organize and regulate human activity. They also provide for smooth interaction between individuals and groups. In the first civilizations, governments were led by rulers—usually monarchs (kings or queens who rule a kingdom)—who organized armies to protect their populations and made laws to regulate their subjects' lives.

The Role of Religion Important religious developments also characterized the new urban civilizations. All of them developed religions to explain the workings of the forces of nature and the fact of their own existence. Gods and goddesses were often believed to be crucial to a community's success. To win their favor, **priests** supervised rituals aimed at pleasing them. This gave the priests special power and made them very important people. Rulers also claimed that their power was based on

HISTORY Online

Web Activity Visit the *Glencoe World History* Web site at tx.wh.glencoe.com and click on **Chapter 1– Student Web Activity** to learn more about early peoples.

divine approval, and some rulers claimed to be divine.

A New Social Structure A new social structure based on economic power also arose. Rulers and an upper class of priests, government officials, and warriors dominated society. Below this upper class was a large group of free people—farmers, artisans, and craftspeople. At the bottom was a slave class.

Abundant food supplies created new opportunities, enabling some people to work in occupations other than farming. The demand of the upper class for luxury items encouraged artisans and craftspeople to create new products. As urban populations exported finished goods to neighboring populations in exchange for raw materials, organized trade began to grow. Because trade brought new civilizations into contact with one another, it often led to the transfer of new technology from one region to another.

By and large, however, the early river valley civilizations developed independently. Each one was based on developments connected to the agricultural revolution of the Neolithic Age and the cities that this revolution helped to produce. Taken together, the civilizations of Mesopotamia, Egypt, India, and China constituted nothing less than a revolutionary stage in the growth of human society.

The Use of Writing Writing was an important feature in the life of these new civilizations. Above all, rulers, priests, merchants, and artisans used writing to keep accurate records. Of course, not all civilizations depended on writing to keep records. The Inca

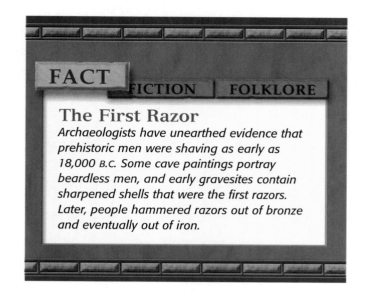

FACT | FICTION | FOLKLORE

The First Razor
Archaeologists have unearthed evidence that prehistoric men were shaving as early as 18,000 B.C. Some cave paintings portray beardless men, and early gravesites contain sharpened shells that were the first razors. Later, people hammered razors out of bronze and eventually out of iron.

in Peru (see Chapter 11), for example, relied on well-trained memory experts to keep track of their important matters. Eventually, all of the first civilizations used writing as a means of creative expression as well as for record keeping. This produced the world's first works of literature.

Artistic Activity Significant artistic activity was another feature of the new civilizations. Temples and pyramids were built as places for worship or sacrifice, or for the burial of kings and other important people. Painting and sculpture were developed to portray gods and goddesses or natural forces.

✓**Reading Check** **Describing** Describe the new social structure that arose in Neolithic cities.

TAKS Practice

SECTION 2 ASSESSMENT

Checking for Understanding

1. **Define** Neolithic Revolution, systematic agriculture, domestication, artisan, Bronze Age, culture, civilization, monarch.

2. **Identify** Mesoamerican, priest.

3. **Locate** Jericho, Çatal Hüyük.

4. **Explain** how some Neolithic people were able to become artisans.

5. **Compare** the roles of men and women in the Neolithic Age.

Critical Thinking

6. **Describe** What was the relationship among artistic activities, religion, and government during the rise of civilization?

7. **Sequencing Information** Create a diagram like the one below to show how changes during the Neolithic Revolution led to the emergence of civilization.

Analyzing Visuals

8. **Examine** the photo of Skara Brae on page 30. What does the village's ocean location tell you about the way its Stone Age inhabitants lived?

Writing About History

9. **Expository Writing** Much disagreement exists about the interpretation of available data on the origins of humankind. Discuss and document at least two different points of view besides the one presented in the text.

Using Key Terms

1. People who combined copper and tin to make tools are said to have entered the _____.

2. The _____ of animals provided humans with a steady source of meat, milk, and wool.

3. The rise of cities, growth of governments, and development of religion are characteristics of _____.

4. The "modern" type of *Homo sapiens* is called _____.

5. _____ focuses mainly on the study of human fossils.

6. The study of past societies by the analysis of the artifacts they have left behind is called _____.

7. The period of time before writing was developed is called _____.

8. The _____ appear to be the first early people to bury their dead.

9. The _____ designates the period when humans used simple stone tools.

10. Humans and other creatures that walk upright are called _____.

11. Remains of human and animal bones preserved in the earth's crust are _____.

12. Skilled workers and craftsmen who made jewelry and weapons were the first _____.

Reviewing Key Facts

13. **Science and Technology** Explain how radiocarbon dating of fossils and artifacts differs from thermoluminescence dating.

14. **History** List the defining characteristics of the Paleolithic Age.

15. **Culture** What do the cave paintings found in both Lascaux, France, and Altamira, Spain, indicate about Paleolithic humans and their culture?

16. **Society** Give four outcomes, or results, of the settlement of humans in villages and towns.

17. **History** What is the Bronze Age and when did it occur?

18. **Economics** Discuss early trade among different groups of people.

19. **Society** Describe the types of shelter and housing that were used by Paleolithic peoples.

20. **History** What is the most significant development of the Neolithic Age?

21. **Science and Technology** What factors would lead scientists to choose DNA analysis, rather than carbon or thermoluminescence dating, to determine the age of fossils and other archaeological remains?

22. **Culture** What evidence has led historians to believe that Neolithic peoples had religious beliefs?

Chapter Summary

Chapter 1 emphasizes cultural change, movement, and technological innovations.

Event	Cultural Change	Movement	Technological Innovation
Early humans migrate to warmer climates during the Ice Ages.		X	
Early humans learn how to control fire and make tools.	X		X
Caves are painted with religious and decorative art.	X		
Neanderthals inhabit Europe and Asia.		X	
Neolithic peoples domesticate animals.	X		X
Early agricultural villages evolve into highly complex societies.	X		

Self-Check Quiz
Visit the *Glencoe World History* Web site at tx.wh.glencoe.com and click on **Chapter 1–Self-Check Quiz** to prepare for the Chapter Test.

Critical Thinking

23. **Evaluating** Explain the importance of cities, government, and religion in the development of a civilization. How are these three related?

24. **Analyzing** Analyze and explain why the development of systematic agriculture by Neolithic peoples deserves to be called a revolution.

Writing About History

25. **Persuasive Writing** Imagine that you are living in southeastern Europe at the beginning of the Neolithic Age. Pretend that you have just learned about the systematic agriculture people in Southwest Asia are practicing. Make an argument for or against the adoption of systematic agriculture in your community.

Analyzing Sources

Louis B. Leakey reminded us years ago,

❝Theories on prehistory and early man constantly change as new evidence comes to light.❞

26. How has history proven Leakey correct in his observation?

27. Why is it necessary for archaeologists and anthropologists to continually consider and assess new ideas, new approaches, and new findings?

Applying Technology Skills

28. **Using the Internet** Use the Internet to explore the most recent archaeological finds of prehistoric humans not mentioned in the text. Present this information in a short essay. Be sure to use authoritative sources and be sure to cite your sources in your bibliography.

Making Decisions

29. Pretend you are a Çatal Hüyük trader who encounters another group of people also interested in trade. Do you trade with them? What steps would you take to reach this decision? Do not forget to take into consideration the possibility of both negative and positive outcomes from your contact with these new people.

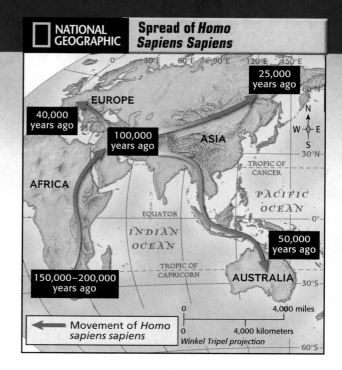

NATIONAL GEOGRAPHIC **Spread of *Homo Sapiens Sapiens***

25,000 years ago

40,000 years ago

100,000 years ago

150,000–200,000 years ago

50,000 years ago

← Movement of *Homo sapiens sapiens*

Winkel Tripel projection

Analyzing Maps and Charts

30. Based on fossil evidence, where did groups of *Homo sapiens sapiens* migrate first, Europe or Australia?

31. What factors would influence migration?

32. Approximately how many miles did *Homo sapiens sapiens* travel from the equator to Australia?

33. From where did *Homo sapiens sapiens* first migrate?

Test Practice

Directions: Choose the best answer to the following question.

The basic change that occurred with the Neolithic Revolution was

A an increase in human population.

B the cultivation of rice.

C the shift to raising animals as a regular source of food.

D an increase in the importance of hunting.

Test-Taking Tip: Always read the question and *all* the answer choices. Do not simply choose the first answer that seems to have something to do with the topic. In this question, you want the choice that comes closest to defining the Neolithic Revolution.

CHAPTER 2

Western Asia and Egypt

3500–500 B.C.

Key Events

As you read, look for the key events in the history of Southwest Asia and Egypt.
- *The Sumerians in Mesopotamia were among the first groups to build a civilization, and they were the first to develop a system of writing.*
- *Due in large part to the Nile, early Egyptian civilization was stable and prosperous. Massive monuments, the pyramids, were built to honor the deaths of the pharaohs.*
- *The Israelites emerged as a distinct people.*
- *Of the other empires that came into being in Southwest Asia, the longest lasting and most powerful were the Assyrian and Persian Empires.*

The Impact Today

The events that occurred during this time period still impact our lives today.
- *The peoples of Mesopotamia and Egypt built cities and struggled with the problems of organized government.*
- *The Israelites developed a major world religion, which influenced the development of Christianity and Islam and has a continuing effect on Western civilization.*

World History Video *The Chapter 2 video, "Egypt," chronicles the rise of Egyptian civilization.*

Hammurabi established a code of law.

3000 B.C.
Sumerian cities emerge in southern Mesopotamia

2700 B.C.
Old Kingdom begins

1792 B.C.
Hammurabi comes to power

1652 B.C.
Middle Kingdom ends

| 3000 B.C. | 2700 B.C. | 2400 B.C. | 2100 B.C. | 1800 B.C. | 1500 B.C. |

3000 B.C.
Cuneiform writing invented

2540 B.C.
Great Pyramid of King Khufu finished

1567 B.C.
New Kingdom begins

Sumerian cuneiform script

The Great Sphinx and the Great Pyramids at Giza, Egypt, symbolize the power and longevity of Egyptian kingdoms.

*Death mask of King
Tutankhamen of Egypt*

539 B.C.
Babylonia
falls

521 B.C.
Darius begins
to expand
Persian
Empire

1200 B.C.　　*900 B.C.*　　*600 B.C.*　　*300 B.C.*　　*100 B.C.*　　*50 B.C.*

970 B.C.
Solomon
becomes
King of Israel

King Solomon's temple in Jerusalem

HISTORY
Online

Chapter Overview
Visit the *Glencoe World History* Web site at
tx.wh.glencoe.com and click
on **Chapter 2–Chapter
Overview** to preview
chapter information.

A Story That Matters

Sumerian ruins at Uruk

The Cradle of the Human Race

*I*n the winter of 1849, a daring young Englishman made a difficult journey into the deserts and swamps of southern Iraq. He moved south down the banks of the river Euphrates while braving high winds and temperatures that reached 120 degrees Fahrenheit (48.9° C). The man, William Loftus, led a small expedition in search of the roots of civilization. As he said, "From our childhood we have been led to regard this place as the cradle of the human race."

Guided by native Arabs into the southernmost reaches of Iraq, Loftus and his small group of explorers were soon overwhelmed by what they saw. He wrote, "I know of nothing more exciting or impressive than the first sight of one of these great piles, looming in solitary grandeur from the surrounding plains and marshes."

One of these "piles" was known to the natives as the mound of Warka. The mound contained the ruins of the ancient city of Uruk, one of the first real cities in the world and part of one of the world's first civilizations. Southern Iraq, known to ancient peoples as Mesopotamia, was one of four areas in the world where civilization began.

Why It Matters

In the fertile river valleys of Mesopotamia, Egypt, India, and China, intensive farming made it possible to support large groups of people. The people in these regions were able to develop the organized societies that we associate with civilization. The beginnings of Western civilization lie in the early civilizations of Southwest Asia and Egypt.

History and You As you read this chapter, analyze the climatic conditions in Mesopotamia that favored certain crops. Compare Mesopotamia's climate and crops to the climate and crops that were grown in the Nile Valley of Egypt. What conclusions can you draw from this information?

SECTION 1
Civilization Begins in Mesopotamia

Guide to Reading

Main Ideas
- Mesopotamia, one of the first civilizations, began between the Tigris and Euphrates Rivers.
- The Sumerians formed city-states and created forms of communication that affect our lives today.

Key Terms
city-state, ziggurat, theocracy, empire, patriarchal, polytheistic, cuneiform

People to Identify
Sumerians, Akkadians, Sargon, Hammurabi

Places to Locate
Tigris River, Euphrates River, Mesopotamia, Fertile Crescent, Uruk, Babylon

Preview Questions
1. How did geography affect the civilizations in Mesopotamia?
2. How did the Akkadian Empire begin?

Reading Strategy
Categorizing Information As you read this section, complete a chart like the one shown below to explain the Sumerians' various contributions to civilization.

Political Life	Cultural Life	Inventions

Preview of Events

♦3000 B.C.	♦2750 B.C.	♦2500 B.C.	♦2250 B.C.	♦2000 B.C.	♦1750 B.C.	♦1500 B.C.

3000 B.C.
Sumerians establish independent cities

2340 B.C.
Akkadians set up the first empire

2100 B.C.
Akkadian Empire falls

1792 B.C.
Hammurabi comes to power

Voices from the Past

The following poem reflects the deep despair of the people of Ur after the burning and sacking of their city:

❝Ur is destroyed, bitter is its lament. The country's blood now fills its holes like hot bronze in a mould. Bodies dissolve like fat in the sun. Our temple is destroyed, the gods have abandoned us, like migrating birds. Smoke lies on our city like a shroud.❞
—*Legacy: The Search for Ancient Cultures,* Michael Wood, 1995

Constant conflict marked early civilization in Mesopotamia. Invaders flowed into the flat land of the region, and city fought city for land and water.

Reconstructed temple at Ur

The Impact of Geography

The ancient Greeks spoke of the valley between the **Tigris** and **Euphrates Rivers** as **Mesopotamia,** the land "between the rivers." Mesopotamia was at the eastern end of an area known as the **Fertile Crescent,** an arc of land from the Mediterranean Sea to the Persian Gulf. Because this land had rich soil and abundant crops, it was able to sustain an early civilization.

Mesopotamia was a region with little rain, but its soil had been enriched over the years by layers of silt—material deposited by the two rivers. In late spring, the Tigris and Euphrates often overflowed their banks and deposited their fertile silt. This flooding, however, depended on the melting of snows in the upland

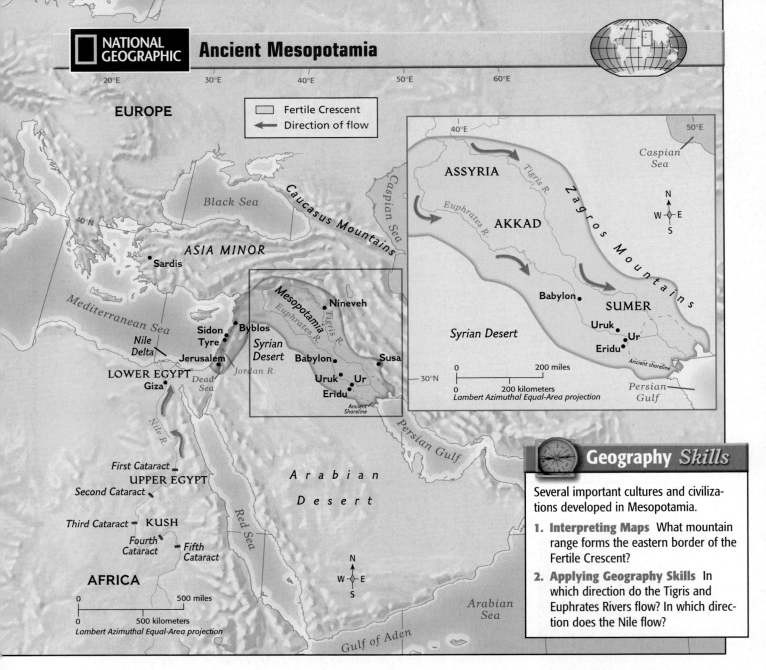

Several important cultures and civilizations developed in Mesopotamia.

1. **Interpreting Maps** What mountain range forms the eastern border of the Fertile Crescent?
2. **Applying Geography Skills** In which direction do the Tigris and Euphrates Rivers flow? In which direction does the Nile flow?

mountains where the rivers began. People in the valley could not tell exactly when the floods would come or how large they would be.

Because of these circumstances, farming in ancient Mesopotamia could be done only when people controlled the flow of the rivers. Irrigation and drainage ditches—part of a large-scale system of water control—made it possible to grow crops on a regular basis. The resulting abundance of food enabled large numbers of people to live together in cities and made possible the emergence of civilization in Mesopotamia.

When we speak of Mesopotamian civilization, we are referring to the achievements of several peoples. Ancient Mesopotamia includes three general areas: Assyria, Akkad, and Sumer. We focus first on the **Sumerians,** the creators of the first Mesopotamian civilization.

✓**Reading Check** **Explaining** What role did geography play in the development of Mesopotamian civilization?

The City-States of Ancient Mesopotamia

The origins of the Sumerian people remain a mystery. By 3000 B.C., they had established a number of independent cities in southern Mesopotamia, including Eridu, Ur, and **Uruk.** As the cities expanded, they came to have political and economic control over the surrounding countryside. They formed city-states, the basic units of Sumerian civilization.

Sumerian Cities
Sumerian cities were surrounded by walls. Uruk, for example, was encircled by a wall six miles (10 km) long with defense towers located along the wall every 30 to 35 feet (9 to 10 m). City dwellings, built of sun-dried bricks, included both the small houses of peasants and the larger buildings of the city officials, priests, and priestesses.

Although Mesopotamia had little stone or wood for building purposes, it did have plenty of mud. Mud bricks, easily shaped by hand, were left to bake in the hot sun until they were hard enough to use for building. People in Mesopotamia were remarkably creative with mud bricks. They invented the arch and the dome, and they built some of the largest brick buildings in the world. Mud bricks are still used in rural areas of Southwest Asia today.

Gods, Goddesses, and Rulers
The most prominent building in a Sumerian city was the temple dedicated to the chief god or goddess of the city. This temple was often built atop a massive stepped tower called a ziggurat. The Sumerians believed that gods and goddesses owned the cities. The people devoted much of their wealth to building temples, as well as elaborate houses for the priests and priestesses who served the gods. The temples and related buildings served as the center of the city physically, economically, and even politically.

Priests and priestesses, who supervised the temples and their property, had a great deal of power. In fact, historians believe that in the early stages of the city-states, priests and priestesses played an important role in ruling. The Sumerians believed that the gods ruled the cities, making the state a theocracy—a government by divine authority. Eventually, however, ruling power passed into the hands of worldly figures, or kings.

Sumerians viewed kingship as divine in origin. Kings, they believed, derived their power from the gods and were the agents of the gods. As one person said in a petition to his king: "You in your judgement, you are the son of Anu [god of the sky]. Your commands, like the work of a god, cannot be reversed. Your words, like rain pouring down from heaven, are without number."

Regardless of their origins, kings had power. They led armies, supervised the building of public works,

History *through Architecture*
Restored ziggurat at Ur, c. 2100 B.C.
At the top of a ziggurat was a shrine, which only the priests and priestesses could enter. Describe the technology and resources needed to build a ziggurat.

and organized workers for the irrigation projects on which Mesopotamian farming depended. The army, the government, and the priests and priestesses all aided the kings in their rule. As befitted their power, Sumerian kings, their wives, and their children lived in large palaces.

Economy and Society Although the economy of the Sumerian city-states was based chiefly on farming, trade and industry became important as well. The peoples of Mesopotamia were well known for their metalwork, but they also made woolen textiles and pottery. The Sumerians imported copper, tin, and timber in exchange for dried fish, wool, barley, wheat, and metal goods. Traders traveled by land to the eastern Mediterranean in the west and by sea to India in the east. The invention of the wheel, around 3000 B.C., led to wheeled carts, which made the transport of goods easier.

Mediterranean Sea
Tigris R.
Euphrates R.
Persian Gulf
Trade route
INDIA
Arabian Sea

Sumerian city-states contained three major social groups: nobles, commoners, and slaves. Nobles included royal and priestly officials and their families. Commoners worked for palace and temple estates and as farmers, merchants, fishers, and craftspeople. Probably 90 percent or more of the people were farmers. Slaves belonged to palace officials, who used them mostly in building projects. Temple officials most often used female slaves to weave cloth and grind grain. Rich landowners also used slaves to farm their lands.

Reading Check **Explaining** Why were the city-states considered to be theocracies?

Empires in Ancient Mesopotamia

As the number of Sumerian city-states grew and the city-states expanded, new conflicts arose. City-state fought city-state for control of land and water. Located on the flat land of Mesopotamia, the Sumerian city-states were also open to invasion by other groups.

To the north of the Sumerian city-states were the **Akkadians** (uh•KAY•dee•uhnz). We call them a *Semitic* people because they spoke a Semitic language. Around 2340 B.C., **Sargon,** leader of the Akkadians, overran the Sumerian city-states and set up the first empire in world history. An empire is a large political unit or state, usually under a single leader, that controls many peoples or territories. Empires are often easy to create but difficult to maintain. The rise and fall of empires is an important part of history.

The Royal Standard of Ur is a box, created about 2700 B.C., that depicts different Sumerian scenes. This panel shows a royal celebration following a military victory.

Attacks from neighboring hill peoples eventually caused the Akkadian Empire to fall. Its end by 2100 B.C. brought a return to the system of warring city-states. It was not until 1792 B.C. that a new empire came to control much of Mesopotamia. Leadership came from **Babylon,** a city-state south of Akkad, where **Hammurabi** (HA•muh•RAH•bee) came to power. He gained control of Sumer and Akkad, thus creating a new Mesopotamian kingdom. After his death in 1750 B.C., however, a series of weak kings was unable to keep Hammurabi's empire united, and it finally fell to new invaders.

✓ **Reading Check** **Evaluating** Why was it so easy for Sargon and his army to invade the Sumerian city-states?

The Code of Hammurabi

⌐TURNING|POINT┐ **Hammurabi is remembered for his law code, a collection of 282 laws. Many of its ideas were similar to later Israelite codes.**

For centuries, laws had regulated people's relationships with one another in the lands of Mesopotamia. Hammurabi's collection of laws provides considerable insight into social conditions in Mesopotamia.

The **Code of Hammurabi** was based on a system of strict justice. Penalties for criminal offenses were severe, and they varied according to the social class of the victim. A crime against a member of the upper class (a noble) by a member of the lower class (a commoner) was punished more severely than the same offense against a member of the lower class. Moreover, the principle of retaliation ("an eye for an eye, tooth for a tooth") was a fundamental part of this system of justice.

Hammurabi's code took seriously the duties of public officials. Officials were expected to catch burglars. If they failed to do so, the officials in the district where the crime was committed had to replace the lost property. If murderers were not found, the officials had to pay a fine to the relatives of the murdered person. Judges could be fined or lose their positions for ruling incorrectly on a case.

The law code also included what we would call consumer protection laws. Builders were held responsible for the buildings they constructed. If a house collapsed and caused the death of the owner, the builder was put to death. If the collapse caused the death of the son of the owner, the son of the builder was put to death. If goods were destroyed,

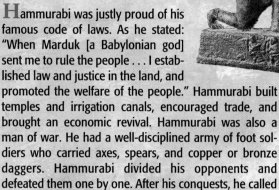

Hammurabi
Ruled 1792–1750 B.C.
Babylonian king

Hammurabi was justly proud of his famous code of laws. As he stated: "When Marduk [a Babylonian god] sent me to rule the people . . . I established law and justice in the land, and promoted the welfare of the people." Hammurabi built temples and irrigation canals, encouraged trade, and brought an economic revival. Hammurabi was also a man of war. He had a well-disciplined army of foot soldiers who carried axes, spears, and copper or bronze daggers. Hammurabi divided his opponents and defeated them one by one. After his conquests, he called himself "the sun of Babylon, the king who has made the four quarters of the world subservient."

they had to be replaced and the house rebuilt at the builder's expense.

The largest category of laws in the Code of Hammurabi focused on marriage and the family. Parents arranged marriages for their children. After marriage, the two parties signed a marriage contract. Without a contract, no one was considered legally married.

Society in ancient Mesopotamia was patriarchal— that is, Mesopotamian society was dominated by men. Hammurabi's code makes it clear that women had far fewer privileges and rights in marriage than did men.

A woman's place was definitely in the home. If she failed to fulfill her duties, her husband had legal grounds for divorce. In addition, if a wife was not able to bear children or tried to leave home to engage in business, her husband could divorce her. Even more harsh, a wife who was a "gadabout . . . neglecting her house [and] humiliating her husband," could be drowned.

Fathers ruled their children as well as their wives. Obedience was expected: "If a son has struck his father, he shall cut off his hand." If a son committed a serious enough offense, his father could disinherit him. Obviously, Hammurabi's law code covered almost every aspect of people's lives.

✓ **Reading Check** **Identifying** Identify at least five aspects of Mesopotamian society as revealed by the Code of Hammurabi.

The Importance of Religion

The physical environment strongly affected the way Mesopotamians viewed the world. Ferocious floods, heavy downpours, scorching winds, and oppressive humidity were all part of the Mesopotamian climate. These conditions, as well as famines, convinced Mesopotamians that this world was controlled by supernatural forces, which often were not kind or reliable. In the presence of nature, Mesopotamians could easily feel helpless, as this poem relates:

> **❝**The rampant flood which no man can oppose,
> Which shakes the heavens and causes earth to
>   tremble,
> In an appalling blanket folds mother and child,
> And drowns the harvest in its time of ripeness.**❞**

To the Mesopotamians, powerful spiritual beings—gods and goddesses—permeated all aspects of the universe. The Mesopotamians identified almost three thousand gods and goddesses. Mesopotamian religion was **polytheistic** because of this belief in many gods. Human beings were supposed to obey and serve the gods. According to Sumerian beliefs, human beings were created to do the manual labor the gods were unwilling to do for themselves. By their very nature, humans were inferior to the gods and could never be sure what the gods might do to help or hurt them.

✓Reading Check **Describing** What role did the physical environment play in the way Mesopotamians viewed the world?

The Creativity of the Sumerians

⌐**TURNING POINT**⌐ **The Sumerians are credited with inventing the oldest writing system, cuneiform, which dates from about 3000 B.C.**

The Sumerians created many inventions that still affect our lives today. Probably their greatest invention was their writing. In addition, historians credit them with many technological innovations.

Writing and Literature Around 3000 B.C., the Sumerians created a **cuneiform** ("wedge-shaped") system of writing. Using a reed stylus (a tool for writing), they made wedge-shaped impressions on clay tablets, which were then baked or dried in the sun. Once dried, these tablets lasted a very long time. Several hundred thousand tablets have been found.

Picturing **History**
The people of Mesopotamia associated gods with different aspects of nature and the universe. What aspect of nature do you think this goddess represents? Explain.

They have been a valuable source of information for modern scholars.

Mesopotamian peoples used writing primarily for record keeping. Cuneiform texts, however, were also used in schools to train scribes, members of the learned class who served as copyists, teachers, and jurists.

For boys of the upper class in Mesopotamia, becoming a scribe was the key to a successful career. Men who began their careers as scribes became the leaders of their cities, temples, and armies. Scribes came to hold the most important positions in Sumerian society.

To become scribes, boys from wealthy families, many of them the sons of scribes, attended the new schools that were in operation by 2500 B.C. Young boys seeking to become scribes began school when they were small children and trained until they were young men. School days began at sunrise and ended at sunset. Discipline was harsh. The following essay, written by a teacher as a copying exercise for pupils, shows that punishments—being caned or beaten with a stick—were frequent:

66In the tablet-house, the monitor said to me:
"Why are you late?" I was afraid, my heart
beat fast. I entered before my teacher, took
my place.
My "school-father" read my tablet to me, said,
"The word is cut off," caned me.
He who was in charge of drawing said "Why
when I was not here did you go out?"
caned me.
He who was in charge of the gate said
"Why when I was not here did you go out?"
caned me.
My teacher said "Your hand is not good,"
caned me.99

Scribal students spent most of their school days following the same routine. They were taught by copying and recopying standard works on clay tablets and reciting from them. Although boring, this was probably the scribe's only way of learning how to form the cuneiform writing signs neatly and correctly.

Writing was important because it allowed a society to keep records and to pass along knowledge from person to person and generation to generation. Writing also made it possible for people to communicate ideas in new ways. This is especially evident in *The Epic of Gilgamesh.*

Gilgamesh is a Mesopotamian epic poem that records the exploits of a legendary king named Gilgamesh. Gilgamesh is wise, strong, and perfect in body. He is part man and part god. Gilgamesh befriends a hairy beast named Enkidu. Together, they set off to do great deeds. When Enkidu dies, Gilgamesh feels the pain of death and begins a search for the secret of immortality. His efforts fail, and Gilgamesh remains mortal. This Mesopotamian epic makes clear that "everlasting life" is only for the gods.

Sumerian Technology The Sumerians invented several tools and devices that made daily life easier and more productive. They developed the wagon wheel, for example, to help transport people and goods from place to place. The potter's wheel to shape containers, the sundial to keep time, and the arch used in construction are other examples of Sumerian technology. The Sumerians were the first to make bronze out of copper and tin, creating finely crafted metalwork. The Sumerians also made outstanding achievements in mathematics and astronomy. In math, they devised a number system based on 60. Geometry was used to measure fields and erect buildings. In astronomy, the Sumerians charted the heavenly constellations. A quick glance at your watch and its division into 60 minutes in an hour should remind you of our debt to the Sumerians.

✓**Reading Check** **Identifying** Name two major inventions of the Sumerians, and tell how those inventions affect our lives today.

TAKS Practice

SECTION 1 ASSESSMENT

Checking for Understanding

1. **Define** city-state, ziggurat, theocracy, empire, patriarchal, polytheistic, cuneiform.

2. **Identify** Sumerians, Akkadians, Sargon, Hammurabi, Code of Hammurabi, *The Epic of Gilgamesh.*

3. **Locate** Tigris River, Euphrates River, Mesopotamia, Fertile Crescent, Uruk, Babylon.

4. **Explain** what the Mesopotamians believed was the relationship between gods and mortals.

5. **List** the three general areas of ancient Mesopotamia.

Critical Thinking

6. **Explain** Which type of government—separate city-states or an empire—would have been most advantageous to the people living in Mesopotamia?

7. **Organizing Information** Create a chart showing the achievements made by the Sumerians and list the effects of these achievements on our lives today.

Achievements	Effects on our lives today

Analyzing Visuals

8. **Examine** the photograph of the Royal Standard of Ur on page 40 of your text. What facts about Mesopotamian life can you identify by studying the picture? How does this box reflect the values of the Sumerian civilization?

Writing About History

9. **Expository Writing** Explain why Hammurabi's code was a significant development. Develop a set of laws based on the Code of Hammurabi that would apply to your community today. Explain why your code differs from that developed by Hammurabi or why it is similar.

Hammurabi's Code

ALTHOUGH THERE WERE EARLIER Mesopotamian law codes, the Code of Hammurabi is the most complete. The law code emphasizes the principle of retribution ("an eye for an eye") and punishments that vary according to social status. Punishments could be severe, as these examples show.

22: If a man has committed highway robbery and has been caught, that man should be put to death.

23: If the highwayman has not been caught, the man that has been robbed shall state on oath what he has lost and the city or district governor in whose territory or district the robbery took place shall restore to him what he has lost.

25: If fire broke out in a free man's house and a free man, who went to extinguish it, cast his eye on the goods of the owner of the house and has appropriated the goods of the owner of the house, that free man shall be thrown into that fire.

196: If a free man has destroyed the eye of a member of the aristocracy, they shall destroy his eye.

198: If he has destroyed the eye of a commoner or broken the bone of a commoner, he shall pay one mina of silver.

199: If he has destroyed the eye of a free man's slave or broken the bone of a free man's slave, he shall pay one-half his value.

229: If a builder constructed a house for a nobleman but did not make his work strong, with the result that the house which he built collapsed and so has caused the death of the owner of the house, that builder shall be put to death.

232: If it has destroyed goods, he shall make good whatever it destroyed; also, because he did not make the house strong that he built and it collapsed, he shall reconstruct the house that collapsed at his own expense.

—The Code of Hammurabi

Hammurabi's code was written on a stone monument, approximately seven feet tall, called a stele. The upper section of the stele shows Hammurabi standing in front of the seated sun god.

Analyzing Primary Sources

1. Explain the principle of retribution.
2. According to the Code of Hammurabi, what was most highly valued in Mesopotamian society? What was the least valued? Explain your answers.
3. What is the guiding principle in the American criminal justice system? How does this compare with Hammurabi's justice?

SECTION 2 Egyptian Civilization: "The Gift of the Nile"

Guide to Reading

Main Ideas
- The Nile was crucial to the development of Egyptian civilization.
- Egyptian history is divided into three major periods.

Key Terms
dynasty, pharaoh, bureaucracy, vizier, mummification, hieroglyphics, hieratic script

People to Identify
Menes, Hyksos, Hatshepsut, Akhenaton, Tutankhamen, Ramses II, Cleopatra VII

Places to Locate
Nile River, Lower Egypt, Upper Egypt, Giza

Preview Questions
1. What was the "Black Land"?
2. Why were the pyramids built and how were they used?

Reading Strategy
Identifying As you read this section, complete a chart like the one below identifying the characteristics of the three major periods of Egyptian history.

The Old Kingdom	The Middle Kingdom	The New Kingdom

Preview of Events

♦3500 B.C.	♦3000 B.C.	♦2500 B.C.	♦2000 B.C.	♦1500 B.C.	♦1000 B.C.	♦500 B.C.

3100 B.C.
King Menes unites villages of Upper and Lower Egypt

2540 B.C.
Great Pyramid built

1652 B.C.
The Hyksos invade Egypt

1085 B.C.
The New Kingdom collapses

Voices from the Past

Shepherd and his sheep on the banks of the Nile River

The Nile was crucial to the development of Egyptian civilization.

❝The Egyptian Nile," wrote one Arab traveler, "surpasses all the rivers of the world in sweetness of taste, in length of course and usefulness. No other river in the world can show such a continuous series of towns and villages along its banks." In their "Hymn to the Nile," Egyptians wrote of their reliance on the river: "The bringer of food, rich in provisions, creator of all good, lord of majesty, sweet of fragrance. . . . [The Nile] makes the granaries wide, and gives things to the poor. He who makes every beloved tree to grow.❞

—*Ancient Near Eastern Texts,* James B. Pritchard, 1969

Egypt, like Mesopotamia, was one of the first river valley civilizations. Like the people of Mesopotamia, the Egyptians left records of their developing civilization.

The Impact of Geography

The **Nile** is a unique river, beginning in the heart of Africa and coursing northward for more than 4,000 miles (6,436 km). It is the longest river in the world. Before it empties into the Mediterranean, the Nile splits into two major branches. This split forms a triangular territory, the delta. The Nile Delta is called **Lower Egypt;** the land upstream, to the south, is called **Upper Egypt.** Egypt's important cities developed at the tip of the delta, the point at which the Nile divides.

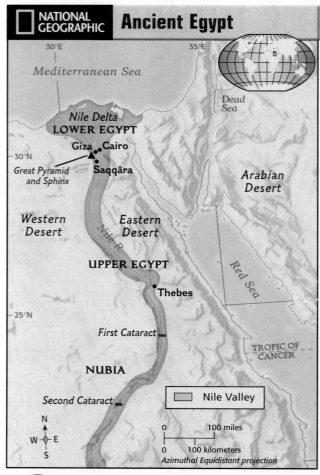

NATIONAL GEOGRAPHIC   Ancient Egypt

Mediterranean Sea

Dead Sea

Nile Delta
LOWER EGYPT

Giza • Cairo
Great Pyramid ▲ • Saqqâra
and Sphinx

Western Desert

Eastern Desert

Nile R.

UPPER EGYPT

Arabian Desert

• Thebes

Red Sea

First Cataract

TROPIC OF CANCER

NUBIA

Second Cataract

[ ] Nile Valley

N
W — E
S

0   100 miles
0   100 kilometers
Azimuthal Equidistant projection

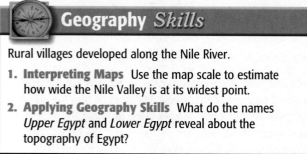

Geography *Skills*

Rural villages developed along the Nile River.

1. **Interpreting Maps** Use the map scale to estimate how wide the Nile Valley is at its widest point.
2. **Applying Geography Skills** What do the names *Upper Egypt* and *Lower Egypt* reveal about the topography of Egypt?

To the ancient Egyptians, the most important feature of the river was its yearly flooding—the "miracle" of the Nile. The river rose in the summer from heavy rains in central Africa, reached its highest point in Egypt in September and October, and left a deposit of mud that created an area of rich soil several miles wide on both sides of the river. The Egyptians called this fertile land, which was dark in color, the "Black Land." Beyond these narrow strips of fertile fields lay the deserts, the "Red Land."

The surpluses of food that the Egyptian farmers grew in the fertile Nile Valley made Egypt prosperous. The river also served as a unifying factor in Egyptian history. In ancient times, the Nile was the fastest way to travel through the land, making both transportation and communication easier. Winds from the north pushed sailboats south, and the current of the Nile carried them north.

Unlike Mesopotamia, which was subject to constant invasion, Egypt was blessed by natural barriers that gave it protection from invasion and a sense of security. These barriers included the deserts to the west and east; the Red Sea to the east; the cataracts (rapids) on the southern part of the Nile, which made defense relatively easy; and the Mediterranean Sea to the north.

The regularity of the Nile floods and the relative isolation of the Egyptians created a feeling of security and changelessness. To the ancient Egyptians, when the Nile flooded each year, "the fields laugh and people's faces light up." Unlike people in Mesopotamia, Egyptians faced life with a spirit of confidence in the stability of things. Ancient Egyptian civilization was marked by a remarkable degree of continuity over thousands of years.

✓ Reading Check **Contrasting** Explain how flooding patterns of rivers in Egypt and Mesopotamia caused the two civilizations to develop differently.

The Importance of Religion

Religion, too, provided a sense of security and timelessness for the Egyptians. Actually, they had no word for religion. For them, religious ideas were an inseparable part of the entire world order. The Egyptians were polytheistic. They had a remarkable number of gods associated with heavenly bodies and natural forces. Two groups, sun gods and land gods, came to have special importance. Is that surprising in view of the importance to Egypt's well-being of the sun and the fertile land along the banks of the Nile?

The sun, the source of life, was of course worthy of worship. The sun god took on different forms and names, depending on his specific role. He was worshiped as Atum in human form and also as Re, who had a human body but the head of a falcon. The Egyptian ruler took the title Son of Re, because he was seen as an earthly form of Re.

River and land gods included Osiris and Isis. A famous Egyptian myth told of the struggle between Osiris, who brought civilization to Egypt, and his evil brother Seth, who killed him, cut his body into 14 parts, and tossed the parts into the Nile. The pieces were found by Osiris's wife, Isis. With help from other gods, Isis brought Osiris back to life.

Osiris took on an important role for the Egyptians as a symbol of resurrection. By identifying with Osiris, people could hope to gain new life, just as Osiris had done. The dead were placed in tombs (in the case of kings, in pyramid tombs); were given the name Osiris; and by a process of magical identification, became Osiris. Like Osiris, they would then be reborn. The flooding of the Nile and the new life it brought to Egypt were symbolized by Isis's bringing all of Osiris's parts together each spring in the festival of the new land.

✓**Reading Check** **Examining**
What is the significance of the famous Egyptian myth of the struggle between Osiris and his evil brother Seth? Why did Osiris take on an important role for the Egyptians?

The Course of Egyptian History

Modern historians have divided Egyptian history into three major periods, known as the Old Kingdom, Middle Kingdom, and New Kingdom. These were periods of long-term stability marked by strong leadership, freedom from invasion, the building of temples and pyramids, and considerable intellectual and cultural activity. Between the periods of stability were ages of political chaos and invasion, known as the Intermediate periods.

The history of Egypt begins around 3100 B.C., when **Menes** (MEE•NEEZ) the king united the villages of Upper (southern) and Lower (northern) Egypt into a single kingdom and created the first Egyptian royal dynasty. A **dynasty** is a family of rulers whose right to rule is passed on within the family.

From then on, the Egyptian ruler would be called "King of Upper and Lower Egypt." The royal crown would be a double crown, indicating the unity of all Egypt. Just as the Nile served to unite Upper Egypt and Lower Egypt physically, kingship united the two areas politically.

The Old Kingdom The Old Kingdom, which lasted from around 2700 to 2200 B.C., was an age of prosperity and splendor. Like the kings of the Sumerian city-states, the monarchs of the Old Kingdom were powerful rulers over a unified state. Among the

Picturing **History**

Osiris (above) ruled the realm of the dead and was associated with rebirth. Horus (above left), the son of Osiris and Isis, was the sky god. What do these depictions reveal about Egyptian belief?

various titles of Egyptian monarchs, that of pharaoh (originally meaning "great house" or "palace") eventually became the most common.

Kingship was a divine institution in ancient Egypt and formed part of a universal cosmic order: "What is the king of Upper and Lower Egypt? He is a god by whose dealings one lives, the father and mother of all men, alone by himself, without an equal." In obeying their pharaoh, subjects believed that they were helping to maintain a stable world order. A breakdown in royal power could only mean that citizens were offending the gods and weakening that order.

Egyptian pharaohs possessed absolute power—that is, they had complete, unlimited power to rule their people. Nevertheless, they had help in ruling.

At first, members of the pharaoh's family aided in running the country. During the Old Kingdom, however, a government **bureaucracy**—an administrative organization with officials and regular procedures—developed. Especially important was the office of **vizier,** the "steward of the whole land." Directly responsible to the pharaoh, the vizier was in charge of the government bureaucracy. In time, Egypt was divided into 42 provinces, which were run by governors appointed by the pharaoh. Each governor was responsible to the pharaoh and vizier.

The Pyramids One of the great achievements of Egyptian civilization, the building of pyramids, occurred in the time of the Old Kingdom. Pyramids were built as part of a larger complex of buildings dedicated to the dead—in effect, a city of the dead. The area included several structures: a large pyramid for the pharaoh's burial; smaller pyramids for his family; and several mastabas, rectangular structures with flat roofs used as tombs for the pharaoh's officials.

The tombs were well prepared for their residents. They contained rooms stocked with

supplies, including chairs, boats, chests, weapons, games, dishes, and a variety of foods. The Egyptians believed that human beings had two bodies—a physical one and a spiritual one, which they called the *ka.* If the physical body was properly preserved and the tomb furnished with all the various objects of regular life, the *ka* could return. Surrounded by earthly comforts, the *ka* could then continue its life despite the death of the physical body.

To preserve the physical body after death, the Egyptians practiced **mummification,** a process of slowly drying a dead body to prevent it from rotting. This process took place in workshops run by priests, primarily for the wealthy families who could afford it. Workers first removed the liver, lungs, stomach, and intestines and placed them in four special jars that were put in the tomb with the mummy. The priests also removed the brain by extracting it through the nose. They then covered the corpse with a natural salt that absorbed the body's water. Later, they filled the body with spices and wrapped it with layers of linen soaked in resin. At the end of the process, which had taken about 70 days, a lifelike mask was placed over the head and shoulders of the mummy. The mummy was then sealed in a case and placed in its tomb.

History *through Architecture*

The mastaba (above) was the forerunner to the pyramid (left) and a simpler burial alternative for people who were not part of the royal court. How would the artifacts and paintings within a mastaba differ from those in a pyramid?

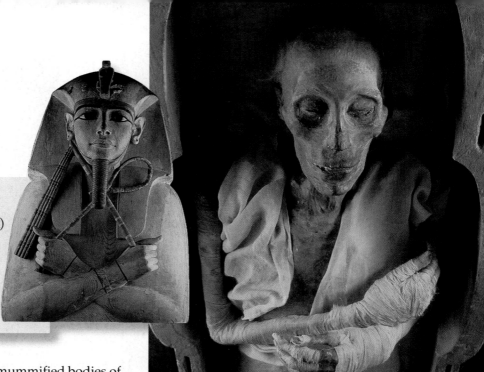

Pyramids were tombs for the mummified bodies of pharaohs. The largest and most magnificent of all the pyramids was built under King Khufu (KOO•FOO). Constructed at **Giza** around 2540 B.C., the famous Great Pyramid of King Khufu covers 13 acres (5.3 ha), measures 756 feet (230 m) at each side of its base, and stands 481 feet (147 m) high.

The building of the Great Pyramid was an enormous construction project. The Greek historian Herodotus reported the traditional story that it took 100,000 Egyptians 20 years to build the Great Pyramid. Herodotus wrote two thousand years after the event, however, and much speculation still surrounds the building of the Great Pyramid. Especially puzzling is how the builders achieved their amazing level of precision. The stone slabs on the outside of the Great Pyramid, for example, fit so closely side by side that even a hair cannot be pushed into the joints between them.

Guarding the Great Pyramid at Giza is a huge statue carved from rock, known as the Great Sphinx. This colossal statue is 240 feet (73 m) long and 66 feet (20 m) high. It has the body of a lion and a human head. The head is believed by many to be a likeness of Khufu's son Khafre, who ordered the statue's construction. Historians do not agree on the purpose of the Great Sphinx. Many Egyptians, however, believed that the mythical sphinx was an important guardian of sacred sites.

The Great Pyramid still stands as a visible symbol of the power of the Egyptian pharaohs of the Old Kingdom. No pyramid built later matched its size or splendor. The pyramid was not only the pharaoh's tomb but also an important symbol of royal power. It could be seen for miles and served to remind people of the glory, might, and wealth of the ruler who was a living god on Earth.

The Middle Kingdom The Old Kingdom eventually collapsed, followed by a period of chaos that lasted about 150 years. Finally, a new royal dynasty gained control of all Egypt and began the Middle Kingdom, a period of stability lasting from about 2050 to 1652 B.C. Egyptians later portrayed the Middle Kingdom as a golden age—an age of stability.

As evidence of its newfound strength, Egypt began a period of expansion. Nubia, which was located south of Egypt, was conquered. Fortresses were built to protect the new southern frontier. The government sent armies into Palestine and Syria, although they did not remain there. Pharaohs also sent traders to Kush, Syria, Mesopotamia, and Crete.

One feature of the Middle Kingdom was a new concern of the pharaohs for the people. In the Old Kingdom, the pharaoh had been seen as a god-king far removed from his people. Now he was portrayed as the shepherd of his people and expected to build public works and provide for the public welfare. Pharaohs of the Middle Kingdom undertook a number of helpful projects. The draining of swampland in the Nile Delta provided thousands of acres of new farmland. The digging of a canal to connect the Nile to the Red Sea aided trade and transportation.

The New Kingdom The Middle Kingdom came to an end around 1652 B.C. with the invasion of Egypt

The Great Sphinx was built more than 4,500 years ago. Today it is crumbling due to wind, humidity, and smog from Cairo.

by a group of people from western Asia known to the Egyptians as the **Hyksos** (HIK•SAHS). The Hyksos used horse-drawn war chariots and overwhelmed the Egyptian soldiers, who fought from donkey carts.

For almost a hundred years, the Hyksos ruled much of Egypt. The conquered Egyptians learned a great deal, however, from their conquerors. From the Hyksos, the Egyptians learned to use bronze in the making of their farming tools and their weapons. The Egyptians also mastered many of the military skills of the Hyksos, especially the use of horse-drawn war chariots.

Eventually, a new dynasty of pharaohs used the new weapons to drive out the Hyksos and reunite Egypt. The New Kingdom was established and lasted approximately from 1567 to 1085 B.C. This reunification launched the Egyptians along a new militaristic path. During the period of the New Kingdom, Egypt created an empire and became the most powerful state in Southwest Asia.

Massive wealth boosted the power of the New Kingdom pharaohs. The Egyptian rulers showed their wealth by building

Web Activity
Visit the *Glencoe World History* Web site at tx.wh.glencoe.com and click on **Chapter 2– Student Web Activity** to learn more about Egypt.

Geography *Skills*

Egypt began a period of commercial and military expansion during the Middle Kingdom that would bring the country stability and wealth until the New Kingdom collapsed in 1085 B.C.

1. **Interpreting Maps** Analyze the patterns of movement for the armies and traders. Explain why they diverge at the Mediterranean Sea.

2. **Applying Geography Skills** Explain how Egypt's location would have been an asset to its expansion, as well as a liability contributing to its downfall.

new temples. **Hatshepsut**—the first woman to become pharaoh—built a great temple at Deir el Bahri, near Thebes. Hatshepsut was succeeded by her nephew, Thutmose (thoot•MOH•suh) III. He led 17 military campaigns into Syria and Palestine and even reached the Euphrates River. His forces occupied Palestine and Syria and moved westward into Libya. Magnificent new buildings and temples were constructed to show the greatness of the empire.

The New Kingdom was not without troubles, however. The pharaoh Amenhotep IV introduced the worship of Aton, god of the sun disk, as the sole god. Amenhotep changed his own name to **Akhenaton** ("It is well with Aton") and closed the temples of other gods. In a society that had always been tolerant of many gods, Akhenaton's actions in destroying the

The Egyptians learned much, including the use of war chariots, from the Hyksos.

old gods meant to many the destruction of Egypt itself. Akhenaton's changes were soon undone after his death by the boy-pharaoh **Tutankhamen,** who restored the old gods.

The upheavals associated with Amenhotep's religious revolution led to a loss of Egypt's empire. Under **Ramses II,** who reigned from 1279 to 1213 B.C., the Egyptians went back on the offensive. They regained control of Palestine but were unable to reestablish the borders of their earlier empire. New invasions in the thirteenth century B.C. by the "Sea Peoples," as Egyptians called them, drove the Egyptians back within their old frontiers and ended the Egyptian Empire. The New Kingdom itself collapsed in 1085 B.C.

For the next thousand years, Egypt was dominated by Libyans, Nubians, Persians, and finally Macedonians after the conquest of Alexander the Great (see Chapter 4). In the first century B.C., the pharaoh **Cleopatra VII** tried to reestablish Egypt's independence. However, her involvement with Rome led to her suicide and defeat, and Egypt became a province in Rome's mighty empire.

✓**Reading Check** **Contrasting** What were the major differences among the Old Kingdom, the Middle Kingdom, and the New Kingdom?

Society in Ancient Egypt

Over a period of thousands of years, Egyptian society maintained a simple structure. It was organized like a pyramid, with the god-king at the top. The pharaoh was surrounded by an upper class of nobles and priests, who joined in the elaborate rituals of the pharaoh's life. The members of this ruling class ran the government and managed their own landed estates, which provided much of their wealth.

Below the upper class were merchants, artisans, scribes, and tax collectors. Middle-class homes, mostly in the city, were comfortable but not elegant. Merchants carried on an active trade up and down the Nile, as well as in town and village markets. Some merchants also engaged in international trade. They were sent by the pharaoh to Crete and Syria, where they obtained wood and other products. Egyptian artisans made an incredible variety of well-built, beautiful goods: stone dishes; painted boxes; wooden furniture; gold, silver, and copper tools and containers; paper and rope made of papyrus; and linen clothes.

By far, the largest number of people in Egypt simply worked the land. In theory, the pharaoh owned all the land but granted portions of it to the subjects. Large sections of land were held by nobles and by the priests who supervised the numerous temples. Most of the lower classes were peasants who farmed the land of these estates. They paid taxes in the form of crops to the pharaoh, nobles, and priests; lived in small villages or towns; and provided military service and forced labor for building projects.

✓**Reading Check** **Summarizing** List the social classes of ancient Egypt and identify the contributions of each to Egyptian society.

People In History

Hatshepsut
Ruled 1503–1482 B.C.
Egyptian pharaoh

Hatshepsut was the daughter of the pharaoh Thutmose I. She married her half-brother, who became the pharaoh Thutmose II. When he died, Hatshepsut assumed the full power of pharaoh. Statues show Hatshepsut clothed and bearded as a king would be. She was addressed as "His Majesty."

Hatshepsut's reign was a prosperous one. She is best known for the temple dedicated to herself at Deir el Bahri on the west bank of the Nile at Thebes. One of the inscriptions she had placed there reads: "Now my heart turns to and fro, in thinking what will the people say, they who shall see my monument in later years, and shall speak of what I have done."

Daily Life in Ancient Egypt

Ancient Egyptians had a very positive attitude toward daily life on Earth. They married young (girls at 12 and boys at 14) and established homes and families. Monogamy (marriage to one person) was the general rule, although a husband was allowed to keep additional wives if his first wife was childless.

The husband was master in the house, but wives were very well respected. Wives were in charge of the household and the education of the children. From a book of wise sayings (which the Egyptians called "instructions") came this advice: "If you are a man of standing, you should love your wife at home as is fitting. Fill her belly; clothe her back. . . . Make her heart glad as long as you live." 📖 *(See page 990 to read excerpts from Vizier Ptah-hotep's* An Egyptian Father's Advice to His Son *in the Primary Sources Library.)*

Women's property and inheritance stayed in their hands, even in marriage. Although most careers and public offices were closed to women, some women did operate businesses. Peasant women, of course, worked long hours in the fields and at numerous tasks in the home. Upper-class women could become priestesses, and four queens became pharaohs.

Parents arranged marriages for their children. Their chief concerns were family and property. The chief purpose of marriage was to produce children, especially sons. Only sons could carry on the family name. Daughters were not ignored, however, and numerous tomb paintings show the close and affectionate relationship parents had with both sons and daughters. Although marriages were arranged, the surviving love poems from ancient Egypt suggest that some marriages included an element of romance.

Egyptian marriages could and did end in divorce. It included compensation for the wife.

✓ Reading Check **Identifying** What were the primary responsibilities of a wife in an Egyptian home?

Writing and Education

Writing in Egypt emerged around 3000 B.C. The Greeks later called this earliest Egyptian writing **hieroglyphics**, meaning "priest-carvings" or "sacred writings." The hieroglyphic system of writing, which used both pictures and more abstract forms, was complex. Learning and practicing it took much time and skill. Hieroglyphic script was used for writing on temple walls and in tombs. A highly simplified version of hieroglyphics, known as **hieratic script**, came into being. It used the same principles as hieroglyphic writing, but the drawings were simplified by using dashes, strokes, and curves to represent them. Hieratic script was used for business transactions, record keeping, and the general needs of daily life.

Egyptian hieroglyphs were at first carved in stone. Later, hieratic script was written on papyrus, a paper made from the papyrus reed that grew along the Nile. Most of the ancient Egyptian literature that has come down to us was written on rolls of papyrus.

The Egyptian scribes were masters of the art of writing and also its teachers. At the age of 10, boys of the upper classes went to schools run by scribes. Training to be a scribe took many years. Students learned to read and write by copying texts. Discipline was strict, as is evident from the following Egyptian saying: "A boy's ears are on his back. He listens only when he is beaten." Girls remained at home and learned housekeeping skills from their mothers.

✓ Reading Check **Contrasting** What are the differences between hieroglyphics and hieratic script?

Achievements in Art and Science

Pyramids, temples, and other monuments bear witness to the architectural and artistic achievements of the Egyptians. Artists and sculptors were expected to follow particular formulas in style. This gave

Architects' tools, amphora (a two-handled jar), and wooden chair belonging to King Tutankhamen

Comparing Life in Mesopotamia and Egypt

	Mesopotamia	Egypt
Geography	Fertile Crescent (Southwest Asia)	Africa
Rivers	Tigris and Euphrates	Nile
Natural Barriers	Flat plains	Deserts, seas, cataracts
Religion	Polytheistic	Polytheistic
Government	City-states; theocracy; large bureaucracy; kings ruled	Rural villages; dynasties; divine kings ruled
Social Structure	Nobles, commoners, slaves	Upper classes, merchants, artisans, peasants
Economy	Farming and trade	Farming and trade
Written Language	Cuneiform	Hieroglyphics

Chart Skills

Ancient civilizations thrived in both Mesopotamia and Egypt.

1. **Making Comparisons** Create a map of Mesopotamia and Egypt. Develop icons to illustrate the differences and similarities in the cultures.

2. **Evaluating** How did geographical differences influence the development of these cultures?

Egyptian art a distinctive look for thousands of years. For example, the human body was often portrayed as a combination of profile, semiprofile, and frontal view to accurately represent each part.

Egyptians also made advances in mathematics. Mathematics helped them in building their massive monuments. Egyptians were able to calculate area and volume and used geometry to survey flooded land.

The Egyptians developed an accurate 365-day calendar by basing their year not only on the movements of the moon, but also the bright star Sirius.

Sirius rises in the sky just before the annual flooding of the Nile River.

The practice of embalming (preserving a dead body to protect it from decay) led to medical expertise in human anatomy. Archeologists have recovered directions from doctors for using splints, bandages, and compresses for treating fractures, wounds, and disease. Other ancient civilizations acquired medical knowledge from the Egyptians.

Reading Check **Describing** What was distinctive about Egyptian art?

TAKS Practice

SECTION 2 ASSESSMENT

Checking for Understanding

1. **Define** dynasty, pharaoh, bureaucracy, vizier, mummification, hieroglyphics, hieratic script.

2. **Identify** Menes, Hyksos, Hatshepsut, Akhenaton, Tutankhamen, Ramses II, Cleopatra VII.

3. **Locate** Nile River, Lower Egypt, Upper Egypt, Giza.

4. **Explain** the significance of the Egyptian ruler's title "Son of Re."

5. **List** the various peoples who dominated Egypt after the collapse of the New Kingdom.

Critical Thinking

6. **Describe** In what ways are the customs of ancient Egypt similar to the customs in your society today?

7. **Organizing Information** Use a diagram like the one below to describe the impact the Nile had on life in ancient Egypt.

Nile River			

Analyzing Visuals

8. **Describe** what the artifacts pictured on page 52 of your text tell you about royal Egyptian life. How do the Egyptian tools compare to the Paleolithic tools shown on page 23 of your text?

Writing About History

9. **Descriptive Writing** Assume you are a tour guide leading a tour of the Great Pyramid. Explain to your tour group why the pyramids were built and what historians believe to be the significance of the Great Pyramid. Create an advertising brochure to promote and sell your tour.

New Centers of Civilization

Guide to Reading

Main Ideas
- The decline of the Hittites and Egyptians allowed a number of small kingdoms and city-states to emerge.
- The Israelites did not create an empire, but they left a world religion, Judaism, that influenced the later religions of Christianity and Islam.

Key Terms
pastoral nomad, monotheistic

People to Identify
Indo-Europeans, Hittites, Phoenicians, Israelites, King Solomon, Isaiah

Places to Locate
Palestine, Jerusalem

Preview Questions
1. How did nomadic peoples affect the centers of civilization?
2. What factors caused the decline of the Hittite kingdom?

Reading Strategy
Summarizing Information Use a diagram like the one below to show how the Phoenicians affected the development of civilization in Southwest Asia.

Phoenicians

Preview of Events

♦1600 B.C.	♦1400 B.C.	♦1200 B.C.	♦1000 B.C.	♦800 B.C.	♦600 B.C.	♦400 B.C.

c. 1600 B.C.
Hittites create empire in western Asia

c. 1200 B.C.
End of Hittite kingdom

c. 1200 B.C.
Israelites emerge as a distinct group of people

722 B.C.
Assyrians overrun the Kingdom of Israel

586 B.C.
Chaldeans destroy Jerusalem

Voices from the Past

According to the biblical account, it was during the flight from Egypt, where they had been enslaved, that the Israelites made a covenant with God:

66And God spoke all these words, 'I am the Lord your God, who brought you out of Egypt, out of the land of slavery. You shall have no other gods before me. You shall not make for yourself an idol in the form of anything in heaven above or on the earth beneath or in the waters below. . . . You shall not murder. You shall not commit adultery. You shall not steal.'99

—Exodus 20:1–17

Obedience to God's law, the Ten Commandments, became an important aspect of the Jewish religious tradition.

Moses receiving the Ten Commandments

The Role of Nomadic Peoples

Our story of civilization so far has focused on Mesopotamia and Egypt. Only recently have archaeologists discovered what they believe is another ancient civilization that flourished in central Asia (in what are now the republics of Turkmenistan and Uzbekistan) around 4,000 years ago. People in this civilization built mud-brick buildings, raised sheep and goats, had bronze tools, and used a system of irrigation to grow wheat and barley. Recently discovered inscriptions show that these early people may have had writing.

On the fringes of these civilizations lived nomadic peoples who depended on hunting and gathering, herding, and sometimes farming for their survival. Most important were the pastoral nomads who on occasion overran settled communities and created their own empires. Pastoral nomads domesticated animals for both food and clothing. They moved along regular migratory routes to provide steady sources of nourishment for their animals.

People who lived in settled communities often viewed nomadic peoples as hostile and barbaric, or uncivilized. The two types of groups did interact, however. Nomads traded animals and animal products for grains and vegetables they were unable to grow. Pastoral nomads also aided long-distance trade by carrying products between civilized centers. In this way, nomads often passed on new technological developments, such as the use of bronze and iron, that provided new sources of strength to the old civilizations. When the normal patterns of the pastoral nomads were disrupted by drought or overpopulation, however, they often attacked the civilized communities to obtain relief.

The **Indo-Europeans** were one of the most important nomadic peoples. The term *Indo-European* refers to a particular group of people who used a language derived from a single parent tongue. Indo-European languages include Greek, Latin, Persian, Sanskrit, and the Germanic languages. The original Indo-European peoples were probably based somewhere in the steppe region north of the Black Sea or in Southwest Asia. Around 2000 B.C. they began to move into Europe, India, and western Asia. One group of Indo-Europeans moved into Asia Minor and Anatolia around 1750 B.C. and combined with the native peoples to form the Hittite kingdom with its capital at Hattusha (Bogazköy in modern Turkey).

Between 1600 and 1200 B.C., the **Hittites** created their own empire in western Asia and even threatened the power of the Egyptians. The Hittites were the first of the Indo-European peoples to make use of iron. This technology enabled them to use weapons that were stronger and cheaper to make because of the widespread availability of iron ore. Around 1200 B.C., however, new waves of invaders known to historians only as the "Sea Peoples" destroyed the Hittite Empire.

The end of the Hittite kingdom and the weakening of Egypt around 1200 B.C. temporarily left no dominant powers in western Asia. This allowed a number of small kingdoms and city-states to emerge, especially in the area of Syria and Palestine. The Phoenicians were one of these peoples.

Reading Check **Identifying** Who were the first Indo-Europeans to make use of iron?

The Phoenicians

The **Phoenicians** lived in the area of Palestine along the Mediterranean coast on a narrow band of land 120 miles (193 km) long. After the downfall of the Hittites and the Egyptians, the newfound

Hebrew, Phoenician, and Latin Alphabets

Hebrew	א ב ג ד ה ו ז ח ט י כ ל מ נ ס ע פ צ ק ר ש ת
Phoenician	𐤀 𐤁 𐤂 𐤃 𐤄 𐤅 𐤆 𐤇 𐤈 𐤉 𐤊 𐤋 𐤌 𐤍 𐤎 𐤏 𐤐 𐤑 𐤒 𐤓 𐤔 𐤕
Imperial Latin	A B C D E F G H I K L M N O P Q R S T V X Y Z

Imperial Latin did not distinguish between I and J or between V and U. There was no W. Y and Z were introduced after 100 B.C. for foreign words only.

Chart *Skills*

Many civilizations developed their own alphabets.

1. **Comparing** What similarities do you see among the three alphabets shown here?

political independence of the Phoenicians helped them expand their trade. Trade had long been the basis of Phoenician prosperity. The chief cities of Phoenicia—Byblos, Tyre, and Sidon—were ports on the eastern Mediterranean. The Phoenicians produced a number of goods for foreign markets, including purple dye, glass, and lumber from the cedar forests of Lebanon.

The Phoenicians improved their ships, became great international sea traders, and thus created a trade empire. They charted new routes not only in the Mediterranean but also in the Atlantic Ocean, where they reached Britain and sailed south along the west coast of Africa. The Phoenicians set up a number of colonies in the western Mediterranean. Carthage, their most famous colony, was located on the North African coast.

The Phoenician culture is best known for its alphabet. The Phoenicians, who spoke a Semitic language, simplified their writing by using 22 different signs to represent the sounds of their speech. These 22 characters, or letters, could be used to spell out all the words in the Phoenician language. Although the Phoenicians were not the only people to invent an alphabet, theirs was important because it was eventually passed on to the Greeks. From the Greek alphabet was derived the Roman alphabet that we still use today.

Reading Check **Identifying**
What was the most significant cultural invention of the Phoenicians?

The "Children of Israel"

To the south of the Phoenicians lived another group of Semitic-speaking people known as the **Israelites.** They were a minor factor in the politics of the region. However, their religion—known today as Judaism—flourished as a world religion and later influenced the religions of Christianity and Islam. Much of the history and the religious beliefs of the Israelites were eventually recorded in written form in the Hebrew Bible, parts of which are known to Christians as the Old Testament. According to their history, the Israelites migrated from Mesopotamia to Palestine, which the Hebrews referred to as Canaan. They followed a lifestyle based on grazing flocks and herds rather than on farming. Then, because of drought, the Israelites migrated to Egypt, where they were enslaved until Moses led them out of Egypt. They wandered for many years in the desert until they returned to Palestine.

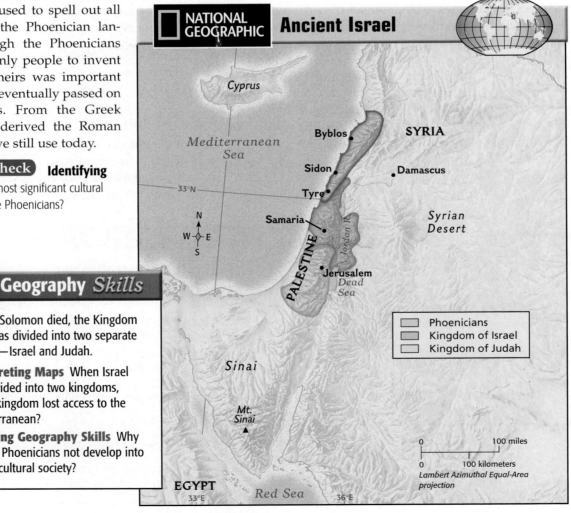

NATIONAL GEOGRAPHIC **Ancient Israel**

Geography *Skills*

After King Solomon died, the Kingdom of Israel was divided into two separate kingdoms—Israel and Judah.

1. **Interpreting Maps** When Israel was divided into two kingdoms, which kingdom lost access to the Mediterranean?

2. **Applying Geography Skills** Why did the Phoenicians not develop into an agricultural society?

Some interpretations of recent archaeological evidence contradict the details of the biblical account. What is generally agreed, however, is that between 1200 and 1000 B.C., the Israelites emerged as a distinct group of people, organized in tribes, who established a united kingdom known as Israel.

The United Kingdom By the time of **King Solomon,** who ruled from about 970 to 930 B.C., the Israelites had established control over all of **Palestine** and made **Jerusalem** into the capital of Israel. Solomon greatly strengthened royal power. He expanded the government and army and encouraged trade. Solomon is best known for building a temple in the city of Jerusalem. The Israelites viewed the temple as the symbolic center of their religion and of the Israelite kingdom itself. Under Solomon, ancient Israel was at the height of its power.

King Solomon was also known for his wisdom. Once, two women brought a child before him, each claiming that she was the child's mother. Solomon ordered his servant to cut the child in half, giving one half to each woman. The first woman objected:

King Solomon

"Please, my lord, give her the living baby! Don't kill him!" The second woman replied, "Neither I nor you shall have him. Cut him in two!" Then Solomon said: "Give the baby to the first woman. Do not kill him; she is his mother." According to the biblical account, "When all Israel heard the verdict the king had given, they held the king in awe, because they saw that he had wisdom from God to administer justice."

The Divided Kingdom After Solomon's death, tension between the northern and southern tribes within Israel led to the creation of two separate kingdoms. The Kingdom of Israel was composed of the ten northern tribes and had its capital at Samaria. To the south, the Kingdom of Judah consisted of two tribes and had its capital at Jerusalem.

In 722 B.C., the Assyrians overran the Kingdom of Israel and sent many Israelites to other parts of the Assyrian Empire. These scattered Israelites (the "ten lost tribes") merged with neighboring peoples and gradually lost their identity.

CONNECTIONS Past To Present

Conflict in Palestine

Conflict in Southwest Asia has a long history. When the Israelites entered Palestine, around 1220 B.C., other peoples were already settled there. One of these peoples was the Philistines. For over two centuries, Israelites and Philistines fought for control.

By 1020 B.C., the Israelites found themselves on the verge of being conquered by the Philistines. The Israelites decided to give up their loose tribal organization, choosing to unite behind one of their members, Saul, who became king.

At first, Saul and the small army he organized were successful. Around 1000 B.C., however, when they dared to meet the Philistines on an open plain, Saul and his army were defeated.

David, the next king of the Israelites, defeated the Philistines and established control over all of Palestine. Although later the Israelites would be conquered and scattered, Palestine remained the Promised Land in the minds of many Jews.

In 1948, the independent Jewish state of Israel was established in Palestine. More than two-thirds of the people there were Arab Muslims who were not eager to be governed by the Israelis. Arab neighbors of the new state were outraged. In 1964, an Arab organization called the Palestine Liberation Organization was founded to bring about an independent Arab state of Palestine. Conflict between Arabs and Israelis over Palestine continues to this day.

▲ *Conflict in the Middle East*

Comparing Past and Present

Research the steps that have been taken to reach a peaceful settlement between the Israelis and Palestinians over the past five years. What actions have been the most successful? What are the most significant reasons that a lasting peace still does not exist?

The Kingdom of Judah managed to retain its independence for a while, but a new enemy soon appeared on the horizon. The Chaldeans (kal•DEE•uhnz) defeated Assyria, conquered the Kingdom of Judah, and completely destroyed Jerusalem in 586 B.C. Many upper-class people of Judah were sent as captives to Babylonia. The memory of their exile is evoked in the words of Psalm 137:

CHALDEAN EMPIRE

Babylon

Jerusalem

BABYLONIA

Persian Gulf

> 66 By the rivers of Babylon, we sat and wept when we remembered Zion. . . . How can we sing the songs of the Lord while in a foreign land? If I forget you, O Jerusalem, may my right hand forget its skill. May my tongue cling to the roof of my mouth if I do not remember you, if I do not consider Jerusalem my highest joy. 99

The Babylonian captivity of the people of Judah did not last. A new set of conquerors, the Persians, destroyed the Chaldean kingdom and allowed the people of Judah to return to Jerusalem and rebuild their city and temple. The revived Kingdom of Judah remained under Persian control until the conquests of Alexander the Great in the fourth century B.C. The people of Judah survived, eventually becoming known as the Jews and giving their name to Judaism. The Babylonian captivity had changed Judaism. It became a stateless religion based on the belief that God was not fixed to one particular land but instead was Creator and Lord of the whole world.

The Spiritual Dimensions of Israel According to Jewish beliefs, there is but one God, called Yahweh (YAH•WAY), the Creator of the world and everything in it. In the Jews' view, God ruled the world; all peoples were his servants, whether they knew it or not. God had created nature but was not in nature. The stars, moon, rivers, wind, and other natural phenomena were not gods, as other ancient peoples believed, but God's handiwork. All of God's creations could be admired for their awesome beauty, but not worshipped as gods.

This powerful creator, however, was not removed from the life he had created. God was just and good, and he expected goodness from his people. If they did not obey his will, they would be punished. However, he was also a God of mercy and love: "The Lord

THE WAY IT WAS

YOUNG PEOPLE IN . . .

Ancient Israel

The primary goal of marriage in ancient Israel was to produce children. Children were the "crown of man." Sons, in particular, were desired. Daughters would eventually leave the family house; sons carried on the family line. According to the Bible, "sons are olive plants around the table, a reward, like arrows in the hand of a hero; happy the man who has his quiver full of them."

Upon his father's death the eldest son became head of the family and was given a double portion of his father's estate. The rights of an eldest son were protected by law, although committing a grave offense, such as murder, could cost him those rights. A father's inheritance passed only to his sons.

Children were named immediately after birth because Israelites believed that one's name defined one's essence and disclosed the destiny and character of the child. The early education of children was placed

The Ark of the Covenant, as depicted here, played an important role in Jewish worship.

is gracious and compassionate, slow to anger and rich in love. The Lord is good to all; he has compassion on all he has made." Each person could have a personal relationship with this powerful being.

The Jews were monotheistic; they believed in one God. The covenant, law, and prophets were three aspects of the Jewish religious tradition. The Jews believed that during the exodus from Egypt, when Moses led his people out of bondage toward the promised land, God made a covenant, or contract, with them. Yahweh promised to guide them if they obeyed the law of God stated in the Ten Commandments. According to the Bible, Yahweh gave these commandments to Moses on Mount Sinai.

The Jews believed that certain religious teachers, called prophets, were sent by God to serve as his voice to his people. The following selection from the biblical book of Isaiah makes clear the prophets' belief that unjust actions would bring God's punishment.

    ❝The Lord enters into judgment against the elders and leaders of his people: 'It is you who have ruined my vineyard; the plunder from the poor is in your houses. What do you mean by crushing my people and grinding the faces of the poor?' declares the Lord, the Lord Almighty. The Lord says, 'The women of Zion are haughty . . . with ornaments jingling on their ankles. Therefore the Lord will bring sores on the heads of the women of Zion; the Lord will make their scalps bald. . . . Instead of fragrance there will be a stench; . . . instead of fine clothing, sackcloth; instead of beauty, branding. Your men will fall by the sword, your warriors in battle. The gates of Zion will lament and mourn; destitute, she will sit on the ground.'❞

The age of prophecy lasted from the eleventh to the fifth centuries B.C., during the time when the people of Israel and Judah faced threats or endured conquests by powerful neighbors. The prophets declared that faithlessness to God would bring punishment and catastrophe, but that turning from evil would bring God's mercy.

From the prophets came new concepts that enriched the Jewish tradition. Later prophets, such as Isaiah, embraced a concern for all humanity. All nations would someday come to the God of Israel. This vision included the end of war and the establishment of peace for all the nations of the world. In the words of the prophet Isaiah:

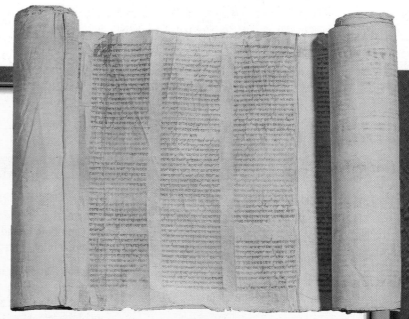

Scribes in ancient Israel carefully copied the Torah by hand.

in the hands of the mother, especially in regard to basic moral principles.

As boys matured, their fathers took over responsibility for their education, which remained largely informal. This included religious instruction as well as a general education for life. Since trades were usually hereditary, fathers also chose trades for their sons. As one rabbi stated, "He who does not teach his son a useful trade is bringing him up to be a thief."

Additional education for boys came from teachers whose sacred mission was to instruct boys in the Torah, the first five books of the Bible. An organized school system was not established until much later, possibly in the second century B.C. The education girls received was from their mothers, who taught them the basic fundamentals of how to be good wives, mothers, and housekeepers.

CONNECTING TO THE PAST

1. **Compare and Contrast** Compare the upbringing and education of the eldest son in an Israelite family to that of an eldest daughter.

2. **Writing about History** "The primary goal of marriage in ancient Israel was to produce children." Explain why this might be. Do you think the primary goal of marriage is the same today?

The Ten Commandments

1. I am the Lord thy God . . . . Thou shalt have no other gods before me.

2. Thou shalt not make unto thee any graven image . . . .

3. Thou shalt not take the name of the Lord thy God in vain . . . .

4. Remember the Sabbath day, to keep it holy.

5. Honor thy father and thy mother . . . .

6. Thou shalt not kill.

7. Thou shalt not commit adultery.

8. Thou shalt not steal.

9. Thou shalt not bear false witness against thy neighbor.

10. Thou shalt not covet . . . anything that is thy neighbor's.

Source: Exodus 20:1–17

❝He will judge between the nations and will settle disputes for many people. They will beat their swords into plowshares and their spears into pruning hooks. Nation will not take up sword against nation, nor will they train for war anymore.❞

The prophets also cried out against social injustice. They condemned the rich for causing the poor to suffer. They denounced luxuries as worthless, and they threatened Israel with prophecies of dire punishments for these sins. They said that God's command was to live justly, share with one's neighbors, care for the poor and the unfortunate, and act with compassion. When God's command was not followed, according to the prophets, the community was threatened. These words of the prophets became a source for universal ideals of social justice.

The religion of Israel was unique among the religions of western Asia and Egypt. The most dramatic difference was the Jewish belief that there is only one God for all peoples (monotheism). In all other religions at that time, only priests (and some rulers) had access to the gods. In the Jewish tradition, God's wishes, though communicated to the people through prophets, had all been written down. No spiritual leader could claim that he alone knew God's will. This knowledge was open to anyone who could read the Torah.

Although the prophets developed a concern for all humanity, the demands of Judaism—the need to obey God—encouraged a separation between Jews and their non-Jewish neighbors. Unlike most other peoples of Southwest Asia, Jews would not accept the gods of their conquerors or neighbors and be made part of another community. To remain faithful to the demands of God, they might even have to refuse loyalty to political leaders.

✓**Reading Check** **Identifying** Which aspect of the Israelite culture had the greatest impact on Western civilization?

✦TAKS Practice

SECTION 3 ASSESSMENT

Checking for Understanding

1. **Define** pastoral nomad, monotheistic.

2. **Identify** Indo-Europeans, Hittites, Phoenicians, Israelites, King Solomon, Isaiah.

3. **Locate** Palestine, Jerusalem.

4. **Explain** why some Israelites came to be known as the "ten lost tribes." How did the fate of the "ten lost tribes" compare to that of the other Israelite kingdom, Judah, at the time?

5. **List** the areas reached by Phoenician traders. Also list the areas that were colonized by the Phoenicians.

Critical Thinking

6. **Evaluate** How did nomadic peoples both contribute to and slow down the development of civilization?

7. **Organizing Information** Use a chart like the one below to show the significance of three major events in the history of the Israelites.

Event	Significance
1.	
2.	
3.	

Analyzing Visuals

8. **Examine** the Torah shown on page 59 of your text. Why is the Torah so important to the Jewish religion? What does the book's appearance tell you about how the book was read?

Writing About History

9. **Informative Writing** Using the Internet, news magazines, and newspapers, research the current conflicts in the Middle East. Prepare a brief research report summarizing what you have learned about current events and movements toward peace in the region.

The Rise of New Empires

Guide to Reading

Main Ideas
- The Hittites and Egyptians were eventually overshadowed by the rise of the Assyrian and Persian Empires.
- The Persian Empire brought many years of peace to Southwest Asia, increasing trade and the general well being of its peoples.

Key Terms
satrapy, satrap, monarchy

People to Identify
Assyrians, Nebuchadnezzar, Persians, Cyrus, Darius, Immortals, Zoroaster

Places to Locate
Assyrian Empire, Persian Empire, Royal Road

Preview Questions
1. What caused the downfall of the Assyrian Empire?
2. Why did the people of his time call Cyrus "the Great"?

Reading Strategy
Compare and Contrast Prepare a Venn diagram listing the characteristics of the Assyrian Empire and the characteristics of the Persian Empire. Identify the similarities and differences of both empires.

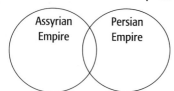

Assyrian Empire   Persian Empire

Preview of Events

♦700 B.C.	♦600 B.C.	♦500 B.C.	♦400 B.C.	♦300 B.C.	♦200 B.C.	♦100 B.C.

559 B.C. Cyrus rules Persian Empire

539 B.C. Babylon falls

330s B.C. Alexander the Great conquers the Persian Empire

Voices from the Past

Darius I

Darius, one of the rulers of the Persian Empire, described the divine source of his power:

❝A great god is Ahuramazda [god of the Persians], who created this earth, who created man, who made Darius king, one king of many, one lord of many. I am Darius the Great King, King of Kings, King of countries containing all kinds of men, King in this great earth far and wide. I am king. This which has been done, all that by the will of Ahuramazda I did.❞

—*Old Persian: Grammar, Texts, Lexicon,* R.G. Kent, 1953

A small and independent Hebrew state could exist only as long as no larger state dominated western Asia. New empires soon arose, however, that conquered vast stretches of the ancient world.

The Assyrian Empire

The first of the new empires was formed in Assyria, located on the upper Tigris River. The **Assyrians** were a Semitic-speaking people who exploited the use of iron weapons to establish an empire by 700 B.C. The **Assyrian Empire** included Mesopotamia, parts of the Iranian Plateau, sections of Asia Minor, Syria, Palestine, and Egypt down to Thebes. Within less than a hundred years, however, internal strife and resentment of Assyrian rule began to tear the Assyrian Empire apart.

In 612 B.C., the empire fell to a coalition of Chaldeans and Medes (people who lived in the East), and was divided between those two powers.

At its height, the Assyrian Empire was ruled by kings whose power was seen as absolute. Under their leadership, the Assyrian Empire came to be well organized. Local officials were directly responsible to the king. The Assyrians also developed an efficient system of communication to administer their empire. A network of posts was established throughout the empire that used relays of horses to carry messages. The system was so effective that a governor anywhere in the empire could send a question and receive an answer from the king within a week. One of the world's first libraries was established at Nineveh by Ashurbanipal, one of the last Assyrian kings. This library has provided abundant information concerning ancient Southwest Asian civilizations.

The Assyrians were good at conquering others. Over many years of practice, they developed effective military leaders and fighters. The Assyrian army was large, well organized, and disciplined. A force of infantrymen was its core, joined by cavalrymen and horse-drawn war chariots that were used as platforms for shooting arrows. Moreover, the Assyrians had the first large armies equipped with iron weapons.

The Assyrians used terror as an instrument of warfare. They regularly laid waste to the land in which they were fighting. They smashed dams; looted and destroyed towns; set crops on fire; and cut down trees, particularly fruit trees. The Assyrians were especially known for committing atrocities on their captives. King Ashurnasirpal recorded this account of his treatment of prisoners: "3,000 of their combat troops I felled with weapons. . . . Many I took alive; from some of these I cut off their hands to the wrist, from others I cut off their noses, ears and fingers; I put out the eyes of many of the soldiers. . . . I burned their young men and women to death."

✓ Reading Check **Summarizing** Why were the Assyrians so successful at conquering others?

The Persian Empire

After the collapse of the Assyrian Empire, the Chaldeans, under their king **Nebuchadnezzar** (NEH•byuh•kuhd•NEH•zuhr) II, made Babylonia the leading state in western Asia. Nebuchadnezzar rebuilt Babylon as the center of his empire and gave it a reputation as one of the great cities of the ancient world. However, the splendor of Chaldean Babylonia proved to be short-lived. Babylon fell to the Persians in 539 B.C.

The Rise of the Persian Empire The **Persians** were an Indo-European people who lived in what is today southwestern Iran. Primarily nomadic, the Persians were organized in groups until one family managed to unify them. One of the family's members, **Cyrus,** created a powerful Persian state that stretched from Asia Minor to western India.

Cyrus ruled from 559 to 530 B.C. In 539 B.C., he entered Mesopotamia and captured Babylon. His treatment of Babylonia showed remarkable restraint and wisdom. Cyrus also issued an edict permitting the Jews, who had been brought to Babylon in the sixth century B.C., to return to Jerusalem.

The people of his time called Cyrus "the Great." Indeed, he must have been an unusual ruler for his time, a man who demonstrated much wisdom and compassion in the conquest and organization of his empire. Unlike the Assyrian rulers, Cyrus had a reputation for mercy. Medes, Babylonians, and Jews all accepted him as their ruler. Cyrus had a genuine respect for other civilizations. In building his palaces,

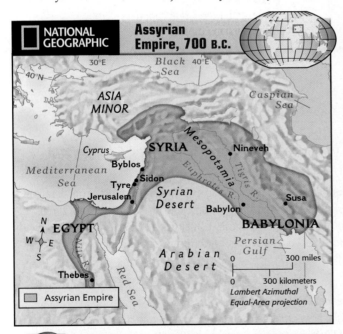

NATIONAL GEOGRAPHIC

Assyrian Empire, 700 B.C.

Black Sea · Caspian Sea · ASIA MINOR · Cyprus · SYRIA · Mesopotamia · Nineveh · Byblos · Tyre · Sidon · Jerusalem · Syrian Desert · Babylon · Susa · BABYLONIA · Mediterranean Sea · EGYPT · Persian Gulf · Arabian Desert · Thebes · Red Sea

0 300 miles
0 300 kilometers
Lambert Azimuthal Equal-Area projection

☐ Assyrian Empire

Geography *Skills*

The Assyrians used iron weapons to conquer an empire that reached from Thebes to Mesopotamia by 700 B.C.

1. **Interpreting Maps** Compare and contrast the geographic features of the Nile, Tigris, and Euphrates Rivers.
2. **Applying Geography Skills** Why did so many civilizations develop in this region?

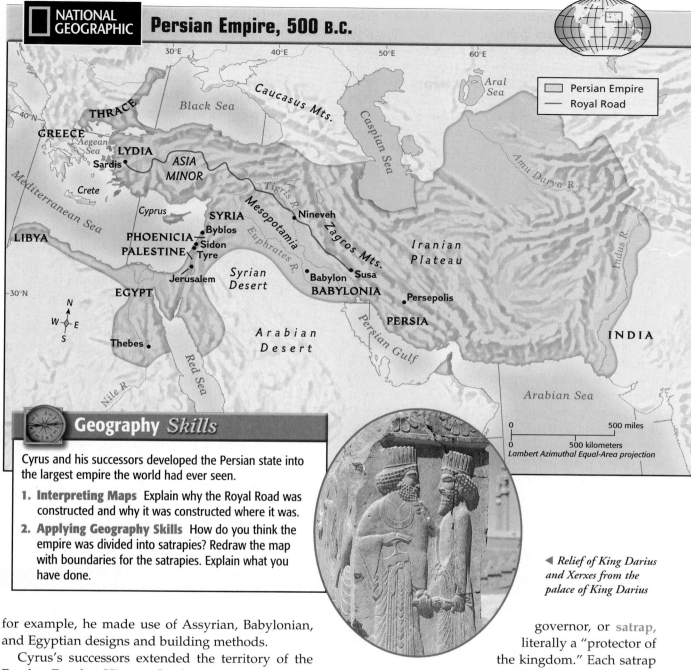

Persian Empire, 500 B.C.

Persian Empire

— Royal Road

THRACE

Black Sea

Caucasus Mts.

GREECE

Aegean Sea

LYDIA

Sardis

ASIA MINOR

Crete

Cyprus

Aral Sea

Caspian Sea

Amu Darya R.

Tigris R.

Nineveh

Mediterranean Sea

LIBYA

SYRIA

PHOENICIA

Byblos

Sidon

PALESTINE

Tyre

Mesopotamia

Euphrates R.

Zagros Mts.

Iranian Plateau

Indus R.

Jerusalem

Syrian Desert

Babylon

Susa

BABYLONIA

Persepolis

EGYPT

N
W—E
S

PERSIA

INDIA

Arabian Desert

Thebes

Red Sea

Persian Gulf

Arabian Sea

Nile R.

0   500 miles
0   500 kilometers
Lambert Azimuthal Equal-Area projection

Geography *Skills*

Cyrus and his successors developed the Persian state into the largest empire the world had ever seen.

1. **Interpreting Maps** Explain why the Royal Road was constructed and why it was constructed where it was.

2. **Applying Geography Skills** How do you think the empire was divided into satrapies? Redraw the map with boundaries for the satrapies. Explain what you have done.

◄ *Relief of King Darius and Xerxes from the palace of King Darius*

for example, he made use of Assyrian, Babylonian, and Egyptian designs and building methods.

Cyrus's successors extended the territory of the **Persian Empire.** His son Cambyses (kam•BY•SEEZ) successfully invaded Egypt. **Darius,** who ruled from 521 to 486 B.C., added a new Persian province in western India that extended to the Indus River. He then moved into Europe, conquering Thrace and creating the largest empire the world had yet seen. Darius's contact with the Greeks led him to undertake an invasion of the Greek mainland (see Chapter 4).

The Structure of the Persian Empire Darius strengthened the Persian government. He divided the empire into 20 provinces, called **satrapies** (SAY•truh•pees). Each province was ruled by a

governor, or **satrap,** literally a "protector of the kingdom." Each satrap collected taxes, provided justice and security, and recruited soldiers for the royal army.

An efficient system of communication was crucial to sustaining the Persian Empire. Well-maintained roads made it easy for officials to travel through the empire. The **Royal Road** stretched from Lydia to Susa, the chief capital of the empire. Like the Assyrians, the Persians set up way stations that provided food and shelter, as well as fresh horses, for the king's messengers.

In this vast system, the Persian king—the "Great King"—occupied an exalted position. The Great King held the power of life and death.

At its height, much of the power of the Persian Empire and its rulers depended upon the military. By the time of Darius, the Persian kings had created a standing army of professional soldiers. This army was composed of people from all over the empire. At its core was a cavalry force of ten thousand and an elite infantry force of ten thousand. These groups were known as the **Immortals** because their numbers were never allowed to fall below ten thousand. When one member was killed, he was immediately replaced.

The Fall of the Persian Empire After Darius, the Persian kings became more and more isolated at their courts, surrounded by luxuries provided by the immense quantities of gold and silver that flowed into their treasuries. As the Persian kings increased taxes to gain more wealth, loyalty to the empire declined. Struggles over the throne weakened the monarchy (rule by a king or queen).

Persian kings had many wives and many children. For example, Artaxerxes (AHR•tuh•ZUHRK•SEEZ) II, who ruled in the fourth century B.C., had 115 sons. The sons had little real power, which only encouraged them to engage in plots to gain the throne. Of the nine rulers after Darius, six were murdered as a result of such plots. Xerxes II, for example, reigned for only 45 days before being murdered in bed by his half-brother. The assassin was soon killed by another half-brother. Over a period of time, this bloody struggle for the throne weakened the empire and led to its conquest by the Greek ruler Alexander the Great during the 330s B.C.

Persian Religion Of all the Persians' cultural contributions, the most original was their religion, Zoroastrianism (ZOHR•uh•WAS•tree•uh•NIH•zuhm). According to Persian tradition, **Zoroaster** was born in 660 B.C. After a period of wandering and solitude, he had visions that caused him to be revered as a prophet of the "true religion." His teachings were eventually written down in the *Zend Avesta*, the sacred book of Zoroastrianism.

Like the Jews, the followers of Zoroaster were monotheistic. To Zoroaster, Ahuramazda (the "Wise Lord") was the supreme god who brought all things into being. Ahuramazda was supreme, but he was not unopposed. At the beginning of the world, the good spirit of Ahuramazda was opposed by the evil spirit known as Ahriman.

Humans also played a role in the struggle between good and evil. Ahuramazda, the creator, gave all humans the freedom to choose between right and wrong. The good person chooses the right way of Ahuramazda. Zoroaster taught that there would be an end to the struggle between good and evil. Ahuramazda would eventually triumph; and at the last judgment at the end of the world, the final separation of good and evil would occur.

✓**Reading Check** **Examining** What caused the Persian Empire to decline after the death of Darius?

🟊**TAKS Practice**

SECTION 4 ASSESSMENT

Checking for Understanding

1. **Define** satrapy, satrap, monarchy.

2. **Identify** Assyrians, Nebuchadnezzar, Persians, Cyrus, Darius, Immortals, Zoroaster.

3. **Locate** Assyrian Empire, Persian Empire, Royal Road.

4. **Describe** Who were the Immortals? What was their significance to the Persian Empire?

5. **List** the duties of the satraps of the Persian government.

Critical Thinking

6. **Compare** How were the Assyrian and Persian systems of government different?

7. **Organizing Information** Create a chart identifying the differences between a religious system based on monotheism and one based on polytheism.

Monotheism	Polytheism

Analyzing Visuals

8. **Examine** the relief of Darius and Xerxes on page 63. Describe what you see in this image. What can you tell about the Persian court from this depiction? Why do you think images such as this were made of the Persian rulers?

Writing About History

9. **Persuasive Writing** Imagine that you are Cyrus ruling the Babylonians, a people you have just conquered. Explain to your government officials why you believe that kindness and tolerance are better policies than harshness.

CRITICAL THINKING
SKILLBUILDER

Understanding Cause and Effect

Why Learn This Skill?

It is important to understand how or why an event occurred. What action or situation caused a particular event? What were the effects or consequences of that particular action or situation?

Learning the Skill

Understanding cause and effect involves considering how or why an event occurred. A cause is the action or situation that produces an event. An effect is the result or consequence of an action or situation. To identify cause-and-effect relationships, follow these steps:

• Identify two or more events or developments.

• Decide whether or not one event caused the other. Look for "clue words" such as *because, led to, brought about, produced, as a result of, so that, since,* and *therefore.*

• Identify the outcomes of events.

Making a graphic organizer can help you understand cause and effect. Study the graphic organizer on this page, and then read the passage below.

Unlike the floods on Mesopotamia's rivers, the flooding of the Nile was gradual and predictable. The river was seen as life-giving, not life-threatening. Whereas massive, state-controlled irrigation and flood control were needed in Mesopotamia, the small villages along the Nile easily managed small irrigation systems that required no state assistance. As a result, Egyptian civilization tended to remain more rural. Many small villages were gathered along a narrow band of land on both sides of the Nile.

Practicing the Skill

On a separate piece of paper, make a cause-and-effect diagram for each of the following statements. Some of the statements may have more than one cause and effect.

❶ Irrigation and drainage ditches made it possible to grow crops on a regular basis. The resulting abundance of food supplies enabled large numbers of people to live together in cities.

❷ Under Hammurabi's code, a son found guilty of striking his father had his hand cut off.

❸ Akhenaton's actions in destroying the old gods meant destruction of Egypt itself. The upheavals associated with his religious revolution led to a loss of Egypt's empire.

Cause and Effect

Cause

• The flooding of the Nile was gradual and predictable.

Effects

• Villages used small irrigation systems that required no state assistance.
• Egyptian civilization tended to remain rural, with many small villages gathered along the Nile.

Applying the Skill

Read an account of a current event in your community as reported in a local newspaper. Determine at least one cause and one effect of that event. Show the cause-and-effect relationship in a chart.

 Glencoe's **Skillbuilder Interactive Workbook, Level 2,** provides instruction and practice in key social studies skills.

Using Key Terms

1. A Sumerian stepped tower is called a _____.

2. In a _____ society, women have fewer privileges and rights than men.

3. The Sumerians invented a system of writing called _____.

4. The Persian ruler Darius divided his empire into provinces called _____, which were ruled by _____.

5. The basic units of Sumerian civilization were _____.

6. If ruling power is passed from one generation to the next, the government of a country could be called a _____.

7. The belief in one god, rather than many gods, is called _____.

8. If citizens believe their city is ruled by gods, they might call their government a _____.

9. To preserve the physical body after death, the Egyptians used a process called _____.

10. A _____ was a government official directly responsible to the Pharaoh.

11. _____ script was used for business transactions and record keeping.

12. An administrative organization with officials and regular procedures is known as a _____.

Reviewing Key Facts

13. **Government** List four examples of the kinds of laws found in Hammurabi's code.

14. **Geography** How was the spring flooding of the Tigris and Euphrates Rivers both beneficial and harmful?

15. **Culture** Which two groups of gods were most important to the Egyptians?

16. **Science and Technology** When was the wheel invented? Explain at least one way in which the invention of the wheel affected the Mesopotamian economy.

17. **History** What people created the first Mesopotamian civilization? What did they contribute to early civilization?

18. **History** Name at least four reasons why the Assyrians were good at conquering others.

19. **Government** What were the main powers and responsibilities of a Sumerian king?

20. **Geography** List three reasons why the Nile was crucial to the development of Egyptian civilization.

21. **Culture** What religion began in the Persian Empire? How was it similar to the Jewish religion?

22. **Science and Technology** Who were the first Indo-Europeans to use iron? In what way was the use of iron advantageous to this group of people?

Chapter Summary

Below are examples of how peoples discussed in Chapter 2 utilized their environment and invented new technologies.

Environment

- Egypt uses floodwaters for farming.
- Phoenicia sets up a trading empire on the sea.
- Mesopotamia creates irrigation and flood control systems.

Cooperation

- Assyria develops an empire-wide communication system.
- Mesopotamia builds temples and houses for religious leaders.
- Palestine adheres to sacred law to maintain separateness.

Cultural Diffusion

- Assyria acquires iron making from the Hittites.
- Persia acquires architecture from the Assyrians, Babylonians, and Egyptians.
- Egypt acquires bronze making from the Hyksos.

Innovation

- Mesopotamia invents the arch, dome, wheel, and a system of writing.
- Phoenicia invents an alphabet.
- Persia creates a standing army.

Critical Thinking

23. **Comparing and Contrasting** Compare and contrast the basic levels of government in the United States today with the Sumerian political structure. What advantages or disadvantages can you identify for each system?

24. **Analyzing** Analyze how the Jewish religion was different from religions of other cultures. How did these differences affect the ways Jews interacted with other peoples?

25. **Interpreting** Restate in your own words the meaning of William Loftus's phrase, "the cradle of civilization."

26. **Making Generalizations** Identify two projects undertaken by the Egyptians at the direction of Middle Kingdom pharaohs. Explain how these projects would have affected the Egyptian economy.

Writing About History

27. **Expository Writing** Imagine that you are a religious scholar examining world religions. Prepare a speech explaining why the Israelites adopted monotheism, while the Egyptian religion was based on polytheism.

Analyzing Sources

Read the following Mesopotamian poem.

> 66The rampant flood which no man can oppose,
> Which shakes the heavens and causes earth to tremble,
> In an appalling blanket folds mother and child,
> And drowns the harvest in its time of ripeness.99

28. How does this poem represent the importance of the physical environment and religion in the lives of the Mesopotamians?

29. Explain the significance of the line: "Which shakes the heavens and causes earth to tremble."

Applying Technology Skills

30. **Using the Internet** Search the Internet for the e-mail address of an Egyptologist from an international museum or university. Compose a letter requesting information about aspects of ancient Egyptian culture such as architecture, religion, or hieroglyphics.

Making Decisions

31. Imagine you are the king's adviser in a newly created empire without a reliable communication system. Explain what potential problems this poses and suggest a solution using the Assyrian and Persian communication networks as models. Include the costs and benefits of your system.

32. Research different interpretations of why the Great Sphinx was built and its purpose, or develop one of your own. Why do historians sometimes arrive at different conclusions? How might these differences be reconciled?

TAKS
Test Practice

Directions: Use the map and your knowledge of world history to choose the best answer to the following question.

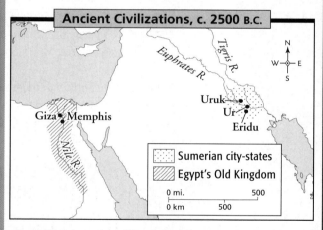

How did geography influence both Egypt and Sumeria?

F Geography provided natural borders for protecting these civilizations.

G Floods from nearby rivers irrigated crops.

H Challenges helped people unite and work together.

J The flooding rivers caused people to have a dark outlook on the world.

Test-Taking Tip: This question asks for an example of how geography influenced history. Eliminate any answer choices that do not mention anything about geography or geographic features. Then study the map thoroughly and choose from the answer choices that remain.

India and China

3000 B.C.–A.D. 500

Key Events

As you read, look for the key events in the history of the early civilizations of India and China.

- *Buddhism, Hinduism, Confucianism, Daoism, and Legalism profoundly affected the way of life of the early Indians and Chinese.*
- *The Silk Road provided a means for prosperous trade.*
- *The ruler of the Zhou overthrew the Shang dynasty and established the longest lasting dynasty in Chinese history.*
- *The Great Wall of China was built to keep out enemies.*

The Impact Today

The events that occurred during this time period still impact our lives today.
- *The well-organized government of the Harappan culture provided a public water supply, wastewater treatment, and trash disposal similar to what many cities provide today.*
- *The difficulties the ancient Chinese experienced in maintaining a strong central government are similar to those facing modern governments.*
- *The early Chinese created a written language and made lasting technological advances.*

World History Video *The Chapter 3 video, "Writings of India and China," chronicles the emergence of civilization and cultural developments in India and China.*

Oxen pulling iron plow

3000 B.C.
Indus River valley
civilization begins

1500 B.C.
Aryans invade
India

3000 B.C.　　　*1600 B.C.*　　　*1000 B.C.*

*Ruins of
Mohenjo-Daro*

The Great Wall of China

551 B.C.
Confucius is born

Confucius

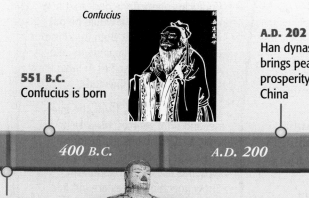

A.D. 202
Han dynasty
brings peace and
prosperity to
China

Han burial suit of jade

400 B.C.   A.D. 200   A.D. 500

563 B.C.
Siddhartha
Gautama, founder
of Buddhism, is
born

The Buddha

HISTORY
Online

Chapter Overview
Visit the *Glencoe World
History* Web site at
tx.wh.glencoe.com and click
on **Chapter 3–Chapter
Overview** to preview
chapter information.

A Story That Matters

The Buddha

Confucius

Two Great Leaders

*I*n the sixth century B.C., two remarkable people appeared in the civilizations of India and China.

In India there lived a man named Siddhartha Gautama. He is better known as the Buddha. In his lifetime, he gained thousands of devoted followers. People would come to him seeking to know more about him, asking, "Are you a god?"

"No," he answered.

"Are you an angel?"

"No."

"Are you a saint?"

"No."

"Then what are you?"

The Buddha replied, "I am awake."

The religion of Buddhism began with a man who claimed that he had awakened and seen the world in a new way.

At about the same time the Buddha was teaching in India, a philosopher named Confucius traveled the length of China observing events and seeking employment as a political counselor. He had little success in his job search and instead became a teacher to hundreds of students who sought his wise advice. He taught by asking questions and expected much of his students. As he said, "Only one who bursts with eagerness do I instruct; only one who bubbles with excitement, do I enlighten." Some disciples of Confucius recorded his sayings, which became guiding principles for Chinese civilization.

Why It Matters

Buddhism was the product of one man, Siddhartha Gautama, whose simple message of achieving wisdom created a new spiritual philosophy in India. In China, the philosophy of Confucius opened the door to a new idea of statecraft that would be put into widespread use. Both Buddhism and Confucianism continue to influence the ways of peoples in India, China, and around the world.

History and You Using the Internet and print sources, prepare a chart that compares the historical origins, central ideas, and the spread of Confucianism and Buddhism. Show how those ideas are put into practice today. Be sure to cite three reliable sources that support the data in your chart.

Early Civilization in India

Guide to Reading

Main Ideas
- India's earliest cities provided the foundation for the Aryans.
- The caste system was a set of rigid social categories in Indian society.

Key Terms
monsoon, Sanskrit, raja, caste system, caste, Hinduism, reincarnation, karma, dharma, yoga, Buddhism, ascetic, nirvana

People to Identify
Aryans, Brahmans, Kshatriyas, Vaisyas, Sudras, Untouchables, Siddhartha Gautama

Places to Locate
Indian subcontinent, Himalaya, Ganges River, Deccan, Persian Gulf, Hindu Kush

Preview Questions
1. How did geographic factors impact the civilization that arose in India?
2. What is a patriarchal family?

Reading Strategy
Sequencing Information As you read this section, use a diagram like the one below to illustrate the process that led Siddhartha Gautama to enlightenment.

```
┌──────────────┐
│              │
└──────────────┘
       │
       ▼
┌──────────────┐
│              │
└──────────────┘
       │
       ▼
┌──────────────┐
│ enlightenment│
└──────────────┘
```

Preview of Events

♦1000 B.C.	♦800 B.C.	♦600 B.C.	♦400 B.C.

1000 B.C.
Aryans begin composing the Vedas

c. 500 B.C.
Buddhism develops

480 B.C.
Gautama (the Buddha) dies

Voices from the Past

Arjuna was in despair as he prepared for battle. Many of his friends were in the opposing army. Some of them he had known since childhood. According to the *Bhagavad Gita,* India's great religious poem, Arjuna appealed to the god Krishna:

❝O Krishna, when I see my own people . . . eager for battle, my limbs shudder, my mouth is dry, my body shivers, and my hair stands on end. I can see no good in killing my own kinsmen." Krishna replied, "Do not despair of your duty. If you do not fight this just battle you will fail in your own law and in your honor.❞

Arjuna understood. He was a warrior, and he must do his duty without regard for the consequences.

— *The Bhagavad Gita*

Krishna supporting Mount Govardhana

Arjuna's decision—to fight no matter what the personal cost—illustrates the importance of Hinduism's concept of divine life. In fact, two religions—Hinduism and Buddhism—were crucial in shaping the civilization of India.

The Land of India

India is a land of diversity. Today, about 110 languages and more than 1,000 dialects (varieties of language) are spoken in India. Diversity is also apparent in India's geography. The **Indian subcontinent,** shaped like a triangle hanging from the southern ridge of Asia, is composed of a number of core regions, including mountain ranges, river valleys, a dry interior plateau, and fertile coastal plains.

In the far north are the **Himalaya,** the highest mountains in the world. Directly south of the Himalaya is the rich valley of the **Ganges** (GAN•JEEZ) **River,** one of the chief regions of Indian culture. To the west is the Indus River valley, a relatively dry plateau that forms the backbone of the modern state of Pakistan. In ancient times, the Indus Valley enjoyed a more moderate climate and served as the cradle of Indian civilization.

South of India's two major river valleys—the valleys of the Ganges and the Indus—lies the **Deccan,** a plateau that extends from the Ganges Valley to the southern tip of India. The interior of the plateau is relatively hilly and dry. India's eastern and western coasts are lush plains. These plains have historically been among the most densely populated regions of India.

The primary feature of India's climate is the monsoon, a seasonal wind pattern in southern Asia. One monsoon blows warm, moist air from the southwest during the summer and another blows cold, dry air from the northeast during the winter. The southwest monsoon brings heavy rains, and throughout history Indian farmers have depended on these rains to grow their crops. If the rains come early or late, or too much or too little rain falls, crops are destroyed and thousands starve.

Reading Check **Describing** How does the monsoon affect Indian farmers?

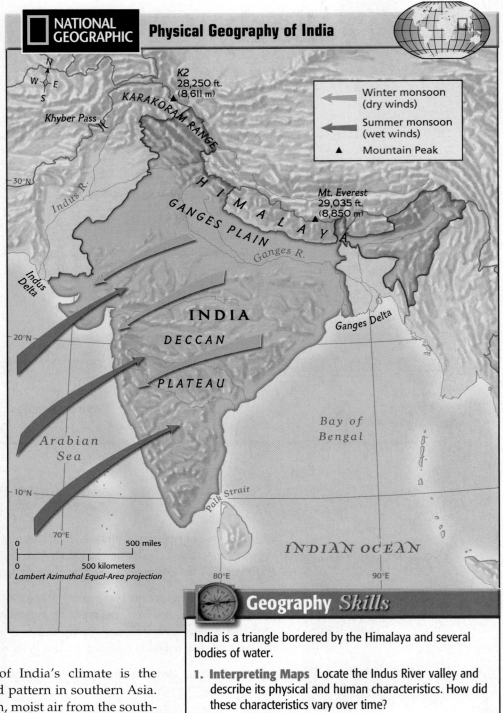

NATIONAL GEOGRAPHIC Physical Geography of India

K2
28,250 ft.
(8,611 m)

KARAKORAM RANGE

Khyber Pass

Winter monsoon (dry winds)
Summer monsoon (wet winds)
▲ Mountain Peak

30°N

Indus R.

H I M A L A Y A

GANGES PLAIN

Mt. Everest
29,035 ft.
▲ (8,850 m)

Ganges R.

Indus Delta

INDIA

20°N

DECCAN

Ganges Delta

PLATEAU

Bay of Bengal

Arabian Sea

10°N

Palk Strait

70°E

0   500 miles

0   500 kilometers
Lambert Azimuthal Equal-Area projection

80°E

INDIAN OCEAN

90°E

Geography *Skills*

India is a triangle bordered by the Himalaya and several bodies of water.

1. **Interpreting Maps** Locate the Indus River valley and describe its physical and human characteristics. How did these characteristics vary over time?

India's First Civilization

As in Mesopotamia and Egypt, early civilization in India and China emerged in river valleys. Between 3000 B.C. and 1500 B.C., the valleys of the Indus River supported a flourishing civilization that extended hundreds of miles from the Himalaya to the coast of the Arabian Sea. Archaeologists have found the remains of more than a thousand settlements in this region. Two of the ruins, about 400 miles (643.6 km) apart, were sites of what once were the major cities of Harappa (huh•RA•puh) and

Mohenjo-Daro (moh•HEHN•joh DAHR•oh). An advanced civilization flourished in these cities for hundreds of years. Historians call it Harappan or Indus civilization.

Harappa and Mohenjo-Daro

At its height, Harappa had 35,000 inhabitants, and Mohenjo-Daro perhaps 35,000 to 40,000. Both cities were carefully planned. The main, broad streets ran in a north-south direction and were crossed by smaller east-west roads. Both cities were divided into large walled neighborhoods, with narrow lanes separating the rows of houses. Houses varied in size, some reaching as high as three stories, but all followed the same plan of a square courtyard surrounded by rooms.

Most buildings were constructed of mud bricks baked in ovens and were square, forming a grid pattern. Public wells provided a regular supply of water for all the inhabitants. Bathrooms featured an advanced drainage system. Wastewater flowed out to drains located under the streets and then was carried to sewage pits beyond the city walls. A system of chutes took household trash from houses to street-level garbage bins. Only a well-organized government could have maintained such carefully structured cities.

Rulers and the Economy

As in Egypt and Mesopotamia, Harappan rulers based their power on a belief in divine assistance. Religion and political power were closely linked. The fact that the royal palace and the holy temple were combined in the citadel, or fortress, at Harappa shows this close connection. Priests at court probably prayed to a god or goddess of fertility to guarantee the annual harvest.

Like those in Mesopotamia and along the Nile, the Harappan economy was based primarily on farming. The Indus River flooded every year, providing rich soil for the growing of wheat, barley, and peas, the chief crops.

This Indus valley civilization also carried on extensive trade with city-states in Mesopotamia. Textiles and food were imported from the Sumerian city-states in exchange for copper, lumber, precious stones, cotton, and various types of luxury goods. Much of this trade was carried by ship via the **Persian Gulf,** although some undoubtedly went by land.

✔ Reading Check **Explaining** What evidence leads us to conclude that there must have been well-organized governments in Harappa and Mohenjo-Daro?

Picturing **History**

A priest-king and the restored city of Mohenjo-Daro are pictured. **What elements of an advanced civilization can you find in these photos?**

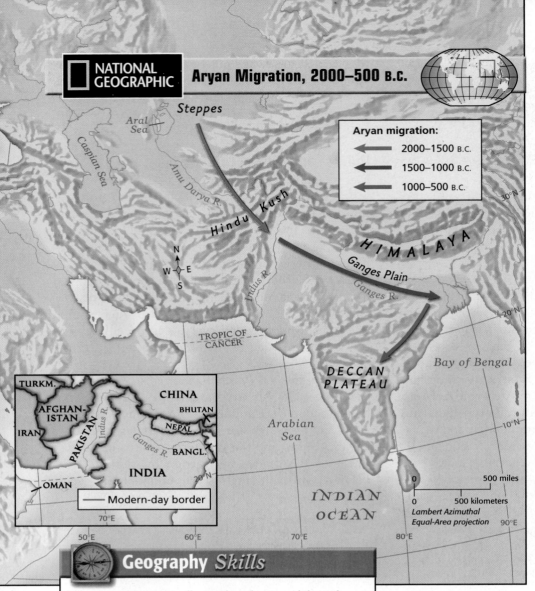

Aryan migration:

← 2000–1500 B.C.

← 1500–1000 B.C.

← 1000–500 B.C.

Steppes

Aral Sea

Caspian Sea

Amu Darya R.

Hindu Kush

HIMALAYA

Ganges Plain

Ganges R.

Indus R.

TROPIC OF CANCER

DECCAN PLATEAU

Bay of Bengal

Arabian Sea

INDIAN OCEAN

500 miles

500 kilometers

Lambert Azimuthal Equal-Area projection

TURKM.

AFGHAN-ISTAN

IRAN

PAKISTAN

Indus R.

CHINA

BHUTAN

NEPAL

Ganges R. BANGL.

INDIA

OMAN

Modern-day border

Geography *Skills*

The Aryans were nomadic peoples who moved through India. Eventually, they controlled most of India.

1. **Interpreting Maps** What geographical feature enabled the Aryans to end their nomadic lifestyle?
2. **Applying Geography Skills** Examine the pattern of Aryan migration. Why do you think the Aryans followed such a route?

The Arrival of the Aryans

Eventually, floods, an earthquake, changes in climate, and even a change in the course of the Indus River weakened the once-flourishing civilization in the Indus River valley. Invaders—the Aryans—brought its final end.

Who Were the Aryans? Around 1500 B.C., a group of Indo-European nomadic peoples began to move out of their original homeland in central Asia. Known as the **Aryans**, they moved south across the **Hindu Kush** mountain range into the plains of northern India. They conquered the Harappans and created a new Indian society based on Aryan culture and institutions.

Like other nomadic peoples, the Aryans excelled at the art of war. Between 1500 and 1000 B.C., the Aryan peoples gradually advanced eastward from the Indus Valley, across the fertile plain of the Ganges. Later they moved southward into the Deccan Plateau. Eventually they extended their control throughout most of India.

Aryan Ways of Life Organized in groups, the Aryans were a pastoral people with a strong warrior tradition. After settling in India, the Aryans gave up the pastoral life for regular farming. The introduction of iron—probably from Southwest Asia, where it had first been used by the Hittites (see Chapter 2)—played a role in this change. The creation of the iron plow, along with the use of irrigation, made it possible for the Aryans and their subject peoples to clear the dense jungle growth along the Ganges River and turn it into a rich farming area.

The basic crops in the north during this period were wheat, barley, and millet. Rice was common in the fertile river valleys. In the south, grain and vegetables were grown, supplemented by cotton and spices such as pepper, ginger, and cinnamon.

Like most nomadic peoples, the Aryans had no written language. The Aryans developed their first writing system, known as Sanskrit, by 1000 B.C. This enabled them to write down the legends and religious chants and rituals that had previously been passed down orally from generation to generation.

The early writings of the Aryans reveal that between 1500 and 400 B.C., India was a world of warring kingdoms and shifting alliances. Various Aryan leaders, known as rajas (princes), carved out small states and fought other Aryan chieftains. They attacked one another's fortresses and seized women, cattle, and treasure.

✓ **Reading Check** **Evaluating** How did the introduction of iron impact the Aryan way of life?

Society in Ancient India

The conquest by the Aryans had a lasting impact on Indian society. Out of the clash between conqueror and conquered came a set of social institutions and class divisions that has lasted in India, with only minor changes, to the present day.

The Caste System The caste system of ancient India was a set of rigid social categories that determined not only a person's occupation and economic potential, but also his or her position in society. It was based in part on skin color.

The Aryan invaders were primarily a light-skinned people. They looked down on their subjects, who were dark skinned, despite the fact that the civilization of the dark-skinned inhabitants of the Indus Valley was much more advanced than the Aryan civilization.

There were five major divisions of Indian classes (known as castes in English) in ancient times. At the top were two castes that were clearly the ruling elites in Aryan society: the priests and the warriors.

The priestly class, whose members were known as **the Brahmans,** was usually considered to be at the top of the social scale. They were in charge of the religious ceremonies that were so important in Indian society.

The second caste was the **Kshatriyas** (KSHA•tree•uhz), or warriors. As Aryan society changed, the Kshatriyas often found new forms of employment. At the same time, families from other castes were sometimes accepted into the ranks of the warriors.

The third-ranked caste in Indian society was the **Vaisyas** (VYSH•yuhz), or commoners. Most Vaisyas were merchants who engaged in commerce, or farmers caring for the land.

CONNECTIONS Past To Present

Aryans in India and Nazi Germany

The Aryans were a group of Indo-European nomadic peoples who began moving into the plains of northern India about 1500 B.C. In the nineteenth century A.D., linguists (people who study languages) borrowed the term *Aryan* to identify people speaking a common set of languages known as Indo-European.

In the twentieth century, Adolf Hitler and the Nazis used the term *Aryan* in a new way. They identified the Aryans as a race that included the Greeks and Romans of the past and the Germans and Scandinavians of the present. They viewed the Germans as the true descendants and chief leaders of the Aryans.

Hitler believed that the Aryan race, to which all "true Germans" belonged, was the highest race of humanity. According to Hitler, "All the human culture, all the results of art, science, and technology that we see before us today, are almost exclusively the creative product of the Aryan." The Aryans, according to Hitler, were once rulers of the earth. The German people were destined to regain the

▲ *Adolf Hitler*

former ruling position of the Aryan race and ensure Aryan world domination.

To Hitler, however, one major obstacle stood in the way of Aryan destiny—the Jews. Hitler thought the Jews were poisoners of the

▲ *Neo-Nazi rally*

blood of the Aryan race. To eliminate them became Hitler's special "higher mission." The Holocaust, the deliberate attempt to kill all of Europe's Jews during World War II, was a result of Hitler's twisted ideas of the Aryans as a race.

In our time, the existence of such organizations as the Aryan Nations shows the continuing influence of Hitler's ideas. The Aryan Nations is but one of a number of neo-Nazi and white supremacist groups in the United States and Europe that continue to follow Hitler's racist ideas.

Comparing Past and Present

Identify ways that Hitler misapplied the term *Aryan*. How does this point out the importance of studying history?

Below these three castes were the **Sudras** (SOO•druhz), who made up the great bulk of the Indian population. The Sudras were not Aryans, and the term probably originally referred to the conquered dark-skinned natives. Most Sudras were peasants and people who worked at other forms of manual labor. They had only limited rights in society.

At the lowest level of Indian society—and in fact not even considered a real part of the caste system—were the **Untouchables.** The Untouchables were given menial, degrading tasks that other Indians would not accept, such as collecting trash and handling dead bodies. The Untouchables probably made up about 5 percent of the total population of ancient India.

The life of the Untouchables was extremely difficult. They were not considered human, and their very presence was considered harmful to members of the other classes. No Indian would touch or eat food handled by an Untouchable. Untouchables lived in separate areas. When they traveled outside their quarters, they were required to tap two sticks together so that others could hear them coming and avoid them.

The Family in Ancient India Life in ancient India centered on the family, the most basic unit in society. The ideal was an extended family, with three generations—grandparents, parents, and children—living under the same roof. The family was basically patriarchal, because in most of India the oldest male held legal authority over the entire family unit.

The superiority of males in ancient Indian society was evident in a number of ways. Only males could inherit property, except in a few cases where there were no sons. Women were not allowed to serve as priests, and generally, only males were educated. In high-class families, young men began their education with a *guru*, or teacher, then went on to higher studies in one of the major cities.

Upper-class young men were not supposed to marry until they completed 12 years of study. Divorce was usually not allowed. Husbands, however, could take a second wife if the first was unable to bear children.

Children were an important product of marriage, primarily because they were expected to take care of their parents as they grew older. Marriage, arranged by the parents, was common for young girls, probably because daughters were seen as an economic drain on their parents.

Perhaps the most vivid symbol of women's dominance by men was the ritual of suttee (suh•TEE). In ancient India, the dead were placed on heaps of material called pyres, which were then set on fire. Suttee required a wife to throw herself on her dead husband's flaming funeral pyre. A Greek visitor reported that "he had heard from some persons of wives burning themselves along with their deceased husbands and doing so gladly; and that those women who refused to burn themselves were held in disgrace."

✓ **Reading Check** **Summarizing** What are the names of the castes in Indian society?

Hinduism

Hinduism had its origins in the religious beliefs of the Aryan peoples who settled in India after 1500 B.C. Evidence about the religious beliefs of the Aryan peoples comes from the Vedas, collections of hymns and religious ceremonies that were passed down orally through the centuries by Aryan priests and then eventually written down.

Early Hindus believed in the existence of a single force in the universe, a form of ultimate reality or God, called *Brahman*. It was the duty of the individual self—called the *atman*—to seek to know this ultimate reality. By doing so, the self would merge with Brahman after death.

By the sixth century B.C., the idea of reincarnation had appeared in Hinduism. Reincarnation is the belief that the individual soul is reborn in a different form after death. As one of the Vedas says, "Worn-out garments are shed by the body/Worn-out bodies are shed by the dweller [the soul]." After a number of existences in the earthly world, the soul reaches its final goal in a union with Brahman. According to Hinduism, all living beings seek to achieve this goal.

Important to this process is the idea of karma, the force generated by a person's actions that determines how the person will be reborn in the next life. According to this idea, what people do in their current lives determines what they will be in their next lives. In the same way, a person's current status is not simply an accident. It is a result of the person's actions in a past existence.

The concept of karma is ruled by the dharma, or the divine law. The law requires all people to do their duty. However, people's duties vary, depending on their status in society. More is expected of those high on the social scale, such as the Brahmans, than of the lower castes.

The system of reincarnation provided a religious basis for the rigid class divisions in Indian society. It justified the privileges of those on the higher end of the scale. After all, they would not have these privileges if they were not deserving. At the same time, the concept of reincarnation gave hope to those lower on the ladder of life. The poor, for example, could hope that if they behaved properly in this life, they would improve their condition in the next.

How does one achieve oneness with God? Hindus developed the practice of yoga, a method of training designed to lead to such union. (In fact, *yoga* means "union.") The final goal of yoga was to leave behind the cycle of earthly life and achieve union with Brahman, seen as a kind of dreamless sleep. As one Hindu writing states, "When all the senses are stilled, when the mind is at rest, that, say the wise, is the highest state."

Most ordinary Indians, however, could not easily relate to this ideal and needed a more concrete form of heavenly salvation. It was probably for this reason that the Hindu religion came to have a number of human-like gods and goddesses.

There are hundreds of deities in the Hindu religion, including three chief ones: Brahma the Creator, Vishnu the Preserver, and Siva (SIH•vuh) the Destroyer. Many Hindus regard the multitude of gods as simply different expressions of the one ultimate reality, Brahman. However, the various gods and goddesses give ordinary Indians a way to express their religious feelings. Through devotion at a Hindu temple, they seek not only salvation but also a means of gaining the ordinary things they need in life. Today, Hinduism is still the religion of the vast majority of the Indian people.

Picturing **History**

Siva is the god of destruction, transformation, and change. Siva creates with the right hand and destroys with the left hand. Compassion and healing are offered with the lower hands. How does this bronze statue illustrate Siva's role in Hinduism?

✓ Reading Check

Comparing How do karma, dharma, and yoga relate to reincarnation?

The Sanchi stupa, third century B.C.
Originally the stupa housed a relic of the Buddha. This stupa has become the greatest Buddhist monument in India. Describe how the decorative architecture reflects the monument's importance to Buddhism.

◀ *The Buddha*

Buddhism

In the sixth century B.C., a new doctrine, called Buddhism, appeared in northern India and soon became a rival of Hinduism. The founder of Buddhism was **Siddhartha Gautama** (sih •DAHR •tuh• GOW• tuh•muh), known as the Buddha, or "Enlightened One."

The Story of the Buddha Siddhartha Gautama came from a small kingdom in the foothills of the Himalaya (in what is today southern Nepal). Born around 563 B.C., he was the son of a ruling family. The young and very handsome Siddhartha was raised in the lap of luxury and lived a sheltered life. At the age of 16, he married a neighboring princess and began to raise a family.

Siddhartha appeared to have everything: wealth, a good appearance, a model wife, a child, and a throne that he would someday inherit. In his late twenties, however, Siddhartha became aware of the pain of illness, the sorrow of death, and the effects of old age on ordinary people. He exclaimed, "Would that sickness, age, and death might be forever bound!" He decided to spend his life seeking the cure for human suffering. He gave up his royal clothes, shaved his head, abandoned his family, and set off to find the true meaning of life.

At first he followed the example of the ascetics, people who practiced self-denial to achieve an understanding of ultimate reality. The abuse of his physical body, however, only led to a close brush with death from not eating. He abandoned asceticism and turned instead to an intense period of meditation. (In Hinduism, this was a way to find oneness with God.) One evening, while sitting in meditation under a tree, Siddhartha reached enlightenment as to the meaning of life. He spent the rest of his life preaching what he had discovered. His teachings became the basic principles of Buddhism.

The Basic Principles of Buddhism Siddhartha denied the reality of the material world. The physical surroundings of humans, he believed, were simply illusions. The pain, poverty, and sorrow that afflict human beings are caused by their attachment to things of this world. Once people let go of their worldly cares, pain and sorrow can be forgotten. Then comes *bodhi,* or wisdom. (The word *bodhi* is the root of the word *Buddhism* and of Siddhartha's usual name—Gautama Buddha.) Achieving wisdom is a key step to achieving nirvana, or ultimate reality— the end of the self and a reunion with the Great World Soul.

Siddhartha preached this message in a sermon to his followers in the Deer Park at Sarnath (outside India's holy city of Banaras). It is a simple message based on the Four Noble Truths:

1. Ordinary life is full of suffering.
2. This suffering is caused by our desire to satisfy ourselves.

3. The way to end suffering is to end desire for selfish goals and to see others as extensions of ourselves.

4. The way to end desire is to follow the Middle Path.

This Middle Path is also known as the Eightfold Path, because it consists of eight steps:

1. *Right view* We need to know the Four Noble Truths.

2. *Right intention* We need to decide what we really want.

3. *Right speech* We must seek to speak truth and to speak well of others.

4. *Right action* The Buddha gave five precepts: "Do not kill. Do not steal. Do not lie. Do not be unchaste. Do not take drugs or drink alcohol."

5. *Right livelihood* We must do work that uplifts our being.

6. *Right effort* The Buddha said, "Those who follow the Way might well follow the example of an ox that arches through the deep mud carrying a heavy load. He is tired, but his steady, forward-looking gaze will not relax until he comes out of the mud."

7. *Right mindfulness* We must keep our minds in control of our senses: "All we are is the result of what we have thought."

8. *Right concentration* We must meditate to see the world in a new way.

Siddhartha accepted the idea of reincarnation, but he rejected the Hindu division of human beings into rigidly defined castes based on previous reincarnations. He taught instead that all human beings could reach nirvana as a result of their behavior in this life. This made Buddhism appealing to the downtrodden peoples at the lower end of the social scale.

Buddhism also differed from Hinduism in its simplicity. Siddhartha rejected the multitude of gods that had become identified with Hinduism. He forbade his followers to worship either his person or his image after his death. For that reason, many Buddhists see Buddhism as a philosophy rather than as a religion.

Siddhartha Gautama died in 480 B.C. at the age of 80 in what is today Nepal. After his death, his followers traveled throughout India, spreading his message. Temples sprang up throughout the countryside. Buddhist monasteries were also established to promote his teaching and provide housing and training for monks dedicated to the simple life and the pursuit of wisdom.

✓ **Reading Check** **Contrasting** How does Buddhism differ from Hinduism?

HISTORY *Online*

Web Activity Visit the *Glencoe World History* Web site at tx.wh.glencoe.com and click on **Chapter 3– Student Web Activity** to learn more about Buddhism.

🏴 **TAKS Practice**

SECTION 1 ASSESSMENT

Checking for Understanding

1. **Define** monsoon, Sanskrit, raja, caste system, caste, Hinduism, reincarnation, karma, dharma, yoga, Buddhism, ascetic, nirvana.

2. **Identify** Aryans, Siddhartha Gautama, Brahmans, Kshatriyas, Vaisyas, Sudras.

3. **Locate** Indian subcontinent, Himalaya, Ganges River, Deccan, Persian Gulf, Hindu Kush.

4. **Describe** the relationship that exists in Hinduism between the caste system and the dharma, or divine law.

Critical Thinking

5. **Evaluate** How did Arjuna's decision to fight illustrate the importance of Hinduism's concept of dharma in Indian life?

6. **Compare and Contrast** Prepare a Venn diagram like the one shown below to show the similarities and differences between Hinduism and Buddhism.

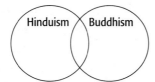

Analyzing Visuals

7. **Examine** the photographs on page 76. Explain how the photos represent the caste system in India. What photos would you take to represent the class system in your community?

Writing About History

8. **Expository Writing** In spite of the difficulties they faced, most Untouchables did not opt to convert to other religions or emigrate to other countries in order to escape their lot in life. What social pressures might prevent a person from converting from the religion of his or her culture?

SOCIAL STUDIES SKILLBUILDER

Finding Exact Location on a Map

Why Learn This Skill?

A friend tells you that she lives at the northwest corner of Vine Street and Oak Avenue. By giving you the names of two streets that cross, she has pinpointed her exact location. We use a similar system to identify the exact location of any place on Earth.

Learning the Skill

Over many centuries, cartographers developed a grid system of imaginary lines—lines of latitude and lines of longitude. Lines of latitude run east and west around the earth. Because they always remain the same distance from each other, they are also called parallels. The parallel lines of latitude measure distance north and south of the Equator, which is located at 0 degrees latitude. Each line of latitude is one degree, or 69 miles (110 km), from the next. There are 90 latitude lines between the Equator and each pole. For example, New York City lies about 41 degrees north of the Equator, or 41°N.

Lines of longitude, or meridians, run north and south from pole to pole. Unlike lines of latitude, lines of longitude are not always the same distance from each other. Lines of longitude are farthest apart at the Equator, and they intersect at the North and South Poles. The prime meridian marks 0 degrees longitude and runs through Greenwich, England, and western Africa. Longitude lines are measured by their distance east and west of the prime meridian up to 180 degrees. New York City, for example, lies about 74 degrees west of the prime meridian, or 74°W.

With this system we can pinpoint the "grid address" of any place on Earth. For example, if we wanted to find a grid address for New York City, we would first find the line of latitude closest to it. Then, by following this line, we would locate the nearest line of longitude to cross it. The point where the lines intersect is the grid address. New York City's grid address would be about 41°N, 74°W.

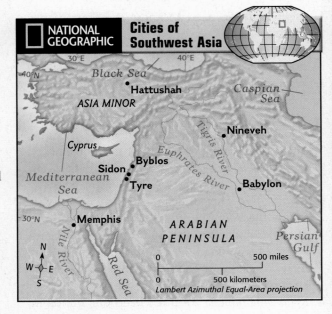

Practicing the Skill

Use the map above to answer the following questions.

1. What is Babylon's approximate grid address?
2. What city sits at approximately 30°N, 31°E?
3. What is Nineveh's approximate grid address?
4. What is Tyre's approximate grid address?

Applying the Skill

Create a travel itinerary for a tour of the ruins of ancient Egypt, Greece, or Southwest Asia. Choose at least 10 sites to visit. Draw a map of each region, including grid lines. On the map, identify each site's approximate grid location.

 Glencoe's **Skillbuilder Interactive Workbook, Level 2,** provides instruction and practice in key social studies skills.

New Empires in India

Main Ideas
- The Mauryan dynasty flourished under Asoka.
- The Kushan kingdom prospered.
- The Gupta Empire left a lasting legacy through literature, architecture, and science.

Key Terms
Silk Road, pilgrim

People to Identify
Asoka, Faxian, Huns, Kalidasa, Aryabhata

Places to Locate
Persia, Changan, Antioch, Syria, Mediterranean Sea

Preview Questions
1. How did the Kushan kingdom become prosperous?
2. In what way did early Indian literature influence the Indian people?

Reading Strategy
Categorizing Information As you read this section, complete a chart identifying the indicated characteristics of the Mauryan and Gupta Empires.

	Mauryan Empire	Gupta Empire
Dates		
Government		
Economy		

Preview of Events

◆300 B.C.	◆200 B.C.	◆100 B.C.	◆A.D. 1	◆A.D. 100	◆A.D. 200	◆A.D. 300

301 B.C.
Chandragupta Maurya dies

232 B.C.
Asoka dies

C. A.D. 100
Silk Road connects China and Mesopotamia

A.D. 320
Gupta kingdom begins

Asoka

Voices from the Past

One of the decrees of Asoka read:

❝By order of the Beloved of the Gods [Asoka] to the officers in charge: Let us win the affection of all people. All people are my children, and as I wish all welfare and happiness in this world and the rest for my own children, so do I wish it for all men . . . . For that purpose many officials are employed among the people to instruct them in righteousness and to explain it to them.❞
— *Asoka Maurya*, **B. G. Gokhale, 1966**

Asoka is remembered as one of India's greatest rulers, one who used Buddhist ideas as a guide to good governing.

The Mauryan Dynasty

Both Hinduism and Buddhism developed out of the Aryan culture in India. As we have seen, however, the Aryans brought little political unity to India. Between 1500 and 400 B.C., warring kingdoms and shifting alliances prevented a lasting peace. After 400 B.C., India faced new threats from the west. First came **Persia,** which extended its empire into western India. Then came the Greeks and Macedonians.

The Macedonian king Alexander the Great had heard of the riches of India. After conquering Persia, he swept into northwestern India in 327 B.C., but his soldiers refused to continue fighting. They departed almost as quickly as they had come. His conquests in western India, however, gave rise to the first dynasty to control much of India.

The Founding of the Mauryan Dynasty The new Indian state was founded by Chandragupta Maurya (CHUN•druh•GUP•tuh MAH•oor•yuh), who ruled from 324 to 301 B.C. He drove out the foreign forces and established the capital of his new Mauryan Empire in northern India at Pataliputra (modern Patna) in the Ganges Valley.

This first Indian Empire was highly centralized. According to the *Arthasastra*, a work on politics written by a Mauryan court official, "It is power and power alone which, only when exercised by the king with impartiality, over his son or his enemy, maintains both this world and the next."

The king divided his empire into provinces which were ruled by governors appointed by him. He had a large army and a secret police that followed his orders. According to Megasthenes, the Greek ambassador to the Mauryan court, Chandragupta Maurya was always afraid of assassination. All food was tasted in his presence, and he made a practice of never sleeping two nights in a row in the same bed in his large palace.

The Reign of Asoka The Mauryan Empire flourished during the reign of **Asoka** (uh•SHOH•kuh), the grandson of Chandragupta Maurya. Asoka is generally considered to be the greatest ruler in the history of India. After his conversion to Buddhism, Asoka used Buddhist ideals to guide his rule. He set up hospitals for both people and animals. He ordered that trees and shelters be placed along the road to provide shade and rest for weary travelers.

Asoka was more than a kind ruler, however. His kingdom prospered as India's role in regional trade began to expand. India became a major crossroads in a vast commercial network that extended from the rim of the Pacific to Southwest Asia and the Mediterranean Sea.

After Asoka's death in 232 B.C., the Mauryan Empire began to decline. In 183 B.C., the last Mauryan ruler was killed by one of his military commanders. India then fell back into disunity.

✓ **Reading Check**

Evaluating Why was Asoka considered a great ruler?

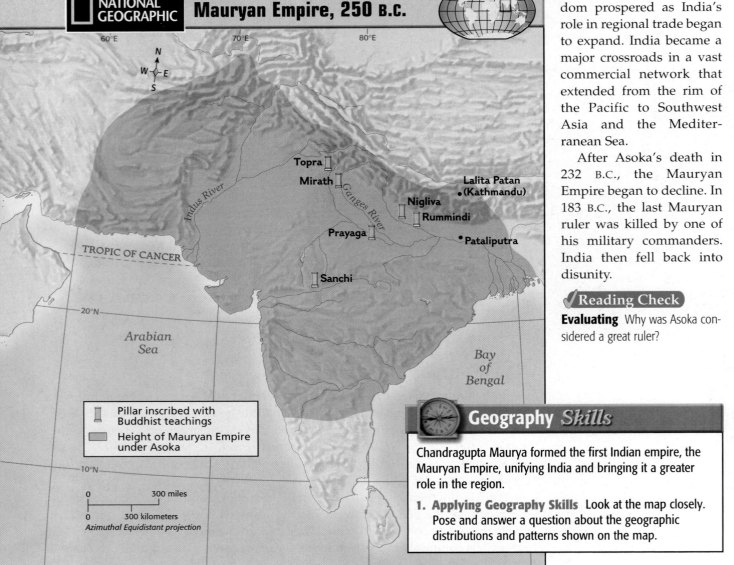

NATIONAL GEOGRAPHIC **Mauryan Empire, 250 B.C.**

Topra
Mirath
Indus River
Ganges River
Lalita Patan (Kathmandu)
Nigliva
Rummindi
Prayaga
Pataliputra
TROPIC OF CANCER
Sanchi
20°N
Arabian Sea
Bay of Bengal

▯ Pillar inscribed with Buddhist teachings
▮ Height of Mauryan Empire under Asoka

10°N

0 — 300 miles
0 — 300 kilometers
Azimuthal Equidistant projection

Geography *Skills*

Chandragupta Maurya formed the first Indian empire, the Mauryan Empire, unifying India and bringing it a greater role in the region.

1. **Applying Geography Skills** Look at the map closely. Pose and answer a question about the geographic distributions and patterns shown on the map.

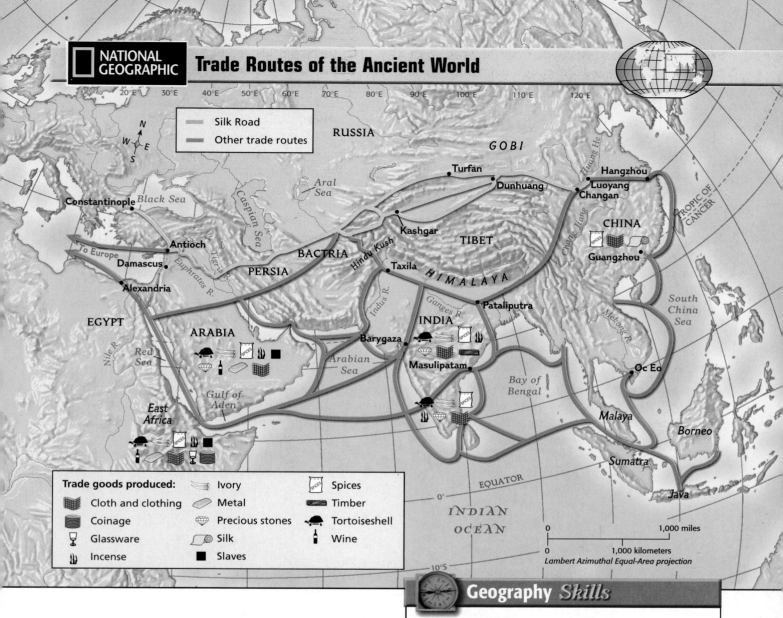

NATIONAL GEOGRAPHIC Trade Routes of the Ancient World

Legend:
- Silk Road
- Other trade routes

RUSSIA

GOBI

Aral Sea

Caspian Sea

Black Sea

Constantinople

Antioch

Damascus

Alexandria

EGYPT

ARABIA

PERSIA

BACTRIA

Hindu Kush

Kashgar

Taxila

TIBET

HIMALAYA

Turfan

Dunhuang

Luoyang
Changan

Hangzhou

CHINA

Guangzhou

TROPIC OF CANCER

Huang He

Chang Jiang

South China Sea

Tigris R.

Euphrates R.

To Europe

Nile R.

Red Sea

Indus R.

Ganges R.

Pataliputra

INDIA

Barygaza

Masulipatam

Oc Eo

Mekong R.

Bay of Bengal

Arabian Sea

Gulf of Aden

East Africa

EQUATOR

INDIAN OCEAN

Malaya

Borneo

Sumatra

Java

Trade goods produced:
- Ivory
- Cloth and clothing
- Coinage
- Glassware
- Incense
- Metal
- Precious stones
- Silk
- Slaves
- Spices
- Timber
- Tortoiseshell
- Wine

0 ____ 1,000 miles
0 ____ 1,000 kilometers
Lambert Azimuthal Equal-Area projection

Geography Skills

Trade in the ancient world brought many cultures and kingdoms together. The Silk Road was one of the main routes of trade, allowing people and camels to move goods across 4,000 miles (6,436 km).

1. **Interpreting Maps** How was the Silk Road different from the other trade routes of the ancient world?

2. **Applying Geography Skills** What pattern do you see behind the placement of the ancient trade routes?

The Kushan Kingdom and the Silk Road

After the collapse of the Mauryan Empire, a number of new kingdoms arose along the edges of India in Bactria, known today as Afghanistan. In the first century A.D., nomadic warriors seized power and established the new Kushan kingdom. For the next two centuries, the Kushans spread over northern India as far as the central Ganges Valley. In the rest of India, other kingdoms fought for control.

The Kushans prospered from the trade that passed through their land on its way between the Mediterranean Sea and the countries bordering the Pacific Ocean. Most of that trade was between the Roman Empire and China. It was shipped along the route known as the Silk Road, so called because silk was China's most valuable product. One section of the

Silk Road passed through the mountains northwest of India.

The Silk Road, which had arisen sometime between 200 B.C. and A.D. 100, reached from the city of **Changan** in China across central Asia to Mesopotamia. It covered a distance of about 4,000 miles (6,436 km). On it, people and camels transported goods through mountains and deserts, winding up at **Antioch** in **Syria,** a port city on the **Mediterranean**

Sea. At Antioch, luxury goods from the West were traded for luxury goods from the East, which were then shipped across the Mediterranean to Greece and Rome. Only luxury goods were carried on the Silk Road because camel caravans were difficult, dangerous, and thus expensive.

Chinese merchants made large fortunes by trading luxury goods, such as silk, spices, teas, and porcelain. Indian merchants sent ivory, textiles, precious stones, and pepper. They were exchanged for woolen and linen clothes, glass, and precious stones from the Roman Empire. Silk was especially desired by the Romans, who considered it worth its weight in gold. In fact, the Romans knew China as Serica, which means "Land of Silk."

☑ **Reading Check** **Explaining** What was the Silk Road and why was it important?

The Kingdom of the Guptas

The Kushan kingdom came to an end in the third century A.D., when invaders from Persia overran it. In 320, a new state was created in the central Ganges Valley by a local prince named Chandragupta (no relation to the earlier Chandragupta Maurya). He located his capital at Pataliputra, the site of the decaying palace of the Mauryas.

His successor, his son Samudragupta, expanded the empire into surrounding areas. A court official wrote of Samudragupta that he "was skillful in waging hundreds of battles with only the strength of his arms. The beauty of his charming body was enhanced by the number of wounds, caused by the blows of battle axes, arrows, spears, pikes, barbed darts, swords, lances, javelins, iron arrows, and many other weapons."

Eventually the new kingdom of the Guptas became the dominant political force throughout northern India. It also established loose control over central India, thus becoming the greatest state in India since the Mauryan Empire.

Under a series of efficient monarchs—especially Chandragupta II, who reigned from 375 to 415—the Gupta Empire created a new age of Indian civilization. The greatness of its culture was reported by a Chinese traveler, **Faxian** (FAY•SYEN), who spent several years there in the fifth century. Faxian, a Buddhist monk, admired the Gupta rulers, their tolerance of Buddhism, and the prosperity of the country.

The Gupta Empire actively engaged in trade with China, Southeast Asia, and the Mediterranean and also encouraged domestic trade in cloth, salt, and iron. Cities famous for their temples as well as for their prosperity rose along the main trade routes

History *through Architecture*

The Sun Temple **at Modhera, India**
Hinduism thrived under the Gupta Empire. How were Hindu beliefs reflected in the architecture of India?

throughout India. Much of their wealth came from religious trade as pilgrims (people who travel to religious places) from across India and as far away as China came to visit the major religious centers.

Much of the trade in the Gupta Empire was managed by the Gupta rulers, who owned silver and gold mines and vast lands. They earned large profits from their dealings. They lived in luxury, awakening to the sound of music and spending much time in dining with followers and guests. It was said that "the king and his companions drank wine out of ruby cups while lutes were strummed."

The good fortunes of the Guptas did not last. Beginning in the late fifth century A.D., invasions by nomadic **Huns** from the northwest gradually reduced the power of the empire. A military commander briefly revived the empire in the middle of the seventh century, but after his death, the empire fell completely apart. North India would not be reunited for hundreds of years.

✓ **Reading Check** **Examining** What characteristics made the Gupta Empire great?

The World of Indian Culture

Few cultures in the world are as rich and varied as that of India. The country produced great works in almost all cultural fields, including literature, architecture, and science.

Literature: A Lasting Legacy The earliest known Indian literature comes from the Aryan tradition in the form of the **Vedas,** which were primarily religious. Originally, these were passed down orally from generation to generation. After the Aryan conquest of India and the development of a writing system, the Vedas were written down in Sanskrit.

With the development of writing, India's great historical epics, the *Mahabharata* (muh•HAH•BAH•ruh•tuh) and the *Ramayana*, were also put into written form. Both of these epics told of the legendary deeds of great warriors.

The *Mahabharata* consists of over ninety thousand stanzas (a series of lines of poetry), making it the longest poem in any written language. Probably written about 100 B.C., it describes a war between cousins in Aryan society for control of the kingdom about 1000 B.C. The most famous section of the book, called the **Bhagavad Gita** (BAH•guh•VAHD GEE•tuh), is a sermon by the god Krishna on the eve of a major battle. In this sermon, he sets forth one of the key points of Indian society: In taking action, one

***Krishna and Maidens*, Mughal period, 1710**
What similarities does this painting share with Hindu architecture?

must not worry about success or failure. One should only be aware of the moral rightness of the act itself.

The *Ramayana*, written at about the same time, is much shorter than the *Mahabharata*. It is an account of the fictional ruler Rama. As a result of a palace plot, he is banished from the kingdom and forced to live as a hermit in the forest. Later, he fights the demon-king of Ceylon, who had kidnapped his beloved wife Sita.

Like the *Mahabharata* (and most works of the ancient world), the *Ramayana* is strongly imbued with religious and moral lessons. Rama is seen as the ideal Aryan hero, a perfect ruler and ideal son. Sita projects the supreme duty of wifely loyalty to her husband. To this day, the *Mahabharata* and *Ramayana* continue to inspire the people of India.

One of ancient India's most famous authors was **Kalidasa,** who lived during the Gupta dynasty. Kalidasa's poem, *The Cloud Messenger,* remains one of the most popular of Sanskrit poems. It tells of an exiled male earth spirit who misses his wife and shares his grief with a passing cloud. He laments:

> ❝I see your body in the sinuous creeper, your gaze
>   in the startled eyes of deer,
> your cheek in the moon, your hair in the
>   plumage of peacocks,
> and in the tiny ripples of the river I see your
>   sidelong glances,
> but alas, my dearest, nowhere do I find your
>   whole likeness!❞

Stone pillars built during the rule of Asoka were topped with decorative capitals. The Lions of Sarnath capital (left) is famous for its beauty and Buddhist symbolism.

Architecture Some of the earliest examples of Indian architecture stem from the time of Asoka, when Buddhism became the religion of the state. The desire to spread the ideas of Gautama Buddha inspired the great architecture of the Mauryan dynasty and the period that followed.

There were three main types of structures, all serving religious purposes: the pillar, the stupa, and the rock chamber. The pillar is the most famous. During Asoka's reign, many stone pillars were erected alongside roads to mark sites related to events in Buddha's life. These polished sandstone pillars weighed up to 50 tons (45.4 t) each and rose as high as 50 feet (15 m). Each was topped with a carving. The carvings usually depicted lions uttering the Buddha's message.

A stupa was originally meant to house a relic of the Buddha, such as a lock of his hair. These structures were built in the form of burial mounds. Eventually, the stupa became a place for devotion and the most familiar form of Buddhist architecture. Each stupa rose to considerable heights and was surmounted by a spire. According to legend, Asoka ordered the construction of eighty-four thousand stupas throughout India.

The final development in early Indian architecture was the rock chamber, carved out of rock cliffs. This structure was developed by Asoka to provide a series of rooms to house monks and to serve as a hall for religious ceremonies.

Science Ancient Indians possessed an impressive amount of scientific knowledge, particularly in astronomy. They charted the movements of the heavenly bodies and recognized that Earth was a sphere that rotated on its axis and revolved around the sun.

Their most important contribution was in the field of mathematics. **Aryabhata,** the most famous mathematician of the Gupta Empire, was one of the first scientists known to have used algebra. Indian mathematicians also introduced the concept of zero and used a symbol (0) for it.

After Arabs conquered parts of India in the eighth century A.D., Arab scholars adopted the Indian system. In turn, European traders borrowed it from the Arabs, and it spread through Europe in the 1200s. Today it is called the Indian-Arabic numerical system.

✓**Reading Check** **Evaluating** How have Indian advances in science and mathematics impacted our world today?

⭐**TAKS Practice**

SECTION 2 ASSESSMENT

Checking for Understanding

1. **Define** Silk Road, pilgrim.

2. **Identify** Asoka, Faxian, Huns, Vedas, Bhagavad Gita, Kalidasa, Aryabhata.

3. **Locate** Persia, Changan, Antioch, Mediterranean Sea.

4. **Explain** what sorts of goods were carried on the Silk Road and why.

5. **List** three examples of early Indian architecture.

Critical Thinking

6. **Analyze** How do the historic epics *Mahabharata* and *Ramayana* reflect real life in early India?

7. **Organizing Information** Create a table showing the main imports and exports of Chinese and Indian merchants.

Country	Imports	Exports
China		
India		

Analyzing Visuals

8. **Examine** the painting of Krishna shown on page 85 of your text. How does this painting reflect Aryan culture? What fundamental ideas are represented in the picture?

Writing About History

9. **Expository Writing** Write a short essay about what would have happened to India's economic development without the Silk Road.

The Good Life in Gupta India

IN THE FIFTH CENTURY A.D., A CHINESE Buddhist monk, Faxian, made a visit to the India of the Guptas in search of documents recording the teachings of the Buddha. He provides a description of life in part of India under the Guptas.

66Beyond the deserts are the territories of western India. The kings of these territories are all firm believers in the law of [the] Buddha. They remove their caps of state when they make offerings to the priests. The members of the royal household and the chief ministers personally direct the food giving. When the distribution of food is over, they spread a carpet on the ground and sit down before it. They dare not sit on couches in the presence of the priests.

Southward from this is the so-called middle-country. The climate of this country is warm and equable, without frost or snow. The people are very well off, without poll-tax or official restrictions. Only those who farm the royal lands return a portion of profit of the land [to the king]. If they desire to go, they go; if they like to stop, they stop. The kings govern without corporal punishment; criminals are fined, according to circumstances, lightly or heavily. Even in cases of repeated rebellion they only cut off the right hand. The king's personal attendants, who guard him on the right and left, have fixed salaries. Throughout the country the people kill no living thing nor drink wine, nor do they eat garlic or onions, with the exception of the [U]ntouchables only. The [U]ntouchables are named 'evil men' and dwell apart from others; if they enter a town or market, they sound a piece of wood in order to separate themselves; then men, knowing who they are, avoid coming in contact with them. In this country they do not keep swine nor fowls, and do not deal in cattle; they have no shambles or wine-shops in their market-places. The [U]ntouchables only hunt and sell flesh.99

—Faxian, Describing Life under the Guptas

▲ *The caves of Ajanta, India, are famous for the paintings and sculptures of the Buddha found inside.*

Gupta painting of Prince Gautama, from Ajanta caves shown above ▶

Analyzing Primary Sources

1. What was good about life in Gupta India?
2. Is there anything that the monk viewed as positive about life in Gupta India that you view as negative? Explain your answer.
3. Analyze your high school community (students, teachers, administrators, and other staff). Is there a caste system? What is the high school good life? Is school life equally good for everyone? Develop your ideas.

SECTION 3 Early Chinese Civilizations

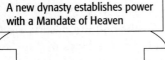
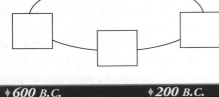
Voices from the Past

Confucius

Confucius wanted to promote good government in China. Confucius said:

❝If the people be led by laws, and uniformity be imposed on them by punishments, they will try to avoid the punishment, but will have no sense of shame. If they be led by virtue, and uniformity be provided for them by the rules of propriety, they will have the sense of shame, and will become good." He also said, "Let the ruler be filial and kind to all people; then they will be faithful to him. Let him advance the good and teach the incompetent; then they will eagerly seek to be virtuous.❞

— *The Chinese Classics*, James Legge, 1893

Confucianism, along with Daoism and Legalism, sought to spell out the principles that would create stability and order in society.

The Geography of China

The **Huang He** (HWONG•HUH), or Yellow River, stretches across China for more than 2,900 miles (4,666.1 km), carrying its rich yellow silt all the way from **Mongolia** to the Pacific Ocean. The **Chang Jiang** (CHONG•JYONG), or Yangtze River, is even longer, flowing for about 3,400 miles (5,470.6 km) across central China before emptying into the **Yellow Sea.** The densely cultivated valleys of these two rivers began to emerge as one of the great food-producing areas of the ancient world.

China, however, is not just a land of fertile fields. In fact, only 10 percent of the total land area is suitable for farming, compared with 19 percent of the United States. Much of the rest of the land in China consists of mountains and deserts, which ring the country on its northern and western frontiers.

This forbidding landscape is a dominant feature of Chinese life and has played an important role in Chinese history. Geographical barriers—mountains and deserts—isolated the Chinese people from peoples in other parts of Asia. In the frontier regions created by these barriers lived peoples of Mongolian, Indo-European, and Turkish backgrounds. The contacts of these groups with the Chinese were often marked by conflict. The northern frontier of China became one of the areas of conflict in Asia as Chinese armies tried to protect their precious farmlands.

✓ **Reading Check** **Describing** What isolated the Chinese people from peoples in other parts of Asia?

The Shang Dynasty

Historians of China have traditionally dated the beginning of Chinese civilization to the founding of the **Xia** (SYAH) **dynasty** over four thousand years ago. Little is known about this dynasty, which was replaced by a second dynasty, the Shang.

China under the **Shang dynasty** (about 1750 to 1122 B.C.) was a mostly farming society ruled by an aristocracy whose major concern was war. An **aristocracy** is an upper class whose wealth is based on land and whose power is passed on from one generation to another.

Archaeologists have found evidence of impressive cities in Shang China. Shang kings may have had at least five different capital cities before settling at Anyang (AHN•YAHNG), just north of the Huang He in north-central China. Excavation of some of these urban centers reveals huge city walls, royal palaces, and large royal tombs.

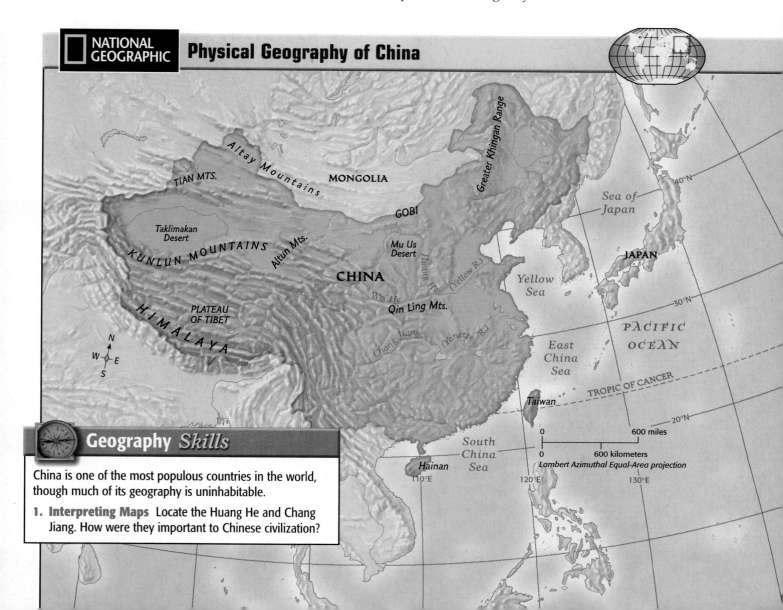

NATIONAL GEOGRAPHIC **Physical Geography of China**

Geography *Skills*

China is one of the most populous countries in the world, though much of its geography is uninhabitable.

1. Interpreting Maps Locate the Huang He and Chang Jiang. How were they important to Chinese civilization?

Political and Social Structures The Shang king ruled from the capital city of Anyang. His realm was divided into territories governed by aristocratic warlords (military leaders), but the king had the power to choose these leaders and could also remove them. The king was also responsible for defending the realm, and he controlled large armies, which often fought on the fringes of the kingdom. The king's importance is evident in the ritual sacrifices undertaken at his death. Like rulers in Mesopotamia and Egypt, early Chinese kings were buried with the corpses of their faithful servants in the royal tombs.

The Chinese believed in supernatural forces with which they could communicate to obtain help in worldly affairs. To communicate with the gods, rulers made use of oracle bones. These were bones on which priests scratched questions asked by the rulers, such as: Will the king be victorious in battle? Will the king recover from his illness? Heated metal rods were then stuck into the bones, causing them to crack. The priests interpreted the shapes of the cracks as answers from the gods. The priests wrote down the answers, then the bones were stored. The inscriptions on the bones have become a valuable source of information about the Shang period.

The king and his family were at the top of Shang society, aided by a number of aristocratic families. The aristocrats not only waged war and served as officials but also were the chief landowners. The great majority of people were peasants who farmed the land of the aristocratic landowners. In addition to the aristocrats and peasants, Shang society also included a small number of merchants and artisans, as well as slaves.

Religion and Culture under the Shang The early Chinese had a strong belief in life after death. Remains of human sacrifices found in royal tombs are evidence of peoples' efforts to win the favor of the gods. The Chinese also wanted to provide companions for the king and members of his family on their journey to the next world.

From this belief in an afterlife would come the idea of the veneration of ancestors (commonly

Oracle bones were inscribed with questions and answers, then preserved in the king's records.

THE WAY IT WAS

FOCUS ON EVERYDAY LIFE

Ancestral Rites

Shang bronzes are one of the great cultural achievements of the ancient world. One reason for the unusual quality of Shang bronze work is the method of casting used. Clay molds made in several sections were tightly fitted together before the liquid bronze was poured. This technique enabled artisans to apply their designs directly to the mold. In this way they could use intricate motifs in a rich surface decoration.

The most important decorative motif on Shang bronzes was the *taotie* mask. It featured a pair of large eyes, nostrils, and fangs, giving it the look of a fantastic beast. Although fierce in appearance, the *taotie* represented a protective force against evil spirits.

These bronze vessels played a significant role in ceremonies for the veneration of ancestors.

Shang bronze

known in the West as "ancestor worship"). The practice of burning replicas (exact copies) of physical objects to accompany the departed on their journey to the next world continues to this day in many Chinese communities. The early Chinese believed that the spirits of family ancestors could bring good or evil fortune to the living members of the family. It was important to treat the spirits well.

The Shang are perhaps best remembered for their mastery of the art of bronze casting. Objects made of bronze have been found in tombs in urban centers throughout the area under Shang influence. More than ten thousand vessels of an incredible variety of form and design survive today. These bronze objects are among the most admired creations of Chinese art.

✓ **Reading Check** **Identifying** How did the Shang rulers communicate with the gods?

The Zhou Dynasty

According to legend, the last of the Shang rulers was a wicked tyrant who swam in "ponds of wine" and ordered the writing of lustful music that "ruined the morale of the nation." This led the aggressive ruler of the state of Zhou (JOH) to revolt against the Shang and establish a new dynasty. The **Zhou dynasty** lasted for almost eight hundred years (1045 to 256 B.C.), making it the longest-lasting dynasty in Chinese history.

Political Structure The Zhou dynasty continued the political system of the rulers it had overthrown. At the head of the government was the Zhou king, who was served by an increasingly large and complex bureaucracy. The king was seen as the link between Heaven and Earth. The correct performance of rituals or ceremonial acts that served to strengthen those links was crucial to a king's duties.

The Shang practice of dividing the kingdom into a number of territories governed by officials appointed by the king was continued under the Zhou. The governing officials of these territories were members of the aristocracy. They were appointed by the king and were subject to his authority. Like the Shang rulers, the Zhou king was in charge of defense and controlled armies that served under his command throughout the country.

The Mandate of Heaven The Zhou kings also made some changes, however, as the Chinese began to develop a theory of government. The Zhou dynasty claimed that it ruled China because it possessed the Mandate of Heaven. What was the Mandate of Heaven? It was believed that Heaven—which was an impersonal law of nature—kept order in the universe through the Zhou king. Thus, he ruled over all humanity by a mandate, or authority to command, from Heaven. The king, who was chosen to rule because of his talent and virtue, was then

The vessels were used as instruments for preparing and serving food in the ancestral rites.

Ancestor veneration was important to the Chinese. They believed that the souls of the dead could bring good or evil fortune to the living members of a family. Thus, ancestral rites had to be properly performed. As one poet observed, "Every custom and rite is observed, every smile, every word is in place."

As part of the ritual, members of the family knelt before several vessels that held offerings of wine and various kinds of food. The quality of the vessels was considered an important part of the ceremony. Well-to-do families, who were the only

ones who could afford bronze vessels, competed to acquire these magnificently crafted pieces.

Once a year, the Chinese also celebrated a major festival called Qingming ("Clear and Bright"). On the day of the festival, people visited their family graves, usually located on hillsides outside their villages. They cleaned the graves and left offerings of food for the spirits of their deceased ancestors.

CONNECTING TO THE PAST

1. **Drawing Inferences** Did death sever familial ties for the Chinese?

2. **Writing about History** Why would rituals and festivals be important to Chinese families? Do you have any family traditions? If so, explain what they are and how they evolved.

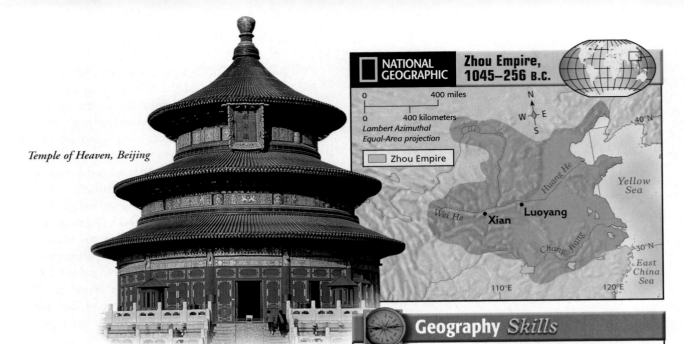

Temple of Heaven, Beijing

Zhou Empire, 1045–256 B.C.

0 ___ 400 miles
0 ___ 400 kilometers
Lambert Azimuthal Equal-Area projection

☐ Zhou Empire

Huang He
Yellow Sea
Wei He
Xian ● Luoyang ●
Chang Jiang
East China Sea
40°N
30°N
110°E
120°E

Geography *Skills*

The ruler of the state of Zhou established the longest-lasting dynasty in Chinese history.

1. **Interpreting Maps** Describe the extent of the Zhou Empire.
2. **Applying Geography Skills** Compare this map to the map on page 89. What do you notice about the location of the Zhou Empire in relation to the rest of China?

responsible for ruling the people with goodness and efficiency. The concept of the heavenly mandate became a basic principle of Chinese statecraft.

The Mandate of Heaven, however, was double-edged. The king was expected to rule according to the proper "Way," called the **Dao** (DOW). It was his duty to keep the gods pleased in order to protect the people from natural disaster or a bad harvest. If the king failed to rule effectively, he could be overthrown and replaced by a new ruler.

This theory has strong political side effects. It sets forth a "right of revolution" to overthrow a corrupt or evil ruler. It also makes clear that the king, though serving as a representative of Heaven, is not a divine being himself. In practice, of course, each founder of a new dynasty would say that he had earned the Mandate of Heaven. Who could disprove it except by overthrowing the king? The saying, "He who wins is the king; he who loses is the rebel," sums up this view.

The Mandate of Heaven was closely tied to the pattern of dynastic cycles. From the beginning of Chinese history to A.D. 1912, China was ruled by a series of dynasties. The Zhou dynasty, as we have seen, lasted for almost eight hundred years. Others did not last as long, but the king of each dynasty ruled with the Mandate of Heaven.

No matter how long the dynasties lasted, all went through a cycle of change. A new dynasty established its power, ruled successfully for many years, and then began to decline. The power of the central government would begin to collapse, giving rise to rebellions or invasion. Finally, the dynasty collapsed and a new dynasty took over, beginning another dynastic cycle.

The Fall of the Zhou Dynasty The Zhou dynasty, too, followed the pattern of rise, decline, and collapse. For centuries the dynasty was ruled by wise and efficient rulers, but later Zhou rulers began to decline, both intellectually and morally. The Zhou kingdom had been divided into several small territories, and some of these territories began to evolve into powerful states that challenged the Zhou ruler. In 403 B.C., civil war broke out, beginning an age known in Chinese historical records as the "Period of the Warring States."

By this time, the nature of warfare had also changed in China. Iron weapons, more powerful than bronze weapons, came into use. Foot soldiers (the infantry) and soldiers on horseback (the cavalry) made their first appearance. Members of the cavalry were now armed with the powerful crossbow, a Chinese invention of the seventh century B.C. Eventually, one of the warring states—that of Qin (CHIN)—took control. In 221 B.C., it created a new dynasty.

Life during the Zhou Dynasty During the Zhou dynasty, the basic features of Chinese economic and social life began to take shape. The Zhou continued the pattern of land ownership that had existed under the Shang. The peasants worked on lands owned by their lord, but they also had land of their own, which they farmed for their own use. A class of artisans and merchants lived in walled towns under the direct control of the local lord. Merchants did not operate freely but were considered the property of the local lord. There was also a class of slaves.

Trade in this period involved the exchange of local products that were used on an everyday basis. Eventually, it increased to include goods brought in from distant regions. Among these goods were salt, iron, cloth, and various luxury items.

Economic and Technological Growth The period from the sixth to the third centuries B.C. was an age of significant economic growth and technological change, especially in farming. For thousands of years, farmers had depended on rainfall to water crops such as rice and millet. By the sixth century B.C., irrigation was in wide use. Large-scale water projects were set in motion to control the flow of rivers and spread water evenly to the fields.

Changes in farming methods also increased food production. By the mid-sixth century B.C., the use of iron had led to the development of iron plowshares, which made it possible to plow land that had not yet been used for farming. This development allowed the Chinese to add to the amount of land available for growing crops. Because of these advances in farming, the population of China rose as high as fifty million people during the late Zhou period.

Improved farming methods were also a major factor in encouraging the growth of trade and manufacturing. One of the most important items of trade in ancient China was silk. Chinese silk fragments from the period have been found throughout central Asia and as far away as Athens, Greece—clear indications of a far-reaching trade network.

The Family in Ancient China Few social institutions have been as closely identified with China as the family. As in most agricultural societies, in ancient China the family served as the basic economic and social unit. However, the family there took on an almost sacred quality as a symbol of the entire social order.

At the heart of the concept of family in China was the idea of filial

piety. *Filial* refers to a son or daughter. *Filial piety*, then, refers to the duty of members of the family to subordinate their needs and desires to those of the male head of the family. More broadly, the term describes a system in which every family member had his or her place. The concept is important in Confucianism, as you will see later in this section.

What explains the importance of the family in ancient China? Certainly, the need to work together on the land was a significant factor. In ancient times, as today, farming in China required the work of many people. Children, too, were essential to the family's needs. They worked in the fields during their early years. Later, sons were expected to take over the burden of physical labor on the family plots and provide for the well-being of their parents.

Male supremacy was a key element in the social system of ancient China, as it was in the other civilizations that we have examined. The male was considered so important because he was responsible for providing food for his family. In ancient China, men worked in the fields. They also governed society and were the warriors, scholars, and government ministers. Women raised the children and worked in the home.

Although women did not hold positions of authority, some did have influence in politics. This was especially true at the royal court, where wives of the ruler or other female members of the royal family played a part in court affairs. These activities were

This photograph from the 1900s illustrates the continuing importance of the family in Chinese culture.

93

clearly looked down upon by males, as this Chinese poem indicates:

> 66A clever man builds a city,
> A clever woman lays one low;
> With all her qualifications, that clever woman
> Is but an ill-omened bird.99

The Chinese Written Language Perhaps the most important cultural contribution of ancient China to later Chinese society was the creation and development of the Chinese written language. By Shang times, the Chinese had developed a simple script that is the ancestor of the highly complex written language of today. Like many other ancient languages, it was primarily pictographic and ideographic in form.

Pictographs are picture symbols, usually called characters, that form a picture of the object to be represented. For example, the Chinese characters for mountain 山, sun 日, and moon 月 were meant to represent the objects themselves. Ideographs are characters that combine two or more pictographs to represent an idea. For example, the word *east* 東 symbolizes the sun coming up behind the trees.

Each character, of course, would be given a sound by the speaker when pronounced. In other cultures, this process eventually led people to stop using pictographs and ideographs and to adopt a written language based on phonetic symbols representing speech sounds, such as the Roman alphabet. The Chinese, too, eventually began to attach phonetic meaning to some of their symbols. However, although the Chinese language has evolved continuously over a period of four thousand years, it has never entirely abandoned its original format.

✓ **Reading Check** **Describing** What is the pattern of dynastic cycles?

The Chinese Philosophies

⌐TURNING POINT⌐ **Confucius believed that the government should be open to all men of superior talent. This concept became a crucial part of Chinese history after his death.**

Between 500 and 200 B.C., toward the end of the Zhou dynasty, three major schools of thought about the nature of human beings and the universe emerged in China—Confucianism, Daoism, and Legalism. While Hindus and Buddhists focused on freeing the human soul from the cycle of rebirth, Chinese philosophers were more concerned about the immediate world in which people lived and how to create a stable order in that world.

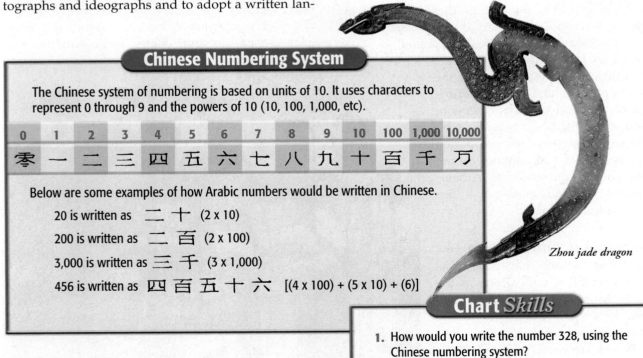

Zhou jade dragon

Chinese Numbering System

The Chinese system of numbering is based on units of 10. It uses characters to represent 0 through 9 and the powers of 10 (10, 100, 1,000, etc).

0	1	2	3	4	5	6	7	8	9	10	100	1,000	10,000
零	一	二	三	四	五	六	七	八	九	十	百	千	万

Below are some examples of how Arabic numbers would be written in Chinese.

20 is written as 二 十 (2 x 10)

200 is written as 二 百 (2 x 100)

3,000 is written as 三 千 (3 x 1,000)

456 is written as 四 百 五 十 六 [(4 x 100) + (5 x 10) + (6)]

Chart *Skills*

1. How would you write the number 328, using the Chinese numbering system?
2. What is the equivalent Arabic numeral for

二 千 六 百 九 十 三 ?

This early nineteenth-century painting illustrates scenes from the life of Confucius, who is shown here with his followers.

Confucianism **Confucius** was known to the Chinese as the First Teacher. (*Confucius* is the western form of the name Kongfuzi [KOONG•FOO•DZUH], meaning "Master Kung," as he was called by his followers.) Confucius was born in 551 B.C. He hoped to get a job as a political adviser, but he had little success in finding a patron.

Upset by the violence and moral decay of his age, Confucius traveled around China in an attempt to persuade political leaders to follow his ideas. Few listened at the time, but a faithful band of followers revered him as a great teacher, recorded his sayings in the *Analects,* and spread his message. Until the twentieth century, almost every Chinese pupil studied his sayings. This made Confucianism, or the system of Confucian ideas, an important part of Chinese history.

Confucius lived at a time of great confusion in China. The chaos in China was largely caused by unceasing warfare among numerous Chinese armies, which did not hesitate to slaughter opposing soldiers and their families. Men, women, and children were beheaded in mass executions. China was faced with one basic question: How do we restore order to this society? Confucius provided a basic set of ideas that eventually came to be widely accepted.

Confucius's interest in philosophy was political and ethical, not spiritual. He believed that it was useless to speculate on spiritual questions. It was better by far to assume that there was an order in the universe and then focus on ordering the affairs of this world. The universe was made in such a way that, if humans would act in harmony with its purposes, their own affairs would prosper. Much of his concern was with human behavior. The key to proper behavior was to behave in accordance with the Dao (Way).

Two elements stand out in the Confucian view of the Dao: duty and humanity. The concept of duty meant that all people had to subordinate their own interests to the broader needs of the family and the community. Everyone should be governed by the Five Constant Relationships: parent and child, husband and wife, older sibling and younger sibling, older friend and younger friend, and ruler and subject. Each person in the relationship had a duty to the other. Parents should be loving, and children should revere their parents. Husbands should fulfill their duties, and wives should be obedient. The elder sibling should be kind, and the younger sibling respectful. The older friend should be considerate, and the younger friend deferential. Rulers should be benevolent, and subjects loyal. Three of these five relationships concern the family, which shows the family's importance to Confucius: "The duty of children to their parents is the foundation from which all virtues spring."

The Confucian concept of duty is often expressed in the form of a "work ethic." If each individual

worked hard to fulfill his or her duties, then the affairs of society as a whole would prosper as well. As Confucius stated,

❝If there is righteousness in the heart, there will be beauty in the character. If there is beauty in the character, there will be harmony in the home. If there be harmony in the home, there will be order in the nation. If there be order in the nation, there will be peace in the world.❞

Above all, the ruler must set a good example. If the king followed the path of goodness and the common good, then subjects would respect him, and society would prosper.

The second key element in the Confucian view of the Dao is the idea of humanity. This consists of a sense of compassion and empathy for others. It is similar in some ways to Christian ideas but with a twist. Christians are taught, "Do unto others as you would have others do unto you." Confucius would say, "Do not do unto others what you would not wish done to yourself." To many Chinese, this meant that others should be tolerated. Confucius urged people to "measure the feelings of others by one's own," for "within the four seas all men are brothers." The ideas of Confucius had a strong appeal to his contemporaries. After his death in 479 B.C., his message spread widely throughout China. Confucius was a harsh critic of his own times. He seemed to stress the need to return to the values of an earlier age—the Golden Age of the early Zhou dynasty. He saw it as an age of perfection that no longer existed. In referring to that age, he is quoted as saying the following:

❝When the Great Way was practiced, the world was shared by all alike. The worthy and the able were promoted to office and practiced good faith and lived in affection. The aged found a fitting close to their lives, the robust their proper employment; the young were provided with an upbringing and the widow and widower, the orphaned and the sick, with proper care. Men had their talks and women their hearths. They hated to see goods lying about in waste, yet they did not hoard them for themselves; they disliked the thought that their energies were not fully used, yet they used them not for private ends. Therefore all evil plotting was prevented and thieves and rebels did not arise, so that people could leave their outer gates unbolted. This was the age of Grand Unity.❞

Confucius was not just living in the past, however. Many of his key ideas looked forward rather than backward. Perhaps his most striking political idea was that the government should not be limited solely to those of noble birth but should be open to all men of superior talent. This concept of rule by merit was, of course, not popular with the aristocrats who held political offices based on their noble birth. Although Confucius's ideas did not have much effect in his lifetime, they opened the door to a new idea of statecraft that would later be put into widespread use.

Daoism Daoism was a system of ideas based on the teachings of **Laozi** (LOW•DZUH). According to tradition, Laozi, or the Old Master, was a contemporary of Confucius. Scholars do not know if Laozi actually existed. Nevertheless, the ideas people associate with him became popular in the fifth and fourth centuries B.C.

The chief ideas of Daoism are discussed in a short work known as *Tao Te Ching (The Way of the Dao)*. Scholars have argued for centuries over its meaning. Nevertheless, the basic ideas of Daoism, as interpreted by followers of the doctrine, are straightforward. Like Confucianism, Daoism does not concern itself with the underlying meaning of the universe. Rather, it tries to set forth proper forms of behavior for human beings on Earth.

Daoism's point of view is quite different from that of Confucianism. Followers of Confucius believe that it is the duty of human beings to work hard to improve life here on Earth. Daoists believe that the true way to follow the will of Heaven is not action but inaction:

> ❝Without going outside, you may
>   know the whole world.
> Without looking through the window,
>   you may see the ways of heaven.
> The farther you go, the less you know.
> Thus the sage [wise man] knows
>   without traveling;
> He sees without looking;
> He works without doing.❞

The best way to act in harmony with the universal order is to act spontaneously and let nature take its course by not interfering with it:

> ❝The universe is sacred.
> You cannot improve it.
> If you try to change it, you will ruin it.
> If you try to hold it, you will lose it.❞

Legalism A third philosophy that became popular in China was **Legalism.** Unlike Confucianism or Daoism, Legalism proposed that human beings were evil by nature. They could only be brought to follow the correct path by harsh laws and stiff punishments. Legalists were referred to as the "School of Law" because they rejected the Confucian view that government by "superior men" could solve society's problems. Instead, they argued for a system of impersonal laws.

The Legalists believed that a strong ruler was required to create an orderly society. Confucius had said, "Lead the people by virtue and restrain them by the rules of good taste, and the people will have a sense of shame, and moreover will become good." The Legalists did not believe this. To them, people were not capable of being good. Fear of harsh punishment would cause the common people to serve the interests of the ruler. The ruler did not have to show compassion for the needs of the people.

✓ **Reading Check** **Summarizing** What three philosophies became popular in early China?

🌟 **TAKS Practice**

SECTION **3** ASSESSMENT

Checking for Understanding

1. **Define** aristocracy, Mandate of Heaven, Dao, filial piety, Confucianism, Daoism, Legalism.

2. **Identify** Xia dynasty, Shang dynasty, Zhou dynasty, Confucius, Laozi.

3. **Locate** Huang He, Mongolia, Chang Jiang, Yellow Sea.

4. **Explain** the importance of filial piety to the Chinese. How does the concept of filial piety relate to the Confucian view of how society should function?

5. **List** some of the agricultural advances developed in ancient China and explain how they increased food production.

Critical Thinking

6. **Evaluate** What are the advantages and disadvantages of a society based on Legalism?

7. **Taking Notes** Using an outline format, describe the Confucian ideas of the Five Constant Relationships.

I. The Five Constant Relationships
   A. Parent and Child
      1. parents should be loving, children should revere their parents
   B.
   C. Older Sibling and Younger Sibling
   D.
   E. Ruler and Subject
      1. rulers should be benevolent, subjects loyal

Analyzing Visuals

8. **Analyze** the Shang bronze vessel shown on page 90. What artistic or cultural ideals are represented? Why are these bronze vessels considered to be among the greatest cultural achievements of the ancient world? How were these vessels used by the Chinese people?

Writing About History

9. **Expository Writing** Write a paper about the philosophical traditions of Confucianism, Daoism, and Legalism. Use newspapers, magazines, and the Internet to identify examples of the influence of these three philosophies in historic and contemporary world events.

Rise and Fall of Chinese Empires

Main Ideas
- The Qin and Han dynasties established strong central governments that were the basis for future dynasties.
- Technical and cultural achievements during the Qin and Han dynasties included the invention of paper and written literary classics.

Key Terms
regime, censorate

People to Identify
Qin Shihuangdi, Xiongnu, Liu Bang, Han Wudi

Places to Locate
Gobi, South China Sea, Indian Ocean

Preview Questions
1. Why was the Great Wall of China built?
2. How did nomadic peoples affect Chinese history?

Reading Strategy
Compare and Contrast As you read this section, compare and contrast the Qin and Han dynasties using a Venn diagram.

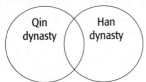

Qin dynasty | Han dynasty

Preview of Events

| ♦ 200 B.C. | ♦ 100 B.C. | ♦ A.D. 1 | ♦ A.D. 100 | ♦ A.D. 200 |

202 B.C.
Han dynasty begins

87 B.C.
Han Wudi dies

A.D. 170
Han dynasty begins collapse

Voices from the Past

Qin Shihuangdi

Faced with the invasion of China's northern frontier, Emperor Qin Shihuangdi responded forcefully. According to an ancient Chinese historian:

❝The emperor dispatched Meng T'ien to lead a force of a hundred thousand men north to attack the barbarians. He seized control of all lands south of the Huang He and established border defenses along the river, constructing forty-four walled district cities overlooking the river and manning them with convict laborers transported to the border for garrison duty. Thus he utilized the natural mountain barriers to establish the border defenses, scooping out the valleys and constructing ramparts and building installations at other points where they were needed.❞

—*Records of the Grand Historian of China,* **Burton Watson, 1961**

The First Qin Emperor unified the Chinese world, though his dynasty was short-lived. The Han dynasty that followed, however, lasted more than four hundred years.

The Qin Dynasty (221–206 B.C.)

As we have seen, from about 400 to 200 B.C., China experienced bloody civil war. Powerful states fought one another and ignored the authority of the Zhou kings. One state—that of Qin—gradually defeated its chief rivals. In 221 B.C., the Qin ruler declared the creation of a new dynasty.

The ruler of Qin was **Qin Shihuangdi** (CHIN SHUR•HWONG•DEE), meaning "the First Qin Emperor." A person of much ambition, Qin Shihuangdi had come to the throne of Qin in 246 B.C. at the age of 13. In 221 B.C., he defeated the last of Qin's rivals and founded a new dynasty, with himself as emperor.

Changes under the Qin Dynasty

The **Qin dynasty** dramatically changed Chinese politics. Legalism was adopted as the regime's (the government in power) official ideology. Those who opposed the policies of the new regime were punished or executed. Books presenting ideas opposed to the official views were publicly burned. 📖 *(See page 991 to read excerpts from Li Su's* The Burning of Books *in the Primary Sources Library.)*

The Qin dynasty made a number of important administrative and political changes, which served as models for future dynasties. In the first place, unlike the Zhou dynasty, the Qin dynasty ruled a highly centralized state. The central bureaucracy was divided into three parts: the civil division, the military division, and the censorate. The censorate had inspectors who checked on government officials to make sure they were doing their jobs. This became standard procedure for future Chinese dynasties.

Below the central government were two levels of administration—provinces and counties. Officials at these levels did not inherit their positions (as was done under the Zhou), but were appointed and

People In History

Qin Shihuangdi
259–210 B.C.—Chinese emperor

Qin Shihuangdi was described by the famous Chinese historian Sima Qian as having "the chest of a bird of prey, the voice of a jackal, and the heart of a tiger." Landed aristocrats and Confucian intellectuals, as well as the common people, groaned under the censorship of speech, harsh taxes, and forced labor projects (instituted by the ruler). Sima Qian said of Qin Shihuangdi, "He killed men as though he thought he could never finish, he punished men as though he were afraid he would never get around to them all, and the whole world revolted against him." Indeed, Qin Shihuangdi was to be his dynasty's only ruler.

dismissed by the emperor. The censors, who reported directly to the throne, kept a close watch over officials. Those found guilty of wrongdoing were executed.

Qin Shihuangdi unified the Chinese world. He created a single monetary system and ordered the building of a system of roads throughout the entire empire. Many of these roads led out from his capital city of Xianyang (SYEN•YONG), just north of modern-day Xian (SYEN).

Qin Shihuangdi was equally aggressive in foreign affairs. His armies advanced to the south, extending the border of China to the edge of the Yuan (YOO•AHN) River, or Red River, in modern-day Vietnam. To supply his armies, he had a canal dug from the Chang Jiang in central China to what is now the modern city of Guangzhou (GWONG•JOH).

The Great Wall

The Qin emperor's major foreign concern was in the north. In the vicinity of the **Gobi,** there resided a nomadic people known to the Chinese as the **Xiongnu** (SYEN•NOO). Mounted on their horses, the Xiongnu ranged far and wide in search of pasture for their flocks of cattle, sheep, or goats. They were organized loosely into tribes, and moved with the seasons from one pasture to another.

The Xiongnu had mastered the art of fighting on horseback. The historian Sima Qian remarked that "the little boys start out by learning to ride sheep and shoot birds and rats with a bow and arrow, and when they get a little older they shoot foxes and rabbits, which are used for food. Thus all the young men are able to use a bow and act as armed cavalry in time of

As a Chinese ruler looks on, books are burned and scholars are killed.

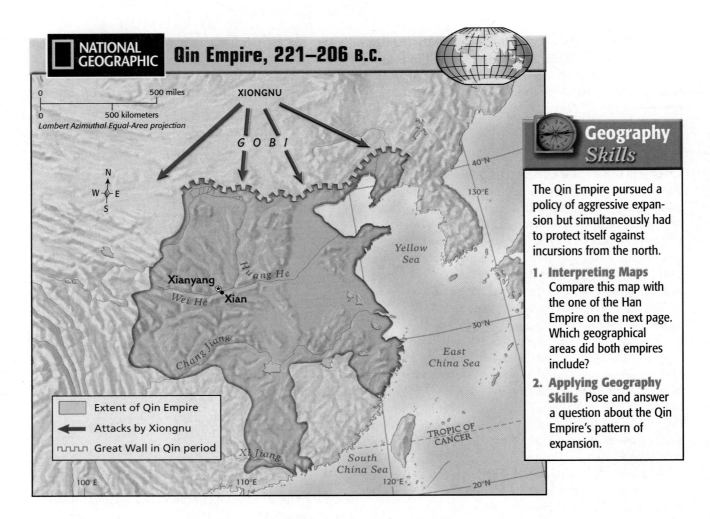

NATIONAL GEOGRAPHIC

Qin Empire, 221–206 B.C.

XIONGNU

GOBI

Xianyang
Xian

Huang He
Wei He
Chang Jiang
Xi Jiang

Yellow Sea
East China Sea
South China Sea

TROPIC OF CANCER

Extent of Qin Empire
Attacks by Xiongnu
Great Wall in Qin period

0   500 miles
0   500 kilometers
Lambert Azimuthal Equal-Area projection

Geography Skills

The Qin Empire pursued a policy of aggressive expansion but simultaneously had to protect itself against incursions from the north.

1. **Interpreting Maps** Compare this map with the one of the Han Empire on the next page. Which geographical areas did both empires include?

2. **Applying Geography Skills** Pose and answer a question about the Qin Empire's pattern of expansion.

war." The Xiongnu soon became a challenge to Chinese communities near the northern frontier. A number of Chinese states in the area began to build walls to keep them out.

Qin Shihuangdi's answer to the problem in the north was to strengthen the existing system of walls to keep the nomads out. Today we know Qin Shihuangdi's project as the **Great Wall of China.** However, the wall that we know today from films and photographs was not built at the order of the First Qin Emperor but 1,500 years later. Some of the walls built by Qin Shihuangdi do remain standing, but many of them were constructed of loose stone, sand, or piled rubble and disappeared long ago. Defensive walls against nomads had existed in parts of North China for years. Qin Shihuangdi linked these sections of walls together to create "The Wall of Ten Thousand *Li*" (a *li* is about a third of a mile, or half a kilometer).

This is not to say, of course, that the wall was not a massive project. It required the efforts of thousands of laborers. Many of them died while working there and, according to legend, are now buried within the

wall. With his wall, the First Qin Emperor enjoyed some success in fighting off the threat of the nomads, but the victory was only temporary.

The Fall of the Qin Dynasty By ruthlessly gathering control over the empire into his own hands, Qin Shihuangdi had hoped to establish a rule that "would be enjoyed by his sons for ten thousand generations." In fact, the First Qin Emperor had angered many Chinese. The emperor died in 210 B.C., and his dynasty was overthrown four years later.

The fall of the Qin dynasty was followed by a period of civil war, but it did not last long. A new dynasty would soon arise.

Reading Check **Identifying** What were the three parts of the central bureaucracy developed by the Qin dynasty?

The Han Dynasty (202 B.C.–A.D. 220)

One of the greatest and most long-lasting dynasties in Chinese history—the **Han** (HAHN) **dynasty**—emerged in 202 B.C. The founder of the Han dynasty was **Liu Bang** (LYOH BONG), a man of peasant

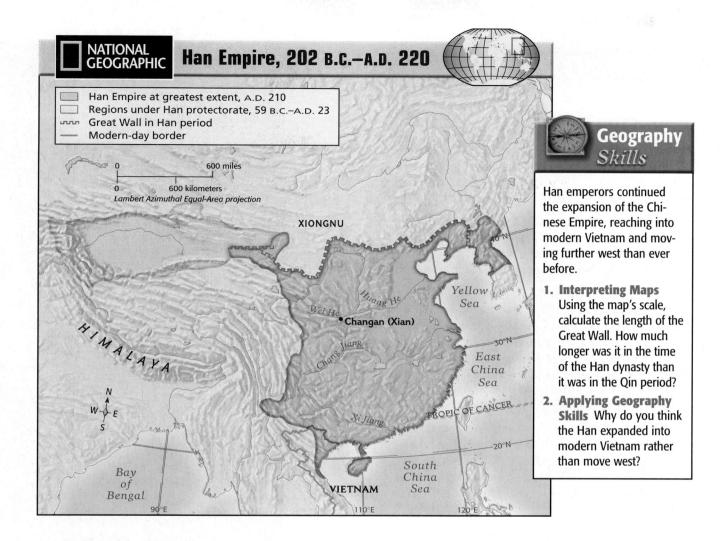

Han Empire, 202 B.C.–A.D. 220

NATIONAL GEOGRAPHIC

Han Empire at greatest extent, A.D. 210
Regions under Han protectorate, 59 B.C.–A.D. 23
Great Wall in Han period
Modern-day border

0   600 miles
0   600 kilometers
Lambert Azimuthal Equal-Area projection

XIONGNU

HIMALAYA

Huang He
Wei He
•Changan (Xian)
Chang Jiang
Xi Jiang

Yellow Sea

East China Sea

TROPIC OF CANCER

Bay of Bengal

VIETNAM

South China Sea

40°N
30°N
20°N
90°E   110°E   120°E

Geography Skills

Han emperors continued the expansion of the Chinese Empire, reaching into modern Vietnam and moving further west than ever before.

1. **Interpreting Maps** Using the map's scale, calculate the length of the Great Wall. How much longer was it in the time of the Han dynasty than it was in the Qin period?

2. **Applying Geography Skills** Why do you think the Han expanded into modern Vietnam rather than move west?

origin who became known by his title of Han Gaozu ("Exalted Emperor of Han"). Under his strong rule and that of his successors, the new dynasty quickly established its control over the empire.

Political Structure The first Han emperor discarded the harsh policies of the Qin dynasty. Confucian principles, rather than Legalism, soon became the basis for the creation of a new state philosophy. However, Han Gaozu and his successors found it convenient to keep some of the practices of the First Qin Emperor, including the division of the central government into three ministries—the military, civil service, and censorate. The Han rulers also kept the system of local government that divided the empire into provinces and counties.

Most important, the Han rulers continued the Qin system of choosing government officials on the basis of merit rather than birth. To create a regular system for new officials, the Han dynasty introduced the civil service examination and established a school to train these candidates. This system for officials

influenced Chinese civilization for two thousand years. Students were expected to learn the teachings of Confucius, as well as Chinese history and law. (For a discussion of the civil service examination system, see Chapter 8.)

China under the Han dynasty was a vast empire. The population increased rapidly—by some estimates rising from about twenty million to over sixty million at the height of the dynasty. The large size of the population created a growing need for a large and efficient bureaucracy to keep the state in proper working order.

Expansion of the Empire In addition to providing a strong central government, the Han emperors continued to expand the Chinese Empire. Han rulers, especially **Han Wudi** (HAHN WOO•DEE) ("Martial Emperor of Han"), added the southern regions below the Chang Jiang into the empire. Along the coast of the **South China Sea,** part of what is today northern Vietnam became part of the empire. Han armies also went westward into central Asia, extending the

Papermaking in Han China

The ancient Chinese were responsible for four remarkable inventions that were crucial to the development of modern technology: the magnetic compass, paper, printing, and gunpowder. How to make paper was one of their early discoveries.

The oldest piece of paper found in China dates from the first century B.C. Made from hemp fibers, it was thick, rough, and useless for writing. That was not a problem for the ancient Chinese, however, because they preferred to write on bamboo or silk.

Paper with writing on it dates from around A.D. 100. By this time, the Chinese had figured out how to make paper of better quality. After hemp or linen rags were soaked in water, they were mixed with potash and mashed into a pulp. A frame with a fine bamboo mesh was lowered into this vat of pulp. When the frame was removed, it held a thin sheet of pulp. Any extra water was removed before the sheets of paper were hung up to dry.

The art of papermaking spread westward from China beginning in the eighth century A.D. First India and then the Arab world developed the technique. The Arab cities of Baghdad, Damascus, and Cairo all had large papermaking industries. Paper was shipped from these centers to the West, but Europeans did not begin their production of paper until the twelfth century.

Describing *What did the Chinese use to make paper?*

Bamboo for paper is lifted out of China's Mekong River.

A contemporary artisan demonstrates ancient papermaking techniques.

Chinese boundary there. Han Wudi also had to deal with the Xiongnu, the nomads beyond the Great Wall to the north. His armies drove the Xiongnu back, and after his death in 87 B.C., China experienced almost another 150 years of relative peace.

Society in the Han Empire The Han period was one of great prosperity. Free peasants, however, began to suffer. Land taxes on land-owning farmers were fairly light, but there were other demands on them, including military service and forced labor of up to one month per year. Then, too, the tripling of the population under the Han dynasty eventually reduced the average size of the individual farm plot to about one acre per person—barely enough for survival.

As time went on, many poor peasants were forced to sell their land and become tenant farmers, who paid rents ranging up to half of the annual harvest. Land once again came to be held in the hands of the powerful landed aristocrats. These nobles often owned thousands of acres worked by tenants. They gathered their own military forces to bully free farmers into becoming tenants.

Technology in the Han Empire New technology added to the economic prosperity of the Han Era. Much progress was made in such areas as textile manufacturing, water mills for grinding grain, and iron casting. Iron casting technology led to the invention of steel. In addition, paper was developed under the Han dynasty.

With the invention of the rudder and fore-and-aft rigging, ships could sail into the wind for the first time. This made it possible for Chinese merchant ships carrying heavy cargoes to travel throughout the islands of Southeast Asia and into the **Indian Ocean,** leading to a major expansion of trade in the Han period. Trade relations were even established with areas as far away as India and the Mediterranean.

An army of life-sized terra-cotta soldiers was found in Qin Shihuangdi's tomb.

The Fall of the Han Empire Over a period of time, the Han Empire began to fall into decay. As weak rulers amused themselves with the pleasures of court life, the power of the central government began to decline. The great noble families filled the gap, amassing vast landed estates and forcing free farmers to become their tenants. Official corruption and the concentration of land in the hands of the wealthy led to widespread peasant unrest. Then, too, nomadic raids on Chinese territory continued in the north.

By A.D. 170, wars, intrigues at the court, and peasant uprisings brought the virtual collapse of the Han dynasty. In 190, rebel armies sacked the Han capital, Luoyang (LWO•YONG). The final blow came in 220, when a general seized control but was unable to maintain his power. China again plunged into civil war, made worse by invasions of northern peoples. The next great dynasty would not arise for four hundred years.

✓**Reading Check** **Identifying** What new technology developed during the Han Era?

Culture in Qin and Han China

The Qin and Han dynasties were also known for their cultural achievements. The key works of the Confucian school, for example, were made into a set of Confucian classics, which became required reading for generations of Chinese schoolchildren. These classics introduced children to the forms of behavior that they would need as adults.

Perhaps the most remarkable artistic achievement of the Qin period was discovered in 1974. Farmers digging a well about 35 miles (56 km) east of Xian discovered an underground pit near the burial mound of the First Qin Emperor. It contained a vast army made of terra-cotta (hardened clay). Chinese archaeologists believed that it was a re-creation of Qin Shihuangdi's imperial guard and was meant to be with the emperor on his journey to the next world.

The army, dressed in uniforms, is contained in four pits. Archaeologists estimate that there are more than six thousand figures in the first pit alone, along with horses, wooden chariots, and seven thousand bronze weapons. The figures are slightly larger than life-size. They were molded, then fired and painted in brilliant colors. To achieve individuality in the faces of the soldiers, ten different head shapes were used, which were finished by hand.

✓**Reading Check** **Describing** What was the purpose of the terra-cotta figures discovered near Xian?

🔶**TAKS Practice**

SECTION 4 ASSESSMENT

Checking for Understanding

1. **Define** regime, censorate.

2. **Identify** Qin Shihuangdi, Qin dynasty, Xiongnu, Great Wall of China, Han dynasty, Liu Bang, Han Wudi.

3. **Locate** Gobi, South China Sea, Indian Ocean.

4. **Explain** how free farmers sometimes became tenant farmers.

5. **Discuss** Qin Shihuangdi's actions for unifying the Chinese world.

Critical Thinking

6. **Explain** What is the importance of the technological advancements in sailing that were made during the Han dynasty?

7. **Organizing Information** Create a flow chart showing the government organization during the Han dynasty and the duties for each division.

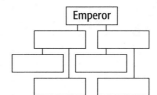

Analyzing Visuals

8. **Examine** the illustration on page 99. What is the significance of the political decision the emperor made to burn books? What else is being depicted?

Writing About History

9. **Expository Writing** Write an essay that explains what the Chinese archaeological site east of Xian tells us about the people of the Qin dynasty. What might future historians conclude about us should they uncover memorials such as the Washington Monument or Lincoln Memorial?

Using Key Terms

1. Aryan leaders known as _____ (princes) fought other Aryan chieftans and seized their property.

2. The major divisions of the Indian classes of people were called _____ in English.

3. The belief that the individual soul is reborn in a different form after death is _____.

4. _____ is a method of training designed to lead to a union with Brahman.

5. In Buddhism, reaching _____, or ultimate reality, is the end of the self and a reunion with the Great World Soul.

6. The Kushan kingdom prospered from trade that passed through their land along the _____.

7. According to Confucius, the key to proper behavior was to behave in accordance with the _____ (Way).

8. The Qin bureaucracy had civil and military divisions and a _____.

Reviewing Key Facts

9. **Geography** Describe the diverse geography of the Indian subcontinent.

10. **Culture** Explain the following statement: "The Harappan rulers were closely linked to their religion."

11. **History** Identify the physical changes that occurred in the Indus River valley that contributed to the collapse of the once-flourishing civilization there.

12. **Culture** Discuss the connection between the Four Noble Truths and the Eightfold Path.

13. **History** "Faxian, a Chinese Buddhist monk, traveled through the Gupta Empire and admired the character of their rule, their tolerance of Buddhism, and the prosperity of the country." Describe what Faxian found in India that supports this quote.

14. **Geography** Describe the geography of China.

15. **Science, Technology, and Society** Identify the ways in which warfare changed in China near the end of the Zhou dynasty.

16. **Culture** Discuss the life of a peasant during the Han Era.

17. **Culture** How does the ancient Chinese system of writing differ from cuneiform and hieroglyphic writing?

18. **Government** The dynastic cycles in China meant each dynasty would eventually fall. What factors caused this to happen?

Critical Thinking

19. **Evaluating** How might Chinese society and culture have evolved differently if there had been more contact with other civilizations?

20. **Compare and Contrast** In what ways are the ideas of the Buddhist Eightfold Path similar to and different from the ideas, beliefs, and practices of other religions or philosophies you may know about?

21. **Analyzing** What do Chinese art forms tell us about technological development in ancient China?

Chapter Summary

Chinese and Indian civilizations are remarkable for their achievement and innovation. This chart shows their accomplishments in several areas.

Country	Religion/Philosophy	Key People	Innovation	Literature	Government/Society
India	Hinduism Buddhism	Siddhartha Gautama Asoka Chandragupta II	Iron plow Caste system Concept of zero Decimal system	*Mahabharata* *Ramayana* *Arthasastra* Vedas	Patriarchal Monarchy
China	Confucianism Daoism Legalism	Confucius Laozi Qin Shihuangdi	Bronze casting Crossbow Paper Iron plowshare Silk	*Analects* Confucian classics *Tao Te Ching* Poetry	Patriarchal Monarchy

Writing About History

22. **Persuasive Writing** Prepare an editorial for a newspaper in which you discuss the philosophies of Confucianism, Legalism, and Daoism. Explain why you think the current government of your country should adopt one of these philosophies in its system of government.

Analyzing Sources

Read the following decree of Asoka, one of India's greatest rulers.

> ❝By order of the Beloved of the Gods [Asoka] to the officers in charge: Let us win the affection of all people. All people are my children, and as I wish all welfare and happiness in this world and the rest for my own children, so do I wish it for all men. . . . For that purpose many officials are employed among the people to instruct them in righteousness and to explain it to them.❞

23. What is the relationship between Asoka and the Beloved of the Gods?

24. How does this quote reflect the Buddhist beliefs that were adopted by Asoka?

Applying Technology Skills

25. **Using the Internet** The Chinese had the Great Wall of China built for protection from enemies. Using the Internet, research how other countries have protected themselves. Using a word processor, write a brief description of two examples. List the name of the country, what it used for protection, and who was being kept out.

Making Decisions

26. In this chapter you read about Chinese pictographs and ideographs. In Chapter 2, you learned about cuneiform, hieroglyphic writing, and hieratic script. How do archaelogists, historians, and linguists decipher (translate) an unknown language?

27. Religion has always played a major role in Indian society. How might religious differences have affected India and its development as a nation?

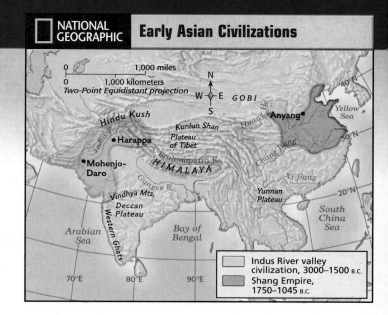

NATIONAL GEOGRAPHIC **Early Asian Civilizations**

Analyzing Maps and Charts

Study the map above to answer the following questions.

28. Compare this map to the maps of the Fertile Crescent and Egyptian civilizations in previous chapters. What geographic features are common to each of these civilizations?

29. In what mountain range does the Indus River originate?

30. What major rivers empty into the Yellow Sea?

31. Name the river valley civilizations studied thus far.

Test Practice

Directions: Choose the best answer to the following question.

In general, women in ancient India

A could not get an education or inherit property.

B passed down the Vedas to the younger generation.

C traded with Chinese merchants.

D became a force in politics.

Test-Taking Tip: Even if you don't know the correct answer, you still may know which answer choices are *wrong.* Eliminating only one or two answer choices improves your chances of answering the question correctly. Using all of your knowledge about ancient India, eliminate the answer choices you know are wrong. Then choose the best answer from the choices that remain.

Ancient Greece

1900–133 B.C.

Key Events

As you read, look for the key events in the history of early Greece.
- *Athens and Sparta emerged as the leading Greek city-states.*
- *The Greek military defeated the Persian army.*
- *Greek theatre, arts, and architecture flourished during the Classical Age.*
- *Greek philosophers such as Socrates, Plato, and Aristotle established the foundations of Western philosophy.*

The Impact Today

- *The Olympic games are held every two years.*
- *Greek architecture is still considered the classical model of grace and symmetry.*
- *Greek plays continue to be performed throughout the world.*
- *Current democratic systems of government and citizenship are based on ideas originally developed by the Greeks.*

World History Video *The Chapter 4 video, "The Early Olympics," chronicles the origins of the Olympic games.*

Mycenaean ceremonial cup

1900 B.C.
Minoan
civilization on
Crete peaks

1300 B.C.
Mycenaean
civilization
reaches its
height

| 1900 B.C. | 1700 B.C. | 1500 B.C. | 1300 B.C. | 1100 B.C. |

c. 1250 B.C.
According
to Homer,
Greeks sack
Troy

Plato's School, a mosaic from the Hellenistic period

The Parthenon in Athens

750 B.C.
Dark Age of
Greece ends

431 B.C.
Great
Peloponnesian
War begins

405 B.C.
Athenian
Empire is
destroyed

900 B.C.   700 B.C.   500 B.C.   300 B.C.   100 B.C.

700 B.C.
Athens
becomes a
unified polis

500 B.C.
Classical
Greece
flourishes

323 B.C.
Alexander the
Great dies at
age 32

Alexander the Great

The goddess Athena

HISTORY
Online
Chapter Overview
Visit the *Glencoe World History* Web site at
tx.wh.glencoe.com and click
on **Chapter 4–Chapter Overview** to preview
chapter information.

A Story That Matters

Pericles giving his famous Funeral Oration

Pericles Addresses Athens

*I*n 431 B.C., war erupted in Greece as two very different Greek states—Athens and Sparta—fought for domination of the Greek world. Strengthened by its democratic ideals, Athens felt secure behind its walls.

In the first winter of the war, the Athenians held a public funeral to honor those who had died in combat. On the day of the ceremony, the citizens of Athens joined in a procession. The relatives of the dead mourned their loved ones.

As was the custom in Athens, one leading citizen was asked to address the crowd. On this day it was Pericles who spoke to the people. He talked about the greatness of Athens and reminded the Athenians of the strength of their political system.

"Our constitution," Pericles said, "is called a democracy because power is in the hands not of a minority but of the whole people. When it is a question of settling private disputes, everyone is equal before the law; when it is a question of putting one person before another in positions of public responsibility, what counts is not membership in a particular class, but the actual ability which the man possesses. No one . . . is kept in political obscurity because of poverty. And, just as our political life is free and open, so is our day-to-day life in our relations with each other. . . . Here each individual is interested not only in his own affairs but in the affairs of the state as well."

Why It Matters

In his famous speech, called the Funeral Oration, Pericles describes the Greek ideal of democracy and the importance of the individual. This is but one example of how the Greeks laid the intellectual foundations of Western civilization. They asked basic questions about the purpose of life, divine forces, and truth. The Greeks not only strove to answer these questions, they also created a system of logical thought for answering such questions. This system of thought remains worthwhile today.

History and You Reread the quote by Pericles. What portions of Athenian democracy described in this passage are found in the Constitution of the United States? Prepare a written report explaining and supporting your position with examples from the United States Constitution.

The First Greek Civilizations

Guide to Reading

Main Ideas
- Mycenaean civilization flourished in Greece between 1600 and 1100 B.C.
- The Greeks used the *Iliad* and *Odyssey* to present role models of the values of courage, honor, and excellence.

Key Terms
epic poem, *arete*

People to Identify
Minoans, Mycenaeans, Homer

Places to Locate
Aegean Sea, Black Sea, Crete, Ionia

Preview Questions
1. How did the geography of Greece affect Greek history?
2. What role did Homer's writings play in the lives of Greeks?

Reading Strategy
Compare and Contrast Use a Venn diagram to compare and contrast the Minoan and Mycenaean civilizations.

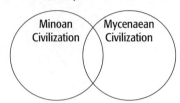

Minoan Civilization / Mycenaean Civilization

Preview of Events

◆1500 B.C. ◆1400 B.C. ◆1300 B.C. ◆1200 B.C. ◆1100 B.C. ◆1000 B.C. ◆900 B.C. ◆800 B.C.

1450 B.C.
Minoan civilization on Crete collapses

1300 B.C.
Mycenaean civilization peaks

750 B.C.
Dark Age of Greece ends

Homer

Voices from the Past

The Trojan War and other adventures had kept Odysseus away from his home for many years. Penelope, his wife, remained faithful to her husband and displayed great courage and intelligence in preserving their household during her husband's long absence. On his return, Odysseus praised her for her excellence:

❝Madame, there is not a man in the wide world who could find fault with you. For your fame has reached heaven itself, like that of some perfect king, ruling a populous and mighty state with the fear of god in his heart, and upholding the right.❞

— *The Odyssey*, Homer, E. V. Rieu, trans., 1946

Homer, Greece's great eighth-century B.C. poet, wrote about heroes. Heroes like Odysseus and Penelope in Homer's *Odyssey* were expected to strive for excellence. Homer's writings identified the ideals that were valued by the Greek ruling class.

The Impact of Geography

Geography played an important role in the development of Greek civilization. Compared with Mesopotamia and Egypt, Greece occupies a small area. It consists of a mountainous peninsula and numerous islands that encompass about fifty thousand square miles of territory—about the size of the state of Louisiana.

The mountains and the sea played especially significant roles in the development of Greek history. Much of Greece consists of small plains and river valleys

Greece's geography helped shape Greek civilization.

surrounded by high mountain ranges. The mountains isolated Greeks from one another, causing different Greek communities to develop their own ways of life. Over a period of time, these communities became fiercely independent. It is probable that the small size of these independent communities encouraged people to participate in political affairs. On the other hand, the rivalry between the communities led to warfare that devastated Greek society.

The sea also influenced the evolution of Greek society. Greece has a long seacoast dotted by bays and inlets that provided many harbors. The Greeks lived on a number of islands to the west, south, and east of the Greek mainland. It was no accident that the Greeks became seafarers. They sailed out into the **Aegean Sea,** the Mediterranean, and the **Black Sea,** making contact with the outside world. Later they established colonies that spread Greek civilization throughout the Mediterranean world.

✓ **Reading Check** **Explaining** What role did the mountains and the sea play in the development of Greek history?

The Minoan Civilization

By 2800 B.C., a Bronze Age civilization that used metals, especially bronze, in making weapons had been established on the large island of **Crete,** southeast of the Greek mainland. Called the Minoan civilization, it flourished between 2700 and 1450 B.C. Arthur Evans, the English archaeologist who first discovered the civilization, named it after Minos, the legendary king of Crete.

NATIONAL GEOGRAPHIC

Greece, 1400 B.C.

Settled areas

N W E S

Mount Olympus ▲

Troy

ASIA MINOR

Aegean Sea

IONIA

GREECE

Mycenae •

Ionian Sea

Mediterranean Sea

Thera

Crete

Knossos

0   100 miles
0   100 kilometers

20°E   25°E   35°N   40°N

Chamberlin Trimetric projection

Geography *Skills*

The physical geography of Greece had a major impact on the development of Greek civilization.

1. **Interpreting Maps** How many miles apart are Mycenae and Troy?
2. **Applying Geography Skills** Using the map, give examples of how Greece's geography affected Greek civilization.

At the beginning of the twentieth century, Evans discovered an enormous palace complex on Crete at Knossos (NAH•suhs). The remains of this complex revealed a rich culture, with Knossos as the center of a far-ranging sea empire based on trade.

The ships of the **Minoans** took them to Egypt as well as southern Greece in search of goods.

The palace at Knossos, the royal seat of the kings, was an elaborate building that included numerous private living rooms for the royal family and workshops for making decorated vases, ivory figurines, and jewelry. Even bathrooms, with elaborate drains, formed part of the complex. The rooms were decorated with brightly colored paintings showing sporting events and nature scenes. Storerooms in the palace held gigantic jars of oil, wine, and grain, items that were paid as taxes to the king.

The centers of Minoan civilization on Crete suffered a sudden and catastrophic collapse around 1450 B.C. Some historians believe that a tidal wave triggered by a powerful volcanic eruption on the island of Thera (THIHR•uh) was responsible for the devastation. Most historians, however, believe that the destruction was the result of invasion by mainland Greeks known as the **Mycenaeans** (MY•suh•NEE•uhnz).

✔ **Reading Check** **Describing** In what ways was the Minoan civilization an advanced civilization?

The First Greek State: Mycenae

The term Mycenaean comes from Mycenae (my•SEE•nee), a fortified site in Greece that was first discovered by the German archaeologist Heinrich Schliemann. Mycenae was one of a number of centers in a Mycenaean Greek civilization that flourished between 1600 and 1100 B.C.

The Mycenaean Greeks were part of the Indo-European family of peoples who spread into southern and western Europe, India, and Iran. One of these groups entered Greece from the north around 1900 B.C. Over a period of time, this group managed to gain control of the Greek mainland and develop a civilization.

Mycenaean civilization, which reached its high point between 1400 and 1200 B.C., was made up of powerful monarchies. Each resided in a fortified palace center. Like Mycenae, these centers were built on hills and surrounded by gigantic stone walls. The various centers of power probably formed a loose alliance of independent states. While the royal families lived within the walls of these complexes, the civilian populations lived in scattered locations outside the walls. Among the noticeable features of these Mycenaean centers were the tombs where members of the royal families were buried. Known as *tholos* tombs, they were built into hillsides. An entryway led into a circular tomb chamber constructed of cut

History *through Architecture*

Heinrich Schliemann discovered six tombs at the royal grave circle near the lion gate at Mycenae. How do these tombs compare to Egyptian tombs?

stone blocks in a domed shape that resembled a beehive in appearance.

The Mycenaeans were, above all, a warrior people who prided themselves on their heroic deeds in battle. Mycenaean wall murals often show war and hunting scenes, the natural occupations of a warrior aristocracy. Archaeological evidence also indicates that the Mycenaean monarchies developed an extensive commercial network. Mycenaean pottery has been found throughout the Mediterranean area, in Syria and Egypt to the east and Sicily and southern Italy to the west. But some historians believe that the Mycenaeans, led by Mycenae itself, also spread outward militarily, conquering Crete and making it part of the Mycenaean world. Some of the Aegean islands also fell subject to Mycenaean control.

The most famous of all their supposed military adventures has come down to us in the poetry of **Homer.** According to Homer, Mycenaean Greeks, led by Agamemnon, king of Mycenae, sacked (plundered) the city of Troy on the northwestern coast of Asia Minor around 1250 B.C. Did this event really occur? Ever since the excavations of Schliemann, begun in 1870, scholars have debated this question. (Schliemann's discovery of Troy was featured in Chapter 1.) Many believe that Homer's account does have a basis in fact.

By the late thirteenth century B.C., Mycenaean Greece was showing signs of serious trouble. Mycenaean states fought one another, and major earthquakes caused widespread damage. In the twelfth century B.C., new waves of Greek-speaking invaders moved into Greece from the north. By 1100 B.C., Mycenaean civilization had collapsed.

✓ **Reading Check** **Explaining** How was Mycenaean government organized?

The Greeks in a Dark Age

After the collapse of Mycenaean civilization, Greece entered a difficult period in which the population declined and food production dropped. Historians call the period from approximately 1100 to 750 B.C. the Dark Age, because few records of what happened exist. Not until 850 B.C. did farming revive. At the same time, the basis for a new Greece was forming.

Developments of the Dark Age During the Dark Age, large numbers of Greeks left the mainland and sailed across the Aegean Sea to various islands. Many went to the western shores of Asia Minor, a strip of territory that came to be called **Ionia** (or Ionian Greece), which is in modern-day Turkey.

Two other major groups of Greeks settled in established parts of Greece. The Aeolian Greeks who were located in northern and central Greece colonized the large island of Lesbos and the

territory near the mainland. The Dorians established themselves in southwestern Greece, especially in the Peloponnesus, as well as on some of the southern Aegean islands, including Crete.

Other important activities occurred in this Dark Age as well. There was a revival of some trade and some economic activity besides agriculture. Iron replaced bronze in the construction of weapons, making them affordable for more people. Farming tools made of iron helped to reverse the decline in food production.

At some point in the eighth century B.C., the Greeks adopted the Phoenician alphabet to give themselves a new system of writing. By reducing all words to a combination of twenty-four letters (both consonants and vowels), the Greeks made learning to read and write simpler. Near the very end of the Dark Age appeared the work of Homer, one of the truly great poets of all time.

Homer The *Iliad* and the *Odyssey* were the first great epic poems of early Greece. An **epic poem** is a long poem that tells the deeds of a great hero. The *Iliad* and the *Odyssey* were based on stories that had been passed from generation to generation.

Homer used stories of the Trojan War to compose the *Iliad* and the *Odyssey.* The war is caused by Paris, a prince of Troy. By kidnapping Helen, the wife of the king of the Greek state of Sparta, Paris outrages all the Greeks. Under the leadership of the Spartan king's brother, King Agamemnon, the Greeks attack Troy. Ten years later, the Greeks devise a plan to take the city. They trick the Trojans by building a huge hollow wooden horse. The best Mycenaean soldiers hide inside the horse, while the rest board their ships and pretend to sail away. The joyful Trojans, thinking themselves victorious, bring the gift horse into the city. That night, the Greeks creep out of the horse, slaughter the Trojan men, enslave the women and children, and burn the city to the ground. The *Iliad* is

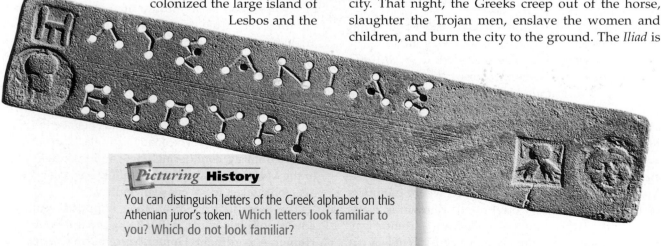

Picturing **History**

You can distinguish letters of the Greek alphabet on this Athenian juror's token. Which letters look familiar to you? Which do not look familiar?

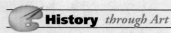
Golden Mask of Agamemnon, c. 1500 B.C.
This gold mask was found by Heinrich Schliemann at the royal grave circle at Mycenae. Who was Agamemnon and what was his role in Greek history?

not so much the story of the war itself, however, as it is the tale of the Greek hero Achilles (uh•KIH•leez) and how the anger of Achilles led to disaster.

The *Odyssey* recounts the journeys of one of the Greek heroes, Odysseus, after the fall of Troy, and his ultimate return to his wife. The *Odyssey* has long been considered Homer's other masterpiece. Some scholars believe that it was composed later than the *Iliad*.

Homer proved to be of great value to later Greeks. He did not so much record history; he created it. The Greeks looked on the *Iliad* and the *Odyssey* as true history and as the works of one poet, Homer. These masterpieces gave the Greeks an ideal past with a cast of heroes. The epics came to be used as basic texts for the education of generations of Greek males. As one ancient Athenian stated, "My father was anxious to see me develop into a good man . . . and as a means to this end he compelled me to memorize all of Homer."

The values Homer taught were courage and honor. A hero strives for excellence, which the Greeks called *arete* (ahr•ah•TEE). Arete is won in a struggle or contest. Through his willingness to fight, the hero protects his family and friends, preserves his own honor and that of his family, and earns his reputation. Homer gave to later generations of Greek males a model of heroism and honor. For example, in an exciting description of men marching to war, the *Iliad* taught students to be proud of their Greek heritage and their heroic ancestors.

✓**Reading Check** **Summarizing** Why is Homer thought to have created, rather than to have recorded, Greek history?

TAKS Practice

SECTION 1 ASSESSMENT

Checking for Understanding

1. **Define** epic poem, *arete*.

2. **Identify** Minoans, Mycenaeans, Homer.

3. **Locate** Aegean Sea, Black Sea, Crete, Ionia.

4. **Explain** why *arete* was important to Greek culture.

5. **List** the troubles affecting Mycenaean Greece before its collapse.

Critical Thinking

6. **Evaluate** Why was the Dark Age of Greece considered "dark"?

7. **Summarizing Information** Using a chart like the one below, identify the changes that occurred in Greece during the Dark Ages.

Dark Ages

Analyzing Visuals

8. **Examine** the funeral mask shown above. Looking at this mask, what conclusions can you draw about how the ancient Mycenaeans approached death? Explain your reasoning.

Writing About History

9. **Expository Writing** What archaeological evidence might support scholars' differing views of the collapse of Minoan and Mycenaean culture? Explain your opinions in a well reasoned essay.

CRITICAL THINKING
SKILLBUILDER

Making Comparisons

Why Learn This Skill?

When making comparisons, you identify the similarities and differences among two or more ideas, objects, or events.

Learning the Skill

Follow these steps to make comparisons:

- Find two subjects that can be compared. They should be similar enough to have characteristics that are common to both. For example, it would be more appropriate to compare a Greek statue to an Egyptian statue than to an abstract modern painting.
- Determine which features the subjects have in common that are suitable for comparison.
- Look for similarities and differences within these areas.
- If possible, find information that explains the similarities and differences.

Practicing the Skill

The following excerpts from the text discuss Spartan and Athenian models for raising children. Read both excerpts, then answer the questions that follow.

Passage A

In Sparta, boys were trained to be soldiers. State officials examined all children at birth and decided whether or not they were fit to live. Those who were judged unfit were left in the open on a mountainside to die. Boys judged fit were put under control of the state at age seven. They lived in military-style barracks and were subjected to harsh discipline to make them tough. Their education stressed military training and obedience to authority.

Passage B

Athenian children were nurtured by their mothers until the age of seven, when boys of the upper class were turned over to a male servant known as a pedagogue. The pedagogue accompanied the child to school and was responsible for teaching his charge good manners. He could punish the child with a birch rod to impose discipline.

The purpose of an education for upper-class Athenian boys was to create a well-rounded person. A boy had three teachers. One taught reading, writing, and arithmetic; a second taught physical education; and a third taught music. Education ended at eighteen, when an Athenian male formally became a citizen.

❶ Make a chart with one column labeled Sparta and one labeled Athens. List the similarities in how the two states raised children, then list the differences.

❷ How did the similarities and differences in raising children suit the needs of each city-state?

Athenian warrior

Applying the Skill

Survey your classmates about an issue in the news. Summarize their opinions and compare the different results in a paragraph.

Glencoe's **Skillbuilder Interactive Workbook, Level 2,** provides instruction and practice in key social studies skills.

The Greek City-States

Main Ideas
- The polis or city-state was the central focus of Greek life.
- The search for farmland and the growth of trade resulted in colonies and the spread of Greek culture and politics.

Key Terms

polis, acropolis, agora, hoplite, phalanx, democracy, oligarchy, helot, ephor

People to Identify

Aristotle, Solon, Cleisthenes

Places to Locate

Athens, Hellespont, Bosporus, Byzantium, Sparta

Preview Questions

1. Who lived in the polis?
2. How did Athens and Sparta differ?
3. What role did tyrants play in Greek history?

Reading Strategy

Categorizing Information Complete a chart showing the three types of government used in Greek city-states, and explain the advantages and disadvantages of each.

	Advantage	Disadvantage
Tyranny		
Democracy		
Oligarchy		

Preview of Events

◆800 B.C.	◆700 B.C.	◆600 B.C.	◆500 B.C.

750 B.C.
The city-state is the central focus of Greek life

700 B.C.
Hoplites become a new military order

600 B.C.
Colonization leads to increased trade and industry

Spartan warrior

Voices from the Past

Greek villages gradually expanded and became independent city-states. The Greek historian Plutarch related how one of these city-states—Sparta—educated its young boys:

❝As soon as they were seven years old they were to be enrolled in certain companies and classes, where they all lived under the same order and discipline, doing their exercises and taking their play together. Of these, he who showed the most courage was made captain; they had their eyes always upon him, obeyed his orders, and underwent patiently whatsoever punishment he inflicted; so that the whole course of their education was one continued exercise of a ready and perfect obedience.❞

— *The Lives of the Noble Grecians and Romans,*
Plutarch, J. Dryden and A. H. Clouth, trans., 1992

It is no surprise that the Spartan city-state became known for its military prowess.

The Polis: Center of Greek Life

By 750 B.C., the city-state—or what the Greeks called a polis—became the central focus of Greek life. Our word *politics* is derived from the Greek word *polis*. In a physical sense, the polis was a town, a city, or even a village, along with its surrounding countryside. The town, city, or village served as the center of the polis where people could meet for political, social, and religious activities.

The main gathering place in the polis was usually a hill. At the top of the hill was a fortified area called an acropolis. The acropolis served as a place of refuge during an attack and sometimes came to be a religious center on which temples and public buildings were built. Below the acropolis was an agora, an open area that served as a place where people could assemble and as a market.

City-states varied greatly in size, from a few square miles to a few hundred square miles. They also varied in population. **Athens** had a population of more than three hundred thousand by the fifth century B.C., but most city-states were much smaller, consisting of only a few hundred to several thousand people.

The polis was, above all, a community of people who shared a common identity and common goals. As a community, the polis consisted of citizens with political rights (adult males), citizens with no political rights (women and children), and noncitizens (slaves and resident aliens).

Citizens of a polis had rights, but these rights were coupled with responsibilities. The Greek philosopher **Aristotle** argued that a citizen did not belong just to himself or herself: "We must rather regard every citizen as belonging to the state." However, the loyalty that citizens had to their city-states had a negative side. City-states distrusted one another, and the division of Greece into fiercely patriotic independent units helped to bring about its ruin.

As the polis developed, so too did a new military system. In earlier times, wars in Greece had been fought by aristocratic cavalry soldiers—nobles on horseback. These aristocrats, who were large landowners, also dominated the political life of their city-states. By 700 B.C., however, the military system was based on hoplites, who were heavily armed infantry soldiers, or foot soldiers. Each carried a round shield, a short sword, and a thrusting spear about nine feet (2.7 m) long.

Hoplites went into battle as a unit, marching shoulder to shoulder in a rectangular formation known as a phalanx. This close formation created a wall of shields to protect the hoplites. As long as they kept their order, it was difficult for enemies to harm them.

☑ **Reading Check** **Identifying** What responsibilities did the citizens of the polis have?

Greek Colonies

Between 750 and 550 B.C., large numbers of Greeks left their homeland to settle in distant lands. A desire for good farmland and the growth of trade were two important factors in the people's decisions to move. Each colony became a new polis. This new polis was usually independent of the polis that had founded it.

Picturing **History**

The Acropolis in Athens is crowned by the Parthenon. How does this classic temple express the Athenians' pride in their city-state?

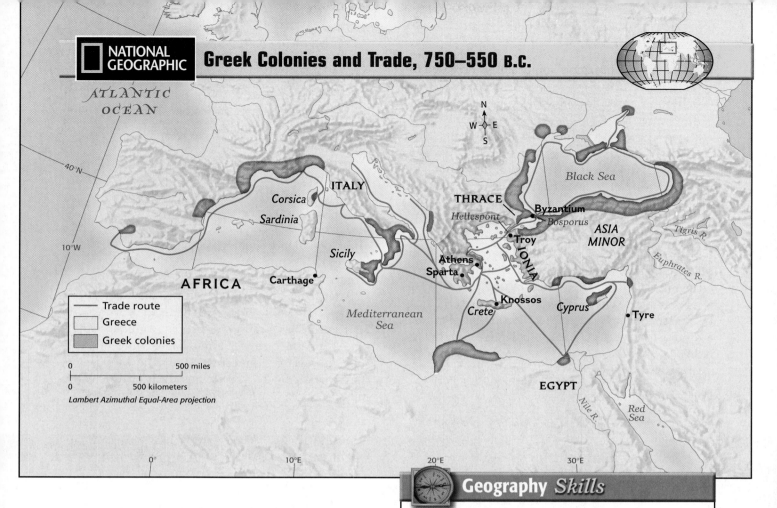

NATIONAL GEOGRAPHIC
Greek Colonies and Trade, 750–550 B.C.

ATLANTIC OCEAN

40°N

10°W

ITALY
Corsica
Sardinia
Sicily
AFRICA
Carthage

THRACE
Hellespont
Byzantium
Bosporus
Troy
ASIA MINOR
IONIA
Athens
Sparta
Crete
Knossos
Cyprus
Tyre
EGYPT

Black Sea

Tigris R.
Euphrates R.

Mediterranean Sea

Nile R.
Red Sea

Legend:
— Trade route
☐ Greece
▨ Greek colonies

0 — 500 miles
0 — 500 kilometers
Lambert Azimuthal Equal-Area projection

0° 10°E 20°E 30°E

Across the Mediterranean, new Greek colonies were established along the coastlines of southern Italy, southern France, eastern Spain, and northern Africa west of Egypt. At the same time, to the north the Greeks set up colonies in Thrace, where they sought good farmland to grow grains. The Greeks also settled along the shores of the Black Sea, setting up cities on the **Hellespont** and the **Bosporus.** The most notable of these cities was **Byzantium** (buh•ZAN•tee•uhm), the site of what later became Constantinople (now Istanbul). In establishing these colonies, the Greeks spread their culture and political ideas throughout the Mediterranean.

Colonization also led to increased trade and industry. The Greeks on the mainland exported pottery, wine, and olive oil. In return, they received grains and metals from the west and fish, timber, wheat, metals, and slaves from the Black Sea region.

The expansion of trade and industry created a new group of wealthy individuals in many of the Greek city-states. These men wanted political power, but found it difficult to gain because of the power of the ruling aristocrats.

✓ Reading Check **Explaining** What political dilemma was caused by the expansion of trade and industry?

Geography *Skills*

Over a period of 200 years, the Greeks spread across Europe and northern Africa, bringing Greek civilization to areas more than 1,500 miles (2,400 km) from Greece.

1. **Interpreting Maps** Analyze the relationship between Greek trading routes and Greek colonies.
2. **Applying Geography Skills** Find a map of the contemporary world. Name all the modern countries where Greece had colonies.

Tyranny in the City-States

The creation of this new group of rich men fostered the rise of tyrants in the seventh and sixth centuries B.C. Tyrants were not necessarily oppressive or wicked, as our word *tyrant* implies. Greek tyrants were rulers who seized power by force from the aristocrats. Support for the tyrants came not only from the new rich who had made their money in trade and industry, but also from poor peasants who were in debt to landholding aristocrats. Both the rich and the peasants were tired of aristocratic domination of their city-states.

The tyrants gained power and kept it by using hired soldiers. Once in power, they built new marketplaces, temples, and walls. These constructions glorified the city but, more importantly, increased the tyrants' popularity. Despite their achievements, however, tyrants had fallen out of favor by the end of the sixth century B.C. Greeks believed in the rule of law, and tyranny was an insult to that ideal.

Although tyranny did not last, it played an important role in Greek history. The rule of the tyrants had ended the rule of the aristocrats in many city-states. The end of tyranny then allowed many new people to participate in government. In some Greek city-states, this led to the development of democracy, which is government by the people or rule of the many. Other city-states remained committed to government by an oligarchy, rule by the few. The differences in how Greek city-states were governed can be understood by examining the two most famous and most powerful Greek city-states, **Sparta** and Athens.

Reading Check **Evaluating** What role did tyrants play in the development of Greek forms of government?

Sparta

Like other Greek city-states, Sparta was faced with the need for more land. Instead of sending its people out to start new colonies, as some states did, the Spartans conquered the neighboring Laconians. Later, beginning around 730 B.C., the Spartans undertook the conquest of neighboring Messenia despite its larger size and population.

After their conquest, the Messenians and Laconians became serfs and were made to work for the Spartans. These captured people were known as helots, a name derived from a Greek word for "capture." To ensure control over the conquered helots, the Spartans made a conscious decision to create a military state.

YOUNG PEOPLE IN . . .

Greece

In Sparta, boys were trained to be soldiers. At birth, each child was examined by state officials, who decided whether the child was fit to live. Those who were judged unfit were left on a mountainside to die. Boys judged fit were taken from their mothers at the age of seven and put under control of the state.

These boys lived in military-style barracks, where they were subjected to harsh discipline to make them tough and mean. Their education stressed military training and obedience to authority. The Greek historian Plutarch described the handling of young Spartans:

“After they were twelve years old, they were no longer allowed to wear any undergarments, they had one coat to serve them a year; their bodies were hard and dry, with but little acquaintance of baths; these human indulgences they were allowed only on some few particular days in the year. They lodged together in little bands upon beds made of the rushes which grew by the banks of the river Eurotas, which they were to break off with their hands with a knife.”

In Sparta girls and boys were trained to be athletes, as is shown by this bronze statue, which was part of a vase lid.

118

A Military State Between 800 and 600 B.C., the lives of Spartans were rigidly organized and tightly controlled (thus, our word *spartan*, meaning "highly self-disciplined"). Males spent their childhood learning military discipline. Then they enrolled in the army for regular military service at age 20. Although allowed to marry, they continued to live in the military barracks until age 30. All meals were eaten in public dining halls with fellow soldiers. Meals were simple; the famous Spartan black broth consisted of a piece of pork boiled in animal blood, salt, and vinegar. A visitor who ate some of the black broth once remarked that he now understood why Spartans were not afraid to die. At 30, Spartan males were allowed to vote in the assembly (to be discussed later) and live at home, but they stayed in the army until the age of 60.

While their husbands lived in the barracks, Spartan women lived at home. Because of this separation, Spartan women had greater freedom of movement and greater power in the household than was common elsewhere in Greece. Spartan women were expected to exercise and remain fit to bear and raise healthy children.

Many Spartan women upheld the strict Spartan values, expecting their husbands and sons to be brave in war. The story is told of a Spartan woman who, as she was handing her son his shield, told him to come back carrying his shield or being carried on it.

Government of Sparta The Spartan government was an oligarchy headed by two kings, who led the Spartan army on its campaigns. A group of five men, known as the ephors (EH•fuhrs), were elected each year and were responsible for the education of youth and the conduct of all citizens. A council of elders, composed of the two kings and 28 citizens over the age of 60, decided on the issues that would be presented to an assembly made up of male citizens. This assembly did not debate; it only voted on the issues.

To make their new military state secure, the Spartans turned their backs on the outside world.

Basically, the Spartan system worked. Spartan males were known for their toughness and their meanness. They were also known as the best soldiers in all of Greece.

Spartan girls received an education similar to that of the boys. Girls, too, underwent physical training, including running, wrestling, and throwing the javelin. The purpose was clear: to strengthen the girls for their roles as healthy mothers.

Well-to-do Athenian citizens raised their children very differently. Athenian children were nurtured by their mothers until the age of seven. At seven, a boy of the upper class was turned over to a male servant, known as a *pedagogue*. The pedagogue, who was usually a slave, accompanied the child to school. He was also responsible for teaching his charge good manners. He could punish the child with a birch rod to impose discipline.

The purpose of an education for upper-class Athenian boys was to create a well-rounded person. To that end, a boy had three teachers. One taught him reading, writing, and arithmetic. Another taught physical education, a necessity to achieve the ideal of a sound mind in a sound body. A third taught him music, which consisted of playing the lyre (a stringed instrument) and singing. Education ended at 18, when an Athenian male formally became a citizen.

Girls of all classes remained at home, as their mothers did. Their mothers taught them how to run a home, which included how to spin and weave—activities expected of a good wife. Only in some wealthy families did girls learn to read, write, and perhaps play the lyre.

CONNECTING TO THE PAST

1. **Summarizing Information** Describe a Spartan upbringing. How does this differ from the childhood of an American child?

2. **Compare and Contrast** Compare a well-educated Spartan boy with a well-educated Athenian and a well-educated American. What are the differences?

3. **Writing about History** Does your education today incorporate any Spartan or Athenian ideas? If so, give specific examples.

Foreigners, who might have brought in new ideas, were discouraged from visiting. Except for military reasons, Spartans were not allowed to travel abroad, where they might encounter ideas dangerous to the stability of the state. Likewise, Spartan citizens were discouraged from studying philosophy, literature, or the arts—subjects that might encourage new thoughts. The art of war was the Spartan ideal. All other arts were frowned upon.

✓**Reading Check** **Summarizing** How did the restrictions placed on Spartan males affect their lives?

Athens

By 700 B.C., Athens had become a unified polis on the peninsula of Attica. Early Athens was ruled by a king. By the seventh century B.C., however, Athens had become an oligarchy under the control of its aristocrats. These aristocrats owned the best land and controlled political life. There was an assembly of all the citizens, but it had few powers.

Aegean Sea

ATTICA
•Athens

PELOPONNESUS

Near the end of the seventh century B.C., Athens faced political turmoil because of serious economic problems. Many Athenian farmers were sold into slavery when they were unable to repay their debts to their aristocratic neighbors. Over and over, there were cries to cancel the debts and give land to the poor. Athens seemed on the verge of civil war.

The ruling Athenian aristocrats reacted to this crisis in 594 B.C. by giving full power to **Solon,** a reform-minded aristocrat. Solon canceled all land debts and freed people who had fallen into slavery for debts. He refused, however, to take land from the rich and give it to the poor.

Solon's reforms, though popular, did not solve the problems of Athens. Aristocrats were still powerful, and poor peasants could not obtain land. Internal strife finally led to the very thing Solon had hoped to avoid—tyranny.

Pisistratus (pih•SIHS•truh•tuhs), an aristocrat, seized power in 560 B.C. He then aided Athenian trade as a way of pleasing the merchants. He also gave aristocrats' land to the peasants in order to gain the favor of the poor.

The Athenians rebelled against Pisistratus's son, who had succeeded him, and ended the tyranny in 510 B.C. Two years later, with the backing of the Athenian people, **Cleisthenes** (KLYS•thuh•neez), another reformer, gained the upper hand.

Cleisthenes created a new council of five hundred that supervised foreign affairs, oversaw the treasury, and proposed the laws that would be voted on by the assembly. The Athenian assembly, composed of male citizens, was given final authority to pass laws after free and open debate. Because the assembly of citizens now had the central role in the Athenian political system, the reforms of Cleisthenes created the foundations for Athenian democracy.

✓**Reading Check** **Explaining** How did Cleisthenes create the foundation for democracy in Athens?

🌟**TAKS Practice**

SECTION 2 ASSESSMENT

Checking for Understanding

1. **Define** polis, acropolis, agora, hoplite, phalanx, democracy, oligarchy, helot, ephor.

2. **Identify** Aristotle, Solon, Cleisthenes.

3. **Locate** Athens, Hellespont, Bosporus, Byzantium, Sparta.

4. **Explain** the different political systems in Athens and Sparta.

5. **Summarize** why the Greeks left their homelands to establish colonies.

Critical Thinking

6. **Compare and Contrast** In what way(s) is Athenian democracy similar to American democracy? In what way(s) is it different?

7. **Sequencing Information** Create a cause-and-effect sequence chart of Greek colonization, trade, and industry.

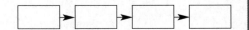

Analyzing Visuals

8. **Examine** the photograph of the Acropolis on page 116 of your text. Why do you think the Athenians decided to place their important buildings on top of a hill?

Writing About History

9. **Descriptive Writing** Imagine that you are a 25-year old male living in Sparta in 700 B.C. Create a diary in which you record your activities for one week. Write one diary page for each day.

Classical Greece

Guide to Reading

Main Ideas
- During the Age of Pericles, Athens became the center of Greek culture.
- The creation of an Athenian empire led to war with Sparta.

Key Terms
Age of Pericles, direct democracy, ostracism

People to Identify
Darius, Xerxes, Pericles

Places to Locate
Asia Minor, Delos, Thebes, Macedonia

Preview Questions
1. How did Pericles expand the involvement of Athenians in their democracy?
2. Why was trade highly important to the Athenian economy?

Reading Strategy
Organizing Information Use a concept map like the one below to show the elements that contributed to the Classical Age of Greece.

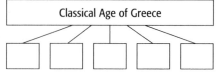

Classical Age of Greece

Preview of Events

♦500 B.C.	♦475 B.C.	♦450 B.C.	♦425 B.C.	♦400 B.C.

500 B.C.
Classical Age of Greece flourishes with Athens at the center

480 B.C.
Persians burn Athens

445 B.C.
Athenian Empire expands

405 B.C.
Athenian Empire destroyed

Voices from the Past

Thucydides

Classical Greece is the name given to the period of Greek history from around 500 B.C. to the conquest of Greece by the Macedonian king Philip II in 338 B.C. This period was marked not only by a brilliant culture but also by a disastrous war among the Greeks, the Peloponnesian War, described here by the Greek historian Thucydides:

66The Peloponnesian War not only lasted for a long time, but throughout its course brought with it unprecedented suffering for Greece. Never before had so many cities been captured and then devastated, whether by foreign armies or by the Greek powers themselves; never had there been so many exiles; never such loss of life—both in the actual warfare and in internal revolutions.99

— *The History of the Peloponnesian War,* Thucydides, R. Warner, trans., 1954

For all their accomplishments, the Greeks were unable to rise above the divisions and rivalries that caused them to fight one another and undermine their own civilization.

The Challenge of Persia

As the Greeks spread throughout the Mediterranean, they came in contact with the Persian Empire to the east. The Ionian Greek cities in western **Asia Minor** had already fallen subject to the Persian Empire by the mid-sixth century B.C. In 499 B.C., an unsuccessful revolt by the Ionian cities—assisted by the Athenian navy—led the Persian ruler **Darius** to seek revenge.

In 490 B.C., the Persians landed on the plain of Marathon, only 26 miles (41.8 km) from Athens. There, an outnumbered Athenian army attacked and defeated the Persians decisively.

According to legend, news of Persia's defeat was brought by an Athenian runner named Pheidippides who raced 26 miles (41.8 km) from Marathon to Athens. With his last breath, he announced, "Victory, we win," before dropping dead. Today's marathon is based on this heroic story.

After Darius died in 486 B.C., **Xerxes** (ZUHRK•SEEZ) became the new Persian monarch. Xerxes vowed revenge and planned to invade Greece. In preparation for the attack, the Athenians began rebuilding their navy. By the time the Persians invaded in 480 B.C., the Athenians had a fleet of about two hundred vessels.

Xerxes led a massive invasion force into Greece. His forces included about 180,000 troops and thousands of warships and supply vessels. The Greeks tried to delay the Persians at the pass of Thermopylae (thuhr•MAH•puh•lee), along the main road into central Greece. A Greek force of about seven thousand held off the Persian army for two days. The three hundred Spartans in the Greek army were especially brave. When told that Persian arrows would darken the sky in battle, one Spartan warrior responded, "That is good news. We will fight in the shade!" Unfortunately for the Greeks, a traitor told the Persians how to use a mountain path to outflank the Greek force.

The Athenians, now threatened by the onslaught of the Persian forces, abandoned their city. Near the island of Salamis, the Greek fleet, though outnumbered, managed to outmaneuver the Persian fleet and defeat it. A few months later, early in 479 B.C., the Greeks formed the largest Greek army up to that time and defeated the Persian army at Plataea (pluh•TEE•uh), northwest of Athens.

Reading Check **Identifying** What did victory over the Persians cost the Greeks?

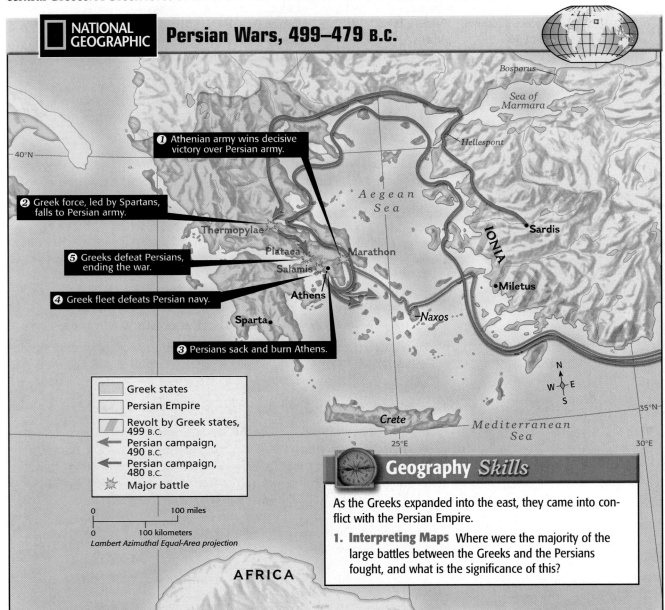

NATIONAL GEOGRAPHIC

Persian Wars, 499–479 B.C.

❶ Athenian army wins decisive victory over Persian army.

❷ Greek force, led by Spartans, falls to Persian army.

❺ Greeks defeat Persians, ending the war.

❹ Greek fleet defeats Persian navy.

❸ Persians sack and burn Athens.

Bosporus
Sea of Marmara
Hellespont
Aegean Sea
Sardis
IONIA
Thermopylae
Plataea
Marathon
Salamis
Athens
•Miletus
Sparta•
Naxos
Crete
Mediterranean Sea

40°N
35°N
25°E
30°E

N
W   E
S

☐ Greek states
☐ Persian Empire
▨ Revolt by Greek states, 499 B.C.
← Persian campaign, 490 B.C.
← Persian campaign, 480 B.C.
✷ Major battle

0   100 miles
0   100 kilometers
Lambert Azimuthal Equal-Area projection

AFRICA

Geography *Skills*

As the Greeks expanded into the east, they came into conflict with the Persian Empire.

1. **Interpreting Maps** Where were the majority of the large battles between the Greeks and the Persians fought, and what is the significance of this?

The Growth of the Athenian Empire

After the defeat of the Persians, Athens took over the leadership of the Greek world. In 478 B.C., the Athenians formed a defensive alliance against the Persians called the **Delian League.** Its main headquarters was on the island of **Delos.** However, its chief  officials, including the treasurers and commanders of the fleet, were Athenian. Under Athenian leadership, the Delian League pursued the attack against the Persian Empire, eventually liberating virtually all of the Greek states in the Aegean from Persian control. In 454 B.C., the Athenians moved the treasury of the league from the island of Delos to Athens. By controlling the Delian League, Athens had created an empire.

Under **Pericles,** who was a dominant figure in Athenian politics between 461 and 429 B.C., Athens expanded its new empire abroad. At the same time, democracy flourished at home. This period of Athenian and Greek history, which historians have called the Age of Pericles, saw the height of Athenian power and brilliance.

Reading Check **Describing** What was the role of the Delian League in the creation of the Athenian Empire?

The Age of Pericles

TURNING POINT Pericles expanded the involvement of Athenians in their democracy. By creating a direct democracy, he enabled every male citizen to play a role in government.

In the Age of Pericles, the Athenians became deeply attached to their democratic system, which was a direct democracy. In a direct democracy, the people participate directly in government decision making through mass meetings. In Athens, every male citizen participated in the governing assembly and voted on all major issues.

Most residents of Athens, however, were not citizens. In the mid-fifth century B.C., the assembly consisted of about forty-three thousand male citizens over 18 years old. Meetings of the assembly were held every 10 days on a hillside east of the Acropolis. Not all attended, and the number present seldom reached six thousand. The assembly passed all laws, elected public officials, and made final decisions on war and foreign policy. Anyone could speak, but usually only respected leaders did so.

However, by making lower-class male citizens eligible for public office and by paying officeholders, Pericles made it possible for poor citizens to take part in public affairs. Pericles believed that Athenians should be proud of their democracy.

A large body of city officials ran the government on a daily basis. Ten officials known as generals were the overall directors of policy. The generals could be reelected, making it possible for individual leaders to play an important political role.

The Athenians also devised the practice of ostracism to protect themselves against overly ambitious politicians. Members of the assembly could write on a broken pottery fragment (*ostrakon*) the name of a person they considered harmful to the city. A person so named by at least six thousand members was banned from the city for 10 years.

Under Pericles, Athens became the center of Greek culture. The Persians had destroyed much of the city during the Persian Wars, but Pericles set in motion a massive rebuilding program. New temples and statues soon signified the greatness of Athens. Art, architecture, and philosophy flourished. Pericles broadly boasted that Athens had become the "school of Greece."

Reading Check **Explaining** Why did Athenians develop and practice ostracism?

This stone relief from the fourth century B.C. shows Democracy crowning a figure that symbolizes Athens. The panel was placed in the marketplace for all to see.

The Great Peloponnesian War

After the defeat of the Persians, the Greek world came to be divided into two major camps: the Athenian Empire and Sparta. Athens and Sparta had built two very different kinds of societies, and neither state was able to tolerate the other's system. Sparta and its allies feared the growing Athenian Empire, and a series of disputes finally led to the outbreak of the **Great Peloponnesian War** in 431 B.C.

At the beginning of the war, both sides believed they had winning strategies. The Athenians planned to remain behind the city's protective walls and receive supplies from their colonies and navy. The Spartans and their allies surrounded Athens, hoping that the Athenians would send out their army to fight beyond the walls. Pericles knew, however, that the Spartan forces could beat the Athenians in open battles. He also believed that Athens was secure behind its walls, so the Athenians stayed put.

In the second year of the war, a plague broke out in overly crowded Athens, killing more than a third of the people. Pericles himself died the following year (429 B.C.). Despite these severe losses, the Athe-

nians fought on in a struggle that lasted for about another 25 years. 📖 *(See page 991 to read excerpts from* Thucydides' Plague in Athens *in the Primary Sources Library.)*

A crushing blow came in 405 B.C., when the Athenian fleet was destroyed at Aegospotami (EE•guh•SPAH•tuh•MEE) on the Hellespont. Within the next year, Athens surrendered. Its walls were torn down, the navy disbanded, and the Athenian Empire destroyed. The great war was finally over.

The Great Peloponnesian War weakened the major Greek states and ruined any possibility of cooperation among them. During the next 66 years, Sparta, Athens, and **Thebes** (a new Greek power) struggled to dominate Greek affairs. In continuing their petty wars, the Greeks ignored the growing power of **Macedonia** to their north. This oversight would cost them their freedom.

✔Reading Check **Explaining** How did the Great Peloponnesian War weaken the Greek states?

Daily Life in Classical Athens

In the fifth century B.C., Athens had the largest population of the Greek city-states. Before the plague

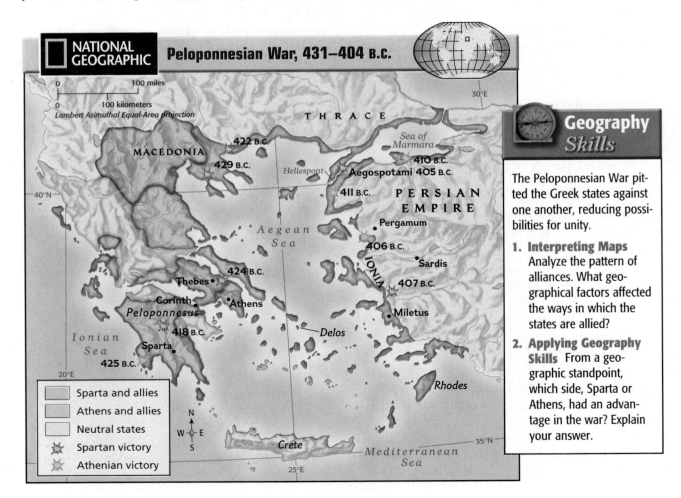

NATIONAL GEOGRAPHIC

Peloponnesian War, 431–404 B.C.

0   100 miles
0   100 kilometers
Lambert Azimuthal Equal-Area projection

THRACE

MACEDONIA

422 B.C.
429 B.C.

Hellespont

Sea of Marmara

410 B.C.
Aegospotami 405 B.C.

411 B.C.

PERSIAN EMPIRE

Pergamum

406 B.C.

Aegean Sea

424 B.C.
Thebes
Corinth
Peloponnesus
Athens

418 B.C.

Sardis

407 B.C.

IONIA

Miletus

Delos

Ionian Sea

Sparta

425 B.C.

Rhodes

Crete

Mediterranean Sea

Sparta and allies
Athens and allies
Neutral states
💥 Spartan victory
💥 Athenian victory

N W E S

Geography Skills

The Peloponnesian War pitted the Greek states against one another, reducing possibilities for unity.

1. **Interpreting Maps** Analyze the pattern of alliances. What geographical factors affected the ways in which the states are allied?

2. **Applying Geography Skills** From a geographic standpoint, which side, Sparta or Athens, had an advantage in the war? Explain your answer.

in 430 B.C., there were about 150,000 citizens living in Athens. About 43,000 of them were adult males with political power. Foreigners living in Athens, who numbered about 35,000, received the protection of the laws. They were also subject to some of the responsibilities of citizens—namely, military service and the funding of festivals. The remaining social group, the slaves, numbered around 100,000.

Slavery was common in the ancient world. Most people in Athens—except the very poor—owned at least one slave. The very wealthy might own large numbers. Those who did usually employed them in industry. Most often, slaves in Athens worked in the fields or in the home as cooks and maids. Some slaves were owned by the state and worked on public construction projects.

The Athenian Economy

The Athenian economy was largely based on farming and trade. Athenians grew grains, vegetables, and fruit for local use. Grapes and olive trees were cultivated for wine and olive oil, which were used locally and also exported. The Athenians raised sheep and goats for wool and milk products.

Because of the number of people and the lack of fertile land, Athens had to import from 50 to 80 percent of its grain, a basic item in the Athenian diet. This meant that trade was highly important to the Athenian economy. The building of a port at nearby Piraievs (PEE•reh•EFS) helped Athens become the leading trade center in the fifth-century Greek world.

The Family and the Role of Women

The family was an important institution in ancient Athens. It was composed of a husband, wife, and children, although other dependent relatives and slaves were also regarded as part of the family. The family's primary social function was to produce new citizens.

Women were citizens who could take part in most religious festivals, but they were otherwise excluded from public life. They could not own property beyond personal items. They always had a male guardian: if unmarried, a father; if married, a husband; if widowed, a son or male relative.

An Athenian woman was expected to be a good wife. Her chief obligation was to bear children, especially male children who would preserve the family line. She was also expected to take care of her family and her house. She either did the housework herself or supervised the slaves who did the actual work.

Women were strictly controlled. Because they married at the age of 14 or 15, they were taught their responsibilities early. Although many managed to learn to read and play musical instruments, they were not provided any formal education.

Women were expected to remain at home, out of sight, unless attending funerals or festivals. If they left the house, they had to have a companion.

✓ **Reading Check** **Examining** What kinds of work did slaves perform in classical Athens?

⬥ TAKS Practice

SECTION 3 ASSESSMENT

Checking for Understanding

1. **Define** Age of Pericles, direct democracy, ostracism.

2. **Identify** Darius, Xerxes, Delian League, Pericles, Great Peloponnesian War.

3. **Locate** Asia Minor, Delos, Thebes, Macedonia.

4. **Describe** the system of direct democracy in Athens.

5. **Identify** which Greek states struggled for power after the Great Peloponnesian War. What area to the north grew in power and threatened the freedom of the Greeks?

Critical Thinking

6. **Analyze** What is meant by the phrase "The Age of Pericles"?

7. **Organizing Information** Create a pie diagram to show the ratio of citizens, foreigners, and slaves in classical Athens.

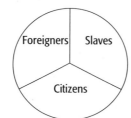

Analyzing Visuals

8. **Examine** the bust of Thucydides shown on page 121 of your text. What does this sculpture tell you about the Greek view of the human individual? Compare this bust to artistic representations of people in earlier chapters of your text. What differences and similarities do you see?

Writing About History

9. **Descriptive Writing** Write three short journal entries about a particular day or event. Write one entry from the perspective of an Athenian male citizen, one as a female citizen, and one as a slave, contrasting their daily lives.

An Athenian Husband Explains His Wife's Duties

IN FIFTH-CENTURY ATHENS, A WOMAN'S PLACE was in the home. She had two major responsibilities: the bearing and raising of children and the care of the household. In his dialogue on estate management, the Greek writer Xenophon relates the advice of an Athenian gentleman on how to train a wife.

Vases are an excellent source of information about everyday life in Greece.

❝[A man addresses his new wife.] For it seems to me, dear, that the gods have coupled together male and female, as they are called, chiefly in order that they may form a perfect partnership in mutual service. For, in the first place, that the various species of living creatures may not fail, they are joined in wedlock for the production of children. Secondly, offspring to support them in old age is provided by this union, to human beings, at any rate. Thirdly, human beings live not in the open air, like beasts, but obviously need shelter. Nevertheless, those who mean to win stores to fill the covered place, have need of someone to work at the open-air occupations; ploughing, sowing, planting and grazing are all such open-air employments; and these supply the needful food. . . . For he made the man's body and mind more capable of enduring cold and heat, and journeys and campaigns; and therefore imposed on him the outdoor tasks. To the woman, since he had made her body less capable of such endurance, I take it that the gods have assigned the indoor tasks. And knowing that he had created in the woman and had imposed on her the nourishment of the infants, he meted out to her a larger portion of affection for new-born babes than to the man. . . .

Your duty will be to remain indoors and send out those servants whose work is outside, and supervise those who are to work indoors, and to receive the incomings, and distribute so much of them as must be spent, and watch over so much as is to be kept in store, and take care that the sum laid by for a year be not spent in a month. And when wool is brought to you, you must see that cloaks are made for those that want them. You must see too that the dry corn is in good condition for making food. One of the duties that fall to you, however, will perhaps seem rather thankless: you will have to see that any servant who is ill is cared for.❞

—Xenophon, *Memorabilia and Oeconomicus*

Analyzing Primary Sources

1. Over what areas of life did an Athenian wife have authority?
2. Do you think the husband respected his wife? Why or why not?
3. How are the roles of men and women in America now different from their roles in ancient Greece? In what ways have these roles remained the same over the centuries?

SECTION 4 The Culture of Classical Greece

Guide to Reading

Main Ideas
- Greek philosophers were concerned with the development of critical or rational thought about the nature of the universe.
- Greeks believed that ritualized religion was necessary for the well-being of the state.

Key Terms
ritual, oracle, tragedy, philosophy, Socratic method

People to Identify
Aeschylus, Sophocles, Pythagoras, Socrates, Plato, Aristotle, Thucydides

Places to Locate
Delphi, Gulf of Corinth

Preview Questions
1. In what ways was religion closely connected to Greek life?
2. How did defeat in the Peloponnesian War change the Athenians?

Reading Strategy
Summarizing Information Create a chart like the one below showing the major Greek contributions to Western civilization.

Major Greek Contributions	

Preview of Events

◆800 B.C.	◆700 B.C.	◆600 B.C.	◆500 B.C.	◆400 B.C.	◆300 B.C.

776 B.C.
The first Olympic Festival is held

c. 550 B.C.
Pythagoras develops geometrical theories

399 B.C.
Socrates placed on trial

c. 387 B.C.
Plato founds Academy in Athens

Voices from the Past

Classical Greece, especially Athens under Pericles' rule, witnessed a period of remarkable intellectual and cultural growth that became the main source of Western culture. Aristotle often wrote about the importance of intellectual life:

❝The activity of the mind is not only the highest . . . but also the most continuous: we are able to study continuously more easily than to perform any kind of action. . . . It follows that the activity of our intelligence constitutes the complete happiness of man. In other words, a life guided by intelligence is the best and most pleasant for man, inasmuch as intelligence, above all else, is man. Consequently, this kind of life is the happiest.❞

— *Western Civilization*, Margaret King, 2000

The philosopher Aristotle, with Socrates and Plato, established the foundations of Western philosophy.

Aristotle

Greek Religion

Religion affected every aspect of Greek life. Greeks considered religion necessary to the well-being of the state. Temples dedicated to gods and goddesses were the major buildings in Greek cities.

Homer described the gods worshiped in the Greek religion. Twelve chief gods and goddesses were thought to live on Mount Olympus, the highest mountain in

The gods worshiped in the Greek religion.

Greece. Among the twelve were Zeus, the chief god and father of the gods; Athena, goddess of wisdom and crafts; Apollo, god of the sun and poetry; Ares, god of war; Aphrodite, goddess of love; and Poseidon, brother of Zeus and god of the seas and earthquakes.

Greek religion did not have a body of doctrine, nor did it focus on morality. The spirits of most people, regardless of what they had done in life, went to a gloomy underworld ruled by the god Hades. Because the Greeks wanted the gods to look favorably upon their activities, rituals became important. **Rituals** are ceremonies or rites. Greek religious rituals involved prayers often combined with gifts to the gods based on the principle "I give so that you [the gods] will give [in return]."

Festivals also developed as a way to honor the gods and goddesses. Certain festivals were held at special locations, such as those dedicated to the worship of Zeus at Olympia or to Apollo at **Delphi.** Numerous events took place in honor of the gods at the great festivals, including athletic games to which all Greeks were invited. The first such games were held at the Olympic festival in 776 B.C.

The Greeks also had a great desire to learn the will of the gods. To do so, they made use of the oracle, a sacred shrine where a god or goddess revealed the future through a priest or priestess. The most famous was the oracle of Apollo at Delphi, located on the side of Mount Parnassus overlooking the **Gulf of Corinth.** At Delphi, a priestess, thought to be inspired by Apollo, listened to questions. Her responses were then interpreted by priests and given in verse form to the persons asking the questions. Representatives of states and individuals traveled to Delphi to consult the oracle of Apollo.

The responses provided by the priests and priestesses were often puzzling and could be interpreted in more than one way. For example, Croesus (KREE•suhs), king of Lydia and known for his incredible wealth, sent messengers to the oracle at Delphi asking "whether he shall go to war with the Persians." The oracle replied that if Croesus attacked

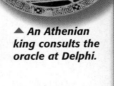

CONNECTIONS Around The World

Rulers and Gods

All of the world's earliest civilizations believed that there was a close connection between rulers and gods. In Egypt, pharaohs were considered gods whose role was to maintain the order and harmony of the universe in their own kingdoms. In Mesopotamia, India, and China, rulers were thought to rule with divine assistance. Kings were often seen as rulers who derived their power from the gods and who were the agents or representatives of the gods. Many Romans certainly believed that their success in creating an empire was a visible sign of divine favor. As one Roman stated, "We have overcome all the nations of the world, because we have realized that the world is directed and governed by the gods."

The rulers' supposed connection to the divine also caused them to seek divine aid in the affairs of the world. This led to the art of *divination*—an organized method to figure out the intentions of the gods. In Mesopotamian and Roman society, divination took the form of examining the livers of sacrificed animals or the flights of birds to determine the will of the gods. The Chinese used oracle bones to receive advice from the gods. The Greeks consulted oracles.

Underlying all of these practices was a belief in a supernatural universe—a world in which divine forces were in charge and human well-being depended on those divine forces. It was not until the scientific revolution of the 1600s that many people began to believe in a natural world that was not governed by spiritual forces.

▲ *An Athenian king consults the oracle at Delphi.*

Comparing Cultures

Why were rulers of early civilizations considered to have divine powers? How did this affect their systems of government?

the Persians, he would destroy a mighty empire. Overjoyed to hear these words, Croesus made war on the Persians but was crushed by his enemy. A mighty empire—that of Croesus—was destroyed!

✓**Reading Check** **Describing** In what ways did the Greeks honor their gods and goddesses?

Greek Drama

Drama as we know it in Western culture was created by the Greeks. Plays were presented in outdoor theaters as part of religious festivals. The first Greek dramas were tragedies, which were presented in a trilogy (a set of three plays) built around a common theme. The only complete trilogy we possess today, called the *Oresteia*, was composed by **Aeschylus.** This set of three plays relates the fate of Agamemnon, a hero in the Trojan War, and his family after his return from the war. In the plays, evil acts are shown to breed evil acts and suffering. In the end, however, reason triumphs over the forces of evil.

Another great Athenian playwright was **Sophocles,** whose most famous play was *Oedipus Rex.* In this play, the oracle of Apollo foretells how Oedipus will kill his own father and marry his mother. Despite all attempts to prevent this, Oedipus does commit these tragic acts.

A third outstanding Athenian dramatist, Euripides, tried to create more realistic characters. His plots became more complex and showed a greater interest in real-life situations. Euripides was controversial. He questioned traditional values. He portrayed war as brutal and barbaric and expressed deep compassion for the women and children who suffered as a result of it.

Greek tragedies dealt with universal themes still relevant today. They examined such problems as the nature of good and evil, the rights of the individual, the nature of divine forces, and the nature of human beings. In the world of the Greek tragedies, striving to do the best thing may not always lead to success, but the attempt is a worthy endeavor. Greek pride in accomplishment and independence was real. As the chorus chanted in Sophocles' *Antigone,* "Is there anything more wonderful on earth, our marvelous planet, than the miracle of man?"

Greek comedy developed later than tragedy. It was used to criticize both politicians and intellectuals. Comedy tried to make a point, intending to both entertain and provoke a reaction. The plays of Aristophanes are good examples.

✓**Reading Check** **Identifying** Name three Greek tragedies that examine universal themes.

Greek Philosophy

Philosophy refers to an organized system of thought. The term comes from a Greek word that means "love of wisdom." Early Greek philosophers were concerned with the development of critical or rational thought about the nature of the universe.

Many early Greek philosophers tried to explain the universe on the basis of unifying principles. In the sixth century B.C., for example, **Pythagoras,** familiar to geometry students for his Pythagorean theorem, taught that the essence of the universe could be found in music and numbers. In the fifth and fourth centuries B.C., Socrates, Plato, and Aristotle raised basic questions that have been debated for two thousand years.

Sophists The Sophists were a group of traveling teachers in ancient Greece who rejected speculation such as that of Pythagoras as foolish. They argued that it was simply beyond the reach of the human mind to understand the universe. It was more important for individuals to improve themselves.

The Sophists sold their services as professional teachers to the young men of Greece, especially those of Athens. The Sophists stressed the importance of rhetoric (the art of persuasive speaking in winning debates and swaying an audience). This skill was especially valuable in democratic Athens.

To the Sophists, there was no absolute right or wrong. What was right for one individual might be wrong for another. True wisdom consisted of being able to perceive and pursue one's own good. Because of these ideas, many people viewed the Sophists as harmful to society and especially dangerous to the values of young people.

Socrates One of the critics of the Sophists was **Socrates,** a sculptor whose true love was philosophy. Because Socrates left no writings, we know about him only what we have learned from the writings of his pupils, such as Plato. Socrates taught many pupils, but he accepted no pay. He believed that the goal of education was only to improve the individual.

Socrates used a teaching method that is still known by his name. The Socratic method of teaching uses a question-and-answer format to lead pupils to see things for themselves by using their own reason. Socrates believed that all real knowledge is already present within each person. Only critical examination is needed to call it forth. This is the real task of

THE WAY IT WAS

SPORTS & CONTESTS

The Olympic Games of the Greeks

The Olympic games were the greatest of all the ancient Greek sports festivals. They were held at Olympia every four years beginning in 776 B.C. to honor Zeus, father of the gods.

At first, the Olympic games consisted only of footraces. Later, wrestling, boxing, javelin and discus throwing, long jumping, and chariot racing were added. Competitions were always between individuals, not groups. Only young men took part until contests for boys were added by 632 B.C. Beginning in 472 B.C., the games were held over a five-day period.

In the Olympic games, each event had only one winner. His prize was simply a wreath made of olive leaves, considered sacred to Zeus. However, the Greeks looked on winning athletes as great heroes and often rewarded them in other ways. The people of a city in Sicily welcomed home the winner of the 200-meter race with a parade of 300 chariots pulled by white horses. Some communities rewarded their winners with money and free rents for life.

The long-held belief that athletes in the Olympic games were amateurs is simply not true. City-states supported both athletes and their trainers. This practice freed them to train for long periods of time in

philosophy, because, as Socrates said, "The unexamined life is not worth living." This belief in the individual's ability to reason was an important contribution of the Greeks.

Socrates questioned authority, and this soon led him into trouble. Athens had had a tradition of free thought and inquiry, but defeat in the Peloponnesian War changed the Athenians. They no longer trusted open debate. Socrates was accused and convicted of corrupting the youth of Athens by teaching them to question and think for themselves. An Athenian jury sentenced him to die by drinking hemlock, a poison.

Plato One of Socrates' students was **Plato,** considered by many the greatest philosopher of Western civilization. Unlike his teacher Socrates, who did not write down his thoughts, Plato wrote a great deal. He was fascinated with the question of reality. How do we know what is real?

According to Plato, a higher world of eternal, unchanging Forms has always existed. These ideal Forms make up reality and only a trained mind—the goal of philosophy—can become aware of or understand these Forms. To Plato, the objects that we perceive with our senses (trees, for example) are simply reflections of the ideal Forms (treeness). They (the trees) are but shadows. Reality is found in the Form (treeness) itself.

Plato explained his ideas about government in a work entitled *The Republic.* Based on his experience in Athens, Plato had come to distrust the workings of democracy. To him, individuals could not achieve a good life unless they lived in a just and rational state.

Plato's search for the just state led him to construct an ideal state in which people were divided into three basic groups. At the top was an upper class of philosopher-kings: "Unless either philosophers become kings in their countries or those who are now called kings and rulers come to be sufficiently inspired with a genuine desire for wisdom; unless, that is to say, political power and philosophy meet together . . . there can be no rest from troubles . . . for states, nor for all mankind."

The second group in Plato's ideal state were warriors who protected society. The third group contained all the rest, the masses, people driven not by wisdom or courage but by desire. They would be the producers of society—artisans, tradespeople, and farmers. Contrary to Greek custom, Plato also believed that men and women should have the same education and equal access to all positions.

the hope that they would bring back victories—and glory—to their communities. Larger city-states even bribed winners from other city-states to move to their communities and compete for them in the next games.

Olympic games could be dangerous. Wrestlers, for example, were allowed to gouge eyes and even pick up their competitors and bring them down head first onto a hard surface. Boxers wrapped their hands and forearms with heavy leather thongs, making their blows damaging. Some athletes were killed during the games.

The Greek Olympic games came to an end in A.D. 393, when a Christian Roman emperor banned them as pagan exercises. Fifteen hundred years later, the games were revived through the efforts of a French baron, Pierre de Coubertin, who was inspired by the ideals of the ancient Greeks. In 1896, the first modern Olympic games were held in Athens, Greece.

Discobolos, a famous Greek statue, pays tribute to athletes and the Greek ideals of sound mind and sound body.

CONNECTING TO THE PAST

1. **Explaining** Why were winning athletes so enthusiastically rewarded by their communities?

2. **Writing about History** How were the Greek Olympics influenced by governments and politics?

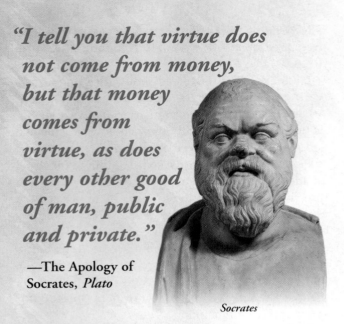

"I tell you that virtue does not come from money, but that money comes from virtue, as does every other good of man, public and private."

—The Apology of Socrates, *Plato*

Socrates

Aristotle Plato established a school in Athens known as the Academy. One of his pupils, who studied at the Academy for 20 years, was **Aristotle.** Aristotle did not accept Plato's theory of ideal forms. He thought that by examining individual objects (trees), we could perceive their form (treeness). However, he did not believe that these forms existed in a separate, higher world of reality beyond material things. Rather, he thought of forms as a part of things themselves. (In other words, we know what treeness is by examining trees.)

Aristotle's interests, then, lay in analyzing and classifying things based on observation and investigation. His interests were wide ranging. He wrote about many subjects, including ethics, logic, politics, poetry, astronomy, geology, biology, and physics. Until the seventeenth century, science in the Western world remained largely based on Aristotle's ideas.

Like Plato, Aristotle wanted an effective form of government that would rationally direct human affairs. Unlike Plato, he did not seek an ideal state but tried to find the best form of government by analyzing existing governments. For his *Politics*, Aristotle looked at the constitutions of 158 states and found three good forms of government: monarchy, aristocracy, and constitutional government. He favored constitutional government as the best form for most people.

✓ **Reading Check** **Contrasting** How did Aristotle's idea of government differ from Plato's?

The Writing of History

History as we know it—as a systematic analysis of past events—was created in the Western world by the Greeks. Herodotus (hih•RAH•duh•tuhs) was the author of *History of the Persian Wars,* a work commonly regarded as the first real history in Western civilization. The central theme of this work is the conflict between the Greeks and the Persians, which Herodotus viewed as a struggle between Greek freedom and Persian despotism.

Herodotus traveled widely and questioned many people as a means of obtaining his information. He was a master storyteller.

Many historians today consider **Thucydides** (thoo•SIH•duh•DEEZ) the greatest historian of the ancient world. Thucydides was an Athenian general who fought in the Great Peloponnesian War. A defeat in battle led the Athenian assembly to send him into exile. This gave him the opportunity to write his *History of the Peloponnesian War.*

Unlike Herodotus, Thucydides was not concerned with divine forces or gods as causal factors in history. He saw war and politics in purely human terms, as the activities of human beings. He examined the causes and the course of the Peloponnesian War clearly and fairly, placing much emphasis on the accuracy of his facts. As he stated, "And with regard to my factual reporting of the events of the war I have made it a principle not to write down the first story that came my way, and not even to be guided by my own general impressions; either I was present myself at the events which I have described or else I heard of them from eye-witnesses whose reports I have checked with as much thoroughness as possible." Thucydides also provided remarkable insight into the human condition. He believed that the study of history is of great value in understanding the present.

✓ **Reading Check** **Contrasting** How did Thucydides' view of history differ from Herodotus's view?

The Classical Ideals of Greek Art

The arts of the Western world have been largely dominated by the standards set by the Greeks of the classical period. Classical Greek art was concerned with expressing eternal ideals. The subject matter of this art was the human being, presented as an object of great beauty. The classic style, based on the ideals of reason, moderation, balance, and harmony in all things, was meant to civilize the emotions.

In architecture, the most important form was the temple dedicated to a god or goddess. At the center of Greek temples were walled rooms that housed both the statues of deities and treasuries in which gifts to the gods and goddesses were safeguarded.

History *through Architecture*

The Erechtheum near the Parthenon has figures of maidens in place of conventional columns. This type of ornamental support is called a caryatid. Why might the architect have decided to use female figures?

These central rooms were surrounded by a screen of columns that made Greek temples open structures rather than closed ones. The columns were originally made of wood. In the fifth century B.C., marble began to be used.

Some of the finest examples of Greek classical architecture were built in Athens in the fifth century B.C. The most famous building, regarded as the greatest example of the classical Greek temple, was the Parthenon. It was built between 447 and 432 B.C. Dedicated to Athena, the patron goddess of Athens, the Parthenon was an expression of Athenian pride in their city-state. Indeed, it was dedicated not only to Athena but also to the glory of Athens and the Athenians. The Parthenon shows the principles of classical architecture: the search for calmness, clarity, and freedom from unnecessary detail.

Greek sculpture also developed a classical style. Lifelike statues of the male nude, the favorite subject of Greek sculptors, showed relaxed attitudes. Their faces were self-assured, their bodies flexible and smooth muscled.

Greek sculptors did not seek to achieve realism, however, but rather a standard of ideal beauty. Polyclitus (PAH•lih•KLY•tuhs), a fifth-century sculptor, wrote down systematic rules for proportions that he illustrated in a work known as the *Doryphoros*. His theory maintained that the use of ideal proportions, based on mathematical ratios found in nature, could produce an ideal human form.

Reading Check **Identifying** What was the most important architectural form in ancient Greece?

TAKS Practice

SECTION 4 ASSESSMENT

Checking for Understanding

1. **Define** ritual, oracle, tragedy, philosophy, Socratic method.

2. **Identify** Aeschylus, Sophocles, Pythagoras, Socrates, Plato, Aristotle, Thucydides.

3. **Locate** Delphi, Gulf of Corinth.

4. **Describe** the themes found in Greek tragedies. Identify one of the dramas discussed in the text, name the playwright who wrote it, and describe the themes it contains.

5. **List** the three basic groups of people in Plato's ideal state.

Critical Thinking

6. **Summarize** How does Plato's theory of ideal forms differ from Aristotle's theory of forms? Which view makes more sense to you? Why?

7. **Organizing Information** Make a web diagram that shows what bodies of knowledge the Greeks explored.

Bodies of Knowledge Explored by the Greeks

Analyzing Visuals

8. **Examine** the photograph of the Erechtheum shown above and identify the building's defining architectural characteristics. In what types of modern buildings would you find examples of classical architecture?

Writing About History

9. **Descriptive Writing** Describe and evaluate the roles of oracles, priestesses, and priests in Greek religion. You may want to research these roles in your school library. After writing your descriptions of the roles, make comparisons to the roles of religious leaders in your community.

MORE THAN
MYTH TO THE *ILIAD*

1

In Homer's epic poem the *Iliad*, the rich and powerful city-state of Mycenae headed a united Greek attack against "windy Ilion"—the wealthy city of Troy—to avenge the kidnapping of "lovely-haired Helen," wife of Sparta's king Menelaus. For centuries, the fabled treasures of these legendary cities were thought to exist—like the Trojan War itself—in imagination only. But modern archaeology suggests there may be more than myth to Homer's classic tale.

Greeks in antiquity considered the *Iliad* to be a historical account of their past. Alexander the Great, for example, traced his mother's family back to the hero Achilles. We know today that the poem is not a true story of a war in Greece's late Bronze Age (about 1600 to 1100 B.C.). For one thing, the *Iliad* was not written during this period. It is the result of more than 500 years of oral tradition, handed down by generations of professional poets. Credit for the final masterpiece went to someone the Greeks called "divine Homer," but they knew nothing more about this person than his supposed name—and neither do we.

Still, myths often spring from a kernel of historical truth, and in the late nineteenth century, the Trojan War's mythic rival cities entered the real world of history. Between 1870 and 1890 German businessman and amateur archaeologist Heinrich Schliemann carried out archaeological digs that put Troy and Mycenae on the map. Since then, archaeologists and scholars have uncovered numerous details suggesting that Homer's *Iliad* records many aspects of the Greek Bronze Age (known to historians as the Mycenaean Age, for the city that dominated the period). The giant walls of Mycenae and its fabulous treasure, for example, and the geography around Troy itself in northwestern Turkey, all support descriptions you can find in the poem's stirring rhythms.

Descendants of Greek-speaking peoples who appeared on the Greek mainland around 1900 B.C., the Mycenaeans eventually developed societies that revolved around a central palace. In addition to Mycenae itself, Schliemann and later archaeologists have discovered major Mycenaean centers whose names appear in the *Iliad:* "sacred" Pylos, Tiryns "of the huge walls," and "thirsty" Argos, to list only a few of them. Researchers have also discovered hundreds of settlements and tombs—all with a shared culture.

The historical Mycenae dominated the plain of Argos, a wealthy region that controlled much of the trade

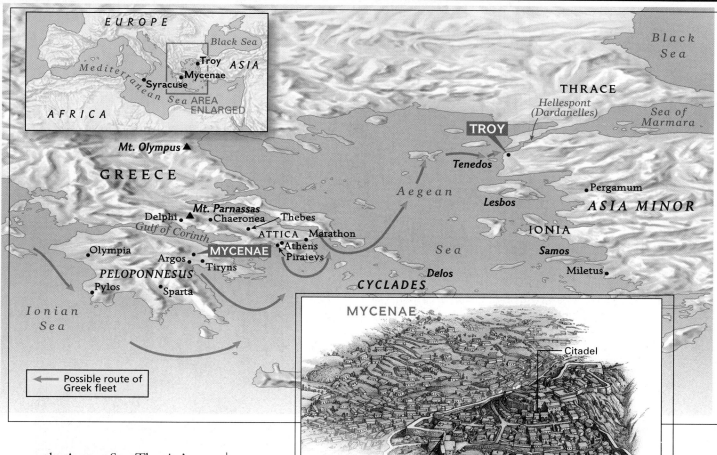

EUROPE

Black Sea

Mediterranean Sea

Troy

ASIA

Mycenae

Syracuse

AFRICA

AREA ENLARGED

Black Sea

THRACE

Hellespont (Dardanelles)

Sea of Marmara

TROY

Tenedos

Mt. Olympus ▲

GREECE

Aegean

Pergamum

Lesbos

ASIA MINOR

Delphi ▲

Mt. Parnassas ▲

Chaeronea

Thebes

IONIA

MYCENAE

ATTICA

Marathon

Sea

Samos

Olympia

Argos

Athens
Piraievs

Tiryns

Miletus

PELOPONNESUS

Delos

Pylos

Sparta

CYCLADES

Ionian Sea

← Possible route of Greek fleet

MYCENAE

Citadel

Lion Gate

Grave circle

Cult center

2

across the Aegean Sea. The city's massive walls enclosed a large administrative complex of royal courts, houses, sanctuaries, and storerooms. Its famous grave circle, unearthed by Schliemann in 1876, revealed rich treasures suggesting that as early as the sixteenth century B.C. the Mycenaean ruling class possessed a treasure trove of silver, gold, and ivory.

From archaeological digs at both Mycenae and Troy came signs that Homer's *Iliad* told of real things in the ancient world. Among the items found at Mycenae, for example, was a small gold ring. Carved on its face is a miniature battle scene showing a man protecting his entire body behind a huge shield, the kind that Homer describes the Greek hero Ajax holding in front of him "like a wall." The *Iliad's* heroes were known across the sea in Asia as well. Tomb art found in Turkey and dating from the fourth century

B.C. depicts a scene from the Trojan siege (opposite page).

◼

Troy's location at the mouth of the Dardanelles, the strait that Homer called the Hellespont, gave it command of the water route into central Asia. From this vantage point, the historical Trojans traded skillfully throughout central Asia. What remains of Troy's walls still overlooks a plain crossed by willow-lined rivers mentioned in the *Iliad*.

Heinrich Schliemann's excavation of Troy was crude and impatient. He sank trenches straight to bedrock, believing Homer's "windy Ilion" would lie at the bottom, thus destroy-

1 A scene etched in stone on a fourth century B.C. tomb found in Turkey suggests the *Iliad's* tragic final battle, between Hector of Troy and Achilles, hero of the Greeks.

2 Prosperous Mycenae traded throughout the Aegean. The reconstruction above shows the city's fortress in the late thirteenth century B.C., at the peak of its power. Some 250 miles (402 km) away, its rival Troy commanded the strait called the Dardanelles (Homer's Hellespont), a key link to the Black Sea. Today Troy's ruins lie 3 miles (4.8 km) inland, but in the late Bronze Age, the city sat on the edge of a bay that opened directly onto the Hellespont.

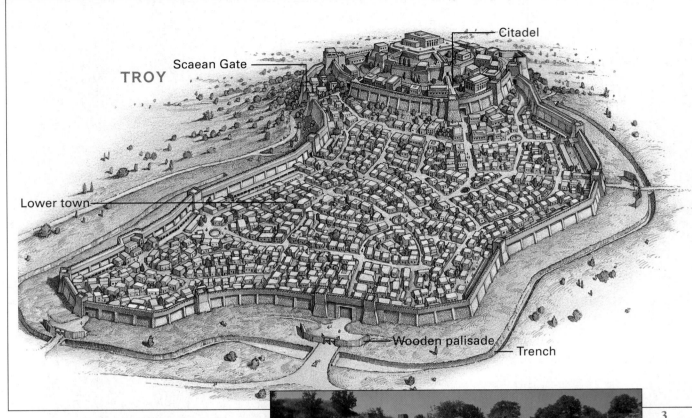

TROY

Scaean Gate

Citadel

Lower town

Wooden palisade — Trench

3

ing several layers of history. Today an international team of archaeologists directed by Manfred Korfmann of Germany's Tubingen University is reexcavating the entire site—nine levels ranging from 3000 B.C. to the Roman city of New Ilium in the early sixth century A.D. The sixth and seventh levels straddle the years 1250 to 1150 B.C., the era of Homer's war.

Whether or not the Greeks actually launched an invasion or entered Troy by means of the famous Trojan horse ruse (opposite page), evidence shows that the two peoples were in trading contact. Mycenaean pottery found at Troy dates back to 1500 B.C.

Some 1,300 feet (396 m) beyond the citadel first uncovered by Schliemann, Korfmann's team of archaeologists has made a most exciting find. They uncovered an extensive trench 8 feet (2.4 m) deep and 10 feet (3 m) wide encircling an entire lower town

of wooden houses. The reconfigured city (reconstruction above)—which increases the known area of the sixth level of Troy by as much as 50 acres (20.25 ha)— is almost ten times as large as the citadel and held a population of at least 6,000. This finding makes Troy an opponent more equal to the mighty Mycenae than Schliemann's hilltop fortress.

Farther afield, in a nearby sand cove, lies evidence to support specula-

tion that the Trojans took advantage of their commanding position at this crossroads of trade between Europe and Asia. Because of prevailing north-easterly winds, shallow-keeled Bronze Age merchant ships would have been forced to wait at Troy for a favorable breeze before proceeding north of the Dardanelles to the Black Sea.

Korfmann's team has located burials in the cove that reflect different cultural influences, suggesting that

4

the crews of stranded vessels may have died while waiting for the wind to change. Korfmann says later texts confirm that "occupants of the region exacted tolls from incoming vessels." If Troy grew rich with this practice, it would have made bitter enemies of merchants like the Mycenaeans.

Indeed, some historians speculate that conflict over trade routes, rather than Helen's legendary beauty, may have sparked the Trojan War. As Korfmann sees it, "It is possible that Troy experienced several commercial skirmishes, if not one Trojan War."

3 Stone walls believed to be the citadel of Troy were first unearthed in the 1870s. Troy holds the remains of at least nine settlements spanning 3,500 years. In the early 1990s, archaeologists discovered several wooden palisades and a 10-foot (3-m) trench encircling a lower town (reconstruction). Earlier only the hilltop citadel was known.

4 The Tumulus of Ajax is one of more than 40 mounds on the plain of Troy said to honor fallen heroes of the Trojan War.

5 A seventh-century B.C. amphora from Mykonos shows the earliest known depiction of the wooden horse that bore "death and doom for the Trojans."

5

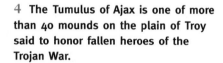

INTERPRETING THE PAST

1. Was there a Trojan War? If so, what was its likely cause?

2. What is significant about the strait called the Dardanelles?

Alexander and the Hellenistic Kingdoms

Guide to Reading

Main Ideas
- Under Alexander, Macedonians and Greeks conquered the Persian Empire.
- Hellenistic cities became centers for the spread of Greek culture.

Key Terms
Hellenistic Era, Epicureanism, Stoicism

People to Identify
Philip II, Alexander the Great, Eratosthenes, Euclid, Archimedes

Places to Locate
Macedonia, Alexandria, Pergamum

Preview Questions
1. What event brought to an end the freedom of Greek city-states?
2. In what ways has Alexander's legacy affected history?

Reading Strategy
Compare and Contrast Use a Venn diagram like the one shown below to compare and contrast the characteristics of the Classical and Hellenistic periods.

Classical Age of Greece | Hellenistic Era

Preview of Events

◆360 B.C.	◆350 B.C.	◆340 B.C.	◆330 B.C.	◆320 B.C.

359 B.C.
Philip II turns Macedonia into the chief power of the Greek world

338 B.C.
Macedonia crushes the Greeks

330 B.C.
Alexander the Great takes possession of the Persian Empire

323 B.C.
Alexander dies at the age of thirty-two

Voices from the Past

Under the leadership of Alexander the Great, Macedonians and Greeks united to invade and conquer the Persian Empire. The ancient historian Diodorus of Sicily gave this account of Alexander's destruction of the Persian palace at Persepolis:

66While they [Alexander's victorious forces] were feasting and the drinking was far advanced, as they began to be drunken a madness took possession of the minds of the intoxicated guests. At this point one of the women present, Thaïs by name and Athenian by origin, said that for Alexander it would be the finest of all his feats in Asia if he . . . set fire to the palaces, and permitted women's hands in a minute to extinguish the famed accomplishments of the Persians. . . . Promptly many torches were gathered. . . . Thaïs was the first, after the king, to hurl her blazing torch into the palace. As the others all did the same, immediately the entire palace area was consumed.99

— *Library of History*, **Diodorus Siculus, C. H. Oldfather, trans., 1967**

In the conquered lands, Greeks and non-Greeks formed a new society in what is known as the Hellenistic Era.

Alexander the Great

The Threat of Macedonia

The Greeks viewed their northern neighbors, the Macedonians, as barbarians. The Macedonians were rural people organized in groups, not city-states. By the end of the fifth century B.C., however, **Macedonia** emerged as a powerful kingdom.

In 359 B.C., **Philip II** came to the throne. He built a powerful army and turned Macedonia into the chief power of the Greek world. Philip was soon drawn into Greek affairs. A great admirer of Greek culture, he longed to unite all of Greece under Macedonia.

Fearing Philip, the Athenians allied with a number of other Greek states and fought the Macedonians at the Battle of Chaeronea (KEHR•uh•NEE•uh), near Thebes, in 338 B.C. The Macedonian army crushed the Greeks.

Philip quickly gained control of all Greece, bringing an end to the freedom of the Greek city-states. He insisted that the Greek states form a league and then cooperate with him in a war against Persia. Before Philip could undertake his invasion of Asia, however, he was assassinated, leaving the task to his son Alexander.

✔**Reading Check** **Identifying** What was Philip II's plan for the conquered Greeks and their city-states?

Alexander the Great

┌**TURNING POINT**┐ **As a result of Alexander's conquests, Greek language, art, architecture, and literature spread throughout Southwest Asia. Today we continue to admire and to imitate Greek art and architecture.**

Alexander the Great was only 20 when he became king of Macedonia. Philip had carefully prepared his son for kingship. By taking Alexander along with him on military campaigns, Philip taught Alexander the basics of military leadership. After his father's death, Alexander moved quickly to fulfill his father's dream—the invasion of the Persian Empire. He was motivated by the desire for glory and empire but also by the desire to avenge the Persian burning of Athens in 480 B.C.

Alexander's Conquests Alexander was taking a chance in attacking the Persian Empire. Although weakened, it was still a strong state in the spring of 334 B.C. when Alexander entered Asia Minor with an army of some thirty-seven thousand men, both Macedonians and Greeks. The cavalry, which would play an important role as a striking force, numbered about five thousand.

By the next year, Alexander had freed the Ionian Greek cities of western Asia Minor from the Persians and defeated a large Persian army at Issus. He then turned south. By the winter of 332 B.C., Syria, Palestine, and Egypt were under his control. He built **Alexandria** as the Greek capital of Egypt. It became,

and remains today, one of the most important cities in both Egypt and the Mediterranean world. It was also the first of a series of cities named after him.

In 331 B.C., Alexander turned east and fought the decisive battle with the Persians at Gaugamela, not far from Babylon. After this victory, Alexander took possession of the rest of the Persian Empire. However, he was not content.

Over the next three years, Alexander moved east and northeast, as far as modern Pakistan. In 326 B.C. he crossed the Indus River and entered India, where he experienced a number of difficult campaigns. Weary of fighting year after year, his soldiers refused to go farther.

Alexander agreed to return home. He led his troops across the desert, through what is now southern Iran. A blazing sun and lack of water led to thousands of deaths. At one point, when a group of Alexander's soldiers found a little water, they scooped it up in a helmet and gave it to him. Then, according to one ancient Greek historian, Alexander, "in full view of his troops, poured the water on the ground. So extraordinary was the effect

Web Activity Visit the *Glencoe World History* Web site at tx.wh.glencoe.com and click on **Chapter 4– Student Web Activity** to learn more about Alexander the Great and his conquests.

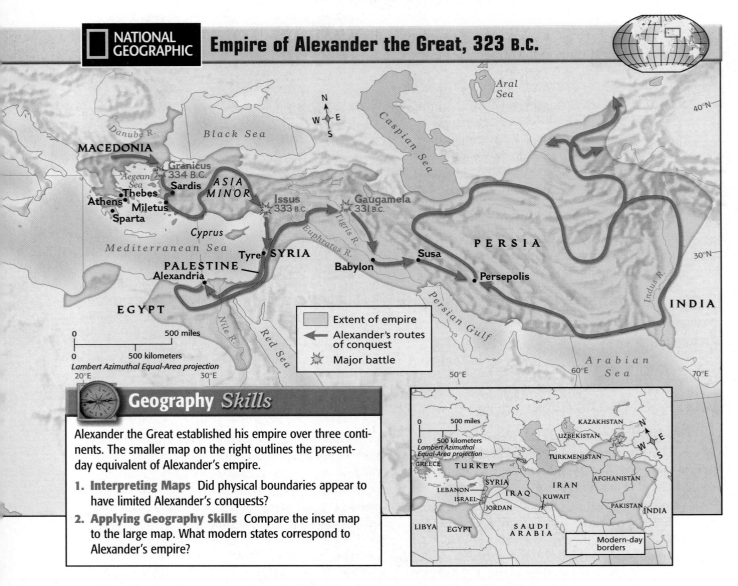

Geography *Skills*

Alexander the Great established his empire over three continents. The smaller map on the right outlines the present-day equivalent of Alexander's empire.

1. **Interpreting Maps** Did physical boundaries appear to have limited Alexander's conquests?

2. **Applying Geography Skills** Compare the inset map to the large map. What modern states correspond to Alexander's empire?

of this action that the water wasted by Alexander was as good as a drink for every man in the army."

Alexander returned to Babylon, where he planned more campaigns. However, in June 323 B.C., exhausted from wounds, fever, and too much alcohol, he died at the age of 32.

The Legacy of Alexander What explains Alexander's extraordinary military success? No doubt, he was a great military leader—a master of strategy and tactics, fighting in every kind of terrain and facing every kind of opponent. Alexander was a brave and even reckless fighter who was quite willing to lead his men into battle and risk his own life. His example inspired his men to follow him into unknown lands and difficult situations. Alexander sought to imitate Achilles, the warrior-hero of Homer's *Iliad*, who was an ideal still important in Greek culture. Alexander kept a copy of the *Iliad*—and a dagger—under his pillow.

Alexander's military skill created an enormous legacy. He had extended Greek and Macedonian rule over a vast area. This brought large quantities of gold and silver to Greece and Macedonia, stimulating their economies.

Alexander's successors tried to imitate him, using force and claims of divine rule to create military monarchies. Although mainland Greeks remained committed to the ideals of the city-state, the creation of the monarchies became part of Alexander's political legacy.

Alexander also left a cultural legacy. Due to his conquests, Greek language, architecture, literature, and art spread throughout Southwest Asia and the Near East. The cultural influences did not, however, flow in only one direction. The Greeks also absorbed aspects of Eastern culture.

✔**Reading Check** **Identifying** What were the different aspects of Alexander's legacy?

Modern Alexandria is the main port of Egypt and its second largest city. It has been a prominent cultural and economic metropolis for thousands of years.

The Hellenistic Kingdoms

Alexander created a new age, the Hellenistic Era. The word *Hellenistic* is derived from a Greek word meaning "to imitate Greeks." It is an appropriate way, then, to describe an age that saw the expansion of the Greek language and ideas to the non-Greek world of Southwest Asia and beyond.

The united empire that Alexander created by his conquests fell apart soon after his death as the most important Macedonian generals engaged in a struggle for power. By 300 B.C., any hope of unity was dead. Eventually, four Hellenistic kingdoms emerged as the successors to Alexander: Macedonia, Syria in the east, the kingdom of **Pergamum** in western Asia Minor, and Egypt. All were eventually conquered by the Romans.

Alexander the Great had planned to fuse Macedonians, Greeks, and Persians in his new empire by using Persians as officials and encouraging his soldiers to marry native women. The Hellenistic monarchs who succeeded him, however, relied only on Greeks and Macedonians to form the new ruling class. Even those easterners who did advance to important government posts had learned Greek, for all government business was transacted in Greek. The Greek ruling class was determined to maintain its privileged position.

In his conquests, Alexander had created a series of new cities and military settlements. Hellenistic kings did likewise. These new population centers varied in size from military settlements of only a few hundred men to cities with thousands of people. Alexandria, which Alexander had founded in Egypt, was the largest city in the Mediterranean region by the first century B.C.

Hellenistic rulers encouraged a massive spread of Greek colonists to Southwest Asia. Greeks (and Macedonians) provided not only new recruits for the army but also a pool of civilian administrators and workers. Architects, engineers, dramatists, and actors were all in demand in the new Greek cities. The Greek cities of the Hellenistic Era became the chief agents in the spread of Greek culture in Southwest Asia—as far, in fact, as modern Afghanistan and India.

Reading Check **Identifying** Which four kingdoms emerged following Alexander's death?

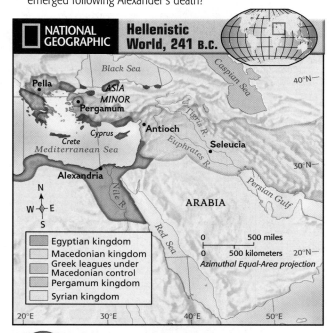

NATIONAL GEOGRAPHIC — Hellenistic World, 241 B.C.

- Egyptian kingdom
- Macedonian kingdom
- Greek leagues under Macedonian control
- Pergamum kingdom
- Syrian kingdom

Geography *Skills*

After Alexander's death, the Greek world separated into four emerging kingdoms.

1. **Interpreting Maps** Which kingdom appears to have had the most extensive territory?

Hellenistic Culture

The Hellenistic Era was a period of considerable cultural accomplishment in many areas, especially science and philosophy. These achievements occurred throughout the Hellenistic world. Certain centers, however—especially the great Hellenistic city of Alexandria—stood out. Alexandria became home to poets, writers, philosophers, and scientists—scholars of all kinds.

The library in Alexandria became the largest in ancient times, with more than five hundred thousand scrolls. The library encouraged the careful study of literature and language. There was also a museum that provided a favorable atmosphere for scholarly research.

Pergamum, the most important city in Asia Minor, also became a leading cultural center. As a result, Pergamum also attracted both scholars and artists. The library at Pergamum was second only to Alexandria's library.

Architecture and Sculpture

The founding of new cities and the rebuilding of old ones presented many opportunities for Greek architects and sculptors. Hellenistic kings were very willing to spend their money to beautify the cities within their states. The buildings characteristic of the Greek homeland—baths, theaters, and temples—lined the streets of these cities.

Both Hellenistic kings and rich citizens patronized sculptors. Thousands of statues were erected in towns and cities all over the Hellenistic world. Hellenistic sculptors maintained the technical skill of the classical period, but they moved away from the idealism of earlier classicism to a more emotional and realistic art. This is especially evident in the numerous statues of old women and little children.

Picturing **History**

Winged Victory was carved from a solid block of marble in the second century B.C. The folds in her garment look almost like real cloth. How does this statue differ from classical Greek sculpture?

Literature

The Hellenistic Age produced an enormous quantity of literature. Writing talent was held in high esteem, especially by Hellenistic leaders who spent large amounts of money subsidizing writers. Unfortunately very little of this literature has survived.

Appolonius of Rhodes wrote the epic poem called *Argonautica*, which tells the story of Jason and his search for the Golden Fleece. Theocritus wrote short poems that expressed a love of nature and an appreciation of nature's beauty. Unlike Appolonius, Theocritus believed that it was best not to attempt epic poems, for which Homer had established a standard that could not be matched according to many Greek scholars.

Athens remained the center of Greek theatre. A new type of comedy developed that sought only to entertain and amuse and avoided political commentary. Menander was perhaps the most successful of these new playwrights.

Science

The Hellenistic Age witnessed considerable advances in the sciences. Astronomy and mathematics were two areas of progress.

One astronomer—Aristarchus (AR•uh•STAHR•kuhs) of Samos—developed the theory that the sun is at the center of the universe while the Earth rotates around the sun in a circular orbit. The prevailing view, in contrast, held that Earth was at the center of the universe. The new theory was not widely accepted. Most scholars continued to believe in the Earth-centered universe.

Another astronomer—**Eratosthenes** (EHR•uh•TAHS•thuh•NEEZ)—determined that Earth was round and calculated Earth's circumference at 24,675 miles (39,702 km), an estimate that was within 185 miles (298 km) of the actual figure. The mathematician **Euclid** wrote the *Elements*, a textbook on plane geometry. This work has been used up to modern times.

By far the most famous of the scientists of the Hellenistic period was **Archimedes** (AHR•kuh•MEE•deez) of Syracuse. Archimedes was especially important because of his work on the geometry of spheres and cylinders, as well as for establishing the value of the mathematical constant pi.

Archimedes was also a practical inventor. He may have devised the Archimedes' screw, a machine used to pump water out of mines and to lift irrigation water. During the Roman siege of his native city of Syracuse, he built a number of devices to repel the attackers.

Archimedes

Archimedes' achievements inspired a number of stories. Supposedly, he discovered specific gravity by observing the water he displaced in his bath. He then became so excited by his realization that he jumped out of the water and ran home naked, shouting, "Eureka!" ("I have found it!") He is said to have emphasized the importance of levers by proclaiming to the king of Syracuse, "Give me a lever and a place to stand on and I will move the earth." The king was so impressed that he encouraged Archimedes to lower his sights and build defensive weapons instead.

Philosophy Athens remained the chief center for philosophy in the Hellenistic world. After the time of Alexander the Great, the home of Socrates, Plato, and Aristotle continued to attract the most famous philosophers from the Greek world, who chose to establish their schools there. New systems of thought—Epicureanism and Stoicism—strengthened Athens' reputation as a philosophical center.

Epicurus, the founder of a philosophy that came to be known as Epicureanism, established a school in Athens near the end of the fourth century B.C. Epicurus believed that human beings were free to follow self-interest as a basic motivating force. Happiness was the goal of life. The means to achieve happiness was the pursuit of pleasure, the only true good.

Epicurus did not speak of the pursuit of pleasure in a physical sense (which is what our word *epicurean* has come to mean). Instead, pleasure was freedom from emotional turmoil and worry. To achieve this, people had to free themselves from public activity. However, they were not to give up all social life. To Epicurus, a life could only be complete when it was centered on the ideal of friendship.

Another school of thought was Stoicism. It became the most popular philosophy of the Hellenistic world and later flourished in the Roman Empire as well. Stoicism was the product of a teacher named Zeno. Zeno came to Athens and began to teach in a building known as the Painted Portico (the *Stoa Poikile*—hence, the word *Stoicism*).

Like Epicureanism, Stoicism was concerned with how people find happiness. However, the Stoics approached the problem differently. To them, happiness could be found only when people gained inner peace by living in harmony with the will of God. They could bear whatever life offered (hence, our word *stoic*).

Unlike Epicureans, Stoics did not believe in the need to separate themselves from the world and politics. Public service was regarded as noble. The real Stoic was a good citizen.

✓**Reading Check** **Contrasting** What were the major differences between Epicureanism and Stoicism?

🌟**TAKS Practice**

SECTION 5 ASSESSMENT

Checking for Understanding

1. **Define** Hellenistic Era, Epicureanism, Stoicism.

2. **Identify** Philip II, Alexander the Great, Eratosthenes, Euclid, Archimedes.

3. **Locate** Macedonia, Alexandria, Pergamum.

4. **Describe** the defining characteristics of the Hellenistic period.

5. **List** the three most famous scientists of the Hellenistic Age and describe their contributions.

Critical Thinking

6. **Evaluate** Why is Alexander called "Great"? Do you think the title is justified? Why or why not?

7. **Organizing Information** Use a cluster diagram to show Alexander's goals for his empire.

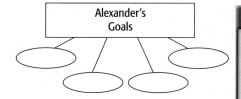

Analyzing Visuals

8. **Examine** the photograph of Alexandria, Egypt, shown on page 141 of your text. What do you notice that you might not have expected about the city? What does the city's location tell you about the importance of ports to Alexander's creation of an empire?

Writing About History

9. **Persuasive Writing** Choose an Epicurean or Stoic perspective and argue whether an individual should participate in government and civic affairs.

Using Key Terms

1. Some Greek city-states were committed to government by the many, called _____, while others ruled by _____, which means rule by the few.

2. The upper fortified part of a city, the _____ , was a place of refuge during an attack.

3. _____ were a heavily armed military order of infantrymen or foot soldiers.

4. Marching shoulder to shoulder in a rectangular formation was known as a _____ .

5. Athenians devised the practice of _____ to protect themselves against overly ambitious politicians.

6. In order to know the will of the gods, the Greeks consulted an _____ , a sacred shrine dedicated to a god or goddess.

7. According to the Greek philosophy of _____ , humans are free to follow self-interest as a basic motivating force.

8. Greek citizens assembled in an open area called an _____ that also served as a market.

9. The term _____ comes from the Greek word that means "love of wisdom."

10. Greek _____ were presented as a set of three plays.

11. The _____ of teaching uses a question-and-answer format to lead pupils to understand ideas for themselves.

Reviewing Key Facts

12. **Culture** What was the basic textbook for the education of Greek males?

13. **Citizenship** What were the rights and responsibilities of Athenian citizens?

14. **Economics** What types of goods were exchanged between the Greek city-states and their colonies?

15. **Government** What caused the Spartans to create a military state?

16. **History** What is significant about the Age of Pericles?

17. **Society** How were Greek women kept under strict control?

18. **History** How did Philip prepare Alexander for kingship?

19. **History** What is the meaning of the term Hellenistic?

20. **Culture** Who were the philosophers of classical Greece?

21. **Science and Technology** What contributions did Pythagorus, Eratosthenes, and Archimedes make to science?

Critical Thinking

22. **Analyzing** How did the formation of the Delian League give proof to the saying that strength lies in unity?

23. **Understanding Cause and Effect** The Peloponnesian War weakened the Greek states, yet later, Greek culture was spread farther than ever. How did this happen?

Chapter Summary

Although each Greek civilization had unique problems, all four faced common challenges.

	Minoans	Mycenaeans	Spartans	Athenians
Environment a. location b. factors	a. Crete b. tidal waves	a. Peloponnesus b. earthquakes	a. Peloponnesus b. farming	a. Attica b. lack of fertile land
Movement a. origin b. trade	a. unknown b. sea trading empire	a. Indo-European b. pottery	a. Greek-speaking invaders b. trade discouraged	a. Greek-speaking invaders b. pottery
Regionalism a. government b. values, interests, beliefs	a. king b. sports, nature	a. monarchies forming a loose alliance of independent states b. heroic deeds	a. military state, oligarchy b. discipline, military arts	a. oligarchy, direct democracy b. philosophy, art, theatre, architecture
Conflict a. with other Greeks b. with foreign invaders	a. invaded by Mycenaeans	a. conquered Minoans b. fell to Greek-speaking invaders	a. conquered other Greeks, fought Athenians b. fought Persians, Macedonians	a. fought Spartans b. fought Persians, Macedonians

Writing About History

24. **Expository Writing** Some classicists translate Sophocles' work on Oedipus as "Oedipus Tyrannus" or "Oedipus the Tyrant." Using what you know about Greek history, explain why some people might want to talk about Oedipus as a tyrant rather than a king.

Analyzing Sources

Read the following excerpt from Pericles' Funeral Oration:

❝Our Constitution is called a democracy because the power is in the hands not of a minority but of the whole people. When it is a question of settling private disputes, everyone is equal before the law. Just as our political life is free and open, so is our day-to-day life in our relations with each other. . . . Here each individual is interested not only in his own affairs but in the affairs of the state as well.❞

25. How does Pericles define a democracy?
26. According to Pericles, what is the relationship between the individual and the state in a democracy?
27. What is the historical significance of this speech in Pericles' own day and now?

Applying Technology Skills

28. **Creating a Multimedia Presentation** Using the Internet and traditional print sources, conduct further research on Greek architecture, especially the design and building of temples. Then, design and construct a small three-dimensional temple, using the type of column you feel is best suited to your building. To which Greek god or goddess will your temple be dedicated? Share your project with the class.

Making Decisions

29. Pretend you are Pericles in Athens facing the possibility of a Spartan assault. Why are you and Sparta at war? Are there any alternatives to battle? Might you choose to negotiate with Sparta? Keep in mind the reasons for Spartan antagonism and the great costs a battle inflicts.

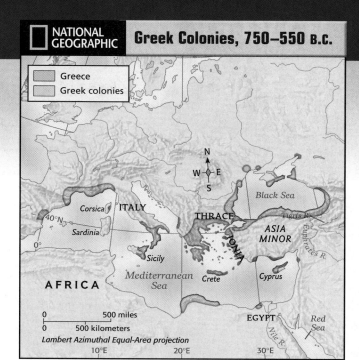

NATIONAL GEOGRAPHIC   Greek Colonies, 750–550 B.C.

Greece
Greek colonies

Black Sea
Corsica ITALY
Sardinia   THRACE
IONIA   ASIA MINOR
Sicily
Mediterranean Sea   Crete   Cyprus
AFRICA
EGYPT   Red Sea

0   500 miles
0   500 kilometers
Lambert Azimuthal Equal-Area projection

Analyzing Maps and Charts

Directions: Study the map above to answer the following questions.

30. Analyze the location of the Greek colonies. What generalizations can you make about their locations?
31. What is the approximate maximum distance that a Greek citizen would have to travel to reach the sea?
32. How important was a navy to the Athenian Empire?

Directions: Choose the best answer to the following question.

The Great Peloponnesian War from 431 B.C. to 405 B.C. immediately resulted in

F the Age of Pericles.
G the Hellenistic Era.
H the weakening of the Athenian city-state.
J a rise of literature and history.

Test-Taking Tip: The key word *immediately* indicates that the correct answer is a direct result of the *Great Peloponnesian War*. Although many of the events stated in the answer choices happened around this time, you want the answer that happened directly after the Great Peloponnesian War.

Rome and the Rise of Christianity

600 B.C.–A.D. 500

Key Events

As you read, look for the key events in the history of Rome and early Christianity.
- Romans overthrew the last Etruscan king and established a republic.
- Romans crushed Hannibal and won the Second Punic War.
- Augustus became the first emperor, signifying the beginning of the Roman Empire.
- Constantine proclaimed official tolerance of Christianity.
- Germanic tribes defeated the Romans, and the empire fell.

The Impact Today

The events that occurred during this time period still impact our lives today.
- Using their practical skills, the Romans made achievements in law, government, language, and engineering that became an important part of Western civilization.
- In the last two hundred years of the Roman Empire, Christianity grew, along with its new ideals of spiritual equality and respect for human life.

 World History Video The Chapter 5 video, "The Roman World," chronicles the emergence and expansion of the Roman Empire.

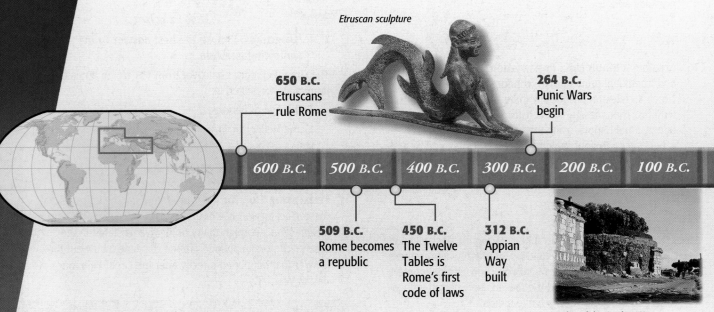

Etruscan sculpture

650 B.C.
Etruscans
rule Rome

264 B.C.
Punic Wars
begin

600 B.C.	500 B.C.	400 B.C.	300 B.C.	200 B.C.	100 B.C.

509 B.C.
Rome becomes
a republic

450 B.C.
The Twelve
Tables is
Rome's first
code of laws

312 B.C.
Appian
Way
built

Ruins of the Appian Way

The Pont du Gard, a Roman aqueduct in southern France

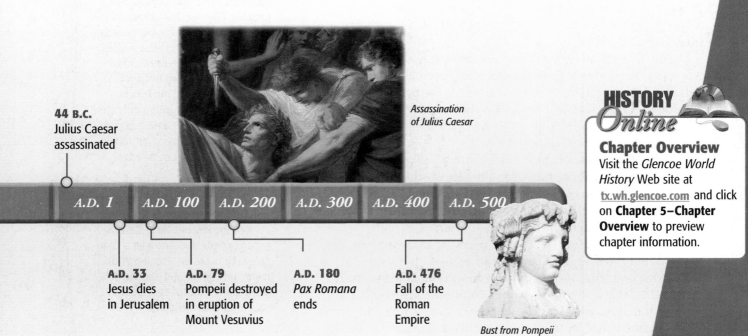

44 B.C.
Julius Caesar
assassinated

*Assassination
of Julius Caesar*

A.D. 1   A.D. 100   A.D. 200   A.D. 300   A.D. 400   A.D. 500

A.D. 33
Jesus dies
in Jerusalem

A.D. 79
Pompeii destroyed
in eruption of
Mount Vesuvius

A.D. 180
Pax Romana
ends

A.D. 476
Fall of the
Roman
Empire

Bust from Pompeii

HISTORY
Online
Chapter Overview
Visit the *Glencoe World
History* Web site at
tx.wh.glencoe.com and click
on **Chapter 5–Chapter
Overview** to preview
chapter information.

A Story That Matters

Horatius at the bridge over the Tiber River

Horatius at the Bridge

*O*ne of the great heroes of early Rome was Horatius, whose bravery in battle made him a legend. As the story goes, Roman farmers, threatened by attack from the neighboring Etruscans, abandoned their fields and moved into the city of Rome, protected by the city's walls. One weak point in the Roman defense was a wooden bridge over the Tiber River. On the day of the Etruscan attack, Horatius was on guard at the bridge.

A surprise attack by the Etruscans caused many Roman troops to throw down their weapons and run. Horatius acted promptly, urging them to make a stand at the bridge in order to protect Rome. As a last resort, he challenged the Roman troops to destroy the bridge while he made a stand at the outer end to give them more time.

At first, the Etruscans held back, astonished at the sight of a single defender. Soon, however, they threw their spears at the lone figure who barred their way. Horatius blocked the spears with his shield and held his ground as the Etruscans advanced on foot, ready to overwhelm him.

Meanwhile, the Roman soldiers used the extra time to bring down the bridge. When Horatius heard the sound of the bridge crashing into the river behind him, he dove, fully armed, into the water and swam. Despite the arrows that fell around him, he safely reached the other side. Rome had been saved by the courageous act of Horatius, a Roman who knew his duty and was determined to carry it out.

Why It Matters

Courage, duty, determination—these were common words to many Romans, who believed that it was their mission to rule nations and peoples. Whereas the Greeks had excelled in philosophy and the arts, the Romans were practical people. They knew how to govern, make laws, and build roads that took them to the ends of the known world. Even after the Roman Empire disappeared, those same gifts continued to play an important role in the civilizations that came after.

History and You Horatius is only one of the famous Romans you will meet in this chapter. To keep track of the key people in Roman history, create and maintain a computerized database that shows the name, time lived, and notable accomplishments of each person you study in this chapter.

The Rise of Rome

Main Ideas
- The Romans conquered the plain of Latium, the Italian peninsula, and then the entire Mediterranean world.
- Their practical political skills allowed the Romans to maintain control over their conquered lands.

Key Terms
republic, patrician, plebeian, consul, praetor

People to Identify
Latins, Etruscans, Livy, Hannibal

Places to Locate
Rome, Sicily, Carthage, Alps

Preview Questions
1. How did the Etruscans impact the development of Roman civilization?
2. How did the Roman Republic gain control of the lands of the Mediterranean?

Reading Strategy
Categorizing Information As you read this section, complete a chart like the one shown below listing the government officials and the legislative bodies of the Roman Republic.

Officials	Legislative Bodies

Preview of Events

♦700 B.C.	♦600 B.C.	♦500 B.C.	♦400 B.C.	♦300 B.C.	♦200 B.C.	♦100 B.C.

650 B.C.
Etruscans control Rome

509 B.C.
Romans overthrow Etruscans

146 B.C.
Rome destroys Carthage

129 B.C.
Rome obtains first province in Asia

Voices from the Past

Judas Maccabeus

Roman history is the story of the Romans' conquest of the area around Rome, then of Italy, and finally of the entire Mediterranean world. Judas Maccabeus, a Jewish military leader, said of the Romans:

❝They had defeated Antiochus the Great, king of Asia, who went to fight against them with one hundred twenty elephants and with cavalry and chariots and a very large army. He was crushed by them. . . . Yet for all this not one of the Romans has put on a crown, but they have built for themselves a senate chamber, and every day three hundred senators constantly deliberate concerning the people, to govern them well.❞
—*Western Civilization*, Margaret L. King, 2000

The Romans were conquerors, but they also governed, using republican forms that have been passed down to us.

The Land and Peoples of Italy

Italy is a peninsula extending about 750 miles (1,207 km) from north to south. It is not very wide, averaging about 120 miles (193 km) across. The Apennine (A•puh•NYN) mountain range forms a ridge from north to south down the middle of Italy that divides west from east. Italy has some fairly large fertile plains ideal for farming. Most important are the Po River valley in the north; the plain of Latium, on which the city of **Rome** is located; and the region of Campania, to the south of Latium.

The Impact of Geography In the same way as the other civilizations we have examined, geography played an important role in the development of Rome. The Apennines are less rugged than the mountain ranges of Greece and did not divide the Italian peninsula into many small, isolated communities. Italy also had more land for farming than did Greece, enabling it to support a large population.

The location of the city of Rome was especially favorable to early settlers. Located about 18 miles (29 km) inland on the Tiber River, Rome had a way to the sea. However, it was far enough inland to be safe from pirates. Because it was built on seven hills, it was easily defended. In addition, it was situated

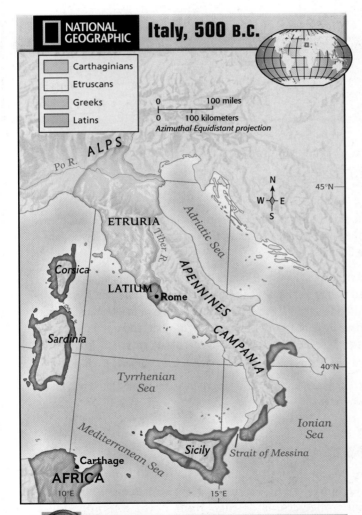

Geography *Skills*

In 500 B.C., the Etruscans and Greeks occupied much of Italy. Note the many cultures that influenced ancient Rome.

1. **Applying Geography Skills** Why was Rome's location important for the Latins' conquest of Italy?

where the Tiber could be easily crossed. Thus, it became a natural crossing point for north-south traffic in western Italy. All in all, Rome had a good central location in Italy from which to expand.

The Italian peninsula juts into the Mediterranean, making it an important crossroads between the western and eastern Mediterranean Sea. Once Rome had unified Italy, it easily became involved in Mediterranean affairs. After the Romans had established their Mediterranean empire, governing it was made easier by Italy's central location.

The Peoples of Italy Indo-European peoples moved into Italy during the period from about 1500 to 1000 B.C. We know little about these peoples, but we do know that one such group was the **Latins,** who lived in the region of Latium. These people spoke Latin, which, like Greek, is an Indo-European language. They were herders and farmers who lived in settlements consisting of huts on the tops of Rome's hills. After about 800 B.C., other people also began settling in Italy—the two most notable being the Greeks and the **Etruscans.**

The Greeks came to Italy in large numbers during the age of Greek colonization (750–550 B.C.). They settled in southern Italy and then slowly moved around the coast and up the peninsula. The eastern two-thirds of **Sicily,** an island south of the Italian peninsula, was also occupied by the Greeks. The Greeks had much influence on Rome. They cultivated olives and grapes, passed on their alphabet, and gave the Romans artistic and cultural models through their sculpture, architecture, and literature.

The early development of Rome, however, was influenced most by the Etruscans, who were located north of Rome in Etruria. After 650 B.C., they expanded into north-central Italy and came to control Rome and most of Latium. The Etruscans found Rome a village but launched a building program that turned it into a city. Etruscan dress—the toga and short cloak—was adopted by the Romans. The organization of the Roman army also was borrowed from the Etruscans.

✓ **Reading Check** **Evaluating** What role did geography play in the prosperity and defensibility of Rome?

The Roman Republic

Roman tradition maintains that early Rome (753–509 B.C.) was under the control of seven kings and that two of the last three kings were Etruscans. Historians know for certain that Rome did fall under Etruscan influence during this time. In 509 B.C., the

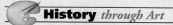

Etruscan mural, c. 500 B.C. Etruscan murals show colorful, lively scenes of Etruscan daily life. Particularly popular subjects were scenes of wrestling matches, religious ceremonies, and people enjoying music and feasts. Why do these murals provide archaeologists and historians with important clues to Etruscan life? What do the murals reveal about Etruscan life?

Romans overthrew the last Etruscan king and established a **republic,** a form of government in which the leader is not a monarch and certain citizens have the right to vote. This was the beginning of a new era in Rome's history.

War and Conquest At the beginning of the republic, Rome was surrounded by enemies. For the next two hundred years, the city was engaged in almost continuous warfare.

In 338 B.C., Rome crushed the Latin states in Latium. During the next 50 years, the Romans waged a fierce struggle against people from the central Apennines, some of whom had settled south of Rome. Rome was again victorious. The conquest gave the Romans control over a large part of Italy.

It also brought them into direct contact with the Greek communities of southern Italy. Soon, the Romans were at war with these Greek cities. By 264 B.C., they had overcome the Greeks and completed their conquest of southern Italy. After defeating the remaining Etruscan states to the north over the next three years, Rome had conquered virtually all of Italy.

To rule Italy, the Romans devised the Roman Confederation. Under this system, Rome allowed some peoples—especially Latins—to have full Roman citizenship. Most of the remaining communities were made allies. They remained free to run their own local affairs but were required to provide soldiers for Rome. The Romans made it clear that loyal allies could improve their status and even become Roman citizens. The Romans made the conquered peoples feel they had a real stake in Rome's success.

Why Rome Was Successful Romans believed that their early ancestors were successful because of their sense of duty, courage, and discipline. The Roman historian **Livy,** writing in the first century B.C., provided a number of stories to teach Romans the virtues that had made Rome great. His account of Cincinnatus (SIHN•suh• NA•tuhs), a simple farmer who was chosen as a temporary ruler to save Rome from attack, is one such example.

Looking back today, how can we explain Rome's success in gaining control of the entire Italian peninsula? First, the Romans were good diplomats. They were shrewd in extending Roman citizenship and allowing states to run their own internal affairs. Although diplomatic, however, they could be firm, and even cruel when necessary, crushing rebellions without mercy.

Second, the Romans excelled in military matters. They were not only accomplished soldiers but also persistent ones. The loss of an army or a fleet did not cause them to quit but instead spurred them on to build new armies and new fleets. In addition, they were brilliant strategists. As they conquered, the Romans built colonies—fortified towns—throughout Italy. By building roads to these towns and thus connecting them, the Romans could move troops quickly throughout their conquered territory.

Finally, in law and politics, as in conquest, the Romans were practical. They did not try to build an ideal government but instead created political institutions in response to problems, as the problems arose.

Reading Check **Examining** How did the Romans gain support for their empire?

The Roman State

The Romans had been ruled by kings under the Etruscans. As a result, they distrusted kingship and devised a very different system of government.

The Government of Rome

Early Rome was divided into two groups or orders—the patricians and the plebeians (plih•BEE•uhns). The patricians were great landowners, who became Rome's ruling class. Less wealthy landholders, craftspeople, merchants, and small farmers were part of a larger group called plebeians.

Men in both groups were citizens and could vote, but only the patricians could be elected to governmental offices. The chief executive officers of the Roman Republic were the consuls and praetors (PREE•tuhrs). Two consuls, chosen every year, ran the government and led the Roman army into battle. The praetor was in charge of civil law—law as it applied to Roman citizens. As the Romans' territory expanded, another praetor was added to judge cases in which one or both people were noncitizens. The Romans also had a number of officials who had special duties, such as supervising the treasury.

The Roman **Senate** came to hold an especially important position in the Roman Republic. It was a select group of about three hundred patricians who served for life. At first, the Senate's only role was to advise government officials. However, the advice of the Senate carried a great deal of weight. By the third century B.C., it had the force of law.

The Roman Republic had several people's assemblies in addition to the Senate. By far the most important of these was the **centuriate assembly.** The centuriate assembly elected the chief officials, such as consuls and praetors, and passed laws. Because it was organized by classes based on wealth, the wealthiest citizens always had a majority. The council of the plebs was the assembly for plebeians only, and it came into being as a result of the struggle between the two social orders in Rome.

The Struggle of the Orders

There was often conflict between the patricians and the plebeians in the early Roman Republic. Children of patricians and plebeians were forbidden to marry each other. Plebeians resented this situation, especially since they served in the Roman army that protected the Republic. They thought that they deserved both political and social equality with the patricians.

The struggle between the patricians and plebeians dragged on for hundreds of years. Ultimately, it led to success for the plebeians. A popular assembly for plebeians only, the **council of the plebs,** was created in 471 B.C. New officials, known as **tribunes of the plebs,** were given the power to protect the plebeians. In the fourth century B.C., plebeians were permitted to become consuls. Finally, in 287 B.C., the council of the plebs received the right to pass laws for all Romans.

By 287 B.C., all male Roman citizens were supposedly equal under the law. In reality, however, a few wealthy patrician and plebeian families formed a new senatorial ruling class that came to dominate the political offices. The Roman Republic had not become a democracy.

Roman Law One of Rome's chief gifts to the Mediterranean world of its day and to later generations was its system of law. Rome's first code of laws was the **Twelve Tables,** which was adopted in 450 B.C. This code was a product of a simple farming society and proved inadequate for later Roman needs. From the Twelve Tables, the Romans developed a more sophisticated system of civil law. This system applied only to Roman citizens, however.

As Rome expanded, legal questions arose that involved both Romans and non-Romans. The Romans found that although some of their rules of civil law could be used in these cases, special rules were often needed. These rules gave rise to a body of law known as the **Law of Nations.** The Romans came to identify the Law of Nations with natural law, or universal law based on reason. This enabled them to establish standards of justice that applied to all people.

These standards of justice included principles still recognized today. A person was regarded as innocent until proved otherwise. People accused of wrongdoing were allowed to defend themselves before a judge. A judge, in turn, was expected to weigh evidence carefully before arriving at a decision. These principles lived on long after the fall of the Roman Empire.

Reading Check **Explaining** How did the differences between plebeians and patricians prevent Rome from becoming a true democracy?

Rome Conquers the Mediterranean

After their conquest of Italy, the Romans found themselves face to face with a strong power in the Mediterranean—the state of **Carthage.** Carthage had been founded around 800 B.C. on the coast of North Africa by Phoenicians. The state had created an enormous trading empire in the western Mediterranean. By the third century B.C., the Carthaginian Empire included the coast of northern Africa, southern Spain, Sardinia, Corsica, and western Sicily. With its control of western Mediterranean trade, Carthage was the largest and richest state in the area.

The presence of Carthaginians in Sicily, an island close to the Italian coast, made the Romans fearful. In 264 B.C., the two powers began a lengthy struggle for control of the western Mediterranean.

The First Punic War Rome's first war with Carthage began in 264 B.C. It is called the First Punic War, after the Latin word for Phoenician, *punicus.* The war started when the Romans sent an army to Sicily. The Carthaginians, who thought of Sicily as part of their empire, considered this an act of war. Both sides became determined to conquer Sicily.

The Romans—a land power—realized that they could not win the war without a navy and created a large naval fleet. After a long struggle, a Roman fleet defeated the Carthaginian navy off the coast of Sicily, and the war came to an end. In 241 B.C., Carthage gave up all rights to Sicily and paid a fine to the Romans. Sicily became the first Roman province.

Carthage vowed revenge, however, and added new lands in Spain to make up for the loss of Sicily. The Romans encouraged one of Carthage's Spanish allies to revolt against Carthage. In response, **Hannibal,** the greatest of the Carthaginian generals, struck back, beginning the Second Punic War (218 to 201 B.C.).

The Second Punic War Hannibal decided that the Carthaginians would bring the war home to the Romans. Hannibal entered Spain, moved east, and crossed the **Alps** with an army of about 46,000 men, a large number of horses, and 37 battle elephants. The Alps took a toll on the Carthaginian army; most of the elephants did not survive. The remaining army, however, posed a real threat to the Romans.

In 216 B.C., the Romans decided to meet Hannibal head on. It was a serious mistake. At Cannae (KA•nee), the Romans lost an army of almost forty thousand men. On the brink of disaster, Rome refused to surrender and raised yet another army.

Hannibal
247–183 B.C.
Carthaginian general

When Hannibal was only nine years old, his father, a Carthaginian general, took him to a temple in Carthage and made him swear that he would always hate the Romans. Hannibal later inflicted terrible losses on the Romans— his army killed or captured thousands of Romans and allied soldiers in Italy. Unable to win the war, Hannibal eventually sought refuge with Rome's enemies.

The Romans never forgave Hannibal. They pursued him for years and finally caught up with him in Bithynia. To avoid capture, Hannibal took poison after remarking, "Let us relieve the Romans of the fear which has so long afflicted them, since it seems to tax their patience too hard to wait for an old man's death."

Rome gradually recovered. Although Hannibal remained free to roam Italy, he had neither the men nor the equipment to attack the major cities, including Rome. The Romans began to reconquer some of the Italian cities that had been taken by Hannibal. More important, they sent troops to Spain and, by 206 B.C., they had pushed the Carthaginians out of Spain.

In a brilliant military initiative, Rome decided to invade Carthage rather than fight Hannibal in Italy. This strategy forced the Carthaginians to recall Hannibal from Italy. At the Battle of Zama (ZAY•muh) in 202 B.C., the Romans crushed Hannibal's forces, and the war was over. Carthage lost Spain, which became a Roman province. Rome had become the dominant power in the western Mediterranean.

More Conquests Fifty years later, the Romans fought their third and final struggle with Carthage, the Third Punic War. For years, a number of prominent Romans had called for the complete destruction of Carthage.

In 146 B.C., Carthage was destroyed. For 10 days, Roman soldiers burned and demolished all of the city's buildings. The inhabitants—fifty thousand men, women, and children—were sold into slavery. The territory of Carthage became a Roman province called Africa.

During its struggle with Carthage, Rome also battled the Hellenistic states in the eastern Mediterranean. The Fourth Macedonian War ended in 148 B.C., and Macedonia was made a Roman province. Two years later, Greece was placed under the control of the Roman governor of Macedonia. In 129 B.C., Pergamum became Rome's first province in Asia. Rome was now master of the Mediterranean Sea.

✓**Reading Check** **Evaluating** What is the historical and cultural significance of the Roman destruction of Carthage?

🐴 TAKS Practice

SECTION 1 ASSESSMENT

Checking for Understanding

1. **Define** republic, patrician, plebeian, consul, praetor.

2. **Identify** Latins, Etruscans, Livy, Senate, centuriate assembly, council of the plebs, tribune of the plebs, Twelve Tables, Law of Nations, Hannibal.

3. **Locate** Rome, Sicily, Carthage, Alps.

4. **Describe** the significance of the Twelve Tables and the Law of Nations.

5. **List** ways in which the Greeks influenced the Romans.

Critical Thinking

6. **Discuss** What was the importance of the Senate and other assemblies to the Roman Republic?

7. **Contrasting Information** Create a chart that shows the major differences between the patricians and the plebeians.

Patricians	Plebeians

Analyzing Visuals

8. **Examine** the picture of Horatius on page 148 of your text. How does this picture represent Roman military values?

Writing About History

9. **Informative Writing** Imagine that you are a journalist covering the Second Punic War. Using the text or outside authoritative sources, write an account of one of the major battles of the war. Be sure to pose and answer questions for both Hannibal and the Roman generals in your account.

Cincinnatus Saves Rome

THERE IS PERHAPS NO BETTER account of how the virtues of duty and simplicity enabled good Roman citizens to succeed during the difficulties of the fifth century B.C. than Livy's account of Cincinnatus.

Lucius Quinctius Cincinnatus, Roman statesman and dictator, is shown here receiving his dictatorship.

❝The city was thrown into a state of turmoil, and the general alarm was as great as if Rome herself were surrounded. The situation evidently called for a dictator [the position of dictator was a temporary one used only in emergencies], and, with no dissenting voice, Lucius Quinctius Cincinnatus was named for the post.

Now I would solicit the particular attention of those numerous people who imagine that money is everything in this world, and that rank and ability are inseparable from wealth: let them observe that Cincinnatus, the one man in whom Rome reposed all her hope of survival, was at that moment working a little three-acre farm west of the Tiber. A delegation from the city found him at work on his land—digging a ditch, maybe, or ploughing. Greetings were exchanged, and he was asked—with a prayer for divine blessing on himself and his country—to put on his toga and hear the Senate's instructions. This naturally surprised him, and, asking if all were well, he told his wife to run to their cottage and fetch his toga. The toga was brought, and wiping the grimy sweat from his hands and face he put it on; at once the envoys from the city saluted him, with congratulations, as Dictator, invited him to enter Rome, and informed him of the terrible danger of the enemy's army. . . .

[Cincinnatus proceeded to raise an army, marched out, and defeated the enemy.]

In Rome the Senate was convened, and a decree was passed inviting Cincinnatus to enter in triumph with his troops. The chariot he rode in was preceded by the enemy commanders and the military flags, and followed by his army loaded with its spoils. . . . Cincinnatus finally resigned after holding office for fifteen days, having originally accepted it for a period of six months. He returned to his farm.❞

—**Livy,** *The Early History of Rome*

Analyzing Primary Sources

1. How did Cincinnatus embody the characteristics of an ideal Roman citizen?
2. What lesson(s) did Livy hope to teach his readers?
3. Compare the position of dictator in this account with present-day dictators.

From Republic to Empire

Main Ideas
- The internal instability of the Roman Empire eventually led to civil wars and increased power for the military.
- Octavian, titled Caesar Augustus, was named emperor, an event that stabilized the Roman Empire and paved the way for expansion and prosperity.

Key Terms
triumvirate, dictator, imperator

People to Identify
Crassus, Pompey, Julius Caesar, Octavian, Antony, Augustus, Nero

Places to Locate
Rubicon River, Dacia, Mesopotamia, Sinai Peninsula, Rhine River, Danube River

Preview Questions
1. What was Marius's political legacy?
2. How did Julius Caesar gain control of the Roman government?

Reading Strategy
Sequencing Information Using a chart like the one shown below, create a sequence of the five good emperors and their accomplishments.

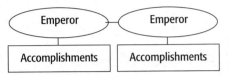

Emperor		Emperor
Accomplishments		Accomplishments

Preview of Events

♦60 B.C.	♦A.D. 1	♦A.D. 60	♦A.D. 120	♦A.D. 180

60 B.C.
First Triumvirate is formed

44 B.C.
Julius Caesar is assassinated

27 B.C.
Octavian is named emperor

A.D. 96
Rule of Five Good Emperors begins

A.D. 180
Pax Romana ends

Voices from the Past

By 133 B.C., Rome stood supreme over the Mediterranean Sea, but problems arose in Rome itself. The Roman historian Sallust tried to explain why:

❝But when our country had grown great through toil, when great kings had been vanquished in war, when Carthage, the rival of Rome's sway, had perished root and branch, then Fortune began to grow cruel. . . . Hence the lust for power first, then for money, grew upon them; these were, I may say, the root of all evils. For greed destroyed honor, integrity, and all other noble qualities. Ambition drove many men to become false; to have one thought locked in the breast, another ready on the tongue; to value friendships and enmities not on their merits but by the standard of self-interest.❞

—*Sallust*, J.C. Rolfe, trans., 1921

Sallust

While Rome was creating an empire, its internal stability was disintegrating.

Growing Inequality and Unrest

By the second century B.C., the Senate had become the real governing body of the Roman state. Members of the Senate were drawn mostly from the landed aristocracy. They remained senators for life and held the chief offices of the republic. The Senate directed the wars of the third and second centuries B.C. and took control of both foreign and domestic policy, including financial affairs. The Senate and political offices were increasingly controlled by a small circle of wealthy and powerful families.

Of course, these aristocrats formed only a tiny minority of the Roman people. The backbone of the Roman state and army had always been the small farmers. Over a period of time, however, many small farmers had found themselves unable to compete with large, wealthy landowners and had lost their lands. As a result, many of these small farmers drifted to the cities, especially Rome, forming a large class of landless poor.

Some aristocrats tried to remedy this growing economic and social crisis. Two brothers, Tiberius and Gaius Gracchus (GRA•kuhs), believed that the basic cause of Rome's problems was the decline of the small farmer. To remedy the problem, they urged the council of the plebs to pass land-reform bills that called for the government to take back public land held by large landowners and give it to landless Romans.

Many senators, themselves large landowners whose estates included large areas of public land, were furious. A group of senators took the law into their own hands and killed Tiberius in 133 B.C. His brother Gaius later suffered the same fate. The attempts of the Gracchus brothers to bring reforms had opened the door to more instability and more violence. Changes in the Roman army soon brought even worse problems.

✓ **Reading Check** **Explaining** What was the sequence of events that led to the deaths of Tiberius and Gaius Gracchus?

A New Role for the Army

In 107 B.C., a Roman general named Marius became consul and began to recruit his armies in a new way. For a long time, the Roman army had been made up of small farmers who were landholders. Now Marius recruited volunteers from the urban and rural poor who owned no property. To recruit them, he promised them land. These volunteers swore an oath of loyalty to the general, not to the Roman state. As a result, Marius created a new type of army that was not under government control. In addition, generals were forced to become involved in politics in order to get laws passed that would provide the land they needed for their veterans.

Julius Caesar

Marius left a powerful legacy. He had created a new system of military recruitment that placed much power in the hands of the individual generals.

Lucius Cornelius Sulla was the next general to take advantage of the new military system. The Senate had given him command of a war in Asia Minor. The council of the plebs tried to transfer command to Marius, and a civil war broke out. Sulla won and seized Rome itself in 82 B.C., conducting a reign of terror to wipe out all opposition. Then Sulla restored power to the hands of the Senate and eliminated most of the powers of the popular assemblies.

Sulla hoped that he had created a firm foundation to restore a traditional Roman republic governed by a powerful Senate. His real legacy was quite different from what he had intended, however. His example of using an army to seize power would prove most attractive to ambitious men.

✓ **Reading Check** **Explaining** Explain the consequences of Sulla's actions, especially his eliminating the power of the popular assemblies.

The Collapse of the Republic

For the next 50 years (82–31 B.C.), Roman history was characterized by civil wars as a number of individuals competed for power. Three men—**Crassus, Pompey,** and **Julius Caesar**—emerged as victors.

Crassus was known as the richest man in Rome. Pompey had returned from a successful command in Spain as a military hero. Julius Caesar also had a military command in Spain. The combined wealth and power of these three men was enormous and enabled them to dominate the political scene and achieve their basic aims.

The First Triumvirate In 60 B.C., Caesar joined with Crassus and Pompey to form the First Triumvirate. A triumvirate is a government by three people with equal power. Pompey received a command in

HISTORY *Online*

Web Activity Visit the *Glencoe World History* Web site at **tx.wh.glencoe.com** and click on **Chapter 5–Student Web Activity** to learn more about the Roman Republic.

Picturing **History**

At the Battle of Actium (shown left), Octavian's forces defeated the combined forces of Antony and Cleopatra. What impact did the Battle of Actium have on the development of the Roman Republic?

Spain, Crassus was given a command in Syria, and Caesar was granted a special military command in Gaul (modern France)—where he achieved success and distinction as a military leader.

When Crassus was killed in battle in 53 B.C., however, only two powerful men were left. Leading senators decided that rule by Pompey alone would be to their benefit. They voted for Caesar to lay down his command.

Caesar refused. During his time in Gaul, he had gained military experience, as well as an army of loyal veterans. He chose to keep his army and moved into Italy by illegally crossing the **Rubicon,** the river that formed the southern boundary of his province. ("Crossing the Rubicon" is a phrase used today to mean being unable to turn back.)

Caesar marched on Rome, starting a civil war between his forces and those of Pompey and his allies. The defeat of Pompey's forces left Caesar in complete control of the Roman government.

Caesar was officially made dictator in 45 B.C. A dictator is an absolute ruler. Realizing the need for reforms, Caesar gave land to the poor and increased the Senate to 900 members. By filling it with many of his supporters and increasing the number of members, he weakened the power of the Senate.

Caesar planned much more in the way of building projects and military adventures to the east. However, in 44 B.C., a group of leading senators assassinated him.

The Second Triumvirate

A new struggle for power followed Caesar's death. Three men—**Octavian,** Caesar's heir and grandnephew; **Antony,** Caesar's ally and assistant; and Lepidus, who had been commander of Caesar's cavalry—joined forces to form the Second Triumvirate. Within a few years after Caesar's death, however, only two men divided the Roman world between them. Octavian took the west; Antony, the east.

The empire of the Romans, large as it was, was still too small for two masters. Octavian and Antony soon came into conflict. Antony allied himself with the Egyptian queen Cleopatra VII. Like Caesar before him, Antony had fallen deeply in love with her. At the Battle of Actium in Greece in 31 B.C., Octavian's  forces smashed the army and the navy of Antony and Cleopatra. Both fled to Egypt, where they committed suicide a year later:

> ❝Antony was the first to commit suicide, by the sword. Cleopatra threw herself at Octavian's feet, and tried her best to attract his gaze: in vain, for his self-control enabled him to ignore her beauty. It was not her life she was after, . . . but a portion of her kingdom. When she realized this was hopeless. . . she took advantage of her guard's carelessness to get herself into the royal tomb. Once there, she put on the royal robes . . . and lay down in a richly perfumed coffin beside her Antony. Then she applied poisonous snakes to her veins and passed into death as though into a sleep.❞

Octavian, at the age of 32, stood supreme over the Roman world. The civil wars had ended. So had the republic. The period beginning in 31 B.C. and lasting until A.D. 14 came to be known as the Age of Augustus.

✓ **Reading Check** **Summarizing** How did Caesar weaken the power of the Senate?

The Age of Augustus

┌TURNING POINT┐ **In this section, you will learn how, after the collapse of Rome's republican institutions and a series of brutal civil wars, Augustus created a new order that began the Roman Empire.**

In 27 B.C., Octavian proclaimed the "restoration of the Republic." He knew that only traditional republican forms would satisfy the Senate. At the same time, he was aware that the republic could not be fully restored. Although he gave some power to the Senate, Octavian in fact became the first Roman emperor. In 27 B.C., the Senate awarded him the title of **Augustus**—"the revered one," a fitting title in view of his power.

Augustus proved to be highly popular, but his continuing control of the army was the chief source of his power. The Senate gave Augustus the title imperator, or commander in chief. Imperator gave us our word *emperor*.

Augustus maintained a standing army of 28 legions, or about 150,000 men. (A legion was a military unit of about 5,000 troops.) Only Roman citizens could be legionnaires (members of a legion). Subject peoples could serve as auxiliary forces, which numbered around 130,000 under Augustus. Augustus also set up a praetorian guard of roughly 9,000 men who had the important task of guarding the emperor.

Augustus stabilized the frontiers of the Roman Empire, conquering many new areas. His attempt to conquer Germany failed, however, when three Roman legions under Varus were massacred by German warriors. These defeats in Germany taught Augustus that Rome's power was not unlimited. This knowledge devastated him. For months, he would beat his head on a door, shouting, "Varus, give me back my legions!"

✓**Reading Check** **Evaluating** Why did the Roman defeat in Germany devastate Augustus?

The Early Empire

Beginning in A.D. 14, a series of new emperors ruled Rome. This period, ending in A.D. 180, is called the Early Empire.

Emperors of the Early Empire
Augustus's new political system allowed the emperor to select his successor from his natural or adopted family. The first four emperors after Augustus came from his family. They were Tiberius, Caligula, Claudius, and Nero. During their reigns, these emperors took over

---

What If...

Roman Legions Had Defeated Germanic Tribes?

The Roman Empire was near its height during the first century A.D. However, in A.D. 9, three Roman legions, approximately 15,000 men, were wiped out by Germanic tribesmen led by Arminius in the Teutoburg Forest. From that point on, Rome made no serious attempts to conquer what we know today as Germany.

Consider the Consequences Identify and explain at least two ways in which European history might have been different if the Romans had defeated the German warriors in the Teutoburg Forest.

---

more and more of the responsibilities that Augustus had given to the Senate. At the same time, as the emperors grew more powerful, they became more corrupt.

Nero, for example, had people killed if he wanted them out of the way—including his own mother. Without troops, the senators were unable to oppose his excesses, but the Roman legions finally revolted. Nero, abandoned by his guards, chose to commit suicide by stabbing himself in the throat after allegedly uttering these final words: "What an artist the world is losing in me."

At the beginning of the second century, a series of five so-called good emperors came to power. They were Nerva, Trajan, Hadrian, Antoninus Pius, and Marcus Aurelius. These emperors created a period of peace and prosperity known as the *Pax Romana*—the "Roman Peace." The *Pax Romana* lasted for almost a hundred years. These rulers treated the ruling classes with respect, ended arbitrary executions, maintained peace in the empire, and supported domestic policies generally helpful to the empire. By adopting capable men as their sons and successors, the first four good emperors reduced the chances of succession problems.

Under the five good emperors, the powers of the emperor continued to expand at the expense of the Senate. Officials who were appointed and directed by the emperor took over the running of the government. The good emperors also created new programs to help the people. Trajan, for example, created a program that provided state funds to assist poor

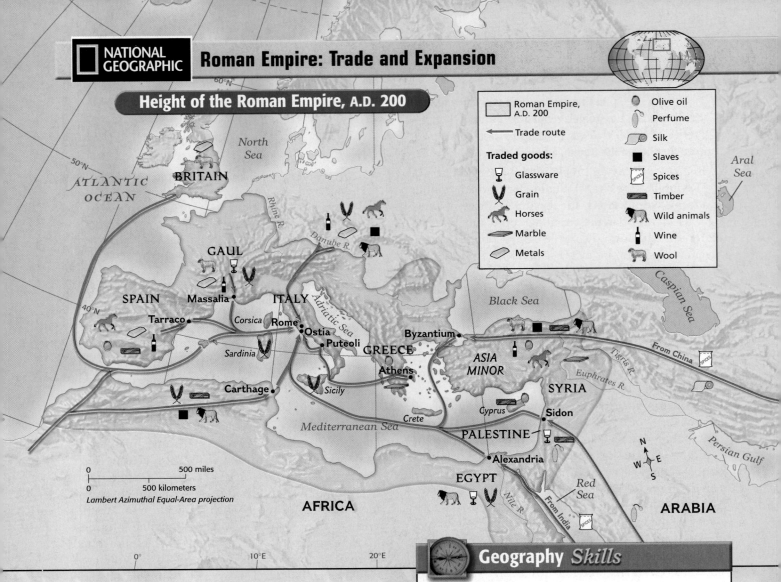

Roman Empire: Trade and Expansion

Height of the Roman Empire, A.D. 200

Legend:
- Roman Empire, A.D. 200
- Trade route
- **Traded goods:**
  - Glassware
  - Grain
  - Horses
  - Marble
  - Metals
  - Olive oil
  - Perfume
  - Silk
  - Slaves
  - Spices
  - Timber
  - Wild animals
  - Wine
  - Wool

Map labels: North Sea, ATLANTIC OCEAN, BRITAIN, Rhine R., GAUL, Danube R., SPAIN, Massalia, ITALY, Tarraco, Corsica, Rome, Ostia, Adriatic Sea, Puteoli, Sardinia, GREECE, Athens, Byzantium, ASIA MINOR, Black Sea, Caspian Sea, Aral Sea, Tigris R., From China, Euphrates R., SYRIA, Cyprus, Sidon, Crete, Carthage, Sicily, Mediterranean Sea, PALESTINE, Persian Gulf, Alexandria, EGYPT, Nile R., Red Sea, From India, AFRICA, ARABIA

500 miles / 500 kilometers
Lambert Azimuthal Equal-Area projection

Geography Skills

In about 350 years, the Romans conquered an area about the size of the present-day United States. Exchange and communication through trade was extensive throughout the vast Roman Empire.

1. **Interpreting Maps** Explain how the trading routes indicated on this map allowed for the areas in the furthest reaches of the Roman Empire to trade with one another.

2. **Applying Geography Skills** How did control of the Mediterranean region contribute to the achievements of the five good emperors? Why would control of the Mediterranean region benefit Rome's economy?

parents in the raising and education of their children. The good emperors were widely praised for their building programs. Trajan and Hadrian were especially active in building public works—aqueducts, bridges, roads, and harbor facilities—throughout the provinces and in Rome.

Extent of the Empire Rome expanded further during the period of the Early Empire. Trajan extended Roman rule into **Dacia** (modern Romania), **Mesopotamia,** and the **Sinai Peninsula.** His successors, however, realized that the empire was too large to be easily governed.

Hadrian withdrew Roman forces from much of Mesopotamia and also went on the defensive in his frontier policy. He strengthened the fortifications along a line connecting the **Rhine** and **Danube**

Rivers. He also built a defensive wall (Hadrian's Wall) about 74 miles (118 km) long across northern Britain to keep out the Picts and the Scots. By the end of the second century, it became apparent that it would be more and more difficult to defend the empire. Roman forces were located in permanent bases behind the frontiers.

At its height in the second century, the Roman Empire was one of the greatest states the world had

Expansion of the Roman Empire

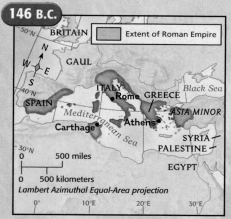

146 B.C.

At the end of the Punic Wars

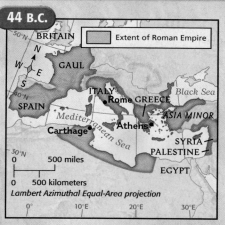

44 B.C.

At Caesar's death

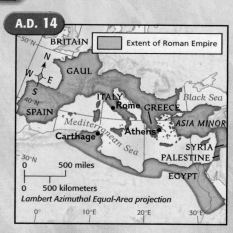

A.D. 14

At Augustus's death

The "Five Good Emperors" of the *Pax Romana*

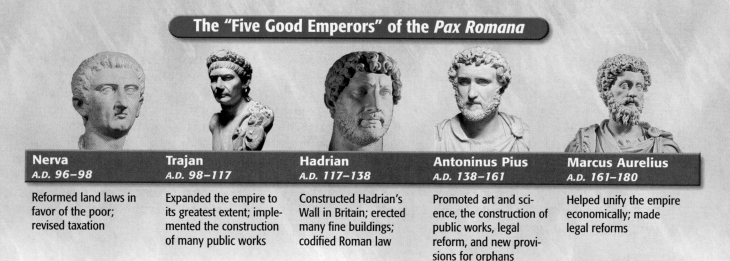

Nerva A.D. 96–98	Trajan A.D. 98–117	Hadrian A.D. 117–138	Antoninus Pius A.D. 138–161	Marcus Aurelius A.D. 161–180
Reformed land laws in favor of the poor; revised taxation	Expanded the empire to its greatest extent; implemented the construction of many public works	Constructed Hadrian's Wall in Britain; erected many fine buildings; codified Roman law	Promoted art and science, the construction of public works, legal reform, and new provisions for orphans	Helped unify the empire economically; made legal reforms

ever seen. It covered about three and a half million square miles (about 9.1 million square km) and had a population that has been estimated at more than fifty million.

The emperors and the imperial government provided a degree of unity. Much leeway was given to local customs, and the privileges of Roman citizenship were granted to many people throughout the empire. In A.D. 212, the emperor Caracalla gave Roman citizenship to every free person in the empire.

Cities were important in the spread of Roman culture, Roman law, and the Latin language. Provincial cities resembled each other with their temples, markets, and public buildings. Local city officials acted as Roman agents, performing many government duties, especially taxation.

Latin was the language of the western part of the empire, whereas Greek was used in the east. Roman culture spread to all parts of the empire and freely mixed with Greek culture. The result has been called Greco-Roman civilization.

Economic and Social Conditions The Early Empire was a period of much prosperity, with internal peace leading to high levels of trade. Merchants from all over the empire came to the chief Italian ports of Puteoli (pyuh•TEE•uh•LY) on the Bay of Naples and Ostia at the mouth of the Tiber. Trade went beyond the Roman frontiers as well and included even silk goods from China. Large quantities of grain were imported, especially from Egypt, to feed the people of Rome. Luxury items poured in to satisfy the wealthy upper classes.

Despite the active trade and commerce, however, farming remained the chief occupation of most people and the underlying basis of Roman prosperity. Large landed estates, called *latifundia* (LA•tuh•FUHN•dee•uh), dominated farming in southern and central Italy. These estates raised sheep and cattle on a large scale using mostly slave labor. Small peasant farms continued to exist in northern Italy.

An enormous gulf separated rich and poor in Roman society. The upper classes lived lives of great leisure and luxury in their villas and on their vast estates. Small farmers often became dependent on the huge estates of their wealthy neighbors. In the cities, many poor citizens worked in shops and markets. Thousands of unemployed people depended on the emperor's handouts of grain to survive.

✓ **Reading Check** **Summarizing** What were the economic conditions and chief occupations in Rome during the Early Empire?

TAKS Practice

SECTION 2 ASSESSMENT

Checking for Understanding

1. **Define** triumvirate, dictator, imperator.

2. **Identify** Crassus, Pompey, Julius Caesar, Octavian, Antony, Augustus, Nero, *Pax Romana.*

3. **Locate** Rubicon River, Dacia, Mesopotamia, Sinai Peninsula, Rhine River, Danube River.

4. **Explain** how Augustus's political system provided for succession of rulers in the empire.

5. **List** the men who made up the Second Triumvirate and explain their fates.

Critical Thinking

6. **Analyze** What qualities made the good emperors good in comparison to Augustus's successors?

7. **Compare and Contrast** Create a Venn diagram like the one shown below to compare and contrast the accomplishments of the three men.

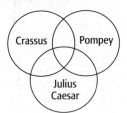

Crassus   Pompey

Julius Caesar

Analyzing Visuals

8. **Analyze** the picture of a Roman woman shown above. The woman is holding a cithera, a type of ancient Greek lyre, or stringed instrument. In what ways do you think that this painting represents the vastly different living conditions between the rich and poor in Roman society?

Writing About History

9. **Persuasive Writing** Pretend you are part of the council of the plebs. Argue for or against the land reforms instituted by Tiberius and Gaius Gracchus.

Culture and Society in the Roman World

Voices from the Past

Virgil

Virgil's masterpiece, the *Aeneid,* was an epic poem clearly meant to rival the work of Homer. It was also meant to express that the art of ruling was Rome's gift, as seen here:

❝Let others fashion from bronze more lifelike, breathing images—
For so they shall—and evoke living faces from marble;
Others excel as orators, others track with their instruments
The planets circling in heaven and predict when stars will appear.
But, Romans, never forget that government is your medium!
Be this your art: to practise men in the habit of peace,
Generosity to the conquered, and firmness against aggressors.❞
—*Aeneid,* **C. Day Lewis, trans., 1952**

One of the most noticeable characteristics of Roman culture and society is the impact of the Greeks.

Roman Art and Architecture

During the third and second centuries B.C., the Romans adopted many features of the Greek style of art. They developed a taste for Greek statues, which they placed not only in public buildings but also in their private houses. Reproductions of Greek statues became popular once the supply of original works ran low.

While Greek sculptors aimed for an ideal appearance in their figures, Roman sculptors produced realistic statues that included even unpleasant physical details.

The Romans excelled in architecture, a highly practical art. Although they continued to use Greek styles such as colonnades and rectangular buildings, the Romans also used forms based on curved lines: the arch, vault, and dome. The Romans were the first people in antiquity to use concrete on a massive scale. Using concrete along with the new architectural forms made it possible for the Romans to construct huge buildings undreamed of by the Greeks.

The remarkable engineering skills of the Romans were also put to use in constructing roads, bridges, and aqueducts. The Romans built a network of some 50,000 miles (80,450 km) of roads throughout the empire. In Rome, almost a dozen aqueducts kept a population of one million supplied with water. The Romans were superb builders.

Reading Check **Contrasting** Why were the Romans able to construct buildings larger than those of the Greeks?

Roman Literature

Although there were many talented writers, the high point of Latin literature was reached in the Age of Augustus. Indeed, the Augustan Age has been called the golden age of Latin literature.

The most distinguished poet of the Augustan Age was **Virgil.** The son of a small landholder in northern Italy near **Mantua,** he welcomed the rule of Augustus and wrote his greatest work, the *Aeneid* (ih• NEE•uhd), in honor of Rome. In the poem, the character of Aeneas is portrayed as the ideal Roman—his virtues are duty, piety, and faithfulness. Virgil's overall purpose was to show that Aeneas had

CONNECTIONS Past To Present

Roman and American Builders

One need only look at many public buildings in the United States to realize that Roman architectural models played an important role in their design. Thomas Jefferson, for example, believed that architecture could be a means for expressing the ideals of the newly founded United States. He wanted the ideals of classical architecture, especially as put into practice by the Romans, to serve as a model for American buildings. Jefferson copied Roman temples for his designs for the buildings of the University of Virginia at Charlottesville.

Concrete enabled the Romans to build mammoth colosseums that held tens of thousands of spectators. The Romans also used concrete to erect domed buildings that created new interior spaces.

American engineers continue to learn from the Romans. For example, all of us are aware of highway potholes, as well as crumbling bridges on American highways. In many cases, these problems are a result of concrete that is not hard and dense enough to survive the ravages of wind, ice, and rain. Recently, however, American engineers have experimented with a form of concrete used by the ancient Romans and have found it to be considerably harder and more durable than the usual concrete. By analyzing Roman concrete, they found that the Romans combined lime with deposits of volcanic ash to form a very hard and durable building material that would set into shape even under water. Almost two thousand years later, American engineers have finally caught up with the Romans.

▼ *Hadrian's Pantheon in Rome*

▲ *Rotunda at the University of Virginia*

Comparing Past and Present

Identify a building in your community or state that has been modeled on Roman architecture. What features are most similar to Roman temples? Describe the similarities and the differences to your class.

fulfilled his mission to establish the Romans in Italy and thereby start Rome on its divine mission to rule the world.

Another prominent Augustan poet was **Horace,** a friend of Virgil's. He was a sophisticated writer who enjoyed pointing out to his fellow Romans the "follies and vices of his age." In the *Satires,* Horace directs attacks against job dissatisfaction and greed. ("How does it happen, Maecenas, that no man alone is content with his lot?") Horace mostly laughs at the weaknesses of humans.

The most famous Latin prose work of the golden age was written by the historian **Livy,** whose masterpiece was the *History of Rome.* In 142 books, Livy traced the history of Rome from the foundation of the city to 9 B.C. Only 35 of the books have survived. Livy saw history in terms of moral lessons. He stated in the preface:

> 66 The study of history is the best medicine for a sick mind; for in history you have a record of the infinite variety of human experience plainly set out for all to see; and in that record you can find for yourself and your country both examples and warnings: fine things to take as models, base things, rotten through and through, to avoid. 99

Livy's history celebrated Rome's greatness. He built scene upon scene that not only revealed the character of the chief figures but also demonstrated the virtues that had made Rome great. Livy had a serious weakness as a historian: he was not always concerned about the factual accuracy of his stories. He did tell a good tale, however, and his work became the standard history of Rome for a long time.

☑ Reading Check **Evaluating** Why are the works of Livy considered to be so invaluable to historians?

The Roman Family

At the heart of the Roman social structure stood the family, headed by the paterfamilias—the dominant male. The household also included the wife, sons with their wives and children, unmarried daughters, and slaves.

Unlike the Greeks, the Romans raised their children at home. All Roman upper-class children (boys and girls) were expected to learn to read. The father was the chief figure in providing for the education of his children. He made the decision whether to teach his children himself, acquire a teacher for them, or send them to school. Teachers were often Greek

A Roman couple

slaves because upper-class Romans had to learn Greek as well as Latin to prosper in the empire.

Roman boys learned reading and writing, moral principles and family values, law, and physical training to prepare them to be soldiers. The end of childhood for Roman males was marked by a special ceremony. At the age of 16, a young Roman man exchanged his purple-edged toga for a plain white toga—the toga of manhood.

Some parents in upper-class families provided education for their daughters by hiring private tutors or sending the girls to primary schools. However, at the age when boys were entering secondary schools, girls were entering into marriage.

Attitudes toward Women Like the Greeks, Roman males believed that the weakness of females made it necessary for women to have male guardians. The paterfamilias had that responsibility. When he died, his sons or nearest male relatives assumed the role of guardian. Fathers also arranged the marriages of their daughters.

For females, the legal minimum age for marriage was 12, although 14 was a more common age in practice (for males, the legal minimum age was 14, although most men married later). Although some Roman doctors warned that pregnancies could be dangerous for young girls, early marriages continued.

Traditionally, Roman marriages were meant to be for life, but divorce was introduced in the third century B.C. and became fairly easy to obtain. Either husband or wife could ask for a divorce. No one needed to prove the breakdown of the marriage.

Changing Roles By the second century A.D., important changes were occurring in the Roman family. The paterfamilias no longer had absolute authority over his children. He could not sell his children into slavery or have them put to death. The husband's absolute authority over his wife also disappeared. By the late second century, women were no longer required to have guardians.

Upper-class Roman women in the Early Empire had considerable freedom and independence. They had the right to own, inherit, and sell property. Unlike Greek wives, Roman wives were not segregated from males in the home. They were appreciated as enjoyable company and were at the center of household social life.

Outside their homes, upper-class women could attend races, the theater, and events in the amphitheater. In the latter two places, however, they were forced to sit in separate female sections. Women of rank were still accompanied by maids and companions when they went out. Women could not officially participate in politics, but a number of important women influenced politics through their husbands.

Reading Check **Contrasting** How were expectations for Roman boys and girls different?

Slavery

Slavery was common throughout the ancient world, but no people had more slaves or relied so much on slave labor as the Romans did. Before the third century B.C., a small Roman farmer might possess one or two slaves, who would help farm his few acres and work in the house. These slaves would most likely be from Italy and be regarded as part of the family household. The very rich would have many slaves.

The Use of Slaves The Roman conquest of the Mediterranean brought a drastic change in the use of slaves. Large numbers of foreign peoples who had been captured in different wars were brought back to Italy as slaves.

Greek slaves were in much demand as tutors, musicians, doctors, and artists. Roman businessmen

---

THE WAY IT WAS

SPORTS & CONTESTS

The Gladiatorial Shows

Gladiatorial shows were an important part of Roman society. They took place in public arenas known as amphitheaters (similar in appearance to our modern football stadiums) and were free to the public. The most famous amphitheater was the Colosseum, constructed in Rome to seat fifty thousand people.

Gladiatorial games were held from dawn to dusk. Contests to the death between trained fighters (gladiators) formed the central focus of these games. Most gladiators were slaves or condemned criminals who had been trained for combat in special gladiatorial schools.

Gladiatorial games included other forms of entertainment as well. Criminals of all ages and both sexes were sent into the arena without weapons to face certain death from wild animals. Numerous kinds of animal contests were also held. It is recorded that nine thousand beasts were killed during 100 days of games when the Emperor Titus inaugurated the Colosseum in A.D. 80.

The Colosseum in Rome

would employ them as shop assistants or craftspeople. Many slaves of all nationalities were used as household workers, such as cooks, valets, waiters, cleaners, and gardeners.

Slaves built roads and public buildings, and farmed the large estates of the wealthy. The conditions under which these slaves lived were often pitiful. One Roman writer argued that it was cheaper to work slaves to death and then replace them than to treat them well.

Slave Revolts Some slaves revolted against their owners and even murdered them, causing some Romans to live in great fear of their slaves. The murder of a master by a slave might mean the execution of all the other household slaves.

The most famous slave revolt in Italy occurred in 73 B.C. Led by the gladiator **Spartacus,** the revolt broke out in southern Italy and involved seventy thousand slaves. Spartacus managed to defeat several Roman armies before being trapped and killed in 71 B.C. Six thousand followers of Spartacus were crucified (put to death by nailing to a cross).

✓ **Reading Check** **Describing** What jobs did the Romans assign to slaves?

Daily Life in The City of Rome

At the center of the colossal Roman Empire was the ancient city of **Rome.** Truly a capital city, Rome had the largest population of any city in the empire—close to one million by the time of Augustus. For anyone with ambitions, Rome was the place to be. People from all over the empire resided there.

Living Conditions Rome was an overcrowded and noisy city. Because of the congestion, cart and wagon traffic was banned from the streets during the day. However, the noise from the traffic at night often made sleep difficult. Walking in Rome at night was also dangerous. Augustus had organized a police force, but people could be assaulted or robbed. They could also be soaked by filth thrown out of the upper-story windows of Rome's massive apartment buildings.

An enormous gulf existed between rich and poor. The rich had comfortable villas, while the poor lived in apartment blocks called *insulae,* which might be six stories high. Constructed of concrete walls with wooden beam floors, these buildings were usually poorly built and often collapsed.

Amphitheaters, which varied greatly in size, were built throughout the empire. Many resources and much ingenuity went into building them. In most cities and towns, amphitheaters came to be the biggest buildings, rivaled only by the circuses and the public baths.

Bloody spectacles were indeed popular with the Roman people. The Roman historian Tacitus said, "Few indeed are to be found who talk of any other subjects in their homes, and whenever we enter a classroom, what else is the conversation of the youths."

To the Romans, the gladiatorial games, as well as the other forms of public entertainment, fulfilled a political need. Certainly, the games served to keep the minds of the idle masses off any political unrest.

Gladiators in battle

CONNECTING TO THE PAST

1. **Drawing Conclusions** What was the appeal of gladiatorial contests?

2. **Writing about History** Explain how the games satisfied the ruling class's political purposes.

Bas-relief of chariot races in the Circus Maximus

Fire was a constant threat in the *insulae* because of the use of movable stoves, torches, candles, and lamps within the rooms for heat and light. Once started, fires were extremely difficult to put out. The famous fire of A.D. 64, which Nero was falsely accused of starting, destroyed a good part of the city.

High rents forced entire families to live in one room. There was no plumbing or central heating. These conditions made homes uncomfortable. As a result, many poor Romans spent most of their time outdoors in the streets.

Public Programs Rome boasted public buildings unequaled anywhere in the empire. Its temples, markets, baths, theaters, governmental buildings, and amphitheaters gave parts of the city an appearance of grandeur and magnificence.

Although it was the center of a great empire, Rome had serious problems. Beginning with Augustus, the emperors provided food for the city poor. About two hundred thousand people received free grain. Even so, conditions remained grim for the poor.

Entertainment was provided on a grand scale for the inhabitants of Rome. The poet Juvenal said of the Roman masses, "But nowadays, with no vote . . . , their motto is 'Couldn't care less.' Time was when their vote elected generals, heads of state, commanders of legions: but now. . . there's only two things that concern them: Bread and Circuses."

Public spectacles were provided by the emperor as part of the great religious festivals celebrated by the state. The festivals included three major types of entertainment. At the Circus Maximus, horse and chariot races attracted hundreds of thousands. Dramatic performances were held in theaters. The most famous of all the public spectacles, however, were the gladiatorial shows.

✓ **Reading Check** **Evaluating** Why did the Roman emperors provide free grain to the poor?

TAKS Practice

SECTION 3 ASSESSMENT

Checking for Understanding

1. **Define** paterfamilias, *insulae.*

2. **Identify** Virgil, Horace, Livy, Spartacus.

3. **Locate** Mantua, Rome.

4. **Explain** how the Romans were able to obtain large numbers of slaves. Why did some Romans live in great fear of their slaves?

5. **Compare and contrast** Greek and Roman sculpture. Do you prefer one style over the other? If so, why?

Critical Thinking

6. **Explain** Why do historians not find Livy a reliable source of information?

7. **Summarizing Information** Create a table like the one below describing the contributions of the Greeks and the Romans to Western civilization.

Greek contributions	Roman contributions

Analyzing Visuals

8. **Examine** the photograph of the Pantheon on page 164 of your text. How does it illustrate the architectural innovations of the Romans and the ideas they borrowed from the Greeks?

Writing About History

9. **Expository Writing** In this section there are several excerpts from Roman writers. What does each passage reveal about Roman life and society?

SECTION 4 | The Development of Christianity

Guide to Reading

Main Ideas
- Jesus, a Jew from Palestine, began his public preaching.
- Christianity spread throughout the empire and eventually became the state religion of Rome.

Key Terms
procurator, New Testament, clergy, laity

People to Identify
Jesus, Simon Peter, Paul of Tarsus, Constantine, Theodosius the Great

Places to Locate
Judaea, Jerusalem, Aegean Sea

Preview Questions
1. What religious climate existed in Rome prior to Christianity?
2. Why were Christians persecuted?
3. Why did Christianity grow so quickly?

Reading Strategy
Summarizing Information In the diagram below, identify the political views held by the three groups.

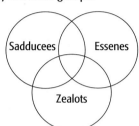

Sadducees — Essenes — Zealots

Preview of Events

◆75 B.C.	◆A.D. 1	◆A.D. 75	◆A.D. 150	◆A.D. 225	◆A.D. 300

A.D. 6
Judaea becomes a Roman province

A.D. 40
The Gospels begin to be written

A.D. 100
Churches are established throughout the Roman world

A.D. 313
Constantine proclaims official tolerance of Christianity

Saint Matthew

Voices from the Past

Christian views on God, human beings, and the world were quite different from those of the Greeks and Romans, as is shown in the Gospel of Matthew:

❝Therefore I tell you, do not worry about your life, what you will eat or drink; or about your body, what you will wear. Is not life more important than food, and the body more important than clothes? . . . So do not worry, saying, What shall we eat? or What shall we drink? or What shall we wear? For the pagans run after all these things, and your heavenly Father knows that you need them. But seek first his kingdom and his righteousness, and all these things will be given to you as well.❞

—*New International Version Bible,* Matthew 6:25–34

The rise of Christianity marked an important break with the dominant values of the Greek and Roman worlds.

Background: Roman Religion

Augustus brought back traditional festivals and ceremonies to revive the Roman state religion, which had declined during the turmoil of the late Roman Republic. The official state religion focused on the worship of a number of gods and goddesses, including Jupiter, Juno, Minerva, and Mars. (In addition, beginning with Augustus, emperors were often officially made gods by the Roman Senate, thus bolstering support for the emperors.)

Greek and Roman Gods

Greek God	Roman God	Role
Ares	Mars	god of war
Zeus	Jupiter	chief god
Hera	Juno	wife of chief god
Aphrodite	Venus	goddess of love
Artemis	Diana	goddess of the hunt
Athena	Minerva	goddess of wisdom
Hermes	Mercury	messenger god
Hades	Pluto	god of the underworld
Poseidon	Neptune	god of the sea
Hephaestus	Vulcan	god of fire

Chart *Skills*

The Romans adopted many of the gods of the peoples they conquered. Eventually the most important gods took on the characteristics of the Greek gods.

1. **Applying Chart Skills** Nike— the Greek goddess of victory—is the name of a sports shoe. What names in the chart do you recognize and what do you associate them with? In your examples, what is the connection to a particular god?

◀ *Minerva*

The Romans believed that the observation of proper ritual by state priests brought them into a right relationship with the gods. This guaranteed peace and prosperity. Indeed, the Romans believed that their success in creating an empire meant that they had earned the favor of the gods. As the politician Cicero claimed in the first century B.C., "We have overcome all the nations of the world, because we have realized that the world is directed and governed by the gods."

At the same time, the Romans were tolerant of other religions. They allowed the worship of native gods and goddesses throughout their provinces. They even adopted some of the local gods.

After the Romans conquered the states of the Hellenistic east, religions from those regions flooded the western Roman world. The desire for a more emotional spiritual experience drew many people to these religions. They promised their followers an entry into a higher world of reality and the promise of a future life superior to the present one. It was believed that, by participating in these ceremonies, a person could communicate with spiritual beings and open the door to life after death.

✓**Reading Check** **Explaining** How were religion and government connected in the Roman Empire?

The Jewish Background

In Hellenistic times, the Jewish people had been given considerable independence. By A.D. 6, however, **Judaea,** which embraced the lands of the old Jewish kingdom of Judah, had been made a Roman province and been placed under the direction of a Roman official called a procurator.

Unrest was widespread in Judaea, but the Jews differed among themselves about Roman rule. The priestly Sadducees (SA·juh·SEEZ) favored cooperation with Rome. The scholarly Pharisees (FA·rah·SEEZ) held that close observance of religious law would protect Jewish identity from Roman influences. The Essenes lived apart from society, sharing goods in common. Like many other Jews, they waited for God to save Israel from oppression. The Zealots, however, called for the violent overthrow of Roman rule. In fact, a Jewish revolt began in A.D. 66, only to be crushed by the Romans four years later. The Jewish temple in **Jerusalem** was destroyed.

✓**Reading Check** **Identifying** Name four of the Jewish groups in Judaea and explain how they differed.

The Rise of Christianity

A few decades before the revolt, a Jewish prophet named Jesus traveled and preached throughout Judaea and neighboring Galilee.

The Message of Jesus Jesus believed that his mission was to complete the salvation that God had promised to Israel throughout its history. He stated:

"Do not think that I have come to abolish the Law or the Prophets; I have not come to abolish them but to fulfill them." According to Jesus, what was important was not strict adherence to the letter of the law but the transformation of the inner person: "So in everything, do to others what you would have them do to you, for this sums up the Law and the Prophets."

God's command was to love God and one another. Jesus said, "Love the Lord your God with all your heart and with all your soul and with all your mind and with all your strength. This is the first commandment. The second is this: Love your neighbor as yourself." Jesus voiced the ethical concepts—humility, charity, and love toward others—that would later shape the value system of Western civilization.

Jesus' preaching eventually stirred controversy. Some people saw Jesus as a potential revolutionary who might lead a revolt against Rome. Jesus' opponents finally turned him over to Roman authorities. The procurator Pontius Pilate ordered Jesus' crucifixion.

After the death of Jesus, his followers proclaimed that he had risen from death and had appeared to them. They believed Jesus to be the Messiah (anointed one), the long expected deliverer who would save Israel from its foes.

The Spread of Christianity Christianity began as a movement within Judaism. After the reports that Jesus had overcome death, the Christian movement won followers in Jerusalem and throughout Judaea and Galilee.

Prominent apostles, or leaders, arose in early Christianity. One was **Simon Peter,** a Jewish fisherman who had become a follower of Jesus during Jesus' lifetime. Peter was recognized as the leader of the apostles. Another major apostle was **Paul,** a highly educated Jewish Roman citizen who joined the movement later. Paul took the message of Jesus to Gentiles (non-Jews) as well as to Jews. He founded Christian communities throughout Asia Minor and along the shores of the **Aegean Sea.**

At the center of Paul's message was the belief that Jesus was the Savior, the Son of God who had come to Earth to save humanity. Paul taught that Jesus' death made up for the sins of all humans. By accepting Jesus as Christ (from *Christos,* the Greek term for Messiah) and Savior, people could be saved from sin and reconciled to God.

The teachings of early Christianity were passed on orally. Written materials also appeared, however. Paul and other followers of Jesus had written letters, or epistles, outlining Christian beliefs for

The Last Supper by Philippe de Champaigne, 1648

Roman mural of Christian disciples

act of treason, punishable by death. The Christians, however, believed there was only one God. To them, the worship of state gods and the emperors meant worshiping false gods and endangering their own salvation.

The Roman government began persecuting (harassing to cause suffering) Christians during the reign of Nero (A.D. 54–68). The emperor blamed the Christians for the fire that destroyed much of Rome and subjected them to cruel deaths. In contrast, in the second century, persecution of Christians diminished. By the end of the reigns of the five good emperors, Christians still represented a small minority, but one of considerable strength.

✔ **Reading Check** **Explaining** Why did the Roman authorities fear Jesus?

communities they had helped found around the eastern Mediterranean. Also, some of Jesus' disciples, or followers, may have preserved some of the sayings of Jesus in writing and passed on personal memories. Later, between A.D. 40 and 100, these accounts became the basis of the written Gospels—the "good news" concerning Jesus. These writings give a record of Jesus' life and teachings, and they form the core of the New Testament, the second part of the Christian Bible.

By 100, Christian churches had been established in most of the major cities of the eastern empire and in some places in the western part of the empire. Most early Christians came from the Jews and the Greek-speaking populations of the east. In the second and third centuries, however, an increasing number of followers were Latin-speaking people.

Roman Persecution The basic values of Christianity differed markedly from those of the Greco-Roman world. In spite of that, the Romans at first paid little attention to the Christians, whom they regarded as simply another sect of Judaism. As time passed, however, the Roman attitude toward Christianity began to change.

The Romans tolerated the religions of other peoples unless these religions threatened public order or public morals. Many Romans came to view Christians as harmful to the Roman state because Christians refused to worship the state gods and emperors. The Romans saw the Christians' refusal to do so as an

The Triumph of Christianity

⌐TURNING POINT¬ **Under Theodosius the Great, who ruled from 378 to 395, the Romans adopted Christianity as the official religion of the Roman Empire.**

The Romans persecuted Christians in the first and second centuries, but this did nothing to stop the growth of Christianity. In fact, it did just the opposite, strengthening Christianity in the second and third

People In History

Perpetua
?–A.D. 203
Christian martyr

Many women found that Christianity offered them new roles. Many also died for their faith. Perpetua was an aristocratic woman who converted to Christianity. Her pagan family begged her to renounce her new faith, but she refused. Arrested by the Roman authorities, she chose instead to die for her faith. She was one of a group of Christians who were slaughtered by wild beasts in the arena at Carthage on March 7, 203. She wrote a diary while she was in prison. The final entry read, "Thus far I have written this, till the day before the games; but the deed of the games themselves let him write who will."

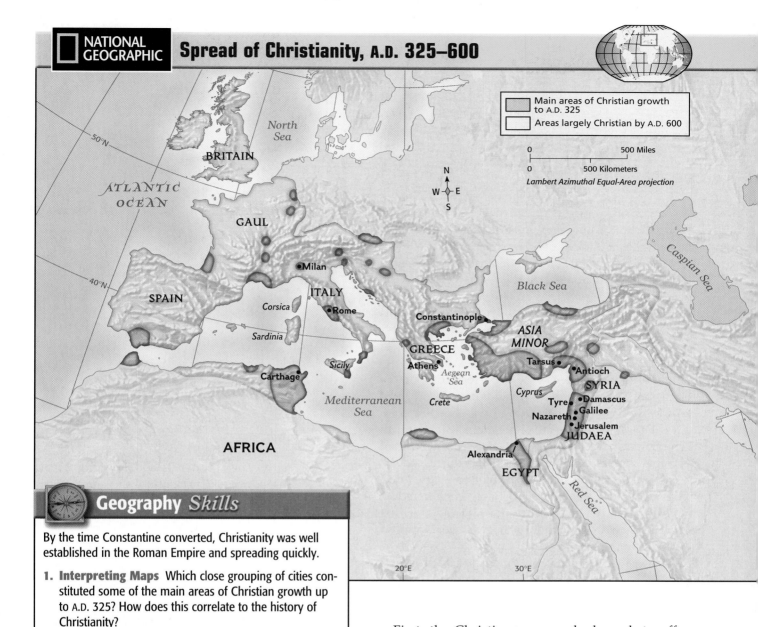

Main areas of Christian growth to A.D. 325

Areas largely Christian by A.D. 600

0   500 Miles
0   500 Kilometers
Lambert Azimuthal Equal-Area projection

Geography *Skills*

By the time Constantine converted, Christianity was well established in the Roman Empire and spreading quickly.

1. **Interpreting Maps** Which close grouping of cities constituted some of the main areas of Christian growth up to A.D. 325? How does this correlate to the history of Christianity?

2. **Applying Geography Skills** What geographical factors both helped and limited the spread of Christianity?

centuries by forcing it to become more organized. Fear of persecution meant that only the most committed individuals would choose to follow the outlawed faith.

Crucial to this change was the emerging role of the bishops, who began to assume more control over church communities. The Christian church was creating a new structure in which the clergy (the church leaders) had distinct functions separate from the laity (the regular church members).

Christianity grew quickly in the first century, took root in the second, and by the third had spread widely. Why was Christianity able to attract so many followers?

First, the Christian message had much to offer the Roman world. The Roman state-based religion was impersonal and existed for the good of Rome. Christianity was personal and offered salvation and eternal life to individuals. Christianity gave meaning and purpose to life.

Second, Christianity seemed familiar. It was viewed by some as similar to other religions, offering immortality as the result of the sacrificial death of a savior-god.

Finally, Christianity fulfilled the human need to belong. Christians formed communities bound to one another. In these communities, people could express their love by helping one another and offering assistance to the poor and the sick. Christianity satisfied the need to belong in a way that the huge Roman Empire could never provide.

Picturing **History**

Early Christians buried their dead in catacombs, underground chambers that sometimes had multiple rooms and levels. This catacomb was built in Rome in the second century. Why might early Christians have wanted an underground sanctuary for their dead?

Christianity proved attractive to all classes, but especially to the poor and powerless. Eternal life was promised to all—rich, poor, aristocrats, slaves, men, and women. As Paul stated in his letters to the Colossians and the Galatians, "And [you] have put on the new self . . . . Here there is no Greek nor Jew . . . barbarian, Scythian, slave or free, but Christ is all, and is in all." Although Christianity did not call for revolution, it stressed a sense of spiritual equality for all people, which was a revolutionary idea.

Some emperors began new persecutions of the Christians in the third century, but their schemes failed. The last great persecution was by Diocletian (DY•uh•KLEE•shuhn) at the beginning of the fourth century. Even he had to admit, however, what had become obvious in the course of the third century: Christianity was too strong to be blotted out by force.

In the fourth century, Christianity prospered as never before when **Constantine** became the first Christian emperor. Although he was not baptized until the end of his life, in 313 Constantine issued the Edict of Milan, which proclaimed official tolerance of Christianity. Then, under **Theodosius the Great,** the Romans adopted Christianity as their official religion.

✓**Reading Check** **Explaining** Why and how did the Christian church become more organized in the second and third centuries?

★**TAKS Practice**

SECTION 4 ASSESSMENT

Checking for Understanding

1. **Define** procurator, New Testament, clergy, laity.

2. **Identify** Jesus, Simon Peter, Paul, Constantine, Theodosius the Great.

3. **Locate** Judaea, Jerusalem, Aegean Sea.

4. **Explain** why the Romans persecuted Christians despite their general religious tolerance.

5. **List** the ethical concepts voiced by Jesus.

Critical Thinking

6. **Drawing Conclusions** Explain why Romans began to accept Christianity and why it took so long for it to be accepted by the state.

7. **Contrasting Information** Use a chart like the one below to contrast the beliefs of the Roman state religion with the beliefs of Christianity.

Roman State Religion	Christianity

Analyzing Visuals

8. **Examine** the photograph of a Roman catacomb shown above. What conclusions can you draw about early Christian practices and beliefs?

Writing About History

9. **Expository Writing** Research reasons why Romans thought Christianity was dangerous to their empire. Compare these arguments to actual Christian doctrine and practices. Present your findings in a carefully prepared essay. Show that your sources corroborate your position.

Decline and Fall

Main Ideas
- Under two strong emperors, Diocletian and Constantine, the Roman Empire gained a new lease on life.
- Ferocious warriors from Asia and Germany finally brought an end to the Roman Empire.

Key Terms
plague, inflation

People to Identify
Diocletian, Constantine, Huns, Visigoths, Vandals, Romulus Augustulus

Places to Identify
Byzantium, Bosporus, Danube River

Preview Questions
1. How did Diocletian and Constantine restore order and stability to the Roman Empire?
2. What became of the Roman Empire after it was divided into two parts?

Reading Strategy
Cause and Effect Complete a chart describing the events that led to the decline and fall of the Roman Empire.

Decline	Fall

Preview of Events

◆A.D. 200	◆A.D. 300	◆A.D. 400	◆A.D. 500

A.D. 193
Severan rule starts

A.D. 235
Military leaders begin to seize throne

A.D. 410
The Visigoths sack Rome

A.D. 476
Deposition of Emperor Romulus Augustulus marks the end of the Western Roman Empire

Jerome

Voices from the Past

In A.D. 410, the unthinkable happened. The city of Rome was sacked by a German tribe, the Visigoths. The scholar Jerome responded in disbelief:

❝A terrible rumor had arrived from the West. Rome is besieged. . . . The City is taken which took the whole world. It had perished of famine before it died by the sword, and only a few captives were found. [As Virgil said in the *Aeneid:*]

What tongue can tell the slaughter of that night?

What eyes can weep the sorrows and affright?

An ancient and imperial city falls.❞

—*Jerome, Letters,* **J. Hillgarth, trans., 1986**

The Western Roman Empire would fall before the end of the century.

The Decline

Marcus Aurelius, the last of the five good emperors, died in A.D. 180. A period of conflict and confusion followed.

Political Upheavals Following a series of civil wars, a military government under the Severan rulers restored order. Septimius Severus told his sons "to pay the soldiers, and ignore everyone else," setting the tone for the new dynasty. After the Severan rulers there was a period of disorder. For almost fifty years, from 235 to 284, the Roman throne was occupied by whoever had military strength to seize it. During this period there were 22 emperors. Many of these emperors met a violent death.

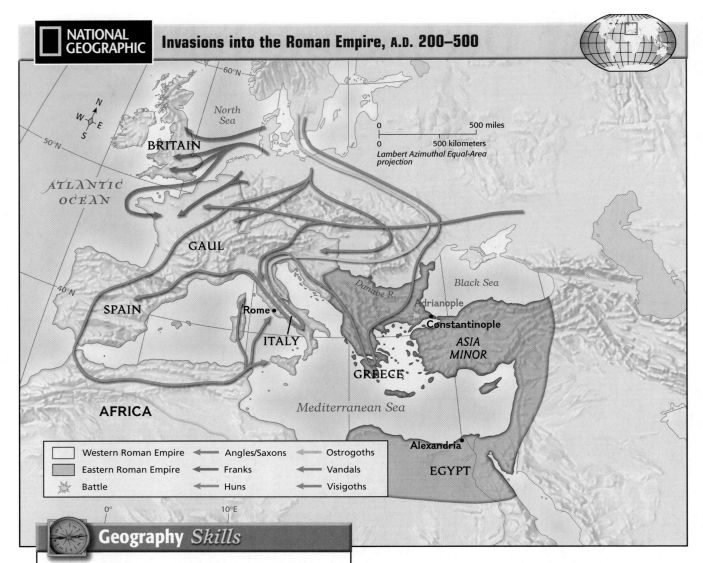

Geography *Skills*

Contributing to the fall of the Roman Empire were invasions that pressed in on all sides of the empire.

1. **Interpreting Maps** Which group of invaders made the most limited incursions?

2. **Applying Geography Skills** Which parts of the Roman Empire seem to have been more secure from the invasion? Why do you think this was?

At the same time, the empire was troubled by a series of invasions. In the east, the Sassanid (suh•SAH•nuhd) Persians made inroads into Roman territory. Germanic tribes poured into the Balkans, Gaul, and Spain. Not until the end of the third century were most of the boundaries restored.

Economic and Military Problems Invasions, civil wars, and plague came close to causing an economic collapse of the Roman Empire in the third century. There was a noticeable decline in trade and small industry. A labor shortage created by plague (an epidemic disease) affected both military recruiting and the economy. Farm production declined as fields were ravaged by invaders or, even more often, by the defending Roman armies. The monetary system began to show signs of collapse.

Armies were needed more than ever, but financial strains made it difficult to pay and enlist more soldiers. By the mid-third century, the state had to rely on hiring Germans to fight under Roman commanders. These soldiers did not understand Roman traditions and had little loyalty to either the empire or the emperors.

The Reforms of Diocletian and Constantine At the end of the third and the beginning of the fourth centuries, the Roman Empire gained a new lease on life through the efforts of two emperors, **Diocletian** and **Constantine.** The empire was changed into a new state: the Late Roman Empire, which included a new governmental structure, a rigid economic and social system, and a new state religion—Christianity.

Believing that the empire had grown too large for a single ruler, Diocletian, who ruled from 284 to 305, divided it into four units, each with its own ruler. Diocletian's military power still enabled him to claim a higher status and to hold the ultimate authority. Constantine, who ruled from 306 to 337, continued and even expanded the policies of Diocletian.

Both rulers greatly strengthened and enlarged the administrative bureaucracies of the Roman Empire. A hierarchy of officials exercised control at the various levels of government. The army was enlarged to five hundred thousand men, including German troops. Mobile units were established to support frontier troops at threatened borders.

The political and military reforms of Diocletian and Constantine greatly enlarged two institutions—the army and civil service—which drained most of the public funds. More revenues were needed to pay for the army and bureaucracy. The population was not growing, however, so the tax base could not be increased.

Diocletian and Constantine devised new economic and social policies to deal with these financial burdens. To fight inflation—a rapid increase in prices—Diocletian issued a price edict in 301 that set wage and price controls for the entire empire. Despite severe penalties, it failed to work.

To ensure the tax base and keep the empire going despite the shortage of labor, the emperors issued edicts that forced people to remain in their designated vocations. Hence, basic jobs, such as bakers and shippers, became hereditary. The fortunes of free tenant farmers also declined. Soon they found themselves bound to the land by large landowners who took advantage of depressed agricultural conditions to enlarge their landed estates.

Constantine began his reign in 306, and by 324 he had emerged as the sole ruler of the empire. Constantine's biggest project was the construction of a new capital city in the east, on the site of the Greek city of **Byzantium** on the shores of the **Bosporus.** The city, eventually renamed Constantinople (modern Istanbul in Turkey), was developed for defensive reasons and had an excellent

Relief showing Roman tax collectors

strategic location. Calling it his "New Rome," Constantine enriched the city with a forum, large palaces, and a vast amphitheater. Constantinople would become the center of the Eastern Roman Empire and one of the great cities of the world.

In general, the economic and social policies of Diocletian and Constantine were based on control and coercion. Although temporarily successful, such policies in the long run stifled the very vitality the Late Empire needed to revive its sagging fortunes.

Reading Check **Describing** Describe the economic and social conditions in the Roman Empire prior to Diocletian and Constantine.

The Fall

The restored empire of Diocletian and Constantine limped along for more than a century. After Constantine, the empire continued to be divided into western and eastern parts. The capital of the Western Roman Empire remained in Rome. Constantinople remained the capital of the Eastern Roman Empire. The Western Roman Empire came under increasing pressure from the invading Germanic tribes. The major breakthrough of invaders into the west came in the second half of the fourth century. The **Huns,** who came from Asia, moved into eastern Europe and put pressure on the Germanic **Visigoths.** The Visigoths, in turn, moved south and west, crossed the **Danube River** into Roman territory, and settled down as Roman allies. However, the Visigoths soon revolted. The Romans' attempt to stop the revolt at Adrianople in 378 led to a crushing defeat for the Romans.

Increasing numbers of Germans now crossed the frontiers. In 410, the Visigoths sacked Rome. Another group, the **Vandals,** poured into southern Spain and Africa. They crossed into Italy from northern Africa and, in 455, they too sacked Rome. (Our modern word *vandal* is taken from this ruthless tribe.)

In 476, the western emperor, **Romulus Augustulus,** was deposed by the Germanic head of the army. This is usually taken as the date of the fall of the Western Roman Empire. As we shall see in Chapter 9, a series of German kingdoms replaced the Western Roman Empire. The Eastern Roman Empire, or the Byzantine Empire, however, continued to thrive with its center at Constantinople.

Emperor Constantine

Many theories have been proposed to explain the decline and fall of the Roman Empire. They include the following:

- Christianity's emphasis on a spiritual kingdom weakened Roman military virtues.
- Traditional Roman values declined as non-Italians gained prominence in the empire.
- Lead poisoning through leaden water pipes and cups caused a mental decline in the population.
- Plague wiped out one-tenth of the population.
- Rome failed to advance technologically because of slavery.
- Rome was unable to put together a workable political system.

There may be an element of truth in each of these theories, but each has also been challenged. History is an intricate web of relationships, causes, and effects. No single explanation can sufficiently explain complex historical events, such as the fall of a great empire.

For example, both the Han dynasty in China and the Roman Empire lasted for centuries. Both of these empires were able to govern large areas of land effectively. They instituted and maintained laws and a language. In spite of their attempts at unifying conquered territories, both empires experienced problems that came from acquiring so much land. Both tried to protect their borders with walls, forts, and troops. Both, however, eventually fell to invaders. The Han dynasty fell to the Xiongnu. The Roman army in the west was not able to fend off the hordes of people invading Italy and Gaul, and the Western Roman Empire fell. In contrast, the Eastern Roman Empire, which would survive for another thousand years, was able to withstand invaders.

✓ **Reading Check** **Identifying** Which groups invaded the Western Roman Empire?

🟥 TAKS Practice

SECTION 5 ASSESSMENT

Checking for Understanding

1. **Define** plague, inflation.

2. **Identify** Diocletian, Constantine, Huns, Visigoths, Vandals, Romulus Augustulus.

3. **Locate** Byzantium, Bosporus, Danube River.

4. **Explain** why the decline in population was so harmful to the Roman Empire.

5. **List** the economic and military problems that contributed to the decline of the Roman Empire.

Critical Thinking

6. **Evaluate** Summarize the theories about why the Roman Empire fell and then tell why some theories seem more possible than others.

7. **Summarizing Information** Create a chart like the one below to list ways that Diocletian and Constantine strengthened the Roman Empire.

Diocletian	Constantine

Analyzing Visuals

8. **Examine** the relief of Roman tax collectors shown on page 177 of your text. What do you think each of the people depicted in the image is doing?

Writing About History

9. **Persuasive Writing** Imagine you are the adviser to a benevolent Roman emperor. Write a letter to the emperor describing the steps he should take to preserve the Roman Empire.

CRITICAL THINKING
SKILLBUILDER

TAKS Practice

Making Decisions

Why Learn This Skill?

A decision is a choice you make from among two or more alternatives. For instance, when choosing which elective class to take, how will you decide? What if you are equally interested in taking computer graphics and band? Following the steps below will help you make more thoughtful decisions.

Learning the Skill

To make decisions more easily, follow the steps below.

- **State the situation or define the problem** Gather all the facts. Ask: Why do I have to make a decision on this matter? Whom will my decision affect? *In the example above, you can only take one elective, so you need to make a choice.*

- **List the options** Ask: What are the alternatives? How can I deal with this situation in a different way? *Is there any way to take both electives? If only one fit your schedule, it would be an easier choice. Can you take one of them at some other time?*

- **Weigh the possible outcomes** What are the positive or negative effects of each? *Which would be more interesting for you? Which would be more useful when you graduate? Which would look more impressive on your college application?*

- **Consider your values** Values are the beliefs and ideas that are important to you. Your values should serve as your guidelines in making all decisions. *You love music, but feel you have to be practical and take the computer class. What is more important to you?*

- **Make a decision and act** Use all the information gathered to make a decision. Then act on your decision. *You decide that this might be your last*

Augustus Caesar

chance to take band. You decide to take computer graphics at the local junior college this summer.

- **Evaluate the decision** Ask: How did the outcome affect you and others? Would you make the same decision again? Why or why not? *If you had taken computer graphics, you would be working at a software company. Instead you play with a jazz band at night and could not be happier.*

Practicing the Skill

Decisions affect not just your daily life, they affect the outcome of history. Each of the following events took place as a result of a decision made by a person or a group of people. Think of an alternative for each event and describe its possible consequences.

❶ During the Third Punic War, in 146 B.C., the Romans burned Carthage.

❷ In 27 B.C., Augustus Caesar became Rome's first emperor.

❸ Roman persecution of Christians in the second and third centuries did nothing to stop the growth of Christianity.

❹ The Emperor Theodosius made Christianity the official religion of the Roman Empire.

Applying the Skill

Read newspapers for articles about an event that affects your community, such as a decision whether or not to tear down a historic landmark to build a new shopping mall. Make a decision about how you would handle the situation. Explain your reasoning.

Glencoe's **Skillbuilder Interactive Workbook, Level 2,** provides instruction and practice in key social studies skills.

Using Key Terms

1. Cases of civil law were applied to citizens and later to non-citizens by judges who were called _____.

2. The term _____ refers to the idea in Roman society that males should be dominant because females were too weak.

3. In the Roman Republic, two _____ ran the government and led the Roman army into battle.

4. Judaea became a Roman province under the direction of an official called a _____.

5. _____ housed the poor in the city of Rome.

6. Caesar, Crassus, and Pompey formed a powerful governmental coalition called the _____ .

Chapter Summary

The history of ancient Rome was a series of causes and effects.

Cause	Effect
Rome defeats Carthage and takes Sicily.	Hannibal brings the Second Punic War into Italy, defeating the Romans at Cannae.
Marius recruits armies by promising them land. He requires an oath of loyalty to him.	The Roman army is no longer under government control; military power rests in the hands of individual generals.
Sulla uses his army to seize governmental power.	Sulla restores power to the government with a strong Senate, but his actions set the precedent for military coups.
Julius Caesar fills the Senate with his own supporters.	The power of the Senate is weakened. Julius Caesar is assassinated in 44 B.C.
Economic and social policies of Diocletian and Constantine are based on control and coercion.	The policies of these two emperors contribute to the empire's eventual collapse.

7. The writings recording Jesus' life and teachings form the core of the _____.

8. The _____ in the Christian church were officials who were separate from regular church members called the _____ .

9. _____ were Roman citizens who wanted political and social equality with the wealthy _____.

10. An epidemic disease that kills thousands is known as a _____.

11. Augustus was a popular ruler who was given the title of _____ , or commander in chief, by the Senate.

12. A form of government in which the leader is not a monarch and certain citizens have the right to vote is called a _____.

Reviewing Key Facts

13. **Geography** List at least three ways in which geography influenced Roman history.

14. **History** Why were the Etruscans considered to be the greatest influence on early Rome?

15. **Government** Who were the patricians and plebeians and why were they in conflict with each other?

16. **Citizenship** Describe the different roles of citizens and non-citizens in the Roman Empire, especially as the roles pertain to civic participation.

17. **History** Who was Hannibal, what happened to him, and why was he important?

18. **Economics** What factors contributed to the high level of trade in the Early Empire?

19. **Science and Technology** Identify new ideas in technology that occurred during the Greco-Roman civilization.

20. **Culture** Name three famous Roman writers. Name their works and explain why these works are important.

Critical Thinking

21. **Compare and Contrast** Compare the historical origins, central ideas, and the spread of Buddhism and Christianity.

22. **Drawing Conclusions** Identify the ways in which the Romans preserved the intellectual heritage of the Greek world.

Writing About History

23. **Expository Writing** Find a picture of Roman architecture. Discuss how it demonstrates Roman culture, including potential influence from other cultures. In what ways do archaeologists and anthropologists analyze Roman culture, based on the limited remains of architecture and artifacts? Justify your answer with outside research.

HISTORY *Online*

Self-Check Quiz
Visit the *Glencoe World History* Web site at tx.wh.glencoe.com and click on **Chapter 5–Self-Check Quiz** to prepare for the Chapter Test.

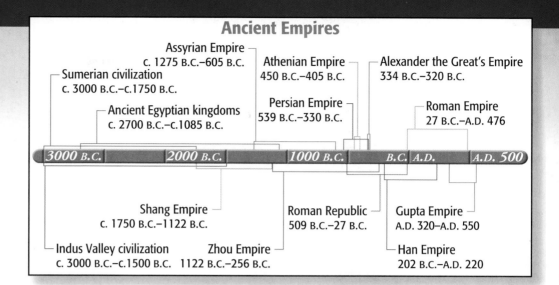

Ancient Empires

Assyrian Empire
c. 1275 B.C.–605 B.C.

Sumerian civilization
c. 3000 B.C.–c.1750 B.C.

Athenian Empire
450 B.C.–405 B.C.

Alexander the Great's Empire
334 B.C.–320 B.C.

Ancient Egyptian kingdoms
c. 2700 B.C.–c.1085 B.C.

Persian Empire
539 B.C.–330 B.C.

Roman Empire
27 B.C.–A.D. 476

3000 B.C.　**2000 B.C.**　**1000 B.C.**　**B.C. A.D.**　**A.D. 500**

Shang Empire
c. 1750 B.C.–1122 B.C.

Roman Republic
509 B.C.–27 B.C.

Gupta Empire
A.D. 320–A.D. 550

Indus Valley civilization
c. 3000 B.C.–c.1500 B.C.

Zhou Empire
1122 B.C.–256 B.C.

Han Empire
202 B.C.–A.D. 220

Analyzing Sources

Read the following poem by Virgil, and answer the questions.

> ❝Let others fashion from bronze more lifelike, breathing images—
>
> For so they shall—and evoke living faces from marble;
>
> Others excel as orators, others track with their instruments
>
> The planet circling in heaven and predict when stars will appear.
>
> But, Romans, never forget that government is your medium!
>
> Be this your art: to practise men in the habit of peace,
>
> Generosity to the conquered, and firmness against aggressors.❞

24. What did the poet feel was Rome's gift? Who are the "others" mentioned in the poem?

25. How does this poem summarize the fundamental ideas of Western civilization that originated in Rome?

Applying Technology Skills

26. Using the Internet Use the Internet and other resources to research the Twelve Tables. Design a similar code of laws using modern-day language.

Making Decisions

27. Pretend you are in a public forum in Rome. In class, debate with another citizen the extent to which the gulf between the patricians and plebeians is straining the Roman Empire. Together, decide on measures that could provide stability to the government and the empire as a whole.

Analyzing Maps and Charts

Study the chart above that shows various empires of the ancient world. Then answer the following questions.

28. Which lasted longer, the Roman Republic or the Zhou Empire?

29. How long did the Roman civilization last? Which lasted longer, the Roman Republic or the Roman Empire?

30. Which empires overlap the Roman period?

31. Is there any correlation between the length of an empire's existence and its impact on later civilizations?

32. Which empire lasted the shortest time period, and which lasted the longest?

The Princeton Review

TAKS Test Practice

Directions: Choose the best answer to the following question.

One lasting contribution of the Roman Empire was

A the idea of the Triumvirate.

B the Christian church.

C the gladiatorial shows.

D its system of law.

Test-Taking Tip: Do not pick an answer just because it sounds good. Sometimes a choice is deliberately meant to sound correct but is not. Read all of the answer choices very carefully before you select the best one and avoid making any hasty decisions.

WORLD LITERATURE

from the Iliad

By Homer, translated by Samuel Butler

Homer is probably one of the best known figures to have emerged from Greek antiquity. Writing in the eighth century B.C., Homer's most famous works are the *Odyssey* and the *Iliad*. These works mark the beginnings of what we know as Greek literature and are used as models even in contemporary work. The *Iliad* is the story of the Trojan War, and the *Odyssey* recounts the challenges of one Greek hero, Odysseus (also known as "Ulysses"), in returning to his homeland.

Read to Discover

In the *Iliad,* Hektor was the Trojans' hero and son of King Priam. Achilles, the Greeks' hero, was the son of Peleus. Hektor killed Achilles' friend Patroklos, and Achilles was determined to avenge the death. What language does Homer use to show Hektor's and Achilles' feelings about each other? Do you see evidence of the heroic tradition in this passage?

Reader's Dictionary

covenant: a binding agreement or promise

spoil: to plunder from an enemy in war

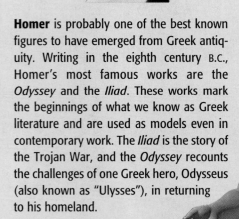

Hektor was first to speak. "I will no longer flee you, son of Peleus," said he, "as I have been doing hitherto. . . .[Let] me either slay or be slain, for I am in the mind to face you. Let us, then, give pledges to one another by our gods; . . . [that if] I take your life, I am not to treat your dead body in any unseemly fashion, but when I have stripped you of your armor, I am to give up your body to the Achaeans, And do you likewise."

Achilles glared at him and answered, "Fool . . . [there] can be no covenants between men and lions, wolves and lambs can never be of one mind, but hate each other out and out . . . . Therefore there can be no understanding between you and me . . . till one or other shall fall. . . . You have no more chance, and Pallas Athena will forthwith vanquish you by my spear: you shall now pay me in full for the grief you have caused me on account of my comrades whom you have killed in battle."

He poised his spear as he spoke and hurled it. Hektor saw it coming and avoided it; he watched it and crouched down so that it flew over his head and stuck in the ground beyond; Athena then snatched it up and gave it back to Achilles without Hektor's seeing her; Hektor thereon said . . . "You have missed your aim, Achilles. . . . [And] now for your own part avoid

◄ *Athena*

my spear if you can—would that you might receive the whole of it into your body; if you were once dead the Trojans would find the war an easier matter, for it is you who have harmed them most."
He poised his spear as he spoke and hurled it. His aim was sure for he hit the middle of Achilles' shield, but the spear rebounded from it, and did not pierce it. Hektor was angry when he saw that the weapon had sped from his hand in vain, and stood there in dismay for he had no second spear . . . . [Then] he said to himself, "Alas! The gods have lured me on to my destruction . . . . [Death] is now indeed exceedingly near at hand and there is no way out of it . . . . My doom has come upon me; let me not then die ingloriously and without a struggle, but let me first do some great thing that shall be told among men hereafter."
As he spoke he drew the keen blade that hung so great and strong by his side, and gathering himself together he sprang on Achilles . . . . Achilles mad with rage darted towards him . . . . He eyed [Hektor's] fair flesh over and over to see where he could best wound it, but all was protected by the goodly armor of which Hektor had spoiled Patroklos after he had slain him, save only the throat where the collar-bones divide the neck from the shoulders, and this is the quickest place for the life-breath to escape: here then did Achilles strike him as he was coming on towards him, and the point of his spear went right through the fleshy part of the neck, but it did not sever his windpipe so that he could still speak. Hektor fell headlong, and Achilles vaunted over him saying, "Hektor, you deemed that you should come off scatheless when you were spoiling Patroklos . . . . Fool that you were: for I, his comrade, mightier far than he, was still left behind him at the ships, and now I have laid you low. The Achaeans

shall give him all due funeral rites, while dogs and vultures shall work their will upon yourself."
Then Hektor said, as the life-breath ebbed out of him, "I pray you . . . , let not dogs devour me at the ships of the Achaeans, but accept the rich treasure of gold and bronze which my father and mother will offer you, and send my body home, that the Trojans and their wives may give me my dues of fire when I am dead."
Achilles glared at him and answered, "Dog . . . [though] Priam . . . should bid them offer me your weight in gold, even so your mother shall never lay you out and make lament over the son she bore, but dogs and vultures shall eat you utterly up."
Hektor with his dying breath then said, "I know you what you are, and was sure that I should not move you, for your heart is hard as iron . . . ."
When he had thus said the shrouds of death's final outcome enfolded him, whereon his life-breath went out of him and flew down to the house of Hades, lamenting its sad fate that it should enjoy youth and strength no longer.

Interpreting World Literature

1. How does Achilles plan to avenge his friend Patroklos' death beyond killing Hektor?

2. Who is Athena supporting in this conflict?

3. Explain Achilles' concern with Hektor's armor.

4. **CRITICAL THINKING** What does Hektor's last request reveal about Greek attitudes towards death?

Applications Activity
Outline a story for a modern epic. Who would be your hero and why?

UNIT
2 New Patterns of Civilization

400–1500

The Period in Perspective

By the beginning of the first millennium A.D., the great states of the ancient world were mostly in decline. On the ruins of these ancient empires, new patterns of civilization began to take shape. Some of these new societies built upon elements of earlier civilizations, even as they moved in unique directions.

At the same time, between 400 and 1500, new civilizations were beginning to appear in a number of other parts of the world—Japan, Southeast Asia, Africa, and the Americas. Like earlier states, most of these civilizations obtained much of their wealth from farming. More striking, however, is that these societies were being increasingly linked through trade.

Primary Sources Library

See pages 992–993 for primary source readings to accompany Unit 2.

💿 *Use The World History **Primary Source Document Library CD-ROM** to find additional primary sources about New Patterns of Civilization.*

▲ Mayan sculpture

▶ Ruins at Chichén Itzá

"*Let there be dawn in the sky and on the earth.*"

—Mayan myth

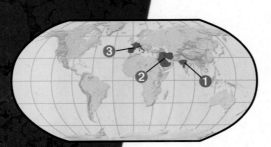

Mathematics

The invention of mathematics changed the course of civilization. Astronomers used mathematics to account for the movements of the sun and moon so they could mark the seasons. Geometry enabled people to calculate the volume of a cylindrical granary. Mathematics supported travel, from the earliest sea travel to the development of the space program. It all began with the Sumerians.

3000 B.C.
Sumerians record numbers on clay tablets

572–212 B.C.
Greeks develop geometric principles

❶ *Indus Valley*

The Use of Numerals

In order to keep accurate records and inventories, the Sumerians, around 3000 B.C., devised one of the world's earliest numbering systems. They used two wedge-like symbols for counting. One symbol stood for 1, the other for 10. These wedge-like symbols—and others that followed—basically came from the Sumerian cuneiform. The wedges served double duty, for they symbolized both words and figures.

Other early peoples who invented numbering systems used letters from their alphabets. Then, around A.D. 500, Hindu people in the Indus River valley abandoned the use of letters and created special number symbols to stand for the figures 1 to 9. Although modernized over time, these nine Hindu symbols are the ones we use today.

Sumerian cuneiform tablet

to See Ahead

al-Khowarizmi

❷ Southwest Asia

The Rise of Algebra

About A.D. 825, an Arab mathematician, al-Khowarizmi of Baghdad, wrote books showing ways to use the Hindu numbering system. *Algebra* comes from *al-jabra*, which he used in the title of his book *al-jabr w'al-muqabalah*, roughly meaning "bringing together unknowns to match a known quantity."

The wonder of the system caught Arab imaginations. They especially liked the concept of zero, which had also been created by the Hindus. With the use of zero, mathematicians could build numbers of astronomical size.

A.D. 500
In India, Hindus create a number system with zero

A.D. 825
Al-Khowarizmi advances the use of Hindu numbers and algebra in the Arab world

A.D. 1202
Leonardo Fibonacci, an Italian merchant, spreads al-Khowarizmi's work to Europe

❸ Europe

The Triumph of Arabic Numerals

Muslims ruled parts of Spain from the A.D. 700s to the A.D. 1400s. Their presence opened the door for European use of the new Hindu-Arabic number system. At first, many Europeans rejected it. They clung instead to Roman numerals.

Later, however, European merchants found knowledge of "Arabic numerals," as they were called, necessary for dealing with merchants in Muslim ports. Influenced by al-Khowarizmi's work, Leonardo Fibonacci published, in 1202, a book of arithmetic and algebraic information. Europeans who learned the new arithmetic also found it easier to do their tallies. By the A.D. 1400s, the numbers could even be found in popular art.

European wool merchants

Why It Matters

Early arithmetic was used at first for business transactions and simple calculations that were part of daily life. How did mathematics make it possible for fifteenth- and sixteenth-century explorers to voyage into unknown regions?

187

CHAPTER 6

The World of Islam

600–1500

Key Events

- *Muhammad and his followers spread the beliefs and practices of Islam.*
- *At its peak, the Arab Empire extended west and north through Spain and into France.*
- *In the seventh century, a split in Islam created two groups, the Shiite and the Sunni Muslims.*

The Impact Today

- *More than one billion people around the world are Muslims who follow the teachings of the Quran, and Islam is one of the world's leading faiths.*
- *The cultural, artistic, and scientific contributions of Muslims continue to enrich our daily lives.*

World History Video *The Chapter 6 video, "Islamic Scientific Advances," chronicles the many contributions of Islamic culture to our world.*

Prayer rug

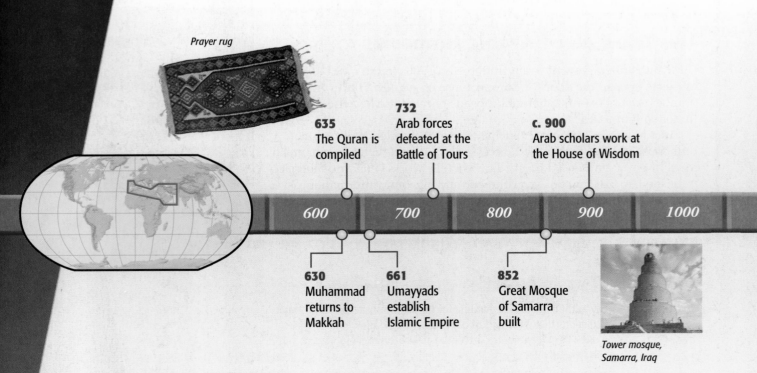

635
The Quran is compiled

732
Arab forces defeated at the Battle of Tours

c. 900
Arab scholars work at the House of Wisdom

600   *700*   *800*   *900*   *1000*

630
Muhammad returns to Makkah

661
Umayyads establish Islamic Empire

852
Great Mosque of Samarra built

Tower mosque, Samarra, Iraq

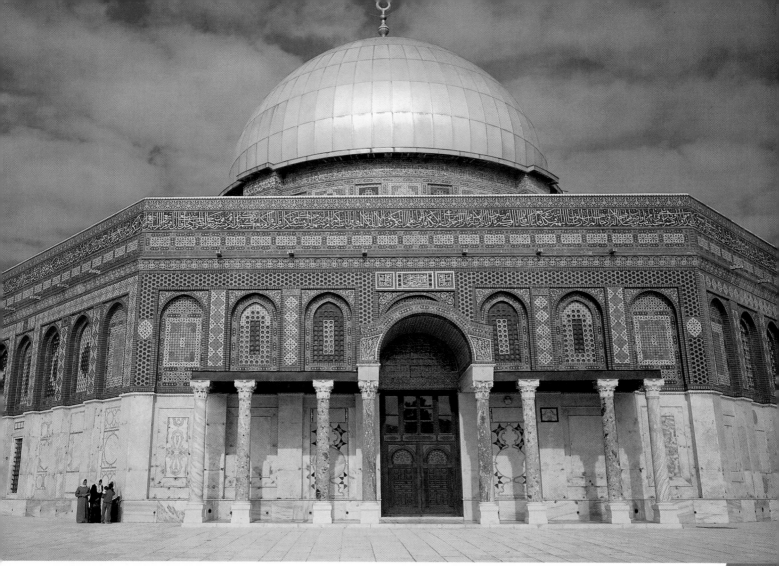

The Dome of the Rock in Jerusalem was built by Muslims in the seventh century. Muslims believe that Muhammad ascended into Paradise from this site.

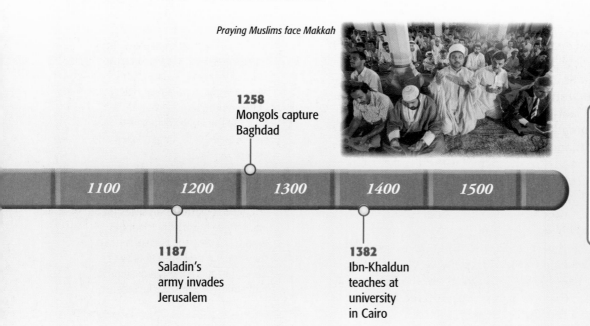

Praying Muslims face Makkah

1258
Mongols capture Baghdad

| 1100 | 1200 | 1300 | 1400 | 1500 |

1187
Saladin's army invades Jerusalem

1382
Ibn-Khaldun teaches at university in Cairo

HISTORY
Online

Chapter Overview
Visit the *Glencoe World History* Web site at tx.wh.glencoe.com and click on **Chapter 6–Chapter Overview** to preview chapter information.

A Story That Matters

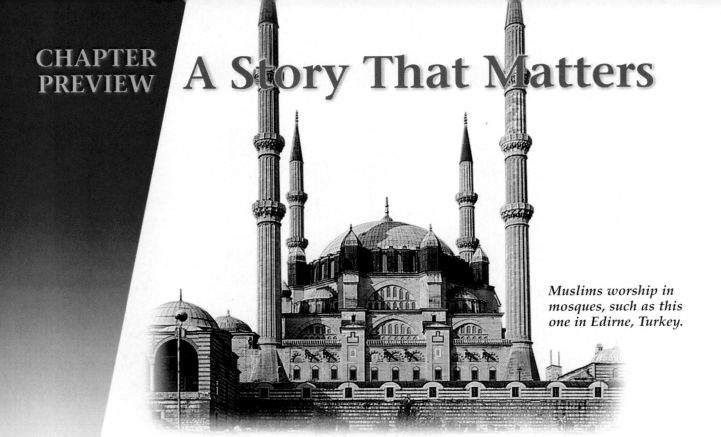

Muslims worship in mosques, such as this one in Edirne, Turkey.

Muhammad's Message

*I*n Makkah, a small town of about three thousand people located in the desert lands of the Arabian Peninsula, a man named Muhammad was born in 570. His father died when he was not yet one; and his mother died when he was only five. He was raised by relatives, from whom he learned how to buy, sell, and transport goods. Intelligent and hardworking, he became a capable merchant. He married, had children, and seemed to have a happy and rewarding life.

Muhammad, however, was not content. Deeply disturbed by problems in society, he spent days on end in a nearby cave, praying and meditating. According to Islamic teachings, one night in 610, while Muhammad was deep in meditation, the voice of the angel Gabriel called out, "Recite!" The voice repeated the proclamation twice more.

A frightened Muhammad replied, "What shall I recite?"

The angel responded, "In the name of thy Lord the Creator, who created mankind from a clot of blood, recite!"

Over the next 23 years, Muhammad received and memorized everything the angel revealed and preached these words to others: "Allah will bring to nothing the deeds of those who disbelieve. . . . As for the faithful who do good works and believe in what is revealed to Muhammad—which is the truth from their Lord—He will forgive them their sins and ennoble their state." These words were gathered together as the Quran, or Koran, the sacred book of Islam.

Why It Matters

Muhammad's life had a lasting impact on world history. When he was born, Southwest Asia was ruled by two competing empires: the Byzantine and the Sassanid Persian. After Muhammad's death, his successors organized the Arabs and began a great expansion. Arab armies marched westward across North Africa and eastward into Mesopotamia and Persia, creating a new empire that stretched from Spain to the Indus River valley. Arab rule brought with it the religion and culture of Islam.

History and You Create a multimedia presentation illustrating the scientific and artistic advances that were made during the Islamic Empire. Show your presentation to the class. Be prepared to answer questions about the Islamic innovations that you chose to include.

SECTION 1 The Rise of Islam

Guide to Reading

Main Ideas
- In the fifth and sixth centuries, the Arabian Peninsula took on a new importance as a result of the caravan trade.
- The religion of Islam arose in the Arabian Peninsula, and its prophet was a man named Muhammad.

Key Terms
sheikh, Quran, Islam, *Hijrah*, hajj, *shari'ah*

People to Identify
Muhammad, Bedouins, Khadija, Muslims

Places to Locate
Arabian Peninsula, Makkah, Madinah

Preview Questions
1. What was the role of Muhammad in the spread of Islam?
2. What are the major beliefs and principles of the religion of Islam?

Reading Strategy
Summarizing Information Create a diagram like the one below to list the main characteristics of the Islamic religion. Your diagram can list more characteristics than this example.

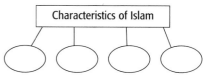

Characteristics of Islam

Preview of Events

◆550	◆575	◆600	◆625	◆650

570
Muhammad is born

610
Muhammad receives the first message

622
Muhammad and his followers journey to Madinah, a journey known as the *Hijrah*

630
The people of Makkah convert to Islam

632
Muhammad dies

Voices from the Past

Arabic illustration of angels

Allah speaks to Muslims through the Quran:

❝God had helped you at Badr, when you were a contemptible little band. So fear God and thus show your gratitude. Remember when you said to the Believers: 'Is it not enough for you that your Lord helped you with 3,000 angels sent down? Yes, and if you remain firm and aright, even if the enemy should come against you here in hot haste, your Lord would help you with 5,000 angels on the attack.'❞

—*Muhammad and the Origins of Islam*, **F.E. Peters, 1994**

From ancient times, Southwest Asia has been the site of great empires. In the seventh century, a new empire was being built by the Arabs—a people who believed that their efforts were aided by Allah.

The Arabs

Like the Hebrews and the Assyrians, the Arabs were a Semitic-speaking people who lived in the **Arabian Peninsula**, a desert land sorely lacking in rivers and lakes. The Arabs were nomads who, because of their hostile surroundings, moved constantly to find water and food for their animals.

Survival in such a harsh environment was not easy, and the Arabs organized into tribes to help one another. Each tribe was ruled by a sheikh (SHAYK) who was chosen from one of the leading families by a council of elders. Although each tribe was independent, all the tribes in the region were loosely connected to one another.

The Arabs lived as farmers and sheepherders on the oases and rain-fed areas of the Arabian Peninsula. After the camel was domesticated in the first millennium B.C., the Arabs populated more of the desert. They also expanded the caravan trade into these regions. Towns developed along the routes as the Arabs became major carriers of goods between the Indian Ocean and the Mediterranean, where the Silk Road ended.

Most early Arabs were polytheistic—they believed in many gods. The Arabs trace their ancestors to Abraham and his son Ishmael, who were believed to have built at **Makkah** (Mecca) the Kaaba (KAH• buh), a house of worship whose cornerstone was a sacred stone, called the Black Stone. The Arabs recognized a supreme god named **Allah** (*Allah* is Arabic for "God"), but they also believed in other tribal gods. They revered the Kaaba for its association with Abraham.

The Arabian Peninsula took on a new importance when political disorder in Mesopotamia and Egypt made the usual trade routes in Southwest Asia too dangerous to travel. A safer trade route that went through Makkah to present-day Yemen and then by ship across the Indian Ocean became more popular.

Communities along this route, such as Makkah, prospered from the increased caravan trade. Tensions arose, however, as increasingly wealthy merchants showed less and less concern for the welfare of their poorer clanspeople and slaves.

Reading Check **Explaining** Why did the communities on the Arabian Peninsula prosper?

The Life of Muhammad

Into this world of tension stepped **Muhammad.** Born in Makkah to a merchant family, he became an orphan at the age of five. He grew up to become a caravan manager and married a rich widow named **Khadija,** who was also his employer.

Over time, Muhammad became troubled by the growing gap between what he saw as the simple honesty and generosity of most Makkans and the greediness of the rich trading elites in the city. Deeply worried, he began to visit the hills to meditate.

During one of these visits, Muslims believe, Muhammad received revelations from God. According to Islamic teachings, the messages were given by the angel Gabriel, who told Muhammad to recite what he heard.

Muhammad came to believe that Allah had already revealed himself in part through Moses and Jesus—and thus through the Hebrew and Christian traditions. He believed, however, that the final revelations of Allah were now being given to him.

A modern caravan in the Niger desert

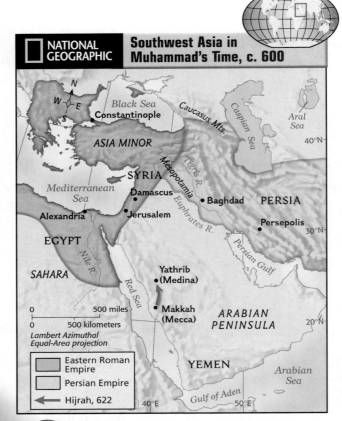

NATIONAL GEOGRAPHIC — **Southwest Asia in Muhammad's Time, c. 600**

Eastern Roman Empire
Persian Empire
← Hijrah, 622

Geography *Skills*

Islamic teachings and Muhammad's influence reshaped the geography and politics of the Arab world.

1. **Interpreting Maps** Calculate the distance from Makkah to Yathrib, using the map's scale.
2. **Applying Geography Skills** Draw a new map, inserting the trade routes that passed through Makkah. What bodies of water did these routes link?

Out of these revelations, which were eventually written down, came the Quran, the holy book of the religion of Islam. (The word *Islam* means "peace through submission to the will of Allah.") The Quran contains the ethical guidelines and laws by which the followers of Allah are to live. Those who practice the religion of Islam are called **Muslims.** Islam has only one God, Allah, and Muhammad is God's prophet.

After receiving the revelations, Muhammad returned home and reflected upon his experience. His wife, Khadija, urged him to follow Gabriel's message, and she became the first convert to Islam. Muhammad then set out to convince the people of Makkah of the truth of the revelations. 📖 *(See page 992 to read excerpts from* Muhammad's Wife Remembers the Prophet *in the Primary Sources Library.)*

People were surprised at his claims to be a prophet. The wealthy feared that his attacks on corrupt society would upset the established social and political order. After three years of preaching, he had only 30 followers.

Muhammad became discouraged by the persecution of his followers, as well as by the failure of the Makkans to accept his message. He and some of his closest supporters left Makkah and moved north to Yathrib, later renamed **Madinah** (Medina; "city of the prophet"). The journey of Muhammad and his followers to Madinah is known as the *Hijrah* (HIH•jruh). The year the journey occurred, 622, became year 1 in the official calendar of Islam.

Muhammad soon began to win support from people in Madinah, as well as from Arabs in the desert, known as **Bedouins.** From these groups, he formed the first community of practicing Muslims.

Muslims saw no separation between political and religious authority. Submission to the will of Allah meant submission to his prophet, Muhammad. For this reason, Muhammad soon became both a religious and a political leader. His political and military skills enabled him to put together a reliable military force to defend himself and his followers. His military victories against the Makkans began to attract large numbers of supporters.

In 630, Muhammad returned to Makkah with a force of ten thousand men. The city quickly surrendered, and most of the townspeople converted to

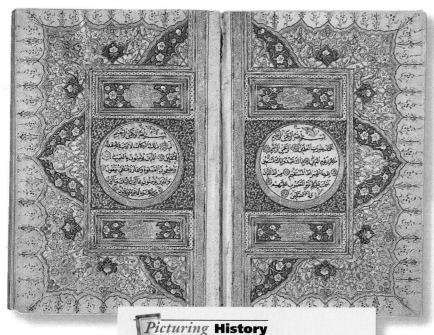

Islam. During a visit to the Kaaba, Muhammad declared it a sacred shrine of Islam. Two years after his triumphal return to Makkah, Muhammad died, just as Islam was beginning to spread throughout the Arabian Peninsula. All Muslims are encouraged to make a pilgrimage to Makkah, known as the hajj (HAJ), if possible.

Reading Check **Identifying** What was the significance of the message given to Muhammad by Gabriel?

The Teachings of Muhammad

Like Christianity and Judaism, Islam is monotheistic. Allah is the all-powerful being who created the universe and everything in it. Islam emphasizes salvation and offers the hope of an afterlife. Those who desire to achieve life after death must subject themselves to the will of Allah.

Unlike Christianity, Islam does not believe that its first preacher was divine. Muhammad is considered a prophet, similar to Moses, but he was also a man like other men. Muslims believe that because human beings rejected Allah's earlier messengers, Allah sent his final revelation through Muhammad.

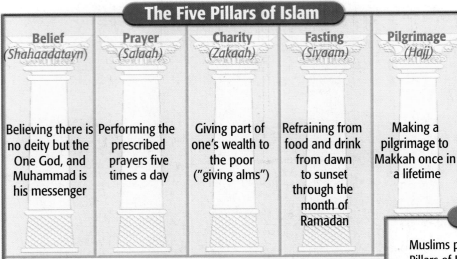

The Five Pillars of Islam

Belief (Shahaadatayn)	Prayer (Salaah)	Charity (Zakaah)	Fasting (Siyaam)	Pilgrimage (Hajj)
Believing there is no deity but the One God, and Muhammad is his messenger	Performing the prescribed prayers five times a day	Giving part of one's wealth to the poor ("giving alms")	Refraining from food and drink from dawn to sunset through the month of Ramadan	Making a pilgrimage to Makkah once in a lifetime

Quran

Chart Skills

Muslims practice acts of worship called the Five Pillars of Islam.

1. **Compare and Contrast** How do the Five Pillars of Islam differ from the Ten Commandments? How are they similar?

2. **Describing** What behaviors are encouraged by the Five Pillars of Islam?

Islam is a direct and simple faith, stressing the need to obey the will of Allah. This means practicing acts of worship known as the Five Pillars of Islam. The faithful who follow the law are guaranteed a place in an eternal paradise.

Islam is not just a set of religious beliefs but a way of life as well. After Muhammad's death, Muslim scholars developed a law code known as the *shari'ah* (shuh•REE•uh). It provides believers with a set of practical laws to regulate their daily lives. It is based on scholars' interpretations of the Quran and the example set by Muhammad in his life. The *shari'ah* applies the teachings of the Quran to daily life. It regulates all aspects of Muslim life including family life, business practice, government, and moral conduct.

The *shari'ah* does not separate religious matters from civil or political law.

Believers are expected to follow sound principles for behavior. In addition to acts of worship called the Five Pillars, Muslims must practice honesty and justice in dealing with others. Muslims are forbidden to gamble, eat pork, drink alcoholic beverages, or engage in dishonest behavior. Family life is based on marriage.

✓ **Reading Check** **Comparing** How is Islam similar to Christianity and Judaism?

TAKS Practice

SECTION 1 ASSESSMENT

Checking for Understanding

1. **Define** sheikh, Quran, Islam, *Hijrah*, hajj, *shari'ah.*

2. **Identify** Allah, Muhammad, Khadija, Muslims, Bedouins.

3. **Locate** Arabian Peninsula, Makkah, Madinah.

4. **Describe** the importance of the *shari'ah* on the daily life of a Muslim.

5. **List** the Five Pillars of Islam.

Critical Thinking

6. **Discuss** What problems did Muhammad encounter while trying to spread the message of Islam?

7. **Organizing Information** Create a chart like the one below showing the changes that Islam brought to the peoples of the Arabian Peninsula.

Early Arabs	Islam

Analyzing Visuals

8. **Examine** the picture of the Quran on page 193 of your text. How does the design of this book reflect the importance of Muhammad's words?

Writing About History

9. **Descriptive Writing** Imagine that you are a former Bedouin who now lives in Makkah. Write a letter to your Bedouin cousin describing how your life has changed since the move to the city.

A Pilgrimage to Makkah

THE PILGRIMAGE TO Makkah is one of the Five Pillars of Islam and is the duty of every Muslim. In this selection, Ibn Jubayr, a twelfth-century Spanish Muslim, describes the final destination in his pilgrimage—the Black Stone, which resides in the Kaaba at Makkah.

Muslim pilgrims circle the Kaaba, which holds the Black Stone.

❝The blessed Black Stone is encased in the corner [of the Kaaba] facing east. The depth to which it penetrates it is not known, but it is said to extend two cubits into the wall. Its breadth is two-thirds of a span, its length one span and a finger joint. It has four pieces, joined together, and it is said that it was the Qarmata—may God curse them—who broke it. Its edges have been braced with a sheet of silver whose white shines brightly against the black sheen and polished brilliance of the Stone, presenting the observer a striking spectacle which will hold his gaze. The Stone, when kissed, has a softness and moistness which so enchants the mouth that he who puts his lips to it would wish them never to be removed. This is one of the special favors of Divine Providence, and it is enough that the Prophet—may God bless and preserve him—declared it to be a covenant of God on earth. May God profit us by the kissing and touching of it. By His favor may all who yearn fervently for it be brought to it. In the sound piece of the stone, to the right of him who presents himself to kiss it, is a small white spot that shines and appears like a mole on the blessed surface.

Concerning this white mole, there is a tradition that he who looks upon it clears his vision, and when kissing it one should direct one's lips as closely as one can to the place of the mole.❞

—Ibn Jubayr, Describing the Black Stone

Analyzing Primary Sources

1. What are the unique properties of the Black Stone?
2. What is the significance of the Black Stone?
3. What are the three units of measurement used in this source?

The Arab Empire and Its Successors

Main Ideas
- After Muhammad's death, his successor organized the Arabs and set in motion a great expansion.
- Internal struggles weakened the empire and, by the close of the thirteenth century, the Arab Empire had ended.

Key Terms
caliph, jihad, Shiite, Sunni, vizier, sultan, mosque

People to Identify
Abu Bakr, Mu'awiyah, Hussein, Harun al-Rashid, Saladin

Places to Locate
Syria, Damascus, Baghdad, Cairo

Preview Questions
1. What major developments occurred under the Umayyads and Abbasids?
2. Why did the Umayyad and the Abbasid dynasties fall?

Reading Strategy
Compare and Contrast Use a chart to compare and contrast the characteristics of the early caliphs with the caliphs of the Umayyad and Abbasid dynasties.

Early Caliphs	Caliphs of the Umayyad and Abbasid dynasties

Preview of Events

◆600	◆700	◆800	◆900	◆1000	◆1100	◆1200	◆1300

632
Abu Bakr becomes the first caliph

732
Arab forces are defeated at the Battle of Tours

750
The Abbasid dynasty comes to power

1055
The Seljuk Turks capture Baghdad and take command of the Abbasid Empire

1258
The Abbasid dynasty comes to an end

Voices from the Past

Interior courtyard of the Alhambra in Granada, Spain

After the death of Muhammad, a caliph became the secular and spiritual leader of the Islamic community. As the empire grew, caliphs became more like kings or emperors, as described by this thirteenth-century Chinese traveler:

❝The king wears a turban of silk brocade and foreign cotton stuff. On each new moon and full moon he puts on an eight-sided flat-topped headdress of pure gold, set with the most precious jewels in the world. His robe is of silk brocade and is bound around him with a jade girdle. On his feet he wears golden shoes. . . . The king's throne is set with pearls and precious stones, and the steps of the throne are covered with pure gold. The various vessels and utensils around the throne are of gold or silver, and precious pearls are knotted in the screen behind it. In great court ceremonies the king sits behind this screen.❞

— *Chau Ju-Kua: His Work on the Chinese and Arab Trade in the Twelfth and Thirteenth Centuries*, **Fredrick Hirth and W.W. Rockhill, trans., 1966**

The jewels and finery of the Arab rulers were indications of the strength and power of the growing Arab Empire.

Creation of an Arab Empire

Muhammad had been accepted as both the political and religious leader of the Islamic community. The death of Muhammad left his followers with a problem: Muhammad had never named a successor. Although he had several daughters, he had left no son. In a male-oriented society, who would lead the community of the faithful?

Shortly after Muhammad's death, some of his closest followers chose **Abu Bakr** (uh•BOO BA•kuhr), a wealthy merchant and Muhammad's father-in-law, to be their leader. He was named caliph (KAY•luhf), or successor to Muhammad.

Arab Conquest

Under Abu Bakr's leadership, the Islamic movement began to grow. As the Romans had slowly conquered Italy, so also the Muslims expanded over Arabia, and beyond.

Muhammad had overcome military efforts by the early Makkans to defeat his movement. The Quran permitted fair, defensive warfare as jihad (jih•HAHD), or "struggle in the way of God." Muhammad's successors expanded their territory.

Unified under Abu Bakr, the Arabs began to turn the energy they had once directed toward each other against neighboring peoples. At Yarmuk in 636, the Arab army defeated the Byzantine army in the midst of a dust storm that enabled the Arabs to take their enemy by surprise. Four years later, they took control of the Byzantine province of **Syria**. By 642, Egypt and other areas of northern Africa had been added to the new Arab Empire. To the east, the Arabs had conquered the entire Persian Empire by 650.

The Arabs, led by a series of brilliant generals, had put together a large, dedicated army. The courage of the Arab soldiers was enhanced by the belief that Muslim warriors were assured a place in Paradise if they died in battle.

Arab Rule

Early caliphs ruled their far-flung empire from Madinah. After Abu Bakr died, problems arose over who should become the next caliph. There were no clear successors to Abu Bakr, and the first two caliphs to rule after his death were assassinated. In 656, Ali, Muhammad's son-in-law, was chosen to be caliph, but he too was assassinated after ruling for five years.

HISTORY Online

Web Activity Visit the *Glencoe World History* Web site at tx.wh.glencoe.com and click on **Chapter 6– Student Web Activity** to learn more about the practice of hajj.

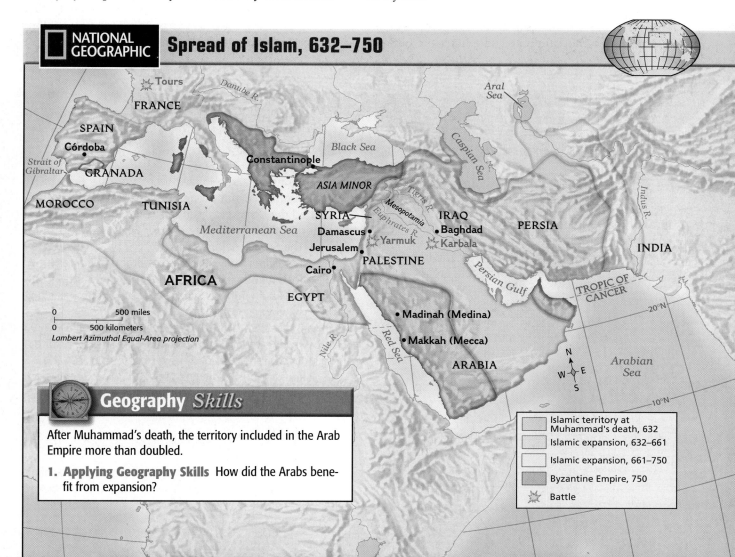

NATIONAL GEOGRAPHIC

Spread of Islam, 632–750

Tours
Danube R.
FRANCE
SPAIN
Córdoba
Strait of Gibraltar
GRANADA
MOROCCO
TUNISIA
Black Sea
Aral Sea
Caspian Sea
Constantinople
ASIA MINOR
SYRIA
Damascus
Jerusalem
Cairo
PALESTINE
EGYPT
Mediterranean Sea
Euphrates R.
Tigris R.
Mesopotamia
Yarmuk
IRAQ
Baghdad
Karbala
PERSIA
Indus R.
INDIA
Persian Gulf
TROPIC OF CANCER
20°N
AFRICA
Nile R.
Red Sea
Madinah (Medina)
Makkah (Mecca)
ARABIA
Arabian Sea
10°N

0 500 miles
0 500 kilometers
Lambert Azimuthal Equal-Area projection

N
W E
S

Legend:
- Islamic territory at Muhammad's death, 632
- Islamic expansion, 632–661
- Islamic expansion, 661–750
- Byzantine Empire, 750
- Battle

Geography *Skills*

After Muhammad's death, the territory included in the Arab Empire more than doubled.

1. **Applying Geography Skills** How did the Arabs benefit from expansion?

In the conquered territories, Arab administrators were quite tolerant, sometimes even allowing local officials to continue to govern. The conquered people were not forced to convert to Islam. Those who chose not to convert were required only to be loyal to Muslim rule and to pay taxes.

✓Reading Check **Identifying** Who was the first caliph to unify the Arabs and begin an expansionist movement?

The Umayyads

►TURNING **POINT**◄ **In this section, you will learn how Arab forces were defeated by the Frankish army at the Battle of Tours in 732. While Spain remained under Muslim rule, this battle marked the end of Arab expansion into Europe.**

In 661, the general **Mu'awiyah** (moo•UH•wee•uh), the governor of Syria and one of Ali's chief rivals, became caliph. He was known for one outstanding virtue: he used force only when absolutely necessary. As he said, "I never use my sword when my whip will do, nor my whip when my tongue will do."

Mu'awiyah moved quickly to make the office of caliph, called the caliphate, hereditary in his own family. In doing this, he established the **Umayyad** (oo•MY•uhd) **dynasty.** He then moved the capital of the Arab Empire from Madinah to **Damascus,** in Syria.

Umayyad Conquests At the beginning of the eighth century, Arab armies conquered and converted the **Berbers**, a pastoral people living along the Mediterranean coast of northern Africa.

Around 710, combined Berber and Arab forces crossed the Strait of Gibraltar and occupied southern Spain. By 725, most of Spain had become a Muslim state with its center at Córdoba. In 732, however, Arab forces were defeated at the Battle of Tours in Gaul (now France). Arab expansion in Europe came to a halt.

In 717, another Muslim force had launched an attack on Constantinople with the hope of defeating the Byzantine Empire. The Byzantines survived, however, by destroying the Muslim fleet. This created an uneasy frontier in southern Asia Minor between the Byzantine Empire and the Islamic world.

The Arab advance had finally come to an end, but not before the southern and eastern Mediterranean parts of the old Roman Empire had been conquered. Arab power also extended to the east in Mesopotamia and Persia and northward into central Asia.

CONNECTIONS Past To Present

The Conflict between Sunnis and Shiites

In 1980, a brutal and bloody war erupted between Iran and Iraq. Border disputes were one cause of the war, but religious differences were another.

Both Iranians and Iraqis are Muslims. The Iranians are largely Shiites. Although the Iraqi people are mostly Shiites as well, the ruling groups in the country are Sunnis. During the war, Iran hoped to defeat Iraq by appealing to the Shiite majority in Iraq for support. The attempt largely failed, however.

The clash between Shiites and Sunnis goes back to the seventh century. The Shiites believed that only the descendants of Ali, Muhammad's son-in-law, were the true leaders of Islam. Sunnis did not all agree with Umayyad rule but accepted the Umayyads as rulers. Over the years, Shiites developed their own body of law, which differed from that of the Sunni majority.

Most Muslims today are Sunnis, although Shiites form majorities in both Iran and Iraq. Shiite minorities continue to exist in Turkey, Syria, Lebanon, India, Pakistan, and east Africa.

The success of the Iranian Revolution in 1978–1979, led by the Ayatollah Khomeini (koh•MAY•nee), resulted in a noticeable revival of Shiism in Iran and in parts of the Islamic world adjacent to Iran. The separation between Shiite and Sunni Muslims still exists.

Iran–Iraq War, 1981

Comparing Past and Present

Research the current relationship between Iraq and Iran. Has the conflict between the Shiites and the Sunnis changed in any way since the war of 1980?

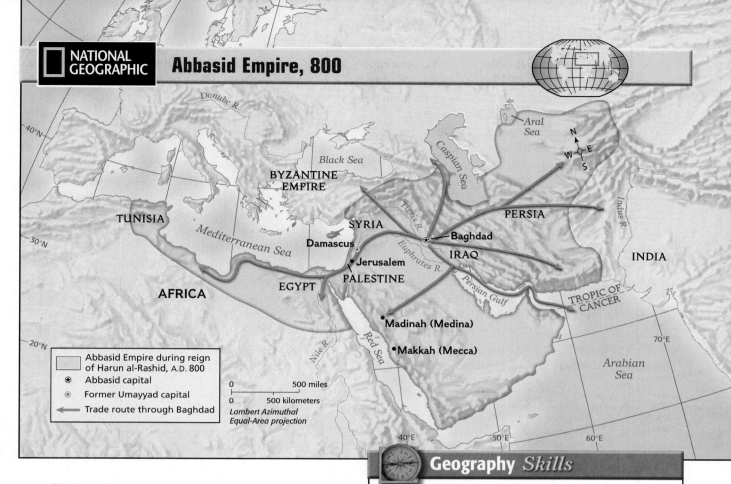

Abbasid Empire, 800

Danube R.

40°N

BYZANTINE EMPIRE

Black Sea

Aral Sea

Caspian Sea

TUNISIA

Mediterranean Sea

PERSIA

Tigris R.

SYRIA

Baghdad

30°N

Damascus

IRAQ

INDIA

Indus R.

Jerusalem

Euphrates R.

PALESTINE

AFRICA

EGYPT

Persian Gulf

TROPIC OF CANCER

70°E

Madinah (Medina)

20°N

Nile R.

Red Sea

Makkah (Mecca)

Arabian Sea

Legend:
- Abbasid Empire during reign of Harun al-Rashid, A.D. 800
- ⊛ Abbasid capital
- ⊛ Former Umayyad capital
- ← Trade route through Baghdad

0   500 miles
0   500 kilometers
Lambert Azimuthal Equal-Area projection

40°E   50°E   60°E

A Split in Islam In spite of Umayyad successes, internal struggles threatened the empire's stability. Many Muslims of non-Arab background, such as Persians and Byzantines, did not like the way local administrators favored the Arabs.

An especially important revolt took place in present-day Iraq early in the Umayyad period. It was led by **Hussein** (hoo•SAYN), second son of Ali—the son-in-law of Muhammad.

Hussein encouraged his followers to rise up against Umayyad rule in 680. He set off to do battle, but his soldiers defected, leaving him with an army of 72 warriors against 10,000 Umayyad soldiers. Hussein's tiny force fought courageously, but all died.

This struggle led to a split of Islam into two groups. The **Shiite** (SHEE•YT) Muslims accept only the descendants of Ali as the true rulers of Islam. The **Sunni** (SU•NEE) Muslims did not all agree with Umayyad rule but accepted the Umayyads as rulers. This political split led to the development of two branches of Muslims that persists to the present. The Sunnis are a majority in the Muslim world, but most of the people in Iraq and neighboring Iran consider themselves to be Shiites.

✓ Reading Check **Evaluating** What weakness in Arab rule led to revolts against the Umayyads?

Geography Skills

The Abbasid dynasty lasted 500 years and saw a period of rising prosperity as Baghdad became the center of an enormous trading empire.

1. **Interpreting Maps** What geographical factors would have influenced the placement of the Abbasid capital?

2. **Applying Geography Skills** Compare this map to the one on page 160 showing the Roman Empire at its height. Identify the geographic factors that would have influenced the expansion of both empires. Create a Venn diagram to compare and contrast the geography of the Roman and the Abbasid Empires.

The Abbasid Dynasty

Resentment against Umayyad rule grew. As mentioned, non-Arab Muslims resented favoritism shown to Arabs. The Umayyads also helped bring about their own end by their corrupt behavior. In 750, Abu al-Abbas, a descendant of Muhammad's uncle, overthrew the Umayyad dynasty and set up the **Abbasid** (uh•BA•suhd) **dynasty,** which lasted until 1258.

Abbasid Rule In 762, the Abbasids built a new capital city at **Baghdad**, on the Tigris River, far to the east of the Umayyad capital at Damascus. The new capital was well placed. It took advantage of river traffic to the Persian Gulf and was located on the caravan route from the Mediterranean to central Asia.

The move eastward increased Persian influence and encouraged a new cultural outlook. Under the Umayyads, warriors had been seen as the ideal citizens. Under the Abbasids, judges, merchants, and government officials were the new heroes. All Muslims, regardless of ethnic background, could now hold both civil and military offices. Many Arabs began to intermarry with conquered peoples.

The Abbasid dynasty experienced a period of splendid rule during the ninth century. Best known of the caliphs of the time was **Harun al-Rashid** (ha•ROON ahl•rah•SHEED), whose reign is often described as the golden age of the Abbasid caliphate. Harun al-Rashid was known for his charity, and he also lavished support on artists and writers. His son al-Ma'mun (ahl•mah•MOON) was a great patron of learning. He supported the study of astronomy and created a foundation for translating classical Greek works.

This was also a period of growing prosperity. The Arabs had conquered many of the richest provinces of the Roman Empire, and they now controlled the trade routes to the East. Baghdad became the center of an enormous trade empire that extended into Asia, Africa, and Europe, greatly adding to the riches of the Islamic world.

Under the Abbasids, the caliph began to act in a more regal fashion. The bureaucracy assisting the caliph in administering the empire grew more complex as well. A council headed by a prime minister, known as a vizier, advised the caliph. The caliph did not attend meetings of the council but instead sat behind a screen listening to the council's discussions and then whispered his orders to the vizier.

*O*pposing *V*iewpoints

How did the Arab Empire Succeed?

During the early eighth century, the Muslims vastly extended their empire. Their swift conquest of Southwest Asia has intrigued many historians. Was their success due to religious fervor or military strength; or, were there other reasons for their military victories that are not so obvious?

❝They were aided by the weakness of the two contemporary empires, the Sassanian (Persian) and the Byzantine, which had largely exhausted themselves by their wars on one another. . . . Nor were these Arabs simply zealots fired by the ideal of a Holy War. They were by long tradition tough fighters, accustomed to raiding out of hunger and want; many or perhaps even most of them were not ardent followers of Mohammed. Yet there can be little question that what got the Arabs started, and kept them going, was mainly the personality and the teaching of the Prophet.❞

—Herbert J. Muller, 1958
The Loom of History

❝Perhaps . . . another kind of explanation can be given for the acceptance of Arab rule by the population of the conquered countries. To most of them it did not much matter whether they were ruled by Iranians, Greeks or Arabs. Government impinged for the most part on the life of cities and . . . city-dwellers might not care much who ruled them,

Decline and Division Despite its prosperity, all was not well in the empire of the Abbasids. There was much fighting over the succession to the caliphate. When Harun al-Rashid died, his two sons fought to succeed him, almost destroying the city of Baghdad.

Vast wealth gave rise to financial corruption. Members of Harun al-Rashid's clan were given large sums of money from the state treasury. His wife was reported to have spent vast amounts on a pilgrimage to Makkah.

The process of disintegration was helped along by a shortage of qualified Arabs for key positions in the army and the civil service. As a result, caliphs began to recruit officials from among the non-Arab peoples within the empire, such as Persians and Turks. These people were trained to serve the caliphs, but gradually they also became a dominant force in the army and the bureaucracy.

Eventually, rulers of the provinces of the Abbasid Empire began to break away from the central authority

provided they were secure, at peace and reasonably taxed. The people of the countryside . . . lived under their own chiefs and . . . with their own customs, and it made little difference to them who ruled the cities. For some, the replacement of Greeks and Iranians by Arabs even offered advantages. **"**

—Albert Hourani, 1991
A History of the Arab Peoples

You Decide

1. Review the information presented in this section carefully. Using the material from the text and information obtained from your own outside research, explain why both of these viewpoints can be considered valid.

2. Compare the information given in the second excerpt to attitudes of other conquered peoples that you have read about. Do you believe that most people easily accept outside rule? What factors lead to acceptance and what factors lead to rebellion against outside rule?

and establish independent dynasties. Spain had established its own caliphate when a prince of the Umayyad dynasty fled there in 750. Morocco became independent, and a new dynasty under the Fatimids was established in Egypt, with its capital at **Cairo**, in 973. The Muslim Empire was now politically divided.

✓ Reading Check **Describing** What changes did the Abbasid rulers bring to the world of Islam?

The Seljuk Turks

The Fatimid dynasty in Egypt soon became the dynamic center of Islamic civilization. From their position in the heart of the Nile delta, the Fatimids played a major role in the trade passing from the Mediterranean to the Red Sea and beyond. They created a strong army by hiring non-native soldiers to fight for them. One such group was the Seljuk (SEHL•JOOK) Turks.

The **Seljuk Turks** were a nomadic people from central Asia. They had converted to Islam and prospered as soldiers for the Abbasid caliphate. As the Abbasids grew weaker, the Seljuk Turks grew stronger, moving gradually into Iran and Armenia. By the eleventh century, they had taken over the eastern provinces of the Abbasid Empire.

In 1055, a Turkish leader captured Baghdad and took command of the empire. His title was sultan—or "holder of power." The Abbasid caliph was still the chief religious authority, but, after they captured Baghdad, the Seljuk Turks held the real military and political power of the state.

By the second half of the eleventh century, the Seljuks were putting military pressure on the Byzantine Empire. In 1071, the Byzantines foolishly challenged the Turks, and the Byzantine army was routed at Manzikert in modern-day eastern Turkey. The Turks now took over most of the Anatolian Peninsula. In desperation, the Byzantine Empire turned to the West for help.

✓ Reading Check **Explaining** How did the Seljuk Turks gradually replace the Abbasids?

The Crusades

The Byzantine emperor Alexius I asked the Christian states of Europe for help against the Turks. Because the Christian states and the Islamic world feared and disliked each other, many Europeans agreed, beginning a series of crusades in 1096.

At first, Muslim rulers were thrown on the defensive by the invading crusaders, who were able to conquer areas and establish crusader states. In 1169, however, **Saladin,** a new Muslim ruler, took control of Egypt and made himself sultan, thus ending the Fatimid dynasty. He also established control over Syria and took the offensive against the Christian states in the area. In 1187, Saladin's army invaded the kingdom of Jerusalem and destroyed the Christian forces there. Soon the Christians were left with only a handful of fortresses along the coast of Palestine. Saladin did not allow a massacre of the population. He even allowed Christian religious services to continue.

The Crusades had little lasting impact on Southwest Asia, except to breed centuries of mistrust between Muslims and Christians. Far more important was the threat posed by new invaders—the Mongols.

✔ **Reading Check** **Identifying** Why did crusaders from Europe invade Southwest Asia?

The Mongols

The **Mongols** were a pastoral people who swept out of the Gobi in the early thirteenth century to seize control over much of the known world (see Chapter 8). These invaders were destructive in their conquests. They burned cities to the ground, destroyed dams, and reduced farming villages to the point of mass starvation. Their goal was to create such terror that people would not fight back.

Beginning with the advances led by Genghis Khan in North China, Mongol armies spread across central Asia. In 1258, under the leadership of Hülegü (hoo•LAY•GOO), brother of the more famous Kublai Khan (KOO•BLUH•KAHN), the Mongols seized Persia and Mesopotamia. The Abbasid caliphate at Baghdad was brought to an end. Hülegü had a strong hatred of Islam. After his forces captured Baghdad in 1258, he decided to destroy the city. Schools, libraries, mosques (Muslim houses of worship), and palaces were burned to the ground.

The Mongols advanced as far as the Red Sea. Their attempt to seize Egypt failed, however, in part because of resistance from the Mamluks. The Mamluks were Turkish slave-soldiers who had overthrown the administration set up by Saladin and seized power for themselves.

Over time, the Mongol rulers converted to Islam and began to intermarry with local peoples. They began to rebuild the cities. By the fourteenth century, the Mongol Empire had begun to split into separate kingdoms. The old Islamic Empire established by the Arabs in the seventh and eighth centuries had come to an end. As a result of the Mongol destruction of Baghdad, the new center of Islamic civilization became Cairo, in Egypt.

✔ **Reading Check** **Describing** How did the Mongols seize control of the Arab Empire in the early thirteenth century?

🟥 **TAKS Practice**

SECTION 2 ASSESSMENT

Checking for Understanding

1. **Define** caliph, jihad, Shiite, Sunni, vizier, sultan, mosque.

2. **Identify** Abu Bakr, Mu'awiyah, Umayyad dynasty, Berbers, Hussein, Abbasid dynasty, Harun al-Rashid, Seljuk Turks, Saladin, Mongols.

3. **Locate** Syria, Damascus, Baghdad, Cairo.

4. **Explain** how General Mu'awiyah created the Umayyad dynasty.

5. **List** the occupations that were given increased respect under the Abbasids.

Critical Thinking

6. **Explain** The initial Mongol reaction to Islam was hatred and destruction, yet over time that changed. Why do you think the Mongols gradually accepted Islam?

7. **Categorizing Information** Create a chart that shows the strengths and weaknesses of the Abbasid dynasty.

Strengths of Abbasid dynasty	Weaknesses of Abbasid dynasty

Analyzing Visuals

8. **Examine** the photograph of the interior courtyard of the Alhambra on page 196. Where is this building located? Can you identify various influences on its architectural style?

Writing About History

9. **Persuasive Writing** Imagine you are General Mu'awiyah and you have just become caliph. Write a speech that outlines how you will rule the empire and explain why you believe the caliphate should be hereditary.

Islamic Civilization

Guide to Reading

Main Ideas
- An extensive trade network brought prosperity to the Islamic world.
- The Quran provided fundamental guidelines for all Muslims, not only in spiritual affairs but also in politics, economics, and social life.

Key Terms
bazaar, dowry

People to Identify
Abbasids, Fatimids

Places to Locate
Morocco, Caspian Sea, Córdoba

Preview Questions
1. List the items traded in the Arab Empire and where they came from.
2. What were the basic characteristics of Islamic society?

Reading Strategy
Compare and Contrast Create a chart like the one below comparing the urban areas of the Arab Empire to the more rural areas of the empire.

Urban areas	Rural areas

Preview of Events

♦600	♦700	♦800	♦900	♦1000

635
The Quran is compiled

750
Trade begins to flourish during the Abbasid dynasty

c. 800
Baghdad reaches its height of prosperity

Voices from the Past

In the late twelfth century, a Spanish rabbi wrote the following account of Baghdad, one of the world's greatest cities, during a visit there:

66The city of Baghdad is twenty miles in circumference, situated in a land of palms, gardens, and plantations, the like of which is not to be found in the whole land of Mesopotamia. People come there with merchandise from all lands. Wise men live there, philosophers who know all manner of wisdom, and magicians expert in all manner of witchcraft. . . . Within the domains of the palace of the caliph there are great buildings of marble and columns of silver and gold, and carvings upon rare stones are fixed in the walls. In the caliph's palace are great riches and towers filled with gold.99
—*The Itinerary of Benjamin of Tudela*, **M.N. Adler, trans., 1907**

The riches of Baghdad symbolized the prosperity of the Arab Empire.

Baghdad

Prosperity in the Islamic World

Overall, the period of the Arab Empire was prosperous. The Arabs carried on extensive trade, not only within the Islamic world but also with China, the Byzantine Empire, India, and Southeast Asia. Trade was carried both by ship and by camel caravans, which traveled from **Morocco** in the far west to the countries beyond the **Caspian Sea.**

Starting around 750, trade flourished under the Abbasid dynasty. From south of the Sahara came gold and slaves; from China, silk and porcelain; from eastern Africa, gold and ivory; and from the lands of Southeast Asia and India, sandalwood and spices. Within the empire, Egypt contributed grain; Iraq provided linens, dates, and precious stones; and western India supplied textile goods. The development of banking and the use of coins made it easier to exchange goods.

The Role of Cities With flourishing trade came prosperous cities. While the **Abbasids** were in power, Baghdad, the Abbasid capital known as the City of Peace, was probably the greatest city in the empire and one of the greatest cities in the world. After the rise of the **Fatimids** in Egypt, however, the focus of trade shifted to Cairo. A traveler described Cairo as "one of the greatest and most famous cities in all the whole world, filled with stately and admirable palaces . . . and most sumptuous temples." Another great trading city was Damascus in modern-day Syria.

Baghdad, Cairo, and Damascus were the centers of administrative, cultural, and economic activity for their regions. Aside from these capital cities, travelers did not find Islamic cities to be especially grand, though the cities did outshine those of mostly rural Europe. This is exemplified by **Córdoba,** the capital of Umayyad Spain. With a population of two hundred thousand, Córdoba was Europe's largest city after Constantinople.

Islamic cities had a distinctive physical appearance. Usually, the most impressive urban buildings were the palaces for the caliphs or the local governors and the great mosques for worship. There were also public buildings with fountains and secluded courtyards, public baths, and bazaars or marketplaces.

The bazaar, or covered market, was an important part of every Muslim city or town. Goods from many regions were available in the bazaar. To guarantee high standards, market inspectors enforced rules, such as the daily washing of counters and containers. Guidelines were established for food prepared for sale at the market. One rule stated, "Grilled meats should only be made with fresh meat and not with meat coming from a sick animal and bought for its cheapness." The bazaar also housed many craftspeople's shops, as well as services such as laundries and bathhouses.

THE WAY IT WAS

FOCUS ON EVERYDAY LIFE

Housing and Food in the Islamic Empire

As might be expected, housing conditions in the Islamic Empire during this period varied widely according to the region and the economic conditions of the individual family. In the cities, houses were often constructed of stone or brick around a wooden frame. The larger houses were often built around an inner courtyard where the residents could retreat from the dust, noise, and heat of the city streets. Sometimes domestic animals like goats and sheep would be stabled there.

The houses of the wealthy often had several

Bedouin woman making bread

stories. Rooms upstairs would have balconies and windows covered with latticed shutters to provide privacy and relief from heat and cold for those inside. Walls would be plastered and decorated with designs.

The poor in both urban and rural areas lived in simpler houses made of clay or unfired bricks. In the cities, the poor often crowded into huts built around an open courtyard. Lesser merchants and artisans might live in apartment houses. The Bedouins, like nomads elsewhere, lived in tents that could be taken down and moved according to the needs of the day.

Eating habits varied considerably, based on one's economic standing. The

The Importance of Farming The Arab Empire was more urban than most other areas of the world at the time. Nevertheless, a majority of people still lived in the countryside, making their living by farming or herding animals.

During the early stages of the empire, most of the farmland was owned by independent peasants. Later, wealthy landowners began to amass large estates. Some lands were owned by the state or the court and were farmed by slave labor. In the Tigris, Euphrates, and Nile River valleys, however, most farmers remained independent peasants. Despite all the changes since the days of ancient Egypt, peasants along the Nile continued to farm the way their ancestors had.

✓ **Reading Check** **Identifying** List the major Islamic cities. What activities were centered there?

Islamic Society

To be a Muslim is not simply to worship Allah but also to live one's life according to Allah's teachings as revealed in the Quran, which was compiled in 635. As Allah has decreed, so must humans live. Questions concerning politics, economics, and social life are answered by following Islamic teachings.

Social Structure According to Islam, all people are equal in the eyes of Allah. In reality, however, this was not strictly the case in the Arab Empire. There was a fairly well defined upper class that consisted of ruling families, senior officials, nomadic elites, and the wealthiest merchants. Even ordinary merchants, however, enjoyed a degree of respect that merchants did not receive in Europe, China, or India.

One group of people in the Islamic world was not considered equal. They were the slaves. As in the other civilizations we have examined so far, slavery was widespread. Because Muslims could not be slaves, most of their slaves came from Africa or from non-Islamic populations elsewhere in Asia. Many had been captured in war.

Slaves often served in the army. This was especially true of slaves recruited from the Turks of central Asia. Many military slaves were freed. Some even came to exercise considerable power.

poor were generally forced to survive on boiled millet or peas, served occasionally with meat. Bread was crucial to the diet of the poor. Usually made of wheat, it could be found on tables throughout the region except in the deserts, where boiled grain was the staple food.

The rich had greater variety in their diet. Muslims do not eat pork, but those who could afford it often served other meats—boiled or roasted—such as lamb, poultry, or fish. A variety of vegetables and fruits, including grapes, oranges, apricots, dates, and peaches, were also found on the tables of the well-to-do. Dairy products, made from the milk of sheep, goats, camels, and cows, included cheese, butter, and yogurt. Mild spices such as pepper and salt were used with some foods. Delicacies included sweets, usually made with honey as a sweetener.

Shoppers at a textile market

CONNECTING TO THE PAST

1. **Summarizing Information** Describe the differences between the lifestyles of the wealthy and the poor.

2. **Writing about History** Pretend you live in the Islamic Empire, and you have just been hired as a servant. Write a description of the living conditions of the rich. How do you think a wealthy citizen of the Islamic Empire would react to seeing the living standards of the poor?

"Our religion and our Empire are Arab and twins."

—al-Biruni, 973–c. 1050
Muslim writer of Iranian origin

An illustrated section of the Quran

Many slaves, especially women, were used as domestic servants. These slaves were sometimes permitted to purchase their freedom. Islamic law made it clear that slaves should be treated fairly, and it was considered a good act to free them.

The Role of Women The Quran granted women spiritual and social equality with men. Believers, men and women, were to be friends and protectors of one another. Women had the right to the fruits of their work and to own and inherit property. Women had played prominent roles in the rise of Islam during the time of Muhammad.

Islamic teachings did account for differences between men and women in the family and social order. Both had duties and responsibilities. As in most societies of the time, however, men were dominant in Muslim society.

Every woman had a male guardian, be it father, brother, or other male relative. Parents or guardians arranged marriages for their children. The Quran allowed Muslim men to have more than one wife, but no more than four. Most men, however, were unable to afford more than one, because they were required to pay a **dowry** (a gift of money or property) to their brides. Women had the right to freely enter into marriage, but they also had the right of divorce under some circumstances. Adultery was forbidden to both men and women.

After the spread of Islam, older customs eroded the rights enjoyed by early Muslim women. For example, some women were secluded in their homes and kept from social contacts with males outside their own families. One jurist wrote that "some . . . have said that a woman should leave her house on three occasions only: when she is conducted to the house of her bridegroom, on the deaths of her parents, and when she goes to her own grave."

The custom of requiring women to cover virtually all parts of their bodies when appearing in public was common in the cities and is still practiced today in many Islamic societies. It should be noted, however, that these customs owed more to traditional Arab practice than to the Quran. Despite the restrictions, the position of women in Islamic society was better than it had been in former times, when women had often been treated like slaves.

✓ **Reading Check** **Describing** Describe how life in the Arab Empire did and did not reflect the principle of equality.

🌟 **TAKS Practice**

SECTION 3 ASSESSMENT

Checking for Understanding

1. **Define** bazaar, dowry.

2. **Identify** Abbasids, Fatimids.

3. **Locate** Morocco, Caspian Sea, Córdoba.

4. **Explain** how high standards were ensured at bazaars. What was sold at the bazaar?

5. **Identify** the basic differences in the roles of Muslim men and women.

Critical Thinking

6. **Analyze** What was the importance of trade to Arab life, both in rural areas and in cities?

7. **Summarizing Information** Use a chart to list the characteristics of farming during the Arab Empire.

Characteristics of Farming	

Analyzing Visuals

8. **Examine** the photograph of a market on page 205 of your text. Describe how this photograph reflects the economic influence of women in Islamic culture.

Writing About History

9. **Descriptive Writing** Imagine that you are an inspector at a bazaar. Describe what is sold at the bazaar. Then describe the types of violations that you are searching for and ways you use to spot violations.

The Culture of Islam

Main Ideas
- Muslim scholars made great advances in the areas of mathematics and the natural sciences.
- Muslim art and architecture incorporated innovative, geometric styles of decoration.

Key Terms
astrolabe, minaret, muezzin, arabesque

People to Identify
Ibn-Rushd, Ibn Sina (Avicenna), Ibn-Khaldun, Omar Khayyám

Places to Locate
Samarra, Granada

Preview Questions
1. What was the House of Wisdom?
2. What are the traits of Islamic art?

Reading Strategy
Summarizing Information Use a chart like the one below to identify the achievements of Islamic civilization.

Achievements of Islam

Preview of Events

♦700	♦750	♦800	♦850	♦900

c. 750
Papermaking introduced to Muslim world

848
Great Mosque of Samarra is begun

c. 920
Córdoba in Spain becomes major cultural center

Voices from the Past

An Arabic manuscript

In his *Autobiography*, the eleventh-century Islamic scholar Ibn Sina, known in the West as Avicenna, described his early training:

❝By the time I was [10] I had mastered the Quran and a great deal of literature. There followed training in philosophy . . . then I took to reading texts by myself . . . mastering logic, geometry and astronomy. I now occupied myself with mastering the various texts and commentaries on natural science and metaphysics, until all the gates of knowledge were open to me. Next I desired to study medicine, and proceeded to read all the books that have been written on this subject. At the same time I continued to study and dispute on law, being now sixteen years of age.❞
—*Autobiography*, **Ibn Sina**

Ibn Sina was one of the Islamic world's greatest scholars.

Preservation of Knowledge

During the first few centuries of the Arab Empire, the ancient Greek philosophers were largely unknown in Europe. The Arabs, however, were not only aware of Greek philosophy, they were translating works by Plato and Aristotle into Arabic. The translations were then put in a library called the House of Wisdom in Baghdad, where they were read and studied by Muslim scholars. Similarly, texts on mathematics were brought to Baghdad from India.

The process of translating works and making them available to scholars was aided by the making of paper, which was introduced from China in the eighth century. By the end of the century, paper factories had been established in Baghdad. Booksellers and libraries soon followed.

It was through the Muslim world that Europeans recovered the works of Aristotle and other Greek philosophers. In the twelfth century, the Arabic translations were translated into Latin, making them available to the West.

✓ **Reading Check** **Explaining** Why was paper manufacturing important to Islamic culture?

Philosophy, Science, and History

The brilliant Islamic civilization contributed more intellectually to the West than translations, however. When Aristotle's works arrived in Europe in the second half of the twelfth century, they were accompanied by commentaries written by outstanding Arabic philosophers. One such philosopher was **Ibn-Rushd** (IH•buhn•RUSHT). He lived in Córdoba and wrote a commentary on virtually all of Aristotle's surviving works.

Islamic scholars also made contributions to mathematics and the natural sciences that were passed on to the West. The Muslims adopted and passed on the numerical system of India, including the use of the zero. In Europe, it became known as the "Arabic" system. A ninth-century Arab mathematician gave shape to the mathematical discipline of algebra, which is still taught in schools today.

In astronomy, Muslims set up an observatory at Baghdad to study the position of the stars. They were aware that Earth was round, and they named many stars. They also perfected the astrolabe, an instrument used by sailors to determine their location by observing the positions of stars and planets. The astrolabe made it possible for Europeans to sail to the Americas.

Muslim scholars developed medicine as a field of scientific study. Especially well known was the philosopher and scientist, **Ibn Sina** (IH•buhn SEE•nuh). He wrote a medical encyclopedia that, among other things, stressed the contagious nature of certain diseases. Ibn Sina showed how diseases could be spread by contaminated water supplies. After it was translated into Latin, Ibn Sina's work became a basic medical textbook for university students in medieval Europe. Ibn Sina was only one of many Arabic scholars whose work was translated into Latin and thus helped the development of intellectual life in Europe in the twelfth and thirteenth centuries.

Islamic scholars also took an interest in writing history. **Ibn-Khaldun** (IH•buhn KAL•DOON), who lived in the fourteenth century, was the most prominent Muslim historian of the age. Disappointed in his career in politics, he began to devote his time to the study and writing of history.

In his most famous work *Muqaddimah (Introduction to History)*, he argued for a cyclical view of history. Civilizations, he believed, go through regular cycles of birth, growth, and decay. He sought to find a scientific basis for the political and social factors that determine the course of history.

✓ **Reading Check** **Identifying** What instrument used by sailors was perfected by Muslim astronomers in Baghdad?

Literature

Islam brought major changes to the culture of Southwest Asia, including its literature. Though Muslims regarded the Quran as their greatest literary work, pre-Islamic traditions continued to influence writers throughout the region.

One of the most familiar works of Middle Eastern literature is the *Rubaiyat* (ROO•bee•AHT) of **Omar Khayyám** (KY•YAHM). Another is *The 1001 Nights* (also called *The Arabian Nights*).

Little is known of the life or the poetry of the twelfth-century Persian poet, mathematician, and astronomer, Omar Khayyám. We do know that he did not write down his poems but composed them orally. His simple, down to earth

Picturing **History**

Islamic doctors could diagnose and treat many illnesses. Muslim astronomers perfected the astrolabe (above). Why was Islamic medicine more advanced than European medicine?

Rumi
1201–1273—Sufi poet and mystic

Whirling dervishes

The thirteenth-century poet Rumi embraced Sufism, a form of Sunni religious belief that focused on a close personal relationship with Allah. Rumi was converted to Sufism by a wandering dervish. (Dervishes try to achieve union with Allah through dancing and chanting.) He then abandoned orthodox Islam to embrace God directly through love.

Rumi sought to achieve union with God through a trance attained in the whirling dance of the dervishes, set to enchanting music. As he twirled, Rumi composed his poems: "Come! But don't join us without music. . . . We are the spirit's treasure, Not bound to this earth, to time or space. . . . Love is our mother. We were born of Love."

poetry was recorded later by friends or scribes. As can be seen in the following lines, Omar Khayyám wondered about the meaning of life, which seemed to pass too quickly. He writes,

> 66They did not ask me, when they planned my life;
> Why then blame me for what is good or bad?
> Yesterday and today go on without us;
> Tomorrow what's the charge against me, pray?
> In youth I studied for a little while;
> Later I boasted of my mastery.
> Yet this was all the lesson that I learned:
> We come from dust, and with the wind are gone.
> Of all the travelers on this endless road
> No one returns to tell us where it leads,
> There's little in this world but greed and need;
> Leave nothing here, for you will not return.99

The anonymous stories of *The Arabian Nights* are a collection of folktales, fables, and romances that blend the natural with the supernatural. The earliest stories were told orally and then written down later, with many additions, in Arabic and Persian. The famous story of Aladdin and the magic lamp, for example, was added in the eighteenth century. *The Arabian Nights* allows the reader to enter a land of wish fulfillment through unusual plots, comic and tragic situations, and a cast of unforgettable characters.

✓**Reading Check** **Comparing** What are the similarities between the *Rubaiyat* and *The Arabian Nights*?

Art and Architecture

Islamic art is a blend of Arab, Turkish, and Persian traditions. The best expression of Islamic art is found in the magnificent Muslim mosques. The mosque represents the spirit of Islam.

The Great Mosque of **Samarra** in present-day Iraq was the world's largest mosque at the time it was built (848 to 852), covering 10 acres (more than 40,000 square m). The most famous section of the Samarra mosque is its **minaret.** This is the tower from which the **muezzin** (moo•EH•zuhn), or crier, calls the faithful to prayer five times a day. The minaret of Samarra, nearly 90 feet (around 27 m) in height, is unusual because of its outside spiral staircase.

One of the most famous mosques is the ninth-century mosque at Córdoba in southern Spain. It is still in remarkable condition today. Its hundreds of columns, which support double-horseshoe arches, transform this building into a unique "forest of trees" pointing upward, giving it a light and airy effect.

The minaret of the Samarra mosque

The Mosque of Córdoba This mosque in Spain is famous for the symmetry of its arches. Intricate arabesque patterns highlight the interior of this mosque and others. Why do mosques use abstract forms of decoration?

Because the Muslim religion combines spiritual and political power in one, palaces also reflected the glory of Islam. Beginning in the eighth century with the spectacular castles of Syria, Islamic rulers constructed large brick palaces with protective walls, gates, and baths.

Designed around a central courtyard surrounded by two-story arcades and massive gate-towers, Islamic castles resembled fortresses as much as palaces. One feature of these castles was a gallery over the entrance gate with holes through which boiling oil could be poured down on the heads of attacking forces. This feature was taken over by the crusaders and became part of European castles.

The finest example of the Islamic palace is the fourteenth-century **Alhambra** in **Granada,** Spain. Every inch of the castle's surface is decorated in floral and abstract patterns. Much of the decoration is plasterwork that is so finely carved that it looks like lace. The Alhambra is considered an excellent expression of Islamic art.

Most decorations on all forms of Islamic art consisted of Arabic letters, natural plants, and abstract figures. These decorations were repeated over and over in geometric patterns called arabesques that completely covered the surfaces of objects.

No representation of the prophet Muhammad ever adorns a mosque, in painting or in any other art form. The Quran does not forbid representational painting. However, the Hadith, an early collection of the prophet's sayings, warns against any attempt to imitate God by creating pictures of living beings. As a result, from early on, no representations of figures appear in Islamic religious art.

✓**Reading Check** **Summarizing** What are the characteristics of the largest mosque ever built?

🌟**TAKS Practice**

SECTION 4 ASSESSMENT

Checking for Understanding

1. **Define** astrolabe, minaret, muezzin, arabesque.

2. **Identify** Ibn-Rushd, Ibn Sina (Avicenna), Ibn-Khaldun, Omar Khayyám, Alhambra.

3. **Locate** Samarra, Granada.

4. **Explain** how the Muslims transmitted ancient literature to other cultures.

5. **List** the other cultures that influenced Islamic art and architecture.

Critical Thinking

6. **Evaluate** Argue against the viewpoint that Islamic civilization was mainly a preserver and transmitter of culture, rather than a creator of culture.

7. **Organizing Information** Create a table like the one below to identify and describe two important Islamic works of literature.

Literary Work	Description

Analyzing Visuals

8. **Examine** the mosque at Samarra on page 209 and the mosque shown on page 190. Compare and contrast how both mosques reflect Islamic architecture.

Writing About History

9. **Descriptive Writing** Imagine that you are a young Muslim Arab corresponding with a European friend. In a brief paragraph describe Islamic accomplishments in art and architecture to your friend.

STUDY & WRITING
SKILLBUILDER

Taking Notes

Why Learn This Skill?

Effective note taking involves more than just writing down everything your teacher says. The information you write down should be meaningful and concise so that it can be understood and remembered when reviewed.

Learning the Skill

To take notes, follow these steps:

- Do not try to write down everything. Listen for the key points. Note these, along with any important facts and figures that support these points.

- Use abbreviations and phrases.

- Copy words, statements, or diagrams drawn on the chalkboard.

- Ask the teacher to repeat important points you have missed or do not understand.

- Organize notes from textbooks into an outline.

- For a research report, take notes on cards. Note the title, author, and page number. Use them as a reference in your report.

Practicing the Skill

Suppose you are writing a research paper on the topic "The Life of Muhammad." First, ask yourself questions about the main ideas of this topic, such as: "Who was Muhammad?", "How did he spread the religion of Islam?", "What were his teachings?" Then, find material that answers each of these questions.

A decorative tile with inscription "Allah is Great"

Using this textbook as a source, read the material on "The Life of Muhammad" in Section 1. After reviewing the material, prepare notes as if you were writing a report. Use the first set of notes as an example.

Topic: The Life of Muhammad

Main Idea: Who was Muhammad?

❶ Born to merchant family but orphaned at age five

❷ Became a caravan manager and married his rich employer

❸ Troubled by gap between poor Bedouins and rich traders and withdrew to hills to meditate

❹ According to Islamic teachings, received revelations from the angel Gabriel

Main Idea: How did Muhammad spread the religion of Islam?

❶

❷

❸

Main Idea: What were Muhammad's teachings?

❶

❷

❸

Applying the Skill

Scan a local newspaper for a short editorial or an article about an important issue or event in the world today. Take notes by writing the main idea and supporting facts. Summarize the article using only your notes.

Glencoe's **Skillbuilder Interactive Workbook, Level 2,** provides instruction and practice in key social studies skills.

ASSESSMENT and ACTIVITIES

Using Key Terms

1. _____ are Muslim houses of worship.

2. The leader of the Seljuk Turks was called a _____, or "holder of power."

3. A crucial part of every Muslim city or town was the covered market, called the _____.

4. The journey of Muhammad from Makkah to Madinah is known in history as the _____.

5. The sacred book of _____ is called the Quran.

6. According to the Quran, _____ means struggle in the way of God.

7. One of the Five Pillars of Islam is making a pilgrimage, called the _____, to Makkah.

8. Islamic geometric designs entwined with natural plants, Arabic letters, and abstract figures are known as _____.

9. Islamic scholars and theologians organized Islamic moral rules into the _____, or code of law.

10. During the Abbasid dynasty, the council that advised the caliph was led by a prime minister known as a _____.

Reviewing Key Facts

11. **Geography** How did the harsh environment of Arabia shape the political and economic life of the people?

12. **Government** Who were caliphs and how did they administer their empire?

13. **History** Identify the changes in the Arabian Peninsula during the 600s.

14. **Economics** How did the caravan trade benefit the Arabian Peninsula in the fifth and sixth centuries and why did the trade routes change during this time?

15. **Culture** What is the significance of the Black Stone and where is it located?

16. **Geography** Trace the expansionist movement of the Arabs from 632 to 1055.

17. **History** What is the basic message of the Quran and when was it compiled?

18. **Culture** What were some of the physical characteristics of Islamic cities?

19. **History** What are the main differences between the Shiites and the Sunnis?

20. **Science and Technology** Name three contributions by Muslim scholars in the fields of mathematics and the natural sciences.

Critical Thinking

21. **Compare and Contrast** Compare and contrast the Islamic religion to Christianity.

22. **Drawing Conclusions** Evaluate the significance in world history of the Battle of Tours in 732 and the destruction of the Muslim fleet in 717.

Writing About History

23. **Expository Writing** *The Arabian Nights* incorporates tales from many cultures. What does this tell us about the diverse nature of Islamic society? Find a story from *The Arabian Nights* and analyze how it reflects Islamic society.

Chapter Summary

Islamic civilization is renowned for its innovation, movement, and cultural diffusion.

Innovation

- irrigation
- astrolabe
- algebra
- large-scale paper manufacturing

Movement

- trade routes
- Arab expansion in Africa, Asia, and Europe
- movement of Arab center of power from Makkah to Baghdad to Cairo

Cultural Diffusion

- Bureaucracy relies on non-Arabs.
- Arabs translate Greek philosophers.
- Ibn Sina's medical textbook is standard in Europe.

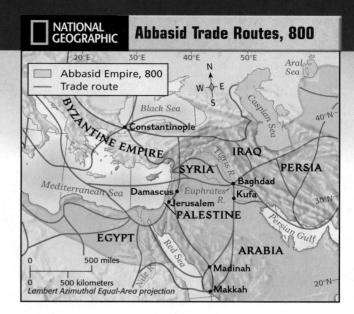

NATIONAL GEOGRAPHIC Abbasid Trade Routes, 800

- ☐ Abbasid Empire, 800
- — Trade route

Analyzing Sources

Read the following poem by Omar Khayyám as translated by Ehsan Yarshater.

    ❝ They did not ask me, when they planned my life;
Why then blame me for what is good or bad?
Yesterday and today go on without us;
Tomorrow what's the charge against me, pray?
In youth I studied for a little while;
Later I boasted of my mastery.
Yet this was all the lesson that I learned;
We come from dust, and with the wind are gone.
Of all the travelers on this endless road
No one returns to tell us where it leads,
There's little in this world but greed and need;
Leave nothing here, for you will not return. ❞

24. How do you think Omar Khayyám viewed life in Southwest Asia in the twelfth century?

25. Find another translation of this poem and compare the two. Are they similar? How do they differ? Can you corroborate which translation is most representative of the original poem? Explain the steps you took to make your decision.

Applying Technology Skills

26. Creating a Database Search the Internet to find information about different modern Islamic countries. Build a database collecting information about the Islamic countries of the world. Include information about beliefs, practices, and demographics of each country. Identify each country's major cities, major imports and exports, and cultural treasures. Choose one country and present your findings to the class.

Making Decisions

27. Imagine that you are a Bedouin, used to living in the desert with your family. You have grown accustomed to the nomadic lifestyle. You are offered the opportunity to join another family in the city, go to school daily, and meet new friends who have grown up in the city. What would you choose to do? Justify your answer with logic and support your position with research from both traditional and electronic sources.

Analyzing Maps and Charts

28. The Umayyads moved their capital from Makkah to Damascus, and the Abbasids then moved it to Baghdad. What were the advantages of these moves?

29. Trade went overland or by sea. What were the advantages and disadvantages of each method?

30. How far did a caravan travel overland from Makkah to Constantinople? Calculate your answer in miles and kilometers using the map's scale.

The Princeton Review

TAKS
Test Practice

Directions: Choose the best answer to the following question.

What is a similarity between the religions of Islam and Christianity?

F They are both monotheistic.

G They both believe that Allah and Muhammad are prophets.

H Both religions forbid the eating of pork.

J Believers of both religions were persecuted by the Romans.

Test-Taking Tip: When a question asks for a similarity, check that your answer is true for both parts of the comparison. In this case, you need something that is true for both faiths. Wrong answer choices often describe only *one half* of the comparison.

WORLD RELIGIONS

How was the universe created? What happens when we die? How do we become good people? These are some of the questions that religions attempt to answer. By creating an organized system of worship, religions help us make sense of our lives and our world.

Religion can be an individual belief. In some nations, religion is also state policy. Throughout history, religions have had the power both to unite people and to create terrible conflict. Today, there are thousands of religions practiced by about 6 billion people around the world.

Major World Religions

Religion	Number of Followers
Christianity	1,974,181,000
Islam	1,155,109,000
Hinduism	799,028,000
Buddhism	356,270,000
Confucianism	154,080,000
Judaism	14,313,000

Source: *Encyclopaedia Britannica Book of the Year.*
Note: The figure for Confucianism includes Chinese followers.

NATIONAL GEOGRAPHIC — World Religions

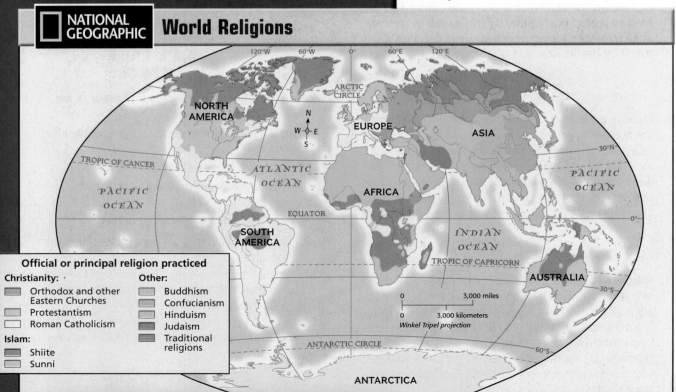

Official or principal religion practiced

Christianity:
- Orthodox and other Eastern Churches
- Protestantism
- Roman Catholicism

Islam:
- Shiite
- Sunni

Other:
- Buddhism
- Confucianism
- Hinduism
- Judaism
- Traditional religions

0   3,000 miles
0   3,000 kilometers
Winkel Tripel projection

Local Religions

Although some religions have spread worldwide, many people still practice religions that originated and developed in their own area.

Australia

There are no deities in the traditional beliefs of the Aborigines of Australia. Their lives revolve around a belief known as the Dreamtime. According to aboriginal mythology, ancestor heroes created the world and all it contains during the Dreamtime. The Aborigines also believe in spirits that inhabit the natural world and can be reborn or return to the earth many times.

Africa

Many Africans south of the Sahara continue traditional religious practices. Because Africa has many ethnic groups, languages, customs, and beliefs, it is not surprising that local religions are just as diverse. Despite the differences, however, most Africans recognize one god whom they consider to be a supreme creator.

Japan

In Japan there are over 80,000 Shinto shrines, such as the one shown to the left. Shintoism, which goes back to prehistoric times, has no formal doctrine. Believers worship *kami,* which are sacred spirits that take on natural forms such as trees or mountains. They also worship ancestors or protectors of families.

North America

The Navajo religion is distinct in that it must be practiced in a particular geographical area. Navajo people believe that the Creator instructed them never to leave the land between four sacred mountains located in Colorado, New Mexico, and Arizona. Navajo dwellings, called hogans (at right), are sacred and constructed to symbolize their land: the four posts represent the sacred mountains, the floor is Mother Earth, and the dome-like roof is Father Sky.

Major Religions —→ History and Beliefs

Buddhism

Buddhism began in India around the sixth century B.C. and today is practiced by over 350 million people throughout Asia. It is based on the teachings of Siddhartha Gautama, known as the Buddha, or Enlightened One. The Buddha taught that to escape the suffering caused by worldly desires, people must follow the Eightfold Path, which prescribes a life of morality, wisdom, and contemplation. The Wheel of Law (at left) is an important Buddhist symbol, representing the endless cycle of life.

Christianity

Christians believe in one God and that Jesus Christ is the Savior, the Son of God, who was sent to Earth and died on the cross to save humanity. Christians believe that faith in Jesus saves believers from God's penalty for sin and bestows eternal life. The cross remains a very potent symbol of the religion. For Christians, the Bible is the inspired word of God. Christianity began approximately 2,000 years ago. It is practiced by almost 2 billion people in nearly all parts of the world.

Confucianism

Although many people consider Confucianism a religion, it is actually a philosophy based on the teachings of Confucius, a Chinese scholar who lived about 500 B.C. He believed that moral character and social responsibility were the way to lead a fulfilling life. Confucianism has been an important influence on Chinese life since its founding, and Confucius is often honored as a spiritual teacher.

Major Religions——⟩ History and Beliefs

Hinduism

Hinduism is the world's oldest organized religion, starting in India about 1500 B.C. It has influenced and absorbed many other religions. This has led to a wide variety of beliefs and practices among its followers, who number about 800 million and still live principally in India. Although Hindus worship a number of gods, today they primarily worship Siva and Vishnu (shown at left). Siva represents both the destructive and creative forces of the universe. Vishnu is considered the preserver of the universe.

Islam

The followers of Islam, known as Muslims, believe in one God, *Allah.* They also accept all the prophets of Judaism and Christianity. Muslims follow the practices and teachings of the Quran, which the prophet Muhammad said was revealed to him by Allah beginning in A.D. 610. In 2000, there were about 1.1 billion Muslims, living mainly in Asia and Africa. Islam is often symbolized by a crescent moon, an important element of Muslim rituals, which depend on the lunar calendar.

Judaism

Jews believe in only one God; in fact, their faith, Judaism, was the first monotheistic religion. Today about 14 million people throughout the world practice Judaism, with most Jews living in Israel and the United States. The main laws and practices of Judaism are contained in the Torah (the *Pentateuch*), the first five books of the Hebrew Bible. The six-pointed star, known as the Star of David (see the Torah mantle at left), was rarely used as a Jewish symbol until the nineteenth century. Today it is widely accepted and appears on the Israeli flag.

Major Religions → *Worship and Celebrations*

Buddhism

The ultimate goal of Buddhism is to reach nirvana, an enlightened state that frees an individual from the suffering that is found in life. Anyone might reach nirvana, but it is considered most attainable by Buddhist monks. These devout believers usually live in monasteries, leading a disciplined life of poverty, meditation, and study. Those who are not monks pursue enlightenment by making offerings and performing rituals such as walking clockwise around sacred domes, called stupas.

Christianity

Christians gather weekly to worship God and pray. Christians also observe important and joyful holidays such as Easter, which celebrates the resurrection of Jesus Christ. Christians believe that his resurrection was the evidence of God's power over sin and death. Holy Week, the week before Easter, begins with Palm Sunday, which celebrates Jesus' arrival into Jerusalem. Maundy Thursday, or Holy Thursday, commemorates Jesus' last meal with his disciples. Good Friday is a somber day in remembrance of Jesus' death.

Confucianism

Confucianism does not have a god or clergy and does not concern itself with what could be considered religious issues. It is more of a guide to ethical behavior and good government. Despite this, Confucius is venerated as a spiritual leader, and there are many temples dedicated to him. His teachings were recorded by his students in a book called the *Analects,* which have influenced Chinese people for generations.

Major Religions—⟶ *Worship and Celebrations*

Hinduism

Hindus believe that after death the soul leaves the body and is reborn in another person, animal, vegetable, or mineral. Where a soul is reborn depends upon its karma, or the accumulated merits or faults of its past lives. One of the ways Hindus increase "good" karma is through rituals such as washing away their sins. The Ganges is considered a sacred river to Hindus, and each year thousands come to bathe in the water to purify themselves.

Islam

Ramadan is the ninth month of the Muslim calendar, commemorating the time during which Muhammad received the Quran from Allah. During Ramadan, Muslims read from the Quran and fast from dawn until sunset. Fasting helps believers focus on spiritual rather than bodily matters. The daily fast is broken with prayers and a meal called the *iftar*. People celebrate the end of Ramadan with the Feast of the Fast, *Eid-ul-Fitr*.

Judaism

Observant Jews follow many strict laws that guide their daily lives and the ways in which they worship. They recite their prayers standing up and often wear a prayer shawl. Their heads are covered as a sign of respect for God. Every synagogue (place of worship) has a Torah, handwritten on a parchment scroll. During services, the Torah is read to the congregation, and the entire text is read in the course of a year.

7 Early African Civilizations

2000 B.C.–A.D. 1500

Key Events

As you read this chapter, look for the key events in the history of the early African civilizations.

- *The continent's immense size and distinct geographical and climatic zones influenced where civilizations developed and how they survived.*
- *The introduction of Christianity and Islam affected the way civilizations developed and interacted.*
- *The development of trade led to the exchange of goods and cultural ideas.*

The Impact Today

The events that occurred during this time period still impact our lives today.
- *The expansion of trade creates a global society, allowing people to exchange goods, services, and ideas throughout the world.*
- *African art, music, and dance remain very influential today.*

 World History Video *The Chapter 7 video, "Early African Empires," chronicles the emergence and development of African culture.*

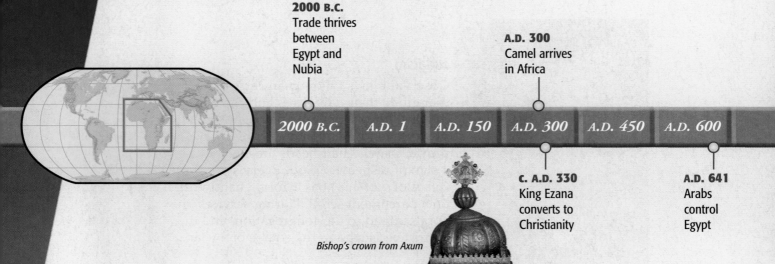

2000 B.C.
Trade thrives between Egypt and Nubia

A.D. 300
Camel arrives in Africa

| 2000 B.C. | A.D. 1 | A.D. 150 | A.D. 300 | A.D. 450 | A.D. 600 |

C. A.D. 330
King Ezana converts to Christianity

A.D. 641
Arabs control Egypt

Bishop's crown from Axum

The great mosque in Djenné, Mali, exemplifies mud architecture of this region of Africa.

Leopard from Benin

A.D. 1250
Mali established

A.D. 1300
Yoruba and Benin produce bronze sculptures

A.D. 1331
Ibn Battuta visits Kilwa

A.D. 750   *A.D. 900*   *A.D. 1050*   *A.D. 1200*   *A.D. 1350*   *A.D. 1500*

A.D. 1100
Problems arise between Christian Axum and its Muslim neighbors

Mosque in Mali

A.D. 1493
Muhammad Ture expands the Songhai Empire

Sixteenth-century sculpture found in modern-day Nigeria

HISTORY
Online

Chapter Overview
Visit the *Glencoe World History* Web site at tx.wh.glencoe.com and click on **Chapter 7–Chapter Overview** to preview chapter information.

A Story That Matters

Great Zimbabwe, the ruins of the capital of Zimbabwe, was the wealthiest city in southern Africa.

Explorer Finds Great Zimbabwe

*I*n 1871, the German explorer Karl Mauch began to search South Africa's Central Plateau for the colossal stone ruins of a legendary lost civilization. In early September, he found what he had been looking for, Great Zimbabwe. He wrote in his diary, "Presently I stood before it and beheld a wall of a height of about 20 feet (6 m) of granite bricks. Very close by there was a place where a kind of foot-path led over rubble into the interior. Following this path I stumbled over masses of rubble and parts of walls and dense thickets. I stopped in front of a towerlike structure. Altogether it rose to a height of about 30 feet (9.1 m)."

Mauch was convinced that "a civilized nation must once have lived here." Like many other nineteenth-century Europeans, however, Mauch was equally convinced that the Africans who had lived there could never have built structures as splendid as the ones he had found at Great Zimbabwe. Mauch and other archaeologists believed that Great Zimbabwe must have been the work of "a northern race closely akin to the Phoenician and Egyptian." Not until the twentieth century did Europeans finally overcome their prejudices and admit that Africans south of Egypt had developed advanced civilizations with spectacular achievements.

Why It Matters

The continent of Africa has played a central role in the long evolution of humankind. It was in Africa that the immediate ancestors of modern human beings—*Homo sapiens sapiens*—emerged between 200,000 and 150,000 years ago. Certainly, one of the first civilizations appeared in Africa: the kingdom of Egypt in the Nile valley. A number of advanced societies took root in other parts of Africa as well.

History and You The origins of Great Zimbabwe remain a mystery. Using the Internet and traditional print sources, investigate and then document your theory about who was responsible for building this city.

The Development of Civilizations in Africa

Main Ideas
- Africa's four distinct climate zones affected the development of African civilizations.
- The mastery of farming gave rise to the first civilizations in Africa: Egypt, Kush, and Axum.

Key Terms
plateau, savanna

People to Identify
Kushites, King Ezana

Places to Locate
Sahara, Great Rift Valley, Congo River, Kalahari Desert, Nubia, Ethiopia

Preview Questions
1. What were the main occupations of early Africans?
2. How did the introduction of Christianity and Islam affect African states?

Reading Strategy
Cause and Effect As you read this section, create a chart that lists a significant event that occurred (cause) and the effect this event had on early African civilization. Refer to this section's main ideas for causes.

Cause	Effect

Preview of Events

♦700 B.C.	♦400 B.C.	♦100 B.C.	♦A.D. 200	♦A.D. 500	♦A.D. 800	♦A.D. 1100

750 B.C.
Kush conquers Egypt

663 B.C.
Assyrians drive Kushites out of Egypt

A.D. 150
Kush declines as Axum emerges

A.D. 1100
Conflicts arise between Christians and Muslims

Voices from the Past

Axum stele with record of King Ezana

One king of the African state of Axum left this description of his conquest of Kush:

❝With the help of the Lord of Heaven, who in heaven and earth conquers all, Ezana, king of Axum . . . by the power of the Lord of the Earth . . . burnt their towns, those with stone houses and those with straw [dwellings], and [my troops] pillaged their [crops] and bronze and iron and copper; they destroyed the [images] in their temples and also their stores of [crops] and cotton, and threw them into the river Seda . . . and the next day I sent my troops on a campaign up the Seda to the towns of stone and of straw.❞

—*The Dawn of African History,* **Roland Oliver, ed., 1968**

After the decline of the Egyptian Empire during the first millennium B.C., the focus of social change moved to other areas of Africa.

The Land of Africa

After Asia, Africa is the largest of the continents. It stretches nearly five thousand miles (around eight thousand km) and is almost completely surrounded by two oceans and two seas.

As diverse as it is vast, Africa includes several distinct geographical zones. The northern fringe, on the coast washed by the Mediterranean Sea, is mountainous. South of the mountains lies the largest desert on Earth, the **Sahara.**

CHAPTER 7   Early African Civilizations   **223**

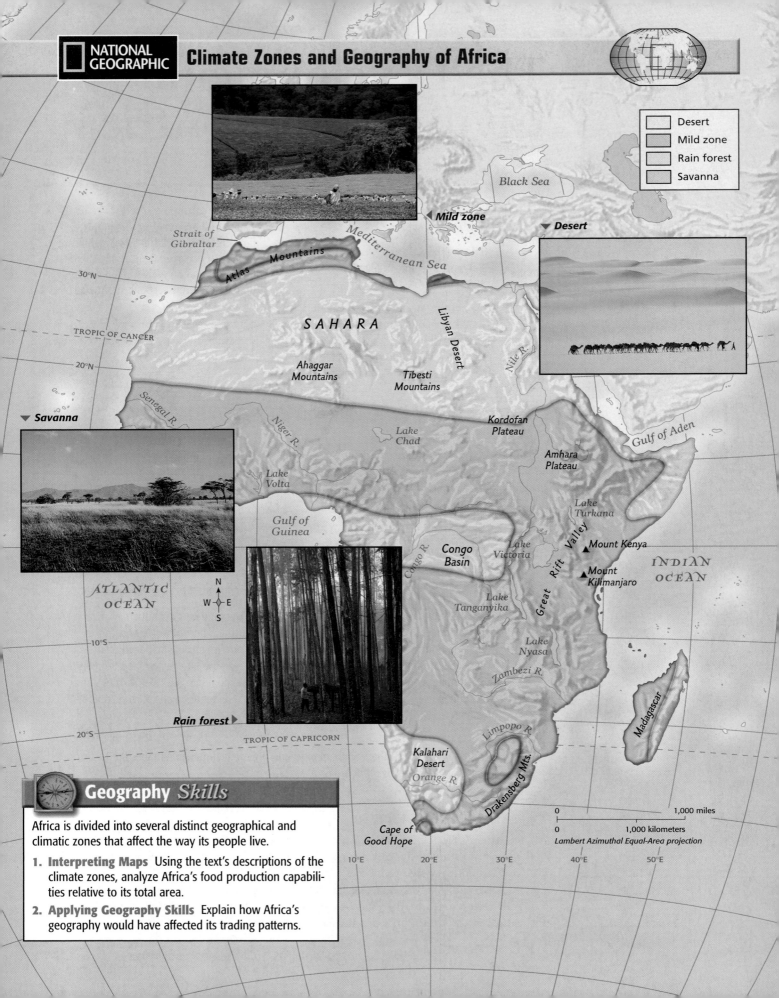

Climate Zones and Geography of Africa

NATIONAL GEOGRAPHIC

Legend:
- Desert
- Mild zone
- Rain forest
- Savanna

◄ **Mild zone**

▼ **Desert**

Black Sea

Strait of Gibraltar

Mediterranean Sea

Atlas Mountains

30°N

TROPIC OF CANCER

SAHARA

Libyan Desert

20°N

Ahaggar Mountains

Tibesti Mountains

Nile R.

Gulf of Aden

Kordofan Plateau

▼ **Savanna**

Senegal R.

Niger R.

Lake Chad

Amhara Plateau

Lake Turkana

Lake Volta

Gulf of Guinea

Congo R.

Congo Basin

Lake Victoria

Great Rift Valley

Lake Tanganyika

▲ Mount Kenya

▲ Mount Kilimanjaro

INDIAN OCEAN

ATLANTIC OCEAN

N
W · E
S

10°S

Lake Nyasa

Zambezi R.

Madagascar

Rain forest ►

Limpopo R.

20°S

TROPIC OF CAPRICORN

Kalahari Desert

Drakensberg Mts.

Orange R.

0 — 1,000 miles
0 — 1,000 kilometers
Lambert Azimuthal Equal-Area projection

Cape of Good Hope

10°E   20°E   30°E   40°E   50°E

Geography Skills

Africa is divided into several distinct geographical and climatic zones that affect the way its people live.

1. **Interpreting Maps** Using the text's descriptions of the climate zones, analyze Africa's food production capabilities relative to its total area.

2. **Applying Geography Skills** Explain how Africa's geography would have affected its trading patterns.

Africa south of the Sahara is divided into a number of major regions. In the west is the so-called hump of Africa, which juts like a massive shoulder into the Atlantic Ocean. Here the Sahara gradually gives way to grasslands in the interior and then to tropical jungles along the coast.

Far to the east is a very different terrain of snow-capped mountains, upland plateaus, and lakes. A distinctive feature is the **Great Rift Valley,** where mountains loom over deep canyons. Much of this region is grassland populated by wild animals. Further to the south lies the Congo basin, with its dense vegetation watered by the mighty **Congo River.** The tropical rain forests of this area then fade gradually into the hills, plateaus (relatively high, flat land areas), and deserts of the south.

✔**Reading Check** **Describing** Describe the distinct geographical zones in Africa.

The Climate of Africa

Africa includes four distinct climate zones, which help to explain the different lifestyles of the peoples of Africa. A mild climate zone stretches across the northern coast and southern tip of Africa. Moderate rainfall and warm temperatures result in fertile land that produces abundant crops. This crop production can support large populations.

Deserts form another climate zone. The Sahara in the north and the **Kalahari** in the south are the two largest deserts. Altogether, deserts cover about 40 percent of Africa.

A third climate zone is the rain forest that stretches along the equator and makes up about 10 percent of the continent. Heavy rains and warm temperatures produce dense forests where little farming and little travel are possible. The rain forest is also home to disease-carrying insects, especially the tsetse (SET• see) fly, which infects both animals and humans with sleeping sickness. As a result, people who live in the rain forest do not raise cattle or use animals, hoping in this way to avoid the tsetse fly.

A final climate zone consists of the savannas, broad grasslands dotted with small trees and shrubs. Savannas stretch across Africa both north and south of the rain forest and cover perhaps 40 percent of Africa's land area. The savannas receive enough rainfall to allow for farming and the herding of animals, but the rain is unreliable.

✔**Reading Check** **Summarizing** How do the four different climate zones affect daily life in Africa?

Emerging Civilization and the Rise of Islam

About seven or eight thousand years ago, hunters and gatherers in Africa began to tame animals and grow crops. The mastery of farming gave rise to the first civilizations in Africa: Egypt (discussed in Chapter 2), Kush, and Axum. Much later, Islam became an important factor in the development of African empires.

Kush By 2000 B.C., a busy trade had arisen between Egypt and the area to the south known as **Nubia.** Egyptian merchants traveled to Nubia to obtain ivory, ebony, frankincense (a fragrant tree resin), and leopard skins. Although Nubia was subject to Egyptian control for many centuries, it freed itself around 1000 B.C. and became the independent state of Kush.

In 750 B.C., Kush conquered Egypt. In 663 B.C., however, the **Kushites,** who were still using bronze and stone weapons, were overwhelmed by the Assyrians, who were armed with iron spears and swords. The Kushites, driven out of Egypt, returned to their original lands in the upper Nile valley.

The economy of Kush was based at first on farming. Kush soon emerged, however, as one of the major trading states in the region, with its center at the city of Meroë (MEHR•oh•EE).

Meroë was well located at the point where a newly opened land route across the desert to the north crossed the Nile. It was also blessed with a large supply of iron ore. Having learned iron ore smelting from the Assyrians, the Kushites made iron weapons and tools.

For the next several hundred years, Kush was a major trading empire with links to other states throughout the region. Kush provided iron products and goods from central and eastern Africa to the Roman Empire, as well as to Arabia and India. Other major exports were ivory, gold, ebony, and slaves. In return, the Kushites received luxury goods, including jewelry and silver lamps from India and Arabia.

Not much is known about Kushite society. It seems likely that it was mostly urban. At first, state authorities probably controlled foreign trade. The presence of extensive luxury goods in the numerous private tombs in the area indicates that at one time material prosperity was relatively widespread. This suggests that at some point a large merchant class prospered from trade activities.

The Rise of Axum Kush flourished from about 250 B.C. to about A.D. 150, but declined because of the rise of a new power in the region. This new power, known as Axum, was located in the highlands of what is now Ethiopia. Axum was founded as a colony by Arabs from the southern tip of the Arabian Peninsula. Eventually, Axum emerged as an independent state that combined Arab and African cultures.

Axum owed much of its prosperity to its location along the Red Sea, on the trade route between India and the Mediterranean. Axum exported ivory, frankincense, myrrh (another aromatic tree resin), and slaves. It imported textiles, metal goods, wine, and olive oil.

This stele is the tallest of many built for King Ezana.

For a time, Axum competed with the neighboring state of Kush for control of the ivory trade. Probably as a result of this competition for ivory, in the fourth century A.D., **King Ezana**, the Axumite ruler, launched an invasion of Kush and conquered it.

Perhaps the most distinctive feature of Axumite civilization was its religion. About A.D. 330, King Ezana converted to Christianity, which was first brought to Axum by shipwrecked Syrians. The king made Christianity the official religion of Axum.

When Ezana died, Axum was a flourishing kingdom. Within a few centuries, however, a new religious force—Islam—brought profound challenges to the kingdom of Axum.

The Coming of Islam The rise of Islam in the Arabian Peninsula had an impact on neighboring areas. In 641, Arab forces took control of Egypt. By the early eighth century, the entire coastal region of North Africa as far west as the Strait of Gibraltar was under Arab rule.

By the eighth century, a number of Muslim trading states had been established on the African coast of the Red Sea. For hundreds of years, relations between Christian Axum and its Muslim neighbors were relatively peaceful.

Beginning in the twelfth century, however, problems arose as the Muslim states along the coast began to move inland to gain control over the trade in slaves and ivory. Axum, which had dominated this trade, fought back. By the early fifteenth century, Axum had become deeply involved in an expanding conflict with the Muslim state of Adal, located at the point where the Indian Ocean meets the Red Sea.

✓**Reading Check** **Summarizing** How did conquest and trade affect the people of Kush and Axum?

🔶**TAKS Practice**

SECTION 1 ASSESSMENT

Checking for Understanding

1. **Define** plateau, savanna.

2. **Identify** Kushites, King Ezana.

3. **Locate** Sahara, Great Rift Valley, Congo River, Kalahari Desert, Nubia, Ethiopia.

4. **Explain** the significance of Christianity in the history of Axum.

5. **List** Axum's exports. What product led to King Ezana's decision to invade Kush?

Critical Thinking

6. **Analyze** Why did the rise of a new power in the region cause the decline of Kush?

7. **Compare and Contrast** Complete the chart below, comparing the occupations, natural resources, imports, and exports of Kush and Axum.

Kush	Axum

Analyzing Visuals

8. **Compare** the stele on this page with those pictured on pages 44 and 86. What are the similarities and differences?

Writing About History

9. **Persuasive Writing** Christian Axum traded peacefully with its Muslim neighbors. Do you think that two major religious groups can be peaceful neighbors? Write an essay explaining your opinion.

TECHNOLOGY
SKILLBUILDER

Using A Computerized Card Catalog

Why Learn This Skill?

How do you find the information you need when you are preparing to write a research paper? The number of books and reference materials might seem overwhelming. You can, however, narrow your search. The place to begin is the library's computerized card catalog.

Learning the Skill

- Go to the computerized card catalog in your school or local library. Type in the name of an author or the title of a book. Often, you might not know any particular sources. If that is the case, enter a general subject. For example, if you are writing a paper on salt mining, you might enter "salt mines" or "salt" as your subject.

- When you enter a subject request, the computer will list all the titles that are filed under that subject category, including books, videotapes, audiocassettes, or CDs. The computer might show additional categories for you to check. You will see other information on the screen, such as the author, the media type, and the date the material was published.

Yoruba queen from Ife

- Choose a book from the list. A new screen will appear that gives more details about that particular book, such as the publisher, how many pages and illustrations it has, and the language it is written in.

- The computer will then allow you to check to see if the material is available. If it is, write down the call number so you can find the material on the library shelf.

Practicing the Skill

Follow the steps below to collect materials on the subject of West African kingdoms in the eighth through sixteenth centuries.

❶ Using the computerized card catalog in the library, conduct a subject search on West African kingdoms. What subject(s) would you look under? How could you broaden or narrow your search?

❷ Follow the on-screen instructions to display all the titles under your subject. Find four titles that you think contain information on West African kingdoms.

❸ Select one title from your list. How do you find more details on this title? What information should you check to make sure it is an appropriate resource?

❹ How many copies of this work are available in the library? Where can you find this work in the library?

Applying the Skill

Use a library computerized card catalog to research and produce a brochure giving step-by-step directions on how to find source material about West African kingdoms in the eighth through sixteenth centuries. Describe at least four of the resources you found and why you chose them.

Kingdoms and States of Africa

Main Ideas
- The expansion of trade led to migration and the growth of new kingdoms.
- Rulers introduced different forms of government.

Key Terms
Bantu, subsistence farming, Swahili, stateless society

People to Identify
Berbers, Sundiata Keita, Mansa Musa, Sunni Ali, Muhammad Ture, Ibn Battuta

Places to Locate
Ghana, Mali, Timbuktu, Morocco, Mogadishu, Mombasa, Kilwa, Zambezi River, Zimbabwe

Preview Questions
1. What were the accomplishments of the West African kingdoms?
2. How did Islam impact East Africa?

Reading Strategy
Categorizing Information As you read this section, complete a chart describing the rulers, government, and economy of each kingdom.

Ghana	Mali	Songhai

Preview of Events

♦300	♦500	♦700	♦900	♦1100	♦1300	♦1500

c. 500
Ghana emerges as a trading state

1240
Sundiata defeats Ghanaians

1300
Zimbabwe emerges as a powerful state

1312
Mansa Musa begins reign as Mali's king

1464
Kingdom of Songhai expands

Clay figure from Mali

Voices from the Past

Ibn Battuta, a fourteenth-century Arab traveler, was clearly impressed by the peace and order in Mali:

❝One of [the] good features [of the people of Mali] is their lack of oppression. They are the farthest removed of people from it and their king does not permit anyone to practice it. Another is the security throughout the entire country, so that neither traveler there nor dweller there has anything to fear from robbers or men of violence.❞
— *Ibn Battuta in Black Africa,* **Said Hamdun and Noel King, eds., 1975**

Mali, established in the mid-thirteenth century, was one of the important trading states of West Africa.

The Kingdom of Ghana

Ghana, the first great trading state in West Africa, emerged as early as A.D. 500. The kingdom of Ghana was located in the upper Niger River valley, a grassland region between the Sahara and the tropical forests along the West African coast. (The modern state of Ghana takes its name from this early state but is located in the forest region to the south.) Most of the people in the area were farmers living in villages under the authority of a local ruler. Together, the villages formed the kingdom of Ghana.

The Kings of Ghana The kings of Ghana were strong rulers who governed without any laws. They played active roles in running the kingdom, and their wealth was vast. Al-Bakri, an eleventh-century Muslim traveler, wrote of the Ghanaian king's court:

> 66The king sits in audience or to hear grievances against officials in a domed pavilion around which stand ten horses covered with gold-embroidered materials. Behind the king stand ten pages holding shields and swords decorated with gold, and on his right are the sons of subordinate kings of his country wearing splendid garments and their hair mixed with gold.99

To protect their kingdom and enforce their wishes, Ghanaian kings relied on a well-trained regular army of thousands of men.

Economy and Trade The people of Ghana had lived off the land for centuries. In addition they prospered from their possession of both iron and gold.

The region had an abundant supply of iron ore. The skilled blacksmiths of Ghana were highly valued because of their ability to turn ore into tools and weapons.

Ghana also had an abundance of gold. The heartland of the state was located near one of the richest gold-producing areas in all of Africa. Ghana's gold made it the center of an enormous trade empire.

Muslim merchants from North Africa brought to Ghana metal goods, textiles, horses, and salt. Salt was a highly desired item for the Ghanaians. It was used to preserve food, as well as to improve the food's taste. Salt was also important because people needed extra salt to replace what their bodies lost in the hot climate.

Ghanaians traded their abundant gold for salt and other products brought from North Africa. The exchange of goods in Ghana was done by a method of silent trade, as described by a tenth-century Arabian traveler:

> 66Great people of the Sudan [the Arab name for West Africa] lived [in Ghana]. They had traced a boundary which no one who sets out to them ever crosses. When the merchants reach this boundary, they place their wares and cloth on the ground and then depart, and so the people of the Sudan come bearing gold which they leave beside the merchandise and then depart. The owners of the merchandise then return, and if they were satisfied with what they had found, they take it. If not, they go away again, and the people of the Sudan return and add to the price until the bargain is concluded.99

Other exports from Ghana, including ivory, ostrich feathers, hides, and slaves, also found their way to the markets of the Mediterranean and beyond.

Much of the trade across the desert was carried by the **Berbers,** nomadic peoples whose camel caravans

Picturing **History**

Camel caravans made it possible for people in different regions of Africa to exchange goods and merchandise. In what different ways was this trade advantageous for the people of Ghana?

became known as the "fleets of the desert." Camels became a crucial factor in trade across the Sahara. They were well adapted to conditions in the desert, since they could drink enormous quantities of water at one time and needed little food for days.

In a typical caravan trek, as many as a hundred camels would be loaded with goods and supplies for the journey across the desert. Accompanied by guards, the caravan moved at a rate of about three miles (4.8 km) per hour. A caravan might take 40 to 60 days to reach its destination.

The trading merchants of Ghana often became wealthy. Kings prospered too, because they imposed taxes on goods that entered or left the kingdom. By the eighth and ninth centuries, however, much of this trade was carried by Muslim merchants. They bought the goods from local traders, using iron or copper or items from as far away as Southwest Asia. They then sold them to Berbers, who carried them across the desert.

☑ **Reading Check** **Examining** How did the arrival of the camel affect African trade?

The Kingdom of Mali

The state of Ghana flourished for several hundred years. Eventually, it was weakened by wars, and it collapsed during the 1100s. In its place rose a number

of new trading societies in West Africa. The greatest of these states was **Mali,** established in the mid-thirteenth century by **Sundiata Keita.**

Founding and Economy Like George Washington in the United States, Sundiata is considered the founder of his nation. Sundiata defeated the Ghanaians and captured their capital in 1240. He united the people of Mali and created a strong government.

Extending from the Atlantic coast inland as far as the famous trading city of **Timbuktu** (TIHM•BUHK• TOO), Mali built its wealth and power on the gold and salt trade. Most of its people, however, were farmers who grew grains such as sorghum, millet, and rice. The farmers lived in villages with local rulers, who served as both religious and administrative leaders. The ruler was responsible for sending tax revenues from the village to the kings of Mali.

Reign of Mansa Musa One of the richest and most powerful kings was **Mansa Musa,** who ruled from 1312 to 1337 (*mansa* means "king"). Mansa Musa doubled the size of the kingdom of Mali. He created a strong central government and divided the kingdom into provinces ruled by governors whom he appointed. Once he felt secure, he decided—as a devout Muslim—to make a pilgrimage to Makkah.

A king, of course, was no ordinary pilgrim. Mansa Musa was joined by thousands of servants and

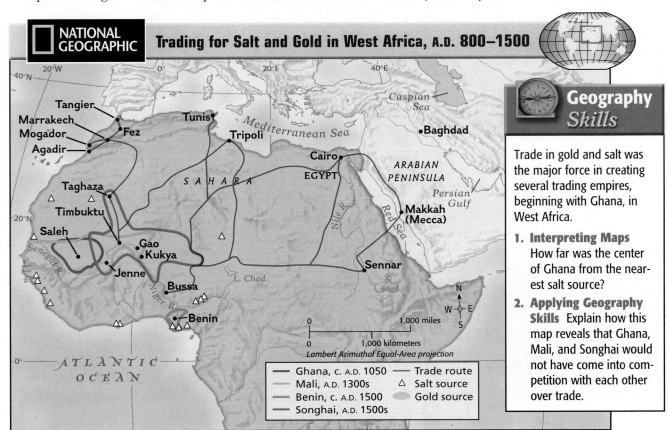

NATIONAL GEOGRAPHIC

Trading for Salt and Gold in West Africa, A.D. 800–1500

Geography Skills

Trade in gold and salt was the major force in creating several trading empires, beginning with Ghana, in West Africa.

1. **Interpreting Maps** How far was the center of Ghana from the nearest salt source?

2. **Applying Geography Skills** Explain how this map reveals that Ghana, Mali, and Songhai would not have come into competition with each other over trade.

Map legend:
- Ghana, c. A.D. 1050
- Mali, A.D. 1300s
- Benin, c. A.D. 1500
- Songhai, A.D. 1500s
- Trade route
- △ Salt source
- Gold source

0 / 1,000 miles
0 / 1,000 kilometers
Lambert Azimuthal Equal-Area projection

soldiers. Accompanying the people were hundreds of camels carrying gold, as well as food, clothing, and other supplies.

Everywhere he went, Mansa Musa lavished gold gifts on his hosts and made hundreds of purchases with gold from merchants. In fact, by putting so much gold into circulation in such a short time, he caused the value of gold to fall. The caravan's route took it through Egypt, and one observer reported, "Gold was at a high price in Egypt until they came in that year. Its value fell and it cheapened in price and has remained cheap till now. . . . This has been the state of affairs for about twelve years until this day by reason of the large amount of gold which they brought into Egypt and spent there."

No doubt, Mansa Musa's great pilgrimage left people with an image of him as a great ruler of a powerful and prosperous kingdom. Mansa Musa also left another legacy. Earlier rulers of Mali had already converted to Islam, but Mansa Musa strongly encouraged the building of mosques and a palace, as well as the study of the Quran in his kingdom.

He imported scholars and books to introduce his subjects to the message of Allah. He brought architects back with him to build mosques like the ones he had seen in Cairo and Arabia. The famous Sankore mosque in Timbuktu was one of the results. Sankore also became an important center of learning.

Mansa Musa proved to be the last powerful ruler of Mali. By 1359, civil war divided Mali. Within another hundred years a new kingdom—that of Songhai—was beginning to surpass Mali.

Reading Check **Summarizing** What were Mansa Musa's accomplishments?

The Kingdom of Songhai

Like the Nile, the Niger River floods and thus provides a rich soil for raising crops and taking care of cattle. East of Timbuktu, the river makes a wide bend. Along the river, south of that bend, a people known as the Songhai established themselves.

In 1009, a ruler named Kossi converted to Islam and established the Dia dynasty. This first Songhai state benefited from the Muslim trade routes linking Arabia, North Africa, and West Africa. An era of prosperity ensued with Gao as the chief trade center.

Under the leadership of **Sunni Ali,** who created a new dynasty—the Sunni—in 1464, Songhai began to expand. Sunni Ali spent much of his reign on horseback and on the march as he led his army in one military campaign after another. Two of Sunni Ali's

People In History

Sundiata Keita
c. 1210–1260—Malian ruler

The name Sundiata means the "lion prince." The lion was the symbol of the Keita clan, of which Sundiata was a member.

Sundiata belonged to a family that had ruled Mali for about two centuries. Born with a disability, he still could not walk when he was seven years old. With the aid of a blacksmith who made braces for his legs, however, Sundiata gradually and painfully learned to walk.

Although he became a Muslim, Sundiata kept his traditional African religion as well. This enabled him to maintain the support of the common people, who believed that the king had magical powers. As a powerful warrior-king and the creator of the kingdom of Mali, Sundiata Keita became revered as the father of his country.

conquests, Timbuktu and Jenne, were especially important. They gave Songhai control of the trading empire—especially trade in salt and gold—that had made Ghana and Mali so prosperous.

The Songhai Empire reached the height of its power during the reign of **Muhammad Ture.** A military commander and devout Muslim, Muhammad Ture overthrew the son of Sunni Ali and seized power in 1493, thus creating a new dynasty, the Askia. (*Askia* means "usurper.")

Muhammad Ture continued Sunni Ali's policy of expansion, creating an empire that stretched a thousand miles along the Niger River. He was an able administrator who divided Songhai into provinces. Muhammad Ture maintained the peace and security of his kingdom with a navy and soldiers on horseback. The chief cities of the empire prospered as never before from the salt and gold trade.

After Muhammad Ture's reign, Songhai entered a period of slow decline. Near the end of the sixteenth century, that decline quickened when the forces of the sultan of **Morocco** occupied much of Songhai. One observer wrote, "From that moment on, everything changed. Danger took the place of security, poverty [took the place] of wealth. Peace gave way to distress, disasters, and violence." By 1600, the Songhai Empire was little more than a remnant of its former glorious self.

Reading Check **Summarizing** What were the key factors in Songhai's rise to power?

African Trading Empires, 1000 B.C.–A.D. 1600

	Kush (Nubia)	Axum	Ghana	Mali	Songhai
Empire	Meroë	Adulis	Saleh	Timbuktu	Gao
Location	East Africa south of Egypt	East Africa (Ethiopia)	West Africa	West Africa	West Africa
Time Period	1000 B.C.–A.D. 150	A.D. 100–1400	A.D. 400–1200	A.D. 1250–1450	A.D. 1000–1600
Goods Traded	Iron products, ivory, gold, ebony, slaves	Ivory, frankincense, myrrh, slaves	Iron products, animal products, gold	Gold, salt	Gold, salt
Key Facts	Kush lost power to Axum.	Axum was founded by Arab traders; the king converted to Christianity in A.D. 324.	Ghana traded for salt from the Saharan salt mines.	Mansa Musa doubled the size of the kingdom and created a Muslim center of learning.	Songhai gained control of trade in West Africa with the conquest of Timbuktu and Jenne.

Societies in East Africa

⌐TURNING POINT⌐ **There is little or no evidence of ironworking in eastern and southern Africa before the arrival of the Bantu, suggesting that the new technology was spread by the migrants.**

In eastern Africa, a variety of states and small societies took root. Islam strongly influenced many of them. Some became extremely wealthy as a result of trade.

Migration of the Bantus South of Axum, along the shores of the Indian Ocean and inland from the mountains of Ethiopia through the lake district of central Africa, lived a mixture of peoples. Some lived by hunting and food gathering, whereas others raised livestock.

Beginning in the first millennium B.C., new peoples began to migrate into eastern Africa from the west. Farming peoples who spoke dialects of the Bantu (BAN•TOO) family of languages began to move from the region of the Niger River into East Africa and the Congo River

basin. They moved slowly, not as invading hordes but as small communities.

Recent archaeological work has provided us with a better idea of the nature of Bantu society. The communities that arose as a result of these population movements were based on subsistence farming—growing just enough crops for personal use, not for sale. The primary crops were grains (millet and sorghum), along with yams, melons, and beans. The land was farmed with both iron and stone tools.

Within the families in the villages, men and women performed different tasks. Women tilled the fields and cared for the children. Men tended the herds or engaged in such tasks as hunting and trade. Most trade was local and involved necessities such as salt and commodities such as animal products, copper, and iron ore.

Chart *Skills*

For thousands of years, African states and kingdoms conducted flourishing trade with surrounding empires and with cultures throughout the Mediterranean world.

1. **Identifying** What was the longest lasting empire of those listed above? What were the two largest kingdoms geographically?

Indian Ocean Trade and Ports On the eastern fringe of the continent, the Bantu-speaking peoples gradually began to take part in the regional trade that moved by sea up and down the East African coast. With the growth in regional trade following the rise of Islam during the seventh and eighth centuries A.D., the eastern coast of Africa became an important part of the trading network along the Indian Ocean. Beginning in the eighth century, Muslims from the Arabian Peninsula and the Persian Gulf began to settle at ports along the coast.

The result was the formation of a string of trading ports that included **Mogadishu** (MAH•guh•DIH•shoo), **Mombasa,** and **Kilwa** in the south. Merchants in these cities grew very wealthy. One of the most magnificent cities of the day was Kilwa.

In the fourteenth century, two monumental buildings were constructed in Kilwa of coral cut from the cliffs along the shore. One was the Great Mosque of Kilwa. Even grander was the Husuni Kubwa palace, an enormous clifftop building of more than a hundred rooms. Members of Kilwa's wealthy elite built their houses near the palace and the Great Mosque. With imported Chinese porcelain and indoor plumbing, these homes provided a luxurious lifestyle.

The Arab traveler **Ibn Battuta** called Kilwa, which he visited in 1331, "one of the most beautiful towns in the world." Kilwa's splendor did not last long,

however. Kilwa began to decline, and the Portuguese finished the job in 1505 by sacking the city and destroying its major buildings.

As time passed, a mixed African-Arabian culture, eventually known as Swahili (swah•HEE•lee), began to emerge throughout the coastal area. Intermarriage was common among the ruling groups. Gradually, the Muslim religion and Arabic architectural styles became part of a society still largely African.

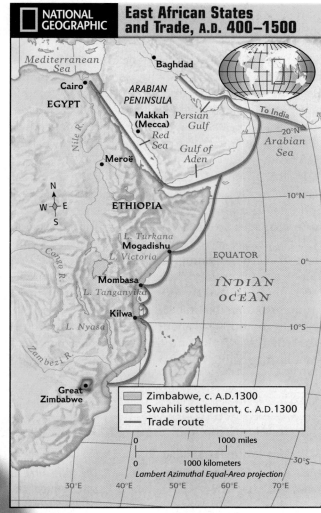

NATIONAL GEOGRAPHIC

East African States and Trade, A.D. 400–1500

Zimbabwe, c. A.D. 1300
Swahili settlement, c. A.D. 1300
— Trade route

0   1000 miles
0   1000 kilometers
Lambert Azimuthal Equal-Area projection

Wealthy merchants in Mombasa built enormous stone houses. Note the Chinese influence in the architecture.

Geography *Skills*

Trade greatly affected East Africa and created prosperous cities such as Kilwa.

1. **Interpreting Maps** Where were the primary Swahili settlements? How was their location related to trade and the trade routes?

2. **Applying Geography Skills** What do you think the trade routes shown in the map reveal about preferred methods of transportation?

The term *Swahili* (from *sahel,* meaning "coast" in Arabic, and thus "peoples of the coast") was also applied to the major language used in the area. Swahili was a mixed language that combined Bantu with a number of Arabic words and phrases. Today it is the national language of **Kenya** and **Tanzania.**

✓ **Reading Check** **Describing** How did the Bantu migrations affect African culture?

States and Stateless Societies in South Africa

In the southern half of the African continent, states formed more slowly than in the north. Until the eleventh century A.D., most of the peoples in this region lived in what are sometimes called stateless societies. A stateless society is a group of independent villages organized by clans and led by a local ruler or clan head.

In the grassland regions south of the **Zambezi River,** a mixed economy of farming, cattle herding, and trade had developed over a period of many centuries. Villages in this area were usually built inside walls to protect the domestic animals from wild animals at night. Beginning in the eleventh century, in some parts of southern Africa, these independent villages gradually began to consolidate. Out of these groupings came the first states.

From about 1300 to about 1450, **Zimbabwe** (zihm•BAH•bwee) was the wealthiest and most powerful state in the region. It prospered from the gold trade with the Swahili trading communities on the eastern coast of the continent. Indeed, Zimbabwe's gold ended up in the court of Kublai Khan, emperor of China.

The ruins of Zimbabwe's capital, known as Great Zimbabwe, illustrate the kingdom's power and influence. The town sits on a hill overlooking the Zambezi River and is surrounded by stone walls. Ten thousand residents would have been able to live in the area enclosed by the walls. Artifacts found at the site include household implements, ornaments made of gold and copper, and porcelain imported from China.

The Great Enclosure, whose exact purpose is not known, dominated the site. It was an oval space surrounded by a wall 800 feet long, 17 feet thick, and 32 feet high (about 244 m long, 5 m thick, and 10 m high). Near the Great Enclosure were smaller walled enclosures that contained round houses built of a mudlike cement on stone foundations. In the valley below was the royal palace, surrounded by a high stone wall.

The massive walls of Great Zimbabwe are unusual. The local people stacked granite blocks together without mortar to build the walls. By the middle of the fifteenth century, however, the city was abandoned, possibly because of damage to the land through overgrazing or natural disasters such as droughts and crop failures.

✓ **Reading Check** **Evaluating** What do the walled enclosures tell us about Great Zimbabwe?

🏴 **TAKS Practice**

SECTION 2 ASSESSMENT

Checking for Understanding

1. **Define** Bantu, subsistence farming, Swahili, stateless society.

2. **Identify** Berbers, Sundiata Keita, Mansa Musa, Sunni Ali, Muhammad Ture, Ibn Battuta.

3. **Locate** Ghana, Mali, Timbuktu, Morocco, Mogadishu, Mombasa, Kilwa, Zambezi River, Zimbabwe.

4. **Explain** the relationship between the king of Mali and his local governors.

5. **List** Sunni Ali's conquests that gave the Songhai control of the trading empire.

Critical Thinking

6. **Describe** How did the religion of Islam spread throughout Africa during the period discussed in this section?

7. **Summarizing Information** Create a chart describing the cultural and technological contributions made by Ghana, Mali, and Zimbabwe.

Kingdom	Contributions
Ghana	
Mali	
Zimbabwe	

Analyzing Visuals

8. **Examine** the figure on page 228 of your text. What is distinctive about this figure? What might the artist be attempting to convey?

Writing About History

9. **Expository Writing** Reread the text description of Mansa Musa's pilgrimage to Makkah, then write a brief account of his journey. Follow up your description with an explanation of how his pilgrimage had both a positive and negative impact on the economies of the countries he visited.

Eyewitness to History

The Salt Mines

IBN BATTUTA WAS BORN IN MOROCCO in 1304. When he was 21 years old, he went on a pilgrimage to Makkah. He spent the next 24 years wandering throughout Africa and Asia. In writing an account of his travels, he provided modern readers with an accurate description of conditions in the fourteenth century.

❝We arrived after 25 days at Taghaza. It is a village with no good in it. Among its curiosities is the fact that the construction of its houses is of

rock salt with camel skin roofing and there are no trees in it, the soil is just sand. In it is a salt mine. It is dug out of the ground and is found there in huge slabs, one on top of another as if it had been carved and put under the ground. A camel can carry two slabs of salt. Nobody lives in the village except slaves who dig for the salt and live on dates and on the meat of camels that is brought from the land of the blacks. The blacks arrive from their country and carry away the salt from there. The blacks exchange the salt as money as one would exchange gold and silver. They cut it up and trade with it in pieces. In spite of the insignificance of the village of Taghaza, much trading goes on in it. We stayed in it 10 days in miserable conditions, because its water is bitter and it is of all places the most full of flies. In it water is drawn for the entry into the desert which comes after it. This desert is a traveling distance of 10 days and there is no water in it except rarely. But we found much water in it in pools left behind by the rains. One day we found a pool of sweet water between two hillocks of rocks. We quenched our thirsts from it and washed our clothes. In that desert truffles are abundant. There are also so

African salt mines were described by Ibn Battuta (inset photo) in the 1300s and still exist today.

many lice in it that people put strings around their necks in which there is mercury which kills the lice. In those days we used to go ahead in front of the caravan. When we found a place suitable for pasture we would let the animals pasture. ❞

—Ibn Battuta, *Ibn Battuta in Black Africa*

Analyzing Primary Sources

1. Why did Ibn Battuta write that the village of Taghaza was a village "with no good in it"?
2. Explain the economic value of Taghaza.

SECTION 3 | African Society and Culture

Guide to Reading

Main Ideas
- Extended family units formed the basis of African villages.
- The arts were important in early African culture.

Key Terms
lineage group, matrilineal, patrilineal, diviner, griot

People to Identify
Yoruba, Ashanti

Places to Locate
Nigeria, Ife, Benin

Preview Questions
1. How were ancestors and family important to early Africans?
2. What roles did storytelling and music play in African culture?

Reading Strategy
Compare and Contrast As you read this section, use the chart below to compare and contrast the duties and rights of women and men in African society.

	Duties	Rights
Women		
Men		

Preview of Events

♦ 600 B.C.	♦ 200 B.C.	♦ A.D. 200	♦ A.D. 600	♦ A.D. 1000	♦ A.D. 1400

500 B.C.
Nok culture begins to flourish along Niger River

A.D. 1300
Yoruba culture produces bronze and iron sculpture

A.D. 1490
Area south of Sahara accepts Islam

Voices from the Past

Benin brass casting honoring the king (top, center)

The Arab traveler Ibn Battuta once described an audience between an African king and his subjects:

❝When [the king] calls one of [his subjects] while he is in session the man invited takes off his clothes and wears patched clothes, takes off his turban, puts on a dirty cap, and goes in raising his clothes and trousers up his legs half-way to his knees. He advances with humility looking like a beggar. He hits the ground with his elbows, he hits it hard. He stands bowed, listening to what the king says. When one of them speaks to the king and he gives him an answer, he removes his clothes from his back and throws dust on his head and back, as a person does when bathing with water. I used to wonder how they do not blind their eyes.❞
— *Ibn Battuta in Black Africa*, **Said Hamdun and Noel King, eds., 1975**

Because most African societies did not have written languages, much of what we know about these societies comes from descriptions recorded by foreign visitors, like Ibn Battuta.

Aspects of African Society

African towns often began as fortified walled villages and gradually grew into larger communities serving several purposes. These towns were the centers of government, and the markets were filled with goods from faraway regions. The towns were also home to artisans skilled in metal-working, woodworking, pottery making, and other crafts, as well as farmers who tilled the soil in the neighboring fields.

Although Ibn Battuta's description on the preceding page might not suggest it, the relationship of African kings to their subjects was beneficial to king and subject. Indeed, African society had several unusual features.

King and Subject
In most Asian societies, the royal family and the aristocracy were largely isolated from the rest of the people. In Africa, the gulf between king and common people was not as great. Frequently, the ruler would hold an audience to allow people to voice their complaints. Nevertheless, the king was still held in a position high above all others.

The relationship between king and subject in many African states helped both sides. Merchants received favors from the king, and the king's treasury was filled with taxes paid by merchants. It was certainly to the benefit of the king to maintain law and order in the kingdom so that the merchants could practice their trade.

Family and Lineage
Few Africans, of course, ever had an audience (meeting) with their kings. Most people lived in small villages in the countryside. Their sense of identity was determined by their membership in an extended family and a lineage group.

At the basic level was the extended family, made up of parents, children, grandparents, and other family dependents. They lived in small, round dwellings made of packed mud and topped with a thatch roof of plant material such as straw. These extended family units were in turn combined into larger communities known as lineage groups.

Lineage groups served as the basic building blocks of African society. All members of a lineage group could claim to be descended from a real or legendary common ancestor. As in China, the elders—the leading members of the lineage group—had much power over the others in the group. A lineage group provided mutual support for all its members. Members of extended families and lineage groups were expected to take care of one another.

The Role of Women
Women were usually subordinate to men in Africa, as they were in most early societies around the world. In some cases, they were valued for the work they could do or for their role in having children and thus increasing the size of the lineage group. Women often worked in the fields while the men of the village tended the cattle or went on hunting expeditions. In some communities, women were merchants.

There were some key differences between the role of women in Africa and elsewhere, however. In many African societies, lineage was based on the mother rather than the father. In other words, these were matrilineal societies (societies in which descent is traced through the mother) rather than patrilineal societies (societies in which descent is traced through the father).

One Arab traveler noted, "A man does not pass on inheritance except to the sons of his sister to the exclusion of his own sons." Women were often permitted to inherit property, and the husband was often expected to move into his wife's house.

Community Education and Initiation
In a typical African village a process existed for educating young people and preparing them to become part of the community. For example, in the Congo, by the fifteenth century, both boys and girls were raised by their mothers until the age of six. From their mothers, they learned language, their family history, and the

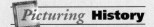

Picturing **History**

A woman and child walk down a road in contemporary Africa. What can you infer about the way they live?

songs that gave meaning to their lives. At six, boys and girls went their separate ways. Girls went to live in the "house of the women," boys in the "house of the men."

Fathers then took control of their sons' education. Boys learned how to hunt and fish, how to grow plants, and how to clear the fields for planting. By experience, young males learned how to live and survive in the natural world.

Girls continued to learn what they needed from their mothers. This included how to take care of the home and work in the fields. Girls also learned what they would need to be good wives and mothers. Marriage and motherhood would be their entry into the world of the community for females.

As the children matured, they played a larger role in the community. Boys cleared the fields, built houses, and took part in village discussions and ceremonies. Girls took over more responsibility for household tasks, took care of younger brothers and sisters, and attended village ceremonies, especially those connected to marriages and funerals.

Finally, young people reached a point in their upbringing where they were expected to enter the community fully. This transition—which occurred at the time of puberty—was marked by an initiation ceremony in which young people were kept isolated from the community. They then underwent a ritual ceremony in which they symbolically died and were reborn. Young females were then fully women; young males were fully men. Both entered completely into the life of the community.

Slavery When we use the term African slavery, we usually think of the period after 1500, when European slave ships carried millions of Africans in bondage to Europe or the Americas (see Chapter 13). Slavery, however, did not begin with the coming of the Europeans. It had been practiced in Africa since ancient times. Furthermore, as we have seen, slavery was not unique to Africa but was common in many societies throughout the world.

Berber groups in North Africa regularly raided farming villages south of the Sahara for captives. The captives were then taken northward and sold throughout the Mediterranean. Some became soldiers. Others were used as domestic servants in the homes of the wealthy.

The use of captives for forced labor or for sale was also common in African societies further south and along the coast of East Africa. Slaves included people captured in war, debtors, and some criminals. They were not necessarily seen as inferior but rather could be trusted servants and might even be respected for their special knowledge or talents.

Life was difficult for most slaves. Those who worked on farmlands owned by the royal family or other wealthy landowners worked hard, long hours. Those enrolled as soldiers were sometimes better off. At least in Muslim societies in Southwest Asia, slaves might at some point win their freedom.

Many slaves were used in the royal household or as domestic servants in private homes. In general, these slaves usually had the best existence. Their living conditions were often decent and sometimes were almost the same as those of the free individuals in the household.

✓ **Reading Check** **Summarizing** Describe the role of lineage groups in African society.

Religious Beliefs in Africa

Early African religious beliefs varied from place to place. Most African societies shared some common religious ideas. One of these was a belief in a single creator god. The **Yoruba** peoples in **Nigeria,** for example, believed that their chief god sent his son Oduduwa down from Heaven in a canoe to create the first humans. The Yoruba religion was practiced by many of the slaves transported to the Americas.

Sometimes, the creator god was joined by a whole group of lesser gods. The **Ashanti** people of Ghana, for example, believed in a supreme being called Nyame, whose sons were lesser gods. Each son served a different purpose: one was the rainmaker, and another brought sunshine. Because the Ashanti gods could not always be trusted, humans needed to appease them to avoid their anger. Some peoples believed that the creator god originally lived on Earth but left in disgust at the behavior of human beings. However, he was also merciful and could be pacified by proper behavior.

One way to communicate with the gods was through ritual. This process was usually carried out by a special class of diviners, people who believe they have the power to foretell events, usually by working with supernatural forces. Many diviners were employed by the king to contact the supreme god. This was done to guarantee a bountiful

This panel shows a family from the Congo at work.

harvest or otherwise protect the interests of the ruler and his subjects.

Another key element in African religion was the importance of ancestors. Each lineage group could trace itself back to a founding ancestor or group of ancestors. Ritual ceremonies dedicated to ancestors were important because the ancestors were believed to be closer to the gods. They had the power to influence, for good or evil, the lives of their descendants.

Many African religions shared a belief in an afterlife. Human life, it was thought, consisted of two stages. The first stage was life on Earth. The second stage was an afterlife in which the soul floated in the atmosphere throughout eternity. Ancestral souls would live on in the afterlife as long as the lineage group continued to perform rituals in their names.

African religious beliefs were challenged, but not always replaced, by the arrival of Islam. Islam swept rapidly across the northern coast of Africa in the wake of the Arab conquest. It was slower to penetrate the lands south of the Sahara. The process probably began as a result of trade, as merchants introduced Muslim beliefs to the trading states in the areas south of the desert. At first, conversion took place on an individual basis. Initially, the rulers did not convert to Islam themselves, although they welcomed Muslim merchants and did not try to keep their subjects from adopting the new faith. The first rulers to convert to Islam were the royal family of Gao at the end of the tenth century. By the end of the fifteenth century, however, much of the population in the grasslands south of the Sahara had accepted Islam.

The process was even more gradual in East Africa. As Islam spread southward, it was adopted by many lowland peoples. It had less success in the mountains of Ethiopia, where, as we have seen, Christianity continued to win followers. Islam was first brought to the coast of East Africa by Muslim merchants from Arabia, but it did not win many adherents there until the twelfth and thirteenth centuries. At that time, Swahili culture emerged, and many members of the upper class converted to the Muslim faith.

In some ways, of course, the beliefs of Islam were in conflict with traditional African beliefs and customs. Islam's rejection of spirit worship ran counter to the beliefs of many Africans and was often ignored in practice. Likewise, Islam's insistence on distinct roles for men and women

Web Activity Visit the *Glencoe World History* Web site at tx.wh.glencoe.com and click on **Chapter 7– Student Web Activity** to learn more about early African culture.

and modesty in dress for both sexes was contrary to the relatively informal relationships that prevailed in many African societies. Thus, this practice was slow to take root. As elsewhere, in Africa imported ideas were combined with native beliefs to create a unique brand of Africanized Islam.

✓ **Reading Check** **Describing** What role do ancestors play in African religion?

African Culture

In early Africa, as in much of the rest of the world at the time, the arts—whether painting, literature, or music—were a means of serving religion. A work of art was meant to express religious conviction.

The earliest art forms in Africa were rock paintings. The most famous examples are in the Tassili Mountains in the central Sahara. These paintings, some of which date back as far as 4000 B.C., show the life of the peoples of the area as they shifted from hunting to cattle herding and eventually to trade.

Some of the later paintings depict the two-horse chariots used to transport goods prior to the introduction of the camel.

Wood carvers throughout Africa made remarkable masks and statues. The carvings often represented gods, spirits, or ancestral figures and were believed to embody the spiritual powers of the subjects. Terracotta (clay) and metal figurines served a similar purpose. For example, impressive terra-cotta human figures and human heads found near the city of Nok in northern Nigeria are believed to have had religious significance. The Nok peoples of the Niger River produced a flourishing culture from 500 B.C. to A.D. 200. In fact, the Nok culture is the oldest known culture in West Africa to have created sculpture.

In the thirteenth and fourteenth centuries, metalworkers at **Ife** (EE•feh), the capital of the Yoruba people, in what is now southern Nigeria, produced handsome bronze and iron statues. The Ife sculptures may have influenced artists in **Benin** in West Africa, who produced equally impressive works in bronze during the same period. The Benin sculptures

CONNECTIONS Past To Present

From African Rhythms to Rock and Roll

Beginning in the 1500s, Africans were brought as slaves to the Western Hemisphere. Their music came with them and became an important ingredient in the development of musical styles in the Americas.

A strong rhythmic pattern was an important feature of African music, an effect achieved through a wide variety of instruments, including drums, bells, harps, gourds, pots, sticks beaten together, and hand clapping. Another important feature of African music was the coming together of voice and instrument. A call and response pattern was common: a leader would sing a short piece and people would repeat it back to the beat of a drum.

As slaves in North America, Africans would use work songs, sung to rhythmic patterns, to make their long work days less burdensome. At rest, others sang folk songs known as spirituals to lament the loss of their homeland and their freedom. Over the years, these African musical forms developed into new forms known as blues, gospel, jazz, and ragtime. In the twentieth century, African American artists inspired new forms of music known as rock and roll and rap.

In Latin America, the beat of African drums was combined with European instruments, such as the Spanish guitar, and Native American instruments, such as the maraca and wooden rhythm sticks. From the combination of these elements came such styles as reggae, calypso, and salsa music.

▼ *Drummers from Burundi*

▲ *Jazz saxophonist*

Comparing Past and Present

Listen to blues, gospel, jazz, and ragtime music. Describe the similarities and the differences, then compare these types of music to contemporary, popular music.

include bronze heads, many of kings, and figures of various types of animals. These works are rivaled only by the sculptures of the Chinese.

Like wood carving and sculpture, African music and dance often served a religious purpose. African dancing, with its heavy rhythmic beat, has strongly influenced modern Western music. Dancing was "the great popular art of the African people." The dances, however, were also a means of communicating with the spirits. The movements seen in African dance were meant to represent spirits expressing themselves through humans.

African music also served a social purpose. It was used to pass on to young people information about the history of the community. In the absence of written language, the words to songs served to transmit folk legends and religious traditions from generation to generation.

Storytelling, usually by priests or a special class of storytellers known as griots (GREE•OHZ), served the same purpose. These storytellers were also historians who kept alive a people's history. For example, much of what we know about Sundiata Keita—the founder of the kingdom of Mali—has come down to us from the oral traditions of the griot.

☑ **Reading Check** **Explaining** Why were storytellers important in African society?

▲ *Benin bronze figures*

▲ *Ife king, bronze*

Delicately carved bronze ▲ *head of Benin, queen mother, from 1500s*

🌟 **TAKS Practice**

SECTION 3 ASSESSMENT

Checking for Understanding

1. **Define** lineage group, matrilineal, patrilineal, diviner, griot.

2. **Identify** Yoruba, Ashanti.

3. **Locate** Nigeria, Ife, Benin.

4. **Discuss** the arts that were developed by the Nok, the Yoruba, and the Benin peoples. What do these works say about the cultures in which they were created?

5. **Describe** the practical consequences of Africa's matrilineal society. Is your society matrilineal or patrilineal? Do you have an opinion as to why one type of society might be better or worse to live in than the other? Support your opinion with facts.

Critical Thinking

6. **Identify Opinions** Explain how art, music, and dance formed an integral part of African society. Explain why you think these subjects should or should not be part of every school's curriculum.

7. **Organizing Information** Create a web diagram listing the ways that religion was expressed in Africa.

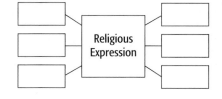

Religious Expression

Analyzing Visuals

8. **Identify** all the tasks being performed in the village scene in the stone panel on page 239 of your text. Are comparable tasks performed by individuals in your family? In your opinion, what was the artist's attitude toward work? Explain your answer.

Writing About History

9. **Expository Writing** Music, dance, and storytelling do not leave a physical archaeological record in the same way as buildings or roads. Describe how historians have been able to determine the significance of the performing arts in African society.

Using Key Terms

1. _____ occurs when farmers only grow enough crops for their personal use.

2. The _____ were the historians of ancient Africa.

3. Farming peoples who spoke dialects of the _____ family of languages migrated into East Africa and the Congo Basin.

4. _____ refers to a mixed African-Arabian culture and a major language spoken by the peoples of coastal Africa.

5. Broad grasslands dotted with trees and shrubs are called _____.

6. A _____ consists of a group of independent villages with a local ruler.

7. A _____ society traces its descent through the mother.

8. Larger communities formed from extended families are known as _____.

9. _____ are people who communicate with the gods and possess the power to foretell the future.

Reviewing Key Facts

10. **Science and Technology** Why do people who live in the rain forest not keep cattle or animals?

11. **Culture** What was the official religion of Axum?

12. **Geography** Name at least four distinct geographic zones or geographic elements of Africa.

13. **Geography** What is the name of a major desert in Africa other than the Sahara?

14. **Economics** What made Meroë a major trading center?

15. **History** Name the major trading states of Africa south of the Sahara.

16. **Economics** What was the highly desired item that Arab traders brought to Ghana from North Africa?

17. **Culture** What was a distinctive feature of the kings of Ghana as noticed by outside observers?

18. **Government** What contributions did Sundiata Keita make to Mali?

19. **Culture** How did Mansa Musa carry on the advances begun by Sundiata?

20. **Citizenship** What caused the decline of Mali?

21. **History** List the dynasties that prevailed in the kingdom of Songhai.

22. **Economics** Name the East African ports vital to the Indian Ocean trade network.

23. **Culture** What roles did slaves play in African society?

24. **Economics** What role did Berbers play in African trade?

25. **Geography** Identify two different trade routes across Africa.

Critical Thinking

26. **Evaluating** Explain the reasons for the devaluation of gold during the reign of Mansa Musa.

27. **Analyzing** Compare the growth of Islam with the expansion of trade between Africa and its Arab neighbors.

Chapter Summary

African civilizations did not develop in a vacuum. As far back as the ancient Egyptians, African civilizations were open to contact with outside groups. Contact came about either through trade, migration, or war, and led to the introduction of new ideas, new ways of living, and the development of multicultural societies. The chart below lists major concepts associated with cultural diffusion and contact.

Trade

- Ghanaian gold is exchanged for salt from the Sahara.
- Muslim traders bring cotton, silk, and Chinese porcelain from India to East Africa.
- Malian farmers produce surplus crops for export.
- Ivory and gold from inland Africa are brought to East Africa.
- Cotton cloth, brass, copper, and olive oil are imported by Axum.
- Mali becomes rich from the profitable salt and gold trades.

Migration

- Bantu peoples slowly migrate into East Africa.
- Arab merchants settle along east coast of Africa.
- Islamic scholars move to Timbuktu, a new center for learning.

Warfare

- Kushites conquer Egyptians.
- Muslim merchants gain control of Axum's trade.
- Moroccan armies occupy Songhai's gold-trading centers.
- Assyrians drive Kushites out of Egypt.

Writing About History

28. Expository Writing Through trade, many civilizations came in contact with each other. What civilizations outside of Africa did African kingdoms and states contact? How did these civilizations influence each other?

Analyzing Sources

Read the following passage written by Tierno Bokar, the sage of Bandiagara.

> ❝If you wish to know who I am,
> If you wish me to teach you what I know
> Cease for the while to be what you are.
> And forget what you know.❞

29. According to the quote, what role does Tierno Bokar want to play in society?

30. Evaluate Bokar's statement that the students must forget who they are and what they know to learn the teacher's lesson. Do you think that it is essential to forget who you are and what you know in order to learn something new? Can you think of situations in which this would be good advice?

Applying Technology Skills

31. Creating a Database Create a database of 5 to 10 primary sources on early African civilization. Evaluate each source based on its language, correlation with other sources, and information about its author. Identify any bias the author reveals through his or her writing. State the reasons why you think the author is biased, and give examples to support your argument.

Making Decisions

32. Why do you think the Ghanaians conducted silent trade? What difficulties of trade might this form of exchange solve? Can you think of another way to accomplish the same purpose?

33. Reread the Eyewitness to History feature on page 235. Decide how valuable first-person accounts are in understanding past cultures. Also decide if a writer's cultural background influences the way in which an event is recorded. Give specific examples to support your decision.

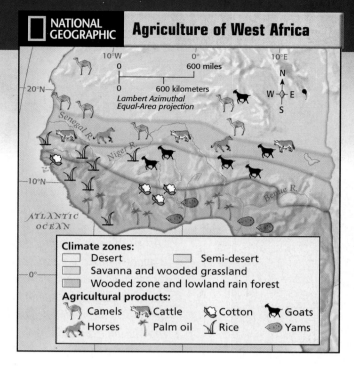

NATIONAL GEOGRAPHIC   Agriculture of West Africa

Climate zones:
☐ Desert   ☐ Semi-desert
☐ Savanna and wooded grassland
☐ Wooded zone and lowland rain forest
Agricultural products:
🐫 Camels   🐄 Cattle   🌿 Cotton   🐐 Goats
🐎 Horses   🌴 Palm oil   🌾 Rice   🍠 Yams

Analyzing Maps and Charts

Study the map above to answer the following questions.

34. The great trade empires of West Africa grew out of the various vegetation zones and the products they produced. For example, yams were better suited to one area, grazing animals to another. How would these differences account for growth in trade?

35. In what zone was palm oil produced?

36. Which zone produced the fewest number of different products? Where were most agricultural products grown?

37. In what zones were animals most plentiful? What geographical features allowed animals to thrive there?

The Princeton Review   ⬆TAKS Test Practice

Directions: Choose the best answer to the following question.

Muhammad Ture expanded his empire. By 1493, it extended one thousand miles along the banks of the Niger River. Which kingdom did he rule?

A Kush   **C** Bantu
B Zimbabwe   **D** Songhai

Test-Taking Tip: Notice the clues in this question before you make an answer choice. Ask yourself what part of Africa and what century the question describes. Use these hints to eliminate answer choices that must be incorrect.

CHAPTER 8 The Asian World
400–1500

Key Events

As you read this chapter, look for the key events in the development of the Asian world.
- Innovations in agricultural production, the reemergence of trade routes, and a unified central government allowed China to prosper under the Sui, Tang, and Song dynasties.
- Japan's geography isolated it from other countries and caused the island nation to develop its own unique culture.
- The Muslim expansion made both Islam and Hinduism powerful religions in the Indian subcontinent.
- Because of the geography of the region, Southeast Asian countries developed into a series of separate states with their own culture, religion, and language.

The Impact Today

The events that occurred during this time period still impact our lives today.
- Gunpowder and printing were invented during the Tang dynasty in China.
- The expansion of Islam into northwestern India is reflected in the current division of the Indian subcontinent into India, which is mostly Hindu, and the two Islamic states of Bangladesh and Pakistan.

 World History Video The Chapter 8 video, "The Great Wall," chronicles the development of Asian cultures.

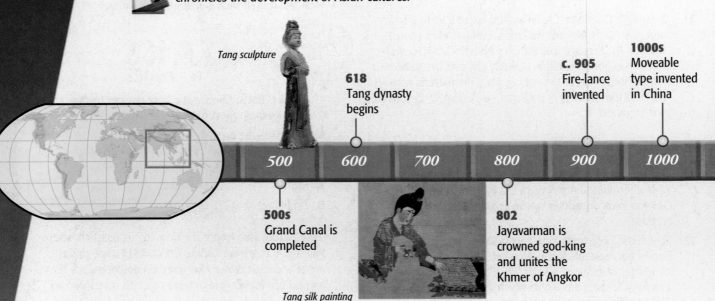

Tang sculpture

618 Tang dynasty begins

c. 905 Fire-lance invented

1000s Moveable type invented in China

500   600   700   800   900   1000

500s Grand Canal is completed

802 Jayavarman is crowned god-king and unites the Khmer of Angkor

Tang silk painting

Heiji Scroll **(detail)** This scroll depicts one of the first samurai battles, the Heiji Insurrection of 1159.

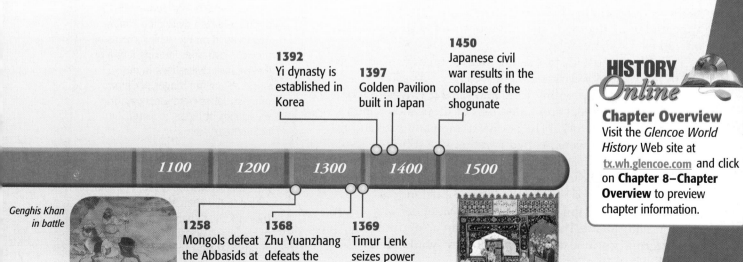

1392
Yi dynasty is established in Korea

1397
Golden Pavilion built in Japan

1450
Japanese civil war results in the collapse of the shogunate

1100   1200   1300   1400   1500

Genghis Khan in battle

1258
Mongols defeat the Abbasids at Baghdad

1368
Zhu Yuanzhang defeats the Mongols and establishes the Ming dynasty

1369
Timur Lenk seizes power and begins conquests

Timur Lenk enthroned

HISTORY
Online

Chapter Overview
Visit the *Glencoe World History* Web site at tx.wh.glencoe.com and click on **Chapter 8–Chapter Overview** to preview chapter information.

A Story That Matters

Kublai Khan, grandson of Genghis Khan

Destruction of the Mongol fleet attacking Japan

Japan Faces Kublai Khan

In 1274, the Mongol emperor of China, Kublai Khan, demanded that the Japanese pay tribute to China or face invasion. When the Japanese refused, the khan sent a force of thirty thousand warriors to teach the Japanese a lesson. Bad weather forced the emperor's forces to retreat, however.

Not until 1281 was the Great Khan prepared to try again. This time he sent a force of two fleets, consisting of 4,400 ships carrying almost 150,000 warriors. The Japanese appeared to be doomed. The emperor ordered prayers to be offered everywhere in Japan.

Then, on August 15, just as the khan's forces were preparing to land, the sky darkened. For two days, massive typhoons struck, uprooting trees and raising waves that battered the Mongol fleet and killed tens of thousands. One Korean observer wrote, "The bodies of men and broken timbers of the vessels were heaped together in a solid mass so that a person could walk across from one point of land to another on the mass of wreckage." Those warriors who made it to shore were cut down by the Japanese defenders.

To the Japanese, this victory over the Mongols was a sign of supernatural aid. They called the storm a "divine wind," or *kamikaze,* and became convinced that they would always be protected from foreign invasion.

Why It Matters

This great confrontation between the ancient and well-established civilization of China and the newly-emerged Japanese state was a turning point in Asia during this period. Chinese civilization continued to build on the achievements of previous dynasties, making it one of the greatest civilizations in the world. Along the fringes of China, other societies were emerging on the islands of Japan, in Korea, and in Southeast Asia.

History and You Using the Internet and a computer, create a database that shows the amount of land added to the khanate during the rule of Kublai Khan. Include dates of conquests and identify the peoples who were conquered. Add illustrations to your database and create a multimedia presentation.

China Reunified

Main Ideas

- The Sui, Tang, and Song dynasties restored peace to China in between periods of chaos and disorder.
- Innovations and reforms in government, agriculture, and technology brought periods of growth and prosperity to China.

Key Terms

scholar-gentry, dowry

People to Identify

Sui Yangdi, Tang Xuanzang, Uighurs, Marco Polo, Wu Zhao

Places to Locate

Tibet, Changan, Hangzhou

Preview Questions

1. What contributions did the Sui, Tang, and Song dynasties make to Chinese civilization?
2. What economic changes occurred under the Tang and Song rulers?

Reading Strategy

Summarizing Information Draw and complete three diagrams like the one below to summarize the time periods, the most important rulers, and the reasons for decline of the Sui, Tang, and Song dynasties.

Sui dynasty

Preview of Events

♦500	♦600	♦700	♦800	♦900	♦1000

581
Sui dynasty begins

618
Tang dynasty begins

868
First complete book printed

907
Tang dynasty ends

960
Song dynasty rises to power

Emperor Yangdi and his fleet

Voices from the Past

A seventh-century Chinese writer described how the emperor Sui Yangdi kept an eye on his empire:

❝Moreover, the Emperor caused to be built dragon boats, war boats of the 'Yellow dragon' style, and multi-decked transports. The Emperor rode in the dragon boat, and civil and military officials rode in the multi-decked transports. . . . The districts through which they passed were ordered to prepare to offer provisions. Those who made bountiful arrangements were given an additional office or title; those who fell short were given punishments up to the death penalty.❞

—*The Sui Dynasty*, **Arthur F. Wright, 1978**

The Sui dynasty had reunified China after hundreds of years of turmoil. Chinese civilization began to flourish once more.

The Sui Dynasty

The Han dynasty came to an end in 220, and China fell into chaos. For the next three hundred years, the Chinese suffered through disorder and civil war. Then, in 581, a new Chinese empire was set up under a dynasty known as the Sui (SWAY). The Sui dynasty (581–618) did not last long, but it managed to unify China once again under the emperor's authority.

Sui Yangdi, the second emperor of the dynasty, completed the Grand Canal, built to link the two great rivers of China, the Huang He (Yellow River) and the Chang Jiang (Yangtze River). Both rivers flowed from west to east. The new canal linked north and south, making it easier to ship rice from the south to the north.

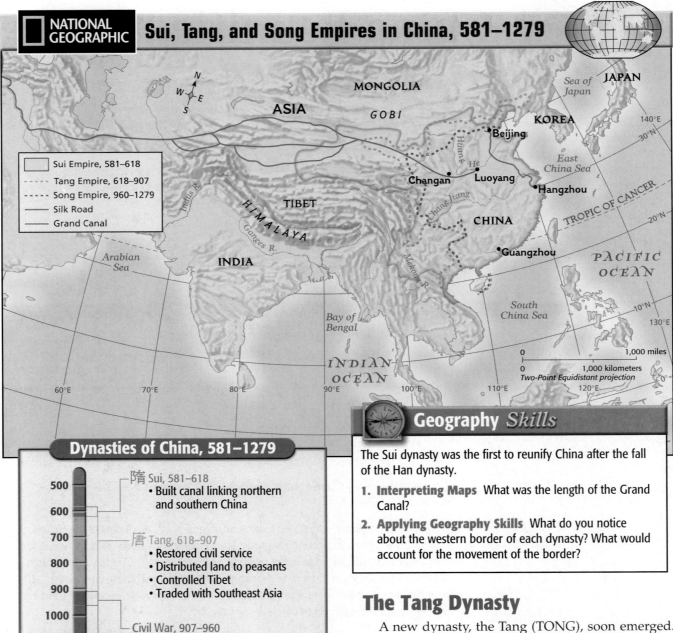

MONGOLIA

Sea of Japan **JAPAN**

ASIA

GOBI

KOREA

•Beijing

140°E

30°N

East China Sea

Changan •Luoyang

•Hangzhou

Sui Empire, 581–618

Tang Empire, 618–907

Song Empire, 960–1279

Silk Road

Grand Canal

TIBET

HIMALAYA

Ganges R.

Indus R.

Chang Jiang

CHINA

TROPIC OF CANCER

20°N

Arabian Sea

INDIA

•Guangzhou

PACIFIC OCEAN

Mekong R.

South China Sea

10°N

130°E

Bay of Bengal

INDIAN OCEAN

0   1,000 miles

0   1,000 kilometers
Two-Point Equidistant projection

60°E   70°E   80°E   90°E   100°E   110°E   120°E

Dynasties of China, 581–1279

500	隋 Sui, 581–618
600	• Built canal linking northern and southern China
700	唐 Tang, 618–907
800	• Restored civil service • Distributed land to peasants
900	• Controlled Tibet • Traded with Southeast Asia
1000	Civil War, 907–960
1100	
1200	宋 Song, 960–1279
1300	• Lost control of Tibet • Formed alliance with Mongols

Geography *Skills*

The Sui dynasty was the first to reunify China after the fall of the Han dynasty.

1. **Interpreting Maps** What was the length of the Grand Canal?
2. **Applying Geography Skills** What do you notice about the western border of each dynasty? What would account for the movement of the border?

The Tang Dynasty

A new dynasty, the Tang (TONG), soon emerged. It would last for almost three hundred years, from 618 until 907. The early Tang rulers began their reigns by instituting reforms, as rulers often did in the early days of new dynasties. They restored the civil service examination from earlier times to serve as the chief method of recruiting officials for the civilian bureaucracy. They also tried to create a more stable economy by giving land to the peasants and breaking up the power of the owners of the large estates.

Tang rulers worked hard to restore the power of China in East Asia. They brought peace to northwestern China and expanded their control to the borders of **Tibet,** an area north of the Himalaya. China claimed to be the greatest power in East Asia. Neighboring states, including Korea, offered tribute

Sui Yangdi was a cruel ruler. He used forced labor to build the Grand Canal. This practice, together with high taxes, his extravagant and luxurious lifestyle, and military failures, caused a rebellion. The emperor was murdered, and his dynasty came to an end.

✓ **Reading Check** **Explaining** What were the principal reasons for the murder of Sui Yangdi and the end of the Sui dynasty?

The Invention of Printing in Tang China

Woodblock printing on paper began in the seventh century A.D. The first printed text in China (and in the world) was a Buddhist prayer, done sometime between 704 and 751. The first complete book was a Buddhist work printed in 868.

Once woodblock printing was developed, it was used to make numerous copies of important works. In the tenth century, a printing of the Confucian classics used over twenty thousand woodblocks and comprised 130 volumes. Over four hundred thousand copies still exist of one Buddhist work printed in the tenth century.

In the eleventh century, the Chinese improved on the art of printing by inventing movable type. An eleventh-century Chinese author described the work of Pi Sheng, who lived from 990 to 1051:

66. . . he took sticky clay and cut in it characters as thin as the edge of a coin. Each character formed, as it were, a single type. He baked them in the fire to make them hard. He had previously prepared an iron plate and he had covered his plate with a mixture of pine resin, wax, and paper ashes. When he wished to print, he took an iron frame and set it on the iron plate. In this he placed the type, set close together. When the frame was full, the whole made one solid block of type. If one were to print only one or three copies, this method would be neither simple nor easy. But for printing hundreds of thousands of copies, it was marvelously quick.99

Drawing Inferences *What did the invention of movable type mean to China and the rest of the world?*

Woodblock printing was used to print *The Diamond Sutra,* which is the earliest printed text with a known printing date (868).

Face
Counter
Beard
Shoulder

Composing stick

to China. The Chinese imperial court also set up trade and diplomatic relations with the states of Southeast Asia.

Like the Han, however, the Tang sowed the seeds of their own destruction. Tang rulers were unable to prevent plotting and government corruption. One emperor was especially unfortunate. Emperor **Tang Xuanzang** (TONG SEE•WAHN•DZONG) is remembered for his devotion to a commoner's daughter. To entertain her, he kept hundreds of dancers and musicians at court. He also ordered riders to travel thousands of miles to bring her fresh fruit.

Finally, the emperor's favorite general led a bloody revolt. The army demanded that someone be held accountable for the war and strife in the country. For this reason the emperor invited his true love to

hang herself from a nearby tree, although it is said that for the rest of his life, the emperor "washed his face everyday with a fountain of tears."

During the eighth century, the Tang dynasty weakened and became prey to rebellions. Tang rulers hired **Uighurs** (WEE•GURZ), a northern tribal group of Turkic-speaking people, to fight for the dynasty. Continued unrest, however, led to the collapse of Tang rule in 907.

Reading Check **Contrasting** How did the Tang and Sui rulers differ?

The Song Dynasty

In 960, a new dynasty known as the Song (SOONG) rose to power. The Song ruled during a period of economic prosperity and cultural achievement, from 960 to 1279. From the start, however, the Song also experienced problems, especially from northern neighbors. These groups crossed into northern China and occupied large parts of Chinese territory. Because of this threat, Song rulers were forced to move the imperial court farther south to **Hangzhou** (HONG•JOH).

The Song dynasty could never overcome the challenge from the north. During the 1200s, the Mongols—a nomadic people from the Gobi—carried out wars of conquest and built a vast empire. Within 70 years, they controlled all of China. As we shall see, the Mongols overthrew the Song and created a new Mongol dynasty in China.

✓ **Reading Check** **Identifying** What problems did the Song dynasty encounter?

Government and the Economy

The era from the beginning of the Sui dynasty to the end of the Song dynasty lasted nearly seven hundred years. During that period, a mature political system based on principles first put into practice during the Qin and Han dynasties gradually emerged in China. As in the Han Era, China was a monarchy that employed a relatively large bureaucracy. Beyond the capital, government was centered around provinces, districts, and villages. Confucian ideals were still the cement that held the system together.

During the long period between the Sui and Song dynasties, the Chinese economy grew in size and complexity. Agriculture flourished, and manufacturing and trade grew dramatically.

China was still primarily a farming society. In the long period of civil war, aristocratic families had taken control of most of the land, and the majority of

---

THE WAY IT WAS

YOUNG PEOPLE IN . . .

Traditional China

By using the civil service examination, a practice started by the Qin dynasty, Tang and Song rulers sought to recruit a class of civil servants based on merit. This undermined the power of the aristocrats and created a new class of scholar-gentry.

To the sons of the scholar-gentry, the civil service examinations were crucial in gaining a civil service position and hence a government career. Consequently, preparing their sons for these examinations became very important to scholar-gentry families.

Education began at a young age. Boys began to learn to write Chinese characters at the age of four. Within three years, they were able to read a number of characters. They were then expected to

memorize their first work, *The Thousand Character Classic* by Confucius. This consisted of a thousand different characters, rhymed in four-character lines. Any mistake in recitation was greeted with a blow on the backside by a boy's teacher.

Over the course of many more years, students memorized many other Confucian classics. Not until a work was completely memorized was a student given an explanation of the work's meaning. Ultimately, students memorized all of the Confucian classics.

Young men who were being educated for the civil service examinations had little time for recreation. They were not allowed to take part in any strenuous physical activities. They could fish, which was considered a scholarly

Confucius

peasants had become serfs or slaves. The Song government, however, worked to weaken the power of the large landholders and help poor peasants obtain their own land. These reform efforts and improved farming techniques led to an abundance of food.

Technology and Trade In Chinese cities, technological developments added new products and stimulated trade. During the Tang dynasty, for example, the Chinese began to make steel by mixing cast iron and wrought iron in a blast furnace heated by the burning of coal. The steel was then used to make swords and sickles. The introduction of cotton made it possible to make new kinds of clothes.

Gunpowder was also invented during the Tang dynasty and was used to make explosives and a primitive flamethrower called a fire-lance. The fire-lance could spit out a mixture of flame and projectiles that could travel as far as 40 yards (almost 37 m).

Long-distance trade had declined between the fourth and sixth centuries as a result of the collapse of both the Han dynasty and the Roman Empire. Trade began to revive under the Tang dynasty and the unification of much of Southwest Asia under the Arabs. The Silk Road was renewed and thrived as caravans carried goods back and forth between China and the countries of Southwest and South Asia.

Trade with regions near China also increased during the Tang and Song dynasties. The Chinese exported tea, silk, and porcelain to the countries beyond the South China Sea. In return, they received exotic woods, precious stones, and various tropical goods. As a result of trade, the city of Changan, with a population estimated at two million, became the wealthiest city in the world during the Tang Era.

✓ **Reading Check** **Comparing** In what ways did trade improve during the time between the Sui and Song dynasties?

sport; play the lute; write poems; paint landscapes; and look at scenery. Students were taught never to use their hands except for painting or writing. Manual labor was strictly forbidden.

After many years of education, young men began to take their civil service examinations. If they passed (only one in five did), they could go on to positions in the civil service. Those who failed could teach, assist officials, or hope for family support. Because of their family connections, few starved.

During the Tang period, people complained that the choice of who would pass the test was made before the tests were graded. In response, the Song instituted the policy of "name covering" so that the test graders would not know whose test they had. Later, they required that each test be copied so that only the copies would be graded. The examiners thus could not tell from the handwriting whose test they had graded.

This silk watercolor shows students taking a civil service examination during the Song dynasty.

CONNECTING TO THE PAST

1. **Summarizing** What skills were Chinese boys required to master in preparation for the civil service exams?

2. **Explaining** What measures were taken to prevent favoritism in the testing process?

3. **Writing about History** How was the use of the civil service examination a departure from the traditional way of placing young men in government service?

Chinese Society

Economic changes had an impact on Chinese society. For wealthier city dwellers, the Tang and Song Eras were an age of prosperity. There was probably no better example than the Song capital of Hangzhou. In the late thirteenth century the Italian merchant **Marco Polo** described the city to European readers as one of the largest and wealthiest cities on Earth. "So many pleasures may be found," he said, "that one fancies himself to be in Paradise."

For rich Chinese during this period, life offered many pleasures. There were new forms of entertainment, such as playing cards and chess (brought from India). The invention of block printing in the eighth century provided new ways to communicate.

The vast majority of the Chinese people still lived off the land in villages. Most peasants never left their villages except for an occasional visit to a nearby market town. Changes were taking place in the countryside, however. Before, there had been a great gulf between wealthy landowners and poor peasants. A more complex mixture of landowners, free peasants, sharecroppers, and landless laborers now emerged.

Most significant was the rise of the landed gentry. This group controlled much of the land and at the same time produced most of the candidates for the civil service. The scholar-gentry, as this class was known, replaced the old landed aristocracy as the political and economic elite of Chinese society.

Few Chinese women had any power. An exception was **Wu Zhao** (WOO JOW), known as Empress Wu.

As in other parts of the world, female children were considered less desirable than male children. In times of famine, female infants might be killed if there was not enough food to feed the whole family. When a female married, she became part of her husband's family. In addition, a girl's parents were expected to provide a dowry (money, goods, or property) to her husband when she married. Poor families often sold their daughters to wealthy villagers.

✓ **Reading Check** **Identifying** Which group in Chinese society replaced the landed aristocracy?

🟠 TAKS Practice

SECTION 1 ASSESSMENT

Checking for Understanding

1. **Define** scholar-gentry, dowry.

2. **Identify** Sui Yangdi, Tang Xuanzang, Uighurs, Marco Polo, Wu Zhao.

3. **Locate** Tibet, Hangzhou.

4. **Describe** the reasons that civil service examinations were instituted by the Tang and Song rulers. Also describe the impact of the use of the exams on the Chinese government.

5. **List** the new social and economic classes that emerged in the countryside during the Tang and Song Eras.

Critical Thinking

6. **Evaluate** The Chinese form of government was adopted by many other countries. Describe the basis for the Chinese form of government and evaluate its effectiveness.

7. **Compare and Contrast** Using a Venn diagram, compare and contrast family life in early China with family life in the United States today.

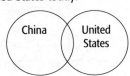

Analyzing Visuals

8. **Describe** in detail the people and activities depicted in the painting shown on page 251. Identify and describe elements in a present-day situation that parallel the situation shown in the painting.

Writing About History

9. **Expository Writing** Imagine that you have just heard about one of the Tang dynasty innovations, perhaps the process of making steel, but you do not understand it. Write a letter of inquiry to the Tang emperor asking for further information.

The Mongols and China

Guide to Reading

Main Ideas
- The Mongols acquired the world's largest land empire.
- With the invention of printing, a golden age of literature and art emerged in China.

Key Terms
khanate, neo-Confucianism, porcelain

People to Identify
Genghis Khan, Kublai Khan, Li Bo, Duo Fu

Places to Locate
Mongolia, Gobi, Beijing, Vietnam, Java, Sumatra

Preview Questions
1. What were the major achievements of the Mongol dynasty?
2. What changes resulted from the Mongol invasions?

Reading Strategy
Cause and Effect Use a chart like the one below to show how the Mongols acquired the world's largest land empire.

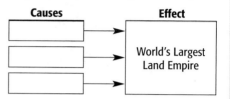

Causes	Effect
	World's Largest Land Empire

Preview of Events

♦1200	♦1220	♦1240	♦1260	♦1280

1206
Temujin elected Genghis Khan of the Mongols

1231
Mongols attack Persia

1279
Kublai Khan defeats the Song and establishes the Yuan dynasty

Voices from the Past

The Mongols were masters of military tactics. John of Plano Carpini, a Franciscan friar, wrote:

❝As soon as they discover the enemy they charge and each one unleashes three or four arrows. If they see that they can't break him, they retreat in order to entice the enemy to pursue, thus luring him into an ambush prepared in advance. If they conclude that the enemy army is stronger, they retire for a day or two and ravage neighboring areas. Or they [set up] camp in a well chosen position, and when the enemy army begins to pass by, they appear unexpectedly.❞

—*L'Empire des Steppes,* **Rene Grousset, 1939**

Due in large part to their military prowess, the Mongols rose to power in Asia with stunning speed.

Mongol horseman

The Mongol Empire

The Mongols were a pastoral people from the region of modern-day **Mongolia** who were organized loosely into clans. Temujin (teh•MOO•juhn), born during the 1160s, gradually unified the Mongols. In 1206, he was elected **Genghis Khan** ("strong ruler") at a massive meeting somewhere in the **Gobi.** From that time on, he devoted himself to conquest.

The Mongols brought much of the Eurasian landmass under a single rule, creating the largest land empire in history. To rule the new Mongol Empire, Genghis Khan set up a capital city at Karakorum. Mongol armies traveled both to the west and to the east. Some went as far as central Europe (see Chapter 9).

Picturing History

In the thirteenth-century battle shown above, Mongol troops storm across the Chang Jiang on a bridge made of boats. Which Chinese dynasty do you think the Mongols were attempting to conquer in this battle?

After the death of Genghis Khan in 1227, the empire began to change. Following Mongol custom, upon the death of the ruling khan, his heirs divided the territory. The once-united empire of Genghis Khan was thus split into several separate territories called khanates, each under the rule of one of his sons.

It may be that only the death of Genghis Khan kept the Mongols from attacking western Europe. In 1231, the Mongols attacked Persia and then defeated the Abbasids at Baghdad in 1258 (see Chapter 6). Mongol forces attacked the Song dynasty in China in the 1260s.

In their attack on the Chinese, the Mongols encountered the use of gunpowder and the fire-lance. By the end of the thirteenth century, the fire-lance had evolved into the much more effective handgun and cannon. By the early fourteenth century, foreigners employed by the Mongol rulers of China had introduced the use of gunpowder and firearms into Europe.

✓ **Reading Check** **Describing** How did the Mongol Empire change after the death of Genghis Khan?

The Mongol Dynasty in China

In 1279, one of Genghis Khan's grandsons, named **Kublai Khan** (KOO•BLUH KAHN), completed the conquest of the Song and established a new Chinese dynasty, the Yuan (YOO•AHN). Kublai Khan, who ruled China until his death in 1294, established his capital at Khanbaliq ("the city of the Khan") in northern China. Later the city would be known by the Chinese name **Beijing.**

Under the leadership of the talented Kublai Khan, the Yuan (or Mongol) dynasty continued to expand the empire. Mongol armies advanced into **Vietnam,** and Mongol fleets were launched against **Java** and **Sumatra** and twice against the islands of Japan. Only Vietnam was conquered, however—and then only for a while. The other campaigns failed. Mongol tactics, such as cavalry charges and siege warfare, were not very effective in tropical and hilly regions.

The Mongols had more success in ruling China. Mongol rulers adapted to the Chinese political system and made use of Chinese bureaucrats. Culturally, however, the Mongols were quite different from the Chinese and became a separate class with their own laws. The highest positions in the bureaucracy were usually staffed by Mongols.

Over time, the Mongol dynasty won the support of many Chinese people. Some came to respect the stability and economic prosperity that the Mongols at first brought to China. The capital at Khanbaliq reflected Mongol prosperity. It was a magnificent city, and foreign visitors were impressed by its splendor.

One such visitor was Marco Polo, who lived in Khanbaliq during the reign of Kublai Khan. According to Polo, "The streets are so straight and wide that you can see right along them from end to end and from one gate to the other. And up and down the city there are beautiful palaces, and many great and fine hostelries, and fine houses in great numbers." Polo's stories of the glories of China seemed unbelievable to the Europeans who heard them.

The Mongol dynasty eventually fell victim to the same problems that had plagued other dynasties: too much spending on foreign conquests, corruption at court, and growing internal instability. In 1368, Zhu Yuanzhang (JOO YOO•AHN•JAHNG), the son of a peasant, put together an army, ended

HISTORY Online

Web Activity Visit the *Glencoe World History* Web site at **tx.wh.glencoe.com** and click on **Chapter 8– Student Web Activity** to learn more about the Mongol dynasty.

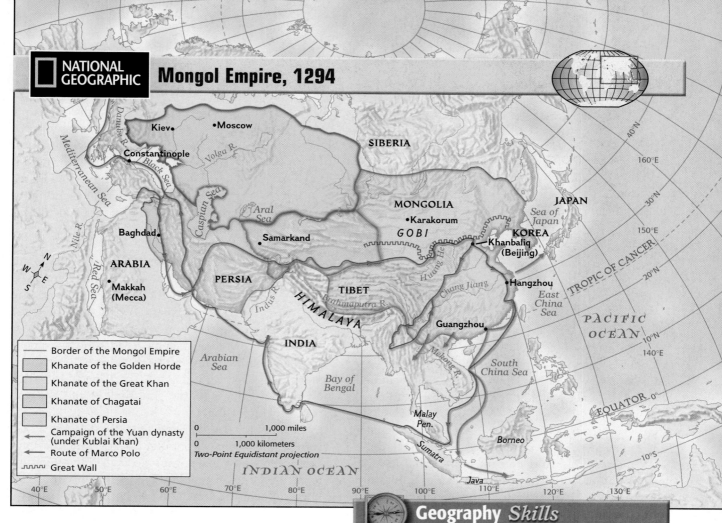

NATIONAL GEOGRAPHIC — Mongol Empire, 1294

Kiev
Moscow
Constantinople
SIBERIA
Mediterranean Sea
Danube R.
Volga R.
Black Sea
Aral Sea
Caspian Sea
MONGOLIA
• Karakorum
JAPAN
Sea of Japan
Baghdad
Samarkand
GOBI
KOREA
Khanbaliq (Beijing)
ARABIA
PERSIA
TIBET
Huang He
Hangzhou
TROPIC OF CANCER
Makkah (Mecca)
Red Sea
Nile R.
Indus R.
HIMALAYA
Brahmaputra R.
Chang Jiang
East China Sea
PACIFIC OCEAN
INDIA
Guangzhou
Arabian Sea
Bay of Bengal
Mekong R.
South China Sea
Malay Pen.
Borneo
Sumatra
Java
INDIAN OCEAN
EQUATOR

Legend:
— Border of the Mongol Empire
Khanate of the Golden Horde
Khanate of the Great Khan
Khanate of Chagatai
Khanate of Persia
← Campaign of the Yuan dynasty (under Kublai Khan)
← Route of Marco Polo
ᴗᴗᴗ Great Wall

0 — 1,000 miles
0 — 1,000 kilometers
Two-Point Equidistant projection

the Mongol dynasty, and set up a new dynasty, the Ming dynasty.

Reading Check **Summarizing** Why were the Mongols so successful in ruling China?

Religion and Government

By the time the Mongols established their dynasty in China, religious preferences in the Chinese court had undergone a number of changes. Confucian principles became the basis for Chinese government during the Han dynasty (202 B.C.–A.D. 220). By the time of the Sui and Tang dynasties, Buddhism and Daoism rivaled the influence of Confucianism. During the Song dynasty, however, Confucian ideas reemerged in a new form. Once again, Confucianism became dominant at court, a position it retained until the early twentieth century.

Buddhism and Daoism Buddhism was brought to China in the first century A.D. by merchants and missionaries from India. At first, only merchants and intellectuals were intrigued by the new ideas. However, as a result of the insecurity that prevailed

Geography *Skills*

Genghis Khan created the largest land empire in history. After his death, according to Mongol custom, the empire was divided among his heirs into regions called khanates.

1. **Interpreting Maps** Can you identify any physical geographic factors that might have determined the boundaries of the khanates?

2. **Applying Geography Skills** This map indicates the campaigns staged by Kublai Khan. Using this map and your text, draw a new map with the borders of Kublai Khan's khanate at the end of his reign.

after the collapse of the Han dynasty, both Buddhism and Daoism became more attractive to many people. Both philosophies gained support among the ruling classes. 📖 *(See page 993 to read excerpts from* The Buddha's Sermon *in the Primary Sources Library.)*

The growing popularity of Buddhism continued into the early years of the Tang dynasty. Early Tang rulers lent their support to Buddhist monasteries that were set up throughout the country. Buddhists became advisers at the imperial court. Ultimately, though, Buddhism lost favor at court and was increasingly subject to attack.

The Buddha, carved about 460, in the Yun-Kang caves in China

Buddhism was criticized for being a foreign religion. Like Christian monasteries in Europe during the Middle Ages, Buddhist monasteries had acquired thousands of acres of land and serfs. With land came corruption.

The government reacted strongly. During the later Tang period, it destroyed countless Buddhist temples and monasteries and forced more than 260,000 monks and nuns to leave the monasteries and return to secular life. Buddhism no longer received support from the state.

Neo-Confucianism Official support went instead to a revived Confucianism. From the Song dynasty to the end of the dynastic system in the twentieth century, Confucianism was at the heart of the state government. However, it was different from the Confucianism established during the Han dynasty.

Neo-Confucianism, as the new doctrine was called, served as a Confucian response to Buddhism and Daoism. Neo-Confucianism teaches that the world is real, not an illusion, and that fulfillment comes not from withdrawal but from participation in the world.

Neo-Confucianists divide the world into a material world and a spiritual world. Humans form the link between the two worlds. Although humans live in the material world, each individual is also linked with the Supreme Ultimate. The goal of individuals is to move beyond the material world to reach union with the Supreme Ultimate. Humans do this through a careful examination of the moral principles that rule the universe.

✓**Reading Check** **Explaining** What caused Buddhism to lose favor with the Chinese government?

A Golden Age in Literature and Art

The period between the Tang and Ming dynasties was in many ways the great age of Chinese literature. The invention of printing during the Tang dynasty helped to make literature more readily available and more popular. Art, too, flourished during this period.

Poetry It was in poetry, above all, that the Chinese of this time best expressed their literary talents. The Tang dynasty is viewed as the great age of poetry in China. At least 48,000 poems were written by 2,200 authors. Chinese poems celebrated the beauty of nature, the changes of the seasons, and the joys of friendship. They expressed sadness at the shortness of life and the necessity of parting.

Li Bo (LEE BWAW) and **Duo Fu** (DWAW FOO) were two of the most popular poets during the Tang Era. Li Bo was a free spirit whose writing often centered on nature. The following is probably the best-known poem in China and has been memorized by schoolchildren for centuries. It is entitled "Quiet Night Thoughts":

❝Beside my bed the bright moonbeams bound
Almost as if there were frost on the ground.
Raising up, I gaze at the Mountain moon;
Lying back, I think of my old home town.❞

FACT FICTION | FOLKLORE

The World's Oldest Restaurant
China has a long history of advanced discoveries, including steel, printing, and gunpowder. It is also home to the world's longest running restaurant. In 1153, Ma Yu Ching opened a restaurant that specialized in chicken dishes. Operating today as Ma Yu Ching's Bucket Chicken, the restaurant offers takeout food.

Where Li Bo was carefree, Duo Fu was a serious Confucian. Many of his works reflect a concern with social injustice and the plight of the poor. In his poem entitled "Spring Prospect," the poet has returned to his home in the capital after a rebellion against the dynasty has left the city in ruins:

66The capital is taken. The hills and streams are left,
And with spring in the city the grass and trees grown
    dense.
Mourning the times, the flowers trickle their tears;
Saddened with parting, the birds make my heart
    flutter.
The army beacons have flamed for three months;
A letter from home would be worth ten thousand
    in gold.
My white hairs have I anxiously scratched ever
    shorter;
But such disarray! Even hairpins will do no good.99

Painting and Ceramics During the Song and Mongol dynasties, landscape painting reached its high point. Influenced by Daoism, Chinese artists went into the mountains to paint and find the Dao, or Way, in nature. This practice explains in part the emphasis on nature in traditional Chinese painting. The word for landscape in Chinese means "mountain-water" and reflects the Daoist search for balance between the earth and water.

Chinese artists tried to reveal the hidden forms of the landscape. Rather than depicting the realistic shape of a specific mountain, for example, they tried to portray the idea of "mountain." Empty spaces were left in the paintings because in the Daoist vision, one cannot know the whole truth.

Daoist influence was also evident in the portrayal of human beings as insignificant in the midst of nature. Chinese artists painted people as tiny figures fishing in small boats or wandering up a hillside trail, living in but not dominating nature.

Next to painting in creative accomplishment was the field of ceramics. In particular, Tang artisans perfected the making of porcelain—a ceramic made of fine clay baked at very high temperatures. As an Arab traveler in 851 described it, "There is in China a very fine clay from which are made vases having the transparency of glass bottles; water in these vases is visible through them, and yet they are made of clay." The technique for making porcelain did not reach Europe until the eighteenth century.

Song ink and watercolor drawing on silk

✓**Reading Check** **Summarizing** What invention helped to make literature both more available and more popular?

TAKS Practice

SECTION 2 ASSESSMENT

Checking for Understanding

1. **Define** khanate, neo-Confucianism, porcelain.

2. **Identify** Genghis Khan, Kublai Khan, Li Bo, Duo Fu.

3. **Locate** Mongolia, Gobi, Beijing, Vietnam, Java, Sumatra.

4. **Explain** how neo-Confucianism differs from Confucianism.

5. **List** the ways in which Daoism is represented in Chinese art of the Song and Mongol dynasties.

Critical Thinking

6. **Explain** What is the difference between the Buddhist and neo-Confucian philosophies? What impact might these two philosophies have had on the way the early Chinese viewed life?

7. **Sequencing Information** Create a time line like the one shown below that illustrates the Mongols' rise to power.

Mongols' rise to power

Analyzing Visuals

8. **Describe** what you see in the landscape painting shown on this page, then describe your emotional reaction to the painting. How do you think the painting reflects the times during which it was created? What artistic ideals did the artist express in the work?

Writing About History

9. **Expository Writing** Evaluate how the poems of Li Bo and Duo Fu reflect their different relationships to Chinese thought and culture.

LORD OF THE MONGOLS
GENGHIS KHAN

Samarkand, Bukhara, Urgench, Balkh, Merv, Nishapur, Herat, Ghazni: The glorious cities of central Asia toppled like dominoes before fierce horsemen who burst from the Mongolian steppe in the thirteenth century. According to one survivor of a Mongol raid, "They came, they sapped, they burnt, they slew, they plundered, and they departed." The leader of this ruthless horde was called Genghis Khan—"strong ruler." But was Genghis Khan only a merciless killer and looter? The answer, say modern historians, is yes—and no.

There is no question that the Mongols blazed a trail of destruction. Some historians think that Genghis Khan stifled development in parts of Asia for centuries. Other scholars point out that Genghis was simply a major player in one of the most war-torn centuries in history. While Crusaders attacked in the Holy Land, and dynasties fought one another in China, central Asia suffered a number of wars even before Genghis invaded.

Whatever opinions historians may hold, present-day Mongolians regard Genghis Khan as a national hero.

After more than six decades of Soviet domination—during which Mongolia's own history was suppressed to destroy any trace of national pride—Mongolians have reclaimed Genghis Khan as the father of their country. In the capital, Ulaanbaatar, the former Lenin Avenue is now Genghis Khan Avenue, and Genghis's face is stamped on the currency.

The boy who would grow up to be the great khan was born in the 1160s some 200 miles (321.8 km) northeast of Ulaanbaatar near the Onon River. It is said that the baby, named Temujin ("blacksmith"), was born with a clot of blood in his hand—a sign of good fortune.

2

Later his shaman (a spiritual leader) told Temujin that the supreme Mongol deity had ordained him to be master of the world.

At this time, the Mongolian population included some 30 nomadic groups that had long vied with one another for power. When Temujin was nine, Tatars poisoned his father, a minor chieftain. To help the family survive, Temujin and his brothers caught fish and snared small animals called marmots. Like other Mongol children, Temujin grew up on horseback, probably learning to ride at age four or five.

In his youth Temujin began to demonstrate the leadership that would make him famous. He made allies with

other leaders, one of whom was Toghril, a leader of the Kereyits. When the Merkit group kidnapped Temujin's young wife, Borte, in a raid, Toghril and other friends helped Temujin rescue her. Later, through conquest or bestowal of gifts, Temujin steadily built a confederation of groups. He did not include the Tatars, who had killed his father. When he defeated them he left only the smallest males alive and enslaved the women and children. This act of vengeance effectively erased the Tatars from the face of the earth. (One of the ironies of history is that Europeans for centuries used a variation of Tatars, "Tartars," to refer to the Mongols.)

Eventually, some of Temujin's former friends began to oppose his growing power, but he crushed them. When he was about 40, the Mongols named him Genghis Khan.

Some historians suggest Genghis did not consciously set out to conquer the world. He acted because he needed to feed his people and supply them with horses, although he may at times have been out for revenge.

Whatever the Mongol leader's

3

1 A Mongol cavalryman, lightly armored in leather, was much more agile than the knights of Europe in their heavy chain mail. He carried a small leather shield that he could raise to protect his face, and under a loose robe he wore a tightly woven silk tunic to blunt enemy arrows. Braced on disk-shaped stirrups he could maneuver easily during battle, firing arrows either forward or backward.

2 A lone horseman rides on the flood-plain of the Onon River in northeastern Mongolia, where a boy named Temujin was born in the 1160s.

3 Bronze plaque of Genghis Khan.

4 Mongol youngsters, like these children racing at a summer festival, learn to ride by the time they are about five—just as their ancestors did eight centuries ago.

motivation, however, warfare was an old tradition among these nomads, and soon Genghis's army was on the move. According to modern researchers, his troops never numbered more than 110,000, but they were molded into a disciplined force. Genghis was a canny judge of men who had survived power struggles. To prevent other leaders from gaining too much influence, Genghis gave command only to those who had proven themselves in campaigns.

Genghis's army moved against two kingdoms in quick succession. His first campaign outside Mongolia was in 1209 against Xi Xia. Xi Xia was a kingdom in northern China that controlled oases along the Silk Road and exacted heavy taxes from Mongol caravans. To reach Ningxia, the capital (now the Chinese city of Yinchuan), Genghis's army had to cross the Gobi, a harsh desert that had discouraged invasions. Crossing was relatively easy for Mongol nomads, however, who could survive on mare's milk and blood drawn from a cut in a horse's hide. After a defeat by Genghis's forces, the emperor of Xi Xia opted for peace in 1210, offering tribute and giving Genghis one of his daughters to marry.

This pattern was repeated with the vastly richer kingdom east of Xi Xia, ruled by the Jin dynasty, which had controlled northern China for more than a century. With much of the 600,000-man Jin army bogged down in a war in the south, Genghis's 70,000 troops slaughtered the remnant force blocking their way into northern China. Chinese texts say disheartened Jin troops changed sides and swore allegiance to the invader.

When the Mongols surrounded the Jin capital of Zhongdu (present-day Beijing) in 1214, the emperor offered gold, silver, and other tribute—including one of his daughters—if Genghis would withdraw his troops.

Returning to Mongolia as he would after each campaign, Genghis began to build a capital at Karakorum. Not one to waste talented artisans, he marched some 30,000 of them back from Xi Xia to put them to work raising his citadel. Genghis also borrowed from other cultures to develop Mongol society. He used a scholar in China to advise him on building a government and recruited Uighurs, his advanced Turkic neighbors, as

5

accountants and scribes. Soon a school was turning out Mongol tax collectors and record keepers.

In 1218, Genghis sent one of his trusted generals, Jebe, to preempt a possible attack by the prince of Kara-Khitai, at Mongolia's western border. The mostly Muslim people rejoiced to be freed of their ruler, who had forbidden them to practice their religion and had crucified a religious leader. Genghis took Kara-Khitai into his protection.

With success in that quarter, Genghis's territory now touched that of the wealthy Khwarizm Empire, ruled by Shah Muhammad in Samarkand. Genghis attempted to establish friendly trade relations with the shah, but the Khwarizm would not cooperate. A caravan of 450 Mongol merchants were murdered by the governor of one of Khwarizm's outlying regions. When Genghis sent an ambassador to the shah to demand the governor be handed over, the shah had the ambassador killed and his head sent back to Genghis. Thus, Genghis aimed to punish his enemies, although the possibility of enormous plunder was surely an added incentive for his campaign. Although the shah's army was much larger than that of the Mongols, he proved a weak adversary. When Genghis appeared outside Samarkand, the shah fled. City nobles opened the gates and begged for mercy, but some of the shah's soldiers refused to surrender. About a thousand took refuge in the mosque hoping for Allah's protection, but flaming Mongol arrows rained on the building. When archaeologists excavated the site centuries later, they found burned bones.

More destruction was to come. In Bukhara, Genghis rode his horse into the courtyard of the Friday Mosque, ordered the nobles to bring him their riches, then turned his troops loose to

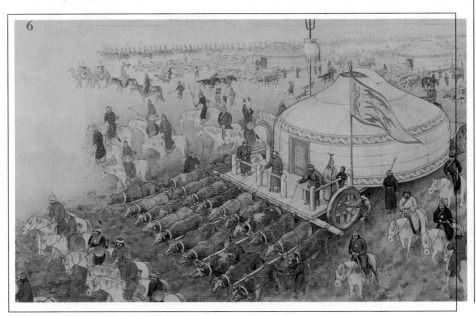

6

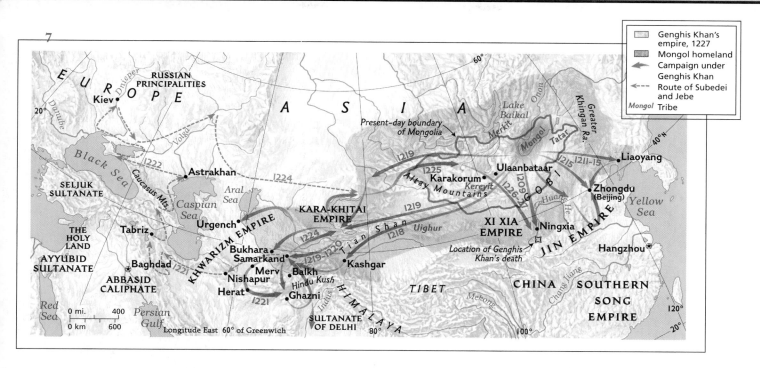

7

Genghis Khan's empire, 1227
Mongol homeland
Campaign under Genghis Khan
Route of Subedei and Jebe
Mongol Tribe

pillage, rape, and burn the city to the ground. Next came the Silk Road cities of Urgench and Merv. By one account, a Muslim holy man and his helpers spent 13 days in Merv counting corpses—tallying 1.3 million in all—"taking into account only those that were plain to see."

Although Muslim accounts of Mongol butchery also report enormous numbers, historians doubt these cities had such large populations. Some cities might have been decimated to frighten others.

While Genghis pursued Muhammad's son Jalal, who had escaped, he sent his generals Jebe and Subedai after the shah. The pair chased Muhammad to the Caspian Sea, where the exhausted shah died. Having now entered new territory, the two generals took 20,000 troops on a reconnaissance of Europe. Living off the land over the next three years and vanquishing every opposing army, they rode 8,000 miles (12,872 km), circling the Caspian in one of the greatest cavalry exploits of all time.

Upon rejoining Genghis in the central Asian steppe, the warriors headed for home. Genghis had a last score to settle. Just before the campaign against the Khwarizm Empire, the Xi Xia had insulted him and they had since been trying to revolt. In 1226 he decided it was time to teach them a lesson. As fate would have it, the lesson would be taught by someone else. One account says that Genghis had an accident and fell when his horse shied, another that he was ill, perhaps with typhus. In any case, the great khan delivered his final orders from his deathbed: the extermination of the Xi Xia people. His army is said to have killed "mothers and fathers down to the offspring of their offspring." Finally, in August 1227, Genghis Khan died. His body is supposed to be buried near a mountain called Burkhan Khaldun. It is said that a thousand horsemen trampled the site so the grave could not be found. Its location is still a mystery.

5 **Many Mongol cavalrymen wore elaborately designed helmets inlaid with silver.**

6 **One of the Mongols' great advantages in warfare was the mobility of its armies. To help sustain the army, the Mongols traveled with their *gers*, or felt tent homes, their families, and thousands of animals. The large *ger* in the center is the khan's, which functioned as his portable court.**

7 **Between 1206 and his death in 1227, Genghis Khan unified Mongolia and conquered kingdoms across central Asia.**

INTERPRETING THE PAST

1. How did Genghis Khan's experiences in his youth prepare him for his later military and political success?

2. What made Mongol armies so much stronger than their enemies?

3. What region suffered the most at the hands of the Mongols? Why was this region so harshly ravaged?

Eyewitness to History

At the Table of the Great Khan

◀ *Detail of historic map showing Marco Polo's journey along the Silk Road*

▼ *Kublai Khan presents golden tablets to Marco Polo.*

THE EUROPEAN VISITOR MARCO POLO was clearly impressed by the court of Kublai Khan. Here he describes the Great Khan at a banquet.

❝And when the great Khan sits at table on any great court occasion, it is in this fashion. His table is elevated a good deal above the others, and he sits at the north end of the hall, looking towards the south, with his chief wife beside him on the left. On his right sit his sons and his nephews, and other kinsmen of the blood imperial, but lower, so that their heads are on a level with the emperor's feet. And then the other barons sit at other tables lower still. So also with the women; for all the wives of the lord's sons, and of his nephews and below them again the ladies of the other barons and knights, each in the place assigned by the lord's order. The tables are so arranged that the emperor can see the whole of them from end to end, many as they are. . . .

And you should know that those who wait upon the great Khan with his dishes and his drink are some of the great barons. They have the mouth and nose muffled with fine napkins of silk and gold, so that no breath nor odor from their person should taint the dish or the goblet presented to the lord. And when the emperor is going to drink, all the musical instruments, of which he has a vast store of every kind, begin to play. And when he takes the

cup all the barons and the rest of the company drop on their knees and make the deepest obeisance [bow] before him, and then the emperor does drink. But each time that he does so the whole ceremony is repeated.❞

—**Marco Polo,** *The Travels of Marco Polo*

Analyzing Primary Sources

1. What did the arrangement of the banquet tables symbolize about the Great Khan's reign?
2. Who was the center of attention at the banquet—the Great Khan or his guests? Why?

Early Japan and Korea

Guide to Reading

Main Ideas
- Japan developed differently from many other countries because of its geography.
- Japan's history has been marked by power struggles between rulers and independent families.

Key Terms
samurai, Bushido, shogun, shogunate, daimyo, Shinto, Zen

People to Identify
Shotoku Taishi, Minamoto Yoritomo, Murasaki Shikibu, Yi Song-gye

Places to Locate
Japan, Hokkaido, Honshu, Kyushu, Shikoku, Osaka, Kyoto, Korea

Preview Questions
1. Why did Japan not develop a centralized government like China's?
2. How was Korea influenced by China?

Reading Strategy
Categorizing Information Use a chart like the one below to identify elements of Chinese culture accepted by Korea and Japan.

Chinese Culture in . . .

Japan	Korea

Preview of Events

◆600	◆800	◆1000	◆1200	◆1400	◆1600

622 Shotoku Taishi dies

794 Capital moved to Heian

1192 Minamoto Yoritomo establishes Kamakura shogunate

1281 Mongols invade Japan

1333 Ashikagas overthrow Kamakura shogunate

1477 Civil war ends in Japan

Voices from the Past

Japanese ruler, possibly Shotoku Taishi

In 604, a new constitution for an early Japanese state was drafted. It read:

❝When an imperial command is given, obey it with reverence. The sovereign is likened to heaven and his subjects are likened to earth. With heaven providing the cover and earth supporting it, the four seasons proceed in orderly fashion, giving sustenance to all that which is nature. If earth attempts to overtake the functions of heaven, it destroys everything. If there is no reverence shown to the imperial command, ruin will automatically result.❞

—*Sources of Japanese History,* **David Lu, ed., 1974**

Reverence for the emperor became an important part of Japanese society.

The Geography of Japan

Chinese and Japanese societies have historically been very different. One of the reasons for these differences is geography. Whereas China is on a vast continent, **Japan** is a chain of many islands. The population is concentrated on four main islands: **Hokkaido,** the main island of **Honshu,** and the two smaller islands of **Kyushu** and **Shikoku.** Japan's total land area is approximately 146,000 square miles (378,000 sq km)—about the size of the state of Montana.

Like China, much of Japan is mountainous. Only about 11 percent of the total land area can be farmed. The mountains are volcanic in origin. On the one hand, volcanic soils are very fertile, which has helped Japanese farming. On the other hand, the area is prone to earthquakes. In 1923, an earthquake almost destroyed the entire city of Tokyo.

NATIONAL GEOGRAPHIC   Early Japan

Geography Skills

The geography of Japan influenced the development of Japanese culture.

1. **Interpreting Maps** List, from north to south, the four major islands that make up Japan. On which island are the major cities of early Japan located?

2. **Applying Geography Skills** Heian (Kyoto) and Osaka were important cities in early Japan. Today Tokyo is a major city. What geographic features contributed to Tokyo's importance?

Because of their geographical isolation, the Japanese developed a number of unique qualities. These qualities contributed to the Japanese belief that they had a destiny separate from that of the peoples on the continent.

☑ **Reading Check** Evaluating How has Japan's geography affected its history?

The Rise of the Japanese State

⌐TURNING POINT⌐ **In this section you will learn how a violent storm destroyed most of the Mongol ships that were sent to attack Japan in 1281. After this Mongol defeat, Japan remained free of foreign invaders until 1945.**

The ancestors of present-day Japanese settled in the Yamato Plain near the modern cities of **Osaka** and **Kyoto** in the first centuries A.D. Their society was made up of clans. The people were divided between a small aristocratic class (the rulers) and a large

population of rice farmers, artisans, and household servants. The local ruler of each clan protected the population in return for a share of the annual harvest.

Eventually, one ruler of the Yamato clan achieved supremacy over the others and became, in effect, ruler of Japan. Other powerful families would, however, continue to compete for power.

Chinese Influences In the early seventh century, **Shotoku Taishi,** a Yamato prince, tried to unify the various clans so that the Japanese could more effectively resist an invasion by the Chinese. To do this, Prince Shotoku sent representatives to the Tang capital of China to learn more about how the Chinese organized their government. He then began to create a new centralized system of government in Japan, based roughly on the Chinese model.

Prince Shotoku wanted a centralized government under a supreme ruler. His objective was to limit the powers of the aristocrats and enhance the Yamato ruler's (his own) authority. As a result, the ruler was portrayed as a divine figure and the symbol of the Japanese nation.

Shotoku Taishi's successors continued to make reforms based on the Chinese model. The territory of Japan was divided into administrative districts, and the senior official of each district was selected from among the local nobles. As in China, the rural village was the basic unit of government. A new tax system was set up. Now all farmland technically belonged to the state. Taxes were to be paid directly to the central government rather than to local aristocrats.

The Nara Period After Shotoku Taishi's death in 622, political power fell into the hands of the Fujiwara clan. A Yamato ruler was still emperor. He was, however, strongly influenced by the Fujiwara family. In 710, a new capital was established at Nara. The emperor began to use the title "son of Heaven."

Though the reforms begun by Prince Shotoku continued during this period, Japan's central government could not overcome the power of the aristocrats. These powerful families were able to keep the taxes from the lands for themselves. Unable to gain tax revenues, the central government steadily lost power and influence.

The Heian Period In 794, the emperor moved the capital from Nara to nearby Heian, on the site of present-day Kyoto. At Heian, the emperor continued to rule in name, but actual power remained in the hands of the Fujiwara clan.

In fact, the government was returning to the decentralized system that had existed before the time of Shotoku Taishi. Powerful families whose wealth was based on the ownership of tax-exempt farmland dominated the rural areas. To avoid paying taxes, peasants often surrendered their lands to a local aristocrat, who then would allow the peasants to farm the land in return for the payment of rent.

With the decline of central power, local aristocrats tended to take justice into their own hands. They turned increasingly to military force as a means of protecting their interests. A new class of military servants emerged whose purpose was to protect the security and property of their employers.

Called the samurai ("those who serve"), these warriors resembled the knights of medieval Europe. Like knights, the samurai fought on horseback, clad in helmet and armor, although a samurai carried a sword and a bow and arrow rather than a lance and shield. Like knights, the samurai were supposed to live by a strict warrior code, known in Japan as Bushido ("the way of the warrior"). Above all, the samurai's code was based on loyalty to his lord.

The Kamakura Shogunate
By the end of the twelfth century, rivalries among Japanese aristocratic families had led to almost constant civil war. Finally, a powerful noble named **Minamoto Yoritomo** defeated several rivals and set up his power near the modern city of Tokyo.

To strengthen the state, he created a more centralized government under a powerful military leader known as the shogun (general). In this new system—called the shogunate—the emperor remained ruler in name only, and the shogun exercised the actual power. The Kamakura shogunate, founded by Yoritomo, lasted from 1192 to 1333.

At first the system worked well. The Japanese were fortunate that it did, because the government soon faced its most serious challenge yet from the Mongols. In 1281 Kublai Khan invaded Japan with an army nearly 150,000 strong. Fortunately for the Japanese, almost the entire fleet was destroyed by a massive typhoon (violent storm). Japan would not again face a foreign invader until American forces landed in the summer of 1945.

Fighting the Mongols put a heavy strain on the political system. In 1333, the Kamakura shogunate was overthrown by a group of powerful families led by the Ashikaga family.

Collapse of Central Rule The power of the local aristocrats grew during the fourteenth and fifteenth centuries. Heads of noble families, now called daimyo (DY•mee•OH), "great names," controlled vast landed estates that owed no taxes to the government. As family rivalries continued, the daimyo relied on the samurai for protection, and political power came into the hands of a loose coalition of noble families.

By 1500, Japan was close to chaos. A disastrous civil war known as the Onin War, which lasted from 1467 to 1477, led to the virtual destruction of the capital city of Kyoto. Armies passed back and forth through the city, burning temples and palaces.

Central authority disappeared. Powerful aristocrats in rural areas seized control over large territories, which they ruled as independent lords. Their rivalries caused almost constant warfare.

✓ **Reading Check** Summarizing What were the results of the Onin War?

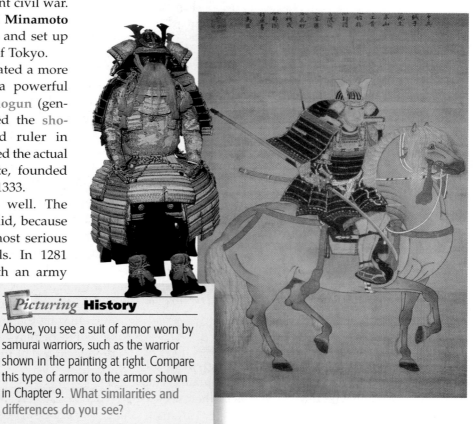

Picturing **History**

Above, you see a suit of armor worn by samurai warriors, such as the warrior shown in the painting at right. Compare this type of armor to the armor shown in Chapter 9. What similarities and differences do you see?

Life in Early Japan

Early Japan was mostly a farming society. Its people took advantage of the limited amount of farmland and abundant rainfall to grow wet rice (rice grown in flooded fields). As we have seen, noble families were able to maintain control over most of the land.

Manufacturing began to develop during the Kamakura period. Markets appeared in the larger towns, and industries such as paper, iron casting, and porcelain emerged. Trade between regions also grew. Foreign trade, mainly with Korea and China, began during the eleventh century. Japan shipped raw materials, paintings, swords, and other manufactured items in return for silk, porcelain, books, and copper coins.

The Role of Women

In early Japan, women may have had a certain level of equality with men. An eighth-century law code, for example, guaranteed the inheritance rights of women. Wives who were abandoned could divorce and remarry. However, later practices make it clear that women were considered subordinate to men. A husband could divorce his wife if she did not produce a

Aristocratic Japanese woman playing musical instrument

male child or if she committed adultery, talked too much, was jealous, or had a serious illness.

Although women did not possess the full legal and social rights of men, they played an active role at various levels of society. Aristocratic women were prominent at court. Some became known for their artistic or literary talents.

Women often appear in the paintings of the period along with men. The women are doing the spring planting, threshing and hulling rice, and acting as salespersons and entertainers.

Religion in Early Japan
Early Japanese people worshiped spirits, called *kami*, whom they believed resided in trees, rivers, streams, and mountains. The Japanese also believed that the spirits of their ancestors were present in the air around them. In Japan, these beliefs evolved into a kind of state religion called Shinto ("the Sacred Way" or "the Way of the Gods"), which is still practiced today.

In time, Shinto evolved into a state doctrine linked to a belief in the divinity of the emperor and the sacredness of the Japanese nation. A national shrine was established at Ise (EE•SAY). There, the emperor paid tribute to the sun goddess, Amaterasu, every year. According to legend, the first emperor was descended from the sun goddess.

Shinto, however, did not satisfy the spiritual needs of all the Japanese people. Some turned to Buddhism, which Buddhist monks from China brought to Japan during the sixth century A.D. Among the aristocrats in Japan, one sect, known as Zen, became the most popular. Zen beliefs became part of the samurai warrior's code of behavior.

In Zen Buddhism, there are different ways to achieve enlightenment (a state of pure being). Some believe that enlightenment can be achieved suddenly. Others claim that it can only be achieved through strong self-discipline, especially a long process of meditation that clears the mind of all thoughts.

Culture in Early Japan
During much of the history of early Japan, aristocratic men believed that prose fiction was merely "vulgar gossip" and was thus beneath them. Consequently, from the ninth to the twelfth centuries, women were the most productive writers of prose fiction in Japanese. Females learned to read and write at home, and they wrote diaries, stories, and novels to pass the time.

From this tradition appeared one of the world's great novels, *The Tale of Genji*. The novel was written by court author **Murasaki Shikibu** around the year 1000. Murasaki Shikibu wrote, "A story happens because the storyteller's own experiences . . . have moved him to an emotion so passionate that he can no longer keep it shut up in his heart." Her novel traces the life of the noble Genji as he tries to remain in favor with those in power. Various aspects of Genji's personality are explored as he moves from youthful adventures to a life of sadness and compassion in his later years.

In Japanese art and architecture, landscape serves as an important means of expression. The landscape surrounding the fourteenth-century Golden Pavilion in Kyoto displays a harmony of garden, water, and architecture that makes it one of the treasures of the world.

☑ **Reading Check** **Summarizing** Give one example of each of these aspects of life in early Japan: economic, social, religious, and cultural.

The Emergence of Korea

The Korean Peninsula, only slightly larger than the state of Minnesota, is relatively mountainous. Its closeness to both China and Japan has greatly affected its history. Indeed, no society in East Asia was more strongly influenced by the Chinese model than **Korea.**

In 109 B.C., the northern part of the Korean Peninsula came under the control of the Chinese. The Koreans, however, drove them out in the third century A.D. Eventually, three separate kingdoms emerged: Koguryo in the north, Paekche (pah•EHK•chee) in the southwest, and Silla in the southeast. From the fourth to the seventh centuries, the three kingdoms were bitter rivals.

Gradually, the kingdom of Silla gained control of the peninsula. After the king of Silla was assassinated, however, Korea sank into civil war. Finally, in the early tenth century, a new dynasty called Koryo (the root of the modern word *Korea*) arose in the north. This kingdom adopted Chinese political institutions in order to unify its territory and remained in power for four hundred years.

In the thirteenth century, the Mongols seized the northern part of Korea. By accepting Mongol authority, the Koryo dynasty managed to remain in power. Mongol rule, however, led to much suffering for the Korean people, especially the thousands of peasants and artisans who were forced to build ships for Kublai Khan's invasion of Japan.

History *through Architecture*

***Golden Pavilion,* Kyoto, 1300s** Landscape architecture has long been an important art form to the Japanese. Describe in your own words the landscaping around the Golden Pavilion.

After the collapse of the Mongol dynasty in China, the Koryo dynasty broke down. In 1392, **Yi Song-gye,** a military commander, seized power and founded the Yi dynasty. The Korean people were once again in charge of their own destiny.

✓**Reading Check** **Identifying** Which Asian country had the greatest influence on Korean political institutions?

⬟ TAKS Practice

SECTION **3** ASSESSMENT

Checking for Understanding

1. **Define** samurai, Bushido, shogun, shogunate, daimyo, Shinto, Zen.

2. **Identify** Shotoku Taishi, Minamoto Yoritomo, Murasaki Shikibu, Yi Song-gye.

3. **Locate** Japan, Hokkaido, Honshu, Kyushu, Shikkoku, Osaka, Kyoto, Korea.

4. **Explain** why women were the most productive writers of prose fiction in Japan between the ninth and twelfth centuries.

5. **List** the reforms in government made by Shotoku Taishi's successors. Which country's system of government was the model for these reforms?

Critical Thinking

6. **Explain** How did the samurai and shogun affect the government of early Japan?

7. **Summarizing Information** Create a cluster diagram like the one below that clarifies the role of women in early Japan.

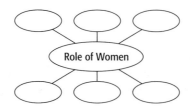

Role of Women

Analyzing Visuals

8. **Examine** the painting of the woman shown on page 266 of your text. What do you think her role was in Japanese society? Identify elements in the painting that support your answer. Do you see any similarities between the tone and mood of the painting and the feelings generated by looking at the landscape architecture shown above?

Writing About History

9. **Descriptive Writing** Imagine that you are a samurai living in Japan during the fourteenth century. Explain why you became a samurai and describe your daily duties.

SECTION 4 / India after the Guptas

Guide to Reading

Main Ideas
- Buddhism, Hinduism, and Islam influenced the development of India.
- Its location made India a center for trade, but conflicts among its states plagued its growth and prosperity.

Key Terms
Theravada, Mahayana

People to Identify
Mahmud of Ghazni, Rajputs, Timur Lenk, Moguls, Dandin

Places to Locate
India, Ghazni, Sultanate of Delhi, Deccan Plateau, Samarkand

Preview Questions
1. What major events marked the Islamic expansion into India?
2. What impact did Muslim rule have on Indian society and culture?

Reading Strategy
Contrasting Information Use a graphic organizer like the one below to diagram the main differences between Theravada and Mahayana Buddhism.

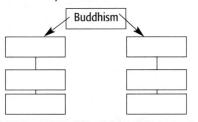

Preview of Events

| ♦900 | ♦1000 | ♦1100 | ♦1200 | ♦1300 | ♦1400 |

997 Mahmud of Ghazni extends Islamic influence into Hindu kingdoms

1200 Muslim power extends to northern India

1369 Timur Lenk begins conquest of northern India

Voices from the Past

Indian warrior seated on his elephant

An Indian poet gave advice to those who wanted to follow a military career:

❝When you see a fight, rush to the front, divide your enemy's forces, stand before them, and get your body scarred by the deep cuts of their swords; thus your fame is pleasant to the ear, not your body to the eye. As for your enemies, when they see you, they turn their backs, and with bodies whole and unscarred, they are pleasant to the eye, not so their shame to the ear.❞

—*Light in the East*, C.A. Bayly et al., eds., 1988

In the centuries that followed the collapse of the Gupta Empire, internal fighting plagued the Indian states. Other changes were occurring at the same time.

The Decline of Buddhism

For hundreds of years, Buddhism had retained its popularity among the Indian people. The teachings of the Buddha came to be interpreted in different ways, however. People did not always agree on the meaning of the Buddha's teachings. As a result, a split developed among the followers of Buddhism in **India.**

One group believed that they were following the original teachings of the Buddha. They called themselves the school of Theravada, "the teachings of the elders." Followers of Theravada see Buddhism as a way of life, not a religion that is centered on individual salvation. They continue to insist that an understanding of one's self is the chief way to gain nirvana, or release from the "wheel of life."

Another view of Buddhist doctrine was emerging in northwest India. Here, Buddhists stressed that nirvana could be achieved through devotion to the Buddha. This school, known as Mahayana Buddhism, said that Theravada teachings were too strict for ordinary people. To Mahayana Buddhists, Buddhism is a religion, not a philosophy. The Buddha is not just a wise man, but also a divine figure. Nirvana is not just a release from the wheel of life, but a true heaven. Through devotion to the Buddha, people can achieve salvation in this heaven after death.

In the end, neither the Mahayana nor the Theravada sect of Buddhism remained popular in Indian society. By the seventh century, Theravada had declined rapidly. Mahayana was absorbed by a revived Hinduism and later by a new arrival, Islam.

Despite their decline in India, though, both schools of Buddhism found success abroad. Carried by monks to China, Korea, Southeast Asia, and Japan, the practice of Buddhism has remained active in all four areas to the present.

Reading Check **Summarizing** What are the two schools of Buddhism?

The Eastward Expansion of Islam

In the early eighth century, Islam became popular in the northwestern corner of the Indian subcontinent. The new religion had a major impact on Indian civilization. This impact is still evident today in the division of the subcontinent into mostly Hindu India and two Islamic states, Bangladesh and Pakistan.

One reason for Islam's success in South Asia is that it arrived at a time when India was in a state of great political disunity. The Gupta Empire had collapsed, and no central authority had replaced it. India was divided into about seventy states, which fought each other constantly.

When the Arab armies reached India in the early eighth century, they did little more than move into the frontier regions. At the end of the tenth century, however, a new phase of Islamic expansion took place when rebellious Turkish slaves founded a new Islamic state known as **Ghazni,** located in present-day Afghanistan.

When the founder of the new state died in 997, his son, **Mahmud of Ghazni,** succeeded him. Mahmud, an ambitious man, began to attack neighboring Hindu kingdoms to the southeast. Before his death in 1030, he was able to extend his rule throughout the upper Indus Valley and as far south as the Indian Ocean.

Resistance against the advances of Mahmud and his successors into northern India was led by the **Rajputs,** who were Hindu warriors. They fought bravely, but their military tactics, based on infantry supported by elephants, were no match for the cavalry of the invaders, which struck with great speed. Mahmud's successors continued their advances. By 1200, Muslim power had reached over the entire plain of northern India, creating a new Muslim state known as the **Sultanate of Delhi.** In the fourteenth century, this state extended its power into the **Deccan Plateau.**

Reading Check **Evaluating** What was the impact of the introduction of Islam in India?

The Impact of Timur Lenk

During the latter half of the fourteenth century, the Sultanate of Delhi began to decline. Near the end of the century, a new military force crossed the Indus River from the northwest, raided the capital of Delhi, and then withdrew. As many as 100,000 Hindu prisoners were massacred before the gates of the city. It was India's first meeting with **Timur Lenk** (Tamerlane).

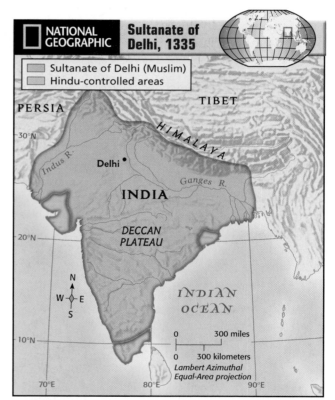

NATIONAL GEOGRAPHIC

Sultanate of Delhi, 1335

- Sultanate of Delhi (Muslim)
- Hindu-controlled areas

PERSIA · TIBET · HIMALAYA · Indus R. · Delhi · Ganges R. · INDIA · DECCAN PLATEAU · INDIAN OCEAN

0 300 miles
0 300 kilometers
Lambert Azimuthal Equal-Area projection

Geography *Skills*

The collapse of the Gupta Empire allowed the rise of the Muslim state known as the Sultanate of Delhi.

1. **Applying Geography Skills** Create a political map of the subcontinent of India today. Use a legend with icons or color to show Hindu and Muslim populations. How does your map compare to the map above?

Timur Lenk was the ruler of a Mongol state based in **Samarkand,** to the north of the Pamir Mountains. Born sometime during the 1330s in Samarkand, Timur Lenk seized power in 1369 and immediately launched a program of conquest. During the 1380s, he placed the entire region east of the Caspian Sea under his authority and then occupied Mesopotamia. After his brief foray into

northern India, he turned to the west. He died in 1405 in the midst of a military campaign.

The death of Timur Lenk removed a major menace from the various states of the Indian subcontinent, but the calm did not last long. By the early sixteenth century, two new challenges had appeared from beyond the horizon. One came from the north in the form of the **Moguls,** a newly emerging nomadic power. The other came from Europe, from Portuguese traders arriving by sea in search of gold and spices.

✓**Reading Check** **Describing** Who seized power in 1369 and launched a program of conquest?

Islam and Indian Society

The Muslim rulers in India viewed themselves as foreign conquerors. They tried to maintain a strict separation between the Muslim ruling class and the mass of the Hindu population.

Picturing **History**

This miniature taken from an Indian manuscript shows Mongol ruler Timur Lenk. What signs of a courageous warrior and conqueror do you see in the image?

Like rulers elsewhere at this time, many Muslim rulers in India were intolerant of other faiths. They generally used peaceful means, however, to encourage people to convert to Islam. Still, some could be fierce when their religious zeal was aroused. Said one, "I forbade the infliction of any severe punishment on the Hindus in general, but I destroyed their idol temples and raised mosques in their place."

Most Muslim rulers realized that there were simply too many Hindus to convert them all. They reluctantly accepted the need to tolerate religious differences. Nevertheless, Muslim rulers did impose many Islamic customs on Hindu society. Overall, the relationship between Muslim and Hindu was that of conqueror and conquered, a relationship marked by suspicion and dislike rather than friendship and understanding.

✓**Reading Check** **Evaluating** What was the relationship between the Muslims and Hindus in India?

Economy and Daily Life

Between 500 and 1500, most Indians lived on the land and farmed their own tiny plots. These peasants paid a share of their harvest each year to a landlord, who in turn sent part of the payment to the local ruler. In effect, the landlord worked as a tax collector for the king, who in theory owned all the land in his state.

Although the vast majority of Indians were peasants, reports by foreign visitors between 500 and 1500 indicate that many people lived in the cities. It was here that the landed elites and rich merchants lived, often in conditions of considerable wealth.

Rulers, of course, had the most wealth. One maharaja (great king) of a small state in southern India, for example, had more than a hundred thousand soldiers in his pay, along with nine hundred elephants and twenty thousand horses. Another ruler kept a thousand high-caste women to serve as sweepers of his palace. Each carried a broom and a brass basin holding a mixture of cow dung and water. "When the King goes from one house to another, or to a house of prayer, he goes on foot, and these women go before him with their brooms and basins in their hands, plastering the path where he is to tread."

Agriculture was not the only source of wealth in India. Since ancient times, India's location had made it a center for trade between Southwest Asia and East Asia. It had also been a source for other goods shipped throughout the world.

CONNECTIONS Past To Present

The Clash between Hindus and Muslims

On December 7, 1992, a mob of Hindu militants in India sacked a Muslim mosque in the town of Ayodhya, in northern India. This mosque had been built in the seventeenth century on a Hindu holy site once occupied by a Hindu temple. For years, militant Hindus had demanded that the mosque, which was not used much, be destroyed.

When the government failed to meet the militants' demands, the Hindu demonstrators pulled down the mosque and began to erect a Hindu temple at the site. These actions in turn led to clashes between Hindus and Muslims throughout the country. In neighboring Pakistan as well, Muslim rioters destroyed a number of Hindu shrines.

Since 1992, the tensions between Hindus and Muslims in India have continued to grow. In the 1990s, a militant Hindu political party led by Balasaheb Thackeray, who calls himself the "Hitler of Bombay," has called for a new Indian state that would only meet the interests of the Hindu majority. This conflict between Hindus and Muslims has been a feature of life in India for over a thousand years.

The invasion of India by Muslim forces began in the eighth century. At the end of the tenth century, however, Muslim invasions became more numerous and more devastating. One Muslim conqueror of northern India, Mahmud of Ghazni, destroyed many Hindu temples. His army massacred thousands of Hindus and caused massive destruction.

Other Muslim conquerors after Mahmud promoted Islamic culture at the expense of India's Hindu heritage. Stones from demolished Hindu temples were often used to build mosques. The actions of these early Muslim conquerors angered Hindus and helped create the bitter rivalries that have lasted in India to this day.

▲ *Riots between Hindus and Muslims in British India*

Comparing Past and Present

Using outside sources, investigate whether there have been any other major clashes between the Hindus and the Muslims in India since 1992. If so, were these clashes rooted in the same tensions? Can you identify any possible resolution to this conflict between the two groups?

Internal trade within India probably declined during this period, primarily because of the fighting among the many states of India. The level of foreign trade, however, remained high, especially in the south and along the northwestern coast. Both areas were located along the traditional trade routes to Southwest Asia and the Mediterranean Sea.

Wealthy Hindu merchants with close ties to the royal courts carried on much of the foreign trade. Others, including Muslims, also participated in this trade.

✓ **Reading Check** **Summarizing** What were the principal sources of wealth in India?

The Wonder of Indian Culture

Between 500 and 1500, Indian artists and writers built on the achievements of their predecessors while making innovations in all fields of creative endeavor. Here, we examine two such fields: architecture and prose literature.

Temple Architecture Between 500 and 1500, religious architecture in India developed from caves to new, magnificent structures. From the eighth century on, Indian architects built monumental Hindu temples. Each temple consisted of a central shrine surrounded

This Hindu temple at Khajuraho (left) was built about 950. The detail above shows the intricate sculpture in the temple's walls.

by a tower, a hall for worshippers, an entryway, and a porch, all set in a rectangular courtyard. Temples became ever more ornate. The towers became higher and the temple complexes more intricate.

Probably the greatest examples of Hindu temple art of this period are found at Khajuraho. Of the 80 temples originally built there in the tenth century, 20 remain standing today. All of the towers on these temples are buttressed (supported by stone walls) at various levels on the sides. This gives the whole temple a sense of unity and creates an upward movement similar to that of Mount Kailasa in the Himalaya, a sacred place to Hindus.

Prose The use of prose was well established in India by the sixth and seventh centuries. This is truly astonishing in light of the fact that the novel did not appear in Japan until the tenth century and in Europe until the seventeenth century.

One of the greatest masters of Sanskrit prose was **Dandin,** a seventh-century author. In *The Ten Princes,* he created a fantastic world, fusing history and fiction. His powers of observation, details of everyday life, and humor give his writing much vitality.

✓ **Reading Check** **Describing** How does Indian architecture reflect Hindu ideals?

🌟 TAKS Practice

SECTION 4 ASSESSMENT

Checking for Understanding

1. **Define** Theravada, Mahayana.

2. **Identify** Mahmud of Ghazni, Rajputs, Timur Lenk, Moguls, Dandin.

3. **Locate** India, Ghazni, Sultanate of Delhi, Deccan Plateau, Samarkand.

4. **Explain** what happened to the spread of Buddhism in India.

5. **List** the two groups that entered India after the death of Timur Lenk.

Critical Thinking

6. **Evaluate** What was the impact of the introduction of Islam into the Indian culture? Give reasons to support whether the impact was negative or positive.

7. **Outlining Information** Use an outline as shown below to describe the impact of Timur Lenk.

   I. Timur Lenk
   A.　　born during 1330s in Samarkand
   B. _____
   C. _____

Analyzing Visuals

8. **Analyze** how the Hindu temple, shown above, reflects the history of the culture in which it was produced.

Writing About History

9. **Persuasive Writing** Assume the role of either a Theravada or a Mahayana Buddhist. Write a persuasive letter to a Buddhist counterpart explaining why your beliefs are more true to Buddhist ideals.

SECTION 5

Civilization in Southeast Asia

Guide to Reading

Main Ideas
- Geography and cultural influences affected the development of Southeast Asia.
- Southeast Asian countries had primarily farming or trading economies that influenced their social structures.

Key Terms
archipelago, agricultural society, trading society

People to Identify
Jayavarman, Thai

Places to Locate
Malay Peninsula, Vietnam, Angkor, Pagan, Thailand, Strait of Malacca, Melaka

Preview Questions
1. What influence did geography have on the development of Southeast Asia?
2. How does Southeast Asia reflect Chinese, Indian, and Muslim influences?

Reading Strategy
Categorizing Information Use a chart like the one below to compare characteristics of the states in Southeast Asia.

	Government	Economy	Culture
Vietnam			
Angkor			
Thailand			
Burma			
Malay			

Preview of Events

♦800	♦1000	♦1200	♦1400	♦1600

802
Jayavarman crowned god-king

c. 1050
Kingdom of Pagan founded in Burma

c. 1400
Islamic state forms in Melaka on Malay Peninsula

1432
Thai destroy Angkor capital

1500s
Dai Viet extend territory to Gulf of Thailand

Voices from the Past

Bas-relief depicting Southeast Asian battle

Although the Chinese invaded Vietnam, the Vietnamese were not easy to defeat, as one Chinese historian related:

❝The Viet people fled into the depths of the mountains and forests, and it was not possible to fight them. The soldiers were kept in garrisons to watch over abandoned territories. This went on for a long time, and the soldiers grew weary. Then the Viet came out and attacked; the Chinese soldiers suffered a great defeat; the dead and wounded were many. After this, the emperor deported convicts to hold the garrisons against the Viet people.❞
— *The Birth of Vietnam,* **Keith W. Taylor, 1983**

The Chinese imposed their culture through conquest. The people of Southeast Asia, however, changed the ideas they adopted from neighboring countries, creating rich, diverse cultures.

The Land and People of Southeast Asia

Between China and India lies the region that today is called Southeast Asia. It has two major parts. One is the mainland region, extending southward from the Chinese border down to the tip of the **Malay Peninsula.** The other is an extensive archipelago, or chain of islands, most of which is part of present-day Indonesia and the Philippines.

Ancient mariners called the area the "golden region" or "golden islands." Located between India and China—two highly advanced and densely populated regions of the world—Southeast Asia is a melting pot of peoples. It contains a vast mixture of races, cultures, and religions.

Mainland Southeast Asia consists of several north-south mountain ranges. Between these ranges are several fertile river valleys that run in a southerly or southeasterly direction. The mountains are densely forested and often infested with malaria-bearing mosquitoes. Thus, the people living in the river valleys were often cut off from one another and had only limited contacts with the people living in the mountains.

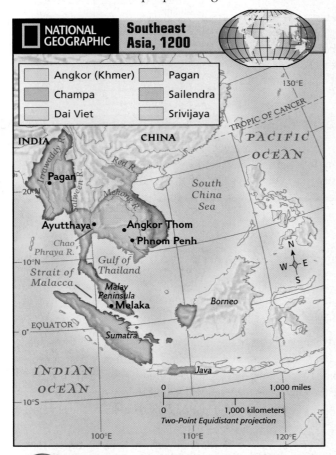

Geography Skills

Southeast Asia is a diverse area, largely due to the region's geographical barriers.

1. **Interpreting Maps** Is the mainland region of Southeast Asia located north or south of the equator?
2. **Applying Geography Skills** Of the kingdoms shown in the map, why were Sailendra and Srivijaya least influenced by Chinese culture? What geographic feature do you think had the greatest influence on their development?

These geographical barriers may help explain why Southeast Asia is one of the few regions in Asia that was never unified under a single government. The geographical barriers encouraged the development of separate, distinctive cultures with diverse cultural practices, such as different religions and languages.

✓ **Reading Check** **Examining** Why was Southeast Asia never unified under a single government?

The Formation of States

Between 500 and 1500, a number of organized states developed throughout Southeast Asia. When the peoples of the region began to form states, they used models from China and India. At the same time, they adapted these models to their own needs and created their own unique states.

Vietnam The Vietnamese were one of the first peoples in Southeast Asia to develop their own state and their own culture. After the Chinese conquered **Vietnam** in 111 B.C., they tried for centuries to make Vietnam part of China. However, Chinese officials were often frustrated by the Vietnamese. As one official said, "The people are like birds and beasts; they wear their hair tied up and go barefoot, while for clothing they simply cut a hole in a piece of cloth for their head or they fasten their garments on the left side. It is useless to try to change them." The Vietnamese clung to their own identity. In the tenth century, they finally overthrew Chinese rule.

Chinese influence remained, however. Vietnamese rulers realized the advantages of taking over the Chinese model of centralized government. The new Vietnamese state, which called itself Dai Viet (Great Viet), adopted state Confucianism. Following the Chinese model, the rulers called themselves emperors and adopted Chinese court rituals. They also introduced the civil service examination as a means of recruiting government officials on the basis of merit.

The state of Dai Viet became a dynamic force on the Southeast Asian mainland. As its population grew, it expanded southward. Several centuries of bitter warfare with its southern neighbor, Champa, ended in Vietnamese victory by 1500. Continuing their march to the south, the Vietnamese reached the Gulf of Thailand (formerly Gulf of Siam) by 1600.

Angkor In the ninth century, the kingdom of **Angkor** arose in the region that is present-day Cambodia. The kingdom was formed when a powerful figure named **Jayavarman** united the Khmer (kuh•MEHR) people and established a capital at Angkor Thom. In 802, Jayavarman was crowned as god-king of his people. For several hundred years, Angkor—or the Khmer Empire—was the most powerful state in mainland Southeast Asia.

Angkor faced enemies on all sides. To the east were the Vietnamese and the kingdom of Champa. To the west was the Burman kingdom of **Pagan** (pah•GAHN). With the arrival in the fourteenth century of new peoples from the north—known today as the **Thai**—Angkor began to decline.

In 1432, the Thai from the north destroyed the Angkor capital. The Angkor ruling class fled to the southeast, where they set up a new capital near Phnom Penh (puh•NAHM PEN), the capital of present-day Cambodia.

Thailand The Thai first appeared in the sixth century as a frontier people in China. Beginning in the eleventh or twelfth century, Thai groups began moving southward. This process was encouraged by the Mongol invasion of China in the mid-thirteenth century. These migrating peoples eventually came into conflict with Angkor, destroying the Angkor capital in 1432.

The Thai set up their own capital at Ayutthaya (ah•YU•tuh•yuh) on the Chao Phraya (chau PRY•uh) River, where they remained as a major force in the region for the next four hundred years.

Although they converted to Buddhism and borrowed Indian political practices as well, they created their own unique blend that evolved into the modern-day culture of **Thailand.**

Burma The Thai were also threatened from the west by the Burman peoples, who had formed their own society in the valleys of the Salween and Irrawaddy (IHR•uh•WAH•dee) Rivers. The Burmans had migrated from the highlands of Tibet beginning in the seventh century A.D., probably to escape advancing Chinese armies.

The Burmans were pastoral peoples, but they adopted farming soon after their arrival in Southeast Asia. In the eleventh century, they founded the first great Burman state, the kingdom of Pagan. Like the Thai, they converted to Buddhism and adopted Indian political institutions and culture.

During the next two hundred years, Pagan became a major force in the western part of Southeast Asia. It played an active role in the sea trade throughout the region. Attacks from the Mongols in the late thirteenth century, however, weakened Pagan, causing it to decline.

The Malay World In the Malay Peninsula and the Indonesian Archipelago, a different pattern emerged. For centuries, this area had been tied to the trade that passed from East Asia into the Indian Ocean. The

History *through Architecture*

Old and new come together as modern-day boats speed past The Temple of Dawn on the Chao Phraya River in Thailand. Examine the closeup view of the temple (below). Do you see any similarities between this architecture and the architecture of other monuments shown in this chapter? Describe the similarities.

area had never been united under a single state, however. The vast majority of the people of the region were of Malay background, but the peoples were divided into numerous separate communities.

Two organized states eventually emerged in the region. In the eighth century, the state of Srivijaya (SHREE•vih•JAY•uh) came to dominate the trade route passing through the **Strait of Malacca.** At the same time, the kingdom of Sailendra emerged in eastern Java. Both states were influenced by Indian culture. Whereas Srivijaya depended on trade, the wealth of Sailendra was based primarily on farming.

In the late thirteenth century, the new kingdom of Majapahit (mah•jah•PAH•heet) was founded. It became the greatest empire the region had yet seen. In the mid-fourteenth century, Majapahit incorporated most of the archipelago and perhaps even parts of the mainland under a single rule. Majapahit did not have long to enjoy its status, however. By the fifteenth century, a new state was beginning to emerge in the region.

After the Muslim conquest of northern India, Muslim merchants—either Arabs or Indian converts—had settled in port cities in the region and had begun to convert the local population. Around 1400, an Islamic state began to form in **Melaka,** a small town on the western coast of the Malay Peninsula.

Melaka soon became the major trading port in the region and a chief rival to Majapahit. From Melaka, Muslim traders and the Muslim faith moved into the interior. Eventually, almost the entire population of the region was converted to Islam and became part of the Sultanate of Melaka.

✓**Reading Check** **Contrasting** How did the development of the Malay Peninsula and the Indonesian Archipelago differ from the development of Southeast Asia?

States of Southeast Asia, 111 B.C.–A.D. 1600

State	Time Frame	Cultural Influence(s)	Economic Base
Vietnam	Conquered by China in 111 B.C.; independent in A.D. 939	China, Confucianism	Agriculture
Angkor	Arose in 9th century; destroyed by Thailand in 1432	India	Agriculture
Thailand	Thai people first appeared in 6th century, settling in area of present-day Thailand in 15th century	India, Buddhism	Agriculture
Burma (Pagan)	11th–13th centuries	India, Buddhism	Agriculture, sea trade
Malay			
Srivijaya	8th century	India	Sea trade
Sailendra	8th century	India	Agriculture
Majapahit	13th–15th centuries	Islam	Trade, agriculture
Melaka	15th century	Islam	Sea trade

Chart *Skills*

The states of Southeast Asia adapted the models of China and India to their own needs.

1. **Summarizing** What religions influenced these states?

2. **Analyzing** Using the map on page 274, explain why the economies of certain states were based on agriculture, while others were based on trade.

Economic Forces

The states of Southeast Asia can be divided into two groups: agricultural societies, whose economies were largely based on farming, and trading societies, which depended primarily on trade for income. Of course, the agricultural states had some trading activities, and the trading societies had some farming. Nevertheless, some states, such as Vietnam, Angkor, Pagan, and Sailendra, drew most of their wealth from the land. Others, such as Srivijaya and the Sultanate of Melaka, supported themselves chiefly through trade.

Trade through Southeast Asia expanded after the emergence of states in the area and reached even greater heights after the Muslim conquest of northern India. The rise in demand for spices also added to the growing volume of trade. As the wealth of Europe and Southeast Asia increased, demand grew for the products of East Asia. Merchant fleets from India and the Arabian Peninsula sailed to the Indonesian islands to buy the cloves, pepper, nutmeg, cinnamon, and precious woods like teak and sandalwood that the wealthy in China and Europe wanted.

Reading Check **Contrasting** What is the difference between an agricultural society and a trading society?

Social Structures

At the top of the social ladder in most Southeast Asian societies were the hereditary aristocrats. They held both political power and economic wealth. Most aristocrats lived in the major cities. Angkor Thom, for example, was a city with royal palaces and parks, a massive parade ground, reservoirs, and numerous temples.

Beyond the major cities lived the rest of the population, which consisted of farmers, fishers, artisans, and merchants. In most Southeast Asian societies, the majority of people were probably rice farmers who lived at a bare level of subsistence and paid heavy rents or taxes to a landlord or local ruler.

Most of the societies in Southeast Asia gave greater rights to women than did their counterparts in China and India. Women worked side by side with men in the fields and often played an active role in trading activities.

Reading Check **Summarizing** Describe the social organization of Southeast Asia.

Culture and Religion

Chinese culture made an impact on Vietnam. In many other areas of Southeast Asia, Indian cultural influence prevailed. The most visible example of this influence was in architecture. Of all the existing structures at Angkor Thom, the temple of **Angkor Wat** is the most famous and most beautiful. It combines Indian architectural techniques with native inspiration in a structure of impressive grace. Surrounded by walls measuring 1,700 by 1,500 feet (518

Stone image of the Buddha from Borobudur temple in Java

by 457 m), Angkor Wat rises like a 200-foot-high (61-m-high) mountain in a series of three great terraces. The construction of Angkor Wat, which took 40 years to complete, required an enormous quantity of stone—as much as it took to build Egypt's Great Pyramid.

Hindu and Buddhist ideas began to move into Southeast Asia in the first millennium A.D. However, the new religions did not entirely replace existing beliefs. In all Southeast Asian societies, as in China and Japan, old beliefs were blended with those of the new faiths. In this process, the king played a central role. The ruler of Angkor, for example, was seen as a living link between the people and the gods, and he helped unite the new Hindu gods with local gods.

Buddhism also spread to Southeast Asia. It made little impact, however, until the introduction of Theravada Buddhism in the eleventh century. From Burma, Theravada spread rapidly to other areas of Southeast Asia.

Eventually, Theravada Buddhism became the religion of the masses in much of Southeast Asia. Why did it have such appeal? For one thing, it teaches that people can seek nirvana through their own efforts; they do not need priests or rulers. Moreover, it tolerated local gods and posed no threat to established faith.

✓ **Reading Check** **Identifying** Which countries most influenced the cultural development of Southeast Asia?

🔻 **TAKS Practice**

SECTION 5 ASSESSMENT

Checking for Understanding

1. **Define** archipelago, agricultural society, trading society.

2. **Identify** Jayavarman, Thai, Angkor Wat.

3. **Locate** Malay Peninsula, Vietnam, Angkor, Pagan, Thailand, Strait of Malacca, Melaka.

4. **Explain** the importance of Islam in the development of Melaka. What other religious and philosophical influences were important in the formation of states in Southeast Asia?

5. **List** the Chinese reforms that were adopted by the Dai Viet.

Critical Thinking

6. **Explain** How would an increase in trade and exporting cause a region to develop more complex forms of political and social organization? Use examples from the text to support your answer.

7. **Organizing Information** Create a graphic organizer like the one below to diagram the social hierarchy in most Southeast Asian societies discussed in this section.

Social Hierarchy

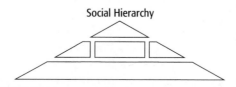

Analyzing Visuals

8. **Compare** the examples of religious temples and their art pictured on pages 275, 277, and on this page. What elements or features are unique in each example? Identify the country where each was built or resides. How do these buildings and sculptures compare to the religious art and architecture in your area?

Writing About History

9. **Expository Writing** Write an essay explaining why the tradition of the nuclear family is common in Burma and Thailand, but the extended family is the rule in Vietnam and the Malay Peninsula.

CRITICAL THINKING
SKILLBUILDER

Identifying Central Issues

Why Learn This Skill?

*If someone asked you what the movie **Star Wars** was about, how would you answer? At first you might want to describe everything that happens in the movie. Identifying central issues is finding the key themes, or major ideas, in a body of information. Central issues are the framework that holds a body of information together.*

Learning the Skill

Follow the steps below to identify a central issue:

• Find out the setting and purpose of the selection.

• Skim the material to identify its general subject.

• Read the information to pinpoint the ideas that the details support.

• Identify the central issue. Ask: What part of the material conveys the main idea?

Read the following excerpt from *Code of the Samurai: A Modern Translation of the Bushido Shoshinshu of Taira Shigesuke* discussing the rules and expectations of Japan's warrior class.

> 66. . . when young people or servants are unmannerly in conversation and other interaction with their employers or parents, and yet this is overlooked as long as they are sincere in their regard for their employers and parents, this is the loyalty and familial duty of the lower three classes. In the way of warriors, no matter how much you may treasure loyalty and familial duty in your heart, without the courteous manners to express respect for your employers and honor for your parents, you cannot be said to be in accord with the way. 99

The Bushido code emphasizes courtesy and respect. The central issue in this excerpt is that warriors must express their respect through actions.

Samurai warrior

Practicing the Skill

Read the excerpt below from *The Travels of Marco Polo the Venetian* about Kublai Khan and answer the questions that follow.

> 66But since the wise men of the idolaters, and especially the baksis [learned astrologers], already mentioned, have represented to his majesty that providing for the poor is a good work and highly acceptable to their deities, he has relieved their wants in the manner stated, and at his court none are denied food who come to ask it. Not a day passes in which there are not distributed, by the regular officers, twenty thousand vessels of rice, millet, and panicum. By reason of this admirable and astonishing liberality which the grand khan exercises towards the poor, the people all adore him as a divinity.99

❶ According to Marco Polo, how do people view Kublai Khan?

❷ Summarize the central issue in one sentence.

Applying the Skill

Find and read a magazine article that contains a first-hand account of a recent national or international event. Identify two central issues that are covered in the article. Write a sentence that identifies each of the central issues.

Glencoe's **Skillbuilder Interactive Workbook, Level 2,** provides instruction and practice in key social studies skills.

Using Key Terms

1. The _____ were a class of people in China who controlled much of the land in the countryside and produced most of the candidates for the civil service.

2. The sons of Genghis Khan divided his empire up into separate territories called _____.

3. Made of fine clay baked at very high temperatures in a kiln, _____ became popular during the Tang Era.

4. The purpose of the _____ in Japan was to protect the security and property of their patrons.

5. The "way of the warrior," or _____, strictly governed the behavior of the Japanese military class.

6. In Japan, a powerful military leader who exercised actual power while ruling under the emperor's name was called a _____.

7. The _____ were the heads of great noble families in Japan who controlled vast land estates and paid no taxes to the government.

8. In India, the teachings of the Buddha came to be interpreted in two different ways: the school of Theravada and the school of _____.

9. Resistance against the advances of Mahmud and his successors into northern India was led by the _____, who were Hindu warriors.

10. Southeast Asia has a mainland region and an extensive _____, or chain of islands.

Reviewing Key Facts

11. **History** Discuss the importance of the *kamikaze,* the "divine wind," in early Japanese history.

12. **Geography** Name the two rivers in China that the Grand Canal connected. Explain why the canal was important.

13. **Science and Technology** Choose three products developed by the Tang and discuss the importance of each.

14. **Government** Explain the circumstances under which the Mongol dynasty ended. Name the dynasty that emerged as a result.

15. **Geography** Compare the geography of Japan and China. How did geography influence the development of their societies?

16. **Economy** Specify the reasons India was successful in world trade.

17. **Culture** State the role that Vietnamese culture played in the eventual overthrow of Chinese rule.

18. **Economy** List the Southeast Asian regions that were considered agricultural societies and the ones considered trading societies. Explain how they influenced each other.

Critical Thinking

19. **Analyzing** How did the civil service examinations aid in the development of a strong central government in China?

20. **Making Comparisons** In what ways were the roles of women of the early Chinese dynasties similar to the roles of women of Southeast Asia? How were they different?

Chapter Summary

In the Asian world, countries developed different political systems and forms of government. Each country, however, had strong leaders, as shown below.

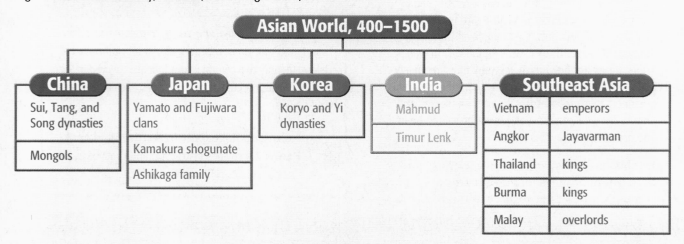

Asian World, 400–1500					
China	**Japan**	**Korea**	**India**	**Southeast Asia**	
Sui, Tang, and Song dynasties	Yamato and Fujiwara clans	Koryo and Yi dynasties	Mahmud	Vietnam	emperors
Mongols	Kamakura shogunate		Timur Lenk	Angkor	Jayavarman
	Ashikaga family			Thailand	kings
				Burma	kings
				Malay	overlords

Writing About History

21. **Descriptive Writing** Pretend that you are a native Chinese citizen traveling through Southeast Asia. Choose a country that you wish to visit, as well as a time period, and write a brief essay about your impressions of the area. Finally, compare the area to your home in China.

Analyzing Sources

Read the following quote about the Japanese samurai.

> ❝I spurred my horse on, careless of death in the face of the foe.
>
> I braved the dangers of wind and wave, not reckoning that my body
>
> might sink to the bottom of the sea, and be devoured by monsters of the deep.❞

22. How does this quote reflect the code of the samurai?

23. How would the ideals expressed in this quote relate to the codes of other warriors, such as the Mongols?

Applying Technology Skills

24. **Using the Internet** Search the Internet for information about Buddhism, Hinduism, Confucianism, and Shintoism, and complete a table comparing the main beliefs of each.

	Buddhism	Hinduism	Confucianism	Shinto
Founder (if any)				
Main God/ Gods/Spirits				
Celebrations/ Rituals				

Making Decisions

25. Imagine that a samurai warrior is able to time travel and meet a knight from medieval Europe. Create a dialogue between the two, showing how each would approach and solve the problem of an invading enemy.

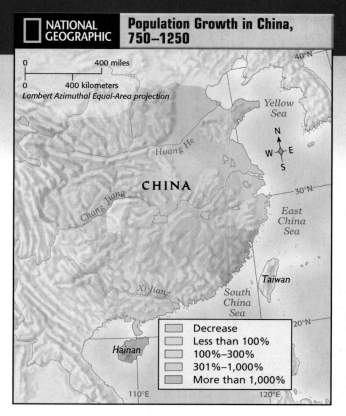

NATIONAL GEOGRAPHIC — **Population Growth in China, 750–1250**

0 ——— 400 miles
0 ——— 400 kilometers
Lambert Azimuthal Equal-Area projection

Legend:
- Decrease
- Less than 100%
- 100%–300%
- 301%–1,000%
- More than 1,000%

Analyzing Maps and Charts

26. From the map determine in which geographic direction the population shifted.

27. Using your text, explain why the population decreased in certain areas of China during this period.

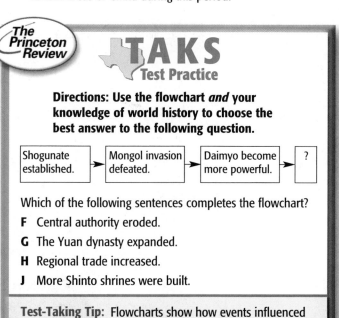

The Princeton Review

TAKS Test Practice

Directions: Use the flowchart *and* your knowledge of world history to choose the best answer to the following question.

Shogunate established. → Mongol invasion defeated. → Daimyo become more powerful. → ?

Which of the following sentences completes the flowchart?

F Central authority eroded.

G The Yuan dynasty expanded.

H Regional trade increased.

J More Shinto shrines were built.

Test-Taking Tip: Flowcharts show how events influenced other events. Study the progression carefully. Think about what cause-and-effect relationship the flowchart illustrates.

CHAPTER 9

Emerging Europe and the Byzantine Empire

400–1300

Key Events

As you read, look for the key events in the history of early Europe and the Byzantine Empire.

- *The new European civilization was formed by the coming together of three major elements: the Germanic tribes, the Roman legacy, and the Christian church.*
- *The collapse of a central authority in the Carolingian Empire led to feudalism.*
- *In the 1100s, European monarchs began to build strong states.*
- *While a new civilization arose in Europe, the Byzantine Empire created its own unique civilization in the eastern Mediterranean.*

The Impact Today

The events that occurred during this time period still impact our lives today.
- *Ancient Roman literary works exist today because they were copied by monks.*
- *The influence of English common law is seen in our American legal system.*
- *Byzantine architecture inspired building styles in eastern Europe and Southwest Asia.*

World History Video The Chapter 9 video, "Charlemagne and His World," chronicles the emergence of the European nations.

Charlemagne

410
Visigoths
sack Rome

c. 510
Clovis
establishes
Frankish
kingdom

400   500   600   700   800

Emperor Justinian

534
Justinian
codifies Roman
law in *The Body
of Civil Law*

768
Charlemagne
becomes Frankish
king

800
Charlemagne
crowned Roman
emperor

Perched above the city, Edinburgh Castle was a residence for Scotland's kings and queens.

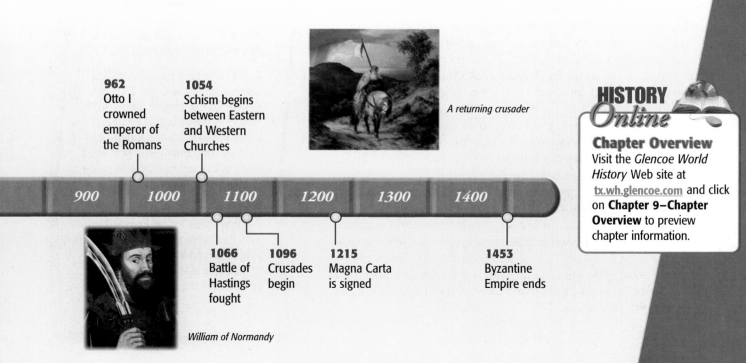

962
Otto I crowned emperor of the Romans

1054
Schism begins between Eastern and Western Churches

A returning crusader

1066
Battle of Hastings fought

1096
Crusades begin

1215
Magna Carta is signed

1453
Byzantine Empire ends

900 1000 1100 1200 1300 1400

William of Normandy

HISTORY
Online
Chapter Overview
Visit the *Glencoe World History* Web site at tx.wh.glencoe.com and click on **Chapter 9–Chapter Overview** to preview chapter information.

A Story That Matters

A medieval depiction of the crowning of Charlemagne

The Crowning of Charlemagne

*I*n the autumn of the year 800, Charles the Great—or Charlemagne—the king of the Franks, entered Rome. His goal was to help Pope Leo III, head of the Catholic Church. The pope was disliked by the Roman people and was barely clinging to power in the face of their hostility.

Charlemagne brought the pope and the Romans together and resolved their differences. To celebrate the newfound peace, Charlemagne, his family, and a host of citizens from the city crowded into Saint Peter's Basilica on Christmas Day to attend mass.

All were surprised, according to an observer, when, "as the king rose from praying before the tomb of the blessed apostle Peter, Pope Leo placed a golden crown on his head." In keeping with ancient tradition, the people in the church shouted, "Long life and victory to Charles Augustus, crowned by God the great and peace-loving Emperor of the Romans."

Charles was not entirely happy being crowned emperor by the pope. He said later that he would not have entered the church if he had known that Leo intended to crown him. To the onlookers, however, it appeared that the Roman Empire in the West had been reborn and Charles had become the first Roman emperor since 476.

Why It Matters

The coronation of Charlemagne did not signal a rebirth of the Roman Empire, but reflected the emergence of a new European civilization. The period during which European civilization developed is called the Middle Ages or the medieval period. It lasted from about 500 to 1500.

At the same time European civilization was emerging in the West, the Eastern Roman Empire continued to survive as the Byzantine Empire. A buffer between Europe and the East, the Byzantine Empire also preserved many of the accomplishments of the Greeks and Romans.

History and You Create a time line that shows events from 800 to 1215 that led to the signing of the Magna Carta. Identify the impact of the political and legal ideas contained in the Magna Carta.

Transforming the Roman World

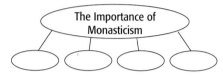
Voices from the Past

In 416, a Byzantine historian named Procopius described the Visigoths:

❝When the barbarians [the Visigoths] met with no opposition they proved the most brutal of mankind. All the cities they took they so destroyed as to leave them unrecognizable, unless a tower or a single gate or some such relic happened to survive. All the people that came their way, young and old, they killed, sparing neither women nor children. That is why Italy is depopulated to this day. They plundered all the money out of all Europe and, most important, in Rome they left nothing of value, public or private, when they moved on to Gaul.❞

—*A History of Rome,* Moses Hadas, ed., 1956

The Visigoths were Germanic peoples. German tribes, like the Visigoths and Ostrogoths, would play an important part in the new European civilization.

Visigoths on the battlefield

The New Germanic Kingdoms

The Germanic peoples had begun to move into the lands of the Roman Empire by the third century. The **Visigoths** occupied Spain and Italy until the **Ostrogoths**, another Germanic tribe, took control of Italy in the fifth century. By 500, the Western Roman Empire had been replaced by a number of states ruled by German kings. The merging of Romans and Germans took different forms in the various Germanic kingdoms.

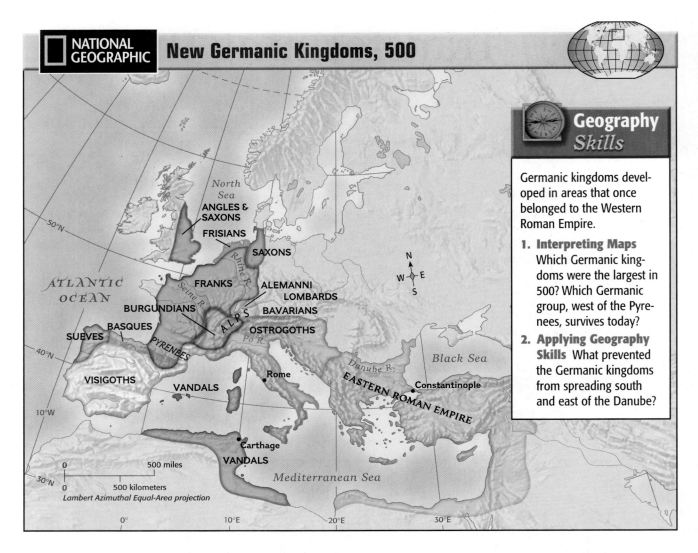

Geography Skills

Germanic kingdoms developed in areas that once belonged to the Western Roman Empire.

1. **Interpreting Maps** Which Germanic kingdoms were the largest in 500? Which Germanic group, west of the Pyrenees, survives today?

2. **Applying Geography Skills** What prevented the Germanic kingdoms from spreading south and east of the Danube?

Both the kingdom of the Ostrogoths in Italy and the kingdom of the Visigoths in Spain retained the Roman structure of government. However, a group of Germanic warriors came to dominate the considerably larger native populations and eventually excluded Romans from holding power.

Roman influence was even weaker in Britain. When the Roman armies abandoned Britain at the beginning of the fifth century, the Angles and Saxons, Germanic tribes from Denmark and northern Germany, moved in and settled there. Eventually, these peoples became the **Anglo-Saxons.**

The Kingdom of the Franks Only one of the German states on the European continent proved long lasting—the kingdom of the Franks. The Frankish kingdom was established by **Clovis,** a strong military leader who around 500 became the first Germanic ruler to convert to Christianity. At first, Clovis had refused the pleas of his Christian wife to adopt Christianity. According to Gregory of Tours, a sixth-century historian, Clovis had remarked to his wife, "Your God can do nothing."

During a battle with another Germanic tribe, however, when Clovis's army faced certain destruction, he cried out, "Jesus Christ, if you shall grant me victory over these enemies, I will believe in you and be baptized." After he uttered these words, the enemy began to flee, and Clovis soon became a Christian.

Clovis found that his conversion to Christianity gained him the support of the Roman Catholic Church, as the Christian church in Rome had become known. Not surprisingly, the Catholic Church was eager to obtain the friendship of a major ruler in the Germanic states.

By 510, Clovis had established a powerful new Frankish kingdom that stretched from the **Pyrenees** in the southwest to German lands in the east (modern-day France and western Germany). After Clovis's death, however, his sons followed Frankish custom and divided his newly created kingdom among themselves.

Germanic Society Over time, Germans and Romans intermarried and began to create a new society. As they did, some of the social customs of the Germanic people came to play an important role.

The crucial social bond among the Germanic peoples was the family, especially the extended family of husbands, wives, children, brothers, sisters, cousins, and grandparents. This extended family worked the land together and passed it down to future generations. The family also provided protection, which was much needed in the violent atmosphere of the time.

The German concept of family affected the way Germanic law treated the problem of crime and punishment. In the Roman system, as in our own, a crime such as murder was considered an offense against society or the state. Thus, a court would hear evidence and arrive at a decision. Germanic law, on the other hand, was personal. An injury by one person against another could mean a blood feud, and the feud could lead to savage acts of revenge.

To avoid bloodshed, a new system developed, based on a fine called **wergild** (WUHR•GIHLD). Wergild was the amount paid by a wrongdoer to the family of the person he or she had injured or killed. Wergild, which means "money for a man," was the value of a person in money. The value varied according to social status. An offense against a member of the nobility, for example, cost considerably more than one against an ordinary person or a slave.

One means of determining guilt in Germanic law was the ordeal. The **ordeal** was based on the idea of divine intervention. All ordeals involved a physical trial of some sort, such as holding a red-hot iron. It was believed that divine forces would not allow an innocent person to be harmed. If the accused person was unharmed after a physical trial, or ordeal, he or she was presumed innocent.

Reading Check **Analyzing** What was the significance of Clovis's conversion to Christianity?

The Role of the Church

By the end of the fourth century, Christianity had become the supreme religion of the Roman Empire. As the official Roman state fell apart, the Church played an increasingly important role in the growth of the new European civilization.

Organization of the Church By the fourth century, the Christian church had developed a system of organization. Local Christian communities called parishes were led by priests. A group of parishes was headed by a bishop, whose area of authority was known as a **bishopric,** or diocese. The bishoprics of the Roman provinces were joined together under the direction of an archbishop.

Over time, one bishop—the bishop of Rome—began to claim that he was the leader of what was now called the Roman Catholic Church. According to Catholic beliefs, Jesus had given the keys to the kingdom of Heaven to Peter, who was considered the chief apostle and the first bishop of Rome. Later bishops of Rome were viewed as Peter's successors. They came to be known as **popes** (from the Latin word *papa,* "father") of the Catholic Church.

Western Christians came to accept the bishop of Rome—the pope—as head of the Church, but they did not agree on how much power the pope should

Picturing **History**

Pope Gregory I promoted the use of chants in the Catholic service. In this painting, Gregory I is shown teaching a group of boys to sing what became known as a Gregorian chant. **Why is Gregory I known as Gregory the Great?**

"Let all things be common to all, as it is written, lest anyone should say that anything is his own."

—*The Rule of St. Benedict*

have. In the sixth century, a strong pope, **Gregory I,** known as Gregory the Great, strengthened the power of the papacy (office of the pope) and the Roman Catholic Church.

Gregory I was pope from 590 to 604. He also served as leader of the city of Rome and its surrounding territories (later called the Papal States), thus giving the papacy a source of political power, and he increased his spiritual authority over the church in the West. He was especially active in converting non-Christian peoples of Germanic Europe to Christianity. He did this through the monastic movement.

The Monks and Their Missions A monk is a man who separates himself from ordinary human society in order to pursue a life of total dedication to God. The practice of living the life of a monk is known as monasticism. At first, Christian monasticism was based on the model of the hermit who pursues an isolated spiritual life. Later, in the sixth century, **Saint Benedict** founded a community of monks for which he wrote a set of rules. This community established the basic form of monasticism in the Catholic Church. The Benedictine rule came to be used by other monastic groups.

Benedict's rule divided each day into a series of activities, with primary emphasis on prayer and manual labor. Physical work of some kind was required of all monks for several hours a day, because idleness was "the enemy of the soul." At the very heart of community practice was prayer, the proper "Work of God." Although prayer included private meditation and reading, all monks gathered together

seven times during the day for common prayer and the chanting of Psalms (sacred songs). A Benedictine life was a communal one. Monks ate, worked, slept, and worshiped together.

Each Benedictine monastery was strictly ruled by an abbot, or "father" of the monastery, who had complete authority over the monks. Obedience to the will of the abbot was expected of each monk. Each Benedictine monastery owned lands that enabled it to be a self-sustaining community, isolated from and independent of the world surrounding it. Within the monastery, however, monks were to fulfill their vow of poverty.

Monks became the new heroes of Christian civilization and were an important force in the new European civilization. The monastic community came to be seen as the ideal Christian society that could provide a moral example to the wider society around it. The monks' dedication to God became the highest ideal of Christian life. They were the social workers of their communities, providing schools for the young, hospitality for travelers, and hospitals for the sick. They taught peasants carpentry and weaving and made improvements in agriculture that they passed on to others.

Monasteries became centers of learning wherever they were located. The monks worked to spread Christianity to all of Europe. English and Irish monks were especially enthusiastic missionaries—people sent out to carry a religious message—who undertook the conversion of non-Christian peoples, especially in German lands. By 1050 most western Europeans had become Catholics.

Although the first monks were men, women, called nuns, also began to withdraw from the world to dedicate themselves to God. These women played an important role in the monastic movement. Nuns lived in convents headed by abbesses. Many of the abbesses belonged to royal houses, especially in Anglo-Saxon England. In the kingdom of Northumbria, for example, Hilda founded the monastery of Whitby in 657. As abbess, she was responsible for giving learning an important role in the life of the monastery. Five future bishops were educated under her direction.

☑ **Reading Check** **Describing** What was the role of the Catholic Church in the growth of the new European civilization?

Charlemagne and the Carolingians

During the 600s and 700s, the kings of the Frankish kingdom gradually lost their power to the **mayors of the palace,** who were the chief officers of the king's household. One of these mayors, **Pepin,** finally took the logical step of assuming the kingship of the Frankish state for himself and his family. Pepin was the son of Charles Martel, the leader who defeated the Muslims at the Battle of Tours in 732. Upon Pepin's death in 768, his son came to the throne of the Frankish kingdom.

This new king was the dynamic and powerful ruler known to history as Charles the Great, or **Charlemagne.** Charlemagne was a determined and decisive man who was highly intelligent and curious. He was a fierce warrior, a strong statesman, and a pious Christian. Although possibly unable to write, he was a wise patron (supporter) of learning.

The Carolingian Empire During his lengthy rule from 768 to 814, Charlemagne greatly expanded the territory of the Frankish kingdom and created what came to be known as the **Carolingian** (KAR•uh•LIN•jee•uhn) **Empire**. At its height, Charlemagne's empire covered much of western and central Europe. Not until the time of Napoleon Bonaparte in the nineteenth century would an empire its size be seen again in Europe.

The administration of the empire depended both on Charlemagne's household staff and on counts (German nobles) who acted as the king's chief representatives in local areas. As an important check on the power of the counts, Charlemagne established the *missi dominici* ("messengers of the lord king")—two men who were sent out to local districts to ensure that the counts were carrying out the king's wishes.

Charlemagne as Roman Emperor As Charlemagne's power grew, so too did his prestige as the most powerful Christian ruler. One monk even described Charlemagne's empire as the "kingdom of Europe." In 800, Charlemagne acquired a new title—emperor of the Romans.

Charlemagne's coronation as Roman emperor demonstrated the strength of the idea of an enduring Roman Empire. After all, his coronation took place three hundred years after the collapse of the Western Roman Empire.

Charlemagne, King of the Franks

Charles the Man	Charles the Administrator	Charles the Conqueror	Charles the Patron of Learning
• Was athletic, well-spoken, and charismatic	• Delegated authority to loyal nobles	• Was an aggressive warrior	• Revived classical studies
• Married four times	• Retained local laws of conquered areas	• Strengthened the Frankish military	• Preserved Latin culture
• Understood Greek, spoke Latin, but possibly could not write	• Divided kingdom into districts	• Expanded and consolidated the Frankish kingdom	• Established monastic and palace schools
• Left empire to his sole surviving son	• Used *missi dominici* ("messengers of the lord king") to inspect and report on provinces		

Chart *Skills*

Charlemagne was a dynamic and powerful ruler.

1. **Examining** What activities helped Charlemagne strengthen his empire?
2. **Evaluating** What event(s) listed above continue(s) to impact civilization today?

Charlemagne

The coronation also symbolized the coming together of Roman, Christian, and Germanic elements. A Germanic king had been crowned emperor of the Romans by the pope, the spiritual leader of western Christendom. A new civilization had emerged.

An Intellectual Renewal Charlemagne had a strong desire to promote learning in his kingdom. This desire stemmed from Charlemagne's own intellectual curiosity and from the need to provide educated clergy for the Church and literate officials for the government. His efforts led to a revival of learning and culture sometimes called the Carolingian Renaissance, or rebirth. This revival involved renewed interest in Latin culture and classical works—the works of the Greeks and Romans.

The monasteries, many of which had been founded by Irish and English missionaries during the seventh and eighth centuries, played a central role in the cultural renewal of this period. By the 800s, the work asked of Benedictine monks included copying manuscripts. Monasteries established **scriptoria,** or writing rooms, where monks copied not only the works of early Christianity, such as the Bible, but also the works of Latin classical authors. Their work was a crucial factor in the preservation of the ancient legacy. Most of the ancient Roman works we have today exist because they were copied by Carolingian monks.

 **Reading Check** **Explaining** What was the importance of the *missi dominici?*

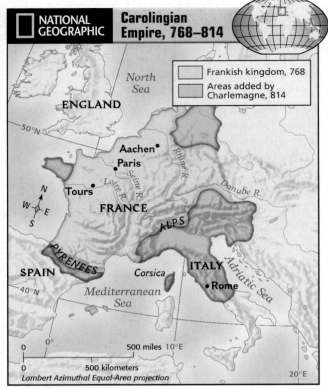

NATIONAL GEOGRAPHIC

Carolingian Empire, 768–814

☐ Frankish kingdom, 768
☐ Areas added by Charlemagne, 814

North Sea
ENGLAND
50°N
Aachen●
●Paris
Tours
Loire R. *Seine R.* *Rhine R.* *Danube R.*
FRANCE
ALPS
PYRENEES
SPAIN   Corsica   ITALY *Adriatic Sea*
40°N   *Mediterranean Sea*   ●Rome

0   0°   500 miles 10°E
0   500 kilometers
Lambert Azimuthal Equal-Area projection   20°E

 **Geography** *Skills*

Charlemagne greatly expanded the Frankish kingdom.

1. **Interpreting Maps** What important city did Charlemagne gain by expanding east of longitude 10°E?

2. **Applying Geography Skills** What important event happened at Tours?

🌟 **TAKS Practice**

SECTION 1 ASSESSMENT

Checking for Understanding

1. **Define** wergild, ordeal, bishopric, pope, monk, monasticism, missionary, nun, abbess.

2. **Identify** Visigoths, Ostrogoths, Anglo-Saxons, Clovis, Gregory I, Saint Benedict, mayor of the palace, Pepin, Charlemagne, scriptoria.

3. **Locate** Pyrenees, Carolingian Empire.

4. **Summarize** the crucial social bond among the Germanic peoples and one area of its application.

5. **List** the daily activities of the Benedictine monks.

Critical Thinking

6. **Explain** What significance did Charlemagne's coronation as Roman emperor have to the development of European civilization?

7. **Summarizing Information** Identify the rulers discussed in the chapter and explain how they were significant both in religious and political realms.

Rulers	Religious Realm	Political Realm

Analyzing Visuals

8. **Examine** the painting of Charlemagne shown on page 289 of your text. How does this representation reflect Charlemagne's dual role as emperor and as Christian leader?

Writing About History

9. **Persuasive Writing** You have been asked to apply Germanic law to modern society. List at least five common crimes that occur today and argue what *wergild* you think should be established for each crime and why.

Feudalism

Guide to Reading

Main Ideas
- Vikings, Magyars, and Muslims invaded Europe during the ninth and tenth centuries.
- The collapse of central authority in the European world led to a new political system known as feudalism.

Key Terms
feudalism, vassal, knight, fief, feudal contract, tournament, chivalry

People to Identify
Magyars, Vikings, Eleanor of Aquitaine

Places to Locate
Hungary, Normandy

Preview Questions
1. What led to the development of the system of feudalism?
2. What was the role of aristocratic women in the Middle Ages?

Reading Strategy
Identifying Information Use a diagram like the one below to show the system of loyalties created under feudalism.

System of Loyalties

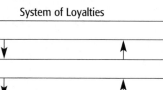

Preview of Events

| ◆800 | ◆900 | ◆1000 | ◆1100 |

814
Charlemagne dies

c. 850
Vikings spread throughout Europe

c. 900
Feudalism takes hold in northern France

c. 1050
Feudalism spreads through western Europe

Voices from the Past

In 1020, Bishop Fulbert of Chartres wrote about the mutual obligations between lord and vassals:

❝[The vassal] who swears loyalty to his lord ought always to have these six things in memory: what is harmless, safe, honorable, useful, easy, practicable. *Harmless*, that is to say, that he should not injure his lord in his body; *safe*, that he should not injure him by betraying his secrets; *honorable*, that he should not injure him in his justice; *useful*, that he should not injure him in his possessions; *easy* and *practicable*, that that good which his lord is able to do easily he make not difficult, nor that which is practicable he make not impossible to him.❞

—*Readings in European History*, James Harvey Robinson, 1934

A system of lords and vassals spread over Europe after the collapse of the Carolingian Empire.

Homage being paid to a medieval lord

The Invaders

The Carolingian Empire began to fall apart soon after Charlemagne's death in 814. Less than 30 years later, it was divided among his grandsons into three major sections: the west Frankish lands, the eastern Frankish lands, and the Middle Kingdom. Local nobles gained power. Invasions in different parts of the old Carolingian world added to the process of disintegration.

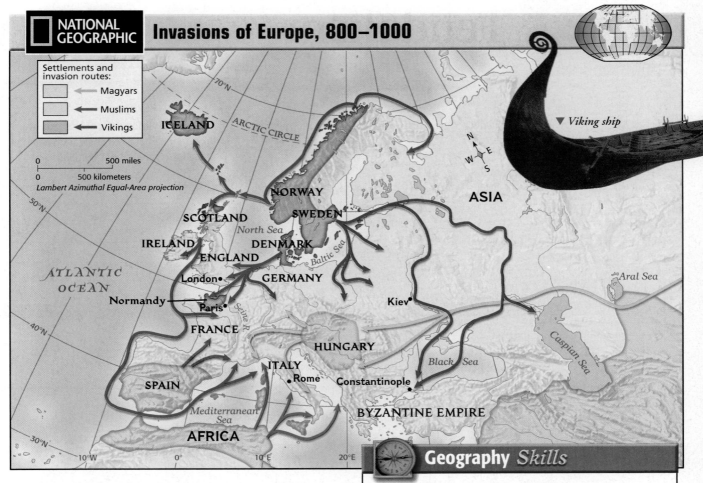

NATIONAL GEOGRAPHIC

Invasions of Europe, 800–1000

Settlements and invasion routes:
- ← Magyars
- ← Muslims
- ← Vikings

ICELAND

ARCTIC CIRCLE

0 — 500 miles
0 — 500 kilometers
Lambert Azimuthal Equal-Area projection

NORWAY

ASIA

▼ Viking ship

SWEDEN

SCOTLAND

North Sea

IRELAND   DENMARK

ENGLAND   Baltic Sea

ATLANTIC   London•   GERMANY   Aral Sea

OCEAN

Normandy —— Paris•   Kiev•   Caspian Sea

Seine R.

FRANCE   HUNGARY   Black Sea

ITALY

SPAIN   •Rome   Constantinople•

Mediterranean Sea   BYZANTINE EMPIRE

AFRICA

Geography Skills

Several different groups invaded and settled in early medieval Europe.

1. **Interpreting Maps** What areas remained free of invasion? What areas experienced multiple invasions?
2. **Applying Geography Skills** Describe how the invaders would have disrupted everyday life in Europe.

In the ninth and tenth centuries, western Europe was beset by a wave of invasions. The Muslims attacked the southern coasts of Europe and sent raiding parties into southern France. The **Magyars,** a people from western Asia, moved into central Europe at the end of the ninth century, settled on the plains of **Hungary,** and invaded western Europe.

The most far-reaching attacks of the time, however, came from the Northmen or Norsemen of Scandinavia, also called the **Vikings.** The Vikings were a Germanic people. Their great love of adventure and their search for spoils of war and new avenues of trade may have been what led them to invade other areas of Europe. In the ninth century, Vikings sacked villages and towns, destroyed churches, and easily defeated small local armies.

The Vikings were warriors, and they were superb shipbuilders and sailors. Their ships were the best of the period. Long and narrow with beautifully carved, arched prows, the Viking dragon ships carried about 50 men. The construction of the ships enabled them to sail up European rivers and attack places far inland. By the mid-ninth century, the Vikings had begun to build various European settlements.

Beginning in 911, the ruler of the west Frankish lands gave one band of Vikings land at the mouth of the Seine River, forming a section of France that came to be known as **Normandy.** The Frankish policy of settling the Vikings and converting them to Christianity was a deliberate one. By their conversion to Christianity, the Vikings were soon made a part of European civilization.

Reading Check **Evaluating** What factors helped the Vikings to successfully invade Europe?

The Development of Feudalism

The Vikings and other invaders posed a large threat to the safety of people throughout Europe. Rulers found it more and more difficult to defend their subjects as centralized governments like the Carolingian Empire were torn apart.

Thus, people began to turn to local landed aristocrats, or nobles, to protect them. To survive, it became important to find a powerful lord who could offer protection in return for service. This led to a new political and social system called **feudalism**.

Knights and Vassals At the heart of feudalism was the idea of vassalage. In Germanic society, warriors swore an oath of loyalty to their leaders and fought for them. The leaders, in turn, took care of the warriors' needs. By the eighth century, a man who served a lord in a military capacity was known as a **vassal.**

The Frankish army had originally consisted of foot soldiers dressed in coats of mail (armor made of metal links or plates) and armed with swords. Horsemen had been throwers of spears. In the eighth century, however, larger horses and the stirrup were introduced. Now, horsemen were armored in coats of mail (the larger horses could carry the weight). They wielded long lances that enabled them to act as battering rams (the stirrups kept them on their horses). For almost five hundred years, warfare in Europe was dominated by heavily armored cavalry, or **knights,** as they came to be

called. The knights had great social prestige and formed the backbone of the European aristocracy.

It was expensive to have a horse, armor, and weapons. With the breakdown of royal governments, the more powerful nobles took control of large areas of land. When these lords wanted men to fight for them, they granted each vassal a piece of land that supported the vassal and his family. In the society of the early Middle Ages, where there was little trade and wealth was based primarily on land, land was the most important gift a lord could give to a vassal.

The Feudal Contract The relationship between lord and vassal was made official by a public ceremony. To become a vassal, a man performed an act of homage to his lord:

> ❝The man should put his hands together as a sign of humility, and place them between the two hands of his lord as a token that he vows everything to him and promises faith to him; and the lord should receive him and promise to keep faith with him. Then the man should say: 'Sir, I enter your homage and faith and become your man by mouth and hands [that is, by taking the oath and placing his hands between those of the lord], and I swear and promise to keep faith and loyalty to you against all others.'❞

CONNECTIONS Around The World

Feudalism

The word *feudalism* usually makes us think of European knights on horseback armed with swords and lances. However, between 800 and 1500, feudal systems developed in various parts of the world.

In Europe, a feudal system based on lords and vassals arose between 800 and 900 and flourished for the next four hundred years.

In Japan, a feudal system much like that found in Europe developed between 800 and 1500. Powerful nobles in the countryside owed only a loose loyalty to the Japanese emperor. The nobles in turn depended on samurai, or warriors who owed loyalty to the nobles and provided military service for them. Like knights in Europe, the samurai fought on horseback, clad in iron.

In the Valley of Mexico, the Aztec developed a political system between 1300 and 1500 that bore some similarities to Japanese and European feudalism. Local rulers of lands outside the capital city were allowed considerable freedom. However, the Aztec king was a powerful ruler and local rulers paid tribute to him and provided him with military forces. Unlike the knights and samurai of Europe and Japan, Aztec warriors were armed with sharp knives and spears of wood, both fitted with razor-sharp blades cut from stone.

▲ *Samurai warrior*

Comparing Cultures

Research two of the three cultures discussed in this feature. What are the similarities and differences in their feudal systems?

In feudal society, loyalty to one's lord was the chief virtue.

By the ninth century, the grant of land made to a vassal had become known as a fief (FEEF). Vassals who held fiefs came to hold political authority within them. As the Carolingian world fell apart, the number of separate powerful lords and vassals increased. Instead of a single government, many different people were now responsible for keeping order.

Feudalism became increasingly complicated. The vassals of a king, who were themselves great lords, might also have vassals who would owe them military service in return for a grant of land taken from their estates. Those vassals, in turn, might likewise have vassals. At that level, the vassals would be simple knights with barely enough land to provide income for their equipment. The lord-vassal relationship, then, bound together both greater and lesser landowners.

The lord-vassal relationship was an honorable relationship between free men and implied no sense of servitude. Feudalism came to be characterized by a set of unwritten rules—known as the feudal contract—that determined the relationship between a lord and his vassal. The major obligation of a vassal to his lord was to perform military service, usually about 40 days a year.

When summoned, a vassal had to appear at his lord's court to give advice to the lord. Vassals were responsible for making financial payments to the lord on a number of occasions as well. These included the knighting of the lord's eldest son, the marriage of the lord's eldest daughter, and the ransom of the lord's person if the lord should be captured.

Under the feudal contract, the lord also had responsibilities toward his vassals. Of course, the lord supported a vassal by granting him land. The lord, however, was also required to protect his vassal, either by defending him militarily or by taking his side in a court of law.

✓Reading Check **Identifying** Why was land the most important gift a lord could give a vassal?

HISTORY *Online*

Web Activity Visit the *Glencoe World History* Web site at **tx.wh.glencoe.com** and click on **Chapter 9– Student Web Activity** to learn more about medieval Europe.

THE WAY IT WAS

FOCUS ON EVERYDAY LIFE

The Castles of the Aristocrats

The growth of the European nobility in the High Middle Ages (1000 to 1300) was made visible by a growing number of castles scattered across the landscape. Castles varied considerably but possessed two common features: they were permanent residences for the noble family, its retainers, and servants, and they were defensible fortifications.

The earliest castles were made of wood. However, by the eleventh century, castles of stone were being built. At first, the basic castle plan had two parts. The *motte* was a man-made or natural steep-sided hill. The *bailey* was an open space next to the motte. Both motte and bailey were encircled by large stone walls. The *keep*, the central building of the castle, was built on the motte.

The keep was a large building with a number of stories constructed of thick stone walls. On the ground floor were the kitchens and stables. The basement housed storerooms for equipment and foodstuffs. Above the ground floor was the great hall. This very large room served a number of purposes.

Bodiam Castle, England

The Nobility of the Middle Ages

In the Middle Ages, European society, like Japanese society during the same period, was dominated by men whose chief concern was warfare. Like the Japanese samurai, many European nobles loved war. As one nobleman wrote in a poem:

> 66And well I like to hear the call of
> 'Help' and see the wounded fall,
> Loudly for mercy praying,
> And see the dead, both great and small,
> Pierced by sharp spearheads one and all.99

The nobles were the kings, dukes, counts, barons, and even bishops and archbishops who had large landed estates and considerable political power. They formed an aristocracy, or nobility, that consisted of people who held political, economic, and social power.

Great lords and ordinary knights came to form a common group within the aristocracy. They were all warriors, and the institution of knighthood united them all. However, there were also social divisions among them based on extremes of wealth and landholdings.

Trained to be warriors but with no adult responsibilities, young knights had little to do but fight. In the twelfth century, tournaments—contests where knights could show their fighting skills—began to appear. By the late twelfth century, the joust—individual combat between two knights—had become the main part of the tournament.

Knights saw tournaments as an excellent way to train for war. As one knight explained: "A knight cannot distinguish himself in war if he has not trained for it in tourneys."

In the eleventh and twelfth centuries, under the influence of the Catholic Church, there gradually evolved among the nobility an ideal of civilized behavior, called chivalry. Chivalry was a code of ethics that knights were supposed to uphold. In addition to their oath to defend the Church and defenseless people, knights were expected to treat captives as honored guests instead of putting them in dungeons. Chivalry also implied that knights should fight only for glory and not for material rewards, an ideal that was not always followed.

✓**Reading Check** **Summarizing** List three features of chivalry.

Here, the lord of the castle held court and received visitors. Here, too, the inhabitants of the castle ate and even slept. Smaller rooms might open off the great hall, including bedrooms with huge curtained beds with straw mattresses, latrines, and possibly a chapel.

The growing wealth of the High Middle Ages made it possible for European nobles to improve their standard of living. Nobles sought to buy more luxury goods, such as jewelry, better clothes, and exotic spices. They also built more elaborate castles with thicker walls and more buildings and towers. Rooms became better furnished and more elaborately decorated.

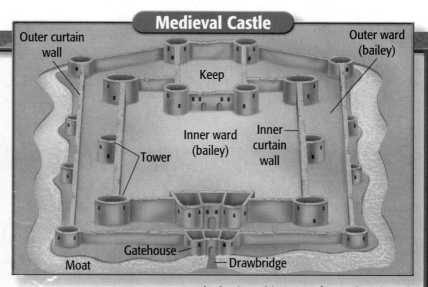

Medieval Castle

Outer curtain wall · Outer ward (bailey) · Keep · Inner ward (bailey) · Inner curtain wall · Tower · Gatehouse · Drawbridge · Moat

The basic architecture of a medieval castle

CONNECTING TO THE PAST

1. **Explaining** What architectural and design features supported the two basic functions of castles?

2. **Describing** What was the lifestyle of the European nobility in the High Middle Ages?

3. **Writing about History** Does a nobility exist today? Where?

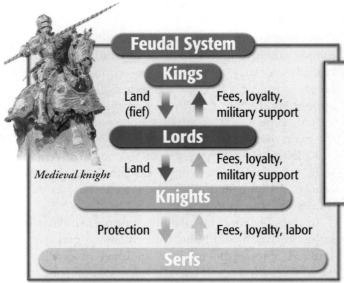

Feudal System

Kings

Land (fief) ↓ ↑ Fees, loyalty, military support

Lords

Medieval knight Land ↓ ↑ Fees, loyalty, military support

Knights

Protection ↓ ↑ Fees, loyalty, labor

Serfs

Chart *Skills*

In the feudal system, the same man could be both a lord and a vassal. Kings, lords, and knights all had serfs.

1. **Compare and Contrast** the obligations of the serfs with those of lords and knights.
2. **Evaluating** What does this chart reveal about what was considered valuable in feudal society?

Aristocratic Women

Although women could legally hold property, most remained under the control of men—of their fathers until they married and of their husbands after they married. Still, aristocratic women had many opportunities to play important roles.

Because the lord was often away at war or court, the lady of the castle had to manage the estate. Households could include large numbers of officials and servants, so this was no small responsibility. Care of the financial accounts alone took considerable knowledge. The lady of the castle was also responsible for overseeing the food supply and maintaining all the other supplies needed for the smooth operation of the household.

Women were expected to be subservient to their husbands, but there were many strong women who advised, and even dominated, their husbands. Perhaps the most famous was **Eleanor of Aquitaine.** Eleanor was one of the most remarkable personalities of twelfth-century Europe. Heiress to the duchy of Aquitaine in southwestern France, she was married at the age of 15 to King Louis VII of France. The marriage was not a happy one, and Louis had their marriage annulled. Eleanor married again, only eight weeks later, to Duke Henry of Normandy, who soon became King Henry II of England.

Henry II and Eleanor had a stormy relationship. She spent much time abroad in her native Aquitaine, where she created a brilliant court dedicated to cultural activities. She and Henry had eight children (five were sons). Two of her sons—Richard and John—became kings of England.

✓**Reading Check** **Summarizing** To whom were aristocratic women subject?

TAKS Practice

SECTION 2 ASSESSMENT

Checking for Understanding

1. **Define** feudalism, vassal, knight, fief, feudal contract, tournament, chivalry.

2. **Identify** Magyars, Vikings, Eleanor of Aquitaine.

3. **Locate** Hungary, Normandy.

4. **Describe** the benefits granted a vassal under feudalism. What was a vassal's primary obligation to his lord?

5. **List** the invasions that besieged the Carolingian Empire in the ninth and tenth centuries.

Critical Thinking

6. **Summarize** What factors helped feudalism develop in western Europe during the ninth and tenth centuries?

7. **Contrasting Information** Use a table like the one below to list the differences between the systems of feudalism and empires.

Feudalism	Empires

Analyzing Visuals

8. **Examine** the image shown on page 291 of your text. How does this image visually represent the medieval system of feudalism?

Writing About History

9. **Descriptive Writing** Write a description of a twelfth-century tournament, using details to create vivid images. Use your local library or the Internet to supplement the information in the text. What questions would you ask about tournaments, knights, and jousting?

The Growth of European Kingdoms

Main Ideas
- During the High Middle Ages, European monarchs began to extend their power and build strong states.
- The Slavic peoples formed three distinct groups, and they settled in different parts of eastern Europe.

Key Terms
common law, Magna Carta, estate

People to Identify
William of Normandy, Henry II, Thomas à Becket, Philip II Augustus, Otto I, Alexander Nevsky

Places to Locate
Paris, Hungary, Kiev

Preview Questions
1. How did centralized monarchies develop in Europe?
2. What caused conflicts between popes and monarchs?

Reading Strategy
Cause and Effect Use a chart like the one below to show the main reasons why eastern Slavs developed separately from western Europe.

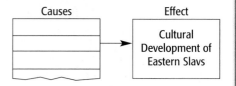

Causes → Effect: Cultural Development of Eastern Slavs

Preview of Events

♦900	♦1000	♦1100	♦1200	♦1300
c. 988 Kiev adopts Eastern Orthodoxy	**1066** William of Normandy invades England	**1180** Philip II Augustus becomes king of France	**1215** King John signs the Magna Carta	**1302** First French parliament assembled

Voices from the Past

The pope crowning Frederick II

A thirteenth-century writer recorded his impressions of Frederick II, king of Germany and Sicily:

❝[Frederick II was] a worthy man, and when he wished to show his good, courtly side, he could be witty, charming, urbane, and industrious. [But he was also strange.] Once he wanted to discover what language a child would use when he grew up if he had never heard anyone speak. Therefore, he placed some infants in the care of nurses, commanding them never to speak or fondle them. For he wanted to discover whether they would speak Hebrew, the first language, or Greek, Latin, Arabic, or the language of their parents. But he worked in vain, because all of the infants died.❞
— *The Chronicle of Salimbene de Adam,* Joseph L. Baird, ed., 1986

Frederick II was one of a number of kings who sought to extend their power during the High Middle Ages—the period from about 1000 to 1300.

England in the High Middle Ages

⌐TURNING POINT⌐ **In this section, you will learn how King John of England was forced to put his seal on the Magna Carta in 1215. By accepting the Magna Carta, John recognized the rights of his nobles, an act that kept the English monarch from ever becoming an absolute ruler.**

NATIONAL GEOGRAPHIC | **Europe, 1160**

Map labels:
20°W, 0°, 10°E, 20°E, 30°E, 40°E, 60°N, 50°N, 40°N

KINGDOM OF NORWAY
KINGDOM OF SWEDEN
KINGDOM OF SCOTLAND
North Sea
ATLANTIC OCEAN
IRELAND
KINGDOM OF ENGLAND
WALES
KINGDOM OF DENMARK
Baltic Sea
KIEVAN RUS
Runnymede · London · Canterbury
Saxony
PRUSSIA
Normandy · Paris
Brittany · Maine
Anjou
KINGDOM OF FRANCE
HOLY ROMAN EMPIRE
KINGDOM OF POLAND
Kiev
Rhine R.
KINGDOM OF NAVARRE
KINGDOM OF LEÓN
Aquitaine
Burgundy
VENETIAN TERRITORIES
Venice
KINGDOM OF HUNGARY
PORTUGAL
KINGDOM OF CASTILE
KINGDOM OF ARAGON
Genoa
Danube R.
Black Sea
Córdoba
Corsica
Rome
Constantinople
BYZANTINE EMPIRE
MUSLIM TERRITORY
Sardinia
PAPAL STATES
KINGDOM OF SICILY
Mediterranean Sea
Sicily
Crete
Cyprus

0 ———— 500 miles
0 ———— 500 kilometers
Lambert Azimuthal Equal-Area projection

Geography Skills

Strong monarchies developed in France and England, while Germany and Italy consisted of independent states.

1. **Interpreting Maps** Locate Runnymede. What event occurred there and why was it significant?

2. **Applying Geography Skills** Create a bar graph comparing the physical sizes of the kingdoms shown on this map.

Angles and Saxons, Germanic peoples from northern Europe, had invaded England early in the fifth century. King Alfred the Great had united various kingdoms in the late ninth century, and since then England had been ruled by Anglo-Saxon kings.

The Norman Conquest On October 14, 1066, an army of heavily armed knights under **William of Normandy** landed on the coast of England and soundly defeated King Harold and his foot soldiers at the **Battle of Hastings.** William was then crowned king of England. Norman knights received parcels of land, which they held as fiefs, from the new king. William made all nobles swear an oath of loyalty to him as sole ruler of England.

The Norman ruling class spoke French, but the marriage of the Normans with the Anglo-Saxon nobility gradually merged Anglo-Saxon and French into a new English culture. The Normans also took over existing Anglo-Saxon institutions, such as the office of sheriff. William took a census, known as the Domesday Book. It was the first census taken in Europe since Roman times and included people, manors, and farm animals. William also developed more fully the system of taxation and royal courts begun by earlier Anglo-Saxon kings.

Henry II The power of the English monarchy was enlarged during the reign of **Henry II,** from 1154 to 1189. Henry increased the number of criminal cases tried in the king's court and also devised means for taking property cases from local courts to the royal courts. By expanding the power of the royal courts, Henry expanded the king's power. In addition, because the royal courts were now found throughout England, a body of common law—law that was common to the whole kingdom—began to replace law codes that varied from place to place.

Henry was less successful at imposing royal control over the Church. He claimed the right to punish clergymen in royal courts. However, **Thomas à Becket,** archbishop of Canterbury and the highest-ranking English cleric, claimed that only Roman Catholic Church courts could try clerics. An angry king publicly expressed the desire to be rid of Becket. "Who will free me of this priest?" he screamed. Four knights took the challenge, went to Canterbury, and murdered the archbishop in the cathedral. Faced with public outrage, Henry backed down in his struggle with the Church.

The Magna Carta and the First Parliament Many English nobles resented the ongoing growth of the king's power and rose in rebellion during the reign of King John. At Runnymede in 1215, John was forced to put his seal on a document of rights called the Magna Carta, or the Great Charter.

The Magna Carta was, above all, a feudal document. Feudal custom had always recognized that the relationship between king and vassals was based on mutual rights and obligations. The Magna Carta gave written recognition to that fact and was used in later years to strengthen the idea that a monarch's power was limited, not absolute.

In the thirteenth century, during the reign of **Edward I,** an important institution in the development of representative government—the English Parliament—also emerged. The Parliament came to be composed of two knights from every county, two people from every town, and all of the nobles and bishops from throughout England. Eventually, nobles and church lords formed the House of Lords; knights and townspeople, the House of Commons. The Parliaments granted taxes and passed laws.

✓**Reading Check** **Analyzing** Why do historians consider 1066 a turning point in history?

The French Kingdom

In 843, the Carolingian Empire was divided into three major sections. One of the sections, the west Frankish lands, formed the core of the eventual kingdom of France. In 987, after the death of the last Carolingian king, the west Frankish nobles chose Hugh Capet as the new king, thus establishing the **Capetian** (kuh•PEE•shuhn) **dynasty** of French kings.

Although they carried the title of king, the Capetians had little real power. The royal domain, or lands that they controlled, only included the area around **Paris,** known as the Île-de-France. As kings,

the Capetians were formally the overlords of the great lords of France. In reality, however, many of the dukes were considerably more powerful than the Capetian kings.

The reign of King **Philip II Augustus,** who ruled from 1180 to 1223, was a turning point in the growth of the French monarchy. Philip waged war against the rulers of England, who also ruled the French territories of Normandy, Maine, Anjou, and Aquitaine. Philip gained control of most of these territories. In doing so, he expanded the income of the French monarchy and greatly increased its power.

Capetian rulers after Philip II continued to add lands to the royal domain. Much of the thirteenth century was dominated by the reign of the saintly Louis IX. Philip IV, called Philip the Fair, ruled from 1285 to 1314. He was especially effective in strengthening the French monarchy by expanding the royal bureaucracy. Indeed, by 1300, France was the largest and best-governed monarchical state in Europe.

Philip IV also brought a French parliament into being by meeting with representatives of the three estates, or classes—the clergy (first estate), the nobles (second estate), and the townspeople and peasants (third estate). The meeting, held in 1302, began the Estates-General, the first French parliament.

✓**Reading Check** **Evaluating** Why was the reign of King Philip II Augustus important to the growth of the French monarchy?

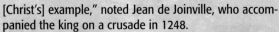

People In History

Louis IX
c. 1214–1270—French king

Louis IX is considered the greatest medieval French king. A deeply religious man, he was later made a saint by the Catholic Church. "This saintly man loved our lord with all his heart and in all his actions followed [Christ's] example," noted Jean de Joinville, who accompanied the king on a crusade in 1248.

Louis was known for his attempts to bring justice to his people. He heard complaints personally in a very informal fashion: "In summer, after hearing mass, the king often went to the wood of Vincennes, where he would sit down with his back against an oak. . . . Those who had any suit to present could come to speak to him without hindrance from an usher or any other person."

The Holy Roman Empire

In the tenth century, the powerful dukes of the Saxons became kings of the eastern Frankish kingdom, which came to be known as Germany. The best-known Saxon king of Germany was **Otto I.** In return for protecting the pope, Otto I was crowned emperor of the Romans in 962. The title had not been used since the time of Charlemagne.

Struggles in Italy As leaders of a new Roman Empire, the German kings attempted to rule both German and Italian lands. Frederick I and Frederick II, instead of building a strong German kingdom, tried to create a new kind of empire. Frederick I planned to get his chief revenues from Italy. He considered Italy the center of a "holy empire," as he called it—hence the name Holy Roman Empire.

Frederick's attempt to conquer northern Italy led to severe problems. The pope opposed him, fearing that he wanted to include Rome and the Papal States as part of his empire. The cities of northern Italy, which had become used to their freedom, were also unwilling to become his subjects. An alliance of these northern Italian cities and the pope defeated the forces of Frederick I in 1176.

The main goal of Frederick II was to establish a strong, centralized state in Italy. However, he too became involved in a deadly struggle with the popes and the northern Italian cities. Frederick II waged a bitter struggle in northern Italy, winning many battles but ultimately losing the war.

Effect on the Empire The struggle between popes and emperors had dire consequences for the Holy Roman Empire. By spending their time fighting in Italy, the German emperors left Germany in the hands of powerful German lords. These nobles ignored the emperor and created their own independent kingdoms. This made the German monarchy weak and incapable of maintaining a strong monarchical state.

In the end, the German Holy Roman Emperor had no real power over either Germany or Italy. Unlike France and England, neither Germany nor Italy created a national monarchy in the Middle Ages. Both Germany and Italy consisted of many small, independent states. Not until the nineteenth century did these states become unified.

✓ **Reading Check** **Explaining** What is the origin of the term *Holy Roman Empire?*

Central and Eastern Europe

The Slavic peoples were originally a single people in central Europe. Gradually, they divided into three major groups: the western, southern, and eastern **Slavs.**

The western Slavs eventually formed the Polish and Bohemian kingdoms. German monks had converted both the **Czechs** in Bohemia and the Slavs in Poland to Christianity by the tenth century. The non-Slavic kingdom of **Hungary** was also converted. The Poles, Czechs, and **Hungarians** all accepted western Christianity and became part of the Roman Catholic Church and its Latin culture.

The southern and eastern Slavic populations took a different path. The eastern Slavic peoples of Moravia were converted to Orthodox Christianity by two Byzantine missionary brothers, Cyril and

NATIONAL GEOGRAPHIC

Slavic Peoples of Central and Eastern Europe

Migration of the Slavic peoples:
- Western Slavs
- Southern Slavs
- Eastern Slavs

Note: Modern country names and borders are shown.

0 — 300 miles
0 — 300 kilometers
Chamberlin Trimetric projection

Geography *Skills*

Slavic groups influenced the development of central and eastern Europe.

1. **Interpreting Maps** Which Slavic groups settled closest to the Adriatic?

2. **Applying Geography Skills** What can you infer from the names of the different Slavic groups and the names of present-day countries?

Methodius, who began their activities in 863. (The Byzantine Empire and its Eastern Orthodox Church are discussed later in this chapter.)

The southern Slavic peoples included the Croats, the Serbs, and the Bulgarians. For the most part, they too embraced Eastern Orthodoxy, although the Croats came to accept the Roman Catholic Church. The acceptance of Eastern Orthodoxy by many southern and eastern Slavic peoples meant that their cultural life was linked to the Byzantine state.

✓ **Reading Check** **Identifying** From where did the Slavic peoples originate?

The Development of Russia

Eastern Slavic peoples had also settled in the territory of present-day Ukraine and Russia. There, beginning in the late eighth century, they began to encounter Swedish Vikings, who moved into their lands in search of plunder and new trade routes. The Vikings eventually came to dominate the native peoples. The native peoples called the Viking rulers the Rus, from which the name Russia is derived.

Kievan Rus One Viking leader, Oleg, settled in **Kiev** at the beginning of the tenth century and created the Rus state known as the principality of Kiev. His successors extended their control over the eastern Slavs and expanded Kiev until it included the territory between the Baltic and Black Seas and the Danube and Volga Rivers. By marrying Slavic wives, the

Viking ruling class was gradually assimilated into the Slavic population.

The growth of the principality of Kiev attracted missionaries from the Byzantine Empire. One Rus ruler, Vladimir, married the Byzantine emperor's sister and officially accepted Eastern Orthodox Christianity for himself and his people in 988. Orthodox Christianity became the religion of the state.

Kievan Rus prospered and reached its high point in the first half of the eleventh century. However, civil wars and new invasions brought an end to the first Russian state in 1169.

Mongol Rule In the thirteenth century, the **Mongols** conquered Russia. They occupied Russian lands and required Russian princes to pay tribute to them.

One prince emerged as more powerful than the others. **Alexander Nevsky,** prince of Novgorod, defeated a German invading army in northwestern Russia in 1242. The khan, leader of the western Mongol Empire, rewarded Nevsky with the title of grand-prince. His descendants became princes of Moscow and eventually leaders of all Russia.

✓ **Reading Check** **Describing** How was the Viking ruling class gradually assimilated into the Slavic population?

🟥 **TAKS Practice**

SECTION ③ ASSESSMENT

Checking for Understanding

1. **Define** common law, Magna Carta, estate.

2. **Identify** William of Normandy, Battle of Hastings, Henry II, Thomas à Becket, Edward I, Capetian dynasty, Philip II Augustus, Otto I, Slavs, Czechs, Hungarians, Mongols, Alexander Nevsky.

3. **Locate** Paris, Hungary, Kiev.

4. **Explain** what Henry II accomplished when he expanded the power of the royal courts in England.

5. **List** the three estates in France.

Critical Thinking

6. **Explain** Unified national monarchies did not develop in Germany and Italy as they did in France and England in the High Middle Ages. Why not?

7. **Organizing Information** Use a chart to identify key achievements of monarchs in England and France.

Monarch/ Country	Achievements
1.	
2.	
3.	
4.	

Analyzing Visuals

8. **Examine** the photograph of the medieval castle shown on page 294 of your text. Identify the major architectural elements that helped inhabitants of the castle to defend themselves against attack.

Writing About History

9. **Informative Writing** Imagine that you are a journalist attending a meeting of the first English Parliament. What questions would you ask? Write a newsletter for people of your town explaining what happened.

A Muslim's Description of the Rus

DESPITE THE DIFFICULTIES THAT TRAVEL presented, early medieval civilization did witness some contact among various cultures. Ibn Fadlan, a Muslim diplomat sent from Baghdad in 921 to a settlement on the Volga River, gave a description of the Swedish Rus. His comments on the filthiness of the Rus reflect the Muslim concern with cleanliness.

Song of the Volga *by Russian artist Wassily Kandinsky*

❝I saw the Rus folk when they arrived on their trading-mission and settled at the river Atul (Volga). Never had I seen people of more perfect physique. They are tall as date-palms, and reddish in color. They wear neither coat or kaftan, but each man carried a cape which covers one half of his body, leaving one hand free. No one is ever parted from his axe, sword, and knife.

They [the Rus] are the filthiest of God's creatures. They do not wash after discharging their natural functions, neither do they wash their hands after meals. They are as lousy as donkeys. They arrive from their distant lands and lay their ships alongside the banks of the Atul, which is a great river, and there they build big houses on its shores. Ten or twenty of them may live together in one house, and each of them has a couch of his own. . . .

They wash their hands and faces every day in incredibly filthy water. Every morning the girl brings her master a large bowl of water in which he washes his hands and face and hair, then blows his nose into it and spits into it. When he has finished the girl takes the bowl to his neighbor—who repeats the performance. Thus the bowl goes the rounds of the entire household. . . .

If one of the Rus folk falls sick they put him in a tent by himself and leave bread and water for him.

They do not visit him, however, or speak to him, especially if he is a serf [peasant laborer]. Should he recover he rejoins the others; if he dies they burn him. But if he happens to be a serf they leave him for the dogs and vultures to devour. If they catch a robber they hang him to a tree until he is torn to shreds by wind and weather.❞

—Ibn Fadlan, on the Swedish Rus

Analyzing Primary Sources

1. How did Ibn Fadlan's impression of the physical attributes of the Swedish Rus differ from his impression of their hygiene?
2. What does the way in which the Rus handled sickness and death tell you about their culture?
3. Why would the Rus way of dealing with hygiene and death be especially repulsive to a Muslim?

The Byzantine Empire and the Crusades

Guide to Reading

Main Ideas
- The Byzantine Empire created its own unique civilization in the eastern Mediterranean.
- The Crusades impacted medieval society in both the East and the West.

Key Terms
patriarch, schism, Crusades, infidel

People to Identify
Justinian, Saint Bernard of Clairvaux, Saladin, Pope Innocent III

Places to Locate
Constantinople, Syria, Palestine, Balkans

Preview Questions
1. What were the major characteristics of the Byzantine Empire?
2. What was the impact of the Crusades?

Reading Strategy
Cause and Effect Use a diagram like the one below to identify ways in which the Byzantine Empire rose to power.

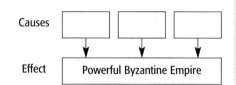

Causes

Effect — Powerful Byzantine Empire

Preview of Events

♦500	♦725	♦950	♦1175	♦1400

527 Justinian's reign begins

537 Hagia Sophia completed

636 Eastern Roman Empire defeated at Yarmuk

867 Macedonian rule begins

1095 Council of Clermont meets

1453 Ottoman Turks conquer the Byzantine Empire

Voices from the Past

During the First Crusade, French knights captured Jerusalem. One commentator, who accompanied the crusaders, described the scene:

66 Then the French entered the city [of Jerusalem] at the noonday hour of Friday, the day of the week when Christ redeemed the whole world on the cross. . . . All the heathen, completely terrified, changed their boldness to swift flight through the narrow streets of the city. . . . Some fled into the Tower of David; others shut themselves in the Temple of the Lord and of Solomon, where in the halls a very great attack was made on them. . . . Within this Temple, about ten thousand were beheaded. Not one of them was allowed to live. They did not spare the women and children. 99
— *Chronicle of the First Crusade*, M.E. McGinty, trans., 1941

Emperor Justinian and his court

While a new civilization struggled to emerge in Europe, the Byzantine Empire created its own civilization in the eastern Mediterranean and continued to flourish. The Crusades, however, eventually weakened the Byzantine Empire.

The Reign of Justinian

During the fifth century, Germanic tribes moved into the western part of the Roman Empire and established their states. In contrast, the Roman Empire in the East, centered on Constantinople, continued to exist, although pressured by powerful Islamic forces.

When **Justinian** became emperor of the Eastern Roman Empire in 527, he was determined to reestablish the Roman Empire in the entire Mediterranean world. By 552, he appeared to have achieved his goals. He had restored the Roman Empire in the Mediterranean. His empire included Italy, part of Spain, North Africa, Asia Minor, Palestine, and Syria. However, only three years after Justinian's death in 565, the Lombards had conquered much of Italy, and other areas were soon lost.

Justinian's most important contribution was his codification of Roman law. The Eastern Roman Empire had inherited a vast quantity of legal materials, which Justinian wished to simplify. The result was *The Body of Civil Law.* This code of Roman laws was the basis of imperial law in the Eastern Roman Empire until its end in 1453. Furthermore, it was also used in the West and became the basis for much of the legal system of Europe.

✔**Reading Check** **Evaluating** What is the significance of *The Body of Civil Law?*

From Eastern Roman Empire to Byzantine Empire

Justinian's accomplishments had been spectacular, but his conquests left the Eastern Roman Empire with serious problems: too much territory to protect far from **Constantinople,** an empty treasury, a decline in population after a plague, and renewed threats to its frontiers. The most serious challenge came from the rise of Islam, which unified Arab groups and created a powerful new force that swept through the Eastern Roman Empire.

Islamic forces defeated an army of the Eastern Roman Empire at Yarmuk in 636. As a result, the empire lost the provinces of **Syria** and **Palestine.** Problems arose along the northern frontier as well, especially in the Balkans. In 679, the Bulgars defeated the Eastern Roman Empire's forces and took possession of the lower Danube Valley, creating a strong Bulgarian kingdom.

By the beginning of the eighth century, the Eastern Roman Empire was much smaller, consisting only of the eastern **Balkans** and Asia Minor. Historians call this smaller Eastern Roman Empire the **Byzantine Empire,** a civilization with its own unique character that lasted until 1453.

The Byzantine Empire was both a Greek and a Christian state. Greek replaced Latin as the official language of the empire. At the same time, the Byzantine Empire was built on a Christian faith that was shared by many of its citizens. The Christian church of the Byzantine Empire came to be known as the Eastern Orthodox Church. An enormous amount of artistic effort and talent was poured into church building, church ceremonies, and church decoration to honor this faith.

The emperor occupied a crucial position in the Byzantine state. Portrayed as chosen by God, he was crowned in sacred ceremonies. His subjects were expected to prostrate themselves in his presence. His power was considered absolute.

NATIONAL GEOGRAPHIC

Justinian's Empire, 527–565

ATLANTIC OCEAN

40°N

10°W

SPAIN

Corsica

Sardinia

Carthage

ITALY
Rome

Sicily

Mediterranean Sea

OSTROGOTHS

Danube R.

LOMBARDS

SLAVS

BALKAN PENINSULA

Crete

Black Sea

Constantinople

ASIA MINOR

Cyprus

PALESTINE

Alexandria

Jerusalem

PERSIAN EMPIRE

Euphrates R.

Tigris R.

SYRIA

ARABIA

EGYPT

Nile R.

Red Sea

N W E S

Before Justinian, 527
After Justinian's conquests, 565

0   500 miles
0   500 kilometers
Lambert Azimuthal Equal-Area projection

0°   10°E   20°E

Geography *Skills*

Emperor Justinian restored the Roman Empire in the Mediterranean.

1. **Interpreting Maps** Locate the city of Carthage. Using the maps in this chapter, list in chronological order the empires or groups that controlled Carthage.

2. **Applying Geography Skills** Using earlier chapters and maps, determine the areas of the original Roman Empire that Justinian did not regain.

Because the emperor appointed the head of the Eastern Orthodox Church, known as the patriarch, he exercised control over church as well as state. The Byzantines believed that God had commanded their state to preserve the true Christian faith. Emperor, church officials, and state officials were all bound together in service to this spiritual ideal.

Reading Check **Evaluating** How did the rise of Islam affect the Eastern Roman Empire?

Life in Constantinople

Riots in Constantinople in 532 caused widespread destruction. Afterward, Emperor Justinian rebuilt the city and gave it the appearance it would keep for almost a thousand years. With a population estimated in the hundreds of thousands, Constantinople was the largest city in Europe during the Middle Ages.

Trade Until the twelfth century, Constantinople was medieval Europe's greatest center of commerce. The city was the chief center for the exchange of products between West and East.

Highly desired in Europe were the products of the East: silk from China, spices from Southeast Asia and India, jewelry and ivory from India (the latter used by Byzantine craftspeople for church items), wheat and furs from southern Russia, and flax and honey from the Balkans. Many of these goods arrived in Constantinople and were then shipped to the Mediterranean area and northern Europe.

Imported raw materials were also used in Constantinople for local industries. In Justinian's reign, silkworms were smuggled from China by two Christian monks to begin a Byzantine silk industry. European demand for silk cloth made it the city's most lucrative product.

Building Much of Constantinople's appearance in the early Middle Ages was due to Justinian's program of rebuilding in the sixth century. The city was dominated by an immense palace complex, hundreds of churches, and a huge arena known as the Hippodrome, where both gladiator fights and chariot races were held. Justinian's public works projects included roads, bridges, walls, public baths, law courts, schools, churches, and colossal underground reservoirs to hold the city's water supply.

His greatest achievement was the famous Hagia Sophia—the Church of the Holy Wisdom—completed in 537. The center of Hagia Sophia consists of four large piers crowned by an enormous dome, which seems to be floating in space. In part, the builders created this impression by ringing the base of the dome with 42 windows, which allows an incredible play of light within the cathedral.

Reading Check **Explaining** Why was Constantinople one of medieval Europe's greatest centers of commerce?

New Heights and New Problems

As we have seen, the size of the Byzantine Empire had been greatly reduced by the beginning of the eighth century. However, the empire recovered and even expanded through the efforts of a new dynasty of Byzantine emperors known as the **Macedonians,** who ruled from 867 to 1081.

The Macedonian emperors expanded the empire to include Bulgaria in the Balkans, the islands of Crete and Cyprus, and Syria. By 1025, the Byzantine Empire was the largest it had been since the beginning of the seventh century.

The Macedonians also fostered a burst of economic prosperity by expanding trade relations with western Europe, especially by selling silks and metalworks. Thanks to this prosperity, the city of Constantinople flourished. Foreign visitors continued to be astounded by its size and wealth.

The Macedonian dynasty of the tenth and eleventh centuries restored much of the power of the Byzantine Empire, but incompetent successors soon undid most of the gains. Struggles for power between ambitious military leaders and aristocratic families led to political and social disorder in the late eleventh century.

The Byzantine Empire was also troubled by a growing split between its church—the Eastern Orthodox Church—and the Catholic Church of the West. The Eastern Orthodox Church was unwilling to accept the pope's claim that he was the sole head of the Christian faith. In 1054, Pope Leo IX and the patriarch Michael Cerularius, head of the Byzantine Church, formally excommunicated each other—each took away the other's rights of church membership. This began a schism, or separation, between the two great branches of Christianity that has not been completely healed to this day.

The Byzantine Empire faced threats from abroad as well. The greatest challenge came from the advance of the **Seljuk Turks** who had moved into Asia Minor—the heartland of the empire and its main source of food and workers. In 1071, a Turkish army disastrously defeated Byzantine forces at

Christian lands, 1095
Muslim lands, 1095
← First Crusade, 1096–1099
← Second Crusade, 1147–1149
← Third Crusade, 1189–1192
← Fourth Crusade, 1202–1204

◄ *Medieval illustration of a battle during the Crusades*

Manzikert. Lacking the resources to undertake new campaigns against the Turks, Emperor Alexius I turned to Europe for military aid.

✓ **Reading Check** **Summarizing** What threats, both internal and external, did the Byzantine Empire face in the eleventh century?

The Crusades

From the eleventh to the thirteenth centuries, European Christians carried out a series of military expeditions to regain the Holy Land from the Muslims. These expeditions are known as the Crusades.

The push for the Crusades came when the Byzantine emperor Alexius I asked the Europeans for help against the Seljuk Turks, who were Muslims. Pope Urban II, who responded to the request, saw a

golden opportunity to provide papal leadership for a great cause. That cause was rallying the warriors of Europe for the liberation of Jerusalem and the Holy Land (Palestine) from the infidels or unbelievers—the Muslims.

At the Council of Clermont in southern France near the end of 1095, Urban II challenged Christians to take up their weapons and join in a holy war. The pope promised: "All who die . . . whether by land or by sea, or in battle against the pagans, shall have immediate remission [forgiveness] of sins." The enthusiastic crowd cried out: "It is the will of God, it is the will of God."

Warriors of western Europe, particularly France, formed the first crusading armies. The knights who made up this first crusading army were mostly motivated by religious fervor, but there were other

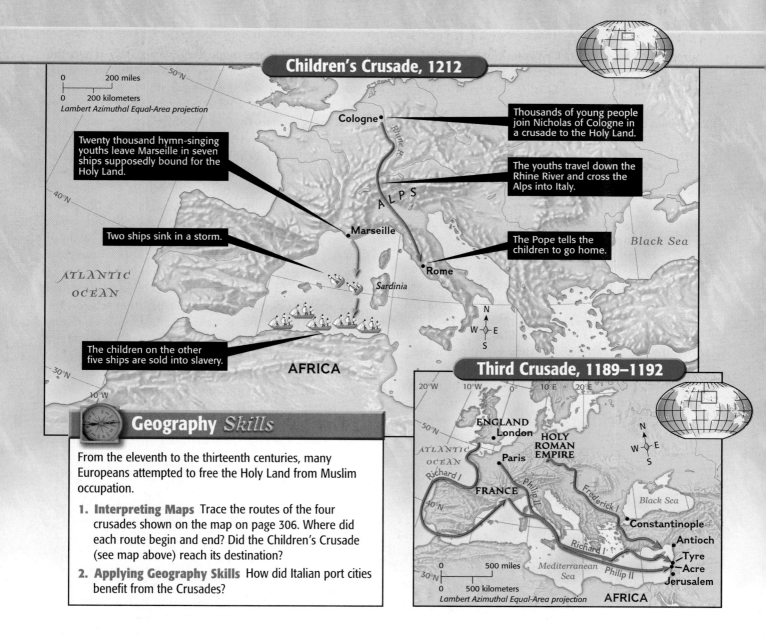

Children's Crusade, 1212

Twenty thousand hymn-singing youths leave Marseille in seven ships supposedly bound for the Holy Land.

Thousands of young people join Nicholas of Cologne in a crusade to the Holy Land.

The youths travel down the Rhine River and cross the Alps into Italy.

Two ships sink in a storm.

The Pope tells the children to go home.

The children on the other five ships are sold into slavery.

Third Crusade, 1189–1192

Geography Skills

From the eleventh to the thirteenth centuries, many Europeans attempted to free the Holy Land from Muslim occupation.

1. **Interpreting Maps** Trace the routes of the four crusades shown on the map on page 306. Where did each route begin and end? Did the Children's Crusade (see map above) reach its destination?

2. **Applying Geography Skills** How did Italian port cities benefit from the Crusades?

attractions as well. Some sought adventure and welcomed the chance to pursue their favorite pastime—fighting. Others saw an opportunity to gain territory, riches, and possibly a title. Merchants in many Italian cities also sought new trading opportunities in Byzantine and Muslim lands.

The Early Crusades The First Crusade began as three organized bands of warriors, most of them French, made their way to the East. The crusading army probably numbered several thousand cavalry and as many as ten thousand infantry. The army captured Antioch in 1098. The crusaders proceeded down the Palestinian coast, avoiding the well-defended coastal cities, and reached Jerusalem in June 1099. The Holy City was taken amid a horrible massacre of the inhabitants.

After further conquests, the crusaders organized four Latin crusader states. Surrounded by Muslims, these crusader kingdoms depended on Italian cities for supplies from Europe. Some Italian port cities, such as Genoa, Pisa, and especially Venice, grew rich and powerful in the process.

It was not easy for the crusader kingdoms to maintain themselves in the East, however. By the 1140s, the Muslims had begun to strike back. The fall of one of the Latin kingdoms led to calls for another crusade, especially from the monastic leader **Saint Bernard of Clairvaux.** Bernard managed to enlist two powerful rulers, King Louis VII of France and Emperor Conrad III of Germany, in a Second Crusade. This campaign, however, was a total failure.

In 1187, the Holy City of Jerusalem fell to Muslim forces under **Saladin.** Three important rulers then agreed to lead a Third Crusade: Emperor Frederick Barbarossa of Germany; Richard I (Richard the Lion-hearted) of England; and Philip II Augustus, King of France.

When members of the Third Crusade arrived in the East in 1189, they encountered problems. Frederick drowned in a local river. The English and French arrived by sea and captured the coastal cities with the aid of their fleets but were unable to move inland against the Muslim forces. After Philip went home, Richard negotiated a settlement with Saladin that permitted Christian pilgrims free access to Jerusalem.

The Later Crusades About six years after the death of Saladin in 1193, **Pope Innocent III** initiated the Fourth Crusade. As it headed east, the crusading army became involved in a fight over the succession to the Byzantine throne. The Venetian leaders of the crusade used the situation to weaken their greatest commercial competitor, the Byzantine Empire. Diverted to Constantinople, the crusaders sacked the city in 1204. Not until 1261 did a Byzantine army recapture the city.

The Byzantine Empire had been reestablished, but it was no longer a great power. The empire now comprised the city of Constantinople and its surrounding lands, as well as some lands in Asia Minor. In this reduced size, the empire limped along for another 190 years, until the Ottoman Turks conquered it in 1453.

Despite failures, the crusading ideal continued. In Germany in 1212, a youth known as Nicholas of Cologne announced that God had inspired him to lead a "children's crusade." Thousands of young people joined Nicholas and made their way to Italy, where the pope told them to go home. At about the same time, some twenty thousand French children headed to Marseille, where two shipowners agreed to take them to the Holy Land. Two of the ships sent perished in a storm. The other five sailed to North Africa, where the children were sold into slavery. The next crusades of adult warriors were hardly more successful.

Did the Crusades have much effect on European civilization? Historians disagree. There is no doubt that the Crusades benefited the Italian port cities, especially Genoa, Pisa, and Venice. Even without the Crusades, however, Italian merchants would have increased trade with the Eastern world.

The Crusades had some unfortunate side effects on European society. The first widespread attacks on the Jews began in the context of the Crusades. Some Christians argued that to fight the Muslims while the "murderers of Christ," as they called the Jews, ran free at home was unthinkable. The massacre of Jews became a feature of medieval European life.

Perhaps the greatest impact of the Crusades was political. They eventually helped to break down feudalism. As kings levied taxes and raised armies, nobles joining the Crusades sold their lands and freed their serfs. As the nobles lost power, the kings were able to create stronger central governments. Taxing trade with the East also provided kings with new wealth. This paved the way for the development of true nation-states. By the mid-1400s, four strong states—Portugal, Spain, England, and France—would emerge in Europe.

✓**Reading Check** **Summarizing** What factors motivated Europeans to participate in a Crusade?

TAKS Practice

SECTION 4 ASSESSMENT

Checking for Understanding

1. **Define** patriarch, schism, Crusades, infidel.

2. **Identify** Justinian, *The Body of Civil Law*, Byzantine Empire, Macedonians, Seljuk Turks, Saint Bernard of Clairvaux, Saladin, Pope Innocent III.

3. **Locate** Constantinople, Syria, Palestine, Balkans.

4. **Explain** how church and state were linked in the Byzantine Empire.

5. **List** Justinian's accomplishments.

Critical Thinking

6. **Explain** Why did cities such as Venice flourish as a result of the Crusades?

7. **Organizing Information** Use a table like the one below to summarize the results of the First, Second, and Third Crusades.

	1st Crusade	2nd Crusade	3rd Crusade
People Involved			
Results			

Analyzing Visuals

8. **Examine** the medieval illustration of one of the battles of the Crusades shown on page 306. How does this visual portrayal of a battle compare to the idealistic goals of the Crusades themselves?

Writing About History

9. **Descriptive Writing** Write a travel brochure encouraging people to visit Constantinople. Identify the features of the city in the early Middle Ages. What sites would you use to illustrate your brochure?

CRITICAL THINKING
SKILLBUILDER

Distinguishing Between Fact and Opinion

Why Learn This Skill?

Imagine that you are watching two candidates for president debate the merits of the college loan program. One says, "In my view, the college loan program must be reformed. Sixty percent of students do not repay their loans on time."

The other replies, "College costs are skyrocketing, but only 30 percent of students default on their loans for more than one year. I believe we should spend more on this worthy program."

How can you tell who or what to believe? You must learn to distinguish fact from opinion in order to effectively evaluate and analyze information acquired from a variety of sources such as books, television, and the Internet.

Learning the Skill

A fact is a statement that can be proved to be true or false. In the example above, the statement "Sixty percent of students do not repay their loans on time" is a fact. By reviewing statistics on the number of student loan recipients who repay their loans, we can determine whether it is true or false. To identify facts, look for words and phrases indicating specific people, places, events, dates, and times.

An opinion, on the other hand, expresses a personal belief, viewpoint, or emotion. Because opinions are subjective, we cannot prove or disprove them. In the opening example, most statements by the candidates are opinions.

Opinions often include qualifying words and phrases such as *I think, I believe, probably, seems to be, may, might, could, ought, in my judgment,* or *in my view.* Also, look for expressions of approval or disapproval such as *good, bad, poor,* and *satisfactory.* Be aware of superlatives such as *greatest, worst, finest,* and *best.* Notice words with negative meanings and implications such as *squander, contemptible,* and

disgrace. Also, identify generalizations such as *none, every, always,* and *never.*

Practicing the Skill

For each pair of statements below, determine which is fact and which is opinion. Give a reason for each choice.

1. a The Byzantine Empire came to a pitiful end at the hands of the savage Turks.

   b The Byzantine Empire ended when Constantine XI died while defending Constantinople in 1453.

2. a The alliance with the Byzantine Empire made Kiev a major trading link between Europe and Asia and between Scandinavia and Southwest Asia.

Byzantine cross

   b In the 900s, Kiev was the most isolated, uncivilized place, and it possessed little in the way of culture.

3. a The Byzantine culture was more advanced than any other of its day.

   b Vladimir's conversion to Eastern Orthodoxy brought Byzantine culture to Kievan Rus.

Applying the Skill

Find a news article and an editorial pertaining to the same subject in your local newspaper. Identify three facts and three opinions from these sources.

Glencoe's **Skillbuilder Interactive Workbook, Level 2,** provides instruction and practice in key social studies skills.

Using Key Terms

1. _____ refers to the practice of living the life of a monk.

2. The _____ determined the relationship between a lord and his vassals.

3. Under the influence of the Church, noblemen followed a code of behavior called _____.

4. _____ was the amount paid by a wrongdoer to the family of an injured person.

5. A Christian bishop headed an area called a _____.

6. A series of Christian military expeditions were called the _____.

7. A _____ developed between the Catholic Church and the Eastern Orthodox Church in 1054.

8. The _____ is the Byzantine counterpart to the pope in Rome.

9. Bishops of Rome became known as _____ of the Catholic Church.

10. A _____ was the grant of land from the lord to a vassal in return for military service.

Reviewing Key Facts

11. **Citizenship** How did the bond of extended family affect the way Germanic law treated the problem of crime and punishment?

12. **Government** How can feudalism be considered a political system?

13. **History** What important English political institution emerged during the reign of Edward I?

14. **History** What two important functions did monks perform?

15. **History** Why are scriptoria so important to the history of western Europe?

16. **Government** Name one basic difference between the Roman and Germanic legal systems.

17. **History** Approximately how long did the Byzantine Empire last?

18. **History** What steps did the Normans take to create a strong, centralized monarchy in England?

19. **Government** How did Henry II enlarge the power of the English monarchy?

20. **Culture** What was the historical context in which the code of chivalry emerged?

Critical Thinking

21. **Analyzing** What factors helped feudalism to develop in western Europe during the ninth and tenth centuries? Describe the major characteristics of the political system of feudalism.

22. **Cause and Effect** What caused the schism in Christianity in the eleventh century? Could the split have been prevented?

Writing About History

23. **Informative Writing** Research the Crusades. Using information you find in this text, your local library, or the Internet, describe the political, economic, and social impact of the Crusades. Which of these areas do you think the Crusades impacted the most? Explain your answers fully, and justify them with factual information.

Chapter Summary

Europe and the Byzantine Empire changed and developed in many ways during the Middle Ages.

Movement

- Angles and Saxons settle in England.
- Monks come to England to convert the Anglo-Saxons to Christianity.
- Vikings, Magyars, and Muslims invade areas of Europe.

Cooperation

- The Frankish ruler Clovis converts to Christianity and gains the support of the Roman Catholic Church.
- Benedictine rule emphasizes the need for monks to work together within the monastery.
- The system of feudalism, based on the granting of land to nobles in exchange for military service, spreads throughout Europe.

Conflict

- Charlemagne's death leads to the decline and division of the Carolingian Empire.
- Schism divides the Eastern Orthodox Church and the Roman Catholic Church.
- William the Conqueror defeats Harold Godwinson in the Battle of Hastings.

Uniformity

- The emperor Justinian restores the Roman Empire in the Mediterranean.
- Eastern Orthodox Christianity becomes the state religion of Kiev.
- The Magna Carta guarantees rights to all English freemen.

Self-Check Quiz

Visit the *Glencoe World History* Web site at
tx.wh.glencoe.com and click on **Chapter 9–Self-Check
Quiz** to prepare for the Chapter Test.

Analyzing Sources

Read the following vow of loyalty:

❝The man should put his hands together as a sign of
humility, and place them between the two hands of
his lord as a token that he vows everything to him and
promises faith to him; and the lord should receive him
and promise to keep faith with him. Then the man should
say: 'Sir, I enter your homage and faith and become your
man by mouth and hands (that is, by taking the oath and placing
his hands between those of the lord), and I swear and promise
to keep faith and loyalty to you against all others.'❞

24. Why is it significant that the vow was given to a particular
person rather than a nation, written constitution, or religion?

25. What is meant by the phrase "and the lord should receive
him and promise to keep faith with him"?

Applying Technology Skills

26. **Using the Internet** Search the Internet for a Web site that
provides information on social history during medieval
times. Use a search engine to help focus your search by
using words such as *medieval, feudalism, vassal*, and
chivalry. Use the information you find to develop a diary
that might have been written by an individual living in
medieval society. In your diary, describe such things as your
daily routine, your family, where you live, and your hopes
and plans for the future.

Making Decisions

27. Pretend you are a knight returning from the First Crusade.
Write a letter to your wife describing the Crusade and its
result. Also, explain why you went on the Crusade, and
whether or not the Crusade lived up to your expectations.

Analyzing Maps and Charts

28. Examine the map showing the expansion of Moscow from
1300 to 1462 at the top of this page. By what year had the
Volga River been added to Russia's holdings?

29. What geographic features enabled the princes of Russia to
expand their holdings?

30. By 1493 Moscow's ruler claimed to be "Sovereign of All
Russia." About how far did Moscow's territory stretch from
north to south in 1462?

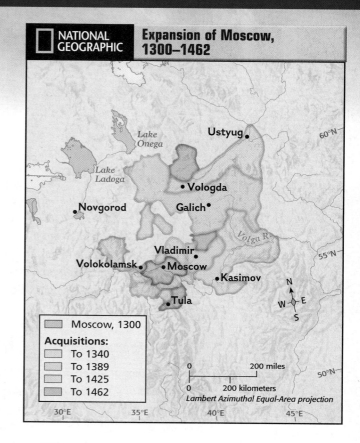

Expansion of Moscow, 1300–1462

Moscow, 1300
Acquisitions:
To 1340
To 1389
To 1425
To 1462

TAKS
Test Practice

**Directions: Choose the best answer to the
following question.**

Between the twelfth and fourteenth centuries, both England
and France

A defeated Frankish rulers and established autonomous
kingdoms.

B were rebuilt by Emperor Justinian.

C established parliaments to help royal authorities rule.

D were accomplished shipbuilders and sailors.

Test-Taking Tip: Questions that ask about a specific fact
can be difficult if you do not know the answer. Increase
your chances of choosing the correct answer by looking at
each answer choice and thinking about the context in which
it was discussed in class and in the textbook. Then, eliminate choices you know are wrong. Finally, ask yourself
which remaining choice makes the most sense and select
that as your answer.

10 Europe in the Middle Ages

1000–1500

Key Events

As you read, look for the key events in the history of medieval Europe.
- *The revival of trade led to the growth of cities and towns, which became important centers for manufacturing.*
- *The Catholic Church was an important part of people's lives during the Middle Ages.*
- *During the fourteenth and early fifteenth centuries, Europeans experienced many problems including the Black Death, the Hundred Years' War, and the decline of the Church.*

The Impact Today

The events that occurred during this time period still impact our lives today.
- *The revival of trade brought with it a money economy and the emergence of capitalism, which is widespread in the world today.*
- *Modern universities had their origins in medieval Europe.*
- *The medieval history of Europe can be seen today in Europe's great cathedrals.*

World History Video *The Chapter 10 video, "Chaucer's England," chronicles the development of civilization in medieval Europe.*

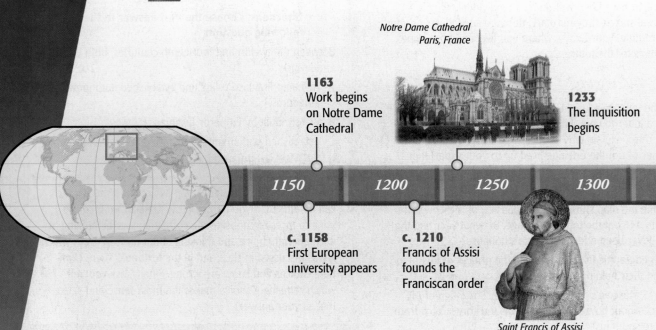

Notre Dame Cathedral
Paris, France

1163
Work begins
on Notre Dame
Cathedral

1233
The Inquisition
begins

1150   1200   1250   1300

c. 1158
First European
university appears

c. 1210
Francis of Assisi
founds the
Franciscan order

Saint Francis of Assisi

The cathedral at Chartres, about 50 miles (80 km) southwest of Paris, is but one of the many great Gothic cathedrals built in Europe during the Middle Ages.

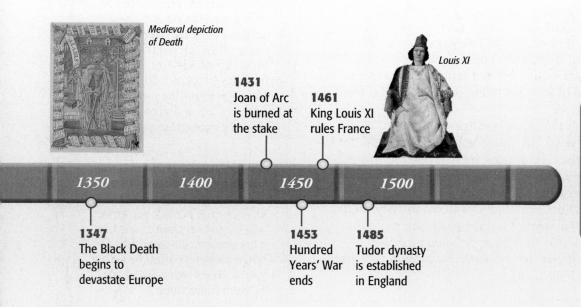

Medieval depiction of Death

Louis XI

1431
Joan of Arc is burned at the stake

1461
King Louis XI rules France

1350   1400   1450   1500

1347
The Black Death begins to devastate Europe

1453
Hundred Years' War ends

1485
Tudor dynasty is established in England

HISTORY
Online

Chapter Overview
Visit the *Glencoe World History* Web site at tx.wh.glencoe.com and click on **Chapter 10–Chapter Overview** to preview chapter information.

A Story That Matters

▲ *Somersaulting was done for entertainment and leisure in medieval London.*

◄ *This medieval manuscript page shows a London scene.*

Life in London

*I*n the twelfth century, William Fitz-Stephen spoke of London as one of the noblest cities of the world: "It is happy in the healthiness of its air, in the Christian religion, in the strength of its defences, the nature of its site, the honor of its citizens, the modesty of its women; pleasant in sports; fruitful of noble men."

To Fitz-Stephen, London offered a number of opportunities and pleasures: "Practically anything that man may need is brought daily not only into special places but even into the open squares, and all that can be sold is loudly advertised for sale." "Any man," according to Fitz-Stephen, "if he is not a good-for-nothing, may earn his living expenses and esteem according to his station."

Sporting events and leisure activities were available in every season of the year: "In Easter holidays they fight battles on water." In summer, "the youths are exercised in leaping, dancing, shooting, wrestling, casting the stone; the maidens dance as long as they can well see." In winter, "when the great fen, or moor, which waters the walls of the city on the north side, is frozen, many young men play upon the ice; some, striding as wide as they may, do slide swiftly."

To Fitz-Stephen, "every convenience for human pleasure is known to be at hand" in London.

Why It Matters

One would hardly know from Fitz-Stephen's cheerful description that medieval cities faced overcrowded conditions, terrible smells from rotting garbage, and the constant threat of epidemics and fires. The rise of cities was one aspect of the new burst of energy and growth that characterized European civilization in the High Middle Ages, the period from about 1000 to 1300. New farming practices, the growth of trade, and a growing population created a vigorous European society.

History and You Research current conditions in the city of London. Compare the city today with the way it was described by Fitz-Stephen. Write an essay in which you explain how London has changed and how it has remained the same. Why do certain problems persist? Document your argument with evidence and include a bibliography.

Peasants, Trade, and Cities

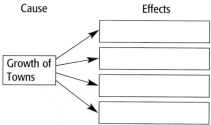
Voices from the Past

Woodcut showing use of elementary watermill

One monk reported in the twelfth century how his monastery used a local stream to grind grain and make cloth:

❝Entering the Abbey under the boundary wall, the stream first hurls itself at the mill where in a flurry of movement it strains itself, first to crush the wheat beneath the weight of the millstones, then to shake the fine sieve which separates flour from bran. . . . The stream is not yet discharged. The fullers [people who finished the manufacture of woolen cloth] located near the mill beckon to it. One by one it lifts and drops the heavy pestles, the fullers' great wooden hammers. How many horses would be worn out, how many men would be weary if this graceful river, to whom we owe our clothes and food, did not labor for us.❞

—*The Medieval Machine*, Jean Gimpel, 1976

Gradually, the growth of trade and manufacturing and the rise of towns laid the foundations for the transformation of Europe from a rural, agricultural society to a more urban, industrial one.

The New Agriculture

In the early Middle Ages, Europe had a relatively small population. In the High Middle Ages, however, population increased dramatically. The number of people almost doubled between 1000 and 1300, from 38 million to 74 million people.

What caused this huge increase in population? For one thing, conditions in Europe were more settled and peaceful after the invasions of the early Middle Ages had stopped. This increased peace and stability also led to a dramatic expansion in food production after 1000.

In part, food production increased because a change in climate during the High Middle Ages improved growing conditions. In addition, more land was cultivated as peasants of the eleventh and twelfth centuries cut down trees and drained swamps. By 1200, Europeans had more land for farming than they do today.

Changes in technology also aided the development of farming. The Middle Ages witnessed an explosion of labor-saving devices. For example, the people of the Middle Ages harnessed the power of water and wind to do jobs once done by human or animal power.

Many of these new devices were made from iron, which was mined in various areas of Europe. Iron was used to make scythes, axes, and hoes for use on farms, as well as saws, hammers, and nails for building. Iron was crucial in making the *carruca,* a heavy, wheeled plow with an iron plowshare. Unlike earlier plows, this plow could easily turn over heavy clay soils.

Because of the weight of the *carruca,* six or eight oxen were needed to pull it. However, oxen were slow. Two new inventions for the horse made it possible to plow faster. A new horse collar spread the weight around the shoulders and chest rather than

SCIENCE, TECHNOLOGY & SOCIETY

Harnessing the Power of Water and Wind

Watermills use the power of running water to do work. The watermill was invented as early as the second century B.C. It was not used much in the Roman Empire because the Romans had many slaves and had no need to mechanize. In the High Middle Ages, watermills became easier to build as the use of metals became more common. In 1086, the survey of English land known as the Domesday Book listed about six thousand watermills in England.

Located along streams, mills powered by water were at first used to grind grains for flour. Gradually, mill operators were able to mechanize entire industries. Waterpower was used in mills for making cloth and in sawmills for cutting wood and stone, as well as in the working of metals.

Rivers, however, were not always available. Where this was the case, Europeans developed windmills to harness the power of the wind. Historians are unsure whether windmills were imported into Europe (they were invented in Persia) or designed independently by Europeans. Like the watermill, the windmill was first used for grinding grains. Later, however, windmills were used for pumping water and even cutting wood. However, they did not offer as great a range of possible uses as watermills.

The watermill and windmill were the most important devices for harnessing power before the invention of the steam engine in the eighteenth century. Their spread had revolutionary consequences, enabling Europeans to produce more food and to more easily manufacture a wide array of products.

Comparing *How are water and wind power used today?*

Watermill on Certovka River in Prague, Czech Republic

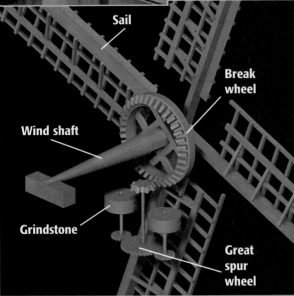
Workings of a basic windmill

Sail

Break wheel

Wind shaft

Grindstone

Great spur wheel

the throat. Now a series of horses could be hitched up, enabling them to pull the new, heavy plow faster and turn over more land. The use of the horseshoe, an iron shoe nailed to the horses' hooves, made it easier for horses to pull the heavy plow through the rocky and heavy clay soil of northern Europe.

The use of the heavy-wheeled plow also led to the growth of farming villages, where people had to work together. Because iron was expensive, a heavy-wheeled plow had to be bought by the entire community. Likewise, one family could not afford a team of animals, so villagers shared their beasts. The size and weight of the plow made it necessary to plow the land in long strips to minimize the amount of turning that would have to be done.

The shift from a two-field to a three-field system of crop rotation added to the increase in food production. In the early Middle Ages, peasants divided their land into two fields of equal size. One field was planted, while the other was allowed to lie fallow, or remain unplanted, to regain its fertility. Now, however, lands were divided into three parts. One field was planted in the fall with grains (such as rye and wheat) that were harvested in summer. The second field was planted in the spring with grains (oats and barley) and vegetables (peas and beans) that were harvested in the fall. The third field was allowed to lie fallow.

The three-field system meant that only one-third, rather than one-half, of the land lay fallow at any time. The rotation of crops also kept the soil from being exhausted so quickly, which allowed more crops to be grown.

✓ **Reading Check** **Analyzing** What were the most important factors leading to the dramatic increase in population during the High Middle Ages?

The Manorial System

You will remember from reading Chapter 9 that feudalism created alliances between nobles (lords and vassals). The landholding nobles were a military elite whose ability to be warriors depended on their having the leisure time to pursue the arts of war. Landed estates, located on the fiefs given to a vassal by his lord, and worked by peasants, provided the economic support that made this way of life possible.

A manor was an agricultural estate run by a lord and worked by peasants. Although free peasants continued to exist, increasing numbers of free peasants became serfs, or peasants legally bound to the land. Serfs had to provide labor services, pay rents,

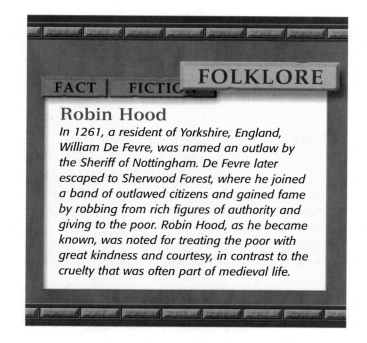

FOLKLORE

FACT | FICTION

Robin Hood

In 1261, a resident of Yorkshire, England, William De Fevre, was named an outlaw by the Sheriff of Nottingham. De Fevre later escaped to Sherwood Forest, where he joined a band of outlawed citizens and gained fame by robbing from rich figures of authority and giving to the poor. Robin Hood, as he became known, was noted for treating the poor with great kindness and courtesy, in contrast to the cruelty that was often part of medieval life.

and be subject to the lord's control. By 800, probably 60 percent of the people of western Europe were serfs.

A serf's labor services included working the lord's land. The lord's land made up one-third to one-half of the cultivated land scattered throughout the manor. The rest of the estate's land was used by the peasants to grow food for themselves. Such tasks as building barns and digging ditches were also part of the labor services. Serfs usually worked about three days a week for their lords.

The serfs paid rents by giving the lords a share of every product they raised. Serfs also paid the lords for the use of the manor's common pasturelands, streams, ponds, and surrounding woodlands. If a serf fished in the pond or stream on a manor, he turned over part of the catch to his lord. Peasants were also obliged to pay a tithe (a tenth of their produce) to their local village churches.

In the feudal contract, lords and vassals were tied together through mutual obligations to each other. On individual estates, lords had a variety of legal rights over their serfs. Serfs could not leave the manor without the lord's permission and could not marry anyone outside the manor without the lord's approval. Lords often had political authority on their lands, which gave them the right to try peasants in their own courts. Peasants were required to pay lords for certain services, such as having their grain ground into flour in the lords' mills.

Even with these restrictions, however, serfs were not slaves. The land assigned to serfs to support themselves usually could not be taken away, and their responsibilities to the lord remained fairly fixed. It was also the lord's duty to protect his serfs, giving them the safety they needed to grow crops.

☑ **Reading Check** **Summarizing** What legal rights did the lords have over the serfs?

Daily Life of the Peasantry

The life of peasants in Europe was simple. Their cottages had wood frames surrounded by sticks, with the spaces between sticks filled with straw and rubble and then plastered over with clay. Roofs were simply thatched.

The houses of poorer peasants consisted of a single room. Others, however, had at least two rooms—a main room for cooking, eating, and other activities and another room for sleeping. There was little privacy in a medieval household.

A hearth in the main room was used for heating and cooking. Because there were few or no windows and no chimney, the smoke created by fires in the hearth went out through cracks in the walls or, more likely, through the thatched roof.

Cycle of Labor The seasons of the year largely determined peasant activities. Each season brought a new round of tasks. Harvest time in August and September was especially hectic. A good harvest of grains for making bread was crucial to survival in the winter months.

A new cycle of labor began in October, when peasants worked the ground for the planting of winter crops. In November came the slaughter of excess livestock, because there was usually not enough food to keep the animals alive all winter. The meat would be salted to preserve it for winter use. In February and March, the land was plowed for the planting of spring crops—oats, barley, peas, and beans. Early summer was a fairly relaxed time, although there was still weeding and sheepshearing to be done.

In every season, of course, the serfs worked not only their own land but also the lords' lands. They also tended the small gardens next to their dwellings, where they grew the vegetables that made up part of their diet.

Peasants did not face a life of constant labor, thanks to the feast days, or holidays, of the Catholic Church. These feast days celebrated the great events of the Christian faith, or the lives of Christian saints or holy persons. The three great feasts of the Catholic Church were Christmas (celebrating the birth of Christ), Easter (celebrating the resurrection of Christ), and Pentecost (celebrating the descent of the Holy Spirit on Christ's disciples 50 days after his resurrection). Other feasts dedicated to saints or the Virgin Mary, the mother of Jesus, were also celebrated. A total of more than 50 days were essentially holidays.

Religious feast days, Sunday mass, baptisms, marriages, and funerals all brought peasants into contact with the village church, a crucial part of manorial life. The village priest taught the peasants the basic ideas of Christianity so that they would gain the Christians' final goal—salvation. However, village priests were often peasants themselves; most were not able to read. It is difficult to know how much church teaching the peasants actually understood. Very likely, they saw

Peasant's Wheel of Life

SUMMER — August, September, October — AUTUMN — November — December — WINTER — February, March — April — SPRING — May, June, July

Harvesting barley and oats
Harvesting peas and beans; breeding cattle
Plowing; sowing wheat and rye; breeding sheep
Slaughtering pigs; collecting firewood
Indoor tasks (spinning, crafts)
Clearing ditches; cutting wood
Pruning trees; lambs and calves born
Plowing; sowing barley and oats
Planting peas, beans, flax, and hemp
Planting vegetables; making repairs
Mowing hay; shearing sheep
Weeding; harvesting flax, wheat, hemp, and rye

Chart Skills

Peasants worked year-round for the lord of the manor. A few days each week were devoted to their own gardens.

1. **Understanding Cause and Effect** Explain how the peasants' activities in one month affected their activities in later months.

2. **Making Inferences** Based on your knowledge of current agricultural technology, how do you think a medieval peasant's yearly routine compares to that of a contemporary farmer?

God as an all-powerful force who needed to be appeased by prayer to bring good harvests.

The position of peasant women in manorial society was both important and difficult. They were expected to work in the fields and at the same time bear children. Their ability to manage the household might determine whether a peasant family would starve or survive in difficult times.

Food and Drink Though simple, a peasant's daily diet was adequate when food was available. The basic staple of the peasant diet, and of the medieval diet in general, was bread. Women made the dough for the bread. The loaves were usually baked in community ovens, which were owned by the lord of the manor. Peasant bread was highly nutritious because it contained not only wheat and rye but also barley, millet, and oats. These ingredients gave the bread a dark appearance and very heavy, hard texture.

Numerous other foods added to the peasant's diet: vegetables from the household gardens; cheese from cow's or goat's milk; nuts and berries from woodlands; and fruits, such as apples, pears, and cherries. Chickens provided eggs and sometimes meat. Peasants usually ate meat only on the great feast days, such as Christmas and Easter.

Grains were important not only for bread but also for making ale. In the Middle Ages, it was not easy to obtain pure sources of water to drink. Consequently, while wine became the choice of drink for members of the upper classes, ale was the most common drink of the poor. If records are accurate, enormous quantities of ale were consumed. A monastery in the twelfth century records a daily allotment to the monks of three gallons of ale a day. Peasants in the field probably consumed even more.

✓ **Reading Check** **Explaining** What role did peasant women play in manorial society?

The Revival of Trade

Medieval Europe was basically an agricultural society in which most people lived in small villages. In the eleventh and twelfth centuries, however, new elements changed the economic foundation of European civilization. The new features included a revival of trade and an associated growth of towns and cities.

The revival of trade in Europe was gradual. During the chaotic times of the early Middle Ages, large-scale trade had declined. By the end of the tenth century, however, people were emerging with both the skills and products for trade.

Picturing **History**

This illustration is from the famous manuscript *Très Riches Heures,* an example of a medieval Book of Hours. Books of Hours were personal prayer books that often contained calendars noting important dates of the year. Using the Wheel of Life on the opposite page, can you tell which month and season are represented in this illustration?

Cities in Italy took the lead. **Venice,** for example, had emerged by the end of the eighth century as a town with close trading ties to the Byzantine Empire. Venice developed a mercantile fleet (a fleet of trading ships) and by the end of the tenth century had become a major trading center.

While Venice and other northern Italian cities were busy trading in the Mediterranean, the towns of **Flanders** were doing the same in northern Europe. Flanders, the area along the coast of present-day Belgium and northern France, was known for its much desired, high-quality woolen cloth.

The location of Flanders made it an ideal center for the traders of northern Europe. Merchants from England, Scandinavia, France, and Germany met there to trade their goods for woolen cloth. Flanders prospered

Geography *Skills*

The revival of trade led to the revival of cities.

1. **Interpreting Maps** What was the most important European trading city for goods being shipped to Asia?

2. **Applying Geography Skills** Assume that you are a trader who has lived and worked in London, Constantinople, and Venice. While conducting trade in each of these cities, what other cities would you have been most likely to visit? Create a table showing your most frequent stops for each of the three base cities.

Slowly, a **money economy**—an economic system based on money, rather than barter—began to emerge. New trading companies and banking firms were set up to manage the exchange and sale of goods. All of these new practices were part of the rise of **commercial capitalism**, an economic system in which people invested in trade and goods in order to make profits.

✔Reading Check **Evaluating** Why were the towns of Flanders busy trading centers?

The Growth of Cities

The revival of trade led to a revival of cities. Towns had greatly declined in the early Middle Ages, especially in Europe north of the Alps. Old Roman cities had continued to exist but had dwindled in size and population.

Cities Old and New With the revival of trade, merchants began to settle in the old Roman cities. They were followed by craftspeople or artisans—people who had developed skills and saw a chance to make goods that could be sold by the merchants. In the course of the eleventh and twelfth centuries, the old Roman cities came alive with new populations and growth.

in the eleventh and twelfth centuries, and such Flemish towns as Bruges and Ghent became centers for the trade and manufacture of woolen cloth.

By the twelfth century, a regular exchange of goods had developed between Flanders and Italy. To encourage this trade, the counts of Champagne, in northern France, initiated a series of trade fairs. Six fairs were held every year in the chief towns of the territory. At these fairs, northern merchants brought the furs, woolen cloth, tin, hemp, and honey of northern Europe and exchanged them for the cloth and swords of northern Italy and the silks, sugar, and spices of the East.

As trade increased, demand for gold and silver coins arose at fairs and trading markets of all kinds.

Many new cities or towns were also founded, especially in northern Europe. Usually, a group of merchants built a settlement near a castle because it was located along a trade route and because the lords of the castle would offer protection. If the settlement prospered and expanded, new walls were built to protect it. The merchants and artisans of these cities later came to be called *burghers* or **bourgeoisie,** from the German word *burg,* meaning "a walled enclosure."

Medieval cities were small in comparison with either ancient or modern cities. A large trading city would number about five thousand inhabitants. By the late 1200s, London—England's largest city—had more than 40,000 people. Italian cities tended to be larger. Venice, Florence, and Milan each had more than 80,000 inhabitants. Even the largest European city, however, seemed small alongside the Byzantine capital of Constantinople or the Arab cities of Damascus, Baghdad, and Cairo.

City Government Most towns were closely tied to the land around them because they depended on the food grown in the surrounding manors. In addition, the towns were often part of the territory belonging to a lord and were subject to his authority. Although lords wanted to treat townspeople as they would their vassals and serfs, the townspeople saw things differently.

Townspeople needed freedom to trade. They needed their own unique laws and were willing to pay for them. Lords and kings, in turn, saw that they could also make money and were willing to sell to the townspeople the liberties they wanted.

By 1100, townspeople were getting numerous rights from local lords. These included the right to buy and sell property, freedom from military service to the lord, a written law that guaranteed the freedom of the townspeople, and the right for an escaped serf to become a free person after living a year and a day in the town.

The people in almost every new town and city gained these basic liberties. Some new towns also received the right to govern themselves by choosing their own officials and having their own courts of law.

Over a period of time, medieval cities developed their own governments for running the affairs of the community. Only males who had been born in the city or who had lived there for some time were citizens. In many cities, these citizens elected the members of a city council, who served as judges and city officials and who passed laws. Elections were carefully rigged to make sure that only **patricians**—members of the wealthiest and most powerful families—were elected.

✔ **Reading Check** **Analyzing** Where did towns tend to be located and why did they appear there?

Daily Life in the Medieval City

Medieval towns were surrounded by stone walls. Because the walls were expensive to build, the space within was precious and tightly filled. Thus, medieval cities had narrow, winding streets. Houses were crowded against one another, and the second and third stories were built out over the streets.

The danger of fire was great. Dwellings were built mostly of wood before the fourteenth century, and candles and wood fires were used for light and heat. Medieval cities burned rapidly once a fire started.

The physical environment of medieval cities was not pleasant. The cities were often dirty and smelled from animal and human waste. Air pollution was also a fact of life. Wood fires, present everywhere, were the usual cause. Even worse pollution, however, came from the burning of cheap grades of coal by brewers, dyers, and people who could not afford to purchase wood.

Cities were also unable to stop water pollution, especially from the tanning and animal-slaughtering industries. Butchers dumped blood and all other waste products from their butchered animals into the rivers. Tanners, who converted animal hides to leather, unloaded tannic acids, dried blood, fat, hair,

Towns and cities grew and prospered during the High Middle Ages.

321

and the other waste products of their operations. Because of the pollution, cities did not use the rivers for drinking water but relied instead on wells.

Private and public baths also existed in medieval towns. Paris, for example, had 32 public baths for men and women. Since nudity was allowed in the baths, city authorities came under pressure to close them down. The great plague of the fourteenth century (discussed later in this chapter) sealed the fate of the baths.

There were considerably more men than women in medieval cities. Women were expected to supervise the household, prepare meals, raise the children, and manage the family's finances. Often, they were expected to help their husbands in their trades. Some women developed their own trades to earn extra money. Sometimes, when a master craftsman died, his widow carried on his trade. It was thus possible for women in medieval towns to lead quite independent lives. In fact, many women became brewers, weavers, and hatmakers.

✓ **Reading Check** **Identifying** List three physical characteristics of medieval cities.

Industry and Guilds

The revival of trade enabled cities and towns to become important centers for manufacturing a wide range of goods, such as cloth, metalwork, shoes, and leather goods. A host of craft activities were carried on in houses located in the narrow streets of the medieval cities.

From the eleventh century on, craftspeople began to organize themselves into guilds, or business associations. Guilds came to play a leading role in the economic life of the cities. By the thirteenth century, there were guilds for almost every craft, such as tanners, carpenters, and bakers. There were also separate guilds for specialized groups of merchants, such as dealers in silk, spices, wool, or money (banking).

Craft guilds directed almost every aspect of the production process. They set the standards for the quality of the articles produced, specified the methods of production to be used, and even fixed the price at which the finished goods could be sold. Guilds also determined the number of people who could enter a specific trade and the procedure they must follow to do so.

A person who wanted to learn a trade first became an **apprentice,** usually at around the age of 10, to a master craftsperson. Apprentices were not paid, but they did receive room and board from their masters. After five to seven years of service during which they learned their craft, apprentices became **journeymen** and worked for wages for other masters. Journeymen aspired to become masters as well. To do so, they were expected to produce a masterpiece, a finished piece in their craft. This piece allowed the master craftspeople of the guild to judge whether a journeyman was qualified to become a master and join the guild.

✓ **Reading Check** **Evaluating** What role did guilds play in the economic life of the cities?

🔶 **TAKS Practice**

SECTION 1 ASSESSMENT

Checking for Understanding

1. **Define** manor, serf, money economy, commercial capitalism, guild, masterpiece.

2. **Identify** *carruca,* bourgeoisie, patricians, apprentice, journeymen.

3. **Locate** Venice, Flanders.

4. **Explain** the process of becoming a master in a guild. What do you think motivated people to participate in and endure this demanding process?

5. **List** the economic developments of the Middle Ages that allowed for the emergence of commercial capitalism.

Critical Thinking

6. **Explain** Why were the three-field system and heavy iron plows so important to increased food production?

7. **Compare and Contrast** Use a chart like the one below to compare and contrast living and working in a medieval city to living and working on a manor.

Medieval Cities	Manor

Analyzing Visuals

8. **Examine** the illustration of peasants working in a field shown on page 319 and the chart of the peasant's year shown on page 318. Use the illustration and chart to help you describe the major characteristics of the economic system of manorialism.

Writing About History

9. **Persuasive Writing** Imagine you are a trader doing business at the beginning of the money economy. Write a letter addressed to other traders convincing them to convert to a money system from bartering.

Christianity and Medieval Civilization

Guide to Reading

Main Ideas
- The Catholic Church played a dominant role in the lives of people during the High Middle Ages.
- Strong leadership by the popes made the Catholic Church a forceful presence in medieval society.

Key Terms
lay investiture, interdict, sacrament, heresy, Inquisition, relic

People to Identify
Pope Gregory VII, Henry IV, Pope Innocent III, Hildegard of Bingen, Saint Francis of Assisi

Places to Locate
Papal States, Assisi

Preview Questions
1. Why were Church leaders often at odds with the European rulers?
2. What role did Christianity play during the Middle Ages?

Reading Strategy
Categorizing Information Use a table like the one below to list characteristics of the Cistercian and Dominican religious orders.

Cistercians	Dominicans

Preview of Events

♦1050	♦1100	♦1150	♦1200	♦1250
1073 Gregory VII is elected pope	**1098** Cistercian order is formed	**1122** Concordat of Worms resolves controversy	**1210** Franciscan order founded	**1216** Dominic de Guzmán founds the Dominicans	**1233** The Inquisition is created to battle heresy

Voices from the Past

Pope Gregory VII, who served as pope from 1073 to 1085

In 1075, Pope Gregory VII issued the following decrees:

66(1) That the Roman [Catholic] Church was founded by God alone. (2) That the pope alone can with right be called universal. (3) That he alone can depose or reinstate bishops. . . . (10) That [the pope's] name alone shall be spoken in the churches. (11) That his name is the only name in the world. (12) That it may be permitted to him to depose emperors. . . . (19) That he himself may be judged by no one. . . . (22) That the Roman Church has never erred; nor will it err to all eternity, the Scripture bearing witness.99

—*Select Historical Documents of the Middle Ages,* **Ernest F. Henderson, ed., 1892**

The popes of the Catholic Church exerted their power, as is evident from these decrees. Christianity was a crucial element in medieval European society.

The Papal Monarchy

Since the fifth century, the popes of the Catholic Church had claimed supremacy over the affairs of the Church. They had also gained control of territories in central Italy that came to be known as the **Papal States.** This control kept the popes involved in political matters, often at the expense of their spiritual duties.

At the same time, the Church became increasingly involved in the feudal system. Chief officials of the Church, such as bishops and abbots, came to hold their offices as grants from nobles. As vassals, they were obliged to carry out the usual feudal services, including military duties. Lords often chose their vassals from other noble families for political reasons. Thus, the bishops and abbots they chose were often worldly figures who cared little about their spiritual duties.

Reform of the Papacy By the eleventh century, church leaders realized the need to be free from the interference of lords in the appointment of church officials. When an individual became a church official in the Middle Ages, he was given a ring and a staff. These objects symbolized the spiritual authority that the official was granted, or invested with, by the Church. Secular, or lay, rulers usually both chose nominees to church offices and gave them the symbols of their office, a practice known as lay investiture. Realizing the need to be free from secular interference in the appointment of church officials, **Pope Gregory VII** decided to fight this practice.

Elected pope in 1073, Gregory was convinced that he had been chosen by God to reform the Church. To pursue this aim, Gregory claimed that he—the pope—was truly God's "vicar on earth" and that the pope's authority extended over all the Christian world, including its rulers. Only by eliminating lay investiture could the Church regain its freedom, by which Gregory meant the right of the Church to appoint clergy and run its own affairs. If rulers did not accept this, the pope would remove them.

Gregory VII soon found himself in conflict with **Henry IV,** the king of Germany, over these claims. For many years, German kings had appointed high-ranking clerics, especially bishops, as their vassals in order to use them as administrators. Without them, the king could not hope to maintain his own power in the face of the powerful German nobles.

In 1075, Pope Gregory issued a decree forbidding high-ranking clerics from receiving their investiture from lay leaders: "We decree that no one of the clergy shall receive the investiture with a bishopric or abbey or Church from the hand of an emperor or king or of any lay person." Henry, however, had no intention of obeying a decree that challenged the very heart of his administration.

The struggle between Henry IV and Gregory VII, which is known as the Investiture Controversy, dragged on until a new German king and a new pope reached an agreement in 1122 called the **Concordat of Worms.** Under this agreement, a bishop in Germany was first elected by Church officials. After election, the new bishop paid homage to the king as his lord. The king in turn invested him with the symbols of temporal (earthly) office. A representative of the pope, however, then invested the new bishop with the symbols of his spiritual office.

History *through Art*

***Meeting with the Pope* by Giovanni Francesco Romanelli** Find descriptions of Gregory VII in the text that seem to match the way in which the artist has portrayed him. Explain your choices.

The Church Supreme Besides his concern over lay investiture, Pope Gregory VII also tried to improve the Church's ability to provide spiritual guidance to the faithful. The popes of the twelfth century did not give up the reform ideals of Pope Gregory VII, but they were even more inclined to strengthen papal power and build a strong administrative system. During the papacy of **Pope Innocent III** in the thirteenth century, the Catholic Church reached the height of its political power. At the beginning of his rule in 1198, in a letter to a priest, the pope made a clear statement of his views on papal supremacy:

❝As God, the creator of the universe, set two great lights in the firmament of heaven, the greater light to rule the day, and the lesser light to rule the night so He set two great dignities in the firmament of the universal Church, . . . the greater to rule the day, that is, souls, and the lesser to rule the night, that is, bodies. These dignities are the papal authority and the royal power. And just as the moon gets her light from the sun, and is inferior to the sun . . . so the royal power gets the splendor of its dignity from the papal authority.❞

Innocent III's actions were those of a man who believed that he, the pope, was the supreme judge of European affairs. He forced the king of France, Philip Augustus, to take back his wife and queen after Philip had tried to have his marriage annulled. The pope also compelled King John of England to accept the pope's choice for the position of archbishop of Canterbury.

To achieve his political ends, Innocent used the spiritual weapons at his command. His favorite was the interdict. An interdict forbids priests from giving the sacraments (Christian rites) of the Church to a particular group of people. The goal was to cause the people under interdiction, who were deprived of the comforts of religion, to exert pressure against their ruler. An interdict is what caused Philip to restore his wife to her rightful place as queen of France.

Reading Check **Explaining** What was the significance of the Concordat of Worms?

New Religious Orders

In the second half of the eleventh century and the first half of the twelfth century, a wave of religious enthusiasm seized Europe. This movement led to a rise in the number of monasteries and the emergence of new monastic orders. Both men and women joined religious orders in increasing numbers.

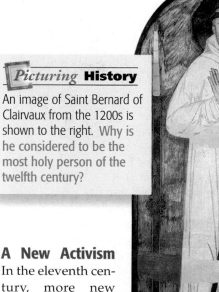

Picturing **History**
An image of Saint Bernard of Clairvaux from the 1200s is shown to the right. Why is he considered to be the most holy person of the twelfth century?

A New Activism

In the eleventh century, more new orders arose and became important. One of the most important new orders of the Middle Ages was the Cistercian (sis•TUHR•shuhn) order. It was founded in 1098 by a group of monks who were unhappy with the lack of discipline at their own Benedictine monastery. Cistercian monasticism spread rapidly from southern France into the rest of Europe.

The **Cistercians** were strict. They ate a simple diet, and each had only a single robe. All decorations were eliminated from their churches and monastic buildings. More time for prayer and manual labor was gained by spending fewer hours at religious services.

The Cistercians played a major role in developing a new, activistic spiritual model for twelfth-century Europe. While Benedictine monks spent hours inside the monastery in personal prayer, the Cistercians took their religion to the people outside the monastery. More than any other person, Saint Bernard of Clairvaux embodied the new spiritual ideal of Cistercian monasticism: "Arise, soldier of Christ, arise! Get up off the ground and return to the battle from which you have fled! Fight more boldly after your flight, and triumph in glory!"

Women in Religious Orders Women were also actively involved in the spiritual movements of the age. The number of women joining religious houses grew dramatically. In the High Middle Ages, most nuns were from the ranks of the landed aristocracy. Convents were convenient for families who were

Hildegard of Bingen
1098–1179 — Medieval abbess

Hildegard entered a religious house for females at the age of eight, took her vows at fourteen, and twenty-four years later became abbess. After becoming abbess, she began to write an account of the mystical visions she had had for years. "A great flash of light from heaven pierced my brain and . . . in that instant my mind was imbued with the meaning of the sacred books," she wrote. Eventually she produced three books based on her visions. Hildegard gained fame as a mystic and prophetess. Popes, emperors, kings, dukes, bishops, abbots, and abbesses eagerly sought her advice. She wrote to them all as an equal and did not hesitate to be critical.

unable or unwilling to find husbands for their daughters, for aristocratic women who did not wish to marry, or for widows.

Female intellectuals found convents a haven for their activities. Most of the learned women of the Middle Ages, especially in Germany, were nuns. This was certainly true of **Hildegard of Bingen,** who became abbess of a religious house for females in western Germany. Hildegard was also one of the first important women composers. She was an important contributor to the body of music known as Gregorian chant. Her work is especially remarkable because she succeeded at a time when music, especially sacred music, was almost exclusively the domain of men.

The Franciscans and the Dominicans

In the thirteenth century, two new religious orders emerged that had a strong impact on the lives of ordinary people. They were the **Franciscans** and the **Dominicans.** The Franciscans were founded by **Saint Francis of Assisi.** Francis was born to a wealthy Italian merchant family in **Assisi.** After having been captured and imprisoned during a local war, he had a series of dramatic spiritual experiences. These experiences led him to abandon all worldly goods and material pursuits and to live and preach in poverty, working and begging for his food. His simplicity, joyful nature, and love for

others soon attracted a band of followers, all of whom took vows of absolute poverty, agreeing to reject all property and live by working and begging for their food.

The Franciscans became very popular. The Franciscans lived among the people, preaching repentance and aiding the poor. Their calls for a return to the simplicity and poverty of the early Church, reinforced by their own example, were especially effective.

Unlike other religious orders, the Franciscans lived in the world. They undertook missionary work, first throughout Italy and then to all parts of Europe and even to the Muslim world.

The Dominican order was founded by a Spanish priest, Dominic de Guzmán. Dominic wanted to defend Church teachings from heresy—the denial of basic Church doctrines. The spiritual revival of the High Middle Ages had led to the emergence of heresies within the Church. Adherents of these movements were called heretics. Heretical movements became especially widespread in southern France.

Dominic believed that a new religious order of men who lived lives of poverty and were capable of preaching effectively would best be able to attack heresy.

The Inquisition

The Church's desire to have a method of discovering and dealing with heretics led to the creation of a court called the Inquisition, or

Saint Francis of Assisi, founder of the Franciscan order, rejected wealth for a life of simplicity and poverty.

CONNECTIONS Past To Present

From Saint Nicholas to Santa Claus

Saint Nicholas was a bishop in Asia Minor (present-day Turkey) who lived during the 300s. He was known as a generous man who was fond of children. During the Middle Ages in Europe, Saint Nicholas became known as the patron saint of children. He brought them simple gifts of fruit, nuts, and candies on his feast day, which was December 6. Saint Nicholas was portrayed as being dressed in a red-and-white bishop's robe and sporting a flowing white beard.

The Dutch brought the tradition of Saint Nicholas with them to their colonies in the Americas. In America, however, changes occurred in the practices associated with Saint Nicholas. For example, in Holland children placed wooden shoes next to the fireplace to be filled with gifts from Saint Nicholas. In America, stockings were hung by the chimney.

The Dutch words for Saint Nicholas were *Sint Nikolass.* In America, they became *Sinte Klaas.* After the English took control of the Dutch colonies, *Sinte Klaas* became *Santa Claus.* Later in the nineteenth century, the physical appearance of Santa Claus also changed. Saint Nicholas had been portrayed as a tall, thin man. By the 1880s, Santa Claus had become the jolly fat man that we still know today.

Saint Nicholas ▶

Comparing Past and Present

Think about a special holiday or event that you celebrate every year. Has your celebration of that holiday changed over the years? If so, how? Can you predict any future changes that might take place?

Holy Office. The job of this court was to find and try heretics, and it developed a regular procedure to deal with them. The Dominicans became especially well known for their roles as examiners of people suspected of heresy.

If an accused heretic confessed, he or she was forced to perform public penance and was subjected to punishment, such as flogging. Beginning in 1252, those who did not confess voluntarily were tortured until they did confess. Many did not confess but were still considered guilty and turned over to the state for execution. Relapsed heretics—those who confessed, did penance, and then reverted to heresy again— were also subject to execution.

The Christians of the thirteenth century believed the only path to salvation was through the Church. To them, heresy was a crime against God and against humanity. In their minds, using force to save souls from damnation was the right thing to do.

✓ Reading Check **Analyzing** What impact did the Franciscans and Dominicans have on the lives of people in the thirteenth century?

Popular Religion in the High Middle Ages

We have witnessed the actions of popes, bishops, monks, and friars. But what of ordinary people? What were their religious hopes and fears? What were their religious beliefs?

The sacraments of the Catholic Church were central in importance to ordinary people. These rites, such as baptism, marriage, and the Eucharist (Communion), made the Church a crucial part of people's lives from birth to death. The sacraments were seen as means for receiving God's grace and were necessary for salvation. Only the clergy could administer the sacraments, so everyone who hoped to gain salvation depended on the clergy to help them achieve this goal.

Other church practices were also important to ordinary people. One practice involved veneration of saints. Saints were men and women who were considered especially holy and who had achieved a special position in Heaven. Their position enabled saints to ask for favors before the throne of God for people who prayed to them. The saints' ability to help and protect people in this way made them very popular with all Christians.

Jesus Christ's apostles, of course, were recognized throughout Europe as saints. There were also numerous local saints who were of special significance to a single area. The Italians, for example, had Saint Nicholas, the patron saint of children, who is known today as Santa Claus. New saints emerged rapidly, especially in the intensely religious atmosphere of the eleventh and twelfth centuries.

Of all the saints, the Virgin Mary, mother of Jesus, was the most highly regarded in the High Middle Ages. Mary was seen as the most important mediator between mortals and her son, Jesus Christ, the judge of all sinners. From the eleventh century on, a fascination with Mary as Jesus' human mother became more evident. A sign of Mary's importance is the number of churches all over Europe that were dedicated to her in the twelfth and thirteenth centuries. (Such churches in France were named *Notre Dame,* or "Our Lady.")

Emphasis on the role of the saints was closely tied to the use of relics. Relics were usually bones of saints or objects connected with saints that were considered worthy of worship because they provided a

The Virgin Mary and child as depicted in a window of the Chartres cathedral

link between the earthly world and God. It was believed that relics could heal people or produce other miracles.

A twelfth-century English monk began his description of an abbey's relics by saying, "There is kept there a thing more precious than gold, . . . the right arm of St. Oswald. . . . This we have seen with our own eyes and have kissed, and have handled with our own hands. . . . There are kept here also part of his ribs and of the soil on which he fell." The monk went on to list additional relics possessed by the abbey, which included two pieces of Jesus' swaddling clothes, pieces of his manger, and part of the five loaves of bread with which he fed five thousand people.

Medieval Christians also believed that a pilgrimage to a holy shrine produced a spiritual benefit. The greatest shrine, but the most difficult to reach, was the Holy City of Jerusalem. On the continent two pilgrim centers were especially popular in the High Middle Ages: Rome, which contained the relics of Saints Peter and Paul, and the Spanish town of Santiago de Compostela, supposedly the site of the tomb of the Apostle James. Local attractions, such as shrines dedicated to the Blessed Virgin Mary, also became pilgrimage centers.

✓ **Reading Check** **Examining** Why were saints important to Christians in the High Middle Ages?

🟊**TAKS Practice**

SECTION 2 ASSESSMENT

Checking for Understanding

1. **Define** lay investiture, interdict, sacrament, heresy, Inquisition, relic.

2. **Identify** Pope Gregory VII, Henry IV, Concordat of Worms, Pope Innocent III, Cistercians, Hildegard of Bingen, Franciscans, Dominicans, Saint Francis of Assisi.

3. **Locate** Papal States, Assisi.

4. **Explain** the use of the interdict.

5. **List** the new religious orders created during the Middle Ages.

Critical Thinking

6. **Explain** Why was the Catholic Church such a powerful influence in lay people's lives during the Middle Ages?

7. **Evaluating Information** Use a diagram like the one below to show the reforms made by the Church that affected the development of medieval civilization.

Church Reforms

Analyzing Visuals

8. **Identify** the figures pictured in the cathedral window shown on this page. What central ideas of the Roman Catholic Church does the window from Chartres illustrate?

Writing About History

9. **Persuasive Writing** Take on the role of either Pope Gregory VII or King Henry IV of Germany. Argue the question of lay investiture from the viewpoint of either the pope or the king and justify the compromise that you reached.

The Culture of the High Middle Ages

Guide to Reading

Main Ideas
- An intellectual revival led to the formation of universities.
- In the High Middle Ages, new technical innovations made it possible to build Gothic cathedrals, which are one of the great artistic triumphs of this age.

Key Terms
theology, scholasticism, vernacular

People to Identify
Aristotle, Saint Thomas Aquinas

Places to Locate
Bologna, Paris, Oxford

Preview Questions
1. What were the major cultural achievements of European civilization in the High Middle Ages?
2. What role did theology play in the European intellectual world?

Reading Strategy
Compare and Contrast Use a table to compare and contrast the Romanesque style of architecture to the Gothic style of architecture. How did the churches built in these two styles differ?

Romanesque	Gothic

Preview of Events

♦1100	♦1200	♦1300	♦1400	♦1500

1100
The Song of Roland is written

c. 1140
Classical works are rediscovered by European scholars

1150
Architects begin to build in the Gothic style

1158
Students in Bologna form a guild

1500
Eighty universities exist in Europe

Engraving showing University of Paris lecture

Voices from the Past

University students in the High Middle Ages were probably quite similar to those of today, as is evident in this letter from a medieval father to his son:

❝I have recently discovered that you live dissolutely and slothfully, preferring license to restraint and play to work and strumming a guitar while the others are at their studies, whence it happens that you have read but one volume of law while your more industrious companions have read several. Wherefore I have decided to exhort you to repent utterly of your dissolute and careless ways, that you may no longer be called a waster and your shame may be turned to good repute.❞
—*The Rise of Universities,* Charles H. Haskins, 1957

The High Middle Ages were a time of intellectual and artistic vitality—a time that witnessed the birth of universities.

The Rise of Universities

The university as we know it today, with faculty, students, and degrees, was a product of the High Middle Ages. The word *university* comes from the Latin word *universitas,* meaning "corporation" or "guild." Medieval universities were educational guilds, or corporations, that produced educated and trained individuals.

The First Universities The first European university appeared in **Bologna** (buh•LOH•nyuh), Italy. A great teacher named Irnerius, who taught Roman law, attracted students to Bologna from all over Europe. Most were men who were administrators for kings and princes.

(Women did not attend universities.) These men were eager to learn more about the law in order to apply it in their own jobs. To protect their own rights, students at Bologna formed a guild. In 1158, the guild was given a charter—a document giving it the right to govern its own affairs—by the ruling authorities.

The first university in northern Europe was the University of Paris. In the second half of the twelfth century, a number of students and masters (teachers) left **Paris** and started their own university at **Oxford,** England. Kings, popes, and princes thought it honorable to found new universities. By 1500, there were 80 universities in Europe.

University Curricula Students began their studies at a medieval university with the traditional liberal arts curriculum, or course of study. This curriculum consisted of grammar, rhetoric, logic, arithmetic, geometry, music, and astronomy.

Teaching at a medieval university was done by a lecture method. The word *lecture* is derived from Latin and means "to read." Before the development of the printing press in the fifteenth century, books were expensive. Few students could afford them, so teachers read from a basic text and then added their explanations.

No exams were given after a series of lectures. When a student applied for a degree, however, he was given an oral examination by a committee of teachers. These examinations were taken after a four- or six-year period of study. The first degree a student could earn was a bachelor of arts. Later, he might receive a master of arts.

After completing the liberal arts curriculum, a student could go on to study law, medicine, or theology. Theology—the study of religion and God—was the most highly regarded subject of the medieval university. The study of law, medicine, or theology could take 10 years or more. A student who passed his final oral examinations in one of these areas was granted a doctor's degree.

Those who had earned doctor's degrees were officially able to teach, although they also pursued other careers. Universities provided the teachers, administrators, lawyers, and medical doctors for medieval society.

Reading Check **Explaining** Why were most early university courses taught as lecture classes?

The Development of Scholasticism

As we have seen, theology was the most highly regarded area of study at medieval universities. Beginning in about the twelfth century, the study of theology in the universities was strongly influenced by a philosophical and theological system known as scholasticism. Scholasticism tried to reconcile faith and reason—to show that what was accepted on faith was in harmony with what could be learned through reason and experience.

The chief task of scholasticism was to harmonize Christian teachings with the works of the Greek philosophers. In the twelfth century, largely because of the work of Muslim and Jewish scholars, western Europe was introduced to the works of **Aristotle.** However, Aristotle's works upset many Christian theologians. He had

A university classroom in fourteenth-century Germany

arrived at his conclusions by rational thought—not by faith—and some of his ideas contradicted the teachings of the Church. In the thirteenth century, **Saint Thomas Aquinas** (uh•KWY•nuhs) made the most famous attempt to reconcile Aristotle with the doctrines of Christianity.

Thomas Aquinas is best known for his *Summa Theologica,* or *A Summa of Theology* (*summa* was a summary of all the knowledge on a given subject). Aquinas's masterpiece was organized according to the logical method of intellectual investigation used by scholars. Aquinas first posed a question such as, "Does God exist?" He then cited sources that offered opposing opinions on the question before finally reconciling them and arriving at his own conclusions. Most scholastic thinkers used this logical process to investigate theological and philosophical questions.

Aquinas's fame is based on his attempt to reconcile the knowledge learned through the Bible and other Christian writings with the knowledge learned through reason and experience. He took it for granted that there were truths arrived at by reason and truths arrived at by faith. He was certain, however, that the two kinds of truths could not be in conflict with each other. The human mind, unaided by faith, could use reason and experience to arrive at truths concerning the physical universe. However, reason alone could not grasp spiritual truths.

Reading Check **Explaining** What was the main goal of scholasticism?

Vernacular Literature

Latin was the universal language of medieval civilization. Used in the Church and schools, Latin enabled learned people to communicate anywhere in Europe. However, in the twelfth century, much new literature was being written in the vernacular—the language of everyday speech in a particular region, such as Spanish, French, English, or German. A new market for vernacular literature appeared in the twelfth century when educated laypeople (religious people who were not clergy) at courts and in the cities took an interest in new sources of entertainment. 📖 *(See page 993 to read excerpts from Christine de Pizan's* A Woman May Need to Have the Heart of a Man *in the Primary Sources Library.)*

Perhaps the most popular vernacular literature of the twelfth century was troubadour poetry, which was chiefly the product of nobles and knights. This poetry told of the love of a knight for a lady, who inspires him to become a braver knight and a better

Picturing **History**

This troubadour is singing for the ladies of the castle. Do you think he is singing in Latin or the vernacular for his area?

poet. For example, the noble Jaufré Rudel cherished a dream woman from afar:

> ❝Most sad, most joyous shall I go away,
> Let me have seen her for a single day,
>   My love afar,
> I shall not see her, for her land and mine
> Are sundered, and the ways are hard to find,
> So many ways, and I shall lose my way,
> So wills it God.
> Yet shall I know no other love but hers,
> And if not hers, no other love at all.❞

Another type of vernacular literature was the **chanson de geste,** or heroic epic. The earliest and finest example is the *Song of Roland,* which appeared around 1100 and was written in French. The chief events described in heroic epic poems are battles and political contests. The epic world is one of combat, in which knights fight courageously for their kings and lords. Women play only a small role or no role at all in this literature.

Reading Check **Identifying** What were two popular types of vernacular literature in the twelfth century?

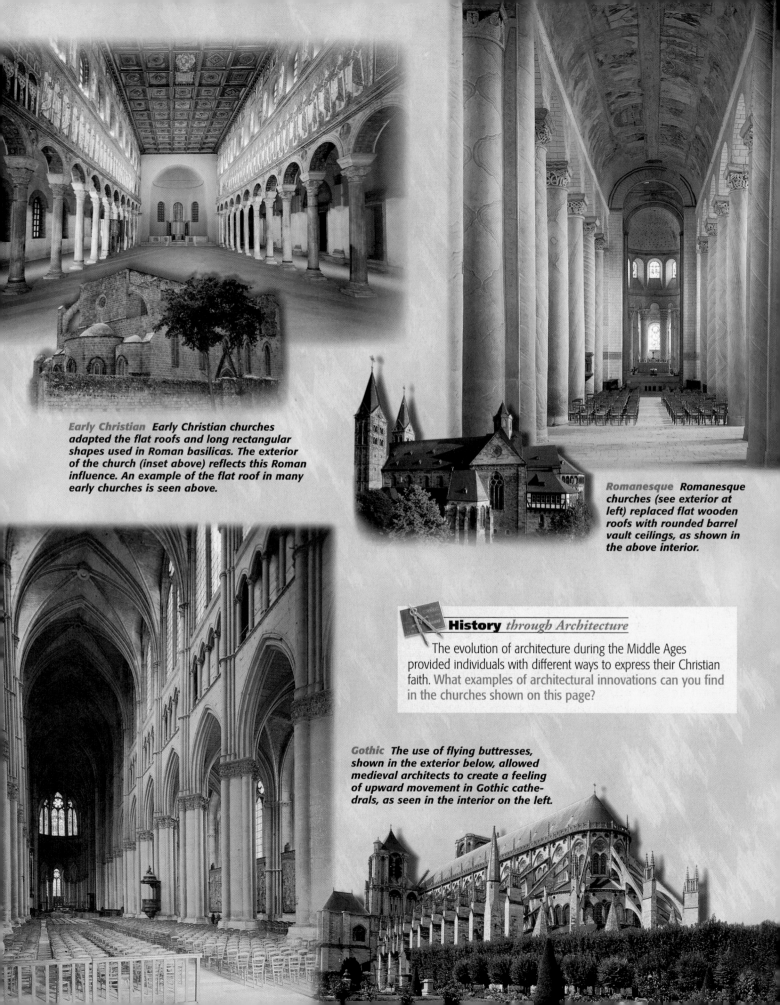

Early Christian *Early Christian churches adapted the flat roofs and long rectangular shapes used in Roman basilicas. The exterior of the church (inset above) reflects this Roman influence. An example of the flat roof in many early churches is seen above.*

Romanesque *Romanesque churches (see exterior at left) replaced flat wooden roofs with rounded barrel vault ceilings, as shown in the above interior.*

History *through Architecture*

The evolution of architecture during the Middle Ages provided individuals with different ways to express their Christian faith. What examples of architectural innovations can you find in the churches shown on this page?

Gothic *The use of flying buttresses, shown in the exterior below, allowed medieval architects to create a feeling of upward movement in Gothic cathedrals, as seen in the interior on the left.*

Architecture

The eleventh and twelfth centuries witnessed an explosion of building in medieval Europe, especially building of churches. The cathedrals of the eleventh and twelfth centuries were built in the Romanesque style. Romanesque churches were normally built in the basilica shape used in the construction of churches in the late Roman Empire.

Basilicas were rectangular buildings with flat wooden roofs. Romanesque builders used this basic plan but replaced the flat wooden roof with a long, round stone arched structure vault (called a barrel vault), or with a cross vault, in which two barrel vaults intersected. The cross vault was used when the builder wanted to create a church plan in the shape of a cross. Although difficult to create, barrel and cross vaults were considered more beautiful than flat roofs.

Because stone roofs were extremely heavy, Romanesque churches required massive pillars and walls to hold them up. This left little space for windows, so Romanesque churches were dark on the inside. Their massive walls and pillars made these churches almost resemble fortresses.

A new style, called Gothic, appeared in the twelfth century and was brought to perfection in the thirteenth. The Gothic cathedral remains one of the greatest artistic triumphs of the High Middle Ages. Two basic innovations of the twelfth century made Gothic cathedrals possible.

One innovation was the replacement of the round barrel vault of Romanesque churches with a combination of ribbed vaults and pointed arches. This change enabled builders to make Gothic churches higher than Romanesque churches. The use of pointed arches and ribbed vaults also creates an impression of upward movement, as if the building is reaching to God.

Another technical innovation was the flying buttress—a heavy, arched support of stone, built onto the outside of the walls. Flying buttresses made it possible to distribute the weight of the church's vaulted ceilings outward and down. This eliminated the heavy walls that were needed in Romanesque churches to hold the weight of the massive barrel vaults.

Gothic cathedrals were built, then, with relatively thin walls. Since they were not supporting great weight, these walls could be filled with magnificent stained glass windows. These windows depict both religious scenes and scenes from daily life. The colored glass windows create a play of light inside the cathedral that varies with the sun at different times of the day. Natural light was believed to be a symbol of the divine light of God. The Gothic cathedral, with its towers soaring toward Heaven, bears witness to an age when most people believed in a spiritual world.

HISTORY Online

Web Activity Visit the *Glencoe World History* Web site at tx.wh.glencoe.com and click on **Chapter 10– Student Web Activity** to learn more about the Middle Ages.

✓ **Reading Check** **Identifying** In what shape were Romanesque churches usually built?

TAKS Practice

SECTION 3 ASSESSMENT

Checking for Understanding

1. **Define** theology, scholasticism, vernacular.

2. **Identify** Aristotle, Saint Thomas Aquinas, *Summa Theologica,* chanson de geste.

3. **Locate** Bologna, Paris, Oxford.

4. **Explain** the origin of universities in Europe.

5. **Describe** the possibilities open to a student who had completed the liberal arts curriculum at a medieval university in Europe.

Critical Thinking

6. **Explain** How did the architecture of the Gothic cathedral reflect medieval religious values?

7. **Compare and Contrast** Use a table like the one below to compare what you know of modern university courses of study with those of the first European universities. What are the similarities and differences?

Similarities	Differences

Analyzing Visuals

8. **Examine** the image on page 331. What does it convey about the role of the troubadour in European society during the Middle Ages?

Writing About History

9. **Persuasive Writing** Create an illustrated brochure to entice students to enroll in a new medieval university opening in Venice. Include information on the method of education and degree and course offerings. Provide a "frequently asked questions" section for students and for parents.

SOCIAL STUDIES
SKILLBUILDER

Analyzing Historical Maps

Why Learn This Skill?

What changes have you noticed in your town the past few years? Has the corner bank been replaced by an ethnic restaurant? Would a map of your town that was drawn today look different from one drawn 15 years ago?

Changes take place on a larger scale across nations and continents. Wars, economic troubles, and natural disasters change borders and land-scapes; once-powerful nations crumble; displaced people move from one country to another, taking their language and their culture with them. These political, social, and cultural changes can be clearly traced and interpreted through the use of historical maps.

Learning the Skill

Follow the steps below to learn how to analyze a historical map.

- Read the title of the map to identify its theme.

- Read the map's key, labels, and captions to determine what time periods and changes appear on the map.

- Identify the chronology or order of events on the map. Many historical maps show changes over time. For example, a map may use colors to show land acquisitions of different rulers over a period of time. On the map of France above, however, the colors represent areas controlled by different rulers at the same time.

- To compare historical maps of the same region in different time periods, first identify the geographic location and time period of each map. Identify the features that have remained the same and those that have changed. For example, has the country's size changed over time?

- After analyzing a map, draw conclusions about the causes and effects of the changes it shows.

Practicing the Skill

Analyze the map on this page and answer these questions:

1. What geographic region and time period are represented in the map?

2. What information is shown in the map's key and labels?

3. Find a present-day map of this region to compare with the map on this page. How has the region changed since the 1400s?

Applying the Skill

Compare a map of Europe today with a map of Europe in 1985 or earlier. Identify at least five changes that have occurred since the early 1980s.

 Glencoe's **Skillbuilder Interactive Workbook, Level 2,** provides instruction and practice in key social studies skills.

SECTION 4 / The Late Middle Ages

Guide to Reading

Main Ideas
- Europe in the fourteenth century was challenged by an overwhelming number of disastrous forces.
- European rulers reestablished the centralized power of monarchical governments.

Key Terms
Black Death, anti-Semitism, Great Schism, new monarchies, *taille*

People to Identify
Pope Boniface VIII, King Philip IV, John Hus, Henry V, Isabella, Ferdinand

Places to Locate
Avignon, Crécy, Agincourt, Orléans

Preview Questions
1. How did the Black Death impact European society?
2. What were the "new monarchies"?

Reading Strategy
Cause and Effect Use a diagram like the one below to identify three reasons for the decline in the power of the papacy.

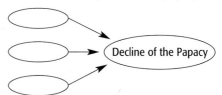

Decline of the Papacy

Preview of Events

♦1300	♦1350	♦1400	♦1450	♦1500

1346
Battle at Crécy is fought

c. 1350
The Black Death spreads

1378
The Great Schism begins

1435
War of the Roses begins

1469
Ferdinand and Isabella marry

Voices from the Past

Detail from the Triumph of Death by Jan Brueghel the Elder

Giovanni Boccaccio, a fourteenth-century Italian writer, described the impact of the Black Death on Florence:

66In the year of our Lord 1348 the deadly plague broke out in the great city of Florence. . . . A great many breathed their last in the public streets, day and night; a large number perished in their homes, and it was only by the stench of their decaying bodies that they proclaimed their death to their neighbors. Everywhere the city was teeming with corpses. . . . Huge trenches were dug in the crowded churchyards and the new dead were piled in them, layer upon layer. A little earth covered the corpses of each row, and the procedure continued until the trench was filled to the top.99
— *The Decameron,* Giovanni Boccaccio, 1348–1351

Florence was only one of many European cities struck by the Black Death.

The Black Death

┌TURNING**POINT**┐ In this section, you will learn how fourteenth-century Europe was devastated by the terrible plague known as the Black Death. This plague greatly decreased the population of Europe and brought about significant economic and social changes in the late Middle Ages.

The Middle Ages in Europe had reached a high point in the thirteenth century. In the fourteenth century, however, some disastrous changes took place. Especially catastrophic was the Black Death.

The Black Death was the most devastating natural disaster in European history. One observer wrote that "father abandoned child, wife [abandoned] husband, one

NATIONAL GEOGRAPHIC
Spread of the Black Death

Extent of spread:
- 1347
- Middle of 1348
- End of 1348
- 1349
- 1350
- 1351
- 1353
- ■ Partially or totally spared
- ▲ Seriously affected

ARCTIC CIRCLE

North Sea

Baltic Sea

ATLANTIC OCEAN

Edinburgh

Stockholm • Novgorod

Hamburg ▲ Lübeck • Danzig

Winchester ▲ London
Bruges • Ghent
Frankfurt •
Paris ▲
Augsburg •
Nuremberg ■
Kraków • Kiev •
Vienna •
Buda
Milan ■ Venice ▲
Genoa ■ Florence ▲ Belgrade
Marseilles ▲
Caffa •
Black Sea
Danube R.
Rome ■
Naples • Constantinople ▲

Bordeaux •
Lyons •
León •
Lisbon •
Toledo •
Valencia •
Córdoba •
Barcelona •
Corsica
Sardinia
Majorca
Mediterranean Sea
Tunis •
Sicily
Crete
Cyprus

0   500 miles
0   500 kilometers
Azimuthal Equidistant projection

Geography *Skills*

By 1353, the Black Death epidemic (bubonic plague) had affected all of Europe.

1. **Interpreting Maps** What questions would you pose to determine the pattern of the spread of the Black Death?

2. **Applying Geography Skills** Create a database of other epidemics in history. Are these diseases a threat today?

brother [abandoned] another, for the plague seemed to strike through breath and sight. And so they died. And no one could be found to bury the dead, for money or friendship." People were horrified by the plague, an evil force they could not understand.

The Plague Spreads Bubonic plague was the most common form of the Black Death. It was spread by black rats infested with fleas carrying a deadly bacterium. Italian merchants brought the plague with them from Caffa, on the Black Sea, to the island of Sicily in October 1347. The plague had spread to parts of southern Italy and southern France by the end of 1347.

Usually, the path of the Black Death followed trade routes. In 1348 and 1349, the plague spread through France, the Low Countries (modern Belgium, Luxembourg, and the Netherlands), and Germany. It ravaged England in 1349 and expanded to northern Europe and Scandinavia. Eastern Europe and Russia were affected by 1351.

Out of a total European population of 75 million, possibly as many as 38 million people died of the plague between 1347 and 1351. Especially hard hit were Italy's crowded cities, where 50 to 60 percent of the people died. In England and Germany, entire villages disappeared.

Social and Economic Consequences People at the time did not know what caused the plague. Many believed that it either had been sent by God as a punishment for their sins or had been caused by the devil. Some reactions became extreme, leading to an outbreak of anti-Semitism—hostility toward Jews. In some towns, Jews were accused of causing the plague by poisoning town wells. The worst attacks occurred in Germany. Many Jews fled eastward, especially to Poland, where the king provided protection.

The death of so many people in the fourteenth century also had severe economic consequences. Trade declined, and a shortage of workers caused a dramatic rise in the price of labor. At the same time, the decline in the number of people lowered the demand for food, resulting in falling prices.

Landlords were now paying more for labor while their incomes from rents were declining. Some peasants bargained with their lords to pay rent instead of owing services. In essence, this change freed them from serfdom, an institution that had been declining throughout the High Middle Ages.

✓ **Reading Check** **Summarizing** What were the economic consequences of the Black Death?

The Decline of Church Power

The popes of the Roman Catholic Church reached the height of their power in the thirteenth century. Then, in the fourteenth century, a series of problems led to a decline in the Church's political position.

The Popes at Avignon The European kings had grown unwilling to accept papal claims of supremacy by the end of the thirteenth century. This is evident in a struggle between **Pope Boniface VIII** and **King Philip IV** of France. Their struggle would have serious consequences for the papacy.

To gain new revenues, Philip said that he had the right to tax the clergy of France. Boniface VIII claimed that the clergy could not pay taxes to their ruler without the pope's consent. He argued that popes were supreme over both the Church and the state.

Philip IV refused to accept the pope's position and sent French forces to Italy to bring Boniface back to France for trial. The pope escaped but died soon after from the shock of his experience. To ensure his position, Philip IV engineered the election of a Frenchman, Clement V, as pope in 1305. The new pope took up residence in **Avignon** (a•veen•YOHN), in southern France.

From 1305 to 1377, the popes lived in Avignon. Sentiments against the papacy grew during this time. The pope was the bishop of Rome, and it seemed improper that he should reside in Avignon instead of Rome. The splendor in which the pope and cardinals were living in Avignon also led to strong criticism of the papacy. The Italian poet Petrarch expressed this feeling when he wrote:

> 66 Here reign the successors of the poor fisherman of Galilee; they have strangely forgotten their origin. I am astounded . . . to see these men loaded with gold and clad in purple, boasting of the spoils of princes and nations. 99

At last, Pope Gregory XI, perceiving the disastrous decline in papal prestige, returned to Rome in 1377.

The Great Schism and Its Aftermath Gregory XI died soon after his return to Rome. When the college of cardinals met to elect a new pope, the citizens of Rome warned that the cardinals would not leave Rome alive unless an Italian was elected pope. The terrified cardinals wisely elected an Italian, who became Pope Urban VI.

Five months later, a group of French cardinals declared the election invalid and chose a Frenchman as pope. This pope promptly returned to Avignon. Because Urban remained in Rome, there were now two popes, beginning what has been called the Great Schism of the Church.

The Great Schism, which lasted from 1378 to 1417, divided Europe. France and its allies supported the pope in Avignon. France's enemy England and England's allies supported the pope in Rome.

In addition to creating political conflict, the Great Schism damaged the Church. The pope was widely believed to be the true leader of Christendom. When each line of popes denounced the other as the Antichrist (one who opposes Christ), people's faith in both the papacy and the Church were undermined.

A church council finally met at Constance, Switzerland, and ended the schism in 1417. The competing popes either resigned or were deposed. A new pope who was acceptable to all parties was then elected.

Meanwhile, the crises in the Catholic Church had led to cries for reform. A group of Czech reformers led by **John Hus** called for an end to the corruption of the clergy and the excessive power of the papacy within the Catholic Church. Hus was accused of heresy by the Council of Constance and burned at the stake in 1415. This angered the Czechs and led to a revolutionary upheaval in Bohemia that was not crushed until 1436.

By the early 1400s, then, the Church had lost much of its political power. The pope no longer had any hope of asserting supremacy over the state. Although Christianity remained a central feature of medieval life, the papacy and the Church had lost much of their spiritual authority.

✓ **Reading Check** **Summarizing** List the problems that led to the decline of the Church's authority in medieval Europe.

The Hundred Years' War

Plague, economic crisis, and the decline of the Catholic Church were not the only problems of the late Middle Ages. War and political instability must also be added to the list. The Hundred Years' War was the most violent struggle during this period.

The War Begins In the thirteenth century, England still held one small possession in France, known as the duchy of Gascony. The English king, who was also the duke of Gascony, pledged his loyalty as a vassal to the French king. However, when King Philip VI of France seized Gascony in 1337 in an attempt to make the duchy part of the French kingdom, the duke of Gascony—King Edward III of England—declared war on Philip. Thus began the Hundred Years' War between England and France. It would go on until 1453.

The war began in a burst of knightly enthusiasm. Trained to be warriors, knights viewed battle as a chance to show their fighting abilities. The Hundred Years' War proved to be an important turning point in the nature of warfare, however. It was peasant foot soldiers, not knights, who won the chief battles of the Hundred Years' War.

The French army of 1337 still relied largely on its heavily armed noble cavalrymen. These knights looked with contempt on foot soldiers, people they viewed as social inferiors. The English, too, used heavily armed cavalry, but they relied more on large numbers of peasants, paid to be foot soldiers. English soldiers were armed not only with pikes, or heavy spears, but also with longbows. The longbow had greater striking power, longer range, and more rapid speed of fire than the crossbow (formerly the weapon of choice).

Crécy and Agincourt The first major battle of the Hundred Years' War occurred in 1346 at **Crécy.** The larger French army followed no battle plan but simply attacked the English lines in a disorderly fashion. The arrows of the English archers devastated the French cavalry.

As the chronicler Froissart described it, "[with their longbows] the English continued to shoot into the thickest part of the crowd, wasting none of their arrows. They impaled or wounded horses and riders, who fell to the ground in great distress, unable to get up again without the help of several men." It was a stunning victory for the English.

The Battle of Crécy was not decisive, however. The English simply did not have enough resources to conquer all France. Nevertheless, they continued to try. The English king, **Henry V,** was especially eager to achieve victory.

Bataille de Crécy

Picturing History

This illustration depicts the Battle of Crécy, in which a much smaller English force under Edward III defeated a French army of approximately 20,000 soldiers. What weapon helped the English defeat the French at Crécy?

At the Battle of **Agincourt** in 1415, the heavy, armor-plated French knights tried to attack Henry's forces across a field turned to mud by heavy rain. They were disastrously defeated, and 1,500 French nobles died on the battlefield. The English were masters of northern France.

Joan of Arc The French cause, now seemingly hopeless, fell into the hands of Charles, the heir to the French throne, who governed the southern two-thirds of the lands of France. Quite unexpectedly, a French peasant woman saved the timid monarch.

Joan of Arc was born in 1412, the daughter of prosperous peasants. She was a deeply religious person who experienced visions and came to believe that her favorite saints had commanded her to free France.

In February 1429, Joan made her way to Charles's court, where her sincerity and simplicity persuaded him to allow her to accompany a French army to **Orléans.** Apparently inspired by Joan's faith, the

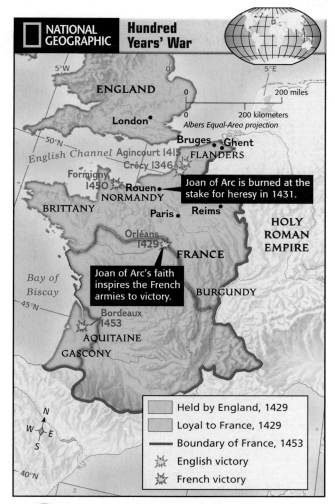

NATIONAL GEOGRAPHIC

Hundred Years' War

Joan of Arc is burned at the stake for heresy in 1431.

Joan of Arc's faith inspires the French armies to victory.

Held by England, 1429
Loyal to France, 1429
Boundary of France, 1453
English victory
French victory

Geography *Skills*

The Hundred Years' War was a series of conflicts between England and France.

1. **Interpreting Maps** Research one of the battles on this map. Create a model illustrating at least two features of the battle (for example, topography and troop deployment).

2. **Applying Geography Skills** Using information from the map, create a chart that shows which nation appears to have the advantage. Take into account the chronology of battles, supply lines, and the amount of land held by each side.

French armies found new confidence in themselves and captured Orléans.

Joan had brought the war to a decisive turning point but did not live to see its end. She was captured in 1430 and turned over by the English to the Inquisition on charges of witchcraft. At that time, spiritual visions were thought to be inspired by either God or the devil. Joan was condemned to death as a heretic.

Joan of Arc's achievements, however, were decisive. Although the war dragged on for another two decades, defeats of English armies in Normandy and Aquitaine led to a French victory by 1453. Also important to the French success was the use of the cannon, a new weapon made possible by the invention of gunpowder.

Reading Check **Analyzing** Why was the Hundred Years' War a turning point in the ways of warfare?

Political Recovery

In the fourteenth century, European rulers faced serious problems. Many dynasties in Europe were unable to produce male heirs. The founders of new dynasties had to fight for their positions when groups of nobles supported opposing candidates for the kingship. Rulers found themselves with financial problems as well.

In the fifteenth century, however, recovery set in as a number of new rulers attempted to reestablish the centralized power of monarchies. Some historians have spoken of these reestablished states as the new monarchies. This term applies especially to the monarchies of France, England, and Spain at the end of the fifteenth century.

Western Europe The Hundred Years' War left France exhausted. However, the war had also developed a strong degree of French national feeling toward a common enemy. The kings used that spirit to reestablish royal power.

The development of a strong French state was greatly advanced by King Louis XI, who ruled from 1461 to 1483. Known as the Spider because of his devious ways, Louis strengthened the use of the *taille*—an annual direct tax, usually on land or property—as a permanent tax imposed by royal authority. This tax gave Louis a sound, regular source of income, which helped him to create the foundations of a strong French monarchy.

The Hundred Years' War had also strongly affected the English. The cost of the war and losses in manpower strained the economy. At the end of the war, England faced even greater turmoil when civil conflicts—known as the War of the Roses—erupted. Noble factions fought to control the monarchy until 1485, when Henry Tudor established a new dynasty.

As the first Tudor king, Henry VII worked to create a strong royal government. Henry ended the wars of the nobles by abolishing their private armies. He was also very thrifty. By not overburdening the nobles and the middle class with taxes, Henry won their favor. They thus provided much support for his monarchy.

Spain, too, experienced the growth of a strong national monarchy at the end of the fifteenth century. Muslims had conquered much of Spain by about 725. During the Middle Ages, Christian rulers in Spain had fought to regain their lands from the Muslims. Several independent Christian kingdoms had emerged in the course of the long reconquest of the Iberian Peninsula.

Two of the strongest kingdoms were Aragon and Castile. When **Isabella** of Castile married **Ferdinand** of Aragon in 1469, it was a major step toward unifying Spain. The two rulers worked to strengthen royal control of the government.

Ferdinand and Isabella also pursued a policy of strict conformity to Catholicism. In 1492, they took the drastic step of expelling all professed Jews from Spain. Muslims, too, after their final loss in 1492 to the armies of Ferdinand and Isabella, were "encouraged" to convert to Catholicism. In 1502, Isabella issued a decree expelling all professed Muslims from her kingdom. To a very large degree, Ferdinand and Isabella, the "most Catholic" monarchs, had achieved their goal of religious uniformity. To be Spanish was to be Catholic.

Central and Eastern Europe Unlike France, England, and Spain, the Holy Roman Empire did not develop a strong monarchical authority. The failures of German emperors in the thirteenth century had made Germany a land of hundreds of states. Almost all of these states acted independently of the German ruler.

After 1438, the position of Holy Roman emperor was held by the Hapsburg dynasty. As rulers of the Austrian lands along the Danube, the house of Hapsburg had become one of the wealthiest landholders in the empire. By the mid-fifteenth century, these rulers had begun to play an important role in European affairs.

In eastern Europe, rulers found it difficult to centralize their states. Religious differences troubled the area as Roman Catholics, Eastern Orthodox Christians, and other groups, including Mongols and Muslims, confronted one another. In Poland, the nobles gained the upper hand and established the right to elect their kings, a policy that drastically weakened royal authority. In Hungary, one king broke the power of the wealthy lords, and created a well-organized central administration. After his death, however, his work was largely undone.

Since the thirteenth century, Russia had been under the domination of the Mongols. Gradually, the princes of Moscow rose to prominence by using their close relationship to the Mongol khans to increase their wealth and expand their possessions. During the reign of the great prince Ivan III, a new Russian state was born. Ivan III annexed other Russian territories. By 1480, he had thrown off the yoke of the Mongols.

Reading Check **Explaining** How did European rulers begin to recover politically after the Hundred Years' War?

🔺TAKS Practice

SECTION 4 ASSESSMENT

Checking for Understanding

1. **Define** Black Death, anti-Semitism, Great Schism, new monarchies, *taille.*

2. **Identify** Pope Boniface VIII, King Philip IV, John Hus, Henry V, Isabella, Ferdinand.

3. **Locate** Avignon, Crécy, Agincourt, Orléans.

4. **Describe** the origins of the Hundred Years' War.

5. **List** the religious groups in conflict in eastern Europe.

Critical Thinking

6. **Analyze** What were the economic and social results of the Black Death in Europe?

7. **Summarizing Information** Use a table like the one below to identify ways in which European monarchs increased their power in the fifteenth century.

France	England	Spain

Analyzing Visuals

8. **Identify** the two armies pictured in the illustration on page 338. How can you tell the two armies apart? What details did the artist include to describe the outcome or significance of the battle?

Writing About History

9. **Informative Writing** Write a newspaper-type obituary for Joan of Arc. Include information on her life and her achievements. Write a tribute or quote that you believe sums up Joan's life.

A Medieval Holocaust—
The Cremation of the Strasbourg Jews

IN THEIR ATTEMPT TO EXPLAIN THE widespread horrors of the Black Death, medieval Christians looked for scapegoats. The Jews were blamed for spreading the plague by poisoning wells. This selection, written in 1349, gives an account of how Christians in the town of Strasbourg in the Holy Roman Empire dealt with the Jewish community.

In this picture, Christian townspeople watch in apparent approval as wood is added to the fire and Jews are burned alive.

**❝In the year 1349 there occurred the greatest epidemic that ever happened. Death went from one end of the earth to the other. . . . This epidemic also came to Strasbourg in the summer of the above-mentioned year, and it is estimated that about sixteen thousand people died.

In the matter of this plague the Jews throughout the world were accused in all lands as having caused it through the poison which they are said to have put into the water and the wells—that is what they were accused of—and for this reason the Jews were burned all the way from the Mediterranean into Germany. . . .

[The account then goes on to discuss the situation of the Jews in the city of Strasbourg.]

On Saturday . . . they burned the Jews on a wooden platform in their cemetery. There were about two thousand people of them. Those who wanted to baptize themselves were spared. [Some say that about a thousand accepted baptism.] Many small children were taken out of the fire and baptized against the will of their fathers and mothers. And everything that was owed to the Jews was canceled, and the Jews had to surrender all pledges and notes that they had taken for debts. The council, however, took the cash that the Jews possessed and divided it among the working-men. The money was indeed the thing that killed the Jews. If they had been poor and if the feudal lords had not been in debt to them, they would not have been burnt.

Thus were the Jews burned at Strasbourg, and in the same year in all the cities of the Rhine, whether Free Cities or Imperial Cities or cities belonging to the lords.❞**

—**Jacob von Königshofen,**
The Cremation of the Strasbourg Jews

Analyzing Primary Sources

1. Who was blamed for causing the Black Death? Were these charges economically motivated? Why or why not?
2. Can you provide examples of discrimination today that are similar to what the Jews experienced in medieval times?

Using Key Terms

1. Governments that attempted to reestablish centralized power were called _____.

2. _____ is the study of religion.

3. Craftspeople began to organize themselves into business organizations called _____ in the twelfth century.

4. _____ were peasants tied to the land.

5. A _____ was an object that provided a link between the earthly world and God.

6. The _____ was an annual direct French tax on land or property.

7. The religious court whose job it was to find and try heretics was called the _____.

8. The school of thought that tried to reconcile faith and reason is called _____.

9. The language of a particular region is called the _____.

10. A Spanish priest founded the Dominicans to defend Church teachings from _____.

Reviewing Key Facts

11. **Culture** Give at least three reasons why medieval cities were not pleasant places to live.

12. **History** How did the Great Schism divide Europe?

13. **Culture** In what role in medieval society might women have had the most chance to be powerful?

14. **History** What new weapon, partly of Chinese origin, helped the French win the Hundred Years' War?

15. **Culture** What was the role of women in medieval cities?

16. **Citizenship** What rights were townspeople given in medieval cities? Who could become citizens?

17. **Science and Technology** Why was the longbow superior to the crossbow?

18. **History** Discuss the major result of the War of the Roses.

19. **Culture** Explain the organization of medieval guilds.

20. **Government** What steps helped Spain to become a strong centralized monarchy?

21. **History** Identify changes that resulted from the revival of trade in Europe during the Middle Ages. What are the origins of the modern economic system of capitalism?

22. **Culture** Identify some examples of religious influence in historic events of the Middle Ages. Why did religious authorities and political rulers clash?

23. **Government** How did the governments of central and eastern Europe evolve differently from those of western Europe after the Hundred Years' War?

24. **History** Explain the significance of the date 1492.

25. **Geography** What impact did geographic factors have on the population of the High Middle Ages?

Critical Thinking

26. **Analyzing** What forces led to Europe's economic growth during the Middle Ages?

27. **Evaluating** How did the continual conflict between England and France strengthen the monarchies of those two countries?

Chapter Summary

The Middle Ages was a period marked by cultural diffusion, innovation, and conflict.

Cultural Diffusion

The Crusades increase the exchange of goods and ideas between European and non-European cultures.

- European monarchs gain strength through new taxes and through the new armies required for the Crusades.
- Increased trade, especially of luxury goods, leads to new importance for Italian cities.
- Classical texts are translated and reintroduced into Europe, leading to a revival in learning.

Innovation

The rise of towns and the middle class leads to advances in all areas of society.

- As trade increases, the importance of towns and guilds grows.
- A money economy replaces bartering.
- Universities are founded.
- Literature and poetry flourish and are increasingly written in the vernacular rather than in Latin.
- The Romanesque style of architecture gives way to the Gothic style.

Conflict

The Hundred Years' War and the Great Schism strengthen the authority of some and weaken the authority of others.

- After the Hundred Years' War, the French monarchy gains power.
- Conflict within the English monarchy leads to the War of the Roses.
- Conflict, corruption, and challenges by reformers weaken the authority of the Catholic Church.

HISTORY Online

Self-Check Quiz
Visit the *Glencoe World History* Web site at
tx.wh.glencoe.com and click on **Chapter 10–Self-Check Quiz** to prepare for the Chapter Test.

Writing About History

28. Expository Writing Identify one medieval innovation and describe its influence on medieval society. Compare this to the impact of a twentieth-century innovation on a modern society. Which innovation, medieval or modern, had the biggest impact on daily life?

Analyzing Sources

Read the following description of an abbey's relics by a twelfth-century English monk:

> ❝There is kept there a thing more precious than gold . . . the right arm of St. Oswald . . . This we have seen with our own eyes and have kissed, and have handled with our own hands. . . . There are kept here also part of his ribs and of the soil on which he fell.❞

29. Why was the arm of St. Oswald preserved as a relic?

30. Why would the relic be considered "a thing more precious than gold"?

Applying Technology Skills

31. Creating a Multimedia Presentation Locate an e-mail address for your local historical society or chamber of commerce. Write a letter requesting information about buildings in your area that reflect the influence of medieval architecture. Using the information you receive, create an illustrated tourist pamphlet filled with information about these buildings.

Making Decisions

32. Pretend you are living in a medieval town when suddenly your fellow townspeople start dying from the plague. You want to stay in the town, but your family wants to leave. Create a dialogue between you and your family giving reasons for why you should stay in the town or leave.

Analyzing Maps and Charts

33. Select an event or invention from each category on the chart at the top of the next column. What was the effect of that event or invention?

34. How did farming practices affect population?

Economic Changes in the Middle Ages

Better Farming Practices

- Climatic change favorable to growing conditions
- Clearing of trees and draining of swamps by peasants
- Use of iron to make labor-saving devices, including scythes, axes, hoes, and wheeled plows
- Harnessing of wind and water power
- Shift from a two-field to a three-field system of crop rotation

Population Increase

- Peaceful conditions following the invasions of the early Middle Ages
- Dramatic expansion in food production

Growth of Cities

- Gradual revival of trade, including the initiation of trade fairs
- Slow emergence of an economy based on money (rather than barter)
- Movement of merchants and artisans to cities; organization of craftspeople into guilds
- Granting of basic liberties to townspeople by local lords
- Rise of city self-government

The Princeton Review

TAKS Test Practice

Directions: Choose the best answer to the following question.

What effect did the Black Death have on Europe?

F The plague resulted in an increase in the number of universities and the rise of scholasticism.

G The plague led to an acute labor shortage that resulted in higher wages and the emancipation of many serfs.

H The plague inspired new ideas about faith that led to the formation of the Cistercian, Franciscan, and Dominican orders.

J The plague sparked the Hundred Years' War between France and England.

Test-Taking Tip: Although these questions mostly ask you about what you've learned in class, using common sense can help you arrive at the correct answers too. For example, to answer this question, think about what you know about the Black Death first and then read the answer choices.

The Americas

400–1500

Key Events

As you read this chapter, look for the key events in the history of the Americas.
- *The early inhabitants of the Americas probably traveled from Asia across a Bering Strait land bridge produced by the Ice Age.*
- *The Mayan, Aztec, and Incan civilizations developed and administered complex societies.*
- *Diseases that Europeans brought to the Americas contributed to the downfall of several cultures.*

The Impact Today

The events that occurred during this time period still impact our lives today.
- *The Anasazi culture and the Anasazi's descendants influenced adobe dwellings and handcrafted pottery made today in the southwestern United States.*
- *The Iroquois League was a model for the British colonies.*
- *As in the Incan Empire, compulsory military service has been used in the United States and is used in other countries of the world.*

World History Video *The Chapter 11 video, "Mesoamerican Civiliza-tions," chronicles the development of cultures and societies in the Americas.*

10,000 B.C.
People migrate from Asia to North and South America

1200 B.C.
Organized societies begin in Central and South America

c. 900 B.C.
Moche culture thrives

| 10,000 B.C. | 5,000 B.C. | 2,500 B.C. | 1500 B.C. | 500 B.C. |

1000 B.C.
Farming villages appear in Eastern Woodlands

400 B.C.
Olmec civilization declines

Olmec ceremonial ax of jade

Archaeologists study the ruins of the ancient Mayan city of Dos Pilas in northern Guatemala.

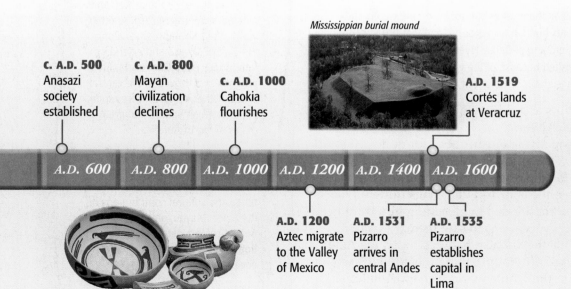

Anasazi pottery with bird motif

C. A.D. 500
Anasazi society established

C. A.D. 800
Mayan civilization declines

C. A.D. 1000
Cahokia flourishes

Mississippian burial mound

A.D. 1519
Cortés lands at Veracruz

A.D. 600   *A.D. 800*   *A.D. 1000*   *A.D. 1200*   *A.D. 1400*   *A.D. 1600*

A.D. 1200
Aztec migrate to the Valley of Mexico

A.D. 1531
Pizarro arrives in central Andes

A.D. 1535
Pizarro establishes capital in Lima

HISTORY
Online

Chapter Overview
Visit the *Glencoe World History* Web site at tx.wh.glencoe.com and click on **Chapter 11–Chapter Overview** to preview chapter information.

A Story That Matters

Mask of an Aztec god

Two Cultures Collide

Bernal Díaz, who accompanied Hernán Cortés on a Spanish expedition to Mexico in 1519, could not believe his eyes when he saw the Aztec city of Tenochtitlán in central Mexico:

> 66When we beheld so many cities and towns on the water, and other large settlements built on firm ground, and that broad causeway running so straight and perfectly level to the city of Tenochtitlán, we were astonished because of the great stone towers and temples and buildings that rose up out of the water.99

To some of the soldiers accompanying Cortés, "All these things seemed to be a dream."

The Aztec were equally astonished, but for quite different reasons. One wrote, "They [the Spanish] came in battle array, as conquerors, and the dust rose in whirlwinds on the roads, their spears glinted in the sun, and their flags fluttered like bats. Some of them were dressed in glistening iron from head to foot; they terrified everyone who saw them."

Within a short time, the Spanish had destroyed the Aztec Empire. Díaz remarked, "I thought that no land like it would ever be discovered in the whole world. But today all that I then saw is overthrown and destroyed; nothing is left standing."

Why It Matters

The first organized societies had begun to take root in Mexico and Central America by 1200 B.C. One key area of development was on the plateau of central Mexico. Another was in the lowland regions along the Gulf of Mexico and extending into modern-day Guatemala. Civilizations also thrived in the central Andes. Other societies were emerging in the river valleys and great plains of North America.

History and You Using the Internet and traditional print sources, research the cities, innovations, and cultural contributions of the Aztec, Mayan, and Incan civilizations. Create a database that shows both the similarities and the differences among the three.

The Peoples of North America

Guide to Reading

Main Ideas
- The first inhabitants of the Americas were hunters and gatherers, while later inhabitants also practiced farming.
- Because of the great variety of climate and geographic features, many different cultures emerged in the Americas.

Key Terms
longhouse, clan, tepee, adobe, pueblo

People to Identify
Inuit, Hopewell, Iroquois, Plains Indians, Anasazi

Places to Locate
Amazon, Bering Strait, Gulf of Mexico, Cahokia, Mesa Verde

Preview Questions
1. Who were the first inhabitants of the Americas?
2. What archaeological evidence remains of the Anasazi culture?

Reading Strategy
Summarizing Information As you read this section, complete a separate chart for each of the five major peoples discussed in this section. Identify the characteristics listed below for each group.

People	
Region	
Types of food	
Shelter	

Preview of Events

♦400	♦500	♦600	♦700	♦800	♦900	♦1000

C. A.D. 500
Anasazi begin farming societies

A.D. 700
Mississippian culture prospers

C. A.D. 850
Cahokia is established as seat of government

Voices from the Past

Sioux warrior shirt with beads and fringe

One Sioux sacred woman said:

❝All of this creation is sacred, and so do not forget. Every dawn as it comes is a holy event, and every day is holy, for the light comes from your Father Wakan-Tanka, and also you must always remember that the two-leggeds and all the other peoples who stand upon this earth are sacred and should be treated as such." A Native American song says, "The whole Southwest was a House Made of Dawn. It was made of pollen and of rain. The land was old and everlasting. There were many colors on the hills and on the plain, and there was a dark wilderness on the mountains beyond. The land was tilled and strong and it was beautiful all around.❞

— *The Native Americans: An Illustrated History,*
Betty and Ian Ballantine, eds.,1993

As these words illustrate, the first peoples who inhabited North America had great respect for the earth and its creatures.

The Lands of the Americas

The Americas make up an enormous land area, stretching about nine thousand miles (more than fourteen thousand km) from the Arctic Ocean in the north to Cape Horn at the tip of South America. Over this vast area are many different landscapes: ice-covered lands, dense forests, fertile river valleys ideal for hunting and farming, coastlines for fishing, lush tropical forests, and hot deserts.

Along the western side of the Americas are two major mountain ranges: the Rocky Mountains in North America and the Andes in South America. Lower ranges, the Appalachian Mountains in North America and the Brazilian Highlands in South America, run along the eastern coasts. Between the mountains of the western and eastern coasts are broad valleys with rich farmland. Through the valleys run great rivers, such as the Mississippi in North America and the **Amazon** in South America.

✔**Reading Check** **Identifying** What different kinds of landscapes are found throughout North and South America?

The First Americans

⌐**TURNING** **POINT**¬ **As you will read in the following section, people gradually spread throughout the North American continent. By 10,000 B.C., people had reached almost as far as the southern tip of South America.**

Between 100,000 and 8,000 years ago, the last Ice Age produced low sea levels that in turn created a land bridge in the **Bering Strait** between the Asian and North American continents. Many scholars believe that small communities of people from Asia crossed this land bridge. Most likely, they were hunters who were pursuing the herds  of bison and caribou that moved in search of grazing land into North America as the glaciers receded. These people became the first Americans. Scholars do not agree on exactly when human beings first began living in the Americas. They do know, however, that these first Americans were hunters and food gatherers.

✔**Reading Check** **Summarizing** According to scholars, why did hunters cross the land bridge into North America?

The Peoples of North America

North America is a large continent with varying climates and geographical features. These different geographical areas became home to various peoples.

Arctic and Northwest: The Inuit About 3000 B.C.,
a group of people called the **Inuit** moved into North America from Asia. They had to learn unique ways to survive in such a cold and harsh environment. Most Inuit settled along the coasts of the tundra region, the treeless land south of the Arctic.

With a variety of harpoons and spears made from antler or narwhal tusk, the Inuit became skilled at hunting seal, caribou, and fish, which provided them with both food and clothing. In winter, the Inuit built homes of stones and turf. The traditional igloo, made out of cut blocks of hard-packed snow, was only a temporary shelter used during traveling.

Eastern Woodlands: The Mound Builders
Around 1000 B.C., farming villages appeared in the Eastern Woodlands, the land in eastern North America from the Great Lakes to the **Gulf of Mexico.** People here grew crops but also continued to gather wild plants for food. Best known are the **Hopewell** peoples in the Ohio River valley, who extended their culture along the Mississippi River. The Hopewell peoples, also known as the Mound Builders, are especially known for the elaborate earth mounds that they built. Mounds were used as tombs or for ceremonies. Some were built in the shape of animals.

A shift to full-time farming around A.D. 700 led to a prosperous culture that was located in the Mississippi River valley from Ohio, Indiana, and Illinois down to the Gulf of Mexico. Among the most commonly grown crops of this Mississippian culture were corn, squash, and beans, grown together to provide plants with nutrients, support, and shade.

Cities began to appear, some of them containing ten thousand people or more. At the site of **Cahokia,** near the modern city of East St. Louis, Illinois, archaeologists found a burial mound over 98 feet (30 m) high with a base larger than that of the Great Pyramid in Egypt. Between A.D. 850 and A.D. 1150, a flourishing Cahokia was the seat of government for much of the Mississippian culture. In the thirteenth century, for reasons unknown, Cahokia collapsed.

Eastern Woodlands: The Iroquois To the northeast of the Mississippian culture were peoples known as the Iroquois. The **Iroquois** lived in villages that consisted of longhouses surrounded by a wooden fence for protection. Each longhouse, built of wooden poles covered with sheets of bark, was 150 to 200 feet (46 to 61 m) in length and housed about a dozen families.

Iroquois men hunted deer, bear, caribou, and small animals like rabbits and beaver. They were also warriors who protected the community. Women owned the dwellings, gathered wild plants, planted the seeds, and harvested the crops, the most important of which were the "three sisters"—corn, beans, and squash. In addition, women cooked, made baskets, and took care of the children.

Wars were common, especially among groups of Iroquois who lived in much of present-day Pennsylvania, New York, and parts of southern Canada. Legend holds that sometime during the 1500s, the Iroquois peoples seemed about to be torn apart by warfare. Deganawida, an elder of one of the Iroquois groups, appeared and preached the need for peace. One who listened was Hiawatha, a member of the Onondaga group.

From the combined efforts of Deganawida and Hiawatha came the Great Peace, which created an alliance of five groups called the Iroquois League. One of the 13 laws of the Great Peace made clear its purpose: "In all of your acts, self-interest shall be cast away. Look and listen for the welfare of the whole people, and have always in view . . . the unborn of the future Nation."

A council of representatives (a group of 50 Iroquois leaders) known as the Grand Council met regularly to settle differences among league members. Representatives were chosen in a special fashion. Each Iroquois group was made up of clans, groups of related families. The women of each clan singled out a well-respected woman as the clan mother. The clan mothers, in turn, chose the male members of the Grand Council.

Much was expected of these men: "With endless patience, they shall carry out their duty. Their firmness shall be tempered with a tenderness for their people. Neither anger nor fury shall find lodging in their minds, and all their words and actions shall be marked by calm deliberation."

The Grand Council, an experiment in democracy, brought the Iroquois a new way to deal with their problems. Some scholars believe that in 1754, Benjamin Franklin used the Iroquois League as a model for a Plan of Union for the British colonies.

Peoples of the Great Plains West of the Mississippi River basin, the **Plains Indians** cultivated beans, corn, and squash along the river valleys of the eastern Great Plains. Every summer, the men left their villages to hunt buffalo, a very important animal to the Plains culture. Hunters worked together to frighten a herd of buffalo, causing them to stampede over a cliff.

The buffalo served many uses for Plains peoples. The people ate the meat, used the skins for clothing, and made tools from the bones. By stretching buffalo skins over wooden poles, they made circular tents called tepees. Tepees provided excellent shelter; they were warm in winter and cool in summer.

Peoples of the Southwest: The Anasazi The Southwest covers the territory of present-day New Mexico, Arizona, Utah, and Colorado. Conditions are dry, but there is sufficient rain in some areas for

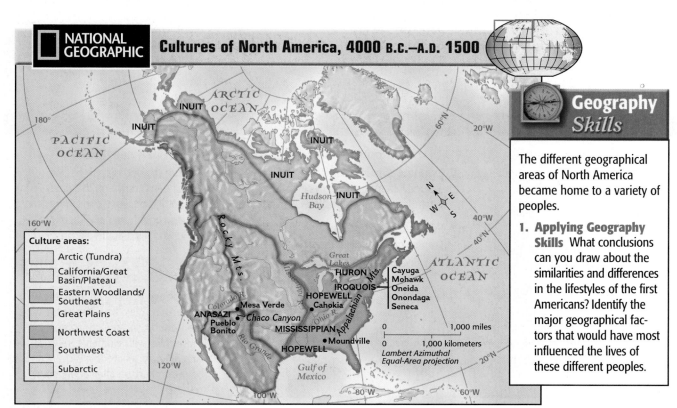

NATIONAL GEOGRAPHIC

Cultures of North America, 4000 B.C.–A.D. 1500

Culture areas:
- Arctic (Tundra)
- California/Great Basin/Plateau
- Eastern Woodlands/Southeast
- Great Plains
- Northwest Coast
- Southwest
- Subarctic

0   1,000 miles
0   1,000 kilometers
Lambert Azimuthal Equal-Area projection

Geography Skills

The different geographical areas of North America became home to a variety of peoples.

1. **Applying Geography Skills** What conclusions can you draw about the similarities and differences in the lifestyles of the first Americans? Identify the major geographical factors that would have most influenced the lives of these different peoples.

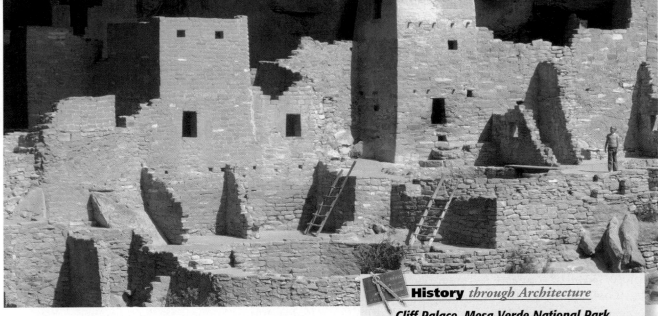

Cliff Palace, Mesa Verde National Park
The group of buildings shown here once housed as many as 400 people. Why do you think the Anasazi built their homes in such inaccessible sites?

farming. The **Anasazi** peoples established an extensive farming society there.

Between A.D. 500 and 1200, the Anasazi used canals and earthen dams to turn parts of the desert into fertile gardens. They were skilled at making baskets and beautifully crafted pottery. They used stone and adobe (sun-dried brick) to build pueblos, multistoried structures that could house many people.

At Chaco Canyon in northwestern New Mexico, they built an elaborate center for their civilization. At the heart of Chaco Canyon was Pueblo Bonito, a large complex that contained some eight hundred rooms housing more than a thousand people. This flourishing center, however, could not survive a 50-year series of droughts, which led the Anasazi to abandon it.

The Anasazi culture itself did not die. To the north, in southern Colorado, a large community had formed at **Mesa Verde** (today a United States national park). Groups of Anasazi there built a remarkable series of buildings in the recesses of the cliff walls. However, a prolonged drought in the late thirteenth century led to the abandonment of Mesa Verde.

✓**Reading Check** **Examining** What caused the Mississippian culture to prosper? What was the result?

🔸**TAKS Practice**

SECTION 1 ASSESSMENT

Checking for Understanding

1. **Define** longhouse, clan, tepee, adobe, pueblo.

2. **Identify** Inuit, Hopewell, Iroquois, Plains Indians, Anasazi.

3. **Locate** Amazon, Bering Strait, Gulf of Mexico, Cahokia, Mesa Verde.

4. **Describe** how settling in the tundra affected Inuit lifestyles.

5. **List** the major sources of food for the Plains Indians. Also list the many different ways in which the Plains peoples made use of the buffalo.

Critical Thinking

6. **Evaluate** The Iroquois League is considered "an experiment in democracy." What do you think this means?

7. **Summarizing Information** Use a graphic organizer like the one below to highlight features of Anasazi culture.

Anasazi Culture

Analyzing Visuals

8. **Examine** the photograph of the Anasazi ruins shown on this page. From this photograph, what conclusions can you draw about the daily life of the people who lived at this site?

Writing About History

9. **Expository Writing** Identify the leadership roles that women took in the Iroquois society and compare those roles with women's roles in American society today. Write a one-page comparison after doing your research.

CRITICAL THINKING
SKILLBUILDER

Analyzing Primary and Secondary Sources

Why Learn This Skill?

Suppose for a moment that a devastating tornado has struck a nearby town. On television that night, you watch an interview with an eyewitness. The eyewitness begins to cry as she describes the destruction of her own home and neighborhood. The next day, you read a newspaper account that describes the tornado's path. Is one of these accounts of the same event more accurate than the other?

Learning the Skill

To determine the accuracy of an account, you must analyze its source. There are two main types of sources—**primary** and **secondary.**

Primary sources are produced by eyewitnesses to events. Diaries, letters, autobiographies, interviews, artifacts, and paintings are primary sources. Because primary sources convey personal experiences, they often include the emotions and opinions of participants in an event.

Secondary sources use information gathered from others. Newspapers, textbooks, and biographies are secondary sources. Secondary sources, written later, help us to understand events in a larger context or time frame.

To determine the reliability of a source, consider the type of source you are using. For a primary source, determine who the author is and when the material was written. An account written during or immediately after an event is often more reliable than one written years later. For a secondary source, look for good documentation. Researchers should cite their sources in footnotes and bibliographies.

For both types of sources, you also need to evaluate the author. Is this author biased? What background and authority does he or she have? Finally, compare two accounts of the same event. If they disagree, you should question the reliability of the material and conduct further research to determine which can be corroborated with other reliable sources.

Practicing the Skill

Read the following excerpts and answer the questions:

❝Finally the two groups met. . . . When all was ready Montezuma placed his feet, shod in gold-soled, gem-studded sandals, on the carpeted pavement and . . . advanced to an encounter that would shape both his own destiny and that of his nation. . . . Montezuma had servants bring forward two necklaces of red shells hung with life-size shrimps made of gold. These he placed around Cortés's neck.❞

—from *Cortés* by William Weber Johnson, 1975

❝When we had arrived at a place not far from the town, the monarch raised himself in his sedan. . . . Montezuma himself was sumptuously attired, had on a species of half boot, richly set with jewels, and whose soles were made of solid gold. . . . Montezuma came up to Cortés, and hung about his neck a chaste necklace of gold, most curiously worked with figures all representing crabs.❞

—from an account by Conquistador Bernal Díaz del Castillo, 1519

1 What is the general topic of the two sources?

2 Identify the primary source.

3 Is one account more reliable than the other? If so, why? How do you know?

Applying the Skill

Find two accounts of a recent event or a historical event. Analyze the reliability of each. Be sure to document how you reached your conclusions about the reliability of the sources.

Glencoe's **Skillbuilder Interactive Workbook, Level 2,** provides instruction and practice in key social studies skills.

Early Civilizations in Mesoamerica

Guide to Reading

Main Ideas
- Early Mesoamerican civilizations flourished with fully-developed political, religious, and social structures.
- The Aztec state succumbed to diseases brought by the Spanish.

Key Terms
Mesoamerica, hieroglyph, tribute

People to Identify
Olmec, Maya, Toltec, Aztec, Hernán Cortés, Montezuma

Places to Locate
Teotihuacán, Yucatán Peninsula, Tikal, Chichén Itzá, Tenochtitlán, Lake Texcoco

Preview Questions
1. What are the principal cultural developments of Mayan civilization?
2. What caused the Aztec to settle in Lake Texcoco?

Reading Strategy
Summarizing Information Create a chart describing the characteristics of the Olmec, Mayan, Toltec, and Aztec cultures.

People	
Location	
Religion	
Architecture	
Year/Reason Declined	

Preview of Events

◆300	◆500	◆700	◆900	◆1100	◆1300	◆1500

A.D. 300
Mayan civilization begins

A.D. 800
Teotihuacán collapses

A.D. 1325
Aztec build Tenochtitlán on Lake Texcoco

A.D. 1520
Aztec begin decline

Voices from the Past

Aztec turquoise mosaic serpent

Bernal Díaz, a Spaniard who arrived in Mexico in 1519, wrote:

❝Let us begin with the dealers in gold, silver, and precious stones, feathers, cloaks, and embroidered goods, and male and female slaves who are also sold [in the markets]. . . . Next there were those who sold coarser cloth, and cotton goods and fabrics made of twisted thread, and there were chocolate merchants with their chocolate. In this way you could see every kind of merchandise to be found anywhere in Mexico, laid out in the same way as goods are laid out in my own district of Medina del Campo, a center for fairs.❞

— *The Conquest of New Spain*, **John M. Cohen, trans., 1975**

Díaz described the city markets of the Aztec with amazement. He and other Spaniards were astonished to find that these markets were larger and better stocked than any markets in Spain.

The Olmec and Teotihuacán

Signs of civilization in Mesoamerica—a name we use for areas of Mexico and Central America that were civilized before the Spaniards arrived—appeared around 1200 B.C. with the **Olmec.** Located in the hot and swampy lowlands along the coast of the Gulf of Mexico south of Veracruz, the Olmec peoples farmed along the muddy riverbanks in the area.

The Olmec had large cities that were centers for their religious rituals. One of these was La Venta, which had a pyramid that towered above the city. The Olmec carved colossal stone heads, probably to represent their gods. Around 400 B.C., the Olmec civilization declined and eventually collapsed.

The first major city in Mesoamerica was **Teotihuacán** (TAY•oh•TEE•wuh•KAHN), or "Place of the Gods." This city was the capital of an early kingdom that arose around 250 B.C. and collapsed about A.D. 800. Most residents were farmers, but the city was also a busy trade center. Tools, weapons, pottery, and jewelry were traded as far as North America.

Located near Mexico City in a fertile valley, Teotihuacán had as many as 200,000 inhabitants at its height. Along its main thoroughfare, known as the Avenue of the Dead, were temples and palaces. All of them, however, were dominated by the massive Pyramid of the Sun, which rose in four tiers to a height of over 200 feet (60 m).

Reading Check **Explaining** What does the term *Mesoamerica* mean, and who were some of the first inhabitants of Mesoamerica?

The Maya and Toltec

Far to the east of Teotihuacán, on the **Yucatán Peninsula,** another major civilization had arisen. This was the civilization of the **Maya,** which flourished between A.D. 300 and 900. It was one of the most sophisticated civilizations in the Americas. The Maya built splendid temples and pyramids and developed a complicated calendar. Mayan civilization came to include much of Central America and southern Mexico.

The Mayan civilization in the central Yucatán Peninsula eventually began to decline. Explanations for the decline include invasion, internal revolt, or a natural disaster such as a volcanic eruption. A more recent theory is that overuse of the land led to reduced crop yields. Whatever the case, Mayan cities were abandoned and covered by dense jungle growth. They were not rediscovered until the nineteenth and twentieth centuries.

Political and Social Structures Mayan cities were built around a central pyramid topped by a shrine to the gods. Nearby were other temples, palaces, and a sacred ball court. Some scholars believe that urban centers such as **Tikal** (in present-day Guatemala) may have had a hundred thousand inhabitants.

Mayan civilization was composed of city-states, each governed by a hereditary ruling class. These Mayan city-states were often at war with each other. Ordinary soldiers who were captured in battle became slaves. Captured nobles and war leaders were used for human sacrifice.

Rulers of the Mayan city-states claimed to be descended from the gods. The Mayan rulers were helped by nobles and a class of scribes who may also have been priests. Mayan society also included townspeople who were skilled artisans, officials, and merchants.

NATIONAL GEOGRAPHIC

Cultures of Mesoamerica, 900 B.C.–A.D. 1500

100°W · 95°W · 90°W · 85°W

Gulf of Mexico

Chichén Itzá

20°N

Lake Texcoco · Tula
Teotihuacán
Tenochtitlán · Tlaxcala · Veracruz
Valley of Mexico

Yucatán Peninsula

Caribbean Sea

La Venta

Palenque · Tikal

15°N

PACIFIC OCEAN

0 · 300 miles
0 · 300 kilometers
Albers Conic Equal-Area projection

- - - - Olmec heartland, 900 B.C.
- - - - Toltec heartland, A.D. 900
Mayan civilization, A.D. 900
Aztec civilization, A.D. 1500

Geography *Skills*

Mesoamerican civilizations developed in Mexico and Central America.

1. **Interpreting Maps** Which cultures developed in the same heartland?
2. **Applying Geography Skills** Identify any pattern(s) you see in the locations of the different cities, and explain why the pattern(s) may have developed.

SPORTS & CONTESTS

The Deadly Games of Central America

Mayan cities contained ball courts. Usually, a court consisted of a rectangular space surrounded by walls with highly decorated stone rings. The walls were covered with images of war and sacrificial victims. The contestants tried to drive a solid rubber ball through these rings. Ball players, usually two or three on a team, used their hips to propel the ball (they were not allowed to use hands or feet). Players donned helmets, gloves, and knee and hip protectors made of hide to protect themselves against the hard rubber balls. Because the stone rings were placed 27 feet (more than 8 m) above the ground, it took considerable skill to score a goal. Some scholars believe that making a goal was so rare

This Mayan athlete is shown wearing protective padding.

Most of the Mayan people were peasant farmers. They lived on tiny plots or on terraced hills in the highlands. There was a fairly clear-cut division of labor. Men did the fighting and hunting, women the homemaking and raising of children. Women also made cornmeal, the basic food of many Mayans.

Crucial to Mayan civilization was its belief that all of life was in the hands of divine powers. The name of their supreme god was Itzamna (eet-SAWM-nuh) (Lizard House). Gods were ranked in order of importance. Some, like the jaguar god of night, were evil rather than good. Like other ancient civilizations in Central America, the Maya practiced human sacrifice as a way to appease the gods. Human sacrifices were also used for special ceremonial occasions. When a male heir was presented to the throne, war captives were tortured and then beheaded. In A.D. 790, one Mayan ruler took his troops into battle to gain prisoners for a celebration honoring his son as his heir apparent.

Writings and Calendar The Maya created a sophisticated writing system based on hieroglyphs, or pictures. Unfortunately, the Spanish conquerors in the sixteenth century made no effort to decipher the language or respect the Maya's writings. Instead, the Spaniards assumed the writings were evil or of no value. Bishop Diego de Landa said, "We found a large number of books in these characters and, as they contained nothing in which there were not to be seen superstition and lies of the devil, we burned them all, which they regretted to an amazing degree, and which caused them much affliction." In their colonization of the New World, the Spanish would repeat this behavior over and over. They would apply their own religious views to the native civilizations with which they came in contact. The Spaniards' subsequent destruction of religious objects, and sometimes entire cities, helped bring an

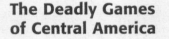

HISTORY Online

Web Activity Visit the *Glencoe World History* Web site at tx.wh.glencoe.com and click on **Chapter 11– Student Web Activity** to learn more about early civilizations in the Americas.

that players were rewarded with clothing and jewelry from the watching crowds.

The exact rules of the game are unknown, but we do know that it was more than a sport. The ball game had a religious meaning. The ball court was a symbol of the world, and the ball represented the sun and the moon. Apparently, it was believed that playing the game often would produce better harvests. The results of the game were deadly. The defeated players were sacrificed in ceremonies held after the end of the game. Similar courts have been found at sites throughout Central America, as well as present-day Arizona and New Mexico.

A present-day soccer match featuring Brazil and Canada

CONNECTING TO THE PAST

1. **Summarizing** Why was great skill required of the athletes who played the Mayan ball game?

2. **Describing** Explain the symbolism of the Mayan ball game.

3. **Writing about History** What other sporting events have you read about that could result in the death of the losing participant?

end to these civilizations. The Maya wrote on bark, folding it like an accordian, then covering the outside with thin plaster. Four of these books have survived. Maya writing was also carved onto clay, jade, bone, shells, and stone monuments.

Mayan hieroglyphs remained a mystery to scholars for centuries. Then, modern investigators discovered that many passages contained symbols that recorded dates in the Mayan calendar known as the Long Count. This calendar was based on a belief in cycles of creation and destruction. According to the Maya, our present world was created in 3114 B.C. and is scheduled to complete its downward cycle on December 23, A.D. 2012.

The Maya used two different systems for measuring time. One was based on a solar calendar of 365 days, divided into 18 months of 20 days each, with an extra 5 days at the end. The other system was based on a sacred calendar of 260 days divided into 13 weeks of 20 days each. Only trained priests could read and use this calendar. They used it to foretell the future and know the omens associated with each day.

Many Mayan hieroglyphs record important events in Mayan history, especially those in the lives of Mayan rulers. One of the most important collections of Mayan hieroglyphs is at Palenque (puh•LEHNG•KAY), deep in the jungles in the neck of the Mexican peninsula. There, archaeologists discovered a royal tomb covered with hieroglyphs that record the accomplishments of a ruler named Pacal, whose body was buried in the tomb.

The Toltec The center of the Toltec Empire was at Tula, built on a high ridge northwest of present-day Mexico City. The **Toltec** were a fierce and warlike people who extended their conquests into the Mayan lands of Guatemala and the northern Yucatán. The Toltec were also builders who constructed pyramids and palaces. They controlled the upper Yucatán Peninsula from another capital at **Chichén Itzá** for several centuries, beginning around A.D. 900. In about 1200 their civilization, too, declined.

✓ **Reading Check** **Describing** How did the Maya measure time?

The Aztec

The origins of the **Aztec** are uncertain. Sometime during the twelfth century A.D., however, they began a long migration that brought them to the Valley of Mexico. They eventually established their capital at **Tenochtitlán** (tay•NAWCH•teet•LAHN), on an island in the middle of **Lake Texcoco,** now the location of Mexico City. There, they would rule until conquered by the Spaniards in the 1500s.

Rise of the Aztec

According to their legends, when the Aztec arrived in the Valley of Mexico, other peoples drove them into a snake-infested region. The Aztec survived, however, strengthened by their belief in a sign that would come from their god of war and of the sun, Huitzilopochtli (wee•tsee•loh• POHKT•lee). The god had told them that when they saw an eagle perched on a cactus growing out of a rock, their journey would end.

In 1325, under attack by another people, they were driven into the swamps and islands of Lake Texcoco. On one of the islands, they saw an eagle standing on a prickly pear cactus on a rock. There they built Tenochtitlán (or "place of the prickly pear cactus"):

"Now we have found the land promised to us. We have found peace for our weary people. Now we want for nothing."

For the next hundred years, the Aztec built their city. They constructed temples, other public buildings, and houses. They built roadways of stone across Lake Texcoco to the north, south, and west, linking the many islands to the mainland.

While they were building their capital city, the Aztec, who were outstanding warriors, consolidated their rule over much of what is modern Mexico. The new kingdom was not a centralized state but a collection of semi-independent territories governed by local lords. The Aztec ruler supported these rulers in their authority in return for tribute, goods or money paid by conquered peoples to their conquerors.

Political and Social Structures

By 1500, as many as four million Aztec lived in the Valley of Mexico and the surrounding valleys of central Mexico.

CONNECTIONS Past To Present

Using the Past to Create a New Future

In the 1920s, after a successful revolution, the new Mexican government sought to create a new image of the Mexican nation and a new sense of national identity for the Mexican people. The revolutionary government enlisted the support of artists to make Mexicans aware of their glorious past.

Diego Rivera, one of Mexico's leading artists, accepted the government's challenge. Between 1920 and 1950, he completed a series of massive paintings on the walls of Mexico's schools and government buildings. In his murals, Rivera used his knowledge of Mexico's past to achieve an imaginative re-creation of the world of the ancient Aztec.

Rivera showed an idealized version of the wonders of the Aztec, as well as their betrayal by the Spaniards: people in the busy markets of the capital city of Tenochtitlán; Aztec doctors performing operations; Aztec people playing instruments and engaged in native arts and crafts; Aztec women grinding corn and preparing tortillas; and Spanish knights armed with guns crushing the Aztec people.

Rivera wanted Mexicans to be aware of their past. He also sought, however, to encourage modern Mexicans to create a civilization as pure, simple, and noble as he imagined that of the Aztec to have been.

▲ *The Aztec World* by Diego Rivera

Comparing Past and Present

Murals and tapestries have long been used to record historical events. Using outside sources, select one well-known historical mural, painting, or tapestry, such as the tapestry of Bayeux. Compare the historic event recorded in the painting or tapestry to a written record of the same event. How are the visual and the written sources similar and different, and why?

Picturing **History**

This mosaic depicts the meeting of Montezuma and Cortés. How has the artist shown that, while offering a gift, Cortés is also a threat to the Aztec?

Power in the Aztec state was vested in the hands of the monarch, who claimed that he was descended from the gods. The Aztec ruler was assisted by a council of lords and government officials.

The rest of the population consisted of commoners, indentured workers, and slaves. Indentured workers were landless laborers who contracted to work on the nobles' estates. Slaves, people captured in war, worked in the households of the wealthy. Most people were commoners, and many commoners were farmers. Others engaged in trade, especially in the densely populated Valley of Mexico, where half of the people lived in cities.

From the beginnings of their lives, boys and girls in Aztec society were given very different roles. As soon as a male baby was born, the midwife who attended the birth said, "You must understand that your home is not here where you have been born, for you are a warrior." To a female infant, the midwife said, "As the heart stays in the body, so you must stay in the house."

Women in Aztec society were not equal to men but they were allowed to own and inherit property and to enter into contracts, something not often allowed in other world cultures at the time. Women were expected to work in the home, weave textiles, and raise children. However, they were also permitted to become priestesses.

Religion and Culture
The Aztec believed in many gods. Huitzilopochtli, the god of the sun and of war, was particularly important. Another important god was the feathered serpent Quetzalcoatl (ket•suhl•KWAH•tul). According to Aztec tradition, this being had left his homeland in the Valley of Mexico in the tenth century, promising to return in triumph. The story of Quetzalcoatl became part of a legend about a Toltec prince whose return from exile would be preceded by the sign of an arrow through a sapling. When the Aztec saw the Spanish with a similar sign—the cross—on their breastplates, the Aztec thought that representatives of Quetzalcoatl had returned.

Aztec religion was based on a belief in an unending struggle between the forces of good and evil throughout the universe. This struggle had led to the creation and destruction of four worlds, or suns. People were living in the time of the fifth sun. However, this world, too, was destined to end with the destruction of the earth by earthquakes.

In an effort to postpone the day of reckoning, the Aztec practiced human sacrifice. They believed that by appeasing the god Huitzilopochtli they could delay the final destruction of their world.

A chief feature of Aztec culture was its monumental architecture. At the center of the capital city of Tenochtitlán was a massive pyramid dedicated to Huitzilopochtli. A platform at the top held shrines to the gods and an altar for performing human sacrifices.

The Destruction of Aztec Civilization
For a century, the Aztec kingdom ruled much of central Mexico from the Gulf of Mexico to the Pacific coasts. Most local officials accepted the authority of the Aztec king in Tenochtitlán. In the region of Tlaxcala to the east, however, the local lords wanted greater independence.

Areas that had never been conquered wanted to remain free of the Aztec.

In 1519, a Spanish force under the command of **Hernán Cortés** landed at Veracruz, on the Gulf of Mexico. Cortés marched to Tenochtitlán at the head of a small body of troops (550 soldiers and 16 horses). As he went, he made alliances with city-states that had tired of the oppressive rule of the Aztec. Particularly important was the alliance with Tlaxcala.

When Cortés arrived at Tenochtitlán, he received a friendly welcome from the Aztec monarch **Montezuma** (also spelled Moctezuma). At first, Montezuma believed that his visitor was a representative of Quetzalcoatl, the god who had departed from his homeland centuries before and had promised that he would return. Montezuma offered gifts of gold to the foreigners and gave them a palace to use while they were in the city.

Eventually, tensions arose between the Spaniards and the Aztec. The Spanish took Montezuma hostage and began to pillage the city. In 1520, one year after Cortés arrived, the local population revolted and drove the invaders from the city. Many of the Spanish were killed.

The Aztec soon experienced new disasters, however. With no natural immunity to the diseases of the Europeans, many of them fell sick and died. Meanwhile, Cortés received fresh soldiers from his new allies, the state of Tlaxcala alone provided fifty thousand warriors. After four months, the city surrendered. The forces of Cortés leveled pyramids,

temples, and palaces and used the stones to build government buildings and churches for the Spanish. The rivers and canals were filled in. As we will see, throughout the Americas, Europeans, using gunpowder first developed in Asia, were able to destroy powerful civilizations weakened by European diseases. The Aztec city of Tenochtitlán was no more.

✓**Reading Check** **Summarizing** What aspect of Aztec culture is reflected in their architecture?

🔲 TAKS Practice

SECTION 2 ASSESSMENT

Checking for Understanding

1. **Define** Mesoamerica, hieroglyph, tribute.

2. **Identify** Olmec, Maya, Toltec, Aztec, Hernán Cortés, Montezuma.

3. **Locate** Teotihuacán, Yucatán Peninsula, Tikal, Chichén Itzá, Tenochtitlán, Lake Texcoco.

4. **Explain** how Mayan hieroglyphs have helped us to understand Mayan culture.

5. **Summarize** the different categories of Aztec society.

Critical Thinking

6. **Evaluate** What was the importance of trade for the early American civilizations?

7. **Summarizing Information** Create a table like the one below listing the major civilizations and principal cities that developed in Mesoamerica.

Mesoamerica	
Civilizations	Cities

Analyzing Visuals

8. **Compare** the sculpture of a Mayan athlete shown on page 354 with the photograph of modern athletes shown on page 355. What inferences can you draw about the status of athletes in Mayan culture? What status do athletes in America have today?

Writing About History

9. **Informative Writing** Imagine that you are the first Aztec warrior to see the perched eagle in Lake Texcoco. Write a paragraph about what the eagle means and why it is important to you and your culture.

Early Civilizations in South America

Guide to Reading

Main Ideas
- The Inca developed a well-organized, militaristic empire.
- Incan communities undertook sophisticated building projects and established a high level of cultural development.

Key Terms
maize, *quipu*

People to Identify
Moche, Inca, Pachacuti, Francisco Pizarro

Places to Locate
Ecuador, Cuzco, Machu Picchu, Urubamba River

Preview Questions
1. What does Moche pottery tell us about the Moche people?
2. What method did the Inca use to enlarge their empire?

Reading Strategy
Organizing Information As you read this section, complete a pyramid diagram showing the hierarchy of the Inca's political organization.

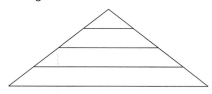

Preview of Events

◆700	◆850	◆1000	◆1150	◆1300	◆1450	◆1600

c. 700
Moche civilization collapses

1440
Incan ruler Pachacuti builds empire

1535
Pizarro conquers the Inca

Voices from the Past

The Sun Temple at Cuzco

In their capital city of Cuzco, the Inca built a temple dedicated to the sun. A Spanish observer described it as follows:

❝[The temple] is built of smooth masonry, very level and smooth. The roof was of wood and very lofty so that there would be plenty of air. It was covered with thatch: they had no tiles. All four walls of the temple were covered from top to bottom with plates and slabs of gold. Over what we have called the high altar they had the image of the Sun on a gold plate twice the thickness of the rest of the wall-plates. The image showed him with a round face and beams and flames of fire all in one piece, just as he is usually depicted by painters. It was so large that it stretched over the whole of that side of the temple from wall to wall.❞

— *Royal Commentaries of the Incas: And General History of Peru,*
Harold V. Livermore, trans., 1966

Known as accomplished builders of impressive structures, the Inca flourished in South America during the 1400s.

Early Civilizations

Caral has been identified as the oldest major city in the Americas. Caral is believed to be one thousand years older than the ancient cities previously known in the Western Hemisphere. Located in the Supe River valley of Peru, the city contains buildings for officials, apartment buildings, and grand residences, all built of stone. The inhabitants of Caral also developed a system of irrigation by diverting a river more than a mile (1.609 km) upstream into their fields. Caral was abandoned between 2000 and 1500 B.C.

Sometime about 200 B.C., another advanced civilization appeared near the Pacific coast not far south of the border of **Ecuador.** At Moche (MOH•cheh), a major urban center arose amid irrigated fields in the valley of the Moche River, which flows from the foothills of the Andes into the Pacific Ocean. Farmers in the area grew enough maize (corn), peanuts, potatoes, and cotton to supply much of the region.

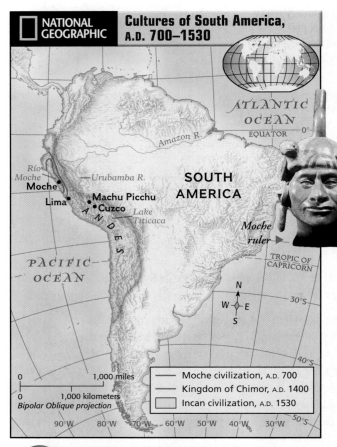

Geography Skills

The Moche, Chimor, and Incan peoples developed advanced civilizations in South America.

1. **Interpreting Maps** Estimate in miles the length of the Incan Empire.
2. **Applying Geography Skills** Create your own map of the Incan Empire. Using your text as a guide, add the Incan system of roads to your map.

Moche was the capital of a powerful state. The authority of the Moche rulers extended far along the coast. The people of Moche had no written language, but their pottery gives us some idea of their interests. Among other things, the pottery shows that the **Moche,** like peoples in Central America, led lives centered around warfare. Paintings and pottery frequently portray warriors, prisoners, and sacrificial victims.

✔ **Reading Check** **Explaining** What was the importance of the Moche River to the people who lived near it?

The Inca

After the collapse of the Moche civilization around A.D. 700, a period of decline set in until the rise of a new power about three hundred years later. This power, the kingdom of Chimor, dominated the area for nearly four centuries. It was finally destroyed by people who created an even more spectacular empire—the **Inca.**

In the late 1300s, the Inca were only a small community in the area of **Cuzco** (KOOS•koh), a city located high, 11,000 feet (3,352.8 m), in the mountains of southern Peru. In the 1440s, however, under the leadership of the powerful ruler **Pachacuti,** the Inca launched a campaign of conquest that eventually brought the entire region under their control.

Political Structures Pachacuti and his immediate successors, Topa Inca and Huayna Inca (the word *Inca* means "ruler"), extended the boundaries of the Incan Empire as far as Ecuador, central Chile, and the edge of the Amazon basin. The empire included perhaps twelve million people.

The Incan state was built on war, so all young men were required to serve in the Incan army. With some two hundred thousand members, the army was the largest and best armed in the region. Because the Inca, like other people in the early Americas, did not make use of the wheel, supplies were carried on the backs of llamas.

Once an area was placed under Incan control, the local inhabitants were instructed in the Quechua (KEH•chuh•wuh) language. Control of new territories was carefully regulated. A noble of high rank was sent out to govern the new region. Local leaders could keep their posts as long as they were loyal to the Inca ruler.

To create a well-organized empire, Pachacuti divided it into four quarters, with each ruled by a

Pachacuti
?–1471—Incan ruler

Pachacuti was the founder of the Incan Empire. Through his conquests, he expanded the small Incan state he inherited into an empire. He also created a highly centralized government and insisted that its officials be honest. He decreed that "any judge who permitted himself to be bribed should be regarded as a thief and, as such, punished with death."

Pachacuti made visits to the various parts of his empire. On these trips, he traveled in litters—covered couches used for carrying passengers—surrounded by guards and carrying jewels and riches with him. Pachacuti was also a builder. The capital of Cuzco was transformed from a city of mud and thatch into an imposing city of stone during his reign.

governor. In turn, the quarters were divided into provinces, each also ruled by a governor. Each province was supposed to contain about ten thousand residents. At the top of the entire system was the emperor, who was believed to be descended from Inti, the sun god.

Forced labor was another important feature of the state. All Incan subjects were responsible for labor service, usually for several weeks each year. Laborers, often with their entire communities, were moved according to need from one part of the country to another to take part in building projects.

The Inca also built roads. A system of some 24,800 miles (around 40,000 km) of roads extended from the border of modern-day Colombia to a point south of modern-day Santiago, Chile. Two major roadways extended in a north-south direction, one through the Andes and the other along the coast, with connecting routes between them.

Rest houses, located a day's walk apart, and storage depots were placed along the roads. Various types of bridges, including some of the finest examples of suspension bridges in premodern times, were built over ravines and waterways.

Social Structures Incan society was highly regimented. So, too, were marriage and the lives of women. Men and women were required to select a marriage partner from within their own social groups. After marriage, women were expected to care for the children and to weave cloth. For women, there was only one alternative to a life of working in the home. Some young girls were chosen to serve as priestesses in temples.

In rural areas, the people lived chiefly by farming. In the mountains, they used terraced farms, watered by irrigation systems that carried precise amounts of water into the fields. These were planted with corn, potatoes, and other crops. The houses of the farmers, built of stone or adobe with thatched roofs, were located near the fields.

Building and Culture The Inca were great builders. The buildings and monuments of the capital city of Cuzco were the wonder of early European visitors. These structures were built of close-fitting stones with no mortar—the better to withstand the frequent earthquakes in the area.

Nothing shows the architectural genius of the Inca more than the ruins of the abandoned city of **Machu Picchu** (MAH•CHOO PEE•CHOO). Machu Picchu, elevation 8,000 feet (2,400 m), was built on a lofty hilltop surrounded by mountain peaks far above the **Urubamba River.** It was a small city, containing only about two hundred buildings.

In one part of Machu Picchu, a long stairway leads to an elegant stone known to the Inca as the "hitching post of the sun." Carved from the mountain, this "hitching post" may have been used as a solar

The 50-foot-tall stone walls of Cuzco were built without mortar by the Inca.

Picturing History

This Peruvian print from 1609 shows an Incan man using the *quipu*. What information about the past can historians gain from this image?

observatory. During the sun festivals held in June and December, the people of Machu Picchu gathered here to chant and say prayers to Inti, the sun god.

The Inca had no writing system but instead kept records using a system of knotted strings called the *quipu*. However, the lack of a fully developed writing system did not prevent the Inca from attaining a high level of cultural achievement.

The Inca had a well-developed tradition of court theater, consisting of both tragic and comic works. Plays often involved the recounting of valiant deeds and other historical events. Actors were not professionals but rather members of the nobility or senior officials who memorized their parts. Poetry was also recited, often accompanied by music played on reed instruments.

Conquest of the Inca The Incan Empire was still flourishing when the first Spanish expeditions arrived in the central Andes. In 1531, **Francisco Pizarro** and a small band of about 180 men landed on the Pacific coast of South America. Pizarro brought steel weapons, gunpowder, and horses. The Inca had seen none of these.

The Incan Empire experienced an epidemic of smallpox. Like the Aztec, the Inca had no immunities to European diseases. All too soon, smallpox was devastating entire villages. Even the Incan emperor was a victim.

When the emperor died, each of his two sons claimed the throne for himself. This led to a civil war. Atahuallpa (AH•tuh•WAHL•puh), one of the sons, defeated his brother's forces. Pizarro took advantage of the situation by capturing Atahuallpa. Armed only with stones, arrows, and light spears, Atahuallpa's soldiers provided little challenge to the charging horses, guns, and cannons of the Spanish.

After executing Atahuallpa, Pizarro and his soldiers, aided by Incan allies, marched on Cuzco and captured the Incan capital. By 1535, Pizarro had established a new capital at Lima for a new colony of the Spanish Empire.

✓ **Reading Check** **Describing** How did the Inca farm in the mountains?

🟥 **TAKS Practice**

SECTION 3 ASSESSMENT

Checking for Understanding

1. **Define** maize, *quipu*.

2. **Identify** Moche, Inca, Pachacuti, Francisco Pizarro.

3. **Locate** Ecuador, Cuzco, Machu Picchu, Urubamba River.

4. **Describe** the Incan system of forced labor.

5. **List** evidence historians use to support the claim that the Moche led lives centered around warfare.

Critical Thinking

6. **Evaluate** How did Pachacuti expand the Incan state into an empire?

7. **Summarizing Information** Create a graphic organizer like the one below to summarize the ways that the Incan system of roads unified the empire.

```
        ○        ○
          \    /
  ○ ─ ( Incan Road System ) ─ ○
          /    \
        ○        ○
```

Analyzing Visuals

8. **Examine** the photograph of the Incan temple at Cuzco, Peru, shown on page 359. What architectural elements does the Incan temple have that are also seen in buildings from other cultures you have read about?

Writing About History

9. **Expository Writing** Write an essay in which you explain the advantages and the disadvantages of the political system of the Inca.

The Quipu

THE INCA DID NOT POSSESS A WRITTEN language. To record events and other aspects of their lives that they wished to remember, they used a system of knotted strings, called the *quipu.* This is a sixteenth-century description of the process.

The **quipu** *was made from woven strands of different-colored yarn.*

❝These men recorded on their knots all the tribute brought annually to the Inca, specifying everything by kind, species, and quality. They recorded the number of men who went to the wars, how many died in them, and how many were born and died every year, month by month. In short they may be said to have recorded on their knots everything that could be counted, even mentioning battles and fights, all the [ambassadors who] had come to visit the Inca, and all the speeches and arguments the king had uttered. But the purpose of the [diplomatic visits] or the contents of the speeches, or any other descriptive matter could not be recorded on the knots, consisting as it did of continuous spoken or written prose, which cannot be expressed by means of knots, since these can only give numbers and not words. To supply this want they used signs that indicated historical events or facts or the existence of any [diplomatic visit], speech, or discussion in time of peace or war. Such speeches were committed to memory and taught by tradition to their successors and descendants from father to son. . . . Another method too was used for keeping alive in the memory of the people their deeds and the [ambassadors] they sent to the Inca and the replies [the king] gave them. The philosophers and sages took the trouble to turn them into stories, no longer than fables, suitable for telling to children, young people, and the rustics of the countryside: they were thus passed from hand to hand and age to age, and preserved in the memories of all. . . . Similarly their poets composed short, compressed poems, embracing a history, or [a diplomatic visit], or the king's reply. In short, everything that could not be recorded on the knots was included in these poems, which were sung at their triumphs. Thus they remembered their history.❞

—**Garcilaso de la Vega,** *Royal Commentaries of the Incas: And General History of Peru*

Analyzing Primary Sources

1. What did the *quipu* record? What was it unable to record?
2. In what other ways and from what other sources was the history of the Inca preserved?

Using Key Terms

1. The Iroquois built _____, made of wooden poles and covered with bark, to house many families.

2. The Inca used knotted strings, called the _____, to keep records.

3. Within each Iroquois group were _____, groups of related families.

4. Circular tents, or _____, were made of buffalo skins stretched over wooden poles.

5. Sun-dried bricks are called _____.

6. _____ were multistoried structures built by the Anasazi.

7. The Aztec ruler allowed others to rule semi-independent territories if they paid _____, goods or money paid by those conquered.

8. The areas of Mexico and Central America that had civilizations before Europeans arrived are called _____.

9. The Mayan system of writing was based on pictures called _____.

Reviewing Key Facts

10. **Geography** Name two major mountain ranges in the western portion of the Americas.

11. **Culture** How many people did some of the urban centers of the Hopewell people contain?

12. **Culture** What were the names of the "three sisters" crops farmed by the Iroquois?

13. **Government** The phrase "self-interest shall be cast away" comes from which Iroquois statement?

14. **History** How did the Plains Indians capture buffalo without using weapons?

15. **History** What did the Spanish bring to the Americas that contributed to the destruction of the early civilizations?

16. **Science and Technology** According to the Mayan calendar, when will the world complete its downward cycle?

17. **Religion** What did the Aztec believe when they saw the crosses on the Spanish breastplates?

18. **Geography** At what altitude did the Inca build Cuzco?

19. **Culture** Why did the Inca use the *quipu?*

Critical Thinking

20. **Making Comparisons** How are the pyramids of the Americas similar to the pyramids of Egypt? Why is this style of building found around the world?

21. **Evaluating** How are the houses of the North American peoples a reflection of the geography of their regions?

22. **Drawing Conclusions** Why did Incan rulers insist that all conquered peoples be taught the Quechua language?

Chapter Summary

The table below summarizes the factors that helped shape early cultures in the Americas.

Location	People	Economics	Architecture
Eastern Woodlands	Mound Builders, Iroquois	Hunting and gathering, some agriculture	Longhouses, some urban centers
Central Plains	Plains	Hunting and gathering	Tepees
Southwest	Anasazi	Extensive farming	Cliff dwellings
Mesoamerica	Olmec, Maya, Aztec	Farming, trade	Large cities, religious and political structures
South America	Moche, Inca	Farming, trade	Large cities, religious and political structures

Writing About History

23. **Expository Writing** Choose a Mesoamerican society from this chapter and write a brief essay describing how geography affected the following: how food was obtained, the materials used for homes and other structures, the size of communities, the need for trade, the impact of natural boundaries such as mountains and bodies of water, and the sources of drinking water.

Analyzing Sources

Read the following quote by Bernal Díaz who accompanied Cortéz on his expedition to Mexico in 1519.

> ❝When we beheld so many cities and towns on the water, and other large settlements built on firm ground, and that broad causeway running so straight and perfectly level to the city of Tenochtitlán, we were astonished because of the great stone towers and temples and buildings that rose up out of the water.❞

24. Which early civilization built the city of Tenochtitlán?

25. Why were the Spanish so "astonished" by what they saw?

26. What was the final result of this encounter between the Spanish and the civilization described in the quote?

Applying Technology Skills

27. **Using the Internet** Access the Internet to locate a Web site that has information about the ancient Incan Empire. Use a search engine to help focus your search by using phrases such as *Incan Empire, Mesoamerican civilization,* or *Native Americans.* Create a bulletin board using the information found on the Web site and incorporate illustrations of Incan culture and artifacts. Include captions with your photos and illustrations.

Making Decisions

28. Early civilizations had to survive with little technology, knowledge of the world, or grocery stores. Imagine that you and a group of friends are stranded on a deserted island. Make a list of things you hope you will find on the island in order to survive, and how you will stay alive until you are rescued.

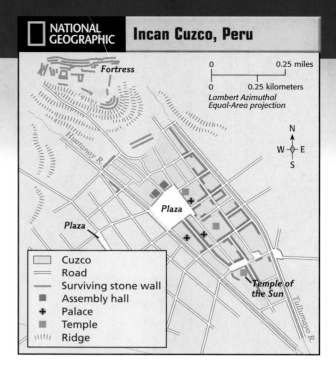

NATIONAL GEOGRAPHIC Incan Cuzco, Peru

Map legend: Cuzco, Road, Surviving stone wall, Assembly hall, Palace, Temple, Ridge

Analyzing Maps and Charts

European visitors were amazed by the buildings and monuments of the Incan capital at Cuzco. Use the above map to answer the following questions.

29. Approximately how long was the city of Cuzco?

30. What natural boundaries surround Cuzco? Where did the Inca build boundaries? Why were man-made boundaries needed?

31. The Inca developed a vast road system. What do you notice about the roads leading out of Cuzco?

32. How might geographical factors have influenced the placement of buildings in Cuzco?

The Princeton Review

TAKS Test Practice

Directions: Choose the best answer to the following question.

The League of Iroquois was important because it

A protected the Aztec from Hernán Cortés.

B was created by Deganawida and Hiawatha.

C was an early American form of the democratic assembly.

D established the Mayan calendar.

Test-Taking Tip: Some answer choices are better than others. Be sure you have read *all* the choices carefully before you pick your answer.

WORLD LITERATURE

Five Poems

by Li Bo

Li Bo was born in A.D. 701 in western China. People began praising his beautiful poems even before he reached adulthood. Throughout his life he traveled extensively in China, amazing people with his ability to compose insightful, touching poems. He wrote about the world around him, the people he met, and the emotions he felt. By the time of his death in A.D. 762, he was regarded as one of China's greatest poets, a distinction he still holds today.

In the following poems, Li Bo interprets parting from a friend, life as a journey, and his experience with his homeland.

Read to Discover

As you read, note the ways in which Li Bo draws the reader into his descriptions. What emotions do his poems evoke in you?

Reader's Dictionary

brooklet: a small brook or creek

sparse: few and scattered

thrush: a type of small to medium sized bird that is an excellent singer

Taking Leave of a Friend

Blue mountains to the north of the walls,
White river winding about them;
Here we must make separation
And go out through a thousand miles
    of dead grass.

Mind like a floating wide cloud,
Sunset like the parting of old acquaintances
Who bow over their clasped hands at a distance.
Our horses neigh to each other as we are departing.

▲ *This painting is titled* Spring Dawn Over Elixir Terrace.

Clearing at Dawn

The fields are chill, the sparse
    rain has stopped;
The colours of Spring teem
    on every side.
With leaping fish the blue pond
    is full;
With singing thrushes the green
    boughs droop.
The flowers of the field have
    dabbled their powdered cheeks;
The mountain grasses are bent
    level at the waist.
By the bamboo stream the last
    fragment of cloud
Blown by the wind slowly
    scatters away.

Hard Is the Journey

Gold vessels of fine wines,
  thousands a gallon,
Jade dishes of rare meats,
  costing more thousands,
I lay my chopsticks down,
  no more can banquet,
And draw my sword and stare
  wildly about me:

Ice bars my way to cross
  the Yellow River,
Snows from dark skies to climb
  the T'ai-hang Mountains!

At peace I drop a hook
  into a brooklet,
At once I'm in a boat
  but sailing sunward . . .

  (Hard is the Journey,
  Hard is the Journey,
  So many turnings,
  And now where am I?)

So when a breeze breaks waves,
  bringing fair weather,
I set a cloud for sails,
  cross the blue oceans!

Landscape of the Four Seasons *by Shen shih-Ch'ung* ▲

In the Mountains on a Summer Day

Gently I stir a white feather fan,
With open shirt sitting in a green wood.
I take off my cap and hang it on a jutting stone;
A wind from the pine-tree trickles on my bare
  head.

Listening to a Flute
in Yellow Crane Pavilion

I came here a wanderer
thinking of home
remembering my far away Ch'ang-an.
And then, from deep in Yellow Crane Pavilion,
I heard a beautiful bamboo flute
play "Falling Plum Blossoms."
It was late spring in a city by the river.

Interpreting World Literature

1. What detail in *Taking Leave of a Friend* reveals a custom specific to Li Bo's times?

2. What happens between the beginning of the first stanza and the end of the second stanza of *Hard Is the Journey?*

3. What is the significance of the last line of *Listening to a Flute in Yellow Crane Pavilion?*

4. **CRITICAL THINKING** Li Bo describes beauty and peace and luxury in *Hard Is the Journey.* Why do you think he calls the journey "hard"?

Applications Activity

Write a poem describing your hometown. Make sure to include a description of something unique to that area.

UNIT 3

The Early Modern World

1400–1800

The **P**eriod in Perspective

Beginning in the late fifteenth century, Europeans engaged in a vigorous period of state building. The result was the creation of independent monarchies in western and central Europe that formed the basis of a new European state system. These European states then began to expand into the rest of the world.

Also during this period, two great new Islamic empires, the Ottomans in Turkey and the Safavids in Persia, arose in Southwest Asia. A third Islamic empire—the Mogul Empire—unified the subcontinent of India. Least affected by the European expansion were the societies of East Asia: China and Japan.

Primary Sources Library

See pages 994–995 for primary source readings to accompany Unit 3.

💿 *Use The World History **Primary Source Document Library CD-ROM** to find additional primary sources about The Early Modern World .*

▲ A model of the Copernican system

▶ A European navigator uses an astrolabe.

> *"Dare to Know."*
>
> —*Immanuel Kant*

Looking Back...

Revolution

In the 1600s and 1700s, revolution traveled back and forth across the Atlantic Ocean. The pattern started with the arrival of the first English colonists in North America. The colonists carried with them ideals born of the English Revolution. They believed that governments existed to protect the rights and freedoms of citizens.

1633
Galileo is tried by the Catholic Church for heresy

1642
The English Revolution begins

1775
The American Revolution begins

❶ *The United States*

Revolutionary Ideas

The spark that sent the spirit of revolution flashing across Europe and the Americas began in the minds of sixteenth-century European scientists. Galileo and others challenged established scientific ideas supported by the Catholic Church. Political authority began to be questioned.

In 1776, American colonists took steps to win their freedom from Great Britain. Thomas Jefferson, the principal author of the Declaration of Independence, clearly stated the reasons for proclaiming independence:

We hold these truths to be self-evident, that all men are created equal, that they are endowed by their Creator with certain unalienable Rights, that among these are Life, Liberty, and the pursuit of Happiness.

Signing of the Declaration of Independence

to See Ahead

French Revolution

❷ *France*

The Expanding Revolution

The revolutionary ideas contained within the Declaration of Independence traveled back across the Atlantic to influence the French Revolution. French rebels fought in defense of *Liberté, Egalité, and Fraternité*. In 1789, French revolutionaries drafted the Declaration of the Rights of Man and the Citizen. Echoing the principles of the Declaration of Independence, the French declaration proclaimed that, "Men are born and remain free and equal in rights."

1776
The Declaration of Independence is signed

1789
The French Revolution begins

1804
Saint Domingue achieves independence

❸ *Haiti*

Exporting Revolution

In 1791, the ideals of the American and French Revolutions traveled across the Atlantic and the Caribbean to the French-held colony of Saint Domingue on the island of Hispaniola. Inspired by talk of freedom, enslaved Africans took up arms. Led by a formerly enslaved man, Toussaint-Louverture, and other island leaders, the rebels fought for thirteen years against the French. On January 1, 1804, Saint Domingue, present-day Haiti, became the second nation in the Americas to achieve independence from colonial rule. "We have asserted our rights," declared the revolutionaries. "We swear never to yield them to any power on earth."

Toussaint-Louverture

Why It Matters

Political and intellectual revolutions changed the way people thought about established ideas and institutions. How did this change in perception eventually lead to the American view of government today?

12 Renaissance and Reformation

1350–1600

Key Events

As you read, look for the key events in the history of the Renaissance and the Reformation in Europe.

- *Between 1350 and 1550, Italian intellectuals began to reexamine the culture of the Greeks and Romans. Historians later referred to this period of European history as the Renaissance.*
- *Martin Luther's break with the Catholic Church led to the emergence of the Protestant Reformation.*
- *During the period known as the Catholic Reformation, the Catholic Church enacted a series of reforms that were successful in strengthening the Church.*

The Impact Today

The events that occurred during this time period still impact our lives today.

- *Western art is founded on classical styles developed by the Greeks and Romans.*
- *Machiavelli's views on politics had a profound influence on later political leaders in the Western world and are still studied in universities today.*
- *The Jesuits have founded many Catholic colleges and universities in the United States.*

World History Video *The Chapter 12 video, "Da Vinci: A Renaissance Man," chronicles Leonardo da Vinci's numerous artistic and scientific innovations.*

c. 1350
The Italian Renaissance begins

Page from the Gutenberg Bible

c. 1455
Gutenberg prints Bible using movable type

1350   1400   1450

Cosimo de' Medici

1434
The de' Medici family takes control of Florence

c. 1450
Christian humanism spreads in northern Europe

Renaissance art and architecture flourished in Florence. The Duomo, a Renaissance church, contains artwork by many important Renaissance artists.

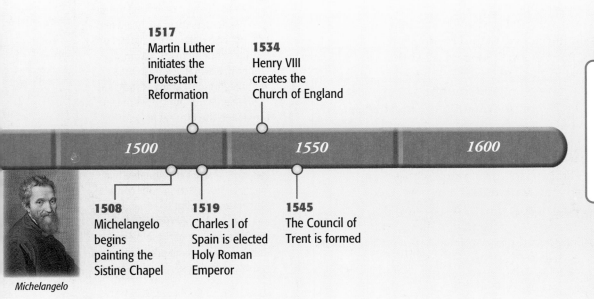

1517
Martin Luther initiates the Protestant Reformation

1534
Henry VIII creates the Church of England

1500   **1550**   **1600**

1508
Michelangelo begins painting the Sistine Chapel

1519
Charles I of Spain is elected Holy Roman Emperor

1545
The Council of Trent is formed

Michelangelo

HISTORY
Online

Chapter Overview
Visit the *Glencoe World History* Web site at tx.wh.glencoe.com and click on **Chapter 12–Chapter Overview** to preview chapter information.

A Story That Matters

This detail from the Sistine Chapel is titled **The Creation of Adam.**

Painting the Sistine Chapel

Around 1500, Pope Julius II wanted the great Italian artist Michelangelo to paint the ceiling of the Sistine Chapel in Rome. "This is not my trade," Michelangelo protested; he was a sculptor, not a painter. He recommended other painters to the pope, but the pope persisted.

Michelangelo needed the money and undertook the project. He worked, on and off, for four years, from May 1508 to October 1512. For a long time he refused to allow anyone, including the pope, to see his work.

Julius grew anxious and pestered Michelangelo on a regular basis about when the ceiling would be finished. Tired of the pope's requests, Michelangelo once replied that the ceiling would be completed "when it satisfies me as an artist." The pope responded, "We want you to finish it soon." He then threatened that if Michelangelo did not "finish the ceiling quickly he would have him thrown down from the scaffolding."

Fearing the pope's anger, Michelangelo quickly completed his work. When he climbed down from the scaffold for the last time, he was tired and worn out. Because he had been on his back so long while painting the ceiling, it was said that he now found it easier to read by holding a book up rather than down. The Sistine Chapel ceiling, however, is one of the great masterpieces in the history of Western art.

Why It Matters

In the fifteenth century, intellectuals in Italy were convinced that they had made a decisive break with the Middle Ages and had entered a new age of human achievement. Today, we call this period of European history the Renaissance. Michelangelo was but one of the great figures of this time. Another was Martin Luther of Germany, whose break with the Roman Catholic Church at the beginning of the sixteenth century led to the Protestant Reformation and a new era in the history of Christianity.

History And You Identify two pieces of public art in your community. Research what commendations or criticism the city received following the unveiling of these pieces. Create a multimedia presentation with your findings.

The Renaissance

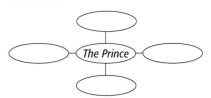
Voices from the Past

Cesare Borgia

Inspired by Cesare Borgia, who conquered central Italy and set up a state, Niccolò Machiavelli wrote *The Prince,* a short work on political power. He said:

❝Everyone realizes how praiseworthy it is for a prince to honor his word and to be straightforward rather than crafty in his dealings; nonetheless experience shows that princes who have achieved great things have been those who have given their word lightly, who have known how to trick men with their cunning, and who, in the end, have overcome those abiding by honest principles. . . . A prince, therefore, need not necessarily have all the good qualities I mentioned above, but he should certainly appear to have them. . . . He should not deviate from what is good, if that is possible, but he should know how to do evil, if that is necessary.❞

—*The Prince,* George Bull, trans., 1981

The Prince reflected the practice of politics in Renaissance Italy.

The Italian Renaissance

The word *renaissance* means rebirth. A number of people who lived in Italy between 1350 and 1550 believed that they had witnessed a rebirth of the ancient Greek and Roman worlds. To them, this rebirth marked a new age. Historians later called this period the Renaissance, or Italian Renaissance—a period of European history that began in Italy and spread to the rest of Europe. What, then, are the most important characteristics of the Italian Renaissance?

First, Renaissance Italy was largely an urban society. As the Middle Ages progressed, powerful city-states became the centers of Italian political, economic, and social life. Within this growing urban society, a secular, or worldly, viewpoint

This painting by Luca Carlevaris, titled The Pier and the Ducal Palace, *shows the wealth associated with Venice.*

emerged as increasing wealth created new possibilities for the enjoyment of material things.

Second, the Renaissance was an age of recovery from the disasters of the fourteenth century such as the plague, political instability, and a decline of Church power. Recovery went hand in hand with a rebirth of interest in ancient culture. Italian thinkers became aware of their own Roman past—the remains of which were to be seen all around them. They also became intensely interested in the culture that had dominated the ancient Mediterranean world. This revival affected both politics and art.

Third, a new view of human beings emerged as people in the Italian Renaissance began to emphasize individual ability. As Leon Battista Alberti, a fifteenth-century Italian, said, "Men can do all things if they will." A high regard for human worth and a realization of what individuals could achieve created a new social ideal. The well-rounded, universal person was capable of achievements in many areas of life. **Leonardo da Vinci** (VIHN•chee), for example, was a painter, sculptor, architect, inventor, and mathematician.

Of course, not all parts of Italian society were directly affected by these three general characteristics of the Italian Renaissance. The wealthy upper classes, who made up a small percentage of the total population, more actively embraced the new ideas and activities. Indirectly, however, the Italian Renaissance did have some impact on ordinary people. Especially in the cities, many of the intellectual and artistic achievements of the period were highly visible and difficult to ignore. The churches, wealthy homes, and public buildings were decorated with art that celebrated religious and secular themes, the human body, and an appreciation of classical antiquity.

✓ Reading Check **Summarizing** What were the characteristics of the Italian Renaissance?

The Italian States

During the Middle Ages, Italy had failed to develop a centralized monarchical state. The lack of a single strong ruler made it possible for a number of city-states in northern and central Italy to remain independent. Three of them—**Milan, Venice,** and

Florence—expanded and played crucial roles in Italian politics.

The Italian city-states prospered from a flourishing trade that had expanded in the Middle Ages. Italian cities traded with both the Byzantine and Islamic civilizations to the east. Italian trading ships had also moved into the western Mediterranean and then north along the Atlantic seaboard. These ships exchanged goods with merchants in both England and the Netherlands. Italian merchants had profited from the Crusades as well and were able to set up new trading centers in eastern ports. There, the Italian merchants obtained silks, sugar, and spices, which they carried back to Italy and the West.

Milan Milan, located in northern Italy at the crossroads of the main trade routes from Italian coastal cities to the Alpine passes, was one of the richest city-states in Italy. In the fourteenth century, members of the Visconti family established themselves as dukes of Milan and extended their power over all of Lombardy.

The last Visconti ruler of Milan died in 1447. **Francesco Sforza** then conquered the city and became its new duke. Sforza was the leader of a band of mercenaries—soldiers who sold their services to the highest bidder.

Both the Visconti and Sforza rulers worked to build a strong

Francesco Sforza, Duke of Milan

centralized state. By creating an efficient tax system, they generated enormous revenues for the government.

Venice Another major northern Italian city-state was the republic of Venice. As a link between Asia and western Europe the city drew traders from all over the world. Officially Venice was a republic with an elected leader called a *Doge*. In reality a small group of merchant-aristocrats, who had become wealthy through their trading activities, ran the government of Venice on behalf of their own interests. Venice's trade empire was tremendously profitable and made Venice an international power.

Florence The republic of Florence dominated the region of Tuscany. In the course of the fourteenth century, a small but wealthy group of merchants established control of the Florentine government. They led the Florentines in a series of successful wars against their neighbors and established Florence as a major city-state in northern Italy.

In 1434, **Cosimo de' Medici** (MEH•duh•chee) took control of the city. The wealthy Medici family controlled the government from behind the scenes. Using their wealth and personal influence, Cosimo, and later **Lorenzo de' Medici,** his

Lorenzo de' Medici

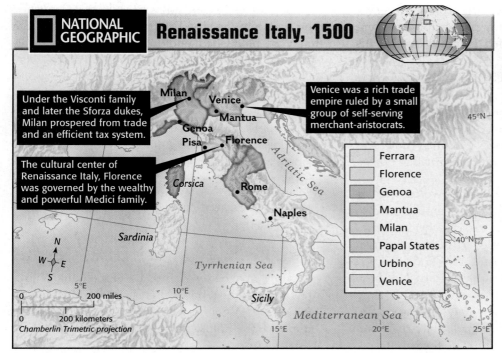

NATIONAL GEOGRAPHIC **Renaissance Italy, 1500**

Under the Visconti family and later the Sforza dukes, Milan prospered from trade and an efficient tax system.

Venice was a rich trade empire ruled by a small group of self-serving merchant-aristocrats.

The cultural center of Renaissance Italy, Florence was governed by the wealthy and powerful Medici family.

Milan
Venice
Mantua
Genoa
Pisa
Florence
Corsica
Rome
Naples
Sardinia
Adriatic Sea
Tyrrhenian Sea
Sicily
Mediterranean Sea

Ferrara
Florence
Genoa
Mantua
Milan
Papal States
Urbino
Venice

N
W E
S

0   200 miles
0   200 kilometers
Chamberlin Trimetric projection

5°E   10°E   15°E   20°E   25°E
45°N
40°N

Geography Skills

Italian city-states prospered during the Renaissance.

1. **Interpreting Maps** Using your text, identify the three most powerful city-states. What geographic features did they have in common?

2. **Applying Geography Skills** Which city-state was in the best location to trade by land and sea with the Byzantine Empire to the east?

grandson, dominated the city at a time when Florence was the cultural center of Italy.

During the late 1400s, Florence experienced an economic decline. Most of its economy was based on the manufacturing of cloth. Increased competition from English and Flemish cloth makers drove down profits.

During this time a Dominican preacher named Girolamo Savonarola began condemning the corruption and excesses of the Medici family. Citizens, tired of Medici rule and frustrated by economic events, turned to Savonarola. So many people followed him that the Medici family turned Florence over to his followers.

Eventually people tired of Savonarola's strict regulations on gambling, horseracing, swearing, painting, music, and books. Savonarola also attacked the corruption of the Church, which angered the pope. In 1498, Savonarola was accused of heresy and sentenced to death. The Medici family returned to power.

The Italian Wars The growth of powerful monarchical states in the rest of Europe eventually led to trouble for the Italian states. Attracted by the riches of Italy, the French king Charles VIII led an army of thirty thousand men into Italy in 1494 and occupied the kingdom of Naples in southern Italy. Northern Italian states turned for help to the Spanish, who gladly agreed to send soldiers to Italy. For the next 30 years, the French and Spanish made Italy their battleground as they fought to dominate the country.

A decisive turning point in their war came in 1527. On May 5, thousands of troops belonging to the Spanish king Charles I arrived at the city of **Rome** along with mercenaries from different countries. They had not been paid for months. When they yelled, "Money! Money!" their leader responded, "If you have ever dreamed of pillaging a town and laying hold of its treasures, here now is one, the richest of them all, queen of the world." The next day the invading forces smashed down the gates and pushed their way into the city. The troops went berserk in a frenzy of bloodshed and looting. Church officials were sold as slaves, and churches and palaces were sacked while drunken soldiers fought over the spoils. The destruction did not end until the authorities were finally forced to establish some order. The terrible sack of Rome in 1527 by the armies of the Spanish king Charles I ended the Italian wars and left the Spanish a dominant force in Italy.

Reading Check **Describing** How did the Visconti and Sforza rulers become powerful in Milan?

Machiavelli and the New Statecraft

No one gave better expression to the Italians' love affair with political power than **Niccolò Machiavelli** (MA•kee•uh•VEH•lee). His book *The Prince* is one of the most influential works on political power in the Western world.

Machiavelli, as portrayed by Santi di Tito

Machiavelli's central thesis in *The Prince* concerns how to acquire—and keep—political power. In the Middle Ages, many writers on political power had stressed the ethical side of a prince's activity—how a ruler ought to behave based on Christian principles. Machiavelli rejected this approach.

From Machiavelli's point of view, a prince's attitude toward power must be based on an understanding of human nature, which he believed was basically self-centered. He wrote, "One can make this generalization about men: they are ungrateful, fickle, liars, and deceivers, they shun danger and are greedy for profit." Political activity, therefore, should not be restricted by moral principles. A prince acts on behalf of the state. For the sake of the state, he must be willing to let his conscience sleep.

Machiavelli was among the first to abandon morality as the basis for analyzing political activity. His views on politics have had a profound influence on political leaders who followed.

✓ **Reading Check** **Explaining** Why was *The Prince* an important work on political power?

Renaissance Society

In the Middle Ages, society was divided into three estates, or social classes (see Chapter 9). Although this social order continued into the Renaissance, some changes became evident. We examine the nobility and the peasants and townspeople here. The clergy are discussed later in the chapter.

The Nobility Throughout much of Europe, land-holding nobles were faced with declining incomes

during the greater part of the fourteenth and fifteenth centuries. Many members of the old nobility, however, retained their lands and titles; new blood also came into their ranks.

By 1500, nobles, old and new, again dominated society. Although they made up only about 2 to 3 percent of the population in most countries, the nobles held important political posts and served as advisers to the king.

By this time, the noble, or aristocrat, was expected to fulfill certain ideals. These ideals were clearly expressed in *The Book of the Courtier,* written by the Italian Baldassare Castiglione (KAHS•teel•YOH•NAY) in 1528.

In his work, Castiglione described the characteristics of a perfect Renaissance noble. First, a noble was born, not made. He was expected to have character, grace, and talent. Second, the perfect noble had to develop two basic skills. Because the chief aim of a noble was to be a warrior, he had to perform military and physical exercises. Unlike the medieval knight, however, who was primarily concerned with acquiring military skill, the Renaissance noble was also expected to gain a classical education and enrich his life with the arts. Third, the noble needed to follow a certain standard of conduct. Nobles were not supposed to hide their achievements but to show them with grace.

A portrait of Baldassare Castiglione by Raphael, c. 1516

The Impact of Printing

The Renaissance saw the development of printing in Europe. In the fifteenth century, Europeans gradually learned how to print with movable metal type. Johannes Gutenberg of Germany played a crucial role in the process. Gutenberg's Bible, printed about 1455, was the first European book produced from movable type.

By 1500, there were over a thousand printers in Europe. Almost forty thousand titles had been published. More than half of these were religious books, including Bibles, prayer books, and sermons. Most others were Latin and Greek classics, legal handbooks, works on philosophy, and popular romances.

The printing of books encouraged scholarly research and increased the public's desire to gain knowledge, which would eventually have an enormous impact on European society. The new religious ideas of the Reformation would not have spread as rapidly as they did in the sixteenth century without the printing press.

Printing allowed European civilization to compete for the first time with the civilization of China. The Chinese had invented printing much earlier, as well as printing with movable type.

Analyzing *Why do you think the printing of books encouraged people's desire to gain knowledge?*

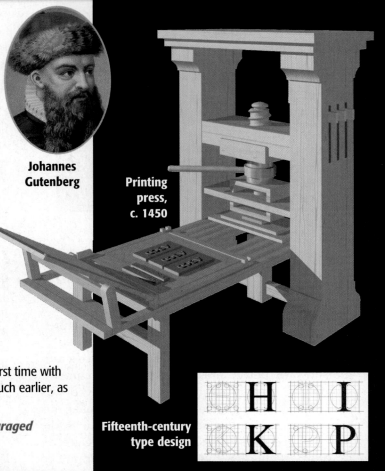

Johannes Gutenberg

Printing press, c. 1450

Fifteenth-century type design

What was the purpose of these standards?

❝I think that the aim of the perfect Courtier is so to win for himself the favor and mind of the prince whom he serves that he may be able to tell him, and always will tell him, the truth about everything he needs to know, without fear or risk of displeasing him; and that when he sees the mind of his prince inclined to a wrong action, he may dare to oppose him . . . so as to dissuade him of every evil intent and bring him to the path of virtue.❞

The aim, then, of the perfect noble was to serve his prince in an effective and honest way. Nobles would adhere to Castiglione's principles for hundreds of years while they continued to dominate European life socially and politically.

Peasants and Townspeople In the Middle Ages, peasants had made up the overwhelming mass of the

third estate. In the Renaissance, they still constituted 85 to 90 percent of the total European population, except in the highly urban areas of northern Italy and Flanders.

Serfdom continued to decrease with the decline of the manorial system. Increasingly, throughout the late Middle Ages, the labor owed by a peasant to a lord was converted into rent on land paid in money. By 1500, especially in western Europe, more and more peasants became legally free.

Townspeople made up the rest of the third estate. In the Middle Ages, townspeople were mostly merchants and artisans. The Renaissance town or city of the fifteenth century, however, was more diverse.

At the top of urban society were the patricians. Their wealth from trade, industry, and banking enabled them to dominate their communities economically, socially, and politically. Below them were the burghers—the shopkeepers, artisans, guild masters, and guild members who provided the goods and services for their fellow townspeople.

Below the patricians and the burghers were the workers, who earned pitiful wages, and the unemployed. Both groups lived miserable lives. These people made up perhaps 30 or 40 percent of the urban population.

During the late 1300s and the 1400s, urban poverty increased dramatically throughout Europe. One rich merchant of Florence, who had little sympathy for the poor, wrote:

> 66Those that are lazy in a way that does harm to the city, and who can offer no just reason for their condition, should either be forced to work or expelled from the city. The city would thus rid itself of that most harmful part of the poorest class.99

Family and Marriage The family bond was a source of great security in the dangerous urban world of Renaissance Italy. To maintain the family, parents carefully arranged marriages, often to strengthen business or family ties. Details were worked out well in advance, sometimes when children were only two or three years old. The most important aspect of the marriage contract was the size of the dowry, a sum of money given by the wife's family to the husband upon marriage.

The father-husband was the center of the Italian family. He gave it his name, managed all finances (his wife had no share in his wealth), and made the deci-

History *through Art*

***Celebration of a Marriage* by Ghirlandaio Domenico** During the Renaissance, a marriage was more of a business arrangement than a matter of love. How does this painting support or contradict that statement?

sions that determined his children's lives. The mother's chief role was to supervise the household.

A father's authority over his children was absolute until he died or formally freed his children. In Renaissance Italy, children did not become adults on reaching a certain age. Instead, adulthood came to children when their fathers went before a judge and formally freed them. The age of adulthood varied from the early teens to the late twenties.

✓**Reading Check** **Contrasting** How was the Renaissance noble different from the medieval knight?

🟥**TAKS Practice**

SECTION 1 ASSESSMENT

Checking for Understanding

1. **Define** urban society, secular, mercenary, dowry.

2. **Identify** Leonardo da Vinci, Francesco Sforza, Cosimo de' Medici, Lorenzo de' Medici, Niccolò Machiavelli.

3. **Locate** Milan, Venice, Florence, Rome.

4. **Explain** how the Spanish became involved in the Italian wars.

5. **Summarize** the characteristics of Castiglione's perfect noble.

Critical Thinking

6. **Explain** Why was a strong family bond so important in Renaissance Italy?

7. **Contrasting Information** Use a table like the one below to describe the differences between the social structure of the Middle Ages and the Renaissance.

	Middle Ages	Renaissance
Nobility		
Peasants		
Townspeople		

Analyzing Visuals

8. **Identify** details in the painting of Venice on page 376 that show it is a major city-state with a profitable trade empire. Find other images of Venice in your school library and compare them to this painting.

Writing About History

9. **Expository Writing** Read a few passages from *The Prince.* Write a brief essay explaining whether or not you agree with Machiavelli's theory of politics.

The Intellectual and Artistic Renaissance

Main Ideas
- The most important intellectual movement associated with the Renaissance was humanism.
- The Renaissance produced many great artists and sculptors such as Michelangelo, Raphael, and Leonardo da Vinci.

Key Terms
humanism, fresco

People to Identify
Petrarch, Dante, Michelangelo, Jan van Eyck, Albrecht Dürer

Places to Locate
Canterbury, Flanders

Preview Questions
1. What were the characteristics of Italian Renaissance humanism?
2. What were the chief achievements of European Renaissance painters?

Reading Strategy
Summarizing Information Use a table like the one below to describe the three pieces of literature written by Dante, Chaucer, and de Pizan. What was the primary importance of each of these works?

Divine Comedy	The Canterbury Tales	The Book of the City of Ladies

Preview of Events

◆1300	◆1350	◆1400	◆1450	◆1500
c. 1310 Dante writes the *Divine Comedy*	**c. 1390** Chaucer writes *The Canterbury Tales*	**c. 1415** Donatello creates his statue of St. George	**c. 1434** Jan van Eyck paints the Arnolfini portrait	**c. 1505** Leonardo da Vinci paints the Mona Lisa

Voices from the Past

Pico della Mirandola

Pico della Mirandola, a Renaissance philosopher, said in his *Oration on the Dignity of Man*:

❝You, constrained by no limits in accordance with your own free will, shall ordain for yourself the limits of your nature. We have set you at the world's center that you may from there more easily observe whatever is in the world. We have made you neither of heaven nor of earth, neither mortal nor immortal, so that with freedom of choice and with honor, as though the maker and molder of yourself, you may fashion yourself in whatever shape you shall prefer.❞

—*The Renaissance Philosophy of Man,* **Ernst Cassirer, Paul Kristeller, and John Randall, Jr., eds., 1948**

There is no better expression of the Renaissance's exalted view of the importance of the individual.

Italian Renaissance Humanism

Secularism and an emphasis on the individual characterized the Renaissance. These characteristics are most noticeable in the intellectual and artistic accomplishments of the period. A key intellectual movement of the Renaissance was humanism.

Humanism was based on the study of the classics, the literary works of ancient Greece and Rome. Humanists studied such things as grammar, rhetoric, poetry, moral philosophy, and history—all of which was based on the works of ancient Greek and Roman authors. Today these subjects are called the humanities.

Petrarch (PEE•TRAHRK), who has often been called the father of Italian Renaissance humanism, did more than any other individual in the fourteenth century to foster the development of humanism. Petrarch looked for forgotten Latin manuscripts and set in motion a search for similar manuscripts in monastic libraries throughout Europe.

He also began the humanist emphasis on using pure classical Latin (Latin as used by the ancient Romans as opposed to medieval Latin). Humanists used the works of Cicero as a model for prose and those of Virgil for poetry.

In Florence, the humanist movement took a new direction at the beginning of the fifteenth century. Fourteenth-century humanists such as Petrarch had described the intellectual life as one of solitude. They rejected family and a life of action in the community. In contrast, humanists in the early 1400s took a new interest in civic life. They believed that it was the duty of an intellectual to live an active life for one's state, and that their study of the humanities should be put to the service of the state. It is no accident that they served as secretaries in the Italian city-states and to princes or popes.

Reading Check **Examining** Why is Petrarch called the father of Italian Renaissance humanism?

Vernacular Literature

The humanist emphasis on classical Latin led to its widespread use in the writings of scholars, lawyers, and theologians. However, some writers wrote in the vernacular (the language spoken in their own regions, such as Italian, French, or German). In the fourteenth century, the literary works of the Italian author **Dante** (DAHN•tay) and the English author Geoffrey Chaucer helped make vernacular literature more popular.

Dante

Dante's masterpiece in the Italian vernacular is the *Divine Comedy.* It is the story of the soul's journey to salvation. The lengthy poem is divided into three major sections: Hell, Purgatory, and Heaven, or Paradise. Dante is led on an imaginary journey through these three realms until he reaches Paradise, where he beholds God, or "the love that moves the sun and the other stars."

Chaucer used the English vernacular in his famous work *The Canterbury Tales.* His beauty of expression and clear, forceful language were important in making his dialect the chief ancestor of the modern English language.

The Canterbury Tales consists of a collection of stories told by a group of 29 pilgrims journeying to the tomb of Saint Thomas à Becket at **Canterbury,** England. This format gave Chaucer the chance to portray an entire range of English society, from the high to the low born.

Another writer who used the vernacular was Christine de Pizan, a Frenchwoman who is best known for her works written in defense of women. In *The Book of the City of Ladies,* written in 1404, she denounced the many male writers who had argued that women, by their very nature, are unable to learn and are easily swayed.

Christine de Pizan

Women, de Pizan argued, could learn as well as men if they could attend the same schools:

> 66Should I also tell you whether a woman's nature is clever and quick enough to learn speculative sciences as well as to discover them, and likewise the manual arts. I assure you that women are equally well-suited and skilled to carry them out and to put them to sophisticated use once they have learned them.99

Reading Check **Explaining** What literary format does Chaucer use to portray English society?

Education in the Renaissance

The humanist movement had a profound effect on education. Renaissance humanists believed that education could dramatically change human beings.

The Tribute Money **by Masaccio, c. 1426**
In this church fresco, Masaccio creates a realistic relationship between the Biblical figures and the background. **Identify the Renaissance artistic elements used by Masaccio in this work.**

They wrote books on education and opened schools based on their ideas.

At the core of humanist schools were the liberal studies. Humanists believed that the liberal studies (what we call today the liberal arts) enabled individuals to reach their full potential. One humanist wrote, "We call those studies liberal by which we attain and practice virtue and wisdom; which calls forth and develops those highest gifts of body and mind which ennoble men."

What, then, were the liberal studies? According to the humanists, students should study history, moral philosophy, eloquence (or rhetoric), letters (grammar and logic), poetry, mathematics, astronomy, and music. In short, the purpose of a liberal education (and thus the reason for studying the liberal arts) was to produce individuals who follow a path of virtue and wisdom. These individuals should also possess rhetorical skills so they can persuade others to take this same path.

Following the Greek ideal of a sound mind in a sound body, humanist educators also stressed physical education. Pupils were taught the skills of javelin throwing, archery, and dancing, and they were encouraged to run, wrestle, hunt, and swim.

Humanist educators thought that a humanist education was a practical preparation for life. Its aim was not to create great scholars but complete citizens. Humanist schools provided the model for the basic education of the European ruling classes until the twentieth century.

Females were largely absent from these schools. The few female students who did attend humanist schools studied the classics and were encouraged to know some history as well as how to ride, dance, sing, play the lute (a stringed instrument), and

appreciate poetry. They were told not to learn mathematics or rhetoric. It was thought that religion and morals should be foremost in the education of "Christian ladies" so that they could become good mothers and wives.

✔**Reading Check** **Explaining** How did a humanist education prepare a student for life?

The Artistic Renaissance in Italy

Renaissance artists sought to imitate nature in their works. They wanted onlookers to see the reality of the objects or events they were portraying. At the same time, these artists were developing a new world perspective. In this new view, human beings became the focus of attention—the "center and measure of all things," as one artist proclaimed.

New Techniques in Painting The frescoes painted by Masaccio (muh•ZAH•chee•oh) in Florence at the beginning of the fifteenth century have long been regarded as the first masterpieces of early Renaissance (1400–1490) art. A **fresco** is a painting done on fresh, wet plaster with water-based paints. Whereas human figures in medieval paintings look flat, Masaccio's have depth and come alive. By mastering the laws of perspective, which enabled him to create the illusion of three dimensions, Masaccio developed a new, realistic style of painting.

This new, or Renaissance, style was used and modified by other Florentine painters in the fifteenth century. Especially important were two major developments. One stressed the technical side of painting—understanding the laws of perspective and the organization of outdoor space and light through geometry. The second development was the investigation of movement and human anatomy. The realistic portrayal of the individual person, especially the human nude, became one of the chief aims of Italian Renaissance art.

Sculpture and Architecture The revolutionary achievements of Florentine painters in the fifteenth century were matched by equally stunning advances in sculpture and architecture. The sculptor Donatello spent time in Rome studying and copying the statues of the Greeks and Romans. Among his numerous works was a statue of Saint George, a realistic, freestanding figure.

The architect Filippo Brunelleschi (BROO•nuhl•EHS•kee) was inspired by the buildings of classical Rome to create a new architecture in Florence. The Medici, the wealthy ruling family of Florence, hired Brunelleschi to design the church of San Lorenzo. The classical columns and rounded arches that Brunelleschi used in the church's design create an environment that does not overwhelm the worshiper, as Gothic cathedrals might. Instead, the church provides comfort as a space created to fit human, and not divine, needs. Like painters and sculptors, Renaissance architects sought to reflect a human-centered world.

By the end of the fifteenth century, Italian painters, sculptors, and architects had created a new artistic world. Many artists had mastered the new techniques

David by Michelangelo

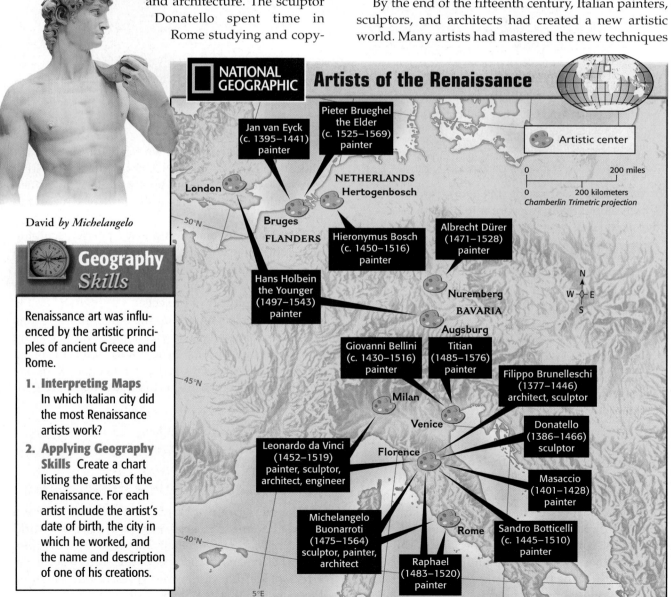

NATIONAL GEOGRAPHIC

Artists of the Renaissance

Artistic center

0   200 miles
0   200 kilometers
Chamberlin Trimetric projection

Pieter Brueghel the Elder (c. 1525–1569) painter

Jan van Eyck (c. 1395–1441) painter

London

NETHERLANDS
Hertogenbosch

Bruges
FLANDERS

Hieronymus Bosch (c. 1450–1516) painter

Albrecht Dürer (1471–1528) painter

Hans Holbein the Younger (1497–1543) painter

Nuremberg
BAVARIA
Augsburg

Giovanni Bellini (c. 1430–1516) painter

Titian (1485–1576) painter

Filippo Brunelleschi (1377–1446) architect, sculptor

Milan

Venice

Donatello (1386–1466) sculptor

Leonardo da Vinci (1452–1519) painter, sculptor, architect, engineer

Florence

Masaccio (1401–1428) painter

Michelangelo Buonarroti (1475–1564) sculptor, painter, architect

Rome

Sandro Botticelli (c. 1445–1510) painter

Raphael (1483–1520) painter

Geography Skills

Renaissance art was influenced by the artistic principles of ancient Greece and Rome.

1. **Interpreting Maps** In which Italian city did the most Renaissance artists work?

2. **Applying Geography Skills** Create a chart listing the artists of the Renaissance. For each artist include the artist's date of birth, the city in which he worked, and the name and description of one of his creations.

Raphael

History *through Art*

***School of Athens* by Raphael** Raphael created this painting for the pope to show the unity of Christian and classical works. Research the painting to discover the identities of the historical figures that Raphael depicted.

for realistically portraying the world around them and were now ready to move into new forms of creative expression.

✓**Reading Check** **Explaining** How did Renaissance paintings differ from medieval paintings?

Masters of the High Renaissance

The final stage of Italian Renaissance painting, which flourished between 1490 and 1520, is called the High Renaissance. The High Renaissance in Italy is associated with three artistic giants, Leonardo da Vinci, Raphael, and Michelangelo.

Leonardo mastered the art of realistic painting and even dissected human bodies to better see how nature worked. However, he also stressed the need to advance beyond such realism. It was Leonardo's goal to create idealized forms that would capture the perfection of nature and the individual—perfection that could not be expressed fully by a realistic style.

At age 25, Raphael was already regarded as one of Italy's best painters. He was especially admired for his numerous madonnas (paintings of the Virgin Mary). In these, he tried to achieve an ideal of beauty far surpassing human standards.

Raphael is also well known for his frescoes in the Vatican Palace. His *School of Athens* reveals a world of balance, harmony, and order—the underlying principles of the art of the classical world of Greece and Rome.

Michelangelo, an accomplished painter, sculptor, and architect, was another artistic master of the High Renaissance. Fiercely driven by his desire to create, he worked with great passion and energy on a remarkable number of projects.

Michelangelo's figures on the ceiling of the Sistine Chapel in Rome reveal an ideal type of human being with perfect proportions. The beauty of this idealized human being is meant to be a reflection of divine beauty. The more beautiful the body, the more godlike the figure.

✓**Reading Check** **Identifying** Name the three Italian artists most closely associated with the High Renaissance.

The Northern Artistic Renaissance

Like the artists of Italy, the artists of northern Europe became interested in portraying their world realistically. However, their approach was different from the Italians'. This was particularly true of the artists of the Low Countries (present-day Belgium, Luxembourg, and the Netherlands).

Circumstance played a role in the differences. The large wall spaces of Italian churches had given rise to the art of fresco painting. Italian artists used these spaces to master the technical skills that allowed them to portray humans in realistic settings. In the north, the Gothic cathedrals with their stained glass windows did not allow for frescoes. Thus, northern artists painted illustrations for books and wooden panels for altarpieces. Great care was needed to depict each object on a small scale.

The most important northern school of art in the fifteenth century was found in **Flanders,** one of the Low Countries. The Flemish painter **Jan van Eyck** (EYEK) was among the first to use oil paint, which enabled the artist to use a wide variety of colors and create fine details as in his painting *Giovanni Arnolfini and His Bride.* Like other Northern Renaissance artists, however, van Eyck imitated nature not by using perspective, as the Italians did, but by simply observing reality and portraying details as best he could.

By 1500, artists from the north had begun to study in Italy and to be influenced by what artists were doing there. One German artist who was greatly affected by the Italians was **Albrecht Dürer.** He made two trips to Italy and absorbed most of what the Italians could teach on the laws of perspective.

As can be seen in his famous *Adoration of the Magi,* Dürer did not reject the use of minute details characteristic of northern artists. He did try, however, to fit

Dürer

In the Adoration of the Magi, *Albrecht Dürer retains the minute details associated with northern European painting, but he also makes use of perspective and proportion.*

those details more harmoniously into his works in accordance with Italian artistic theories. Like the Italian artists of the High Renaissance, Dürer tried to achieve a standard of ideal beauty that was based on a careful examination of the human form.

✓**Reading Check** **Examining** Why was Jan van Eyck's use of oil paint significant?

🔷**TAKS Practice**

SECTION 2 ASSESSMENT

Checking for Understanding

1. **Define** humanism, fresco.

2. **Identify** Petrarch, Dante, Michelangelo, Jan van Eyck, Albrecht Dürer.

3. **Locate** Canterbury, Flanders.

4. **Summarize** Christine de Pizan's main argument in *The Book of the City of Ladies.* Why did her ideas receive so much attention?

5. **Compare** the underlying principles of both classical Greek and Roman art with Italian Renaissance art. How are the principles similar? How are they different?

Critical Thinking

6. **Compare and Contrast** How do the humanist goals and philosophy of education developed during the Renaissance compare with the goals of your high school education?

7. **Summarizing Information** Use a table like the one below to describe the greatest accomplishments of Leonardo da Vinci, Raphael, and Michelangelo.

Leonardo da Vinci	Raphael	Michelangelo

Analyzing Visuals

8. **Compare** the paintings of Raphael and Dürer, shown on page 386 and above. What themes does each artist explore? How does each painting reflect the history of the culture in which it was produced?

Writing About History

9. **Expository Writing** Assume the role of an art docent (a person who guides people through museums). Prepare a lecture to be given to a group of students on the works of Jan van Eyck and how they differ from Italian Renaissance paintings.

The Genius of Leonardo da Vinci

Leonardo da Vinci

DURING THE RENAISSANCE, artists came to be viewed as creative geniuses with almost divine qualities. The painter Giorgio Vasari helped create this image by writing a series of brief biographies of Italy's great artists, including Leonardo da Vinci.

❝In the normal course of events many men and women are born with various remarkable qualities and talents; but occasionally, in a way that transcends nature, a single person is marvelously endowed by heaven with beauty, grace, and talent in such abundance that he leaves other men far behind, all his actions seem inspired, and indeed everything he does clearly comes from God rather than from human art.

Everyone acknowledged that this was true of Leonardo da Vinci, an artist of outstanding physical beauty who displayed infinite grace in everything he did and who cultivated his genius so brilliantly that all problems he studied he solved with ease. He possessed great strength and dexterity; he was a man of regal spirit and tremendous breadth of mind; and his name became so famous that not only was he esteemed during his lifetime but his reputation endured and became even greater after his death. . . .

He was marvelously gifted, and he proved himself to be a first-class geometrician in his work as a sculptor and architect. In his youth, Leonardo made in clay several heads of women with smiling faces, of which plaster casts are still being made, as well as some children's heads executed as if by a mature artist. He also did many architectural drawings both of ground plans and of other elevations, and, while still young, he was the first to propose reducing the Arno River to a navigable canal between Pisa and Florence. He made designs for mills, . . . and engines that could be driven by water-power;

and as he intended to be a painter by profession he carefully studied drawing from life. . . . Altogether, his genius was so wonderfully inspired by the grace of God, his powers of expression were so powerfully fed by a willing memory and intellect, and his writing conveyed his ideas so precisely, that his arguments and reasonings confounded the most formidable critics. In addition, he used to make models and plans showing how to excavate and tunnel through mountains without difficulty, so as to pass from one level to another; and he demonstrated how to lift and draw great weights by means of levers and hoists and ways of cleaning harbors and using pumps to suck up water from great depths.❞

—Giorgio Vasari, *Lives of the Artists*

*A detail from da Vinci's **Last Supper**, shown as the painting was being restored in the late 1990s*

Analyzing Primary Sources

1. Name the qualities that Vasari admires in Leonardo da Vinci.
2. How does Vasari's description of da Vinci reflect the ideals of Italian Renaissance humanism?

The Protestant Reformation

Voices from the Past

Martin Luther addressing the emperor in Worms

On April 18, 1521, Martin Luther stood before the emperor and princes of Germany in the city of Worms and declared:

❝Since then Your Majesty and your lordships desire a simple reply, I will answer without horns and without teeth. Unless I am convicted by Scripture and plain reason—I do not accept the authority of popes and councils, for they have contradicted each other—my conscience is captive to the Word of God. I cannot and I will not recant anything, for to go against conscience is neither right nor safe. Here I stand, I cannot do otherwise. God help me. Amen.❞

—*Here I Stand: A Life of Martin Luther,* Roland Bainton, 1950

With these words Martin Luther refused to renounce his new religious ideas. Luther's words became the battle cry of the Protestant Reformation.

Erasmus and Christian Humanism

The Protestant Reformation is the name given to the religious reform movement that divided the western Church into Catholic and Protestant groups. Although **Martin Luther** began the Reformation in the early sixteenth century, several earlier developments had set the stage for religious change.

One such development grew from widespread changes in intellectual thought. During the second half of the fifteenth century, the new classical learning that was part of Italian Renaissance humanism spread to northern Europe. From that came a movement called Christian humanism, or Northern Renaissance humanism. The major goal of this movement was the reform of the Catholic Church.

The Christian humanists believed in the ability of human beings to reason and improve themselves. They thought that if people read the classics, and especially the basic works of Christianity, they would become more pious. This inner piety, or inward religious feeling, would bring about a reform of the Church and society. Christian humanists believed that in order to change society, they must first change the human beings who make it up.

The best known of all the Christian humanists was **Desiderius Erasmus** (ih•RAZ•muhs). He called his view of religion "the philosophy of Christ." By this, he meant that Christianity should show people how to live good lives on a daily basis rather than provide a system of beliefs that people have to practice to be saved. Erasmus stressed the inwardness of religious feeling. To him, the external forms of medieval religion (such as pilgrimages, fasts, and relics) were not all that important.

To reform the Church, Erasmus wanted to spread the philosophy of Christ, provide education in the works of Christianity, and criticize the abuses in the Church. In his work *The Praise of Folly*, written in 1509, Erasmus humorously criticized aspects of his society that he believed were most in need of reform. He singled out the monks for special treatment. Monks, he said, "insist that everything be done in precise detail. . . . Just so many knots must be on each shoe and the shoelace must be of only one color."

Erasmus sought reform within the Catholic Church. He did not wish to break away from the Church, as later reformers would. His ideas, however, did prepare the way for the Reformation. As people of his day said, "Erasmus laid the egg that Luther hatched."

Reading Check **Examining** How did Erasmus pave the way for the Reformation?

Religion on the Eve of the Reformation

Why were Erasmus and others calling for reform? Corruption in the Catholic Church was one reason. Between 1450 and 1520, a series of popes—known as the Renaissance popes—failed to meet the Church's spiritual needs. The popes were supposed to be the spiritual leaders of the Catholic Church. As leaders of the Papal States, however, they were all too often more concerned with Italian politics and worldly interests than with spiritual matters.

Julius II, the fiery "warrior-pope," personally led armies against his enemies. This disgusted Christians who viewed the pope as a spiritual, not a military, leader. One critic wrote, "How, O bishop standing in the room of the Apostles, dare you teach the people the things that pertain to war?"

Many church officials were also concerned with money and used their church offices to advance their careers and their wealth. At the same time, many ordinary parish priests seemed ignorant of their spiritual duties. People wanted to know how to save their souls, and many parish priests were unable to offer them advice or instruction.

While the leaders of the Church were failing to meet their responsibilities, ordinary people desired meaningful religious expression and assurance of their **salvation** or acceptance into Heaven. As a result, for some, the process of obtaining salvation became almost mechanical. Collections of relics grew more popular as a means to salvation. According to church practice at that time, through veneration of a

Raphael's depiction of Pope Julius II

relic, a person could gain an indulgence—release from all or part of the punishment for sin. Frederick the Wise, Luther's prince, had amassed over five thousand relics. Indulgences attached to them could reduce time in purgatory by 1,443 years. The Church also sold indulgences, in the form of certificates.

Other people sought certainty of salvation in the popular mystical movement known as the Modern Devotion. The Modern Devotion downplayed religious dogma and stressed the need to follow the teachings of Jesus. This deepening of religious life was done within the Catholic Church. However, many people soon found that the worldly-wise clergy had little interest in the spiritual needs of their people. It is this environment that helps to explain the tremendous impact of Luther's ideas.

✓ **Reading Check** **Explaining** What was the Modern Devotion?

Martin Luther

⌐TURNING POINT⌐ **In this section, you will learn how, on October 31, 1517, Martin Luther presented a list of Ninety-five Theses that objected to the Church practice of indulgences. The publication of Luther's theses began the Protestant Reformation.**

Martin Luther was a monk and a professor at the University of Wittenberg, in Germany, where he lectured on the Bible. Through his study of the Bible, Luther arrived at an answer to a problem—the certainty of salvation—that had bothered him since he had become a monk.

Catholic teaching had stressed that both faith and good works were needed to gain personal salvation. In Luther's eyes, human beings were powerless in the sight of an almighty God and could never do enough good works to earn salvation.

Through his study of the Bible, Luther came to believe that humans are not saved through their good works but through their faith in God. If an individual has faith in God, then God makes that person just, or worthy of salvation. God will grant salvation because God is merciful. God's grace cannot be earned by performing good works. This idea, called justification

Indulgence box

The advent of the printing press allowed Luther's views to spread beyond Wittenberg.

(being made right before God) by faith alone, became the chief teaching of the Protestant Reformation. Because Luther had arrived at his understanding of salvation by studying the Bible, the Bible became for Luther, as for all other Protestants, the only source of religious truth.

The Ninety-five Theses Luther did not see himself as a rebel, but he was greatly upset by the widespread selling of indulgences. Especially offensive in his eyes was the monk Johann Tetzel, who sold indulgences with the slogan: "As soon as the coin in the coffer [money box] rings, the soul from purgatory springs." People, Luther believed, were simply harming their chances for salvation by buying these pieces of paper.

On October 31, 1517, Luther, who was greatly angered by the Church's practices, sent a list of Ninety-five Theses to his church superiors, especially the local bishop. The theses were a stunning attack on abuses in the sale of indulgences. Thousands of copies of the Ninety-five Theses were printed and spread to all parts of Germany. Pope Leo X did not take the issue seriously, however. He said that Luther was simply "some drunken German who will amend his ways when he sobers up."

A Break with the Church By 1520, Luther had begun to move toward a more definite break with the Catholic Church. He called on the German princes to overthrow the papacy in Germany and establish a reformed German church. Luther also attacked the Church's system of sacraments. In his view, they were the means by which the pope and the Church had destroyed the real meaning of the gospel for a thousand years. He kept only two sacraments—baptism and the Eucharist (also known as Communion). Luther also called for the clergy to marry. This went against the long-standing Catholic requirement that the clergy remain celibate, or unmarried.

Through all these calls for change, Luther continued to emphasize his new doctrine of salvation. It is faith alone, he said, and not good works, that justifies and brings salvation through Christ.

Unable to accept Luther's ideas, the Church excommunicated him in January 1521. He was also summoned to appear before the imperial diet—or legislative assembly—of the Holy Roman Empire, which was called into session at the city of Worms by the newly elected emperor Charles V. The emperor thought he could convince Luther to change his ideas, but Luther refused.

The young emperor was outraged. "A single friar who goes counter to all Christianity for a thousand years," he declared, "must be wrong!" By the **Edict of Worms,** Martin Luther was made an outlaw within the empire. His works were to be burned and Luther himself captured and delivered to the emperor. However, Luther's ruler, Elector Frederick of Saxony, was unwilling to see his famous professor killed. He sent Luther into hiding and then protected him when he returned to Wittenberg at the beginning of 1522.

The Rise of Lutheranism During the next few years, Luther's religious movement became a revolution. Luther was able to gain the support of many of the German rulers among the numerous states that made up the Holy Roman Empire. These rulers quickly took control of the Catholic churches in their territories, forming state churches whose affairs were supervised by the government.

As part of the development of these state-dominated churches, Luther also set up new religious services to replace the Catholic mass. These featured a worship service consisting of Bible readings, preaching of the word of God, and song. The doctrine developed by Luther soon came to be known as Lutheranism, and the churches as Lutheran churches. Lutheranism was the first Protestant faith.

In June 1524, Luther faced a political crisis when German peasants revolted against their lords. The peasants looked to Luther to support their cause, but Luther instead supported the lords. To him, the state and its rulers were called by God to maintain the peace necessary for

NATIONAL GEOGRAPHIC

Political Europe, 1555

IRELAND
DENMARK
North Sea
Baltic Sea
ENGLAND
NETHERLANDS
London
FLANDERS
HOLY
Wittenberg
POLAND
SAXONY
ROMAN
Paris
Worms EMPIRE BOHEMIA
Augsburg
FRANCE
Geneva
HUNGARY
ATLANTIC OCEAN
PORTUGAL
Madrid
Corsica
Rome
Constantinople
SPAIN
Sardinia
Naples
NAPLES
Mediterranean Sea
Sicily
Black Sea
Crete

— Boundary of the Holy Roman Empire
◻ Hapsburg territories of Holy Roman Emperor Charles V
◻ Major German secular states
◻ Papal States
◻ Ottoman Empire

0   300 miles
0   300 kilometers
Lambert Azimuthal Equal-Area projection

Geography Skills

Charles V wanted to keep his vast territories Catholic.

1. **Interpreting Maps** In which city was Luther declared an outlaw?

2. **Applying Geography Skills** How did the location of Wittenberg benefit the Protestant cause?

the spread of the gospel. It was the duty of princes to stop revolt. By the following spring, the German princes had crushed the peasants. Luther found himself even more dependent on state authorities for the growth of his church.

✓ **Reading Check** **Contrasting** How did Luther's theory of salvation differ from what the Catholic Church believed was necessary for salvation?

Politics in the German Reformation

From its very beginning, the fate of Luther's movement was closely tied to political affairs. **Charles V,** the Holy Roman emperor (who was also Charles I, the king of Spain), ruled an immense empire consisting of Spain and its colonies, the Austrian lands, **Bohemia, Hungary,** the Low Countries, the duchy of Milan in northern Italy, and the kingdom of Naples in southern Italy.

Politically, Charles wanted to keep this enormous empire under the control of his dynasty—the Hapsburgs. Religiously, he hoped to preserve the unity of his empire by keeping it Catholic. However, a number of problems kept him busy and cost him both his dream and his health. These same problems helped Lutheranism survive by giving Lutherans time to organize before having to face the Catholic forces.

The chief political concern of Charles V was his rivalry with the king of France, Francis I. Their conflict over disputed territories in a number of areas led to a series of wars that lasted more than 20 years. At the same time, Charles faced opposition from Pope Clement VII. Guided by political considerations, the pope had joined the side of the French king. The advance of the Ottoman Turks into the eastern part of Charles's empire forced the emperor to send forces there as well.

Finally, the internal political situation in the Holy Roman Empire was not in Charles's favor. Germany was a land of several hundred territorial states. Although all owed loyalty to the emperor, Germany's development in the Middle Ages had enabled these states to free themselves from the emperor's authority. Many individual rulers of the German states supported Luther as a way to assert their own local authority over the authority of the empire and Charles V.

By the time Charles V was able to bring military forces to Germany, the Lutheran princes were well organized. Unable to defeat them, Charles was forced to seek peace.

An end to religious warfare in Germany came in 1555 with the Peace of Augsburg. This agreement formally accepted the division of Christianity in Germany. The German states were now free to choose between Catholicism and Lutheranism. Lutheran states were to have the same legal rights as Catholic states. The peace settlement did not recognize the principle of religious toleration for individuals, however. The right of each German ruler to determine the religion of his subjects was accepted, but not the right of the subjects to choose their own religion.

✓ **Reading Check** **Evaluating** How did the Peace of Augsburg influence the political and religious development of Germany?

TAKS Practice

SECTION 3 ASSESSMENT

Checking for Understanding

1. **Define** Christian humanism, indulgence, salvation.

2. **Identify** Martin Luther, Desiderius Erasmus, Edict of Worms, Charles V, The Peace of Augsburg.

3. **Locate** Wittenberg, Bohemia, Hungary.

4. **Explain** the impact of the Edict of Worms.

5. **List** the ways Erasmus wanted to reform the Catholic Church.

Critical Thinking

6. **Discuss** What were the consequences of Luther's Ninety-five Theses?

7. **Sequencing Information** Use a diagram like the one below to show Luther's actions leading to the emergence of Protestantism.

Luther's Actions

▢ → ▢ → ▢ Protestantism

Analyzing Visuals

8. **Identify** the event illustrated in the painting on page 391. Why was this event significant? How has the painter portrayed Martin Luther?

Writing About History

9. **Persuasive Writing** Martin Luther's father wanted him to become a lawyer. Write a letter in which Martin Luther tries to convince his father that the path he chose was better than the law.

Summarizing Information

Why Learn This Skill?

Imagine you have been assigned a chapter on the Renaissance for a midterm. After taking a short break, you discover that you cannot recall important information. What can you do to avoid this problem?

When you read a long selection, it is helpful to take notes. Summarizing information—reducing large amounts of information to a few key phrases—can help you remember the main ideas and important facts.

Learning the Skill

To summarize information, follow these guidelines when you read:

- Distinguish the main ideas from the supporting details. Use the main ideas in the summary.

- Use your own words to describe the main ideas. Do not copy the selection word for word.

- Summarize the author's opinion if you think it is important.

- If the summary is almost as long as the reading selection, you are including too much information. The summary should be very short.

Practicing the Skill

Read the selection below, and then answer the questions that follow.

> For the next 30 years, the French and Spanish made Italy their battleground as they fought to dominate the country. A decisive turning point in their war came in 1527. On May 5, thousands of troops belonging to the Spanish king Charles I arrived at the city of Rome along with mercenaries from different countries. They had not been paid for months. When they yelled, "Money! Money!" their leader responded, "If you have ever dreamed of pillaging a town and laying hold of its treasures, here now is one, the richest of them all, queen of the world."

The next day the invading forces smashed down the gates and pushed their way into the city. The terrible sack of Rome in 1527 by the armies of the Spanish king Charles I ended the Italian wars and left the Spanish a dominant force in Italy.

1. What are the main ideas of this paragraph?
2. What are the supporting details of the main ideas?
3. Write a brief summary of two or three sentences that will help you remember what the paragraph is about.

St. Peter's Square, sixteenth-century Rome

Applying the Skill

Read and summarize two articles from the front page of a newspaper. Have a classmate ask you questions about them. How much were you able to remember after summarizing the information?

Glencoe's **Skillbuilder Interactive Workbook, Level 2,** provides instruction and practice in key social studies skills.

The Spread of Protestantism and the Catholic Response

Guide to Reading

Main Ideas
- Different forms of Protestantism emerged in Europe as the Reformation spread.
- The Catholic Church underwent a religious rebirth.

Key Terms
predestination, annul

People to Identify
Ulrich Zwingli, John Calvin, Henry VIII, Ignatius of Loyola

Places to Locate
Zürich, Geneva, Trent

Preview Questions
1. What different forms of Protestantism emerged in Europe?
2. What were the contributions of the Jesuits, the papacy, and the Council of Trent to the revival of Catholicism?

Reading Strategy
Cause and Effect Use a diagram like the one below to list some of the reforms proposed by the Council of Trent. Beside each, give the Protestant viewpoint to which it responded.

Council of Trent		Protestant Viewpoint
	←	
	←	
	←	

Preview of Events

♦1530	♦1535	♦1540	♦1545	♦1550	♦1555

1531
War between the Protestant and Catholic states in Switzerland

1534
The Act of Supremacy is passed in England

1540
The Society of Jesus becomes a religious order

1545
The Council of Trent is formed

1553
Mary Tudor, "Bloody Mary," becomes Queen of England

Ignatius Loyola

Voices from the Past

In order to fight Protestantism, the Catholic Ignatius Loyola founded a new religious order. He insisted on certain principles:

❝We must put aside all judgment of our own, and keep the mind ever ready and prompt to obey in all things the true Spouse of Jesus Christ, our holy Mother, the Roman Catholic Church. . . . If we wish to proceed securely in all things, we must hold fast to the following principle: What seems to me white, I will believe black if the Catholic Church so defines. For I must be convinced that in Christ our Lord, the bridegroom, and in His spouse the Catholic Church, only one Spirit holds sway, which governs and rules for the salvation of souls.❞
— *Spiritual Exercises of Ignatius Loyola,* **Louis J. Puhl, trans., 1951**

Loyola's ideal of complete obedience to the church was the cornerstone of his fight against the spread of Protestant groups.

The Zwinglian Reformation

With the Peace of Augsburg, what had at first been merely feared was now certain: the ideal of Christian unity was forever lost. Even before the Peace of Augsburg, however, division had appeared in Protestantism. One of these new groups appeared in Switzerland.

Ulrich Zwingli was a priest in **Zürich.** The city council of Zürich, strongly influenced by Zwingli, began to introduce religious reforms. Relics and images were abolished. All paintings and decorations were removed from the churches and replaced by whitewashed walls. A new church service consisting of scripture reading, prayer, and sermons replaced the Catholic mass.

As his movement began to spread to other cities in Switzerland, Zwingli sought an alliance with Martin Luther and the German reformers. Both the German and Swiss reformers realized the need for unity to defend themselves against Catholic authorities, but they were unable to agree on the meaning of the sacrament of Communion. 📖 *(See page 994 to read excerpts from Martin Luther and Ulrich Zwingli's* A Reformation Debate *in the Primary Sources Library.)*

In October 1531, war broke out between the Protestant and Catholic states in Switzerland. Zürich's army was routed, and Zwingli was found wounded on the battlefield. His enemies killed him, cut up his body, and burned the pieces, scattering the ashes. The leadership of Protestantism in Switzerland now passed to John Calvin.

✓**Reading Check** **Describing** What religious reforms were introduced in Zürich?

Calvin and Calvinism

John Calvin was educated in his native France. After his conversion to Protestantism, however, he was forced to flee Catholic France for the safety of Switzerland. In 1536, he published the *Institutes of the Christian Religion,* a summary of Protestant thought. This work immediately gave Calvin a reputation as one of the new leaders of Protestantism.

On most important doctrines, Calvin stood very close to Luther. He, too, believed in the doctrine of justification by faith alone to explain how humans achieved salvation. However, Calvin also placed much emphasis on the all-powerful nature of God— what Calvin called the "power, grace, and glory of God."

Calvin's emphasis on the all-powerful nature of God led him to other ideas. One of these ideas was predestination. This "eternal decree," as Calvin called it, meant that God had determined in advance who would be saved (the elect) and who would be damned (the reprobate). According to Calvin, "He has once for all determined, both whom he would admit to salvation, and whom he would condemn to destruction."

The belief in predestination gave later Calvinists the firm conviction that they were doing God's work

Picturing **History**

John Calvin is shown speaking before leaders in Geneva. What attitudes about Calvin and the Protestant movement does the artist convey in this painting?

on Earth. This conviction, in turn, made them determined to spread their faith to other people. Calvinism became a dynamic and activist faith.

In 1536, Calvin began working to reform the city of **Geneva.** He created a church government that used both clergy and laity in the service of the church. The Consistory, a special body for enforcing moral discipline, was set up as a court to oversee the moral life and doctrinal purity of Genevans. The Consistory had the right to punish people who deviated from the church's teachings and moral principles. Citizens in Geneva were punished for such varied "crimes" as dancing, singing obscene songs, drunkenness, swearing, and playing cards.

Calvin's success in Geneva made the city a powerful center of Protestantism. Following Calvin's lead, missionaries trained in Geneva were sent to all parts of Europe. Calvinism became established in France, the Netherlands, Scotland, and central and eastern Europe.

By the mid-sixteenth century, Calvinism had replaced Lutheranism as the most important and dynamic form of Protestantism. Calvin's Geneva stood as the fortress of the Protestant Reformation. John Knox, the Calvinist reformer of Scotland, called it "the most perfect school of Christ on earth."

✔ **Reading Check** **Explaining** How did the Consistory enforce moral discipline in Geneva?

The Reformation in England

The English Reformation was rooted in politics, not religion. **King Henry VIII** wanted to divorce his first wife, Catherine of Aragon, with whom he had a daughter, Mary, but no son. Since he needed a male heir, Henry wanted to marry Anne Boleyn. Impatient with the pope's unwillingness to annul (declare invalid) his marriage to Catherine, Henry turned to England's own church courts.

As the archbishop of Canterbury, head of the highest church court in England, Thomas Cranmer ruled in May 1533 that the king's marriage to Catherine was "null and absolutely void." At the beginning of June, Anne was crowned queen. Three months later a child was born. Much to the king's disappointment, the baby was a girl. She would later become Queen Elizabeth I.

In 1534, at Henry's request, Parliament moved to finalize the break of the Catholic Church in England with the pope in Rome. The Act of Supremacy of 1534 declared that the king was "taken, accepted, and reputed the only supreme head on earth of the [new] Church of England." This position gave the king control over religious doctrine, clerical appointments, and discipline. Thomas More, a Christian humanist and devout Catholic, opposed the king's action and was beheaded.

Henry used his new powers to dissolve the monasteries and sell their land and possessions to wealthy landowners and merchants. The king received a great boost to his treasury and a group of supporters who now had a stake in the new order. In matters of doctrine, however, Henry remained close to Catholic teachings.

When Henry died in 1547, he was succeeded by Edward VI, a sickly nine-year-old, the son of his third wife. During Edward's reign, church officials who favored Protestant doctrines moved the Church of England, also called the Anglican Church, in a Protestant direction. New acts of Parliament gave the clergy the right to marry and created a new Protestant church service. These rapid changes aroused much opposition. When Mary, Henry's daughter by Catherine of Aragon, came to the throne in 1553, England was ready for a reaction.

Henry VIII disagreed with Luther's theology but found it politically convenient to break with the Catholic Church.

There was no doubt that Mary was a Catholic who wanted to restore England to Roman Catholicism. However, the way she went about it had the opposite effect. Among other actions, she had more than three hundred Protestants burned as heretics, earning her the nickname "Bloody Mary." As a result of her policies, England was even more Protestant by the end of Mary's reign than it had been at the beginning.

 Reading Check **Examining** Why did Henry VIII form the Church of England?

The Anabaptists

Reformers such as Luther had allowed the state to play an important, if not dominant, role in church affairs. However, some people strongly disliked giving such power to the state. These were radicals known as the Anabaptists.

To Anabaptists, the true Christian church was a voluntary community of adult believers who had undergone spiritual rebirth and had then been baptized. This belief in adult baptism separated Anabaptists from Catholics and Protestants who baptized infants.

Anabaptists also believed in following the practices and the spirit of early Christianity. They considered all believers to be equal, a belief they based on the accounts of early Christian communities in the New Testament. Each Anabaptist church chose its own minister, or spiritual leader. Because all Christians were considered priests, any member of the community was eligible to be a minister (though women were often excluded).

Finally, most Anabaptists believed in the complete separation of church and state. Not only was government to be kept out of the realm of religion, it was not even supposed to have any political authority over real Christians. Anabaptists refused to hold political office or bear arms, because many took literally the biblical commandment "Thou shall not kill."

Their political beliefs, as much as their religious beliefs, caused the Anabaptists to be regarded as dangerous radicals who threatened the very fabric of sixteenth-century society. Indeed, the chief thing

CONNECTIONS Past To Present

The Descendants of the Anabaptists

Despite being persecuted for their belief in the complete separation of church and state, Anabaptists managed to survive.

Menno Simons was a popular leader of Anabaptism in the Netherlands. He dedicated his life to the spread of a peaceful Anabaptism that stressed separation from the world as the means for living a truly Christ-like life. Because of persecution, Menno Simons's followers, known as Mennonites, spread from the Netherlands into Germany and Russia. In the nineteenth century, many moved to Canada and the United States, where Mennonite communities continue to flourish.

In the 1690s, Jacob Ammann took the lead in encouraging a group of Swiss Mennonites to form their own church. They came to be known as the Amish (after the name Ammann). By the end of the seventeenth century, many of the Amish had come to North America in search of a land where they could practice their religion freely.

Today, Amish communities exist throughout Canada and the United States. One of the largest groups of Amish can be found in Pennsylvania, where they are known as the Pennsylvania Dutch. The Amish continue to maintain the Anabaptist way of life as it first developed in the sixteenth century. They live simple lives and refuse to use any modern devices, including cars and electricity.

▲ *The Amish are religious descendants of the Anabaptists.*

Comparing Past and Present

Today, many people living in the United States, such as the Amish, live without modern conveniences. Which appliances and conveniences would you be willing to give up? What cause or belief today might encourage people to give up a modern lifestyle?

NATIONAL GEOGRAPHIC Major European Religions, 1600

Legend:
- Anabaptist
- Anglican
- Calvinist
- Eastern Orthodox Christian
- Jewish
- Lutheran
- Muslim
- Roman Catholic

SWEDEN
NORWAY
SCOTLAND
North Sea
IRELAND
DENMARK
Baltic Sea
ENGLAND
NETHERLANDS
GERMAN STATES
RUSSIA
Canterbury
Wittenberg
SPANISH NETHERLANDS
POLAND
Worms
BOHEMIA
Paris
ATLANTIC OCEAN
BAVARIA
Augsburg
Zürich
AUSTRIA
Geneva
SWITZERLAND
HUNGARY
FRANCE
Trent
Avignon
ITALY
Black Sea
SPAIN
PORTUGAL
Rome
OTTOMAN EMPIRE
Mediterranean Sea

0 ___ 300 miles
0 ___ 300 kilometers
Lambert Azimuthal Equal-Area projection

Geography Skills

Less than 100 years after Luther posted the Ninety-five Theses, the religious affiliations of Europeans were greatly altered.

1. **Interpreting Maps** What religions would not have been on this map prior to 1517?

2. **Applying Geography Skills** Summarize why Protestant religions spread as shown on the map.

other Protestants and Catholics could agree on was the need to persecute Anabaptists.

Reading Check **Describing** Why were the Anabaptists considered to be dangerous political radicals?

Effects on the Role of Women

The Protestants were important in developing a new view of the family. Protestantism had eliminated the idea that special holiness was associated with

celibacy and had abolished both monasticism and the requirement of celibacy for the clergy. The family could now be placed at the center of human life. The "mutual love between man and wife" could be extolled.

Were idea and reality the same, however? More often, reality reflected the traditional roles of husband as the ruler and wife as the obedient servant whose chief duty was to please her husband. Luther stated it clearly:

❝The rule remains with the husband, and the wife is compelled to obey him by God's command. He rules the home and the state, wages war, defends his possessions, tills the soil, builds, plants, etc. The woman on the other hand is like a nail driven into the wall . . . so the wife should stay at home and look after the affairs of the household, as one who has been deprived of the ability of administering those affairs that are outside and that concern the state. She does not go beyond her most personal duties. **99**

Obedience to her husband was not a woman's only role. Her other important duty was to bear children. To Calvin and Luther, this function of women was part of the divine plan. Family life was the only destiny for most Protestant women. Overall, then, the Protestant Reformation did not change women's subordinate place in society.

✔ **Reading Check** **Evaluating** What impact did the Protestant Reformation have on women?

The Catholic Reformation

By the mid-sixteenth century, Lutheranism had become rooted in Germany and Scandinavia, and Calvinism had taken hold in Switzerland, France, the Netherlands, and eastern Europe. In England, the split from Rome had resulted in the creation of a national church. The situation in Europe did not look particularly good for the Catholic Church.

However, the Catholic Church also had a revitalization in the sixteenth century, giving it new strength and enabling it to regain much that it had lost. This Catholic Reformation was supported by three chief pillars: the Jesuits, reform of the papacy, and the Council of Trent.

The Society of Jesus, known as the Jesuits, was founded by a Spanish nobleman, **Ignatius of Loyola.** Loyola gathered together a small group of followers, which was recognized as a religious order by the pope in 1540. All Jesuits took a special vow of absolute obedience to the pope, making them an important instrument for papal policy. Jesuits used education to spread their message. Jesuit missionaries were very successful in restoring Catholicism to parts of Germany and eastern Europe and in spreading it to other parts of the world.

HISTORY *Online*

Web Activity Visit the *Glencoe World History* Web site at tx.wh.glencoe.com and click on **Chapter 12– Student Web Activity** to learn more about the Reformation.

🎨 **History** *through Art*

***Council of Trent* by Titian** The Council of Trent is thought to be the foundation of the Catholic Reformation. How does Titian's painting convey this idea?

Reform of the papacy was another important factor in the Catholic Reformation. The participation of Renaissance popes in dubious financial transactions and Italian political and military affairs had created many sources of corruption. It took the jolt of the Protestant Reformation to bring about serious reform.

Pope Paul III perceived the need for change and took the bold step of appointing a Reform Commission in 1537 to determine the Church's ills. The commission blamed the Church's problems on the corrupt policies of the popes. Paul III (who recognized the Jesuits as a new religious order) also began the Council of Trent, another pillar of the Catholic Reformation.

In March 1545, a group of cardinals, archbishops, bishops, abbots, and theologians met in the city of **Trent,** on the border between Germany and Italy. There, they began the Council of Trent, which met off and on for 18 years.

The final decrees of the Council of Trent reaffirmed traditional Catholic teachings in opposition to Protestant beliefs. Both faith and good works were declared necessary for salvation. The seven sacraments, the Catholic view of the Eucharist, and clerical celibacy were all upheld. Belief in purgatory and in the use of indulgences was strengthened, although the selling of indulgences was forbidden.

After the Council of Trent, the Roman Catholic Church possessed a clear body of doctrine and was unified under the supreme leadership of the pope.

PAVLO · III · PONTIFICI · MAXIMO

Picturing **History**

Ignatius of Loyola, founder of the Jesuits, is shown kneeling before Pope Paul III. What role did the Jesuits play in the Catholic Reformation?

With a renewed spirit of confidence, Catholics entered a new phase, as well prepared as Calvinists to do battle for their faith.

Reading Check **Describing** What was the relationship between the Jesuits and the pope?

🔺 **TAKS Practice**

SECTION 4 ASSESSMENT

Checking for Understanding

1. **Define** predestination, annul.

2. **Identify** Ulrich Zwingli, John Calvin, Henry VIII, Ignatius of Loyola.

3. **Locate** Zürich, Geneva, Trent.

4. **Describe** the results of "Bloody Mary's" religious policies. How might Mary's actions have indirectly affected the history of the United States?

5. **List** which countries had adopted Calvinism and which had adopted Lutheranism by the mid-sixteenth century.

Critical Thinking

6. **Analyze** How were the religious reforms in Zürich consistent with the aims of the Reformation?

7. **Contrasting Information** Use a diagram like the one below to describe how the Calvinists and the Anabaptists differed in their attitudes toward church members participating in government activities.

Calvinists — Church Participation in Government — Anabaptists

Analyzing Visuals

8. **Identify** the details shown in the portrait of Henry VIII on page 397 that illustrate his power and authority. How did the king use his position as "the only supreme head on earth of the Church of England"? Based on what you have read in your text, do you think that Henry was a religious man? Explain your answer.

Writing About History

9. **Expository Writing** Compose an unbiased account of the Council of Trent. Include who was involved, why it was convened, when it happened, and its final results.

Chapter Summary

The Renaissance was a period of great intellectual and artistic achievement. Religious rebirth followed in the 1500s.

1. Italy experiences an artistic, intellectual, and commercial awakening.

VENICE: The city becomes an international trading power.

FLORENCE: The Medici family improves city life and sponsors humanists and artists.

2. Ideas quickly spread from Italy to northern Europe.

ENGLAND: King Henry VIII invites humanists to court.

FLANDERS: Artists use oil paints to depict fine detail in their paintings.

FRANCE: Architects create elegant castles that combine Gothic and classical styles.

3. Reformers begin to challenge both secular and religious rules and practices.

GERMANY: Martin Luther begins the Protestant Reformation. The Peace of Augsburg divides Germany into Catholic and Protestant states.

ENGLAND: King Henry VIII breaks with the pope to create the Church of England. Catholic Queen Mary executes Protestants.

SWITZERLAND: John Calvin promotes the concept of predestination.

4. The Catholic Church enacts reforms.

ITALY: The Council of Trent defines Catholic Church doctrine and tries to end Church abuses. The Jesuits, who take special vows of obedience to the pope, help spread Catholicism.

Using Key Terms

1. Soldiers who sell their services to the highest bidder are called _____.

2. The study of grammar, rhetoric, moral philosophy, and history was the basis of the intellectual movement called _____.

3. A movement whose major goal was the reform of Christendom was called _____.

4. John Calvin emphasized _____ , the belief that God chose who would be saved and who would be damned.

5. A _____ society places less emphasis on religion and more emphasis on a worldly spirit.

6. An _____ is one in which a great many people live in cities.

7. The money and goods given by the wife's family at the time of marriage is called a _____.

8. A remission, after death, from all or part of the punishment due to sin is called an _____.

9. An image painted on fresh, wet plaster is called a _____.

Reviewing Key Facts

10. **History** Which family dominated Florence during the Renaissance?

11. **Culture** Who wrote *The Canterbury Tales?*

12. **Culture** The Renaissance was a rebirth of the ideas of which ancient civilizations?

13. **History** According to Erasmus, what should be the chief concerns of the Christian church?

14. **Culture** How did Renaissance artists portray the human body?

15. **Government** How were the city-states of Renaissance Italy governed? What social classes were present in the typical city-state?

16. **History** How did Ignatius of Loyola help to reform Catholicism?

17. **History** Why did the Renaissance begin in Italy?

18. **Culture** Name the title and the author of one of the most influential works on political power.

19. **Culture** When were children considered adults in Renaissance Italy?

Critical Thinking

20. **Analyzing** Why did Martin Luther split with the Catholic Church? Identify the causes that led to the Protestant Reformation.

21. **Explaining** List one masterpiece of Renaissance literature or art and explain how it reflects Renaissance ideals.

Writing About History

22. **Expository Writing** Analyze how the Reformation shaped the political and religious life of Europe. Be sure to identify the historical effects of the Reformation.

Analyzing Sources

Read the following description by Luther of a woman's role in marriage.

> ❝The rule remains with the husband, and the wife is compelled to obey him by God's command. He rules the home and the state, wages war, defends his possessions, tills the soil, builds, plants, etc. The woman on the other hand is like a nail driven into the wall . . . so the wife should stay at home and look after the affairs of the household, as one who has been deprived of the ability of administering those affairs that are outside and that concern the state. She does not go beyond her most personal duties.❞

23. What does this quote reveal about the woman's role in Protestant society?

24. What do you think Luther meant by the statement "The woman on the other hand is like a nail driven into the wall"?

Applying Technology Skills

25. Using the Internet Use the Internet to research a Renaissance artist. Find information about the person's life and achievements. Using your research, take on the role of that person and create an autobiography about your life and your contributions to the Renaissance.

Making Decisions

26. Select two of the following types of Renaissance people: a noble, merchant, shopkeeper, or peasant. Research what life was like for these individuals. How did their lives vary? Who had the more comfortable lifestyle? Take into account economic and social factors.

Analyzing Maps and Charts

27. Study the map at the top of the page. What are two of the bodies of water that border the Holy Roman Empire?

28. Using a contemporary atlas, name the modern countries that are within the boundaries of what was the Holy Roman Empire.

29. According to this map, was Rome a part of the Holy Roman Empire in 1400?

NATIONAL GEOGRAPHIC **Holy Roman Empire, 1400**

Directions: Use the passage below *and* your knowledge of world history to answer the following question.

> **from the Ninety-five Theses (1517)**
>
> Ignorant and wicked are the doings of those priests who, in the case of the dying, reserve canonical penances for purgatory.

Martin Luther's famous document attacked the Catholic Church for which practice?

F The Catholic Church had allowed humanism to spread through Europe.

G Luther disagreed with the doctrine of predestination.

H Many religious leaders sold indulgences.

J The Catholic popes were too concerned with worldly affairs.

Test-Taking Tip: If the question asks you to read a quote, look for clues that reveal its historical context. Such clues can be found in the title and date of the text as well as in the quote itself. Determining the historical context will help you to determine the quote's *historical significance* or the importance it has gained over time.

CHAPTER 13

The Age of Exploration

1500–1800

Key Events

As you read this chapter, look for the key events of the Age of Exploration.
- Europeans risked dangerous ocean voyages to discover new sea routes.
- Early European explorers sought gold in Africa then began to trade slaves.
- Trade increased in Southeast Asia, and the Dutch built a trade empire based on spices in the Indonesian Archipelago.

The Impact Today

The events that occurred during this time period still impact our lives today.
- European trade was a factor in producing a new age of commercial capitalism that was one of the first steps toward today's world economy.
- The consequences of slavery continue to impact our lives today.
- The Age of Exploration led to a transfer of ideas and products, many of which are still important in our lives today.

World History Video *The Chapter 13 video, "Magellan's Voyage," chronicles European exploration of the world.*

Amerigo Vespucci

Hernán Cortés

1497
John Cabot and Amerigo Vespucci explore the Americas

1519
Spanish begin conquest of Mexico

1595
First Dutch fleet arrives in India

1480   1510   1540   1570   1600

1492
Christopher Columbus reaches the Americas

1518
First boatload of slaves brought directly from Africa to the Americas

1520
Magellan sails into Pacific Ocean

Shackled African slaves

Ships of the Dutch East India Company

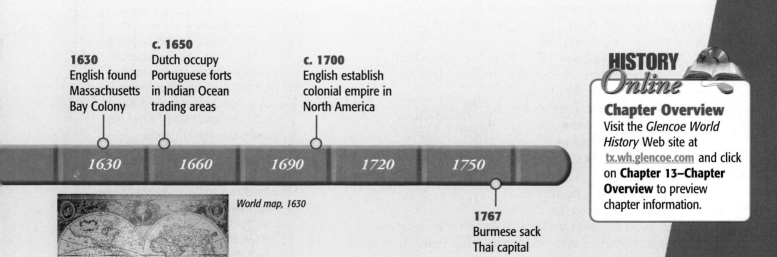

1630
English found
Massachusetts
Bay Colony

c. 1650
Dutch occupy
Portuguese forts
in Indian Ocean
trading areas

c. 1700
English establish
colonial empire in
North America

1630   1660   1690   1720   1750

World map, 1630

1767
Burmese sack
Thai capital

HISTORY
Online
Chapter Overview
Visit the *Glencoe World
History* Web site at
tx.wh.glencoe.com and click
on **Chapter 13–Chapter
Overview** to preview
chapter information.

A Story That Matters

Ferdinand Magellan

Discovery of Magellan Strait *by an unknown artist*

Magellan Sails Around the World

Convinced that he could find a sea passage to Asia through the Western Hemisphere, the Portuguese explorer Ferdinand Magellan persuaded the king of Spain to finance his voyage. On September 20, 1519, Magellan set sail on the Atlantic Ocean with five ships and a Spanish crew of about 250 men.

After reaching South America, Magellan's fleet moved down the coast in search of a strait, or sea passage, that would take them through America. His Spanish ship captains thought he was crazy: "The fool is obsessed with his search for a strait," one remarked.

At last, in November 1520, Magellan passed through a narrow waterway (later named the Strait of Magellan) and emerged in the Pacific Ocean, which he called the Pacific Sea. Magellan reckoned that it would be a short distance from there to the Spice Islands of the East.

Week after week he and his crew sailed on across the Pacific as their food supplies dwindled. At last they reached the Philippines (named after the future King Philip II of Spain). There, Magellan was killed by the native peoples. Only one of his original fleet of five ships returned to Spain, but Magellan is still remembered as the first person to sail around the world.

SOUTH AMERICA
ATLANTIC OCEAN
Strait of Magellan
PACIFIC SEA

Why It Matters

At the beginning of the sixteenth century, European adventurers launched their small fleets into the vast reaches of the Atlantic Ocean. They were hardly aware that they were beginning a new era, not only for Europe but also for the peoples of Asia, Africa, and the Americas. These European voyages marked the beginning of a process that led to radical changes in the political, economic, and cultural life of the entire non-Western world.

History and You Create a map to scale that shows Spain, South America, and the Philippines. Draw the route Magellan took from Spain to the Philippines. If the voyage took about 20 months, how many miles each day, on average, did Magellan travel? How long would a similar sea voyage take today?

Exploration and Expansion

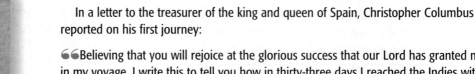

Voices from the Past

Christopher Columbus

In a letter to the treasurer of the king and queen of Spain, Christopher Columbus reported on his first journey:

❝Believing that you will rejoice at the glorious success that our Lord has granted me in my voyage, I write this to tell you how in thirty-three days I reached the Indies with the first fleet which the most illustrious King and Queen, our Sovereigns, gave me, where I discovered a great many thickly-populated islands. Without meeting resistance, I have taken possession of them all for their Highnesses. . . . When I reached [Cuba], I followed its coast to the westward, and found it so large that I thought it must be the mainland—the province of [China], but I found neither towns nor villages on the seacoast, save for a few hamlets.❞

—*Letters from the First Voyage*, **edited 1847**

To the end of his life, despite the evidence, Columbus believed he had found a new route to Asia.

Motives and Means

The dynamic energy of Western civilization between 1500 and 1800 was most apparent when Europeans began to expand into the rest of the world. First Portugal and Spain, then later the Dutch Republic, England, and France, all rose to new economic heights through their worldwide trading activity.

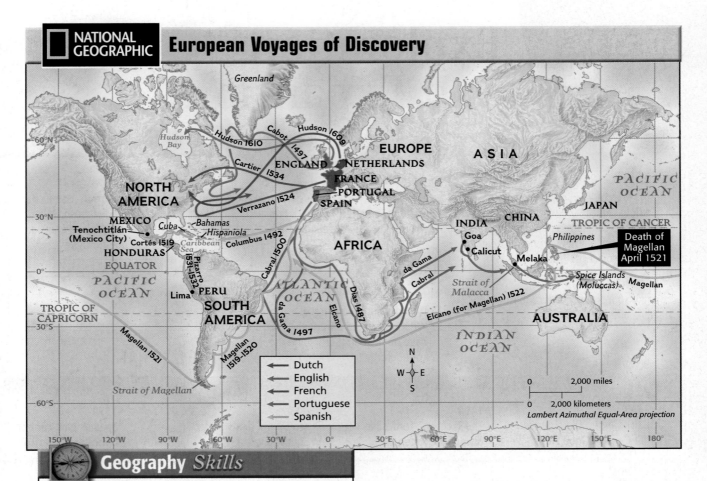

NATIONAL GEOGRAPHIC — European Voyages of Discovery

Geography *Skills*

For more than a hundred years European explorers sailed the globe searching for wealth and glory.

1. **Interpreting Maps** Which continents were left untouched by European explorers?

2. **Applying Geography Skills** Create a table that organizes the information on this map. Include the explorer, date, sponsoring country, and area explored.

For almost a thousand years, Europeans had mostly remained in one area of the world. At the end of the fifteenth century, however, they set out on a remarkable series of overseas journeys. What caused them to undertake such dangerous voyages to the ends of the earth?

Europeans had long been attracted to Asia. In the late thirteenth century, Marco Polo had traveled with his father and uncle to the Chinese court of the great Mongol ruler Kublai Khan. He had written an account of his experiences, known as *The Travels*. The book was read by many, including Columbus, who were fascinated by the exotic East. In the fourteenth century, conquests by the Ottoman Turks reduced the ability of westerners to travel by land to the East. People then spoke of gaining access to Asia by sea.

Economic motives loom large in European expansion. Merchants, adventurers, and state officials had high hopes of expanding trade, especially for the spices of the East. The spices, which were needed to preserve and flavor food, were very expensive after being shipped to Europe by Arab middlemen. Europeans also had hopes of finding precious metals. One Spanish adventurer wrote that he went to the Americas "to give light to those who were in darkness, and to grow rich, as all men desire to do."

This statement suggests another reason for the overseas voyages: religious zeal. Many people shared the belief of Hernán Cortés, the Spanish conqueror of Mexico, that they must ensure that the natives "are introduced into the holy Catholic faith."

There was a third motive as well. Spiritual and secular affairs were connected in the sixteenth century. Adventurers such as Cortés wanted to convert the natives to Christianity, but grandeur, glory, and a spirit of adventure also played a major role in European expansion.

"God, glory, and gold," then, were the chief motives for European expansion, but what made the voyages possible? By the second half of the fifteenth century, European monarchies had increased their power and their resources. They could now turn their energies beyond their borders. Europeans had also reached a level of technology that enabled them to make a regular series of voyages beyond Europe. A new global age was about to begin.

✓ **Reading Check** **Explaining** What does the phrase "God, glory, and gold" mean?

The Portuguese Trading Empire

Portugal took the lead in European exploration. Beginning in 1420, under the sponsorship of Prince Henry the Navigator, Portuguese fleets began probing southward along the western coast of **Africa.** There, they discovered a new source of gold. The southern coast of West Africa thus became known to Europeans as the Gold Coast.

Portuguese sea captains heard reports of a route to India around the southern tip of Africa. In 1488, Bartholomeu Dias rounded the tip, called the Cape of Good Hope. Later, **Vasco da Gama** went around the cape and cut across the Indian Ocean to the coast of India. In May of 1498, he arrived off the port of Calicut, where he took on a cargo of spices. He returned to Portugal and made a profit of several thousand percent. Is it surprising that da Gama's voyage was the first of many along this route?

Portuguese fleets returned to the area to destroy Muslim shipping and to gain control of the spice trade, which had been controlled by the Muslims. In

SCIENCE, TECHNOLOGY & SOCIETY

Sea Travel in an Age of Exploration

European voyagers acquired much of their knowledge about sailing from the Arabs. For example, sailors used charts that Arab navigators and mathematicians had drawn in the thirteenth and fourteenth centuries. Known as *portolani,* these charts recorded the shapes of coastlines and distances between ports. They were very valuable in European waters. Because the charts were drawn on a flat scale and took no account of the curvature of the earth, however, they were of little help on overseas voyages.

Only as sailors began to move beyond the coasts of Europe did they gain information about the actual shape of the earth. By 1500, cartography—the art and science of mapmaking—had reached the point where Europeans had fairly accurate maps of the areas they had explored.

Europeans also learned new navigational techniques from the Arabs. Previously, sailors had used the position of the North Star to determine their latitude. Below the Equator, though, this technique was useless. The compass and the astrolabe (also perfected by the Arabs) greatly aided exploration. The compass showed in what direction a ship was moving. The astrolabe used the sun or a star to ascertain a ship's latitude.

Finally, European shipmakers learned how to use lateen (triangular) sails, which were developed by the Arabs. New ships, called caravels, were more maneuverable and could carry heavy cannon and more goods.

Evaluating *Which one advance was the most important for early explorers? Why?*

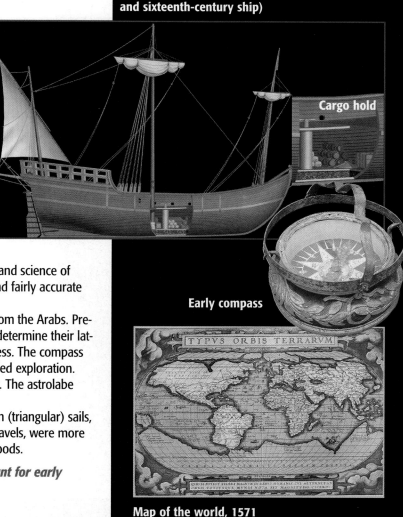

Caravel (small fifteenth- and sixteenth-century ship)

Cargo hold

Early compass

Map of the world, 1571

1509, a Portuguese fleet of warships defeated a combined fleet of Turkish and Indian ships off the coast of India. A year later, Admiral Afonso de Albuquerque set up a port at Goa, on the western coast of India.

The Portuguese then began to range more widely in search of the source of the spice trade. Soon, Albuquerque sailed into **Melaka** on the Malay Peninsula. Melaka was a thriving port for the spice trade. For Albuquerque, control of Melaka would help to destroy Arab control of the spice trade and provide the Portuguese with a way station on the route to the Moluccas, then known as the Spice Islands.

From Melaka, the Portuguese launched expeditions to China and the Spice Islands. There, they signed a treaty with a local ruler for the purchase and export of cloves to the European market. This treaty established Portuguese control of the spice trade. The Portuguese trading empire was complete. However, it remained a limited empire of trading posts. The Portuguese had neither the power, the people, nor the desire to colonize the Asian regions.

Why were the Portuguese the first successful European explorers? Basically it was a matter of guns and seamanship. Later, however, the Portuguese would be no match for other European forces—the English, Dutch, and French.

✓ **Reading Check** **Explaining** Why did Afonso de Albuquerque want control of Melaka?

Voyages to the Americas

The Portuguese sailed eastward through the Indian Ocean to reach the source of the spice trade. The Spanish sought to reach it by sailing westward across the Atlantic Ocean. With more people and greater resources, the Spanish established an overseas empire that was quite different from the Portuguese trading posts.

*O*pposing *V*iewpoints

What Was the Impact of Columbus on the Americas?

Historians have differed widely over the impact of Columbus on world history. Was he a hero who ushered in economic well being throughout the world? Or, was he a prime mover in the destruction of the people and cultures of the Americas?

❝The whole history of the Americas stems from the Four Voyages of Columbus. . . . Today a core of independent nations unite in homage to Christopher, the stout-hearted son of Genoa, who carried Christian civilization across the Ocean Sea.❞

—**Samuel Eliot Morison, 1942**
Admiral of the Ocean Sea,
A Life of Christopher Columbus

❝Just twenty-one years after Columbus's first landing in the Caribbean, the vastly populous island that the explorer had re-named Hispaniola was effectively desolate; nearly 8,000,000 people. . . had been killed by violence, disease, and despair. [W]hat happened on Hispaniola was the equivalent of more than fifty Hiroshimas.* And Hispaniola was only the beginning.❞

—**David E. Stannard, 1992**
American Holocaust: Columbus
and the Conquest of the New World

*The atom bomb dropped on Hiroshima, Japan, killed at least 130,000 people.

The Voyages of Columbus An important figure in the history of Spanish exploration was an Italian, **Christopher Columbus.** Educated Europeans knew that the world was round, but had little understanding of its circumference or of the size of the continent of Asia. Convinced that the circumference of Earth was not as great as others thought, Columbus believed that he could reach Asia by sailing west instead of east around Africa.

Columbus persuaded Queen Isabella of Spain to finance an exploratory expedition. In October 1492, he reached the Americas, where he explored the coastline of **Cuba** and the island of Hispaniola.

Columbus believed he had reached Asia. Through three more voyages, he sought in vain to find a route through the outer islands to the Asian mainland. In his four voyages, Columbus reached all the major islands of the Caribbean and Honduras in Central America—all of which he called the Indies.

Columbus petitions Queen Isabella for financial support of his explorations.

❝When the two races first met on the eastern coast of America, there was unlimited potential for harmony. The newcomers could have adapted to the hosts' customs and values. . . . But this did not happen . . . [Columbus] viewed the natives of America with arrogance and disdain . . . Columbus wrote of gold, . . . and of spices, . . . and 'slaves, as many as they shall order to be shipped. . . .'❞

—**George P. Horse Capture, 1992**
"An American Indian Perspective," *Seeds of Change*

You Decide

1. Using information from the text and outside sources, write an account of Columbus's voyages from his point of view. If Columbus were to undertake his voyages today, would he do anything differently? If not, why not?

2. Using the information in the text and your own research, evaluate the validity of these three excerpts. Which excerpt corroborates the information of the other? What might account for the difference in the viewpoints expressed here?

A Line of Demarcation By the 1490s, then, the voyages of the Portuguese and Spanish had already opened up new lands to exploration. Both Spain and Portugal feared that the other might claim some of its newly discovered territories. They resolved their concerns by agreeing on a line of demarcation, an imaginary line that divided their spheres of influence.

According to the Treaty of Tordesillas (TAWR•duh•SEE•yuhs), signed in 1494, the line would extend from north to south through the Atlantic Ocean and the easternmost part of the South American continent. Unexplored territories east of the line would be controlled by Portugal, and those west of the line by Spain. This treaty gave Portugal control over its route around Africa, and it gave Spain rights to almost all of the Americas.

Race to the Americas Other explorers soon realized that Columbus had discovered an entirely new frontier. Government-sponsored explorers from many countries joined the race to the Americas. A Venetian seaman, **John Cabot,** explored the New England coastline of the Americas for England. The Portuguese sea captain Pedro Cabral landed in South America in 1500. **Amerigo Vespucci** (veh•SPOO•chee), a Florentine, went along on several voyages and wrote letters describing the lands he saw. These letters led to the use of the name *America* (after Amerigo) for the new lands.

Europeans called these territories the New World, but the lands were hardly new. They already had flourishing civilizations made up of millions of people when the Europeans arrived. The Americas were, of course, new to the Europeans, who quickly saw opportunities for conquest and exploitation.

✓ **Reading Check** **Examining** Why did the Spanish and Portuguese sign the Treaty of Tordesillas?

The Spanish Empire

The Spanish conquerors of the Americas—known as conquistadors—were individuals whose guns and determination brought them incredible success. The forces of Hernán Cortés took only three years to overthrow the mighty Aztec Empire in Central Mexico (see Chapter 11). By 1550, the Spanish had gained control of northern Mexico. In South America, an expedition led by **Francisco Pizarro** took control of the Incan Empire high in the Peruvian Andes. Within 30 years, the western part of Latin America, as these lands in Mexico and Central and South America were called, had been brought under Spanish control. (The Portuguese took over Brazil, which fell on their side of the line of demarcation.)

By 1535, the Spanish had created a system of colonial administration in the Americas. Queen Isabella declared Native Americans (then called Indians, after the Spanish word *Indios*, "inhabitants of the Indies") to be her subjects. She granted the Spanish *encomienda*, or the right to use Native Americans as laborers.

The Spanish were supposed to protect Native Americans, but the settlers were far from Spain and largely ignored their rulers. Native Americans were put to work on sugar plantations and in gold and silver mines. Few Spanish settlers worried about protecting them.

Forced labor, starvation, and especially disease took a fearful toll on Native American lives. With little natural resistance to European diseases, the native peoples were ravaged by smallpox, measles, and typhus, and many of them died. Hispaniola, for example, had a population of 250,000 when Columbus arrived. By 1538, only 500 Native Americans had survived. In Mexico, the population dropped from 25 million in 1519 to 1 million in 1630.

In the early years of the conquest, Catholic missionaries converted and baptized hundreds of

Incan mask

thousands of native peoples. With the arrival of the missionaries came parishes, schools, and hospitals—all the trappings of a European society. Native American social and political structures were torn apart and replaced by European systems of religion, language, culture, and government.

✓ **Reading Check** **Evaluating** What was the impact of the Spanish settlement on the Native Americans?

Economic Impact and Competition

⌐TURNING POINT⌐ **International trade was crucial in creating a new age of commercial capitalism, one of the first steps in the development of the world economy.**

Spanish conquests in the Americas affected not only the conquered but also the conquerors. This was especially true in the economic arena. Wherever they went, Europeans sought gold and silver. One Aztec commented that the Spanish conquerors "longed and lusted for gold. Their bodies swelled with greed; they hungered like pigs for that gold." Rich silver deposits were found and exploited in Mexico and southern Peru (modern Bolivia).

Colonists established plantations and ranches to raise sugar, cotton, vanilla, livestock, and other products introduced to the Americas for export to Europe. Agricultural products native to the Americas, such as potatoes, cocoa, corn, and tobacco, were also shipped to Europe. The extensive exchange of plants and animals between the Old and New Worlds—known as the Columbian Exchange—transformed economic activity in both worlds.

At the same time, Portuguese expansion in the East created its own economic impact. With their Asian trading posts, Portugal soon challenged the Italian states as the chief entry point of the eastern trade in spices, jewels, silk, and perfumes. Other European nations soon sought similar economic benefits.

New Rivals Enter the Scene

By the end of the sixteenth century, several new European rivals had entered the scene for the eastern trade. The Spanish established themselves in the Philippine Islands, where **Ferdinand Magellan** had landed earlier. They turned the Philippines into a major Spanish base for trade across the Pacific. Spanish ships carried silver from Mexico to the Philippines and returned to Mexico with silk and other luxury goods.

At the beginning of the seventeenth century, an English fleet landed on the northwestern coast of India and established trade relations with the people there. Trade with Southeast Asia soon followed.

The first Dutch fleet arrived in India in 1595. Shortly after, the Dutch formed the East India Company and began competing with the English and the Portuguese.

The Dutch also formed the West India Company to compete with the Spanish and Portuguese in the Americas. The Dutch colony of New Netherland stretched from the mouth of the Hudson River as far north as Albany, New York. Present-day names such as *Staten Island, Harlem,* and the *Catskill Mountains* remind us that it was the Dutch who initially settled the Hudson River valley.

After 1660, however, rivalry with the English and the French (who had also become active in North America) brought the fall of the Dutch commercial empire in the Americas. The English seized the colony of New Netherland and renamed it New York.

During the 1600s, the French colonized parts of what is now Canada and Louisiana. English settlers, meanwhile, founded Virginia and the Massachusetts Bay Colony. By 1700, the English had established a colonial empire along the eastern seaboard of North America. They also had set up sugar plantations on various islands in the Caribbean Sea.

Trade, Colonies, and Mercantilism Led by Portugal and Spain, European nations in the 1500s and 1600s established many trading posts and colonies in the Americas and the East. A colony is a settlement of people living in a new territory, linked with the parent country by trade and direct government control.

With the development of colonies and trading posts, Europeans entered an age of increased international trade. Colonies played a role in the theory of mercantilism, a set of principles that dominated economic thought in the seventeenth century. According to mercantilists, the prosperity of a nation depended on a large supply of bullion, or gold and silver. To bring in gold and silver payments, nations tried to have a favorable balance of trade. The balance of trade is the difference in value between what a nation imports and what it exports over time. When the balance is favorable, the goods exported are of greater value than those imported.

To encourage exports, governments stimulated export industries and trade. They granted subsidies, or payments, to new industries and improved transportation systems by building roads, bridges, and canals. By placing high tariffs, or taxes, on foreign goods, they tried to keep these goods out of their own countries. Colonies were considered important both as sources of raw materials and markets for finished goods.

✓ **Reading Check** **Identifying** What products were sent from the Americas to Europe?

🔹**TAKS Practice**

SECTION 1 ASSESSMENT

Checking for Understanding

1. **Define** conquistador, colony, mercantilism, balance of trade.

2. **Identify** Vasco da Gama, Christopher Columbus, John Cabot, Amerigo Vespucci, Francisco Pizarro, Ferdinand Magellan.

3. **Locate** Portugal, Africa, Melaka, Cuba.

4. **Explain** why the Spanish were so hungry for gold.

5. **List** the institutions of European society that were brought to the Americas by European missionaries.

Critical Thinking

6. **Describe** Identify and briefly describe the negative consequences of the Spanish *encomienda* system. Were there any positive consequences?

7. **Identifying Information** Use a web diagram like the one below to list motives for European exploration.

Analyzing Visuals

8. **Examine** the photograph of the Incan mask shown on page 412 of your text. How could artifacts such as this have increased the European desire to explore and conquer the Americas?

Writing About History

9. **Descriptive Writing** Research one of the expeditions discussed in this section. Write a journal entry describing your experiences as a sailor on the expedition. Provide details of your daily life on the ship and what you found when you first reached land.

Columbus Lands in the Americas

ON RETURNING FROM HIS VOYAGE TO THE Americas, Christopher Columbus wrote a

letter describing his experience. In this passage from the letter, he tells of his arrival on the island of Hispaniola.

Columbus landing in the Americas

❝The people of this island and of all the other islands which I have found and of which I have information, all go naked, men and women, as their mothers bore them. They have no iron or steel or weapons, nor are they fitted to use them. This is not because they are not well built and of handsome stature, but because they are very marvelously timid. They have no other arms than spears made of canes, cut in seeding time, to the end of which they fix a small sharpened stick.

They refuse nothing that they possess, if it be asked of them; on the contrary, they invite any one to share it and display as much love as if they would give their hearts. They are content with whatever trifle of whatever kind they may be given to them, whether it be of value or valueless. I forbade that they should be given things so worthless as fragments of broken crockery, scraps of broken glass and lace tips, although when they were able to get them, they fancied that they possessed the best jewel in the world. So it was found that for a leather strap a soldier received gold to the weight of two and half castellanos, and others received much more for other things which were worthless. . . . I gave them a thousand handsome good things, which I had brought, in order that they might conceive affection for us and, more than that, might become Christians and be inclined to the love and service of Your Highnesses [king and queen of Spain], and strive to collect and give us of the things which they have in abundance and what are necessary to us.

They practice no kind of idolatry, but have a firm belief that all strength and power, and indeed all good things, are in heaven, and that I had descended from thence with these ships and sailors, and under this impression was I received after they had thrown aside their fears. Nor are they slow or stupid, but of very clear understanding; and those men who have crossed to the neighbouring islands give an abominable description of everything they observed; but they never saw any people clothed, nor any ships like ours.❞

—Christopher Columbus, *The Journal of Christopher Columbus*

Analyzing Primary Sources

1. Why did Columbus give the peoples of Hispaniola "a thousand handsome good things"?
2. How did the explorers take advantage of Native Americans?

Africa in an Age of Transition

Voices from the Past

Captured Africans, yoked and shackled

Early European explorers sought gold in Africa but were soon involved in the slave trade. One Dutch trader noted:

❝As the slaves come down to Fida [a port on the west coast of Africa] from the inland country, they are put into a booth, or prison, built for that purpose, near the beach, all of them together; and when the Europeans are to receive them, they are brought out into a large plain, where the surgeons examine every part of them, men and women being all stark naked. Such as are found good and sound are set on one side. Each of those which have passed as good is marked . . . with a red-hot iron, imprinting the mark of the French, English, or Dutch companies, so that each nation may distinguish its own and prevent their being changed by the natives for worse.❞

—*Documents Illustrative of the Slave Trade to America*, Elizabeth Dorman, ed.,1930

The exchange of slaves became an important part of European trading patterns.

The Slave Trade

Traffic in slaves was not new, to be sure. As in other areas of the world, slavery had been practiced in Africa since ancient times. In the fifteenth century, it continued at a fairly steady level.

The primary market for African slaves was Southwest Asia, where most slaves were used as domestic servants. Slavery also existed in some European countries.

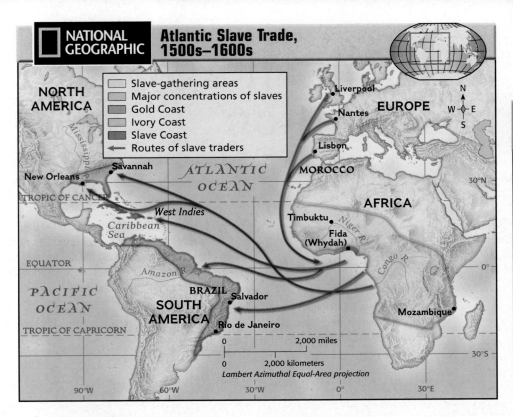

NATIONAL GEOGRAPHIC

Atlantic Slave Trade, 1500s–1600s

Legend:
- Slave-gathering areas
- Major concentrations of slaves
- Gold Coast
- Ivory Coast
- Slave Coast
- ← Routes of slave traders

NORTH AMERICA

EUROPE

Liverpool

Nantes

Lisbon

MOROCCO

ATLANTIC OCEAN

New Orleans

Savannah

TROPIC OF CANCER

West Indies

Caribbean Sea

AFRICA

Timbuktu

Niger R.

Fida (Whydah)

30°N

EQUATOR

Amazon R.

Congo R.

0°

PACIFIC OCEAN

BRAZIL

SOUTH AMERICA

Salvador

Mozambique

TROPIC OF CAPRICORN

Rio de Janeiro

0   2,000 miles

0   2,000 kilometers
Lambert Azimuthal Equal-Area projection

30°S

90°W   60°W   30°W   0°   30°E

Geography Skills

From 1450 to 1600, about 275,000 Africans were exported as slaves to the Americas.

1. **Interpreting Maps** What part of Africa was the greatest source of slaves? Why?

2. **Applying Geography Skills** What, if any, adjustments to climate would African slaves have to make in North America and Europe?

During the last half of the fifteenth century, for example, about a thousand slaves were taken to Portugal each year. Most wound up serving as domestic servants. The demand for slaves changed dramatically, however, with the discovery of the Americas in the 1490s and the planting of sugarcane there.

Cane sugar was introduced to Europe from Southwest Asia during the Middle Ages. During the sixteenth century, plantations, large agricultural estates, were set up along the coast of **Brazil** and on islands in the Caribbean to grow sugarcane. Growing cane sugar demands much labor. The small Native American population, much of which had died of diseases imported from Europe, could not provide the labor needed. Thus, African slaves were shipped to Brazil and the Caribbean to work on the plantations.

Growth of the Slave Trade In 1518, a Spanish ship carried the first boatload of African slaves directly from Africa to the Americas. During the next two centuries, the trade in slaves grew dramatically and became part of the triangular trade that marked the emergence of a new world economy. The pattern of triangular trade connected Europe, Africa and Asia, and the American continents. European merchant ships carried European manufactured goods, such as guns and cloth, to Africa, where they were traded for a cargo of slaves. The slaves were then shipped to the Americas and sold. European merchants then bought tobacco, molasses, sugar, and raw cotton and shipped them back to Europe to be sold in European markets.

An estimated 275,000 African slaves were exported during the sixteenth century. Two thousand went every year to the Americas alone. In the seventeenth century, the total climbed to over a million and jumped to six million in the eighteenth century. By then the trade had spread from West Africa and central Africa to East Africa. Altogether, as many as ten million African slaves were brought to the Americas between the early sixteenth and the late nineteenth centuries.

One reason for these astonishing numbers, of course, was the high death rate. The journey of slaves from Africa to the Americas became known as the Middle Passage, the middle portion of the triangular trade route. Many slaves died on the journey. Those who arrived often died from diseases to which they had little or no immunity.

Death rates were higher for newly arrived slaves than for those born and raised in the Americas. The new generation gradually developed at least a partial immunity to many diseases. Owners, however, rarely encouraged their slaves to have children. Many slave owners, especially on islands in the Caribbean, believed that buying a new slave was less expensive than raising a child from birth to working age.

Sources of Slaves Before the coming of Europeans in the fifteenth century, most slaves in Africa were prisoners of war. When Europeans first began to take part in the slave trade, they bought slaves from local African merchants at slave markets on the coasts in return for gold, guns, or other European goods.

At first, local slave traders obtained their supplies of slaves from the coastal regions nearby. As demand increased, however, they had to move farther inland to find their victims.

Local rulers became concerned about the impact of the slave trade on the well-being of their societies. In a letter to the king of Portugal in 1526, **King Afonso** of Congo (Bakongo) said, "so great is the corruption that our country is being completely depopulated."

Protests from Africans were generally ignored by Europeans, however, as well as by other Africans. As a rule, local rulers who traded slaves viewed the slave trade as a source of income. Many sent raiders into defenseless villages in search of victims.

Effects of the Slave Trade The effects of the slave trade varied from area to area. Of course, it always had tragic effects on the lives of individual victims and their families. The slave trade led to the depopulation of some areas, and it deprived many African communities of their youngest and strongest men and women.

The desire of local slave traders to provide a constant supply of slaves led to increased warfare in Africa. Coastal or near-coastal African leaders and their followers, armed with guns acquired from the trade in slaves, increased their raids and wars on neighboring peoples.

Slaves were kept in the ship's cargo deck, called the hold.

Only a few Europeans lamented what they were doing to traditional African societies. One Dutch slave trader remarked, "From us they have learned strife, quarrelling, drunkenness, trickery, theft, unbridled desire for what is not one's own, misdeeds unknown to them before, and the accursed lust for gold."

HISTORY *Online*

Web Activity Visit the *Glencoe World History* Web site at tx.wh.glencoe.com and click on **Chapter 13– Student Web Activity** to learn more about the Age of Exploration.

The slave trade had a devastating effect on some African states. The case of **Benin** in West Africa is a good example. A brilliant and creative society in the sixteenth century, Benin was pulled into the slave trade.

As the population declined and warfare increased, the people of Benin lost faith in their gods, their art deteriorated, and human sacrifice became more common. When the British arrived there at the end of the nineteenth century, they found a corrupt and brutal place. It took years to discover the brilliance of the earlier culture destroyed by slavery.

✓ **Reading Check** **Describing** Describe the purpose and path of the triangular trade.

Political and Social Structures

The slave trade was one of the most noticeable effects of the European presence in Africa between 1500 and 1800. Generally, European influence did not extend beyond the coastal regions. Only in a few areas, such as **South Africa** and **Mozambique,** were there signs of a permanent European presence.

Traditional Political Systems In general, traditional African political systems continued to exist. By the sixteenth century, monarchy had become a common form of government throughout much of the continent. Some states, like the kingdom of Benin in West Africa, were highly centralized, with the king regarded as almost divine.

Other African states were more like collections of small principalities knit together by ties of kinship or other loyalties. The state of Ashanti on the Gold Coast was a good example. The kingdom consisted of a number of previously independent small states linked together by kinship ties and subordinated to the king. To provide visible evidence of this unity, each local ruler was given a ceremonial stool of office as a symbol of the kinship ties that linked the rulers

King Afonso I
c.1456–c.1545—African king

Afonso I was the greatest king of Congo (present-day Angola and the Democratic Republic of the Congo). He was born Mvemba Nzinga, son of the king of Congo. After the Portuguese arrived in the kingdom, Mvemba converted to Catholicism and changed his name to Afonso. After he became king in 1506, Afonso sought friendly relations with the Portuguese. In return for trade privileges, the Portuguese sent manufactured goods, missionaries, and craftspeople to Congo. Afonso soon found, however, that the Portuguese could not be trusted. They made more and more raids for African slaves and even attempted to assassinate King Afonso when they thought that the king was hiding gold from them. Afonso remained a devout Christian, building churches and schools.

together. The king had an exquisite golden stool to symbolize the unity of the entire state.

Many Africans continued to live in small political units in which authority rested in a village leader. For example, the **Ibo** society of eastern Nigeria was based on independent villages. The Ibo were active traders, and the area produced more slaves than practically any other in the continent.

Foreign Influences Many African political systems, then, were affected little by the European presence.

Nevertheless, the Europeans were causing changes, sometimes indirectly. In the western Sahara, for example, trade routes shifted toward the coast. This led to the weakening of the old Songhai trading empire and the emergence of a vigorous new Moroccan dynasty in the late sixteenth century.

Morocco had long hoped to expand its influence into the Sahara in order to seize control over the trade in gold and salt. In 1591, after a 20-week trek across the desert, Moroccan forces defeated the Songhai army and then occupied the great trading center of Timbuktu. Eventually, the Moroccans were forced to leave, but Songhai was beyond recovery. Its next two centuries were marked by civil disorder.

Foreigners also influenced African religious beliefs. Here, however, Europeans had less impact than the Islamic culture. In North Africa, Islam continued to expand. Muslim beliefs became dominant along the northern coast and spread southward into the states of West and East Africa.

Although their voyages centered on trade with the East, Europeans were also interested in spreading Christianity. The Portuguese engaged in some missionary activity, but the English, the Dutch, and the French made little effort to combine their trading activities with the Christian message. Except for a tiny European foothold in South Africa and the isolated kingdom of Ethiopia, Christianity did not stop the spread of Islam in Africa.

Reading Check **Describing** What was the most common form of government throughout Africa? What other political systems existed?

TAKS Practice

SECTION 2 ASSESSMENT

Checking for Understanding

1. **Define** plantation, triangular trade, Middle Passage.

2. **Identify** King Afonso, Ibo.

3. **Locate** Brazil, Benin, South Africa, Mozambique.

4. **Explain** how the Europeans obtained access to slaves. To what port cities in Europe and the Americas were the African slaves shipped?

5. **Identify** the effects of the slave trade on the culture of Benin.

Critical Thinking

6. **Analyze** Why did Africans engage in slave trade? Did they have a choice?

7. **Compare and Contrast** Use a table like the one below to compare and contrast the political systems of Benin, the state of Ashanti, and the Ibo peoples.

Benin	Ashanti	Ibo

Analyzing Visuals

8. **Examine** the picture of the inside of a slave ship shown on page 417. From looking at this picture, what conclusions can you draw about the conditions that slaves endured during their voyage to the Americas?

Writing About History

9. **Persuasive Writing** Does the fact that Africans participated in enslaving other Africans make the European involvement in the slave trade any less reprehensible? Write an editorial supporting your position.

Southeast Asia in the Era of the Spice Trade

Main Ideas
- The Portuguese occupied the Moluccas in search of spices but were pushed out by the Dutch.
- The arrival of the Europeans greatly impacted the Malay Peninsula.

Key Terms
mainland states, bureaucracy

People to Identify
Khmer, Dutch

Places to Locate
Moluccas, Sumatra, Java, Philippines

Preview Questions
1. How did the power shift from the Portuguese to the Dutch in the control of the spice trade?
2. What religious beliefs were prevalent in Southeast Asia?

Reading Strategy
Summarizing Information Use a chart like the one below to list reasons why, unlike in Africa, the destructive effects of European contact in Southeast Asia were only gradually felt.

European Contact in Southeast Asia

Preview of Events

♦1510	♦1530	♦1550	♦1570	♦1590	♦1610	♦1630

1511
Portuguese seize Melaka

c. 1600
Dutch enter spice trade

1619
Dutch establish a fort at Batavia (present-day Jakarta)

Voices from the Past

After establishing control of the island of Java, the Dutch encountered a problem in ruling it. One observer explained:

66 The greatest number of the Dutch settlers in Batavia [present-day Jakarta, Indonesia], such as were commonly seen at their doors, appeared pale and weak, and as if laboring with death. . . . Of the fatal effects of the climate upon both sexes, however, a strong proof was given by a lady there, who mentioned, that out of eleven persons of her family who had come to Batavia only ten months before, her father, brother-in-law, and six sisters had already died. The general reputation of the unhealthiness of Batavia for Europeans, deter most of those, who can reside at home with any comfort, from coming to it, notwithstanding the temptations of fortunes to be quickly amassed in it. 99

—*Lives and Times: A World History Reader,*
James P. Holoka and Jiu-Hwa L. Upsher, eds., 1995

A parasol shades a European from the sun.

Such difficult conditions kept Southeast Asia largely free of European domination.

Emerging Mainland States

In 1500, mainland Southeast Asia was a relatively stable region. Throughout mainland Southeast Asia, from Burma in the west to Vietnam in the east, kingdoms with their own ethnic, linguistic, and cultural characteristics were being formed.

Conflicts did erupt among the emerging states on the Southeast Asian mainland. The Thai peoples had secured their control over the lower Chao Phraya River valley. Conflict between the Thai and the Burmese was bitter until a Burmese army sacked the Thai capital in 1767, forcing the Thai to create a new capital at Bangkok, farther to the south.

Across the mountains to the east, the Vietnamese had begun their "March to the South." By the end of the fifteenth century, they had subdued the rival state of Champa on the central coast. The Vietnamese then gradually took control of the Mekong delta from the **Khmer.** By 1800, the Khmer monarchy (the successor of the old Angkor kingdom—see Chapter 8) had virtually disappeared.

The situation was different in the Malay Peninsula and the Indonesian Archipelago. The area was gradually penetrated by Muslim merchants attracted to the growing spice trade. The creation of an Islamic trade network had political results as new states arose along the spice route. Islam was accepted first along the coast and then gradually moved inland.

The major impact of Islam, however, came in the fifteenth century, with the rise of the new sultanate at Melaka. Melaka owed its new power to its strategic location astride the strait of the same name, as well as to the rapid growth of the spice trade itself. Within a few years, Melaka had become the leading power in the region.

✔ **Reading Check** **Examining** How did Muslim merchants affect the peoples of Southeast Asia?

The Arrival of Europeans

In 1511, the Portuguese seized Melaka and soon occupied the **Moluccas.** Known to Europeans as the Spice Islands, the Moluccas were the chief source of the spices that had originally attracted the Portuguese to the Indian Ocean.

The Portuguese, however, lacked the military and financial resources to impose their authority over broad areas. Instead, they set up small settlements along the coast, which they used as trading posts or as way stations en route to the Spice Islands.

A Shift in Power The situation changed with the arrival of the English and **Dutch** traders, who were better financed than were the Portuguese. The shift in

CONNECTIONS Around The World

Gunpowder and Gunpowder Empires

Gunpowder and guns were invented in China in the tenth century and spread to Europe and Southwest Asia in the fourteenth century. However, the full impact of gunpowder was not felt until after 1500.

Between 1500 and 1650, the world experienced a dramatic increase in the manufacture of weapons based on gunpowder. Large-scale production of cannons was especially evident in Europe, the Ottoman Empire, India, and China. By 1650, guns were also being made in Korea, Japan, Thailand, Iran, and, to a lesser extent, in Africa.

▲ *Spanish galleon with cannons*

Firearms were a crucial element in the creation of new empires after 1500. Spaniards armed with firearms devastated the civilizations of the Aztec and Inca and carved out empires in Central and South America. The Ottoman Empire, the Mogul Empire in India, and the Safavid Empire in Persia also owed much of their success in creating and maintaining their large empires to the use of the new weapons. Historians have labeled these empires the "gunpowder empires."

◄ Seventeenth-century pistol

The success of Europeans in creating new trade empires in the East owed much to the use of cannons as well. Portuguese ships, armed with heavy guns that could sink enemy ships at a distance of 100 yards (91 m) or more, easily defeated the lighter fleets of the Muslims in the Indian Ocean.

Comparing Cultures

Although gunpowder was invented in China, it was the Europeans who used it most effectively to establish new empires. Evaluate the reasons why this occurred. In your explanation, be sure to include the historical impact of European expansion throughout the world.

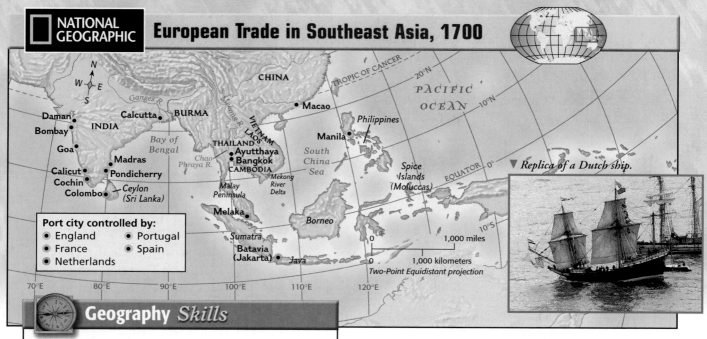

NATIONAL GEOGRAPHIC
European Trade in Southeast Asia, 1700

Port city controlled by:
- England
- France
- Netherlands
- Portugal
- Spain

▼ *Replica of a Dutch ship.*

0 — 1,000 miles
0 — 1,000 kilometers
Two-Point Equidistant projection

Geography *Skills*

Trading forts were established in port cities of India and Southeast Asia.

1. **Interpreting Maps** According to this map, which country controlled the most ports?
2. **Applying Geography Skills** Do outside research to create your own map of European trade. Show the trade routes each country used. What route do ships take today between Europe and Southeast Asia?

power began in the early 1600s when the Dutch seized a Portuguese fort in the Moluccas and then gradually pushed the Portuguese out of the spice trade.

During the next 50 years, the Dutch occupied most of the Portuguese coastal forts along the trade routes throughout the Indian Ocean, including the island of Ceylon (today's Sri Lanka) and Melaka. The aggressive Dutch traders drove the English traders out of the spice market, reducing the English influence to a single port on the southern coast of **Sumatra.**

The Dutch also began to consolidate their political and military control over the entire area. They tried to dominate the clove trade by limiting cultivation of the crop to one island and forcing others to stop growing and trading the spice. Then the Dutch turned their attention to the island of **Java,** where they established a fort at Batavia in 1619. The purpose of the fort was to protect Dutch possessions in the East. Gradually the Dutch brought the entire island under their control.

Impact on the Mainland Portuguese and then Dutch influence was mostly limited to the Malay Peninsula and the Indonesian Archipelago.

The arrival of the Europeans had less impact on mainland Southeast Asia. The Portuguese established limited trade relations with several mainland states (part of the continent, as distinguished from peninsulas or offshore islands), including Thailand, Burma, Vietnam, and the remnants of the old Angkor kingdom in Cambodia. By the early seventeenth century, other European nations had begun to compete actively for trade and missionary privileges. In general, however, the mainland states were able to unite and drive the Europeans out.

In Vietnam, a civil war temporarily divided the country into two separate states, one in the south and one in the north. After their arrival in the mid-seventeenth century, the European powers began to take sides in local politics. The Europeans also set up trading posts for their merchants.

By the end of the seventeenth century, however, it had become clear that economic opportunities were limited. Most of the posts were abandoned at that time. French missionaries tried to stay, but their efforts were blocked by the authorities, who viewed converts to Catholicism as a threat to the prestige of the Vietnamese emperor.

Why were the mainland states better able to resist the European challenge than the states in the Malay Peninsula and the Indonesian Archipelago? The mainland states of Burma, Thailand, and Vietnam had begun to define themselves as distinct political entities. They had strong monarchies that resisted foreign intrusion.

In the non-mainland states, there was less political unity. Moreover, these states were victims of their own resources. The spice trade there was enormously profitable. European merchants and rulers were determined to gain control of the sources of the spices.

✓**Reading Check** **Evaluating** Why were Europeans so interested in Southeast Asia?

Religious and Political Systems

Religious beliefs changed in Southeast Asia during the period from 1500 to 1800. Particularly in the nonmainland states and the **Philippines,** Islam and Christianity were beginning to attract converts. Buddhism was advancing on the mainland, where it became dominant from Burma to Vietnam. Traditional beliefs, however, survived and influenced the new religions.

The political systems in Southeast Asian states evolved into four styles of monarchy. Buddhist kings, Javanese kings, Islamic sultans, and Vietnamese emperors all adapted foreign models of government to local circumstances.

The Buddhist style of kingship became the chief form of government in the mainland states of Burma, Thailand, Laos, and Cambodia. In the Buddhist model, the king was considered superior to other human beings, and served as the link between human society and the universe.

The Javanese style of kingship was rooted in the political traditions of India and shared many of the characteristics of the Buddhist system. Like Buddhist rulers, Javanese kings were believed to have a sacred quality, and they maintained the balance between the

Thai king

sacred and the material world. The royal palace was designed to represent the center of the universe. Rays spread outward to the corners of the realm.

Islamic sultans were found on the Malay Peninsula and in the small coastal states of the Indonesian Archipelago. In the Islamic pattern, the head of state was a sultan. He was viewed as a mortal, although he still possessed some special qualities. He was a defender of the faith and staffed his **bureaucracy** (a body of nonelective government officials) mainly with aristocrats.

In Vietnam, kingship followed the Chinese model. Like the Chinese emperor, the Vietnamese emperor ruled according to the teachings of Confucius. He was seen as a mortal appointed by Heaven to rule because of his talent and virtue. He also served as the intermediary between Heaven and Earth.

✓**Reading Check** **Comparing** How did the Javanese style of kingship compare to the Buddhist style of kingship?

🔺**TAKS Practice**

SECTION 3 ASSESSMENT

Checking for Understanding

1. **Define** mainland states, bureaucracy.

2. **Identify** Khmer, Dutch.

3. **Locate** Moluccas, Sumatra, Java, Philippines.

4. **Explain** why the Portuguese decided to set up only small settlements in the Moluccas.

5. **List** the places where the Dutch established their forts. What were the major objectives of the Dutch? How did they go about accomplishing their objectives?

Critical Thinking

6. **Evaluate** Why did the Malay world fall to foreign traders, while the countries of mainland Southeast Asia retained their independence?

7. **Categorizing Information** Use a table like the one below to describe the four types of political systems that developed in Southeast Asia.

Region	Political System

Analyzing Visuals

8. **Examine** the picture of the Thai king shown above. How does this picture reflect the Buddhist model of kingship practiced in Southeast Asian states such as Thailand?

Writing About History

9. **Expository Writing** Pretend that you are a Portuguese merchant trying to establish trade relations with Southeast Asia. Write a letter to the authorities in Portugal explaining the particular difficulties you are encountering in Southeast Asia.

CRITICAL THINKING
SKILLBUILDER

Making Inferences and Drawing Conclusions

Why Learn This Skill?

While driving, you hear a news report about a fire downtown. As you approach downtown, traffic is very heavy. You cannot see any smoke, but you infer that the traffic is caused by the fire.

*To **infer** means to evaluate information and arrive at a conclusion. When you make inferences, you draw conclusions that are not stated directly.*

Learning the Skill

Follow the steps below to help make inferences and draw conclusions:

- Read carefully to determine the main facts and ideas.

- Write down the important facts.

- Consider any information you know that relates to this topic.

- Determine how your own knowledge adds to or changes the material.

- What inferences can you make about the material that are not specifically stated in the facts that you gathered from your reading?

- Use your knowledge and reason to develop conclusions about the facts.

- If possible, find specific information that proves or disproves your inference.

Practicing the Skill

Read the passage below, then answer the questions that follow.

In 1511, the Portuguese seized Melaka and soon occupied the Moluccas. Known to Europeans as the Spice Islands, the Moluccas were the chief source of the spices that had originally attracted the Portuguese to the Indian Ocean.

The Portuguese, however, lacked the military and financial resources to impose their authority over broad areas. Instead, they set up small settlements along the coast, which they used as trading posts or as way stations en route to the Spice Islands.

Bags of spices for sale

The situation changed with the arrival of the English and Dutch traders, who were better financed than were the Portuguese. The shift in power began in the early 1600s, when the Dutch seized a Portuguese fort in the Moluccas and drove out the Portuguese.

During the next fifty years, the Dutch occupied most of the Portuguese coastal forts along the trade routes throughout the Indian Ocean. The aggressive Dutch traders also drove the English traders out of the spice market, reducing the English influence to a single port on the southern coast of Sumatra.

❶ What events does the writer describe?

❷ What facts are presented?

❸ What can you infer about the Dutch traders during this period?

❹ What conclusion can you make about the spice market, other than those specifically stated by the author?

Applying the Skill

Scan the newspaper or a magazine for a political cartoon. Paste the cartoon on a piece of paper or poster board. Underneath, list three valid inferences based on the work.

Glencoe's **Skillbuilder Interactive Workbook, Level 2,** provides instruction and practice in key social studies skills.

Using Key Terms

1. A set of principles that dominated economic thought in the seventeenth century was called _____.

2. _____ were Spanish conquerors who were motivated by religious zeal and the desire for glory and riches.

3. A body of nonelective government officials is called a _____.

4. Many Africans were removed from their homes and shipped to large landed estates in the Americas called _____.

5. States that form part of a continent are called _____.

6. The _____ is the difference in value between what a nation imports and what it exports.

7. A settlement in a new territory, linked to the parent country, is called a _____.

8. _____ is the route between Europe, Africa, and America.

9. The journey of slaves from Africa to America on the worst portion of the triangular trade route was called the _____.

Reviewing Key Facts

10. **History** What did the Europeans want from the East?

11. **History** Who was the conquistador who overthrew the Aztec Empire? Who conquered the Inca?

12. **Economics** What did Europeans want from the Americas?

13. **Geography** What was the name of the city located on the Malay Peninsula that was the central point in the spice trade?

14. **Economics** When Vasco da Gama reached India, what cargo did he bring back? How profitable was his voyage?

15. **History** How did most Africans become slaves?

16. **History** What European country conquered Brazil?

17. **Science and Technology** How did the Portuguese make effective use of naval technology?

18. **Geography** What did Christopher Columbus believe about the size and shape of Earth?

19. **History** Why were European diseases devastating to the peoples of America?

Chapter Summary

Listed below are the major European explorers of the fifteenth and sixteenth centuries. Marco Polo is the one explorer listed who predates the Age of Exploration.

Explorer	Date	Sponsoring Country	Discovery
Marco Polo	Late 13th cent.	Italy	Asia
Bartholomeu Dias	1488	Portugal	Cape of Good Hope
Christopher Columbus	1492	Spain	Bahamas, Cuba, Hispaniola
John Cabot	1497	England	New England coastline
Vasco da Gama	1498	Portugal	India
Amerigo Vespucci	1499	Portugal, Spain	South American coast
Pedro Cabral	1500	Portugal	Brazil
Afonso de Albuquerque	1511	Portugal	Melaka
Vasco de Balboa	1513	Spain	Pacific Ocean
Juan Ponce de León	1513	Spain	Florida
Hernán Cortés	1519	Spain	Mexico
Ferdinand Magellan	1520	Spain	Sailed around the world
Giovanni da Verrazano	1524	France	East coast of North America
Francisco Pizarro	1531	Spain	Peru
Jacques Cartier	1534	France	St. Lawrence River
Hernando de Soto	1539	Spain	North America's southeast
Francisco de Coronado	1540	Spain	North America's southwest
João Cabrilho	1542	Spain	California
Samuel de Champlain	1603	France	Great Lakes and Quebec
Henry Hudson	1609	Netherlands, England	Hudson River, Hudson Bay

Critical Thinking

20. **Drawing Conclusions** What might have resulted from the fact that many slave owners believed it was more economical to buy a new slave than to raise a child to working age?

21. **Making Generalizations** Describe the impact on history of the voyages of Christopher Columbus.

Writing About History

22. **Informative Writing** Write an essay in which you analyze the reasons why Native Americans in both North and South America might be offended by the term *New World*. What does the use of the term suggest about European attitudes toward the rest of the world? Refer to the Treaty of Tordesillas and use other specific examples.

Analyzing Sources

Read the following comment by an Aztec describing the Spanish conquerors:

> ❝[They] longed and lusted for gold. Their bodies swelled with greed, and their hunger was ravenous; they hungered like pigs for that gold.❞

23. Based on this quote, what might the Aztec have inferred about the Spaniards and their civilization?

24. What do you think is meant by "they hungered like pigs for that gold"?

Applying Technology Skills

25. **Using the Internet** Search the Internet for additional information about early European explorers and their achievements. Organize your information by creating a spreadsheet. Include headings such as name, regions of exploration, types of technology used, and contributions.

Making Decisions

26. Pretend that you are the leader of a country and must decide whether or not to explore outer space. What are the benefits and risks involved in undertaking space exploration? Compare and contrast modern space explorations with European voyages of exploration. Consider the technologies used, the ways explorations were funded, and the impact of these ventures on human knowledge.

Analyzing Maps and Charts

Study the chart on the opposite page to answer the following questions.

27. Approximately how many years separated the explorations of Marco Polo and those of Vasco da Gama?

28. Which countries sponsored the most explorations?

29. The voyages of discovery began in Europe. What continents did the explorers visit?

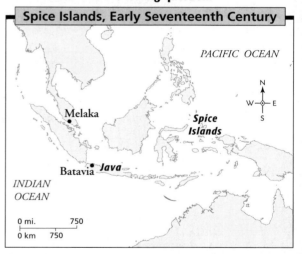

TAKS Test Practice

Directions: Use the map and your knowledge of world history to choose the best answer to the following question.

Spice Islands, Early Seventeenth Century

The Dutch established Batavia as a fort in 1619 to help them edge the Portuguese traders out of the area now called Indonesia. Today, which city is located where Batavia was established?

A New Delhi

B Jakarta

C Phnom Penh

D Beijing

Test-Taking Tip: If a test question involves reading a map, make sure you read the title of the map and look at the map carefully for information before you try to answer the question.

CHAPTER 14

Crisis and Absolutism in Europe

1550–1715

Key Events

As you read this chapter, look for these key events in the history of Europe during the sixteenth, seventeenth, and early eighteenth centuries.
- The French religious wars of the sixteenth century pitted Protestant Calvinists against Catholics.
- From 1560 to 1650, wars, including the devastating Thirty Years' War, and economic and social crises plagued Europe.
- European monarchs sought economic and political stability through absolutism and the divine right of kings.
- Concern with order and power was reflected in the writings of Thomas Hobbes and John Locke.

The Impact Today

The events that occurred during this time period still impact our lives today.
- The ideas of John Locke are imbedded in the Constitution of the United States.
- The works of William Shakespeare continue to be read and dramatized all over the world.

 World History Video The Chapter 14 video, "Louis XIV: The Sun King," chronicles the practice of absolutism in France during the 1600s.

Elizabeth I

c. 1520
Mannerism movement begins in Italy

1558
Elizabeth I becomes queen of England

1500

1550

1566
Violence erupts between Calvinists and Catholics in the Netherlands

St. Francis, as painted by Mannerist El Greco

Versailles was the center of court life during the reign of Louis XIV.

John Locke

1598
French Wars of
Religion end

1648
Peace of
Westphalia ends
Thirty Years' War

1690
John Locke
develops
theory of
government

1600

1650

1700

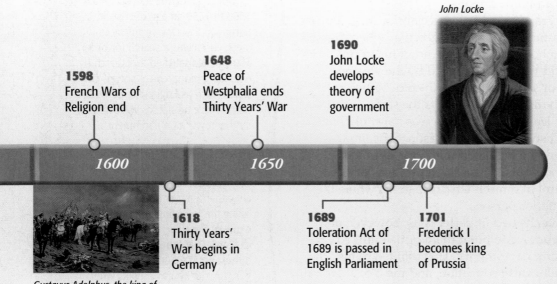

*Gustavus Adolphus, the king of
Sweden, on the battlefield*

1618
Thirty Years'
War begins in
Germany

1689
Toleration Act of
1689 is passed in
English Parliament

1701
Frederick I
becomes king
of Prussia

HISTORY
Online

Chapter Overview
Visit the *Glencoe World
History* Web site at
tx.wh.glencoe.com and click
on **Chapter 14–Chapter
Overview** to preview
chapter information.

A Story That Matters

Louis XIV with his army

Louis XIV holding court

The Majesty of Louis XIV

Louis XIV has been regarded by some as the perfect embodiment of an absolute monarch. Duc de Saint-Simon, who had firsthand experience of French court life, said in his memoirs that Louis was "the very figure of a hero, so imbued with a natural majesty that it appeared even in his most insignificant gestures and movements."

The king's natural grace gave him a special charm: "He was as dignified and majestic in his dressing gown as when dressed in robes of state, or on horseback at the head of his troops." He excelled at exercise and was never affected by the weather: "Drenched with rain or snow, pierced with cold, bathed in sweat or covered with dust, he was always the same."

He spoke well and learned quickly. He was naturally kind, and "he loved truth, justice, order, and reason." His life was orderly: "Nothing could be regulated with greater exactitude than were his days and hours." His self-control was evident: "He did not lose control of himself ten times in his whole life, and then only with inferior persons."

Even absolute monarchs had imperfections, however, and Saint-Simon had the courage to point them out: "Louis XIV's vanity was without limit or restraint." This trait led to his "distaste for all merit, intelligence, education, and most of all, for all independence of character and sentiment in others." It led as well as "to mistakes of judgment in matters of importance."

Why It Matters

The religious upheavals of the sixteenth century left Europeans sorely divided. Wars, revolutions, and economic and social crises haunted Europe, making the 90 years from 1560 to 1650 an age of crisis in European life. One response to these crises was a search for order. Many states satisfied this search by extending monarchical power. Other states, such as England, created systems where monarchs were limited by the power of a parliament.

History and You As you read through this chapter, you will learn about a number of monarchs. Create either a paper or electronic chart listing the following information: name of the ruler; country; religion; challenges; accomplishments. Using outside sources, add another category to your chart to reflect what you learn about the personal life and family of each king.

Europe in Crisis: The Wars of Religion

Guide to Reading

Main Ideas
- In many European nations, Protestants and Catholics fought for political and religious control.
- During the sixteenth and seventeenth centuries, many European rulers extended their power and their borders.

Key Terms
militant, armada

People to Identify
Huguenots, Henry of Navarre, King Philip II, William the Silent, Elizabeth Tudor

Places to Locate
Netherlands, Scotland, Ireland

Preview Questions
1. What were the causes and results of France's wars of religion?
2. How do the policies of Elizabeth I of England and Philip II of Spain compare?

Reading Strategy
Compare and Contrast As you read this section, complete a chart like the one below comparing the listed characteristics of France, Spain, and England.

	France	Spain	England
Government			
Religion			
Conflicts			

Preview of Events

◆1560	◆1570	◆1580	◆1590	◆1600

1562
French Wars of Religion begin

1571
Spain defeats Turks in Battle of Lepanto

1588
England defeats the Spanish Armada

1598
Edict of Nantes recognizes rights of Huguenots in Catholic France

Voices from the Past

Saint Bartholomew's Day massacre

In August of 1572, during the French Wars of Religion, the Catholic party decided to kill Protestant leaders gathered in Paris. One Protestant described the scene:

66In an instant, the whole city was filled with dead bodies of every sex and age, and indeed amid such confusion and disorder that everyone was allowed to kill whoever he pleased. . . . Nevertheless, the main fury fell on our people [the Protestants]. . . . The continuous shooting of pistols, the frightful cries of those they slaughtered, the bodies thrown from windows . . . the breaking down of doors and windows, the stones thrown against them, and the looting of more than 600 homes over a long period can only bring before the eyes of the reader an unforgettable picture of the calamity appalling in every way.99

—*The Huguenot Wars,* **Julian Coudy, 1969**

Conflict between Catholics and Protestants was at the heart of the French Wars of Religion.

The French Wars of Religion

By 1560, Calvinism and Catholicism had become highly **militant** (combative) religions. They were aggressive in trying to win converts and in eliminating each other's authority. Their struggle for the minds and hearts of Europeans was the chief cause of the religious wars that plagued Europe in the sixteenth century.

However, economic, social, and political forces also played an important role in these conflicts.

Of the sixteenth-century religious wars, none was more shattering than the French civil wars known as the French Wars of Religion (1562–1598). Religion was at the center of these wars. The French kings persecuted Protestants, but the persecution did little to stop the spread of Protestantism.

Huguenots (HYOO•guh•NAWTS) were French Protestants influenced by John Calvin. They made up only about 7 percent of the total French population, but 40 to 50 percent of the nobility became Huguenots. Included in this group of nobles was the house of Bourbon, which ruled the southern French kingdom of Navarre and stood next to the Valois dynasty in the royal line of succession. The conversion of so many nobles made the Huguenots a powerful political threat to the Crown.

Still, the Catholic majority greatly outnumbered the Huguenot minority, and the Valois monarchy was strongly Catholic. In addition, an extreme Catholic party—known as the ultra-Catholics—strongly opposed the Huguenots. Possessing the loyalty of sections of northern and northwestern France, the ultra-Catholics could recruit and pay for large armies.

Although the religious issue was the most important issue, other factors played a role in the French civil wars. Towns and provinces, which had long resisted the growing power of the French monarchy, were willing to assist nobles in weakening the monarchy. The fact that so many nobles were Huguenots created an important base of opposition to the king.

For 30 years, battles raged in France between the Catholic and Huguenot sides. Finally, in 1589, **Henry of Navarre,** the political leader of the Huguenots and a member of the Bourbon dynasty, succeeded to the throne as Henry IV. He realized that as a Protestant he would never be accepted by Catholic France, so he converted to Catholicism. When he was crowned king in 1594, the fighting in France finally came to an end.

Henry of Navarre

To solve the religious problem, the king issued the **Edict of Nantes** in 1598. The edict recognized Catholicism as the official religion of France, but it also gave the Huguenots the right to worship and to enjoy all political privileges, such as holding public offices.

✓**Reading Check** **Identifying** List the sequence of events that led to the Edict of Nantes.

Philip II and Militant Catholicism

The greatest supporter of militant Catholicism in the second half of the sixteenth century was **King Philip II** of Spain, the son and heir of Charles V. The reign of King Philip II, which extended from 1556 to 1598, ushered in an age of Spanish greatness, both politically and culturally.

The first major goal of Philip II was to consolidate the lands he had inherited from his father. These included Spain, the **Netherlands,** and possessions in Italy and the Americas. To strengthen his control, Philip insisted on strict conformity to Catholicism and strong monarchical authority.

The Catholic faith was important to both Philip II and the Spanish people. During the late Middle Ages, Catholic kingdoms in Spain had reconquered Muslim areas within Spain and expelled the Spanish Jews. Driven by this crusading heritage, Spain saw itself as a nation of people chosen by God to save Catholic Christianity from the Protestant heretics.

Philip II, the "Most Catholic King," became a champion of Catholic causes, a role that led to spectacular victories and equally spectacular defeats. Spain's leadership of a Holy League against the Turks, for example, resulted in a stunning victory over the Turkish fleet in the Battle of Lepanto in 1571. Philip was not so fortunate in his conflicts with England (discussed in the following section) and the Netherlands.

The Spanish Netherlands, which consisted of 17 provinces (modern Netherlands and Belgium), was one of the richest parts of Philip's empire. Philip attempted to strengthen his control in this important region. The nobles of the Netherlands, who resented the loss of their privileges, strongly opposed Philip's efforts. To make matters worse, Philip tried to crush Calvinism in the Netherlands. Violence erupted in 1566 when Calvinists—especially nobles—began to destroy statues in Catholic churches. Philip sent ten thousand troops to crush the rebellion.

In the northern provinces, the Dutch, under the leadership of **William the Silent,** the prince of

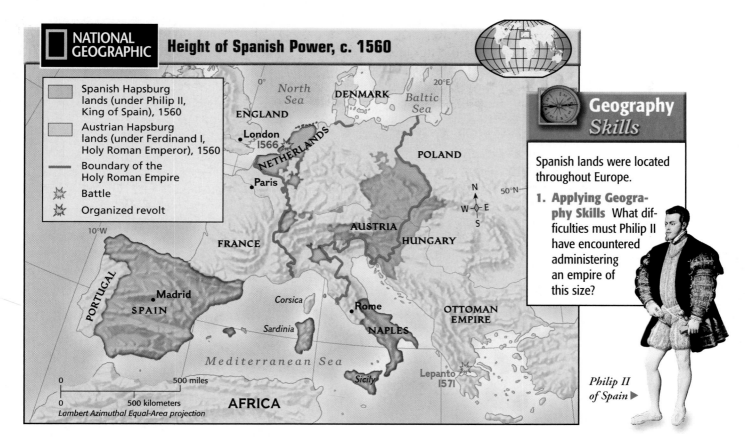

NATIONAL GEOGRAPHIC

Height of Spanish Power, c. 1560

Legend:
- Spanish Hapsburg lands (under Philip II, King of Spain), 1560
- Austrian Hapsburg lands (under Ferdinand I, Holy Roman Emperor), 1560
- Boundary of the Holy Roman Empire
- Battle
- Organized revolt

Geography Skills

Spanish lands were located throughout Europe.

1. **Applying Geography Skills** What difficulties must Philip II have encountered administering an empire of this size?

Philip II of Spain ▶

Orange, offered growing resistance. The struggle dragged on until 1609, when a 12-year truce ended the war. The northern provinces began to call themselves the United Provinces of the Netherlands and became the core of the modern Dutch state. In fact, the seventeenth century has often been called the golden age of the Dutch Republic because the United Provinces held center stage as one of Europe's great powers.

Philip's reign ended in 1598. At that time, Spain had the most populous empire in the world. Spain controlled almost all of South America and a number of settlements in Asia and Africa. To most Europeans, Spain still seemed to be the greatest power of the age.

In reality, however, Spain was not the great power that it appeared to be. Spain's treasury was empty. Philip II had gone bankrupt from spending too much on war, and his successor did the same by spending a fortune on his court. The armed forces were out-of-date, and the government was inefficient. Spain continued to play the role of a great power, but real power in Europe had shifted to England and France.

Reading Check **Describing** How important was Catholicism to Philip II and the Spanish people?

The England of Elizabeth

TURNING POINT In this section, you will learn how the defeat of the Spanish Armada guaranteed that England would remain a Protestant country and signaled the beginning of Spain's decline as a sea power.

When **Elizabeth Tudor** ascended the throne in 1558, England had fewer than four million people. During her reign, the small island kingdom became the leader of the Protestant nations of Europe and laid the foundations for a world empire.

Intelligent, careful, and self-confident, Elizabeth moved quickly to solve the difficult religious problem she inherited from her Catholic half-sister, Queen Mary Tudor. She repealed the laws favoring Catholics. A new Act of Supremacy named Elizabeth as "the only supreme governor" of both church and state. The Church of England under Elizabeth was basically Protestant, but it followed a moderate Protestantism that kept most people satisfied.

Elizabeth was also moderate in her foreign policy. She tried to keep Spain and France from becoming too powerful by balancing power. If one nation seemed to be gaining in power, England would support the weaker nation. The queen feared that war would be disastrous for England and for her own rule, but she could not escape a conflict with Spain.

Philip II of Spain had toyed for years with the idea of invading England. His advisers assured him that the people of England would rise against their queen when the Spaniards arrived. In any case, a successful invasion of England would mean the overthrow of Protestantism and a return to Catholicism.

In 1588, Philip ordered preparations for an armada—a fleet of warships—to invade England. The fleet that set sail had neither the ships nor the manpower that Philip had planned to send. An officer of the Spanish fleet reveals the basic flaw: "It is well known that we fight in God's cause. . . . But unless God helps us by a miracle, the English, who have faster and handier ships than ours, and many more long-range guns . . . will . . . stand aloof and knock us to pieces with their guns, without our being able to do them any serious hurt."

Defeat of the Spanish Armada

The hoped-for miracle never came. The Spanish fleet, battered by a number of encounters with the English, sailed back to Spain by a northward route around **Scotland** and **Ireland,** where it was pounded by storms. Many of the Spanish ships sank.

 **Reading Check** **Explaining** Why was Philip II confident that the Spanish could successfully invade England?

NATIONAL GEOGRAPHIC Defeat of the Spanish Armada, 1588

Route of the Spanish Armada
✦ Battle
✧ Shipwreck

SCOTLAND
North Sea
IRELAND
ENGLAND
Isle of Wight
Portland
Plymouth • Gravelines
Calais
English Channel
ATLANTIC OCEAN
FRANCE
La Coruña • Santander
SPAIN
PORTUGAL
Lisbon
0   200 miles
0   200 kilometers
Chamberlin Trimetric projection

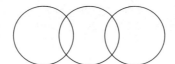 **Geography** *Skills*

England defeated the Spanish Armada in 1588.

1. **Interpreting Maps** Use the map's scale to estimate in miles the length and width of the English Channel.
2. **Applying Geography Skills** What were the Spanish hoping to avoid by taking the northern route back to Spain?

🤠 **TAKS Practice**

SECTION 1 ASSESSMENT

Checking for Understanding

1. **Define** militant, armada.

2. **Identify** Huguenots, Henry of Navarre, Edict of Nantes, King Philip II, William the Silent, Elizabeth Tudor.

3. **Locate** Netherlands, Scotland, Ireland.

4. **Describe** how the Edict of Nantes appeased both Catholics and Huguenots.

5. **List** the ways Elizabeth demonstrated moderation in her religious policy.

Critical Thinking

6. **Making Generalizations** Why did Philip II send out his fleet knowing he did not have enough ships or manpower?

7. **Compare and Contrast** Use a Venn diagram like the one below to compare and contrast the reigns of Henry of Navarre, Philip II, and Elizabeth Tudor.

Analyzing Visuals

8. **Examine** the painting of the Saint Bartholomew's Day massacre shown on page 429 of your text. Is the work an objective depiction of the event, or can you find evidence of artistic bias in the painting?

Writing About History

9. **Persuasive Writing** Write a persuasive essay arguing whether or not it was a good idea for Philip II to sail against England. Identify the main reason the king of Spain decided to launch the invasion.

Queen Elizabeth's Golden Speech

IN 1601, NEAR THE END OF her life, Queen Elizabeth made a speech to Parliament, giving voice to the feeling that existed between the queen and her subjects.

66 I do assure you there is no prince that loves his subjects better, or whose love can contradict our love. There is no jewel, be it of never so rich a price, which I set before this jewel; I mean your love. For I do esteem it more than any treasure or riches.

And, though God has raised me high, yet this I count the glory of my crown, that I have reigned with your love. This makes me that I do not so much rejoice that God has made me to be a Queen, as to be a Queen over so thankful a people.

Queen Elizabeth of England, Faced with the Spanish Armada 1588, Reviews Her Troops *by Ferdinand Piloty the Younger, 1861*

Of myself I must say this: I never was any greedy, scraping grasper, nor a strait, fast-holding Prince, nor yet a waster. My heart was never set on any worldly goods, but only for my subjects' good. What you bestow on me, I will not hoard it up, but receive it to bestow on you again. Yea, mine own properties I account yours, to be expended for your good. . . .

I have ever used to set the Last-Judgement Day before mine eyes, and so to rule as I shall be judged to answer before a higher Judge, to whose judgement seat I do appeal, that never thought was cherished in my heart that tended not unto my people's good. . . .

There will never Queen sit in my seat with more zeal to my country, care for my subjects, and that will sooner with willingness venture her life for your good and safety, than myself. For it is my desire to live nor reign no longer than my life and reign should be for your good. And though you have had and may have many princes more mighty and wise sitting in this seat, you never had nor shall have any that will be more careful and loving. 99

—Queen Elizabeth I, *The Golden Speech*

Analyzing Primary Sources

1. Identify phrases that convey Queen Elizabeth's feeling for her subjects.
2. To whom does Elizabeth feel accountable?
3. Which is more important: how subjects and rulers feel about each other or the policies and laws that rulers develop?

Social Crises, War, and Revolution

Main Ideas
- The Thirty Years' War ended the unity of the Holy Roman Empire.
- Democratic ideals were strengthened as a result of the English and Glorious Revolutions.

Key Terms
inflation, witchcraft, divine right of kings, commonwealth

People to Identify
James I, Puritans, Charles I, Cavaliers, Roundheads, Oliver Cromwell, James II

Places to Locate
Holy Roman Empire, Bohemia

Preview Questions
1. What problems troubled Europe from 1560 to 1650?
2. How did the Glorious Revolution undermine the divine right of kings?

Reading Strategy
Summarizing Information As you read this section, use a chart like the one below to identify which conflicts were prompted by religious concerns.

Religious Conflicts

Preview of Events

◆1600	◆1620	◆1640	◆1660	◆1680	◆1700

1603
Elizabeth I dies

1642
Civil war in England begins

1649
Charles I is executed

1688
Glorious Revolution

Voices from the Past

The Thirty Years' War (1618–1648) was a devastating religious war. A resident of Magdeburg, Germany, a city sacked ten times during the war, reported:

❝There was nothing but beating and burning, plundering, torture, and murder. Most especially was every one of the enemy bent on securing [riches]. . . . In this frenzied rage, the great and splendid city was now given over to the flames, and thousands of innocent men, women and children, in the midst of heartrending shrieks and cries, were tortured and put to death in so cruel and shameful a manner that no words would suffice to describe. Thus in a single day this noble and famous city, the pride of the whole country, went up in fire and smoke.❞
—*Readings in European History*, **James Harvey Robinson, 1934**

Destruction of the city of Magdeburg

This destruction of Magdeburg was one of the disasters besetting Europe during this time.

Economic and Social Crises

From 1560 to 1650, Europe witnessed severe economic and social crises. One major economic problem was inflation, or rising prices. What caused this rise in prices? The great influx of gold and silver from the Americas was one factor. Then, too, a growing population in the sixteenth century increased the demand for land and food and drove up prices for both.

By 1600, an economic slowdown had begun in parts of Europe. Spain's economy, grown dependent on imported silver, was seriously failing by the 1640s. The mines were producing less silver, fleets were subject to pirate attacks, and the loss of Muslim and Jewish artisans and merchants hurt the economy. Italy, the financial center of Europe in the Renaissance, was also declining economically.

Population figures in the sixteenth and seventeenth centuries reveal Europe's worsening conditions. Population grew in the sixteenth century. The number of people probably increased from 60 million in 1500 to 85 million by 1600. By 1620, population had leveled off. It had begun to decline by 1650, especially in central and southern Europe. Warfare, plague, and famine all contributed to the population decline and to the creation of social tensions.

✓ **Reading Check** **Explaining** Explain the causes for inflation in Europe in the 1600s.

The Witchcraft Trials

A belief in witchcraft, or magic, had been part of traditional village culture for centuries. The religious zeal that led to the Inquisition and the hunt for heretics was extended to concern about witchcraft. During the sixteenth and seventeenth centuries an intense hysteria affected the lives of many Europeans. Perhaps more than a hundred thousand people were charged with witchcraft. As more and more people were brought to trial, the fear of witches grew, as did the fear of being accused of witchcraft.

Common people—usually the poor and those without property—were the ones most often accused of witchcraft. More than 75 percent of those accused were women. Most of them were single or widowed and over 50 years old.

Under intense torture, accused witches usually confessed to a number of practices. Many said that they had sworn allegiance to the devil and attended sabbats, nightly gatherings where they feasted and danced. Others admitted using evil spells and special ointments to harm their neighbors.

By 1650, the witchcraft hysteria had begun to lessen. As governments grew stronger, fewer officials were willing to disrupt their societies with trials of witches. In addition, attitudes were changing. People found it unreasonable to believe in the old view of a world haunted by evil spirits.

✓ **Reading Check** **Describing** What were the characteristics of the majority of those accused of witchcraft?

The Thirty Years' War

Religious disputes continued in Germany after the Peace of Augsburg in 1555. One reason for the disputes was that Calvinism had not been recognized by the peace settlement. By the 1600s, Calvinism had spread to many parts of Europe. Religion played an important role in the outbreak of the Thirty Years' War, called the "last of the religious wars," but political and territorial motives were evident as well. The war began in 1618 in the lands of the **Holy Roman Empire.** At first, it was a struggle between Catholic forces, led by the Hapsburg Holy Roman emperors, and Protestant (primarily Calvinist) nobles in **Bohemia** who rebelled against Hapsburg authority. Soon, however, the conflict became a political one as Denmark, Sweden, France, and Spain entered the war. Especially important was the struggle between France and the rulers of Spain and the Holy Roman Empire for European leadership.

Geography *Skills*

The Thirty Years' War was fought primarily in the German states within the Holy Roman Empire.

1. **Interpreting Maps** List the towns that were sacked or plundered during the war.

2. **Applying Geography Skills** Research one of the battles on the map and describe its impact on the course of the war.

The Thirty Years' War was the most destructive conflict that Europeans had yet experienced. Although most of the battles of the war were fought on German soil, all major European powers except England became involved. For 30 years Germany was plundered and destroyed. Rival armies destroyed the German countryside as well as entire towns. Local people had little protection from the armies. The Peace of Westphalia officially ended the war in Germany in 1648. The major contenders gained new territories, and one of them—France—emerged as the dominant nation in Europe.

The Peace of Westphalia stated that all German states, including the Calvinist ones, could determine their own religion. The more than three hundred states that had made up the Holy Roman Empire were virtually recognized as independent states, since each received the power to conduct its own foreign policy. This brought an end to the Holy Roman Empire as a political entity. Germany would not be united for another two hundred years.

✔**Reading Check** **Summarizing** How did the Peace of Westphalia impact the Holy Roman Empire?

SCIENCE, TECHNOLOGY & SOCIETY

The Changing Face of War

Gunpowder was first invented by the Chinese in the eleventh century and made its appearance in Europe by the fourteenth century. During the seventeenth century, firearms developed rapidly and increasingly changed the face of war.

By 1600, the flintlock musket had made firearms more deadly on the battlefield. Muskets were loaded from the front with powder and ball. In the flintlock musket, the powder that propelled the ball was ignited by a spark caused by a flint striking on metal. This mechanism made it easier to fire and more reliable than other muskets. Reloading techniques also improved, making it possible to make one to two shots per minute. The addition of the bayonet to the front of the musket made the musket even more deadly as a weapon. The bayonet was a steel blade used in hand-to-hand combat.

A military leader who made effective use of firearms during the Thirty Years' War was Gustavus Adolphus, the king of Sweden. The infantry brigades of Gustavus's army, six men deep, were composed of equal numbers of musketeers and pikemen. The musketeers employed the salvo, in which all rows of the infantry fired at once instead of row by row. These salvos of fire, which cut up the massed ranks of the opposing infantry squadrons, were followed by pike charges. Pikes were heavy spears 18 feet (about 5.5 m) long, held by pikemen massed together in square formations. Gustavus also used the cavalry in a more mobile fashion. After shooting a pistol volley, the cavalry charged the enemy with swords.

The increased use of firearms, combined with greater mobility on the battlefield, demanded armies that were better disciplined and trained. Governments began to fund regularly paid standing armies. By 1700, France had a standing army of four hundred thousand.

Analyzing *How did the invention of gunpowder change the way wars were fought?*

Austrian flintlock pistol, c. 1680

Soldier firing a musk

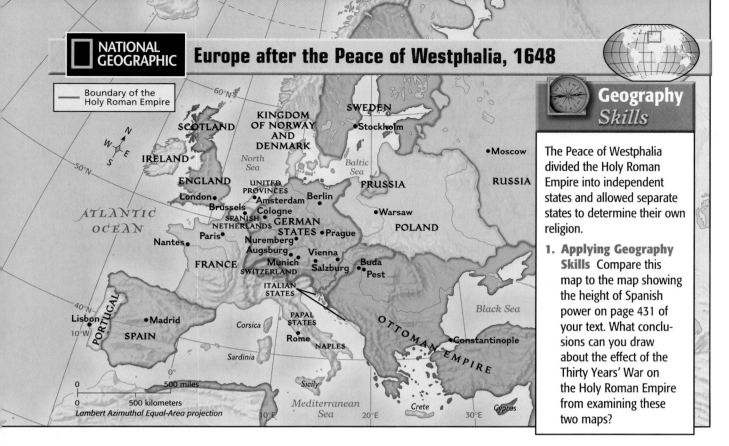

Europe after the Peace of Westphalia, 1648

NATIONAL GEOGRAPHIC

— Boundary of the Holy Roman Empire

Geography Skills

The Peace of Westphalia divided the Holy Roman Empire into independent states and allowed separate states to determine their own religion.

1. **Applying Geography Skills** Compare this map to the map showing the height of Spanish power on page 431 of your text. What conclusions can you draw about the effect of the Thirty Years' War on the Holy Roman Empire from examining these two maps?

Revolutions in England

⌐**TURNING POINT**⌐ **As you read this section, you will discover that Parliament held the real authority in the English system of constitutional monarchy.**

In addition to the Thirty Years' War, a series of rebellions and civil wars rocked Europe in the seventeenth century. By far the most famous struggle was the civil war in England known as the English Revolution. At its core was a struggle between king and Parliament to determine what role each should play in governing England. It would take another revolution later in the century to finally resolve this struggle.

The Stuarts and Divine Right With the death of Queen Elizabeth I in 1603, the Tudor dynasty came to an end. The Stuart line of rulers began with the accession to the throne of Elizabeth's cousin, the king of Scotland, who became **James I** of England.

James believed in the divine right of kings—that is, that kings receive their power from God and are responsible only to God. Parliament did not think much of the divine right of kings. It had come to assume that the king or queen and Parliament ruled England together.

Religion was an issue as well. The **Puritans** (Protestants in England inspired by Calvinist ideas) did not like the king's strong defense of the Church of England. The Puritans were members of the Church

of England but wished to make the church more Protestant. Many of England's gentry, mostly well-to-do landowners, had become Puritans. The Puritan gentry formed an important part of the House of Commons, the lower house of Parliament. It was not wise to alienate them.

The conflict that began during the reign of James came to a head during the reign of his son, **Charles I.** Charles also believed in the divine right of kings. In 1628, Parliament passed a petition that prohibited the passing of any taxes without Parliament's consent. Although Charles I initially accepted this petition, he later changed his mind, realizing that it put limits on the king's power.

Charles also tried to impose more ritual on the Church of England. To the Puritans, this was a return to Catholic practices. When Charles tried to force the Puritans to accept his religious policies, thousands of them chose to go to America instead.

Civil War and the Commonwealth Complaints grew until England slipped into a civil war in 1642 between the supporters of the king (the **Cavaliers** or Royalists) and the parliamentary forces (called the **Roundheads** because of their short hair). Parliament proved victorious, due largely to the New Model Army of **Oliver Cromwell,** a military genius. The New Model Army was made up chiefly of more extreme Puritans, known as the Independents. These men believed they were doing battle for God. As Cromwell wrote, "This is none other but the hand of God; and to Him alone belongs the glory." We might also give some credit to Cromwell; his soldiers were well disciplined and trained in the new military tactics of the seventeenth century.

The victorious New Model Army lost no time in taking control. Cromwell purged Parliament of any members who had not supported him. What was left—the so-called Rump Parliament—had Charles I executed on January 30, 1649. The execution of the king horrified much of Europe. Parliament next abolished the monarchy and the House of Lords and declared England a republic, or commonwealth.

Cromwell found it difficult to work with the Rump Parliament and finally dispersed it by force. As the members of Parliament departed, he shouted, "It is you that have forced me to do this, for I have sought the Lord night and day that He would slay me rather than put upon me the doing of this work." After destroying both king and Parliament, Cromwell set up a military dictatorship.

The Restoration Cromwell ruled until his death in 1658. More than a year later, Parliament restored the monarchy in the person of Charles II, the son of Charles I. With the return of monarchy in 1660, England's time of troubles seemed at an end.

After the restoration of the Stuart monarchy, Parliament kept much of the power it had gained earlier and continued to play an important role in government. One of its actions was to pass laws restoring the Church of England as the state religion and restricting some rights of Catholics and Puritans.

Charles II was sympathetic to Catholicism, and his brother James, heir to the throne, did not hide the fact that he was a Catholic. Parliament was suspicious about their Catholic leanings, especially when Charles suspended the laws that Parliament had passed against Catholics and Puritans. Parliament forced the king to back down on his action.

In 1685, **James II** became king. James was an open and devout Catholic, making religion once more a cause of conflict between king and Parliament. James named Catholics to high positions in the government, army, navy, and universities.

Parliament objected to James's policies but stopped short of rebellion. Members knew that James was an old man, and his successors were his Protestant daughters Mary and Anne, born to his first wife.

CONNECTIONS Around The World

Natural Disasters in History

The religious wars in Europe, which led to many deaths, were manmade disasters that created economic, social, and political crises. Between 1500 and 1800, natural disasters around the world also took many lives and led to economic and social crises.

One of the worst disasters occurred in China in 1556. A powerful earthquake in northern China buried alive hundreds of thousands of peasants who had made their homes in cave dwellings carved out of soft clay hills.

In later years, earthquakes shattered other places around the world. On the last day of 1703, a massive earthquake struck the city of Tokyo. At the same time, enormous tidal waves caused by earthquakes flooded the Japanese coastline, sweeping entire villages out to sea. An earthquake that struck Persia in 1780 killed 100,000 people in the city of Tabriz.

Europe, too, had its share of natural disasters. A massive earthquake leveled the city of Lisbon, Portugal, in 1755, killing over 50,000 people and destroying more than 80 percent of the buildings in the city. The massive eruption of Mount Etna on the island of Sicily in 1669 devastated Catania, a nearby port city.

Earthquake ▶ at Lisbon in 1755

Comparing Cultures

1. How do natural disasters lead to economic and social crises?
2. What natural disasters can occur where you live?

Picturing History

Here Cromwell is shown dismissing Parliament. After Cromwell's death, Parliament restored the monarchy. In 1689, Parliament offered the throne to William and Mary, shown above right. Why did English nobles want William and Mary to rule England, and not the heirs of James II?

However, in 1688, a son was born to James and his second wife, a Catholic. Now, the possibility of a Catholic monarchy loomed large.

A Glorious Revolution A group of English noblemen invited the Dutch leader, William of Orange, husband of James's daughter Mary, to invade England. William and Mary raised an army and in 1688 "invaded" England, while James, his wife, and his infant son fled to France. With almost no bloodshed,

England had undergone a "Glorious Revolution." The issue was not if there would be a monarchy but who would be monarch.

In January 1689, Parliament offered the throne to William and Mary. They accepted it, along with a Bill of Rights. The Bill of Rights set forth Parliament's right to make laws and levy taxes. It also stated that standing armies could be raised only with Parliament's consent, thus making it impossible for kings to oppose or to do without Parliament. The rights of citizens to keep arms and have a jury trial were also confirmed. The Bill of Rights helped create a system of government based on the rule of law and a freely elected Parliament. This bill laid the foundation for a limited, or constitutional, monarchy.

Another important action of Parliament was the Toleration Act of 1689. This act granted Puritans, but not Catholics, the right of free public worship. Few English citizens, however, would ever again be persecuted for religion.

By deposing one king and establishing another, Parliament had destroyed the divine-right theory of kingship. William was, after all, king by the grace of Parliament, not the grace of God. Parliament had asserted its right to be part of the government.

☑ **Reading Check** **Describing** Trace the sequence of events that led to the English Bill of Rights.

⬥**TAKS Practice**

SECTION 2 ASSESSMENT

Checking for Understanding

1. **Define** inflation, witchcraft, divine right of kings, commonwealth.

2. **Identify** James I, Puritans, Charles I, Cavaliers, Roundheads, Oliver Cromwell, James II.

3. **Locate** Holy Roman Empire, Bohemia.

4. **Explain** why Oliver Cromwell first purged Parliament and then declared a military dictatorship.

5. **List** the countries involved in the Thirty Years' War.

Critical Thinking

6. **Drawing Conclusions** Which nation emerged stronger after the Thirty Years' War? Did thirty years of fighting accomplish any of the original motives for waging the war?

7. **Cause and Effect** Use a graphic organizer like the one below to illustrate the causes and effects of the Thirty Years' War.

Thirty Years' War	
Cause	Effect

Analyzing Visuals

8. **Examine** the cameo of William and Mary shown above. How does this painting compare to portraits of other rulers, such as the one of Louis XIV on page 444? How is the purpose of this painting different from the purpose of other royal portraits?

Writing About History

9. **Expository Writing** Write an essay analyzing the population figures in sixteenth- and seventeenth-century England. What accounts for the increases and decreases? Include a graph showing population.

CRITICAL THINKING
SKILLBUILDER

Making Generalizations

Why Learn This Skill?

Generalizations are broad statements or principles derived from specific facts. Here are some facts about Michigan and Florida:

Average monthly temperature (°F)

	January	April	July	October
Grand Rapids, Michigan	22	46.3	71.4	50.9
Vero Beach, Florida	61.9	71.7	81.1	75.2

One generalization that can be made from these facts is that Florida is warmer than Michigan. Generalizations are useful when you want to summarize large amounts of information and when detailed information is not required.

Learning the Skill

To make a valid generalization, follow these steps:

- **Identify the subject matter.** The example above compares Michigan to Florida.

- **Gather related facts and examples.** Each fact is about the climate of Michigan or Florida.

- **Identify similarities among these facts.** In each of the examples, the climate of Florida is more moderate than the climate of Michigan.

- **Use these similarities to form a general statement about the subject.** You can state either that Florida is warmer than Michigan or that Michigan is colder than Florida.

Practicing the Skill

Europe experienced economic crises and political upheaval from 1560 to 1650. Read the following excerpt from the text, then identify valid and invalid generalizations about what you have read.

Sixteenth-century gold coins

From 1560 to 1650, Europe witnessed severe economic and social crises, as well as political upheaval. The so-called price revolution was a dramatic rise in prices (inflation) that was a major economic problem in all of Europe in the sixteenth and early seventeenth centuries. What caused this price revolution? The great influx of gold and silver from the Americas was one factor. Perhaps even more important was an increase in population in the sixteenth century. A growing population increased the demand for land and food and drove up prices for both.

By the beginning of the seventeenth century, an economic slowdown had begun in some parts of Europe. Spain's economy, which had grown dependent on imported silver, was seriously failing by the decade of the 1640s. Italy, once the financial center of Europe in the age of the Renaissance, was also declining economically.

Identify each following generalization as valid or invalid based on the information presented:

❶ Multiple factors can contribute to inflation.

❷ If the government had taken measures to control an increase in population, inflation would have been prevented.

❸ Nations should refrain from importing goods from other countries.

❹ Less dependency on the importing of silver would have helped Spain's economy.

Applying the Skill

Over the next three weeks, read the editorials in your local newspaper. Write a list of generalizations about the newspaper's position on issues that have been discussed, either national or local.

Glencoe's **Skillbuilder Interactive Workbook, Level 2,** provides instruction and practice in key social studies skills.

Response to Crisis: Absolutism

King Louis XIV

Voices from the Past

Jacques Bossuet, a seventeenth-century French bishop, explained a popular viewpoint:

❝It is God who establishes kings. They thus act as ministers of God and His lieutenants on earth. It is through them that he rules. This is why we have seen that the royal throne is not the throne of a man, but the throne of God himself. It appears from this that the person of kings is sacred, and to move against them is a crime. Since their power comes from on high, kings . . . should exercise it with fear and restraint as a thing which has come to them from God, and for which God will demand an account.❞

— *Western Civilization,* **Margaret L. King, 2000**

Bossuet's ideas about kings became reality during the reign of King Louis XIV.

France under Louis XIV

One response to the crises of the seventeenth century was to seek more stability by increasing the power of the monarch. The result was what historians have called absolutism.

Absolutism is a system in which a ruler holds total power. In seventeenth-century Europe, absolutism was tied to the idea of the divine right of kings. It was thought that rulers received their power from God and were responsible to no one except God. Absolute monarchs had tremendous powers. They had the ability to make laws, levy taxes, administer justice, control the state's officials, and determine foreign policy.

The reign of **Louis XIV** has long been regarded as the best example of the practice of absolutism in the seventeenth century. French culture, language, and manners reached into all levels of European society. French diplomacy and wars dominated the political affairs of western and central Europe. The court of Louis XIV was imitated throughout Europe.

Richelieu and Mazarin French history for the 50 years before Louis was a period of struggle as governments fought to avoid the breakdown of the state. The situation was made more difficult by the fact that both Louis XIII and Louis XIV were only boys when they came to the throne. The government was left in the hands of royal ministers. In France, two ministers played important roles in preserving the authority of the monarchy.

Cardinal Richelieu (RIH•shuh•LOO), Louis XIII's chief minister, strengthened the power of the monarchy. Because the Huguenots were seen as a threat to the king's power, Richelieu took away their political and military rights while preserving their religious rights. Richelieu also tamed the nobles by setting up a network of spies to uncover plots by nobles against the government. He then crushed the conspiracies and executed the conspirators.

Louis XIV came to the throne in 1643 at the age of four. Due to the king's young age, Cardinal Mazarin, the chief minister, took control of the government. During Mazarin's rule, a revolt led by nobles unhappy with the growing power of the monarchy broke out. This revolt was crushed. With its end, many French people concluded that the best hope for stability in France lay with a strong monarch.

Louis Comes to Power When Mazarin died in 1661, Louis XIV took over supreme power. The day after Cardinal Mazarin's death, the new king, at the age of 23, stated his desire to be a real king and the sole ruler of France:

THE WAY IT WAS

FOCUS ON EVERYDAY LIFE

At the Court of Versailles

In 1660, Louis XIV of France decided to build a palace at Versailles, near Paris. Untold sums of money were spent and tens of thousands of workers labored incessantly to complete the work. The enormous palace housed thousands of people.

Life at Versailles became a court ceremony, with Louis XIV at the center of it all. The king had little privacy. Only when he visited his wife, mother, or mistress or met with ministers was he free of the nobles who swarmed about the palace.

Most daily ceremonies were carefully staged, such as the king's rising from bed, dining, praying, attending mass, and going to bed. A mob of nobles competed to assist the king in carrying out these solemn activities. It was considered a great honor, for example, for a noble to be chosen to hand the king his shirt while dressing.

Why did the nobles take part in these ceremonies? Louis had made it clear that anyone who hoped to obtain an office, title, or pension from the king had to participate. This was Louis XIV's way of controlling their behavior.

Court etiquette became very complex. Nobles and royal princes were expected to follow certain rules. Who could sit where

View of the vast grounds and palace of Versailles

> 66Up to this moment I have been pleased to entrust the government of my affairs to the late Cardinal. It is now time that I govern them myself. You [secretaries and ministers of state] will assist me with your counsels when I ask for them. I request and order you to seal no orders except by my command. I order you not to sign anything, not even a passport without my command; to render account to me personally each day and to favor no one.99

The king's mother, who was well aware of her son's love of fun and games and his affairs with the maids in the royal palace, laughed aloud at these words. Louis was serious, however. He established a strict routine from which he seldom deviated. He also fostered the myth of himself as the Sun King—the source of light for all of his people.

Government and Religion One of the keys to Louis's power was his control of the central policy-making machinery of government. The royal court that Louis established at Versailles (VUHR•SY) served three purposes. It was the personal household of the king. In addition, the chief offices of the state were located there, so Louis could watch over them. Finally, Versailles was the place where powerful subjects came to find favors and offices for themselves.

The greatest danger to Louis's rule came from very high nobles and royal princes. They believed they should play a role in the government of France. Louis got rid of this threat by removing them from the royal council. This council was the chief administrative body of the king, and it supervised the government. At the same time, Louis enticed the nobles and royal princes to come to his court, where he could keep them busy with court life and keep them out of politics.

Louis's government ministers were expected to obey his every wish. Said Louis, "I had no intention of sharing my authority with them." As a result, Louis had complete authority over the traditional areas of royal power: foreign policy, the Church, and taxes.

at meals with the king was carefully regulated. Once, at a dinner, the wife of a minister sat closer to the king than did a duchess. Louis XIV became so angry that he did not eat for the rest of the evening.

Daily life at Versailles included many forms of entertainment. Louis and his nobles hunted once a week. Walks through the Versailles gardens, boating trips, plays, ballets, and concerts were all sources of pleasure.

One form of entertainment—gambling—became an obsession at Versailles. Many nobles gambled regularly and lost enormous sums of money. One princess described the scene: "Here in France as soon as people get together they do nothing but play cards; they play for frightful sums, and the players seem bereft of their senses. One shouts at the top of his voice, another strikes the table with his fist. It is horrible to watch them." However, Louis did not think so. He was pleased by an activity that kept the Versailles nobles busy and out of politics.

The bedroom of Louis XIV at Versailles

CONNECTING TO THE PAST

1. **Summarizing** How did Louis XIV attempt to control the behavior of his nobles?

2. **Explaining** Why did Louis like the gambling that went on at Versailles?

3. **Writing about History** In what way was the system of court etiquette another way in which Louis controlled his nobles?

Louis XIV, shown here, had a clear vision of himself as a strong monarch. He had no intention of sharing his power with anyone. What effect did his views on monarchical government have on the development of the French state?

Although Louis had absolute power over France's nationwide policy making, his power was limited at the local level. The traditional groups of French society—the nobles, local officials, and town councils—had more influence than the king in the day-to-day operation of the local governments. As a result, the king bribed important people in the provinces to see that his policies were carried out.

Maintaining religious harmony had long been a part of monarchical power in France. The desire to keep this power led Louis to pursue an anti-Protestant policy aimed at converting the Huguenots to Catholicism. Early in his reign, Louis ordered the destruction of Huguenot churches and the closing of their schools. Perhaps as many as two hundred thousand Huguenots fled to England, the United Provinces, and the German states.

The Economy and War The cost of building palaces, maintaining his court, and pursuing his wars made finances a crucial issue for Louis XIV. He was most fortunate in having the services of Jean-Baptiste Colbert (kohl•BEHR) as controller-general of finances.

Colbert sought to increase the wealth and power of France by following the ideas of mercantilism. To decrease imports and increase exports, he granted subsidies to new industries. To improve communications and the transportation of goods within France, he built roads and canals. To decrease imports directly, Colbert raised tariffs on foreign goods and created a merchant marine to carry French goods.

The increase in royal power that Louis pursued led the king to develop a standing army numbering four hundred thousand in time of war. He wished to achieve the military glory befitting the Sun King. He also wished to ensure the domination of his Bourbon dynasty over European affairs.

To achieve his goals, Louis waged four wars between 1667 and 1713. His ambitions caused many nations to form coalitions to prevent him from dominating Europe. Through his wars, Louis added some territory to France's northeastern frontier and set up a member of his own dynasty on the throne of Spain.

Legacy of Louis XIV In 1715, the Sun King died. He left France with great debts and surrounded by enemies. On his deathbed, the 76-year-old monarch seemed remorseful when he told his successor (his great-grandson), "Soon you will be King of a great kingdom. . . . Try to remain at peace with your neighbors. I loved war too much. Do not follow me in that or in overspending. . . . Lighten your people's burden as soon as possible, and do what I have had the misfortune not to do myself."

Did Louis mean it? We do not know. In any event, the advice to his successor was probably not remembered; his great-grandson was only five years old.

Reading Check **Describing** What steps did Louis XIV take to maintain absolute power?

Absolutism in Central and Eastern Europe

After the Thirty Years' War, there was no German state, but over three hundred "Germanies." Of these states, two—**Prussia** and **Austria**—emerged in the seventeenth and eighteenth centuries as great European powers.

The Emergence of Prussia Frederick William the Great Elector laid the foundation for the Prussian state. Realizing that Prussia was a small, open territory with no natural frontiers for defense, Frederick William built a large and efficient standing army. He had a force of forty thousand men, which made the Prussian army the fourth-largest in Europe.

Expansion of Prussia, 1618–1720
NATIONAL GEOGRAPHIC

- East Prussia and possessions, 1618
- Acquisitions/possessions, 1619–1699
- Acquisitions/possessions, 1700–1720

Frederick I ▶

Expansion of Austria, 1525–1720
NATIONAL GEOGRAPHIC

- Austrian Hapsburg lands, 1525
- Acquisitions/possessions, 1526–1699
- Acquisitions/possessions, 1700–1720

Geography Skills

Prussia and Austria emerged as great powers in the seventeenth and eighteenth centuries.

1. **Interpreting Maps** What did Austria gain by expanding south?
2. **Applying Geography Skills** What destructive war happened during the time period covered by these maps?

To maintain the army and his own power, Frederick William set up the General War Commissariat to levy taxes for the army and oversee its growth. The Commissariat soon became an agency for civil government as well. The new bureaucratic machine became the elector's chief instrument to govern the state. Many of its officials were members of the Prussian landed aristocracy, known as the Junkers, who also served as officers in the army.

In 1701, Frederick William's son Frederick officially gained the title of king. Elector Frederick III became King Frederick I.

The New Austrian Empire The Austrian Hapsburgs had long played a significant role in European politics as Holy Roman emperors. By the end of the Thirty Years' War, their hopes of creating an empire in Germany had been dashed. The Hapsburgs made a difficult transition in the seventeenth century. They had lost the German Empire, but now they created a new empire in eastern and southeastern Europe.

The core of the new Austrian Empire was the traditional Austrian lands in present-day Austria, the Czech Republic, and Hungary. After the defeat of the Turks in 1687 (see Chapter 15), Austria took control of all of Hungary, Transylvania, Croatia, and Slavonia as well. By the beginning of the eighteenth century, the Austrian Hapsburgs had gained a new empire of considerable size.

The Austrian monarchy, however, never became a highly centralized, absolutist state, chiefly because it was made up of so many different national groups. The Austrian Empire remained a collection of territories held together by the Hapsburg emperor, who was archduke of Austria, king of Bohemia, and king of Hungary. Each of these areas had its own laws and political life. No common sentiment tied the regions together other than the ideal of service to the Hapsburgs, held by military officers and government officials.

Reading Check **Examining** Why was the Austrian monarchy unable to create a highly centralized, absolutist state?

Russia under Peter The Great

A new Russian state had emerged in the fifteenth century under the leadership of the principality of Muscovy and its grand dukes. In the sixteenth century, **Ivan IV** became the first ruler to take the title of *czar,* the Russian word for caesar.

Expansion of Russia, 1462–1796

NATIONAL GEOGRAPHIC

Map Legend:
- Russia, 1462
- Acquisitions:
  - by 1505 (Ivan III)
  - by 1584 (Ivan the Terrible)
  - by 1725 (Peter the Great)
  - by 1796 (Catherine the Great)

0   1,000 miles
0   1,000 kilometers
Two-Point Equidistant projection

Geography Skills

Peter the Great organized Russia into provinces in an attempt to strengthen the power of the central government.

1. **Interpreting Maps** What did Russia gain by acquiring lands on the Baltic coast?

2. **Applying Geography Skills** Why are most cities in eastern Russia located near or south of 60°N latitude?

Ivan expanded the territories of Russia eastward. He also crushed the power of the Russian nobility, known as the **boyars.** He was known as Ivan the Terrible because of his ruthless deeds, among them stabbing his own son to death in a heated argument.

When Ivan's dynasty came to an end in 1598, a period of anarchy known as the Time of Troubles followed. This period did not end until the Zemsky Sobor, or national assembly, chose **Michael Romanov** as the new czar in 1613.

The Romanov dynasty lasted until 1917. One of its most prominent members was **Peter the Great.** Peter the Great became czar in 1689. Like the other Romanov czars who preceded him, Peter was an absolutist monarch who claimed the divine right to rule.

A few years after becoming czar, Peter made a trip to the West. When he returned to Russia, he was determined to westernize, or Europeanize, Russia.

He was especially eager to borrow European technology. Only this kind of modernization could give him the army and navy he needed to make Russia a great power. Under Peter, Russia became a great military power. By his death in 1725, Russia was an important European state.

Military and Governmental Changes One of Peter's first goals was to reorganize the army. He employed both Russians and Europeans as officers. He drafted peasants for 25-year stints of service to build a standing army of 210,000 men. Peter has also been given credit for forming the first Russian navy, which was his overriding passion.

To impose the rule of the central government more effectively throughout the land, Peter divided Russia into provinces. He hoped to create a "police state," by which he meant a well-ordered community governed by law. However, few of his bureaucrats shared his concept of honest service and duty to the state. Peter hoped for a sense of civic duty, but his own personality created an atmosphere of fear that prevented it. He wrote to one administrator, "According to these orders act, act, act. I won't write more, but you will pay with your head if you interpret orders again." Peter wanted the impossible—that his administrators be slaves and free men at the same time.

Cultural Changes After his first trip to the West, Peter began to introduce Western customs, practices, and manners into Russia. He ordered the preparation of the first Russian book of etiquette to teach Western manners. Among other things, the book pointed out that it was not polite to spit on the floor or to scratch oneself at dinner.

Because Westerners did not wear beards or the traditional long-skirted coat, Russian beards had to be shaved and coats shortened. At the royal court, Peter shaved off his nobles' beards and cut their coats at the knees with his own hands. Outside the court, barbers and tailors planted at town gates cut the beards and cloaks of those who entered.

One group of Russians—upper-class women—gained much from Peter's cultural reforms. Having watched women mixing freely with men in Western courts, Peter insisted that Russian upper-class women remove the veils that had traditionally covered their faces and move out into society. Peter also held gatherings in which both sexes could mix for conversation and dancing, a practice he had learned in the West.

St. Petersburg The object of Peter's domestic reforms was to make Russia into a great state and military power. An important part of this was to "open a window to the West," meaning a port with ready access to Europe. This could be achieved only on the Baltic Sea. At that time, however, the Baltic coast was controlled by Sweden, the most important power in northern Europe.

People In History

Peter the Great
1672–1725—Russian czar

Peter the Great, the man who made Russia a great power, was an unusual character. He was a towering, strong man 6 feet, 9 inches (2 m) tall. He was coarse in his tastes and rude in his behavior. He enjoyed a low kind of humor (belching contests and crude jokes) and vicious punishments (flogging, impaling, and roasting). Peter often assisted dentists and enjoyed pulling their patients' teeth.

During his first visit to the West, Peter immersed himself in the life of the people. He once dressed in the clothes of a Dutch sea captain and spent time with Dutch sailors. A German princess said of him: "He told us that he worked in building ships, showed us his hands, and made us touch the callous places that had been caused by work."

A long and hard-fought war with Sweden enabled Peter to acquire the lands he sought. On a marshland on the Baltic in 1703, Peter began the construction of a new city, **St. Petersburg,** his window on the West. St. Petersburg was finished during Peter's lifetime and remained the Russian capital until 1918.

✓ **Reading Check** **Evaluating** Why was it so important that Peter the Great have a seaport on the Baltic?

🔺 TAKS Practice

SECTION 3 ASSESSMENT

Checking for Understanding

1. **Define** absolutism, czar, boyar.

2. **Identify** Louis XIV, Cardinal Richelieu, Frederick William the Great Elector, Ivan IV, Michael Romanov, Peter the Great.

3. **Locate** Prussia, Austria, St. Petersburg.

4. **Describe** the Western customs, practices, and manners that Peter the Great introduced to Russia.

5. **List** the purposes of the royal court at Versailles.

Critical Thinking

6. **Explain** What were Cardinal Richelieu's political goals? How did he reduce the power of the nobility and the Huguenots in France?

7. **Summarizing Information** Use a chart like the one below to summarize the reign of Louis XIV of France.

Government	Wars	Economics	Religion

Analyzing Visuals

8. **Examine** the photograph of the king's bedroom shown on page 443. How does this room reflect the nature of kingship under Louis XIV?

Writing About History

9. **Expository Writing** Historians have long considered the reign of Louis XIV to be the best example of the practice of absolute monarchy in the seventeenth century. Do you believe the statement is true? Why or why not? Write an essay supporting your opinion.

The World of European Culture

Guide to Reading

Main Ideas
• The artistic movements of Mannerism and the baroque began in Italy and both reflected the spiritual perceptions of the time.
• Shakespeare and Lope de Vega were prolific writers of dramas and comedies that reflected the human condition.

Key Terms
Mannerism, baroque, natural rights

People to Identify
El Greco, Gian Lorenzo Bernini, William Shakespeare, Lope de Vega, Miguel de Cervantes, Thomas Hobbes, John Locke

Places to Locate
Madrid, Prague, Vienna, Brussels

Preview Questions
1. What two new art movements emerged in the 1500s?
2. Why are Shakespeare's works considered those of a "genius"?

Reading Strategy
Summarizing Information As you read this section, complete a chart like the one below summarizing the political thoughts of Thomas Hobbes and John Locke.

Thomas Hobbes	John Locke

Preview of Events

♦1575	♦1590	♦1605	♦1620	♦1635	♦1650	♦1665

1575
Baroque movement begins in Italy

1580
Golden Age of English theater begins

1599
Globe Theater built

1615
Cervantes completes *Don Quixote*

1651
Leviathan by Hobbes is published

Voices from the Past

William Shakespeare

In the play *Richard II,* William Shakespeare wrote the following lines about England:

❝This royal throne of kings, this sceptered isle,
This earth of majesty, this seat of Mars,
This other Eden, demi-Paradise,
This fortress built by Nature for herself
Against infection and the hand of war,
This happy breed of men, this little world,
This precious stone set in the silver sea,
Which serves it in the office of a wall
Or as a moat defensive to a house
Against the envy of less happier lands—
This blessed plot, this earth, this realm, this England.❞

— *Richard II,* **William Shakespeare**

In this play, one of the greatest playwrights of the English world expressed his patriotic enthusiasm.

Mannerism

The artistic Renaissance came to an end when a new movement, called **Mannerism**, emerged in Italy in the 1520s and 1530s. The Reformation's revival of religious values brought much political turmoil. Especially in Italy, the worldly enthusiasm of the Renaissance declined as people grew anxious and uncertain and wished for spiritual experience.

Mannerism in art reflected this new environment by deliberately breaking down the High Renaissance principles of balance, harmony, and moderation. The rules of proportion were deliberately ignored as elongated figures were used to show suffering, heightened emotions, and religious ecstasy.

Mannerism spread from Italy to other parts of Europe and perhaps reached its high point in the work of **El Greco** ("the Greek"). El Greco was from the island of Crete. After studying in Venice and Rome, he moved to Spain.

In his paintings, El Greco used elongated and contorted figures, portraying them in unusual shades of yellow and green against an eerie background of stormy grays. The mood he depicts reflects well the tensions created by the religious upheavals of the Reformation.

Reading Check **Describing** What did the mood of El Greco's paintings reflect?

The Baroque Period

Mannerism was eventually replaced by a new movement—the baroque. This movement began in Italy in the last quarter of the sixteenth century and eventually spread to the rest of Europe and even Latin America. The Catholic reform movement most wholeheartedly adopted the baroque style. This can be seen in the buildings at Catholic courts, especially those of the Hapsburgs in **Madrid, Prague, Vienna,** and **Brussels.**

Baroque artists tried to bring together the classical ideals of Renaissance art with the spiritual feelings of the sixteenth-century religious revival. The baroque painting style was known for its use of dramatic effects to arouse the emotions. In large part, though, baroque art and architecture reflected the search for power that was such a part of the seventeenth century. Baroque churches and palaces were magnificent and richly detailed. Kings and princes wanted other kings and princes as well as their subjects to be in awe of their power.

Perhaps the greatest figure of the baroque period was the Italian architect and sculptor **Gian Lorenzo Bernini,** who completed Saint Peter's Basilica in Rome. Action, exuberance, and dramatic effects mark the work of Bernini in the interior of Saint Peter's.

Bernini's *Throne of Saint Peter* is a highly decorated cover for the pope's medieval wooden throne. The

History *through Art*

Throne of Saint Peter **by Bernini, 1666**
It took Bernini eleven years to complete this monumental throne. How do you think Bernini wanted his work to impact the viewer?

throne seems to hover in midair, held by the hands of the four great theologians of the early Catholic Church. Above the chair, rays of heavenly light drive a mass of clouds and angels toward the spectator.

Artemisia Gentileschi is less well-known than the male artists who dominated the seventeenth-century art world in Italy but prominent in her own right. Born in Rome, she studied painting with her father. In 1616, she moved to Florence and began a successful career as a painter. At the age of 23, she became the first woman to be elected to the Florentine Academy of Design. Although she was known internationally in her day as a portrait painter, her fame now rests on a series of pictures of heroines from the Old Testament. Most famous is her *Judith Beheading Holofernes.*

Reading Check **Identifying** How did baroque art and architecture reflect the seventeenth-century search for power?

A Golden Age of Literature

In both England and Spain, writing for the theater reached new heights between 1580 and 1640. Other forms of literature flourished as well.

England's Shakespeare

A cultural flowering took place in England in the late sixteenth and early seventeenth centuries. The period is often called the Elizabethan Era, because so much of it fell within the reign of Queen Elizabeth. Of all the forms of Elizabethan literature, none expressed the energy of the era better than drama. Of all the dramatists, none is more famous than **William Shakespeare.**

When Shakespeare appeared in London in 1592, Elizabethans already enjoyed the stage. Elizabethan theater was a very successful business. London theaters ranged from the Globe, which was a circular, unroofed structure holding three thousand people, to the Blackfriars, a roofed structure that held only five hundred.

The Globe's admission charge of one or two pennies enabled even the lower classes to attend. The higher prices of the Blackfriars brought an audience of the well-to-do. Because Elizabethan audiences varied greatly, playwrights had to write works that pleased nobles, lawyers, merchants, and vagabonds alike.

William Shakespeare was a "complete man of the theater." Although best known for writing plays, he was also an actor and shareholder in the chief theater company of the time, the Lord Chamberlain's Men.

Shakespeare has long been viewed as a universal genius. He was a master of the English language and his language skills were matched by his insight into human psychology. Whether in his tragedies or his comedies, Shakespeare showed a remarkable understanding of the human condition.

Spanish Literature The theater was one of the most creative forms of expression during Spain's golden century as well. The first professional theaters, created in Seville and Madrid, were run by actors' companies, as they were in England. Soon, every large town had a public playhouse, including Mexico City in the New World. Touring companies brought the latest Spanish plays to all parts of the Spanish Empire.

Beginning in the 1580s, the standard for playwrights was set by **Lope de Vega.** He wrote an extraordinary number of plays, perhaps 1,500 in all. Almost 500 of them survive. They have been characterized as witty, charming, action-packed, and realistic.

Lope de Vega made no apologies for the fact that he wrote his plays to please his audiences and satisfy public demand. He remarked once that if anyone thought he had written his plays for fame, "undeceive him and tell him that I wrote them for money."

One of the crowning achievements of the golden age of Spanish literature was the work of **Miguel de Cervantes** (suhr•VAN•TEEZ). His novel *Don Quixote* has been hailed as one of the greatest literary works of all time.

In the two main characters of this famous work, Cervantes presented the dual nature of the Spanish character. The knight, Don Quixote from La Mancha, is the visionary so involved in his lofty ideals that he does not see the hard realities around him. To him, for example, windmills appear to be four-armed giants. In contrast, the knight's fat and earthy squire, Sancho Panza, is a realist. Each of these characters finally comes to see the value of the other's perspective. We are left with the conviction that both visionary dreams and the hard work of reality are necessary to the human condition.

✓ **Reading Check** **Describing** When was the "golden age" of Spanish literature? Who set the standard for playwrights?

Don Quixote and Sancho Panza

Political Thought

The seventeenth-century concerns with order and power were reflected in the political thought of the time. The English revolutions of the seventeenth century prompted very different responses from two English political thinkers, Thomas Hobbes and John Locke.

Hobbes Thomas Hobbes was alarmed by the revolutionary upheavals in England. He wrote *Leviathan,* a work on political thought, to try to deal with the problem of disorder. *Leviathan* was published in 1651.

Hobbes claimed that before society was organized, human life was "solitary, poor, nasty, brutish, and short." Humans were guided not by reason and moral ideals but by a ruthless struggle for self-preservation.

To save themselves from destroying one another, people made a social contract and agreed to form a state. Hobbes called the state "that great Leviathan to which we owe our peace and defense." People in the state agreed to be governed by an absolute ruler who possessed unlimited power. Rebellion must be suppressed. To Hobbes, such absolute power was needed to preserve order in society.

Locke John Locke, who wrote a political work called *Two Treatises of Government,* 1690, viewed the exercise of political power quite differently. He argued against the absolute rule of one person.

Unlike Hobbes, Locke believed that before society was organized, humans lived in a state of equality and freedom rather than a state of war. In this state of nature, humans had certain natural rights—rights with which they were born. These included rights to life, liberty, and property.

Like Hobbes, however, Locke believed that problems existed in the state of nature. People found it difficult to protect their natural rights. For that reason, they agreed to establish a government to ensure the protection of their rights.

The contract between people and government involved mutual obligations. Government would protect the rights of the people, and the people would act reasonably toward government. However, if a government broke the contract—if a monarch, for example, failed to live up to the obligation to protect subjects' natural rights—the people might form a new government.

To Locke, people meant the landholding aristocracy, not landless masses. Locke was not an advocate of democracy, but his ideas proved important to both Americans and French in the eighteenth century. These ideas were used to support demands for constitutional government, the rule of law, and the protection of rights. Locke's ideas can be found in the American Declaration of Independence and the United States Constitution.

✓ **Reading Check** Explaining According to Hobbes, why was absolute power needed?

🏴 **TAKS Practice**

SECTION 4 ASSESSMENT

Checking for Understanding

1. **Define** Mannerism, baroque, natural rights.

2. **Identify** El Greco, Gian Lorenzo Bernini, William Shakespeare, Lope de Vega, Miguel de Cervantes, Thomas Hobbes, John Locke.

3. **Locate** Madrid, Prague, Vienna, Brussels.

4. **Describe** what *Don Quixote* reveals about the nature of Spanish character.

5. **Summarize** the mutual obligations between people and government as understood by Locke.

Critical Thinking

6. **Describe** How did the Elizabethan theater experience provide a full reflection of English society?

7. **Compare and Contrast** Using a Venn diagram, compare and contrast Mannerism and baroque art.

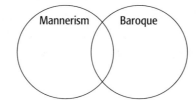

Mannerism   Baroque

Analyzing Visuals

8. **Examine** the photograph of Bernini's *Throne of Saint Peter* shown on page 449 of your text. How does Bernini's artistic masterpiece reflect the political and social life of the period in which it was created?

Writing About History

9. **Persuasive Writing** In an essay, argue whether Shakespeare is stereotyping in this quote: "Frailty, thy name is woman." Support your position with quotes from other authors who either corroborate or disagree with Shakespeare.

Using Key Terms

1. Philip II sent a fleet of warships called an _____ to invade England in 1588.

2. Parliament abolished the monarchy and declared England a republic or _____.

3. The _____ hysteria began to end in 1650.

Chapter Summary

The rulers of Europe during the sixteenth, seventeenth, and early eighteenth centuries battled to expand their borders, power, and religion. The chart below summarizes some of the events of this chapter.

Conflict

Spanish and English monarchs engage in a dynastic struggle.
• Philip II, a champion of Catholicism, resents English tolerance of Protestants.
• The defeat of the Spanish Armada in 1588 means that England will remain Protestant.

Change

Tudor monarchs bring stability and prosperity to England.
• The Act of Supremacy is passed.
• Foreign policy is moderate.
• Spain is defeated in 1588.

Uniformity

France's Louis XIV strengthens absolute monarchy in France and limits the rights of religious dissenters.
• He removes nobles and princes from royal council and keeps them busy with court life.
• He bribes people to make sure his policies are followed in the provinces.

Conflict

Dynastic and religious conflicts divide the German states.
• Two German states emerge as great powers in the seventeenth and eighteenth centuries: Prussia and Austria.
• Prussia has to build an army to protect its borders. Austria is diverse with no common culture or political rule.

Innovation

Peter the Great attempts to modernize Russian society.
• He introduces Western customs, practices, and manners.
• He prepares a Russian book of etiquette to teach Western manners.
• He mixes the sexes for conversation and dancing.

4. The belief that the monarch receives power directly from God is called _____.

5. In _____, elongated figures show suffering and heightened emotions.

6. _____ refers to the political system in which ultimate authority rests with the monarch.

7. _____ artists paired ideals of Renaissance art with sixteenth-century spiritual feelings.

8. The Russian monarch was called a _____.

9. The _____ were Russian nobility defeated by Ivan the Terrible.

10. John Locke believed people had certain _____—to life, liberty, and property.

Reviewing Key Facts

11. **Religion** What is the name given to French Calvinists?

12. **Government** Why is the Edict of Nantes sometimes called the Edict of Tolerance?

13. **History** Whom did Spain defeat in the Battle of Lepanto in 1571?

14. **Geography** At the beginning of the seventeenth century, Spain controlled territory on which continents?

15. **History** When and where was the Thirty Years' War fought?

16. **History** After the Thirty Years' War, which country emerged as the most dominant in Europe?

17. **Government** On his deathbed, what advice did Louis XIV give to his great-grandson, the future king?

18. **Culture** What reason for writing did Lope de Vega give those who asked?

19. **Culture** What is the essential message of *Don Quixote* by Cervantes?

20. **Philosophy** According to John Locke, what was the purpose of government?

Critical Thinking

21. **Analyzing** Baroque art and architecture reflected a search for power. How can a particular style of art be more powerful than another? (Consider the palace at Versailles.)

22. **Explaining** "Repression breeds rebellion." Explain how this quote relates to the history of the Netherlands during the reign of Philip II.

23. **Compare and Contrast** Compare the political thought of John Locke to the American form of government. What would Locke support? What would he not support?

Writing About History

24. **Persuasive Writing** Which of the monarchs described in this chapter do you most and least admire? Why? Write an essay supporting your answer with logic and reason.

Analyzing Sources

Read the following quote about absolutism by Jacques Bossuet, a seventeenth-century French bishop.

> ❝It is God who establishes kings. They thus act as ministers of God and His lieutenants on earth. It is through them that he rules. This is why we have seen that the royal throne is not the throne of man, but the throne of God himself. It appears from this that the person of kings is sacred, and to move against them is a crime. Since their power comes from on high, kings . . . should exercise it with fear and restraint as a thing which has come to them from God, and for which God will demand an account.❞

25. According to the quote, how should kings rule?

26. How do these words justify divine right of kings, and what does it mean that God will demand an account? What questions would you ask Bossuet about his ideas? How might he answer?

Applying Technology Skills

27. **Using the Internet** or library, research the current political status of France, Great Britain, Spain, and Germany. List the name of the current leader and the type of government (for example: Mexico, President Fox, constitutional democracy).

Making Decisions

28. Assume the role of King Louis XIV, or Queen Elizabeth I. Write a speech to your people about raising taxes and religion. Assess the needs of the state, the military, the court, and the people. Is it necessary to raise taxes? Which group is demanding the increase? How will this action affect each of these groups? Who will benefit the most, and who will suffer the most from the increase? After you have weighed options and considered the consequences, write a speech to your subjects announcing your decision. Persuade them that the increase is in the best interest of all.

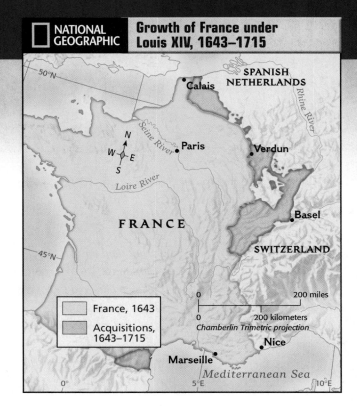

NATIONAL GEOGRAPHIC Growth of France under Louis XIV, 1643–1715

Analyzing Maps and Charts

29. What natural borders help to define France during this period?

30. Study the map carefully. What means of transportation do you think most French people used for trade?

31. Using this map and your text, describe how Louis XIV expanded France. What was the legacy of Louis XIV's expansion for his successor?

32. How does the extent of France in 1715 compare to the extent of France today? Use an atlas to research your answer.

The Princeton Review TAKS Test Practice

Directions: Choose the best answer to the following question.

The controversy that led to the English "Glorious Revolution" was

F a Tudor-Stuart struggle for the throne.

G the restoration of a monarch in England.

H increased religious freedom for Catholics.

J a power struggle between Parliament and the king.

Test-Taking Tip: Remember the date of the Glorious Revolution to help eliminate answers.

CHAPTER 15

The Muslim Empires

1450–1800

Key Events

As you read this chapter, look for the key events in the history of the Muslim empires.
- *Muslim conquerors captured vast territory in Europe and Asia using firearms.*
- *Religion played a major role in the establishment of the Ottoman, Safavid, and Mogul Empires.*
- *Trade and the arts flourished under the Muslim empires.*

The Impact Today

The events that occurred during this time period still impact our lives today.
- *Muslim art and architectural forms have endured, and examples can be found throughout the world.*
- *Since the territory once occupied by the Ottoman and Safavid dynasties produces one-third of the world's oil supply, these regions continue to prosper.*

 World History Video *The Chapter 15 video, "Constantinople to Istanbul," chronicles the spread of Islam and Muslim cultural achievements.*

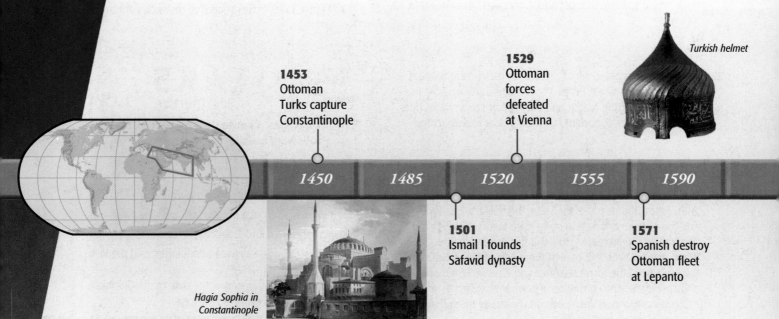

Turkish helmet

1453
Ottoman Turks capture Constantinople

1529
Ottoman forces defeated at Vienna

1450   1485   1520   1555   1590

1501
Ismail I founds Safavid dynasty

1571
Spanish destroy Ottoman fleet at Lepanto

Hagia Sophia in Constantinople

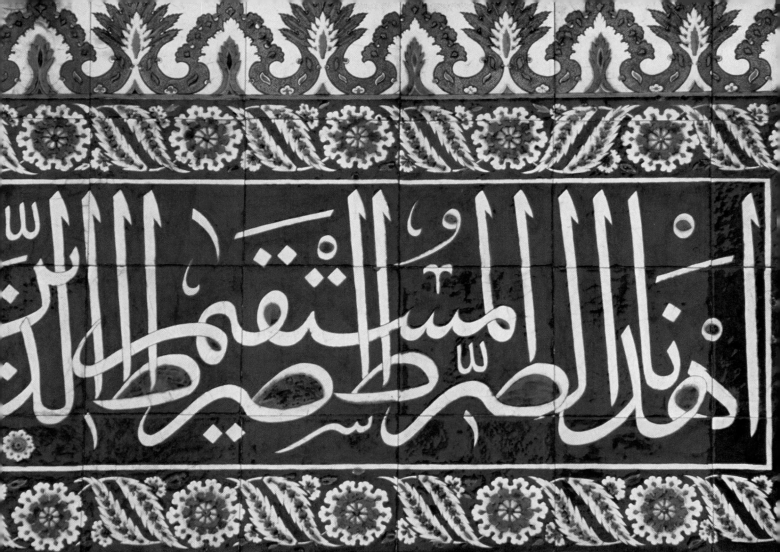

This tilework features an inscription from the Quran, the sacred book of Islam.

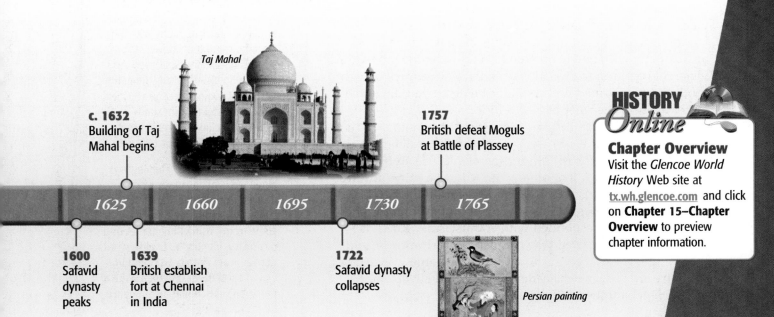

Taj Mahal

c. 1632
Building of Taj
Mahal begins

1757
British defeat Moguls
at Battle of Plassey

1625   1660   1695   1730   1765

1600
Safavid
dynasty
peaks

1639
British establish
fort at Chennai
in India

1722
Safavid dynasty
collapses

Persian painting

HISTORY
Online
Chapter Overview
Visit the *Glencoe World
History* Web site at
tx.wh.glencoe.com and click
on **Chapter 15–Chapter
Overview** to preview
chapter information.

A Story That Matters

The Fortress of Gwalior in India greatly impressed Babur.

The Conquests of Babur

At the beginning of the sixteenth century, to the north of India in present-day Afghanistan, lived a military adventurer named Babur, a descendant of the great Asian conqueror Timur Lenk (Tamerlane). Babur began with a pitifully small following: "The greater part of my followers (about 250 men) were on foot with sandals on their feet, clubs in their hands, and long frocks over their shoulders."

After seizing Kabul in 1504, Babur increased his forces, armed them with newly invented firearms, and extended his vision of conquest to the lands of India. With a force of eight thousand men armed with artillery, he destroyed the much larger army of the ruler of North India.

Nine months later, Babur's army faced yet another Indian prince with a considerably larger army. Babur rallied his forces with these words: "Let us, then, with one accord, swear on God's holy word, that none of us will even think of turning his face from this warfare, nor desert from the battle and slaughter that ensues, till his soul is separated from his body."

Babur's troops responded with enthusiasm. "Towards evening," he wrote later, "the confusion was complete, and the slaughter was dreadful. The fate of the battle was decided . . . I ordered the [enemy leader] to be flayed alive." Babur had won yet another decisive victory.

Why It Matters

During Europe's age of exploration, between 1500 and 1800, the world of Islam experienced new life with the rise of three great Muslim empires. With his victories, Babur created one of them—the Mogul Empire—in India. Along with the Ottomans and the Safavids, the Moguls dominated Southwest Asia and the South Asian subcontinent. For about two hundred years, these three powerful Muslim states brought stability to a region that had been in turmoil for centuries.

History and You

The English language contains many words derived from Arabic. Research the subject of etymology (where words come from), using the Internet or a dictionary. Identify 25 English words derived from Arabic. List them in alphabetical order and then write a paragraph describing the influence of Arabic on English.

The Ottoman Empire

Main Ideas
- Ottoman Turks used firearms to expand their lands and appointed local rulers to administer conquered regions.
- The Ottomans created a strong empire with religious tolerance and artistic achievements.

Key Terms
janissary, pasha, gunpowder empire, sultan, harem, grand vizier, ulema

People to Identify
Mehmet II, Sultan Selim I, Sinan

Places to Locate
Anatolian Peninsula, Bosporus, Dardanelles, Sea of Marmara, Makkah

Preview Questions
1. What were the major events in the growth of the Ottoman Empire?
2. What role did religion play in the Ottoman Empire?

Reading Strategy
Organizing Information Create a chart to show the structure of Ottoman society. List groups in order of importance.

Sultan

Preview of Events

♦1450	♦1475	♦1500	♦1525	♦1550	♦1575	♦1600

1453
Ottoman Turks capture Constantinople

1520
Süleyman I becomes Ottoman ruler

1526
Ottomans defeat Hungarians

1529
Austria defeats Ottomans at Vienna

1571
Spanish defeat Ottomans at Lepanto

Voices from the Past

In 1453, the Ottoman Turks conquered Constantinople, the Byzantine capital. One Greek described the scene:

❝The soldiers fell on the citizens with anger and great wrath. They were driven by the hardships of the siege, and some foolish people had hurled taunts and curses at them from the battlements all through the siege. Now they killed so as to frighten all the city, and to terrorize and enslave all by the slaughter. When they had had enough of murder, some of the troops turned to the mansions of the mighty, for plunder and spoil. Others went to the robbing of churches, and others dispersed to the simple homes of the common people, stealing, robbing, plundering, killing, insulting, taking and enslaving men, women, and children, old and young, priests, monks—in short, every age and class.❞
—*The Islamic World,* William H. McNeill and M.R. Waldham, 1973

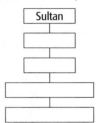

The siege of Constantinople

After this siege, Constantinople became the capital of the new Ottoman Empire.

Rise of the Ottoman Turks

In the late thirteenth century, a new group of Turks under their leader Osman began to build power in the northwest corner of the **Anatolian Peninsula.** That land had been given to them by the Seljuk Turk rulers as a reward for helping the rulers to defend their lands against the Mongols in the late thirteenth century.

At first, the Osman Turks were relatively peaceful and engaged in pastoral activities. However, as the Seljuk Empire began to decline in the early fourteenth century, the Osman Turks began to expand. This was the beginning of the Ottoman dynasty.

From their location in the northwestern corner of the peninsula, the Ottomans expanded westward and eventually con-

trolled the **Bosporus** and the **Dardanelles.** These two straits (narrow passageways), separated by the **Sea of Marmara,** connect the Black Sea and the Aegean Sea, which leads to the Mediterranean. The Byzantine Empire had controlled this area for centuries.

In the fourteenth century, the Ottoman Turks expanded into the **Balkans.** Ottoman rulers claimed the title of sultan and began to build a strong military by developing an elite guard called janissaries. Recruited from the local Christian population in the Balkans, the janissaries were converted to Islam and trained as foot soldiers or administrators to serve the sultan.

As knowledge of firearms spread in the late fourteenth century, the Ottomans began to master the new technology. The janissaries, trained as a well-armed infantry, began to spread Ottoman control in the Balkans. With their new forces, the Ottomans defeated the Serbs at the Battle of Kosovo in 1389. During the 1390s, they advanced northward and annexed Bulgaria.

Reading Check **Identifying** What strategic lands and bodies of water did the Ottomans take from the Byzantine Empire?

Expansion of the Empire

Over the next three hundred years, Ottoman rule expanded to include large areas of Western Asia, as well as North Africa and additional lands in Europe.

The Fall of Constantinople Under the leadership of **Mehmet II,** the Ottomans moved to end the Byzantine Empire. With eighty thousand troops ranged against only seven thousand defenders, Mehmet laid siege to Constantinople. In their attack on the city, the Ottomans used massive cannons with 26-foot (8-m) barrels that could launch stone balls weighing up to 1,200 pounds (545 kg) each.

The attack began on April 6, 1453, with an Ottoman bombardment. The Byzantines took their final stand behind the walls along the western edge

CONNECTIONS Past To Present

Conflict in Yugoslavia

In 1919, Yugoslavia was formed as a new state in the Balkans. It consisted of six territories that had little interest in being part of a single nation. From 1945 to 1980, the dictator Marshal Tito held the country together.

In 1992, Yugoslavia began to disintegrate. Slovenia, Croatia, Bosnia-Herzegovina, and Macedonia declared their independence. When Serbia refused to accept the breakup of Yugoslavia, conflict erupted. The Serbs invaded Bosnia and pursued a policy of "ethnic

▼ *Ethnic Albanian refugees cross the Albanian border in 1999.*

cleansing," in which they killed Muslims or forcibly removed them from their homes.

Ethnic and religious struggles in Yugoslavia had deep roots in the past. In the Middle Ages, the Slavic peoples had accepted Christianity. While the Croats and Slovenes became Roman Catholics, the Serbs and the others became Eastern Orthodox. In the fourteenth century, the Ottoman conquest of the Balkans brought the Muslims. Many Christians chose to convert to Islam. By 1500, the area that later became Yugoslavia was a land where Muslim, Catholic, and Eastern Orthodox groups maintained an uneasy peace.

Comparing Past and Present

Using outside sources, research the current political situation in the Balkan states. How did the Balkan wars of the early 1990s end? How have those wars influenced the development of that region since 1992? What is the current political and economic situation in the Balkans?

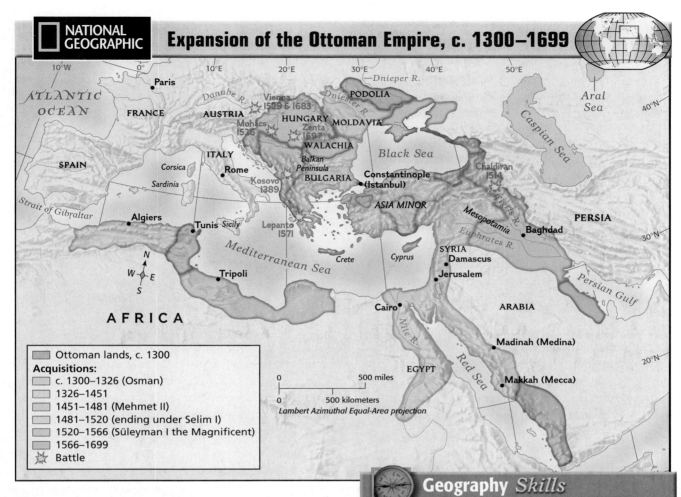

NATIONAL GEOGRAPHIC
Expansion of the Ottoman Empire, c. 1300–1699

Legend:
- Ottoman lands, c. 1300
- **Acquisitions:**
  - c. 1300–1326 (Osman)
  - 1326–1451
  - 1451–1481 (Mehmet II)
  - 1481–1520 (ending under Selim I)
  - 1520–1566 (Süleyman I the Magnificent)
  - 1566–1699
  - ✶ Battle

Lambert Azimuthal Equal-Area projection

of the city. They fought desperately for almost two months to save their city. Finally, on May 29, the walls were breached, and Ottoman soldiers poured into the city.

The Byzantine emperor died in the final battle, and a great three-day sack of the city began. When Mehmet II saw the ruin and destruction of the city, he was filled with regret and lamented, "What a city we have given over to plunder and destruction."

Western Asia and Africa
With their new capital at Constantinople (later renamed **Istanbul**), the Ottoman Turks now dominated the Balkans and the Anatolian Peninsula. From approximately 1514 to 1517, **Sultan Selim I** took control of Mesopotamia, Egypt, and Arabia—the original heartland of Islam. Controlling several of the holy cities of Islam, including **Jerusalem, Makkah** (Mecca), and **Madinah,** Selim declared himself to be the new caliph, defender of the faith and successor to Muhammad.

After their victories in the east, Ottoman forces spent the next few years advancing westward along the African coast, eventually almost reaching the Strait

Geography *Skills*

For nearly four hundred years, the Ottoman Empire continued to expand.

1. **Interpreting Maps** Name the places and dates for three battles that stopped Ottoman expansion into Europe.
2. **Applying Geography Skills** The Ottomans conquered Constantinople in 1453. How did that event impact their expansion?

of Gibraltar. The impact of Ottoman rule on the peoples of North Africa was relatively light, however.

Like their predecessors, the Ottomans were Muslims. Where possible, they preferred to administer their conquered regions through local rulers. The central government appointed officials, called pashas, who collected taxes, maintained law and order, and were directly responsible to the sultan's court in Constantinople.

Europe
After their conquest of Constantinople in 1453, the Ottoman Turks tried to complete their conquest of the Balkans. They took the Romanian territory of Walachia, but the Hungarians stopped their advance up the Danube Valley.

The reign of Süleyman I, beginning in 1520, led to new Ottoman attacks on Europe. Advancing up the Danube, the Ottomans seized Belgrade. In 1526, at the Battle of Mohacs (MOH•hach) on the Danube, they won a major victory over the Hungarians.

The Ottomans then conquered most of Hungary, moved into Austria, and advanced as far as Vienna, where they were finally defeated in 1529. At the same time, they extended their power into the western Mediterranean until a large Ottoman fleet was destroyed by the Spanish at Lepanto in 1571 (see Chapter 14).

During the first half of the seventeenth century, the Ottoman Empire in eastern Europe remained a "sleeping giant." Occupied with internal problems, the Ottomans were content with the status quo in eastern Europe. However, in the second half of the seventeenth century, they again went on the offensive.

HISTORY Online

Web Activity Visit the *Glencoe World History* Web site at tx.wh.glencoe.com and click on **Chapter 15– Student Web Activity** to learn more about the Ottoman Empire.

By mid-1683, the Ottomans had marched through the Hungarian plain and laid siege to Vienna. Repulsed by an army of Europeans, the Ottomans retreated and were pushed out of Hungary. Although they retained the core of their empire, the Ottoman Turks would never again be a threat to central Europe.

✓ **Reading Check** **Summarizing** List the sequence of events that led to the expansion of the Ottoman Empire.

The Nature of Ottoman Rule

Like the other Muslim empires in Persia and India, the Ottoman Empire is often labeled a "gunpowder empire." Gunpowder empires were formed by outside conquerors who unified the regions that they conquered. As the name suggests, such an empire's success was largely based on its mastery of the technology of firearms.

At the head of the Ottoman system was the sultan, who was the supreme authority in both a political and a military sense. The position of the sultan was hereditary. A son, although not necessarily the eldest, always succeeded the father. This practice led to struggles over succession upon the death of individual sultans. The losers in these struggles were often executed.

THE WAY IT WAS

YOUNG PEOPLE IN . . .

The Ottoman Empire

Every few years, as need arose, government commissioners went into the provinces of the Ottoman Empire to recruit a special class of slaves. Those chosen were usually Christian boys, because Muslims were not allowed to enslave other Muslims. This collecting of boys was known as the Devshirme—literally, the "boy levy." (The word *levy*, as used here, means the enlistment of people for military service.)

Most of the boys who were selected were from Christian peasant families in the Balkans. Recruits, usually between the ages of 10 and 20, were selected on the basis of good appearance and good physical build. These boys were brought to Constantinople, now the city of Istanbul, where most of them remained for training.

The boys were first converted to Islam. The brightest were then made pages (attendants) for the sultan and put into palace schools for a special education. Royal servants taught them languages (Turkish, Persian, and Arabic), literature, history, and of course, the Quran. The young boys also received physical and military training.

The boys were strictly disciplined. Sleep, study, and play were all done at very specific times. The boys were told to regard

As the empire expanded, the status and prestige of the sultan increased, and the position took on the trappings of imperial rule. A centralized administrative system was adopted, and the sultan became increasingly isolated in his palace.

The Topkapi ("iron gate") Palace in Istanbul, the new name for Constantinople, was the center of the sultan's power. The palace was built in the fifteenth century by Mehmet II. Like Versailles in France, it had an administrative purpose and served as the private residence of the ruler and his family.

The private domain of the sultan was called the harem ("sacred place"). Here, the sultan and his wives resided. Often a sultan chose four wives as his favorites.

When a son became a sultan, his mother became known as the queen mother and acted as a major adviser to the throne. This tradition often gave considerable power to the queen mother in the affairs of state.

The sultan controlled his bureaucracy through an imperial council that met four days a week. A chief minister, known as the grand vizier, led the meetings of the council. The sultan sat behind a screen and privately indicated his desires to the grand vizier.

The empire was divided into provinces and districts, each governed by officials. They were assisted by bureaucrats who had been trained in a palace school for officials in Istanbul. Senior officials were given land by the sultan. They were then responsible for collecting taxes and supplying armies for the empire from this landed area.

✓ **Reading Check** **Describing** What was the relationship among the grand vizier, the sultan, and the imperial council?

Religion in the Ottoman World

Like most Turkic-speaking peoples in the Anatolian Peninsula and throughout Western Asia, the Ottomans were Sunni Muslims (see Chapter 6). Ottoman sultans had claimed the title of caliph since the early sixteenth century. In theory, they were responsible for guiding the flock and maintaining Islamic law.

In practice, the sultans gave their religious duties to a group of religious advisers known as the ulema. This group administered the legal system and schools for educating Muslims. Islamic law and customs were applied to all Muslims in the empire.

their families as dead and were kept isolated from the outside world. Punishments were severe. Any boy who broke the rules was beaten on the soles of his feet with a thin wooden rod.

At the age of 25, the young men were assigned different roles. Some who were well-trained in the use of firearms became janissaries. These foot soldiers also served as guards for the person of the sultan. Some became members of the regular cavalry, and others became government officials. Some of the latter even rose in importance to become chief ministers to the sultan.

The janissaries were an elite group who served the sultan.

CONNECTING TO THE PAST

1. **Explaining** Why were Christian boys chosen to be the special class of slaves?

2. **Writing about History** Muslim boys could not be made into slaves, but Christian slaves could be converted to Muslims. What do you think about the logic of this system? Explain your answer.

History *through Architecture*

Built by Mehmet II, the Topkapi Palace was the center of the sultan's power. This photo of the Fruit Room of Ahmet III in the palace is a beautiful reminder of the splendor of Islamic architecture and painting. How do you think this room acquired its name?

The Ottoman system was generally tolerant of non-Muslims, who made up a significant minority within the empire. Non-Muslims paid a tax, but they were allowed to practice their religion or to convert to Islam. Most people in the European areas of the empire remained Christian. In some areas, however, such as present-day Bosnia, large numbers converted to the Islamic faith.

✔ **Reading Check** **Identifying** What religious responsibilities did the sultans have in their role as caliphs?

Ottoman Society

The subjects of the Ottoman Empire were divided by occupation. In addition to the ruling class, there were four main occupational groups: peasants, artisans, merchants, and pastoral peoples. Peasants

farmed land that was leased to them by the state. Ultimate ownership of all land resided with the sultan. Artisans were organized according to craft guilds. Each guild provided financial services, social security, and training to its members. Outside the ruling elite, merchants were the most privileged class in Ottoman society. They were largely exempt from government regulations and taxes and were able, in many cases, to amass large fortunes. Pastoral peoples—nomadic herders—were placed in a separate group with their own regulations and laws.

Technically, women in the Ottoman Empire were subject to the same restrictions as women in other Muslim societies, but their position was somewhat better. As applied in the Ottoman Empire, Islamic law was more tolerant in defining the legal position of women. This relatively tolerant attitude was probably due to traditions among the Turkish peoples, which regarded women as almost equal to men.

Women were allowed to own and inherit property. They could not be forced into marriage and, in certain cases, were permitted to seek divorce. Women often gained considerable power within the palace. In a few instances, women even served as senior officials, such as governors of provinces.

✔ **Reading Check** **Contrasting** How did the position of women in the Ottoman Empire contrast to that of women in other Muslim societies?

Problems in the Ottoman Empire

The Ottoman Empire reached its high point under Süleyman the Magnificent, who ruled from 1520 to 1566. It may also have been during Süleyman's rule that problems began to occur, however. Having executed his two most able sons on suspicion of treason, Süleyman was succeeded by his only surviving son, Selim II.

The problems of the Ottoman Empire did not become visible until 1699, when the empire began to lose some of its territory. However, signs of internal disintegration had already appeared at the beginning of the 1600s.

After the death of Süleyman, sultans became less involved in government and allowed their ministers to exercise more power. The training of officials declined, and senior positions were increasingly assigned to the sons or daughters of elites. Members of the elite soon formed a privileged group seeking wealth and power. The central bureaucracy lost its links with rural areas. As a result, local officials grew corrupt, and taxes rose. Constant wars depleted the imperial treasury. Corruption and palace intrigue grew.

Another sign of change within the empire was the exchange of Western and Ottoman ideas and customs. Officials and merchants began to imitate the habits and lifestyles of Europeans. They wore European clothes and bought Western furniture and art objects. Europeans borrowed Ottoman military technology and decorated their homes with tiles, tulips, pottery, and rugs. During the sixteenth and seventeenth centuries, coffee was introduced to Ottoman society and spread to Europe.

Some sultans attempted to counter these trends. One sultan in the early seventeenth century issued a decree outlawing both coffee and tobacco. He even began to patrol the streets of Constantinople at night. If he caught any of his subjects in immoral or illegal acts, he had them immediately executed.

✓ **Reading Check** **Summarizing** What changes ultimately led to the disintegration of the Ottoman Empire?

Ottoman Art

The Ottoman sultans were enthusiastic patrons of the arts. The period from Mehmet II to the early eighteenth century witnessed a flourishing production of pottery; rugs, silk, and other textiles; jewelry; and arms and armor. All of these adorned the palaces of the rulers. Artists came from all over the world to compete for the generous rewards of the sultans.

By far the greatest contribution of the Ottoman Empire to world art was in architecture, especially the magnificent mosques of the last half of the sixteenth century. The Ottoman Turks modeled their mosques on the open floor plan of Constantinople's Byzantine church of Hagia Sophia, creating a prayer hall with an open central area under one large dome.

In the mid-sixteenth century, the greatest of all Ottoman architects, **Sinan,** began building the first of his 81 mosques. One of Sinan's masterpieces was the Suleimaniye Mosque in Istanbul. Each of his mosques was topped by an imposing dome, and often the entire building was framed with four towers, or minarets.

The sixteenth century also witnessed the flourishing of textiles and rugs. The Byzantine emperor Justinian had introduced silk cultivation to the West in the sixth century. Under the Ottomans the silk industry resurfaced. Factories produced silks for wall hangings, sofa covers, and especially court costumes. Rugs were a peasant industry. The rugs, made of wool and cotton in villages from different regions, each boasted their own distinctive designs and color schemes.

✓ **Reading Check** **Explaining** How were the arts tied to religion in Ottoman society?

⬥ TAKS Practice

SECTION 1 ASSESSMENT

Checking for Understanding

1. **Define** janissary, pasha, gunpowder empire, sultan, harem, grand vizier, ulema.

2. **Identify** Mehmet II, Sultan Selim I, Sinan.

3. **Locate** Anatolian Peninsula, Bosporus, Dardanelles, Sea of Marmara, Makkah.

4. **Evaluate** how the problems in the Ottoman Empire may have begun during the reign of Süleyman the Magnificent.

5. **Identify** the four main occupational groups in the Ottoman Empire.

Critical Thinking

6. **Drawing Inferences** Describe the organization of Ottoman government and explain why it was effective.

7. **Compare and Contrast** Create a chart like the one below to compare and contrast the contributions of Mehmet II, Selim I, and Süleyman I to the Ottoman Empire.

Ruler	Contributions	Effect on Empire
Mehmet II		
Selim I		
Süleyman I		

Analyzing Visuals

8. **Compare** the room shown on page 462 with the room from the palace of Versailles shown on page 443 of your text. How do the two rooms reflect the power of the rulers who had them built?

Writing About History

9. **Expository Writing** The Ottoman Empire was considered a "gunpowder empire." Research the history of gunpowder and write an essay explaining how the Ottomans acquired it. What impact did this acquisition have on the expansion of the Ottoman Empire? Use both primary and secondary sources for your research.

THE WORLD OF
SÜLEYMAN

1

Called "the Magnificent" by Europeans who both feared and admired him, Süleyman I was a brilliant sixteenth-century military strategist who raised the Ottoman Empire to the height of its glory—more than doubling the landholdings he inherited from his father. During his 46-year reign (1520–1566), he personally led his armies on 13 campaigns, encouraged the growth of architecture and the fine arts, and played a key role in European politics of the day.

Yet in spite of his power and his many achievements, Süleyman also endured great tragedy—driven to execute not only his dearest friend but also two of his own sons.

Arising from a nomadic Turkic-speaking tribe in western Anatolia (today's Turkey) in the late thirteenth century, the Ottomans were zealous Muslims who regarded the *jihad*, or holy war, against non-believers as their religious duty. Over the next century, they conquered Anatolia and ever larger portions of Byzantine territories in eastern Europe. In 1453, Süleyman's great-grandfather, Mehmet the Conqueror, delivered the final blow to the Byzantine Empire when he captured its capital, Constantinople. Renamed Istanbul, it became the rich Ottoman capital.

The fall of Constantinople sent a shock wave through Europe and confirmed the Ottomans as a European power. During Süleyman's reign, the empire would extend from Buda in central Europe to Basra in Asia. Süleyman would also greatly expand the practice begun by Mehmet the Conqueror of supporting the arts and architecture, building public baths, bridges, religious schools, and grand mosque complexes. One of the most famous still standing today is Istanbul's Süleimaniye Mosque.

Süleyman lived and ruled from the ornate palace of Topkapi. Also housed here were the empire's treasury, a school for training high officials, the sultan's advisers, and the harem. The women of the sultan's harem were drawn from non-Muslim enslaved women either captured or given as tribute by vassal states.

A small guard of janissaries, the sultan's elite army, also lived at the palace. Founded in the late fourteenth century—long before any standing army in Europe—the janissaries were recruited exclusively from Christian boys who were then brought up in the Islamic faith and trained in the use of arms. The sultan's high officials were also recruited as children from Christian families. After rigorous training, they gained their positions by their own skill. This system was so unusual for the times that one foreign ambassador who was granted an audience with Süleyman observed with astonishment that "there was not in all that great assembly a single man who

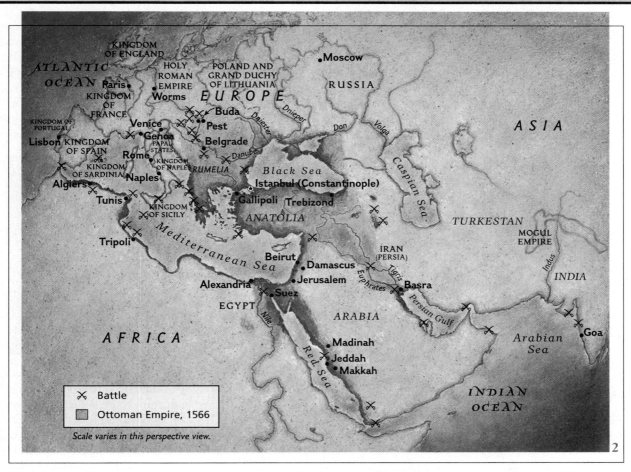

Battle
Ottoman Empire, 1566

Scale varies in this perspective view.

owed his position to aught save his valor and his merit."

Süleyman held absolute power and the right of life or death over his subjects. Yet one of his first official acts as sultan was to free 1,500 Egyptian and Iranian captives. He also paid merchants for any goods his father had confiscated, and ordered the execution of governors who were hated for their cruel abuses. This earned him a reputation as a just ruler who would protect the powerless among his people from illegal acts of corrupt officials.

His grateful subjects called Süleyman *Kanuni*, the Lawgiver. "I know of no State which is happier than this one," reported the Venetian ambassador. "It is furnished with all God's gifts. It controls war and peace with all; it is rich in gold, in people, in ships, and in obedience; no State can be compared with it." At the heart of

this well-ordered system, however, lay the seeds of its eventual downfall.

■

"Whichever of my sons inherits the sultan's throne," declared Mehmet the Conqueror, "it behooves him to kill his brothers in the interest of the world order." Killing off all contenders early in a sultan's reign could protect the regime from the kind of civil wars that disrupted other monarchies during the sixteenth century. Because it was sacrilege to shed royal blood, the deed was carried out by strangling with a silken bowstring.

Mehmet himself began his rule by killing his infant brother. And according to one chronicler, Süleyman's father, Selim, claimed the throne by killing "his father and two brothers, and many nephews and sixty-two other relatives." Selim the Grim, as he was called, knew that failure to carry

out the executions would have meant his own death—and that of Süleyman, his heir.

When his father became sultan, 18-year-old Prince Süleyman intensified his own training. Ottoman princes were assigned to serve as governors of provincial capitals, and to serve on military campaigns, ensuring

1 Süleyman's elaborate monogram endorsed many official documents issued during his 46-year reign.

2 Occupying a strategic position at the junction of three continents, the Ottoman Empire under Süleyman became a major world power. The broad sweep of the empire at the time of Süleyman's death in 1566 (shown in orange) included peoples of many religious and ethnic backgrounds.

that whoever survived the battle for the throne would be well prepared to lead the empire. According to custom, the prince of the house was supposed to be skilled in crafts as well as in government and war. Süleyman was trained as a goldsmith and was knowledgeable about science and poetry.

4

During his teens, he was educated with Ibrahim, a page at the prince's miniature court. A Greek fisherman's son who had been enslaved during a raid, Ibrahim was fluent in languages, charming, and intelligent. He and Süleyman were soon close friends. So high was Süleyman's opinion of his childhood friend that when he became sultan he made Ibrahim his grand vizier, the sultan's deputy and the general supervisor of the administration. He also put Ibrahim in charge of military campaigns when he himself did not ride into battle.

Süleyman set about producing several heirs to the throne. Three of his sons died in infancy, but the first to reach adulthood was Mustafa, whose mother was an enslaved girl named Gulbahar. Several sons by another concubine also reached adulthood. Their mother was a captive Russian bought for the sultan's harem at the slave market in Istanbul. Known in the West as Roxelana, she was nicknamed Hürrem—"Laughing One"—for her high spirits and lively storytelling. Much to Gulbahar's dis-

3

may, Roxelana became one of Süleyman's favorites, appearing with him on some public occasions. His sons meant a lot to Süleyman at the beginning of his reign. He went hunting with them in many parts of his far-flung empire.

This abundance of male heirs set up a deadly rivalry between Gulbahar and Roxelana. Each mother knew that her sons would die if the other's ascended the throne. Roxelana seems to have taken every opportunity to strengthen her position with Süleyman and to undermine that of anyone she perceived as a rival. The rivals included not only Gulbahar but also the grand vizier, Ibrahim, who had openly opposed Süleyman's relationship with Roxelana. Süleyman's mother, who favored Ibrahim, was also a rival.

Then, in 1534, Süleyman's mother died. Two years later, convinced by Roxelana that Ibrahim was plotting against him, Süleyman ordered his lifelong friend executed. In addition, Roxelana managed to get her son-in-law, Rustem Pasha, appointed grand vizier.

Meanwhile, all of Süleyman's sons were being trained just as he had been. Historians have speculated that he favored one or another of them at different times, but the record is hard to interpret. What is known is that Mustafa, Mehmet, Selim, and Bayezid each were assigned to governorships or military campaigns, and that Mehmet died of natural causes in 1543, only a year into his first governorship. Losing a son in adulthood was a great shock to Süleyman, who was, nonetheless, steadily conquering territory and using his influence to unsettle and destabilize Christian Europe.

Then in 1553, Rustem Pasha convinced Süleyman that Mustafa was plotting a rebellion. There may have been something to the rumor. Süleyman, at 59, was showing signs of his age and had recently been seriously ill. Mustafa, 39, had 20 years experience as a governor. He was respected by the soldiers he led and by the people, who considered him the best successor to his father.

Whatever the truth, Süleyman believed Mustafa to be a danger to the state. On campaign in Iran, he killed his oldest son. Very shortly thereafter, another son, Cihangir, died, leaving only Bayezid and Selim.

The battle for the throne turned into a decade-long civil war between Süleyman's two remaining sons and came to involve the empire's war with its longtime enemy, the Safavid dynasty of Iran. For the sultan, law and order in his empire was more important than any personal family ties. In 1561, Süleyman sided with Selim. He had Bayezid and all his sons—Süleyman's grandsons—killed.

Thus it happened that on Süleyman's death five years later, Selim II was the undisputed heir to the throne. Many date the slow decline of the

empire to Selim's reign. Known as the Drunkard, he left the actual running of the state to his advisers. He also started the practice of choosing only one of his sons for training, thereby reducing the jockeying for power among sons, mothers, and palace officials.

In the seventeenth century, the sultans stopped killing their male relatives and began instead to imprison them. Thus, when a sultan was overthrown, or died without a male heir, the next person to sit on the throne would have spent years —and in some cases, their entire lives—in prison. Ill-equipped to lead, these sultans were easy prey for a corrupt bureaucracy.

3 The soaring dome of Selimiye Mosque in Edirne is decorated with intricate patterns and phrases from the Quran. The vast mosque was built for Süleyman's son and successor, Selim II.

4 Transcribed by a court calligrapher, Süleyman's verses were often decorated with flecks of gold.

5 Solid gold and studded with rubies, emeralds, and other gems, this canteen was carried into battle for the sultan.

6 Ottoman armor, like this grand vizier's helmet, was frequently very ornate.

INTERPRETING THE PAST

1. Why was Süleyman known as the Lawgiver? What kind of ruler was he?

2. What were Süleyman's main accomplishments?

3. What factors contributed to the decline of the Ottoman Empire after Süleyman's death?

The Rule of the Safavids

Guide to Reading

Main Ideas
- The Safavids used their faith as a unifying force to bring Turks and Persians together.
- The Safavid dynasty reached its height under Shah Abbas.

Key Terms
shah, orthodoxy, anarchy

People To Identify
Safavids, Shah Ismail, Shah Abbas, Riza-i-Abbasi

Places To Locate
Azerbaijan, Caspian Sea, Tabriz, Isfahan

Preview Questions
1. What events led to the creation and growth of the Safavid dynasty?
2. What cultural contributions were made by the Safavid dynasty?

Reading Strategy
Compare and Contrast Fill in the table below listing the key features of the Ottoman and Safavid Empires.

Ottoman Empire	Safavid Empire

Preview of Events

◆1500	◆1535	◆1570	◆1605	◆1640	◆1675	◆1710

1501
Ismail captures Iran and Iraq

1508
Safavid shah conquers Baghdad

1588
Shah Abbas becomes Safavid ruler

1612
Azerbaijan returned to Safavids

1722
Safavid Empire collapses

Voices from the Past

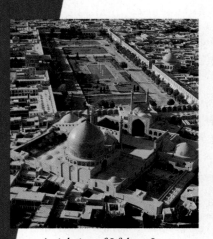

Aerial view of Isfahan, Iran

Under the Safavid dynasty of Persia, the capital city of Isfahan was known for its beauty. One English traveler reported:

❝The magnificently-arched bazaars, which form the Noble Square to the Palace, the several public inns, the stately rows of sycamore trees, which the world cannot parallel, the glorious summer-houses, the pleasant gardens, the stupendous bridges, sumptuous temples, the religious convents, the college for the professors of astronomy, are so many lasting monuments of Shah Abbas' fame. . . . Few cities in the world surpass Isfahan for wealth, and none come near it for those stately buildings, which for that reason are kept entire.❞
—*A New Account of East India and Persia, Being Nine Years' Travels, 1672–1681,*
John Fryer, edited 1911

Isfahan was a planned city created by Shah Abbas the Great, ruler of the Safavids.

Rise of the Safavid Dynasty

After the collapse of the empire of Timur Lenk (Tamerlane) in the early fifteenth century, the area extending from Persia into central Asia fell into anarchy. At the beginning of the sixteenth century, however, a new dynasty known as the **Safavids** (sah•FAH•weedz) took control. Unlike many of their Islamic neighbors who were Sunni Muslims, the Safavids became ardent Shiites. (As discussed in

Chapter 6, the Sunnis and Shiites were the two major groups in the Islamic religion.)

The Safavid dynasty was founded by **Shah Ismail** (ihs•MAH•EEL), the descendant of Safi al-Din (thus the name *Safavid*). In the early fourteenth century, Safi al-Din had been the leader of a community of Turkish ethnic groups in **Azerbaijan,** near the **Caspian Sea.**

In 1501, Ismail used his forces to seize much of Iran and Iraq. He then called himself the shah, or king, of a new Persian state. Ismail sent Shiite preachers into Anatolia to convert members of Turkish tribes in the Ottoman Empire. The Ottoman sultan tried to halt this activity, but Ismail refused to stop. He also ordered the massacre of Sunni Muslims when he conquered Baghdad in 1508.

Alarmed by these activities, the Ottoman sultan, Selim I, advanced against the Safavids in Persia and won a major battle near **Tabriz.** However, Selim could not maintain control of the area. A few years later, Ismail regained Tabriz.

During the following decades, the Safavids tried to consolidate their rule throughout Persia and in areas to the west. Faced with the problem of integrating various Turkish peoples with the settled Persian-speaking population of the urban areas, the Safavids used the Shiite faith as a unifying force. Like the Ottoman sultan, the shah himself claimed to be the spiritual leader of all Islam.

In the 1580s, the Ottomans went on the attack. They placed Azerbaijan under Ottoman rule and controlled the Caspian Sea with their fleet. This forced the new Safavid shah, Abbas, to sign a peace treaty in which he lost much territory. The capital of the Safavids was moved from the northwestern city of Tabriz to the more centrally located city of **Isfahan.**

Reading Check **Identifying** What led to fighting between the Ottomans and the Safavids?

Glory and Decline

Under **Shah Abbas,** who ruled from 1588 to 1629, the Safavids reached the high point of their glory. A system similar to that of the janissaries in the Ottoman Empire was created to train administrators to run the kingdom. Shah Abbas also strengthened his army, which he armed with the latest weapons.

In the early seventeenth century, Shah Abbas moved against the Ottomans to regain lost territories. He was helped by European states, whose leaders viewed the Safavids as useful allies against their chief enemies, the Ottoman Turks. The Safavids had some initial success, but they could not hold all their territorial gains against the Ottoman armies. Nevertheless, in 1612, a peace treaty was signed that returned Azerbaijan to the Safavids.

After the death of Shah Abbas in 1629, the Safavid dynasty gradually lost its vigor. Most of his successors lacked his talent and political skills. The power of Shiite religious elements began to increase at court and in Safavid society at large.

While intellectual freedom had marked the height of the empire, the pressure to conform to traditional religious beliefs, called religious orthodoxy, increased. For example, Persian women who had considerable freedom during the early empire were now forced into seclusion and required to adopt the wearing of the veil.

In the early eighteenth century, during the reign of Shah Hussein, Afghan peoples invaded and seized the capital of Isfahan. The remnants of the Safavid ruling family were forced to retreat to Azerbaijan,

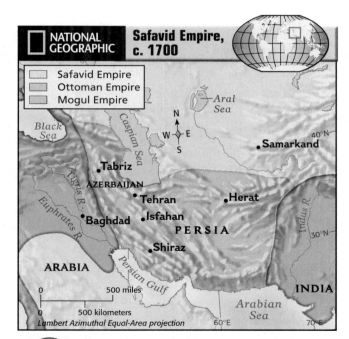

NATIONAL GEOGRAPHIC **Safavid Empire, c. 1700**

- Safavid Empire
- Ottoman Empire
- Mogul Empire

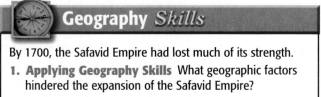

Geography *Skills*

By 1700, the Safavid Empire had lost much of its strength.

1. **Applying Geography Skills** What geographic factors hindered the expansion of the Safavid Empire?

Ottoman and Safavid Empires

Ottoman Empire

Arose in early 14th century

Expanded from northwest Anatolian Peninsula to western Asia, eastern Europe, and North Africa

Attempted to conquer central Europe

Sunni Muslims

Ruler: Sultan

Was generally tolerant of non-Muslims in empire

Began slow decline in 17th century

(Both)

Conquered surrounding territory

Strong military used latest weapons

Muslims

Political and religious ruler inherited position and owned all land

Mixed ethnicities and religions in society

Encouraged trade and arts

Safavid Empire

Arose in early 16th century

Controlled area from Persia into central Asia; lost territory to Ottomans

Allied with European states against Ottomans

Shiite Muslims

Ruler: Shah

Used Shiite faith to unify peoples in empire

Collapsed in 1722

Graphic Organizer → Skills

Both the Ottomans and the Safavids created strong empires.

Compare and Contrast Which empire had a greater influence on Europe? What factors do you think most influenced the ability of both empires to expand?

their original homeland. The Turks took advantage of the situation to seize territories along the western border. Persia sank into a long period of political and social **anarchy** (lawlessness and disorder).

☑ **Reading Check** **Evaluating** How did the Safavid Empire reach its pinnacle under Shah Abbas? Why did it decline after his death?

Political and Social Structures

Persia under the Safavids was a mixed society. The Safavids had come to power with the support of nomadic Turkish groups, but the majority of the people were Persian. Most of them were farmers or townspeople. The combination of Turkish and Persian elements affected virtually all aspects of Safavid society.

The Safavid political system, like that in most empires, was organized in the shape of a pyramid. The shah was at the top, the bureaucracy and landed classes were in the middle, and the common people were below.

The Role of the Shah
The Safavid rulers were eagerly supported by Shiites, who believed that the founder of the empire (Shah Ismail) was a direct successor of the prophet Muhammad. In return, the shahs declared Shia Islam to be the state religion.

Visitors reported that the shahs were more available to their subjects than were rulers elsewhere. "They show great familiarity to strangers," remarked one visitor, "and even to their own subjects, eating and drinking with them pretty freely." Indeed, the shahs even had their physical features engraved inside drinking cups so that people throughout their empire would know them.

Strong-minded shahs firmly controlled the power of the landed aristocracy. The shahs seized the large landed estates of the aristocrats and brought them under the control of the Crown. In addition, appointment to senior positions in the bureaucracy was based on merit rather than birth. To avoid competition between Turkish and non-Turkish elements, Shah Abbas, for example, hired a number of foreigners from neighboring countries for positions in his government.

Economy and Trade
The Safavid shahs played an active part in trade and manufacturing activity. There

was also a large and affluent urban middle class involved in trade.

Most goods in the empire traveled by horse or camel caravans. Although the road system was poor, the government provided resting places for weary travelers. In times of strong rulers, the roads were kept fairly clear of thieves and bandits.

At its height, Safavid Persia was a worthy successor to the great Persian empires of the past. However, it was probably not as prosperous as its neighbors to the east and west—the Moguls and the Ottomans. Hemmed in by the sea power of the Europeans to the south and the land power of the Ottomans to the west, the Safavids found trade with Europe difficult.

✓**Reading Check** **Describing** Describe the shah's power and its effect on society.

Safavid Culture

Knowledge of science, medicine, and mathematics under the Safavids was equal to that of other societies in the region. In addition, Persia witnessed an extraordinary flowering of the arts during the reign of Shah Abbas from 1588 to 1629.

The capital of Isfahan, built by Shah Abbas, was a grandiose planned city with wide spaces and a sense of order. Palaces, mosques, and bazaars were arranged around a massive polo ground. The immense mosques were richly decorated, and the palaces were delicate structures with slender wooden columns. To adorn the buildings, craftspeople created imaginative metalwork, elaborate tiles, and

The Royal Academy of Isfahan

delicate glass vessels. Much of the original city still stands and is a gem of modern-day Iran.

Silk weaving based on new techniques flourished throughout the empire. The silks were a brilliant color, with silver and gold threads. The weavings portrayed birds, animals, and flowers.

Above all, carpet weaving flourished, stimulated by the great demand for Persian carpets in the West. Made primarily of wool, these carpets are still highly prized all over the world.

Persian painting enjoyed a long tradition, which continued in the Safavid Era. **Riza-i-Abbasi,** the most famous artist of this period, created exquisite works on simple subjects, such as oxen plowing, hunters, and lovers. Soft colors and flowing movement were the dominant features of the painting of this period.

✓**Reading Check** **Describing** What subjects were portrayed in many works of art from the Safavid Era?

🔺**TAKS Practice**

SECTION 2 ASSESSMENT

Checking for Understanding

1. **Define** shah, orthodoxy, anarchy.

2. **Identify** Safavids, Shah Ismail, Shah Abbas, Riza-i-Abbasi.

3. **Locate** Azerbaijan, Caspian Sea, Tabriz, Isfahan.

4. **Describe** how the Safavids tried to bring the various Turkish and Persian peoples together.

5. **Summarize** how the increased pressures of religious orthodoxy influenced women's lives in the late Safavid dynasty.

Critical Thinking

6. **Explain** What was the shah's role in Safavid society and government?

7. **Organizing Information** Create a chart like the one below listing the Safavid shahs and significant developments that occurred during their administrations.

Shah	Significant Events

Analyzing Visuals

8. **Examine** the photograph of the Royal Academy of Isfahan shown on this page. Why would mosques have included schools like this academy?

Writing About History

9. **Expository Writing** Analyze the impact of the Safavid Empire's geographical location on its economy (what goods could be traded, trading partners, goods in high demand). Compare and contrast the Safavid economy with that of another economy.

STUDY & WRITING SKILLBUILDER

Using Library Resources

Why Learn This Skill?

You have been assigned a major research report. At the library, you wonder: Where do I start my research? Which reference works should I use?

Learning the Skill

Libraries contain many reference works. Here are brief descriptions of important reference sources:

Reference Books Reference books include encyclopedias, biographical dictionaries, atlases, and almanacs.

- An encyclopedia is a set of books containing short articles on many subjects arranged alphabetically.

- A biographical dictionary includes brief biographies listed alphabetically by last names.

- An atlas is a collection of maps and charts for locating geographic features and places. An atlas can be general or thematic.

Many libraries contain print and electronic resource materials.

- An almanac is an annually updated reference that provides current statistics and historical information on a wide range of subjects.

Card Catalogs Every library has a card catalog (on actual cards, computerized, or both), which lists every book in the library. Search for books by author, subject, or title. Computerized card catalogs can also advise you on the book's availability.

Periodical Guides A periodical guide lists topics covered in magazines and newspapers and tells you where the articles can be found.

Computer Databases Computer databases provide collections of information organized for rapid search and retrieval. For example, many libraries carry reference materials on CD-ROM.

Practicing the Skill

Decide which source(s) described in this skill you would use to answer each of these questions for a report on the Safavid dynasty of Persia.

1. During what time period was the Safavid dynasty in control?
2. What present-day geographical area constitutes the territory occupied by the Safavids?
3. What type of leader was Shah Ismail?
4. What event was instrumental in moving the capital to Isfahan?

Application Activity

Using your school or local library, research the following and write a brief report to present your findings: Who established the East India Company and when? What was the work of the East India Company? Why was it important?

Glencoe's **Skillbuilder Interactive Workbook, Level 2,** provides instruction and practice in key social studies skills.

The Grandeur of the Moguls

Guide to Reading

Main Ideas
- The Moguls united India under a single government with a common culture.
- The introduction of foreigners seeking trade opportunities in India hastened the decline of the Mogul Empire.

Key Terms
zamindar, suttee

People to Identify
Babur, Akbar, Shah Jahan, Aurangzeb

Places to Locate
Khyber Pass, Delhi, Deccan Plateau, Calcutta, Chennai, Agra

Preview Questions
1. How did Mogul rulers develop the empire's culture?
2. What were the chief characteristics of Mogul society?

Reading Strategy
Summarizing Information As you read this section, create a chart listing the accomplishments and weaknesses of the Mogul rulers.

Ruler	Accomplishments	Weaknesses

Preview of Events

♦1500	♦1545	♦1590	♦1635	♦1680	♦1725	♦1770

1517
Babur crosses Khyber Pass into India

1556
Akbar becomes Mogul ruler

1605
Moguls rule most of India

1739
Persians sack Delhi

1763
Treaty of Paris gives British control in India

Voices from the Past

The Mogul rulers of India lived in great splendor, as is evident in this report by an English traveler:

*Persian cotton rug,
c. 1630*

66The first of September was the king's birthday. . . . Here attended the nobility all sitting on carpets until the king came; who at last appeared clothed, or rather laden with diamonds, rubies, pearls, and other vanities, so great, so glorious! His head, neck, breast, arms, above the elbows at the wrists, his fingers every one, with at least two or three rings; fettered with chains of diamonds; rubies as great as walnuts, and pearls, such as my eyes were amazed at. . . . He ascended his throne, and had basins of nuts, almonds, fruits, and spices made in thin silver, which he cast about.99

—*Eyewitness to History*, John Carey, ed.,1987

Mogul rulers united most of India under a single government with a common culture.

The Mogul Dynasty

In 1500, the Indian subcontinent was still divided into a number of Hindu and Muslim kingdoms. However, the Moguls established a new dynasty and brought a new era of unity to the region. The Moguls were not natives of India, but came from the mountainous region north of the Indus River valley.

The founder of the Mogul dynasty was **Babur.** His father was descended from the great Asian conqueror Timur Lenk, and his mother, from the Mongol

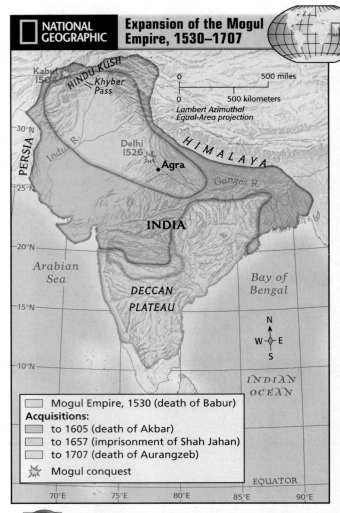

Expansion of the Mogul Empire, 1530–1707

Kabul 1504
HINDU KUSH
Khyber Pass
PERSIA
Indus R.
Delhi 1526
Agra
HIMALAYA
Ganges R.
INDIA
Arabian Sea
DECCAN PLATEAU
Bay of Bengal
INDIAN OCEAN
EQUATOR

0   500 miles
0   500 kilometers
Lambert Azimuthal Equal-Area projection

N
W   E
S

☐ Mogul Empire, 1530 (death of Babur)
Acquisitions:
☐ to 1605 (death of Akbar)
☐ to 1657 (imprisonment of Shah Jahan)
☐ to 1707 (death of Aurangzeb)
✳ Mogul conquest

30°N 25°N 20°N 15°N 10°N
70°E 75°E 80°E 85°E 90°E

Geography *Skills*

Most of the people the Moguls encountered as they expanded into India were Hindu.

1. **Interpreting Maps** Why did the southern tip of India remain free from Mogul expansion?
2. **Applying Geography Skills** How does the map support the text's assertion that Akbar was the greatest of the conquering Mogul monarchs?

conqueror Genghis Khan. Babur had inherited a part of Timur Lenk's empire in an upland river valley of the Syr Darya. As a youth, he commanded a group of warriors who seized Kabul in 1504. Thirteen years later, his forces crossed the **Khyber Pass** to India.

Babur's forces were far smaller than those of his enemies, but they had advanced weapons, including artillery, and used them to great effect. With twelve thousand troops against an enemy force nearly ten times that size, Babur captured **Delhi** and established his power in the plains of North India. He

continued his conquests in North India until his death in 1530 at the age of 47.

✓**Reading Check** **Summarizing** How did Babur begin the Mogul dynasty in India?

The Reign of Akbar

Babur's grandson **Akbar** was only 14 when he came to the throne. Highly intelligent and industrious, Akbar set out to extend his domain. By 1605, he had brought Mogul rule to most of India.

How was Akbar able to place almost all of India under his rule? By using heavy artillery, Akbar's armies were able to overpower the stone fortresses of their rivals. The Moguls were also successful negotiators.

Akbar's conquests created the greatest Indian empire since the Mauryan dynasty nearly two thousand years earlier. The empire appeared highly centralized but was actually a collection of semi-independent states held together by the power of the emperor.

Akbar was probably the greatest of the conquering Mogul monarchs, but he is best known for the humane character of his rule. Like all Mogul rulers, Akbar was born a Muslim, but he adopted a policy of religious tolerance. As emperor, he showed a keen interest in other religions and tolerated Hindu practices. He even welcomed the expression of Christian views by his Jesuit advisers at court. By taking a Hindu princess as one of his wives, Akbar put his policy of religious tolerance into practice.

Akbar was also tolerant in his administration of the government. The upper ranks of the government bureaucracy were filled with non-native Muslims, but many of the lower-ranking officials were Hindus.

It became common practice to give the lower-ranking officials plots of farmland for their temporary use. These local officials, known as zamindars, kept a portion of the taxes paid by the peasants in lieu of a salary. They were then expected to forward the rest of the taxes from the lands under their control to the central government. Zamindars came to exercise considerable power in their local districts.

Overall, the Akbar Era was a time of progress, at least by the standards of the day. All Indian peasants were required to pay about one-third of their annual harvest to the state but the system was applied justly. When bad weather struck in the 1590s, taxes were reduced, or suspended altogether. Thanks to a long period of peace and political stability, trade and manufacturing flourished.

The era was an especially prosperous one in the area of foreign trade. Indian goods, notably textiles, tropical food products and spices, and precious stones, were exported in exchange for gold and silver. Much of the foreign trade was handled by Arab traders, because the Indians, like their Mogul rulers, did not care for travel by sea.

✓ **Reading Check** **Explaining** How did Akbar's religious policy affect his government?

Decline of the Moguls

Akbar died in 1605 and was succeeded by his son Jahangir (juh•HAHN•GIHR). Jahangir was able and ambitious. During the early years of his reign, he continued to strengthen the central government's control over his vast empire.

Eventually, however, his grip began to weaken when he fell under the influence of one of his wives, Persian-born Nur Jahan. The empress used her position to enrich her own family. She arranged the marriage of her niece to her husband's third son and ultimate successor, **Shah Jahan.**

During his reign from 1628 to 1658, Shah Jahan maintained the political system established by earlier Mogul rulers. He also expanded the boundaries of the empire through successful campaigns in the **Deccan Plateau** and against the city of Samarkand, north of the Hindu Kush.

Shah Jahan's rule was marred by his failure to deal with growing domestic problems, however. He had inherited a nearly empty treasury. His military campaigns and expensive building projects put a heavy strain on the imperial finances and compelled him to raise taxes. Meanwhile, the majority of his subjects lived in poverty.

Shah Jahan's troubles worsened with his illness in the mid-1650s, which led to a struggle for power between two of his sons. One of Shah Jahan's sons, **Aurangzeb,** had his brother put to death and imprisoned his father. Aurangzeb then had himself crowned emperor in 1658.

Aurangzeb is one of the most controversial rulers in the history of India. A man of high principle, he attempted to eliminate many of what he considered to be India's social evils. He forbade both the Hindu custom of suttee (cremating a widow on her husband's funeral pyre) and the levying of illegal taxes. He tried to forbid gambling and drinking as well.

Aurangzeb was a devout Muslim and adopted a number of measures that reversed the Mogul policies of religious tolerance. The building of new Hindu temples was prohibited, and Hindus were forced to convert to Islam.

Aurangzeb's policies led to Hindu outcries and domestic unrest. In addition, a number of revolts against imperial authority broke out in provinces throughout the empire. Rebellious groups threatened the power of the emperor, leaving an increasingly divided India vulnerable to attack from abroad. In 1739, Delhi was sacked by the Persians, who left it in ashes.

✓ **Reading Check** **Explaining** Why was Aurangzeb one of the most controversial rulers in the history of India?

The British in India

┌TURNING POINT┐ **In this section, you will learn how a small British force defeated a Mogul army at the Battle of Plassey in 1757. A few years later, a similar victory over the French made the British a dominant presence in India until after World War II.**

The arrival of the British hastened the decline of the Mogul Empire. By 1650, British trading forts had been established at Surat, Fort William (now the city of **Calcutta**), and **Chennai** (Madras). From Chennai, British ships carried Indian-made cotton goods to the East Indies, where they were traded for spices.

British success in India attracted rivals, especially the French. The French established their own forts on the east coast at Pondicherry, south of Chennai, at Surat, and in the Bay of Bengal. For a brief period, the French went on the offensive, even capturing the British fort at Chennai.

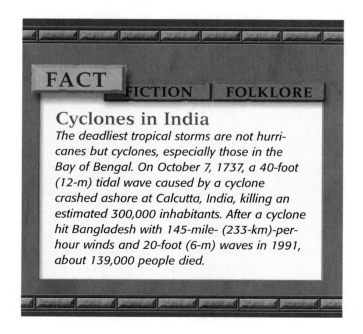

FACT FICTION FOLKLORE

Cyclones in India
The deadliest tropical storms are not hurricanes but cyclones, especially those in the Bay of Bengal. On October 7, 1737, a 40-foot (12-m) tidal wave caused by a cyclone crashed ashore at Calcutta, India, killing an estimated 300,000 inhabitants. After a cyclone hit Bangladesh with 145-mile- (233-km)-per-hour winds and 20-foot (6-m) waves in 1991, about 139,000 people died.

The British were saved by the military genius of Sir Robert Clive, an aggressive British empire builder. Clive eventually became the chief representative in India of the East India Company, a private company empowered by the British Crown to act on its behalf. As chief representative, it was Clive's job to fight any force, French or Indian, that threatened the East India Company's power in India. Owing to Clive's efforts, the French were ultimately restricted to the fort at Pondicherry and a handful of small territories on the southeastern coast.

While fighting the French, Clive was also consolidating British control in Bengal, the state in which Fort William was located. The Indian ruler of Bengal had attacked Fort William in 1756. He had imprisoned the British garrison overnight in what became known as the "Black Hole of Calcutta," an underground prison. The intense heat in the crowded space had led to disaster. Only 23 people (out of 146) had walked out alive.

In 1757, Clive led a small British force numbering about three thousand to victory over a Mogul-led army more than ten times its size in the Battle of

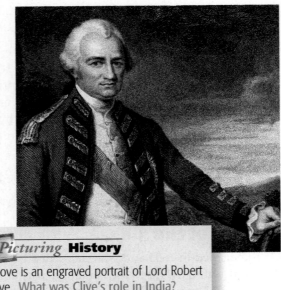

Plassey in Bengal. As part of the spoils of victory, the failing Mogul court gave the British East India Company the power to collect taxes from lands in the area surrounding Calcutta.

Britain's rise to power in India, however, was not a story of constant success. Officials of the East India Company, from the governor-general on down, often combined arrogance with incompetence. They offended both their Indian allies and the local population, who were taxed heavily to meet the growing expenses of the East India Company. Intelligent Indian commanders avoided direct pitched battles with well-armed British troops. They preferred to harass and ambush them in the manner of modern-day guerrillas. Said one of India's commanders:

> 66Shall I risk my cavalry which cost a thousand rupees each horse, against your cannon ball which cost two pice? No! I will march your troops until their legs swell to the size of their bodies. You shall not have a blade of grass, nor a drop of water. I will hear of you every time your drum beats, but you shall not know where I am once a month. I will give your army battle, but it must be when I please, and not when you choose.99

In the late eighteenth century, the East India Company moved inland from the great coastal cities. British expansion brought great riches to individual British merchants, as well as to British officials who found they could obtain money from local rulers by selling trade privileges. The British were in India to stay.

✔ **Reading Check** **Examining** How did the East India Company, a private company, become involved in the struggle over control of India?

NATIONAL GEOGRAPHIC

British in India, c.1700

- ■ British trading fort
- ■ French trading fort
- ✳ British victory over Moguls
- – – – Extent of Mogul Empire, 1700

30°N

Delhi

INDIA

BENGAL

Plassey 1757

Fort William (Calcutta)

Surat

20°N

Arabian Sea

0   300 miles

0   300 kilometers

Two-Point Equidistant projection

10°N

Bay of Bengal

Chennai (Madras)

Pondicherry

Sri Lanka (Ceylon)

70°E   80°E   90°E

Geography *Skills*

The British East India Company gradually took over more and more land in India.

1. **Interpreting Maps** What do you notice about the placement of foreign trading forts in India?

2. **Applying Geography Skills** Create a map that shows the route British and French ships sailed to India.

What If...

Britain's East India Company had been a financial disaster?

Chartered companies were the main instruments of imperial expansion for much of eighteenth-century Europe. They were private companies granted certain royal privileges—such as monopolies—that brought their rulers territorial and military dominance even as they sought their own commercial gains. However, some chartered companies did not prosper. The French East India Company, for example, did not survive.

Consider the Consequences Consider what would have happened to the political landscape of both India and Europe if Britain's East India Company had been a financial failure. What other country or company could have filled Britain's role in India?

Society and Daily Life in Mogul India

The Moguls were foreigners in India. In addition, they were Muslims ruling a largely Hindu population. The resulting blend of influences on the lives of ordinary Indians could be complicated. The treatment of women in Mogul India is a good example of this complexity.

Women had long played an active role in Mogul tribal society, and some actually fought on the battlefield alongside the men. Mogul rulers often relied on female relatives for political advice.

To a degree, these Mogul attitudes toward women affected Indian society. Women from aristocratic families frequently received salaries and were allowed to own land and take part in business activities.

At the same time, the Moguls placed certain restrictions on women under their interpretations of Islamic law. These practices sometimes were compatible with existing tendencies in Indian society and were adopted by Hindus. The practice of isolating women, for example, was followed by many upper-class Hindus.

In other ways, however, Hindu practices remained unchanged by Mogul rule. The custom of suttee continued despite efforts by the Moguls to abolish it. Child marriage also remained common.

The Mogul era saw the emergence of a wealthy landed nobility and a prosperous merchant class. During the late eighteenth century, this economic prosperity was shaken by the decline of the Mogul Empire and the coming of the British. However, many prominent Indians established trading ties with the foreigners, a relationship that temporarily worked to the Indians' benefit.

Most of what we know about the daily lives of ordinary Indians outside of the cities comes from the observations of foreign visitors. One such foreign visitor provided the following description of Indian life:

> 66 Their houses are built of mud with thatched roofs. Furniture there is little or none except some earthenware pots to hold water and for cooking and two beds, one for the man, the other for his wife; their bed cloths are scanty, merely a sheet or perhaps two, serving as under- and over-sheet. This is sufficient for the hot weather, but the bitter cold nights are miserable indeed, and they try to keep warm over little cow-dung fires. 99

✓ **Reading Check** **Contrasting** How did women's lives under Islamic and Hindu religious laws differ from women's lives in Mogul society?

Mogul Culture

The Moguls brought together Persian and Indian influences in a new and beautiful architectural style. This style is best symbolized by the **Taj Mahal,** which was built in **Agra** by the emperor Shah Jahan in the mid-seventeenth century. The emperor built the Taj Mahal in memory of his wife, Mumtaz Mahal, who had died at the age of 39 giving birth to her fourteenth child. The project employed twenty thousand workers and lasted more than twenty years. To finance it, the government raised land taxes, thus driving many Indian peasants into complete poverty.

The Taj Mahal is widely considered to be the most beautiful building in India, if not in the entire world. All the exterior and interior surfaces are decorated with cut-stone geometric patterns, delicate black stone tracery, or intricate inlays of colored precious stones in floral mosaics. The building seems to have monumental size, nearly blinding brilliance, and delicate lightness, all at the same time.

Another major artistic achievement of the Mogul period was in painting. Like architecture, painting in Mogul India resulted from the blending of two cultures: Persian and Indian. Akbar established a state

History *through Architecture*

Of all the buildings in India, none is more famous than the Taj Mahal. Its simple symmetry and the placement of the long reflecting pool create a timeless image of beauty. **Why was the Taj Mahal built?**

workshop for artists, mostly Hindus, who worked under the guidance of Persian masters to create the Mogul school of painting. The "Akbar style" combined Persian with Indian motifs. It included the portrayal of humans in action, for example—a characteristic not usually seen in Persian art. Akbar also encouraged his artists to imitate European art forms, including the use of perspective and lifelike portraits.

The Mogul emperors were dedicated patrons of the arts, and going to India was the goal of painters, poets, and artisans from as far away as the Mediterranean. Apparently, the generosity of the Moguls made it difficult to refuse a trip to India. It is said that the Moguls would reward a poet with his weight in gold.

✓**Reading Check** **Describing** What was the "Akbar style" of art?

🌟**TAKS Practice**

SECTION 3 ASSESSMENT

Checking for Understanding

1. **Define** zamindar, suttee.

2. **Identify** Babur, Akbar, Shah Jahan, Aurangzeb.

3. **Locate** Khyber Pass, Delhi, Deccan Plateau, Calcutta, Chennai, Taj Mahal, Agra.

4. **Describe** the impact of the Moguls on the Hindu and Muslim peoples of the Indian subcontinent. How did the reign of Aurangzeb weaken Mogul rule in India?

5. **Summarize** the problems Shah Jahan faced during his rule. How did the rule of Shah Jahan come to an end?

Critical Thinking

6. **Evaluate** What role did the British play in the decline of the Mogul Empire in India?

7. **Cause and Effect** Create a chart like the one below listing the events that led to the decline of the Mogul Empire and tell how each contributed to the empire's decline.

```
┌──────────┐    ┌──────────┐
│          │ →  │          │
└──────────┘    └──────────┘
┌──────────┐    ┌──────────┐
│          │ →  │          │
└──────────┘    └──────────┘
┌──────────┐    ┌──────────┐
│          │ →  │          │
└──────────┘    └──────────┘
┌──────────┐    ┌──────────┐
│          │ →  │          │
└──────────┘    └──────────┘
┌──────────┐    ┌──────────┐
│          │ →  │          │
└──────────┘    └──────────┘
```

Analyzing Visuals

8. **Examine** the photograph above of the Taj Mahal, built as a tomb for the wife of Shah Jahan. How does the Taj Mahal compare to other buildings created to house the dead, such as the pyramids of Egypt? Which type of tomb is more impressive, in your opinion?

Writing About History

9. **Descriptive Writing** When the British established trading posts in India, their influence spread throughout the country. Present a speech describing how India would have developed if the British had not colonized the country.

An Elephant Fight for the King's Entertainment

FRANÇOIS BERNIER WAS A WELL-TRAVELED Frenchman who visited India during the mid-seventeenth century. In this excerpt from his account of the visit, he describes a festival just outside the Red Fort at Delhi for the amusement of the emperor.

This woodcut captures the fierceness of elephant fights.

❝The festivals generally conclude with an amusement unknown in Europe—a combat between two elephants; which takes place in the presence of all the people on the sandy space near the river: the King, the principal ladies of the court, and the nobles viewing the spectacle from different apartments in the fortress.

A wall of earth is raised three or four feet wide and five or six high. The two ponderous beasts meet one another face to face, on opposite sides of the wall, each having a couple of riders, that the place of the man who sits on the shoulders, for the purpose of guiding the elephant with a large iron hook, may immediately be supplied if he should be thrown down. The riders animate the elephants either by soothing words, or by chiding them as cowards, and urge them on with their heels, until the poor creatures approach the wall and are brought to the attack. The shock is tremendous, and it appears surprising that they ever survive the dreadful wounds and blows inflicted with their teeth, their heads, and their trunks. The stronger or more courageous elephant passes on and attacks his opponent, and, putting him to flight, pursues and fastens upon him with so much obstinacy, that the animals can be separated only by means of fire-works, which are made to explode between them; for they are naturally timid, and have a particular dread of fire, which is the reason why elephants have been used with so very little advantage in armies since the use of fire-arms.

The fight of these noble creatures is attended with much cruelty. It frequently happens that some of the riders are trodden underfoot; and killed on the spot. . . . So imminent is the danger considered, that on the day of combat the unhappy men take the same formal leave of their wives and children as if condemned to death. . . . The mischief with which this amusement is attended does not always end with the death of the rider: it happens that some spectators are knocked down and trampled upon by the elephants.❞

—François Bernier, *Travels in the Mogul Empire*

Analyzing Primary Sources

1. What was the purpose of the elephant fights?
2. Did the elephant riders enjoy the sport? Explain your answer.
3. What other examples of animal fights can you think of? Why do you think people across cultures are entertained by watching such spectacles?

Using Key Terms

1. Mogul officials called _____ kept a portion of the taxes paid by peasants as their salaries.
2. The _____ led the meetings of the sultan's imperial council and served as his chief minister.
3. The _____ was the ruler of the Safavid Empire.
4. Boys from Christian families were recruited and trained as _____, the elite of the army.
5. The _____ administered the sultan's legal system and schools for educating Muslims.
6. The sultan's private living quarters was called the _____.
7. _____ collected taxes for the sultan.
8. The _____ was the political and military leader of the Ottoman Empire.
9. Adherence to traditional religious beliefs, called religious _____, increased as the Safavid dynasty started to decline.
10. A state of lawlessness or political disorder due to the absence of governmental authority is called _____.
11. _____ were formed by conquerors who had mastered the technology of firearms.

Reviewing Key Facts

12. **Geography** What effect did the capture of Constantinople have on Ottoman expansion?
13. **Culture** List and describe the Ottoman Empire's main contributions to world art.
14. **History** What two major ethnic groups were included in Safavid society?
15. **Government** Why did the shah have his physical features engraved in drinking cups?
16. **Economics** What Safavid goods were prized throughout the world?
17. **Science and Technology** How was Babur able to capture an enemy force nearly 10 times the size of his forces?
18. **Culture** What were the social evils Aurangzeb tried to eliminate?
19. **History** What happened at the Black Hole of Calcutta?
20. **Economics** Why was the British East India Company empowered to act on behalf of the British Crown? What other countries had financial interests in India?
21. **Culture** List the artistic contributions of Mogul society.

Chapter Summary

The following table shows the characteristics of the Ottoman, Safavid, and Mogul Empires.

	Ottomans	Safavids	Moguls
Warfare	• Train janissaries • Conquer Constantinople	• Battle Ottomans • Ally with European states	• Conquer India • Battle Persians and British
Arts	• Make magnificent mosques, pottery, rugs, and jewelry	• Blend Persian and Turkish influences • Excel at carpet making and painting	• Combine Persian and Indian motifs • Excel at architecture and painting
Government	• The sultan governs through local rulers called pashas.	• The shah trains administrators.	• The emperor controls semi-independent states.
Trade	• Merchants are the privileged class.	• Geography limits trade.	• Trade with Europeans
Religion	• Sunni Muslim • Religious tolerance	• Shiite Muslim • Religious orthodoxy	• Muslim, Hindu • Religious tolerance
Women	• Social restrictions • Can own land, inherit property, seek divorce, and hold senior government posts	• Social restrictions • Are kept secluded and made to wear veils	• Some social restrictions • Serve as warriors, landowners, political advisers, and businesspeople

Critical Thinking

22. **Compare and Contrast** Compare the role of religion in Ottoman and Safavid societies.

23. **Analyzing** How did women play prominent roles in the Ottoman and Mogul cultures?

Writing About History

24. **Expository Writing** The acquisition of new technology can affect a country's development in many ways. Explain how the use of firearms affected the establishment of the three Muslim empires and tell how that same technology affects present-day society in the United States.

Analyzing Sources

Read a foreign visitor's description of Indian life:

> ❝Their houses are built of mud with thatched roofs. Furniture there is little or none except some earthenware pots to hold water and for cooking and two beds, one for the man, the other for his wife; their bed cloths are scanty, merely a sheet or perhaps two, serving as under- and over-sheet. This is sufficient for the hot weather, but the bitter cold nights are miserable indeed, and they try to keep warm over little cow-dung fires.❞

25. What type of furnishings did Indian families have?

26. From reading this passage, what can you conclude about the lives of Indian people during the Mogul Empire? Find two other sources describing Indian life during this time period. Do they corroborate this description? How is the information in the other passages similar to or different from this?

Making Decisions

27. The struggles to become the next sultan were often bitter and prolonged. Sometimes, those who lost were executed by the person who successfully gained the position and the power. Why do you think this occurred? Can you think of a better alternative, one that would have smoothly paved the way for the future sultan and guaranteed the security of the position without eliminating competitors? Explain your plan clearly and persuasively.

Expansion of the Ottoman Empire, 1451–1566

Sultan	Dates	Conquered Territory
Mehmet II	1451–1481	• Anatolian Peninsula • Balkans • Constantinople (Istanbul)
Selim I	1512–1520	• Arabia • Egypt • Mesopotamia
Süleyman I	1520–1566	• Austria • Hungary • Libya

Analyzing Maps and Charts

28. Which sultan ruled the longest?

29. Which sultan did *not* expand the empire in Europe?

30. Do you think the Ottoman army or navy made more conquests? Explain your reasoning.

Applying Technology Skills

31. **Using the Internet** Religion was one of the unifying forces in the creation of the Ottoman, Safavid, and Mogul Empires. Using the Internet, research the history of Iran, a country established on a religious basis. Write an essay explaining the role religion plays in present-day Iran.

Directions: Choose the best answer to the following question.

How were the Ottoman and the Mogul rulers similar?

A They controlled the Indian subcontinent.

B They were principally Shiite Muslims.

C Although Muslims, they tolerated other religions.

D They invaded and then controlled the Balkans for about a century.

Test-Taking Tip: Look at each answer choice carefully and ask yourself, "Is this statement true for *both* empires?" By eliminating answer choices you know are incorrect, you can improve your chances of identifying the correct answer.

CHAPTER 16

The East Asian World

1400–1800

Key Events

As you read this chapter, look for the key events in the history of the East Asian world.
- China closed its doors to the Europeans during the period of exploration between 1500 and 1800.
- The Ming and Qing dynasties produced blue-and-white porcelain and new literary forms.
- Emperor Yong Le began renovations on the Imperial City, which was expanded by succeeding emperors.

The Impact Today

The events that occurred during this time still impact our lives today.
- China today exports more goods than it imports.
- Chinese porcelain is collected and admired throughout the world.
- The Forbidden City in China is an architectural wonder that continues to attract people from around the world.
- Relations with China today still require diplomacy and skill.

World History Video The Chapter 16 video, "The Samurai," chronicles the role of the warrior class in Japanese history.

Chinese sailing ship

1514
Portuguese arrive in China

| 1400 | 1435 | 1470 | 1505 | 1540 | 1575 |

1405
Zheng He begins voyages of exploration

Ming dynasty porcelain bowl

1550
Ming dynasty flourishes

The Forbidden City in the heart of Beijing contains hundreds of buildings.

1598
Japanese
unification
begins

1644
Last Ming
emperor
dies

1750
Edo is one of
the world's
largest cities

1796
White Lotus
rebellion
weakens Qing
dynasty

1610 *1645* *1680* *1715* *1750* *1785*

1603
Tokugawa
rule begins
"Great
Peace"

1661
Emperor
Kangxi begins
61-year reign

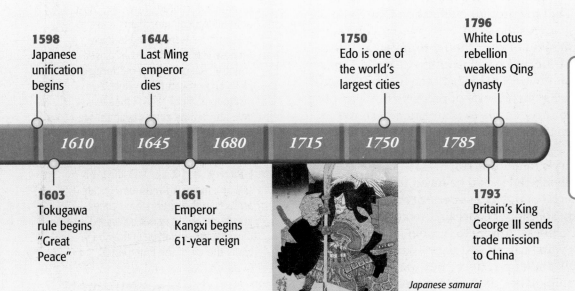

Japanese samurai

1793
Britain's King
George III sends
trade mission
to China

HISTORY Online

Chapter Overview
Visit the *Glencoe World
History* Web site at
tx.wh.glencoe.com and click
on **Chapter 16–Chapter
Overview** to preview
chapter information.

A Story That Matters

Emperor Qianlong

The meeting of Emperor Qianlong and Lord George Macartney

Mission to China

*I*n 1793, a British official named Lord George Macartney led a mission on behalf of King George III to China. Macartney carried with him British products that he thought would impress the Chinese so much that they would be eager to open their country to trade with Great Britain. King George wrote in his letter to the Chinese emperor: "No doubt the exchange of goods between nations far apart tends to their mutual convenience, industry, and wealth."

Emperor Qianlong, however, was not impressed: "You, O King, are so inclined toward our civilization that you have sent a special envoy across the seas . . . to present your native products as an expression of your thoughtfulness. . . . As a matter of fact, the virtue and prestige of the Celestial Dynasty having spread far and wide, the kings of the myriad nations come by land and sea with all sorts of precious things. Consequently, there is nothing we lack, as your principal envoy and others have themselves observed. We have never set much store on strange or ingenious objects, nor do we need any more of your country's manufactures."

Macartney was shocked. He had believed that the Chinese would recognize, as he said, "that superiority which Englishmen, wherever they go, cannot conceal." An angered Macartney compared the Chinese Empire to "an old, crazy, first-rate man-of-war [naval warship]." It had once awed its neighbors "merely by [its] bulk and appearance" but was now destined, under poor leadership, to be "dashed to pieces on the shore."

Why It Matters

Between 1500 and 1800, China experienced one of its most glorious eras. The empire expanded, and Chinese culture flourished. In 1514, Portuguese ships arrived on the coast of China. At first, the new arrivals were welcomed. During the seventeenth century, however, most of the European merchants and missionaries were forced to leave. Chinese leaders adopted a "closed country" policy to keep out foreign ideas and protect their values and institutions. Until 1800, China was little affected by events taking place outside the region. Japan and Korea, too, remained isolated.

History and You Visit the Web site of a major art museum. Locate artifacts in their permanent collection from the dynasties discussed in this chapter, and explain how they typify the art of the time period.

SECTION 1 / China at Its Height

Guide to Reading

Main Ideas
- China opened its doors to Europeans but closed those doors when it observed the effect of Western ideas on Chinese society.
- Between 1500 and 1800, Chinese art and culture flourished.

Key Terms
queue, banner

People to Identify
Ming, Zheng He, Manchu, Qing, Kangxi

Places to Locate
Guangzhou, Beijing, Manchuria, Taiwan

Preview Questions
1. What was remarkable about the naval voyages under Emperor Yong Le?
2. How did the Manchus gain the support of the Chinese?

Reading Strategy
Compare and Contrast As you read this section, complete a diagram like the one below to compare and contrast the achievements of the two dynasties.

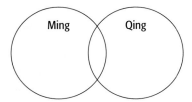

Ming   Qing

Preview of Events

♦1500   ♦1540   ♦1580   ♦1620   ♦1660   ♦1700   ♦1740

1551
China allows Portuguese to occupy Macao

1630
Major epidemic reduces the population in many areas

1736
Emperor Qianlong begins reign

Voices from the Past

Emperor Kangxi

Ferdinand Verbiest, a European missionary, reported on his experience with the Chinese emperor:

66 This emperor [Kangxi] [punishes] offenders of the highest as well as lowest class with marvelous impartiality, according to their misdeeds, depriving them of rank and dignity. . . . On this account men of all ranks and dignities whatsoever, even the nearest to him in blood, stand in his presence with the deepest awe, and recognize him as sole ruler. . . . The same goodwill he showed us on many other occasions, to wit, in frequently sending us dishes from his own table to ours. He even ordered us sometimes to be entertained in his own tent. 99

—*Sources of World History*, **Mark A. Kishlansky, ed.,1995**

Kangxi was one of the greatest of the many strong emperors who ruled China during the Ming and Qing dynasties.

The Ming Dynasty

⌐TURNING POINT⌐ **As you read this section, you will discover how the decision to stop the voyages of exploration in the 1400s caused China to turn inward for four centuries, away from foreign trade and toward agriculture.**

The Mongol dynasty in China was overthrown in 1368. The founder of the new dynasty took the title of Ming Hong Wu (the Ming Martial Emperor). This was the beginning of the **Ming** dynasty, which lasted until 1644.

Under Ming emperors, China extended its rule into Mongolia and central Asia and briefly reconquered Vietnam. Along the northern frontier, the Chinese strengthened the Great Wall and made peace with the nomadic tribes that had troubled them for centuries.

At home, Ming rulers ran an effective government using a centralized bureaucracy staffed with officials chosen by the civil service examination system. They set up a nationwide school system. Manufactured goods were produced in workshops and factories in vastly higher numbers. New crops were introduced, which greatly increased food production. The Ming rulers also renovated the Grand Canal, making it possible to ship grain and other goods from southern to northern China. The Ming dynasty truly began a new era of greatness in Chinese history.

The Voyages of Zheng He

Ming Hong Wu, founder of the dynasty, ruled from 1368 until 1398. After his death, his son Yong Le became emperor. This was after a four-year campaign to defeat the rightful heir. To establish the legitimacy of his rule, Yong Le built large monuments, strengthened the Great Wall, and restored Chinese rule over Vietnam.

In 1406, Yong Le began construction of the Imperial City in Beijing. In 1421 he moved the capital from Nanjing to Beijing, after construction was sufficiently far along. The Imperial City (known today as the Forbidden City) was created to convey power and prestige. For nearly 500 years the Imperial City was home to China's emperors. Yong Le died in 1424 and was buried with his wife and 16 concubines in a new cemetery for emperors outside of Beijing.

During his reign, Yong Le also sent a series of naval voyages into the Indian Ocean that sailed as far west as the eastern coast of Africa. Led by the court official **Zheng He** (JUNG HUH), seven voyages of exploration were made between 1405 and 1433. On the first voyage, nearly 28,000 men embarked on 62 ships. The largest ship was over 440 feet (134.1 m) long. (Columbus's Santa Maria was only 75 feet [22.9 m] long.) The fleet passed through Southeast Asia and visited the western coast of India and the city-states of East Africa. It returned with items unknown in China and information about the outside world. The emperor was especially fascinated by the giraffes from Africa, and he placed them in the imperial zoo.

The voyages led to enormous profits, which alarmed traditionalists within the bureaucracy. Some of them held the Confucian view that trading activities were unworthy. Shortly after Yong Le's death, the voyages were halted, never to be revived. One can only guess what difference it would have made if Zheng He's fleet had reached the Americas before Columbus did.

First Contacts with the West

In 1514, a Portuguese fleet arrived off the coast of China. It was the first direct contact between the Chinese Empire and Europe since the journeys of Marco Polo.

At the time, the Ming government thought little of the arrival of the Portuguese. China was at the height of its power as the most magnificent civilization on

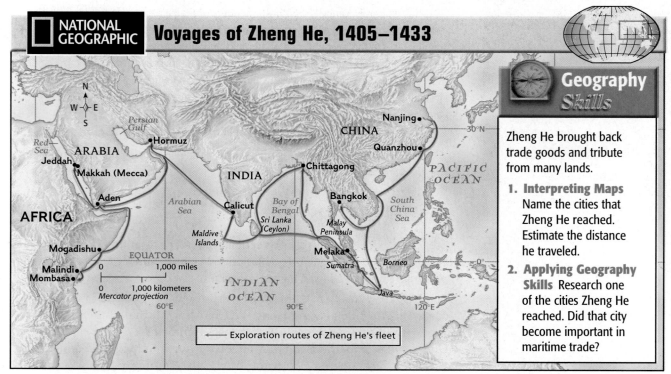

NATIONAL GEOGRAPHIC

Voyages of Zheng He, 1405–1433

Geography Skills

Zheng He brought back trade goods and tribute from many lands.

1. **Interpreting Maps** Name the cities that Zheng He reached. Estimate the distance he traveled.

2. **Applying Geography Skills** Research one of the cities Zheng He reached. Did that city become important in maritime trade?

← Exploration routes of Zheng He's fleet

Earth. From the perspective of the emperor, the Europeans were only an unusual form of barbarian. To the Chinese ruler, the rulers of all other countries were simply "younger brothers" of the Chinese emperor, who was seen as the Son of Heaven.

The Portuguese soon outraged Chinese officials with their behavior. They were expelled from **Guangzhou** (Canton) but were allowed to occupy Macao.

At first, the Portuguese had little impact on Chinese society. Portuguese ships did carry goods between China and Japan but direct trade between Europe and China remained limited. Perhaps more important than trade, however, was the exchange of ideas.

Christian missionaries had also made the long voyage to China on European merchant ships. The Jesuits were among the most active. Many of them were highly educated men who brought along instruments, such as clocks, that impressed Chinese officials and made them more receptive to Western ideas.

Both sides benefited from this early cultural exchange. Chinese scholars marveled at their ability to read better with European eyeglasses. Christian missionaries were impressed with many aspects of Chinese civilization, such as the teachings of Confucius, the printing and availability of books, and Chinese architecture. Reports back home soon made Europeans even more curious about this great civilization on the other side of the world.

Fall of the Ming Dynasty After a period of prosperity and growth, the Ming dynasty gradually began to decline. During the late sixteenth century, a series of weak rulers led to a period of government corruption. High taxes, caused in part by this corruption, led to peasant unrest. Crop yields declined because of harsh weather.

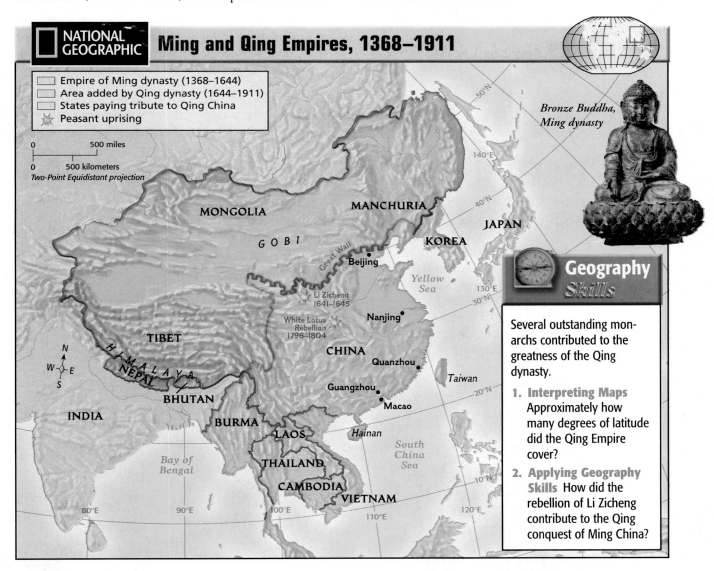

NATIONAL GEOGRAPHIC — Ming and Qing Empires, 1368–1911

- Empire of Ming dynasty (1368–1644)
- Area added by Qing dynasty (1644–1911)
- States paying tribute to Qing China
- Peasant uprising

0 500 miles
0 500 kilometers
Two-Point Equidistant projection

Bronze Buddha, Ming dynasty

Geography Skills

Several outstanding monarchs contributed to the greatness of the Qing dynasty.

1. **Interpreting Maps** Approximately how many degrees of latitude did the Qing Empire cover?

2. **Applying Geography Skills** How did the rebellion of Li Zicheng contribute to the Qing conquest of Ming China?

In the 1630s, a major epidemic greatly reduced the population in many areas. One observer in a major city wrote, "There were few signs of human life in the streets and all that was heard was the buzzing of flies."

The suffering caused by the epidemic helped spark a peasant revolt led by Li Zicheng (LEE DZUH•CHUNG). The revolt began in central China and then spread to the rest of the country. In 1644, Li and his forces occupied the capital of **Beijing** (BAY• JING). The last Ming emperor committed suicide by hanging himself from a tree in the palace gardens.

The overthrow of the Ming dynasty created an opportunity for the **Manchus,** a farming and hunting people who lived northeast of the Great Wall in the area known today as **Manchuria.** The Manchus conquered Beijing, and Li Zicheng's army fell. The victorious Manchus then declared the creation of a new dynasty called the **Qing** (CHING), meaning "pure." This dynasty, created in 1644, remained in power until 1911.

✔**Reading Check** **Describing** What were the achievements of the Ming dynasty?

The Qing Dynasty

At first, the Chinese resisted the new rulers. At one point, rebels seized the island of **Taiwan** just off the coast of China. The new Manchu government evacuated the coastline across from the island in preparation for an attack on the rebels. To make it easier to identify the rebels, the government ordered all men to adopt Manchu dress and hairstyles. All Chinese males were to shave their foreheads and braid their hair into a pigtail called a queue. Those who refused were to be executed: "Lose your hair or lose your head."

The Manchus eventually adopted the Chinese political system and were gradually accepted as the legitimate rulers of the country. The Qing flourished under a series of strong early rulers. The emperors pacified the country, corrected serious social and economic ills, and restored peace and prosperity.

Qing Adaptations The Qing maintained the Ming political system but faced one major problem: the Manchus were ethnically and culturally different from their subject population. The Qing dealt with this reality in two ways.

SPORTS & CONTESTS

The Martial Arts in China

The phrase *martial arts* refers to arts of combat and self-defense. Martial arts are a significant part of Asian history and culture. In recent years, they have become part of Western culture as well. Throughout the United States, for example, one can learn Japanese karate and judo, Korean tae kwon do, and Chinese kung fu and tai chi. Chinese martial arts are especially well known because of films featuring actors trained in the martial arts.

Chinese martial arts were already highly visible during the Han dynasty. Later, in 495, a Zen Buddhist monastery in Henan province developed methods of physical training that became Shaolin Quan. This style of boxing is known to the world today as kung fu.

Archery contest

First, the Qing tried to preserve their distinct identity within Chinese society. The Manchus, who made up only 1 percent of the population, were defined legally as distinct from everyone else in China. The Manchu nobility maintained large landholdings and received revenues from the state treasury. Other Manchus were organized into separate military units, called **banners.** The "bannermen" were the chief fighting force of the empire.

Second, the Qing dealt with the problem of ethnic differences by bringing Chinese into the imperial administration. More than 80 percent of lower posts were filled by Chinese, although they held a much smaller share of the top positions. The Manchus' sharing of power won the support of many Chinese.

Reign of Kangxi

Kangxi (KONG•SEE), who ruled from 1661 to 1722, was perhaps the greatest emperor in Chinese history. A person with political skill and a strong character, Kangxi took charge of the government while still in his teens and reigned for 61 years.

Kangxi rose at dawn and worked until late at night. He wrote, "One act of negligence may cause sorrow all through the country, and one moment of negligence may result in trouble for thousands of generations." Kangxi calmed the unrest along the northern and western frontiers by force. As a patron of the arts and letters, he gained the support of scholars throughout the country.

During Kangxi's reign, the efforts of Christian missionaries reached their height. The emperor was quite tolerant of the Christians. Several hundred officials became Catholics, as did an estimated three hundred thousand ordinary Chinese. The Christian effort was undermined by squabbling among the Western religious orders who opposed the Jesuit policy of accommodating local beliefs and practices in order to facilitate conversion. Although Kangxi tried to resolve the problem, no solution was reached. After the death of Kangxi, however, his successor began to suppress Christian activities throughout China.

Westerners in China

Qianlong, who ruled from 1736 to 1795, was another outstanding Qing ruler. During his reign, however, the first signs of internal decay began to appear in the Qing dynasty. As the emperor grew older, he fell under the influence of

Tai chi practice outside the Forbidden City

Martial arts in China fell into five groups: empty-hand boxing, sparring, training in pairs, group exercises involving six or more athletes, and weapons training. Weapons included bows and arrows, swords, spears, and chains with a pointed tip.

The Tang dynasty began to select military officials through martial arts contests and established regular competitions. During the Ming dynasty, the martial arts became even more developed. The classic work on martial arts, *Treatise on Armament Technology,* was published, and martial arts techniques were organized into schools.

One method developed during the Ming era was tai chi. This method focused on providing for better health and longer life by unlocking the flow of energy (chi) in the body. Today, martial arts such as tai chi are used as methods of exercise.

After Communists came to power in China in 1949, the government again fostered the martial arts as a competitive sport. Martial arts teams have spread throughout the world. In 1991, an International Wushu (Martial Arts) Association was formed, consisting of representatives from 38 nations. That same year, the First World Martial Arts Championship took place in Beijing.

CONNECTING TO THE PAST

1. **Summarizing Information** Identify at least five martial arts and the five groups of Chinese martial arts.

2. **Writing about History** Martial arts are very popular in the United States today. Why do you think this is so? Write a persuasive essay in which you present a case for offering martial arts classes as part of the physical educational program at your school.

Sixteenth-century farming in China

destructive elements at court. Corrupt officials and higher taxes led to unrest in rural areas. Growing pressure on the land because of population growth also led to economic hardship for many peasants. In central China, unhappy peasants launched a revolt known as the White Lotus Rebellion (1796–1804). The revolt was suppressed, but the enormous expenses of fighting the rebels weakened the Qing dynasty.

Unfortunately for China, the Qing dynasty was declining just as Europe was seeking more trade. At first, the Qing government sold trade privileges to the Europeans. However, to limit contacts between Europeans and Chinese, the Qing confined all European traders to a small island just outside Guangzhou. The traders could reside there only from October through March and could deal only with a limited number of Chinese firms licensed by the government.

For a while, the British accepted this system. By the end of the eighteenth century, however, some British traders had begun to demand access to additional cities along the Chinese coast. At the same time, the Chinese government was under pressure from its own merchants to open China to British manufactured goods.

In 1793, a British mission led by Lord George Macartney visited Beijing to seek more liberal trade policies. However, Emperor Qianlong wrote to King George III that China had no need of "your country's manufactures." The Chinese would later pay for their rejection of the British request.

✓**Reading Check** **Predict Consequences** Predict the consequences of the Chinese attitude toward trade with Europe.

🟥 TAKS Practice

SECTION 1 ASSESSMENT

Checking for Understanding

1. **Define** queue, banner.

2. **Identify** Ming, Zheng He, Manchu, Qing, Kangxi.

3. **Locate** Guangzhou, Beijing, Manchuria, Taiwan.

4. **Explain** how the pigtail became a political symbol under the Qing dynasty.

5. **List** the ways the Ming and Qing dynasties tried to limit contacts between Europeans and the Chinese people. Why did the British initially accept the restrictions?

Critical Thinking

6. **Make Generalizations** What was the general attitude of the Chinese regarding trade with the Western world? Give examples from the text to support your answer.

7. **Summarizing Information** Create a chart like the one below to show how both the Europeans and Chinese benefited from their early cultural exchange.

European Benefits	Chinese Benefits

Analyzing Visuals

8. **Examine** the picture of the Chinese peasants farming shown above. What conclusions can you draw about peasant life in China from looking at this picture? How do your conclusions compare and contrast with the depictions of peasant life found in other cultures you have already read about?

Writing About History

9. **Expository Writing** Using the Internet or print resources, research the voyages of Zheng He and Columbus. Write an essay comparing the technology, equipment, purpose, and results of the explorations of Zheng He and Columbus.

Chinese Society and Culture

Guide to Reading

Main Ideas
• A rapid increase in population led to rural land shortages.
• Chinese society was organized around the family.
• Architecture, decorative arts, and literature flourished during this period.

Key Terms
commercial capitalism, clan, porcelain

People to Identify
Cao Xuegin, Emperor Yong Le

Places to Locate
Imperial City, Beijing

Preview Questions
1. Why did the population increase between 1500 and 1800?
2. Why did commercial capitalism not develop in China during this period?

Reading Strategy
Organizing Information Use a concentric circle diagram like the one below to show the organization of the Chinese family.

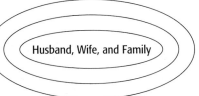

Husband, Wife, and Family

Preview of Events

```
♦1400      ♦1475      ♦1550      ♦1625      ♦1700      ♦1775      ♦1850
```

1368
Ming dynasty begins a new era of greatness in China

1406
Renovations are begun on the Imperial City

1791
Popular novel, *The Dream of the Red Chamber,* is published

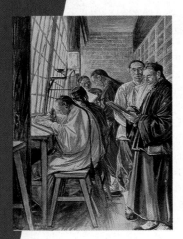

Chinese printers at work

Voices from the Past

In the sixteenth century, an Italian named Matteo Ricci expressed a great appreciation of Chinese printing:

❝The Chinese method of printing has one decided advantage, namely, that once these tablets are made, they can be preserved and used for making changes in the text as often as one wishes. . . . The simplicity of Chinese printing is what accounts for the exceedingly large numbers of books in circulation here and the ridiculously low prices at which they are sold.❞
—*China in the Sixteenth Century,* **Louis J. Gallagher, trans., 1942**

Europeans who lived in China found much to admire in Chinese civilization.

Economic Changes

Between 1500 and 1800, China remained a mostly agricultural society. Nearly 85 percent of the people were small farmers. Nevertheless, the Chinese economy was changing.

The first change involved an increase in population, from less than 80 million in 1390 to more than 300 million at the end of the 1700s. The increase had several causes. A long period of peace and stability under the early Qing dynasty was one. Improvements in the food supply were another. A faster growing species of rice from Southeast Asia increased the food supply.

The population increase meant there was less land available for each family. The imperial court tried to make more land available by limiting the amount wealthy landowners could hold. By the eighteenth century, however, almost all the land that could be farmed was already being farmed. Shortages of land in rural areas led to unrest and revolts.

Another change in this period was a steady growth in manufacturing and increased trade between provinces. Taking advantage of the long era of peace and prosperity, merchants and manufacturers expanded their trade in silk, porcelain, cotton goods, and other products. 📖 *(See page 995 to read excerpts from Sung Ying-Hsing's* The Silk Industry in China *in the Primary Sources Library.)*

Despite the growth in trade and manufacturing, China did not develop the kind of commercial capitalism—private business based on profit—that was emerging in Europe. Some key differences between China and Europe explain this fact.

In the first place, middle-class merchants and manufacturers in China were not as independent as those in Europe. Trade and manufacturing remained under the firm control of the government. Many Chinese looked down on trade and manufacturing as inferior to farming. The state reflected this attitude by levying heavy taxes on manufacturing and trade and low taxes on farming.

✓ **Reading Check** **Contrasting** What was the key difference in government policy toward trade and manufacturing in Europe and in China?

Daily Life

Daily life in China remained similar to what it had been in earlier periods. The emphasis on family relationships, based on Confucian ideals, contributed stability to Chinese society.

The Chinese Family Chinese society was organized around the family. The family was expected to provide for its members' needs, including the education of children, support of unmarried daughters, and care of the elderly. At the same time, all family members were expected to sacrifice their individual desires for the benefit of the family as a whole.

CONNECTIONS Around The World

A Population Explosion

Between 1700 and 1800, many areas in the world experienced a population explosion. In Europe, China, India, and the Muslim world, the number of people grew dramatically. Europe, for example, went from 120 million people in 1700 to almost 200 million by 1800; China, from less than 200 million to 300 million during the same period.

Four factors were important in causing this population explosion. First, better agricultural growing conditions affected wide areas of the world and enabled people to produce more food. Second, new foods provided additional sources of nutrition. Food crops were introduced in new areas: sweet potatoes in China, corn in Africa and Europe, and potatoes in northern Europe and Russia. Third, states controlled larger territories

and were able to ensure a higher degree of order. Less violence led to fewer deaths.

Finally, by the eighteenth century, people had begun to develop immunities to epidemic diseases. The migration of people after 1500 had led to devastating epidemics. For example, the arrival of Europeans in Mexico led to millions of deaths from smallpox, measles, and chicken pox among a native population that had no immunities to European diseases. By 1750, however, the number and effects of plagues and epidemic diseases had decreased in Europe, India, China, and Southwest Asia.

◀ *Many cities experienced a growth in population.*

Comparing Cultures

Many demographers believe that the world is currently experiencing another population boom. Research current population figures and predictions for the next 50 years. Check at least three sources. Is the information corroborated in three sources? If not, what reasons can explain the differences? How can you assess the reliability of the sources you used?

The ideal family unit in Qing China was the extended family, in which as many as three or four generations lived under the same roof. When sons married, they brought their wives to live with them in the family home. Unmarried daughters also remained in the house, as did parents and grandparents. Chinese society held the elderly in high regard. Aging parents knew they would be cared for by their children.

Beyond the extended family was the clan, which consisted of dozens, or even hundreds, of related families. These families were linked by a clan council of elders and a variety of common social and religious activities. The clan system made it possible for wealthier families to help poorer relatives.

The Role of Women Women were considered inferior to men in Chinese society. Only males could have a formal education and pursue a career in government or scholarship. Within the family, capable women often played strong roles. Nevertheless, the wife was clearly subordinate to the husband. Legally, she could not divorce her husband or inherit property. The husband, in contrast, could divorce his wife if she did not produce sons. He could also take a second wife. Husbands were expected to provide support for their wives and children. In many cases, the head of the family would also be responsible for providing for more than just his own wife and children.

A feature of Chinese society that restricted the mobility of women was the practice of footbinding. The origins of footbinding are not clear. Scholars believe it began among the wealthiest class of women and was later adopted by all classes. Bound feet were a status symbol. Women who had bound feet were more marriageable than those who did not, thus there was a status incentive as well as an economic incentive. An estimated one-half to two-thirds of the women in China bound their feet.

The process, begun in childhood, was very painful. Women who had their feet bound could not walk, they were carried. Not all clans looked favorably on footbinding. Women who worked in the fields or in occupations that required mobility did not bind their feet.

✓ **Reading Check** **Describing** What was the legal status of women in China?

Cultural Developments

During the late Ming and the early Qing dynasties, traditional culture in China reached new heights.

The Chinese Novel During the Ming dynasty, a new form of literature arose that eventually evolved into the modern Chinese novel. Works in this literary form were enormously popular, especially among well-to-do urban dwellers.

One Chinese novel, *The Golden Lotus*, is considered by many to be the first realistic social novel. *The Golden Lotus* depicts the corrupt life of a wealthy landlord in the late Ming period who cruelly manipulates those around him for sex, money, and power.

The Dream of the Red Chamber, by **Cao Xuegin**, is generally considered even today to be China's most distinguished popular novel. Published in 1791, it tells of the tragic love between two young people caught in the financial and moral disintegration of a powerful Chinese clan.

Ming and Qing Art During the Ming and the early Qing dynasties, China experienced an outpouring of artistic brilliance.

In architecture, the most outstanding example is the **Imperial City** in **Beijing. Emperor Yong Le** began construction of the Imperial City—a complex of palaces and temples—in 1406. Succeeding emperors continued to add to the palace.

The Imperial City is an immense compound surrounded by six and one-half miles (10.5 km) of walls. It includes a maze of private apartments and offices, as well as stately halls for imperial audiences and banquets and spacious gardens. Because it was off-limits to commoners, the compound was known as the Forbidden City.

The decorative arts also flourished in this period. Perhaps the most famous of all the arts of the Ming Era was blue-and-white porcelain. Europeans admired the beauty of this porcelain and collected it in great quantities. Different styles of porcelain were produced during the reign of individual emperors.

The Gate of Supreme Harmony at the Forbidden City is guarded by a centuries-old lion.

✓ **Reading Check** **Describing** What were the artistic accomplishments of the Ming and Qing dynasties?

🔺**TAKS Practice**

SECTION 2 ASSESSMENT

Checking for Understanding

1. **Define** commercial capitalism, clan, porcelain.

2. **Identify** Cao Xuegin, Emperor Yong Le.

3. **Locate** Imperial City, Beijing.

4. **Explain** the significance of the Chinese extended family.

5. **Summarize** the plot of *The Dream of the Red Chamber*.

Critical Thinking

6. **Draw Conclusions** Although legally inferior to men, what important roles did women in the peasant class have?

7. **Identifying Information** Use a diagram to identify the economic changes in China from 1500 to 1800.

Economic Change

Analyzing Visuals

8. **Examine** the picture of women spinning silk shown on page 493 of your text. How does this picture reflect the role of women in Chinese society during the eighteenth century?

Writing About History

9. **Persuasive Writing** Pretend you are a Chinese mother talking to your daughter in 1700. Using research or your own ideas, convince her that footbinding is necessary and beneficial.

SKILLBUILDER

Using E-mail

Why Learn This Skill?

Less than one hundred years ago, people could only communicate long distances by mail or messenger. Today, electronic mail, or e-mail, enables users to send and receive messages worldwide.

E-mail is a useful way to instantaneously exchange information with a variety of sources. Most agencies and businesses have e-mail addresses so that they can be contacted easily by anyone who needs their services.

Learning the Skill

- Your computer is ready for e-mailing after two items are added to it. The first piece of equipment is a device that enables the computer to communicate with other computers. This can be either a modem, which connects the computer to a telephone line, or a wideband connection through cable or fiber-optics lines that does not need to connect to the telephone. The second necessary item is communications software, which lets your computer prepare and send information through the modem or wideband connection. It also allows your computer to receive and understand the information it receives.

- Once the computer is ready, you must subscribe to an *Internet Service Provider* (ISP), which receives and stores your messages in an electronic "mailbox" until you choose to access it. When you subscribe to an e-mail network, you have a specific address. This address identifies the location of your electronic "mailbox"—the place where you receive your e-mail. To send e-mail, you must write in the address of the recipient, but your address is automatically attached to the document. When the message is sent, the e-mail system places the message in the receiver's mailbox. He or she may read the message at any time and send you a return message.

Practicing the Skill

To send an e-mail message, complete the following steps:

❶ Access your e-mail server by clicking on the icon on your desktop display.

❷ Select the "New Message" or "Write" function from your communications software.

❸ Type in the e-mail address of the recipient.

❹ Write your message—remember to proofread it for errors.

❺ Select the "Send" button. Some e-mail systems will allow you to select an option that will notify you when your message has been delivered and opened.

Applying the Skill

Silkworm farming and the wearing of silk began in the East Asian world. Using e-mail, contact a librarian and ask for recommendations of books about the silk industry. Share the list of resources you receive from the librarian with your class.

Tokugawa Japan and Korea

Guide to Reading

Main Ideas
- Japan was unified by three powerful political figures.
- Between 1500 and 1800, Japan experienced many peasant uprisings.
- Korea could not withstand invasions by the Japanese and Manchus.

Key Terms
daimyo, han, hostage system, eta

People to Identify
Oda Nobunaga, Toyotomi Hideyoshi, Tokugawa Ieyasu, Matsuo Basho

Places to Locate
Kyoto, Osaka, Edo, Korea

Preview Questions
1. What economic changes took place under the Tokugawa shoguns?
2. How did Japanese culture change during the Tokugawa Era?

Reading Strategy
Categorizing Information Using a diagram like the one below, categorize the different elements of Japanese culture.

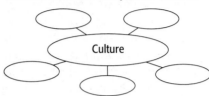
Culture

Preview of Events

| ♦1450 | ♦1500 | ♦1550 | ♦1600 | ♦1650 | ♦1700 | ♦1750 |

c. 1450
Power of shogun collapses

1568
Japan's unification begins

1750
Edo is one of the largest cities in the world

Voices from the Past

Japanese rice farmers

In 1649, the Japanese government issued an edict to be read in every village:

❝Peasants are people without sense or forethought. Therefore they must not give rice to their wives and children at harvest time, but must save food for the future. They should eat millet, vegetables, and other coarse food instead of rice. Even the fallen leaves of plants should be saved. The husband must work in the fields, the wife must work at the loom. However good-looking a wife may be, if she neglects her household duties by drinking tea or sightseeing or rambling on the hillsides, she must be divorced. Peasants must wear only cotton or hemp. They may not smoke tobacco. It is harmful to health, it takes up time and costs money.❞
—*A History of World Societies*, J.P. McKay, B.D. Hill, and J. Buckler, eds., 1996

The life of the Japanese peasant was a difficult one, and there were many peasant revolts between 1500 and 1800.

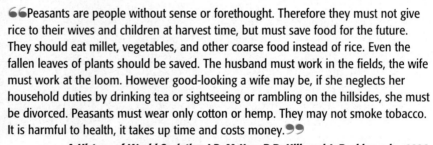

The Three Great Unifiers

At the end of the fifteenth century, Japan was in chaos. The centralized power of the shogunate had collapsed. Daimyo, heads of noble families, controlled their own lands and warred with their neighbors. Soon, however, a dramatic reversal would unify Japan. The process of unification began in the late sixteenth century with three powerful political figures.

The first was **Oda Nobunaga** (oh•DAH noh•boo•NAH•gah). Nobunaga seized the imperial capital of **Kyoto** and placed the reigning shogun under his control. During the next few years, he tried to consolidate his rule throughout the central plains.

Nobunaga was succeeded by **Toyotomi Hideyoshi** (toh•yoh•TOH•mee HEE•day•YOH•shee), a farmer's son who had become a military commander. Hideyoshi located his capital at **Osaka.** By 1590, he had persuaded most of the daimyo on the Japanese islands to accept his authority.

After Hideyoshi's death in 1598, **Tokugawa Ieyasu** (toh•kuh•GAH•wah ee•YAH•soo), the powerful daimyo of **Edo** (modern-day Tokyo), took control of Japan. Ieyasu took the title of shogun in 1603. The Tokugawa rulers completed the restoration of central authority begun by Nobunaga and Hideyoshi. Tokugawa shoguns remained in power at their capital at Edo until 1868. Tokugawa rule brought a long period of peace known as the "Great Peace."

✓**Reading Check** **Identifying** Sequence the events that led to the unification of Japan.

Europeans in Japan

⌐TURNING POINT┐ **As you read this section, note how Japan's "closed country" policy removed European influence, allowing Japan to remain in isolation for centuries.**

As the three great commanders were unifying Japan, the first Europeans began to arrive. Portuguese traders landed on the islands in 1543. In a few years, Portuguese ships began stopping regularly at Japanese ports to take part in the regional trade between Japan, China, and Southeast Asia.

At first, the visitors were welcomed. The Japanese were fascinated by tobacco, clocks, eyeglasses, and other European goods. Daimyo were interested in buying all types of European weapons. Oda Nobunaga and Toyotomi Hideyoshi found the new firearms helpful in defeating their enemies and unifying the islands.

The first Jesuit missionary, Francis Xavier, arrived in 1549. The Jesuits converted a number of local daimyo. By the end of the sixteenth century, thousands of Japanese had become Christians. However, the Jesuit practice of destroying shrines caused a severe reaction. In 1587, Hideyoshi issued an edict prohibiting Christian activities within his lands.

Hideyoshi's edict was at first not strictly enforced. The Jesuits were allowed to continue their activities. Under Tokugawa Ieyasu, however, all missionaries were expelled, and Japanese Christians were persecuted.

European merchants were the next to go. Only a small Dutch community in Nagasaki was allowed to remain in Japan. Dutch ships were permitted to dock at Nagasaki harbor only once a year and could remain for only two or three months.

HISTORY Online

Web Activity Visit the *Glencoe World History* Web site at tx.wh.glencoe.com and click on **Chapter 16– Student Web Activity** to learn more about the role of the shogun in Japan.

✓**Reading Check** **Explaining** What was the effect of the Jesuit practice of destroying shrines?

Tokugawa Rule

The Tokugawa rulers set out to establish control of the feudal system that had governed Japan for over three hundred years. As before, the state was divided into about 250 separate territories called hans, or domains. Each was ruled by a daimyo. In theory, the

Jesuit priests in Japan

daimyo were independent, because they were able to support themselves from taxes on their lands. In actuality, the shogunate controlled the daimyo by a hostage system.

In this system, the daimyo were required to maintain two residences—one in their own lands and one in Edo, where the court of the shogun was located. When the daimyo was absent from his residence in Edo, his family was forced to stay there.

During this long period of peace—known as the "Great Peace"—brought by Tokugawa rule, the samurai who had served the daimyo gradually ceased to be a warrior class. Many of them became managers on the lands of the daimyo.

Reading Check **Explaining** What was the hostage system? What was its effect on the daimyo?

Economic and Social Changes

A major economic change took place under the Tokugawa. Since the fourteenth century, many upper-class Japanese, influenced by Confucianism, had considered trade and industry beneath them. Under the Tokugawa, trade and industry began to flourish as never before, especially in the growing cities of Edo, Kyoto, and Osaka.

By 1750, Edo had a population of over a million and was one of the largest cities in the world. Banking flourished, and paper money became the normal medium of exchange in business transactions. A Japanese merchant class emerged and began to play a significant role in the life of the Japanese nation.

What effect did these economic changes have on Japanese peasants, who made up most of the population? Some farm families benefited by exploiting the growing demand for cash crops (crops grown for sale). Most peasants, however, experienced both declining profits and rising costs and taxes. Many were forced to become tenants or to work as hired help.

When rural conditions became desperate, some peasants revolted. Almost seven thousand peasant revolts and demonstrations against high taxes took place during the Tokugawa Era.

The Class System Social changes also marked the Tokugawa Era. These changes affected the class system and the role of women. During this era, Japan's class system became rigid. Rulers established strict

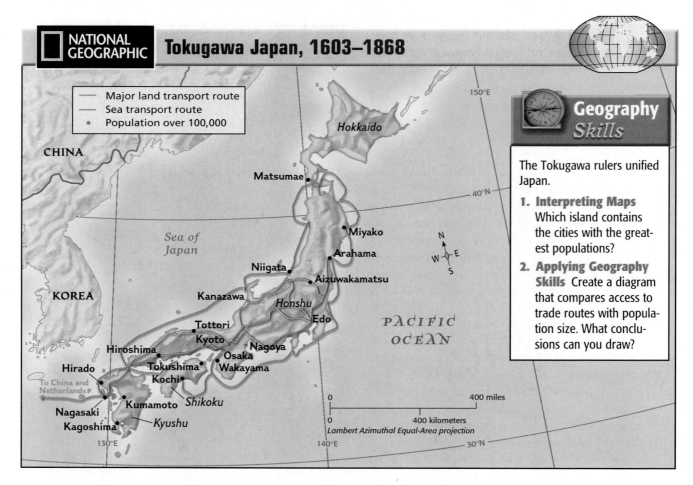

NATIONAL GEOGRAPHIC

Tokugawa Japan, 1603–1868

— Major land transport route
— Sea transport route
• Population over 100,000

CHINA

Hokkaido

Matsumae

150°E

40°N

Sea of Japan

Miyako

Arahama

Niigata

Aizuwakamatsu

KOREA

Kanazawa

Honshu

Edo

Tottori

Kyoto

Nagoya

Hiroshima

Osaka

Wakayama

Hirado

Tokushima

Kochi

To China and Netherlands

Kumamoto

Shikoku

Nagasaki

Kagoshima

Kyushu

130°E

140°E

30°N

PACIFIC OCEAN

0   400 miles
0   400 kilometers
Lambert Azimuthal Equal-Area projection

Geography Skills

The Tokugawa rulers unified Japan.

1. **Interpreting Maps** Which island contains the cities with the greatest populations?

2. **Applying Geography Skills** Create a diagram that compares access to trade routes with population size. What conclusions can you draw?

legal distinctions among the four main classes: warriors, peasants, artisans, and merchants. Intermarriage between classes was forbidden.

The emperor and imperial court families were at the very top of the political and social structure. Next came the warrior class composed of the shogun, daimyo, samurai, and ronin. The shogun was supreme ruler below the emperor and distributor of the national rice crop. The local daimyo received land and rice from the shogun in exchange for military service. Samurai received rice from the daimyo in exchange for their services as advisers, castle guards, and government officials. Finally, the ronin were warriors without masters who traveled the countryside seeking employment.

Below the warriors were the farmers (peasants). Farmers produced rice and held a privileged position in society but were often poor. The artisan class included craftspeople such as swordmakers and carpenters. Finally, the merchant class distributed food and essential goods. This class was at the bottom of the social hierarchy because they profited from the labor of others.

Below these classes were Japan's outcasts, the eta. The Tokugawa enacted severe laws to regulate the places of residence, the dress, and even the hairstyles of the eta.

The Role of Women The role of women in Tokugawa society became somewhat more restricted. Especially in the samurai class, where Confucian values were highly prized, the rights of females were restricted. Male heads of households had broad authority over property, marriage, and divorce.

Among the common people, women were also restricted. Parents arranged marriages, and a wife was expected to move in with her husband's family. A wife who did not meet the expectations of her husband or his family was likely to be divorced. Still, women were generally valued for their roles as childbearers and homemakers among the common people. Both sexes worked in the fields as well, although men did the heavier labor.

Reading Check **Explaining** In what ways were the rights of women of the common class restricted?

Tokugawa Culture

In the Tokugawa Era, a new set of cultural values began to appear, especially in the cities. It included the rise of popular literature written by and for the townspeople.

People In History

Matsuo Basho
1644–1694—Japanese poet

Basho was one of the chief literary figures in Tokugawa Japan. Although he lived most of his life in Kyoto and Edo, he also traveled to many other parts of the country. He was concerned with the search for the meaning of life and found answers to his quest in nature. His poems, called haiku, are grounded in natural images. This feature is evident in the following examples, which are among his most famous poems:

> The ancient pond
> A frog leaps in
> The sound of the water.
>
> On the withered branch
> A crow has alighted—
> The end of autumn.

Literature The best examples of the new urban fiction in the seventeenth century are the works of Ihara Saikaku, considered one of Japan's greatest writers. Saikaku's greatest novel, *Five Women Who Loved Love*, tells of a search for love by five women of the merchant class. The women are willing to die for love—and all but one eventually do.

Much of the popular literature of the Tokugawa Era was lighthearted and intended to please its audiences. Poetry remained a more serious form of literary expression. Exquisite poetry was written in the seventeenth century by the greatest of all Japanese poets, **Matsuo Basho.**

Theater and Art A new world of entertainment in the cities gave rise in the theater to Kabuki, which emphasized action, music, and dramatic gestures to entertain its viewers. Early Kabuki dramas dealt with the world of teahouses and dance halls in the cities.

Government officials feared that such activities could corrupt the nation's morals. Thus, the government forbade women to appear on stage. Officials therefore created a new professional class of male actors to impersonate female characters.

Art also reflected the changes in Japanese culture under the Tokugawa regime. The shogun's order that all daimyo and their families have residences in Edo sparked an increase in building. Nobles competed to erect the most magnificent mansions with lavish and beautiful furnishings. The abundant use of gold foil on walls and ceilings helped reflect the light in dark castle rooms, where windows were often small.

Japanese art was enriched by ideas from other cultures. Japanese pottery makers borrowed techniques and designs from Korea to create handsome ceramic pieces. The Japanese studied Western medicine, astronomy, languages, and even painting styles. In turn, Europeans wanted Japanese ceramics, which were prized as highly as the ceramics of the Chinese.

✓**Reading Check** **Summarizing** Why were government officials concerned about Kabuki theater?

Korea: The Hermit Kingdom

The Yi dynasty in **Korea,** founded at the end of the fourteenth century, remained in power during the entire Tokugawa Era in Japan. From their capital at Hanyang (modern-day Seoul), Yi rulers patterned their society after that of their powerful Chinese neighbors to the north.

Korean rulers tried to keep the country isolated from the outside world, earning it the name "the Hermit Kingdom." They were not always successful, however. A Japanese force under Toyotomi Hideyoshi invaded Korea in the late sixteenth century. Although the Japanese invaders were defeated, Korea was devastated, and the Yi dynasty was weakened. In the

Kabuki actor

1630s, a Manchu army invaded northern Korea and forced the Yi dynasty to become subject to China. Korea remained largely untouched by European merchants and Christian missionaries.

✓**Reading Check** **Summarizing** Why was Korea called "the Hermit Kingdom"?

🔶**TAKS Practice**

SECTION 3 ASSESSMENT

Checking for Understanding

1. **Define** daimyo, han, hostage system, eta.

2. **Identify** Oda Nobunaga, Toyotomi Hideyoshi, Tokugawa Ieyasu, Matsuo Basho.

3. **Locate** Kyoto, Osaka, Edo, Korea.

4. **Sequence** the events that led to Japan's policy of isolation.

5. **List** the four main social classes that existed during the Tokugawa Era. Who was at the top of the social structure, and who was at the bottom?

Critical Thinking

6. **Draw Inferences** How were most peasants affected by the economic changes in Japan?

7. **Organizing Information** Using a chart like the one below, show how the new urban centers in Japan influenced the arts and entertainment.

urban centers	_____
	_____
	_____
	_____
	_____

Analyzing Visuals

8. **Examine** the photograph of a Kabuki actor shown above. What does this photograph tell you about Japanese Kabuki theater, and how does this theater compare to and contrast with the different forms of theater (opera, pantomime, realistic drama) that developed in the West?

Writing About History

9. **Descriptive Writing** Imagine that you are the literate wife of a samurai. Write a journal entry that describes your relationship to your husband, your children, and your mother-in-law.

The Japanese Discover Firearms

THE PORTUGUESE BROUGHT guns to Japan in the sixteenth century. In this selection, the daimyo of a small island off the southern tip of Japan provides an explanation of how to use the new weapons. Obviously, he is fascinated by the results.

This detail from a late sixteenth-century Japanese painting records the arrival of the first Portuguese traders at the port city of Nagasaki, Japan.

❝There are two leaders among the traders. In their hands they carried something two or three feet [.6 or .9 m] long, straight on the outside with a passage inside, and made of a heavy substance. The inner passage runs through it although it is closed at the end. At its side, there is an opening which is the passageway for fire. Its shape defies comparison with anything I know. To use it, fill it with powder and small lead pellets. Set up a small target on a bank. Grip the object in your hand, compose your body, and closing one eye, apply fire to the opening. Then the pellet hits the target squarely. The explosion is like lightning and the report like thunder. Bystanders must cover their ears. This thing with one blow can smash a mountain of silver and a wall of iron. If one sought to do mischief in another man's domain and he was touched by it, he would lose his life instantly. . . . Lord Tokitaka saw it and thought it was the wonder of wonders. He did not know its name at first nor the details of its use. Then someone called it 'ironarms.'

Disregarding the high price of the arms, Tokitaka purchased from the aliens two pieces of the firearms for his family treasure. As for the art of grinding, sifting, and mixing of the powder, Tokitaka let his retainer learn it. Tokitaka occupied himself, morning and night, and without rest in handling the arms. As a result, he was able to convert the misses of his early experiments into hits—a hundred hits in a hundred attempts.**❞**

—Lord Tokitaka, On the Use of Firearms

Analyzing Primary Sources

1. Who introduced firearms to Japan in the sixteenth century?
2. Considering the description of the firearm the Portuguese brought, what do you think we would call it today?
3. In the last paragraph, to whom does the term *aliens* refer?

Using Key Terms

1. Military units called _____ were strategically placed throughout China as the chief fighting force of the Manchu Empire.

2. Trade and manufacturing in China did not develop into _____ as it did in Europe.

3. Chinese pottery makers were famous for their blue and white _____.

4. Heads of noble Japanese families, _____, controlled their own lands.

5. The shogunate controlled the daimyo by what has been called a _____, forcing the daimyo lords to leave their families in their Edo residence when the daimyo lords were away.

6. Japan was divided into 250 separate territories called _____, each ruled by a daimyo lord.

7. During the Tokugawa Era, Japan's class system became rigid with four classes and an underclass of outcasts, called the _____.

Reviewing Key Facts

8. **Culture** What was the Chinese view of Europeans, and how did interactions with Europeans impact Chinese society?

9. **Government** How did the Qing government solve the problem of being ethnically and culturally different from the people they governed?

10. **Culture** Why is the Imperial City in Beijing called the Forbidden City?

11. **Society** Explain how the samurai gradually ceased to be a warrior class.

12. **Government** How did the completion of the Grand Canal impact China?

13. **Economics** What was the Chinese attitude toward European products?

14. **Society** Why did Toyotomi Hideyoshi turn against the Jesuit missionaries?

15. **History** What year did the Portuguese make official contact with China?

16. **Geography** What is the current name of Edo, Japan? Why was Edo an important city to the Tokugawa rulers?

17. **Geography** Where was the ancient capital of Korea located?

Critical Thinking

18. **Making Generalizations** Do you believe that the plots of *The Golden Lotus* and *The Dream of the Red Chamber* would appeal to Western readers? Give your reasons.

19. **Analyzing** How might the Surgeon General of the United States today respond to the portion of the Japanese government's edict in 1649 that said, "They [peasants] should eat millet and vegetables and other coarse food instead of rice. . . . They may not smoke tobacco. It is harmful to health. . . ."?

Chapter Summary

By the nineteenth century, Japanese and Chinese societies had changed as a result of the decisions and policies of their leaders.

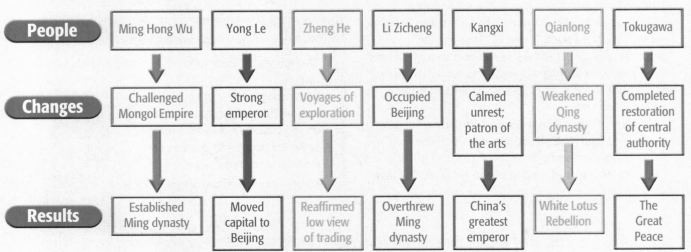

People	Ming Hong Wu	Yong Le	Zheng He	Li Zicheng	Kangxi	Qianlong	Tokugawa
Changes	Challenged Mongol Empire	Strong emperor	Voyages of exploration	Occupied Beijing	Calmed unrest; patron of the arts	Weakened Qing dynasty	Completed restoration of central authority
Results	Established Ming dynasty	Moved capital to Beijing	Reaffirmed low view of trading	Overthrew Ming dynasty	China's greatest emperor	White Lotus Rebellion	The Great Peace

Self-Check Quiz

Visit the *Glencoe World History* Web site at
tx.wh.glencoe.com and click on **Chapter 16–Self-Check Quiz** to prepare for the Chapter Test.

Writing About History

20. **Expository Writing** Compare the isolationist periods of China and Japan. Discuss each government's reasons for isolation, as well as the impact of isolation on their societies.

Analyzing Sources

Read the following excerpts from A Story That Matters, page 484.

❝. . . there is nothing we lack. We have never set much store on strange or ingenious objects, nor do we need any more of your country's manufactures.❞

—Emperor Qianlong

❝. . . that superiority which Englishmen, wherever they go, cannot conceal.❞

—Lord George Macartney

21. Compare the attitudes of Lord Macartney and Emperor Qianlong.

22. What have been some of the historical results of the political views of China and Britain?

Applying Technology Skills

23. **Creating an Electronic Database** Conduct outside research to learn more about the Tokugawa emperors in Japan. Then create an electronic database listing names of the emperors, dates each ruled, their significant accomplishments, and any problems that arose in Japan during their reigns. Share your database with your class.

Making Decisions

24. Imagine you are a Jesuit missionary in Japan. What would lead you to destroy Japanese religious shrines? When it becomes evident that the Japanese are outraged by your actions, what would you do and why?

Analyzing Maps and Charts

Study the map on this page to answer the following questions.

25. How many major daimyo clans existed during the Tokugawa Era?

26. How many miles separate Uesugi and Shimazu?

27. Which clans are located at the same latitudes?

NATIONAL GEOGRAPHIC **Japan, 1572**

— Boundaries of daimyo domains
Colors indicate the most powerful daimyo clans.

TAKS Test Practice

The Princeton Review

Directions: Use the passage *and* your knowledge of world history to answer the following question.

❝[I]t seems to be quite remarkable . . . that in a kingdom of almost limitless expanse and innumerable population . . . [that has] a well-equipped army and navy . . . neither the King nor his people ever think of waging a war of aggression.❞

—Journals of Matteo Ricci

The author suggests that people in the Ming dynasty

F lived in a militaristic society.

G adopted a "closed country" policy.

H were impoverished and starving.

J were prosperous but focused inward.

Test-Taking Tip: Do not rely on your memory of the passage to answer this question. Instead, look at each answer choice and check it against the quote.

WORLD LANGUAGES

Language not only allows us to communicate, it affects the way we think and even how we may view ourselves. It creates an identity for a community of people and shapes their experiences.

Today about 6,500 languages are spoken around the world. Hundreds of these will disappear in this century because younger generations no longer speak them. Others will be overpowered by the influence of English, a language that has spread through technology, global commerce, telecommunications, and tourism.

World Languages

Language(s)	Native Speakers
Chinese languages	1,223,307,000
Spanish	332,000,000
English	322,000,000
Hindi/Urdu	240,000,000
Bengali	189,000,000
Arabic languages	174,950,000
Portuguese	170,000,000
Russian	170,000,000
Japanese	125,000,000
German	98,000,000
French	72,000,000

Source: SIL International, 1999.

NATIONAL GEOGRAPHIC Major World Languages

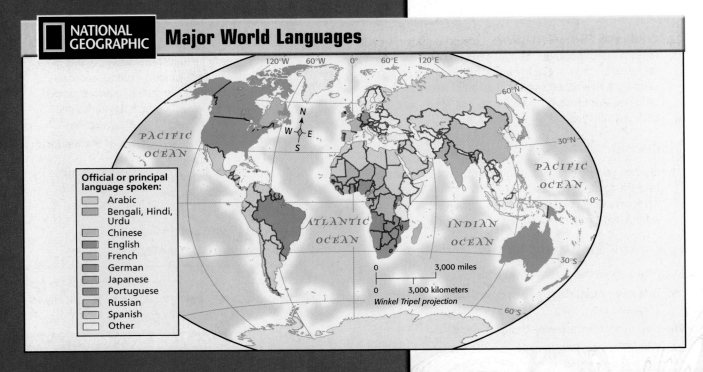

Official or principal language spoken:
- Arabic
- Bengali, Hindi, Urdu
- Chinese
- English
- French
- German
- Japanese
- Portuguese
- Russian
- Spanish
- Other

0   3,000 miles
0   3,000 kilometers
Winkel Tripel projection

English Spoken Here

Old English (5th–11th Centuries)

If you were to travel back in time to visit Robin Hood, you would not be able to understand him. Even though you would both be speaking English, the language you speak has changed a great deal since the days of Robin and his merry men. Can you recognize any words from this old English conversation?

"Hast thu hafoc?"
> *Do you have a hawk?*

"Ic habbe."
> *I have.*

"Canst thu temian hig?"
> *Do you know how to tame them?*

"Gea, ic cann. Hwat sceoldon hig me buton ic cuthe temian hig?"
> *Yes, I do. What use would they be to me if I could not tame them?*

—From a tenth-century lesson

Middle English (11th–15th Centuries)

Middle English evolved when the Normans conquered England, bringing their language, French, with them. Many different dialects of English were spoken, but the dialect spoken in London became dominant. Geoffrey Chaucer's *Canterbury Tales* (1390) is an example.

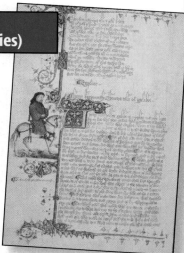

**In this viage shal telle tales tweye
To Caunterbury-ward I mene it so,
And homward he shal tellen othere two,
Of aventures that whilom han bifalle.**

*On this trip [you each] shall tell two tales
On the way to Canterbury,
And homeward [you] shall tell another two,
Of adventures that once had happened.*

—From the Prologue of *Canterbury Tales*

Modern English (15th Century–Present)

Although you might find Shakespeare difficult to understand, his English is essentially the language that evolved into the way we speak and read today.

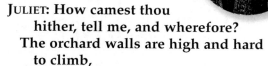

JULIET: **How camest thou hither, tell me, and wherefore?
The orchard walls are high and hard to climb,
And the place death, considering who thou art,
If any of my kinsmen find thee here.**

ROMEO: **With love's light wings did I o'er perch these walls,
For stony limits cannot hold love out,
And what love can do, that dares love attempt,
Therefore thy kinsmen are no stop to me.**

—From *Romeo and Juliet*

The ABCs of Language

How did writing begin? Early writing systems were derived from pictures. Every word would correspond to one or more symbols. For example, the word *house* might be written as a symbol that looked like a simplified house. Ancient Egyptian and Mayan hieroglyphics are examples.

The Phoenicians were among the first to develop an alphabet with characters that could be combined to make different sounds. The Greeks adapted it and passed it on to the Romans. The Roman alphabet is the alphabet most Western languages, such as English, use today.

How would you write "How are you?" to the people you meet around the world through the Internet?

"How Are You?"

Languages written from left to right →	
Danish	Hvordan gaar det?
Greek	Πως ειστε:
Hindi	आप कैसे है ?
Russian	Как поживаете?
Spanish	¿Cómo está usted?
Swahili	Hujambo?
Tagalog (Philippines)	Kumusta po kayo?
Thai	สบายดีหรือ
Vietnamese	Anh (Chi) có khoe không?

Languages written from right to left ←	
Arabic	كيف حالك؟
Hebrew	מה שלומך?
Persian	چطورید؟

Languages written from top to bottom ↓		
Chinese 你好吗？	Japanese お元気ですか	Korean 어떻게지내십니까?

Reading Chinese Characters

Chinese characters are combined in thousands of ways to make new words. In this example, when the character for tree is inserted into the character for box, you have a tree growing in a box, which is the character for "be in trouble."

Here are some other Chinese words divided into their elements. See if you can figure out what these characters mean.

EXAMPLE

木　□　困

tree　+　box　=　be in trouble

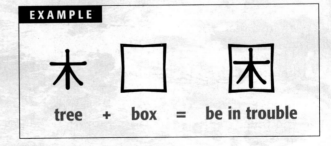

1. 火　山　火山

fire + mountain = _____

2. 木　木　木　森

tree + tree + tree = _____

Disappearing Languages

Before World War II, it is estimated that over 11 million Jews spoke Yiddish, a language based on German, Hebrew, and other languages. Many Yiddish speakers were killed in the Holocaust. Children of Holocaust survivors often forgot the language or chose not to use it in their new homelands. Today, the number of speakers is approximately 2 million, most of whom are elderly. When these people die, there will be few people left who speak the language, even though it's preserved in literature and oral records.

Many minority cultures around the world face the same problem. Often, these people live in areas that were once subjugated or conquered by other countries. The new rulers forced native peoples to adopt a new culture, often by prohibiting the use of the local language. In the United States, Native American children were frequently sent to boarding schools where they were forced to speak English and were punished if they spoke their own language. Not surprisingly, where there had once been hundreds of Native American languages, today there are only 175, and many of those will soon be extinct.

Fortunately, many struggling languages are making a comeback. In places like Ireland, northern Spain, and even Hawaii, schools are teaching traditional languages, and their usage is becoming widely accepted. Native Americans are also taking steps to revive their languages, as demonstrated by the Navajo newspaper at right. With language comes renewed interest in culture, and many ethnic groups who revive their language also find that they revive hope and self-worth within their people.

English As an International Language

Mahesh is an Indian who lives in Trinidad. His wife is from Venezuela. To communicate they speak English. He works for an international oil company where he conducts business worldwide in English. On TV he watches CNN news, and he enjoys going to American movies.

English was first spread through colonization. Though usually unwelcome, English eventually became a way of communicating between ethnic groups who shared a country but not a common language. In the late twentieth century, English became even more dominant as American language and culture spread through global business (think Coca-Cola and McDonald's), media, and technology. The Israeli sign with English translations at left is an example of how English is being used worldwide.

Today, English is spoken in 115 countries as either the official language or as an important minority language. Although many people do not like it, the globalization of English has made communication and interaction between peoples easier. On the other hand, many smaller languages and cultures are being lost as the world becomes more homogeneous.

CHAPTER 17 Revolution and Enlightenment

1550–1800

Key Events

As you read this chapter, look for the key events in the history of the Scientific Revolution and the Enlightenment.
- *The ideas of the Scientific Revolution and the Enlightenment laid the foundation for a modern worldview based on rationalism and secularism.*
- *Enlightenment thought led some rulers to advocate such natural rights as equality before the law and freedom of religion.*
- *The American colonies formed a new nation and ratified the Constitution of the United States.*

The Impact Today

The events that occurred during this time period still impact our lives today.
- *Scientists use research techniques that are based on the scientific method.*
- *The intellectuals of the Enlightenment advocated the rights of the individual, paving the way for the rise of democracy.*
- *Montesquieu's idea of separation of powers strongly influenced the writing of the Constitution of the United States.*

World History Video *The Chapter 17 video, "New Scientific Thinking," chronicles the origins of the Scientific Revolution in Europe and its impact on scientific thinking worldwide.*

Francis Bacon

1620
Francis Bacon publishes the *Novum Organum*

1633
The Church condemns Galileo's teachings

1687
Isaac Newton publishes the *Principia*

1550	1575	1600	1625	1650	1675

1543
Nicholas Copernicus presents a new view of the universe

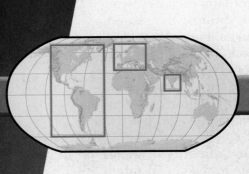

1666
Royal Academy of Science founded in France

Engraving of Copernican system, 1661

Louis XIV at the French Royal Academy of Sciences

Denis Diderot

1751
Diderot becomes editor of the *Encyclopedia*

1763
The Seven Years' War ends

1788
The Constitution of the United States is ratified by nine states

1759
James Wolfe dies in battle outside Quebec, Canada

1776
American colonies declare independence from Britain

1792
Mary Wollstonecraft publishes *A Vindication of the Rights of Women*

| 1700 | 1725 | 1750 | 1775 | 1800 | 1825 |

British general, James Wolfe

HISTORY
Online

Chapter Overview
Visit the *Glencoe World History* Web site at tx.wh.glencoe.com and click on **Chapter 17–Chapter Overview** to preview chapter information.

A Story That Matters

Galileo sits before the Inquisition in Rome.

Galileo on Trial

The Italian scientist Galileo found himself in trouble with the authorities of the Catholic Church. Galileo believed in a new worldview. He explained to a friend, "I hold the Sun to be situated motionless in the center of the revolution of the celestial bodies, while . . . Earth rotates on its axis and revolves about the Sun." Moreover, "nothing physical that sense-experience puts before our eyes . . . ought to be called in question (much less condemned) upon the testimony of passages from the Bible."

The Catholic Church had a different view. In 1632, Galileo, 68 years old and in ill health, was called before the dreaded Inquisition in Rome. He was kept waiting for two months before he was tried and found guilty of heresy and disobedience. The report of the Inquisition said: "The view that the Sun stands motionless at the center of the universe is foolish, philosophically false, and utterly heretical, because contrary to Holy Scripture."

Completely shattered by the experience, Galileo recanted in 1633: "With a sincere heart I curse and detest the said errors contrary to the Holy Church, and I swear that I will nevermore in future say or assert anything that may give rise to a similar suspicion of me." Legend holds that when he left the trial room, Galileo muttered to himself, "And yet it [Earth] does move!"

Why It Matters

Galileo was one of the scientists of the seventeenth century who set the Western world on a new path. That path, known as the Scientific Revolution, developed a new way of viewing the universe.

In the eighteenth century, a group of intellectuals used the ideas of the Scientific Revolution to reexamine all aspects of life and began what came to be called the Age of Enlightenment. The ideas of the Enlightenment helped foster the American and French Revolutions.

History and You The philosopher Adam Smith used Enlightenment ideas to identify economic laws. Read the front page, business section, and classifieds of a newspaper. Create a poster with articles and advertisements reflecting Smith's economic principles.

The Scientific Revolution

Guide to Reading

Main Idea

• The Scientific Revolution gave Europeans a new way to view humankind's place in the universe.

Key Terms

geocentric, Ptolemaic system, heliocentric, universal law of gravitation, rationalism, scientific method, inductive reasoning

People to Identify

Ptolemy, Nicholas Copernicus, Galileo Galilei, Isaac Newton, Robert Boyle, Margaret Cavendish, Maria Winkelmann, René Descartes, Francis Bacon

Places to Locate

Poland, Padua

Preview Questions

1. How did the Scientific Revolution begin?
2. What is the scientific method?

Reading Strategy

Summarizing Information Use a table like the one below to identify the contributions of Copernicus, Kepler, Galileo, and Newton to the development of a new concept of the universe.

Copernicus	
Kepler	
Galileo	
Newton	

Preview of Events

♦1545　　♦1560　　♦1575　　♦1590　　♦1605　　♦1620　　♦1635

1543
Vesalius publishes *On the Fabric of the Human Body*

1610
Galileo's discoveries are published

1628
Harvey publishes *On the Motion of the Heart and Blood*

1632
Galileo faces the Inquisition

1637
Descartes publishes *Discourse on Method*

Voices from the Past

Galileo Galilei

In 1610, Galileo described what he had observed with his newly devised telescope:

❝Now let us review the observations made during the past two months. . . . Let us speak first of that surface of the Moon which faces us. For greater clarity I distinguish two parts of this surface, a lighter and a darker. . . . [T]he darker part makes the Moon appear covered with spots. . . . From observation of these spots . . . I have been led to the opinion and conviction that the surface of the Moon is not smooth, uniform, and precisely spherical as a great number of philosophers believe it and the other heavenly bodies to be, but is uneven, rough, and full of cavities, not unlike the face of . . . Earth, relieved by chains of mountains and deep valleys. ❞

—*Discoveries and Opinions of Galileo*, Stillman Drake, ed., 1957

Galileo's observations helped to create a new view of the universe in the seventeenth century.

Background to the Revolution

In the Middle Ages, many educated Europeans took an intense interest in the world around them. However, these "natural philosophers," as medieval scientists were known, did not make observations of the natural world. These scientists relied on a few ancient authorities—especially Aristotle—for their scientific knowledge. A number of changes in the fifteenth and sixteenth centuries caused the natural philosophers to abandon their old views and develop new ones.

Renaissance humanists had mastered Greek as well as Latin and thus had access to newly discovered works by **Ptolemy** (TAH•luh•mee), Archimedes, and Plato. These writings made it obvious that some ancient thinkers had disagreed with Aristotle and other accepted authorities of the Middle Ages.

Other developments also encouraged new ways of thinking. Technical problems that required careful observation and accurate measurements, such as calculating the amount of weight that ships could hold, served to stimulate scientific activity. Then, too, the invention of new instruments, such as the telescope and microscope, made fresh scientific discoveries possible. Above all, the printing press helped spread new ideas quickly and easily.

Mathematics played a very important role in the scientific achievements of the sixteenth and seventeenth centuries. The study of mathematics was promoted in the Renaissance by the rediscovery of the works of ancient mathematicians. Nicholas Copernicus, Johannes Kepler, Galileo Galilei, and Isaac Newton were all great mathematicians who believed that the secrets of nature were written in the language of mathematics. After studying and, sometimes, discarding the ideas of the ancient mathematicians, these intellectuals developed new theories that became the foundation of the Scientific Revolution.

✓ **Reading Check** **Evaluating** What changes in the fifteenth and sixteenth centuries helped the natural philosophers develop new views?

A Revolution in Astronomy

Especially significant in the Scientific Revolution were discoveries in astronomy. These discoveries would overturn the conception of the universe held by Westerners in the Middle Ages.

The Ptolemaic System Ptolemy, who lived in the second century A.D., was the greatest astronomer of antiquity. Using his ideas, as well as those of Aristotle and of Christianity, the philosophers of the Middle

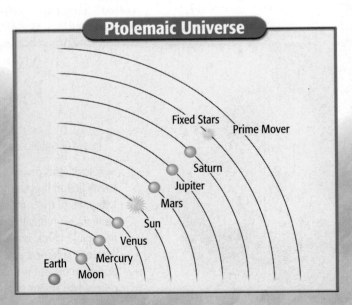

Ptolemaic Universe

Prime Mover
Fixed Stars
Saturn
Jupiter
Mars
Sun
Venus
Mercury
Earth
Moon

Picturing **History**

These astronomers, Ptolemy (left) and Copernicus (shown on page 513), were separated in time by approximately 1,400 years. Both men had a major impact on the way people viewed their place in the universe. What elements do you see in the two illustrations that help to convey to the viewer the importance of the two men and their scientific discoveries?

Ages had constructed a model of the universe known later as the Ptolemaic (TAH•luh•MAY•ik) system. This system is called geocentric because it places Earth at the center of the universe.

In the Ptolemaic system, the universe is a series of concentric spheres—spheres one inside the other. Earth is fixed, or motionless, at the center of these spheres. The spheres are made of a crystal-like, transparent substance, in which the heavenly bodies—pure orbs of light—are embedded. For example, the Moon is embedded in the first sphere, Mercury in the second, Venus in the third, and the Sun in the fourth. The rotation of the spheres makes these heavenly bodies rotate about the earth and move in relation to one another.

The tenth sphere in the Ptolemaic system was the "prime mover," which moved itself and gave motion to the other spheres. Beyond the tenth sphere was Heaven, where God and all the saved souls resided. God was at one end of the universe, then, and humans were at the center. Humans had been given power over the earth, but their real purpose was to achieve salvation.

Copernicus and Kepler In May 1543, **Nicholas Copernicus,** a native of **Poland,** published his famous book, *On the Revolutions of the Heavenly Spheres.* Copernicus, a mathematician, felt that the geocentric system was too complicated. He believed that his heliocentric, or sun-centered, conception of the universe offered a more accurate explanation than did the Ptolemaic system.

Copernicus argued that the Sun, not Earth, was at the center of the universe. The planets revolved around the Sun. The Moon, however, revolved around Earth. Moreover, according to Copernicus, the apparent movement of the Sun around Earth was really caused by the daily rotation of Earth on its axis and the journey of Earth around the Sun each year.

The next step in destroying the Ptolemaic system was taken by the German mathematician Johannes Kepler. Kepler used detailed astronomical data to arrive at his laws of planetary motion. His observations confirmed that the Sun was at the center of the universe and also added new information. In his first law, Kepler showed that the orbits of the planets around the Sun were not circular, as Copernicus

Copernican Universe

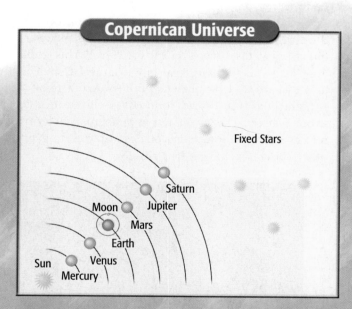

Fixed Stars

Saturn
Jupiter
Moon
Mars
Earth
Venus
Sun
Mercury

Chart *Skills*

Compare the illustrations of two different models of the universe on the previous page and this page, then answer the questions below.

1. **Compare and Contrast** Identify as many specific similarities and differences as you can find in the two models.

2. **Explaining** Explain the changes in the way people viewed the universe that resulted from the mathematical and scientific discoveries of Copernicus.

NICOLAS COPERNICVS

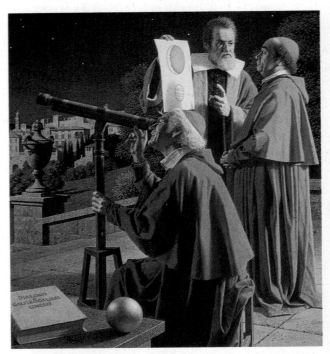

Galileo displays his drawings to the clergy.

had thought. Rather, the orbits were elliptical (egg-shaped), with the Sun toward the end of the ellipse instead of at the center. This finding, known as Kepler's First Law, contradicted the circular orbits and crystal-like spheres that were central to the Ptolemaic system.

Galileo

Scientists could now think in terms of planets revolving around the Sun in elliptical orbits. Important questions remained unanswered, however. What are the planets made of? How does one explain motion in the universe? An Italian scientist answered the first question.

Galileo Galilei taught mathematics. He was the first European to make regular observations of the heavens using a telescope. With this tool, Galileo made a remarkable series of discoveries: mountains on the Moon, four moons revolving around Jupiter, and sunspots.

Galileo's observations seemed to destroy yet another aspect of the Ptolemaic conception. Heavenly bodies had been seen as pure orbs of light. Instead, it appeared that they were composed of material substance, just as Earth was.

Galileo's discoveries, published in *The Starry Messenger* in 1610, did more to make Europeans aware of the new view of the universe than did the works of Copernicus and Kepler. In the midst of his newfound fame, however, Galileo found himself under suspicion by the authorities of the Catholic Church.

The Church ordered Galileo to abandon the Copernican idea. The Copernican system threatened the Church's entire conception of the universe and seemed to contradict the Bible. In the Copernican view, the heavens were no longer a spiritual world but a world of matter. Humans were no longer at the center of the universe, and God was no longer in a specific place.

In spite of the Church's position, by the 1630s and 1640s, most astronomers had come to accept the heliocentric conception of the universe. However, the problem of explaining motion in the universe had not been solved, and the ideas of Copernicus, Kepler, and Galileo had yet to be tied together. This would be done by an Englishman who has long been considered the greatest genius of the Scientific Revolution.

Newton Born in 1642, **Isaac Newton** showed few signs of brilliance until he attended **Cambridge University.** Later, he became a professor of mathematics at the university and wrote his major work, *Mathematical Principles of Natural Philosophy.* This work is known simply as the *Principia,* by the first word of its Latin title.

In the first book of the *Principia,* Newton defined the three laws of motion that govern the planetary bodies, as well as objects on Earth. Crucial to his whole argument was the universal law of gravitation. This law explains why the planetary bodies do not go off in straight lines but instead continue in elliptical orbits about the Sun. The law states, in mathematical terms, that every object in the universe is attracted to every other object by a force called gravity.

Isaac Newton analyzing light rays

Newton had shown that one universal law, mathematically proved, could explain all motion in the universe. At the same time, Newton's ideas created a new picture of the universe. It was now seen as one huge, regulated, uniform machine that worked according to natural laws. Newton's world-machine concept dominated the modern worldview until the twentieth century, when Albert Einstein's concept of relativity created a new picture of the universe.

✓ **Reading Check** **Identifying** Name the four great mathematicians who had a profound impact on astronomy.

Breakthroughs in Medicine and Chemistry

A revolution in medicine also began in the sixteenth century. Medicine in the Late Middle Ages was dominated by the teachings of the Greek physician Galen, who had lived in the second century A.D. Galen had relied on animal, rather than human, dissection to arrive at a picture of human anatomy, and he was wrong in many instances.

The new anatomy of the sixteenth century was based on the work of Andreas Vesalius. In his 1543 book, *On the Fabric of the Human Body,* Vesalius discussed what he had found when dissecting human bodies while he was a professor of surgery at the University of **Padua.**

Vesalius presented a careful and accurate examination of the individual organs and general structure of the human body. His "hands-on" approach enabled him to overthrow some of Galen's theories. Nevertheless, Vesalius still clung to Galen's erroneous idea that two kinds of blood flowed in the veins and arteries.

William Harvey's reputation rests on his book *On the Motion of the Heart and Blood,* published in 1628. Harvey's work was based on close observations and experiments. Harvey showed that the heart—not the liver, as Galen had thought—was the beginning point for the circulation of blood in the body. He also proved that the same blood flows in both veins and arteries. Most important, he showed that the blood makes a complete circuit as it passes through the body.

Drawings such as this from Vesalius's On the Fabric of the Human Body *did much to revolutionize knowledge of human anatomy and medicine.*

A science of chemistry also arose in the seventeenth and eighteenth centuries. **Robert Boyle** was one of the first scientists to conduct controlled experiments. His pioneering work on the properties of gases led to Boyle's Law. This generalization states that the volume of a gas varies with the pressure exerted on it. In the eighteenth century, Antoine Lavoisier invented a system of naming the chemical elements, much of which is still used today. He is regarded by many as the founder of modern chemistry.

✓ **Reading Check** **Describing** How did Vesalius and Harvey disprove many of Galen's theories?

Women and the Origins of Modern Science

Women as well as men were involved in the Scientific Revolution. One of the most prominent female scientists of the seventeenth century, **Margaret Cavendish,** came from an aristocratic family. She wrote a number of works on scientific matters, including *Observations Upon Experimental Philosophy.*

In her work, Cavendish was especially critical of the growing belief that humans, through science, were the masters of nature: "We have no power at all over natural causes and effects . . . for man is but a small part, his powers are but particular actions of Nature, and he cannot have a supreme and absolute power."

In Germany, many of the women who were involved in science were astronomers. These women had received the opportunity to become astronomers from working in family observatories, where they had been trained by their

Margaret Cavendish

fathers or husbands. Between 1650 and 1710, women made up 14 percent of all German astronomers.

The most famous of the female astronomers in Germany was **Maria Winkelmann.** She received training in astronomy from a self-taught astronomer. Her chance to be a practicing astronomer came when she married Gottfried Kirch, Prussia's foremost astronomer, and became his assistant.

Winkelmann made some original contributions to astronomy, including the discovery of a comet. Her husband described the discovery:

> ❝Early in the morning (about 2:00 A.M.) the sky was clear and starry. Some nights before, I had observed a variable star, and my wife (as I slept) wanted to find and see it for herself. In so doing, she found a comet in the sky. At which time she woke me, and I found that it was indeed a comet. . . . I was surprised that I had not seen it the night before.❞

When her husband died, Winkelmann applied for a position as assistant astronomer at the Berlin Academy. She was highly qualified, but as a woman—

with no university degree—she was denied the post. Members of the Berlin Academy feared that they would set a bad example by hiring a woman. "Mouths would gape," they said.

Winkelmann's problems with the Berlin Academy reflect the obstacles women faced in being accepted as scientists. Such work was considered to be chiefly for males. In the view of most people in the seventeenth century, a life devoted to any kind of scholarship was at odds with the domestic duties women were expected to perform.

✓ **Reading Check** **Summarizing** What did Margaret Cavendish and Maria Winkelmann contribute to the Scientific Revolution?

Descartes and Reason

The new conception of the universe brought about by the Scientific Revolution strongly influenced the Western view of humankind. Nowhere is this more evident than in the work of the seventeenth-century French philosopher **René Descartes** (day•KAHRT). Descartes began by thinking and writing about the doubt and uncertainty that seemed to be everywhere in the confusion of the seventeenth century. He ended with a philosophy that dominated Western thought until the twentieth century.

The starting point for Descartes's new system was doubt. In his most famous work, *Discourse on Method,* written in 1637, Descartes decided to set aside all that he had learned and to begin again. One fact seemed to him to be beyond doubt—his own existence:

> ❝But I immediately became aware that while I was thus disposed to think that all was false, it was absolutely necessary that I who thus thought should be something; and noting that this truth I think, therefore I am, was so steadfast and so assured . . . I concluded that I might without scruple accept it as being the first principle of the philosophy I was seeking.❞

Descartes emphasized the importance of his own mind and asserted that he would accept only those things that his reason said were true.

From his first principle—"I think, therefore I am"—Descartes used his reason to arrive at a second principle. He argued that because "the mind cannot be doubted but the body and material world can, the two must be radically different."

From this idea came the principle of the separation of mind and matter (and of mind and body).

Picturing **History**

René Descartes is pictured here with Queen Christina of Sweden, who invited Descartes to her court. What philosophical principles did Descartes establish in his famous work *Discourse on Method?*

Descartes's idea that mind and matter were completely separate allowed scientists to view matter as dead or inert—as something that was totally detached from themselves and that could be investigated independently by reason.

Descartes has rightly been called the father of modern rationalism. This system of thought is based on the belief that reason is the chief source of knowledge.

✓ **Reading Check** Explaining What is the significance of Descartes's principle of the separation of mind and matter?

The Scientific Method

During the Scientific Revolution, people became concerned about how they could best understand the physical world. The result was the creation of a scientific method—a systematic procedure for collecting and analyzing evidence. The scientific method was crucial to the evolution of science in the modern world.

The person who developed the scientific method was actually not a scientist. **Francis Bacon,** an English philosopher with few scientific credentials, believed that instead of relying on the ideas of ancient authorities, scientists should use inductive reasoning to learn about nature. In other words,

Scientific advances helped to produce a vaccine for smallpox.

scientists should proceed from the particular to the general. Systematic observations and carefully organized experiments to test hypotheses (theories) would lead to correct general principles.

Bacon was clear about what he believed his scientific method could accomplish. He stated that "the true and lawful goal of the sciences is none other than this: that human life be endowed with new discoveries and power." He was much more concerned with practical matters than pure science.

Bacon wanted science to benefit industry, agriculture, and trade. He said, "I am laboring to lay the foundation, not of any sect or doctrine, but of human utility and power."

How would this "human power" be used? Bacon believed it could be used to "conquer nature in action." The control and domination of nature became an important concern of science and the technology that accompanied it.

✓ **Reading Check** Summarizing What are the characteristics of the scientific method?

🔺 **TAKS Practice**

SECTION 1 ASSESSMENT

Checking for Understanding

1. **Define** geocentric, Ptolemaic system, heliocentric, universal law of gravitation, rationalism, scientific method, inductive reasoning.

2. **Identify** Ptolemy, Nicholas Copernicus, Galileo Galilei, Isaac Newton, Cambridge University, Robert Boyle, Margaret Cavendish, Maria Winkelmann, René Descartes, Francis Bacon.

3. **Locate** Poland, Padua.

4. **Contrast** the Ptolemaic, or geocentric, system of the universe to the heliocentric system developed by Copernicus.

5. **List** the pioneers of modern chemistry who lived during the seventeenth and eighteenth centuries.

Critical Thinking

6. **Analyze** Why did the Catholic Church condemn the work of Galileo during the seventeenth century?

7. **Identifying Information** Use a diagram to identify examples of new ideas in the form of mathematical discoveries, scientific discoveries, or technological innovations that appeared during the 1500s and 1600s. Then show in the diagram the changes produced by these discoveries or innovations.

```
            New Scientific Ideas
     ┌────┬────┬────┬────┬────┐
   (idea)(idea)(idea)(idea)(idea)
     │     │     │     │     │
     ▼     ▼     ▼     ▼     ▼
 [change][change][change][change][change]
```

Analyzing Visuals

8. **Examine** the painting of Galileo on page 514. Why do you think that Galileo is showing his drawings to the clergyman standing beside him? Why might the other man be looking through Galileo's telescope? Based on what you have read in this section, do you think these men will support Galileo's views? Why or why not?

Writing About History

9. **Expository Writing** Do some research and then write an essay about either Copernicus, Galileo, or Newton. For the scientist you choose, discuss that person's individual contributions to the Scientific Revolution and how his ideas have influenced the development of modern society.

The Enlightenment

Guide to Reading

Main Ideas
- Eighteenth-century intellectuals used the ideas of the Scientific Revolution to reexamine all aspects of life.
- People gathered in salons to discuss the ideas of the philosophes.

Key Terms
philosophe, separation of powers, deism, laissez-faire, social contract, salon

People to Identify
John Locke, Montesquieu, Voltaire, Denis Diderot, Adam Smith, Jean-Jacques Rousseau, Mary Wollstonecraft, John Wesley

Places to Locate
Paris, London

Preview Questions
1. What was the Enlightenment?
2. What role did religion play during the Enlightenment?

Reading Strategy
Summarizing Information Use a diagram like the one below to list some of the main ideas introduced during the Enlightenment.

Major Ideas of the Enlightenment

Preview of Events

◆1700	◆1715	◆1730	◆1745	◆1760	◆1775	◆1790

1702
The first daily newspaper is published in London

1748
Baron de Montesquieu publishes *The Spirit of the Laws*

1762
Rousseau publishes *The Social Contract*

1763
Voltaire writes his *Treatise on Toleration*

1776
Adam Smith publishes *The Wealth of Nations*

Voices from the Past

Voltaire

The French intellectual Voltaire attacked religious intolerance in *The Ignorant Philosopher:*

❝I say, there is scarce any city or borough in Europe, where blood has not been spilled for religious quarrels; I say, that the human species has been perceptibly diminished, because women and girls were massacred as well as men. I say that Europe would have a third larger population if there had been no theological disputes. In fine, I say, that so far from forgetting these abominable times, we should frequently take a view of them, to inspire an eternal horror for them. . . . It is for our age to make amends by toleration, for this long collection of crimes, which has taken place through the lack of toleration during sixteen barbarous centuries.❞
— *From Absolutism to Revolution* 1648–1848, Herbert H. Rowen, ed., 1963

Religious toleration was one of the major themes of the Enlightenment.

Path to the Enlightenment

The Enlightenment was an eighteenth-century philosophical movement of intellectuals who were greatly impressed with the achievements of the Scientific Revolution. One of the favorite words of these intellectuals was *reason.* By this, they meant the application of the scientific method to an understanding of all life. They hoped that by using the scientific method, they could make progress toward a better society than the one they had inherited. *Reason, natural law, hope, progress*— these were common words to the thinkers of the Enlightenment.

The Enlightenment was especially influenced by the ideas of two seventeenth-century Englishmen, Isaac Newton and **John Locke.** To Newton, the physical world and everything in it was like a giant machine (the Newtonian world-machine). If Newton could discover the natural laws that governed the physical world, then by using his methods, the intellectuals of the Enlightenment thought they could discover the natural laws that governed human society.

John Locke's theory of knowledge also greatly affected eighteenth-century intellectuals. In his *Essay Concerning Human Understanding,* Locke argued that every person was born with a tabula rasa, or blank mind:

> ❝Let us then suppose the mind to be, as we say, white paper, void of all characters, without any ideas. How comes it to be furnished? Whence has it all the materials of reason and knowledge? To this I answer, in one word, from experience. . . . Our observation, employed either about external sensible objects or about the internal operations of our minds perceived and reflected on by ourselves, is that which supplies our understanding with all the materials of thinking.❞

Locke's ideas suggested that people were molded by the experiences that came through their senses from the surrounding world. If environments were changed and people were exposed to the right influences, then people could be changed and a new society created.

How should the environment be changed? Using Newton's methods, people believed that they could discover the natural laws that all institutions should follow to produce the ideal society.

✓ **Reading Check** Explaining
What was Newton's main contribution to Enlightenment thought?

Philosophes and Their Ideas

The intellectuals of the Enlightenment were known by the French name **philosophe** (FEE•luh•ZAWF), meaning "philosopher." Not all philosophes were French, however, and few were philosophers in the strict sense of the term. They were writers, professors, journalists, economists, and above all, social reformers. They came chiefly from the nobility and the middle class.

Most of the leaders of the Enlightenment were French, but even the French would have acknowledged that the English had provided the philosophical inspiration for the Enlightenment. It was definitely these French philosophes, however, who affected intellectuals elsewhere and created a movement that influenced the entire Western world. The Enlightenment was a truly international movement.

To the philosophes, the role of philosophy was to change the world. One writer said that the philosophe is one who "applies himself to the study of society with the purpose of making his kind better and happier." One conducts this study by using reason, or an appeal to facts. A spirit of rational criticism was to be applied to everything, including religion and politics.

𝒫*icturing* **History**

Leaders of the American Revolution, such as Franklin, Adams, and Jefferson (pictured here left to right), were greatly influenced by the ideas of John Locke (shown above) and eighteenth-century Enlightenment thinkers. By what means or methods did Locke believe a new society could be created?

***Madame de Geoffrin's Salon* by Anicet Lemonnier** shows the first reading of one of Voltaire's works. Describe the different reactions to Voltaire's ideas that you might hear from a typical Parisian eighteenth-century salon audience.

The philosophes often disagreed. The Enlightenment spanned almost a century, and it evolved over time. Each succeeding generation became more radical as it built on the contributions of the previous one. A few people, however, dominated the landscape. We begin our survey of the ideas of the philosophes by looking at the three French giants—Montesquieu (MAHN•tuhs•KYOO), Voltaire, and Diderot (dee• DROH).

Montesquieu Charles-Louis de Secondat, the Baron de **Montesquieu,** came from the French nobility. His most famous work, *The Spirit of the Laws,* was published in 1748. In this study of governments, Montesquieu tried to use the scientific method to find the natural laws that govern the social and political relationships of human beings.

Montesquieu identified three basic kinds of governments: (1) republics, suitable for small states; (2) despotism, appropriate for large states; and (3) monarchies, ideal for moderate-size states. He used England as an example of a monarchy.

Montesquieu believed that England's government had three branches: the executive (the monarch), the legislative (parliament), and the judicial (the courts of law). The government functioned through a **separation of powers.** In this separation, the executive, legislative, and judicial powers of the government limit and control each other in a system of checks and balances. By preventing any one person or group from gaining too much power, this system provides the greatest freedom and security for the state.

Montesquieu's analysis of the system of checks and balances through separation of powers was his most lasting contribution to political thought. The translation of Montesquieu's work into English made it available to American philosophes, who took his principles and worked them into the United States Constitution.

Voltaire The greatest figure of the Enlightenment was François-Marie Arouet, known simply as **Voltaire.** A Parisian, Voltaire came from a prosperous middle-class family. He wrote an almost endless stream of pamphlets, novels, plays, letters, essays, and histories, which brought him both fame and wealth.

Voltaire was especially well known for his criticism of Christianity and his strong belief in religious toleration. He fought against religious intolerance in France. In 1763, he penned his *Treatise on Toleration,* in which he reminded governments that "all men are brothers under God."

Throughout his life, Voltaire championed deism, an eighteenth-century religious philosophy based on reason and natural law. Deism built on the idea of the Newtonian world-machine. In the Deists' view, a mechanic (God) had created the universe. To Voltaire and most other philosophes, the universe was like a clock. God, the clockmaker, had created it, set it in motion, and allowed it to run without his interference, according to its own natural laws.

Diderot **Denis Diderot** went to the University of **Paris** to fulfill his father's hopes that he would be a lawyer or pursue a career in the Church. He did neither. Instead, he became a freelance writer so that he could study and read in many subjects and languages. For the rest of his life, Diderot remained dedicated to new ideas.

Diderot's most famous contribution to the Enlightenment was the *Encyclopedia, or Classified Dictionary of the Sciences, Arts, and Trades,* a 28-volume collection of knowledge that he edited. Published between 1751 and 1772, the purpose of the *Encyclopedia,* according to Diderot, was to "change the general way of thinking."

The *Encyclopedia* became a major weapon in the philosophes' crusade against the old French society. Many of its articles attacked religious superstition and supported religious toleration. Others called for social, legal, and political improvements that would lead to a society that was more tolerant and more humane. The *Encyclopedia* was sold to doctors, clergymen, teachers, and lawyers, thus spreading the ideas of the Enlightenment.

✓ **Reading Check** **Comparing** What were the major contributions of Montesquieu, Voltaire, and Diderot to the Enlightenment?

Toward a New Social Science

The philosophes, as we have seen, believed that Newton's methods could be used to discover the natural laws underlying all areas of human life. This led to what we would call the social sciences—areas such as economics and political science.

Economics The Physiocrats and Scottish philosopher Adam Smith have been viewed as the founders of the modern social science of economics. The Physiocrats, a French group, were interested in identifying the natural economic laws that governed human society. They maintained that if individuals were free to pursue their own economic self-interest, all society would ultimately benefit.

The state, then, should not interrupt the free play of natural economic forces by imposing government regulations on the economy. The state should leave the economy alone. This doctrine became known by its French name, **laissez-faire** (LEH•SAY FEHR), meaning "to let (people) do (what they want)."

The best statement of laissez-faire was made in 1776 by **Adam Smith** in his famous work *The Wealth of Nations.* Like the Physiocrats, Smith believed that the state should not interfere in economic matters. Indeed, Smith gave to government only three basic roles: protecting society from invasion (the army); defending citizens from injustice (the police); and keeping up certain public works, such as roads and canals, that private individuals could not afford.

History *through Art*

***Port of Marseille* by Claude-Joseph Vernet, 1754** Vernet was commissioned by the French king to paint the military and commercial seaports of France. What characteristic activities of a commercial port are included here? What information about the past could historians learn from this painting?

Beccaria and Justice By the eighteenth century, most European states had developed a system of courts to deal with the punishment of crime. Punishments were often cruel. The primary reason for extreme punishments was the need to deter crime in an age when a state's police force was too weak to ensure the capture of criminals.

One philosophe who proposed a new approach to justice was Cesare Beccaria. In his essay *On Crimes and Punishments*, written in 1764, Beccaria argued that punishments should not be exercises in brutality. He also opposed capital punishment. He did not believe that it stopped others from committing crimes. Moreover, it set an example of barbarism: "Is it not absurd, that the laws, which punish murder, should, in order to prevent murder, publicly commit murder themselves?"

✓ **Reading Check** **Explaining** What is the concept of laissez-faire?

The Later Enlightenment

By the late 1760s, a new generation of philosophes had come to maturity. Most famous was **Jean-Jacques Rousseau** (ru•SOH). The young Rousseau wandered through France and Italy holding various jobs. Eventually he made his way to Paris, where he was

introduced into the circle of the philosophes. He did not like city life, however, and often withdrew into long periods of solitude.

In his *Discourse on the Origins of the Inequality of Mankind,* Rousseau argued that people had adopted laws and government in order to preserve their private property. In the process, they had become enslaved by government. What, then, should people do to regain their freedom?

In his famous work *The Social Contract,* published in 1762, Rousseau presented his concept of the **social contract.** Through a social contract, an entire

Jean-Jacques Rousseau

society agrees to be governed by its general will. Individuals who wish instead to follow their own self-interests must be forced to abide by the general will. "This means nothing less than that [they] will be forced to be free," said Rousseau. Thus, liberty is achieved by being forced to follow what is best for "the general will," because the general will represents what is best for the entire community.

Another important work by Rousseau is *Emile.* Written in the form of a novel, the work is a general discussion "on the education of the natural man." Rousseau argues that education should foster, and not restrict, children's natural instincts.

Unlike many Enlightenment thinkers, Rousseau believed that emotions, as well as reason, were important to human development. He sought a balance between heart and mind, between emotions and reason.

Rousseau did not necessarily practice what he preached. His own children were sent to orphanages, where many children died at a young age. Rousseau also viewed women as being "naturally" different from men: "To fulfill her functions, . . . [a woman] needs a soft life. . . . How much care and tenderness does she need to hold her family together." To Rousseau, women should be educated for their roles as wives and mothers by learning obedience and the nurturing skills that would enable them to provide loving care for their husbands and children. Not everyone in the eighteenth century agreed with Rousseau, however.

✓ **Reading Check** **Summarizing** What were Rousseau's basic theories as presented in *The Social Contract* and *Emile?*

People In History

Mary Wollstonecraft
1759–1797—English writer

Mary Wollstonecraft is considered by many to be the founder of the European and American movements for women's rights. Wollstonecraft was largely self-educated. For a while, she earned a living as a governess but soon moved to a writing career and worked for a magazine publisher.

All along, Wollstonecraft continued to develop her ideas on education and women's rights. She wrote in 1792: "Make women rational creatures, and free citizens, and they will quickly become good wives; that is—if men do not neglect the duties of husbands and fathers!"

Mary Wollstonecraft married the philosopher William Godwin in 1797. She died shortly after the birth of their daughter—Mary Wollstonecraft Godwin Shelley—who wrote the famous novel *Frankenstein.*

CONNECTIONS Past To Present

Magazines, Then and Now

Bookstores and newsstands carry thousands of magazines that appeal to an enormous variety of interests. We can find magazines on fishing, car racing, fashion, politics, television, furniture making, tourism, wrestling, and a host of other subjects.

The first magazines in Europe were a product of a growing reading public in the seventeenth and eighteenth centuries, especially among the middle classes. The first magazine was published in Germany in 1633. It contained poems and articles on religion, the chief interest of its editor, Johann Rist.

Many early magazines had serious goals. Joseph Addison and Richard Steele's *Spectator,* begun in 1711, aimed to "bring Philosophy out of the closets and libraries, schools and colleges, to dwell in clubs and assemblies, at tea-tables and coffeehouses." It did not last long.

Some publishers began to broaden the appeal of their magazines. One goal was to attract women readers. *Ladies' Mercury,* published in Britain, provided advice on marriage and child rearing as well as sewing patterns and gossip. Its success brought forth a host of similar magazines.

Many early magazines failed because customers did not always pay for them on time. Isaiah Thomas, editor of the *Worcester Magazine,* became so desperate that he wrote: "The editor requests all those who are indebted to him for magazines, to make payment—butter will be received in small sums, if brought within a few days."

◀ Argentine magazine stand

Comparing Past and Present

Pretend you are an eighteenth-century magazine editor assigned to write an article for the next edition. Choose a person or an event discussed in Chapter 17 to be the subject of your article (use outside resources if necessary). You could also select one Enlightenment idea and present it to your readers.

Rights of Women

For centuries, male intellectuals had argued that the nature of women made them inferior to men and made male domination of women necessary. By the eighteenth century, however, female thinkers began to express their ideas about improving the condition of women. The strongest statement for the rights of women was advanced by the English writer **Mary Wollstonecraft.** Many see her as the founder of the modern European and American movement for women's rights.

In *A Vindication of the Rights of Women,* Wollstonecraft identified two problems with the views of many Enlightenment thinkers. She noted that the same people who argued that women must obey men also said that government based on the arbitrary power of monarchs over their subjects was wrong.

Wollstonecraft pointed out that the power of men over women was equally wrong.

Wollstonecraft further argued that the Enlightenment was based on an ideal of reason in all human beings. Because women have reason, then they are entitled to the same rights as men. Women, Wollstonecraft declared, should have equal rights in education, as well as in economic and political life.

✓ **Reading Check** **Evaluating** How did Mary Wollstonecraft use the Enlightenment ideal of reason to advocate rights for women?

Social World of the Enlightenment

The Enlightenment was not a movement belonging exclusively to the nobles and aristocrats. For example, philosophes such as Diderot and Rousseau came from

Geography Skills

The intellectuals of the Enlightenment created a movement that influenced the entire Western world.

1. **Interpreting Maps** Examine the keys of the two maps. What kind of information does each map contain?

2. **Applying Geography Skills** Pose and answer two questions about the geographic distributions shown on one of the maps on this page. Create a thematic chart that represents the same information.

the lower middle class. The movement did, however, have its greatest appeal with the aristocrats and upper classes in the larger cities. The common people, especially the peasants, were mostly unaware and little affected by the Enlightenment.

The Growth of Reading Of great importance to the Enlightenment was the spread of its ideas to the literate elite of European society. Especially noticeable in the eighteenth century was the growth of both publishing and the reading public. The number of titles issued each year by French publishers rose from 300 in 1750 to about 1,600 in the 1780s. Books had previously been aimed at small groups of the educated elite. Now, many books were directed at the

new reading public of the middle classes, which included women and urban artisans.

An important aspect of the growth of publishing and reading in the eighteenth century was the development of magazines for the general public. In Great Britain, an important center for the new magazines, 25 periodicals were published in 1700, 103 in 1760, and 158 in 1780.

Along with magazines came daily newspapers. The first was printed in **London** in 1702. Newspapers were relatively cheap and were even provided free in many coffeehouses.

The Salon Enlightenment ideas were also spread through the salon. Salons were the elegant drawing rooms of the wealthy upper class's great urban houses. Invited guests gathered in these salons and took part in conversations that were often centered on the new ideas of the philosophes. The salons brought writers and artists together with aristocrats, government officials, and wealthy middle-class people.

The women who hosted the salons found themselves in a position to sway political opinion and influence literary and artistic taste. At her fashionable home in Paris, for example, Marie-Thérèse de

Geoffrin, wife of a wealthy merchant, held gatherings that became the talk of France and of all Europe. Distinguished foreigners, including a future king of Sweden and a future king of Poland, competed to receive invitations. These gatherings helped spread the ideas of the Enlightenment.

Reading Check **Examining** What was the importance of the salons?

Religion in the Enlightenment

Although many philosophes attacked the Christian churches, most Europeans in the eighteenth century were still Christians. Many people also sought a deeper personal devotion to God.

The Catholic parish church remained an important center of life for the entire community. How many people went to church regularly cannot be known. It has been established that 90 to 95 percent of Catholic populations did go to mass on Easter Sunday.

After the initial religious fervor that created Protestantism in the sixteenth century, Protestant churches settled into well-established patterns controlled by state authorities. Many Protestant churches were lacking in religious enthusiasm. The desire of ordinary Protestants for greater depths of religious experience led to new religious movements.

In England, the most famous new religious movement—Methodism—was the work of **John Wesley,** an Anglican minister. Wesley had a mystical

John Wesley

experience in which "the gift of God's grace" assured him of salvation. This experience led him to become a missionary to the English people to bring them the "glad tidings" of salvation.

Wesley preached to the masses in open fields. He appealed especially to the lower classes. He tried, he said, "to lower religion to the level of the lowest people's capacities."

Wesley's powerful sermons often caused people to have conversion experiences. Many of these converts joined Methodist societies in which they helped each other do good works. In this way Wesley's Methodism gave the lower and middle classes in English society a sense of purpose and community. The Methodists stressed the importance of hard work and encouraged behaviors that led to spiritual contentment, which took the place of political equality.

After Wesley's death, Methodism became a separate Protestant group. Methodism proved that the need for spiritual experience had not been eliminated by the eighteenth-century search for reason.

Reading Check **Describing** What are some of the central ideas of Methodism?

TAKS Practice

SECTION 2 ASSESSMENT

Checking for Understanding

1. **Define** philosophe, separation of powers, deism, laissez-faire, social contract, salon.

2. **Identify** John Locke, Montesquieu, Voltaire, Denis Diderot, Adam Smith, Jean-Jacques Rousseau, Mary Wollstonecraft, John Wesley.

3. **Locate** Paris, London.

4. **Explain** the influence of Isaac Newton and John Locke on Enlightenment thinkers.

5. **List** the primary occupations of the philosophes.

Critical Thinking

6. **Discuss** What did Rousseau mean when he stated that if any individual wants to pursue his own self-interests at the expense of the common good, "He will be forced to be free"? Do you agree or disagree with Rousseau's ideas? Why?

7. **Summarizing Information** Use a diagram like the one below to identify factors that helped spread Enlightenment ideas throughout Europe.

Factors that Spread Enlightenment

Analyzing Visuals

8. **Describe** the scene in the painting shown on page 521. What activities depicted in the painting are related to economics? What elements of the picture illustrate the economic principle of laissez-faire?

Writing About History

9. **Persuasive Writing** Mary Wollstonecraft argued that women are entitled to the same rights as men. Do you believe this premise to be true? Do you believe women are accorded equal rights today? Present your argument in an essay supported with evidence and logic.

The Impact of the Enlightenment

Main Ideas

- Enlightenment beliefs were reflected in the art, music, and literature of the time.
- Enlightenment thought impacted the politics of Europe in the eighteenth century.

Key Terms

rococo, enlightened absolutism

People to Identify

Bach, Handel, Haydn, Mozart, Frederick the Great, Maria Theresa, Catherine the Great

Places to Locate

Prussia, Austria, Russia, Silesia

Preview Questions

1. What innovations in the arts occurred during the eighteenth century?
2. What were the causes and results of the Seven Years' War?

Reading Strategy

Describing Use a chart like the one below to list the conflicts of the Seven Years' War. Include the countries involved and where the conflicts were fought.

Conflicts of the Seven Years' War

Preview of Events

♦1735	♦1740	♦1745	♦1750	♦1755	♦1760	♦1765
1730s Rococo style spreads through Europe	**1740** War of the Austrian Succession begins	**1748** The Treaty of Aix-la-Chapelle is signed	**1756** The Seven Years' War erupts		**1762** Catherine the Great becomes ruler of Russia	**1763** The Treaty of Paris is signed

Voices from the Past

Prussian soldiers

The eighteenth-century Prussian king Frederick II once said:

66[The services a monarch must provide for his people] consisted in the maintenance of the laws; a strict execution of justice; . . . and defending the state against its enemies. It is the duty of this magistrate to pay attention to agriculture; it should be his care that provisions for the nation should be in abundance, and that commerce and industry should be encouraged. He is a perpetual sentinel, who must watch the acts and the conduct of the enemies of the state. . . . If he be the first general, the first minister of the realm, it is not that he should remain the shadow of authority, but that he should fulfill the duties of such titles. He is only the first servant of the state.99

— *The Western Tradition,* Eugen Weber, 1972

These comments reveal the impact of the ideas of the Enlightenment on the rulers of the period.

The Arts

The ideas of the Enlightenment also had an impact on the world of culture. Eighteenth-century Europe witnessed both traditional practices and important changes in art, music, and literature.

Architecture and Art The palace of Louis XIV at Versailles, in France, had made an enormous impact on Europe. The Austrian emperor, the Swedish king, and other rulers also built grandiose residences. These palaces were modeled more on the Italian baroque style of the 1500s and 1600s than they were on the seventeenth-century French classical style of Versailles. Thus, a unique architectural style was created.

One of the greatest architects of the eighteenth century was Balthasar Neumann. Neumann's two masterpieces are the Church of the Fourteen Saints in southern Germany and the Residence, the palace of the prince-bishop of Würzburg. In these buildings, secular and spiritual become one, as lavish and fanciful ornament, light, bright colors, and elaborate detail greet the visitor. Inside the church, a pilgrim in search of holiness is struck by the incredible richness of detail.

The baroque and neoclassical styles that had dominated seventeenth-century art continued into the eighteenth century. By the 1730s, however, a new artistic style, known as rococo, had spread all over Europe.

Unlike the baroque style, which stressed grandeur and power, rococo emphasized grace, charm, and gentle action. Rococo made use of delicate designs colored in gold with graceful curves. The rococo style was highly secular. Its lightness and charm spoke of the pursuit of pleasure, happiness, and love.

Rococo's appeal is evident in the work of Antoine Watteau. In his paintings, gentlemen and ladies in elegant dress reveal a world of upper-class pleasure and joy. Underneath that exterior, however, is an element of sadness, as the artist suggests the fragility and passing nature of pleasure, love, and life.

Another aspect of rococo was a sense of enchantment and enthusiasm, especially evident in the work of Giovanni Battista Tiepolo. Many of Tiepolo's paintings came to adorn the walls and ceilings of churches and palaces. His masterpiece is the ceiling of the bishop's residence at Würzburg, a massive scene representing the four continents.

Music The eighteenth century was one of the greatest periods in the history of European music. In the first half of the century, two composers—Johann Sebastian Bach and George Frederick Handel—stand out as musical geniuses.

Bach, a renowned organist as well as a composer, spent his entire life in Germany. While he was music director at the Church of Saint Thomas in Leipzig, he composed his *Mass in B Minor* and other works that gave him the reputation of being one of the greatest composers of all time.

Handel was a German who spent much of his career in England. He is probably best known for his religious music. Handel's *Messiah* has been called a rare work that appeals immediately to everyone and yet is a masterpiece of the highest order.

HISTORY *Online*

Web Activity Visit the *Glencoe World History* Web site at tx.wh.glencoe.com and click on **Chapter 17– Student Web Activity** to learn more about the rococo style.

History *through Art*

***Danse dans un Pavillon* by Antoine Watteau**
Watteau began his career as an interior decorator and rose to become the court painter to King Louis XV. What details in this painting by Watteau are examples of the rococo style of painting?

Bach and Handel perfected the baroque musical style. Two geniuses of the second half of the eighteenth century—Franz Joseph Haydn and Wolfgang Amadeus Mozart—were innovators who wrote music called classical rather than baroque.

Haydn spent most of his adult life as musical director for wealthy Hungarian princes. Visits to England introduced him to a world where musicians wrote for public concerts rather than princely patrons. This "liberty," as he called it, led him to write two great works, *The Creation* and *The Seasons.*

Mozart was truly a child prodigy. His failure to get a regular patron to support him financially made his life miserable. Nevertheless, he wrote music passionately. His *The Marriage of Figaro, The Magic Flute,* and *Don Giovanni* are three of the world's greatest operas. Haydn remarked to Mozart's father, "Your son is the greatest composer known to me."

Literature The eighteenth century was also important in the development of the European novel. The novel was especially attractive to a growing number of middle-class readers.

The Englishman Henry Fielding wrote novels about people without morals who survive by their wits. Fielding's best-known work is *The History of Tom Jones, a Foundling,* which describes the adventures of a young scoundrel. In a number of hilarious episodes, Fielding presents scenes of English life from the slums of London to the country houses of the English aristocracy. His characters reflect real types in eighteenth-century English society.

☑ **Reading Check** **Identifying** What are the characteristics of the rococo style?

Enlightenment and Enlightened Absolutism

Enlightenment thought had an effect on the political life of European states in the eighteenth century. The philosophes believed in natural rights for all people. These rights included equality before the law; freedom of religious worship; freedom of speech; freedom of the press; and the right to assemble, hold property, and pursue happiness. As the American Declaration of Independence expressed, "We hold these truths to be self-evident, that all men are created equal; that they are endowed by their creator with certain unalienable rights; that among these are life, liberty and the pursuit of happiness."

How were these natural rights to be established and preserved? Most philosophes believed that people needed to be governed by enlightened rulers. What are enlightened rulers? They allow religious toleration, freedom of speech and of the press, and the rights of private property. They nurture the arts, sciences, and education. Above all, enlightened

Picturing **History**

In this painting, c. 1763, a seven-year-old Mozart is shown with his father and sister. Above is the original manuscript of Mozart's first attempt at writing choral music. What is a child prodigy? Do you know anyone who could be described as a child prodigy?

rulers obey the laws and enforce them fairly for all subjects. Only strong, enlightened monarchs could reform society.

Many historians once assumed that a new type of monarchy emerged in the later eighteenth century, which they called enlightened absolutism. In the system of enlightened absolutism, rulers tried to govern by Enlightenment principles while maintaining their royal powers.

Did Europe's rulers, however, actually follow the advice of the philosophes and become enlightened? To answer this question, we can examine three states—**Prussia, Austria,** and **Russia**.

Prussia: Army and Bureaucracy

Two able Prussian kings, Frederick William I and Frederick II, made Prussia a major European power in the eighteenth century. Frederick William I strove to maintain a highly efficient bureaucracy of civil service workers. The supreme values of the bureaucracy were obedience, honor, and, above all, service to the king. As Frederick William asserted: "One must serve the king with life and limb, . . . and surrender all except salvation. The latter is reserved for God. But everything else must be mine."

Frederick William's other major concern was the army. By the end of his reign in 1740, he had doubled the army's size. Although Prussia was tenth in physical size and thirteenth in population in Europe, it had the fourth largest army after France, Russia, and Austria. The Prussian army, because of its size and its reputation as one of the best armies in Europe, was the most important institution in the state.

Members of the nobility, who owned large estates with many serfs, were the officers in the Prussian army. These officers, too, had a strong sense of service to the king or state. As Prussian nobles, they believed in duty, obedience, and sacrifice.

Frederick II, or **Frederick the Great,** was one of the best educated and most cultured monarchs in the eighteenth century. He was well versed in the ideas of the Enlightenment and even invited Voltaire to live at his court for several years. Frederick was a dedicated ruler. He, too, enlarged the Prussian army, and he kept a strict watch over the bureaucracy.

For a time, Frederick seemed quite willing to make enlightened reforms. He abolished the use of torture except in treason and murder cases. He also granted limited freedom of speech and press, as well as greater religious toleration. However, he kept Prussia's serfdom and rigid social structure intact and avoided any additional reforms.

The Austrian Empire The Austrian Empire had become one of the great European states by the beginning of the eighteenth century. It was difficult to rule, however, because it was a sprawling empire composed of many different nationalities, languages, religions, and cultures. Empress **Maria Theresa,** who inherited the throne in 1740, worked to centralize the Austrian Empire and strengthen the power of the state. She was not open to the philosophes' calls for reform, but she worked hard to alleviate the condition of the serfs.

Her son, Joseph II, believed in the need to sweep away anything standing in the path of reason: "I have made Philosophy the lawmaker of my empire."

Joseph's reform program was far reaching. He abolished serfdom, eliminated the death penalty, established the principle of equality of all before the law, and enacted religious reforms, including religious toleration. In his effort to change Austria, Joseph II issued thousands of decrees and laws.

Joseph's reform program, however, largely failed. He alienated the nobles by freeing the serfs. He alienated the Catholic Church with his religious reforms. Even the serfs were unhappy, because they were unable to make sense of the drastic changes in Joseph's policies. Joseph realized his failure when he

Pictured from left to right are Catherine the Great, a carriage used by Catherine, and Joseph II. How might the carriage symbolize the differences between Catherine's and Joseph's attempts at reform?

wrote his own epitaph for his gravestone: "Here lies Joseph II who was unfortunate in everything that he undertook." His successors undid almost all of Joseph II's reforms.

Russia under Catherine the Great

In Russia, Peter the Great was followed by six weak successors who were often put in power and deposed by the palace guard. After the last of these six successors, Peter III, was murdered by a group of nobles, his German wife emerged as ruler of all the Russians.

Catherine II, or **Catherine the Great,** ruled Russia from 1762 to 1796. She was an intelligent woman who was familiar with the works of the philosophes and seemed to favor enlightened reforms. She invited the French philosophe Denis Diderot to Russia and, when he arrived, urged him to speak frankly, "as man to man." He did so, outlining an ambitious program of political and financial reform.

Catherine, however, was skeptical about what she heard. Diderot's impractical theories, she said, "would have turned everything in my kingdom upside down." She did consider the idea of a new law code that would recognize the principle of the equality of all people in the eyes of the law. In the end, however, she did nothing, because she knew that her success depended on the support of the Russian nobility.

Catherine's policy of favoring the landed nobility led to worse conditions for the Russian peasants and eventually to rebellion. Led by an illiterate Cossack (a Russian warrior), Emelyan Pugachev, the rebellion spread across southern Russia, but soon collapsed. Catherine took stronger measures against the peasants. All rural reform was halted, and serfdom was expanded into newer parts of the empire.

Catherine proved to be a worthy successor to Peter the Great in her policies of territorial expansion. Russia spread southward to the Black Sea by defeating the Turks under Catherine's rule. To the west, Russia gained about 50 percent of Poland's territory.

Enlightened Absolutism?

Of the rulers we have discussed, only Joseph II sought truly radical changes based on Enlightenment ideas. Both Frederick II and Catherine II liked to talk about enlightened reforms. They even attempted some, but their interest in strengthening the state and maintaining the existing system took priority.

In fact, all three rulers were chiefly guided by a concern for the power and well-being of their states. In the final analysis, heightened state power in Prussia, Austria, and Russia was not used to undertake enlightened reforms. Rather, it was used to collect more taxes and thus to create armies, to wage wars, and to gain more power.

The philosophes condemned war as a foolish waste of life and resources. Despite their words, the rivalry among states that led to costly struggles remained unchanged in eighteenth-century Europe. Europe's self-governing, individual states were chiefly guided by the self-interest of the rulers.

The eighteenth-century monarchs were concerned with the balance of power, the idea that states should have equal power in order to prevent any one from dominating the others. This desire for a balance of power, however, did not imply a desire for peace. Large armies created to defend a state's security were often used to conquer new lands as well. As Frederick the Great of Prussia remarked, "The fundamental rule of governments is the principle of extending their territories."

✓ **Reading Check** **Evaluating** What effect did enlightened reforms have in Prussia, Austria, and Russia?

War of the Austrian Succession

In 1740, a major war broke out in connection with the succession to the Austrian throne. When the Austrian emperor Charles VI died, he was succeeded by his daughter, Maria Theresa. King Frederick II of Prussia took advantage of the succession of a woman to the throne of Austria by invading Austrian **Silesia.** France then entered the war against Austria, its traditional enemy. In turn, Maria Theresa made an alliance with Great Britain.

The War of the Austrian Succession (1740 to 1748) was fought in three areas of the world. In Europe, Prussia seized Silesia while France occupied the Austrian Netherlands. In the Far East, France took Madras (today called Chennai) in India from the British. In North America, the British captured the French fortress of Louisbourg at the entrance to the St. Lawrence River.

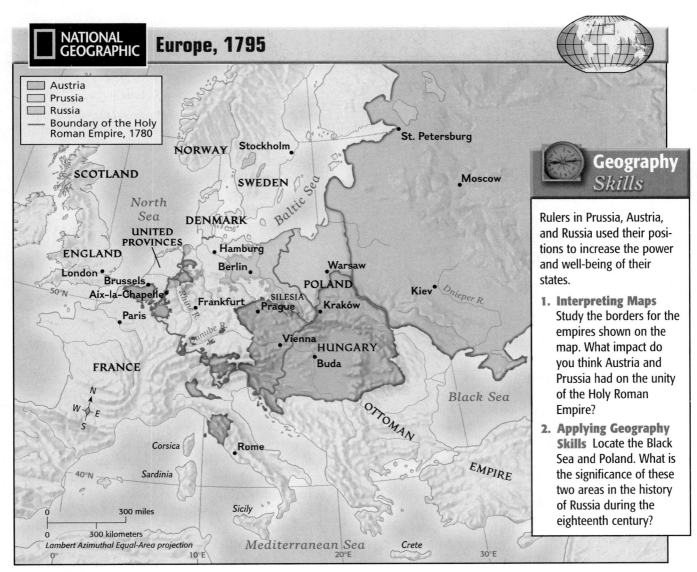

NATIONAL GEOGRAPHIC **Europe, 1795**

Austria
Prussia
Russia
— Boundary of the Holy Roman Empire, 1780

Geography Skills

Rulers in Prussia, Austria, and Russia used their positions to increase the power and well-being of their states.

1. **Interpreting Maps** Study the borders for the empires shown on the map. What impact do you think Austria and Prussia had on the unity of the Holy Roman Empire?

2. **Applying Geography Skills** Locate the Black Sea and Poland. What is the significance of these two areas in the history of Russia during the eighteenth century?

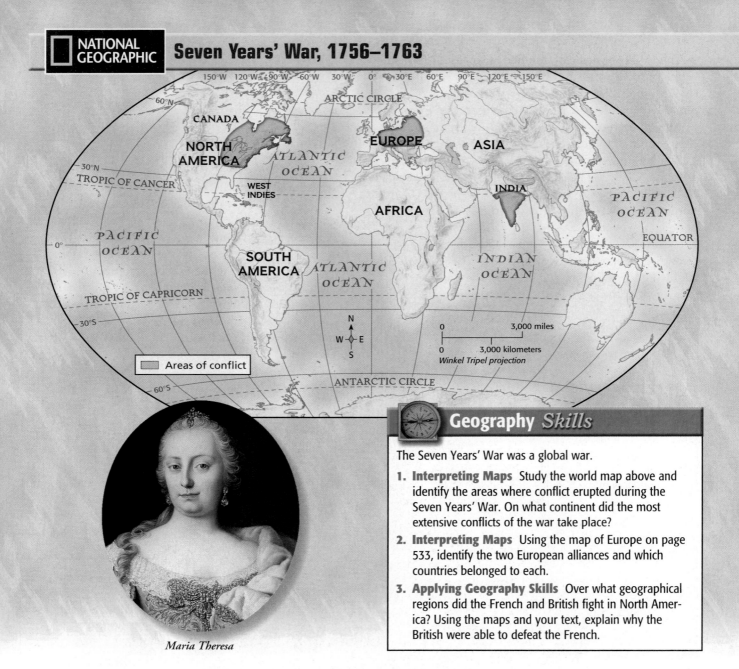

Maria Theresa

Geography *Skills*

The Seven Years' War was a global war.

1. **Interpreting Maps** Study the world map above and identify the areas where conflict erupted during the Seven Years' War. On what continent did the most extensive conflicts of the war take place?

2. **Interpreting Maps** Using the map of Europe on page 533, identify the two European alliances and which countries belonged to each.

3. **Applying Geography Skills** Over what geographical regions did the French and British fight in North America? Using the maps and your text, explain why the British were able to defeat the French.

After seven years of warfare, all parties were exhausted and agreed to the Treaty of Aix-la-Chapelle in 1748. This treaty guaranteed the return of all occupied territories except Silesia to their original owners. Prussia's refusal to return Silesia meant yet another war between Prussia and Austria.

✓ **Reading Check** **Describing** Name the countries which fought on each side during the War of the Austrian Succession.

The Seven Years' War

Maria Theresa refused to accept the loss of Silesia. She rebuilt her army while working diplomatically to separate Prussia from its chief ally, France. In 1756,

Austria achieved what was soon labeled a diplomatic revolution.

New Allies French-Austrian rivalry had been a fact of European diplomacy since the late sixteenth century. However, two new rivalries now replaced the old one: the rivalry of Britain and France over colonial empires and the rivalry of Austria and Prussia over Silesia. France abandoned Prussia and allied with Austria. Russia, which saw Prussia as a major threat to Russian goals in central Europe, joined the new alliance with France and Austria. In turn, Britain allied with Prussia. This diplomatic revolution of 1756 led to another worldwide war. The war had

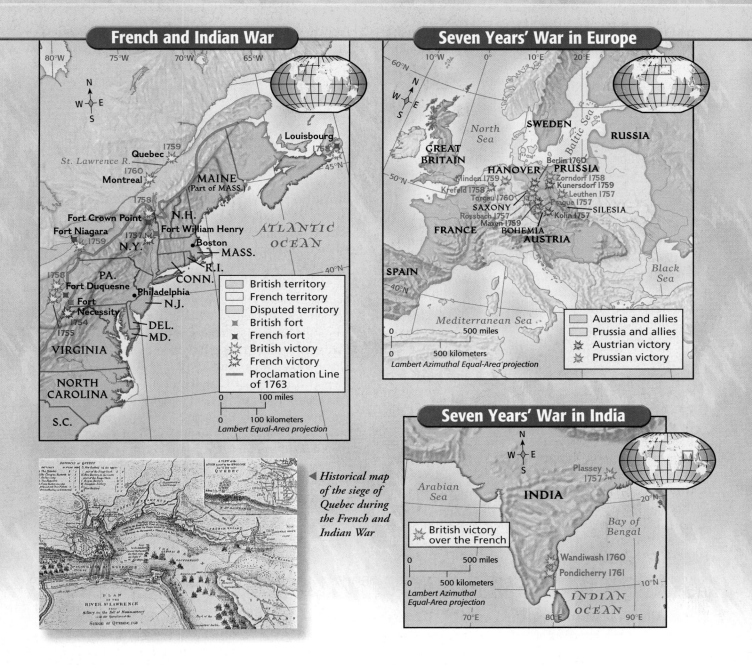

French and Indian War

British territory
French territory
Disputed territory
★ British fort
■ French fort
✳ British victory
✳ French victory
━ Proclamation Line of 1763

0   100 miles
0   100 kilometers
Lambert Equal-Area projection

Historical map of the siege of Quebec during the French and Indian War

Seven Years' War in Europe

0   500 miles
0   500 kilometers
Lambert Azimuthal Equal-Area projection

Austria and allies
Prussia and allies
✳ Austrian victory
✳ Prussian victory

Seven Years' War in India

✳ British victory over the French

0   500 miles
0   500 kilometers
Lambert Azimuthal Equal-Area projection

three major areas of conflict: Europe, India, and North America.

The War in Europe Europe witnessed the clash of the two major alliances: the British and Prussians against the Austrians, Russians, and French. With his superb army and military skill, Frederick the Great of Prussia was able for some time to defeat the Austrian, French, and Russian armies. His forces were under attack from three different directions, however, and were gradually worn down.

Frederick faced disaster until Peter III, a new Russian czar who greatly admired Frederick, withdrew Russian troops from the conflict and from the Prussian lands that the Russians had occupied. This withdrawal created a stalemate and led to the desire for peace. The European war ended in 1763. All occupied territories were returned to their original owners, while Austria officially recognized Prussia's permanent control of Silesia.

The War in India The struggle between Britain and France in the rest of the world had more decisive results. Known as the Great War for Empire, it was fought in India and North America. The French had returned Madras to Britain after the War of the Austrian Succession, but the struggle in India continued. The British ultimately won out, not because they had better forces but because they were more persistent. With the Treaty of Paris in 1763, the French withdrew and left India to the British.

The War in North America The greatest conflicts of the Seven Years' War took place in North America. On the North American continent, the French and British colonies were set up differently. French North America (Canada and Louisiana) was run by the French government as a vast trading area. It was valuable for its fur, leather, fish, and timber. The French state was unable to get people to move to North America, so its colonies were thinly populated.

British North America consisted of 13 prosperous colonies on the eastern coast of the present United States. Unlike the French colonies, the British colonies were more populated, containing more than one million people by 1750.

The British and French fought over two primary areas in North America. One consisted of the waterways of the Gulf of St. Lawrence, which were protected by the fortress of Louisbourg and by forts that guarded French Quebec. The other area that was fought over was the unsettled Ohio River valley. The French began to move down from Canada and up from Louisiana to establish forts in the Ohio River valley. This French activity threatened to cut off the British settlers in the 13 colonies from expanding into this vast area. The French were able to gain the support of the Indians. As traders and not settlers, the French were viewed by the Indians with less hostility than the British.

The French scored a number of victories, at first. British fortunes were revived, however, by the efforts of William Pitt the Elder, Britain's prime minister. Pitt was convinced that the French colonial empire would have to be destroyed for Britain to create its own colonial empire. Pitt's policy focused on doing little in the European theater of war while putting resources into the colonial war, especially through the use of the British navy. The French had more troops in North America but not enough naval support. The defeat of French fleets in major naval battles gave the British an advantage, because the French could no longer easily reinforce their garrisons.

A series of British victories soon followed. In 1759, British forces under General Wolfe defeated the French under General Montcalm on the Plains of Abraham, outside Quebec. Both generals died in the battle. The British went on to seize Montreal, the Great Lakes area, and the Ohio River Valley. The French were forced to make peace. By the Treaty of Paris, they transferred Canada and the lands east of the Mississippi to England. Their ally Spain transferred Spanish Florida to British control. In return, the French gave their Louisiana territory to the Spanish. By 1763, Great Britain had become the world's greatest colonial power.

✓**Reading Check** **Explaining** How did Great Britain become the world's greatest colonial power?

🦅 **TAKS Practice**

SECTION 3 ASSESSMENT

Checking for Understanding

1. **Define** rococo, enlightened absolutism.

2. **Identify** Bach, Handel, Haydn, Mozart, Frederick the Great, Maria Theresa, Catherine the Great.

3. **Locate** Prussia, Austria, Russia, Silesia.

4. **Describe** the characteristics of an ideal enlightened ruler. Do any of the eighteenth-century rulers discussed in this section have the characteristics of an ideal ruler?

5. **List** all the countries in the world that fought in the Seven Years' War. Which country gained the most territory?

Critical Thinking

6. **Analyze** Why were Enlightenment ideals never fully practiced by eighteenth-century rulers?

7. **Compare and Contrast** Use a table like the one below to compare and contrast the reforms of Joseph II of Austria with those of Frederick II of Prussia and Catherine II of Russia.

Joseph II	Frederick II	Catherine II

Analyzing Visuals

8. **Identify** the theme of the Watteau painting on page 527. Find another example of rococo painting in an art history book in your school's library (such as a work by Giovanni Battista Tiepolo). Compare this painting to Watteau's. How are they similar?

Writing About History

9. **Expository Writing** Listen to a selection of medieval religious music and of Mozart's *The Magic Flute.* Write an essay describing how the two pieces are similar and different. What kind of emotion does each piece convey?

STUDY & WRITING SKILLBUILDER

Outlining

Why Learn This Skill?

Outlining is a useful skill for both taking notes and writing papers. When you are studying written material, use outlining to organize information. This not only helps you absorb the material, but later you will have useful notes to review for class or tests. When you are writing a paper, outlining is a good starting point for putting information in a logical order. Then use the material in the outline to write your paragraphs and arrange your essay.

Learning the Skill

There are two kinds of outlines—formal and informal. An informal outline is similar to taking notes and is useful for reviewing for a test.

- Write only words and phrases needed to remember ideas.

- Note related but less important details under the main ideas.
  A formal outline has a standard format. In a formal outline:

- Label main heads with Roman numerals, subheads with capital letters, and details with Arabic numerals.

- Have at least two entries for each level.

- Indent each level from the level above.

- Use the same grammatical form for all entries. If one entry is a complete sentence, all other entries at that level must be complete sentences.

Practicing the Skill

Study the following outline and then answer these questions.

I. Changes in Astronomy
  A. Galileo Galilei
    1. Used the telescope to observe the heavens
    2. Condemned by the Catholic Church
  B. Isaac Newton
    1. Tied together the work of Copernicus, Kepler, and Galileo

    2. Published the *Principia*
      a. Defined the three laws of motion
      b. Proved the universal law of gravitation
II. Changes in Medicine
  A. Andreas Vesalius
    1. Dissected human bodies for the first accurate descriptions of human anatomy
    2. Published *On the Fabric of the Human Body*
  B. William Harvey
    1. Wrote the theory of blood circulation
    2. Published *Motion of the Heart and Blood*

❶ Is this a formal or an informal outline?

❷ What are the two main headings?

❸ How does each subhead under "Isaac Newton" support the topic of the level above it?

❹ Give two examples of grammatical consistency.

Nicholas Copernicus observing an eclipse of the moon

Applying the Skill

Using the guidelines above, create a formal outline for Section 3 of this chapter.

 Glencoe's **Skillbuilder Interactive Workbook, Level 2,** provides instruction and practice in key social studies skills.

Colonial Empires and the American Revolution

Voices from the Past

Thomas Jefferson

On July 4, 1776, the Second Continental Congress adopted a resolution declaring the independence of the American colonies. It read:

❝We hold these truths to be self-evident, that all men are created equal, that they are endowed by their Creator with certain unalienable Rights, that among these are Life, Liberty, and the pursuit of Happiness. That to secure these rights, Governments are instituted among Men, deriving their just powers from the consent of the governed. That whenever any Form of Government becomes destructive of these ends, it is the Right of the People to alter or to abolish it and to institute new Government.❞
— *The Declaration of Independence*

The ideas of the Enlightenment had clearly made an impact on the colonies in North America. Despite their close ties to their European mother countries, the colonies of Latin America and British North America were developing in ways that sometimes differed significantly from those of Europe.

Colonial Empires in Latin America

In the sixteenth century, Portugal came to dominate **Brazil.** At the same time, Spain established an enormous colonial empire in the Western Hemisphere that included parts of North America, Central America, and most of South America. Within the lands of Central America and South America, a new civilization arose, which we call Latin America.

Latin America was a multiracial society. Already by 1501, Spanish rulers permitted intermarriage between Europeans and Native Americans, whose offspring became known as mestizos (meh•STEE•zohz). In addition, over a period of three centuries, possibly as many as 8 million African slaves were brought to Spanish and Portuguese America to work the plantations. Mulattoes—the offspring of Africans and Europeans—joined mestizos and other descendants of Europeans, Africans, and Native Americans to produce a unique society in Latin America.

Economic Foundations Both the Portuguese and the Spanish sought ways to profit from their colonies in Latin America. One source of wealth came from abundant supplies of gold and silver, which were sent to Europe. Farming, however, proved to be a more long-lasting and rewarding source of prosperity for Latin America.

A noticeable feature of Latin American agriculture was the dominant role of the large landowner. Both Spanish and Portuguese landowners created immense estates. Native Americans either worked on the estates or worked as poor farmers on marginal lands. This system of large landowners and dependent peasants has remained a lasting feature of Latin American society.

Trade provided another avenue for profit. In addition to gold and silver, a number of other natural products were shipped to Europe, including sugar, tobacco, diamonds, and animal hides. In turn, the mother countries supplied their colonists with manufactured goods.

Both Spain and Portugal closely regulated the trade of their American colonies to keep others out. By the beginning of the eighteenth century, however, both the British and the French had become too powerful to be kept out of the lucrative Latin American markets.

State and Church Portuguese Brazil and Spanish Latin America were colonial empires that lasted over three hundred years. The difficulties of

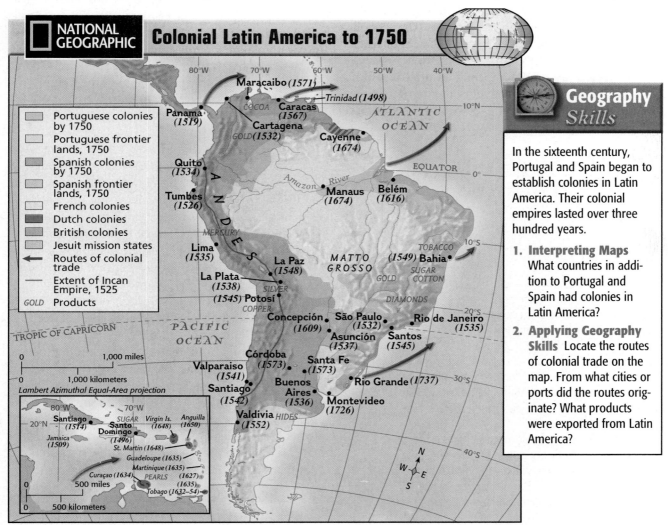

Colonial Latin America to 1750

Portuguese colonies by 1750
Portuguese frontier lands, 1750
Spanish colonies by 1750
Spanish frontier lands, 1750
French colonies
Dutch colonies
British colonies
Jesuit mission states
Routes of colonial trade
Extent of Incan Empire, 1525
GOLD Products

Maracaibo (1571)
Trinidad (1498)
Panama (1519)
Caracas (1567)
COCOA
Cartagena (1532)
GOLD
Cayenne (1674)
ATLANTIC OCEAN
Quito (1534)
Amazon River
EQUATOR
Tumbes (1526)
Manaus (1674)
Belém (1616)
MERCURY
Lima (1535)
La Paz (1548)
MATTO GROSSO
Bahia (1549)
TOBACCO
La Plata (1538)
SILVER
Potosí (1545)
GOLD SUGAR COTTON
COPPER
DIAMONDS
Concepción (1609)
São Paulo (1532)
Rio de Janeiro (1535)
Córdoba (1573)
Asunción (1537)
Santos (1545)
Santa Fe (1573)
Valparaíso (1541)
Buenos Aires (1536)
Rio Grande (1737)
Santiago (1542)
Montevideo (1726)
Valdivia (1552) HIDES
TROPIC OF CAPRICORN
PACIFIC OCEAN
0   1,000 miles
0   1,000 kilometers
Lambert Azimuthal Equal-Area projection

Santiago (1514)
SUGAR Virgin Is. (1648) Anguilla (1650)
Santo Domingo (1496)
Jamaica (1509)
St. Martin (1648)
Guadeloupe (1635)
Martinique (1635)
Curaçao (1634) PEARLS (1627) (1635)
Tobago (1632–54)
0   500 miles
0   500 kilometers
N W E S

Geography Skills

In the sixteenth century, Portugal and Spain began to establish colonies in Latin America. Their colonial empires lasted over three hundred years.

1. **Interpreting Maps** What countries in addition to Portugal and Spain had colonies in Latin America?

2. **Applying Geography Skills** Locate the routes of colonial trade on the map. From what cities or ports did the routes originate? What products were exported from Latin America?

communication and travel between the Americas and Europe made the attempts of the Spanish and Portuguese monarchs to provide close regulation of their empires virtually impossible. As a result, colonial officials in Latin America had much freedom in carrying out imperial policies.

From the beginning of their conquest of the New World, Spanish and Portuguese rulers were determined to Christianize the native peoples. This policy gave the Catholic Church an important role to play in the Americas—a role that added considerably to the Church's power.

Catholic missionaries—especially the Dominicans, Franciscans, and Jesuits—fanned out to different parts of the Spanish Empire. To make their efforts easier, the missionaries brought Native Americans together into villages, or missions, where the native peoples could be converted, taught trades, and encouraged to grow crops. Missions enabled missionaries to control the lives of the Native Americans and keep them as docile members of the empire.

The Catholic Church built cathedrals, hospitals, orphanages, and schools in the colonies. The schools taught Native American students the basics of reading, writing, and arithmetic. The Catholic Church also provided an outlet other than marriage for women. They could enter convents and become nuns.

As in Europe, women in colonial religious orders—many of them of aristocratic background—often lived well. Many nuns worked outside their convents by running schools and hospitals. Indeed, one of these nuns, **Sor Juana Inés de la Cruz,** urged that women be educated.

✓ Reading Check **Explaining** How did the Portuguese and the Spanish profit from their colonies in Latin America?

Britain and British North America

The United Kingdom of Great Britain came into existence in 1707, when the governments of England and Scotland were united. The term *British* came to refer to both the English and the Scots.

In eighteenth-century Britain, the monarch and the Parliament shared power, with Parliament gradually gaining the upper hand. The monarch chose ministers who were responsible to the Crown and who set policy and guided Parliament. Parliament had the power to make laws, levy taxes, pass the budget, and indirectly influence the ministers of the monarch.

In 1714, a new dynasty—the **Hanoverians**—was established when the last Stuart ruler, Queen Anne, died without an heir. The crown was offered to her nearest relatives, Protestant rulers of the German state of Hanover. The first Hanoverian king, George I, did not speak English, and neither the first nor the second George knew the British system very well. Therefore, their chief ministers were allowed to handle Parliament.

Robert Walpole served as head of cabinet (later called prime minister) from 1721 to 1742 and pursued a peaceful foreign policy. However, growing trade and industry led to an ever-increasing middle class. The middle class favored expansion of trade and of Britain's world empire. They found a spokesman in William Pitt the Elder, who became head of cabinet in 1757. He expanded the British Empire by acquiring Canada and India in the Seven Years' War.

In North America, then, Britain controlled Canada as well as 13 colonies on the eastern coast of the present United States. The British colonies were thickly populated, containing more than one million people by 1750. They were also prosperous.

The colonies were supposedly run by the British Board of Trade, the Royal Council, and Parliament, but the colonies actually had legislatures that tended to act independently. Merchants in port cities such as Boston, Philadelphia, New York, and Charleston did not want the British government to run their affairs.

✓ Reading Check **Explaining** What countries made up Great Britain in the 1700s? To whom does the term *British* refer?

People In History

Sor Juana Inés de la Cruz
1651–1695—Mexican poet

Juana Inés de la Cruz was one of seventeenth-century Latin America's best-known literary figures. She was an avid learner but was denied admission to the University of Mexico because she was a woman. As a result of this rejection, she chose to enter a convent, where she could write poetry and plays. She said, "Who has forbidden women to engage in private and individual studies? Have they not a rational soul as men do?"

By her late thirties, she had become famous as a great poet. Denounced by her bishop for writing secular literature, she agreed to stop writing and devote herself to purely religious activities. She died at the age of 43 while nursing the sick during an epidemic in Mexico City.

The American Revolution

After the Seven Years' War, British leaders wanted to get new revenues from the colonies. These revenues would be used to cover war costs, as well as to pay for the expenses of maintaining an army to defend the colonies.

In 1765, the Parliament imposed the Stamp Act on the colonies. The act required that certain printed materials, such as legal documents and newspapers, carry a stamp showing that a tax had been paid to Britain. Opposition was widespread and often violent, and the act was repealed in 1766. The crisis was over, but the cause of the dispute was not resolved.

Lord Cornwallis surrendering to George Washington (left of the American flag)

The War Begins Crisis followed crisis in the 1770s. To counteract British actions, the colonies organized the First Continental Congress, which met in Philadelphia in September 1774. Outspoken members urged colonists to "take up arms and organize militias."

Fighting finally erupted between colonists and the British army in April 1775 in Lexington and Concord, Massachusetts. The Second Continental Congress met soon afterward and formed an army, called the Continental Army, with George Washington as commander in chief. Still, the colonists did not rush headlong into war. After the fighting in Lexington and Concord, more than a year passed before the decision was made to declare independence from the British Empire.

On July 4, 1776, the Second Continental Congress approved a declaration of independence written by Thomas Jefferson. A stirring political document, the Declaration of Independence declared the colonies to be "free and independent states absolved from all allegiance to the British Crown." The American Revolution had formally begun.

The war against Great Britain was a great gamble. Britain was a strong military power with enormous financial resources. The Continental Army of the Americans was made up of undisciplined amateurs who agreed to serve for only a short time.

Foreign Support and British Defeat Of great importance to the colonies' cause was support from foreign countries. These nations were eager to gain revenge for earlier defeats at the hands of the British.

The French supplied arms and money to the rebels from the beginning of the war. French officers and soldiers also served in Washington's army. In February 1778, following a British defeat, the French granted diplomatic recognition to the American state.

Spain and the Dutch Republic also entered the war against Great Britain. Now, the British were faced with war against much of Europe, as well as against the Americans.

When the army of General Cornwallis was forced to surrender to combined American and French forces under Washington at **Yorktown** in 1781, the British decided to end the war. The Treaty of Paris, signed in 1783, recognized the independence of the American colonies and granted the Americans control of the western territory from the Appalachians to the Mississippi River.

✔ **Reading Check** **Explaining** Why did foreign countries support the American cause?

The Birth of a New Nation

▸**TURNING POINT**◂ **Americans created a new social contract in 1788. The creation of the Constitution made Enlightenment concepts of liberty and representative government a reality for the first time.**

The 13 American colonies had gained their independence. The former colonies were now states. The states feared concentrated power, however, and each one was primarily concerned for its own interests. For these reasons, they had little enthusiasm for creating a united nation with a strong central government.

The Articles of Confederation, the American nation's first constitution, thus did little to provide for a strong central government. It soon became clear that the government under the Articles lacked the power to deal with the new nation's problems. A movement for a different form of national government arose.

The Articles of Confederation had been approved in 1781. In the summer of 1787, 55 delegates met in Philadelphia to revise the Articles. That meeting became known as the Constitutional Convention. The convention's delegates decided to write a plan for an entirely new national government.

The Constitution

The proposed Constitution created a federal system in which power would be shared between the national government and the state governments. The national, or federal, government was given the power to levy taxes, raise an army, regulate trade, and create a national currency.

The federal government was divided into three branches, each with some power to check the workings of the others. The first branch was the executive branch. A president served as the chief executive. The president had the power to execute laws, veto the legislature's acts, supervise foreign affairs, and direct military forces.

The second branch of government was the legislative branch. It consisted of two houses—the Senate, with members elected by the state legislatures, and the House of Representatives. Representatives were elected directly by the people.

The Supreme Court and other courts "as deemed necessary" by Congress provided the third branch of government, the judicial branch. The courts would enforce the Constitution as the "supreme law of the land."

According to the Constitutional Convention, the Constitution would have to be ratified, or approved, by nine states before it could take effect. The Constitution was eventually approved, but in several states the margin was slim.

The Bill of Rights

Important to the eventual adoption of the Constitution was a promise to add a bill of rights. In 1789 the new Congress proposed 12 amendments, and the 10 that were approved by the states became known as the Bill of Rights.

These 10 amendments guaranteed freedom of religion, speech, press, petition, and assembly. They gave Americans the right to bear arms and to be protected against unreasonable searches and arrests. They guaranteed trial by jury, due process of law, and the protection of property rights.

Many of the rights in the Bill of Rights were derived from the natural rights proposed by the eighteenth-century philosophes. Many European intellectuals saw the American Revolution as the embodiment of the Enlightenment's political dreams. The premises of the Enlightenment seemed confirmed. A new age and a better world could be achieved.

✓ **Reading Check** **Contrasting** What was the main difference between the Articles of Confederation and the Constitution?

TAKS Practice

SECTION 4 ASSESSMENT

Checking for Understanding

1. **Define** mestizo, mulatto, federal system.

2. **Identify** Sor Juana Inés de la Cruz, Hanoverians, Robert Walpole.

3. **Locate** Brazil, Yorktown.

4. **Explain** the role of the Catholic Church and its missionaries in colonial Latin America.

5. **List** the freedoms guaranteed under the American Bill of Rights.

Critical Thinking

6. **Summarize** Why did the American colonies declare their independence from the British Empire?

7. **Summarizing Information** Use a chart like the one below to identify the significant events and conflicts between the British and the colonists leading to the American Revolution.

Conflicts Between British and Colonists

Analyzing Visuals

8. **Examine** the depiction of the signing of the Declaration of Independence on page 370. What principles of government and citizenship are illustrated in the painting?

Writing About History

9. **Expository Writing** Do further research on how the French supported the colonies during the American Revolution. Based on your research, write an essay analyzing the importance of the French assistance to the American colonists.

The Mission

IN 1609, TWO JESUIT PRIESTS set out as missionaries to the Guarani Indians in eastern Paraguay. Eventually, the Jesuits established more than 30 missions in the region. This description of a Jesuit mission in Paraguay was written by Félix de Azara, a Spanish soldier and scientist.

Seventeenth-century mission in Paraguay

66Having spoken of the towns founded by the Jesuit fathers, and of the manner in which they were founded, I shall discuss the government which they established in them. . . . In each town resided two priests, a curate and a sub-curate, who had certain assigned tasks.

The curate allowed no one to work for personal gain; he compelled everyone, without distinction of age or sex, to work for the community, and he himself saw to it that all were equally fed and dressed. For this purpose the curates placed in storehouses all the fruits of agriculture and the products of industry, selling in the Spanish towns their surplus of cotton, cloth, tobacco, vegetables, skins, and wood, transporting them in their own boats down the nearest rivers, and returning with whatever was required.

From the foregoing one may infer that the curates disposed of the surplus funds of the Indian towns, and that no Indian could aspire to own private property. This deprived them of any incentive to use reason or talent, since the most industrious, able, and worthy person had the same food, clothing, and pleasures as the most wicked, dull, and indolent. It also follows that although this form of government was well designed to enrich the communities it also caused the Indian to work at a languid pace, since the wealth of his community was of no concern to him.

It must be said that although the Jesuit fathers were supreme in all respects, they employed their authority with a mildness and restraint that command admiration. They supplied everyone with abundant food and clothing. They compelled the men to work only half a day, and did not drive them to produce more. Even their labor was given a festive air, for they went in procession to the fields, to the sound of music. . . . They gave them many holidays, dances, and tournaments, dressing the actors and the members of the municipal councils in gold or silver tissue and the most costly European garments, but they permitted the women to act only as spectators.99

—Félix de Azara, *Description and History of Paraguay and Rio de la Plata*

Analyzing Primary Sources

1. How is the mission town's government and economic system structured?
2. According to Azara, what are some of the problems with the town's system?
3. How might a Native American's description of the mission differ from Azara's European perspective?

Using Key Terms

1. The _____ is a systematic procedure for collecting and analyzing evidence.

2. The idea that Earth is at the center of the universe is called a _____ or _____ system.

3. In the Americas, the offspring of European and American native peoples were called _____.

4. A new type of monarchy called _____ was influenced by reform-minded philosophes.

5. In the _____, power is shared between the national government and the state government.

6. When scientists proceed from the particular to the general they are using _____.

7. The belief that the Sun is at the center of the universe is called a _____ theory.

8. The intellects, or thinkers, of the Enlightenment, were generally called _____.

9. Descartes is known as the father of _____.

10. The doctrine that maintains that the state should not intervene in economics is called _____.

Reviewing Key Facts

11. **History** What was the Enlightenment?

12. **Government** Name two of the three groups that officially ran the 13 British colonies in North America.

13. **Government** According to Adam Smith, what is the proper role of government in society?

14. **Culture** Name two early eighteenth-century composers who have stood out as musical geniuses of the baroque style.

15. **History** What country challenged Spanish power in the Americas?

16. **Culture** What did Henry Fielding write about in his novels? What was his most popular work?

17. **Science and Technology** How did Newton explain the universal law of gravitation?

18. **Culture** Why is Mary Wollstonecraft often considered the founder of the modern women's movement?

19. **Culture** In his *Essay Concerning Human Understanding,* what ideas did John Locke propose?

20. **History** What was the major accomplishment of the Second Continental Congress?

Critical Thinking

21. **Making Generalizations** Describe inductive reasoning and give an example of finding scientific truth by using inductive principles.

22. **Summarizing** Explain how separation of powers works in the American government today and give specific examples.

Chapter Summary

As the Scientific Revolution and the ideas of the Enlightenment spread across Europe, innovations based on science and reason came into conflict with traditional beliefs, as shown in the chart below.

Innovation	Conflict or Reaction
Copernicus theorizes that Earth revolves around the Sun.	The Church teaches that Earth is the center of the universe.
Vesalius makes discoveries in anatomy.	French lawmakers consider dissecting human bodies illegal.
Boyle discovers that air is not a basic element.	Alchemists believe that all matter is made from four elements: earth, water, fire, and air.
Philosophes believe that the universe is structured, orderly, and governed by systematic laws.	Rousseau criticizes the emphasis on reason and promotes acting upon instinct.
Deism, a new religious concept based on reason and natural law, emerges.	Traditional views of established, organized religions are widespread.
Diderot publishes new scientific theories in the *Encyclopedia*.	The Catholic Church bans the *Encyclopedia,* and its editor is sent to prison.
Enlightened rulers implement political and humanitarian reforms.	Powerful nobles and church leaders fear losing power and reject most political reforms.

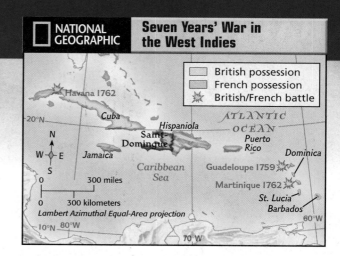

NATIONAL GEOGRAPHIC

Seven Years' War in the West Indies

British possession
French possession
British/French battle

Havana 1762
Cuba
Hispaniola
Saint-Domingue
Jamaica
Puerto Rico
Dominica
Guadeloupe 1759
Martinique 1762
St. Lucia
Barbados
Caribbean Sea
ATLANTIC OCEAN

300 miles
300 kilometers
Lambert Azimuthal Equal-Area projection

Writing About History

23. **Expository Writing** Analyze how the ideas of John Locke, Montesquieu, Rousseau, and Voltaire influenced the development of the United States Constitution. Which thinker(s) had the most impact on the writers of the Constitution? Why has the Constitution remained so strong while so many reform efforts of the eighteenth century failed?

Analyzing Sources

Read the following quote from John Locke's *Essay Concerning Human Understanding:*

❝Let us then suppose the mind to be, as we say, white paper, void of all characters, without any ideas. How comes it to be furnished? Whence has it all the materials of reason and knowledge? To this I answer, in one word, from experience. . . . Our observation, employed either about external sensible objects or about the internal operations of our minds perceived and reflected on by ourselves, is that which supplies our understanding with all the materials of thinking.❞

24. According to Locke, how did the blank mind become knowledgeable?

25. How did one gain the experience necessary to nurture the mind?

Applying Technology Skills

26. **Creating a Database** Search the Internet for information about the great thinkers of the Enlightenment. Use a word processor to organize your research into a chart. Include headings such as name of philosopher, country, and ideas. Write a paragraph explaining which philosopher you believe had the greatest impact on modern civilization. Support your selection with facts and examples.

Making Decisions

27. As the reigns of Joseph II and Catherine the Great illustrate, it was very difficult to put the ideas of the Enlightenment into practice. Imagine that you are an enlightened monarch who wants to reform your country. What reforms will you initiate? Which thinker will most influence your reform plans? What problems might you encounter?

Analyzing Maps and Charts

28. What are the two largest islands in the Caribbean?

29. Name the battles fought in the West Indies during the Seven Years' War.

30. What is the approximate distance from Havana to Martinique?

The Princeton Review

TAKS Test Practice

Directions: Use the time line *and* your knowledge of world history to answer the following question.

Selected Milestones in Political Thought

1762 *The Social Contract* describes Rousseau's belief that governments should reflect the people's general will

1760 1765 1770 1775 1780 1785 1790 1795

1776 The Declaration of Independence asserts the right to overthrow an unjust king

1792 Mary Wollstonecraft argues for equal rights for women

Which one of the following statements is supported by the information on the time line?

A Most Europeans supported their monarchs completely.

B Many people questioned the nature of their governments.

C There were few political problems in the 1750s.

D Only men thought and wrote about politics.

Test-Taking Tip: With a time line question, you may need to make an inference. Look for clues in the test question and time line. In this case, think about what the events on the time line have in common. These clues can help you make an inference that is supported by the time line.

CHAPTER 18

The French Revolution and Napoleon

1789–1815

Key Events

As you read this chapter, look for the key events of the French Revolution and French Empire.
• The fall of the Bastille marked the beginning of the French Revolution.
• The Committee of Public Safety began the Reign of Terror.
• Napoleon Bonaparte created the French Empire.
• Allied forces defeated Napoleon at Waterloo.

The Impact Today

The events that occurred during this time period still impact our lives today.
• The French Revolution became the model for revolution in the modern world.
• The power of nationalism was first experienced during the French Revolution, and it is still powerful in existing nations and emerging nations today.
• The French Revolution spread the principles of liberty and equality, which are held dear by many nations and individuals today.

 World History Video The Chapter 18 video, "Napoleon," chronicles the rise and fall of Napoleon Bonaparte.

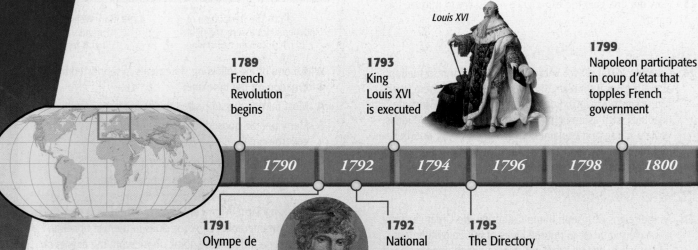

Louis XVI

1789
French Revolution begins

1793
King Louis XVI is executed

1799
Napoleon participates in coup d'état that topples French government

1790   1792   1794   1796   1798   1800

1791
Olympe de Gouges writes declaration of rights for women

Olympe de Gouges

1792
National Convention establishes French Republic

1795
The Directory is formed

Napoleon Crossing the Great St. Bernard by Jacques-Louis David David was the leading artist of the French Revolution.

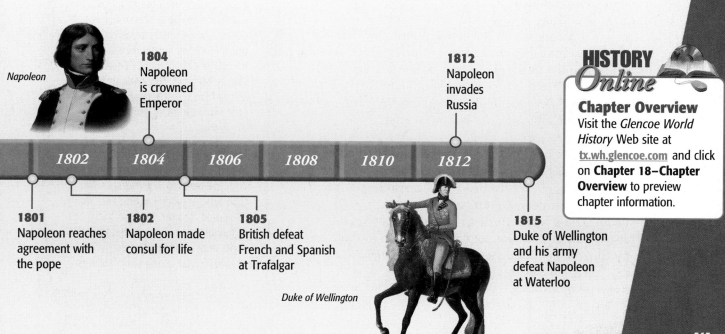

Napoleon

1804
Napoleon
is crowned
Emperor

1812
Napoleon
invades
Russia

1802   *1804*   *1806*   *1808*   *1810*   *1812*

1801
Napoleon reaches
agreement with
the pope

1802
Napoleon made
consul for life

1805
British defeat
French and Spanish
at Trafalgar

Duke of Wellington

1815
Duke of Wellington
and his army
defeat Napoleon
at Waterloo

HISTORY
Online

Chapter Overview
Visit the *Glencoe World
History* Web site at
tx.wh.glencoe.com and click
on **Chapter 18–Chapter
Overview** to preview
chapter information.

A Story That Matters

The storming of the Bastille

Fall of the Bastille

On the morning of July 14, 1789, a Parisian mob of some eight thousand men and women in search of weapons streamed toward the Bastille, a royal armory filled with arms and ammunition. The Bastille was also a state prison. Although it contained only seven prisoners at the time, in the eyes of those angry Parisians it was a glaring symbol of the government's harsh policies. The armory was defended by the Marquis de Launay and a small garrison of 114 men.

The assault began at one o'clock in the afternoon when a group of attackers managed to lower two drawbridges over the moat surrounding the fortress. The mob was joined by members of the French Guard, who began to bombard the fortress with cannon balls. After four hours of fighting, 98 attackers lay dead or dying. Only one defender had been killed.

As more attackers arrived, de Launay realized that he and his troops could not hold out much longer and surrendered. Angered by the loss of its members, the victorious mob beat de Launay to death, cut off his head, and carried it aloft in triumph through the streets of Paris.

When King Louis XVI returned to his palace at Versailles after a day of hunting, he was told about the fall of the Bastille by the duc de La Rochefoucauld-Liancourt. Louis exclaimed, "Why, this is a revolt." "No, Sire," replied the duke, "It is a revolution."

Why It Matters

The French Revolution began a new age in European political life. The old political order in France was destroyed. The new order was based on individual rights, representative institutions, and loyalty to the nation rather than the monarch. The revolutionary upheaval of the era, especially in France, created new political ideals, summarized in the French slogan, "Liberty, Equality, and Fraternity." These ideals transformed France, then spread to other European countries and the rest of the world.

History and You Using print or Internet sources, familiarize yourself with the lyrics to *The Marseillaise, God Save the Queen,* and *The Star Spangled Banner.* How do they vary in subject matter, tone, theme, and style, and how are they similar? Create a chart listing your findings.

The French Revolution Begins

Guide to Reading

Main Ideas
- Social inequality and economic problems contributed to the French Revolution.
- Radicals, Catholic priests, nobles, and the lower classes opposed the new order.

Key Terms
estate, relics of feudalism, bourgeoisie, *sans-culottes*

People to Identify
Louis XVI, Olympe de Gouges

Places to Locate
Versailles, Paris, Austria, Prussia

Preview Questions
1. How was the population of France divided into three estates?
2. How did the fall of the Bastille save the National Assembly?

Reading Strategy
Cause and Effect As you read this section, use a web diagram like the one below to list the factors that contributed to the French Revolution.

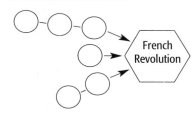

Preview of Events

♦1780	♦1790	♦1800

1787
Bad harvests lead to food shortages

1789
National Assembly adopts Declaration of the Rights of Man

1791
National Assembly completes new constitution

Voices from the Past

A correspondent with the London *Times* sent this report to his newspaper editor on July 20, 1789:

❝The number of armed men in Paris is supposed to amount to 300,000 men, and they called themselves the Militia. The way by which so many people have procured arms is, that all the public storehouses where weapons were lodged, have been broken open, as well as several private houses plundered, which they thought contained them. The Archbishop of Paris is among the number of those who have been sacrificed to the people's rage. He was assassinated at Versailles on Tuesday night. The city of Paris is entirely surrounded with a guard, and not a soul suffered to go out who has an appearance of wealth.❞

—*History in the First Person*, Louis L. Snyder and Richard B. Morris, eds., 1951

The correspondent may not have realized the full significance of the events he reported, but the French Revolution had begun.

Conquerors of the Bastille

Background to the Revolution

The year 1789 witnessed two far-reaching events: the beginning of a new United States of America and the beginning of the French Revolution. Compared with the American Revolution, the French Revolution was more complex, more violent, and far more radical. It tried to create both a new political order and a new social order. Indeed, it has often been seen as a major turning point in European political and social history.

The causes of the French Revolution include both long-range problems and immediate forces. The long-range causes are to be found in the condition of French society. Before the revolution, French society was based on inequality. France's population of 27 million was divided, as it had been since the Middle Ages, into three orders, or estates.

The Three Estates The First Estate consisted of the clergy and numbered about 130,000 people. These people owned approximately 10 percent of the land. They were exempt from the *taille* (TAH•yuh), France's chief tax. The clergy were radically divided. The higher clergy, members of aristocratic families, shared the interests of the nobility. The parish priests were often poor and from the class of commoners.

The Second Estate, the nobility, included about 350,000 people. Nobles owned about 25 to 30 percent of the land. They played an important, and even a crucial, role in French society in the eighteenth century. They held many of the leading positions in the government, the military, the law courts, and the higher church offices. Moreover, they possessed many privileges, including tax exemptions. Like the clergy, they were exempt from the *taille*.

The nobles sought to expand their power at the expense of the monarchy. Many nobles said they were defending liberty by resisting the arbitrary actions of the monarchy. They also sought to keep their control over positions in the military, the Church, and the government.

The Third Estate, or the commoners of society, made up the overwhelming majority of the French population. Unlike the First and Second Estates, the Third Estate was divided by vast differences in occupation, level of education, and wealth.

The peasants, who constituted 75 to 80 percent of the total population, were by far the largest segment of the Third Estate. As a group, they owned about 35 to 40 percent of the land. However, landholdings varied from area to area, and over half of the peasants had little or no land on which to survive.

Serfdom no longer existed on any large scale in France, but French peasants still had obligations to their local landlords that they deeply resented. These relics of feudalism, or aristocratic privileges, were obligations that survived from an earlier age. They included the payment of fees for the use of village facilities such as the flour mill, community oven, and winepress, as well as contributions to the clergy.

Another part of the Third Estate consisted of skilled craftspeople, shopkeepers, and other wage earners in the cities. In the eighteenth century, a rise in consumer prices that was greater than the increase in wages left these urban groups with a decline in buying power. The struggle for survival led many of these people to play an important role in the revolution, especially in Paris.

The bourgeoisie (BURZH•WAH•ZEE), or middle class, was another part of the Third Estate. This group included about 8 percent of the population, or 2.3 million people. They owned about 20 to 25 percent of the land. This group included merchants, bankers, and industrialists, as well as professional people—lawyers, holders of public offices, doctors, and writers.

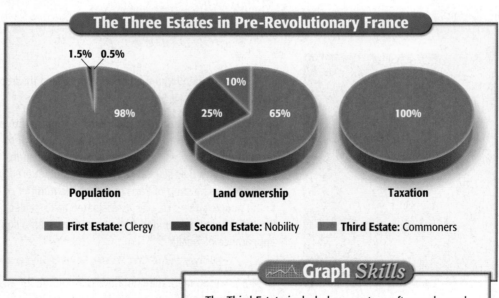

The Three Estates in Pre-Revolutionary France

1.5% 0.5% 98% — Population
10% 25% 65% — Land ownership
100% — Taxation

First Estate: Clergy Second Estate: Nobility Third Estate: Commoners

Graph Skills

The Third Estate included peasants, craftspeople, and the bourgeoisie. In the Third Estate, peasants owned about 40 percent of the land in France, and the bourgeoisie owned about 25 percent.

1. **Drawing Inferences** From looking at these circle graphs, what inferences can you draw about why a revolution occurred in France?

Members of the middle class were unhappy with the privileges held by nobles. At the same time, they shared a great deal with the nobility. Indeed, by obtaining public offices, wealthy middle-class individuals could enter the ranks of the nobility. In the eighteenth century, thousands of new noble families were created.

In addition, both aristocrats and members of the bourgeoisie were drawn to the new political ideas of the Enlightenment. Both groups were increasingly upset with a monarchical system resting on privileges and on an old and rigid social order. The opposition of these elites to the old order ultimately led them to drastic action against the monarchy.

Financial Crisis Social conditions, then, formed a long-range background to the French Revolution. The immediate cause of the revolution was the near collapse of government finances.

The French economy, although it had been expanding for 50 years, suffered periodic crises. Bad harvests in 1787 and 1788 and a slowdown in manufacturing led to food shortages, rising prices for food, and unemployment. The number of poor, estimated by some at almost one-third of the population, reached crisis proportions on the eve of the revolution.

An English traveler noted the misery of the poor in the countryside: "All the country girls and women are without shoes or stockings; and the plowmen at their work have neither shoes nor stockings to their feet. This is a poverty that strikes at the root of national prosperity."

In spite of these economic problems, the French government continued to spend enormous sums on costly wars and court luxuries. The queen, Marie Antoinette, was especially known for her extravagance. The government had also spent large amounts to help the American colonists against Britain.

On the verge of a complete financial collapse, the government of **Louis XVI** was finally forced to call a meeting of the Estates-General to raise new taxes. This was the French parliament, and it had not met since 1614.

✓Reading Check **Identifying** What groups were part of the Third Estate?

From Estates-General to National Assembly

The Estates-General was composed of representatives from the three orders of French society. The First and Second Estates had about three hundred delegates each. The Third Estate had almost six hundred delegates, most of whom were lawyers from French towns. To fix France's financial problems, most members of the Third Estate wanted to set up a constitutional government that would abolish the tax exemptions of the clergy and nobility.

The meeting of the Estates-General opened at **Versailles** on May 5, 1789. It was troubled from the start with a problem about voting. Traditionally, each estate had one vote. That meant that the First and Second Estates together could outvote the Third Estate two to one.

The Third Estate demanded that each deputy have one vote. With the help of a few nobles and clerics, that would give the Third Estate a majority. The king, however, declared he was in favor of the current system, in which each estate had one vote.

The Third Estate reacted quickly. On June 17, 1789, it called itself a National Assembly and decided to draft a constitution. Three days later, on June 20, the deputies of the Third Estate arrived at their meeting place, only to find the doors locked.

The deputies then moved to a nearby indoor tennis court and swore that they would continue to meet

History *through Art*

The Tennis Court Oath by Jacques-Louis David Members of the National Assembly swore that they would produce a French constitution. What caused members to fear that the National Assembly would be dissolved by force?

until they had produced a French constitution. The oath they swore is known as the **Tennis Court Oath.**

Louis XVI prepared to use force against the Third Estate. The common people, however, saved the Third Estate from the king's forces. On July 14, a mob of Parisians stormed the Bastille (ba•STEEL), an armory and prison in **Paris,** and dismantled it, brick by brick. Paris was abandoned to the rebels.

Louis XVI was soon informed that he could no longer trust the royal troops. Royal authority had collapsed. Louis XVI could enforce his will no more. The fall of the Bastille had saved the National Assembly.

At the same time, popular revolutions broke out throughout France, both in the cities and in the countryside. A growing hatred of the entire landholding system, with its fees and obligations, led to the popular uprisings.

Peasant rebellions took place throughout France and became part of the Great Fear, a vast panic that spread quickly through France in the summer of 1789. Citizens, fearing invasion by foreign troops that would support the French monarchy, formed militias.

☑ **Reading Check** **Examining** Why did the Third Estate object to each estate's having one vote in the Estates-General?

The Destruction of the Old Regime

The peasant revolts and fear of foreign troops had a strong effect on the National Assembly, which was meeting in Versailles. One of the assembly's first acts was to destroy the relics of feudalism, or aristocratic privileges. On the night of August 4, 1789, the National Assembly voted to abolish the rights of landlords, as well as the financial privileges of nobles and clergy.

Declaration of the Rights of Man On August 26, the National Assembly adopted the **Declaration of the Rights of Man and the Citizen.** Inspired by the American Declaration of Independence and Constitution, and the English Bill of Rights, this charter of basic liberties began with a ringing affirmation of "the natural and imprescriptible rights of man" to "liberty, property, security, and resistance to oppression."

Reflecting Enlightenment thought, the declaration went on to proclaim freedom and equal rights for all men, access to public office based on talent, and an end to exemptions from taxation. All citizens were to have the right to take part in the making of laws. Freedom of speech and the press were affirmed.

The declaration also raised an important issue. Did its ideal of equal rights for all men also include women? Many deputies insisted that it did, provided that, as one said, "women do not hope to exercise political rights and functions."

Olympe de Gouges, a woman who wrote plays and pamphlets, refused to accept this exclusion of women from political rights. Echoing the words of the official declaration, she penned a Declaration of the Rights of Woman and the Female Citizen. In it, she insisted that women should have all the same rights as men.

She wrote:

> ❝Believing that ignorance, omission, or scorn for the rights of woman are the only causes of public misfortunes and of the corruption of governments, the women have resolved to set forth in a solemn declaration the natural, inalienable, and sacred rights of woman in order that this declaration, constantly exposed before all the members of the society, will ceaselessly remind them of their rights and duties.❞

The National Assembly ignored her demands. 📖 *(See page 995 to read excerpts from Olympe de Gouges's* Declaration of the Rights of Woman and the Female Citizen *in the Primary Sources Library.)*

The King Concedes In the meantime, Louis XVI had remained at Versailles. He refused to accept the National Assembly's decrees on the abolition of feudalism and the Declaration of Rights. On October 5, however, thousands of Parisian women—described by one eyewitness as "detachments of women coming up from every direction, armed with broomsticks, lances, pitchforks, swords, pistols and muskets"—marched to Versailles. A delegation of the women met with Louis XVI and described how their children were starving from a lack of bread. They forced the king to accept the new decrees.

The crowd now insisted that the royal family return to Paris to show the king's support of the National Assembly. On October 6, the family journeyed to Paris. As a goodwill gesture, Louis XVI brought along wagonloads of flour from the palace

CONNECTIONS Around The World

A National Holiday

The French Revolution gave rise to the concept of the modern nation-state. With the development of the modern state came the celebration of one day a year as a national holiday—usually called Independence Day. The national holiday is a day that has special significance in the history of the nation-state.

In France, the fall of the Bastille on July 14, 1789, has been celebrated ever since as the beginning of the French nation-state. Independence Day in the United States is celebrated on July 4. On July 4, 1776, the Second Continental Congress approved the Declaration of Independence.

In Norway, people celebrate Constitution Day as a national holiday on May 17. On that day in 1814, Norway received a constitution, although it did not gain its independence from Sweden until 1905.

Most Latin American countries became independent of Spain or Portugal in the early nineteenth century. Mexico, for example, celebrates its Independence Day on September 16 with a colorful festival. On September 16, 1810, a crowd of local people attacked Spanish authorities in a small village north of Mexico City. They

were crushed, but their action eventually led to Mexico's independence from Spanish control in 1821.

Most nations in Africa and Asia gained their independence from Western colonial powers after World War II. India celebrates Independence Day on August 15. On that day in 1947, India won its independence from the British Empire.

Bastille Day parade ▶

Comparing Cultures

Every nation celebrates its Independence Day with different kinds of festivities. For example, in the United States, many people have barbecues and watch firework displays. Choose two other nations and research how each nation and its people celebrate their Independence Day. Create an illustrated poster or chart showing your results.

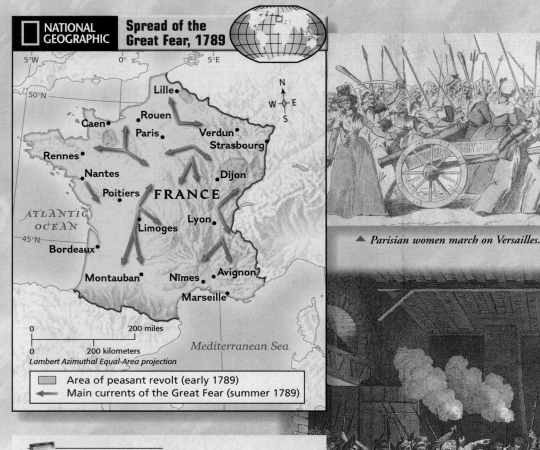

NATIONAL GEOGRAPHIC

Spread of the Great Fear, 1789

FRANCE

Lille
Rouen
Caen
Paris
Verdun
Strasbourg
Rennes
Nantes
Dijon
Poitiers
ATLANTIC OCEAN
Limoges
Lyon
Bordeaux
Montauban
Nîmes
Avignon
Marseille

Mediterranean Sea

0   200 miles
0   200 kilometers
Lambert Azimuthal Equal-Area projection

    Area of peasant revolt (early 1789)
⟵ Main currents of the Great Fear (summer 1789)

▲ *Parisian women march on Versailles.*

▲ *Louis XVI is arrested at Varennes.*

Picturing History

Louis XVI remained at Versailles during the great panic that swept through France in the summer of 1789. On October 5, 1789, thousands of women marched to Versailles and persuaded Louis to return to Paris with his family. Louis later tried to escape from France in 1791 but was captured at Varennes and returned to Paris. **What happened to the royal family after their capture?**

stores. The royal family and the supplies were escorted by women armed with pikes. The women sang, "We are bringing back the baker, the baker's wife, and the baker's boy" (the king; Marie Antoinette, the queen; and their son). The king and his family became virtual prisoners in Paris.

Church Reforms Because the Catholic Church was seen as an important pillar of the old order, it, too, was subject to change. Because of the need for money, the National Assembly seized and sold the lands of the Church.

The Church was also secularized. A new Civil Constitution of the Clergy was put into effect. Both bishops and priests were to be elected by the people

and paid by the state. The French government now controlled the Church. Many Catholics became enemies of the revolution.

A New Constitution and New Fears The National Assembly completed a new constitution, the Constitution of 1791, which set up a limited monarchy. According to the constitution, there would still be a king, but a Legislative Assembly would make the laws.

The Assembly was to consist of 745 representatives. The way they were to be chosen ensured that only the more affluent members of society would be elected. Though all male citizens had the same rights, only men over 25 who paid a specified amount in taxes could vote.

By 1791, the old order had been destroyed. However, many people—including Catholic priests, nobles, lower classes hurt by a rise in the cost of living, and radicals who wanted more drastic solutions—opposed the new order. Louis XVI also made things difficult for the new government. He attempted to flee France in June 1791. He almost succeeded but was recognized, captured, and brought back to Paris.

In this unsettled situation, with a seemingly disloyal monarch, the new Legislative Assembly held its first session in October 1791. France's relations with the rest of Europe would soon lead to the downfall of Louis XVI.

War with Austria Over time, some European leaders began to fear that revolution would spread to their countries. The rulers of **Austria** and **Prussia** even threatened to use force to restore Louis XVI to full power. Insulted by this threat, the Legislative Assembly declared war on Austria in the spring of 1792.

The French fared badly in the initial fighting. A frantic search for scapegoats began. One observer noted, "Everywhere you hear the cry that the king is betraying us, the generals are betraying us, that nobody is to be trusted; . . . that Paris will be taken in six weeks by the Austrians . . . we are on a volcano ready to spout flames."

Rise of the Paris Commune Defeats in war, coupled with economic shortages at home in the spring of 1792, led to new political demonstrations, especially against Louis XVI. In August, radical political groups in Paris, declaring themselves a commune, organized a mob attack on the royal palace and Legislative Assembly.

Members of the new Paris Commune took the king captive. They forced the Legislative Assembly to suspend the monarchy and call for a National Convention, chosen on the basis of universal male suffrage, to decide on the nation's future form of government. (Under a system of universal male suffrage, all adult males had the right to vote.)

The French Revolution was about to enter a more radical and violent stage. Power now passed from the Assembly to the Paris Commune. Many of its members proudly called themselves the *sans-culottes*, ordinary patriots without fine clothes. (They wore long trousers instead of knee-length breeches; *sans-culottes* means "without breeches.") It has become customary to equate the more radical *sans-culottes* with working people or the poor. However, many were small traders and better-off artisans who were the elite of their neighborhoods.

Parisian sans-culottes

✓ **Reading Check** **Evaluating** What was the significance of the Constitution of 1791?

🤠 **TAKS Practice**

SECTION 1 ASSESSMENT

Checking for Understanding

1. **Define** estate, relics of feudalism, bourgeoisie, *sans-culottes*.

2. **Identify** Louis XVI, Tennis Court Oath, Declaration of the Rights of Man and the Citizen, Olympe de Gouges.

3. **Locate** Versailles, Paris, Austria, Prussia.

4. **Explain** why the Catholic Church was targeted for reform.

5. **List** the reasons for the near collapse of government finances in France.

Critical Thinking

6. **Summarize** What were the main affirmations of the Declaration of the Rights of Man and the Citizen?

7. **Organizing Information** Equality was one of the slogans of the French Revolution. In a web diagram, identify five occasions when different groups expressed concern for equality during the revolution.

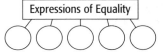

Analyzing Visuals

8. **Examine** the painting of the Tennis Court Oath shown on page 550. How does David's painting reflect the ideals of the French Revolution?

Writing About History

9. **Persuasive Writing** Olympe de Gouges wrote, "ignorance, omission, or scorn for the rights of woman are the only causes of public misfortune and corruption of governments." Do you agree or disagree? Write a paragraph supporting your point of view.

Declaration of the Rights of Man and the Citizen

ONE OF THE MOST IMPORTANT DOCUMENTS of the French Revolution, the Declaration of the Rights of Man and the Citizen, was adopted in August 1789 by the National Assembly.

❝The representatives of the French people, organized as a national assembly, considering that ignorance, neglect, and scorn of the rights of man are the sole causes of public misfortunes and of corruption of governments, have resolved to display in a solemn declaration the natural, inalienable, and sacred rights of man, so that this declaration, constantly in the presence of all members of society, will continually remind them of their rights and their duties . . . Consequently, the National Assembly recognizes and declares, in the presence and under the auspices of the Supreme Being, the following rights of man and citizen:

1. Men are born and remain free and equal in rights; social distinctions can be established only for the common benefit.

2. The aim of every political association is the conservation of the natural . . . rights of man; these rights are liberty, property, security, and resistance to oppression. . . .

4. Liberty consists in being able to do anything that does not harm another person. . . .

6. The law is the expression of the general will; all citizens have the right to concur personally or through their representatives in its formation; it must be the same for all, whether it protects or punishes.

7. No man can be accused, arrested, or detained except in cases determined by the law, and according to the forms which it has prescribed. . . .

10. No one may be disturbed because of his opinions, even religious, provided that their public demonstration does not disturb the public order established by law.

Painting of the declaration

11. The free communication of thoughts and opinions is one of the most precious rights of man: every citizen can therefore freely speak, write, and print . . .

16. Any society in which guarantees of rights are not assured nor the separation of powers determined has no constitution.❞

—Declaration of the Rights of Man and the Citizen

Analyzing Primary Sources

1. According to this document, what are the natural, inalienable rights of man?

2. According to this document, can a person be arrested or otherwise "disturbed" because of his religious beliefs?

3. How do the rights listed in number 2 of the document compare to the rights listed in the U.S. Bill of Rights?

Radical Revolution and Reaction

Guide to Reading

Main Ideas
- Radical groups and leaders controlled the Revolution.
- The new French Republic faced enemies at home and abroad.

Key Terms
faction, elector, coup d'état

People to Identify
Georges Danton, Jean-Paul Marat, Jacobins, Maximilien Robespierre

Places to Locate
Lyon, Nantes, Austrian Netherlands

Preview Questions
1. Why did a coalition of European countries take up arms against France?
2. Why did the Reign of Terror occur?

Reading Strategy
Summarizing Information As you read the section, list in a table like the one shown below the actions taken by the National Convention.

Actions taken by the National Convention
1.
2.
3.
4.

Preview of Events

♦1792	♦1793	♦1794	♦1795
1792 National Convention splits into factions	**1793** King Louis XVI is executed	**1794** Reign of Terror ends	**1795** New constitution is created

King Louis XVI

Voices from the Past

Henry de Firmont reported on the major event of January 21, 1793:

❝The path leading to the scaffold was extremely rough and difficult to pass; the King was obliged to lean on my arm, and from the slowness with which he proceeded, I feared for a moment that his courage might fail; but what was my astonishment, when arrived at the last step, he suddenly let go of my arm, and I saw him cross with a firm foot the breadth of the whole scaffold; and in a loud voice, I heard him pronounce distinctly these words: 'I die innocent of all the crimes laid to my charge; I pardon those who had occasioned my death; and I pray to God that the blood you are going to shed may never be visited on France.'❞

—*Eyewitness to History*, John Carey, ed., 1987

The execution of King Louis XVI in 1793 pushed the French Revolution into a new radical stage.

The Move to Radicalism

The Paris Commune had forced the Legislative Assembly to call a National Convention. Before the Convention met, the Paris Commune dominated the political scene. Led by the newly appointed minister of justice, **Georges Danton,** the *sans-culottes* sought revenge on those who had aided the king and resisted the popular will. Thousands of people were arrested and then massacred. New leaders of the people emerged, including **Jean-Paul Marat,** who published a radical journal called *Friend of the People.*

The Fate of the King
In September 1792, the newly elected National Convention began its sessions. Although it had been called to draft a new constitution, it also acted as the sovereign ruling body of France.

The Convention was dominated by lawyers, professionals, and property owners. Two-thirds of its deputies were under the age of 45. Almost all had had political experience as a result of the revolution. Almost all distrusted the king. It was therefore no surprise that the National Convention's first major step on September 21 was to abolish the monarchy and establish a republic, the French Republic.

That, however, was as far as members of the convention could agree. They soon split into factions (dissenting groups) over the fate of the king. The two most important factions were the Girondins (juh•RAHN•duhns) and the Mountain. Both factions were members of the **Jacobin** (JA•kuh•buhn) club, a large network of political groups throughout France. The Girondins represented the provinces, areas outside the cities. Girondins feared the radical mobs in Paris and leaned toward keeping the king alive. The Mountain represented the interests of radicals in the city of Paris.

The Mountain won at the beginning of 1793 when it convinced the National Convention to pass a decree condemning Louis XVI to death. On January 21, 1793, the king was beheaded on the guillotine. Revolutionaries had adopted this machine because it killed quickly and, they believed, humanely. The execution of the king created new enemies for the revolution, both at home and abroad. A new crisis was at hand.

Crises and Response
Disputes between Girondins and the Mountain were only one aspect of France's domestic crisis in 1792 and 1793. Within Paris, the local government—the Commune—favored radical change and put constant pressure on the National Convention to adopt ever more radical positions. Moreover, the National Convention itself still did not rule all of France. Peasants in western France as well as inhabitants of France's major provincial cities refused to accept the authority of the National Convention.

People In History

Jean-Paul Marat
1743–1793
French revolutionary

Jean-Paul Marat was a popular revolutionary leader in Paris at the beginning of the radical stage of the French Revolution. Born in Switzerland, he practiced medicine in London before returning to France in 1777. Marat was an intense man, always in a hurry: "I allot only two of the twenty-four hours to sleep. I have not had fifteen minutes play in over three years." He often worked in the bathtub because the water soothed the pain of a severe skin disorder.

In his journal, *Friend of the People,* Marat expressed his ideas, which were radical for his time. He called for mob violence and the right of the poor to take by force whatever they needed from the rich. He helped make the Jacobins more radical, especially by condemning the Girondins. This also led to his death: Charlotte Corday, a Girondin, stabbed him to death in his bathtub.

Maximilien Robespierre
1758–1794
French revolutionary

Robespierre was one of the most important French revolutionary leaders. He received a law degree and later became a member of the National Convention, where he preached democracy and advocated suffrage (the right to vote) for all adult males. He lived simply and was known to be extremely honest. In fact, he was often known as "The Incorruptible." A believer in Rousseau's social contract idea, Robespierre thought that anyone opposed to being governed by the general will, as he interpreted it, should be executed.

One observer said of Robespierre, "That man will go far; he believes all that he says." Robespierre himself said, "How can one reproach a man who has truth on his side?" His eagerness and passion in pursuing the Reign of Terror frightened many people. Eventually, he was arrested and guillotined.

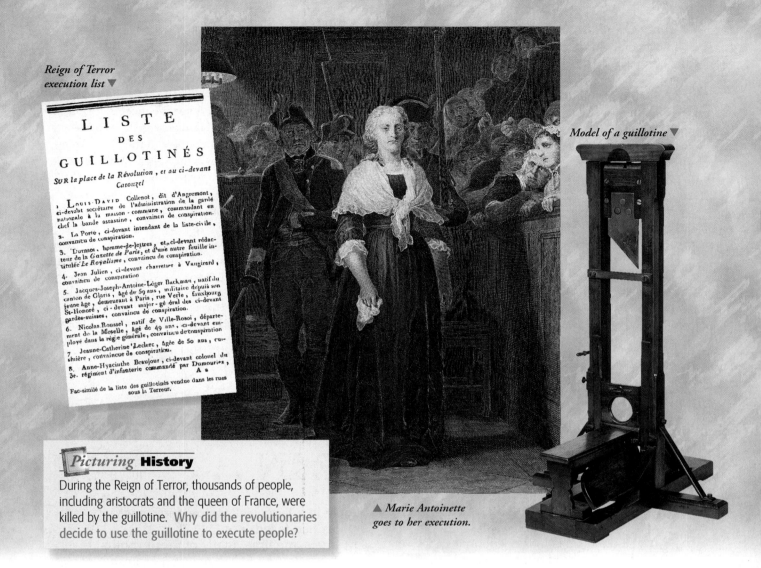

Reign of Terror execution list ▼

LISTE DES GUILLOTINÉS

SUR la place de la Révolution, et au ci-devant Carouzel

Model of a guillotine ▼

Picturing History

During the Reign of Terror, thousands of people, including aristocrats and the queen of France, were killed by the guillotine. **Why did the revolutionaries decide to use the guillotine to execute people?**

▲ *Marie Antoinette goes to her execution.*

A foreign crisis also loomed large. The execution of Louis XVI had outraged the royalty of most of Europe. An informal coalition of Austria, Prussia, Spain, Portugal, Britain, and the Dutch Republic took up arms against France. The French armies began to fall back.

By late spring of 1793, the coalition was poised for an invasion of France. If successful, both the revolution and the revolutionaries would be destroyed, and the old regime would be reestablished. The revolution had reached a decisive moment.

To meet these crises, the National Convention gave broad powers to a special committee of 12 known as the **Committee of Public Safety.** It was dominated at first by Georges Danton, then by **Maximilien Robespierre.**

✓ **Reading Check** **Examining** What were the differences between the Girondins and the Mountain?

The Reign of Terror

For roughly a year during 1793 and 1794, the Committee of Public Safety took control. The Committee acted to defend France from foreign and domestic threats.

To meet the crisis at home, the National Convention and the Committee of Public Safety set in motion an effort that came to be known as the **Reign of Terror.** Revolutionary courts were set up to prosecute internal enemies of the revolutionary republic. During the course of the Reign of Terror, close to 40,000 people were killed. Of those, 16,000 people, including Marie Antoinette and Olympe de Gouges, died under the blade of the guillotine. Peasants and persons who had opposed the *sans-culottes* were among the victims. Most executions were held in places that had openly rebelled against the authority of the National Convention.

Crushing Rebellion Revolutionary armies were set up to bring rebellious cities back under the control of the National Convention. The Committee of Public Safety decided to make an example of **Lyon.** Some 1,880 citizens of that city were executed. When guillotining proved too slow, grapeshot (a cluster of small iron balls) was used to shoot the condemned into open graves. A German observer noted the terror of the scene:

> 66Whole ranges of houses, always the most handsome, burnt. The churches, convents, and all the dwellings of the former patricians were in ruins. When I came to the guillotine, the blood of those who had been executed a few hours beforehand was still running in the street . . . I said to a group of *sans-culottes* that it would be decent to clear away all this human blood. Why should it be cleared? one of them said to me. It's the blood of aristocrats and rebels. The dogs should lick it up.99

In western France, too, revolutionary armies were brutal in defeating rebel armies. The commander of the revolutionary army ordered that no mercy be given: "The road is strewn with corpses. Women, priests, monks, children, all have been put to death. I have spared nobody." Perhaps the most notorious act of violence occurred in **Nantes,** where victims were executed by being sunk in barges in the Loire River.

People from all classes were killed during the Terror. Clergy and nobles made up about 15 percent of the victims, while the rest were from the bourgeoisie and peasant classes. The Committee of Public Safety held that all this bloodletting was only temporary. Once the war and domestic crisis were over, the true "Republic of Virtue" would follow, and the Declaration of the Rights of Man and the Citizen would be fully realized.

The Republic of Virtue Along with the terror, the Committee of Public Safety took other steps both to control France and to create a new order, called by

THE WAY IT WAS

YOUNG PEOPLE IN . . .

Revolutionary France

In 1794, deputies in the National Convention proposed a new military school that would train several thousand young males aged 16 and 17 in the arts of war and the love of country. A few months later, the *École de Mars*, or School of Mars (the Roman god of war), opened on the outskirts of Paris.

Much was expected of the 3,400 young recruits. They were expected to maintain high moral standards and become enthusiastic patriots. Students, however, ignored discipline and expressed the desire to return home. After the death of Robespierre, authorities shut the school down. The plan to train young people in a few weeks to be dedicated patriots had failed.

At the same time, many of these youths now became part of the reaction against the Reign of Terror. They formed what were called "golden youth," gangs of young men who attacked Jacobins and destroyed public statues of revolutionary figures, such as Jean-Paul Marat.

For many young people who had shared in the revolutionary enthusiasm, however,

Young Men Off to Practice Using the Cannon, *c. 1789*

Robespierre the Republic of Virtue—a democratic republic composed of good citizens. In the new French Republic, the titles "citizen" and "citizeness" had replaced "mister" and "madame." Women wore long dresses inspired by the clothing worn in the great republic of ancient Rome.

By spring 1793, the Committee was sending "representatives on mission" as agents of the central government to all parts of France to implement laws dealing with the wartime emergency. A law aimed at primary education for all was passed but not widely implemented. Slavery was abolished in France's colonies.

The committee also attempted to provide some economic controls by establishing price limits on goods considered necessities, ranging from food and drink to fuel and clothing. The controls failed to work very well, since the government lacked the machinery to enforce them.

In 1789, it had been a group of women who convinced Louis XVI to return to Paris from Versailles. Women remained actively involved in the revolution, even during its more radical stage. Women observed sessions of the National Convention and made their demands known to those in charge. In 1793, two women founded the Society for Revolutionary Republican Women. This Parisian group, which was mainly composed of working-class women, stood ready to defend the new French Republic. Many men, however, continued to believe that women should not participate in political or military affairs.

In its attempts to create a new order that reflected its belief in reason, the National Convention pursued a policy of dechristianization. The word *saint* was removed from street names, churches were pillaged and closed by revolutionary armies, and priests were encouraged to marry. In Paris, the cathedral of Notre Dame was designated a "temple of reason." In

the reaction against the Reign of Terror was a disaster. One good example is Marc-Antoine Jullien. At 18, he had been an assistant to Robespierre. After the execution of Robespierre, he was hunted down and put in prison for two years.

While in prison, Jullien wrote a diary expressing the hardships of a young revolutionary who had grown old before his time. He wrote: "I was born in a volcano, I lived in the midst of its eruption. I will be buried in its lava." He expressed his pain: "My life is a dark and terrible story, but one that is touching and educational for inexperienced youth."

When Jullien was released from prison, he wrote, "I am leaving, I never wish to see Paris again, I want cows and milk. I am twenty-one years old, may the dawn of my life no longer be clouded by dark images."

Disillusioned by his troubles, Jullien came to long for a savior who would restore the freedom of the republic. When Napoleon came along, he believed that he had found his savior.

Closing of the Salle des Jacobins in Paris, symbolizing the end of the Reign of Terror

CONNECTING TO THE PAST

1. **Examine** Why did the National Convention choose to open a school dedicated to training patriots? Are there comparable schools in the United States today?

2. **Writing about History** Marc-Antoine Jullien lived during troubled times. In the world today, many young people are undergoing similar experiences. Research an area of political unrest. Write a one-page paper describing the effect of that unrest on a person your age.

November 1793, a public ceremony dedicated to the worship of reason was held in the former cathedral. Patriotic maidens in white dresses paraded before a temple of reason where the high altar had once stood.

Another example of dechristianization was the adoption of a new calendar. Years would no longer be numbered from the birth of Christ but from September 22, 1792—the first day of the French Republic. The calendar contained 12 months. Each month consisted of three 10-day weeks, with the tenth day of each week a day of rest. This eliminated Sundays and Sunday worship services, as well as church holidays.

The anti-Christian purpose of the calendar was reinforced in the naming of the months of the year. The months were given names that were supposed to invoke the seasons, the temperature, or the state of the vegetation (for example, the month of *Vendémiaire,* or "seed time"). As Robespierre came to realize, however, dechristianization failed to work because France was still overwhelmingly Catholic.

✓ Reading Check **Identifying** Whom did the Committee of Public Safety consider to be enemies of the state?

A Nation in Arms

⌐TURNING POINT⌐ **As you will learn, the French Republic created a new kind of army that would ultimately change the nature of modern warfare.**

As you read earlier, France was threatened by external forces during this time. To save the republic from its foreign enemies, the Committee of Public Safety decreed a universal mobilization of the nation on August 23, 1793:

> ❝Young men will fight, young men are called to conquer. Married men will forge arms, transport military baggage and guns and will prepare food supplies. Women, who at long last are to take their rightful place in the revolution and follow their true destiny, will forget their futile tasks: their delicate hands will work at making clothes for soldiers; they will make tents and they will extend their tender care to shelters where the defenders of the Patrie [homeland] will receive the help that their wounds require. Children will make lint of old cloth. It is for them that we are fighting: children, those beings destined to gather all the fruits of the revolution, will raise their pure hands toward the skies. And old men, performing their missions again, as of yore, will be guided to the public squares of the cities where they will kindle the courage of young warriors and preach the doctrines of hate for kings and the unity of the Republic.❞

In less than a year, the French revolutionary government had raised a huge army. By September 1794, it was over one million. The republic's army was the largest ever seen in European history. It pushed the allies invading France back across the Rhine and even conquered the **Austrian Netherlands.**

The French revolutionary army was an important step in the creation of modern nationalism. Previously, wars had been fought between governments or ruling dynasties by relatively small armies of professional soldiers. The new French army was the creation of a people's government. Its wars were people's wars. When dynastic wars became people's wars, however, warfare became more destructive.

End of the Terror By the summer of 1794, the French had largely defeated their foreign foes. There was less need for the Reign of Terror, but it continued nonetheless. Robespierre, who had become very powerful, was obsessed with ridding France of all its corrupt elements. Only then could the Republic of Virtue follow.

Many deputies in the National Convention who feared Robespierre decided to act. They gathered enough votes to condemn him, and Robespierre was guillotined on July 28, 1794.

After the death of Robespierre, revolutionary fervor began to cool. The Jacobins lost power and more moderate middle-class leaders took control. Much to the relief of many in France, the Reign of Terror came to a halt.

✓ Reading Check **Evaluating** How did the French revolutionary army help to create modern nationalism?

The Directory

With the terror over, the National Convention reduced the power of the Committee of Public Safety. Churches were allowed to reopen for public worship. In addition, a new constitution was created in August 1795 that reflected the desire for more stability.

In an effort to keep any one governmental group from gaining control, the Constitution of 1795 established a national legislative assembly consisting of two chambers: a lower house, known as the Council of 500, which initiated legislation; and an upper house, the Council of Elders, which accepted or rejected the

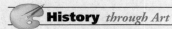
The Eighteenth of Brumaire by Francois Bouchot
This painting depicts Napoleon's coup d'état, November 10, 1799. What factors helped Napoleon (shown center) overthrow the Directory?

proposed laws. The 750 members of the two legislative bodies were chosen by electors (individuals qualified to vote in an election). The electors had to be owners or renters of property worth a certain amount, a requirement that limited their number to 30,000.

From a list presented by the Council of 500, the Council of Elders elected five directors to act as the executive committee, or Directory. The Directory, together with the legislature, ruled. The period of the revolution under the government of the Directory (1795–1799) was an era of corruption and graft. People reacted against the sufferings and sacrifices that had been demanded in the Reign of Terror. Some of them made fortunes in property by taking advantage of the government's severe money problems.

At the same time, the government of the Directory was faced with political enemies. Royalists who desired the restoration of the monarchy, as well as radicals unhappy with the turn toward moderation, plotted against the government. The Directory was unable to find a solution to the country's continuing economic problems. In addition, it was still carrying on wars left from the Committee of Public Safety.

Increasingly, the Directory relied on the military to maintain its power. In 1799, a coup d'état (KOO day•TAH), a sudden overthrow of the government, led by the successful and popular general Napoleon Bonaparte, toppled the Directory. Napoleon seized power.

☑ **Reading Check** **Describing** Describe the government that replaced the National Convention.

🟥 **TAKS Practice**

SECTION 2 ASSESSMENT

Checking for Understanding

1. Define faction, elector, coup d'état.

2. Identify Georges Danton, Jean-Paul Marat, Jacobins, Committee of Public Safety, Maximilien Robespierre, Reign of Terror.

3. Locate Lyon, Nantes, Austrian Netherlands.

4. Explain both the similarities and the differences between the Girondins and the Mountain.

5. List the members of the informal coalition that took up arms against France. What was the result of this conflict?

Critical Thinking

6. Drawing Conclusions Did the French Republic live up to the revolution's ideals of Liberty, Equality, and Fraternity? Write a paragraph in support of your opinion.

7. Contrasting Information Using a table like the one below, contrast the changes in French governmental policy during and after Robespierre's possession of power.

During	After

Analyzing Visuals

8. Examine the painting shown on page 557. Explain whether or not you think this is a realistic depiction of Marie Antoinette before her execution, or whether the artist is promoting a particular version of her death.

Writing About History

9. Expository Writing Propaganda is the spreading of information for the purpose of helping or injuring a cause. How does the decree of universal mobilization quoted on page 560 fit the definition of propaganda? Use examples from the decree to support your argument in an essay.

SOCIAL STUDIES
SKILLBUILDER

Interpreting Graphs

Why Learn This Skill?

Graphs are one method of illustrating dates, facts, and figures. With a graph, you can compare change or differences easily. For example, your parents say you are spending too much money on clothes. You disagree, but they show you a bar graph of your weekly expenses. The bar for each week shows how the money you have spent on clothes is higher than the week before. With a quick glance, you immediately see that they are right. You decide to make a graph of your own to show them how your allowance is not keeping up with inflation.

Learning the Skill

There are basically three types of graphs:

- **Circle graphs** They look like a pizza that has been divided into different size slices. They are useful for showing comparisons and percentages.

- **Bar graphs** Individual bars are drawn for each item being graphed. The length of the bars easily illustrates differences or changes over time.

- **Line graph** Each item is indicated by a point on the graph. The points are then connected by a line. You can tell how values have changed by whether the line is going up or down.

Most graphs also use words to identify or label information. The steps below will help you interpret graphs.

- **Read the title** If the graph is called "Randy's Weekly Clothing Expenses," then it will be plotting Randy's expenses every week.

- **Read the captions and text** In Randy's graph, each bar would be captioned with a weekly date, and the amounts that each bar represents would be clearly marked.

- **Determine the relationships among all sections of the graph** By looking at each bar, you can see the amount spent for that week. By comparing the bars with each other, you can see how Randy's expenses have changed from week to week.

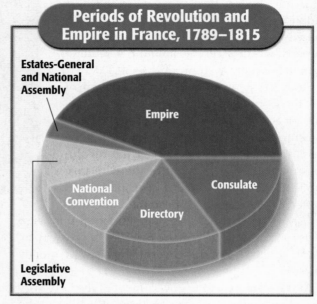

Periods of Revolution and Empire in France, 1789–1815

Estates-General and National Assembly

Empire

Consulate

National Convention

Directory

Legislative Assembly

Practicing the Skill

The circle graph above visually compares the length of time for different periods discussed in this chapter. Study the graph and answer the following:

❶ What was the longest of the six periods of the French Revolution?

❷ What was the shortest of the six periods?

❸ About what percentage of the total time did Napoleon rule France (he ruled during the Consulate and Empire)?

❹ About what percentage of the time did the Directory rule?

Applying the Skill

Pick a recent day and make a list of all of your activities in a 24-hour period. Now create a circle graph that shows the division of the day.

Glencoe's **Skillbuilder Interactive Workbook, Level 2,** provides instruction and practice in key social studies skills.

SECTION 3 | The Age of Napoleon

Guide to Reading

Main Ideas
• Napoleon built and lost an empire.
• Nationalism spread as a result of the French Revolution.
• Napoleon was exiled first to Elba, and then to St. Helena, where he died.

Key Terms
consulate, nationalism

People to Identify
Napoleon Bonaparte, Anne-Louise-Germaine de Staël, Duke of Wellington

Places to Locate
Corsica, Moscow, Elba, Waterloo

Preview Questions
1. Why did Napoleon want to stop British goods from reaching Europe?
2. What were two reasons for the collapse of Napoleon's empire?

Reading Strategy
Summarizing Information In a table like the one below, list the achievements of Napoleon's rule.

Achievements of Napoleon's Rule

Preview of Events

◆1790	◆1800	◆1810	◆1820

1799 Napoleon takes part in coup d'état

1804 Napoleon is crowned emperor

1805 French are defeated at Trafalgar

1815 Napoleon is defeated at Waterloo

Voices from the Past

Napoleon Bonaparte

Napoleon once wrote:

❝But let that impatiently awaited savior give a sudden sign of his existence, and the people's instinct will divine him and call upon him. The obstacles are smoothed before his steps, and a whole great nation, flying to see him pass, will seem to be saying: 'Here is the man.' . . . A consecutive series of great actions never is the result of chance and luck; it always is the product of planning and genius. Great men are rarely known to fail in their most perilous enterprises. . . . Is it because they are lucky that they become great? No, but being great, they have been able to master luck.❞
— *The Mind of Napoleon,* J. Christopher Herold, 1955

Napoleon possessed an overwhelming sense of his own importance. He was convinced that he was the man of destiny who would save the French people.

The Rise of Napoleon

Napoleon Bonaparte dominated French and European history from 1799 to 1815. In a sense, he brought the French Revolution to an end in 1799, but he was also a child of the revolution. The French Revolution made possible his rise first in the military and then to supreme power in France. Indeed, Napoleon once said, "I am the revolution." He never ceased to remind the French that they owed to him the preservation of all that was beneficial in the revolutionary program.

Early Life Napoleon was born in 1769 in **Corsica,** an island in the Mediterranean Sea, only a few months after France had annexed the island. He was the son of a lawyer whose family came from the Florentine nobility. The young Napoleon received a royal scholarship to study at a military school in France.

Napoleon's education in French military schools led to his commission in 1785 as a lieutenant in the French army. He was not well liked by his fellow officers because he was short, spoke with an Italian accent, and had little money.

For the next seven years, Napoleon read the works of the philosophes and educated himself in military matters by studying the campaigns of great military leaders from the past. The revolution and the European war that followed gave him new opportunities to use his knowledge.

Military Successes

Napoleon rose quickly through the ranks of the French army. In 1792, he became a captain. Two years later, at the age of only 24, he was made a brigadier general by the Committee of Public Safety. In 1796, he was made commander of the French armies in Italy, where he used speed, deception, and surprise to win a series of victories.

Throughout his Italian campaigns, Napoleon won the confidence of his men with his energy, charm, and ability to make quick decisions. These qualities, combined with his keen intelligence, ease with words, and supreme confidence in himself, enabled him to influence people and win their firm support.

In 1797, Napoleon returned to France as a conquering hero. He was given command of an army in training to invade Britain. Knowing that the French were not ready for such an invasion, Napoleon proposed instead to strike indirectly at Britain by taking Egypt and threatening India, a major source of British wealth.

The British, however, controlled the seas. By 1799, they had cut off Napoleon's army in Egypt. Seeing certain defeat, Napoleon abandoned his army and returned to Paris.

Consul and Emperor

In Paris, Napoleon took part in the coup d'état that overthrew the government of the Directory. He was only 30 years old at the time. With the coup d'état of 1799, a new government—called the consulate—was proclaimed. Although theoretically it was a republic, in fact Napoleon held absolute power.

As first consul, Napoleon controlled the entire government. He appointed members of the bureaucracy, controlled the army, conducted foreign affairs, and influenced the legislature.

In 1802, Napoleon was made consul for life. Two years later, he crowned himself Emperor Napoleon I.

Reading Check **Describing** What personal qualities did Napoleon possess that gained him popular support?

Picturing **History**

In this painting, Napoleon is shown crowning his wife Josephine empress. During his own coronation, Napoleon seized the crown from Pope Pius VII and placed it on his own head. How had Napoleon earlier made peace with the Catholic Church?

Napoleon's Domestic Policies

Napoleon once claimed that he had preserved the gains of the revolution for the French people. The ideal of republican liberty had, of course, been destroyed by Napoleon's takeover of power. However, were the ideals of the French Revolution maintained in other ways? An examination of his domestic policies will enable us to judge the truth or falsehood of Napoleon's claim.

Peace with the Church One of Napoleon's first moves at home was to establish peace with the oldest enemy of the revolution, the Catholic Church. Napoleon himself had no personal religious faith. He was an eighteenth-century believer in reason who regarded religion at most as a convenience. In Egypt, he called himself a Muslim; in France, a Catholic. However, he saw the need to restore stability to France, and most of the French were Catholic.

In 1801, Napoleon made an agreement with the pope. The agreement recognized Catholicism as the religion of a majority of the French people. In return, the pope agreed not to ask for the return of the church lands seized in the revolution.

With this agreement, the Catholic Church was no longer an enemy of the French government. At the same time, those who had bought church lands during the revolution became avid supporters of the Napoleonic regime.

Codification of the Laws Napoleon's most famous domestic achievement was his codification of the laws. Before the revolution, France did not have a single set of laws but rather had almost 300 different legal systems. During the revolution, efforts were made to prepare a single law code for the entire nation. However, it remained for Napoleon to bring the work to completion in seven codes of law.

The most important of the codes was the **Civil Code,** or Napoleonic Code. This code preserved most of the gains of the revolution by recognizing the principle of the equality of all citizens before the law, the right of the individual to choose a profession, religious toleration, and the abolition of serfdom and feudalism. Property rights continued to be carefully protected, and the interests of employers were safeguarded by outlawing trade unions and strikes.

The rights of some people were strictly curtailed by the Civil Code, however. During the radical phase of the French Revolution, new laws had made divorce an easy process for both husbands and wives and had allowed all children (including daughters)

French marriage ceremony, nineteenth century

to inherit property equally. Napoleon's Civil Code undid these laws.

Divorce was still allowed, but the Civil Code made it more difficult for women to obtain divorces. Women were now "less equal than men" in other ways as well. When they married, their property was brought under the control of their husbands. In lawsuits, they were treated as minors, and their testimony was regarded as less reliable than that of men.

A New Bureaucracy Napoleon also developed a powerful, centralized administrative machine. He worked hard to develop a bureaucracy of capable officials. Early on, the regime showed that it cared little whether the expertise of officials had been gained in royal or revolutionary bureaucracies. Promotion, whether in civil or military offices, was to be based not on rank or birth but on ability only. Opening government careers to individuals based on their ability was one change the middle class had wanted before the revolution.

Napoleon also created a new aristocracy based on merit in the state service. Napoleon created 3,263 nobles between 1808 and 1814. Nearly 60 percent were military officers, while the remainder came from the upper ranks of the civil service and other state and local officials. Socially, only 22 percent of Napoleon's aristocracy came from the nobility of the old regime. Almost 60 percent were middle class in origin.

Preserver of the Revolution? In his domestic policies, then, Napoleon did preserve aspects of the revolution. The Civil Code preserved the equality of all citizens before the law. The concept of opening government careers to more people was another gain of the revolution that he retained.

On the other hand, Napoleon destroyed some revolutionary ideals. Liberty was replaced by a despotism that grew increasingly arbitrary, in spite of protests by such citizens as the prominent writer **Anne-Louise-Germaine de Staël.** Napoleon shut down 60 of France's 73 newspapers. He insisted that all manuscripts be subjected to government scrutiny before they were published. Even the mail was opened by government police.

✓ **Reading Check** **Evaluating** What was the significance of Napoleon's Civil Code?

Napoleon's Empire

Napoleon is, of course, known less for his domestic policies than for his military leadership. His conquests began soon after he rose to power.

Building the Empire When Napoleon became consul in 1799, France was at war with a European

People In History

Anne-Louise-Germaine de Staël

1766–1817—French writer

Anne-Louise-Germaine de Staël was a prominent writer of the revolutionary and Napoleonic eras in France. She established a salon for the powerful that lasted from 1790 until 1804. It was said of her that she was "so spoiled by admiration for her wit that it [would] be hard to make her realize her shortcomings." During the Reign of Terror, she helped friends escape France. She also left France but returned in 1795.

Although she at first supported Napoleon, she clashed repeatedly with him. She once asked him, "Who was the greatest woman of history?" Napoleon responded, "The one who had the most children." Eventually, she denounced Napoleon's rule as tyrannical. Napoleon banned her books in France and exiled her to the German states, where she continued to write.

coalition of Russia, Great Britain, and Austria. Napoleon realized the need for a pause in the war. He remarked that "the French Revolution is not finished so long as the scourge of war lasts. . . . I want peace, as much to settle the present French government, as to save the world from chaos."

Napoleon achieved a peace treaty in 1802, but it did not last long. War was renewed in 1803 with Britain. Gradually, Britain was joined by Austria, Russia, Sweden, and Prussia. In a series of battles at Ulm, Austerlitz, Jena, and Eylau from 1805 to 1807, Napoleon's Grand Army defeated the Austrian, Prussian, and Russian armies. Napoleon now had the opportunity to create a new European order.

From 1807 to 1812, Napoleon was the master of Europe. His Grand Empire was composed of three major parts: the French Empire, dependent states, and allied states.

The French Empire was the inner core of the Grand Empire. It consisted of an enlarged France extending to the Rhine in the east and including the western half of Italy north of Rome.

Dependent states were kingdoms under the rule of Napoleon's relatives. These came to include Spain, Holland, the kingdom of Italy, the Swiss Republic, the Grand Duchy of Warsaw, and the Confederation of the Rhine (a union of all German states except Austria and Prussia).

Allied states were those defeated by Napoleon and forced to join his struggle against Britain. The allied states included Prussia, Austria, Russia, and Sweden.

Spreading the Principles of the Revolution

Within his empire, Napoleon sought to spread some of the principles of the French Revolution, including legal equality, religious toleration, and economic freedom. He explained to his brother Jerome after he had made Jerome king of Westphalia:

❝What the peoples of Germany desire most impatiently is that talented commoners should have the same right to your esteem and to public employments as the nobles, that any trace of serfdom and of an intermediate hierarchy between the sovereign and the lowest class of the people should be completely abolished. The benefits of the Code Napoleon, the publicity of judicial procedure, the creation of juries must be so many distinguishing marks of your monarchy. . . . The peoples of Germany, the peoples of France, of Italy, of Spain all desire equality and liberal ideas. . . . the buzzing of the privileged classes is contrary to the general opinion. Be a constitutional king.❞

Napoleonic Europe, 1799–1815

NATIONAL GEOGRAPHIC

Map legend:
- France, 1799
- French Empire, 1812
- Dependent states, 1812
- States allied with Napoleon, 1812
- States allied against Napoleon, 1812
- ☼ French victory
- ☼ French defeat
- ← Napoleon's invasion of Russia, June–December 1812

0 — 300 miles
0 — 300 kilometers
Lambert Azimuthal Equal-Area projection

Map labels: KINGDOM OF DENMARK AND NORWAY, SWEDEN, North Sea, Baltic Sea, UNITED KINGDOM, PRUSSIA, GRAND DUCHY OF WARSAW, RUSSIAN EMPIRE, Moscow, Borodino 1812, Smolensk, Minsk, Kovno, Neman, Friedland 1807, Kiev, Dnieper R., London, Berlin, Leipzig 1813, Jena 1806, Brussels, Rhine R., CONFEDERATION OF THE RHINE, Dniester R., ATLANTIC OCEAN, Waterloo 1815, Paris, Versailles, Seine R., Danube R., Austerlitz 1805, AUSTRIAN EMPIRE, Ulm 1805, Vienna, Wagram 1809, Black Sea, FRENCH EMPIRE, SWITZ., ILLYRIAN PROVINCES, OTTOMAN EMPIRE, Marengo 1800, KINGDOM OF ITALY, Elba, Corsica, Rome, KINGDOM OF NAPLES, PORTUGAL, Madrid, SPAIN, Sardinia, Sicily, Mediterranean Sea, Trafalgar 1805, Strait of Gibraltar

In the inner core and dependent states of his Grand Empire, Napoleon tried to destroy the old order. The nobility and clergy everywhere in these states lost their special privileges. Napoleon decreed equality of opportunity with offices open to talents, equality before the law, and religious toleration. The spread of French revolutionary principles was an important factor in the development of liberal traditions in these countries.

✓ **Reading Check** **Identifying** What were the three parts of Napoleon's Grand Empire?

The European Response

Like Hitler 130 years later, Napoleon hoped that his Grand Empire would last for centuries. Like Hitler's empire, it collapsed almost as rapidly as it had been

Geography *Skills*

From 1807 to 1812, Napoleon controlled a vast empire in Europe.

1. **Interpreting Maps** Compare the map of Napoleon's Grand Empire to the map of the Roman Empire shown on page 160 of your text. How were these two empires similar, and how were they different? What geographic factors could help to account for these similarities and differences?

2. **Applying Geography Skills** Examine the locations of the states that were allied against Napoleon in 1812. What geographic factors would have helped these states to remain independent from Napoleon's control?

formed. Two major reasons help to explain this: the survival of Great Britain and the force of nationalism.

Britain's Survival Britain's survival was due primarily to its sea power. As long as Britain ruled the waves, it was almost invulnerable to military attack.

Napoleon hoped to invade Britain and even collected ships for the invasion. The British navy's decisive defeat of a combined French-Spanish fleet at Trafalgar in 1805 destroyed any thought of an invasion, however.

Napoleon then turned to his Continental System to defeat Britain. The aim of the Continental System was to stop British goods from reaching the European continent to be sold there. By weakening Britain economically, Napoleon would destroy its ability to wage war.

The Continental System, too, failed. Allied states resented being told by Napoleon that they could not trade with the British. Some began to cheat. Others resisted. Furthermore, new markets in the Middle East and in Latin America gave Britain new outlets for its goods. Indeed, by 1809–1810, British overseas exports were at near-record highs.

Nationalism A second important factor in the defeat of Napoleon was nationalism. Nationalism is the unique cultural identity of a people based on common language, religion, and national symbols. The spirit of French nationalism had made possible the mass armies of the revolutionary and Napoleonic eras. However, Napoleon's spread of the principles of the French Revolution beyond France indirectly brought a spread of nationalism as well.

The French aroused nationalism in two ways. First, they were hated as oppressors. This hatred stirred the patriotism of others in opposition to the French. Second, the French showed the people of Europe what nationalism was and what a nation in arms could do. It was a lesson not lost on other peoples and rulers.

✓ **Reading Check** **Explaining** Why did being a sea power help Britain to survive an attack by the French?

The Fall of Napoleon

The beginning of Napoleon's downfall came in 1812 with his invasion of Russia. Within only a few years, the fall was complete.

Disaster in Russia The Russians had refused to remain in the Continental System, leaving Napoleon with little choice but to invade. He knew the risks in invading such a large country. However, he also knew that if the Russians were allowed to challenge the Continental System unopposed, others would soon follow suit.

In June 1812, a Grand Army of over six hundred thousand men entered Russia. Napoleon's hopes for victory depended on a quick defeat of the Russian armies. The Russian forces, however, refused to give battle. They retreated for hundreds of miles. As they retreated, they burned their own villages and countryside to keep Napoleon's army from finding food. When the Russians did stop to fight at Borodino, Napoleon's forces won an indecisive and costly victory.

When the remaining Grand Army arrived in **Moscow**, they found the city ablaze. Lacking food

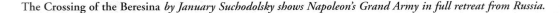

The Crossing of the Beresina by January Suchodolsky shows Napoleon's Grand Army in full retreat from Russia.

The Final Defeat The new king had little support, and Napoleon, bored on the island of Elba, slipped back into France. Troops were sent to capture him. Napoleon opened his coat and addressed them: "Soldiers of the 5th regiment, I am your Emperor. . . . If there is a man among you [who] would kill his Emperor, here I am!"

No one fired a shot. Shouting "Vive l'Empereur! Vive l'Empereur!" ("Long Live the Emperor! Long Live the Emperor!") the troops went over to his side. Napoleon made his entry into Paris in triumph on March 20, 1815.

The powers that had defeated Napoleon pledged once more to fight this person they called the "Enemy and Disturber of the Tranquility of the World." Napoleon raised yet another army and moved to attack the nearest allied forces stationed in Belgium.

At **Waterloo** in Belgium on June 18, 1815, Napoleon met a combined British and Prussian army under the **Duke of Wellington** and suffered a bloody defeat.

This time, the victorious allies exiled him to St. Helena, a small island in the South Atlantic. Only Napoleon's memory would continue to haunt French political life.

Reading Check **Examining** Why did Napoleon invade Russia?

and supplies, Napoleon abandoned Moscow late in October and began the "Great Retreat" across Russia. The retreat proceeded in terrible winter conditions. Less than forty thousand out of the original army managed to arrive back in Poland in January 1813.

This military disaster led other European states to rise up and attack the crippled French army. Paris was captured in March 1814. Napoleon was soon sent into exile on the island of **Elba,** off the coast of Tuscany. The Bourbon monarchy was restored to France in the person of Louis XVIII, brother of the executed king, Louis XVI.

TAKS Practice

SECTION 3 ASSESSMENT

Checking for Understanding

1. **Define** consulate, nationalism.

2. **Identify** Napoleon Bonaparte, Civil Code, Anne-Louise-Germaine de Staël, Duke of Wellington.

3. **Locate** Corsica, Moscow, Elba, Waterloo.

4. **Explain** how nationalism contributed to Napoleon's defeat. Be sure to discuss how French nationalism produced nationalism outside of France.

5. **List** the powers Napoleon exercised as first consul.

Critical Thinking

6. **Describe** How did the principles of the French Revolution spread throughout Europe?

7. **Sequencing Information** Using a diagram like the one below, identify the reasons for the rise and fall of Napoleon's Grand Empire.

Napoleon's Rise and Fall

Rise ↑ _____ Fall ↓

Analyzing Visuals

8. **Examine** the portrait shown on page 545 of your text. Napoleon commissioned this painting in 1800. How does David portray Napoleon, and why do you think Napoleon wanted artists to produce portraits like the one created by David?

Writing About History

9. **Persuasive Writing** In your opinion, was Napoleon an enlightened ruler or a tyrant? Write a position paper supporting your view. Be sure to include pertinent information about Napoleon's Civil Code.

Chapter Summary

The French Revolution was one of the great turning points in history. The years from 1789 to 1815 in France were chaotic, and change came in unexpected ways. The chart below will help you understand and remember some of the major events of this time and the changes they caused.

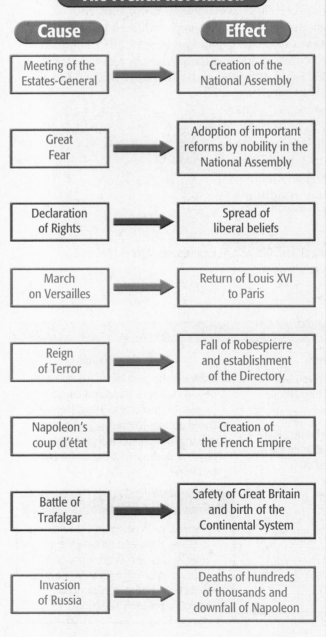

The French Revolution

Cause → **Effect**

Cause	Effect
Meeting of the Estates-General	Creation of the National Assembly
Great Fear	Adoption of important reforms by nobility in the National Assembly
Declaration of Rights	Spread of liberal beliefs
March on Versailles	Return of Louis XVI to Paris
Reign of Terror	Fall of Robespierre and establishment of the Directory
Napoleon's coup d'état	Creation of the French Empire
Battle of Trafalgar	Safety of Great Britain and birth of the Continental System
Invasion of Russia	Deaths of hundreds of thousands and downfall of Napoleon

Using Key Terms

1. Aristocratic privileges, or _____, were obligations of the French peasants to local landlords.

2. From the period of the Middle Ages until the creation of the French Republic, France's population was divided into three orders or _____.

3. Members of the French middle class, the _____, were part of the Third Estate.

4. Members of the Paris Commune were called _____ because of their clothing.

5. During the National Convention of 1792, dissenting groups or _____ disagreed over the fate of Louis XVI.

6. Napoleon seized power during an overthrow of the French government, which is called a _____.

7. In 1799, Napoleon controlled the _____, a new government in which Napoleon had absolute power.

8. _____ is the cultural identity of a people based on common language, religion, and national symbols.

Reviewing Key Facts

9. **Government** What was the Declaration of the Rights of Man and the Citizen?

10. **History** What event started the French Revolution?

11. **Government** What reforms did the National Assembly make between 1789 and 1791?

12. **History** Why was Louis XVI executed?

13. **Government** How did Robespierre and the Committee of Public Safety deal with opponents of the government? What was the effect of their policies?

14. **Government** How did Napoleon assume power in France and become emperor?

15. **Geography** How did the French Revolution lead to war with other European nations?

16. **Economics** What was the purpose of the Continental System? Did it succeed? Explain.

17. **History** Why was the French invasion of Russia a failure?

Critical Thinking

18. **Making Comparisons** Examine the different systems of government in France from 1789 to 1812. Which was the most democratic? Which form of government was the most effective and why?

19. **Evaluating** Evaluate which Enlightenment ideals affected the French Revolution.

Self-Check Quiz

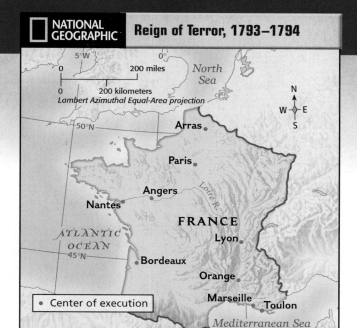

Visit the *Glencoe World History* Web site at tx.wh.glencoe.com and click on **Chapter 18–Self-Check Quiz** to prepare for the Chapter Test.

Writing about History

20. Expository Writing Look ahead to Section 3 in Chapter 23. Compare and contrast the American, French, and Russian Revolutions. Consider their causes and effects and summarize the principles of each revolution regarding ideas such as democracy, liberty, separation of powers, equality, popular sovereignty, human rights, constitutionalism, and nationalism.

Analyzing Sources

Read the following quotation by Napoleon, then answer the questions below.

> 66What the peoples of Germany desire most impatiently is that talented commoners should have the same right to your esteem and to public employments as the nobles, that any trace of serfdom and of an intermediate hierarchy between the sovereign and the lowest class of the people should be completely abolished. The benefits of the Code Napoleon, the publicity of judicial procedure, the creation of juries must be so many distinguishing marks of your monarchy.99

21. What does Napoleon say that the people of Germany want and do not want?

22. What were Napoleon's views about how civil and military workers should be hired and promoted? Where in this quote does Napoleon refer to these views?

Applying Technology Skills

23. Using the Internet Use the Internet to do a keyword search for "Declaration of the Rights of Man." Identify the places where the ideals of liberty, equality, and fraternity are still being debated today. Are there places where these ideals are not being discussed and should be?

Making Decisions

24. Think about the execution of Robespierre. Why did the National Convention decide to execute Robespierre? Can you think of another solution that would have addressed their concerns?

Analyzing Maps and Charts

Study the map above to answer the following questions.

25. What cities served as centers of execution?

26. Approximately how far from Paris were centers of execution established?

27. Research one of the towns on the map and write a brief essay that describes the impact of the Reign of Terror on the people who lived there.

Directions: Choose the best answer to the following question.

The rule of Robespierre was a time when the French Revolution

F was controlled by royalists who supported King Louis XVI.

G established a long-lasting constitutional monarchy.

H became a centralized military force under Napoleon.

J grew more violent as extremists took control.

Test-Taking Tip: If you do not know the answer to a question, eliminate any answer choices that you know are incorrect. Then choose the best answer from the remaining choices.

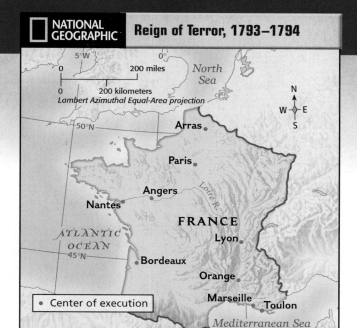

Reign of Terror, 1793–1794

North Sea

Arras

Paris

Angers

Nantes

FRANCE

ATLANTIC OCEAN

Lyon

Bordeaux

Orange

Marseille

Toulon

Mediterranean Sea

• Center of execution

200 miles
200 kilometers
Lambert Azimuthal Equal-Area projection

*W*ORLD LITERATURE

from Candide

by Voltaire

Voltaire was born François-Marie Arouet on November 21, 1694. He assumed the pen name "Voltaire" in 1718. Voltaire was a critical and satirical writer who used his wit to attack both church and state. *Candide* is one of Voltaire's most brilliant and most well-known works.

Read to Discover

Candide has been taught that "everything is for the best." However, his adventures usually prove the opposite. Here, he has just been cast out of a castle. The "men in blue" he meets are army recruiters for Frederick the Great, king of Prussia, who was at war with the French when Voltaire wrote *Candide.* How can you tell that Voltaire is making fun of the Prussian king and his army?

Reader's Dictionary

bulwark: strong support or protection

summarily: done without delay or formality

*C*andide . . . dragged himself into the neighboring village, which was called Waldberghofftrarbkdikdorff; he was penniless, famished, and exhausted. At the door of a tavern he paused forlornly. Two men dressed in blue [Prussian soldiers] took note of him:

—Look, chum, said one of them, there's a likely young fellow of just about the right size.

They approached Candide and invited him very politely to dine with them.

—Gentlemen, Candide replied with charming modesty, I'm honored by your invitation, but I really don't have enough money to pay my share.

—My dear sir, said one of the blues, people of your appearance and your merit don't have to pay; aren't you five feet five inches tall?

—Yes, gentlemen, that is indeed my stature, said he, making a bow.

—Then, sire, you must be seated at once; not only will we pay your bill this time, we will never allow a man like you to be short of money; for men were made only to render one another mutual aid.

—You are quite right, said Candide; it is just as Dr. Pangloss always told me, and I see clearly that everything is for the best.

They beg him to accept a couple of crowns, he takes them, and offers an I.O.U.; they won't hear of it, and all sit down at table together.

—Don't you love dearly . . . ?

—I do indeed, says he, I dearly love Miss Cunégonde.

▲ **Prussian soldiers**

—No, no, says one of the gentlemen, we are asking if you don't love dearly the King of the Bulgars [Frederick the Great].

—Not in the least, says he, I never laid eyes on him

—What's that you say? He's the most charming of kings, and we must drink his health.

—Oh, gladly, gentlemen; and he drinks.

—That will do, they tell him; you are now the bulwark, the support, the defender, the hero of the Bulgars; your fortune is made and your future assured.

▲ **Frederick the Great, king of Prussia**

Promptly they slip irons on his legs and lead him to the regiment. There they cause him to right face, left face, present arms, order arms, aim, fire, doubletime, and they give him thirty strokes of the rod. Next day he does the drill a little less awkwardly and gets only twenty strokes; the third day, they give him only ten, and he is regarded by his comrades as a prodigy.

Candide, quite thunderstruck, did not yet understand very clearly how he was a hero. One fine spring morning he took it into his head to go for a walk, stepping straight out as if it were a privilege of the human race, as of animals in general, to use his legs as he chose. He had scarcely covered two leagues when four other heroes [Prussian soldiers], each six feet tall, overtook him, bound him, and threw him into a dungeon. At the court-martial they asked which he preferred, to be flogged thirty-six times by the entire regiment or to receive summarily a dozen bullets in the brain. In vain did he argue that the human will is free and insist that he preferred neither alternative; he had to choose; by virtue of the divine gift called "liberty" he decided to run the gauntlet thirty-six times, and actually endured two floggings. The regiment was composed of two thousand men. That made four thousand strokes. As they were preparing for the third beating, Candide, who could endure no more, begged as a special favor that they would have the goodness to smash his head. His plea was granted; they bandaged his eyes and made him kneel down. The King of the Bulgars [Frederick the Great], passing by at this moment, was told of the culprit's crime; and as this king had a rare genius, he understood, from everything they told him of Candide, that this was a young metaphysician, extremely ignorant of the ways of the world, so he granted his royal pardon, with a generosity which will be praised in every newspaper in every age. A worthy surgeon cured Candide in three weeks with the ointments described by Dioscorides. He already had a bit of skin back and was able to walk when the King of the Bulgars went to war with the King of the Abares.

Nothing could have been so fine, so brisk, so brilliant, so well-drilled as the two armies. The trumpets, the fifes, the oboes, the drums, and the cannon produced such a harmony as was never heard in hell. First the cannons battered down about six thousand men on each side; then volleys of musket fire removed from the best of worlds about nine or ten thousand rascals who were cluttering up its surface.

Interpreting World Literature

1. Why do the men choose Candide to kidnap into the army?

2. Explain the irony of the soldiers' statement, "your fortune is made and your future assured."

3. Why is Candide punished? How does this relate to the philosophy of the Enlightenment?

4. **CRITICAL THINKING** What is Voltaire's attitude toward the "King of the Bulgars"?

Applications Activity

Write a satirical piece criticizing something about a television show or movie. Remember that a satire does not directly attack but criticizes by showing how ridiculous something is.

UNIT 4

An Era of European Imperialism

1800–1914

The Period in Perspective

The period of world history from 1800 to 1914 was characterized by two major developments: the growth of industrialization and Western domination of the world. The Industrial Revolution became one of the major forces for change, leading Western civilization into the industrial era that has characterized the modern world. At the same time, the Industrial Revolution created the technological means, including new weapons, by which the West achieved domination over much of the rest of the world.

Primary Sources Library

See pages 996–997 for primary source readings to accompany Unit 4.

Use The World History **Primary Source Document Library CD-ROM** to find additional primary sources about An Era of European Imperialism.

▲ Zulu lodging

► Zulu king Cetewayo meeting with British ambassadors

"The world's surface is limited, therefore the great object should be to take as much of it as possible."

—Cecil John Rhodes

Looking Back...

Industrialization

The rise of industry changed the world forever. So dramatic were the changes that historians have labeled the period the Industrial Revolution. Although the revolution began in Britain, it eventually touched every nation on Earth.

1705
Thomas Newcomen perfects the steam engine

1769
James Watt patents a more efficient steam engine

1787
Edmund Cartwright patents a power loom

❶ *Great Britain*

Workshop of the World

The birth of industry needed certain preconditions: the technology, incentive, and money to build machines; a labor force to run them; raw materials and markets to make the system profitable; and efficient farms to feed a new group of workers. By the early 1700s, Great Britain possessed all these conditions.

Industry grew from the innovations of individuals who developed machines to do work formerly done by humans and animals. Inventors built upon each other's ideas. For example, in 1769 James Watt improved upon Thomas Newcomen's primitive steam engine. Other inventors then adapted Watt's engine to run cloth-making machines. Business owners soon brought machines and workers together in factories.

By the 1800s, industry had catapulted Great Britain into a position of world leadership. "[Britain has] triumphantly established herself as the workshop of the world," boasted one leader. Soon, however, America would be humming with its own workshops.

James Watt's steam engine

to See Ahead

Samuel Slater's mill

❷ *The United States*

The Revolution Spreads

Great Britain prohibited the export of machines and machine operators. In 1789, however, a factory supervisor named Samuel Slater escaped by disguising himself as a farmhand and boarding a ship to New York. Working from memory, Slater built a cotton mill in Rhode Island in 1793.

Soon after, the United States began churning out its own industrial inventors. Standardized parts and the assembly line led to mass production—a concept that would revolutionize people's lives around the globe.

1793
Samuel Slater opens the first machine-run cotton mill in the U.S.

1855
Henry Bessemer patents an inexpensive method of producing steel

1913
Henry Ford uses assembly lines to mass produce cars

1914
Japan expands foreign trade

❸ *Japan*

The Search for Markets

In 1853, the Industrial Revolution traveled to Japan in the form of a fleet of United States steamships sent to open the islands to trade. "What we had taken as a fire at sea," recalled one Japanese observer, "was really smoke coming out of the smokestacks."

The military power produced by United States industry shook the Japanese. They temporarily gave in to American trade demands, but they also vowed that they too would possess industry. By 1914, Japan's merchant fleet was the sixth largest in the world, and its trade had increased one hundredfold in value in 50 years.

Matthew Perry's steamship in Tokyo Bay

Why It Matters

The increase in industry made it necessary to find new sources of raw materials and new markets for manufactured goods. How could competition for resources and markets lead to the wars of the twentieth century?

19 Industrialization and Nationalism

1800–1870

Key Events

As you read this chapter, look for the key events in the development of industrialization and nationalism.

- *The Industrial Revolution saw a shift from an economy based on farming and handi-crafts to an economy based on manufacturing by machines and industrial factories.*
- *Three important ideologies—conservatism, nationalism, and liberalism—emerged to play an important role in world history.*
- *Romanticism and realism reflected changes in society in Europe and North America.*

The Impact Today

The events that occurred during this time period still impact our lives today.

- *The early conflicts between workers and employers produced positive effects for workers in modern society.*
- *The Industrial Revolution replaced many handcrafted items with mass-produced items, many of which we still use today.*
- *Nationalism has had a profound effect on world developments in the twentieth century.*

World History Video *The Chapter 19 video, "The Romantic Era," chronicles cultural and social changes in nineteenth-century Europe.*

The Clermont, *built by Robert Fulton*

1807
Robert Fulton builds the first paddle-wheel steamboat

| 1800 | 1810 | 1820 | 1830 |

1814
Congress of Vienna meets

1830
First public railway line opens in Britain

Coalbrookedale by Night by Philippe Jacques de Loutherbourg Artists painted the dramatic changes brought on by the Industrial Revolution.

Francis I, Austrian emperor

1848 Revolutions erupt in Europe

1865 U.S. Confederate troops surrender

1871 German unification achieved

1840

1850

1860

1870

1837 Victoria becomes queen of Great Britain

Queen Victoria

1853 Crimean War begins

1861 Czar Alexander II frees the Russian serfs

Czar Alexander II of Russia

HISTORY Online

Chapter Overview Visit the *Glencoe World History* Web site at tx.wh.glencoe.com and click on **Chapter 19–Chapter Overview** to preview chapter information.

A Story That Matters

Austrian emperor Francis I (left) hosted the Congress of Vienna.

The Congress of Vienna

*I*n the fall of 1814, hundreds of foreigners began to converge on Vienna, the capital city of the Austrian Empire. Many of these foreigners were members of European royalty—kings, archdukes, princes, and their wives—accompanied by their political advisers and scores of servants.

Their congenial host was the Austrian emperor Francis I, who was quite willing to spend a fortune to entertain the visitors. A Festivals Committee arranged entertainment on a daily basis for nine months. Francis I never tired of providing Vienna's guests with glittering balls, hunting parties, picnics, hot-air balloon displays, and sumptuous feasts.

A banquet for forty tables of guests was held every night in the Hofburg Palace. Then, too, there were the concerts. Actors, actresses, singers, and composers were engaged to entertain, and Beethoven even composed a new piece of music for the event. One participant remembered, "Eating, fireworks, public illuminations. For eight or ten days, I haven't been able to work at all. What a life!"

Of course, not every waking hour was spent in pleasure during this gathering of notables, known to history as the Congress of Vienna. These people were representatives of all the states that had fought Napoleon. Their real business was to arrange a final peace settlement after almost 10 years of war.

Why It Matters

The Congress of Vienna tried to find a way to undo the changes brought about by the French Revolution and Napoleon. However, the new forces of change had become too powerful to be contained. They called forth political revolutions that would shake Europe for years to come. At the beginning of the nineteenth century, another kind of revolution began to transform the economic and social structure of Europe. The Industrial Revolution led to the industrialization that shaped the modern world.

History and You List several inventions developed during your lifetime. What are their purposes? Do they save time or make manual work easier? Have they impacted society as a whole? Have there been any negative consequences to any of these inventions? Write a paper summarizing your thoughts.

The Industrial Revolution

Guide to Reading

Main Ideas
- Coal and steam replaced wind and water as new sources of energy and power.
- Cities grew as people moved from the country to work in factories.

Key Terms
capital, entrepreneur, cottage industry, puddling, industrial capitalism, socialism

People to Identify
James Watt, Robert Fulton

Places to Locate
Liverpool, Manchester

Preview Questions
1. What technological changes led to the development of industrialization?
2. What was the social impact of the Industrial Revolution in Europe, especially on women and children?

Reading Strategy
Categorizing Information Use a table like the one below to name important inventors mentioned in this section and their inventions.

Inventors	Inventions

Preview of Events

♦1750	♦1770	♦1790	♦1810	♦1830	♦1850

1764
James Hargreaves invents spinning jenny

1782
James Watt builds steam engine that can drive machinery

1807
Steamboats make transportation easier

1833
Factory Act reduces child labor in Britain

1840
Steamships begin to cross the Atlantic

Voices from the Past

In 1844, a factory in Berlin posted the following rules for its workers:

❝The normal working day begins at all seasons at 6 A.M. precisely and ends, after the usual break of half an hour for breakfast, an hour for dinner and half an hour for tea, at 7 P.M. . . . Workers arriving 2 minutes late shall lose half an hour's wages; who-ever is more than 2 minutes late may not start work until after the next break, or at least shall lose his wages until then. . . . No worker may leave his place of work other-wise than for reasons connected with his work. . . . All conversation with fellow-workers is prohibited . . . ❞

—*Documents of European Economic History,* **Sidney Pollard and Colin Holmes, 1968**

The new factories of the Industrial Revolution demanded a rigorous discipline to force employees to become accustomed to a new kind of work life.

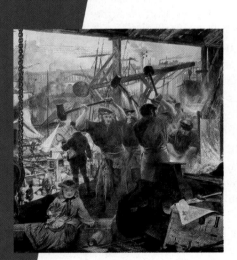
Factory workers

The Industrial Revolution in Great Britain

⌐TURNING POINT¬ **As you will learn, during the Industrial Revolution, Europe saw a shift from an economy based on farming and handicrafts to an economy based on man-ufacturing by machines in factories.**

The Industrial Revolution began in Great Britain in the 1780s and took several decades to spread to other Western nations. Several factors contributed to make Great Britain the starting place.

Young woman at work in a textile mill

Contributing Factors First, agricultural practices in the eighteenth century had changed. Expansion of farmland, good weather, improved transportation, and new crops, such as the potato, led to a dramatic increase in the food supply. More people could be fed at lower prices with less labor. Now even ordinary British families could use some of their income to buy manufactured goods.

Second, with more abundant food supplies, the population grew. This increase created a large labor force to work in the new factories that were emerging in Britain.

Third, Britain had a ready supply of money, or capital, to invest in the new industrial machines and the factories needed to house them. Many British people were very wealthy. Some, called entrepreneurs, were interested in finding new business opportunities and new ways to make profits.

Fourth, natural resources were plentiful in Britain. The country's many rivers provided water power and a means for transporting raw materials and finished products from one place to another. Britain also had abundant supplies of coal and iron ore, essential in manufacturing processes.

Finally, a supply of markets gave British manufacturers a ready outlet for their goods. Britain had a vast colonial empire, and British ships could transport goods anywhere in the world. In addition, because of population growth and cheaper food at home, domestic markets were increasing. A growing demand for cotton cloth led British manufacturers to begin to look for ways to increase production.

Changes in Cotton Production In the eighteenth century, Great Britain had surged ahead in the production of inexpensive cotton goods. The manufacture of cotton cloth was a two-step process. First, spinners made cotton thread from raw cotton. Then, weavers wove the thread into cloth on looms. In the eighteenth century, these tasks were done by individuals in their rural homes—a production method known as cottage industry.

A series of technological advances in the eighteenth century made cottage industry inefficient. First, the invention of the "flying shuttle" made weaving faster. Now, weavers needed more thread from spinners because they could produce cloth at a faster rate.

In 1764 James Hargreaves had invented a spinning machine called the spinning jenny, which met this need. Other inventors made similar contributions. The spinning process became much faster. In fact, thread was being produced faster than weavers could use it.

Another invention made it possible for the weaving of cloth to catch up with the spinning of thread. This was a water-powered loom invented by Edmund Cartwright by 1787. It now became more efficient to bring workers to the new machines and have them work in factories near streams and rivers, which were used to power many of the early machines.

The cotton industry became even more productive when the steam engine was improved in the 1760s by a Scottish engineer, **James Watt.** In 1782, Watt made changes that enabled the engine to drive machinery. Steam power could now be used to spin and weave cotton. Before long, cotton mills using steam engines were found all over Britain. Because steam engines were fired by coal, they did not need to be located near rivers.

British cotton cloth production increased dramatically. In 1760, Britain had imported 2.5 million pounds (1.14 million kg) of raw cotton, which was used to produce cloth in cottage industries. In 1787, the British imported 22 million pounds (10 million kg) of cotton, most of it spun on machines. By 1840, 366 million pounds (166 million kg) of cotton were imported each year. By this time, cotton cloth was Britain's most valuable product. British cotton goods were sold everywhere in the world and were produced mainly in factories.

The Coal and Iron Industries The steam engine was crucial to Britain's Industrial Revolution. For fuel, the engine depended on coal, a substance that seemed then to be unlimited in quantity. The success of the steam engine increased the need for coal and led to an expansion in coal production. New processes using coal aided the transformation of another industry—the iron industry.

Britain's natural resources included large supplies of iron ore. At the beginning of the eighteenth century, the basic process of producing iron had changed little since the Middle Ages. It became possible to produce a better quality of iron in the 1780s, when Henry Cort developed a process called puddling.

In this process, coke, which was derived from coal, was used to burn away impurities in crude iron, called pig iron, and produce an iron of high quality. The British iron industry boomed. In 1740, Britain had produced 17,000 tons (15,419 t) of iron. After Cort's process came into use in the 1780s, production jumped to nearly 70,000 tons (63,490 t). In 1852, Britain produced almost 3 million tons (2.7 million t)—more iron than was produced by the rest of the world combined. The high-quality iron was used to build new machines, especially new means of transportation.

Railroads In the eighteenth century, more efficient means of moving resources and goods developed. Railroads were particularly important to the success of the Industrial Revolution.

In 1804, the first steam-powered locomotive ran on an industrial rail-line in Britain. It pulled 10 tons (9 t) of ore and 70 people at 5 miles (8.05 km) per hour. Better locomotives followed. One called the *Rocket* was used on the first public railway line, which opened in 1830 and extended 32 miles

(51.5 km) from **Liverpool** to **Manchester,** England. The *Rocket* sped along at 16 miles (25.7 km) per hour while pulling a 40-ton (36-t) train. Within 20 years, locomotives were able to reach 50 miles (80.5 km) per hour, an incredible speed to passengers. In 1840, Britain had almost 2,000 miles (3,218 km) of railroads. By 1850, more than 6,000 miles (9,654 km) of railroad track crisscrossed much of that country.

Building railroads created new jobs for farm laborers and peasants. Less expensive transportation led to lower-priced goods, thus creating larger markets. More sales meant more factories and more machinery. Business owners could reinvest their profits in new equipment, adding to the growth of the economy. This type of regular, ongoing economic growth became a basic feature of the new industrial economy.

The New Factories The factory was another important element in the Industrial Revolution. From its beginning, the factory created a new labor system. Factory owners wanted to use their new machines constantly. So, workers were forced to work in shifts to keep the machines producing at a steady rate.

Early factory workers came from rural areas, where they were used to periods of hectic work, followed by periods of inactivity. Early factory owners therefore had to create a system of work discipline in which employees became used to working regular hours and doing the same work over and over. For example, adult workers were fined for being late and were dismissed for serious misconduct, especially for being drunk. Child workers were often beaten. One early industrialist said that his aim was "to make the men into machines that cannot err."

✓ **Reading Check** Describing
How were adult and child factory workers disciplined?

Picturing **History**

In the *Rocket* (left), it took just two hours to travel 32 miles (51.5 km). How does this picture capture people's sense of wonder about train travel?

The Spread of Industrialization

By the mid-nineteenth century, Great Britain had become the world's first and richest industrial nation. It produced one-half of the world's coal and manufactured goods. Its cotton industry alone in 1850 was equal in size to the industries of all other European countries combined.

Europe The Industrial Revolution spread to the rest of Europe at different times and speeds. First to be industrialized in continental Europe were Belgium, France, and the German states.

In these places, governments were very active in encouraging the development of industrialization. For example, governments provided funds to build roads, canals, and railroads. By 1850, a network of iron rails had spread across Europe.

North America An Industrial Revolution also occurred in the new nation of the United States. In 1800, six out of every seven American workers were farmers, and there were no cities with more than 100,000 people. Between 1800 and 1860, the population in the United States grew from about 5 million to 30 million people. Cities grew, too. Nine cities had populations over 100,000. Only 50 percent of American workers were farmers.

The United States was a large country in the 1800s. A transportation system to move goods across the nation was vital. Thousands of miles of roads and canals were built to link east and west. **Robert Fulton** built the first paddle-wheel steamboat, the *Clermont,* in 1807. By 1860, a thousand steamboats plied the Mississippi River and made transportation easier on the Great Lakes and along the Atlantic coast.

Most important in the development of an American transportation system was the railroad. It began with fewer than 100 miles (160.9 km) of track in 1830. By 1860, about 30,000 miles (48,270 km) of railroad track covered the United States. The railroad turned the United States into a single massive market for the manufactured goods of the Northeast.

Labor for the growing number of factories in the Northeast came chiefly from the farm population. Many of the workers in the new factories of New England were women. Indeed, women and girls made up a substantial majority of the workers in large textile (cotton and wool) factories.

Factory owners sometimes sought entire families, including children, to work in their factories. One advertisement in a newspaper in the town of Utica, New York, read: "Wanted: A few sober and industrious families of at least five children each, over the age of eight years, are wanted at the cotton factory in Whitestown. Widows with large families would do well to attend this notice."

✔ Reading Check **Evaluating** Why was the railroad important to the American Industrial Revolution?

Comparing Britain and the United States*

Britain

Population (in millions)

Year	Population
1830	24.0
1870	31.0
1900	41.0

United States

Population (in millions)

Year	Population
1830	12.9
1870	38.6
1900	76.0

Britain

Railroad Track (in thousands of miles)

Year	Track
1830	.032
1870	11.0
1900	18.6

United States

Railroad Track (in thousands of miles)

Year	Track
1830	.023
1870	53.0
1900	195.0

*As you study these comparisons, keep in mind the vast difference in area encompassed by Britain and the United States. Britain (England, Scotland, Wales, and Ireland) totals 94,548 square miles (244,879 sq km); the continental United States totals 3,717,796 square miles (9,629,091 sq km).

Graph Skills

Britain was the leading industrial nation in the early and mid-nineteenth century, but countries such as the United States eventually surpassed Britain in industrial production.

1. **Comparing** How did Britain's population growth, from 1830 to 1870 and 1870 to 1900, compare to the United States's growth? How did Britain's expansion in railroad tracks compare to that of the United States during the same period?

2. **Problem Solving** Which country had the highest percentage of railroad track miles in comparison to total square miles in 1870? In 1900?

NATIONAL GEOGRAPHIC — Industrialization of Europe by 1870

Geography *Skills*

The Industrial Revolution spread throughout nineteenth-century Europe.

1. **Interpreting Maps** What was the predominate industry in the United Kingdom?

2. **Applying Geography Skills** What patterns do you see in the distribution of the major industries? What geographical factors could account for these patterns?

Legend:

- Manufacturing and industrial area
- • Major industrial center
- ++++ Major railways by 1870

Industry:
- Coal mining
- Iron working
- Textile production

Social Impact in Europe

The Industrial Revolution drastically changed the social life of Europe and the world. This change was evident in the first half of the nineteenth century in the growth of cities and the emergence of two new social classes: the industrial middle class and the industrial working class.

Growth of Population and Cities In 1750, European population stood at an estimated 140 million. By 1850, the population had almost doubled to 266 million. The key to this growth was a decline in death rates, wars, and diseases, such as smallpox and plague. Because of an increase in the food supply, more people were better fed and resistant to disease. Famine largely disappeared from western Europe. The 1840s Irish potato famine proved an exception. The Irish depended on the potato for food. When a fungus infected the crops, almost a million died. A million more emigrated, many to the United States.

Cities and towns in Europe grew dramatically in the first half of the nineteenth century. The growth was directly related to industrialization. By 1850, especially in Great Britain and Belgium, cities were rapidly becoming home to many industries. With the steam engine, factory owners did not need water power and could locate their plants in cities. People moved from the country to the cities to find work, traveling on the new railroads.

In 1800, Great Britain had one major city, London, with a population of about 1 million, and six cities with populations between 50,000 and 100,000. Fifty years later, London's population had swelled to about 2,500,000. Nine cities had populations over 100,000, and 18 cities had populations between 50,000 and 100,000. Over 50 percent of the British population lived in towns and cities by 1850. Urban populations also grew in other European countries, but less dramatically.

The rapid growth of cities in the first half of the nineteenth century led to pitiful living conditions for many of the inhabitants. Eventually, these conditions prompted urban reformers to call on local governments to clean up their cities. The calls for reform would be answered in the second half of the nineteenth century.

The Industrial Middle Class The Middle Ages had seen the rise of commercial capitalism, an economic system based on trade. With the Industrial Revolution came the rise of industrial capitalism, an economic system based on industrial production. Industrial capitalism produced a new middle-class group—the industrial middle class.

In the Middle Ages, the bourgeois, or middle-class person, was the burgher or town dweller, who may have been active as a merchant, official, artisan, lawyer, or intellectual. Later, the term *bourgeois* came to include people involved in industry and banking, as well as professionals, such as lawyers, teachers, doctors, and government officials.

The new industrial middle class was made up of the people who built the factories, bought the machines, and figured out where the markets were.

THE WAY IT WAS

YOUNG PEOPLE IN . . .

The Industrial Revolution

Children had been an important part of the family economy in preindustrial times. They worked in the fields or at home in cottage industries. In the Industrial Revolution, however, child labor was exploited.

Children represented a cheap supply of labor. In 1821, 49 percent of the British people were under 20 years of age. Hence, children made up a large pool of workers. Children were paid only about one-sixth to one-third of what a man was paid.

The owners of cotton factories in England found child labor especially useful.

Young laborers

Children had a delicate touch as spinners of cotton. Their smaller size made it easier for them to move under machines to gather loose cotton. Furthermore, they were more easily trained to factory work than adults.

In the cotton factories in 1838, children under the age of 18 made up 29 percent of the total workforce. In cotton mills, children as young as age seven worked 12 to 15 hours per day, six days a week.

Discipline was often harsh. A report from a British parliamentary inquiry into the condition of child factory workers in 1838 stated:

Their qualities included initiative, vision, ambition, and often, greed. One manufacturer said, "Getting of money . . . is the main business of the life of men."

The Industrial Working Class

The Industrial Revolution also created an industrial working class. Industrial workers faced wretched working conditions. Work hours ranged from 12 to 16 hours a day, six days a week, with a half-hour for lunch and dinner. There was no security of employment and no minimum wage.

The worst conditions were in the cotton mills, where temperatures were especially harmful. One report noted that "in the cotton-spinning work, these creatures are kept, 14 hours in each day, locked up, summer and winter, in a heat of from 80 to 84 degrees." Mills were also dirty, dusty, dangerous, and unhealthy.

Conditions in the coal mines were also harsh. Although steam-powered engines were used to lift coal from the mines to the top, inside the mines men still bore the burden of digging the coal out. Horses, mules, women, and children hauled coal carts on rails to the lift. Dangerous conditions, including cave-ins, explosions, and gas fumes (called "bad air"), were a way of life. The cramped conditions in mines—tunnels were often only three or four feet high—and their constant dampness led to deformed bodies and ruined lungs.

In Britain, women and children made up two-thirds of the cotton industry's workforce by 1830. However, the number of children declined under the Factory Act of 1833, which set 9 as the minimum age for employment. Children between 9 and 13 could work only 9 hours a day; those between 13 and 18 could work 12 hours.

As the number of children employed declined, their places were taken by women. Women made up 50 percent of the labor force in British textile factories before 1870. They were mostly unskilled labor and

66It is a very frequent thing at Mr. Marshall's . . . for Mr. Horseman to start the mill earlier in the morning than he formerly did; and provided a child should be drowsy, the over-looker walks round the room with a stick in his hand, and he touches that child on the shoulder, and says, 'Come here.' In a corner of the room there is an iron cistern; it is filled with water; he takes this boy, and takes him up by the legs, and dips him over head in the cistern, and sends him to work for the remainder of the day. . . . What means were taken to keep the children to their work?—Sometimes they would tap them over the head, or nip them over the nose, or give them a pinch of snuff, or throw water in their faces, or pull them off where they were, and job them about to keep them awake.99

The same inquiry also reported that, in some factories, children were often beaten with a rod or whip to keep them at work.

Supervisors made sure children worked continuously.

CONNECTING TO THE PAST

1. **Identifying** What kind of working conditions did children face in the factories during the early Industrial Revolution?

2. **Analyzing** Why did factory owners permit such conditions and such treatment of children?

3. **Writing about History** What are conditions like today for factory workers? Write an essay contrasting current conditions with those of 100 years ago.

were paid half or less than half of what men received. Excessive working hours for women were outlawed in 1844.

The employment of children and women was in large part carried over from an earlier pattern. Husband, wife, and children had always worked together in cottage industry. The laws that limited the work hours of children and women thus gradually led to a new pattern of work.

Men were now expected to earn most of the family income by working outside the home. Women, in contrast, took over daily care of the family and performed low-paying jobs, such as laundry work, that could be done in the home. Working at home for pay made it possible for women to continue to help with the family's financial survival.

Early Socialism In the first half of the nineteenth century, the pitiful conditions created by the Industrial Revolution gave rise to a movement known as socialism. Socialism is a system in which society, usually in the form of the government, owns and controls some means of production, such as factories and utilities.

Early socialism was largely the idea of intellectuals who believed in the equality of all people and who wanted to replace competition with cooperation in industry. To later socialists, especially the followers of Karl Marx, such ideas were merely impractical dreams. The later socialists contemptuously labeled the earlier theorists utopian socialists. The term has lasted to this day.

Robert Owen, a British cotton manufacturer, was one utopian socialist. He believed that humans would show their natural goodness if they lived in a cooperative environment. At New Lanark in Scotland, Owen transformed a squalid factory town into a flourishing community. He created a similar community at New Harmony, Indiana, in the United States in the 1820s, which failed.

✔ **Reading Check** **Describing** What type of working conditions did the industrial workers face?

⬥TAKS Practice

SECTION 1 ASSESSMENT

Checking for Understanding

1. **Define** capital, entrepreneur, cottage industry, puddling, industrial capitalism, socialism.

2. **Identify** James Watt, Robert Fulton.

3. **Locate** Liverpool, Manchester.

4. **Describe** the importance of the railroads in the growth of cities in Europe and North America.

5. **List** the members of the new industrial middle class.

Critical Thinking

6. **Cause and Effect** Analyze how the Industrial Revolution changed the way families lived and worked.

7. **Cause and Effect** Use a diagram like the one below to list the causes and effects of the Industrial Revolution.

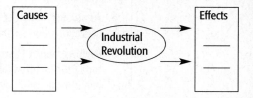

Analyzing Visuals

8. **Examine** the picture of a female textile worker shown on page 582 of your text. How does this picture reflect the role that women played in the Industrial Revolution?

Writing About History

9. **Informative Writing** You are a nineteenth-century journalist. Write a brief article depicting the working conditions in cotton mills and an explanation of how owners defend such conditions.

SECTION 2 / Reaction and Revolution

Guide to Reading

Main Ideas
- The great powers worked to maintain a conservative order throughout Europe.
- The forces of liberalism and nationalism continued to grow and led to the revolutions of 1848.

Key Terms
conservatism, principle of intervention, liberalism, universal male suffrage

People to Identify
Klemens von Metternich, Louis-Napoleon

Places to Locate
Vienna, Prague

Preview Questions
1. What did the Congress of Vienna try to accomplish?
2. Why did revolutions occur in 1848?

Reading Strategy
Cause and Effect Use a chart like the one below to identify the causes of the revolutions in France in 1830 and 1848.

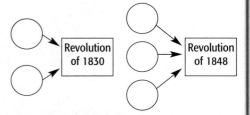

Preview of Events

| ◆1810 | ◆1820 | ◆1830 | ◆1840 | ◆1850 | ◆1860 |

1814
Congress of Vienna meets to create balance of power

1830
Liberals overthrow Charles X and establish a constitutional monarchy in France

1848
Revolutions sweep through Europe

1849
Austria reestablishes control over Lombardy

Klemens von Metternich confers with Napoleon.

Voices from the Past

Prince Klemens von Metternich, the foreign minister of the Austrian Empire, wrote:

❝The first principle to be followed by the monarchs, united as they are by the coincidence of their desires and opinions, should be that of maintaining the stability of political institutions against the disorganized excitement which has taken possession of men's minds. . . . The first and greatest concern for the immense majority of every nation is the stability of the laws, and their uninterrupted action—never their change. Therefore, let the governments govern, let them maintain the groundwork of their institutions, both ancient and modern; for it is at all times dangerous to touch them.❞

—*Memoirs,* Alexander Napler, trans., 1881

Metternich worked tirelessly for 30 years to repress the "revolutionary seed," as he called it, that had been spread by Napoleon Bonaparte.

The Congress of Vienna

After the defeat of Napoleon, European rulers moved to restore the old order. This was the goal of the great powers—Great Britain, Austria, Prussia, and Russia—when they met at the **Congress of Vienna** in September 1814 to arrange a final peace settlement. The leader of the congress was the Austrian foreign minister, Prince **Klemens von Metternich** (MEH•tuhr•NIHK).

Metternich claimed that he was guided at **Vienna** by the principle of legitimacy. This meant that lawful monarchs from the royal families that had ruled before Napoleon would be restored to their positions of power in order to keep peace and stability in Europe. This had already been done in France with the

NATIONAL GEOGRAPHIC
Europe after the Congress of Vienna, 1815

KINGDOM OF NORWAY AND SWEDEN

North Sea

UNITED KINGDOM

DENMARK

Baltic Sea

RUSSIAN EMPIRE

ATLANTIC OCEAN

NETH.

PRUSSIA

GERMAN STATES

FRANCE

SWITZ.

Vienna

AUSTRIAN EMPIRE

Black Sea

PORTUGAL

SPAIN

ITALIAN STATES

OTTOMAN EMPIRE

Constantinople

Mediterranean Sea

0   400 miles
0   400 kilometers
Lambert Azimuthal Equal-Area projection

— German Confederation

---

restoration of the Bourbon monarchy. However, the principle of legitimacy was largely ignored elsewhere.

Practical considerations of power were addressed at the Congress of Vienna. The great powers rearranged territories in Europe, believing that this would form a new balance of power. The powers at Vienna wanted to keep any one country from dominating Europe. This meant balancing political and military forces that guaranteed the independence of the great powers. To balance Russian territorial gains, for example, new territories were given to Prussia and Austria.

Reading Check **Explaining** What was the "principle of legitimacy"?

The Conservative Order

The arrangements worked out at the Congress of Vienna were a victory for rulers who wanted to contain the forces of change unleashed by the French Revolution. These rulers, like Metternich, believed in the political philosophy known as **conservatism.**

Geography *Skills*

The Congress of Vienna tried to create a new balance of power in Europe.

1. **Interpreting Maps** Within what political boundries is Vienna located? Of what nation is Vienna the capital today?

2. **Applying Geography Skills** Compare this map to the map of Napoleonic Europe shown on page 567 of your text. What territories that belonged to the French Empire in 1812 were *not* part of France after the Congress of Vienna? What land did Russia gain?

Conservatism is based on tradition and social stability. Most conservatives at that time favored obedience to political authority and believed that organized religion was crucial to order in society. Conservatives hated revolutions and were unwilling to accept demands from people who wanted either individual rights or representative governments.

To maintain the new balance of power, Great Britain, Russia, Prussia, and Austria (and later France) agreed to meet at times in conferences to take steps that would maintain the peace in Europe. These meetings came to be called the Concert of Europe.

Eventually, the great powers adopted a principle of intervention. According to this principle, the great powers had the right to send armies into countries where there were revolutions in order to restore legitimate monarchs to their thrones. Britain refused to accept the principle, arguing that the great powers should not interfere in the internal affairs of other states. Austria, Prussia, Russia, and France, however, used military forces to crush revolutions in Spain and Italy, as well as to restore monarchs to their thrones.

✓ **Reading Check** **Summarizing** What were the views of the conservative movement?

Forces of Change

Between 1815 and 1830, conservative governments throughout Europe worked to maintain the old order. However, powerful forces for change—known as liberalism and nationalism—were also at work.

Liberalism Liberalism, a political philosophy based largely on Enlightenment principles, held that people should be as free as possible from government restraint.

Liberals had a common set of political beliefs. Chief among them was the protection of civil liberties, or the basic rights of all people. These civil liberties included equality before the law and freedom of assembly, speech, and press. Liberals believed that all these freedoms should be guaranteed by a written document, such as the American **Bill of Rights.**

Most liberals wanted religious toleration for all, as well as separation of church and state. Liberals also demanded the right of peaceful opposition to the government. They believed that laws should be made by a representative assembly (legislature) elected by qualified voters.

Many liberals, then, favored government ruled by a constitution such as in a constitutional monarchy, in which a king is regulated by a constitution. They believed that written constitutions would guarantee the rights they sought to preserve.

Liberals did not, however, believe in a democracy in which everyone had a right to vote. They thought that the right to vote and hold office should be open only to men of property. Liberalism, then, was tied to middle-class men, especially industrial middle-class men, who wanted voting rights for themselves so that they could share power with the landowning classes. The liberals feared mob rule and had little desire to let the lower classes share that power.

Nationalism Nationalism was an even more powerful force for change in the nineteenth century than was liberalism. Nationalism arose out of people's awareness of being part of a community with common institutions, traditions, language, and customs. This community is called a nation. For nationalists, people owe their chief political loyalty to the nation rather than to a dynasty, city-state, or other political unit.

Nationalism did not become a popular force for change until the French Revolution. From then on, nationalists came to believe that each nationality should have its own government. Thus, the Germans, who were separated into many principalities, wanted national unity in a German nation-state with one central government. Subject peoples, such as the Hungarians, wanted the right to establish their own governments rather than be subject to the Austrian emperor.

Nationalism, then, was a threat to the existing political order. A united Germany, for example, would upset the balance of power set up at the Congress of Vienna in 1815. At the same time, an independent Hungarian state would mean the breakup of the Austrian Empire. Conservatives feared such change and thus tried hard to repress nationalism.

In the first half of the nineteenth century, nationalism found a strong ally in liberalism. Most liberals

People In History

Klemens von Metternich
1773–1859—Austrian statesman

There was no greater symbol of conservatism in the first half of the nineteenth century than Prince Klemens von Metternich. Born in the Rhineland of Germany, he fled to Austria in 1794 and joined the Austrian diplomatic service. He was made Austrian foreign minister in 1809.

An experienced diplomat, Metternich was conceited and self-assured. He described himself in his memoirs in 1819: "There is a wide sweep about my mind. I am always above and beyond the preoccupation of most public men; I cover a ground much vaster than they can see. I cannot keep myself from saying about twenty times a day: 'How right I am, and how wrong they are.'" When revolution erupted in 1848, Metternich fled to England.

Picturing **History**

In 1830, Charles X of France dissolved the French legislature and suspended freedom of the press. Revolution followed. The rebels (left) demanded a republic. **How was Louis-Philippe involved in these events?**

Louis-Philippe

believed that freedom could only be possible in people who ruled themselves. Each group of people should have its own state: no state should attempt to dominate another state. The association with liberalism meant that nationalism had a wider scope.

Revolutionary Outbursts Beginning in 1830, the forces of change—liberalism and nationalism—began to break through the conservative domination of Europe. In France, liberals overthrew the Bourbon monarch Charles X in 1830 and established a constitutional monarchy. Political support for the new monarch, Louis-Philippe, a cousin of Charles X, came from the upper middle class.

Nationalism was the chief force in three other revolutions the same year. Belgium, which had been annexed to the former Dutch Republic in 1815, rebelled and created an independent state. Revolutions in Poland and Italy were less successful. Russian forces crushed the Poles' attempt to free themselves from foreign domination. Austrian troops marched into Italy and put down revolts in a number of Italian states.

✔**Reading Check** **Evaluating** How did liberalism and nationalism begin to break through the conservative domination of Europe?

The Revolutions of 1848

Despite liberal and nationalist successes in France and Belgium, the conservative order still dominated much of Europe as the midpoint of the nineteenth

century approached. However, the forces of liberalism and nationalism continued to grow. These forces of change erupted once more in the revolutions of 1848.

Another French Revolution Revolution in France was again the spark for revolution in other countries. Severe economic problems beginning in 1846 brought untold hardship in France to the lower middle class, workers, and peasants. At the same time, members of the middle class clamored for the right to vote. The government of Louis-Philippe refused to make changes, and opposition grew.

The monarchy was finally overthrown in 1848. A group of moderate and radical republicans set up a provisional, or temporary, government. The republicans were people who wished France to be a republic—a government in which leaders are elected.

The provisional government called for the election of representatives to a Constituent Assembly that would draw up a new constitution. Election was to be by **universal male suffrage**—that is, all adult men could vote.

The provisional government also set up national workshops to provide work for the unemployed. From March to June, the number of unemployed enrolled in the national workshops rose from about 66,000 to almost 120,000. This emptied the treasury and frightened the moderates, who reacted by closing the workshops on June 21.

The workers refused to accept this decision and poured into the streets. In four days of bitter and bloody fighting, government forces crushed the working-class revolt. Thousands were killed, and thousands more were sent to the French prison colony of Algeria in northern Africa.

The new constitution, ratified on November 4, 1848, set up a republic, called the Second Republic. The Second Republic had a single legislature elected by universal male suffrage. A president, also chosen by universal male suffrage, served for four years. In the elections for the presidency held in December 1848, Charles Louis Napoleon Bonaparte (called **Louis-Napoleon**), the nephew of the famous French ruler, won a resounding victory.

Trouble in the German States

News of the 1848 revolution in France led to upheaval in other parts of Europe. The Congress of Vienna in 1815 had recognized the existence of 38 independent German states (called the **German Confederation**). Of these, Austria and Prussia were the two great powers. The other states varied in size.

In 1848, cries for change led many German rulers to promise constitutions, a free press, and jury trials. Indeed, an all-German parliament, called the Frankfurt Assembly, was held to fulfill a liberal and nationalist dream—the preparation of a constitution for a new united Germany. Deputies to the parliament were elected by universal male suffrage.

Ultimately, however, the Frankfurt Assembly failed to achieve its goal. The members drafted a constitution but had no real means of forcing the German rulers to accept it. German unification was not achieved.

Revolutions in Central Europe

The Austrian Empire also had its problems. The empire was a **multinational state**—a collection of different peoples, including Germans, Czechs, Magyars (Hungarians), Slovaks, Romanians, Slovenes, Poles, Croats, Serbians, and Italians. Only the Hapsburg emperor provided a common bond. The Germans, though only a quarter of the population, played a leading role in governing the Austrian Empire.

In March 1848, demonstrations in the major cities led to the dismissal of Metternich, the Austrian foreign minister. In Vienna, revolutionary forces took control of the capital and demanded a liberal constitution. To appease the revolutionaries, the government gave Hungary its own legislature. In Bohemia, the Czechs clamored for their own government.

Austrian officials had made concessions to appease the revolutionaries but were determined to reestablish their control over the empire. In June 1848, Austrian

CONNECTIONS Past To Present

Russian Troops in Hungary

On November 1, 1956, Imre Nagy, leader of Hungary, declared Hungary a free nation and promised new elections. Hungary was at that time under the control of the Soviet Union. Fearing that these elections would mean the end of Communist rule in Hungary, Nikita Khrushchev, leader of the Soviet Union, reacted dramatically.

On November 4, two hundred thousand Soviet (mostly Russian) troops and four thousand Soviet tanks invaded Budapest, Hungary's capital city. An estimated fifty thousand Hungarians died on that day. Nagy fled but was later arrested and executed. The Hungarian Revolution of 1956 had failed.

To Hungarians who knew their country's history, the use of Russian troops to crush their independence had an all-too-familiar ring. In 1848, Louis Kossuth had led a revolt that forced Hungary's Austrian rulers to grant Hungary its own legislature and a separate national army. In April 1849, the Hungarian legislature declared Hungary a republic. Kossuth was made the new president.

Meanwhile, the Austrians were unwilling to give up their control of Hungary. Unable to subdue the Hungarians, the Austrian government asked the Russians for help. Czar Nicholas I of Russia, who feared revolution anywhere, gladly agreed. A Russian army of 140,000 men crushed the Hungarian forces, and Kossuth fled abroad. The Hungarian Revolution of 1848–1849 had failed.

▲ *Soviet tanks in Hungary*

Comparing Past and Present

There have been other, more recent revolts against repressive governments that have been met with force, violence, and loss of life. Review recent newsmagazines to locate one such event. Write a historical account of the event, using both primary and secondary sources.

NATIONAL GEOGRAPHIC
Revolutions in Europe, 1848–1849

✳ Center of revolution

0   300 miles
0   300 kilometers
Chamberlin Trimetric projection

BELGIUM
FRANCE
Paris
Lyon
Corsica
Sardinia
Mediterranean Sea
Berlin PRUSSIA
Frankfurt
Dresden
GERMANY Prague
Munich
Vienna Buda
AUSTRIAN EMPIRE
Milan Venice
Florence
Livorno
PAPAL
STATES
Rome
Naples
KINGDOM OF
THE TWO
SICILIES
Palermo
Sicily
RUSSIA
Warsaw
Kraków
OTTOMAN
EMPIRE
GREECE
50°N
45°N
40°N
5°E
10°E
20°E

Geography *Skills*

In 1848 and 1849, revolution spread through Europe.

1. **Interpreting Maps** How far south did the revolutions of 1848 to 1849 extend?

2. **Applying Geography Skills** Pose and answer one question about the pattern in world history shown on this map.

---

military forces crushed the Czech rebels in **Prague.** By the end of October, the rebels in Vienna had been defeated as well. With the help of a Russian army of 140,000 men, the Hungarian revolutionaries were finally subdued in 1849. The revolutions in the Austrian Empire had failed.

Revolts in the Italian States The Congress of Vienna had set up nine states in Italy, including the Kingdom of Piedmont in the north; the Kingdom of the Two Sicilies (Naples and Sicily); the Papal States; a handful of small states; and the northern provinces of Lombardy and Venetia, which were now part of the Austrian Empire.

In 1848, a revolt broke out against the Austrians in Lombardy and Venetia. Revolutionaries in other Italian states also took up arms and sought to create liberal constitutions and a unified Italy. By 1849, however, the Austrians had reestablished complete control over Lombardy and Venetia. The old order also prevailed in the rest of Italy.

Throughout Europe in 1848, popular revolts started upheavals that had led to liberal constitutions and liberal governments. However, moderate liberals and more radical revolutionaries were soon divided over their goals, and so conservative rule was reestablished. Even with the reestablishment of conservative governments, however, the forces of nationalism and liberalism continued to influence political events.

✓**Reading Check** **Identifying** What countries experienced revolutions in 1848?

🔶 TAKS Practice

SECTION 2 ASSESSMENT

Checking for Understanding

1. **Define** conservatism, principle of intervention, liberalism, universal male suffrage.

2. **Identify** Congress of Vienna, Klemens von Metternich, Bill of Rights, Louis-Napoleon, German Confederation, multinational state.

3. **Locate** Vienna, Prague.

4. **Explain** the effect of conservatism in 1848.

5. **List** the different peoples living in the Austrian Empire.

Critical Thinking

6. **Analyze** How did the social and economic changes from the Industrial Revolution contribute to the spread of liberalism?

7. **Compare and Contrast** Use a table like the one below to compare and contrast the ideologies of conservatism, liberalism, and nationalism.

Conservatism	Liberalism	Nationalism

Analyzing Visuals

8. **Examine** the portrait of Louis-Philippe shown on page 592. How does this portrait reflect Louis-Philippe's position in France? How is this portrait different from that of earlier French rulers like Louis XIV or Napoleon?

Writing About History

9. **Expository Writing** Select one of the following ideologies: conservatism, liberalism, or nationalism. Write an essay in which you identify contemporary ideas that are influenced by that ideology.

Revolutionary Excitement

THE EXCITEMENT WITH WHICH GERMAN liberals and nationalists received the news of the revolution in France are captured well in the *Reminiscences* of Carl Schurz. After the failure of the German revolution of 1848, Schurz went to the United States, where he fought in the Civil War and became secretary of the interior.

Carl Schurz and the Frankfurt Assembly

❝One morning, toward the end of February, 1848, I sat quietly in my attic-chamber, working hard at my tragedy of "Ulrich von Hutten" [a sixteenth-century German knight], when suddenly a friend rushed breathlessly into the room, exclaiming: "What, you sitting here! Do you not know what has happened?"

"No; what?"

"The French have driven away Louis Philippe and proclaimed the republic."

I threw down my pen—and that was the end of "Ulrich von Hutten." I never touched the manuscript again. We tore down the stairs, into the street, to the market-square, the accustomed meeting-place for all the student societies after their midday dinner. Although it was still forenoon, the market was already crowded with young men talking excitedly. . . . We were dominated by a vague feeling as if a great outbreak of elemental forces had begun, as if an earthquake was impending of which we had felt the first shock, and we instinctively crowded together. . . .

The next morning there were the usual lectures to be attended. But how profitless! The voice of the professor sounded like a monotonous drone coming from far away. What he had to say did not seem to concern us. At last we closed with a sigh the notebook and went away, pushed by a feeling that now we had something more important to do—to devote ourselves to the affairs of the fatherland. . . . Now had arrived in Germany the day for the establishment of "German Unity," and the founding of a great, powerful national German Empire. In the first line the meeting of a national parliament. Then the demands for civil rights and liberties, free speech, free press, the right of free assembly, equality before the law, a freely elected representation of the people with legislative power . . . the word *democracy* was soon on all tongues. . . . Of course the regeneration of the fatherland must, if possible, be accomplished by peaceable means. Like many of my friends, I was dominated by the feeling that at last the great opportunity had arrived for giving to the German people the liberty which was their birthright and to the German fatherland its unity and greatness, and that it was now the first duty of every German to do and to sacrifice everything for this sacred object.❞

—Carl Schurz, *Reminiscences*

Analyzing Primary Sources

1. Why were Schurz and other Germans so excited about the revolution in France?
2. Would you be willing to sacrifice everything for your freedom and liberty? Why or why not?

National Unification and the National State

Guide to Reading

Main Ideas
- The rise of nationalism contributed to the unification of Italy and Germany.
- While nationalism had great appeal, not all peoples achieved the goal of establishing their own national states.

Key Terms
militarism, kaiser, plebiscite, emancipation, abolitionism, secede

People to Identify
Giuseppe Garibaldi, Otto von Bismarck, Queen Victoria, Czar Alexander II

Places to Locate
Piedmont, Alsace, Lorraine, Budapest

Preview Questions
1. What were the roles of Camillo di Cavour and Otto von Bismarck in the unification of their countries?
2. What caused the American Civil War?

Reading Strategy
Summarizing Information Use a table like the one below to list the changes that took place in the indicated countries during the nineteenth century.

Great Britain	France	Austrian Empire	Russia

Preview of Events

♦1850	♦1855	♦1860	♦1865	♦1870	♦1875

1852
Second Empire begins in France

1861
Kingdom of Italy proclaimed

1867
The British North America Act is passed

1870
Franco-Prussian War begins

1871
William I becomes kaiser of a united Germany

Giuseppe Garibaldi

Voices from the Past

On June 13, 1860, the *Times* of London made the following report:

❝In the afternoon, Garibaldi made a tour of inspection round [Palermo]. The popular idol [Garibaldi], in his red flannel shirt, with a loose colored handkerchief around his neck, was walking on foot among those cheering, laughing, crying, mad thousands; and all his few followers could do was to prevent him from being bodily carried off the ground. The people threw themselves forward to kiss his hands, or at least, to touch the hem of his garment. Children were brought up, and mothers asked on their knees for his blessing.❞

—The *Times* of London, June 13, 1860

Garibaldi, hailed by the Italians as a great hero, was one of the most colorful figures involved in the unification of Italy.

Breakdown of the Concert of Europe

The revolutions of 1848 had failed. By 1871, however, both Germany and Italy would be unified. The changes that made this possible began with the Crimean War.

The Crimean War was the result of a long-standing struggle between Russia and the Ottoman Empire. The Ottoman Empire had long controlled much of the territory in the Balkans in southeastern Europe. By the beginning of the nineteenth century, however, the Ottoman Empire was in decline, and its authority over its territories in the Balkans began to weaken.

Russia was especially interested in expanding its power into Ottoman lands in the Balkans. This expansion would give Russia access to the Dardanelles and thus the Mediterranean Sea. Russia would become the major power in eastern Europe and could challenge British naval control of the eastern Mediterranean. Other European powers feared Russian ambitions and had their own interest in the decline of the Ottoman Empire.

In 1853, the Russians invaded the Turkish Balkan provinces of Moldavia and Walachia. In response, the Ottoman Turks declared war on Russia. Great Britain and France, fearful of Russian gains, declared war on Russia the following year. This conflict came to be called the Crimean War.

The Crimean War was poorly planned and poorly fought. Eventually, heavy losses caused the Russians to seek peace. By the Treaty of Paris, signed in March 1856, Russia agreed to allow Moldavia and Walachia to be placed under the protection of all the great powers.

The effect of the Crimean War was to destroy the Concert of Europe. Austria and Russia had been the two chief powers maintaining the status quo in the first half of the nineteenth century. They were now enemies because Austria, which had its own interests in the Balkans, had refused to support Russia in the Crimean War. A defeated and humiliated Russia withdrew from European affairs for the next 20 years. Austria was now without friends among the great powers. This new international situation opened the door for the unification of both Italy and Germany.

Reading Check Explaining How did the Crimean War destroy the Concert of Europe?

Italian Unification

In 1850, Austria was still the dominant power on the Italian Peninsula. After the failure of the revolution of 1848, people began to look to the northern Italian state of **Piedmont** for leadership in achieving the unification of Italy. The royal house of Savoy ruled the Kingdom of Piedmont, which included Piedmont, the island of Sardinia, Nice, and Savoy. The ruler of the kingdom, beginning in 1849, was King Victor Emmanuel II.

The king named Camillo di Cavour his prime minister in 1852. Cavour was a dedicated political leader. As prime minister, he pursued a policy of economic expansion that increased government revenues and enabled the kingdom to equip a large army. Cavour, however, knew that Piedmont's army was not strong enough to defeat the Austrians. He would need help, so he made an alliance with the French emperor Louis-Napoleon. He then provoked the Austrians into declaring war in 1859.

The final result of the conflict that followed was a peace settlement that gave the French Nice and Savoy. Cavour had promised Nice and Savoy to the French for making the alliance. Lombardy, which had been under Austrian control, was given to Piedmont, while Austria retained control of Venetia. Cavour's success caused nationalists in some other northern Italian states (Parma, Modena, and Tuscany) to overthrow their governments and join their states to Piedmont.

NATIONAL GEOGRAPHIC

Unification of Italy, 1859–1870

Kingdom of Piedmont before 1859
Added to Kingdom of Piedmont, 1859
Added to Kingdom of Piedmont, 1860
Added to Kingdom of Italy, 1866
Added to Kingdom of Italy, 1870

Geography Skills

From 1859 to 1870, Italy struggled to become a unified country.

1. **Interpreting Maps** Looking at the map, explain the sequence of events in Italian unification.
2. **Applying Geography Skills** What geographic factors help to explain why the state of Piedmont became the leader in the struggle to unify Italy?

Meanwhile, in southern Italy, a new leader of Italian unification had arisen. **Giuseppe Garibaldi,** a dedicated Italian patriot, raised an army of a thousand volunteers—called Red Shirts because of the color of their uniforms.

The Kingdom of the Two Sicilies (Sicily and Naples) was ruled by a branch of the Bourbon dynasty, and a revolt had broken out in Sicily against the king. Garibaldi's forces landed in Sicily and, by the end of July 1860, controlled most of the island. In August, Garibaldi and his forces crossed over to the mainland and began a victorious march up the Italian Peninsula. Naples and the entire Kingdom of the Two Sicilies fell in early September.

Garibaldi chose to turn over his conquests to Piedmont. On March 17, 1861, a new kingdom of Italy was proclaimed under King Victor Emmanuel II. The task of unification was not yet complete, however. Venetia in the north was still held by Austria, and Rome was under the control of the pope, supported by French troops.

The Italians gained control of Venetia as a result of a war between Austria and Prussia. In the Austro-Prussian War of 1866, the new Italian state became an ally of Prussia. Prussia won the war, and the Italians were given Venetia.

In 1870, during the Franco-Prussian War, French troops withdrew from Rome. Their withdrawal enabled the Italian army to annex Rome on September 20, 1870. Rome became the capital of the united Italian state.

Reading Check **Explaining** How did Giuseppe Garibaldi contribute to Italian unification?

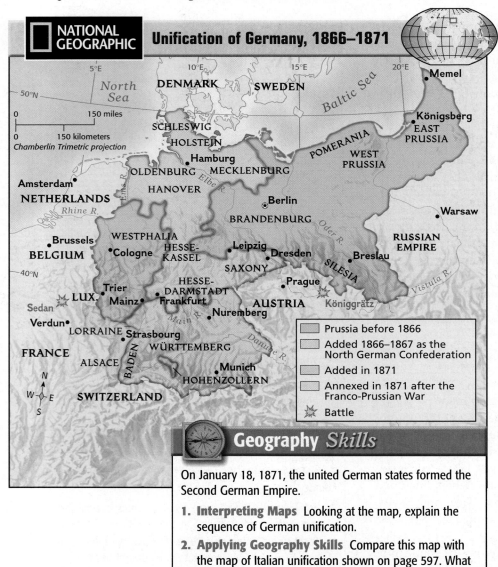

NATIONAL GEOGRAPHIC

Unification of Germany, 1866–1871

- Prussia before 1866
- Added 1866–1867 as the North German Confederation
- Added in 1871
- Annexed in 1871 after the Franco-Prussian War
- ✳ Battle

Geography Skills

On January 18, 1871, the united German states formed the Second German Empire.

1. **Interpreting Maps** Looking at the map, explain the sequence of German unification.
2. **Applying Geography Skills** Compare this map with the map of Italian unification shown on page 597. What geographic factors influenced the process of unification for both Germany and Italy?

German Unification

After the failure of the Frankfurt Assembly to achieve German unification in 1848 and 1849, Germans looked to Prussia for leadership in the cause of German unification. In the course of the nineteenth century, Prussia had become a strong and prosperous state. Its government was authoritarian. The Prussian king had firm control over both the government and the army. Prussia was also known for its militarism, or reliance on military strength.

In the 1860s, King William I tried to enlarge the Prussian army. When the Prussian legislature refused to levy new taxes for the proposed military changes, William I appointed a new prime minister, Count **Otto von Bismarck.**

Bismarck has often been seen as the foremost nineteenth-century practitioner of *realpolitik*—the "politics of reality," or politics based on practical matters rather than on theory or ethics. Bismarck was open about his strong dislike of anyone who opposed him.

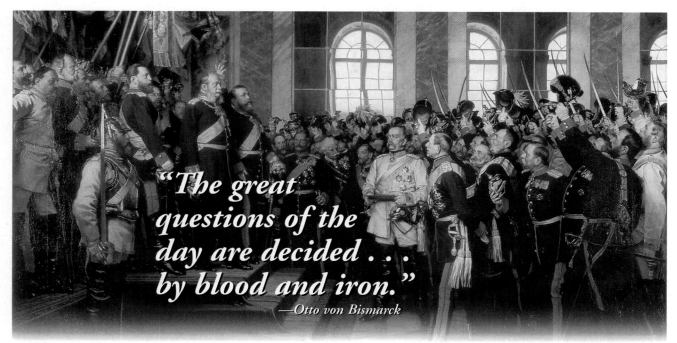

"The great questions of the day are decided . . . by blood and iron."

—*Otto von Bismarck*

Bismarck stands at the center as William I is named Emperor William I of the Second German Empire.

After his appointment, Bismarck ignored the legislative opposition to the military reforms. He argued instead that "Germany does not look to Prussia's liberalism but to her power."

Bismarck proceeded to collect taxes and strengthen the army. From 1862 to 1866, Bismarck governed Prussia without approval of the parliament. In the meantime, he followed an active foreign policy, which soon led to war.

After defeating Denmark with Austrian help in 1864 and gaining control of the duchies of Schleswig and Holstein, Bismarck created friction with the Austrians and forced them into a war on June 14, 1866. The Austrians, no match for the well-disciplined Prussian army, were decisively defeated on July 3.

Prussia now organized the German states north of the Main River into a North German Confederation. The southern German states, which were largely Catholic, feared Protestant Prussia. However, they also feared France, their western neighbor. As a result, they agreed to sign military alliances with Prussia for protection against France.

Prussia now dominated all of northern Germany, but problems with France soon arose. Bismarck realized that France would never be content with a strong German state to its east because of the potential threat to French security.

In 1870, Prussia and France became embroiled in a dispute over the candidacy of a relative of the Prussian king for the throne of Spain. Bismarck took advantage of the misunderstandings between the French and Prussians to goad the French into declaring war on Prussia on July 19, 1870. This conflict was called the Franco-Prussian War.

The French proved to be no match for the better led and better organized Prussian forces. The southern German states honored their military alliances with Prussia and joined the war effort against the French. Prussian armies advanced into France. At Sedan, on September 2, 1870, an entire French army and the French ruler, Napoleon III, were captured.

Paris finally surrendered on January 28, 1871, and an official peace treaty was signed in May. France had to pay 5 billion francs (about $1 billion) and give up the provinces of **Alsace** and **Lorraine** to the new German state. The loss of these territories left the French burning for revenge.

Even before the war had ended, the southern German states had agreed to enter the North German Confederation. On January 18, 1871, Bismarck and six hundred German princes, nobles, and generals filled the Hall of Mirrors in the palace of Versailles, 12 miles outside Paris. William I of Prussia was proclaimed kaiser, or emperor, of the Second German Empire (the first was the medieval Holy Roman Empire).

German unity had been achieved by the Prussian monarchy and the Prussian army. The authoritarian and militaristic values of Prussia were triumphant in the new German state. With its industrial resources and military might, the new state had become the strongest power on the European continent.

Reading Check **Summarizing** What events led to German unification?

Nationalism and Reform in Europe

While Italy and Germany were being unified, other states in Europe were also experiencing changes.

Great Britain Great Britain managed to avoid the revolutionary upheavals of the first half of the nineteenth century. In 1815, Great Britain was governed by aristocratic landowning classes, which dominated both houses of Parliament. In 1832, Parliament passed a bill that increased the number of male voters. The new voters were chiefly members of the industrial middle class. By giving the industrial middle class an interest in ruling Britain, Britain avoided revolution in 1848. In the 1850s and 1860s, Parliament continued to make both social and political reforms that helped the country to remain stable.

Another reason for Britain's stability was its continuing economic growth. By 1850, the British middle class was already prosperous as a result of the Industrial Revolution. After 1850, the working classes at last began to share some of this prosperity. Real wages for laborers increased more than 25 percent between 1850 and 1870.

The British feeling of national pride was well reflected in **Queen Victoria,** whose reign from 1837 to 1901 was the longest in English history. Her sense of duty and moral respectability reflected the attitudes of her age, which has ever since been known as the Victorian Age.

France In France, events after the revolution of 1848 moved toward the restoration of the monarchy. Four years after his election as president in 1848, Louis-Napoleon returned to the people to ask for the restoration of the empire. In this *plebiscite,* or popular vote, 97 percent responded with a yes vote. On December 2, 1852, Louis-Napoleon assumed the title of Napoleon III, Emperor of France. (The first Napoleon had named his son as his successor and had given him the title of Napoleon II. Napoleon II never ruled France, however.) The Second Empire had begun.

The government of Napoleon III was clearly authoritarian. As chief of state, Napoleon III controlled the armed forces, police, and civil service. Only he could introduce legislation and declare war. The Legislative Corps gave an appearance of representative government, because the members of the group were elected by universal male suffrage for six-year terms. However, they could neither initiate legislation nor affect the budget.

Napoleon III completely controlled the government and limited civil liberties. Nevertheless, the

HISTORY Online

Web Activity Visit the *Glencoe World History* Web site at tx.wh.glencoe.com and click on **Chapter 19– Student Web Activity** to learn more about Queen Victoria.

Napoleon III

History *through Art*

La Place Clichy by **Eugene Galien-Laloue**
To distract citizens from their loss of civil liberties, Napoleon III beautified the city of Paris. How successful was this policy?

first five years of his reign were a spectacular success. To distract the public from their loss of political freedom, he focused on expanding the economy. Government subsidies helped foster the rapid construction of railroads, harbors, roads, and canals. Iron production tripled.

In the midst of this economic expansion, Napoleon III also carried out a vast rebuilding of the city of Paris. The old Paris of narrow streets and walls was replaced by a modern Paris of broad boulevards, spacious buildings, public squares, an underground sewage system, a new public water supply system, and gaslights. The new Paris served a military purpose as well. Broad

Peasants had to pay for the poor-quality land they received from the Russian government.

streets made it more difficult for would-be rebels to throw up barricades and easier for troops to move rapidly through the city in the event of revolts.

In the 1860s, opposition to some of Napoleon's economic and governmental policies arose. In response, Napoleon III began to liberalize his regime. For example, he gave the legislature more power. In a plebiscite held in 1870, the French people gave Napoleon another victory. This triumph was short-lived, however. After the French were defeated in the Franco-Prussian War in 1870, the Second Empire fell.

The Austrian Empire As we have seen, nationalism was a major force in nineteenth-century Europe. However, one of Europe's most powerful states—the Austrian Empire—was a multinational empire that had been able to frustrate the desire of its ethnic groups for independence.

After the Hapsburg rulers crushed the revolutions of 1848 and 1849, they restored centralized, autocratic government to the empire. Austria's defeat at the hands of the Prussians in 1866, however, forced the Austrians to make concessions to the fiercely nationalistic Hungarians.

The result was the Compromise of 1867. This compromise created the dual monarchy of Austria-Hungary. Each of these two

components of the empire now had its own constitution, its own legislature, its own government bureaucracy, and its own capital (Vienna for Austria and **Budapest** for Hungary). Holding the two states together were a single monarch (Francis Joseph was both emperor of Austria and king of Hungary) and a common army, foreign policy, and system of finances.

In domestic affairs, then, the Hungarians had become an independent nation. The compromise, of course, did not satisfy the other nationalities that made up the multinational Austro-Hungarian Empire.

Russia At the beginning of the nineteenth century, Russia was overwhelmingly rural, agricultural, and autocratic. The Russian czar was still regarded as a divine-right monarch with unlimited power. The Russian government, based on soldiers, secret police, repression, and censorship, withstood the revolutionary fervor of the first half of the nineteenth century.

In 1856, however, as described earlier, the Russians suffered a humiliating defeat in the Crimean War. Even staunch conservatives now realized that Russia was falling hopelessly behind the western European powers. **Czar Alexander II** decided to make serious reforms.

Serfdom was the largest problem in czarist Russia. On March 3, 1861, Alexander issued an emancipation edict, which freed the serfs. Peasants could now own property and marry as they chose. The government provided land for the peasants by buying it from the landlords. 📖 (*See page 996 to read excerpts from Czar Alexander II's* Imperial Decree to Free the Serfs *in the Primary Sources Library.*)

The new land system, however, was not that helpful to the peasants. The landowners often kept the best lands for themselves. The Russian peasants soon found that they did not have enough good land to support themselves. Emancipation of the serfs, then, led not to a free, landowning peasantry, but to an unhappy, land-starved peasantry that largely followed old ways of farming.

Alexander II attempted other reforms as well, but he soon found that he could please no one. Reformers wanted more changes and a faster pace for change. Conservatives thought that the czar was trying to destroy the basic institutions of Russian society. When a group of radicals assassinated Alexander II in 1881, his son and successor, Alexander III, turned against reform and returned to the old methods of repression.

✓ **Reading Check** **Examining** How was Great Britain able to avoid a revolution in 1848?

Nationalism in the United States

The government under the U.S. Constitution had committed the United States to two of the major forces of the first half of the nineteenth century: liberalism and nationalism. National unity had not come easily, however.

Two factions had fought bitterly about the division of power in the new government. The Federalists had favored a strong central government. The Republicans, fearing central power, had wanted the federal government to be subordinate to the state governments. These early divisions had ended with the War of 1812 against the British. A surge of national feeling had served to cover over the nation's divisions.

The election of Andrew Jackson as president in 1828 had opened a new era in American politics. Property qualifications for voting had been reduced. The right to vote was eventually extended to almost all adult white males.

By the mid-nineteenth century, the issue of American national unity had reemerged. Slavery had become a threat to that unity. Although the importation of slaves had been banned in 1808, there were four million African American slaves in the South by 1860, compared with one million in 1800.

The South's economy was based on growing cotton on plantations, chiefly by slave labor. The cotton economy and plantation-based slavery were closely related. The South was determined to maintain them. At the same time, abolitionism, a movement to end slavery, arose in the North and challenged the Southern way of life.

As opinions over slavery grew more divided, compromise became less possible. Abraham Lincoln said in a speech in Illinois in 1858 that "this government cannot endure permanently half slave and half free."

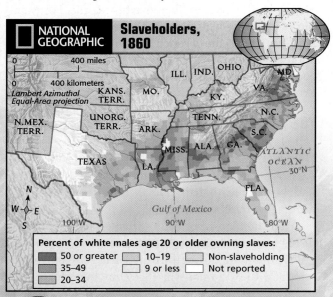

NATIONAL GEOGRAPHIC **Slaveholders, 1860**

Percent of white males age 20 or older owning slaves:
- 50 or greater
- 35–49
- 20–34
- 10–19
- 9 or less
- Non-slaveholding
- Not reported

Geography *Skills*

By 1860, there were four million African American slaves in the South.

1. **Applying Geography Skills** What conclusions can you draw about economic conditions in the southern United States in 1860 from looking at this map?

Slavery challenged national unity in the United States.

When Lincoln was elected president in November 1860, the die was cast.

On December 20, 1860, a South Carolina convention voted to secede, or withdraw, from the United States. In February 1861, six more Southern states did the same, and a rival nation—the Confederate States of America—was formed. In April, fighting erupted between North and South—the Union and the Confederacy.

The American Civil War (1861 to 1865) was an extraordinarily bloody struggle. Over 600,000 soldiers died, either in battle or from deadly diseases spawned by filthy camp conditions. The Union, with more men and resources, gradually wore down the Confederacy. On January 1, 1863, Lincoln's Emancipation Proclamation declared most of the nation's slaves "forever free." The surrender of Confederate forces on April 9, 1865, meant that the United States would be "one nation, indivisible." National unity had prevailed in the United States.

✔ **Reading Check** **Explaining** How did the election of Andrew Jackson influence American politics?

The Emergence of a Canadian Nation

By the Treaty of Paris in 1763, signed at the end of the Seven Years' War, Canada passed from the French to the British. By 1800, most of the Canadian people

favored more freedom from British rule. However, there were also serious differences among the colonists. Upper Canada (now Ontario) was mostly English speaking, whereas Lower Canada (now Quebec) was mostly French speaking.

After two short rebellions against the government broke out in Upper and Lower Canada in 1837 and 1838, the British moved toward change. In 1840, the British Parliament formally joined Upper and Lower Canada into the United Provinces of Canada. The United Provinces was not self-governed.

The head of Upper Canada's Conservative Party, John Macdonald, became a strong voice for self-government. The British, fearful of American designs on Canada, finally gave in. In 1867, Parliament passed the **British North America Act,** which established a Canadian nation—the Dominion of Canada—with its own constitution. John Macdonald became the first prime minister of the Dominion. Canada now possessed a parliamentary system and ruled itself, although foreign affairs remained in the hands of the British government.

✔ **Reading Check** **Describing** How did the British North America Act change the government of Canada?

🏴 **TAKS Practice**

SECTION 3 ASSESSMENT

Checking for Understanding

1. **Define** militarism, kaiser, plebiscite, emancipation, abolitionism, secede.

2. **Identify** Giuseppe Garibaldi, Otto von Bismarck, Queen Victoria, Czar Alexander II, British North America Act.

3. **Locate** Piedmont, Alsace, Lorraine, Budapest.

4. **Explain** why you think Alexander III turned against the reforms of his father.

5. **List** the Prussian values and assets that caused the Second German Empire to become the strongest European state.

Critical Thinking

6. **Drawing Inferences** Explain how the forces of liberalism and nationalism affected events in the United States during the nineteenth century.

7. **Compare and Contrast** Use a Venn diagram to compare and contrast Bismarck's and Cavour's methods for achieving unification in Germany and Italy.

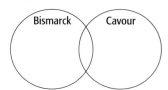

Analyzing Visuals

8. **Examine** the photographs of a peasant and a slave family shown on pages 601 and 602. Based on the visual evidence of the two photographs, how do you think the living conditions of Russian peasants compared to living conditions of slaves in the United States?

Writing About History

9. **Expository Writing** Write an essay comparing the events and outcomes of the rules of Bismarck and Napoleon III. What personal characteristics did each man have that contributed to his accomplishments?

SKILLBUILDER

Identifying an Argument

Why Learn This Skill?

In everyday conversation, the word argument refers to a conflict involving two or more opinions. However, in writing and in formal debate, an argument is the full presentation of a single opinion. An argument uses facts to support a particular opinion. After hearing these facts, it is then up to you to determine whether the argument is valid or not.

Learning the Skill

There are three basic elements to consider in an argument.

- **What is the thesis?** The main idea of an argument is its thesis, or the writer's basic position or viewpoint on the subject. In some arguments the thesis is stated explicitly. In others, you must read carefully to determine the writer's position.

- **What are the supporting reasons, examples, and facts?** The writer supports the thesis with reasons and supports the reasons with examples or facts.

- **What are its strengths and weaknesses?** Before accepting or rejecting an argument, evaluate its strengths and weaknesses. How well is each reason supported by facts and examples? Does the author's bias invalidate the argument?

Practicing the Skill

Read the following quotation published in 1842 in *L'Atelier (The Workshop)*, a Parisian newspaper. Then answer the following questions.

> 66Who has not heard of the women silkworkers . . . working fourteen to sixteen hours (except for one hour for both meals); always standing, without a single minute for repose [rest], putting forth an enormous amount of effort. And many of them have to walk a league or more, morning and evening, to get home, which is often a cause for moral disorder. Nor should we neglect to mention the danger that exists merely from working in these large factories, surrounded by wheels, gears, enormous leather belts that always threaten to seize you and pound you to

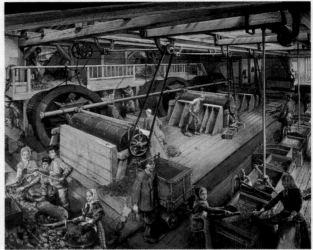

Men, women, and children working in a factory

pieces. There is not a factory in which some kind of accident has not happened—some woman worker caught by the hair or her clothing, and thereby pulverized; some mutilation of the fingers or the hands.99

❶ What is the writer's thesis?

❷ What reasons does the writer give to support this thesis?

❸ What facts support the statement that danger exists for the workers in the workplace?

❹ What is your reaction to the author's argument?

Applying the Skill

Find a recent article that states an argument about a political or historical issue. Identify the thesis of the argument and the major reasons and evidence supporting it. Decide whether you accept or reject this argument and explain why.

Glencoe's **Skillbuilder Interactive Workbook, Level 2,** provides instruction and practice in key social studies skills.

Culture: Romanticism and Realism

Guide to Reading

Main Ideas
- At the end of the eighteenth century, romanticism emerged as a reaction to the ideas of the Enlightenment.
- The Industrial Revolution created a new interest in science and helped produce the realist movement.

Key Terms
romanticism, secularization, organic evolution, natural selection, realism

People to Identify
Ludwig van Beethoven, Louis Pasteur, Charles Darwin, Charles Dickens

Places to Locate
London, France

Preview Questions
1. What were the major features of romanticism and realism?
2. How did the Scientific Revolution lead to secularization?

Reading Strategy
Summarizing Information Use a table like the one below to list popular literature from the romantic and realist movements.

Romanticism	Realism

Preview of Events

♦1820	♦1830	♦1840	♦1850	♦1860	♦1870	♦1880

1820
Walter Scott writes *Ivanhoe*

1849
Courbet paints *The Stonebreakers*

1859
Charles Darwin publishes *On the Origin of Species by Means of Natural Selection*

1869
Mendeleyev presents classification of material elements

Voices from the Past

Charles Dickens

In *The Old Curiosity Shop,* Charles Dickens described the English mill town of Birmingham:

❝A long suburb of red brick houses—some with patches of garden ground, where coal-dust and factory smoke darkened the shrinking leaves, and coarse rank flowers; and where the struggling vegetation sickened and sank under the hot breath of kiln and furnace . . . —a long, flat, straggling suburb passed, they came by slow degrees upon a cheerless region, where not a blade of grass was seen to grow; where not a bud put forth its promise in the spring; where nothing green could live but on the surface of the stagnant pools, which here and there lay idly sweltering by the black roadside.❞

—**Charles Dickens, *The Old Curiosity Shop,* 1840–1841**

Dickens, a highly successful English novelist, realistically portrayed the material surroundings of his time, but an element of romanticism still pervaded his novels.

Romanticism

At the end of the eighteenth century, a new intellectual movement, known as romanticism, emerged as a reaction to the ideas of the Enlightenment. The Enlightenment had stressed reason as the chief means for discovering truth. The romantics emphasized feelings, emotion, and imagination as sources of knowing.

The romantics believed that emotion and sentiment were only understandable to the person experiencing them. In their novels, romantic writers created figures who were often misunderstood and rejected by society but who continued to believe in their own worth through their inner feelings.

Romantics also valued individualism, the belief in the uniqueness of each person. Many romantics rebelled against middle-class conventions. Male romantics grew long hair and beards and both men and women wore outrageous clothes to express their individuality.

Many romantics had a passionate interest in the past. They revived medieval architecture and built castles, cathedrals, city halls, parliamentary buildings (such as the Houses of Parliament in **London**), and even railway stations in a style called neo-Gothic. Literature, too, reflected this interest in the past. The novels of Walter Scott became best-sellers in the first half of the nineteenth century. *Ivanhoe*, in which Scott tried to evoke clashes between knights in medieval England, became his most popular novel. By focusing on their nations' past, many romantic

writers created literature that reflected the nineteenth century's fascination with nationalism.

The exotic and unfamiliar also attracted many romantics. This attraction gave rise to Gothic literature. Chilling examples are Mary Shelley's *Frankenstein* in Britain and Edgar Allen Poe's short stories of horror in the United States. Some romantics even sought the unusual in their own lives by exploring their dreams and nightmares and seeking altered states of consciousness.

The romantics viewed poetry as the direct expression of the soul. Romantic poetry gave expression to one of the most important characteristics of romanticism—its love of nature. Romantics believed that nature served as a mirror into which humans could look to learn about themselves. This is especially evident in the poetry of William Wordsworth, the foremost English romantic poet of nature. His experience of nature was almost mystical:

> ❝One impulse from a vernal wood
> May teach you more of man,
> Of moral evil and of good,
> Than all the sages can.❞

The worship of nature also caused Wordsworth and other romantic poets to be critical of eighteenth-century science, which, they believed, had reduced nature to a cold object of study. To Wordsworth, the scientists' dry, mathematical approach left no room for the imagination or for the human soul. The poet who left to the world "one single moral precept," or principle, said Wordsworth, did more for the world than did scientists, who were soon forgotten. The monster created by Frankenstein in Mary Shelley's novel was a symbol of the danger of science's attempt to conquer nature. Many romantics were convinced that the emerging industrialization would cause people to become alienated from their inner selves and the natural world around them.

Like the literary arts, the visual arts were deeply affected by romanticism. Romantic artists shared at least two features. First, to them, all art was a reflection of

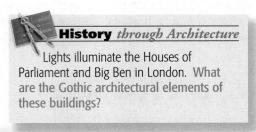

History *through Architecture*

Lights illuminate the Houses of Parliament and Big Ben in London. What are the Gothic architectural elements of these buildings?

Like his contemporary William Wordsworth, English artist John Constable sought to capture nature's dramatic beauty in his works. Constable's watercolor of Stonehenge from 1835 reflects the romantic emphasis on emotion over reason.

the artist's inner feelings. A painting should mirror the artist's vision of the world and be the instrument of the artist's own imagination. Second, romantic artists abandoned classical reason for warmth and emotion.

Eugène Delacroix (DEH•luh•KWAH) was one of the most famous romantic painters from **France.** His paintings showed two chief characteristics: a fascination with the exotic and a passion for color. His works reflect his belief that "a painting should be a feast to the eye."

To many romantics, music was the most romantic of the arts, because it enabled the composer to probe deeply into human emotions. Music historians have called the nineteenth century the age of romanticism. One of the greatest composers of all time, **Ludwig van Beethoven,** was the bridge between the classical and romantic periods in music.

Beethoven was one of the few composers who was able singlehandedly to transform the art of music. For Beethoven, music had to reflect his deepest inner feelings: "I must write, for what weighs on my heart, I must express." Beethoven's early work fell largely within the classical framework of the eighteenth century. However, his Third Symphony embodied the elements of romanticism with its use of powerful melodies to create dramatic intensity.

☑ **Reading Check** **Examining** How did the popularity of *Ivanhoe* reflect the interests of the nineteenth century?

A New Age of Science

The Scientific Revolution had created a modern, rational approach to the study of the natural world. For a long time, only the educated elite understood its importance. With the Industrial Revolution, however, came a heightened interest in scientific research. By the 1830s, new discoveries in science had led to many practical benefits that affected all Europeans. Science came to have a greater and greater impact on people.

In biology, the Frenchman **Louis Pasteur** proposed the germ theory of disease, which was crucial to the development of modern scientific medical practices. In chemistry, the Russian Dmitry Mendeleyev in the 1860s classified all the material elements then known on the basis of their atomic weights. In Great Britain, Michael Faraday put together a primitive generator that laid the foundation for the use of electric current.

The dramatic material benefits often provided by science and technology led Europeans to have a growing faith in science. This faith, in turn, undermined the religious faith of many people. It is no accident that the nineteenth century was an age of increasing secularization (indifference or rejection of religion or religious consideration). For many people, truth was now to be found in science and the concrete material existence of humans. No one did more to create a picture of humans as material beings that were simply part of the natural world than Charles Darwin.

In 1859, **Charles Darwin** published *On the Origin of Species by Means of Natural Selection.* The basic idea of this book was that each kind of plant and animal had evolved over a long period of time from earlier and simpler forms of life. Darwin called this principle **organic evolution.**

How did this natural process work? According to Darwin, in every species, "many more individuals of each species are born than can possibly survive." This results in a "struggle for existence." Darwin believed that some organisms are more adaptable to the environment than others, a process that Darwin called **natural selection.**

Those that are naturally selected for survival ("survival of the fittest") reproduce and thrive. The unfit do not survive. The fit who survive pass on the variations that enabled them to survive until, according to Darwin, a new, separate species emerges. In *The Descent of Man,* published in 1871, Darwin argued that human beings had animal origins and were not an exception to the rule governing other species.

Darwin's ideas raised a storm of controversy. Some people objected that Darwin's theory made human beings ordinary products of nature rather than unique beings. Others were bothered by his idea of life as a mere struggle for survival. "Is there a place in the Darwinian world for moral values?" they asked. Many people also condemned Darwin for denying God's role in creation. Gradually, however, many scientists and other intellectuals came to accept Darwin's theory.

✓**Reading Check** **Describing** How did Darwin's theory of natural selection influence the way in which people viewed the world?

Realism

The belief that the world should be viewed realistically, a view frequently expressed after 1850, was closely related to the scientific outlook. In politics, Bismarck had practiced the "politics of reality." **Realism** became a movement in the literary and visual arts as well.

The literary realists of the mid-nineteenth century rejected romanticism. They wanted to write about ordinary characters from actual life rather than romantic heroes in exotic settings. They also tried to avoid emotional language by using precise description. They preferred novels to poems.

Many literary realists combined their interest in everyday life with an examination of social issues. These artists expressed their social views through their characters. Although this type of realistic writing occurred worldwide, the French led the way.

The realist novel was perfected by the French author Gustave Flaubert, who was a leading novelist of the 1850s and 1860s. His work *Madame Bovary* presents a critical description of small-town life in France. The British novelist **Charles Dickens** became very successful with his realistic novels focusing on the lower and middle classes in Britain's early Industrial Age. In such novels as *Oliver Twist* and *David Copperfield,* Dickens described the urban poor and the brutal life they led with vivid realism.

Picturing **History**

Louis Pasteur developed a vaccine against rabies. In 1983, the Louis Pasteur Institute researchers were the first to isolate the AIDS virus. Research other medical advances that were made during the 1800s.

History *through Art*

***The Stonebreakers* by Gustave Courbet, 1849** As an artist of the realist school, Courbet broke with the mystical and imaginative romantic period. Which style do you prefer?

In art, too, realism became dominant after 1850. Realist artists sought to show the everyday life of ordinary people and the world of nature with photographic realism. The French became leaders in realist painting, as they had become leaders in realist writing.

Gustave Courbet was the most famous artist of the realist school. He loved to portray scenes from everyday life. His subjects were factory workers, peasants, and the wives of saloon keepers. "I have never seen either angels or goddesses, so I am not interested in painting them," Courbet said.

One of his famous works, *The Stonebreakers*, shows two roadworkers engaged in the deadening work of breaking stones to build a road. There were those who objected to Courbet's "cult of ugliness" and who found such scenes of human misery scandalous. To Courbet, however, no subject was too ordinary, too harsh, or too ugly.

✔ **Reading Check** **Evaluating** What factors helped to produce the movement known as realism?

🔺**TAKS Practice**

SECTION 4 ASSESSMENT

Checking for Understanding

1. **Define** romanticism, secularization, organic evolution, natural selection, realism.

2. **Identify** Ludwig van Beethoven, Louis Pasteur, Charles Darwin, Charles Dickens.

3. **Locate** London, France.

4. **Explain** how scientific developments affected the cultural movements of the nineteenth century.

5. **List** the values of the romantics.

Critical Thinking

6. **Compare and Contrast** How did romanticism compare to the ideas of the Enlightenment?

7. **Organizing Information** Use a table to list scientists and their discoveries in the mid-nineteenth century.

Scientist	Discovery
Pasteur	
Mendeleyev	
Faraday	
Darwin	

Analyzing Visuals

8. **Examine** the painting by John Constable shown on page 607 of your text. How does this painting reflect the characteristics of the romantic movement?

Writing About History

9. **Expository Writing** Read poetry by two different poets of romanticism. Write a paper describing the elements of romanticism found in the poems. Be sure to include quotations.

Using Key Terms

1. _____ was the movement to end slavery in the United States.

2. At the Congress of Vienna in 1814, the _____ became the guiding political principle for the great powers.

3. _____ means that all adult men have the right to vote.

4. The process invented by Henry Cort to produce high quality iron is called _____.

5. The basic idea of Charles Darwin's book, *On the Origin of Species*, was the principle of _____.

6. Obedience to political authority, emphasis on organized religion to maintain the social order, and resistance to the ideas of individual rights and representative government are characteristics of _____.

7. Before the Industrial Revolution, goods were often produced by individuals working in their own homes, a method known as _____.

8. Louis-Napoleon became president when 97 percent of the _____ responded with a yes vote.

9. A system in which society and not individuals owns the means of production is called _____.

10. _____ emphasized feeling, emotion, and imagination as sources of knowing.

Reviewing Key Facts

11. **History** The Concert of Europe was destroyed by which war?

12. **History** What four nations were prepared to use military forces to crush revolts in other nations?

13. **Government** Which governments supported the ideology of conservatism?

14. **Culture** What features can be found in paintings of the romantic style?

15. **History** What countries were involved in the Crimean War? What were the causes of the war?

16. **Economics** How did the Industrial Revolution affect Great Britain's social structure?

17. **Science and Technology** Explain the role of the steam engine in the development of the factory system.

18. **Government** What were the provisions of the British voting bill in 1832?

19. **Government** Why did the reforms of Czar Alexander II satisfy few Russians?

20. **History** Between 1815 and 1830, what forces for change threatened the conservative governments throughout Europe?

21. **Culture** Name the social classes that tended to support conservatism.

22. **Science and Technology** How did new discoveries in science in the 1800s provide practical benefits to Europeans?

23. **Government** Identify and describe the Compromise of 1867. To what was the compromise a response, and how successful was it?

24. **Government** Describe how Otto von Bismarck contributed to German unification.

25. **Economics** What was the economic impact of railroads on the Industrial Revolution?

Chapter Summary

In this chapter, you have studied developments from industry to art, faith to science, and liberalism to conservatism. The chart below summarizes some of these developments.

Advances	Conflict	Change	Reaction	Diversity
• Steam and coal are new sources of power. • Higher-quality iron leads to better railroads.	• Nationalism and liberalism become forces for change. • Conservatives attempt to suppress nationalism.	• People move to cities for factory work. • Italy unifies. • Germany emerges as a strong European power.	• Russian czars oppose the forces of liberalism and nationalism. • Science has a greater impact on people, undermining religious faith.	• Austria-Hungary contains many different ethnic groups seeking self-rule. • Romanticism and realism are opposite artistic styles.

Critical Thinking

26. **Making Comparisons** Compare the motives for Czar Alexander II's emancipation of the serfs with Abraham Lincoln's motives for issuing the Emancipation Proclamation in 1863.

27. **Cause and Effect** Describe how the Crimean War indirectly contributed to the unification of the Italian and German states.

Writing about History

28. **Expository Writing** How did the political, economic, and social injustices that existed during the nineteenth century contribute to romanticism and realism?

Analyzing Sources

Read the following excerpt from the poetry of William Wordsworth:

> ❝One impulse from a vernal wood
> May teach you more of man,
> Of moral evil and of good,
> Than all the sages can.❞

29. What characteristic of romantic poetry is evident in Wordsworth's poem?

30. What message is Wordsworth trying to convey? Do you agree?

Applying Technology Skills

31. **Using the Internet** Search the Internet to find information about Charles Dickens. Use a search engine to help focus your search by using words such as *Charles Dickens, Industrial Revolution, London,* and *Oliver Twist.* Prepare a report on the life of Charles Dickens, including his views on the working conditions in Britain and how he portrayed the lower and middle classes in his novels.

Making Decisions

32. Pretend that you are a monarch in Europe in 1847. You can tell that agitation is spreading in your country and you fear revolution. Using what you know about the causes of revolution and how other countries (such as Britain) have been able to avoid it, what reforms might you choose to enact? What steps or policies would you avoid?

33. Evaluate the political choices and decisions that European rulers made at the Congress of Vienna in 1814. What were the consequences of the decisions these leaders made?

Analyzing Maps and Charts

Study the map, Industrialization of Europe by 1870, on page 585 to answer the following questions.

34. In which part of the United Kingdom is industrialization concentrated?

35. What relationship exists between railways and industrial centers?

Directions: Choose the best answer to the following question.

Use the information in the box *and* your knowledge of world history to answer the following question.

> British Economic Conditions During the Early 1800s
> • Canal miles tripled between 1760 and 1830.
> • Britain had built more than 6,000 miles (9,654 km) of railroad tracks by 1850.
> • Britain produced nearly 3 million tons (2.7 million t) of iron ore by 1852.
> • London's population grew by 236 percent between 1800 and 1850.

Which of the following statements is based on the information in this box?

A The Industrial Revolution led to greater urbanization.

B London neighborhoods in the 1800s were sharply divided between rich and poor.

C A boom in railroad and canal construction made transportation more difficult.

D Parliament disagreed with the king over taxes and spending.

Test-Taking Tip: This question asks for an answer that is supported by the facts provided in the box. Find the answer choice that is *proven true* by the information listed in the box.

Mass Society and Democracy

1870–1914

Key Events

As you read this chapter, look for the key events in the development of mass society.
- *The Second Industrial Revolution resulted in changes in political, economic, and social systems.*
- *After 1870, higher wages and improved conditions in cities raised the standard of living for urban workers.*
- *The late 1800s and early 1900s were a time of political conflict that led to the Balkan crises and, eventually, World War I.*
- *New discoveries radically changed scientific thought, art, architecture, and social consciousness between 1870 and 1914.*

The Impact Today

The events that occurred during this time period still impact our lives today.
- *Because of poor working conditions, labor unions were organized to fight for improvements. Millions of workers are members of various unions today.*
- *Many of the inventions produced during this time, such as telephones and automobiles, are still used today.*

World History Video *The Chapter 20 video, "The Industrial Movement," chronicles the impact of the development and advancements of the Second Industrial Revolution.*

Transmitter and receiver used for first telephone call

1876
Alexander Graham Bell invents the telephone

1835   1845   1855   1865   1875

Karl Marx

1848
The Communist Manifesto is published

1861
First Civil War battle fought in United States

1871
British unions gain legal recognition

The Gare Saint-Lazare: Arrival of a Train by Claude Monet, 1877 This painting illustrates Monet's fascination with light as it is reflected and absorbed by the sky, clouds, windows, and trains.

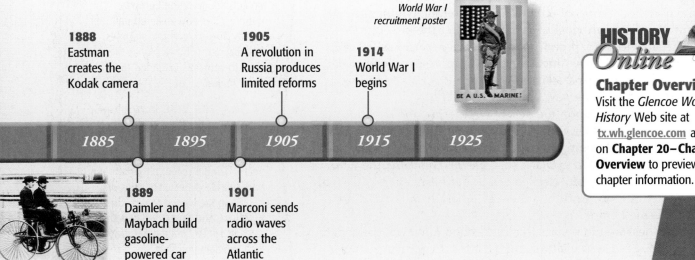

World War I recruitment poster

1888
Eastman creates the Kodak camera

1905
A revolution in Russia produces limited reforms

1914
World War I begins

| 1885 | 1895 | 1905 | 1915 | 1925 |

1889
Daimler and Maybach build gasoline-powered car

1901
Marconi sends radio waves across the Atlantic

Early German automobile, Daimler-Stahlradwagen, 1889

HISTORY
Online

Chapter Overview
Visit the *Glencoe World History* Web site at tx.wh.glencoe.com and click on **Chapter 20–Chapter Overview** to preview chapter information.

A Story That Matters

Steeplechase swimming pool at Coney Island, New York, c. 1919

The New Leisure

By the second half of the nineteenth century, new work patterns had established the concept of the weekend as a distinct time of recreation and fun. New forms of transportation—railroads and streetcars—enabled workers to make brief trips to amusement parks. Coney Island was only eight miles from central New York City; Blackpool, in England, was a short train ride from nearby industrial towns.

With their Ferris wheels and other daring rides that threw young men and women together, amusement parks offered a whole new world of entertainment. Before leaving, people purchased picture postcards to remember the day's fun.

Thanks to the railroad, seaside resorts—once visited only by the wealthy—became accessible to more people for weekend visits. One upper-class seaside resort regular expressed his disgust with the new "day-trippers":

"They swarm upon the beach, wandering about with apparently no other aim than to get a mouthful of fresh air. You may see them in groups of three or four—the husband, a pale man, dressed in black coat, carries the baby; the wife, equally pale and thin, decked out in her best, labors after with a basket of food. And then there is generally another child . . . wandering behind."

Businessmen in resorts like Blackpool, however, welcomed the crowds of new visitors and built for them boardwalks laden with food, drink, and entertainment.

Why It Matters

A new leisure was one part of the mass society that emerged in the late nineteenth century. The development of this new mass society helped improve the lives of the lower classes, who benefited from extended voting rights, a better standard of living, and public education. In addition, the European nation-states now fostered national loyalty and created mass armies. Political democracy grew as the right to vote was extended to all adult males.

History and You In 1850, a person born in the West could expect to live about 40 years. By 1910, life expectancy had increased to 54 years. Using a recent almanac, compare the life expectancy rates of people in the United States, United Kingdom, and Russia today with the rates in 1910. Create a bar graph with the data you find.

The Growth of Industrial Prosperity

Guide to Reading

Main Ideas
- New sources of energy and consumer products transformed the standard of living for all social classes in many European countries.
- Working-class leaders used Marx's ideas to form socialist parties and unions.

Key Terms
bourgeoisie, proletariat, dictatorship, revisionist

People to Identify
Thomas Edison, Alexander Graham Bell, Guglielmo Marconi, Karl Marx

Places to Locate
Netherlands, Austria-Hungary, Spain, Portugal, Russia

Preview Questions
1. What was the Second Industrial Revolution?
2. What were the chief ideas of Karl Marx?

Reading Strategy
Cause and Effect As you read this section, complete a diagram like the one below showing the cause and effect relationship between the resources and the products produced.

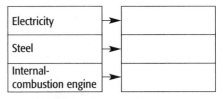

Electricity	→	
Steel	→	
Internal-combustion engine	→	

Preview of Events

♦1845	♦1855	♦1865	♦1875	♦1885	♦1895	♦1905

1848
Marx and Engels publish *The Communist Manifesto*

1875
Creation of German Social Democratic Party

1879
Thomas Edison invents the light bulb

1889
The Second International socialist association forms

1903
Wright brothers make first flight

Voices from the Past

On December 12, 1901, Guglielmo Marconi reported a remarkable discovery:

66 Shortly before mid-day I placed the single earphone to my ear and started listening. . . . I was at last on the point of putting . . . my beliefs to test. The answer came at 12:30 when I heard, faintly but distinctly, *pip-pip-pip.* I handed the phone to Kemp: 'Can you hear anything?' I asked. 'Yes,' he said, 'the letter S'—he could hear it. . . . The electric waves sent out into space from Britain had traversed the Atlantic—the distance, enormous as it seemed then, of 1,700 miles [2,735 km] — It was an epoch in history. I now felt for the first time absolutely certain the day would come when mankind would be able to send messages without wires . . . between the farthermost ends of the earth. 99

—*Eyewitness to History,* John Carey, ed., 1987

Guglielmo Marconi and his wireless apparatus, 1896

Marconi's discovery of radio waves was one of the many advances of the Second Industrial Revolution.

The Second Industrial Revolution

Westerners in the late 1800s worshiped progress. At the heart of this belief in progress was the stunning material growth produced by what is called the Second Industrial Revolution. The first Industrial Revolution had given rise to textiles, railroads, iron, and coal. In the Second Industrial Revolution, steel, chemicals, electricity, and petroleum led the way to new industrial frontiers.

New Products The first major change in industry between 1870 and 1914 was the substitution of steel for iron. New methods for shaping steel made it useful in the building of lighter, smaller, and faster machines and engines, as well as railways, ships, and weapons. In 1860, Great Britain, France, Germany, and Belgium produced 125,000 tons (112,500 t) of steel. By 1913, the total was an astounding 32 million tons (29 million t).

Electricity was a major new form of energy that proved to be of great value. It could be easily converted into other forms of energy, such as heat, light, and motion, and moved easily through space by means of wires. In the 1870s, the first practical generators of electrical current were developed. By 1910, hydroelectric power stations and coal-fired steam-generating plants enabled homes and factories to be tied to a single, common source of power.

Electricity gave birth to a series of inventions. The creation of the light bulb by **Thomas Edison** in the United States and Joseph Swan in Great Britain opened homes and cities to electric lights. A revolution in communications began when **Alexander Graham Bell** invented the telephone in 1876 and **Guglielmo Marconi** sent the first radio waves across the Atlantic in 1901.

By the 1880s, streetcars and subways powered by electricity had appeared in major European cities. Electricity transformed the factory as well. Conveyor belts, cranes, and machines could all be powered by electricity. With electric lights, factories could remain open 24 hours a day.

The development of the internal-combustion engine, fired by oil and gasoline, provided a new source of power in transportation. This engine gave rise to ocean liners with oil-fired engines, as well

SCIENCE, TECHNOLOGY & SOCIETY

The Automobile

Many new forms of transportation were created in the Industrial Revolution, but none affected more people on a daily basis than the automobile. It was the invention of the internal-combustion engine that made the automobile possible.

A German engineer, Gottlieb Daimler, invented a light, portable internal-combustion engine in 1885. In 1889, Daimler and Wilhelm Maybach produced an automobile powered by a gasoline engine that reached a speed of 10 miles [16 km] per hour. In 1926, Daimler and Karl Benz, another German, merged to form Daimler-Benz, an automotive company that would later manufacture the Mercedes-Benz.

Early cars were handmade and expensive. Only several hundred were sold between 1893 and 1901. Their slow speed, 14 miles [22.5 km] per hour, was a problem, too. Early models were not able to climb steep hills.

An American, Henry Ford, revolutionized the car industry in 1908 by using an assembly line to mass-produce his Model T. Before, it had taken a group of workers 12 hours to build a single car. Now, the same number of workers could build a car in an hour and a half. By cutting production costs, Ford lowered the price of the automobile. A Model T cost $850 in 1908 but only $360 by 1916. By 1916, Ford's factories were producing 735,000 cars a year. By 1925, Ford's Model T cars would make up half of the automobiles in the world.

Analyzing *Why were early cars expensive?*

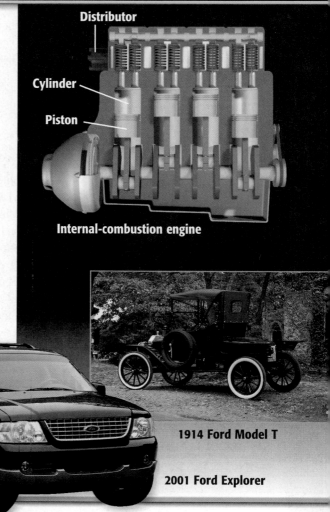

Distributor

Cylinder

Piston

Internal-combustion engine

1914 Ford Model T

2001 Ford Explorer

Industrial concentration:
- Area
- City

Industry:
- ⚗ Chemicals
- ⚡ Electricity
- ⊙ Engineering
- ⛏ Oil production
- Steel

0 _____ 500 miles

0 _____ 500 kilometers

Lambert Azimuthal Equal-Area projection

Geography *Skills*

Steel, electricity, and chemicals were some of the products of the Second Industrial Revolution.

1. **Interpreting Maps** Locate the areas shown on the map that have the heaviest concentrations of industry. What geographic factors could have helped these areas become heavily industrialized?

2. **Applying Geography Skills** Use the information provided in this map to create a chart that shows the type of industry in each European country.

as to the airplane and the automobile. In 1903, Orville and Wilbur Wright made the first flight in a fixed-wing plane at Kitty Hawk, North Carolina. In 1919, the first regular passenger air service was established.

New Patterns Industrial production grew at a rapid pace because of greatly increased sales of manufactured goods. Europeans could afford to buy more consumer products for several reasons. Wages for workers increased after 1870. In addition, prices for manufactured goods were lower because of reduced transportation costs.

In the cities, the first department stores began to sell a new range of consumer goods made possible by the development of the steel and electrical industries. Clocks, bicycles, electric lights, and typewriters were sold in great quantities.

Not all nations benefited from the Second Industrial Revolution. By 1900, Europe was divided into two economic zones. Great Britain, Belgium, France, the **Netherlands,** Germany, the western part of the

Austro-Hungarian Empire, and northern Italy made up an advanced industrialized core. These nations had a high standard of living and decent systems of transportation.

Another part of Europe was still largely agricultural. This was the little-industrialized area to the south and east, consisting of southern Italy, most of **Austria-Hungary, Spain, Portugal,** the Balkan kingdoms, and **Russia.** These countries provided food and raw materials for the industrial countries.

Toward a World Economy The Second Industrial Revolution, combined with the growth of transportation by steamship and railroad, fostered a true world economy. By 1900, Europeans were receiving beef and wool from Argentina and Australia, coffee from Brazil, iron ore from Algeria, and sugar from Java.

European capital was also invested abroad to develop railways, mines, electrical power plants, and banks. Of course, foreign countries also provided markets for the manufactured goods of Europe. With its capital, industries, and military might, Europe dominated the world economy by the beginning of the twentieth century.

Reading Check **Explaining** Why did Europe dominate the world economy by the beginning of the twentieth century?

Organizing the Working Classes

The desire to improve their working and living conditions led many industrial workers to form socialist political parties and socialist trade unions. These organizations emerged after 1870, but the theory on which they were based had been developed earlier by Karl Marx.

Marx's Theory In 1848, *The Communist Manifesto* was published. It was written by two Germans, **Karl Marx** and Friedrich Engels, who were appalled at the horrible conditions in factories. They blamed the system of industrial capitalism for these conditions. Their solution was a new social system. One form of Marxist socialism was eventually called communism (see Chapter 23).

Marx believed that all of world history was a "history of class struggles." According to Marx, oppressor and oppressed have "stood in constant opposition to one another" throughout history.

One group of people—the oppressors—owned the means of production (land, raw materials, money, and so forth) and thus had the power to control government and society. Indeed, government itself was an instrument of this ruling class. The other group, which depended on the owners of the means of production, were the oppressed.

In the industrialized societies of Marx's day, the class struggle continued. According to Marx, "society as a

CONNECTIONS Past To Present

May Day

On May 1, 1997, parades and demonstrations took place around the world. Mexican workers poured into the streets of Mexico City to denounce the North American Free Trade Agreement (NAFTA). Workers believed it had caused a decline in their wages. In Seoul, Korean workers hurled rocks at police to protest government corruption in South Korea. In Berlin and Leipzig, union workers marched to protest high unemployment in Germany. In Beijing, people filled Tiananmen Square to praise workers at the beginning of a three-day vacation. In Japan, two million workers attended rallies across the country. Fifteen thousand workers marched in the streets of San Salvador to demand that the government pass laws to benefit the workers of El Salvador.

Why did these marches and demonstrations occur around the world on May 1? In the nineteenth century, the rise of socialist parties in Europe led to a movement to form an international organization. The purpose of this organization was to strengthen the position of socialist parties against international capitalism.

In 1889, leaders of various socialist parties formed the Second International, a loose association of national groups. Its first action was to declare May 1 as May Day, an international labor day to be marked by strikes and mass labor demonstrations. Although the Second International no longer exists, workers around the world still observe May Day.

◀ *May Day rally near St. Basil's cathedral in Moscow, May 1, 1997*

Comparing Past and Present

Using outside sources, research what occurred last May 1. Were May Day celebrations held, and if so, where? Is May 1 still an international labor day or has the meaning of the date changed?

whole is more and more splitting up into two great hostile camps, into two great classes directly facing each other: Bourgeoisie and Proletariat." The bourgeoisie —the middle class—were the oppressors. The proletariat—the working class—were the oppressed.

Marx predicted that the struggle between the two groups would finally lead to an open revolution where the proletariat would violently overthrow the bourgeoisie. After their victory, the proletariat would form a dictatorship (government in which a person or group has absolute power) to organize the means of production. However, since the proletariat victory would essentially abolish the economic differences that create separate social classes, Marx believed that the final revolution would ultimately produce a classless society. The state—which had been an instrument of the bourgeois interests—would wither away.

Socialist Parties

In time, working-class leaders formed socialist parties based on Marx's ideas. Most important was the German Social Democratic Party (SPD), which emerged in 1875. Under the direction of its Marxist leaders, the SPD advocated revolution while organizing itself into a mass political party that competed in elections for the German parliament. Once in the parliament, SPD delegates worked to pass laws that would improve conditions for the working class.

Despite government efforts to destroy it, the German Social Democratic Party grew. When it received four million votes in the 1912 elections, it became the largest single party in Germany.

Socialist parties also emerged in other European states. In 1889, leaders of the various socialist parties joined together and formed the Second International, an association of national socialist groups that would fight against capitalism worldwide. (The First International had failed in 1872.)

Marxist parties were divided over their goals. Pure Marxists thought that capitalism would be overthrown in a violent revolution. Other Marxists, called revisionists, rejected the revolutionary approach and argued that workers must continue to organize in mass political parties and even work with other parties to gain reforms. As workers received the right to vote, they could achieve their aims by working within democratic systems.

Trade Unions

Another force working for evolutionary rather than revolutionary socialism was the trade union. In Great Britain, unions won the right to strike in the 1870s. (A strike is a work stoppage called by members of a union to pressure an employer into meeting their demands.) Soon after, workers in factories were organized into trade unions so they could use strikes to achieve reforms.

By 1900, there were two million workers in British trade unions. By 1914, there were almost four million. Trade unions in the rest of Europe had varying degrees of success. By 1914, however, they had made considerable progress in bettering both the living and the working conditions of the working classes.

Reading Check Summarizing How would you summarize Marx's theory as expressed in *The Communist Manifesto?*

TAKS Practice

SECTION 1 ASSESSMENT

Checking for Understanding

1. **Define** bourgeoisie, proletariat, dictatorship, revisionist.

2. **Identify** Thomas Edison, Alexander Graham Bell, Guglielmo Marconi, Karl Marx.

3. **Locate** Netherlands, Austria-Hungary, Spain, Portugal, Russia.

4. **Explain** how Marx's ideas came to directly impact society.

5. **List** the European nations that were still largely agricultural in 1900.

Critical Thinking

6. **Drawing Inferences** Do you think there is a relationship between the large number of technical innovations made during this period and the growing need for labor reforms and unions?

7. **Compare and Contrast** Use a Venn diagram like the one below to compare and contrast the first and second Industrial Revolutions.

First Industrial Revolution

Second Industrial Revolution

Analyzing Visuals

8. **Compare** the photos of the two Ford vehicles on page 616. Identify the differences and similarities.

Writing About History

9. **Expository Writing** After Marconi's first transmission across radio waves, he said, "I now felt for the first time absolutely certain the day would come when mankind would be able to send messages without wires. . . ." Write a paragraph about how this was a prophecy of technology to come.

Marx and Engels Proclaim the Classless Society

IN *THE COMMUNIST MANIFESTO,* Karl Marx and Friedrich Engels expressed their view that a classless society would be the end product of the struggle between the bourgeoisie and the proletariat.

German poster proclaiming "Proletarians of the World, Unite!"

66We have seen above, that the first step in the revolution by the working class, is to raise the proletariat to the position of ruling class. . . . The proletariat will use its political supremacy to wrest, by degrees, all capital from the bourgeoisie, to centralize all instruments of production in the hands of the State, i.e., of the proletariat organized as the ruling class; and to increase the total of productive forces as rapidly as possible. . . .

When, in the course of development, class distinctions have disappeared, and all production has been concentrated in the whole nation, the public power will lose its political character. Political power, properly so called, is merely the organized power of one class for oppressing another. If the proletariat during its contest with the bourgeoisie is compelled, by the force of circumstances, to organize itself as a class, if, by means of a revolution, it makes itself the ruling class, and, as such, sweeps away by force the old conditions of production, then it will, along with these conditions, have swept away the conditions for the existence of class antagonisms and of classes generally, and will thereby have abolished its own supremacy as a class.

In place of the old bourgeois society, with its classes and class antagonisms, we shall have an association, in which the free development of each is the condition for the free development of all. . . .

The Communists disdain to conceal their views and aims. They openly declare that their ends can be attained only by the forcible overthrow of all existing social conditions. Let the ruling classes tremble at a Communist revolution. The proletarians have nothing to lose but their chains. They have a world to win. Workingmen of all countries, unite!99

—Karl Marx and Friedrich Engels,
The Communist Manifesto

Analyzing Primary Sources

1. Do you agree with Marx's definition of political power? Why or why not?
2. Do you think Marx's idea of a classless society is realistic? Why or why not?

SECTION 2 The Emergence of Mass Society

Guide to Reading

Main Ideas
- A varied middle class in Victorian Britain believed in the principles of hard work and good conduct.
- New opportunities for women and the working class improved their lives.

Key Terms
feminism, literacy

People to Identify
Amalie Sieveking, Florence Nightingale, Clara Barton, Emmeline Pankhurst

Places to Locate
London, Frankfurt

Preview Questions
1. What were the chief characteristics of the middle class in the nineteenth century?
2. How did the position of women change between 1870 and 1914?

Reading Strategy
Summarizing Information As you read this section, complete a graphic organizer like the one below summarizing the divisions among the social classes.

Social Classes		
Working	Middle	Wealthy

Preview of Events

◆1870	◆1875	◆1880	◆1885	◆1890	◆1895	◆1900

1870
British wives gain greater property rights

1881
First publication of London's *Evening News*

1885
10,000 people watch British Soccer Cup finals

1903
Women's Social and Political Union established

Voices from the Past

Sylvia Pankhurst, feminist and daughter of Emmeline Pankhurst

In *History of the Suffrage Movement,* Sylvia Pankhurst described the efforts of women to enter the House of Commons to petition for the right to vote:

❝Those of us who took refuge in doorways were dragged roughly down the steps and hurled back in front of the horses. When even this failed to banish us, the foot constables rushed at us and, catching us fiercely by the shoulders, turned us round again and then seizing us by the back of the neck and thumping us cruelly between the shoulders forced us at a running pace along the streets until we were far from the House of Commons. They had been told to drive us away and to make as few arrests as possible. Still we returned, until at last sixty-five women, all of them bruised, had been taken to the police station.❞

—*Sources of the West,* Mark A. Kishlansky, ed., 1998

The movement for women's rights was one aspect of the new mass society.

The New Urban Environment

By the end of the nineteenth century, the new industrial world had led to the emergence of a mass society in which the concerns of the majority of the population—the lower classes—were central. More and more people lived in cities. In the early 1850s, urban dwellers made up about 40 percent of the English population, 15 percent of the French, 10 percent of the population in Prussia (the largest

German state), and 5 percent in Russia. By 1890, urban dwellers had increased to some 60 percent in England, 25 percent in France, 30 percent in Prussia, and 10 percent in Russia. The size of cities also grew, especially in industrialized countries. Between 1800 and 1900, the population in **London** grew from 960,000 to 6,500,000.

Urban populations grew quickly because of the vast migration to cities from rural areas. Lack of jobs and lack of land drove people from the countryside to the city. There, they found jobs in factories and, later, in service trades and professions.

Cities also grew faster in the second half of the nineteenth century because living conditions improved so much that more people could survive there longer. In the 1840s, a number of urban reformers had pointed to filthy living conditions as the chief cause of deadly epidemic diseases in the cities. Cholera, for example, had ravaged Europe in the early 1830s and 1840s, especially in the overcrowded cities.

Following the advice of reformers, city governments created boards of health to improve the quality of housing. City medical officers and building inspectors now inspected dwellings for public health hazards. New building regulations required running water and internal drainage systems for all new buildings.

Essential to the public health of the modern European city was the ability to bring in clean water and to expel sewage. The need for fresh water was met by a system of dams and reservoirs that stored the water and by aqueducts and tunnels that carried it from the countryside to the city and into individual dwellings. Gas heaters in the 1860s, and later electric heaters, made regular hot baths available to many people.

The treatment of sewage was improved by building mammoth underground pipes that carried raw sewage far from the city for disposal. The city of **Frankfurt,** Germany, began its program for sewers with a lengthy public campaign featuring the slogan "from the toilet to the river in half an hour."

✓ **Reading Check** **Explaining** Why did cities grow so quickly in the nineteenth century?

Social Structure of Mass Society

After 1871, most people enjoyed an improved standard of living. Even so, great poverty remained a part of Western society. Between the few who were rich and the many who were very poor existed several middle-class groups.

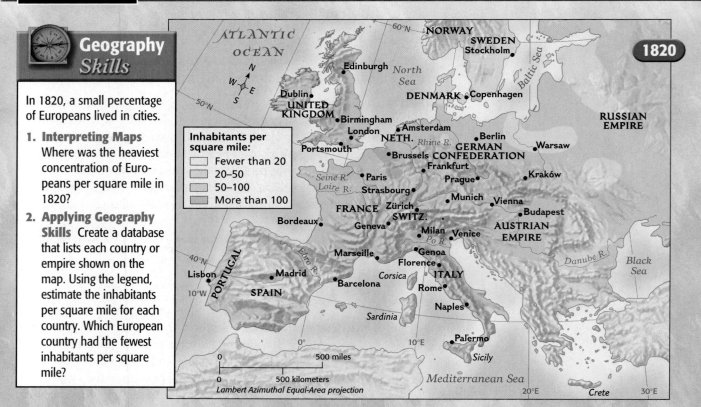

NATIONAL GEOGRAPHIC **European Population Growth and Relocation, 1820–1900**

Geography Skills

In 1820, a small percentage of Europeans lived in cities.

1. **Interpreting Maps** Where was the heaviest concentration of Europeans per square mile in 1820?

2. **Applying Geography Skills** Create a database that lists each country or empire shown on the map. Using the legend, estimate the inhabitants per square mile for each country. Which European country had the fewest inhabitants per square mile?

Inhabitants per square mile:
- Fewer than 20
- 20–50
- 50–100
- More than 100

The New Elite At the top of European society stood a wealthy elite. This group made up only 5 percent of the population but controlled between 30 and 40 percent of the wealth. During the nineteenth century, landed aristocrats had joined with the most successful industrialists, bankers, and merchants—the wealthy upper middle class—to form this new elite. Members of the elite, whether aristocratic or upper middle class in background, became leaders in the government and military.

Marriage also served to unite the two groups. Daughters of business tycoons gained aristocratic titles and aristocratic heirs gained new sources of cash. For example, when wealthy American Consuelo Vanderbilt married the British duke of Marlborough, the new duchess brought approximately $10 million to her husband.

The Middle Classes The middle classes consisted of a variety of groups. Below the upper middle class, which formed part of the new elite, was a middle group that included lawyers, doctors, members of the civil service, business managers, engineers, architects, accountants, and chemists. Beneath this solid and comfortable middle group was a lower middle class of small shopkeepers, traders, and prosperous peasants. The members of this group provided goods and services for the classes above them.

The Second Industrial Revolution produced a new group of white-collar workers between the lower middle class and the lower classes. This group included traveling salespeople, bookkeepers, telephone operators, department store salespeople, and secretaries. Although not highly paid, these white-collar workers were often committed to middle-class ideals.

The middle classes shared a certain lifestyle with values that tended to dominate much of nineteenth-century society. The members of the middle class liked to preach their worldview both to their children and to the upper and lower classes of their society. This was especially evident in Victorian Britain, often considered a model of middle-class society.

The European middle classes believed in hard work, which was open to everyone and guaranteed to have positive results. They were also regular churchgoers who believed in the good conduct associated with Christian morality. The middle class was concerned with the right way of doing things, which gave rise to such best-selling manners and etiquette books as *The Habits of Good Society*.

Geography Skills

Two population changes occurred in Europe from 1820 to 1900: the overall population increased, and it shifted from rural to urban areas.

1. **Interpreting Maps** Which country has the greater population density: Spain or Italy?

2. **Applying Geography Skills** Analyze the relationship between the increased urban populations shown here and the areas of industrial concentration shown on the map on page 617.

Map labels: 1900 · ATLANTIC OCEAN · NORWAY · SWEDEN · Stockholm · Baltic Sea · Edinburgh · North Sea · Dublin · DENMARK · Copenhagen · RUSSIAN EMPIRE · UNITED KINGDOM · Birmingham · Amsterdam · London · NETH. · Rhine R. · Berlin · Warsaw · Portsmouth · GERMAN EMPIRE · Brussels · BELG. · Frankfurt · Seine R. · Paris · Prague · Kraków · Loire R. · Strasbourg · Munich · Vienna · FRANCE · Zürich · SWITZ. · Budapest · Bordeaux · Geneva · Milan · Venice · AUSTRIAN EMPIRE · Marseille · Genoa · Florence · Po R. · Danube R. · Black Sea · Lisbon · Madrid · Corsica · ITALY · Rome · PORTUGAL · SPAIN · Barcelona · Naples · Sardinia · Palermo · Sicily · Mediterranean Sea · Crete

Legend: Inhabitants per square mile: Fewer than 20 · 20–50 · 50–100 · More than 100

500 miles · 500 kilometers · Lambert Azimuthal Equal-Area projection

The Working Classes Below the middle classes on the social scale were the working classes, which made up almost 80 percent of the European population. Many of the members of these classes were landholding peasants, farm laborers, and sharecroppers, especially in eastern Europe.

The urban working class consisted of many different groups, including skilled artisans and semi-skilled laborers. At the bottom of the urban working class were the unskilled laborers. They were the largest group of workers and included day laborers and large numbers of domestic servants. One out of every seven employed persons in Great Britain in 1900 was a domestic servant. Most domestic servants were women.

Urban workers experienced an improvement in the material conditions of their lives after 1870. Reforms created better living conditions in cities. In addition, a rise in wages, along with a decline in many consumer costs, made it possible for workers to buy more than just food and housing. Workers now had money for more clothes and even leisure activities. At the same time, strikes were leading to 10-hour workdays and Saturday afternoons off.

✓Reading Check **Identifying** Name the major groups in the social structure of the late nineteenth century.

The Experiences of Women

In 1800, women were mainly defined by family and household roles. They remained legally inferior and economically dependent upon men. In the course of the nineteenth century, women struggled to change their status.

New Job Opportunities During much of the nineteenth century, working-class groups maintained the belief that women should remain at home to bear and nurture children and should not be allowed in the industrial workforce. Working-class men argued that keeping women out of industrial work would ensure the moral and physical well-being of families.

The Second Industrial Revolution, however, opened the door to new jobs for women. A high demand for relatively low paid white-collar workers, coupled with a shortage of male workers, led many

Women worked as operators and secretaries at the Paris telephone exchange in 1904.

employers to hire women. Both industrial plants and retail shops needed clerks, typists, secretaries, file clerks, and salesclerks.

The expansion of government services created opportunities for women to be secretaries and telephone operators, and to take jobs in the fields of education, health, and social services. While some middle-class women held these jobs, they were mainly filled by the working class who aspired to a better quality of life.

Marriage and the Family Many people in the nineteenth century believed in the ideal expressed in Lord Tennyson's *The Princess,* published in 1847:

❝Man for the field and woman for the hearth:
Man for the sword and for the needle she:
Man with the head and woman with the heart:
Man to command and woman to obey. . . .❞

This view of the sexes was strengthened during the Industrial Revolution. As the chief family wage earners, men worked outside the home. Women were left with the care of the family.

Throughout the 1800s, marriage remained the only honorable and available career for most women. There was also one important change. The number of children born to the average woman began to decline—the most significant development in the modern family. This decline in the birthrate was tied to improved economic conditions, as well as increased use of birth control. In 1882, Europe's first birth control clinic was founded in Amsterdam.

The family was the central institution of middle-class life. With fewer children in the family, mothers could devote more time to child care and domestic leisure.

The middle-class family fostered an ideal of togetherness. The Victorians created the family Christmas with its Yule log, tree, songs, and exchange of gifts. By the 1850s, Fourth of July celebrations in the United States had changed from wild celebrations to family picnics.

The lives of working-class women were different from those of their middle-class counterparts. While they may have aspired to middle-class ideals, most working-class women had to earn money to help support their families. Daughters in working-class families were expected to work until they married. After marriage, they often did small jobs at home to support the family. For the children of the working classes, childhood was over by the age of nine or ten, when children became apprentices or were employed in odd jobs. 📖 *(See page 997 to read excerpts from L'Atelier's* The Unfortunate Situation of Working Women *in the Primary Sources Library.)*

Between 1890 and 1914, however, family patterns among the working class began to change. Higher-paying jobs in heavy industry and improvements in the standard of living made it possible for working-class families to depend on the income of husbands alone.

By the early twentieth century, some working-class mothers could afford to stay at home, following the pattern of middle-class women. At the same time, working-class families aspired to buy new consumer products, such as sewing machines and cast-iron stoves.

The Movement for Women's Rights

Modern **feminism**, or the movement for women's rights, had its beginnings during the Enlightenment, when some women advocated equality for women based on the doctrine of natural rights. In the 1830s, a number of women in the United States and Europe argued for the right of women to divorce and own property. (By law, a husband had almost complete control over his wife's property.) These early efforts were not very successful, and married women in Britain did not win the right to own some property until 1870.

The fight for property rights was only the beginning of the women's movement. Some middle- and upper-middle-class women fought for and gained access to universities, and others sought entry into occupations dominated by men.

Though training to become doctors was largely closed to women, some entered the medical field by becoming nurses. In Germany, **Amalie Sieveking** was a nursing pioneer who founded the Female Association for the Care of the Poor and Sick in Hamburg. More famous is the British nurse **Florence Nightingale.** Her efforts during the Crimean War (1853–1856), combined with those of **Clara Barton** in the U.S. Civil War (1861–1865), transformed nursing into a profession of trained, middle-class "women in white."

By the 1840s and 1850s, the movement for women's rights expanded as women called for equal political rights. Many feminists believed that the right to vote was the key to improving the overall position of women.

The British women's movement was the most active in Europe. The Women's Social and Political Union, founded in 1903 by **Emmeline Pankhurst** and her daughters, used unusual publicity stunts to call attention to its demands. Its members pelted

Picturing **History**

Shown below are Emmeline Pankhurst, her daughters, and a fellow suffragist. Why do you think women such as these had to fight so hard and long to obtain the right to vote?

SPORTS & CONTESTS

The New Team Sports

Sports were by no means a new activity in the late nineteenth century. Soccer games had been played by peasants and workers, and these games had often been bloody and even deadly. However, in the late nineteenth century, sports became strictly organized. The English Football Association (founded in 1863) and the American Bowling Congress (founded in 1895), for example, provided strict rules and officials to enforce them.

The new sports were not just for leisure or fun. Like other forms of middle-class recreation, they were intended to provide excellent training, especially for youth.

Woodcut of scene from 1886 baseball game between New York and Boston

The participants could not only develop individual skills but also acquire a sense of teamwork useful for military service.

These characteristics were already evident in British schools in the 1850s and 1860s. Such schools as Harrow and Loretto placed organized sports at the center of education. At Loretto, for example, education was supposed to instill "First—Character. Second—Physique. Third—Intelligence. Fourth—Manners. Fifth—Information."

The new team sports rapidly became professionalized as well. The English Football Association, mentioned above, regulated professional soccer. In the United States, the first national association to recognize professional baseball players was

government officials with eggs, chained themselves to lampposts, burned railroad cars, and smashed the windows of department stores on fashionable shopping streets. These suffragists (people who advocate the extension of political rights, such as voting rights) had one basic aim: the right of women to full citizenship in the nation-state.

Before World War I, demands for women's rights were being heard throughout Europe and the United States. Before 1914, however, women had the right to vote in only a few nations like Norway and Finland, along with some American states. It would take the dramatic upheaval of World War I to make male-dominated governments give in on this basic issue of the rights of women.

Reading Check **Identifying** What was the basic aim of the suffragists?

Universal Education

Universal education was a product of the mass society of the late nineteenth and early twentieth centuries. Education in the early nineteenth century was primarily for the elite and the wealthier middle class. However, between 1870 and 1914, most Western governments began to set up state-financed primary schools. Both boys and girls between the ages of 6 and 12 were required to attend these schools. States also took responsibility for training teachers by setting up teacher-training schools.

Why did Western nations make this commitment to public education? One reason was industrialization. In the first Industrial Revolution, unskilled labor (workers without training or experience) was able to meet factory needs. The new firms of the Second Industrial Revolution, however, needed trained,

formed in 1863. By 1900, the National League and the American League had complete control over professional baseball.

Mass spectator sports became a big business. In 1872, two thousand people watched the British Soccer Cup finals. By 1885, the crowd had increased to ten thousand and by 1901, to a hundred thousand. Spectator sports even reflected class differences. Upper-class soccer teams in Britain viewed working-class teams as vicious and inclined to "money-grubbing, tricks, sensational displays, and utter rottenness."

Sports in the late nineteenth century were mostly for men, who believed that females were not well suited for "vigorous physical activity." Nevertheless, middle-class women could play "easy" sports—croquet and lawn tennis. Eventually, some sports began to appear at women's colleges and girls' public schools in England.

Late nineteenth-century game of croquet

CONNECTING TO THE PAST

1. **Describing** What did sports offer middle-class men of the late nineteenth century?

2. **Evaluating** Why do you think spectator sports became such a big business?

3. **Writing about History** Write a brief essay comparing the educational goals at your school with those at Loretto. What are the differences and similarities?

---

skilled labor. Both boys and girls with an elementary education now had new job possibilities beyond their villages or small towns. These included white-collar jobs in railways, post offices, and the teaching and nursing fields.

The chief motive for public education, however, was political. Giving more people the right to vote created a need for better-educated voters. Even more important was the fact that primary schools instilled patriotism. As people lost their ties to local regions and even to religion, nationalism gave them a new faith.

Compulsory elementary education created a demand for teachers, and most of them were women. Many men saw teaching as a part of women's "natural role" as nurturers of children. Females were also paid lower salaries, which in itself was a strong incentive for states to set up teacher-training schools

for women. The first female colleges were really teacher-training schools.

The most immediate result of public education was an increase in literacy, or the ability to read. In western and central Europe, most adults could read by 1900. Where there was less schooling, the story was very different. Nearly 79 percent of adults in Serbia and Russia still could not read by 1900.

With the increase in literacy after 1870 came the rise of mass newspapers, such as the *Evening News* (1881) and the *Daily Mail* (1896) in London. Millions of copies were sold each day. These newspapers were all written in an easily understood style. They were also sensationalistic—that is, they provided gossip and gruesome details of crimes.

✓ **Reading Check** **Explaining** Why did states make a commitment to provide public education?

This English train (c. 1845) was an early form of the mass transportation that enabled more people to participate in leisure activities.

New Forms of Leisure

The Second Industrial Revolution allowed people to pursue new forms of leisure. The new forms of popular mass leisure both entertained large crowds and distracted them from the realities of their work lives. Leisure came to be viewed as what people do for fun after work. The industrial system gave people new times—evening hours, weekends, and a week or two in the summer—to indulge in leisure activities.

Amusement parks introduced people to exciting new experiences and technology. By the late nineteenth century, team sports had developed into yet another form of leisure. Subways and streetcars meant that even the working classes could make their way to athletic games, amusement parks, and dance halls.

The new mass leisure was quite different from earlier forms of popular culture. The earlier festivals and fairs had been based on community participation. The new forms of leisure were standardized for largely passive audiences. Amusement parks and professional sports teams were essentially big businesses organized to make profits.

✔ **Reading Check** **Explaining** How did innovations in transportation change leisure activities during the Second Industrial Revolution?

🔻**TAKS Practice**

SECTION 2 ASSESSMENT

Checking for Understanding

1. Define feminism, literacy.

2. Identify Amalie Sieveking, Florence Nightingale, Clara Barton, Emmeline Pankhurst.

3. Locate London, Frankfurt.

4. Explain what is meant by the term *universal education*. How did industrialization help propel the movement for universal education?

5. List the explanations given in this section for the decline in birthrate during the 1800s.

Critical Thinking

6. Explain Why have certain occupations such as elementary teaching and nursing historically been dominated by women?

7. Summarizing Information Use a graphic organizer like the one below to summarize the results of urban reforms.

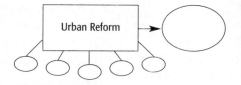

Analyzing Visuals

8. Examine the clothing worn by the women in the photos on pages 624, 625, and 627. How have women's fashions changed since the late nineteenth century? How have women's political rights changed? In what ways might these changes be related?

Writing About History

9. Persuasive Writing The feminist movement changed the role of women. In an essay, argue whether these changes had a positive or negative impact on society.

The National State and Democracy

Guide to Reading

Main Ideas
- The governments of western Europe were challenged by the development of new political parties and labor unions.
- International rivalries led to conflicts in the Balkans and to World War I.

Key Terms
ministerial responsibility, Duma

People to Identify
Otto von Bismarck, William II, Francis Joseph, Nicholas II, Queen Liliuokalani

Places to Locate
St. Petersburg, Montenegro

Preview Questions
1. What domestic problems did the United States and Canada face?
2. What issues sparked the crises in the Balkans?

Reading Strategy
Summarizing Information As you read this section, complete a diagram like the one below listing the countries in each alliance.

Triple Alliance 1882   Triple Entente 1907

Preview of Events

◆1860	◆1870	◆1880	◆1890	◆1900	◆1910

1867
Dual monarchy of Austria-Hungary created

1870
France establishes the Third Republic

1882
Triple Alliance created

1900
Labour Party emerges in Great Britain

1907
Triple Entente formed

Voices from the Past

Czar Nicholas II

On January 22, 1905, a group of peaceful demonstrators tried to present a petition of grievances to Czar Nicholas II. One described the result:

❝We were not more than thirty yards from the soldiers, being separated from them only by the bridge over the Tarakanovskii Canal, when suddenly, without any warning and without a moment's delay, was heard the dry crack of many rifle-shots. . . . A little boy of ten years, who was carrying a church lantern, fell pierced by a bullet. Both the [black]smiths who guarded me were killed, as well as all those who were carrying the icons and banners; and all these emblems now lay scattered on the snow. The soldiers were actually shooting into the courtyards of the adjoining houses, where the crowd tried to find refuge.❞

— *Eyewitness to History,* John Carey, ed., 1987

As a result of the massacre of peaceful demonstrators, the czar faced a revolution. In Russia and other parts of central and eastern Europe, many groups struggled for independence. Throughout much of the western world, however, the national state had become the focus of people's loyalties.

Western Europe and Political Democracy

By the late nineteenth century, progress had been made toward establishing constitutions, parliaments, and individual liberties in the major European states.

Austria-Hungary
French Empire
German Empire
Kingdom of Italy
Ottoman Empire
Russian Empire

0   500 miles
0   500 kilometers
Lambert Equal-Area projection

Political democracy, characterized by universal male suffrage and ministerial responsibility, expanded. As more and more men (and later, women) were able to vote, political parties needed to create larger organizations and to find ways to appeal to the masses of people who were now part of the political process.

Great Britain By 1871, Great Britain had long had a working two-party parliamentary system. For the next 50 years, these two parties—the Liberal Party and the Conservative Party—alternated in power at regular intervals. Both parties were led by a ruling class composed of aristocratic landowners and upper-middle-class businesspeople.

The Liberals and Conservatives competed with each other in passing laws that expanded the right to vote. Reform acts in 1867 and 1884 increased the number of adult males who could vote. By the end of World War I (1918), all males over age 21 and women over age 30 could vote.

At the end of the nineteenth century, then, political democracy was becoming well established in Britain. Social reforms for the working class soon followed. The working class in Great Britain supported the Liberal Party. Two developments made Liberals

Geography Skills

Various empires dominated the European political scene in the late nineteenth century.

1. **Interpreting Maps** Which three empires extend beyond the boundaries shown on this map?
2. **Applying Geography Skills** Pose and answer your own question about how the geographic relationships shown on this map might result in major conflicts, such as the impending world war.

fear that they would lose this support. First, trade unions grew, and they began to favor a more radical change of the economic system. Second, in 1900, a new party—the Labour Party, which dedicated itself to the interests of workers—emerged.

The Liberals held the government from 1906 to 1914. To retain the support of the workers, they voted for a series of social reforms. The National Insurance Act of 1911 provided benefits for workers in case of sickness and unemployment. Additional laws provided a small pension for those over 70 and compensation for those injured in accidents while at work.

France In France, the collapse of Louis-Napoleon's Second Empire left the country in confusion. In 1875, five years after it was proclaimed, the Third Republic gained a republican constitution. The new government had a president and a legislature made up of two houses. Members of the upper house, called the Senate, were elected indirectly. In the lower house, called the Chamber of Deputies, members were elected by universal male suffrage.

The powers of the president were not well defined in the constitution. A premier (or prime minister) actually led the government. The premier and his ministers were responsible to the Chamber of Deputies, not to the president. This principle of ministerial responsibility—the idea that the prime minister is responsible to the popularly elected legislative body and not to the executive officer—is crucial for democracy.

France failed to develop a strong parliamentary system. The existence of a dozen political parties forced the premier to depend on a coalition of parties to stay in power. Frequent changes of government leadership plagued the republic. Nevertheless, by 1914, the Third Republic commanded the loyalty of most French people.

Italy Italy had emerged by 1870 as a united national state. The nation had little sense of unity, however, because a great gulf separated the poverty-stricken south from the industrialized north. Constant turmoil between labor and industry weakened the social fabric of the nation. Widespread corruption among government officials prevented the government from dealing with these problems. Universal male suffrage was granted in 1912 but did little to stop corruption and weakness in the government.

✓ **Reading Check** **Summarizing** What is the principle of ministerial responsibility?

Central and Eastern Europe: The Old Order

Germany, Austria-Hungary (or the Austro-Hungarian Empire), and Russia pursued policies that were quite different from those of some western European nations.

Germany The constitution of the new imperial Germany begun by **Otto von Bismarck** in 1871 provided for a two-house legislature. The lower house of the German parliament, the Reichstag, was elected on the basis of universal male suffrage.

Ministers of government, however, were responsible not to the parliament, but to the emperor. The emperor also controlled the armed forces, foreign policy, and the government bureaucracy. As chancellor (prime minister), Bismarck worked to keep Germany from becoming a democracy.

By the reign of **William II,** emperor from 1888 to 1918, Germany had become the strongest military and industrial power in Europe. With the expansion of industry and cities came demands for democracy.

Conservative forces—especially the landowning nobility and big industrialists, two powerful ruling groups in imperial Germany—tried to block the movement for democracy by supporting a strong

Analyzing *Political Cartoons*

In 1890, Emperor William II fired Otto von Bismarck and took control of Germany's relations with other countries. In this scene, the emperor is shown relaxing on a throne made of cannonballs and artillery, while Bismarck bids him good-bye. The woman watching represents Germany. What do you think the cartoonist is trying to say?

foreign policy. They believed that expansion abroad would not only increase their profits, but would also divert people from pursuing democratic reforms.

Austria-Hungary After the creation of the dual monarchy of Austria-Hungary in 1867, Austria enacted a constitution that, in theory, set up a parliamentary system with ministerial responsibility. In reality, the emperor, **Francis Joseph,** largely ignored this system. He appointed and dismissed his own ministers and issued decrees, or laws, when the parliament was not in session.

Austria remained troubled by conflicts between the various nationalities in the state. The German minority that governed Austria felt increasingly threatened by Czechs, Poles, and other Slavic groups within the empire. Representatives of these groups in the parliament agitated for their freedom, which further encouraged the emperor to ignore the parliament and govern by imperial decrees.

Unlike Austria, Hungary had a parliament that worked. It was controlled by Magyar landowners who dominated the peasants and ethnic groups.

Russia In Russia, **Nicholas II** began his rule in 1894 believing that the absolute power of the czars should be preserved: "I shall maintain the principle of autocracy just as firmly and unflinchingly as did my unforgettable father." Conditions were changing, however.

Industrialization began late in Russia but progressed rapidly after 1890. By 1900, Russia had become the fourth largest producer of steel behind the United States, Germany, and Great Britain. With industrialization came factories, an industrial working class, and pitiful working and living conditions. Socialist parties developed, including the Marxist Social Democratic Party and the Social Revolutionaries, but government repression forced both parties to go underground. Growing discontent and opposition to the czarist regime finally exploded into the Revolution of 1905.

On January 22, 1905, a massive procession of workers went to the Winter Palace in **St. Petersburg** to present a petition of grievances to the czar. Troops foolishly opened fire on the peaceful demonstration, killing hundreds. This "Bloody Sunday" caused workers throughout Russia to call strikes.

Nicholas II was eventually forced to grant civil liberties and create a legislative assembly, called the **Duma.** These reforms, however, proved short-lived. By 1907, the czar had already curtailed the power of the Duma, and again used the army and bureaucracy to rule Russia.

✓**Reading Check** **Identifying** What was the role of the Duma in the Russian government?

Scene at the Narva Gate in St. Petersburg, January 22, 1905, the day known as "Bloody Sunday"

The United States and Canada

Between 1870 and 1914, the United States became an industrial power with a foreign empire. Canada faced problems of national unity during this period.

Aftermath of the Civil War Four years of bloody civil war had preserved American national unity, but the old South had been destroyed. One-fifth of the adult white male population in the South had been killed, and four million African American slaves had been freed.

In 1865, the Thirteenth Amendment to the Constitution was passed, abolishing slavery. Later, the Fourteenth and Fifteenth Amendments gave citizenship to African Americans and the right to vote to African American males. However, new state laws in southern states soon stripped African Americans of their right to vote. By 1880, supporters of white supremacy were in power everywhere in the South.

Economy Between 1860 and 1914, the United States shifted from an agrarian to an industrial nation. In 1860, 20 percent of Americans lived in cities, but by 1900, 40 percent lived in cities. American steel and iron production was the best in the world in 1900, with Carnegie Steel Company alone producing more steel than all of Great Britain.

Migration patterns were an important factor. Europeans migrated to both North and South America, but they migrated to the United States in massive numbers—almost 11 million did so between 1870 and 1900. Some left to escape European conditions. Others were drawn by new opportunities.

In 1900, the United States was the world's richest nation, but the richest 9 percent of Americans owned 71 percent of the wealth. Many workers labored in unsafe factories, and devastating cycles of unemployment made them insecure. Many tried to organize unions, but the American Federation of Labor represented only 8.4 percent of the labor force.

Expansion Abroad At the end of the nineteenth century, the United States began to expand abroad. The Samoan Islands in the Pacific became the first important United States colony. By 1887, American settlers had gained control of the sugar industry on the Hawaiian Islands.

As more Americans settled in Hawaii, they sought to gain political power. When **Queen Liliuokalani** (lee•lee•oo•oh•kah•LAH•nee) tried to strengthen the power of the monarchy to keep the islands under her peoples' control, the United States government sent military forces to the islands. The queen was deposed, and Hawaii was annexed by the United States in 1898.

In 1898, the United States also defeated Spain in the Spanish-American War. As a result, the United States acquired the formerly Spanish possessions of Puerto Rico, Guam, and the Philippines.

The Filipino people hoped for independence, but the United States refused to grant it. It took the United States three years to pacify the Philippines and establish control. By the beginning of the twentieth century, the United States, the world's richest nation, had an empire.

Canada At the beginning of 1870, the Dominion of Canada had four provinces: Quebec, Ontario, Nova Scotia, and New Brunswick. With the addition in 1871 of two more provinces—Manitoba and British Columbia—the Dominion of Canada extended from the Atlantic to the Pacific.

Real unity was difficult to achieve, however, because of distrust between the English-speaking and French-speaking peoples of Canada. Wilfred Laurier, who became the first French-Canadian prime minister in 1896, was able to reconcile these two major groups. During his administration, industrialization boomed, and immigrants from Europe helped populate Canada's vast territories.

Reading Check **Identifying** Name the territories acquired by the United States in 1898.

International Rivalries

Otto von Bismarck realized that Germany's emergence in 1871 as the most powerful state in continental Europe had upset the balance of power established at Vienna in 1815. Fearing that France intended to create an anti-German alliance, Bismarck made a defensive alliance with Austria-Hungary in 1879. In 1882, Italy joined this alliance.

The Triple Alliance of 1882 united the powers of Germany, Austria-Hungary, and Italy in a defensive alliance against France. At the same time, Bismarck maintained a separate treaty with Russia and tried to remain on good terms with Great Britain.

In 1890, Emperor William II fired Bismarck and took control of Germany's foreign policy. The emperor embarked on an activist policy dedicated to enhancing German power. He wanted, as he put it, to find Germany's rightful "place in the sun."

One of the changes he made in Bismarck's foreign policy was to drop the treaty with Russia. The ending of that alliance brought France and Russia together. In 1894, these two powers formed a military alliance.

Over the next 10 years, German policies abroad caused the British to draw closer to France. By 1907, an alliance of Great Britain, France, and Russia—known as the Triple Entente—stood opposed to the Triple Alliance of Germany, Austria-Hungary, and Italy.

Europe was now dangerously divided into two opposing camps that became more and more unwilling to compromise. A series of crises in the Balkans between 1908 and 1913 set the stage for World War I.

✓ **Reading Check** **Summarizing** What countries formed the Triple Alliance and the Triple Entente?

Crises in the Balkans

Over the course of the nineteenth century, the Balkan provinces of the Ottoman Empire had gradually gained their freedom, although regional rivalries between Austria-Hungary and Russia had complicated the process. By 1878, Greece, Serbia, Romania, and **Montenegro** had become independent states. Bulgaria did not become totally independent, but was allowed to operate under Russian protection. The Balkan territories of Bosnia and Herzegovina were placed under the protection of Austria-Hungary.

In 1908, Austria-Hungary took the drastic step of annexing Bosnia and Herzegovina. Serbia was outraged. The annexation of these two Slavic-speaking

territories dashed the Serbians' hopes of creating a large Serbian kingdom that would include most of the southern Slavs.

The Russians, as protectors of their fellow Slavs, supported the Serbs and opposed the annexation. Backed by the Russians, the Serbs prepared for war against Austria-Hungary. At this point, Emperor William II of Germany demanded that the Russians accept Austria-Hungary's annexation of Bosnia and Herzegovina or face war with Germany.

Weakened from their defeat in the Russo-Japanese War in 1905, the Russians backed down but vowed revenge. Two wars between Balkan states in 1912 and 1913 further embittered the inhabitants and created more tensions among the great powers.

The Serbians blamed Austria-Hungary for their failure to create a large Serbian kingdom. Austria-Hungary was convinced that Serbia was a mortal threat to its empire and must at some point be crushed. As Serbia's chief supporters, the Russians were angry and determined not to back down again in the event of another confrontation with Austria-Hungary or Germany in the Balkans. The allies of Austria-Hungary and Russia were determined to support their respective allies more strongly in another crisis. By the beginning of 1914, these countries viewed each other with suspicion.

✓ **Reading Check** **Explaining** Why were the Serbs outraged when Austria-Hungary annexed Bosnia and Herzegovina?

🔶**TAKS Practice**

SECTION 3 ASSESSMENT

Checking for Understanding

1. **Define** ministerial responsibility, Duma.

2. **Identify** Otto von Bismarck, William II, Francis Joseph, Nicholas II, Queen Liliuokalani.

3. **Locate** St. Petersburg, Montenegro.

4. **Explain** how the United States became an industrial power. What problems did industrialization cause in the United States and how did people attempt to solve some of these problems?

5. **List** the series of events leading to unrest in Russia at the turn of the century. What were the consequences of "Bloody Sunday"?

Critical Thinking

6. **Analyze** Which country do you think had a stronger democracy at the end of the nineteenth century, France or England? Why?

7. **Compare and Contrast** Use this chapter and Chapter 17 to create a Venn diagram like the one below comparing and contrasting the systems of government in France and the United States.

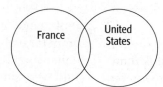

France / United States

Analyzing Visuals

8. **Examine** the illustration of "Bloody Sunday" on page 632. What does the artist seem to be saying about the events that occurred on January 22, 1905? Does the picture reflect a particular point of view? Where might an illustration such as this have been exhibited and why?

Writing About History

9. **Expository Writing** Do some research about recent conflicts in the Balkans. Write one or two paragraphs comparing the causes of the recent conflicts with the causes of the conflicts between Balkan countries in the early twentieth century.

SKILLBUILDER

**★ TAKS
Practice**

Detecting Bias

Why Learn This Skill?

Suppose you see an ad showing two happy customers shaking hands with a used-car salesman. The ad says, "Visit Honest Harry for the best deal on wheels." That evening you see a television program that investigates used-car sales businesses. The report says that many of these businesses cheat their customers.

Each message expresses a bias—an inclination or prejudice that inhibits impartiality. Harry wants

to sell cars; the television program wants to attract viewers. Most people have preconceived feelings, opinions, and attitudes that affect their judgment on many topics. Ideas stated as facts may be opinions. Detecting bias enables us to evaluate the accuracy of information.

Learning the Skill

In detecting bias:

- Identify the writer's or speaker's purpose.

- Watch for emotionally charged language such as *exploit, terrorize,* and *cheat.*

- Look for visual images that provoke a strong emotional response.

- Look for overgeneralizations such as *unique, honest,* and *everybody.*

- Notice italics, underlining, and punctuation that highlight particular ideas.

- Examine the material to determine whether it presents equal coverage of differing views.

Practicing the Skill

Industrialization produced widespread changes in society and widespread disagreement on its effects. Karl Marx and Friedrich Engels presented their viewpoint on industrialization in *The Communist Manifesto* in 1848. Read the following excerpt and then answer these questions.

> 66 The bourgeoisie . . . has put an end to all feudal, patriarchal, idyllic relations. It has pitilessly torn asunder the motley feudal ties that bound man to his 'natural superiors,' and has left remaining no other nexus [link] between man and man than naked self-interest, than callous 'cash payment.' It has drowned the most heavenly of ecstasies of religious fervor, of chivalrous enthusiasm . . . in the icy water of egotistical calculation. . . . In one word, for exploitation, veiled by religious and political illusions, it has substituted naked, shameless, direct, brutal exploitation. 99

❶ What is the purpose of this quote?

❷ What are three examples of emotionally charged language?

❸ According to Marx and Engels, which is more inhumane—the exploitation by feudal lords or by the bourgeoisie? Why?

❹ What bias about the bourgeoisie is expressed in this excerpt?

Applying the Skill

Find written material about a topic of interest in your community. Possible sources include editorials, letters to the editor, and pamphlets from political candidates and interest groups. Write a short report analyzing the material for evidence of bias.

 Glencoe's **Skillbuilder Interactive Workbook, Level 2,** provides instruction and practice in key social studies skills.

Toward the Modern Consciousness

Main Ideas
- Innovative artistic movements during the late 1800s and early 1900s rejected traditional styles.
- Extreme nationalism and racism led to an increase in anti-Semitism.
- Developments in science changed how people saw themselves and their world.

Key Terms
psychoanalysis, pogrom, modernism

People to Identify
Marie Curie, Albert Einstein, Sigmund Freud, Claude Monet, Pablo Picasso

Places to Locate
Vienna, France

Preview Questions
1. How did Einstein and Freud challenge people's views of the world?
2. How did modernism revolutionize architecture?

Reading Strategy
Identifying Information As you read this section, complete a chart like the one below that lists an artist and a characteristic of the art movement indicated.

Impressionism		
Post-Impressionism		
Cubism		
Abstract Expressionism		

Preview of Events

♦1890	♦1895	♦1900	♦1905	♦1910	♦1915	♦1920

1896
Herzl publishes *The Jewish State*

1900
Freud publishes *The Interpretation of Dreams*

1905
Einstein publishes his special theory of relativity

1913
Stravinsky's *The Rite of Spring* performed in Paris

Voices from the Past

Self-Portrait by Camille Pissarro

Camille Pissarro, a French artist, expressed his philosophy of painting in this way:

❝Do not define too closely the outlines of things; it is the brush stroke of the right value and color which should produce the drawing. . . . The eye should not be fixed on one point, but should take in everything, while observing the reflections which the colors produce on their surroundings. Work at the same time upon sky, water, branches, ground, keeping everything going on an equal basis. . . . Don't proceed according to rules and principles, but paint what you observe and feel. Paint generously unhesitatingly, for it is best not to lose the first impression.❞

—*History of Impressionism*, John Rewald, 1961

Pissarro was part of a revolution in the arts. Between 1870 and 1914, radical ideas in the arts and sciences opened the way to a modern consciousness.

A New Physics

⌐TURNING POINT⌐ **As you will learn, Albert Einstein challenged the Newtonian idea of a mechanical universe, thus introducing an element of uncertainty into humankind's perception of space and time.**

Before 1914, many people in the Western world continued to believe in the values and ideals that had been put forth by the Scientific Revolution and the Enlightenment. *Reason, science,* and *progress* were still important words to Europeans.

Science was one of the chief pillars supporting the optimistic view of the world that many Westerners shared in the nineteenth century. Science, which was supposedly based on hard facts and cold reason, offered a certainty of belief in the orderliness of nature. Many believed that by applying already known scientific laws, humans could arrive at a complete understanding of the physical world and an accurate picture of reality.

Throughout much of the nineteenth century, Westerners believed in a mechanical conception of the universe that was based on the ideas of Isaac Newton. In this perspective, the universe was viewed as a giant machine. Time, space, and matter were objective realities that existed independently of those observing them. Matter was thought to be composed of solid material bodies called atoms.

Marie Curie, c. 1910

These views were seriously questioned at the end of the nineteenth century. The French scientist **Marie Curie** discovered that an element called radium gave off energy, or radiation, that apparently came from within the atom itself. Atoms were not simply hard material bodies but small, active worlds.

At the beginning of the twentieth century, **Albert Einstein,** a German-born scientist working in Switzerland, provided a new view of the universe. In 1905, Einstein published his special theory of relativity, which stated that space and time are not absolute but are relative to the observer.

According to this theory, neither space nor time has an existence independent of human experience. As Einstein later explained to a journalist, "It was formerly believed that if all material things disappeared out of the universe, time and space would be left. According to the relativity theory, however, time and space disappear together with the things."

Moreover, matter and energy reflect the

Albert Einstein, 1940

relativity of time and space. Einstein concluded that matter is nothing but another form of energy. This idea led to an understanding of the vast energies contained within the atom and to the Atomic Age. To some, however, a relative universe—unlike Newton's universe—was a universe without certainty.

Reading Check **Explaining** How did Marie Curie's discovery change people's ideas about the atom?

Freud and Psychoanalysis

At the turn of the century, **Sigmund Freud** (FROYD), a doctor from **Vienna,** proposed a series of theories that raised questions about the nature of the human mind. Freud's ideas, like the new physics, added to the uncertainties of the age. His major theories were published in 1900 in *The Interpretation of Dreams.*

Sigmund Freud, c. 1938

According to Freud, human behavior was strongly determined by past experiences and internal forces of which people were largely unaware. Freud argued that painful and unsettling experiences were repressed, or hidden from a person's conscious awareness. Freud believed that these hidden feelings continued to influence behavior, however, because they were part of the unconscious.

According to Freud, repression of such experiences began in childhood, so he devised a method—known as psychoanalysis—by which a therapist and patient could probe deeply into the patient's memory. In this way, they could retrace the chain of repressed thoughts all the way back to their childhood origins. If the patient's conscious mind could be made aware of the unconscious and its repressed contents, the patient could be healed.

The full importance of Sigmund Freud's thought was not felt until after World War I. In the 1920s, his ideas gained worldwide acceptance. Freudian terms, such as *unconscious* and *repression,* became standard vocabulary words. Psychoanalysis, pioneered by Freud, developed into a major profession.

Reading Check **Summarizing** What is Freud's theory of the human unconscious?

		Old View	New View
	Architecture	Ornamentalism	Functionalism
	Literature	Naturalism	Symbolism
	Music	Romanticism	• Impressionism • Chromaticism • Expressionism
	Painting	Realism	• Impressionism • Postimpressionism • Cubism • Abstract expressionism
	Physics	Newton's mechanical universe	Einstein's relative universe
	Psychology	Conscious awareness	Freud's unconscious mind

Chart Skills

In the late nineteenth century, major changes occurred in the arts and sciences.

1. **Identifying** Review earlier chapters of your text and identify artists and scientists whose work exemplified the "Old Views," as listed above.

2. **Evaluating** After reading about the changes that took place in each of the areas listed above, write a paragraph or two explaining which area of change you think had the biggest impact on societies and cultures of the early twentieth century.

Social Darwinism and Racism

In the late nineteenth and early twentieth centuries, scientific theories were sometimes applied inappropriately to achieve desired results. For example, Charles Darwin's theories were applied to human society in a radical way by nationalists and racists. Their ideas are known as Social Darwinism.

The most popular exponent of Social Darwinism was the British philosopher Herbert Spencer. He argued that social progress came from "the struggle for survival" as the "fit"—the strong—advanced while the weak declined. Some prominent businessmen used Social Darwinism to explain their success. To them, the strong and fit—the able and energetic—had risen to the top; the stupid and lazy had fallen by the wayside.

In their pursuit of national greatness, extreme nationalists often insisted that nations, too, were engaged in a "struggle for existence" in which only the fittest (the strongest) survived. The German general Friedrich von Bernhardi argued in 1907, "War is a biological necessity of the first importance, . . . since without it an unhealthy development will follow, which excludes every advancement of the race, and therefore all real civilization. War is the father of all things."

Perhaps nowhere was the combination of extreme nationalism and racism more evident than in Germany. One of the chief exponents of German racism was Houston Stewart Chamberlain, a Briton who became a German citizen. He believed that modern-day Germans were the only pure successors of the Aryans, who were portrayed as the original creators of Western culture. Chamberlain singled out Jews as the racial enemy who wanted to destroy the Aryan race.

Reading Check **Explaining** What does the theory of Social Darwinism state?

Anti-Semitism and Zionism

Anti-Semitism—hostility toward and discrimination against Jews—was not new to European civilization. Since the Middle Ages, the Jews had been portrayed as the murderers of Christ and subjected to mob violence. Their rights had been restricted, and they had been physically separated from Christians by being required to live in areas of cities known as ghettos.

In the nineteenth century, Jews were increasingly granted legal equality in many European countries. Many Jews now left the ghettos and became assimilated into the cultures around them. Many became successful as bankers, lawyers, scientists, scholars, and journalists.

These achievements were only one side of the picture, however, as is evident from the Dreyfus affair in France. Alfred Dreyfus, a Jew, was a captain in the French general staff. In 1894, a secret military court found him guilty of selling army secrets and condemned him to life imprisonment. During his trial, angry right-wing mobs yelled anti-Semitic sayings such as, "Death to the Jews."

Soon after the trial, however, evidence emerged that pointed to Dreyfus's innocence. Another officer, a Catholic aristocrat, was more obviously the traitor. The army refused a new trial. A wave of public outrage finally forced the government to pardon Dreyfus in 1899.

In Germany and Austria-Hungary during the 1880s and 1890s, new parties arose that used anti-Semitism to win the votes of people who felt threatened by the changing economic forces of the times. However, the worst treatment of Jews at the turn of the century occurred in eastern Europe, where a majority of the world Jewish population lived. Russian Jews were forced to live in certain regions of the country. Persecutions and pogroms (organized massacres) were widespread.

Hundreds of thousands of Jews decided to emigrate to escape the persecution. Many went to the United States. Some (probably about 25,000) moved to Palestine, which became home for a Jewish nationalist movement called Zionism.

For many Jews, Palestine, the land of ancient Israel, had long been the land of their dreams. A key figure in the growth of political Zionism was Theodor Herzl, who stated in his book *The Jewish State* (1896), "The Jews who wish it will have their state."

Settlement in Palestine was difficult, however, because it was then part of the Ottoman Empire, which was opposed to Jewish immigration. Although three thousand Jews went annually to Palestine between 1904 and 1914, the Zionist desire for a homeland in Palestine remained only a dream on the eve of World War I.

✓ **Reading Check** **Explaining** Why did Jews begin to move to Palestine?

The Culture of Modernity

Between 1870 and 1914, many writers and artists rebelled against the traditional literary and artistic styles that had dominated European cultural life since the Renaissance. The changes that they produced have since been called modernism.

Literature Throughout much of the late nineteenth century, literature was dominated by naturalism. Naturalists felt that literature should be realistic and address social problems. These writers, such as Henrik Ibsen and Émile Zola, explored issues such as the role of women in society, alcoholism, and the problems of urban slums.

At the beginning of the twentieth century, a group of writers known as the **symbolists** caused a literary revolution. Primarily interested in writing poetry and strongly influenced by the ideas of Freud, the symbolists believed that objective knowledge of the world was impossible. The external world was only a collection of symbols that reflected the true reality—the individual human mind. Art, the symbolists believed, should function for its own sake instead of serving, criticizing, or seeking to understand society.

Painting The period from 1870 to 1914 was one of the most productive in the history of art. Since the Renaissance, the task of artists had been to represent reality as accurately as possible. By the late nineteenth century, artists were seeking new forms of expression to reflect their changing views of the world.

HISTORY Online

Web Activity Visit the *Glencoe World History* Web site at tx.wh.glencoe.com and click on **Chapter 20– Student Web Activity** to learn more about Impressionism.

Starry Night by **Vincent van Gogh, 1889**
During the last two years of his life, van Gogh painted many night scenes such as this one. What adjectives would you use to describe the feelings van Gogh conveyed in this painting?

Impressionism was a movement that began in **France** in the 1870s, when a group of artists rejected the studios where artists had traditionally worked and went out into the countryside to paint nature directly. One important Impressionist is **Claude Monet** (moh•NAY), who painted pictures in which he sought to capture the interplay of light, water, and sky. Other Impressionist painters include Pierre-Auguste Renoir (REHN• WAHR) and Berthe Morisot.

In the 1880s, a new movement, known as Postimpressionism, arose in France and soon spread to other European countries. A famous Postimpressionist is Vincent van Gogh (GOH). For van Gogh, art was a spiritual experience. He was especially interested in color and believed that it could act as its own form of language. Van Gogh maintained that artists should paint what they feel.

By the beginning of the twentieth century, the belief that the goal of art was to represent reality had lost much of its meaning. This was especially true in the visual arts. Perhaps the most important factor in the decline of realism in painting was the spread of photography to the mass markets. Photography had been invented in the 1830s and became widespread after George Eastman created the first Kodak camera in 1888. Now, anyone could take a photograph that looked exactly like the subject.

Artists came to realize that their strength was not in mirroring reality, which the camera could do, but in creating reality. The visual artists, like the symbolist writers of the time, sought meaning in individual consciousness. Between 1905 and 1914, this search for individual expression created modern art. One of the most outstanding features of modern art is the attempt of the artist to avoid "visual reality."

By 1905, one of the most important figures in modern art was beginning his career. **Pablo Picasso** was from Spain but settled in Paris in 1904. He painted in a remarkable variety of styles. He created a new style, called cubism, that used geometric designs to recreate reality in the viewer's mind. In his paintings, Picasso attempted to view human form from many sides. In this aspect he seems to have been influenced by the increasingly popular theory of relativity.

History *through Architecture*

***Fallingwater* by Frank Lloyd Wright, 1936** Why do you think this Pennsylvania house is a good example of modern architecture?

In 1910, abstract painting began. Wassily Kandinsky, a Russian who worked in Germany, was one of the founders of abstract expressionism. Kandinsky sought to avoid visual reality altogether. He believed that art should speak directly to the soul. To do so, it must use only line and color.

Architecture Modernism in the arts revolutionized architecture and gave rise to a new principle known as functionalism. Functionalism was the idea that buildings, like the products of machines, should be functional, or useful. They should fulfill the purpose for which they were built. All unnecessary ornamentation should be stripped away.

The United States was a leader in the new architecture. The country's rapid urban growth and lack of any architectural tradition allowed for new building methods. The Chicago School of the 1890s, led by Louis H. Sullivan, used reinforced concrete, steel frames, and electric elevators to build skyscrapers virtually free of external ornamentation.

One of Sullivan's most successful pupils was Frank Lloyd Wright. Wright's private houses, built chiefly for wealthy patrons, were geometric structures with long lines and overhanging roofs. Wright pioneered the modern American house.

Music At the beginning of the twentieth century, developments in music paralleled those in painting. The music of the Russian composer Igor Stravinsky was the first to reflect expressionist theories.

Stravinsky's ballet *The Rite of Spring* revolutionized music. When it was performed in Paris in 1913, the sounds and rhythms of the music and dance caused a near riot by an outraged audience.

☑ **Reading Check** **Explaining** How did the Impressionists radically change the art of painting in the 1870s?

⭐ TAKS Practice

SECTION 4 ASSESSMENT

Checking for Understanding

1. **Define** psychoanalysis, pogrom, modernism.

2. **Identify** Marie Curie, Albert Einstein, Sigmund Freud, symbolists, Claude Monet, Pablo Picasso.

3. **Locate** Vienna, France.

4. **Explain** why photography caused some artists to reject realism.

5. **List** some of the modernist movements in art, music, and architecture and an individual associated with each of the movements.

Critical Thinking

6. **Analyze** Why are times of political and economic change often associated with times of artistic change?

7. **Organizing Information** Use a web diagram to summarize the problems the Jews faced during the time period discussed in this section.

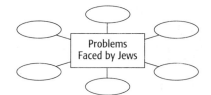

Problems Faced by Jews

Analyzing Visuals

8. **Compare** the painting by van Gogh on page 640 to other paintings of night scenes in art history books. Pick one such painting and tell why you enjoy that painting either more or less than the van Gogh painting.

Writing About History

9. **Expository Writing** Research the symbolist writers. Who were they and what did they write about? Write a short biography about one of the symbolists who interests you. Include the titles of this symbolist's best-known works.

Using Key Terms

1. The _____ were Marxists who rejected the revolutionary approach of pure Marxists.

2. According to Marx, the middle-class oppressors were the _____, and the working-class oppressed were the _____.

3. _____ is the movement for gaining women's rights.

4. The principle by which a prime minister is directly answerable to a popularly elected representative body is _____.

5. The _____ is the Russian legislative assembly.

6. _____ is a method by which a therapist and a patient probe for repressed experiences.

7. A literary and artistic style that rejected traditional styles was called _____.

8. _____ were organized massacres of helpless people, such as the acts against the Jews.

9. A _____ is a government in which a person or group has absolute power.

10. The introduction of universal education in the late nineteenth century led to an increase in _____.

Reviewing Key Facts

11. **Science and Technology** List one invention each of Guglielmo Marconi, Thomas Edison, and Alexander Graham Bell.

12. **Government** Who wrote *The Communist Manifesto?*

13. **Culture** How did Florence Nightingale and Clara Barton transform nursing?

14. **Culture** What purposes were served by compulsory education?

15. **Government** What was the name given to France's government after the adoption of a new constitution in 1875?

16. **Government** What was the result of "Bloody Sunday" in St. Petersburg in 1905?

17. **Economics** Why did American workers organize unions?

18. **Culture** What did Louis H. Sullivan contribute to the field of architecture?

19. **Government** Who was the emperor of Germany at the end of the nineteenth century?

20. **Culture** Who was Vincent van Gogh and why was he important?

21. **Government** What basic right were women denied until World War I?

22. **Economics** By 1900, Russia had become the fourth largest producer of what product?

Critical Thinking

23. **Evaluating** Why was revisionist socialism more powerful in western Europe than in eastern Europe?

24. **Drawing Conclusions** Was the Revolution of 1905 in Russia a success or a failure? Why?

25. **Summarizing** Identify changes that resulted from the Second Industrial Revolution.

Chapter Summary

Innovations in technology and production methods created great economic, political, social, and cultural changes between 1870 and 1914, as shown in the chart below. The development of a mass society led to labor reforms and the extension of voting rights. New scientific theories radically changed people's vision of the world. Change also brought conflict as tensions increased in Europe and new alliances were formed.

Economics	Politics	Society	Culture	Conflict
• Industrial growth and the development of new energy resources lead to increased production of consumer goods.	• Growth of mass politics leads to the development of new political parties. • Labor leaders use ideas of socialism and Marxism to form unions.	• Women fight for equal rights. • Society adopts middle-class values. • Unions fight for labor reforms. • Mass leisure develops.	• Many artists reject traditional styles and develop new art movements. • New scientific ideas radically change people's perception of the world.	• Nationalism and imperialism create conflict in the Balkans and eventually lead to World War I. • Growth of nationalism leads to increased anti-Semitism.

Self-Check Quiz
Visit the *Glencoe World History* Web site at tx.wh.glencoe.com and click on **Chapter 20– Self-Check Quiz** to prepare for the Chapter Test.

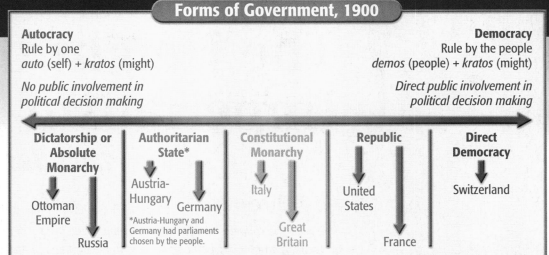

Forms of Government, 1900

Autocracy
Rule by one
auto (self) + *kratos* (might)

No public involvement in political decision making

Democracy
Rule by the people
demos (people) + *kratos* (might)

Direct public involvement in political decision making

Dictatorship or Absolute Monarchy
Ottoman Empire
Russia

Authoritarian State*
Austria-Hungary
Germany
*Austria-Hungary and Germany had parliaments chosen by the people.

Constitutional Monarchy
Italy
Great Britain

Republic
United States
France

Direct Democracy
Switzerland

Writing About History

26. Expository Writing Compare and contrast Einstein's and Newton's understandings of the universe. Explain how they differ and how they are related.

Analyzing Sources

Read the following quote from a regular visitor to an upper-class seaside resort.

❝They swarm upon the beach, wandering about with apparently no other aim than to get a mouthful of fresh air. You may see them in groups of three or four—the husband, a pale man, dressed in black coat, carries the baby; the wife, equally pale and thin, decked out in her best, labors after with a basket of food. And then there is generally another child . . . wandering behind.❞

27. What can you infer about the husband and the wife from the way in which they are described?

28. In what way do the ideas expressed in this quote reflect the class-consciousness of this time period?

Applying Technology Skills

29. Using the Internet Use the Internet to find examples of paintings by Monet and Picasso. Carefully examine the paintings, then describe their main differences and similarities. Some features to look for include each artist's subject matter, use of color, and method of painting.

Making Decisions

30. Assume the role of a working-class laborer at a newly unionized factory. What demands would you present to management? Do these demands cover everything that is wrong with the factory? If not, how did you decide what to present?

31. Reread the information in your text and do further research on similarities and differences among the British Conservative, Liberal, and Labour parties of 1914. Decide which of these three parties you would belong to if you lived in England at that time. Explain your choice of parties.

Analyzing Maps and Charts

Use the chart above to answer the following questions.

32. According to the chart, what is the major difference between an autocratic and a democratic form of government?

33. How are a constitutional monarchy and a republic similar? How do they differ?

34. Where was direct democracy practiced in 1900? Which earlier civilizations also practiced direct democracy?

Directions: Choose the best answer to the following question.

The emergence of different factions in the Balkan Peninsula at the end of the nineteenth century was a result of

F shifting power as the Ottoman Empire waned.

G Serbia's dominance of the region.

H America's victory in the Spanish-American War.

J Nicholas II of Russia's repressive regime.

Test-Taking Tip: This question asks you for a *cause.* Because causes always happen before effects, think about which answer choices happened *before* the disintegration of the Balkan Peninsula.

The Height of Imperialism

1800–1914

Key Events

As you read this chapter, look for the key events in the history of imperialism.
- *Competition among European nations led to the partition of Africa.*
- *Colonial rule created a new social class of Westernized intellectuals.*
- *British rule brought order and stability to India, but with its own set of costs.*
- *As a colonial power, the United States practiced many of the same imperialist policies as European nations.*

The Impact Today

The events that occurred during this time period still impact our lives today.
- *Rhodesia became the nation of Zimbabwe.*
- *India adopted a parliamentary form of government like that of Great Britain.*
- *The United States gave up rights to the Panama Canal Zone on December 31, 1999.*
- *Europeans migrated to the Americas, Australia, New Zealand, and South Africa.*

World History Video *The Chapter 21 video, "Imperialism," chronicles imperialism on three continents.*

Sir Thomas Raffles, founder of Singapore

1848
Mexico loses almost half of its territory to the United States

1855
David Livingstone is first European to see Victoria Falls

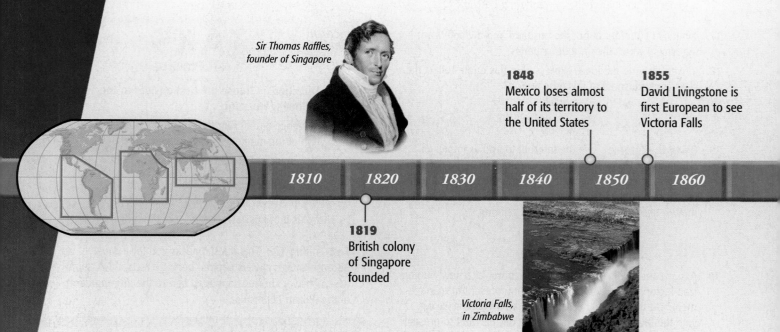

1810   1820   1830   1840   1850   1860

1819
British colony of Singapore founded

Victoria Falls, in Zimbabwe

British family celebrating Christmas in India, c. 1900

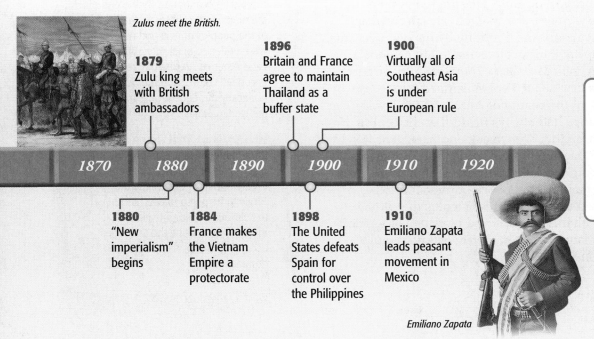

Zulus meet the British.

1879
Zulu king meets with British ambassadors

1896
Britain and France agree to maintain Thailand as a buffer state

1900
Virtually all of Southeast Asia is under European rule

1870   1880   1890   1900   1910   1920

1880
"New imperialism" begins

1884
France makes the Vietnam Empire a protectorate

1898
The United States defeats Spain for control over the Philippines

1910
Emiliano Zapata leads peasant movement in Mexico

Emiliano Zapata

HISTORY
Online

Chapter Overview
Visit the *Glencoe World History* Web site at tx.wh.glencoe.com and click on **Chapter 21–Chapter Overview** to preview chapter information.

A Story That Matters

David Livingstone

Livingstone expedition in Africa, c. 1855

Livingstone in Africa

*I*n 1841, the Scottish doctor and missionary David Livingstone began a series of journeys that took him through much of central and southern Africa. Livingstone was a gentle man whose goal was to find locations for Christian missions on behalf of the London Missionary Society. He took great delight in working with the African people.

Livingstone's travels were not easy. Much of his journey was done by foot, canoe, or mule. He suffered at times from rheumatic fever, dysentery, and malaria. He survived an attack by armed warriors and a mutiny by his own servants.

Back in Great Britain, his exploits made Livingstone a national hero. His book *Missionary Travels and Researches in South Africa* was a best-seller. People jammed into lecture halls to hear him speak of the beauty of Africa. As the *London Journal* reported, "Europe had always heard that the central regions of southern Africa were bleak and barren, heated by poisonous winds, infested by snakes . . . [but Livingstone spoke of] a high country, full of fruit trees, abounding in shade, watered by a perfect network of rivers."

Livingstone tried to persuade his listeners that Britain needed to send both missionaries and merchants to Africa. Combining Christianity and commerce, he said, would achieve civilization for Africa.

Why It Matters

During the nineteenth and early twentieth centuries, Western colonialism spread throughout the non-Western world. Great Britain, Spain, Holland, France, Germany, Russia, and the United States competed for markets and raw materials for their expanding economies. By the end of the nineteenth century, virtually all of the peoples of Asia and Africa were under colonial rule. Although Latin America successfully resisted European control, it remained economically dependent on Europe and the United States.

History and You Territorial and trade dominance are among the primary goals of imperialist nations. Create a map of either Asia or Africa to help you understand how the various imperialists viewed those regions. Code the territories according to exports or European dominance.

Colonial Rule in Southeast Asia

Guide to Reading

Main Ideas
- Through the "new imperialism," Westerners sought to control vast territories.
- Colonial export policies exploited native populations and opened up markets for European manufactured goods.

Key Terms
imperialism, protectorate, indirect rule, direct rule

People to Identify
King Mongkut, King Chulalongkorn, Commodore George Dewey, Emilio Aguinaldo

Places to Locate
Singapore, Burma, Thailand, Philippines

Preview Questions
1. Why were Westerners so determined to colonize Southeast Asia?
2. What was the chief goal of the Western nations?

Reading Strategy
Identifying Information Make a chart showing which countries controlled what parts of Southeast Asia.

Spain (until 1898)	
Holland	
United States (after 1898)	
France	
Great Britain	

Preview of Events

♦1850	♦1870	♦1890	♦1910	♦1930	♦1950

1887
France completes its control of Indochina

1896
France and Great Britain agree to maintain Thailand as a buffer state

1930
Saya San leads Burma uprising

Voices from the Past

Dutch plantation in Java, mid-1800s

In 1860, E. Douwes Dekker wrote a book on the Dutch colonial system on the island of Java. He said:

❝The [Dutch government] compels [the Javanese farmer] to cultivate certain products on his land; it punishes him if he sells what he has produced to any purchaser but itself; and it fixes the price actually paid. The expenses of transport to Europe through a privileged trading company are high; the money paid to the chiefs for encouragement increases the prime cost; and because the entire trade must produce profit, that profit cannot be got in any other way than by paying the Javanese just enough to keep him from starving, which would lessen the producing power of the nation.❞
— *The World of Southeast Asia: Selected Historical Readings,*
Harry J. Benda and John A. Larkin, eds., 1967

Dekker, a Dutch colonial official, was critical of the havoc the Dutch had wreaked on the native peoples of Java.

The New Imperialism

In the nineteenth century, a new phase of Western expansion into Asia and Africa began. European nations began to view Asian and African societies as a source of industrial raw materials and a market for Western manufactured goods. No longer were Western gold and silver traded for cloves, pepper, tea, and silk. Now the products of European factories were sent to Africa and Asia in return for oil, tin, rubber, and the other resources needed to fuel European industries.

Beginning in the 1880s, European states began an intense scramble for overseas territory. Imperialism, the extension of a nation's power over other lands, was not new. Europeans had set up colonies in North and South America and trading posts around Africa and the Indian Ocean by the sixteenth century.

However, the imperialism of the late nineteenth century, called the "new imperialism" by some, was different. Earlier, European states had been content, especially in Africa and Asia, to set up a few trading posts where they could carry on trade and perhaps some missionary activity. Now they sought nothing less than direct control over vast territories.

Why did Westerners begin to increase their search for colonies after 1880? There was a strong economic motive. Capitalist states in the West were looking for both markets and raw materials, such as rubber, oil, and tin, for their industries. Europeans also wanted more direct control of the areas with the raw materials and markets.

The issue was not simply an economic one, however. European nation-states were involved in heated rivalries. As European affairs grew tense, states sought to acquire colonies abroad in order to gain an advantage over their rivals.

Colonies were also a source of national prestige. To some people, in fact, a nation could not be great without colonies. One German historian wrote that "all great nations in the fullness of their strength have the desire to set their mark upon barbarian lands and those who fail to participate in this great rivalry will play a pitiable role in time to come."

In addition, imperialism was tied to Social Darwinism and racism. Social Darwinists believed that in the struggle between nations, the fit are victorious. Racism is the belief that race determines traits and capabilities. Racists erroneously believe that particular races are superior or inferior. Racist beliefs have led to the use of military force against other nations. One British professor argued in 1900, "The path of progress is strewn with the wrecks of nations; traces are everywhere to be seen of the [slaughtered remains] of inferior races. Yet these dead people are, in very truth, the stepping stones on which mankind has arisen to the higher intellectual and deeper emotional life of today."

Some Europeans took a more religious and humanitarian approach to imperialism. They argued that Europeans had a moral responsibility to civilize primitive people. They called this responsibility the "white man's burden."

These people believed that the nations of the West should help the nations of Asia and Africa. To some, this meant bringing the Christian message to the "heathen masses." To others, it meant bringing the benefits of Western democracy and capitalism to these societies.

✓ **Reading Check** **Describing** What were four primary motivations for the "new imperialism"?

Major Regions of European Control

	Southeast Asia	Africa	India
Britain	✓	✓	✓
Belgium		✓	
France	✓	✓	
Germany		✓	
Italy		✓	
Netherlands	✓	✓	
Portugal	✓	✓	
Spain	✓	✓	

Chart Skills

In the late 1800s a "new imperialism" flourished, with most of the major European countries attempting to take control of territories in Asia and Africa.

1. **Identifying** Look at a political map of Europe in Chapter 20. Which European countries did *not* try to colonize parts of Asia or Africa?

2. **Analyzing** It has been said about one of the countries identified in the chart that "the sun never sets" on this particular empire. To which country does this phrase refer? What do you think the phrase means?

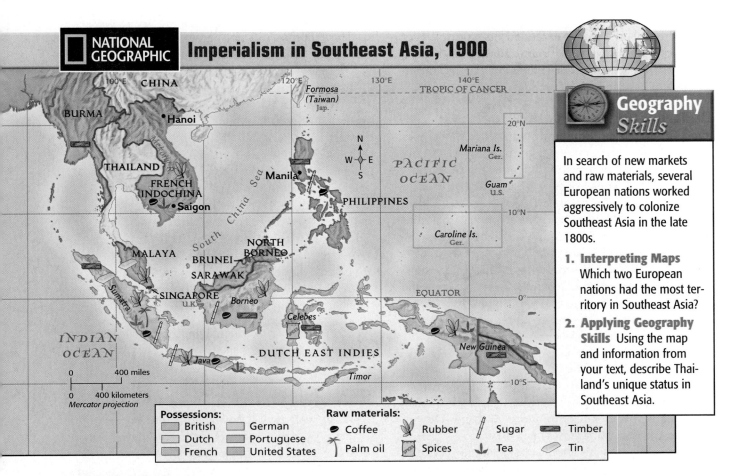

NATIONAL GEOGRAPHIC Imperialism in Southeast Asia, 1900

Geography Skills

In search of new markets and raw materials, several European nations worked aggressively to colonize Southeast Asia in the late 1800s.

1. **Interpreting Maps** Which two European nations had the most territory in Southeast Asia?

2. **Applying Geography Skills** Using the map and information from your text, describe Thailand's unique status in Southeast Asia.

Possessions: British, Dutch, French, German, Portuguese, United States

Raw materials: Coffee, Palm oil, Rubber, Spices, Sugar, Tea, Timber, Tin

Colonial Takeover in Southeast Asia

The new imperialism of the late nineteenth century was evident in Southeast Asia. In 1800, only two societies in this area were ruled by Europeans: the Spanish Philippines and the Dutch East Indies. By 1900, virtually the entire area was under Western rule.

Great Britain The process began with Great Britain. In 1819, Great Britain, under Sir Thomas Stamford Raffles, founded a new colony on a small island at the tip of the Malay Peninsula called **Singapore** ("city of the lion"). In the new age of steamships, Singapore soon became a major stopping point for traffic going to or from China. Raffles was proud of his new city and wrote to a friend in England, "Here all is life and activity; and it would be difficult to name a place on the face of the globe with brighter prospects."

During the next few decades, the British advance into Southeast Asia continued. Next to fall was the kingdom of **Burma** (modern Myanmar). Britain wanted control of Burma in order to protect its possessions in India. It also sought a land route through Burma into South China. Although the difficult terrain along the frontier between Burma and China caused this effort to fail, British activities in Burma led to the collapse of the Burmese monarchy. Britain soon established control over the entire country.

France The British advance into Burma was watched nervously by France, which had some missionaries operating in Vietnam. The French missionaries were persecuted by the local authorities, who viewed Christianity as a threat to Confucian doctrine. However, Vietnam failed to stop the Christian missionaries. Vietnamese internal rivalries divided the country into two separate governments, in the north and the south.

France was especially alarmed by British attempts to monopolize trade. To stop any British move into Vietnam, the French government decided in 1857 to force the Vietnamese to accept French protection.

The French eventually succeeded in making the Vietnamese ruler give up territories in the Mekong River delta. The French occupied the city of Saigon and, during the next 30 years, extended their control over the rest of the country. In 1884, France seized the city of Hanoi and later made the Vietnamese Empire a French protectorate—a political unit that depends on another government for its protection.

In the 1880s, France extended its control over neighboring Cambodia, Annam, Tonkin, and Laos. By 1887, France included all of its new possessions in a new Union of French Indochina.

Thailand—The Exception After the French conquest of Indochina, **Thailand** (then called Siam) was the only remaining free state in Southeast Asia. During the last quarter of the nineteenth century, British and French rivalry threatened to place Thailand, too, under colonial rule.

Two remarkable rulers were able to prevent that from happening. One was **King Mongkut** (known to theatergoers as the king in *The King and I*), and the other was his son **King Chulalongkorn.** Both promoted Western learning and maintained friendly relations with the major European powers. In 1896, Britain and France agreed to maintain Thailand as an independent buffer state between their possessions in Southeast Asia.

The United States One final conquest in Southeast Asia occurred at the end of the nineteenth century. In 1898, during the Spanish-American War, United States naval forces under **Commodore George Dewey** defeated the Spanish fleet in Manila Bay.

Believing it was his moral obligation to "civilize" other parts of the world, President William McKinley decided to turn the **Philippines,** which had been under Spanish control, into an American colony. This action would also prevent the area from falling into the hands of the Japanese. In fact, the islands gave the United States a convenient jumping-off point for trade with China.

This mixture of moral idealism and desire for profit was reflected in a speech given in the Senate in January 1900 by Senator Albert Beveridge of Indiana:

66Mr. President, the times call for candor. The Philippines are ours forever. And just beyond the Philippines are China's unlimited markets. We will not retreat from either. We will not abandon an opportunity in [Asia]. We will not renounce our part in the mission of our race, trustee, under God, of the civilization of the world.99

The Filipinos did not agree with the American senator. **Emilio Aguinaldo** (ah•gee•NAHL•doh) was the leader of a movement for independence in the Philippines. He began his revolt against the Spanish. When the United States acquired the Philippines, Aguinaldo continued the revolt and set himself up as the president of the Republic of the Philippines. Led by Aguinaldo, the guerrilla forces fought bitterly against the United States troops to establish their independence. However, the United States defeated the guerrilla forces, and President McKinley had his stepping-stone to the rich markets of China.

Emilio Aguinaldo

✓**Reading Check** **Identifying** What spurred Britain to control Singapore and Burma?

Colonial Regimes in Southeast Asia

Western powers governed their new colonial empires by either indirect or direct rule. Their chief goals were to exploit the natural resources of these lands and open up markets for their own manufactured goods. To justify their actions, they often spoke of bringing the blessings of Western civilizations to their colonial subjects.

Scene from decisive Manila Bay battle

Indirect and Direct Rule Sometimes, a colonial power could realize its goals most easily through cooperation with local political elites. In these cases, indirect rule was used. Local rulers were allowed to maintain their positions of authority and status in a new colonial setting.

In Southeast Asia, colonial powers, wherever possible, tried to work with local elites. This made it easier to gain access to the region's natural resources. Indirect rule also lowered the cost of government, because fewer officials had to be trained. Moreover, indirect rule had less effect on local culture.

One example of indirect rule was in the Dutch East Indies. Officials of the Dutch East India Company allowed local landed aristocrats in the Dutch East Indies to control local government. These local elites maintained law and order and collected taxes in return for a payment from the Dutch East India Company.

Indirect rule, then, was convenient and cost less. Indirect rule was not always possible, however, especially when local elites resisted the foreign conquest. In such cases, the local elites were removed from power and replaced with a new set of officials brought from the mother country. This system is called direct rule.

In Burma, for example, the monarchy staunchly opposed colonial rule. As a result, Great Britain abolished the monarchy and administered the country directly through its colonial government in India.

In Indochina, France used both direct and indirect rule. It imposed direct rule on the southern provinces in the Mekong delta, which had been ceded to France as a colony after the first war in 1858 to 1862. The northern parts of Vietnam, seized in the 1880s, were governed as a protectorate. The emperor still ruled from his palace in Hue, but he had little power.

To justify their conquests, Western powers had spoken of bringing the blessings of advanced Western civilization to their colonial subjects. Many colonial powers, for example, spoke of introducing representative institutions and educating the native peoples in the democratic process. However, many Westerners came to fear the idea of native peoples (especially educated ones) being allowed political rights.

Colonial Economies The colonial powers did not want their colonists to develop their own industries. Thus, colonial policy stressed the export of raw materials—teak wood from Burma; rubber and tin from Malaya; spices, tea, coffee, and palm oil from the East

Local peasants, shown here in Ceylon in the late 1800s, worked at poverty-level wages for foreign plantation owners during the colonial period.

Indies; and sugar from the Philippines. In many cases, this policy led to some form of plantation agriculture, in which peasants worked as wage laborers on plantations owned by foreign investors.

Plantation owners kept the wages of their workers at poverty levels in order to increase the owners' profits. Conditions on plantations were often so unhealthy that thousands died. In addition, high taxes levied by colonial governments to pay for their administrative costs were a heavy burden for peasants.

Nevertheless, colonial rule did bring some benefits to Southeast Asia. It led to the beginnings of a modern economic system. Colonial governments built railroads, highways, and other structures that could benefit native peoples as well as colonials. The development of an export market helped to create an entrepreneurial class in rural areas. In the Dutch East Indies, for example, small growers of rubber, palm oil, coffee, tea, and spices began to share in the profits of the colonial enterprise. Most of the profits, however, were taken back to the colonial mother country.

Reading Check **Explaining** Why did colonial powers prefer that colonists not develop their own industries?

Resistance to Colonial Rule

Many subject peoples in Southeast Asia were quite unhappy with being governed by Western powers. At first, resistance came from the existing ruling class. In Burma, for example, the monarch himself fought Western domination. By contrast, in Vietnam, after

In 1907, Vietnamese prisoners await trial for plotting against the French.

the emperor had agreed to French control of his country, a number of government officials set up an organization called Can Vuoug ("Save the King"). They fought against the French without the emperor's help.

Sometimes, resistance to Western control took the form of peasant revolts. Under colonial rule, peasants were often driven off the land to make way for plantation agriculture. Angry peasants then vented their anger at the foreign invaders. For example, in Burma, in 1930, the Buddhist monk Saya San led a peasant uprising against the British colonial regime many years after the regime had completed its takeover.

Early resistance movements failed, overcome by Western powers. At the beginning of the twentieth century, a new kind of resistance began to emerge that was based on the force of nationalism. The leaders were often a new class that had been created by colonial rule: westernized intellectuals in the cities.

In many cases, this new urban middle class—composed of merchants, clerks, students, and professionals—had been educated in Western-style schools. They were the first generation of Asians to understand the institutions and values of the West. Many spoke Western languages and worked in jobs connected with the colonial regimes.

At first, many of the leaders of these movements did not focus clearly on the idea of nationhood but simply tried to defend the economic interests or religious beliefs of the natives. In Burma, for example, the first expression of modern nationalism came from students at the University of Rangoon. They formed an organization to protest against official persecution of the Buddhist religion and British lack of respect for local religious traditions. They protested against British arrogance and failure to observe local customs in Buddhist temples. Not until the 1930s, however, did these resistance movements begin to demand national independence.

✓**Reading Check** **Summarizing** Explain three forms of resistance to Western domination.

🔺**TAKS Practice**

SECTION 1 ASSESSMENT

Checking for Understanding

1. **Define** imperialism, protectorate, indirect rule, direct rule.

2. **Identify** King Mongkut, King Chulalongkorn, Commodore George Dewey, Emilio Aguinaldo.

3. **Locate** Singapore, Burma, Thailand, Philippines.

4. **Explain** how the "new imperialism" differed from old imperialism. Also explain how imperialism came to be associated with social Darwinism.

5. **List** some of the benefits colonial rule brought to Southeast Asia. Do you think these benefits outweighed the disadvantages? Why or why not?

Critical Thinking

6. **Making Inferences** Why were resistance movements often led by natives who had lived and been educated in the West? Initially, what were the goals of these resistance leaders? How did their goals change over time?

7. **Cause and Effect** In a diagram like the one below, identify the effects of colonial rule on the colonies.

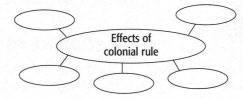

Analyzing Visuals

8. **Describe** the situation being endured by the Vietnamese prisoners in the photo above. Be specific in your description of their confinement. Based on your reading of the living conditions in Southeast Asian colonies at this time, do you think you would have risked this type of punishment if you had been in their position? Explain.

Writing About History

9. **Expository Writing** Use varied media to determine what the United States's relationship is today with the Philippines and how Filipino political groups view this relationship. Write an essay based on your findings.

A Call to Arms

IN 1862, THE VIETNAMESE emperor granted three provinces in southern Vietnam to the French. In outrage, many patriotic Vietnamese military officers and government officials appealed to their fellow Vietnamese to rise up and resist the foreigners. The following lines were written in 1864.

French troops battle Vietnamese resistance fighters.

❝This is a general proclamation addressed to the scholars and the people. . . .
Our people are now suffering through a period of anarchy and disorder. . . .
Let us now consider our situation with the French today.
We are separated from them by thousands of mountains and seas.
By hundreds of differences in our daily customs.
Although they were very confident in their copper battleships surmounted by chimneys,
Although they had a large quantity of steel rifles and lead bullets,
These things did not prevent the loss of some of their best generals in these last years, when they attacked our frontier in hundreds of battles. . . .
You, officials of the country,
Do not let your resistance to the enemy be blunted by the peaceful stand of the court,
Do not take the lead from the three subjected provinces and leave hatred unavenged.
So many years of labor, of energy, of suffering—shall we now abandon all?
Rather, we should go to the far ends of jungles or to the high peaks of mountains in search of heroes.
Rather, we should go to the shores of the sea in search of talented men.
Do not envy the scholars who now become provincial or district magistrates [in the French administration]. They are decay, garbage, filth, swine.
Do not imitate some who hire themselves out to the enemy. They are idiots, fools, lackeys, scoundrels.❞

—An Appeal to Vietnamese Citizens to Resist the French

Analyzing Primary Sources

1. What do the writers of the quoted lines want their fellow Vietnamese to do?
2. What are the writer's feelings toward those who worked with the French administration? How can you tell?

Empire Building in Africa

Guide to Reading

Main Ideas
- Great Britain, France, Germany, Belgium, and Portugal placed virtually all of Africa under European rule.
- Native peoples sought an end to colonial rule.

Key Terms
annex, indigenous

People to Identify
Muhammad Ali, David Livingstone, Henry Stanley, Zulu

Places to Locate
Suez Canal, Rhodesia, Union of South Africa

Preview Questions
1. What new class of Africans developed in many African nations?
2. What was the relationship between the Boers and the Zulu?

Reading Strategy
Categorizing Information Make a chart like the one below showing what countries controlled what parts of Africa.

Controlling Country	Part of Africa
	West Africa
	North Africa (including Egypt)
	Central Africa
	East Africa
	South Africa

Preview of Events

◆1860	◆1870	◆1880	◆1890	◆1900	◆1910	◆1920

1869
Suez Canal completed

1884-1885
Berlin Conference divides Africa among Europeans

1896
Ethiopia defeats Italian forces

1914
Egypt becomes British protectorate

Voices from the Past

King Lobengula, seated, c. 1880

A southern African king, Lobengula, wrote a letter to Queen Victoria about how he had been cheated:

❝Some time ago a party of men came to my country, the principal one appearing to be a man called Rudd. They asked me for a place to dig for gold, and said they would give me certain things for the right to do so. I told them to bring what they could give and I would show them what I would give. A document was written and presented to me for signature. I asked what it contained, and was told that in it were my words and the words of those men. I put my hand to it. About three months afterwards I heard from other sources that I had given by the document the right to all the minerals of my country.❞

— ***The Imperialism Reader,*** **Louis L. Snyder, ed., 1962**

Europeans did not hesitate to deceive native Africans in order to get African lands.

West Africa

Before 1880, Europeans controlled little of the African continent directly. They were content to let African rulers and merchants represent European interests. Between 1880 and 1900, however, fed by intense rivalries among themselves, Great Britain, France, Germany, Belgium, Italy, Spain, and Portugal placed virtually all of Africa under European rule.

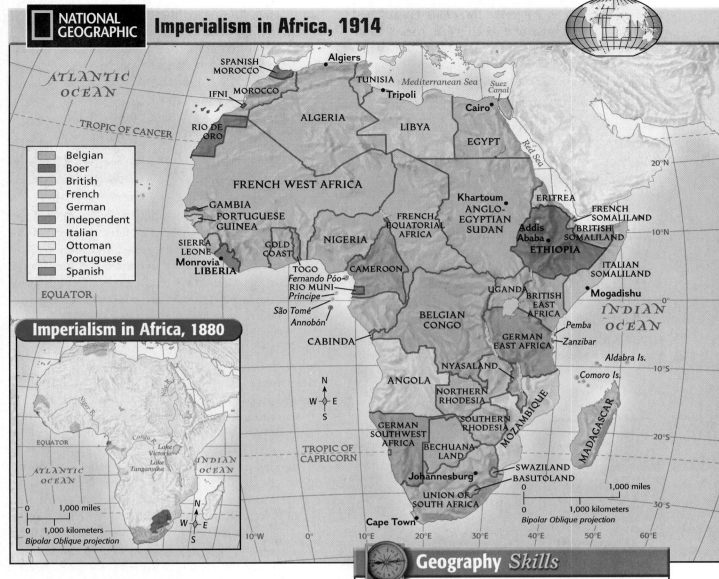

NATIONAL GEOGRAPHIC — Imperialism in Africa, 1914

Legend:
- Belgian
- Boer
- British
- French
- German
- Independent
- Italian
- Ottoman
- Portuguese
- Spanish

Imperialism in Africa, 1880

0   1,000 miles
0   1,000 kilometers
Bipolar Oblique projection

0   1,000 miles
0   1,000 kilometers
Bipolar Oblique projection

Geography Skills

More so in Africa than in Asia, European countries competed against each other in their attempts to colonize new territories.

1. **Interpreting Maps** Identify the two independent countries in Africa in 1914.
2. **Applying Geography Skills** Describe the changes that occurred in Africa from 1880 to 1914 for the Ottoman Empire, France, Britain, and the Boers.

West Africa had been particularly affected by the slave trade, but that had begun to decline by 1800. By 1808, both Great Britain and the United States had declared the slave trade illegal. Other European countries eventually followed suit. Slavery was abolished in the United States in 1865 and in Cuba and Brazil within the next 25 years. By the 1890s, slavery had been abolished in all major countries of the world.

As slavery declined, Europe's interest in other forms of trade increased. Europeans sold textiles and other manufactured goods in exchange for such West African natural resources as peanuts, timber, hides, and palm oil. Encouraged by this growing trade, European governments began to push for a more permanent presence along the coast. Early in the nineteenth century, the British set up settlements along the Gold Coast and in Sierra Leone.

The growing European presence in West Africa led to increasing tensions with African governments in the area. For a long time, most African states were able to maintain their independence. However, in 1874, Great Britain stepped in and annexed (incorporated a country within a state) the west coastal states as the first British colony of Gold Coast. At about the same time, Britain established a protectorate over warring groups in Nigeria. By 1900, France had added the huge area of French West Africa to its colonial empire. This left France in control of the largest part of West Africa. In addition, Germany controlled Togo, Cameroon, German Southwest Africa, and German East Africa.

☑ **Reading Check** **Explaining** Why did the slave trade decline in the 1800s?

North Africa

Egypt had been part of the Ottoman Empire, but as Ottoman rule declined, the Egyptians sought their independence. In 1805, an officer of the Ottoman army named **Muhammad Ali** seized power and established a separate Egyptian state.

During the next 30 years, Muhammad Ali introduced a series of reforms to bring Egypt into the modern world. He modernized the army, set up a public school system, and helped create small industries in refined sugar, textiles, munitions, and ships.

The growing economic importance of the Nile Valley in Egypt, along with the development of steam-

General Gordon's Last Stand by George William Joy

ships, gave Europeans the desire to build a canal east of Cairo to connect the Mediterranean and Red Seas. In 1854, a French entrepreneur, Ferdinand de Lesseps, signed a contract to begin building the **Suez Canal.** The canal was completed in 1869.

The British took an active interest in Egypt

Ferdinand de Lesseps

after the Suez Canal was opened. Believing that the canal was its "lifeline to India," Great Britain sought as much control as possible over the canal area. In 1875, Britain bought Egypt's share in the Suez Canal. When an Egyptian army revolt against foreign influence broke out in 1881, Britain suppressed the revolt. Egypt became a British protectorate in 1914.

The British believed that they should also control the Sudan, south of Egypt, to protect their interests in Egypt and the Suez Canal. In 1881, Muslim cleric Muhammad Ahmad, known as the Mahdi ("the rightly guided one," in Arabic), launched a revolt that brought much of the Sudan under his control.

Britain sent a military force under General Charles Gordon to restore Egyptian authority over the Sudan. However, Gordon's army was wiped out at Khartoum in 1885 by Muhammad Ahmad's troops. Gordon himself died in the battle. Not until 1898 were British troops able to seize the Sudan.

The French also had colonies in North Africa. In 1879, after about 150,000 French people had settled in the region of Algeria, the French government established control there. Two years later, France imposed a protectorate on neighboring Tunisia. In 1912, France established a protectorate over much of Morocco.

Italy joined in the competition for colonies in North Africa by attempting to take over Ethiopia, but Italian forces were defeated by Ethiopia in 1896. Italy now was the only European state defeated by an African state. This humiliating loss led Italy to try again in 1911. Italy invaded and seized Turkish Tripoli, which it renamed Libya.

☑ **Reading Check** **Explaining** Great Britain was determined to have complete control of the Suez Canal. Why?

Central Africa

Territories in Central Africa were also added to the list of European colonies. Explorers aroused popular interest in the dense tropical jungles of Central Africa. **David Livingstone,** as we have seen, was one such explorer. He arrived in Africa in 1841. For 30 years he trekked through unchartered regions. He spent much of his time exploring the interior of the continent.

When Livingstone disappeared for a while, the *New York Herald* hired a young journalist, **Henry Stanley,** to find him. Stanley did, on the eastern shore of Lake Tanganyika, and greeted the explorer with the now famous words, "Dr. Livingstone, I presume."

After Livingstone's death in 1873, Stanley remained in Africa to carry on the great explorer's work. Unlike Livingstone, however, Stanley had a strong dislike of Africa. He once said, "I detest the land most heartily."

In the 1870s, Stanley explored the Congo River in Central Africa and sailed down it to the Atlantic Ocean. Soon, he was encouraging the British to send settlers to the Congo River basin. When Britain refused, he turned to King Leopold II of Belgium.

King Leopold II was the real driving force behind the colonization of Central Africa. He rushed enthusiastically into the pursuit of an empire in Africa. "To open to civilization," he said, "the only part of our globe where it has not yet penetrated, to pierce the darkness which envelops whole populations, is a crusade, if I may say so, a crusade worthy of this century of progress." Profit, however, was equally important to Leopold. In 1876, he hired Henry Stanley to set up Belgian settlements in the Congo.

Leopold's claim to the vast territories of the Congo aroused widespread concern among other European states. France, in particular, rushed to plant its flag in the heart of Africa. Leopold ended up with the territories around the Congo River. France occupied the areas farther north.

✔ **Reading Check** **Examining** What effect did King Leopold II of Belgium have on European colonization of the Congo River basin?

East Africa

By 1885, Britain and Germany had become the chief rivals in East Africa. Germany came late to the ranks of the imperialist powers. At first, the German chancellor Otto von Bismarck had downplayed the importance of colonies. As more and more Germans called for a German empire, however, Bismarck became a convert to colonialism. As he expressed it, "All this colonial business is a sham, but we need it for the elections."

CONNECTIONS Around The World

The Role of Quinine

Before 1850, the fear of disease was a major factor in keeping Europeans from moving into Africa. Especially frightening was malaria, an often fatal disease spread by parasites. Malaria is especially devastating in tropical and subtropical regions, which offer good conditions for breeding the mosquitoes that carry and spread the malaria parasites.

By 1850, European doctors had learned how to treat malaria with quinine, a drug that greatly reduced the death rate from the disease. Quinine is a bitter drug obtained from the bark of the cinchona tree, which is native to the slopes of the Andes in South America. The Indians of Peru were the first people to use the bark of the cinchona tree to treat malaria.

The Dutch took the cinchona tree and began to grow it in the East Indies. The East Indies eventually became the chief source of quinine. With the use of quinine and other medicines, Europeans felt more secure about moving into Africa.

By the beginning of the twentieth century, more than 90 percent of African lands were under the control of the European powers. A drug found in the bark of Latin American trees, which were then grown in Asia, had been used by Europeans to make possible their conquest of Africa.

The bark from cinchona ▶ trees dries in the sun.

Comparing Cultures

Fear of disease kept Europeans from moving into Africa. Once quinine was discovered, Europeans felt safer about Africa.

1. What fears do we have today that prevent or inhibit exploration or research?
2. What technological advances would be required to overcome those fears?

In addition to its West African holdings, Germany tried to develop colonies in East Africa. Most of East Africa had not yet been claimed by any other power. However, the British were also interested in the area because control of East Africa would connect the British Empire in Africa from South Africa to Egypt. Portugal and Belgium also claimed parts of East Africa.

To settle conflicting claims, the Berlin Conference met in 1884 and 1885. The conference officially recognized both British and German claims for territory in East Africa. Portugal received a clear claim on Mozambique. No African delegates were present at this conference.

✓ **Reading Check** **Evaluating** What was significant about the Berlin Conference?

South Africa

Nowhere in Africa did the European presence grow more rapidly than in the south. By 1865, the total white population of the area had risen to nearly two hundred thousand people.

The Boers, or Afrikaners—as the descendants of the original Dutch settlers were called—had occupied Cape Town and surrounding areas in South Africa since the seventeenth century. During the Napoleonic Wars, however, the British seized these lands from the Dutch. Afterward, the British encouraged settlers to come to what they called Cape Colony.

In the 1830s, disgusted with British rule, the Boers fled northward on the Great Trek to the region between the Orange and Vaal (VAHL) Rivers and to the region north of the Vaal River. In these areas, the Boers formed two independent republics—the Orange Free State and the Transvaal (later called the South African Republic). The Boers, who believed white superiority was ordained by God, put many of the indigenous (native to a region) peoples in these areas on reservations.

The Boers had frequently battled the indigenous Zulu people. In the early nineteenth century, the

Opposing Viewpoints

Who Benefited from the New Imperialism?

Europeans justified colonization of Africa and Asia in many ways. Native peoples viewed the takeover of their lands differently. Rudyard Kipling and Edward Morel were British journalists who held opposing viewpoints about imperialism.

❝Take up the White Man's burden—
Send forth the best ye breed—
Go bind your sons to exile
To serve your captives' needs;
To wait in heavy harness,
On fluttered folk and wild—
Your new-caught sullen peoples,
Half-devil and half-child. . . .
Take up the White Man's burden—
And reap his old reward:
The blame of those ye better,
The hate of those ye guard—
The cry of hosts ye humour
(Ah, slowly;) toward the light: —
'Why brought he us from bondage,
Our loved Egyptian night?'❞

—**Rudyard Kipling, 1899**
The White Man's Burden

❝It is [the Africans] who carry the 'Black man's burden. . . . ' In hewing out for himself a fixed abode in Africa, the white man has massacred the African in heaps. . . .

Zulu, under a talented ruler named Shaka, had carved out their own empire. After Shaka's death, the Zulu remained powerful. Finally, in the late 1800s, the British became involved in conflicts with the Zulu, and the Zulu were defeated.

In the 1880s, British policy in South Africa was influenced by Cecil Rhodes. Rhodes had founded diamond and gold companies that had made him a fortune. He gained control of a territory north of the Transvaal, which he named **Rhodesia** after himself.

Rhodes was a great champion of British expansion. He said once, "I think what [God] would like me to do is to paint as much of Africa British red as possible." One of Rhodes's goals was to create a series of British colonies "from the Cape to Cairo"—all linked by a railroad.

Rhodes's ambitions eventually led to his downfall in 1896. The British government forced him to resign as prime minister of Cape Colony after discovering that he planned to overthrow the Boer government of the South African Republic without his government's approval. The British action was too late to avoid a war between the British and the Boers, however.

This war, called the Boer War, dragged on from 1899 to 1902. Fierce guerrilla resistance by the Boers angered the British. They responded by burning crops and herding about 120,000 Boer women and children into detention camps, where lack of food caused some 20,000 deaths. Eventually, the vastly larger British army won.

In 1910, the British created an independent **Union of South Africa,** which combined the old Cape Colony and the Boer republics. The new state would be a self-governing nation within the British Empire. To appease the Boers, the British agreed that only whites, with a few propertied Africans, would vote.

✔ **Reading Check** **Describing** What happened to the Boers at the end of the Boer War?

Colonial Rule in Africa

By 1914, Great Britain, France, Germany, Belgium, Italy, Spain, and Portugal had divided up Africa. Only Liberia, which had been created as a homeland for freed United States slaves, and Ethiopia remained free states. Native peoples who dared to resist were simply devastated by the superior military force of the Europeans.

As was true in Southeast Asia, most European governments ruled their new territories in Africa with the least effort and expense possible. Indirect rule meant relying on existing political elites and institutions. The British especially followed this approach. At first, in some areas, the British simply asked a local ruler to accept British authority and to fly the British flag over official buildings.

The concept of indirect rule was introduced in the Islamic state of Sokoto, in northern Nigeria, beginning in 1903. This system of indirect rule in Sokoto had one good feature: it did not disrupt local customs and institutions. However, it did have some unfortunate consequences.

The system was basically a fraud because British administrators made all major decisions. The native authorities served chiefly to enforce those decisions. Another problem was that indirect rule kept the old African elite in power. Such a policy provided few opportunities for ambitious and talented young Africans from outside the old elite. In this way British indirect rule sowed the seeds for class and tribal tensions, which erupted after independence came in the twentieth century.

What the partial occupation of his soil by the white man has failed do; . . . what the [machine gun] and the rifle, the slave gang, labour in the bowels of the earth and the lash, have failed to do; what imported measles, smallpox and syphilis have failed to do; whatever the overseas slave trade failed to do; the power of modern capitalistic exploitation, assisted by modern engines of destruction, may yet succeed in accomplishing. . . .

Thus the African is really helpless against the material gods of the white man, as embodied in the trinity of imperialism, capitalistic exploitation, and militarism. **"**

—**Edward Morel, 1903**
The Black Man's Burden

You Decide

1. What was the impact of imperialism on the colonized territories in Africa, according to Morel?

2. Quote lines in Rudyard Kipling's poem that reflect his view of colonized peoples. What values did Kipling assume his readers shared with him?

Most other European nations governed their African possessions through a form of direct rule. This was true in the French colonies. At the top was a French official, usually known as a governor-general. He was appointed from Paris and governed with the aid of a bureaucracy in the capital city of the colony.

The French ideal was to assimilate African subjects into French culture rather than preserve native traditions. Africans were eligible to run for office and even serve in the French National Assembly in Paris. A few were appointed to high positions in the colonial administration.

✓**Reading Check** **Comparing** How did the French system of colonial rule differ from that of Great Britain?

Rise of African Nationalism

As in Southeast Asia, a new class of leaders emerged in Africa by the beginning of the twentieth century. Educated in colonial schools or in Western nations, they were the first generation of Africans to know a great deal about the West.

On the one hand, the members of this new class admired Western culture and sometimes disliked the ways of their own countries. They were eager to introduce Western ideas and institutions into their own societies.

On the other hand, many came to resent the foreigners and their arrogant contempt for African peoples. These intellectuals recognized the gap between theory and practice in colonial policy. Westerners had exalted democracy, equality, and political freedom but did not apply these values in the colonies.

There were few democratic institutions. Native peoples could have only low-paying jobs in the colonial bureaucracy. To many Africans, colonialism had meant the loss of their farmlands or employment on plantations or in factories run by foreigners.

Middle-class Africans did not suffer as much as poor African peasant plantation workers. However, members of the middle class also had complaints. They usually qualified only for menial jobs in the government or business. Even then, their salaries were lower than those of Europeans in similar jobs.

Europeans expressed their superiority over Africans in other ways. Segregated clubs, schools, and churches were set up as more European officials brought their wives and began to raise families. Europeans also had a habit of addressing Africans by their first names or calling an adult male "boy."

Such conditions led many members of the new urban educated class to feel great confusion toward their colonial masters and the civilization the colonists represented. The educated Africans were willing to admit the superiority of many aspects of Western culture. However, these intellectuals fiercely hated colonial rule and were determined to assert their own nationality and cultural destiny. Out of this mixture of hopes and resentments emerged the first stirrings of modern nationalism in Africa.

During the first quarter of the twentieth century, resentment turned to action. Across Africa, native peoples began to organize political parties and movements seeking the end of foreign rule.

✓**Reading Check** **Evaluating** Why were many African intellectuals frustrated by colonial policy?

🟥**TAKS Practice**

SECTION 2 ASSESSMENT

Checking for Understanding

1. **Define** annex, indigenous.

2. **Identify** Muhammad Ali, David Livingstone, Henry Stanley, Zulu.

3. **Locate** Suez Canal, Rhodesia, Union of South Africa.

4. **Explain** why the British were interested in East Africa. What other countries claimed parts of East Africa?

5. **List** the ways in which the French system of direct rule included Africans.

Critical Thinking

6. **Drawing Conclusions** What can you conclude from the fact that African delegates were not included in the Berlin Conference of 1884?

7. **Organizing Information** Using a chart like the one below, identify key figures of African resistance to colonial rule.

Leader	Country opposed	Dates of resistance

Analyzing Visuals

8. **Examine** the painting on page 656. What was the painter trying to say about the hostilities between the British and the people of the Sudan? If forced to choose, whom would you support in this confrontation?

Writing About History

9. **Expository Writing** Research the importance of the Suez Canal today. Write a paper comparing the present-day significance of the canal to its historical significance.

TECHNOLOGY
SKILLBUILDER
Evaluating a Web Site

Why Learn This Skill?

Your little sister has developed a strange rash on her back, so you decide to check the Internet to see whether or not it might be chicken pox and how the rash should be treated. When you look for a Web site, however, you find dozens, and they are all giving different advice. How do you determine which site is giving the most accurate and up-to-date information?

The Internet has become a valuable research tool. It is convenient to use and contains plentiful information. Unfortunately, some Web site information is not necessarily correct or reliable. When using the Internet as a research tool, the user must distinguish between quality information and inaccurate or incomplete information.

Learning the Skill

To evaluate a Web site, ask yourself the following questions:

- Where does the site originate? If it is a university, a well-known organization or agency, or a respected publication, then the information is likely to be trustworthy.

- Are the facts on the site documented? Where did this information originally come from? Is the author clearly identified?

- Are the links to other parts of the site appropriate? Do they take you to information that helps you learn more about the subject?

- Is more than one source used for background information within the site? If so, does the site contain a bibliography?

- When was the last time the site was updated?

- Does the site explore the topic in-depth?

- Does the site contain links to other useful and up-to-date resources? Although many legitimate sites have products to sell, some sites are more interested in sales than in providing accurate information.

- Is the information easy to access? Is it properly labeled?

- Is the design appealing?

Practicing the Skill

Visit the Web site about Mohandas Gandhi at *http://www.mkgandhi.org* featured on this page. Then, answer the following questions.

M o h a n d a s K a r a m c h a n d G a n d h i
Man of Millennium

❶ Who is the author or sponsor of the Web site?

❷ What information does the home page link you to? Are the links appropriate to the topic?

❸ What sources were used for the information contained on the site? When was it last updated?

❹ Does the site explore the topic in-depth? Why or why not?

❺ Are there links to other useful sources and are they up-to-date?

❻ Is the design of the site appealing? Why or why not? When was Gandhi born? How easy or difficult was it to locate this information?

Applying the Skill

Comparing Web Sites Locate two other Web sites that provide information about Mohandas Gandhi. Evaluate each one for accuracy and usefulness, and then compare them to the site featured above (http://www.mkgandhi.org).

STANLEY AND LIVINGSTONE
IN AFRICA

AFRICA.—THE MEETING BETWEEN STANLEY AND LIVINGSTONE, AT UJIJI.

1

More than three years had passed with no word from Dr. David Livingstone. The renowned Scottish missionary and explorer had left Britain in August 1865, bound for East Africa, where the Royal Geographical Society had asked him, among other things, to try to determine the source of the Nile River. The explorer Richard Burton favored Lake Tanganyika while the late John Hanning Speke had been certain the Nile arose in Lake Victoria. The 52-year-old Livingstone had arrived at the island of Zanzibar in January 1866. He and his party of about 60 men were taken to the mainland some six weeks later and were known to have headed into the interior. Months later, the first rumors of his death reached the coast.

In October 1869, James Gordon Bennett, son of the publisher of the *New York Herald*, met with reporter Henry M. Stanley in the Grand Hotel in Paris. "Go and find him wherever you may hear that he is and get what news you can of him," Bennett told Stanley. "And perhaps the old man may be in want; take enough with you to help him should he require it. Of course, you will act according to your own plans, and do what you think best—but find Livingstone!"

The man Stanley was supposed to find was known and admired both for his achievements as an explorer and for his dedicated efforts to end the slave trade. Since going out to Africa in 1841 as a 27-year-old medical missionary, David Livingstone had covered thousands of miles of territory previously unexplored by Europeans. Sometimes he traveled by canoe or on the back of an ox, but mostly he went on foot. In the early years he traveled with his wife, Mary, and their young children.

Though he suffered from malaria and had lost the use of his left arm after being attacked by a wounded lion, Livingstone remained determined. He made detailed notes and reports, which he sent to London whenever he could. The information he sent was used to revise the maps of Africa.

All the exploration that Livingstone did in the mid-1850s had one goal: to find a navigable river that would open the center of Africa to legitimate European commerce and to Christianity. In so doing, Livingstone hoped to drive out the slave trade, an evil that he called "this open sore of the world."

In the spring of 1852, Livingstone sent his family back to England. Then, starting from Cape Town, South Africa, he trekked north to the Upper Zambezi and then west to Luanda on the Atlantic coast (in present-day Angola). After a brief rest, he headed to Quelimane on the east coast (now in Mozambique). The trip of some 4,300 miles (6,919 km) finally ended in May 1856. Livingstone traveled with a small party of 25 or so

SPECIAL REPORT

3

Africans. In contrast to other European expedition leaders, the missionary regarded the men not as his servants but as his friends. His loyalty to them was returned manyfold.

The expedition traveled light, although Livingstone always carried his navigational instruments, a Bible, a nautical almanac, and his journal. He also carried a magic lantern (an early slide projector) and slides, so he could tell Bible stories to any who would listen. On the second half of the journey, from the interior to the mouth of the Zambezi River, Livingstone became the first European to see the spectacular waterfall the Africans called "Mosi-oa-tunya" (the smoke that thunders).

Livingstone named it Victoria Falls, after the British queen.

When the missionary got back to Britain in late 1856, he found that word of his explorations and discoveries had preceded him. He was now famous. The following year Livingstone turned his journals into a book—*Missionary Travels and Researches in South Africa*—which quickly became a best-seller. In his book and at every public opportunity he could find, he raised the issue of the slave trade. He condemned those who tolerated it and profited by it.

When he sailed back to Africa in the spring of 1858, Dr. Livingstone was the newly appointed British Con-

1 Tipping his pith helmet, Henry Morton Stanley greets the explorer with his restrained inquiry: "Dr. Livingstone, I presume?"

2 The scarcity of paper did not prevent Livingstone from recording his observations in meticulous detail, as seen in this fragment from his journals. He would also record topographical measurements taken with the sextant.

3 "It had never been seen before by European eyes," Livingstone wrote of his first view of Victoria Falls, "but scenes so lovely must have been gazed upon by angels in their flight." His drawing of the falls and the meandering Zambezi River below it (inset) hardly does the scene justice.

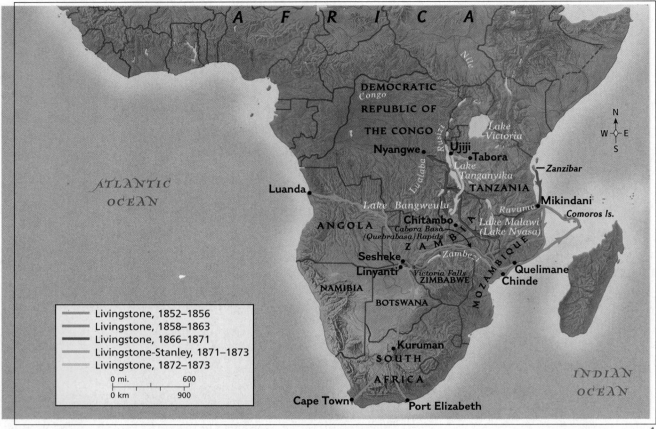

AFRICA

ATLANTIC OCEAN

DEMOCRATIC REPUBLIC OF THE CONGO

Nyangwe · Ujiji · Tabora

Luanda ·

Zanzibar

TANZANIA

Lake Bangweulu

Chitambo · Cabora Basa (Quebrabasa) Rapids

ANGOLA

ZAMBIA

Lake Malawi (Lake Nyasa)

Mikindani

Comoros Is.

Zambezi

Sesheke · Linyanti · Victoria Falls

ZIMBABWE

Quelimane
Chinde

MOZAMBIQUE

NAMIBIA

BOTSWANA

Kuruman ·

SOUTH AFRICA

INDIAN OCEAN

Cape Town · Port Elizabeth ·

Livingstone, 1852–1856
Livingstone, 1858–1863
Livingstone, 1866–1871
Livingstone-Stanley, 1871–1873
Livingstone, 1872–1873

0 mi. 600
0 km 900

4

sul for the East Coast of Africa. With substantial government backing and far more equipment and personnel than he had previously enjoyed, he continued to explore the Zambezi and its tributaries. His wife sailed with him but then fell ill and went to rest in Cape Town.

Despite its advantages, this expedition was plagued with problems. There was quarreling among Livingstone's six European assistants, and the fuel-eating boat he had been given was more trouble than it was worth.

Worst of all was the discovery that on his previous trip down the Zambezi he had bypassed a bend in the river that held big problems. When the party headed upriver from the east coast of Africa, they came around that bend only to be stopped by the Quebrabasa Rapids. Try as he might—and Livingstone insisted on trying, until

everyone in his expedition was exhausted— this was an obstacle no boat could get past.

Even though his efforts were adding daily to European knowledge of the African interior and would be of benefit to all who came after him, Livingstone was frustrated at not finding the navigable river that would surely bring an end to the slave trade.

Then, tragedy struck. In early 1862, Mary Livingstone was well enough to join her husband, but a few months later she fell ill again. In April, she died. Grief stricken, Livingstone threw himself into his work, but his increased efforts did not pay off. In July 1863, the expedition was ordered to return home.

Livingstone stayed in Britain only long enough to write a second book, *The Zambezi and Its Tributaries,* and to drum up support for his next expedi-

tion. On his third and final trip to Africa, the great explorer disappeared.

Henry Stanley left to carry out his employer's orders soon after the Paris meeting. He took a roundabout route to Africa to cover other stories for the *Herald,* including the opening of the Suez Canal in Egypt. James Bennett hoped that by delaying Stanley's arrival in Africa, the reporter would come back with definite news of Livingstone—that he was dead or alive and not just missing. ("If he is dead," Bennett had said, "bring back every possible proof of his death.")

By the time Stanley finally reached Africa in late January 1871, Livingstone had been struggling with near-starvation, chronic dysentery, sore-covered feet, and hostile groups. Of the 60 men he had started with, only a small handful remained, including Chuma, a freed slave, and

Susi, a Yao servant. Both of them had been with him for years. Desperately sick and without medicine, Livingstone had been repeatedly nursed back to relatively good health by Arab slave traders. The passionate antislavery activist owed his life to the very people he wished to banish from Africa.

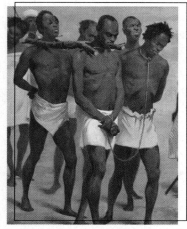

5 In July 1871, ill and discouraged, Livingstone headed to Ujiji, on the east bank of Lake Tanganyika. He expected to find several months' worth of supplies, medicine, and mail waiting for him there. In late October, "reduced to a skeleton," as he put it, he hobbled into the village—only to learn that all his supplies and precious medicines had been plundered by the headman of the place. Extremely depressed, he felt he couldn't do anything but wait for a miracle.

Several weeks later, the miracle arrived under a waving Stars and Stripes. Henry Stanley could hardly contain his emotion as he approached the pale white man. "I would have run to him, only I was a coward in the presence of such a mob," Stanley later wrote, "[I] would have embraced him, only he being an Englishman, I did not know how he would receive me; so I did what cowardice and false pride suggested was the best thing—walked deliberately to him, took off my hat, and said: 'Dr. Livingstone, I presume?' 'Yes,' said he, with a kind smile, lifting his cap slightly."

Stanley remained with Livingstone for five months and explored Lake Tanganyika with him. That trip proved that Burton was wrong about the Ruzizi, the river he thought led from the lake to become the Nile. Livingstone was now determined to prove his own theory, which was that the Nile originated with the headwaters of a river called the Lualaba. (As it turns out, the Lualaba is actually part of the Congo River system. Speke was right all along: The Nile's source is Lake Victoria.)

Unable to persuade the older man to return to Britain, Stanley left in March 1872. Reaching the coast in May, his news of finding Livingstone reached Europe and America in August. At about that time, Livingstone received the fresh supplies and men that Stanley had promised to send back to him. He promptly set off toward Lakes Tanganyika and Bangweulu.

The old explorer's will was great, but his long-suffering body was no longer up to the demands of the trip. By April 22, 1873, he was being carried in a litter. On the night of April

6

30, in the village of Chitambo, Susi helped him to bed, last speaking with him at midnight. The next morning, his companions found Livingstone kneeling by the bed, his head in his hands in prayer—dead.

Resolving that Livingstone should be returned to Britain, they buried his heart under a large tree near the hut where he died. Then they filled the body with salt, smeared it with brandy, and left it to dry for two weeks before beginning the long journey to the coast. Eight months and a thousand miles (1,609 km) later, they delivered Livingstone's body to the British Consul in Zanzibar. April 18, 1874, was declared a national day of mourning and all of London came to a halt as Dr. Livingstone was buried in Westminster Abbey.

4 Livingstone made two significant crossings of the African continent—from the interior west to Luanda in 1853–1854, and then east to Quelimane in 1855–1856. On his expedition in 1866 to find the source of the Nile, illness and other difficulties hampered his progress. Henry Stanley found him at Ujiji on November 10, 1871.

5 The all-too familiar sight of captives in chains drove Livingstone to denounce the collaboration of European authorities in the widespread traffic in slaves.

6 Henry Morton Stanley developed a great interest in exploring Africa after he found Livingstone.

INTERPRETING THE PAST

1. What were two of Dr. Livingstone's reasons for exploring Africa?

2. What waterfall did Livingstone encounter on his trip from the interior to the mouth of the Zambezi River?

3. What were the main obstacles that Livingstone faced?

British Rule in India

Main Ideas
- British rule brought stability to India but destroyed native industries and degraded Indians.
- Mohandas Gandhi advocated non-violent resistance to gain Indian independence from Great Britain.

Key Terms
sepoy, viceroy

People to Identify
Queen Victoria, Indian National Congress, Mohandas Gandhi

Places to Locate
Kanpur, Mumbai

Preview Questions
1. What was the goal of the Indian National Congress?
2. Why was India called the "Jewel in the Crown" of the Empress of India?

Reading Strategy
Cause and Effect Using a chart like the one below, identify some causes and effects of British influence on India.

Cause	Effect
1. British textiles	
2. cotton crops	
3. school system	
4. railroad, telegraph, telephone services	

Preview of Events

♦1840	♦1850	♦1860	♦1870	♦1880	♦1890	♦1900

1857
Sepoy Mutiny fails

1876
Queen Victoria is named "Empress of India"

1885
Indian National Congress forms

Voices from the Past

Thomas Macaulay

Thomas Macaulay, who was charged with the task of introducing an educational system into India, decided that it would use the English language:

❝What, then shall the language of education be? [Some] maintain that it should be the English. The other half strongly recommend the Arabic and Sanskrit. The whole question seems to me to be, which language is the best worth knowing? . . . It is, I believe, no exaggeration to say that all the historical information which has been collected from all the books written in the Sanskrit language is less valuable than what may be found in short textbooks used at preparatory schools in England.❞
— *A New History of India*, Stanley Wolpert, 1977

Macaulay's attitude reflects the sense of superiority that the British brought with them to India.

The Sepoy Mutiny

Over the course of the eighteenth century, British power in India had increased while the power of the Mogul rulers had declined (see Chapter 15). A trading company, the British East India Company, was given power by the British government to become actively involved in India's political and military affairs.

To rule India, the British East India Company had its own soldiers and forts. It also hired Indian soldiers, known as sepoys, to protect the company's interests in the region.

In 1857, a growing Indian distrust of the British led to a revolt. The revolt was known to the British as the Great Rebellion or the Sepoy Mutiny. Indians call it the First War of Independence.

British viceroy

Indian sepoy

Picturing History

After the 1857 revolt, officials of the British government ruled India. The sepoys were unsuccessful and paid dearly, as is shown by the British execution of Indian soldiers above. **Why did the Indian revolt fail?**

The major immediate cause of the revolt was the spread of a rumor that the British were issuing their Indian troops new bullets that were greased with cow and pig fat. The cow was sacred to Hindus; the pig was taboo to Muslims. A group of sepoys at an army post near Delhi refused to load their rifles with the new bullets. When the British arrested them, the sepoys went on a rampage and killed 50 European men, women, and children.

From this beginning, the revolt quickly spread. Within a year, however, Indian troops loyal to the British, along with fresh British troops, had crushed the rebellion. Although Indian troops fought bravely and outnumbered the British by about 230,000 to 40,000, they were not well organized. Rivalries between Hindus and Muslims kept Indians from working together.

Atrocities were terrible on both sides. At **Kanpur** (Cawnpore), Indians armed with swords and knives massacred two hundred defenseless women and children in a building known as the House of the Ladies. When the British recaptured Kanpur, they took their revenge before executing the Indians.

As a result of the uprising, the British Parliament transferred the powers of the East India Company directly to the British government. In 1876, the title of Empress of India was bestowed on **Queen Victoria.** The people of India were now her colonial subjects, and India became her "Jewel in the Crown."

Reading Check **Describing** What were two effects of the Great Rebellion?

Colonial Rule

The British government ruled India directly through a British official known as a viceroy (a governor who ruled as a representative of a monarch), who was assisted by a British civil service staff. This staff of about 3,500 officials ruled almost 300 million people, the largest colonial population in the world. British rule involved both benefits and costs for Indians.

Benefits of British Rule British rule in India had several benefits for subjects. It brought order and stability to a society that had been badly divided by civil war. It also led to a fairly honest and efficient government.

Through the efforts of the British administrator and historian Lord Thomas Macaulay, a new school system was set up. Its goal was to train Indian children to serve in the government and army. The new system served only elite, upper-class Indians, however. Ninety percent of the population remained illiterate.

Railroads, the telegraph, and a postal service were introduced to India shortly after they appeared in Great Britain. In 1853 the first trial run of a passenger train traveled the short distance from Bombay to Thane. By 1900, 25,000 miles (40,225 km) of railroads crisscrossed India. *(See page 997 to read excerpts from Dadabhai Naroji's* The Impact of British Rule in India *in the Primary Sources Library.)*

Costs of British Rule The Indian people, however, paid a high price for the peace and stability brought by British rule. Perhaps the greatest cost was economic. British entrepreneurs and a small number of Indians reaped financial benefits from British rule, but it brought hardship to millions of others in both the cities and the countryside. British manufactured goods destroyed local industries. The introduction of British textiles put thousands of women out of work and severely damaged the Indian textile industry.

In rural areas, the British sent the zamindars to collect taxes. The British believed that using these local officials would make it easier to collect taxes from the peasants. However, the zamindars in India took advantage of their new authority. They increased taxes and forced the less fortunate peasants to become tenants or lose their land entirely. Peasant unrest grew.

The British also encouraged many farmers to switch from growing food to growing cotton. As a result, food supplies could not keep up with the growing population. Between 1800 and 1900, thirty million Indians died of starvation.

Finally, British rule was degrading, even for the newly educated upper classes, who benefited the

THE WAY IT WAS

FOCUS ON EVERYDAY LIFE

British Official's Home in India

During the time that India was a British colony, many British government officials spent a considerable amount of time there fulfilling their administrative duties. Their families usually came with them during their tours of duty, bringing their Victorian lifestyle and many of the furnishings that went with it.

British officials in India built comfortable bungalows, as they were called. Bungalows (The name comes from the Indian word *bungla*, which means *Bengali*.) were elegant and spacious country houses. Many had large porches that were open to breezes while protecting the inhabitants from the sun. Surrounding the bungalows were cottages where dozens of Indian servants lived with their families.

The official was the sahib—the master. The official's wife was the memsahib, or madam-sahib. The memsahib was expected to oversee the running of the household on a daily basis, especially since the sahib was often away on official business. At the beginning of each day, she assigned duties to all the servants. For example, she fixed the menu for the day with the cook and directed the gardeners about how to plant the gardens with seeds from home. In the evening, she was expected to entertain. Supper parties with other British families were the usual form of entertainment.

most from it. The best jobs and the best housing were reserved for Britons. Although many British colonial officials sincerely tried to improve the lot of the people in India, British arrogance cut deeply into the pride of many Indians.

Despite their education, the Indians were never considered equals of the British. Lord Kitchener, one of Britain's military commanders in India, said, "It is this consciousness of the inherent superiority of the European which has won for us India. However well educated and clever a native may be, and however brave he may prove himself, I believe that no rank we can bestow on him would cause him to be considered an equal of the British officer."

The British also showed disrespect for India's cultural heritage. The Taj Mahal, for example, a tomb for the beloved wife of an Indian ruler, became a favorite site for English weddings and parties. Many partygoers even brought hammers to chip off pieces as souvenirs. British racial attitudes led to the rise of an Indian nationalist movement.

✓ **Reading Check** **Examining** How was British rule degrading to Indians?

An Indian Nationalist Movement

The first Indian nationalists were upper class and English-educated. Many of them were from urban areas, such as **Mumbai** (then called Bombay), Chennai (Madras), and Calcutta. Some were trained in British law and were members of the civil service.

At first, many preferred reform to revolution, but the slow pace of reform convinced many Indian nationalists that relying on British goodwill was futile. In 1885, a small group of Indians met in Mumbai to form the **Indian National Congress** (INC). The INC did not demand immediate independence but did call for a share in the governing process.

The INC had difficulties because of religious differences. The goal of the INC was to seek independence for all Indians, regardless of class or religious background. However, many of its leaders were Hindu and reflected Hindu concerns. Eventually, Muslims began to call for the creation of a separate Muslim League to represent the interests of the millions of Muslims in Indian society.

In 1915, the return of a young Hindu from South Africa brought new life to India's struggle for

A British officer receives a pedicure from an Indian servant.

The wife of a British officer is attended by Indian servants. A British merchant waits to speak to her.

Many British officials had a high standard of living and were expected to have a large number of servants. One woman wrote in 1882: "It is one of the social duties of Indian life that you must keep three servants to do the work of one." A well-to-do family had at least 25 servants. Even bachelors had at least a dozen. Indians served as cooks, maids, butlers, gardeners, tailors, and nursemaids for the children. All household servants wore uniforms—usually white with bands on their turbans—and went barefoot in the house.

CONNECTING TO THE PAST

1. **Identifying** What were the responsibilities of the wife of a British officer in India?

2. **Writing about History** What do you learn about British-Indian social relations from this reading?

independence. **Mohandas Gandhi** was born in 1869 in Gujarat, in western India. He studied in London and became a lawyer. In 1893, he went to South Africa to work in a law firm serving Indian workers there. He soon became aware of the racial exploitation of Indians living in South Africa.

On his return home to India, Gandhi became active in the independence movement. Using his experience in South Africa, he set up a movement based on nonviolent resistance. Its aim was to force the British to improve the lot of the poor and grant independence to India. Ultimately, Gandhi's movement would lead to Indian independence.

✓ **Reading Check** **Summarizing** What were the two goals of Mohandas Gandhi?

Colonial Indian Culture

The love-hate tension in India that arose from British domination led to a cultural, as well as a political, awakening. The cultural revival began in the early nineteenth century with the creation of a British college in Calcutta. A local publishing house was opened. It issued textbooks on a variety of subjects, including the sciences, Sanskrit, and Western literature. The publisher also printed grammars and dictionaries in the various Indian languages.

This revival soon spread to other regions of India, leading to a search for modern literary expression and a new national identity. Indian novelists and poets began writing historical romances and epics. Some wrote in English, but most were uncomfortable with a borrowed colonial language. They preferred to use their own regional tongues.

The most illustrious Indian author was Rabindranath Tagore. A great writer and poet, Tagore was also a social reformer, spiritual leader, educator, philosopher, singer, painter, and international spokesperson for the moral concerns of his age. He liked to invite the great thinkers of the time to his country estate. There he set up a school that became an international university.

Tagore's life mission was to promote pride in a national Indian consciousness in the face of British domination. He wrote a widely read novel in which he portrayed the love-hate relationship of India toward its colonial mentor. The novel depicted a country that admired and imitated the British model while also agonizing over how it could establish a modern identity separate from that of Great Britain.

Tagore, however, was more than an Indian nationalist. His life's work was one long prayer for human dignity, world peace, and the mutual understanding and union of East and West. As he once said, "It is my conviction that my countrymen will truly gain their India by fighting against the education that teaches them that a country is greater than the ideals of humanity."

✓ **Reading Check** **Comparing** How did the nationalist movement parallel cultural developments in India?

🌟 TAKS Practice

SECTION 3 ASSESSMENT

Checking for Understanding

1. **Define** sepoy, viceroy.

2. **Identify** Queen Victoria, Indian National Congress, Mohandas Gandhi.

3. **Locate** Kanpur, Mumbai.

4. **Explain** why the Muslim League was created. What were the advantages of its formation? What were the disadvantages?

5. **List** the economic costs to the Indian people that resulted from India being ruled by the British. What benefits to the Indian population, if any, resulted from British rule?

Critical Thinking

6. **Predict Consequences** Many British lived in India for decades. Do you think living in India would have changed British attitudes toward Indians? Explain.

7. **Organizing Information** Draw a graph like the example below to show the percentage of India's population that died of starvation in the 1800s.

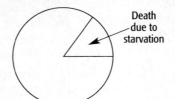
Death due to starvation

Analyzing Visuals

8. **Interpret** the messages conveyed by the two images on page 669. Describe your reactions to the paintings. Why might your reactions be the same as or different from reactions of English teenagers viewing these paintings in the late 1800s?

Writing About History

9. **Descriptive Writing** Imagine you are a member of India's upper-class. You have just attended a reception at the home of a British official. Describe in writing your impressions of the home, making a comparison to your own residence.

Nation Building in Latin America

Guide to Reading

Main Ideas
- Latin American countries served as a source of raw materials for Europe and the United States.
- Because land remained the basis of wealth and power, landed elites dominated Latin American countries.

Key Terms
creole, *peninsulare,* mestizo, Monroe Doctrine, caudillo

People to Identify
José de San Martín, Simón Bolívar, Antonio López de Santa Anna, Benito Juárez

Places to Locate
Puerto Rico, Panama Canal, Haiti, Nicaragua

Preview Question
1. How did the American Revolution inspire political changes in Latin America?

Reading Strategy
Compare and Contrast Create a Venn diagram comparing and contrasting colonial rule in Africa and in Latin America.

Africa   Latin America

Preview of Events

♦1800   ♦1805   ♦1810   ♦1815   ♦1820   ♦1825   ♦1830

1810
Mexico experiences its first revolt

1821
Mexico declares independence

1825
Most of Latin America becomes independent

Voices from the Past

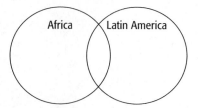

On August 10, 1819, Simón Bolívar issued a proclamation to the people of New Granada (present-day Colombia):

❝Granadans! America's day is come; no human power can stay the course of nature guided by the hand of Providence. Join your efforts to those of your brothers: Venezuela marches with me to free you, as in past years you marched with me to free Venezuela. Already our advance guard fills whole provinces of your territory with the luster of its arms; and the same advance guard, powerfully aided, will hurl the destroyed of New Granada into the seas. The sun will not have completed the course of its present round through the heavens without beholding in all your territory the proud altars of liberty.❞

— *World Civilizations,* Philip J. Adler, 1996

Portrait of Simón Bolívar

Bolívar was one of the leaders in liberating South America from Spanish and Portuguese control.

Nationalist Revolts

By the end of the eighteenth century, the new political ideals stemming from the successful revolution in North America were beginning to influence Latin America. European control would soon be in peril.

Father Hidalgo leads Mexicans in revolt against the Spaniards.

Social classes based on privilege divided colonial Latin America. *Peninsulares*, at the top, held all important positions. Creoles controlled land and business but were regarded as second-class citizens by *peninsulares*. Mestizos were the largest group but worked as servants or laborers.

Prelude to Revolution

The creole elites were especially influenced by revolutionary ideals. Creoles were descendants of Europeans born in Latin America who lived there permanently. They found the principles of the equality of all people in the eyes of the law, free trade, and a free press very attractive. In addition, they, along with a growing class of merchants, disliked the domination of their trade by Spain and Portugal.

Creoles deeply resented the *peninsulares,* Spanish and Portuguese officials who resided temporarily in Latin America for political and economic gain and then returned to their mother countries. These Europeans dominated Latin America and drained the Americas of their wealth.

The creole elites soon began to denounce the rule of the Spanish and Portuguese. At the beginning of the nineteenth century, Napoleon's wars provided them with an opportunity for change. When Napoleon overthrew the monarchies of Spain and Portugal, the authority of the Spaniards and Portuguese in their colonial empires was severely weakened. Between 1807 and 1825, a series of revolts enabled most of Latin America to become independent.

Before the main independence movements began, an unusual revolution took place in the French colony of Saint Domingue, on the island of Hispaniola. Led by François-Dominique Toussaint-Louverture (TOO•SAN LOO•vuhr•TYUR), more than a hundred thousand slaves rose in revolt and seized control of all of Hispaniola. On January 1, 1804, the western part of Hispaniola, now called Haiti, announced its freedom and became the first independent state in Latin America.

✓ **Reading Check** **Describing** How did Napoleon's wars affect Latin America?

Revolt in Mexico

Beginning in 1810, Mexico, too, experienced a revolt. The first real hero of Mexican independence was Miguel Hidalgo, a parish priest in a small village about a hundred miles (160 km) from Mexico City.

Hidalgo, who had studied the French Revolution, roused the local Indians and mestizos (people of European and Indian descent) to free themselves from the Spanish: "My children, this day comes to us as a new dispensation. Are you ready to receive it? Will you be free? Will you make the effort to recover from the hated Spaniards the lands stolen from your forefathers 300 years ago?"

On September 16, 1810, a crowd of Indians and mestizos, armed with clubs, machetes, and a few guns, formed a mob army to attack the Spaniards. Hidalgo was an inexperienced military leader, however, and his forces were soon crushed. A military court sentenced Hidalgo to death, but his memory lived on. In fact, September 16, the first day of the uprising, is Mexico's Independence Day.

The participation of Indians and mestizos in Mexico's revolt against Spanish control frightened both creoles and *peninsulares* there. Afraid of the masses, they cooperated in defeating the popular revolutionary forces. Conservative elites—both creoles and *peninsulares*—then decided to overthrow Spanish rule as a way of

HISTORY Online

Web Activity Visit the *Glencoe World History* Web site at tx.wh.glencoe.com and click on **Chapter 21– Student Web Activity** to learn more about independence movements in Latin America.

preserving their own power. They selected a creole military leader, Agustín de Iturbide (EE•TUR•BEE•thay), as their leader.

In 1821, Mexico declared its independence from Spain. Iturbide named himself emperor in 1822 but was deposed in 1823. Mexico then became a republic.

Revolts in South America José de San Martín of Argentina and Simón Bolívar of Venezuela, both members of the creole elite, were hailed as the "Liberators of South America." These men led revolutions throughout the continent. San Martín believed that the Spaniards must be removed from all of South America if any South American nation was to be free.

By 1810, the forces of San Martín had liberated Argentina from Spanish authority. Bolívar began the struggle for independence in Venezuela in 1810 and then went on to lead revolts in New Granada (Colombia) and Ecuador.

In January 1817, San Martín led his forces over the Andes to attack the Spanish in Chile. The journey was an amazing feat. Two-thirds of the pack mules and horses died during the trip. Soldiers suffered from lack of oxygen and severe cold while crossing mountain passes that were more than two miles (3.218 km) above sea level.

The arrival of San Martín's forces in Chile completely surprised the Spaniards. Spanish forces were badly defeated at the Battle of Chacabuco on February 12, 1817. In 1821, San Martín moved on to Lima, Peru, the center of Spanish authority.

Convinced that he could not complete the liberation of Peru alone, San Martín welcomed the arrival of Bolívar and his forces. The "Liberator of Venezuela" took on the task of crushing the last significant Spanish army at Ayacucho on December 9, 1824.

By the end of 1824, Peru, Uruguay, Paraguay, Colombia, Venezuela, Argentina, Bolivia, and Chile had all become free of Spain. Earlier, in 1822, the prince regent of Brazil had declared Brazil's independence from Portugal. The Central American states had become independent in 1823. In 1838 and 1839, they divided into five republics: Guatemala, El Salvador, Honduras, Costa Rica, and Nicaragua.

In the early 1820s, only one major threat remained to the newly won independence of the Latin American states. Members of the Concert of Europe favored the use of troops to restore Spanish control in Latin

Painting of early twentieth-century coffee plantation by Candido Portinari

America. The British, who wished to trade with Latin America, disagreed. They proposed joint action with the United States against any European moves in Latin America.

Distrustful of British motives, United States president James Monroe acted alone in 1823. In the **Monroe Doctrine,** he guaranteed the independence of the new Latin American nations and warned against any European intervention in the Americas.

More important to Latin American independence than American words, however, was Britain's navy. Other European powers feared British naval power, which stood between Latin America and any European invasion force.

✓Reading Check **Evaluating** How did the French Revolution affect Mexico?

Difficulties of Nation Building

The new Latin American nations faced a number of serious problems between 1830 and 1870. The wars for independence had resulted in a staggering loss of people, property, and livestock. Unsure of their precise boundaries, the new nations went to war with one another to settle border disputes. Poor roads, a lack of railroads, thick jungles, and mountains made communication, transportation, and national unity difficult. During the course of the nineteenth century, the new Latin American nations would become economically dependent on Western nations once again.

Canal
Railroad

ATLANTIC OCEAN

Gulf of Mexico

Alajuela Lake

MADDEN DAM — *Chagres R.* **Gamboa** *Gold Hill* **San Miguelito** **Panama**

Breakwater

Colón
GATUN LOCKS
PANAMA RAILROAD
CULEBRA CUT
MIRAFLORES LOCKS
PEDRO MIGUEL LOCKS

Breakwater

Chagres R. *Spillway*
GATUN DAM
Gatun Lake

Scale varies in this perspective.

Geography *Skills*

The United States's intervention in Latin America in the early 1900s led to the building of the Panama Canal (opened in 1914). The United States controlled the canal throughout most of the twentieth century.

1. **Interpreting Maps** The Panama Canal provides a shorter route between which two oceans?

2. **Interpreting Maps** What is the difference in miles between the two routes from New York City to San Francisco?

3. **Applying Geography Skills** Nicaragua was an alternate site for the canal. Determine why Panama was selected.

Travel Distance

San Francisco
New York City
ATLANTIC OCEAN
30°N
12,600 miles
4,900 miles
Panama Canal
EQUATOR
PACIFIC OCEAN
N W E S
0 1,000 miles
0 1,000 kilometers
Lambert Azimuthal Equal-Area projection
30°S
Strait of Magellan
90°W 60°W
120°W 30°W 0°
60°S

Route via the Strait of Magellan
Route via the Panama Canal

Rule of the Caudillos Most of the new nations of Latin America began with republican governments, but they had had no experience in ruling themselves. Soon after independence, strong leaders known as caudillos came into power.

Caudillos ruled chiefly by military force and were usually supported by the landed elites. Many kept the new national states together. Some were also modernizers who built roads and canals, ports, and schools. Others were destructive.

Antonio López de Santa Anna, for example, ruled Mexico from 1833 to 1855. He misused state funds, halted reforms, and created chaos. In 1835, American settlers in the Mexican state of Texas revolted against Santa Anna's rule.

Texas gained its independence in 1836 and United States statehood in 1845. War between Mexico and the United States soon followed (1846–1848). Mexico was defeated and lost almost one-half of its territory to the United States in the Mexican War.

Fortunately for Mexico, Santa Anna's disastrous rule was followed by a period of reform from 1855 to 1876. This era was dominated by **Benito Juárez,** a Mexican national hero. The son of Native American peasants, President Juárez brought liberal reforms to Mexico, including separation of church and state, land distribution to the poor, and an educational system for all of Mexico.

Other caudillos, such as Juan Manual de Rosas in Argentina, were supported by the masses, became extremely popular, and brought about radical change. Unfortunately, the caudillo's authority depended on his personal power. When he died or lost power, civil wars for control of the country often erupted.

Panama Canal Locks

1. A ship arrives from the Atlantic Ocean or the Pacific Ocean.

2. The ship enters the first lock and steel gates close behind it. Water flows into the lock from an artificial lake. When the water reaches the level of the next higher lock, gates open and the ship moves forward.

3. Electric towing locomotives called mules pull the ship by cables through the locks.

4. In a descending lock, water is drained to the level of the next lower lock and the ship advances.

Workers building the Panama Canal

Panama Canal Facts

• In 1534, Holy Roman Emperor Charles V ordered the first survey of a proposed canal route across the Isthmus of Panama. The survey came back "impossible."

• The canal was constructed in two stages: between 1881 and 1888 by a French company and between 1904 and 1914 by the United States.

• The canal is 51 miles (82 km) long. The average time a ship spends in transit is 8 to 10 hours.

• There are 6 pairs of locks, or a total of 12 locks. Each lock is 1,000 feet (305 m) long and 110 feet (34 m) wide. The lock system lifts ships 85 feet (26 m) above sea level.

• About 140 million tons (127 million t) of commercial cargo pass through the canal each year.

A New Imperialism Political independence brought economic independence, but old patterns were quickly reestablished. Instead of Spain and Portugal, Great Britain now dominated the Latin American economy. British merchants moved into Latin America in large numbers, and British investors poured in funds. Old trade patterns soon reemerged.

Latin America continued to serve as a source of raw materials and foodstuffs for the industrial nations of Europe and the United States. Exports included wheat, tobacco, wool, sugar, coffee, and hides. At the same time, finished consumer goods, especially textiles, were imported.

The emphasis on exporting raw materials and importing finished products ensured the ongoing domination of the Latin American economy by foreigners. Latin American countries remained economic colonies of Western nations, even though they were no longer political colonies.

Persistent Inequality A fundamental, underlying problem for all of the new Latin American nations was the domination of society by the landed elites. Large estates remained a way of life in Latin America. By 1848, for example, the Sánchez Navarro family in Mexico possessed 17 estates made up of 16 million acres (6,480,000 ha). Estates were often so large that they could not be farmed efficiently.

Land remained the basis of wealth, social prestige, and political power throughout the nineteenth century. Landed elites ran governments, controlled courts, and kept a system of inexpensive labor. These landowners made enormous profits by growing single, specialized crops, such as coffee, for export. The masses, with no land to grow basic food crops, experienced dire poverty.

✓**Reading Check** **Describing** What were some of the difficulties faced by the new Latin American republics?

Political Change in Latin America

→**TURNING POINT**← One hundred years of direct United States involvement in the Panama Canal ended on December 31, 1999, when the canal reverted to Panamanian control.

After 1870, Latin American governments, led by large landowners, wrote constitutions similar to those of the United States and European democracies. The ruling elites were careful to keep their power by limiting voting rights, however.

The United States in Latin America
By 1900, the United States, which had emerged as a world power, had begun to intervene in the affairs of its southern neighbors. As a result of the Spanish-American War (1898), Cuba became a United States protectorate, and **Puerto Rico** was annexed to the United States.

In 1903, the United States supported a rebellion that enabled Panama to separate itself from Colombia and establish a new nation. In return, the United States was granted control of a strip of land 10 miles (16.09 km) wide running from coast to coast in Panama. There, the United States built the **Panama Canal,** which was opened in 1914.

American investments in Latin America soon followed, as did American resolve to protect those investments. Beginning in 1898, American military forces were sent to Cuba, Mexico, Guatemala, Honduras, Nicaragua, Panama, Colombia, Haiti, and the Dominican Republic to protect American interests.

Some expeditions remained for many years. United States Marines were in **Haiti** from 1915 to 1934, and **Nicaragua** was occupied from 1909 to 1933. Increasing numbers of Latin Americans began to resent this interference from the "big bully" to the north.

Revolution in Mexico
In some countries, large landowners supported dictators who looked out for the interests of the ruling elite. Porfirio Díaz, who ruled Mexico between 1877 and 1911, created a conservative, centralized government with the support of the army, foreign capitalists, large landowners, and the Catholic Church. All these groups benefited from their alliance. However, forces for change in Mexico led to a revolution.

During Díaz's dictatorial reign, the wages of workers had declined. Ninety-five percent of the rural population owned no land, whereas about a thousand families owned almost all of Mexico. When a liberal landowner, Francisco Madero, forced Díaz from power in 1911, he opened the door to a wider revolution.

Madero's ineffectiveness created a demand for agrarian reform. This new call for reform was led by Emiliano Zapata. Zapata aroused the masses of landless peasants and began to seize the estates of wealthy landholders.

Between 1910 and 1920, the Mexican Revolution caused great damage to the Mexican economy. Finally, a new constitution enacted in 1917 set up a government led by a president, created land-reform policies, established limits on foreign investors, and set an agenda to help the workers. The revolution also led to an outpouring of patriotism. Intellectuals and artists sought to capture what was unique about Mexico, with special emphasis on its past.

✓**Reading Check** **Describing** What was the United States's role as a colonial power?

Picturing **History**

United States marines hoist the American flag following a United States victory in the Spanish-American War. What territory in addition to Cuba came under American control as a result of the Spanish-American War?

Economic Change in Latin America

After 1870, Latin America began an age of prosperity based to a large extent on the export of a few basic items. These included wheat and beef from Argentina, coffee from Brazil, coffee and bananas from Central America, and sugar and silver from Peru. These foodstuffs and raw materials were largely exchanged for finished goods—textiles, machines, and luxury items—from Europe and the United States. After 1900, Latin Americans also increased their own industrialization, especially by building textile, food-processing, and construction material factories.

One result of the prosperity that came from increased exports was growth in the middle sectors (divisions) of Latin American society—lawyers, merchants, shopkeepers, businesspeople, schoolteachers, professors, bureaucrats, and military officers. These middle sectors accounted for only 5 to 10 percent of the population, hardly enough in numbers to make up a true middle class. Nevertheless, after 1900, the middle sectors of society continued to expand.

Regardless of the country in which they lived, middle-class Latin Americans shared some common characteristics. They lived in the cities; sought educa-

Picturing **History**

This photo shows Montevideo, Uruguay, in the early twentieth century. What signs of increasing prosperity do you see in this photo?

tion and decent incomes; and saw the United States as a model, especially in regard to industrialization.

The middle sectors in Latin America sought liberal reform, not revolution. Once they had the right to vote, they generally sided with the landholding elites.

✓**Reading Check** **Evaluating** What caused the growth of a middle class in Latin America?

TAKS Practice

SECTION 4 ASSESSMENT

Checking for Understanding

1. **Define** creole, *peninsulare,* mestizo, Monroe Doctrine, caudillo.

2. **Identify** José de San Martín, Simón Bolívar, Antonio López de Santa Anna, Benito Juárez.

3. **Locate** Puerto Rico, Panama Canal, Haiti, Nicaragua.

4. **Describe** British motives for protecting Latin American states.

5. **List** the powers and privileges of the landed elites.

Critical Thinking

6. **Examine** Why did eliminating European domination from Latin America not bring about significant economic and social change?

7. **Organizing Information** Fill in the chart below to identify which country exported each product listed.

Product	Country
coffee	
bananas and coffee	
beef and wheat	
sugar and silver	

Analyzing Visuals

8. **Describe** the painting on page 672. What action is taking place? How would you describe the emotions of the people in the scene? How has the painter tried to convey the importance of the event?

Writing About History

9. **Expository Writing** Why did Latin American countries remain economic colonies of Western nations when they were no longer political colonies? Write a brief essay explaining why this happened.

Chapter Summary

The Age Of Imperialism

The imperialist powers of the nineteenth century conquered weaker countries and carved up the lands they seized. Their actions had a lasting effect on the world, especially the conquered peoples of Asia and Africa. The chart below organizes selected events that occurred during the age of imperialism according to four themes.

Movement

- Imperialistic nations set up colonies and protectorates.
- Christian missionaries preach in Africa and Asia.
- Cecil Rhodes makes a fortune in South Africa.

Change

- Ferdinand de Lesseps completes the Suez Canal in 1869.
- King Leopold II of Belgium colonizes the Congo Basin.
- The United States gains new territory after the Spanish-American War.
- The Panama Canal opens in 1914.

Reaction

- The British East India Company controls India.
- Afrikaners set up independent republics.

Nationalism

- The United States creates the Monroe Doctrine in 1823.
- In May 1857, the sepoys rebel against British commanders.
- Afrikaners fight the British in the Boer War from 1899 to 1902.

Using Key Terms

1. The establishment of overseas colonies is called _____.
2. A _____ is a political unit that depends on another state for its protection, such as Cambodia in its relationship with France in the 1880s.
3. The method of colonial government in which local rulers maintain their authority is called _____.
4. When foreigners govern the colony instead of locals it is called _____.
5. Puerto Rico was _____ by the United States.
6. The people who are native to a country are also known as _____.
7. Indian soldiers in the service of the British East India Company were called _____.
8. The _____ of India was assisted by a large British civil service staff.
9. To prevent foreign interference in Latin America, the president of the United States issued the _____.
10. The _____ elite led the fight for independence in South America.

Reviewing Key Facts

11. **Economics** Why did European states wish to establish colonies?
12. **Geography** What African state was founded as a refuge for former slaves?
13. **History** By 1914, what European countries had divided up Africa?
14. **Culture** What were the effects of British rule in India?
15. **Government** Describe the zamindar system, which was used by the British in India.
16. **History** What were the goals of Mohandas Gandhi?
17. **History** Why was the Haitian revolution unique?
18. **History** What arrangement did the United States make with Panama?
19. **Geography** What country in Southeast Asia remained independent? Why?

Critical Thinking

20. **Analyzing** Explain the circumstances surrounding the building of the Panama Canal. How did the United States benefit?
21. **Making Comparisons** Discuss the various concerns of people under colonial rule. Did social class affect how they viewed colonial power? How were the concerns of different social classes similar? How were they different?

Writing About History

22. Persuasive Writing Pretend you are a British colonist who
has been living abroad for a year. Decide whether you are
for or against colonialism and write a letter to your family
convincing them of your views. Use examples from the text
or your own research.

Analyzing Sources

Read the following quote by Miguel Hidalgo:

> 66My children, this day comes to us as a new dispen-
> sation. Are you ready to receive it? Will you be free?
> Will you make the effort to recover from the hated
> Spanish the lands stolen from your forefathers 300
> years ago?99

23. Describe the tone of this quote. What emotions is Hidalgo
trying to arouse? Is Hidalgo correct when he claims that the
Spanish stole the land?

24. Do you think Native Americans in North America are justified in feeling that their lands were stolen? Why or why not?

Applying Technology Skills

25. Using the Internet Use the Internet to research Emilio
Aguinaldo and the Philippine quest for independence.
Create a map showing the various battle sites.

Making Decisions

26. You are a local ruler in your country. You deeply resent the
colonial power that has asked you to rule in its interest. Do
you continue to rule or do you resign? What are the
consequences of your decision?

27. Originally the Panama Canal was a French project. When the
French ran into difficulties, they attempted to sell their project to the United States. As a United States senator, decide
whether or not the United States should take over the
project. Give reasons for your decision.

28. Simón Bolívar is considered to be the George Washington of
South America. Do further research on Bolívar in your
school library. If necessary, review information you have
previously learned about George Washington. Decide
whether or not you think the comparison between Bolívar
and Washington is fair. Explain your decision.

 Suez Canal

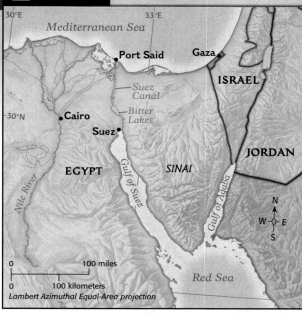

Analyzing Maps and Charts

Use your text and the map above to answer the following
questions.

29. Approximately how long is the Suez Canal?

30. Why is control of the Suez Canal so important?

31. What two seas are connected by the Suez Canal?

32. What route was used for trade and transportation in this area
prior to the building of the Suez Canal?

 **Test Practice**

Directions: Choose the best answer to the following question.

Which of the following was a consequence of British colonial rule in India?

A the defeat of the Mogul dynasty

B the popularity of the joint-stock company

C the exploitation of resources

D the Berlin Conference of 1884

Test-Taking Tip: If you do not immediately know the right
answer to a question, look at each answer choice carefully.
Try to recall the context in which these events were discussed in class. Remembering this context may help you
eliminate incorrect answer choices.

22 East Asia Under Challenge

1800–1914

Key Events

As you read this chapter, look for the key events in the development of East Asia.
- *Western nations used political persuasion and military strength to gain trading privileges with China and Japan.*
- *China's internal problems made it easier for Western nations to penetrate the country and strengthen their influence.*
- *Japan's ability to adopt Western ways and to maintain its own traditions enabled it to develop into a modern, powerful nation.*

The Impact Today

The events that occurred during this time period still impact our lives today.
- *The issues raised by the Opium War continue to be addressed, since drug addiction is still a major international problem.*
- *Japan has one of the world's largest industrialized, free-market economies.*
- *China's large market continues to attract Western business and trade.*

 World History Video The Chapter 22 video, "The Russo-Japanese War," chronicles the conflict between Russia and Japan.

Chinese workers pack tea for export.

1854
Treaty of Kanagawa initiates United States–Japanese relations

1860
Europeans seize Chinese capital of Beijing

1830   1840   1850   1860   1870

1841
British forces seize island of Hong Kong

1842
Treaty of Nanjing establishes trade between China and Great Britain

1868
Meiji Restoration begins

A British steamship attacks Chinese naval forces off the coast of China during the Opium War.

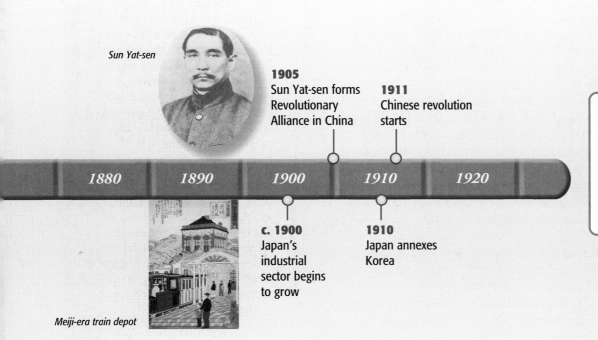

Sun Yat-sen

1905
Sun Yat-sen forms Revolutionary Alliance in China

1911
Chinese revolution starts

1880   1890   1900   1910   1920

c. 1900
Japan's industrial sector begins to grow

1910
Japan annexes Korea

Meiji-era train depot

HISTORY
Online

Chapter Overview
Visit the *Glencoe World History* Web site at tx.wh.glencoe.com and click on **Chapter 22–Chapter Overview** to preview chapter information.

A Story That Matters

The Summer Palace in Beijing today

Palace interior

Looting of the Summer Palace

Like the countries of South Asia, Southeast Asia, and Africa, the nations of East Asia faced a growing challenge from the power of the West in the nineteenth century. In China, Westerners used their military superiority to pursue their goals.

In 1860, for example, Great Britain and France decided to retaliate against the Chinese, who had tried to restrict British and French activities. In July, combined British and French forces arrived on the outskirts of Beijing. There, they came upon the Old Summer Palace of the Chinese emperors. The soldiers were astounded by the riches they beheld and could not resist the desire to steal them.

Beginning on October 6, British and French troops moved through the palace. They took anything that looked valuable and smashed what they could not cart away. One British observer wrote, "You would see several officers and men of all ranks with their heads and hands brushing and knocking together in the same box." In another room, he said, "a scramble was going on over a collection of handsome state robes . . . others would be amusing themselves by taking shots at chandeliers."

Lord Elgin, leader of the British forces in China, soon restored order. After the Chinese took hostage and then murdered some 20 British and French soldiers, however, Lord Elgin ordered the Old Summer Palace to be burned. Intimidated, the Chinese government agreed to Western demands.

Why It Matters

The events of 1860 were part of a regular pattern in East Asia in the nineteenth century. Backed by European guns, European merchants and missionaries pressed for the right to carry out their activities in China and Japan. The Chinese and Japanese resisted but were eventually forced to open their doors to the foreigners. Unlike other Asian societies, however, both Japan and China were able to maintain their national independence.

History and You International contact continues to shrink differences among nations. Using the information in this chapter and outside research, create a chart comparing the development of the United States and Japan during the twentieth century. Include data on material goods as well as economic, political, or social trends.

The Decline of the Qing Dynasty

Guide to Reading

Main Ideas
- The Qing dynasty declined because of internal and external pressures.
- Western nations increased their economic involvement with China.

Key Terms
extraterritoriality, self-strengthening, spheres of influence, indemnity

People to Identify
Hong Xiuquan, Guang Xu, Empress Dowager Ci Xi, John Hay

Places to Locate
Guangzhou, Chang Jiang, Hong Kong

Preview Questions
1. What internal problems led to the decline of the Qing dynasty?
2. What role did Western nations play in the Qing dynasty's decline?

Reading Strategy
Compare and Contrast Create a chart comparing and contrasting the Tai Ping and Boxer Rebellions.

	Tai Ping	Boxer
Reforms Demanded		
Methods Used to Obtain Reforms		
Outcomes		

Preview of Events

◆1840	◆1850	◆1860	◆1870	◆1880	◆1890	◆1900

1839
Opium War begins

1850
Tai Ping Rebellion begins

1898
Ci Xi opposes reforms

1900
Boxer Rebellion defeated

Nobleman, Qing dynasty

Voices from the Past

In the second half of the nineteenth century, calls for political reform were heard in China. However, a leading court official, Zhang Zhidong, argued:

❝The doctrine of people's rights will bring us not a single benefit but a hundred evils. Are we going to establish a parliament? Among the Chinese scholars and people there are still many today who are content to be vulgar and rustic. They are ignorant of the general situation in the world, they do not understand the basic system of the state. They have not the most elementary idea about foreign countries. . . . Even supposing the confused and clamorous people are assembled in one house, for every one of them who is clear-sighted, there will be a hundred others whose vision is clouded; they will converse at random and talk as if in a dream—what use will it be?❞

— *China's Response to the West: A Documentary Survey, 1839–1923,*
Ssu-yu Teng and John K. Fairbank, eds., 1970

Zhang's view prevailed, and no reforms were enacted.

Causes of Decline

In 1800, after a long period of peace and prosperity, the Qing dynasty of the Manchus was at the height of its power. A little over a century later, however, humiliated and harassed by the Western powers, the Qing dynasty collapsed.

One important reason for the abrupt decline and fall of the Qing dynasty was the intense external pressure applied to Chinese society by the modern West. However, internal changes also played a role in the dynasty's collapse.

After an extended period of growth, the Qing dynasty began to suffer from corruption, peasant unrest, and incompetence. These weaknesses were made worse by rapid growth in the country's population. By 1900, there were 400 million people in China. Population growth created a serious food shortage. In the 1850s, one observer wrote, "Not a year passes in which a terrific number of persons do not perish of famine in some part or other of China."

The ships, guns, and ideas of foreigners highlighted the growing weakness of the Qing dynasty and probably hastened its end.

✓ **Reading Check** **Examining** What factors led to the decline of the Qing dynasty?

The Opium War

By 1800, Europeans had been in contact with China for more than two hundred years. European merchants, however, were restricted to a small trading outlet at **Guangzhou** (GWONG•JO), or Canton. The British did not like this arrangement.

The British also had an unfavorable trade balance in China. That is, they imported more goods from China than they exported to China. For years, Britain had imported tea, silk, and porcelain from the Chinese and sent Indian cotton to China to pay for these imports. The cotton, however, did not cover the entire debt, and the British were forced to pay for their imports with silver. The British sent increasing quantities of silver to China, especially in exchange for tea, which was in great demand by the British.

At first, the British tried to negotiate with the Chinese to improve the trade imbalance. When negotiations failed, the British turned to trading opium.

Opium was grown in northern India under the sponsorship of the British East India Company and then shipped directly to Chinese markets. Demand for opium—a highly addictive drug—in South China jumped dramatically. Soon, silver was flowing out of China and into the pockets of the officials of the British East India Company.

The Chinese reacted strongly. The British were not the first to import opium into China. The Chinese government had already seen opium's dangerous qualities, and had made its trade illegal. They appealed to the British government on moral grounds to stop the traffic in opium. A government official wrote to Queen Victoria: "Suppose there were

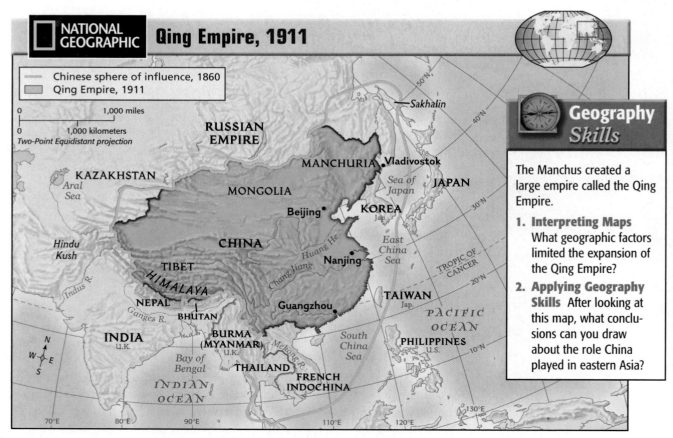

NATIONAL GEOGRAPHIC **Qing Empire, 1911**

Chinese sphere of influence, 1860
Qing Empire, 1911

0 — 1,000 miles
0 — 1,000 kilometers
Two-Point Equidistant projection

RUSSIAN EMPIRE

KAZAKHSTAN
Aral Sea

MANCHURIA • Vladivostok
Sea of Japan
JAPAN

MONGOLIA

Beijing •
KOREA
Jap.

Hindu Kush

CHINA
Huang He
East China Sea

TIBET
HIMALAYA
Chang Jiang
Nanjing •

Indus R.

NEPAL
Ganges R.
BHUTAN

TROPIC OF CANCER

TAIWAN
Jap.

INDIA
U.K.

BURMA (MYANMAR)
U.K.
Mekong R.

Bay of Bengal

THAILAND

South China Sea

PACIFIC OCEAN

PHILIPPINES
U.S.

FRENCH INDOCHINA

INDIAN OCEAN

N W E S

70°E 80°E 90°E 110°E 120°E

Sakhalin

Geography Skills

The Manchus created a large empire called the Qing Empire.

1. **Interpreting Maps** What geographic factors limited the expansion of the Qing Empire?

2. **Applying Geography Skills** After looking at this map, what conclusions can you draw about the role China played in eastern Asia?

people from another country who carried opium for sale to England and seduced your people into buying and smoking it; certainly your honorable ruler would deeply hate it and be bitterly aroused."

The British refused to halt their activity, however. As a result, the Chinese government blockaded the foreign area in Guangzhou in order to force traders to surrender their chests of opium. The British responded with force, starting the Opium War (1839–1842).

The Chinese were no match for the British. British warships destroyed Chinese coastal and river forts. When a British fleet sailed almost unopposed up the **Chang Jiang** (Yangtze River) to Nanjing, the Qing dynasty made peace.

In the Treaty of Nanjing in 1842, the Chinese agreed to open five coastal ports to British trade, limit taxes on imported British goods, and pay for the costs of the war. China also agreed to give the British the island of **Hong Kong.** Nothing was said in the treaty about the opium trade. Moreover, in the five ports, Europeans lived in their own sections and were subject not to Chinese laws but to their own laws—a practice known as extraterritoriality.

The Opium War marked the beginning of the establishment of Western influence in China. For the time being, the Chinese tried to deal with the problem by pitting foreign countries against one another. Concessions granted to the British were offered to other Western nations, including the United States. Soon, thriving foreign areas were operating in the five treaty ports along the southern Chinese coast.

HISTORY *Online*

Web Activity Visit the *Glencoe World History* Web site at tx.wh.glencoe.com and click on **Chapter 22– Student Web Activity** to learn more about Western influence in China.

✓ **Reading Check** **Summarizing** What did the British do to adjust their trade imbalance with China?

The Tai Ping Rebellion

In the meantime, the failure of the Chinese government to deal with pressing internal economic problems led to a peasant revolt, known as the Tai Ping (TIE PING) Rebellion (1850–1864). It was led by

CONNECTIONS Past To Present

The Return of Hong Kong to China

In 1984, Great Britain and China signed a joint declaration in which Britain agreed to return its colony of Hong Kong to China on July 1, 1997. China promised that Hong Kong would keep its free market, its capitalist economy, and its way of life. The formula was "one country, two systems."

In 1841, Hong Kong was a small island with a few fishing villages on the southeastern coast of China. A British naval force seized the island and used it as a port for shipping opium into China. A year later, after a humil-

iating defeat in the Opium War, China agreed to give the island of Hong Kong to Britain.

Later, the British took advantage of the declining power of China's Qing dynasty to gain additional lands next to Hong Kong. In 1860, the Chinese government granted the Kowloon Peninsula to Britain. In 1898, the Chinese granted the British a 99-year lease on the nearby New Territories, an area that provided much of the food for the colony of Hong Kong.

In the 1950s and 1960s, Hong Kong was filled with refugees from the new Communist regime in mainland China. The population of Hong Kong swelled to six million. The economy of Hong Kong boomed. Today, Hong Kong is the eighth largest trading nation in the world.

◀ *Troops take down the British flag in Hong Kong in 1997.*

Comparing Past and Present

Using outside sources, research the current political and cultural situation in Hong Kong. Explain what the formula "one country, two systems" means. Evaluate whether or not the formula has been successful since Hong Kong was returned to China.

Hong Xiuquan, a Christian convert who viewed himself as a younger brother of Jesus Christ.

Hong was convinced that God had given him the mission of destroying the Qing dynasty. Joined by great crowds of peasants, Hong captured the town of Yongan and proclaimed a new dynasty, the Heavenly Kingdom of Great Peace (*Tai Ping Tianguo* in Chinese—hence the name *Tai Ping Rebellion*).

The Tai Ping Rebellion appealed to many people because it called for social reforms. These reforms included giving land to all peasants and treating women as equals of men. Women even served in their own units in the Tai Ping army.

Hong's rebellion also called for people to give up private possessions. Peasants were to hold lands and farms in common, and money, food, and clothing were to be shared equally by all. Hong outlawed alcohol and tobacco and eliminated the practice of binding women's feet. The Chinese Communist Revolution of the twentieth century (see Chapter 31) would have similar social goals.

In March 1853, the rebels seized Nanjing, the second largest city of the empire, and massacred 25,000 men, women, and children. The revolt continued for 10 more years but gradually began to fall apart. Europeans came to the aid of the Qing dynasty when they realized the destructive nature of the Tai Ping forces. As one British observer noted, there was no hope "of

European troops battle Tai Ping soldiers in Guangzhou during the Tai Ping Rebellion.

any good ever coming of the rebel movement. They do nothing but burn, murder, and destroy."

In 1864, Chinese forces, with European aid, recaptured Nanjing and destroyed the remaining rebel force. The Tai Ping Rebellion proved to be one of the most devastating civil wars in history. As many as twenty million people died in the course of the 14-year struggle.

One reason for the Qing dynasty's failure to deal effectively with the internal unrest was its ongoing struggle with the Western powers. Beginning in 1856, the British and the French applied force to gain greater trade privileges. As a result of the Treaty of Tianjin in 1858, the Chinese agreed to legalize the opium trade and open new ports to foreign trade. They also surrendered the Kowloon Peninsula to Great Britain. When the Chinese resisted parts of the treaty, the British seized Beijing in 1860.

✓ **Reading Check** **Summarizing** What social reforms did the Tai Ping Rebellion demand?

Efforts at Reform

By the late 1870s, the Qing dynasty was in decline. Unable to restore order themselves, government troops had relied on forces recruited by regional warlords to help fight the Tai Ping Rebellion. To finance their private armies, warlords had collected taxes from local people. After crushing the revolt, many of these warlords refused to dismiss their units. With the support of the local gentry, they continued to collect local taxes for their own use.

In its weakened state, the Qing court finally began to listen to the appeals of reform-minded officials. The reformers called for a new policy they called "self-strengthening." By this, they meant that China

⌛ **Then** *and* **Now**

Victoria served as the capital of Britain's Hong Kong colony.
How did the presence of the British impact the island of Hong Kong?

Victoria Harbor, c. 1840 ▶

▼ *Modern Hong Kong*

should adopt Western technology while keeping its Confucian values and institutions. Under this policy, factories were built to produce modern weapons and ships, increasing China's military strength. However, the traditional Chinese imperial bureaucracy was also retained, and civil service examinations based on Confucian writers were still used to select government staff members. This new policy guided Chinese foreign and domestic policy for the next 25 years.

Some reformers wanted to change China's traditional political institutions by introducing democracy. However, such ideas were too radical for most reformers. During the last quarter of the nineteenth century, the Chinese government tried to modernize China's military forces and build up industry without touching the basic elements of Chinese civilization. Railroads, weapons factories, and shipyards were built, but the Chinese value system remained unchanged.

Reading Check **Explaining** What was China's policy of "self-strengthening"?

The Advance of Imperialism

In the end, however, the changes did not help the Qing stay in power. The European advance into China continued during the last two decades of the nineteenth century, while internal conditions continued to deteriorate.

Mounting Pressures In the north and northeast, Russia took advantage of the Qing dynasty's weakness to force China to give up territories north of the Amur River in Siberia. In Tibet, a struggle between Russia and Great Britain kept both powers from seizing the territory outright. This allowed Tibet to become free from Chinese influence.

Even more ominous changes were taking place in the Chinese heartland. European states began to create spheres of influence, areas where the imperial powers had exclusive trading rights. After the Tai Ping Rebellion, warlords in the provinces began to negotiate directly with foreign nations. In return for money,

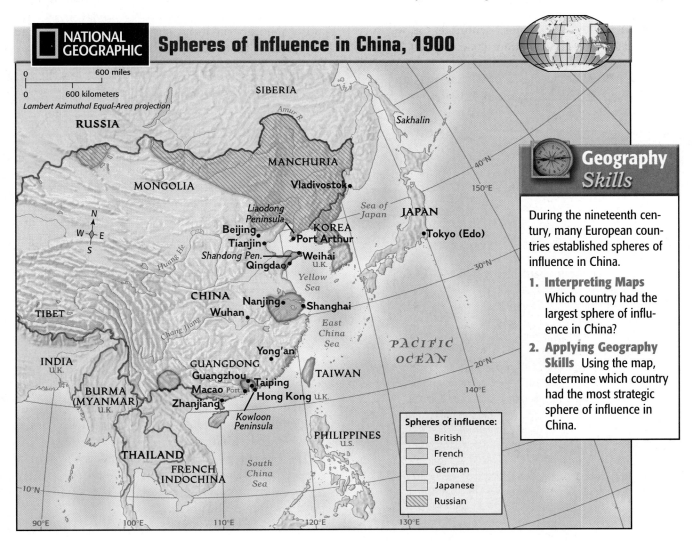

NATIONAL GEOGRAPHIC

Spheres of Influence in China, 1900

600 miles
600 kilometers
Lambert Azimuthal Equal-Area projection

Geography Skills

During the nineteenth century, many European countries established spheres of influence in China.

1. **Interpreting Maps** Which country had the largest sphere of influence in China?

2. **Applying Geography Skills** Using the map, determine which country had the most strategic sphere of influence in China.

Spheres of influence:
- British
- French
- German
- Japanese
- Russian

the warlords granted these nations exclusive trading rights or railroad-building and mining privileges. In this way, Britain, France, Germany, Russia, and Japan all established spheres of influence in China.

In 1894, another blow further disintegrated the Qing dynasty. The Chinese went to war with Japan over Japanese inroads into Korea, a land that the Chinese had controlled for a long time. The Chinese were soundly defeated. As a reward, Japan demanded and received the island of Taiwan (known to Europeans at the time as Formosa), and the Liaodong (LYOW•DOONG) Peninsula. Fearing Japan's growing power, however, the European powers forced Japan to give the Liaodong Peninsula back to China.

New pressures for Chinese territory soon arose. In 1897, two German missionaries were murdered by Chinese rioters. Germany used this pretext to demand territories in the Shandong (SHON•DOONG) Peninsula. When the Chinese government approved the demand, other European nations made new claims on Chinese territory.

Internal Crisis This latest scramble for territory took place at a time of internal crisis in China. In June 1898, the young emperor **Guang Xu** (GWANG SHYOO) launched a massive reform program based on changes in Japan (see the discussion later in this chapter). During the following weeks, known as the One Hundred Days of Reform, the emperor issued edicts calling for major political, administrative, and educational reforms. With these reforms, the emperor intended to modernize government bureaucracy by following Western models; to adopt a new educational system that would replace the traditional civil service examinations; to adopt Western-style schools, banks and a free press; and to train the military to use modern weapons and Western fighting techniques.

Many conservatives at court, however, opposed these reforms. They saw little advantage in copying the West. As one said, "An examination of the causes of success and failure in government reveals that . . . the adoption of foreignism leads to disorder." According to this conservative, traditional Chinese rules needed to be reformed and not rejected in favor of Western changes.

Most important, the new reform program was opposed by the emperor's aunt, **Empress Dowager Ci Xi** (TSUH•SEE). She became a dominant force at court and opposed the emperor's reforms. With the aid of the imperial army, she eventually imprisoned the emperor and ended his reform efforts.

✔ **Reading Check** **Identifying** What countries claimed Chinese lands between 1880 and 1900?

People In History

Ci Xi
1835–1908—Chinese empress

Empress Dowager Ci Xi, through her unwillingness to make significant reforms, helped bring about the overthrow of the Qing dynasty. Ci Xi was at first a low-ranking concubine to Emperor Xian Feng. Her position became influential in 1856, when she gave birth to the emperor's first and only son.

When the emperor died, Ci Xi ruled China on behalf of her son. Later, she ruled on behalf of her nephew Guang Xu. With the aid of conservatives at court and the imperial army, she had Guang Xu jailed in the palace.

Empress Dowager Ci Xi ruled China for almost 50 years, during a crucial period in the nation's history. She was well aware of her own power. "I have often thought that I am the cleverest woman who ever lived . . . I have 400 million people all dependent on my judgement."

Opening the Door to China

As foreign pressure on the Qing dynasty grew stronger, both Great Britain and the United States feared that other nations would overrun the country should the Chinese government collapse. In 1899, U.S. secretary of state **John Hay** presented a proposal that ensured equal access to the Chinese market for all nations and preserved the unity of the Chinese Empire. When none of the other imperialist governments opposed the idea, Hay proclaimed that all major states with economic interests in China had agreed that the country should have an **Open Door policy.**

In part, the Open Door policy reflected American concern for the survival of China. However, it also reflected the interests of some trading companies in the United States. These companies wanted to operate in open markets and disliked the existing division of China into separate spheres of influence dominated by individual states.

The Open Door policy did not end the system of spheres of influence. However, it did reduce restrictions on foreign imports imposed by the dominating power within each sphere.

The Open Door policy also helped to reduce imperialist hysteria over access to the China market. The policy lessened fears in Britain, France, Germany, and Russia that other powers would take advantage of China's weakness and attempt to dominate the China market for themselves.

✓**Reading Check** **Analyzing** Why did the United States want an Open Door policy in China?

The Boxer Rebellion

The Open Door policy came too late to stop the Boxer Rebellion. *Boxer* was the popular name given to members of a secret organization called the Society of Harmonious Fists. Members practiced a system of exercise—a form of shadowboxing, or boxing with an imaginary opponent—that they thought would protect them from bullets.

The Boxers were upset by the foreign takeover of Chinese lands. Their slogan was "destroy the foreigner." They especially disliked Christian missionaries and Chinese converts to Christianity who seemed to threaten Chinese traditions. At the beginning of 1900, Boxer bands roamed the countryside and slaughtered foreign missionaries and Chinese Christians. Their victims also included foreign businessmen and even the German envoy to Beijing.

Response to the killings was immediate and overwhelming. An allied army consisting of twenty thousand British, French, German, Russian, American,

Boxers are rounded up after the failed rebellion.

and Japanese troops attacked Beijing in August 1900. The army restored order and demanded more concessions from the Chinese government. The Chinese government was forced to pay a heavy indemnity— a payment for damages—to the powers that had crushed the uprising. The imperial government was now weaker than ever.

✓**Reading Check** **Explaining** How did the Boxers get their name?

🤠**TAKS Practice**

SECTION 1 ASSESSMENT

Checking for Understanding

1. **Define** extraterritoriality, self-strengthening, spheres of influence, indemnity.

2. **Identify** Hong Xiuquan, Guang Xu, Empress Dowager Ci Xi, John Hay, Open Door policy.

3. **Locate** Guangzhou, Chang Jiang, Hong Kong.

4. **Analyze** how the Tai Ping Rebellion helped to weaken the Qing dynasty.

5. **List** the countries that supplied troops for the allied army, which was formed to fight the Boxers in 1900.

Critical Thinking

6. **Drawing Inferences** Why did European nations agree to follow the Open Door policy proposed by the United States?

7. **Organizing Information** Create a diagram listing the factors that led to the decline of the Qing dynasty.

Analyzing Visuals

8. **Examine** the illustration of the Tai Ping Rebellion shown on page 686 of your text. What visual evidence in this picture shows that both the British and the Chinese were determined to win the battle?

Writing About History

9. **Expository Writing** Using outside sources, research, write, and present a report explaining the effects of population on modern China. Remember to include government laws enacted to curtail population growth and explain the consequences of disobeying these laws.

STUDY & WRITING SKILLBUILDER

Writing a Report

Why Learn This Skill?

You have learned about taking notes, making outlines, and finding sources for researching a paper. Now how do you put all those skills together to actually write a report?

Learning the Skill

Use the following guidelines to help you in writing a report:

- **Select an interesting topic.** As you identify possible topics, focus on resources that are available. Do preliminary research to determine whether your topic is too broad or too narrow. For example, writing about Japan in the nineteenth century is very broad. There is too much information to research and write about. Narrowing it down to one event in the nineteenth century, such as the Treaty of Kanagawa, is much more practical. If, however, you cannot find enough information about your topic, it is probably too narrow.

- **Write a thesis statement.** The thesis defines what you want to prove, discover, or illustrate in your report.

- **Prepare and do research on your topic.** Make a list of main idea questions, and then do research to answer those questions. Prepare note cards on each main idea question, listing the source information.

- **Organize your information.** Use an outline or another kind of organizer. Then follow your outline or organizer in writing a rough draft of your report.

- **Include an introduction, main body, and conclusion.** The introduction briefly presents the topic and gives your topic statement. The main body should follow your outline to develop the important ideas in your argument. The conclusion summarizes and restates your findings.

- **Revise the first draft.** Before writing the final draft of your report, wait one day and then reread and revise your first draft.

Practicing the Skill

Suppose you are writing a report on the decline of the Qing dynasty. Answer the following questions about the writing process.

1. What is a possible thesis statement?
2. What are three main idea questions?
3. What are three possible sources of information?
4. What are the next two steps in the process of writing a report?

Applying the Skill

Review the thesis, questions, and resources you came up with for the report on the Qing dynasty. Using this information, continue your research on this topic, organize your information, and write a short report.

 Glencoe's **Skillbuilder Interactive Workbook, Level 2,** provides instruction and practice in key social studies skills.

Revolution in China

Main Ideas
- Sun Yat-sen introduced reforms that led to a revolution in China.
- The arrival of Westerners brought changes to the Chinese economy and culture.

Key Terms
provincial, commodity

People to Identify
Sun Yat-sen, Henry Pu Yi, General Yuan Shigai

Places to Locate
Shanghai, Wuhan

Preview Questions
1. What was Sun Yat-sen's role in the collapse of the Qing dynasty?
2. How did Western influence affect the Chinese economy and culture?

Reading Strategy
Compare and Contrast Create a chart like the one below listing the reforms requested by Sun Yat-sen and those implemented by Empress Dowager Ci Xi.

Sun Yat-sen's Proposals	Empress Dowager Ci Xi's Reforms

Preview of Events

♦1902	♦1905	♦1908	♦1911	♦1914	♦1917	♦1920

1905
Sun Yat-sen issues reform program

1908
Emperor Guang Xu and Empress Dowager Ci Xi die

1911
Qing dynasty collapses

1916
General Yuan Shigai dies

Voices from the Past

Sun Yat-sen presides over the parliament.

In 1905, a reformer named Sun Yat-sen presented a program that called for the following changes:

❝Establish the Republic: Now our revolution is based on equality, in order to establish a republican government. All our people are equal and all enjoy political rights. The president will be publicly chosen by the people of the country. The parliament will be made up of members publicly chosen by the people of the country. Equalize land ownership: The good fortune of civilization is to be shared equally by all the people of the nation. We should assess the value of all the land in the country. Its present price shall be received by the owner, but all increases in value resulting from reform and social improvements after the revolution shall belong to the state, to be shared by all the people.❞
— **Sources of Chinese Tradition,** William Theodore de Bary et al., eds., 1960

These ideas helped start a revolution in China in 1911.

The Fall of the Qing

After the Boxer Rebellion, the Qing dynasty in China tried desperately to reform itself. Empress Dowager Ci Xi, who had long resisted her advisers' suggestions for change, now embraced a number of reforms in education, administration, and the legal system.

The civil service examination system was replaced by a new educational system based on the Western model. In 1909, legislative assemblies were formed at the provincial, or local, level. Elections for a national assembly were even held in 1910.

The emerging new elite, composed of merchants, professionals, and reform-minded gentry, soon became impatient with the slow pace of political change. They were angry when they discovered that the new assemblies were not allowed to pass laws but could only give advice to the ruler.

Moreover, the recent reforms had done nothing for the peasants, artisans, and miners, whose living conditions were getting worse as taxes increased. Unrest grew in the countryside as the dynasty continued to ignore deep-seated resentments.

The Rise of Sun Yat-sen The first signs of revolution appeared during the last decade of the nineteenth century, when the young radical **Sun Yat-sen** formed the Revive China Society. Sun Yat-sen believed that the Qing dynasty was in a state of decay and could no longer govern the country. Unless the Chinese were united under a strong government, they would remain at the mercy of other countries.

Although Sun believed that China should follow the pattern of Western countries, he also knew that the Chinese people were hardly ready for democracy. He instead developed a three-stage reform process that included: (1) a military takeover, (2) a transitional phase in which Sun's own revolutionary party would prepare the people for democratic rule, and (3) the final stage of a constitutional democracy.

In 1905, at a convention in Tokyo, Sun united radical groups from across China and formed the Revolutionary Alliance, which eventually became

the Nationalist Party. The new organization advocated Sun's Three People's Principles, which promoted nationalism, democracy, and the right for people to pursue their own livelihoods. Although the new organization was small, it benefited from the rising discontent generated by the Qing dynasty's failure to improve conditions in China.

Picturing **History**

Sun Yat-sen's Nationalist soldiers arrive at a village in search of bandits. Sun Yat-sen's revolutionary forces rose against the Qing dynasty in 1911. What stage(s) in his reform process was Sun attempting to undertake with his army?

The Revolution of 1911 The Qing dynasty was near its end. In 1908, Empress Dowager Ci Xi died. Her nephew Guang Xu, a prisoner in the palace, died one day before his aunt. The throne was now occupied by China's "last emperor," the infant **Henry Pu Yi.**

In October 1911, followers of Sun Yat-sen launched an uprising in central China. At the time, Sun was traveling in the United States. Thus, the revolt had no leader, but the government was too weak to react. The Qing dynasty collapsed, opening the way for new political forces.

Sun's party had neither the military nor the political strength to form a new government. The party was forced to turn to a member of the old order, **General Yuan Shigai** (YOO•AHN SHUR•GIE), who controlled the army.

Yuan was a prominent figure in military circles, and he had been placed in charge of the imperial army sent to suppress the rebellion. Instead, he abandoned the government and negotiated with members of Sun Yat-sen's party. General Yuan agreed to serve as president of a new Chinese republic and to allow the election of a legislature. Sun himself arrived in China in January 1912, after reading about the revolution in a Denver, Colorado, newspaper.

In the eyes of Sun Yat-sen's party, the events of 1911 were a glorious revolution that ended two thousand years of imperial rule. However, the 1911 uprising was hardly a revolution. It produced no new political or social order. Sun Yat-sen and his followers still had much to accomplish.

The Revolutionary Alliance was supported mainly by an emerging urban middle class, and its program was based largely on Western liberal democratic principles. However, the urban middle class in China was too small to support a new political order. Most of the Chinese people still lived on the land, and few peasants supported Sun Yat-sen's party. In effect, then, the events of 1911 were less a revolution than a collapse of the old order.

✓ Reading Check **Evaluating** What changes did the Revolution of 1911 actually produce in China?

An Era of Civil War

After the collapse of the Qing dynasty, the military took over. Sun Yat-sen and his colleagues had accepted General Yuan Shigai as president of the new Chinese republic in 1911 because they lacked the military force to compete with his control over the army. Many feared that if the revolt lapsed into chaos, the Western powers would intervene. If that happened, the last shreds of Chinese independence would be lost. However, even the general's new allies distrusted his motives.

"As Heaven has unified [the earth] under one sky, it will harmonize the various teachings of the world and bring them back to the same source."
—*Wang Tao on the need for reform in China, 1800s*

Picturing **History**
Sun Yat-sen and his wife, third and second from the left, stand with other members of the Revolutionary Alliance in Hangzhou, China. How does the clothing of the people in the photograph reflect Sun Yat-sen's beliefs about the future of China and Wang Tao's thoughts on the process of reform in the country?

Yuan understood little of the new ideas sweeping into China from the West. He ruled in a traditional manner and even tried to set up a new imperial dynasty. Yuan was hated by reformers for using murder and terror to destroy the new democratic institutions. He was hated by traditionalists (those who supported the Qing) for being disloyal to the dynasty he had served.

Yuan's dictatorial efforts rapidly led to clashes with Sun's party, now renamed the *Guomindang*, or Nationalist Party. When Yuan dissolved the new parliament, the Nationalists launched a rebellion. The rebellion failed, and Sun Yat-sen fled to Japan.

Yuan was strong enough to brush off the challenge from the revolutionary forces, but he could not turn back history. He died in 1916 and was succeeded by one of his officers. For the next several years, China slipped into civil war as the power of the central government disintegrated and military warlords seized power in the provinces. Their soldiers caused massive destruction throughout China.

✓ **Reading Check** **Explaining** Why were there rebellions in China after General Yuan Shigai became president?

Chinese Society in Transition

When European traders began to move into China in greater numbers in the mid-1800s, Chinese society was already in a state of transition. The growth of industry and trade was especially noticeable in the cities, where a national market for such **commodities**—marketable products—as oil, copper, salt, tea, and porcelain had appeared. Faster and more reliable transportation and a better system of money and banking had begun to create the foundation for a money economy. New crops brought in from abroad increased food production and encouraged population growth. The Chinese economy had never been more productive.

The coming of Westerners to China affected the Chinese economy in three ways. Westerners: (1) introduced modern means of transportation and communications; (2) created an export market; and (3) integrated the Chinese market into the nineteenth-century world economy.

To some, these changes were beneficial. Shaking China out of its old ways quickened a process of change that had already begun in Chinese society. Western influences forced the Chinese to adopt new ways of thinking and acting.

THE WAY IT WAS

YOUNG PEOPLE IN . . .

China

In traditional China, children were thought of not as individuals but as members of a family. Indeed, children were valued because they—especially the sons—would help with the work in the fields, carry on the family name, and care for their parents in old age. By the beginning of the twentieth century, however, these attitudes had changed in some parts of Chinese society.

Some of the changes resulted from the new educational system. After the government abolished the civil service examinations in 1905, a Confucian education was no longer the key to a successful career. New schools based on the Western model were set up. Especially in the cities, both public and private schools educated a new generation of Chinese, who began to have less respect for the past.

By 1915, educated youth had launched an intense attack on the old system and old values. The main focus of the attack was the Confucian concept of the family. Young people rejected the old family ideas of respect for elders, supremacy of men over women, and sacrifice of individual needs to the demands of the family.

Chinese youth in Western-style clothing

At the same time, however, China paid a heavy price for the new ways. Its local industry was largely destroyed. Also, many of the profits in the new economy went to foreign countries rather than back into the Chinese economy.

During the first quarter of the twentieth century, the pace of change in China quickened even more. After World War I, which temporarily drew foreign investment out of the country, Chinese businesspeople began to develop new ventures. **Shanghai, Wuhan,** Tianjin, and Guangzhou became major industrial and commercial centers with a growing middle class and an industrial working class.

✓ **Reading Check** **Evaluating** How did the arrival of Westerners affect China?

China's Changing Culture

In 1800, daily life for most Chinese was the same as it had been for centuries. Most were farmers, living in millions of villages in rice fields and on hillsides throughout the countryside. A farmer's life was governed by the harvest cycle, village custom, and family ritual. A few men were educated in the Confucian classics. Women remained in the home or in the fields. All children were expected to obey their parents, and wives were expected to submit to their husbands.

A visitor to China 125 years later would have seen a different society, although it would still have been recognizably Chinese. The changes were most striking in the cities. Here the educated and wealthy had been visibly affected by the growing Western cultural presence. Confucian social ideals were declining rapidly in influence and those of Europe and North America were on the rise.

Nowhere in China was the struggle between old and new more visible than in the field of culture. Radical reformers wanted to eliminate traditional culture, condemning it as an instrument of oppression. They were interested in creating a new China that would be respected by the modern world.

The first changes in traditional culture came in the late nineteenth century. Intellectuals began to introduce Western books, paintings, music, and ideas to China. By the first quarter of the twentieth century, China was flooded by Western culture as intellectuals called for a new culture based on that of the modern West.

Western literature and art became popular in China, especially among the urban middle class.

A spirit of individualism emerged out of the revolt of the youth. Many urban youth now saw themselves as important in and for themselves. They no longer believed they had to sacrifice their wishes for the concerns of the larger family. They demanded the right to choose their own mates and their own careers.

Young Chinese also demanded that women have rights and opportunities equal to those enjoyed by men. They felt that women no longer should be subject to men.

The effect of the young people's revolt could be seen mainly in the cities. There, the tyranny of the old family system began to decline. Women sought education and jobs alongside men. Free choice in marriage became commonplace among affluent families in the cities. The teenage children of Westernized elites copied the clothing and even the music of young people in Europe and America.

These changes generally did not reach the villages, where traditional attitudes and customs persisted. Marriages arranged by parents continued to be the rule rather than the exception. According to a survey taken in the 1930s, well over two-thirds of marriages were still arranged, even among urban couples. In one rural area, only 3 villagers out of 170 had even heard of the idea of "modern marriage," or a marriage in which people freely choose their marriage partners.

CONNECTING TO THE PAST

1. **Contrasting** Contrast the traditional way of life with life after 1915 for young people in China.

2. **Writing about History** How do the teenagers in China during the early twentieth century compare to the young people in the United States today? What common problems might both experience? Write a one-page essay explaining your ideas. Give specific examples to support your point of view.

Traditional culture, however, remained popular with the more conservative elements of the population, especially in rural areas. Most creative artists followed foreign trends, while traditionalists held on to Chinese culture.

Literature in particular was influenced by foreign ideas. Western novels and short stories began to attract a larger audience. Although most Chinese novels written after World War I dealt with Chinese subjects, they reflected the Western tendency toward a realistic portrayal of society. Often, they dealt with the new Westernized middle class. Mao Dun's *Midnight*, for example, described the changing customs of Shanghai's urban elites. Most of China's modern authors showed a clear contempt for the past.

Ba Jin, the author of numerous novels and short stories, was one of China's foremost writers at the turn of the century. Born in 1904, Ba Jin was well attuned to the rigors and expected obedience of Chinese family life. In his trilogy, *Family, Spring*, and *Autumn*, he describes the distintegration of traditional Confucian ways as the younger members of a large family attempt to break away from their elders.

✓**Reading Check** **Describing** What effects did Western culture have on China?

🌟 TAKS Practice

SECTION 2 ASSESSMENT

Checking for Understanding

1. **Define** provincial, commodity.

2. **Identify** Sun Yat-sen, Henry Pu Yi, General Yuan Shigai.

3. **Locate** Shanghai, Wuhan.

4. **Describe** the attitudes toward Western culture held by Chinese in rural and urban areas. Which of these two groups do you think benefited more from Western involvement in the Chinese economy and society?

5. **List** the stages in Sun Yat-sen's three-stage process for reform. What principles did he hope to promote in China?

Critical Thinking

6. **Analyze** Why did the reforms introduced by Empress Dowager Ci Xi and General Yuan Shigai fail to improve the way China was governed?

7. **Cause and Effect** Create a diagram like the one below showing the changes resulting from European traders' contact with China in the mid-nineteenth century.

Contact		Effects
☐	→	☐
☐	→	☐
☐	→	☐

Analyzing Visuals

8. **Examine** the photograph of Sun Yat-sen's soldiers shown on page 692. What inferences can you draw about his army from looking at the photo? How important was this army in overthrowing the Qing dynasty?

Writing About History

9. **Expository Writing** Research and compare the reasons why both the United States and China experienced civil war. Write an essay offering alternatives to war that might have solved the internal problems of one of the two nations.

Rise of Modern Japan

Guide to Reading

Main Ideas
- Western intervention opened Japan, an island that had been isolated for 200 years, to trade.
- The interaction between Japan and Western nations gave birth to a modern industrial society.

Key Terms
concession, prefecture

People to Identify
Matthew Perry, Millard Fillmore, Mutsuhito, Ito Hirobumi

Places to Locate
Edo Bay, Kyoto, Edo, Port Arthur

Preview Questions
1. What effect did the Meiji Restoration have on Japan?
2. What steps did Japan take to become an imperialist nation?

Reading Strategy
Categorizing Information Create a table like the one below listing the promises contained in the Charter Oath of 1868 and the provisions of the Meiji constitution of 1890.

Charter Oath	Constitution

Preview of Events

♦1850	♦1860	♦1870	♦1880	♦1890	♦1900	♦1910

1853
Commodore Perry arrives in Japan

1871
Government seizes daimyo's lands to strengthen executive power

1874
Japan pursues imperialist policy

1889
Adoption of Meiji constitution

1905
Japan defeats Russia

Voices from the Past

Hand-colored photograph of Japanese children, c. 1890

In 1890, Japanese leaders issued a decree to be read to every schoolchild:

❝You, our subjects, be filial to your parents, affectionate to your brothers and sisters, as husbands and wives be harmonious, as friends true; bear yourselves in modesty and moderation; extend your goodness to all; pursue learning and cultivate arts, and thereby develop intellectual faculties and perfect moral powers; furthermore, advance public good and promote common interests; always respect the Constitution and observe the laws; should emergency arise, offer yourselves to the State; and thus guard and maintain the prosperity of our imperial throne.❞
— ***Sources of Japanese Tradition*, Ryusaku Tsunoda et al., eds., 1958**

Obedience and the community were valued in Japan.

An End to Isolation

⌐TURING POINT¬ **In this section, you will learn how the Treaty of Kanagawa brought Japan out of isolation and started its development into an imperialist nation.**

By 1800, the Tokugawa shogunate had ruled the Japanese islands for two hundred years. It had driven out foreign traders and missionaries and isolated the country from virtually all contact with the outside world. The Tokugawa maintained formal relations only with Korea. Informal trading links with Dutch and Chinese merchants continued at Nagasaki. Foreign ships, which were beginning to prowl along the Japanese coast in increasing numbers, were driven away.

To the Western powers, the continued isolation of Japanese society was a challenge. Western nations were convinced that the expansion of trade on a global basis would benefit all nations. They now began to approach Japan in the hope of opening it up to foreign economic interests.

The first foreign power to succeed with Japan was the United States. In the summer of 1853, an American fleet of four warships under Commodore **Matthew Perry** arrived in **Edo Bay** (now Tokyo Bay). They sought, as Perry said, "to bring a singular and isolated people into the family of civilized nations."

Perry brought with him a letter from President **Millard Fillmore.** The U.S. president asked for better treatment of sailors shipwrecked on the Japanese islands. (Foreign sailors shipwrecked in Japan were treated as criminals and exhibited in public cages.) He also requested the opening of foreign relations between the United States and Japan.

About six months later, Perry, accompanied by an even larger fleet, returned to Japan for an answer. Shogunate officials had been discussing the issue. Some argued that contacts with the West would hurt Japan. Others pointed to the military superiority of the United States and recommended concessions, or political compromises. The question was ultimately decided by the guns of Commodore Perry's ships.

Under military pressure, Japan agreed to the Treaty of Kanagawa. This treaty between Japan and the United States provided for the return of shipwrecked American sailors, the opening of two ports to Western traders, and the establishment of a U.S. consulate in Japan.

In 1858, U.S. consul Townsend Harris signed a more detailed treaty. It called for the opening of several new ports to U.S. trade and residence, as well as an exchange of ministers. Similar treaties were soon signed by Japan and several European nations.

✓ **Reading Check** **Identifying** What benefits did the Treaty of Kanagawa grant the United States?

Resistance to the New Order

The decision to open relations with the Western powers was highly unpopular in parts of Japan. Resistance was especially strong among the samurai warriors in two territories in the south, Satsuma and Choshu. Both had strong military traditions, and neither had been exposed to heavy Western military pressure. In 1863, the Sat-Cho alliance (from Satsuma-Choshu) forced the shogun to promise to end relations with the West.

Picturing History

This Japanese painting records Commodore Perry's arrival in Edo Bay in July 1853. **What was the economic and political impact of Perry's visits on Japan?**

The rebellious groups soon showed their own weakness, however. When Choshu troops fired on Western ships in the Strait of Shimonoseki, which leads into the Sea of Japan, the Westerners fired back and destroyed the Choshu fortifications.

The incident convinced the rebellious forces of the need to strengthen their military. They also became more determined not to give in to the West. As a result, Sat-Cho leaders urged the shogun to take a stronger position against the foreigners.

The Sat-Cho leaders demanded that the shogun resign and restore the power of the emperor. In January 1868, their armies attacked the shogun's palace in **Kyoto** and proclaimed that the authority of the emperor had been restored. After a few weeks, the shogun's forces collapsed, ending the shogunate system.

✓ **Reading Check** **Identifying** What events led to the collapse of the shogunate system in Japan?

The Meiji Restoration

The Sat-Cho leaders had genuinely mistrusted the West, but they soon realized that Japan must change to survive. The new leaders embarked on a policy of reform that transformed Japan into a modern industrial nation.

The symbol of the new era was the young emperor **Mutsuhito.** He called his reign the Meiji (MAY•jee), or "Enlightened Rule." This period has thus become known as the Meiji Restoration.

Emperor Mutsuhito

Of course, the Meiji ruler was controlled by the Sat-Cho leaders, just as earlier emperors had been controlled by the shogunate. In recognition of the real source of political power, the capital was moved from Kyoto to **Edo** (now named Tokyo), the location of the new leaders. The imperial court was moved to the shogun's palace in the center of the city.

Transformation of Japanese Politics

Once in power, the new leaders moved first to abolish the old order and to strengthen power in their hands. To undercut the power of the daimyo—the local nobles—the new leaders stripped these great lords of the titles to their lands in 1871. As compensation, the lords were given government bonds and were named governors of the territories formerly under their control. The territories were now called prefectures.

The Meiji reformers set out to create a modern political system based on the Western model. In 1868, the new leaders signed a Charter Oath, in which they promised to create a new legislative assembly within the framework of continued imperial rule. Although senior positions in the new government were given to the daimyo, the key posts were held by modernizing leaders from the Sat-Cho group. The country was divided into 75 prefectures. (The number was reduced to 45 in 1889 and remains at that number today.)

During the next 20 years, the Meiji government undertook a careful study of Western political systems. A commission under **Ito Hirobumi** traveled to Great Britain, France, Germany, and the United States to study their governments.

As the process evolved, two main factions appeared, the Liberals and the Progressives. The Liberals wanted political reform based on the Western liberal democratic model, with supreme authority vested in the parliament as the representative of the people. The Progressives wanted power to be shared between the legislative and executive branches, with the executive branch having more control.

During the 1870s and 1880s, these factions fought for control. In the end, the Progressives won. The Meiji constitution, adopted in 1889, was modeled after that of Imperial Germany. Most authority was given to the executive branch.

In theory, the emperor exercised all executive authority, but in practice he was a figurehead. Real executive authority rested in the hands of a prime minister and his cabinet of ministers. These ministers were handpicked by the Meiji leaders.

Under the new constitution, the upper house included royal appointments and elected nobles, while the lower house was elected. The two houses were to have equal legislative powers.

The final result was a political system that was democratic in form but authoritarian in practice. Although modern in external appearance, it was still traditional, because power remained in the hands of a ruling oligarchy (the Sat-Cho leaders). Although a new set of institutions and values had emerged, the system allowed the traditional ruling class to keep its influence and economic power.

Meiji Economics

The Meiji leaders also set up a new system of land ownership. A land reform program made the traditional lands of the daimyo into the private property of the peasants. The daimyo, as mentioned, were compensated with government bonds.

The Meiji leaders levied a new land tax, which was set at an annual rate of 3 percent of the estimated value of the land. The new tax was an excellent source of revenue for the government. However, it was quite burdensome for the farmers.

Under the old system, farmers had paid a fixed percentage of their harvest to the landowners. In bad

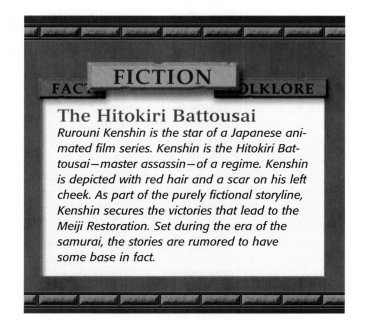

FICTION

FACT ~ ~ OLKLORE

The Hitokiri Battousai

Rurouni Kenshin is the star of a Japanese animated film series. Kenshin is the Hitokiri Battousai—master assassin—of a regime. Kenshin is depicted with red hair and a scar on his left cheek. As part of the purely fictional storyline, Kenshin secures the victories that lead to the Meiji Restoration. Set during the era of the samurai, the stories are rumored to have some base in fact.

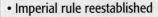

Meiji Restoration: Birth of Modern Japan

Politics

Changes and Events

- Imperial rule reestablished
- Capital moved to Edo
- Most power in executive branch (emperor, prime minister, cabinet)

Economics

- Daimyo's lands given to peasants
- Many farmers, unable to pay new land tax, forced into tenancy
- Industrialization encouraged

Social Structure

- New imperial army created
- Universal system of education developed
- Western practices adopted

Chart Skills

The Meiji government began reforms that transformed Japan's political, economic, and social structures.

1. **Cause and Effect** What changes noted on the chart most reflect the influence of Western ideas upon Japan?
2. **Making Generalizations** How are the changes in the three areas of politics, economics, and social structure interrelated?

harvest years, they had owed little or nothing. Under the new system, the farmers had to pay the land tax every year, regardless of the quality of the harvest.

As a result, in bad years, many peasants were unable to pay their taxes. This forced them to sell their lands to wealthy neighbors and become tenant farmers who paid rent to the new owners. By the end of the nineteenth century, about 40 percent of all farmers were tenants.

With its budget needs met by the land tax, the government turned to the promotion of industry. The chief goal of the reformers was to create a "rich country and a strong state" to guarantee Japan's survival against the challenge of Western nations.

The Meiji government gave subsidies to needy industries, provided training and foreign advisers, improved transportation and communications, and started a new educational system that stressed applied science. In contrast to China, Japan was able to achieve results with little reliance on foreign money. By 1900, Japan's industrial sector was beginning to grow. Besides tea and silk, other key industries were weapons, shipbuilding, and sake (SAH•kee), or Japanese rice wine.

From the start, a unique feature of the Meiji model of industrial development was the close relationship between government and private business. The government encouraged the development of new industries by providing businesspeople with money and privileges. Once an individual enterprise or industry was on its feet, it was turned over entirely to private ownership. Even then, however, the government continued to play some role in the industry's activities.

Building a Modern Social Structure The Meiji reformers also transformed other institutions. A key focus of their attention was the military. The reformers were well aware that Japan would need a modern military force to compete with the Western powers. Their motto was "Strengthen the Army."

A new imperial army based on compulsory military service was formed in 1871. All Japanese men now served for three years. The new army was well equipped with modern weapons.

Education also changed. The Meiji leaders realized the need for universal education, including instruction in modern technology. A new ministry of education, established in 1871, guided the changes.

After a few years of experimentation, the education ministry adopted the American model of elementary schools, secondary schools, and universities. It brought foreign specialists to Japan to teach in the new schools. In the meantime, it sent bright students to study abroad.

Much of the content of the new educational system was Western in inspiration. However, a great deal of emphasis was still placed on the virtues of loyalty to the family and community. Loyalty to the emperor was especially valued. Both teachers and students were required to bow before a portrait of the emperor each day.

Daily Life and Women's Rights Japanese society in the late Tokugawa Era, before the Meiji reforms, could be described by two words: *community* and *hierarchy.* The lives of all Japanese people were determined by their membership in a family, village, and social class. At the same time, Japanese society was highly hierarchical. Belonging to a particular social class determined a person's occupation and social relationships with others. Women were especially limited by the "three obediences": child to father, wife to husband, and widow to son. Whereas husbands could easily obtain a divorce, wives could not. Marriages were arranged, and the average marital age of females was sixteen years. Females did not share inheritance rights with males. Few received any education outside the family.

The Meiji Restoration had a marked effect on the traditional social system in Japan. Special privileges for the aristocracy were abolished. For the first time, women were allowed to seek an education. As the economy shifted from an agricultural to an industrial base, thousands of Japanese began to get new jobs and establish new social relationships.

Western fashions became the rage in elite circles. The ministers of the first Meiji government were known as the "dancing cabinet" because of their love for Western-style ballroom dancing. The game of baseball was imported from the United States.

Young people were increasingly influenced by Western culture and values. A new generation of modern boys and girls began to imitate the clothing styles, eating habits, hairstyles, and social practices of European and American young people.

The social changes brought about by the Meiji Restoration also had a less attractive side. Many commoners were ruthlessly exploited in the coal mines and textile mills. Workers labored up to 20 hours a day, often under conditions of incredible hardship. Coal miners employed on a small island in the harbor of Nagasaki worked in temperatures up to 130 degrees Fahrenheit (54 degrees C). When they tried to escape, they were shot.

Resistance to such conditions was not unknown. In many areas, villagers sought new political rights. In some cases, they demanded increased attention to human rights. A popular rights movement of the 1870s laid the groundwork for one of Japan's first political parties. It campaigned for a government that would reflect the will of the people.

Picturing **History**

For a recital at a music school in 1889, Japanese musicians played Western music and wore Western clothing. In what other ways did Japanese culture change under the Meiji government?

The transformation of Japan into a "modern society" did not detach the country entirely from its old values, however. Traditional values based on loyalty to the family and community were still taught in the new schools. Traditional values were also given a firm legal basis in the 1889 constitution, which limited the right to vote to men. The Civil Code of 1898 played down individual rights and placed women within the context of their family role.

✓ **Reading Check** **Explaining** How was Japan's government structured under the Meiji constitution?

Joining the Imperialist Nations

We have seen that the Japanese modeled some of their domestic policies on Western practices. They also copied the imperialist Western approach to foreign affairs. Japan, after all, is small, lacking in resources, and densely populated. There is no natural room for expansion. To some Japanese, the lessons of history were clear. Western nations had amassed wealth and power not only because of their democratic, economic, and educational systems, but also because of their colonies. Colonies had provided the Western powers with sources of raw materials, inexpensive labor, and markets for their manufactured products. To compete, Japan would also have to expand.

Beginnings of Expansion The Japanese began their program of territorial expansion close to home. In 1874, Japan claimed control of the Ryukyu (ree•YOO•KYOO) Islands, which had long been subject to the Chinese Empire. Two years later, Japan's navy forced the Koreans to open their ports to Japanese trade.

The Chinese had long controlled Korea and were concerned by Japan's growing influence there. During the 1880s, Chinese-Japanese rivalry over Korea intensified. In 1894, the two nations went to war. Japanese ships destroyed the Chinese fleet and seized the Manchurian city of **Port Arthur.**

In the treaty that ended the war, the Manchu rulers of China recognized the independence of Korea. They also ceded (transferred) Taiwan and the Liaodong Peninsula, with its strategic naval base at Port Arthur, to Japan.

Shortly thereafter, the Japanese gave the Liaodong Peninsula back to China. In the early twentieth century, however, the Japanese returned to the offensive.

Rivalry with Russia over influence in Korea had led to increasingly strained relations between Japan and Russia. The Russians thought little of the Japanese and even welcomed the possibility of war. One

adviser to Nicholas II said, "We will only have to throw our caps at them and they will run away."

War with Russia In 1904, Japan launched a surprise attack on the Russian naval base at Port Arthur, which Russia had taken from China in 1898. When Japanese forces moved into Manchuria and the Liaodong Peninsula, Russian troops proved to be no match for them. The Russian commander in chief said, "It is impossible not to admire the bravery and

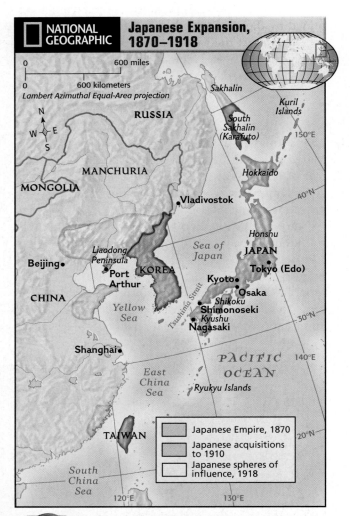

NATIONAL GEOGRAPHIC

Japanese Expansion, 1870–1918

0 — 600 miles
0 — 600 kilometers
Lambert Azimuthal Equal-Area projection

Japanese Empire, 1870
Japanese acquisitions to 1910
Japanese spheres of influence, 1918

🧭 **Geography** *Skills*

In the late nineteenth century, Japan transformed itself into an imperialist nation.

1. **Interpreting Maps** Between 1870 and 1910, approximately how much land did Japan acquire through expansion?

2. **Applying Geography Skills** What geographic factors might have influenced Japan's expansion?

Picturing **History**
The Japanese surprise attack on Port Arthur in 1904 reflected the growing power of Japan and its navy. What impact did the Japanese victory have on Russia? How did it affect relations between Japan and the United States?

activity of the Japanese. The attack of the Japanese is a continuous succession of waves, and they never relax their efforts by day or by night."

In the meantime, Russia had sent its Baltic fleet halfway around the world to East Asia, only to be defeated by the new Japanese navy off the coast of Japan. After their defeat, the Russians agreed to a humiliating peace in 1905. They gave the Liaodong Peninsula back to Japan, as well as the southern part of Sakhalin (SA•kuh•LEEN), an island north of Japan. The Japanese victory stunned the world. Japan had become one of the great powers.

U.S. Relations During the next few years, Japan consolidated its position in northeastern Asia. It established a sphere of influence in Korea. In 1905, the United States recognized Japan's role in Korea in return for Japanese recognition of American authority in the Philippines. In 1910, Japan annexed Korea outright.

Mutual suspicion between the two countries was growing, however. The Japanese resented U.S. efforts to restrict immigration. Moreover, some Americans began to fear the rise of Japanese power in East Asia. In 1907, President Theodore Roosevelt made a "gentlemen's agreement" with Japan that essentially stopped Japanese immigration to the United States.

Reading Check **Explaining** Why did Japan turn itself into an imperialist power?

Culture in an Era of Transition

The wave of Western technology and ideas that entered Japan in the last half of the nineteenth century greatly altered the shape of traditional Japanese culture. Literature was especially affected. Dazzled by European literature, Japanese authors began translating and imitating the imported models.

The novel showed the greatest degree of change. People began to write novels that were patterned after the French tradition of realism. Naturalist Japanese authors tried to present existing social conditions and the realities of war as objectively as possible.

Other aspects of Japanese culture were also changed. The Japanese invited technicians, engineers, architects, and artists from Europe and the United States to teach their "modern" skills to eager Japanese students. The Japanese copied Western artistic techniques and styles. Huge buildings of steel and reinforced concrete, adorned with Greek columns, appeared in many Japanese cities.

A national reaction had begun by the end of the nineteenth century, however. Many Japanese artists

began to return to older techniques. In 1889, the Tokyo School of Fine Arts was established to promote traditional Japanese art. Japanese artists searched for a new but truly Japanese means of expression. Some artists tried to bring together native and foreign techniques. Others returned to past artistic traditions for inspiration.

Cultural exchange also went the other way. Japanese arts and crafts, porcelains, textiles, fans, folding screens, and woodblock prints became fashionable in Europe and North America. Japanese art influenced Western painters. Japanese gardens, with their close attention to the positioning of rocks and falling water, became especially popular in the United States.

✓ **Reading Check** **Describing** What effect did Japanese culture have on other nations?

TAKS Practice

SECTION 3 ASSESSMENT

Checking for Understanding

1. **Define** concession, prefecture.

2. **Identify** Matthew Perry, Millard Fillmore, Mutsuhito, Ito Hirobumi.

3. **Locate** Edo Bay, Kyoto, Edo, Port Arthur.

4. **Explain** how the Japanese educational system promoted traditional values even as it adopted Western educational models.

5. **List** the professionals that the Japanese invited from abroad to teach "modern" skills.

Critical Thinking

6. **Explain** How did the Japanese land reform program create internal problems?

7. **Cause and Effect** Create a diagram listing the results of Western influence on Japanese culture.

Western Influence on Japanese Culture

Analyzing Visuals

8. **Examine** the photograph on page 700. What characteristics of modern Japan does it illustrate?

Writing About History

9. **Persuasive Writing** Pretend that you wish to study abroad in China or Japan. Write a letter of application stating which country you would like to visit and why. State what you hope to learn while abroad, and how you would overcome or minimize the drawbacks of being a foreign student.

EYEWITNESS TO HISTORY

A Letter to the Emperor

WHEN U.S. COMMODORE MATTHEW C. Perry arrived in Tokyo Bay on his first visit to Japan in July 1853, he carried a letter from Millard Fillmore, the president of the United States. This excerpt is from Fillmore's letter.

Millard Fillmore

Japanese officials greet Commodore Perry.

❝Millard Fillmore, President of the United States of America, To His Imperial Majesty, The Emperor of Japan. Great and Good Friend! . . .

I have directed Commodore Perry to assure your Imperial Majesty that I entertain the kindest feelings towards your Majesty's person and government; and that I have no other object in sending him to Japan, but to propose to your Imperial Majesty that the United States and Japan should live in friendship, and have [trade] with each other. . . . I have particularly charged Commodore Perry to abstain from any act, which could possibly disturb the peace of your Imperial Majesty's lands.

The United States of America reaches from ocean to ocean, and our territory of Oregon and state of California lie directly opposite to the dominions of your Imperial Majesty. Our steam-ships can go from California to Japan in eighteen days. Our great state of California produces about sixty millions of dollars in gold, every year, besides silver, quicksilver, precious stones, and many other valuable articles.

Japan is also a rich and fertile country, and produces many very valuable articles. . . . I am desirous that our two countries should trade with each other, for the benefit both of Japan and the United States.

We know that the ancient laws of your Imperial Majesty's government do not allow of foreign trade except with the Dutch. But as the state of the world changes, and new governments are formed, it seems to be wise from time to time to make new laws. . . . If your Imperial Majesty were so far to change the ancient laws, as to allow a free trade between the two countries, it would be extremely beneficial to both.

Many of our ships pass every year from California to China; and great numbers of our people pursue the whale fishery near the shores of Japan. It sometimes happens in stormy weather that one of our ships is wrecked on your Imperial Majesty's shores. In all such cases we ask and expect that our unfortunate people should be treated with kindness, and that their property should be protected, till we can send a vessel and bring them away.

Your Good Friend,
Millard Fillmore❞
—Letter from President Fillmore to the Emperor of Japan

Analyzing Primary Sources

1. What did President Fillmore want from the Japanese?
2. Why can his letter be seen as a masterful combination of salesmanship, diplomacy, and firmness?
3. From the perspective of President Fillmore and others in the United States, the emperor's decision may have looked like an easy one. Explain why this would not have been a simple decision for the emperor.

CHAPTER

22 ASSESSMENT and ACTIVITIES

Using Key Terms

1. The daimyo governed _____ after the Meiji Restoration seized their lands.

2. Europeans who lived by their own laws while on Chinese soil practiced _____.

3. European traders established _____ in which they negotiated directly with Chinese warlords.

4. The presence of Commodore Perry's fleet pressured the Japanese to make _____.

5. The policy of _____ called for the Chinese people to adopt Western technology while retaining their Confucian values and institutions.

6. The Chinese government was forced to pay heavy _____ to the powers that crushed the Boxer Rebellion.

7. After 1905, Chinese legislative assemblies were formed at the _____ level.

8. When Westerners visited China in the mid-1800s, a market for _____ such as oil, copper, salt, tea, and porcelain already existed.

Reviewing Key Facts

9. **Economics** What items did the British import from China, and how did they pay for them?

10. **Government** List the terms of the Treaty of Nanjing.

11. **Culture** Explain the One Hundred Days of Reform and their outcome.

12. **Citizenship** Summarize the terms of Sun Yat-sen's reform program and tell whether or not they were implemented.

13. **Government** What was the role of the Revolutionary Alliance?

14. **Government** What opposing forces formed in China after the civil war?

15. **History** Who was the first foreign power to penetrate Japan?

16. **Economics** What were the terms of the Treaty of Kanagawa?

17. **Citizenship** Which Japanese groups opposed Japanese relations with Western powers?

18. **Government** What was the Meiji Restoration?

19. **Economics** In what three ways did Westerners affect the Chinese economy during the mid-1800s?

20. **Economics** Identify the sequence of events that led to the Opium War of 1839 to 1842.

21. **History** In chronological order, list the territories and countries Japan took control of in its program of expansion.

Critical Thinking

22. **Summarizing** Summarize the effects of imperialism on nineteenth-century China.

23. **Analyzing** How effective was Japan's territorial expansion program?

24. **Identifying Options** Instead of importing opium to China, what else might the British have done to restore the balance of trade?

Chapter Summary

Imperialist powers advanced into China and Japan in the nineteenth century. China's government fell, but Japan's modernized and endured.

Movement
- British secure trade outlets at five coastal ports in China.
- Commodore Perry sails into Edo Bay.
- Japan invades Port Arthur, Manchuria.

Change
- Japan's Tokugawa shogunate and China's Qing dynasty collapse.
- Meiji reformers institute compulsory military service in Japan.
- United States initiates Open Door policy in China.

Reaction
- Tai Ping Rebellion breaks out in China.
- Sat-Cho leaders demand the resignation of Japan's shogun.
- Boxer Rebellion occurs in China.

Nationalism
- Meiji government reforms Japan.
- Japan adopts the Meiji constitution.
- Sun Yat-sen establishes the Republic of China.

HISTORY Online

Self-Check Quiz
Visit the *Glencoe World History* Web site at
tx.wh.glencoe.com and click on **Chapter 22–Self-Check Quiz** to prepare for the Chapter Test.

Writing About History

25. Persuasive Writing Imagine you are a court official living in China during the reign of Emperor Guang Xu. The emperor is planning his reform program and needs advice concerning how to help strengthen China. Write a letter to the emperor telling him how you think China should either change or stay the same. Choose two or three specific issues such as the educational system, the development of the military, or the structure of the government to discuss in your letter.

Analyzing Sources

Zhang Zhidong, a leading Chinese court official, argued:

66The doctrine of people's rights will bring us not a single benefit but a hundred evils. Are we going to establish a parliament? Among the Chinese scholars and people there are still many today who are content to be vulgar and rustic. They are ignorant of the general situation in the world, they do not understand the basic system of the state.99

26. Does Zhang Zhidong think that the Chinese people are well informed?

27. How does Zhang Zhidong's quote apply to China today?

Applying Technology Skills

28. Using the Internet Use the Internet to research the causes of revolution in the world. Research specific examples, such as the American, French, and Russian Revolutions, to determine why they occurred. Compare the causes of these revolutions to those of the 1911 revolution in China.

Making Decisions

29. To build a "rich country and a strong state," the Japanese government subsidized (provided funds for) its industries. Evaluate the reasons for Japan's decision. The potential need for subsidy is not unique to Japan. Imagine that you are the president of a newly colonized island. Write a brief essay explaining how you would promote the growth of industry on your island.

Analyzing Maps and Charts

Examine the chart of the Meiji Restoration shown on page 700 of your text. Then answer the following questions.

30. What impact did the Meiji Restoration have on the social structure of Japan?

31. How do you think the daimyo felt about the Meiji Restoration?

32. What effect did the Meiji Restoration have on industry?

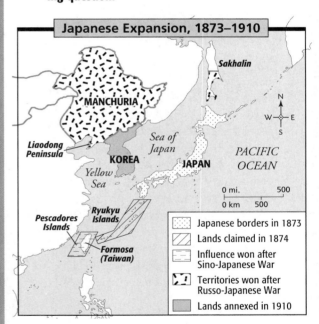

Directions: Use the map *and* your knowledge of world history to answer the following question.

Which of the following resulted from Japanese expansion?

F Japan was humiliated by its losses.

G Japan became an important military force.

H Russia and Japan competed for control of China.

J China's government was strengthened and reformed.

Test-Taking Tip: Any time you get a map, pay careful attention to the title and to the map legend. The legend gives information crucial to understanding the map. The information in the legend may also help you eliminate answer choices that are incorrect.

WORLD LITERATURE

from Shooting an Elephant

George Orwell

George Orwell was the pen name of English author Eric Arthur Blair, who was born in Motihari, India, on June 25, 1903. He lived for 46 years, and during that time, he wrote many influential essays, novels, and newspaper articles. His two most famous works are *1984* and *Animal Farm,* both of which are commentaries against totalitarianism. He served for several years as an assistant superintendent in the Indian Imperial Police but resigned due to his distaste of imperialism. In *Shooting an Elephant,* Orwell describes an incident that happened to him, and he satirizes the problems of colonial rule.

Read to Discover

Examine the ways in which George Orwell describes the relationship between the British colonial officer and the "natives." Can you think of a modern parallel to this situation?

Reader's Dictionary

mahout: a keeper and driver of an elephant

dominion: rule, control

sahib: title meaning "sir" or "master"

I had halted on the road. As soon as I saw the elephant I knew with perfect certainty that I ought not to shoot him. It is a serious matter to shoot a working elephant—it is comparable to destroying a huge and costly piece of machinery—and obviously one ought not to do it if it can possibly be avoided. And at that distance, peacefully eating, the elephant looked no more dangerous than a cow. I thought then and I think now that his attack of "must" was already passing off; in which case he would merely wander harmlessly about until the mahout came back and caught him. Moreover, I did not in the least want to shoot him. I decided that I would watch him for a little while to make sure that he did not turn savage again, and then go home.

But at that moment I glanced round at the crowd that had followed me. It was an immense crowd, two thousand at the least and growing every minute. It blocked the road for a long distance on either side. I looked at the sea of yellow faces above the garish clothes—faces all happy and excited over this bit of fun, all certain that the elephant was going to be shot. They were watching me as they would watch a conjurer about to perform a trick. They did not like me, but with the magical rifle in my hands I was momentarily worth watching. And suddenly I realized that I should have to shoot the elephant after all. The people expected it

◀ **Colonial hunter**

708

▲ *Working elephants, 1890s*

of me and I had got to do it; I could feel their two thousand wills pressing me forward irresistibly. And it was at this moment, as I stood there with the rifle in my hands, that I first grasped the hollowness, the futility of the white man's dominion in the East. Here was I, the white man with his gun, standing in front of the unarmed native crowd—seemingly the leading actor of the piece; but in reality I was only an absurd puppet pushed to and fro by the will of those yellow faces behind. I perceived in this moment that when the white man turns tyrant it is his own freedom that he destroys. He becomes a sort of hollow, posing dummy, the conventionalized figure of a sahib. For it is the condition of his rule that he shall spend his life in trying to impress the "natives," and so in every crisis he has got to do what the "natives" expect of him. He wears a mask, and his face grows to fit it. I had got to shoot the elephant. I had committed myself to doing it when I sent for the rifle. A sahib has got to act like a sahib; he has got to appear resolute, to know his own mind and do definite things. To come all that way, rifle in hand, with two thousand people marching at my heels, and then to trail feebly away, having done nothing—no, that was impossible. The crowd would laugh at me. And my whole life,

every white man's life in the East, was one long struggle not to be laughed at.

. . . But I did not want to shoot the elephant. . . . The sole thought in my mind was that if anything went wrong those two thousand Burmese would see me . . . trampled on, and reduced to a grinning corpse. And if that happened it was quite probable that some of them would laugh. That would never do.

Interpreting World Literature

1. What is the context of this story? Why is the narrator following an elephant?

2. Why does the narrator ultimately decide that he must shoot the elephant?

3. What does this story reveal about Orwell's attitudes about imperialism? How can you tell?

4. **CRITICAL THINKING** According to Orwell in this piece, who held the power in colonial India?

Applications Activity

Write a narrative account of an incident when you felt people were pushing you to act in opposition to your original intentions.

UNIT 5

The Twentieth-Century Crisis

1914–1945

The Period in Perspective

The period between 1914 and 1945 was one of the most destructive in the history of humankind. As many as 60 million people died as a result of World Wars I and II, the global conflicts that began and ended this era. As World War I was followed by revolutions, the Great Depression, totalitarian regimes, and the horrors of World War II, it appeared to many that European civilization had become a nightmare. By 1945, the era of European domination over world affairs had been severely shaken. With the decline of Western power, a new era of world history was about to begin.

Primary Sources Library

See pages 998–999 for primary source readings to accompany Unit 5.

*Use The World History **Primary Source Document Library** CD-ROM to find additional primary sources about The Twentieth-Century Crisis.*

▲ Gate, Dachau Memorial

▶ Former Russian prisoners of war honor the American troops who freed them.

"Never in the field of human conflict was so much owed by so many to so few."

—Winston Churchill

Looking Back...

International Peacekeeping

Until the 1900s, with the exception of the Seven Years' War, never in history had there been a conflict that literally spanned the globe. The twentieth century witnessed two world wars and numerous regional conflicts. As the scope of war grew, so did international commitment to collective security, where a group of nations join together to promote peace and protect human life.

1914–1918
World War I
is fought

1919
League of Nations
created to prevent wars

1939–1945
World War II
is fought

❶ *Europe*

The League of Nations

At the end of World War I, the victorious nations set up a "general association of nations" called the League of Nations, which would settle international disputes and avoid war. By 1920, 42 nations had sent delegates to the League's headquarters in Geneva, Switzerland, and they were eventually joined by another 21.

The United States never joined. Opponents in the U.S. Senate argued that membership in the League went against George Washington's advice to avoid "entangling alliances." When the League failed to halt warlike acts in the 1930s, the same opponents pointed to the failure of collective security.

The League of Nations was seen as a peacekeeper without a sword—it possessed neither a standing army nor members willing to stop nations that used war as diplomacy.

The League of Nations and Uncle Sam

to See Ahead

UN membership flags

❷ *The United States*

The United Nations

After World War II, the United States hosted a meeting to create a new peace-keeping organization. Delegates from 50 nations hammered out the Charter of the United Nations. To eliminate the root causes of war, the UN created agencies that promoted global education and the well-being of children. In 1948, United States delegate Eleanor Roosevelt convinced the UN to adopt the Universal Declaration of Human Rights, which committed the UN to eliminate oppression. The headquarters for the UN are located in New York City.

1945
United Nations
is founded

1948
UN adopts the Universal
Declaration of Human Rights

1950–1953
UN troops participate
in the Korean War

1988
Nobel Peace Prize awarded
to UN peacekeeping forces

❸ *South Africa*

The Power of World Opinion

By 1995, the UN had taken part in 35 peacekeeping missions—some successful, some not. It also had provided protection for over 30 million refugees.

The UN used world opinion to promote justice. In 1977, it urged nations to enforce economic sanctions and an arms embargo against South Africa until apartheid was lifted. In 1994, South Africa held its first all-race elections. Many believed this was a major triumph for collective international action.

Casting a vote in South Africa

Why It Matters

The UN hopes to use collective international actions to promote peace around the world. Often this involves preventing injustice and improving living conditions. What are some recent UN actions that support these principles?

23 War and Revolution

1914–1919

Key Events

As you read this chapter, look for the key events of World War I, the Russian Revolution, and the Paris Peace Conference.
- *Archduke Francis Ferdinand was assassinated by a Serbian nationalist.*
- *Militarism, nationalism, and alliances drew nations into war.*
- *The United States's entry into the war helped the Allies.*
- *The impact of the war at home led to an increase in the federal government's powers and changed the status of women.*
- *The Russian Revolution ended with the Communists in power.*
- *Peace settlements caused lingering resentment.*
- *The League of Nations was formed.*

The Impact Today

The events that occurred during this period still impact our lives today.
- *World War I led to the disintegration of empires and the creation of new states.*
- *Communism became a factor in global conflict as other nations turned to its ideology.*
- *The Balkans continue to be an area of political unrest.*

 World History Video *The Chapter 23 video, "Modern Warfare," chronicles innovations in warfare during the twentieth century.*

1914
Assassination of
Archduke Ferdinand
sparks World War I

1914   *1915*   *1916*

1915
German
submarine
sinks the
Lusitania

German U-boat

Battle of the Somme by Richard Woodville The Battle of the Somme was one of the bloodiest battles of World War I.

Bolsheviks in Russia

1917
Russian
Revolution
begins

1917

1917
United States
enters the war

1918

1918
Germany
agrees to
truce

*People celebrating
the end of the war*

1919
Allies sign
Treaty of
Versailles

1919

HISTORY *Online*

Chapter Overview
Visit the *Glencoe World
History* Web site at
tx.wh.glencoe.com and click
on **Chapter 23–Chapter
Overview** to preview
chapter information.

A Story That Matters

Advancing troops in the Battle of the Somme

British artillery firing on the Germans at the Battle of the Somme

The Battle of the Somme

On July 1, 1916, British and French infantry forces attacked German defensive lines along a front about 25 miles (40 km) long near the Somme River in France. Each soldier carried almost 70 (32 kg) pounds of equipment, including a rifle, ammunition, grenades, a shovel, a mess kit, and a full water bottle. This burden made it "impossible to move much quicker than a slow walk."

German machine guns soon opened fire. "We were able to see our comrades move forward in an attempt to cross No-Man's-Land, only to be mown down like meadow grass," recalled one British soldier. Another wrote later, "I felt sick at the sight of this carnage and remember weeping."

Philip Gibbs, an English journalist with the troops, reported on what he found in the German trenches that the British forces overran: "Victory! . . . Groups of dead lay in ditches which had once been trenches, flung into chaos by that bombardment I had seen. . . . Some of the German dead were young boys, too young to be killed for old men's crimes, and others might have been old or young. One could not tell because they had no faces, and were just masses of raw flesh in rags of uniforms. Legs and arms lay separate without any bodies thereabouts."

In the first day of the Battle of the Somme, about 21,000 British soldiers died. After four months of fighting, the British had advanced five miles (eight km). About one million Allied and German soldiers lay dead or wounded.

Why It Matters

World War I (1914–1918) devastated the economic, social, and political order of Europe. People at the time, overwhelmed by the size of the war's battles and the number of casualties, simply called it the Great War. The war was all the more disturbing to Europeans because it came after a period that many believed to have been an age of progress. World War I and the revolutions it spawned can properly be seen as the first stage in the crisis of the twentieth century.

History and You Look online or in the library for a speech delivered by Woodrow Wilson or another leader, explaining the reasons for entering the war. Analyze the arguments. How might someone opposed to the war counter those arguments?

The Road to World War I

Main Ideas
- Militarism, nationalism, and a crisis in the Balkans led to World War I.
- Serbia's determination to become a large, independent state angered Austria-Hungary and initiated hostilities.

Key Terms
conscription, mobilization

People to Identify
Archduke Francis Ferdinand, Gavrilo Princip, Emperor William II, Czar Nicholas II, General Alfred von Schlieffen

Places to Locate
Serbia, Bosnia

Preview Questions
1. How did the assassination of Archduke Francis Ferdinand lead to World War I?
2. How did the system of alliances help cause the war?

Reading Strategy
Cause and Effect Use a diagram like the one below to identify the factors that led to World War I.

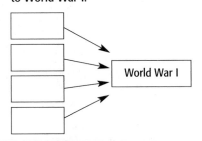

Preview of Events

| ◆1860 | ◆1870 | ◆1880 | ◆1890 | ◆1900 | ◆1910 | ◆1920 |

1882
Triple Alliance forms

1907
Triple Entente forms

1914
World War I begins

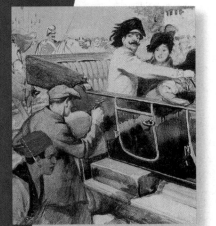

Assassination at Sarajevo

On June 28, 1914, the heir to the Austro-Hungarian throne, Archduke Francis Ferdinand, was assassinated in the Bosnian city of Sarajevo. One of the conspirators described the scene:

❝As the car came abreast, [the assassin] stepped forward from the curb, drew his automatic pistol from his coat and fired two shots. The first struck the wife of the Archduke, the Archduchess Sophia, in the abdomen. She was an expectant mother. She died instantly. The second bullet struck the Archduke close to the heart. He uttered only one word: 'Sophia'—a call to his stricken wife. Then his head fell back and he collapsed. He died almost instantly.❞

—*Eyewitness to History*, John Carey, ed., 1987

This event was the immediate cause of World War I, but underlying forces had been moving Europeans toward war for some time.

Nationalism and the System of Alliances

In the first half of the nineteenth century, liberals believed that if European states were organized along national lines, these states would work together and create a peaceful Europe. They were wrong.

The system of nation-states that emerged in Europe in the last half of the nineteenth century led not to cooperation but to competition. Rivalries over colonies

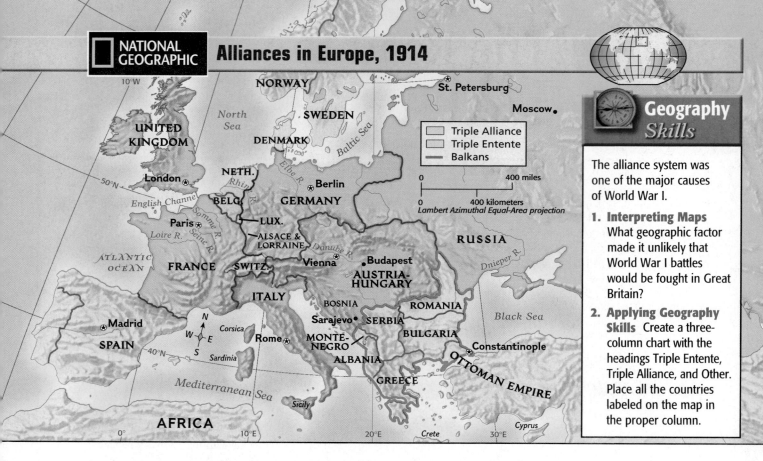

NATIONAL GEOGRAPHIC — Alliances in Europe, 1914

Legend:
- Triple Alliance
- Triple Entente
- Balkans

0 — 400 miles
0 — 400 kilometers
Lambert Azimuthal Equal-Area projection

and trade grew during an age of frenzied nationalism and imperialist expansion.

At the same time, Europe's great powers had been divided into two loose alliances. Germany, Austria-Hungary, and Italy formed the **Triple Alliance** in 1882. France, Great Britain, and Russia created the **Triple Entente** in 1907.

In the early years of the twentieth century, a series of crises tested these alliances. Especially troublesome were the crises in the Balkans between 1908 and 1913. These events left European states angry at each other and eager for revenge. Each state was guided by its own self-interest and success. They were willing to use war as a way to preserve the power of their national states.

The growth of nationalism in the nineteenth century had yet another serious result. Not all ethnic groups had become nations. Slavic minorities in the Balkans and the Hapsburg Empire, for example, still dreamed of creating their own national states. The Irish in the British Empire and the Poles in the Russian Empire had similar dreams.

Reading Check **Identifying** Did the growth of nationalism in the first half of the nineteenth century lead to increased competition or increased cooperation among European nations?

Internal Dissent

National desires were not the only source of internal strife at the beginning of the twentieth century. Socialist labor movements also had grown more powerful. The Socialists were increasingly inclined to use strikes, even violent ones, to achieve their goals.

Some conservative leaders, alarmed at the increase in labor strife and class division, feared that European nations were on the verge of revolution. In the view of some historians, the desire to suppress internal disorder may have encouraged various leaders to take the plunge into war in 1914.

Reading Check **Explaining** According to some historians, how might internal disorder have been one of the causes of World War I?

Militarism

The growth of mass armies after 1900 heightened the existing tensions in Europe. The large size of these armies also made it obvious that if war did come, it would be highly destructive.

Conscription, a military draft, had been established as a regular practice in most Western countries before 1914. (The United States and Britain were exceptions.) European armies doubled in size between 1890 and 1914.

With its 1.3 million men, the Russian army had grown to be the largest. The French and German armies were not far behind, with 900,000 each. The British, Italian, and Austro-Hungarian armies numbered between 250,000 and 500,000 soldiers each.

Militarism—aggressive preparation for war— was growing. As armies grew, so too did the influence of military leaders. They drew up vast and complex plans for quickly mobilizing millions of men and enormous quantities of supplies in the event of war.

Military leaders feared that any changes in these plans would cause chaos in the armed forces. Thus, they insisted that their plans could not be altered. In the 1914 crises, this left European political leaders with little leeway. They were forced to make decisions for military instead of political reasons.

✓ **Reading Check** **Examining** What was the effect of conscription on events leading up to World War I?

The Outbreak of War: Summer 1914

Militarism, nationalism, and the desire to stifle internal dissent may all have played a role in the starting of World War I. However, it was the decisions made by European leaders in response to another crisis in the Balkans in the summer of 1914 that led directly to the conflict.

The Serbian Problem As we have seen, states in southeastern Europe had struggled for many years to free themselves of Ottoman rule. Furthermore, the rivalry between Austria-Hungary and Russia for domination of these new states created serious tensions in the region.

By 1914, **Serbia,** supported by Russia, was determined to create a large, independent Slavic state in the Balkans. Austria-Hungary, which had its own Slavic minorities to contend with, was equally determined to prevent that from happening.

Many Europeans saw the potential danger in this explosive situation. The British ambassador to Vienna anticipated war in 1913:

> ❝Serbia will some day set Europe by the ears, and bring about a universal war on the Continent. . . . I cannot tell you how exasperated people are getting here at the continual worry which that little country causes to Austria under encouragement from Russia. . . . It will be lucky if Europe succeeds in avoiding war as a result of the present crisis.❞

It was against this backdrop of mutual distrust and hatred that the events of the summer of 1914 were played out.

Assassination in Sarajevo On June 28, 1914, **Archduke Francis Ferdinand,** the heir to the throne of Austria-Hungary, and his wife Sophia, visited the Bosnian city of Sarajevo (SAR•uh•YAY•VOH). A group of conspirators waited there in the streets. The conspirators were members of the Black Hand, a Serbian terrorist organization that wanted **Bosnia** to be free of Austria-Hungary and to become part of a large Serbian kingdom.

The conspirators planned to kill the archduke, along with his wife. That morning, one of the conspirators threw a bomb at the archduke's car, but it glanced off and exploded against the car behind him. Later in the day, however, **Gavrilo Princip,** a 19-year-old Bosnian Serb, succeeded in shooting both the archduke and his wife.

Austria-Hungary Responds The Austro-Hungarian government did not know whether or not the Serbian government had been directly involved in the archduke's assassination, but it did not care. It saw an opportunity to "render Serbia innocuous [harmless] once and for all by a display of force," as the Austrian foreign minister put it.

Austrian leaders wanted to attack Serbia but feared Russian intervention on Serbia's behalf, so they sought the backing of their German allies. **Emperor William II** of Germany and his chancellor responded with a "blank check," saying that Austria-

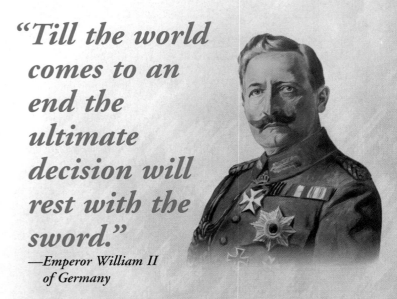

"Till the world comes to an end the ultimate decision will rest with the sword."
—*Emperor William II of Germany*

Hungary could rely on Germany's "full support," even if "matters went to the length of a war between Austria-Hungary and Russia."

Strengthened by German support, Austrian leaders sent an ultimatum to Serbia on July 23. In it, they made such extreme demands that Serbia had little choice but to reject some of them in order to preserve its sovereignty. On July 28, Austria-Hungary declared war on Serbia.

Russia Mobilizes Russia was determined to support Serbia's cause. On July 28, **Czar Nicholas II** ordered partial mobilization of the Russian army against Austria-Hungary. Mobilization is the process of assembling troops and supplies and making them ready for war. In 1914, mobilization was considered an act of war.

Leaders of the Russian army informed the czar that they could not partially mobilize. Their mobilization plans were based on a war against both Germany and Austria-Hungary. Mobilizing against only Austria-Hungary, they claimed, would create chaos in the army. Based on this claim, the czar ordered full mobilization of the Russian army on July 29, knowing that Germany would consider this order an act of war.

The Conflict Broadens Indeed, Germany reacted quickly. The German government warned Russia that it must halt its mobilization within 12 hours. When Russia ignored this warning, Germany declared war on Russia on August 1.

Like the Russians, the Germans had a military plan. It had been drawn up under the guidance of **General Alfred von Schlieffen** (SHLEE•fuhn), so was known as the Schlieffen Plan. The plan called for a two-front war with France and Russia, who had formed a military alliance in 1894.

According to the Schlieffen Plan, Germany would conduct a small holding action against Russia while most of the German army would carry out a rapid invasion of France. This meant invading France by moving quickly along the level coastal area through Belgium. After France was defeated, the German invaders would move to the east against Russia.

Under the Schlieffen Plan, Germany could not mobilize its troops solely against Russia. Therefore, it declared war on France on August 3. About the same time, it issued an ultimatum to Belgium demanding the right of German troops to pass through Belgian territory. Belgium, however, was a neutral nation.

On August 4, Great Britain declared war on Germany, officially for violating Belgian neutrality. In fact, Britain, which was allied with the countries of France and Russia, was concerned about maintaining its own world power. As one British diplomat put it, if Germany and Austria-Hungary won the war, "what would be the position of a friendless England?" By August 4, all the great powers of Europe were at war.

✓**Reading Check** **Evaluating** What was the Schlieffen Plan and how did it complicate the events leading to World War I?

🌟 TAKS Practice

SECTION 1 ASSESSMENT

Checking for Understanding

1. **Define** conscription, mobilization.

2. **Identify** Triple Alliance, Triple Entente, Archduke Francis Ferdinand, Gavrilo Princip, Emperor William II, Czar Nicholas II, General Alfred von Schlieffen.

3. **Locate** Serbia, Bosnia.

4. **Explain** why Great Britain became involved in the war.

5. **List** the ethnic groups that were left without nations after the nationalist movements of the nineteenth century.

Critical Thinking

6. **Analyze** How did the creation of military plans help draw the nations of Europe into World War I? In your opinion, what should today's national and military leaders have learned from the military plans that helped initiate World War I? Explain your answer.

7. **Sequencing Information** Using a diagram like the one below, identify the series of decisions made by European leaders in 1914 that led directly to the outbreak of war.

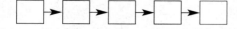

Analyzing Visuals

8. **Examine** the painting of Emperor William II of Germany shown on page 719 of your text. How does this portrait of the emperor reflect the nature of leadership before World War I?

Writing About History

9. **Expository Writing** Some historians believe that the desire to suppress internal disorder may have encouraged leaders to take the plunge into war. As an adviser, write a memo to your country's leader explaining how a war might be advantageous with regard to domestic policy.

SECTION 2 | The War

Guide to Reading

Main Ideas
- The stalemate at the Western Front led to new alliances, a widening of the war, and new weapons.
- Governments expanded their powers, increased opportunities for women, and made use of propaganda.

Key Terms
propaganda, trench warfare, war of attrition, total war, planned economies

People to Identify
Lawrence of Arabia, Admiral Holtzendorff, Woodrow Wilson

Places to Locate
Marne, Tannenberg, Masurian Lakes, Verdun, Gallipoli

Preview Questions
1. How did trench warfare lead to a stalemate?
2. Why did the United States enter the war?

Reading Strategy
Organizing Information Identify which countries belonged to the Allies and the Central Powers. What country changed allegiance? What country withdrew from the war?

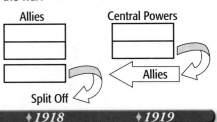

Allies | Central Powers

Split Off | Allies

Preview of Events

♦1914   ♦1915   ♦1916   ♦1917   ♦1918   ♦1919

1915
Lusitania sunk by German forces

1916
Battle of Verdun

1917
United States enters the war

Voices from the Past

Troops going to war

Stefan Zweig, an Austrian writer, described the excitement Austrians felt going to war in 1914:

66What did the people know of war in 1914, after nearly half a century of peace? They did not know war; they had hardly given it a thought. They still saw it in the perspective of their school readers and of paintings in museums; brilliant cavalry attacks in glittering uniforms, the fatal shot always straight through the heart, the entire campaign a resounding march of victory—'We'll be home at Christmas,' the recruits shouted laughingly to their mothers in August of 1914. . . . The young people were honestly afraid that they might miss this most wonderful and exciting experience of their lives; . . . that is why they shouted and sang in the trains that carried them to the slaughter.99

— ***The World of Yesterday**, Helmut Ripperger and B. W. Buebsch, trans., 1943*

Europeans went to war in 1914 with remarkable enthusiasm.

1914 to 1915: Illusions and Stalemate

Before 1914, many political leaders had thought that war involved so many political and economic risks that it would not be worth fighting. Others had believed that diplomats could easily control any situation and prevent war. At the beginning of August 1914, both ideas were shattered. However, the new illusions that replaced them soon proved to be equally foolish.

Government propaganda—ideas spread to influence public opinion for or against a cause—had worked in stirring up national hatreds before the war. Now, in August 1914, the urgent pleas of European governments for defense against aggressors fell on receptive ears in every nation at war. Most people seemed genuinely convinced that their nation's cause was just.

A new set of illusions also fed the enthusiasm for war. In August 1914, almost everyone believed that the war would be over in a few weeks. People were reminded that almost all European wars since 1815 had, in fact, ended in a matter of weeks. Both the soldiers who boarded the trains for the war front in August 1914, and the jubilant citizens who showered them with flowers as they left, believed that the warriors would be home by Christmas.

The Western Front German hopes for a quick end to the war rested on a military gamble. The Schlieffen Plan had called for the German army to make a vast encircling movement through Belgium into northern France. According to the plan, the German forces would sweep around Paris. This would enable them to surround most of the French army.

The German advance was halted a short distance from Paris at the First Battle of the **Marne** (September 6–10). To stop the Germans, French military leaders loaded two thousand Parisian taxicabs with fresh troops and sent them to the front line.

The war quickly turned into a stalemate, as neither the Germans nor the French could dislodge each other from the trenches they had dug for shelter. These trenches were ditches protected by barbed wire. Two lines of trenches soon reached from the English Channel to the frontiers of Switzerland. The Western Front had become bogged down in trench warfare that kept both sides in virtually the same positions for four years.

The Eastern Front In contrast to the Western Front, the war on the Eastern Front was marked by mobility. The cost in lives, however, was equally enormous.

At the beginning of the war, the Russian army moved into eastern Germany but was decisively defeated at the Battle of **Tannenberg** on August 30 and the Battle of **Masurian Lakes** on September 15. As a result of these defeats, the Russians were no longer a threat to German territory.

THE WAY IT WAS

FOCUS ON EVERYDAY LIFE

Trench Warfare

Warfare in the trenches of the Western Front produced unimaginable horrors. Battlefields were hellish landscapes of barbed wire, shell holes, mud, and injured and dying men. The introduction of poison gas in 1915 produced new forms of injuries. One British writer described them:

"I wish those people who write so glibly about this being a holy war could see a case of mustard gas . . . could see the poor things burnt and blistered all over with great mustard-coloured suppurating [pus-forming] blisters with blind eyes all sticky . . . and stuck together, and always fighting for breath, with voices a mere whisper, saying that their throats are closing and they know they will choke.**"**

Soldiers in the trenches also lived with the persistent presence of death. Because combat went on for months, soldiers had to carry on in the midst of countless bodies of dead men or the remains of men blown apart by artillery barrages. Many soldiers remembered the stench of decomposing bodies and the swarms of rats that grew fat in the trenches.

Daily life in the trenches was predictable. Thirty minutes before sunrise, troops had to "stand to," or be combat-ready to repel any attack. If no attack came that day,

British gas mask and pack

Austria-Hungary, Germany's ally, fared less well at first. The Austrians had been defeated by the Russians in Galicia and thrown out of Serbia as well. To make matters worse, the Italians betrayed their German and Austrian allies in the Triple Alliance by attacking Austria in May 1915. Italy thus joined France, Great Britain, and Russia, who had formed the Triple Entente, but now were called the Allied Powers, or Allies.

By this time, the Germans had come to the aid of the Austrians. A German-Austrian army defeated the Russian army in Galicia and pushed the Russians far back into their own territory. Russian casualties stood at 2.5 million killed, captured, or wounded. The Russians had almost been knocked out of the war.

Buoyed by their success, Germany and Austria-Hungary, joined by Bulgaria in September 1915, attacked and eliminated Serbia from the war. Their successes in the east would enable the Germans to move back to the offensive in the west.

✓ **Reading Check** **Contrasting** How did the war on the Eastern Front differ from the war on the Western Front?

1916 to 1917: The Great Slaughter

On the Western Front, the trenches dug in 1914 had by 1916 become elaborate systems of defense. The lines of trenches for both sides were protected by barbed wire entanglements up to 5 feet (about 1.5 m) high and 30 yards (about 27 m) wide, concrete machine-gun nests, and other gun batteries, supported further back by heavy artillery. Troops lived in holes in the ground, separated from each other by a strip of territory known as no-man's-land.

Tactics of Trench Warfare The unexpected development of trench warfare baffled military leaders. They had been trained to fight wars of movement and maneuver. The only plan generals could devise was to attempt a breakthrough by throwing masses of men against enemy lines that had first been battered by artillery. Once the decisive breakthrough had been achieved, they thought, they could return to the war of movement that they knew best.

At times, the high command on either side would order an offensive that would begin with an artillery

the day's routine consisted of breakfast followed by inspection, sentry duty, work on the trenches, care of personal items, and attempts to pass the time. Soldiers often recalled the boredom of life in the dreary, lice-ridden, and muddy or dusty trenches.

At many places along the opposing lines of trenches, a "live and let live" system evolved. It was based on the realization that neither side was going to drive out the other. The "live and let live" system resulted in such arrangements as not shelling the latrines and not attacking during breakfast.

On both sides, troops produced their own humor magazines to help pass the time and fulfill the need to laugh in the midst of their daily madness. The British trench magazine, the *B. E. F. Times*, devoted one of its issues to defining military terms, including "DUDS—These are of two kinds. A shell on impact failing to explode is called a dud. They are unhappily not as plentiful as the other kind, which often draws a big salary and explodes for no reason."

British soldiers in the trenches

CONNECTING TO THE PAST

1. **Explain** What was the rationale behind the "live and let live" system?

2. **Writing about History** Write several journal entries as if you were a soldier in the trenches.

barrage to flatten the enemy's barbed wire and leave the enemy in a state of shock. After "softening up" the enemy in this fashion, a mass of soldiers would climb out of their trenches with fixed bayonets and hope to work their way toward the enemy trenches.

The attacks rarely worked because men advancing unprotected across open fields could be fired at by the enemy's machine guns. In 1916 and 1917, millions of young men died in the search for the elusive breakthrough. In 10 months at **Verdun,** France, in 1916, seven hundred thousand men lost their lives over a few miles of land. World War I had turned into a war of attrition, a war based on wearing the other side down by constant attacks and heavy losses. 📖 *(See page 998 to read an excerpt from Arthur Guy Empey's* Over the Top *in the Primary Sources Library.)*

War in the Air By the end of 1915, airplanes had appeared on the battlefront for the first time in history. At first, planes were used to spot the enemy's position. However, planes soon began to attack ground targets, especially enemy communications.

Fights for control of the air occurred and increased over time. At first, pilots fired at each other with handheld pistols. Later, machine guns were mounted on the noses of planes, which made the skies considerably more dangerous.

The Germans also used their giant airships—the zeppelins—to bomb London and eastern England. This caused little damage but frightened many people. Germany's enemies, however, soon found that zeppelins, which were filled with hydrogen gas, quickly became raging infernos when hit by antiaircraft guns.

✓ **Reading Check** **Explaining** Why were military leaders baffled by trench warfare?

Widening of the War

Because of the stalemate on the Western Front, both sides sought to gain new allies who might provide a winning advantage. The Ottoman Empire had already come into the war on Germany's side in August 1914. Russia, Great Britain, and France—the Allies—declared war on the Ottoman Empire in November.

The Allies tried to open a Balkan front by landing forces at **Gallipoli** (guh•LIH•puh•lee), southwest of Constantinople, in April 1915. However, Bulgaria entered the war on the side of the Central Powers, as Germany, Austria-Hungary, and the Ottoman Empire were called. A disastrous campaign at Gallipoli forced the Allies to withdraw.

In return for Italy entering the war on the Allied side, France and Great Britain promised to let Italy have some Austrian territory. Italy on the side of the Allies opened up a front against Austria-Hungary.

By 1917, the war that had started in Europe had truly become a world conflict. In the Middle East, a British officer known as **Lawrence of Arabia,** in 1917, urged Arab princes to revolt against their Ottoman overlords. In 1918, British forces from Egypt destroyed the Ottoman Empire in the Middle East. For their Middle East campaigns, the British mobilized forces from India, Australia, and New Zealand.

The Allies also took advantage of Germany's preoccupations in Europe and lack of naval strength to seize German colonies in the rest of the world. Japan, a British ally beginning in 1902, seized a number of German-held islands in the Pacific. Australia seized German New Guinea.

✓ **Reading Check** **Describing** What caused the widening of the war?

⧗ **Then** *and* **Now**

The introduction of airplanes greatly changed the nature of warfare during the twentieth century. What kind of aircraft did the Germans use during World War I?

British fighter plane, c. 1917 ▶

U.S. jet fighter, 2001 ▼

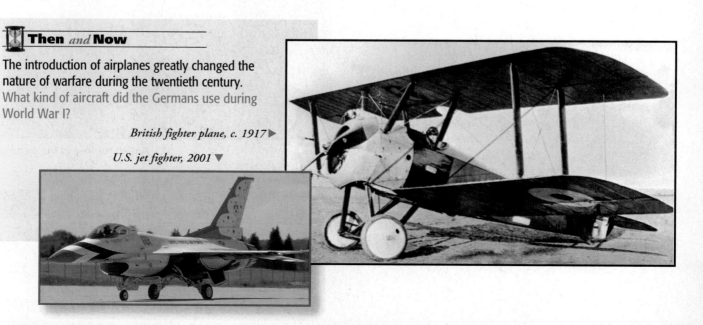

Allies
Central Powers
Neutral nations
‑‑‑‑ Line of trench warfare, 1915–1917
──── Farthest advance of Allies with date
──── Farthest advance of Central Powers with date
British naval blockade
‑ ‑ ‑ Allied mine barrier
German submarine war zone
Sinking of the *Lusitania*, May 7, 1915
‑ ‑ ‑ Armistice line, Nov. 11, 1918
‑ ‑ ‑ Treaty line of Brest-Litovsk
Allied victory
Central Powers victory
Indecisive
Schlieffen Plan

Entry of the United States

At first, the United States tried to remain neutral. As World War I dragged on, however, it became more difficult to do so. The immediate cause of United States involvement grew out of the naval war between Germany and Great Britain.

Britain had used its superior naval power to set up a naval blockade of Germany. The blockade kept war materials and other goods from reaching Germany by sea. Germany had retaliated by setting up its own blockade of Britain. Germany enforced its blockade with the use of unrestricted submarine warfare, which included the sinking of passenger liners.

On May 7, 1915, the British ship *Lusitania* was sunk by German forces. There were about 1,100 civilian casualties, including over 100 Americans. After strong United States protests, the German government suspended unrestricted submarine warfare in September 1915 to avoid antagonizing the United States further. Only once did the German and British naval forces actually engage in direct battle—at the Battle of Jutland on May 31, 1916, when neither side won a conclusive victory.

Geography *Skills*

Trench warfare produced a stalemate on the Western Front.

1. **Applying Geography Skills** Create a bar graph with dates as one axis and miles as the other. Using Berlin as the starting point, plot the Central Powers advances from the earliest to the latest dates shown on the map.

By January 1917, however, the Germans were eager to break the deadlock in the war. German naval officers convinced Emperor William II that resuming the use of unrestricted submarine warfare could starve the British into submission within six months.

When the emperor expressed concern about the United States, he was told not to worry. The British would starve before the Americans could act. Even if the Americans did intervene, **Admiral Holtzendorff** assured the emperor, "I give your Majesty my word as an officer that not one American will land on the continent."

The German naval officers were quite wrong. The British were not forced to surrender, and the return to unrestricted submarine warfare brought the United States into the war in April 1917. United States troops

American troops leave for war.

did not arrive in large numbers in Europe until 1918. However, the entry of the United States into the war not only gave the Allied Powers a psychological boost, but also brought them a major new source of money and war goods.

Reading Check **Evaluating** Why did the Germans resort to unrestricted submarine use?

The Home Front: The Impact of Total War

As World War I dragged on, it became a total war, involving a complete mobilization of resources and people. It affected the lives of all citizens in the warring countries, however remote they might be from the battlefields.

Masses of men had to be organized and supplies had to be manufactured and purchased for years of combat. (Germany alone had 5.5 million men in uniform in 1916.) This led to an increase in government powers and the manipulation of public opinion to keep the war effort going. The home front was rapidly becoming a cause for as much effort as the war front.

Increased Government Powers

Most people had expected the war to be short, so little thought had been given to long-term wartime needs. Governments had to respond quickly, however, when the war machines failed to achieve their goals. Many more men and supplies were needed to continue the war. To meet these needs, governments expanded their powers. Countries drafted tens of millions of young men for that elusive breakthrough to victory.

Throughout Europe, wartime governments also expanded their power over their economies. Free-market capitalistic systems were temporarily put aside. Governments set up price, wage, and rent controls; rationed food supplies and materials; regulated imports and exports; and took over transportation systems and industries. In effect, in order to mobilize all the resources of their nations for the war effort, European nations set up planned economies—systems directed by government agencies.

Under conditions of total war mobilization, the differences between soldiers at war and civilians at home were narrowed. In the view of political leaders, all citizens were part of a national army dedicated to victory. As United States president **Woodrow Wilson** said, the men and women "who remain to till the soil and man the factories are no less a part of the army than the men beneath the battle flags."

Manipulation of Public Opinion

As the war continued and casualties grew worse, the patriotic enthusiasm that had marked the early stages of World War I waned. By 1916, there were signs that civilian morale was beginning to crack under the pressure of total war. War governments, however, fought back against the growing opposition to the war.

Authoritarian regimes, such as those of Germany, Russia, and Austria-Hungary, relied on force to subdue their populations. Under the pressures of the war, however, even democratic states expanded their police powers to stop internal dissent. The British Parliament, for example, passed the Defence of the Realm Act (DORA). It allowed the government to arrest protestors as traitors. Newspapers were censored, and sometimes their publication was even suspended.

Wartime governments made active use of propaganda to arouse enthusiasm for the war. At the beginning, public officials needed to do little to achieve this goal. The British and French, for example, exaggerated German atrocities in Belgium and found that their citizens were only too willing to believe these accounts.

As the war progressed and morale sagged, governments were forced to devise new techniques for motivating the people. In one British recruiting poster, for example, a small daughter asked her father, "Daddy, what did YOU do in the Great War?" while her younger brother played with toy soldiers.

Total War and Women

World War I created new roles for women. Because so many men left to fight at the front, women were asked to take over jobs that had not been available to them before. Women were employed in jobs that had once been considered beyond their capacity. These included such occupations as chimney sweeps, truck drivers, farm laborers, and factory workers in heavy industry. For example, 38 percent of the workers in the Krupp Armaments works in Germany in 1918 were women.

The place of women in the workforce was far from secure, however. Both men and women seemed to expect that many of the new jobs for women were only temporary. This was evident in the British poem "War Girls," written in 1916:

> 66 There's the girl who clips your ticket for the train,
> And the girl who speeds the lift [elevator] from floor
>   to floor,
> There's the girl who does a milk-round [milk delivery]
>   in the rain,
> And the girl who calls for orders at your door.
> Strong, sensible, and fit,
> They're out to show their grit,
> And tackle jobs with energy and knack.
> No longer caged and penned up,
> They're going to keep their end up
> Till the khaki soldier boys come marching back. 99

At the end of the war, governments would quickly remove women from the jobs they had encouraged them to take earlier. The work benefits for women from World War I were short-lived as men returned to the job market. By 1919, there would be 650,000 unemployed women in Great Britain. Wages for the women who were still employed would be lowered.

Nevertheless, in some countries the role played by women in wartime economies had a positive impact

People In History

Edith Cavell
1865–1915—British nurse

Edith Cavell was born in Norfolk, England. She trained as a nurse and moved to Brussels in 1907 to head the Berkendael Medical Institute. After the outbreak of war, the institute became a Red Cross hospital. Cavell worked to shelter French and British soldiers and help them reach safety in the Netherlands.

Outraged, German military authorities in Brussels put her on trial for aiding the enemy and ordered her to be shot. Before her execution, Cavell said, "I am glad to die for my country." To arouse anti-German sentiment, both the French and British used her as an example of German barbarism. The Germans insisted they had the right to execute a traitor—whether man or woman.

on the women's movement for social and political emancipation. The most obvious gain was the right to vote, which was given to women in Germany, Austria, and the United States immediately after the war. Most British women gained the vote in 1918.

Many upper- and middle-class women had also gained new freedoms. In ever-larger numbers, young women from these groups took jobs; had their own apartments; and showed their new independence.

✓ **Reading Check** **Summarizing** What was the effect of total war on ordinary citizens?

🔺 **TAKS Practice**

SECTION 2 ASSESSMENT

Checking for Understanding

1. **Define** propaganda, trench warfare, war of attrition, total war, planned economies.

2. **Identify** Lawrence of Arabia, Admiral Holtzendorff, Woodrow Wilson.

3. **Locate** Marne, Tannenberg, Masurian Lakes, Verdun, Gallipoli.

4. **Explain** why World War I required total warfare.

5. **List** some of the occupations opened to women by the war.

Critical Thinking

6. **Identify** What methods did governments use to counter the loss of enthusiasm and opposition to the war at home?

7. **Organizing Information** Use a diagram like the one below to identify ways in which government powers increased during the war.

Government Powers

Analyzing Visuals

8. **Examine** the photograph of British soldiers shown on page 723. How does this photograph illustrate the type of warfare that emerged during World War I? What aspects of trench warfare are *not* shown in the photo?

Writing About History

9. **Expository Writing** What lasting results occurred in women's rights due to World War I? What were the temporary results? Write an essay discussing the effect of the war on women's rights.

THE LUSITANIA

Passengers boarding the British liner *R.M.S. Lusitania* in New York on May 1, 1915, for the voyage to Liverpool, England, knew of Germany's threat to sink ships bound for the British Isles. Britain and Germany had been fighting for nine months. Still, few passengers imagined that a civilized nation would attack an unarmed passenger steamer without warning.

Built eight years earlier, the *Lusitania* was described as a "floating palace." German authorities, however, saw her as a threat. They accused the British government of using the *Lusitania* to carry ammunition and other war supplies across the Atlantic.

With her four towering funnels, the liner looked invincible as she left New York on her last voyage. Six days later, at 2:10 P.M. on May 7, 1915, Walther Schwieger, the 30-year-old commander of the German submarine U 20, fired a single torpedo at the *Lusitania* from a range of about 750 yards (686 m).

Captain William Turner of the *Lusitania* saw the torpedo's wake from the navigation bridge just before impact. It sounded like a "million-ton hammer hitting a steam boiler a hundred feet high," one passenger said. A second, more powerful explosion followed, sending a geyser of water, coal, and debris high above the deck.

Listing to starboard, the liner began to sink rapidly at the bow, sending passengers tumbling down her slanted decks. Lifeboats on the port side were hanging too far inboard to be readily launched, those on the starboard side too far out to be easily boarded. Several overfilled lifeboats spilled occupants into the

sea. The great liner disappeared under the waves in only 18 minutes, leaving behind a jumble of swimmers, corpses, deck chairs, and wreckage. Looking back upon the scene from his submarine, even the German commander Schwieger was shocked. He later called it the most horrible sight he had ever seen.

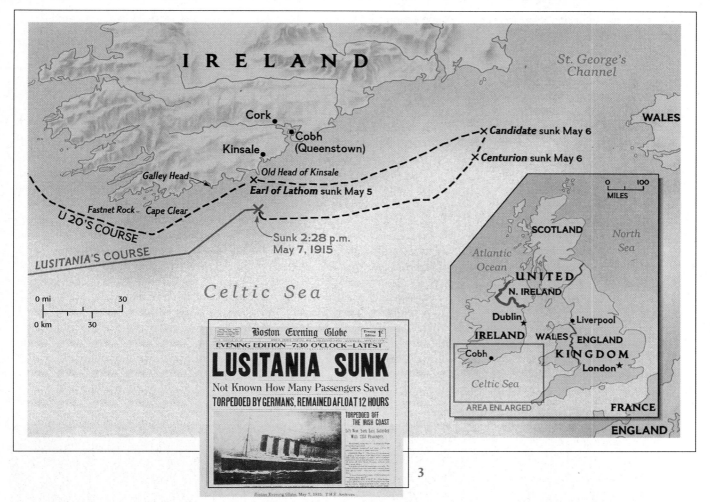

IRELAND

St. George's Channel

WALES

Cork

Cobh (Queenstown)

Kinsale

× Candidate sunk May 6

× Centurion sunk May 6

Old Head of Kinsale

Galley Head

× Earl of Lathom sunk May 5

Fastnet Rock   Cape Clear

U 20'S COURSE

LUSITANIA'S COURSE

Sunk 2:28 p.m. May 7, 1915

Celtic Sea

0 mi   30
0 km   30

0   100
MILES

SCOTLAND

North Sea

Atlantic Ocean

UNITED

N. IRELAND

Dublin   Liverpool

IRELAND   WALES   ENGLAND

Cobh   KINGDOM   London

Celtic Sea

AREA ENLARGED

FRANCE

ENGLAND

Boston Evening Globe Evening 1¢

EVENING EDITION—7:30 O'CLOCK—LATEST

LUSITANIA SUNK

Not Known How Many Passengers Saved

TORPEDOED BY GERMANS, REMAINED AFLOAT 12 HOURS

TORPEDOED OFF THE IRISH COAST

Boston Evening Globe, May 7, 1915; T.H.S. Archives

News of the disaster raced across the Atlantic. Of 1,959 people aboard, only 764 were saved. The dead included 94 children and infants.

Questions were immediately raised. Did the British Admiralty give the *Lusitania* adequate warning? How could one torpedo have sunk her? Why did she go down so fast? Was there any truth to the German claim that the *Lusitania* had been armed?

From the moment the *Lusitania* sank, she was surrounded by controversy. Americans were outraged by the attack, which claimed the lives of 123 U.S. citizens. Newspapers called the attack "deliberate murder" and a "foul deed," and former President Theodore Roosevelt demanded

revenge against Germany. The attack on the *Lusitania* is often credited with drawing the United States into World War I. However, President Woodrow Wilson—though he had vowed to hold Germany responsible for its submarine attacks—knew that the American people were not ready to go to war. It was almost two years before the United States joined the conflict in Europe.

A British judge laid full blame on the German submarine commander, while the German government claimed that the British had deliberately made her a military target. Tragically, inquiries following the sinking of the *Lusitania* revealed that Captain Turner had received warnings by wireless from the British Admiralty,

1 The *Lusitania* arrives in New York on her maiden voyage in 1907 (opposite page).

2 Captain William Turner of the *Lusitania,* (opposite page, center); Walther Schwieger, commander of the German submarine U 20 (opposite page, right).

3 Headlines in Boston and New York (above) report the terrible news of the sinking of the *Lusitania* on May 7, 1915. In the two days prior to the attack on the *Lusitania,* the German submarine U 20 had sunk three ships off Ireland's southern coast. Yet the captain of the *Lusitania,* who had received warnings by wireless from the British Admiralty, took only limited precautions as he approached the area.

but took only limited precautions as he approached the area where the U 20 was waiting.

Rumors of diamonds, gold, and valuables locked away in *Lusitania's* safes have prompted salvage attempts over the years. To date, no treasure has ever been reported.

Perhaps the biggest puzzle has been the hardest to solve: Why did the liner sink so fast? Newspapers speculated that the torpedo had struck munitions in a cargo hold, causing the strong secondary explosion. Divers later reported a huge hole in the port side of the bow, opposite where munitions would have been stored.

Hoping to settle the issue, a team from the Woods Hole Oceanographic Institution, sponsored by the National Geographic Society, sent their robot vehicle Jason down to photograph the damage. Fitted with cameras and powerful lights, the robot sent video images of the wreck by fiber-optic cable to a control room on the surface ship, *Northern Horizon*. A pilot maneuvered Jason with a joystick, while an engineer relayed instructions to the robot's computers. Other team members watched for recognizable objects on the monitors. In addition to using Jason to make a visual survey of the *Lusitania*, the team of researchers and scientists also used sonar to create a computerized, three-dimensional diagram of how the wreck looks today.

From this data, it was discovered that the *Lusitania's* hull had been flattened—in part by the force of gravity—to half its original width. But when Jason's cameras swept across the hold, looking for the hole reported by divers shortly after the sinking, there was none to be found. Indeed, no evidence was found that would indicate that the torpedo had detonated an explosion in a cargo hold, undermining one theory of why the liner sank.

Questions about her cargo have haunted the *Lusitania* since the day she went down. Was she carrying illegal munitions as the Germans have always claimed? In fact, she was. The manifest for her last voyage included wartime essentials such as motorcycle parts, metals, cotton goods, and food, as well as 4,200 cases of rifle ammunition, 1,250 cases of shrapnel (not explosive), and 18 boxes of percussion fuses. However, the investigation conducted by the Woods Hole team and Jason suggested that these munitions did not cause the secondary blast that sent the *Lusitania* to the bottom. So what did?

One likely possibility was a coal-dust explosion. The German torpedo struck the liner's starboard side about 10 feet (3 m) below the waterline, rupturing one of the long coal

4

4 Homer, a small robot, (opposite page) explores a hole in the stern of the *Lusitania* that was cut by a salvage crew to recover silverware and other items.

5 A provocative poster (left) depicted drowning innocents and urged Americans to enlist in the armed forces.

6 Alice Drury (above left) was a young nanny for an American couple on the *Lusitania*. She and another nanny were caring for the couple's children: Audrey (above right), Stuart, Amy, and Susan. Alice was about to give Audrey a bottle when the torpedo hit. Alice wrapped Audrey in a shawl, grabbed Stuart, and headed for the lifeboats. A crewman loaded Stuart, but when Alice tried to board, the sailor told her it was full. Without a life jacket and with Audrey around her neck, Alice jumped into the water. A woman in the lifeboat grabbed her hair and pulled her aboard. Audrey's parents were rescued too, but Amy, Susan, and the other nanny were lost. Alice and Audrey Lawson Johnston have remained close ever since.

bunkers [storage bins] that stretched along both sides. If that bunker, mostly empty by the end of the voyage, contained explosive coal dust, the torpedo might have ignited it. Such an occurrence would explain all the coal that was found scattered on the seafloor near the wreck.

The *Lusitania's* giant funnels have long since turned to rust, an eerie marine growth covers her hull, and her superstructure is ghostly wreckage. Yet the horror and fascination surrounding the sinking of the great liner live on. With today's high-technology tools, researchers and scientists at Woods Hole and the National Geographic Society have provided another look—and some new answers—to explain the chain of events that ended with the *Lusitania* at the bottom of the sea.

INTERPRETING THE PAST

1. How did the *Lusitania* contribute to drawing the United States into World War I?

2. Describe the *Lusitania's* route. Where was it when it sank?

3. What mysteries were researchers able to solve by using underwater robot technology?

The Russian Revolution

Guide to Reading

Main Ideas
- The czarist regime in Russia fell as a result of poor leadership.
- The Bolsheviks under Lenin came to power.
- Communist forces triumphed over anti-Communist forces.

Key Terms
soviets, war communism

People to Identify
Alexandra, Grigori Rasputin, Alexander Kerensky, Bolsheviks, V. I. Lenin, Leon Trotsky

Places to Locate
Petrograd, Ukraine, Siberia, Urals

Preview Questions
1. What promises did the Bolsheviks make to the Russian people?
2. Why did civil war break out in Russia after the Russian Revolution?

Reading Strategy
Categorizing Information Using a chart like the one below, identify the factors and events that led to Lenin coming to power in 1917.

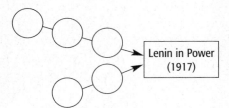

Lenin in Power (1917)

Preview of Events

♦1916	♦1917	♦1918	♦1919	♦1920	♦1921

1916
Rasputin assassinated

1917
Czar Nicholas II steps down

1918
Lenin signs Treaty of Brest-Litovsk

1921
Communists control Russia

Voices from the Past

John Reed

John Reed, an American journalist, described an important event that took place in St. Petersburg, Russia, on the night of November 6, 1917:

❝After a few minutes huddling there, some hundreds of men began again to flow forward. By this time, in the light that streamed out of the Winter Palace windows, I could see that the first two or three hundred men were Red Guards [revolutionaries], with only a few scattered soldiers. Over the barricade of firewood we clambered, and leaping down inside gave a triumphant shout as we stumbled on a heap of rifles thrown down by the guards who had stood there. On both sides of the main gateway the doors stood wide open, and from the huge pile came not the slightest sound.❞
—*Eyewitness to History,* **John Carey, ed., 1987**

Reed was describing the Bolshevik seizure of the Winter Palace, seat of the Russian Government, by Bolshevik revolutionaries. This act led to a successful revolution in Russia.

Background to Revolution

⎡TURNING **POINT**⎤ **As you will learn, out of Russia's collapse in 1917 came the Russian Revolution. Its impact would be felt all over the world.**

Russia was unprepared both militarily and technologically for the total war of World War I. Russia had no competent military leaders. Even worse, Czar

Picturing **History**

Rasputin (shown upper right corner) had great influence over Czar Nicholas II and his family, shown here in a 1913 photograph. **Why was Rasputin able to influence Russian political affairs?**

Nicholas II insisted on taking personal charge of the armed forces despite his obvious lack of ability and training.

In addition, Russian industry was unable to produce the weapons needed for the army. Many soldiers trained using broomsticks. Others were sent to the front without rifles and told to pick one up from a dead comrade.

Given these conditions, it is not surprising that the Russian army suffered incredible losses. Between 1914 and 1916, two million soldiers were killed, and another four to six million wounded or captured. By 1917, the Russian will to fight had vanished.

Beginnings of Upheaval Czar Nicholas II was an autocratic ruler who relied on the army and bureaucracy to hold up his regime. Furthermore, he was increasingly cut off from events by his German-born wife, **Alexandra.** She was a willful and stubborn woman who had fallen under the influence of **Grigori Rasputin** (ra•SPYOO•tuhn), an uneducated Siberian peasant who claimed to be a holy man. Alexandra believed that Rasputin was holy, for he alone seemed able to stop the bleeding of her son Alexis. Alexis, the heir to the throne, had hemophilia (a deficiency in the ability of the blood to clot).

With the czar at the battlefront, Alexandra made all of the important decisions. She insisted on first consulting Rasputin, the man she called "her beloved, never-to-be-forgotten teacher, savior, and mentor." Rasputin's influence made him an important power behind the throne. He did not hesitate to interfere in government affairs.

As the leadership at the top stumbled its way through a series of military and economic disasters, the Russian people grew more and more upset with the czarist regime. Even conservative aristocrats who supported the monarchy felt the need to do something to save the situation.

For a start, they assassinated Rasputin in December 1916. It was not easy to kill this man of incredible physical strength. They shot him three times and then tied him up and threw him into the Neva River. He drowned, but not before he had managed to untie the knots underwater. The killing of Rasputin occurred too late, however, to save the monarchy.

The March Revolution At the beginning of March 1917, a series of strikes led by working-class women broke out in the capital city of **Petrograd** (formerly St. Petersburg). A few weeks earlier, the government had started bread rationing in Petrograd after the price of bread had skyrocketed.

Many of the women who stood in the lines waiting for bread were also factory workers who worked 12-hour days. A police report warned the government:

> ❝Mothers of families, exhausted by endless standing in line at stores, distraught over their half-starving and sick children, are today perhaps closer to revolution than [the liberal opposition leaders] and of course they are a great deal more dangerous because they are the combustible material for which only a single spark is needed to burst into flame.❞

On March 8, about 10,000 women marched through the city of Petrograd demanding "Peace and Bread" and "Down with Autocracy." Soon the women were joined by other workers. Together they called for a general strike. The strike shut down all the factories in the city on March 10.

Alexandra wrote her husband Nicholas II at the battlefront, "This is a hooligan movement. If the weather were very cold they would all probably stay at home." Nicholas ordered troops to break up the crowds by shooting them if necessary. Soon, however, large numbers of the soldiers joined the demonstrators and refused to fire on the crowds.

The Duma, or legislative body, which the czar had tried to dissolve, met anyway. On March 12, it established the provisional government, which mainly consisted of middle-class Duma representatives. This government urged the czar to step down. Because he no longer had the support of the army or even the aristocrats, Nicholas II did step down, on March 15, ending the 300-year-old Romanov dynasty.

The provisional government, headed by **Alexander Kerensky** (keh•REHN•skee), now decided to carry on the war to preserve Russia's honor. This decision to remain in World War I was a major blunder. It satisfied neither the workers nor the peasants, who, tired and angry from years of suffering, wanted above all an end to the war.

The government was also faced with a challenge to its authority—the soviets. The soviets were councils composed of representatives from the workers and soldiers. The soviet of Petrograd had been formed in March 1917. At the same time, soviets sprang up in army units, factory towns, and rural areas. The soviets, largely made up of socialists, represented the more radical interests of the lower classes. One group—the Bolsheviks—came to play a crucial role.

√ **Reading Check** **Identifying** Develop a sequence of events leading to the March Revolution.

HISTORY Online

Web Activity Visit the *Glencoe World History* Web site at tx.wh.glencoe.com and click on **Chapter 23– Student Web Activity** to learn more about the Russian royal family.

CONNECTIONS Past To Present

The Mystery of Anastasia

Czar Nicholas II, his wife Alexandra, and their five children were murdered on the night of July 16, 1918. Soon after, rumors began to circulate that some members of the family had survived.

In 1921, a young woman in Dalldorf, Germany, claimed to be the Grand Duchess Anastasia, youngest daughter of Nicholas II. Some surviving members of the Romanov family became convinced that she was Anastasia. Grand Duke Andrew, Nicholas II's first cousin, said after meeting with her, "For me there is definitely no doubt; it is Anastasia."

Later, the woman claiming to be Anastasia came to the United States. While in New York, she registered at a Long Island hotel as Anna Anderson and soon became known by that name. In 1932, she returned to Germany. During the next 30 years, she pursued a claim in German courts for part of the estate left to Empress Alexandra's German relatives. In the 1960s in the United States, she became even better known as a result of a popular play and film, *Anastasia*.

In 1968, Anna Anderson returned to the United States, where she died in 1984. In 1994, DNA testing of tissues from Anna Anderson revealed that she was not the Grand Duchess Anastasia. In all probability, Anna Anderson was Franziska Schanzkowska, a Polish farmer's daughter who had always dreamed of being an actress.

▲ **Grand Duchess Anastasia**

◄ **Anna Anderson**

Comparing Past and Present

The woman claiming to be Anastasia convinced many people of the authenticity of her claim. What do you think might have motivated her to act out the part of Anastasia for so many years?

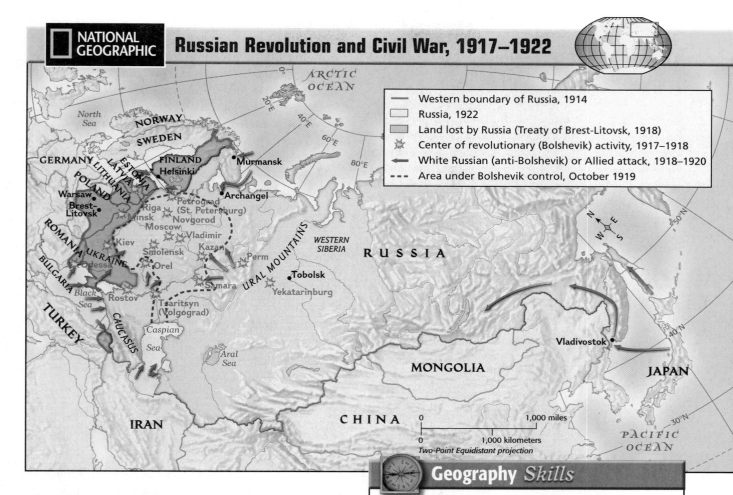

NATIONAL GEOGRAPHIC — **Russian Revolution and Civil War, 1917–1922**

- ——— Western boundary of Russia, 1914
- ☐ Russia, 1922
- ▨ Land lost by Russia (Treaty of Brest-Litovsk, 1918)
- ✳ Center of revolutionary (Bolshevik) activity, 1917–1918
- ← White Russian (anti-Bolshevik) or Allied attack, 1918–1920
- --- Area under Bolshevik control, October 1919

The Rise of Lenin

The **Bolsheviks** began as a small faction of a Marxist party called the Russian Social Democrats. The Bolsheviks came under the leadership of Vladimir Ilyich Ulianov (ool•YAH•nuhf), known to the world as **V. I. Lenin.**

Under Lenin's direction, the Bolsheviks became a party dedicated to violent revolution. Lenin believed that only violent revolution could destroy the capitalist system. A "vanguard" (forefront) of activists, he said, must form a small party of well-disciplined professional revolutionaries to accomplish the task.

Between 1900 and 1917, Lenin spent most of his time abroad. When the provisional government was formed in March 1917, he saw an opportunity for the Bolsheviks to seize power. In April 1917, German military leaders, hoping to create disorder in Russia, shipped Lenin to Russia. Lenin and his associates were in a sealed train to prevent their ideas from infecting Germany.

Lenin's arrival in Russia opened a new stage of the Russian Revolution. Lenin maintained that the soviets of soldiers, workers, and peasants were ready-made instruments of power. He believed that the Bolsheviks should work toward gaining control of

Geography *Skills*

The Russian Revolution and civil war resulted in significant changes to Russia's boundaries.

1. **Interpreting Maps** Compare the area of Russia under Bolshevik control in 1919 with the area *not* under Bolshevik control. Which is larger? Which contained Russia's main cities?

2. **Applying Geography Skills** Pose two questions for your classmates to determine whether or not they can describe the changes in Russia's boundaries resulting from the Russian Revolution and World War I.

these groups and then use them to overthrow the provisional government.

At the same time, the Bolsheviks reflected the discontent of the people. They promised an end to the war, the redistribution of all land to the peasants, the transfer of factories and industries from capitalists to committees of workers, and the transfer of government power from the provisional government to the soviets. Three simple slogans summed up the Bolshevik program: "Peace, Land, Bread," "Worker Control of Production," and "All Power to the Soviets."

✔ **Reading Check** **Examining** What was Lenin's plan when he arrived in Russia?

CHAPTER 23   War and Revolution   **735**

The Bolsheviks Seize Power

By the end of October, Bolsheviks made up a slight majority in the Petrograd and Moscow soviets. The number of party members had grown from 50,000 to 240,000. With Leon Trotsky, a dedicated revolutionary, as head of the Petrograd soviet, the Bolsheviks were in a position to claim power in the name of the soviets. During the night of November 6, Bolshevik forces seized the Winter Palace, the seat of the provisional government. The government quickly collapsed with little bloodshed.

V. I. Lenin

This overthrow of the provisional government coincided with a meeting in Petrograd of the all-Russian Congress of Soviets, which represented local soviets from all over the country. Outwardly, Lenin turned over the power of the provisional government to the Congress of Soviets. The real power, however, passed to a Council of People's Commissars, headed by Lenin.

The Bolsheviks, who soon renamed themselves the Communists, still had a long way to go. Lenin had promised peace, and that, he realized, would not be an easy task. It would mean the humiliating loss of much Russian territory. There was no real choice, however.

On March 3, 1918, Lenin signed the Treaty of Brest-Litovsk with Germany and gave up eastern Poland, **Ukraine,** Finland, and the Baltic provinces. To his critics, Lenin argued that it made no difference. The spread of the socialist revolution throughout Europe would make the treaty largely irrelevant. In any case, he had promised peace to the Russian people. Real peace did not come, however, because the country soon sank into civil war.

✔ **Reading Check** **Describing** What was the impact of the Treaty of Brest-Litovsk on Russia?

Civil War in Russia

Many people were opposed to the new Bolshevik, or Communist, regime. These people included not only groups loyal to the czar but also liberals and anti-Leninist socialists. These groups were joined by the Allies, who were extremely concerned about the Communist takeover. The Allies sent thousands of troops to various parts of Russia in the hope of bringing Russia back into the war. The Allied forces rarely fought on Russian soil, but they did give material aid to anti-Communist forces.

Between 1918 and 1921, the Communist (Red) Army was forced to fight on many fronts against these opponents. The first serious threat to the Communists came from **Siberia.** Here an anti-Communist (White) force attacked westward and advanced almost to the Volga River before being stopped.

Attacks also came from the Ukrainians in the southwest and from the Baltic regions. In mid-1919, White forces swept through Ukraine and advanced almost to Moscow before being pushed back.

By 1920, however, the major White forces had been defeated and Ukraine retaken. The next year, the Communist regime regained control over the independent nationalist governments in Georgia, Russian Armenia, and Azerbaijan (A•zuhr•BY•JAHN).

The royal family was another victim of the civil war. After the czar abdicated, he, his wife, and their five children had been taken into captivity. In April 1918, they were moved to Ekaterinburg, a mining town in the **Urals.** On the night of July 16, members of the local soviet murdered the czar and his family and burned their bodies in a nearby mine shaft.

✔ **Reading Check** **Identifying** Who opposed the new Bolshevik regime?

Triumph of the Communists

How had Lenin and the Communists triumphed in the civil war over what seemed to be overwhelming forces? One reason was that the Red Army was a well-disciplined fighting force. This was largely due to the organizational genius of **Leon Trotsky.** As commissar of war, Trotsky reinstated the draft and insisted on rigid discipline. Soldiers who deserted or refused to obey orders were executed on the spot.

Furthermore, the disunity of the anti-Communist forces weakened their efforts. Political differences created distrust among the Whites and prevented them from cooperating effectively with one another. Some Whites insisted on restoring the czarist regime. Others believed that only a more liberal and democratic program had any chance of success.

The Whites, then, had no common goal. The Communists, in contrast, had a single-minded sense of purpose. Inspired by their vision of a new socialist order, the Communists had the determination that comes from revolutionary zeal and convictions.

The Communists were also able to translate their revolutionary faith into practical instruments of power. A policy of war communism, for example, was used to ensure regular supplies for the Red Army. War communism meant government control of banks and most industries, the seizing of grain from peasants, and the centralization of state administration under Communist control.

Another Communist instrument was revolutionary terror. A new Red secret police—known as the Cheka—began a Red Terror aimed at the destruction of all those who opposed the new regime (much like the Reign of Terror in the French Revolution). The Red Terror added an element of fear to the Communist regime.

Finally, the presence of foreign armies on Russian soil enabled the Communists to appeal to the powerful force of Russian patriotism. At one point, over a

hundred thousand foreign troops—mostly Japanese, British, American, and French—were stationed in Russia in support of anti-Communist forces. Their presence made it easy for the Communist government to call on patriotic Russians to fight foreign attempts to control the country.

By 1921, the Communists were in total command of Russia. In the course of the civil war, the Communist regime had transformed Russia into a centralized state dominated by a single party. The state was also largely hostile to the Allied powers, because the Allies had tried to help the Communists' enemies in the civil war.

✓ **Reading Check** **Contrasting** Why did the Red Army prevail over the White Army?

SECTION 3 ASSESSMENT

Checking for Understanding

1. **Define** soviets, war communism.

2. **Identify** Alexandra, Grigori Rasputin, Alexander Kerensky, Bolsheviks, V.I. Lenin, Leon Trotsky.

3. **Locate** Petrograd, Ukraine, Siberia, Urals.

4. **Explain** why Lenin accepted the loss of so much Russian territory in the Treaty of Brest-Litovsk.

5. **List** some of the different opinions that split the White forces.

Critical Thinking

6. **Explain** How did the presence of Allied troops in Russia ultimately help the Communists?

7. **Organizing Information** Using a chart like the one below, sequence the steps the Communists took to turn Russia into a centralized state dominated by a single party.

Steps to Communist control
1.
2.

Analyzing Visuals

8. **Examine** the photograph of Czar Nicholas II and his family shown on page 733 of your text. Is this photograph an idealized view of royalty? Do you think the people of Russia would have agreed with this view of the royal family as portrayed in this photograph, especially during World War I?

Writing About History

9. **Expository Writing** Write an essay comparing the economic, political, and social causes of the American, French, and Russian Revolutions.

Ten Days That Shook the World

Lenin speaks to the troops in Moscow.

JOHN REED WAS AN AMERICAN JOURNALIST sympathetic to socialism. In *Ten Days That Shook the World*, he left an eyewitness account of the Russian Revolution. Inspired by the Bolsheviks, he helped found the American Communist Labor Party in Chicago. Accused of treason, he returned to the Soviet Union, dying there in 1920.

❝It was just 8:40 when a thundering wave of cheers announced the entrance of the presidium [executive committee], with Lenin—great Lenin— among them. A short, stocky figure, with a big head set down in his shoulders, bald and bulging. Little eyes, a snubbish nose, wide, generous mouth, and heavy chin. Dressed in shabby clothes, his trousers much too long for him. Unimpressive, to be the idol of a mob, loved and revered as perhaps few leaders in history have been. . . .

Now Lenin, gripping the edge of the reading stand, letting his little winking eyes travel over the crowd as he stood there waiting, apparently oblivi- ous to the long-rolling ovation, which lasted several minutes. When it finished, he said simply, 'We shall now proceed to construct the socialist order!' Again that over- whelming human roar.

'The first thing is the adoption of practical measures to realize peace. . . . We shall offer peace to the peoples of all the warring countries upon the basis of the Soviet terms—no annexations, no indemnities, and the right of self-determination of peoples. . . . This proposal of peace will meet with resistance on the part of the imperialist governments—we don't fool our- selves on that score. But we hope that revolution will soon break out in all the warring countries; that is why we address ourselves especially to the workers of France, England and Germany. . . .'

'The revolution of November 6th and 7th,' he ended, 'has opened the era of the Social Revolu- tion. . . . The labour movement, in the name of peace and socialism, shall win, and fulfill its destiny. . . .'

There was something quiet and powerful in all this, which stirred the souls of men. It was understandable why people believed when Lenin spoke.❞

—John Reed, *Ten Days That Shook the World*

Analyzing Primary Sources

1. Did John Reed agree or disagree with Lenin?
2. How do you know that Reed's account of Lenin is biased?

SECTION 4 End of the War

Guide to Reading

Main Ideas
- Combined Allied forces stopped the German offensive.
- Peace settlements brought political and territorial changes to Europe and created bitterness and resentment in several nations.

Key Terms
armistice, reparation, mandate

People to Identify
Erich von Ludendorff, Friedrich Ebert, David Lloyd George, Georges Clemenceau

Places to Locate
Kiel, Alsace, Lorraine, Poland

Preview Questions
1. What were the key events in bringing about an end to the war?
2. What was the intended purpose of the League of Nations?

Reading Strategy
Organizing Information At the Paris Peace Conference, the leaders of France, Britain, and the United States were motivated by different concerns. Using a chart, identify the national interests of each country as it approached the peace deliberations.

France	Britain	United States

Preview of Events

| ◆1917 | ◆1918 | ◆1919 | ◆1920 |

1918
Germany agrees to an armistice

1919
Treaty of Versailles signed at the Paris Peace Conference

Voices from the Past

On September 15, 1916, on the Western Front, a new weapon appeared:

❝We heard strange throbbing noises, and lumbering slowly towards us came three huge mechanical monsters such as we had never seen before. My first impression was that they looked ready to topple on their noses, but their tails and the two little wheels at the back held them down and kept them level. . . . Instead of going on to the German lines the three tanks assigned to us straddled our front line, stopped and then opened up a murderous machine-gun fire. . . . They finally realized they were on the wrong trench and moved on, frightening the Germans out of their wits and making them scuttle like frightened rabbits.❞

—*Eyewitness to History*, **John Carey, ed., 1987**

The tank played a role in bringing an end to World War I and foreshadowed a new kind of warfare.

British tank

The Last Year of the War

The year 1917 had not been a good one for the Allies. Allied offensives on the Western Front had been badly defeated. The Russian Revolution, which began in November 1917, led to Russia's withdrawal from the War a few months later. The cause of the Central Powers looked favorable, although war weariness was beginning to take its toll.

On the positive side, the entry of the United States into the war in 1917 gave the Allies a much-needed psychological boost, along with fresh men and material. In 1918, American troops would prove crucial.

A New German Offensive For Germany, the withdrawal of the Russians offered new hope for a successful end to the war. Germany was now free to concentrate entirely on the Western Front. **Erich von Ludendorff,** who guided German military operations, decided to make one final military gamble—a grand offensive in the west to break the military stalemate.

The German attack was launched in March 1918. By April, German troops were within about 50 miles (80 km) of Paris. However, the German advance was stopped at the Second Battle of the Marne on July 18. French, Moroccan, and American troops (140,000 fresh American troops had just arrived), supported by hundreds of tanks, threw the Germans back over the Marne. Ludendorff's gamble had failed.

With more than a million American troops pouring into France, Allied forces began a steady advance toward Germany. On September 29, 1918, General Ludendorff informed German leaders that the war was lost. He demanded that the government ask for peace at once.

Collapse and Armistice German officials soon discovered that the Allies were unwilling to make peace with the autocratic imperial government of Germany. Reforms were begun to create a liberal government, but these efforts came too late for the exhausted and angry German people.

On November 3, sailors in the town of **Kiel,** in northern Germany, mutinied. Within days, councils of workers and soldiers were forming throughout northern Germany and taking over civilian and military offices. William II gave in to public pressure and left the country on November 9.

After William II's departure, the Social Democrats under **Friedrich Ebert** announced the creation of a democratic republic. Two days later, on November 11, 1918, the new German government signed an armistice (a truce, an agreement to end the fighting).

Opposing Viewpoints

Who Caused World War I?

Immediately after World War I, historians began to assess which nation was most responsible for beginning the war. As these four selections show, opinions have varied considerably.

❝The Allied and Associated Governments affirm and Germany accepts the responsibility of Germany and her allies for causing all the loss and damage to which the Allied and Associated Governments have been subjected as a consequence of the war imposed upon them by the aggression of Germany and her allies.❞

Treaty of Versailles, Article 231, 1919

❝None of the powers wanted a European War. . . . But the verdict of the Versailles Treaty that Germany and her allies were responsible for the War, in view of the evidence now available, is historically unsound. It should therefore be revised.❞

—**Sidney Bradshaw Fay**
Origins of the World War, 1930

Revolutionary Forces The war was over, but the revolutionary forces it had set in motion in Germany were not yet exhausted. A group of radical socialists, unhappy with the moderate policies of the Social Democrats, formed the German Communist Party in December 1918. A month later, the Communists tried to seize power in Berlin.

The new Social Democratic government, backed by regular army troops, crushed the rebels and murdered Rosa Luxemburg and Karl Liebknecht (LEEP• KNEHKT), leaders of the German Communists. A similar attempt at Communist revolution in the city of Munich, in southern Germany, was also crushed.

The new German republic had been saved from radical revolution. The attempt at revolution, however, left the German middle class with a deep fear of communism.

Austria-Hungary, too, experienced disintegration and revolution. As war weariness took hold of the empire, ethnic groups increasingly sought to achieve their independence. By the time the war ended, the Austro-Hungarian Empire was no more.

The empire had been replaced by the independent republics of Austria, Hungary, and Czechoslovakia, along with the large monarchical state called Yugoslavia. Rivalries among the nations that succeeded Austria-Hungary would weaken eastern Europe for the next 80 years.

☑️ **Reading Check** **Describing** What happened within Germany after the armistice?

The Peace Settlements

In January 1919, representatives of 27 victorious Allied nations met in Paris to make a final settlement of the Great War. Over a period of years, the reasons for fighting World War I had changed dramatically. When European nations had gone to war in 1914 they sought territorial gains. By the beginning of 1918, more idealistic reasons were also being expressed.

Wilson's Proposals No one expressed these idealistic reasons better than the U.S. president, Woodrow Wilson. Even before the end of the war, Wilson outlined "Fourteen Points" to the United States Congress—his basis for a peace settlement that he believed justified the enormous military struggle being waged.

Wilson's proposals for a truly just and lasting peace included reaching the peace agreements openly rather than through secret diplomacy; reducing armaments (military forces or weapons) to a "point consistent with domestic safety"; and ensuring self-determination (the right of each people to have its own nation).

Wilson portrayed World War I as a people's war against "absolutism and militarism." These two enemies of liberty, he argued, could be eliminated only by creating democratic governments and a "general association of nations." This association would guarantee "political independence and territorial integrity to great and small states alike."

Wilson became the spokesperson for a new world order based on democracy and international cooperation. When he arrived in Europe for the peace conference, he was enthusiastically cheered by many Europeans. Wilson soon found, however, that more practical motives guided other states.

The Paris Peace Conference Delegates met in Paris in early 1919 to determine the peace settlement. At the Paris Peace Conference, complications became obvious. For one thing, secret treaties and agreements that had been made before the war had raised

❝In estimating the order of guilt of the various countries we may safely say that the only direct and immediate responsibility for the World War falls upon Serbia, France and Russia, with the guilt about equally divided.❞

—**Harry Elmer Barnes**
The Genesis of the World War, 1927

❝As Germany willed and coveted the Austro-Serbian war and, in her confidence in her military superiority, deliberately faced the risk of a conflict with Russia and France, her leaders must bear a substantial share of the historical responsibility for the outbreak of general war in 1914.❞

—**Fritz Fischer,**
Germany's Aims in the First World War, 1961

You Decide

1. Write a quote of your own that reflects your views on which nation caused World War I. Support your quote with passages from the text.

the hopes of European nations for territorial gains. These hopes could not be totally ignored, even if they did conflict with the principle of self-determination put forth by Wilson.

National interests also complicated the deliberations of the Paris Peace Conference. **David Lloyd George,** prime minister of Great Britain, had won a decisive victory in elections in December of 1918. His platform was simple: make the Germans pay for this dreadful war.

France's approach to peace was chiefly guided by its desire for national security. To **Georges Clemenceau** (KLEH•muhn•SOH), the premier of France, the French people had suffered the most from German aggression. The French desired revenge and security against future German aggression. Clemenceau wanted Germany stripped of all weapons, vast German payments—reparations—to cover the costs of the war, and a separate Rhineland as a buffer state between France and Germany.

The most important decisions at the Paris Peace Conference were made by Wilson, Clemenceau, and Lloyd George. Italy, as one of the Allies, was considered one of the so-called Big Four powers. However, it played a smaller role than the other key powers—the United States, France, and Great Britain, called the Big Three. Germany was not invited to attend, and Russia could not be present because of its civil war.

People In History

Georges Clemenceau
1841–1929—French statesman

Georges Clemenceau was one of France's wartime leaders. He had a long political career before serving as French premier (prime minister) from 1906 to 1909 and from 1917 to 1920.

When Clemenceau became premier in 1917, he suspended basic civil liberties for the rest of the war. He had the editor of an antiwar newspaper executed on a charge of helping the enemy. Clemenceau also punished journalists who wrote negative war reports by having them drafted.

Clemenceau strongly disliked and distrusted the Germans and blamed them for World War I. "For the catastrophe of 1914 the Germans are responsible," he said. "Only a professional liar would deny this."

In view of the many conflicting demands at the peace conference, it was no surprise that the Big Three quarreled. Wilson wanted to create a world organization, the League of Nations, to prevent future wars. Clemenceau and Lloyd George wanted to punish Germany. In the end, only compromise made it possible to achieve a peace settlement.

Wilson's wish that the creation of an international peacekeeping organization be the first order of business was granted. On January 25, 1919, the conference accepted the idea of a League of Nations. In return, Wilson agreed to make compromises on territorial arrangements. He did so because he believed that the League could later fix any unfair settlements.

Clemenceau also compromised to obtain some guarantees for French security. He gave up France's wish for a separate Rhineland and instead accepted a defensive alliance with Great Britain and the United States. The U.S. Senate refused to ratify this agreement, which weakened the Versailles peace settlement.

The Treaty of Versailles The final peace settlement of Paris consisted of five separate treaties with the defeated nations—Germany, Austria, Hungary, Bulgaria, and Turkey. The Treaty of Versailles with Germany, signed at Versailles near Paris, on June 28, 1919, was by far the most important.

The Germans considered it a harsh peace. They were especially unhappy with Article 231, the so-called War Guilt Clause, which declared that Germany (and Austria) were responsible for starting the war. The treaty ordered Germany to pay reparations for all the damage to which the Allied governments and their people had been subjected as a result of the war "imposed upon them by the aggression of Germany and her allies."

The military and territorial provisions of the Treaty of Versailles also angered the Germans. Germany had to reduce its army to a hundred thousand men, cut back its navy, and eliminate its air force. **Alsace** and **Lorraine,** taken by the Germans from France in 1871, were now returned. Sections of eastern Germany were awarded to a new Polish state.

German land along both sides of the Rhine was made a demilitarized zone and stripped of all weapons and fortifications. This, it was hoped, would serve as a barrier to any future German military moves westward against France. Outraged by the "dictated peace," the new German government complained but, unwilling to risk a renewal of the war, they accepted the treaty.

Territory lost by:
- Austria-Hungary
- Bulgaria
- Germany
- Ottoman Empire
- Russia

500 miles

500 kilometers

Lambert Azimuthal Equal-Area projection

0   100 mi.

0   100 km

Lambert Azimuthal Equal-Area projection

Rhineland

Geography Skills

World War I dramatically changed political boundaries.

1. **Interpreting Maps** Rank the countries and empires listed in the map legend according to the amount of lost territory, from largest loss to smallest loss.

2. **Applying Geography Skills** Look back at the map on page 718, then examine the map above. Now, knowing the outcome of the war, predict which countries would lose the most territory. Why does the actual loss of territory, as shown above, differ from (or match) your predictions?

A New Map of Europe As a result of the war, the Treaty of Versailles, and the separate peace treaties made with the other Central Powers—Austria, Hungary, Bulgaria, and Turkey—the map of Eastern Europe was largely redrawn. Both the German and Russian empires lost much territory in eastern Europe. The Austro-Hungarian Empire disappeared.

New nation-states emerged from the lands of these three empires: Finland, Latvia, Estonia, Lithuania, Poland, Czechoslovakia, Austria, and Hungary. New territorial arrangements were also made in the Balkans. Romania acquired additional lands from Russia, Hungary, and Bulgaria. Serbia formed the nucleus of a new state, called Yugoslavia, which combined Serbs, Croats, and Slovenes.

The Paris Peace Conference was supposedly guided by the principle of self-determination. However, the mixtures of peoples in eastern Europe made it impossible to draw boundaries along neat ethnic lines. Compromises had to be made, sometimes to satisfy the national interests of the victors. France, for

example, had lost Russia as its major ally on Germany's eastern border. Thus, France wanted to strengthen and expand Poland, Czechoslovakia, Yugoslavia, and Romania as much as possible. Those states could then serve as barriers against Germany and Communist Russia.

As a result of compromises, almost every eastern European state was left with ethnic minorities: Germans in Poland; Hungarians, Poles, and Germans in Czechoslovakia; Hungarians in Romania, and the

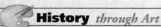

***Signing of the Treaty of Versailles* by John Christen Johansen, 1919** A peace settlement with Germany was signed at Versailles on June 28, 1919. What were the names of the representatives of the Big Three powers at the Paris Peace Conference?

combination of Serbs, Croats, Slovenes, Macedonians, and Albanians in Yugoslavia. The problem of ethnic minorities within nations would lead to later conflicts.

Yet another centuries-old empire—the Ottoman Empire—was broken up by the peace settlement. To gain Arab support against the Ottoman Turks during the war, the Western Allies had promised to recognize the independence of Arab states in the Ottoman Empire. Once the war was over, however, the Western nations changed their minds. France took control of Lebanon and Syria, and Britain received Iraq and Palestine.

These acquisitions were officially called mandates. Woodrow Wilson had opposed the outright annexation of colonial territories by the Allies. As a result, the peace settlement created the mandate system. According to this system, a nation officially governed another nation as a mandate on behalf of the League of Nations but did not own the territory.

The War's Legacy World War I shattered the liberal, rational society that had existed in late nineteenth- and early twentieth-century Europe. The death of almost 10 million people, as well as the incredible destruction caused by the war, undermined the whole idea of progress. Entire populations had participated in a devastating slaughter.

World War I was a total war—one that involved a complete mobilization of resources and people. As a result, the power of governments over the lives of their citizens increased. Freedom of the press and speech were limited in the name of national security. World War I made the practice of strong central authority a way of life.

The turmoil created by the war also seemed to open the door to even greater insecurity. Revolutions broke up old empires and created new states, which led to new problems. The hope that Europe and the rest of the world would return to normalcy was, however, soon dashed.

Reading Check **Identifying** What clause in the Treaty of Versailles particularly angered the Germans?

TAKS Practice

SECTION 4 ASSESSMENT

Checking for Understanding

1. **Define** armistice, reparation, mandate.

2. **Identify** Erich von Ludendorff, Friedrich Ebert, David Lloyd George, Georges Clemenceau.

3. **Locate** Kiel, Alsace, Lorraine, Poland.

4. **Explain** why the mandate system was created. Which countries became mandates? Who governed them?

5. **List** some of President Wilson's proposals for creating a truly just and lasting peace. Why did he feel the need to develop these proposals?

Critical Thinking

6. **Making Generalizations** Although Woodrow Wilson came to the Paris Peace Conference with high ideals, the other leaders had more practical concerns. Why do you think that was so?

7. **Compare and Contrast** Using a Venn diagram like the one below, compare and contrast Wilson's Fourteen Points to the Treaty of Versailles.

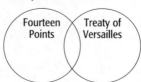

Fourteen Points — Treaty of Versailles

Analyzing Visuals

8. **Compare** the photograph of troops going to war on page 721 with the painting on page 715. How do you think the soldiers' expectations compared to their actual experiences?

Writing About History

9. **Informative Writing** You are a reporter for a large newspaper, sent to the Paris Peace Conference to interview one of the leaders of the Big Three. Prepare a written set of questions you would like to ask the leader you have selected.

CRITICAL THINKING
SKILLBUILDER

Interpreting Military Movements on Maps

Why Learn This Skill?

Although wars begin over many different issues, they end as fights to control territory. Because wars are basically fought over land, maps are particularly useful tools for seeing the "big picture" of a war.

Learning the Skill

The map key is essential in interpreting military maps. The key explains what the map's colors and symbols represent. Use the following steps to study the key:

- Determine the meanings of the colors on the map. Usually, colors represent different sides in the conflict.

- Identify all symbols. These may include symbols for battle sites, victories, and types of military units and equipment.

- Study the arrows, which show the direction of military movements. Because these movements occur over time, some maps give dates showing when and where troops advanced and retreated.

Once you have studied the key and the map, follow the progress of the campaign that is shown. Notice where each side began, in which direction it moved, where the two sides fought, and which side claimed victory.

Practicing the Skill

The map on this page shows the Middle East front during World War I. Study the map and then answer the following questions.

❶ On which side did Arabia and Egypt fight?

❷ Who won the battle at the Dardanelles?

❸ Describe the movement of the Central Powers offensives.

❹ When did the Allies win the most battles in the Middle East?

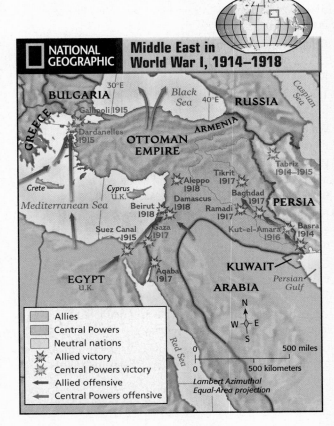

NATIONAL GEOGRAPHIC
Middle East in World War I, 1914–1918

Allies
Central Powers
Neutral nations
Allied victory
Central Powers victory
Allied offensive
Central Powers offensive

0 — 500 miles
0 — 500 kilometers
Lambert Azimuthal Equal-Area projection

Applying the Skill

Choose a military map from this text or select one from another source. Study the map selection carefully. Write a paragraph about the war or conflict as it is depicted in the map. You should respond to issues such as where most of the fighting occurred; the year in which the most significant advance was made, and by whom; and whether or not there was a decisive victory by either side. Attach a copy of the map to your report.

Glencoe's **Skillbuilder Interactive Workbook, Level 2,** provides instruction and practice in key social studies skills.

Using Key Terms

1. The practice of requiring young people to join the military, which was followed by many nations before World War I, was called _____.

2. Before World War I, many European nations completed the _____ of their military by assembling troops and supplies for war.

3. The development of _____ baffled military leaders who had been trained to fight wars of movement.

4. World War I became a _____, or war based on wearing the other side down by constant attacks and heavy losses.

5. World War I involved a complete mobilization of resources and people that affected the lives of all citizens in the warring countries—a situation called _____.

6. European nations set up _____, or systems directed by government agencies to mobilize the entire resources of their nations.

7. Councils of workers and soldiers called _____ challenged the provisional government established after Nicholas II stepped down.

8. _____ is the term used to describe the Communists' centralization of control over its economy.

9. Germany was required by the Treaty of Versailles to make payments called _____ to the nations that won the war.

Reviewing Key Facts

10. **Government** How did the British government try to eliminate opposition from the people who were opposed to World War I?

11. **Culture** Explain the social changes promised by the Bolshevik slogans.

12. **History** State the significance of the following dates: 1914, 1917, and 1918.

13. **Culture** Describe the role and contribution of women during World War I. What was their status after the war?

14. **History** Why were Alexandra and Rasputin able to control the czar's government during much of World War I?

15. **Government** How did international alliances help to draw nations into World War I?

16. **History** Why was a "breakthrough" such an important military goal during the war?

17. **Government** What did the creation of a League of Nations have to do with Woodrow Wilson's willingness to sign the Treaty of Versailles?

18. **History** Why did Russia withdraw from the war? How did that affect Germany?

19. **Science and Technology** What innovations in military warfare occurred during World War I?

Chapter Summary

The outline below shows four themes of the chapter.

Cooperation: Alliance System

- Two loose alliances form in Europe: the Triple Alliance (Germany, Austria-Hungary, and Italy) and the Triple Entente (France, Great Britain, and Russia).

- Alliances draw France and Great Britain into a conflict in which they have no direct interest.

Conflict: World War I

- Combat takes the forms of trench warfare on the Western Front, a war of movement on the Eastern Front, and German submarine warfare in the waters surrounding Great Britain.

- For the first time in history, airplanes are used for reconnaissance, combat, and bombing.

Revolution: Russian Revolution

- Military and economic crises lead to a spontaneous revolution that ends the reign of the czars.

- The Bolsheviks overthrow the provisional government and establish a Communist regime.

Internationalism: Peace of Paris

- The peace is a compromise between international and national interests.

- Germany's reparation payments, military reductions, and territorial losses create a lasting bitterness that helps spark World War II.

HISTORY Online

Self-Check Quiz
Visit the *Glencoe World History* Web site at
tx.wh.glencoe.com and click on **Chapter 23–Self-Check Quiz** to prepare for the Chapter Test.

Critical Thinking

20. **Decision Making** Compare Lenin's beliefs and goals with those of Woodrow Wilson. Which leader has had the greater impact on world history? Why?

21. **Analyzing** Why do some people feel that it is unlikely that a lasting peace could have been created at the end of World War I?

Writing about History

22. **Persuasive Writing** Both Britain and the United States passed laws during the war to silence opposition and censor the press. Are the ideals of a democratic government consistent with such laws? Provide arguments for and against.

Analyzing Sources

Reread the quote below, which appears on page 719, then answer the questions below.

> ❝I cannot tell you how exasperated people are getting here at the continual worry which that little country [Serbia] causes to Austria under encouragement from Russia. . . . It will be lucky if Europe succeeds in avoiding war as a result of the present crisis.❞

23. Where is Vienna located? Is the ambassador neutral in his comments or does he favor one country over another?

24. Compare the ways in which the actual events that started World War I mirror this ambassador's concerns.

Applying Technology Skills

25. **Interpreting the Past** Use the Internet to research the total costs of World War I. Determine how many people, both military and civilian, were killed or wounded on both sides. Also find the monetary costs of the war for both sides. Create a table that clearly shows your findings.

Making Decisions

26. Some historians argue that the heavy psychological and economic penalties placed on Germany by the Treaty of Versailles created the conditions for World War II. How might the treaty have been written to alleviate worldwide concern over German militarism without exacting such a heavy toll?

Paris Peace Conference: The Big Three

Country	United States	Great Britain	France
Leader	Wilson	Lloyd George	Clemenceau
Goal	Lasting peace	Germany pays	French security

Treaty of Versailles

International Relations	• League of Nations is formed.
Responsibility	• Germany accepts responsibility for starting the war and agrees to make reparations to the Allies.
Territory	• New nations are formed. • Germany returns Alsace and Lorraine to France. • France and Great Britain acquire mandates in the Middle East.
Military Strength	• Germany will reduce its army and navy and eliminate its air force. • German land along the Rhine River is demilitarized.

Analyzing Maps and Charts

Using the chart above, answer the following questions:

27. Which of the Big Three nations at the Treaty of Versailles wanted to punish Germany for World War I?

28. What was the effect of the Treaty of Versailles on Germany's military?

29. What territory did France regain after the war?

The Princeton Review — TAKS Test Practice

Directions: Choose the best answer to the following statement.

The role Russia played in World War I can best be described as

A a strong supporter of Germany and Austria.

B a strong supporter of France and Great Britain.

C a weak role due to the Russian Revolution.

D militarily strong because of its vast army.

Test-Taking Tip: An important word in this question is *best*. Although it is true that Russia entered on the side of France and Great Britain, it could never provide strong support due to internal weaknesses.

The West Between the Wars

1919–1939

Key Events

As you read this chapter, look for the key events in the history of the Western countries between the wars.
- *Europe faced severe economic problems after World War I, including inflation and the Great Depression.*
- *Dictatorial regimes began to spread into Italy, Germany, and across eastern Europe.*
- *The uncertainties and disillusionment of the times were reflected in the art and literature of the 1920s and 1930s.*

The Impact Today

The events that occurred during this time period still impact our lives today.
- *The current debate over the federal government's role in local affairs and social problems developed in part from Franklin D. Roosevelt's solution to the Great Depression.*
- *Automobiles, motion pictures, and radios transformed the ways in which people lived during the 1920s and 1930s and still impact how we live our lives today.*

 World History Video The Chapter 24 video, "The Rise of Dictators," chronicles the growth of dictatorial regimes in Europe after 1918.

Dorothea Lange's famous photograph, Migrant Mother, *1936, captured the human hardship and suffering resulting from the Great Depression.*

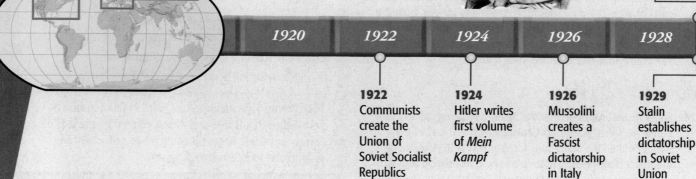

1929
The Great Depression begins

1920   1922   1924   1926   1928

1922
Communists create the Union of Soviet Socialist Republics

1924
Hitler writes first volume of *Mein Kampf*

1926
Mussolini creates a Fascist dictatorship in Italy

1929
Stalin establishes dictatorship in Soviet Union

Hitler and the Nazi Party used rallies, such as this one at Nuremberg in 1937, to create support for their policies.

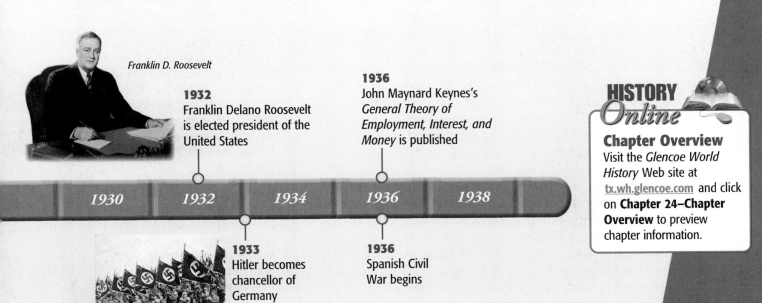

Franklin D. Roosevelt

1932
Franklin Delano Roosevelt is elected president of the United States

1936
John Maynard Keynes's *General Theory of Employment, Interest, and Money* is published

1930   1932   1934   1936   1938

1933
Hitler becomes chancellor of Germany

1936
Spanish Civil War begins

Flags of the Hitler Youth organization

HISTORY
Online

Chapter Overview
Visit the *Glencoe World History* Web site at tx.wh.glencoe.com and click on **Chapter 24–Chapter Overview** to preview chapter information.

A Story That Matters

During the Great Depression, many people had to resort to desperate measures to find food.

The Great Depression

After World War I, Europe was faced with severe economic problems. Most devastating of all was the Great Depression that began at the end of 1929. The Great Depression brought misery to millions of people. Begging for food on the streets became widespread, especially when soup kitchens were unable to keep up with the demand.

More and more people were homeless and moved around looking for work and shelter. One observer in Germany reported, "An almost unbroken chain of homeless men extends the whole length of the great Hamburg-Berlin highway . . . [w]hole families had piled all their goods into baby carriages and wheelbarrows that they were pushing along as they plodded forward in dumb despair." In the United States, the homeless set up shantytowns they named "Hoovervilles" after President Herbert Hoover.

In their misery, some people saw suicide as the only solution. One unemployed person said, "Today, when I am experiencing this for the first time, I think that I should prefer to do away with myself, to take gas, to jump into the river, or leap from some high place. . . . Would I really come to such a decision? I do not know."

Social unrest spread rapidly. Some of the unemployed staged hunger marches to get attention. In democratic countries, people began to listen to, and vote for, radical voices calling for extreme measures.

Why It Matters

In the 1920s, many people assumed that Europe and the world were about to enter a new era of international peace, economic growth, and political democracy. These hopes were not realized, however. Most people wanted peace but were unsure how to maintain it. Plans for economic revival gave way to inflation and then to the Great Depression. Making matters worse, economic hard times gave rise to dictatorial regimes across much of Europe. The world was filled with uncertainty.

History and You Make a diagram listing the problems faced by the United States, Germany, and France during the Great Depression. Indicate how the problems were interrelated. Using what you learn from your diagram, explain how recovery would also have a chain effect.

The Futile Search for Stability

Guide to Reading

Main Ideas
- Peace and prosperity were short-lived after World War I.
- After 1929, a global economic depression weakened the Western democracies.

Key Terms
depression, collective bargaining, deficit spending

People to Identify
John Maynard Keynes, Franklin Delano Roosevelt

Places to Locate
Ruhr Valley, Switzerland

Preview Questions
1. What was the significance of the Dawes Plan and the Treaty of Locarno?
2. How was Germany affected by the Great Depression?

Reading Strategy
Compare and Contrast Use a table like the one below to compare France's Popular Front with the New Deal in the United States.

Popular Front	New Deal

Preview of Events

♦1920	♦1925	♦1930	♦1935	♦1940

1921	1924	1925	1929	1935	1936
German debt determined	German debt restructured	Treaty of Locarno	U.S. stock market crashes	WPA is established	Popular Front is formed in France

Voices from the Past

On October 27, 1932, a group of workers marched in London to protest government policies. One observer reported:

❝By mid-day approximately 100,000 London workers were moving towards Hyde Park from all parts of London, to give the greatest welcome to the hunger marchers that had ever been seen in Hyde Park. . . . As the last contingent of marchers entered the park gates, trouble broke out with the police. It started with the special constables [police officers]; not being used to their task, they lost their heads, and, as the crowds swept forward on to the space where the meetings were to be held, the specials drew their truncheons [billy clubs] in an effort to control the sea of surging humanity. This incensed the workers, who turned on the constables and put them to flight.❞

—*Eyewitness to History,* John Carey, ed., 1987

Hunger marchers in London, 1932

Worker unrest was but one of the social problems in Europe in the 1920s and 1930s.

Uneasy Peace, Uncertain Security

The peace settlement at the end of World War I had tried to fulfill nineteenth-century dreams of nationalism by creating new boundaries and new states. From the beginning, however, the settlement left nations unhappy. Border disputes poisoned relations in eastern Europe for years. Many Germans vowed to revise the terms of the Treaty of Versailles.

A Weak League of Nations President Woodrow Wilson had realized that the peace settlement included unwise provisions that could serve as new causes for conflict. He had placed many of his hopes for the future in the League of Nations. This organization, however, was not very effective in maintaining the peace.

One problem was the failure of the United States to join the league. Most Americans did not wish to be involved in European affairs. The U.S. Senate, despite Wilson's wishes, refused to ratify, or approve, the Treaty of Versailles. That meant the United States could not be a member of the League of Nations, which automatically weakened the organization's effectiveness. As time would prove, the remaining League members could not agree to use force against aggression.

French Demands Between 1919 and 1924, desire for security led the French government to demand strict enforcement of the Treaty of Versailles. This tough policy toward Germany began with the issue of reparations, which were the payments that the Germans were supposed to make for the damage they had done in the war.

In April 1921, the Allied Reparations Commission determined that Germany owed 132 billion German marks (33 billion U.S. dollars) for reparations, payable in annual installments of 2.5 billion marks. The new German republic made its first payment in 1921.

North Sea

Ruhr Valley

Ruhr River

Rhine River

GERMANY

By the following year, however, the German government, faced with financial problems, announced that it was unable to pay any more. France was outraged and sent troops to occupy the **Ruhr Valley,** Germany's chief industrial and mining center. France planned to collect reparations by operating and using the Ruhr mines and factories.

Inflation in Germany The German government adopted a policy of passive resistance to French occupation. German workers went on strike, and the government mainly paid their salaries by printing more paper money. This only added to the inflation (rise in prices) that had already begun in Germany by the end of the war.

CONNECTIONS Around The World

The Great Flu Epidemic

A flu epidemic at the end of World War I proved disastrous to people all over the world. Some observers believe that it began among American soldiers in Kansas. When they were sent abroad to fight, they carried the virus to Europe. By the end of 1918, many soldiers in European armies had been stricken with the flu.

The disease spread quickly throughout Europe. The three chief statesmen at the peace conference— the American president Woodrow Wilson, the British prime minister David Lloyd George, and the French premier Georges Clemenceau— all were sick with the flu during the negotiations that led to the Treaty of Versailles.

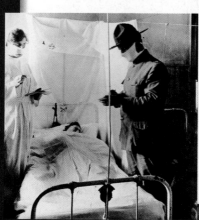

◄ *Flu victim*

The Spanish flu, as this strain of influenza was called, was known for its swift and deadly action. Many people died within a day of being infected. Complications also arose from bacterial infections in the lungs, which caused a deadly form of pneumonia.

In 1918 and 1919, the Spanish flu spread around the world with devastating results. Death tolls were enormous: in Russia, 450,000; in India, at least 6,000,000; in the United States, 550,000. It has been estimated that 22 million people, or more than twice the number of people killed in World War I, died from the great flu epidemic between 1918 and 1919.

Comparing Cultures

Using outside sources, research the medical advancements made since 1919 in treating and preventing influenza viruses. Could another flu epidemic occur today? Has the flu danger been replaced by other medical concerns?

The German mark soon became worthless. In 1914, 4.2 marks equaled 1 U.S. dollar. By November 1, 1923, it took 130 billion marks to equal 1 dollar. By the end of November, the ratio had increased to an incredible 4.2 trillion marks to 1 dollar.

Evidence of runaway inflation was everywhere. Workers used wheelbarrows to carry home their weekly pay. One woman left a basket of money outside while she went into a store. When she came out, the money was there, but the basket had been stolen.

Economic adversity led to political upheavals, and both France and Germany began to seek a way out of the disaster. In August 1924, an international commission produced a new plan for reparations. **The Dawes Plan,** named after the American banker who chaired the commission, first reduced reparations. It then coordinated Germany's annual payments with its ability to pay.

The Dawes Plan also granted an initial $200 million loan for German recovery. This loan soon opened the door to heavy American investment in Europe. A brief period of European prosperity followed, but it only lasted from 1924 to 1929.

The Treaty of Locarno With prosperity came a new European diplomacy. A spirit of cooperation was fostered by the foreign ministers of Germany and France, Gustav Stresemann and Aristide Briand. In 1925, they signed the **Treaty of Locarno,** which guaranteed Germany's new western borders with France and Belgium.

The Locarno pact was viewed by many as the beginning of a new era of European peace. On the day after the pact was concluded, the headlines in *The New York Times* read "France and Germany Ban War Forever." The London *Times* declared "Peace at Last."

The new spirit of cooperation grew even stronger when Germany joined the League of Nations in March 1926. Two years later, the Kellogg-Briand pact brought even more hope. Sixty-three nations signed this accord

NATIONAL GEOGRAPHIC — Europe, 1923

Territories administered by the League of Nations

Territory administered by the League of Nations

Lambert Azimuthal Equal-Area projection

Geography *Skills*

The new nationalism, as reflected by the European political map of the 1920s, did not solve Europe's problems after the war.

1. **Interpreting Maps** Compare the map above to the map of Europe before World War I on page 718. List all the countries shown on this map that are *not* shown on the earlier map. What does your list tell you about the political results of World War I?

2. **Applying Geography Skills** Again, compare the map above to the one on page 718. Create a two-column table. Label one column Changed Boundaries, and the other Unchanged Boundaries. List countries under the appropriate column.

written by U.S. secretary of state Frank B. Kellogg and French foreign minister Aristide Briand. These nations pledged "to renounce war as an instrument of national policy." Nothing was said, however, about what would be done if anyone violated the pact.

Unfortunately, the spirit of Locarno was based on little real substance. Promises not to go to war were worthless without a way to enforce these promises. Furthermore, not even the spirit of Locarno could convince nations to cut back on their weapons. The League of Nations Covenant had suggested that nations reduce their military forces to make war less probable. Germany, of course, had been forced to reduce its military forces. At the time, it was thought that other states would later do the same. However, states were simply unwilling to trust their security to anyone but their own military forces.

✓ **Reading Check** **Explaining** Why was the League of Nations unable to maintain peace?

The Great Depression

⌐TURNING**POINT**⌐ **In this section, you will learn how Western nations suffered a major economic collapse in the 1930s. This collapse, called the Great Depression, devastated morale, led to extremist political parties, and created the conditions for World War II.**

The brief period of prosperity that began in Europe in 1924 ended in an economic collapse that came to be known as the Great Depression. A depression is a period of low economic activity and rising unemployment.

Causes of the Depression Two factors played a major role in the start of the Great Depression. One important factor was a series of downturns in the economies of individual nations in the second half of the 1920s. By the mid-1920s, for example, prices for farm products, especially wheat, were falling rapidly because of overproduction.

The second factor in the coming of the Great Depression was an international financial crisis involving the U.S. stock market. We have seen that

much of the European prosperity between 1924 and 1929 was built on U.S. bank loans to Germany. Germany needed the U.S. loans to pay reparations to France and Great Britain.

During the 1920s, the U.S. stock market was booming. By 1928, American investors had begun to pull money out of Germany to invest it in the stock market. Then, in October 1929, the U.S. stock market crashed, and the prices of stocks plunged.

In a panic, U.S. investors withdrew even more funds from Germany and other European markets. This withdrawal weakened the banks of Germany and other European states. The Credit-Anstalt, Vienna's most famous bank, collapsed in May 1931. By then, trade was slowing down, industrial production was declining, and unemployment was rising.

Responses to the Depression Economic depression was by no means new to Europe. However, the extent of the economic downturn after 1929 truly made this the Great Depression. During 1932, the worst year of the depression, nearly one British worker in every four was unemployed. About six million Germans, or roughly 40 percent of the German labor force, were out of work at the same time. The unemployed and homeless filled the streets.

Governments did not know how to deal with the crisis. They tried a traditional solution of cutting costs by lowering wages and raising tariffs to exclude foreign goods from home markets. These measures made the economic crisis worse, however, and had serious political effects.

One effect of the economic crisis was increased government activity in the economy. This occurred even in countries that, like the United States, had a strong laissez-faire tradition—a belief that the government should not interfere in the economy.

Another effect was a renewed interest in Marxist doctrines. Marx's prediction that capitalism would destroy itself through overproduction seemed to be coming true. Communism thus became more popular, especially among workers and intellectuals.

Finally, the Great Depression led masses of people to follow political leaders who offered simple solutions in return for dictatorial power. Everywhere, democracy seemed on the defensive in the 1930s.

✓ **Reading Check** **Summarizing** What were the results of the Great Depression?

Economic downturns led to labor unrest in many countries.

Democratic States after the War

President Woodrow Wilson had claimed that the war had been fought to make the world safe for democracy. In 1919, his claim seemed justified. Most major European states and many minor ones had democratic governments.

In a number of states, women could now vote. Male political leaders had rewarded women for their contributions to the war effort by granting them voting rights. (Exceptions were France, Italy, and **Switzerland.** Women gained the right to vote in 1944 in France, 1945 in Italy, and 1971 in Switzerland.)

In the 1920s, Europe seemed to be returning to the political trends of the prewar era—parliamentary regimes and the growth of individual liberties. This was not, however, an easy process. Four years of total war and four years of postwar turmoil made a "return to normalcy" difficult.

Germany The Imperial Germany of William II had come to an end in 1918 with Germany's defeat in the war. A German democratic state known as the **Weimar** (VY•MAHR) **Republic** was then created. The Weimar Republic was plagued by problems.

For one thing, the republic had no truly outstanding political leaders. In 1925, Paul von Hindenburg, a World War I military hero, was elected president at the age of 77. Hindenburg was a traditional military man who did not fully endorse the republic he had been elected to serve.

The Weimar Republic also faced serious economic problems. As we have seen, Germany experienced runaway inflation in 1922 and 1923. With it came serious social problems. Widows, teachers, civil servants, and others who lived on fixed incomes all watched their monthly incomes become worthless, or their life savings disappear. These losses increasingly pushed the middle class toward political parties that were hostile to the republic.

To make matters worse, after a period of relative prosperity from 1924 to 1929, Germany was struck by the Great Depression. In 1930, unemployment had grown to 3 million people by March and to 4.38 million by December. The depression paved the way for fear and the rise of extremist parties.

France After the defeat of Germany, France became the strongest power on the European continent. Its greatest need was to rebuild the areas that had been devastated in the war. However, France, too, suffered financial problems after the war.

This German woman is using her worthless money to start a fire in her kitchen stove.

Because it had a more balanced economy than other nations, France did not begin to feel the full effects of the Great Depression until 1932. The economic instability it then suffered soon had political effects. During a nineteen-month period in 1932 and 1933, six different cabinets were formed as France faced political chaos. Finally, in June 1936, a coalition of leftist parties—Communists, Socialists, and Radicals—formed the Popular Front government.

The Popular Front started a program for workers that some have called the French New Deal. This program was named after the New Deal in the United States (discussed later in this section). The French New Deal gave workers the right to collective bargaining (the right of unions to negotiate with employers over wages and hours), a 40-hour workweek in industry, a two-week paid vacation, and a minimum wage.

The Popular Front's policies, however, failed to solve the problems of the depression. By 1938, the French had little confidence in their political system.

Great Britain During the war, Britain had lost many of the markets for its industrial products to the United

States and Japan. Such industries as coal, steel, and textiles declined after the war, leading to a rise in unemployment. In 1921, 2 million Britons were out of work. Britain soon rebounded, however, and experienced limited prosperity from 1925 to 1929.

By 1929, Britain faced the growing effects of the Great Depression. The Labour Party, which had become the largest party in Britain, failed to solve the nation's economic problems and fell from power in 1931. A new government, led by the Conservatives, claimed credit for bringing Britain out of the worst stages of the depression. It did so by using the traditional policies of balanced budgets and protective tariffs.

John Maynard Keynes

Political leaders in Britain largely ignored the new ideas of a British economist, **John Maynard Keynes,** who published his *General Theory of Employment, Interest, and Money* in 1936. He condemned the old theory that, in a free economy, depressions should be left to resolve themselves without governmental interference.

Keynes argued that unemployment came not from overproduction, but from a decline in demand. Demand, in turn, could be increased by putting people back to work building highways and public buildings. The government should finance such projects even if it had to engage in deficit spending, or had to go into debt.

The United States After Germany, no Western nation was more affected by the Great Depression than the United States. By 1932, U.S. industrial production had fallen almost 50 percent from its 1929 level. By 1933, there were more than 12 million unemployed.

Under these circumstances, the Democrat **Franklin Delano Roosevelt** was able to win a landslide victory in the 1932 presidential election. A believer in free enterprise, Roosevelt realized that capitalism had to be reformed if it was to be "saved." He pursued a policy of active government intervention in the economy known as the **New Deal.**

The New Deal included an increased program of public works, including the Works Progress Administration (WPA). The WPA, established in 1935, was a government organization that employed about 3 million people at its peak. They worked at building bridges, roads, post offices, and airports.

The Roosevelt administration was also responsible for new social legislation that began the U.S. welfare system. In 1935, the Social Security Act created a system of old-age pensions and unemployment insurance.

The New Deal provided reforms that perhaps prevented a social revolution in the United States. However, it did not solve the unemployment problems of the Great Depression. In 1938, American unemployment still stood at more than 10 million. Only World War II and the growth of weapons industries brought U.S. workers back to full employment.

✔️**Reading Check** **Explaining** What did John Maynard Keynes think would resolve the Great Depression?

🔶**TAKS Practice**

SECTION 1 ASSESSMENT

Checking for Understanding

1. **Define** depression, collective bargaining, deficit spending.

2. **Identify** Dawes Plan, Treaty of Locarno, John Maynard Keynes, Weimar Republic, Franklin Delano Roosevelt, New Deal.

3. **Locate** Ruhr Valley, Switzerland.

4. **Summarize** the intent of the Roosevelt administration's New Deal.

5. **List** the provisions of the Dawes Plan.

Critical Thinking

6. **Evaluate** Determine the validity of the following quotation: "Promises not to go to war were worthless without a way to enforce these promises."

7. **Cause and Effect** Use a diagram like the one below to list the causes of the Great Depression.

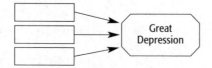

Analyzing Visuals

8. **Examine** the photograph on page 755. How would you survive if currency became worthless? Who would be at an advantage?

Writing About History

9. **Informative Writing** Research and write an essay that explains how the Great Depression caused extremist political parties to emerge throughout the world. Identify which parties are still active in the United States.

TAKS Practice

Analyzing Political Cartoons

Why Learn This Skill?

What is your favorite comic strip? Why do you read it? Many people enjoy comics because they use interesting or amusing visuals to convey a story or idea.

Cartoons do not only appear in the newspaper's funny pages. They are also in the editorial section, where they give opinions on political issues. Political cartoons have been around for centuries and are good historical sources because they reflect the popular views on current affairs.

Learning the Skill

Using caricature and symbols, political cartoonists help readers see relationships and draw conclusions about events. A caricature exaggerates a detail such as a subject's features. Cartoonists use caricature to create a positive or negative impression. For example, if a cartoon shows one figure three times larger than another, it implies that one figure is more powerful than the other.

A symbol is an image or object that represents something else. For example, a cartoonist may use a crown to represent monarchy. Symbols often represent nations or political parties. Uncle Sam is a common symbol for the United States.

To analyze a political cartoon:

- Examine the cartoon thoroughly.
- Identify the topic and principal characters.
- Read labels and messages.
- Note relationships between the figures and symbols.
- Determine what point the cartoon is making.

Practicing the Skill

In the next section of this chapter, you will be reading about several dictators who rose to power in Europe in the years following World War I.

The political cartoon on this page, published in 1938, makes a statement about these dictators and the reaction of the Western democracies toward them. Study the cartoon and then answer these questions.

❶ What do the figures represent?

❷ Why is the standing figure so large?

❸ What is the standing figure holding and what is it attached to?

❹ What is the sitting figure doing?

❺ What is the message of the cartoon?

WOULD YOU OBLIGE ME WITH A MATCH PLEASE?

David Low, *London Evening Standard*

Applying the Skill

Choose a current issue on which you hold a strong opinion. Draw a political cartoon expressing your opinion on this issue. Show it to a friend to find out if the message is clear. If not, revise the cartoon to clarify its point.

 Glencoe's **Skillbuilder Interactive Workbook, Level 2,** provides instruction and practice in key social studies skills.

The Rise of Dictatorial Regimes

Guide to Reading

Main Ideas
- Mussolini established a modern totalitarian state in Italy.
- As leader of the Soviet Union, Stalin eliminated people who threatened his power.

Key Terms
totalitarian state, fascism, New Economic Policy, Politburo, collectivization

People to Identify
Benito Mussolini, Joseph Stalin, Francisco Franco

Places to Locate
Russia, Madrid

Preview Questions
1. To what extent was Fascist Italy a totalitarian state?
2. How did Joseph Stalin establish a totalitarian regime in the Soviet Union?

Reading Strategy
Categorizing Information Use a web diagram like the one below to list methods used by Mussolini to create a Fascist dictatorship.

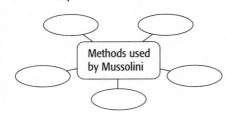

Methods used by Mussolini

Preview of Events

◆1920	◆1925	◆1930	◆1935	◆1940

1919
Mussolini creates the *Fascio di Combattimento*

1924
Lenin dies

1928
Stalin launches his First Five-Year Plan

1929
Mussolini recognizes independence of Vatican City

1939
The Spanish Civil War ends

Voices from the Past

Benito Mussolini

In 1932, Benito Mussolini, the dictator of Italy, published a statement of his movement's principles:

❝Anti-individualistic, the Fascist conception of life stresses the importance of the State and accepts the individual only in so far as his interests coincide with those of the State. . . . The Fascist conception of the State is all-embracing; outside of it no human or spiritual values can exist. Thus understood, fascism is totalitarian, and the Fascist State . . . interprets, develops, and potentiates [makes effective] the whole life of a people . . . fascism does not, generally speaking, believe in the possibility or utility of perpetual peace. . . . War alone keys up all human energies to their maximum tension and sets the seal of nobility on those people who have the courage to face it.❞
—**Benito Mussolini, "The Doctrine of Fascism,"** *Italian Fascisms,*
Adrian Lyttleton, ed., 1973

These were the principles of the movement Mussolini called fascism.

The Rise of Dictators

The apparent triumph of democracy in Europe in 1919 was extremely short-lived. By 1939, only two major European states—France and Great Britain—remained democratic. Italy, the Soviet Union, Germany, and many other European states adopted dictatorial regimes. These regimes took both old and new forms.

A new form of dictatorship was the modern totalitarian state. A totalitarian state is a government that aims to control the political, economic, social, intellectual, and cultural lives of its citizens. New totalitarian regimes pushed the power of the central state far beyond what it had been in the past.

These totalitarian states wanted more than passive obedience. They wanted to conquer the minds and hearts of their subjects. They achieved this goal through mass propaganda techniques and high-speed modern communication. Modern technology also provided totalitarian states with an unprecedented ability to impose their wishes on their subjects.

The totalitarian states that emerged were led by a single leader and a single party. They rejected the ideal of limited government power and the guarantee of individual freedoms. Instead, individual freedom was subordinated to the collective will of the masses. This collective will of the masses, however, was organized and determined by the leader. The totalitarian state expected the active involvement of the masses in the achievement of its goals, whether those goals included war, a socialist state, or a thousand-year empire like the one Adolf Hitler wanted to establish.

Reading Check **Summarizing** What is the goal of a totalitarian state?

Fascism in Italy

In the early 1920s, **Benito Mussolini** (MOO•suh•LEE•nee) established the first European fascist movement in Italy. Mussolini began his political career as a Socialist. In 1919, he created a new political group, the *Fascio di Combattimento,* or League of Combat. The term *fascism* is derived from that name.

As a political philosophy, fascism (FA•SHIH•zuhm) glorifies the state above the individual by emphasizing the need for a strong central government led by a dictatorial ruler. In a fascist state, people are controlled by the government, and any opposition is suppressed.

Rise of Fascism Like other European countries, Italy experienced severe economic problems after World War I. Inflation grew, and both industrial and agricultural workers staged strikes. Socialists spoke of revolution. The middle class began to fear a Communist takeover like the one that had recently occurred in **Russia.** Industrial and agricultural strikes created more division. Mussolini emerged from this background of widespread unrest.

NATIONAL GEOGRAPHIC

Politics of Europe, 1930s

- ☐ Authoritarian
- ☐ Democratic
- ☐ Fascist

Geography *Skills*

Many European countries adopted dictatorial regimes to solve their problems in the 1920s and 1930s.

1. **Interpreting Maps** Which countries shown on the map above are Fascist? Which are authoritarian? Which are democratic states?

2. **Applying Geography Skills** Pose and answer a question that creates a comparison between a country's political status as shown on this map and the side that country fought on in World War I.

In 1920 and 1921, Mussolini formed bands of black-shirted, armed Fascists called *squadristi* or Blackshirts. These bands attacked socialist offices and newspapers. They also used violence to break up strikes. Both middle-class industrialists who feared working-class strikes and large landowners who objected to agricultural strikes began to support Mussolini's Fascist movement.

By 1922, Mussolini's movement was growing quickly. The middle-class fear of socialism, communism, and disorder made the Fascists increasingly attractive to many people. In addition, Mussolini realized that the Italian people were angry over Italy's failure to receive more land in the peace settlement that followed the war. He understood that nationalism was a powerful force. Thus, he demanded more land for Italy and won thousands of converts to fascism with his patriotic and nationalistic appeals.

Benito Mussolini
1883–1945—Italian dictator

Benito Mussolini was the founder of the first Fascist movement. He was an unruly and rebellious child who was expelled from school once for stabbing a fellow pupil. Ultimately, he received a diploma and worked for a short time as an elementary school teacher.

Mussolini became a Socialist and gradually became well known in Italian Socialist circles. In 1912, he obtained the important position of editor of *Avanti (Forward)*, the official Socialist daily newspaper.

After being expelled from the Socialist Party, he formed his own political movement, the Fascist movement. When the Fascists did poorly in the Italian election of November 1919, Mussolini said that fascism had "come to a dead end." He then toyed with the idea of emigrating to the United States to become a journalist.

In 1922, Mussolini and the Fascists threatened to march on Rome if they were not given power. Mussolini exclaimed, "Either we are allowed to govern, or we will seize power." Victor Emmanuel III, the king of Italy, gave in and made Mussolini prime minister.

Mussolini used his position as prime minister to create a Fascist dictatorship. New laws gave the government the right to suspend any publications that criticized the Catholic Church, the monarchy, or the state. The prime minister was made head of the government with the power to make laws by decree. The police were given unrestricted authority to arrest and jail anyone for either nonpolitical or political crimes.

In 1926, the Fascists outlawed all other political parties in Italy and established a secret police, known as the OVRA. By the end of the year, Mussolini ruled Italy as *Il Duce* (eel DOO•chay), "The Leader."

The Fascist State   Since Mussolini believed that the Fascist state should be totalitarian, he used various means to establish complete control over the Italian people. As we have seen, Mussolini created a secret police force, the OVRA, whose purpose was to watch citizens' political activities and enforce government policies. Police actions in Italy, however, were never as repressive or savage as those in Nazi Germany (discussed later in this chapter).

The Italian Fascists also tried to exercise control over all forms of mass media, including newspapers, radio, and film. The media was used to spread propaganda. Propaganda was intended to mold Italians into a single-minded Fascist community. Most Italian Fascist propaganda, however, was fairly unsophisticated and mainly consisted of simple slogans like "Mussolini Is Always Right."

The Fascists also used organizations to promote the ideals of fascism and to control the population. For example, by 1939, Fascist youth groups included about 66 percent of the population between the ages of 8 and 18. These youth groups particularly focused on military activities and values.

With these organizations, the Fascists hoped to create a nation of new Italians who were fit, disciplined, and war-loving. In practice, however, the Fascists largely maintained traditional social attitudes. This is especially evident in their policies regarding women. The Fascists portrayed the family as the pillar of the state and women as the foundation of the family. Women were to be homemakers and mothers, which was "their natural and fundamental mission in life," according to Mussolini.

Despite his attempts, Mussolini never achieved the degree of totalitarian control seen in Hitler's Germany or Stalin's Soviet Union (discussed later in this chapter). The Italian Fascist Party did not completely destroy the country's old power structure. Some institutions, including the armed forces, were not absorbed into the Fascist state but managed to keep most of their independence. Victor Emmanuel was also retained as king.

Mussolini's compromise with the traditional institutions of Italy was especially evident in his relationship with the Catholic Church. In the Lateran Accords of February 1929, Mussolini's regime recognized the sovereign independence of a small area within Rome known as Vatican City. The Church had claimed this area since 1870. When Mussolini formally recognized that claim, the pope then recognized the Italian state.

Mussolini's regime also gave the Church a large grant of money and recognized Catholicism as the "sole religion of the state." In return, the Catholic Church urged Italians to support the Fascist regime.

In all areas of Italian life under Mussolini and the Fascists, there was a large gap between Fascist ideals and practices. The Italian Fascists promised

HISTORY Online

Web Activity Visit the *Glencoe World History* Web site at tx.wh.glencoe.com and click on **Chapter 24– Student Web Activity** to learn more about the rise of fascism.

much but delivered considerably less. They would soon be overshadowed by a much more powerful Fascist movement to the north—that of Adolf Hitler, a student and admirer of Mussolini.

✓ **Reading Check** **Examining** How did Mussolini gain power in Italy?

A New Era in the Soviet Union

As we have seen, Lenin followed a policy of war communism during the civil war in Russia. The government controlled most industries and seized grain from peasants to ensure supplies for the army.

Once the war was over, peasants began to sabotage the communist program by hoarding food. The situation became even worse when drought caused a great famine between 1920 and 1922. As many as 5 million lives were lost. With agricultural disaster came industrial collapse. By 1921, industrial output was only 20 percent of its 1913 level.

Russia was exhausted. A peasant banner proclaimed, "Down with Lenin and horseflesh. Bring back the czar and pork." As Leon Trotsky said, "The country, and the government with it, were at the very edge of the abyss."

Lenin's New Economic Policy In March 1921, Lenin pulled Russia back from the abyss. He abandoned war communism in favor of his New Economic Policy (NEP). The NEP was a modified version of the old capitalist system. Peasants were allowed to sell their produce openly. Retail stores, as well as small industries that employed fewer than 20 workers, could be privately owned and operated. Heavy industry, banking, and mines, however, remained in the hands of the government.

In 1922, Lenin and the Communists formally created a new state called the Union of Soviet Socialist Republics, which is also known as the USSR (by its initials), or as the Soviet Union (by its shortened form). By that time, a revived market and a good harvest had brought an end to famine. Soviet agricultural production climbed to 75 percent of its prewar level.

Overall, the NEP saved the Soviet Union from complete economic disaster. Lenin and other leading Communists, however, only intended the NEP to be a temporary retreat from the goals of communism.

The Rise of Stalin Lenin died in 1924. A struggle for power began at once among the seven members of the Politburo (PAH•luht•BYOOR•OH)—a commit-tee that had become the leading policy-making body of the Communist Party. The Politburo was severely divided over the future direction of the Soviet Union.

One group, led by Leon Trotsky, wanted to end the NEP and launch Russia on a path of rapid industrialization, chiefly at the expense of the peasants. This group also wanted to spread communism abroad and believed that the revolution in Russia would not survive without other communist states.

Another group in the Politburo rejected the idea of worldwide communist revolution. Instead, it wanted to focus on building a socialist state in Russia and to continue Lenin's NEP. This group believed that rapid industrialization would harm the living standards of the Soviet peasants.

These divisions were underscored by an intense personal rivalry between Leon Trotsky and another Politburo member, **Joseph Stalin.** In 1924, Trotsky held the post of commissar of war. Stalin held the bureaucratic job of party general secretary. Because the general secretary appointed regional, district, city, and town party officials, this bureaucratic job actually became the most important position in the party.

Stalin used his post as general secretary to gain complete control of the Communist Party. The thousands of officials Stalin appointed provided him with support in his bid for power. By 1929, Stalin had eliminated from the Politburo the Bolsheviks of the revolutionary era and had established a powerful

People In History

Joseph Stalin
1879–1953—Soviet dictator

Joseph Stalin established a strong personal dictatorship over the Soviet Union. He joined the Bolsheviks in 1903 and came to Lenin's attention after staging a daring bank robbery to get funds for the Bolshevik cause. His real last name was Dzhugashvili, but he adopted the name Stalin, which means "man of steel."

Stalin was neither a dynamic speaker nor a forceful writer. He was a good organizer, however. His fellow Bolsheviks called him "Comrade Index-Card."

Like Hitler, Stalin was one of the greatest mass murderers in human history. It is estimated that his policies and his deliberate executions led to the death of as many as 25 million people. At the time of his death in 1953, he was planning yet another purge of party members.

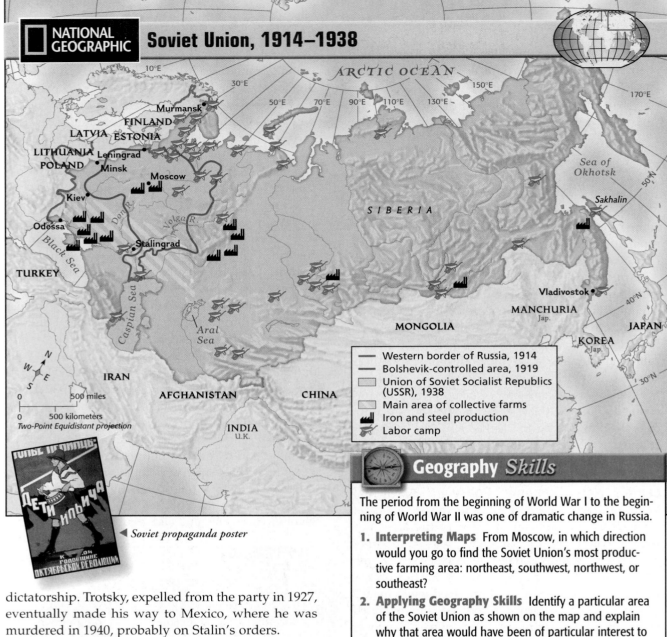

Soviet Union, 1914–1938

Map legend:
- Western border of Russia, 1914
- Bolshevik-controlled area, 1919
- Union of Soviet Socialist Republics (USSR), 1938
- Main area of collective farms
- Iron and steel production
- Labor camp

◀ *Soviet propaganda poster*

Geography Skills

The period from the beginning of World War I to the beginning of World War II was one of dramatic change in Russia.

1. **Interpreting Maps** From Moscow, in which direction would you go to find the Soviet Union's most productive farming area: northeast, southwest, northwest, or southeast?
2. **Applying Geography Skills** Identify a particular area of the Soviet Union as shown on the map and explain why that area would have been of particular interest to Stalin during his First Five-Year Plan.

dictatorship. Trotsky, expelled from the party in 1927, eventually made his way to Mexico, where he was murdered in 1940, probably on Stalin's orders.

Five-Year Plans The Stalinist Era marked the beginning of an economic, social, and political revolution that was more sweeping in its results than were the revolutions of 1917. Stalin made a significant shift in economic policy in 1928 when he ended the NEP and launched his First Five-Year Plan. The **Five-Year Plans** set economic goals for five-year periods. Their purpose was to transform Russia virtually overnight from an agricultural into an industrial country.

The First Five-Year Plan emphasized maximum production of capital goods (goods devoted to the production of other goods, such as heavy machines) and armaments. The plan quadrupled the production of heavy machinery and doubled oil production. Between 1928 and 1937, during the first two Five-Year Plans, steel production in Russia increased from 4 million to 18 million tons (3.628 to 16.326 million t) per year.

The social and political costs of industrialization were enormous. Little provision was made for caring for the expanded labor force in the cities. The number of workers increased by millions between 1932 and 1940, but total investment in housing actually declined after 1929. The result was that millions of workers and their families lived in pitiful conditions. Real wages in industry also declined by 43 percent between 1928 and 1940. Strict laws even limited where workers could move. To keep workers content, government propaganda stressed the need for sacrifice to create the new socialist state.

With rapid industrialization came an equally rapid collectivization of agriculture. **Collectivization** was a system in which private farms were eliminated. Instead, the government owned all of the land, while the peasants worked it.

Strong resistance to Stalin's plans came from peasants, who responded by hoarding crops and killing livestock. However, these actions only led Stalin to step up the program. By 1930, 10 million peasant households had been collectivized. By 1934, 26 million family farms had been collectivized into 250,000 units.

Costs of Stalin's Programs Collectivization was done at tremendous cost. The hoarding of food and the slaughter of livestock produced widespread famine. Stalin himself is supposed to have said that 10 million peasants died in the famines of 1932 and 1933. The only concession Stalin made to the peasants was that each collective farm worker was allowed to have one tiny, privately owned garden plot.

Stalin's programs had other costs as well. To achieve his goals, Stalin strengthened his control over the party bureaucracy. Those who resisted were sent into forced labor camps in Siberia.

Stalin's desire to make all decisions by himself also led to purges, or removals, of the Old Bolsheviks—those who had been involved in the early days of the movement. Between 1936 and 1938, the most promi-nent Old Bolsheviks were put on trial and condemned to death.

During this same time, Stalin purged army officers, diplomats, union officials, party members, intellectuals, and numerous ordinary citizens. An estimated eight million Russians were arrested. Millions were sent to forced labor camps in Siberia, from which they never returned. Others were executed.

The Stalin Era also overturned much of the permissive social legislation that was enacted in the early 1920s. To promote equal rights for women, the Communists had made the divorce process easier, and they had also encouraged women to work outside the home. After Stalin came to power, the family was praised as a small collective in which parents were responsible for teaching the values of hard work, duty, and discipline to their children. Divorced fathers who did not support their children were heavily fined.

Reading Check **Summarizing** What was Lenin's New Economic Policy?

Authoritarian States in the West

A number of governments in the Western world were not totalitarian but were authoritarian. These states adopted some of the features of totalitarian states, in particular, their use of police powers. However, the main concern of these authoritarian governments was not to create a new kind of mass society, but to preserve the existing social order.

Eastern Europe Some of these governments were found among the new states of eastern Europe. At first, it seemed that political democracy would become well established in eastern Europe after the war. Austria, Poland, Czechoslovakia, Yugoslavia (known as the kingdom of the Serbs, Croats, and Slovenes until 1929), Romania, Bulgaria, and Hungary all adopted parliamentary systems. However, most of these systems were soon replaced by authoritarian regimes.

Parliamentary systems failed in most eastern European states for several reasons. These states had little tradition of political democracy. In addition, they were mostly rural and agrarian. Many of the peasants were illiterate, and much of the land was still dominated by large landowners who feared the peasants. Ethnic conflicts also threatened these countries.

Powerful landowners, the churches, and even some members of the small middle class feared land

What If...

Trotsky had succeeded Lenin?

Lenin's death in 1924 caused a bitter political struggle to determine his successor. Although he had no influence over the final outcome, Lenin's testament, written in December 1922, predicted a split between Trotsky and Stalin. In his testament, read to delegates at the Thirteenth Congress, Lenin advised removing Stalin from his post as general secretary to prevent a power struggle.

Consider the Consequences Consider what would have happened if Stalin had not maintained his position of influence and had lost to Trotsky. Research Trotsky's beliefs, then write a short essay describing the direction the Soviet Union would have taken under his leadership.

Guernica **by Pablo Picasso, 1937**
This famous painting is a strong anti-war statement. What do the images say about the realities of war?

reform, communist upheaval, and ethnic conflict. For this reason these groups looked to authoritarian governments to maintain the old system. Only Czechoslovakia, which had a large middle class, a liberal tradition, and a strong industrial base, maintained its political democracy.

Spain In Spain, too, political democracy failed to survive. Led by General **Francisco Franco,** Spanish military forces revolted against the democratic government in 1936. A brutal and bloody civil war began.

Foreign intervention complicated the Spanish Civil War. The Fascist regimes of Italy and Germany aided Franco's forces with arms, money, and men. Hitler used the Spanish Civil War as an opportunity to test the new weapons of his revived air force. The horrible destruction of Guernica by German bombers

in April 1937 was immortalized in a painting by the Spanish artist Pablo Picasso.

The Spanish republican government was aided by forty thousand foreign volunteers and by trucks, planes, tanks, and military advisers from the Soviet Union.

The Spanish Civil War came to an end when Franco's forces captured **Madrid** in 1939. Franco established a dictatorship that favored large landowners, businesspeople, and the Catholic clergy. Because it favored traditional groups and did not try to control every aspect of people's lives, Franco's dictatorship is an example of a regime that was authoritarian rather than totalitarian.

Reading Check **Explaining** How did Czechoslovakia maintain its political democracy?

TAKS Practice

SECTION 2 ASSESSMENT

Checking for Understanding

1. **Define** totalitarian state, fascism, New Economic Policy, Politburo, collectivization.

2. **Identify** Benito Mussolini, Joseph Stalin, Five-Year Plan, Francisco Franco.

3. **Locate** Russia, Madrid.

4. **Explain** how Stalin gained control of the Communist Party after Lenin died.

5. **List** the countries that participated in the Spanish Civil War.

Critical Thinking

6. **Evaluate** What was the major purpose of the Five-Year Plans during the 1920s and 1930s in the Soviet Union?

7. **Organizing Information** Use a diagram like the one below to identify ways in which Stalin changed the Soviet Union. Include the economic, social, and political results of his programs.

> How Stalin Changed the Soviet Union

Analyzing Visuals

8. **Contrast** the above painting with the rally photo on page 749. Both images make political statements about war and militarism. How do they differ? How are they similar? Which makes the strongest statement?

Writing About History

9. **Persuasive Writing** What were the pros and cons of Mussolini's rule? In an essay, argue whether or not Mussolini was good for Italy. Conduct research to support your position and base your statements on fact.

The Formation of Collective Farms

THE COLLECTIVIZATION OF AGRICULTURE transformed Russia's 26 million family farms into 250,000 collective farms (*kolkhozes*). In this first-hand account, we see how the process worked.

❝General collectivization in our village was brought about in the following manner: Two representatives of the [Communist] Party arrived in the village. All the inhabitants were summoned by the ringing of the church bell to a meeting at which the policy of general collectivization was announced. . . . Although the meeting lasted two days, from the viewpoint of the Party representatives, nothing was accomplished.

After this setback, two more officials were sent to reinforce the first two. A meeting of our section of the village was held in a stable which had previously belonged to a kulak [wealthy peasant farmer]. The meeting dragged on until dark. Suddenly someone threw a brick at the lamp, and in the dark the peasants began to beat the Party representatives who jumped out the window and escaped from the village barely alive. The following day seven people were arrested. The militia was called in and stayed in the village until the peasants, realizing their helplessness, calmed down. . . .

By the end of 1930 there were two kolkhozes in our village. Though at first these collectives embraced at most only 70 percent of the peasant households, in the months that followed they gradually absorbed more and more of them.

In these kolkhozes the great bulk of the land was held and worked communally, but each peasant household owned a house of some sort, a small plot of ground and perhaps some livestock. All the members of the kolkhoz were required to work on the kolkhoz a certain number of days each month; the rest of the time they were allowed to work on their own holdings. They derived their income partly from what they grew on their garden strips and partly from their work in the kolkhoz.

When the harvest was over, and after the farm had met its obligations to the state and to various

Russian peasants using scythes to harvest grain

special funds and had sold on the market whatever undesignated produce was left, the remaining produce and the farm's monetary income were divided among the kolkhoz members according to the number of 'labor days' each one had contributed to the farm's work. . . . After they had received their earnings, one of them remarked, 'You will live, but you will be very, very thin. . . .' By late 1932 more than 80 percent of the peasant households had been collectivized.❞

—Max Belov, *The History of a Collective Farm*

Analyzing Primary Sources

1. Why did the peasants resist the collective farms?
2. How would you characterize the writer's description of the collectivization process in his village? Was he fair and objective; or, do you think that he reveals a bias either for or against the process? Explain and support your answer using excerpts from his description.

Hitler and Nazi Germany

Guide to Reading

Main Ideas
- Hitler and the Nazi Party established a totalitarian state in Germany.
- Many Germans accepted the Nazi dictatorship, while other Germans suffered greatly under Hitler's rule.

Key Terms
Reichstag, concentration camp

People to Identify
Adolf Hitler, Heinrich Himmler

Places to Locate
Munich, Nuremberg

Preview Questions
1. How did Adolf Hitler rise to power?
2. What were the chief features of the Nazi totalitarian state?
3. How did the rise of Nazism affect Germany?

Reading Strategy
Categorizing Information Use a chart like the one below to list anti-Semitic policies enforced by the Nazi Party.

Anti-Semitic Policies

Preview of Events

♦1880	♦1890	♦1900	♦1910	♦1920	♦1930	♦1940

1889
Hitler is born

1921
Hitler takes control of the National Socialist German Workers' Party

1933
Reichstag passes Enabling Act

1935
Nazis enact Nuremberg laws

1938
The Kristallnacht occurs

Voices from the Past

Adolf Hitler

In September 1936, Adolf Hitler spoke to a mass rally in the city of Nuremberg:

❝Do we not feel once again in this hour the miracle that brought us together? Once you heard the voice of a man, and it struck deep into your hearts; it awakened you, and you followed this voice. . . . When we meet each other here, the wonder of our coming together fills us all. Not everyone of you sees me, and I do not see everyone of you. But I feel you, and you feel me. It is the belief in our people that has made us small men great, that has made brave and courageous men out of us wavering, timid folk; this belief . . . joined us together into one whole! . . . You come, that you may, once in a while, gain the feeling that now we are together; we are with him and he with us, and we are now Germany!❞

— ***The Speeches of Adolf Hitler,*** Norman Baynes, ed., **1942**

Hitler worked to create an emotional bond between himself and the German people.

Hitler and His Views

Adolf Hitler was born in Austria on April 20, 1889. A failure in secondary school, he eventually traveled to Vienna to become an artist but was rejected by the Vienna Academy of Fine Arts. He stayed in the city, supported at first by an inheritance. While in Vienna, however, Hitler developed his basic ideas, which he held for the rest of his life.

At the core of Hitler's ideas was racism, especially anti-Semitism. Hitler was also an extreme nationalist who understood how political parties could effectively use propaganda and terror. Finally, during his Viennese years, Hitler came to believe firmly in the need for struggle, which he saw as the "granite foundation of the world."

At the end of World War I, after four years of service on the Western Front, Hitler remained in Germany and decided to enter politics. In 1919, he joined the little-known German Workers' Party, one of several right-wing extreme nationalist parties in **Munich.**

By the summer of 1921, Hitler had taken total control of the party, which by then had been renamed the **National Socialist German Workers' Party** (NSDAP), or Nazi for short. Within two years, party membership had grown to 55,000 people, with 15,000 in the party militia. The militia was variously known as the SA, the Storm Troops, or the Brownshirts, after the color of their uniforms.

An overconfident Hitler staged an armed uprising against the government in Munich in November 1923. This uprising, called the Beer Hall Putsch, was quickly crushed, and Hitler was sentenced to prison. During his brief stay in jail, Hitler wrote *Mein Kampf,* or *My Struggle,* an account of his movement and its basic ideas.

In *Mein Kampf,* extreme German nationalism, strong anti-Semitism, and anticommunism are linked together by a social Darwinian theory of struggle. This theory emphasizes the right of superior nations to lebensraum (LAY•buhnz•ROWM)—living space—through expansion. It also upholds the right of superior individuals to gain authoritarian leadership over the masses.

✔**Reading Check** **Summarizing** What main ideas does Hitler express in his book *Mein Kampf?*

Rise of Nazism

While he was in prison, Hitler realized that the Nazis would have to attain power by legal means, and not by a violent overthrow of the Weimar Republic. This meant that the Nazi Party would have to be a mass political party that could compete for votes with the other political parties.

After his release from prison, Hitler expanded the Nazi Party to all parts of Germany. By 1929, it had a national party organization. Three years later, it had 800,000 members and had become the largest party in the Reichstag—the German parliament.

No doubt, Germany's economic difficulties were a crucial factor in the Nazi rise to power. Unemployment had risen dramatically, growing from 4.35 million in 1931 to 6 million by the winter of 1932. The economic and psychological impact of the Great Depression made extremist parties more attractive.

Hitler promised to create a new Germany. His appeals to national pride, national honor, and traditional militarism struck an emotional chord in his listeners. After attending one of Hitler's rallies, a schoolteacher in Hamburg said, "When the speech was over, there was roaring enthusiasm and applause. . . . —How many look up to him with

Picturing **History**

In *Mein Kampf,* Hitler wrote that mass meetings were important because individuals who feel weak and uncertain become intoxicated with the power of the group. **How do you think Hitler viewed the average person?**

touching faith as their helper, their saviour, their deliverer from unbearable distress."

✓ **Reading Check** **Explaining** What factors helped the Nazi Party to gain power in Germany?

Victory of Nazism

After 1930, the German government ruled by decree with the support of President Hindenburg. The Reichstag had little power, and thus Hitler clearly saw that controlling the parliament was not very important.

More and more, the right-wing elites of Germany—the industrial leaders, landed aristocrats, military officers, and higher bureaucrats—looked to Hitler for leadership. He had the mass support to create a right-wing, authoritarian regime that would save Germany and people in privileged positions from a Communist takeover. In 1933, Hindenburg, under pressure, agreed to allow Hitler to become chancellor and create a new government.

Within two months, Hitler had laid the foundation for the Nazis' complete control over Germany. The crowning step of Hitler's "legal seizure" of power came on March 23, 1933, when a two-thirds vote of the Reichstag passed the **Enabling Act.** This law gave the government the power to ignore the constitution for four years while it issued laws to deal with the country's problems.

The Enabling Act gave Hitler's later actions a legal basis. He no longer needed the Reichstag or President Hindenburg. In effect, Hitler became a dictator appointed by the parliamentary body itself.

With their new source of power, the Nazis acted quickly to bring all institutions under Nazi control. The civil service was purged of Jews and democratic elements. Large prison camps called concentration camps were set up for people who opposed the new regime. Trade unions were dissolved. All political parties except the Nazis were abolished.

By the end of the summer of 1933, only seven months after being appointed chancellor, Hitler had established the basis for a totalitarian state. When Hindenburg died in 1934, the office of president was abolished. Hitler became sole ruler of Germany. Public officials and soldiers were all required to take a personal oath of loyalty to Hitler as their *Führer* (FYUR•uhr), or "Leader."

✓ **Reading Check** **Examining** Why was the Enabling Act important to Hitler's success in controlling Germany?

THE WAY IT WAS

YOUNG PEOPLE IN . . .

Nazi Germany

In setting up a totalitarian state, the Nazis recognized the importance of winning young people over to their ideas. The Hitler Youth, an organization for young people between the ages of 10 and 18, was formed in 1926 for that purpose.

By 1939, all German young people were expected to join the Hitler Youth. Upon entering, each took an oath: "In the presence of this blood banner [Nazi flag], which represents our Führer, I swear to devote all my energies and my strength to the savior of our country, Adolf Hitler. I am

Young Germans waving flags

willing and ready to give up my life for him, so help me God."

Members of the Hitler Youth had their own uniforms and took part in a number of activities. For males, these included camping and hiking trips, sports activities, and evenings together in special youth "homes." Almost all activities were competitive and meant to encourage fighting and heroic deeds.

Above all, the Hitler Youth organization worked to foster military values and virtues, such as duty, obedience, strength, and ruthlessness. Uniforms and drilling became

The Nazi State, 1933–1939

Hitler wanted to develop a totalitarian state. He had not simply sought power for power's sake. He had a larger goal—the development of an **Aryan** racial state that would dominate Europe and possibly the world for generations to come. (*Aryan* was a term linguists used to identify people speaking Indo-European languages. The Nazis misused the term and identified the Aryans with the ancient Greeks and Romans and twentieth-century Germans and Scandinavians.) Nazis thought the Germans were the true descendants and leaders of the Aryans and would create another empire like the one ruled by the ancient Romans. The Nazis believed that the world had already seen two German empires or Reichs: the Holy Roman Empire and the German Empire of 1871 to 1918. It was Hitler's goal to create a Third Reich, the empire of Nazi Germany.

To achieve his goal, Hitler needed the active involvement of the German people. Hitler stated:

> ❝We must develop organizations in which an individual's entire life can take place. Then every activity and every need of every individual will be regulated by the collectivity represented by the party. There is no longer any arbitrary will, there are no longer any free realms in which the individual belongs to himself. . . . The time of personal happiness is over.❞

The Nazis pursued the creation of the totalitarian state in a variety of ways. Economic policies, mass spectacles, and organizations—both old and new—were employed to further Nazi goals. Terror was freely used. Policies toward women and, in particular, Jews reflected Nazi aims.

The State and Terror Nazi Germany was the scene of almost constant personal and institutional conflict. This resulted in administrative chaos. Struggle was a basic feature of relationships within the party, within the state, and between party and state. Hitler, of course, was the ultimate decision maker and absolute ruler.

For those who needed coercion, the Nazi totalitarian state used terror and repression. The *Schutzstaffeln* ("Guard Squadrons"), known simply as the SS, were an important force for maintaining order. The SS was originally created as Hitler's personal bodyguard. Under the direction of **Heinrich Himmler,** the SS came to control not only the secret police forces that Himmler had set up, but also the regular police forces.

a way of life. By 1938, training in the military arts was also part of the routine. Even boys 10 to 14 years old were given small-arms drill and practice with dummy hand grenades. Those who were 14 to 18 years old bore army packs and rifles while on camping trips in the countryside.

The Hitler Youth had a female division, known as the League of German Girls, for girls aged 10 to 18. They, too, had uniforms: white blouses, blue ankle-length skirts, and sturdy hiking shoes. Camping and hiking were also part of the girls' activities. More important, however, girls were taught domestic skills—how to cook, clean houses, and take care of children. In Nazi Germany, women were expected to be faithful wives and dutiful mothers.

Many German children were proud of being part of the Hitler Youth.

CONNECTING TO THE PAST

1. **Explaining** What ideals and values did the Hitler Youth promote?

2. **Analyzing** How did the Hitler Youth help support the Nazi attempt to create a total state?

3. **Writing about History** Do organizations like the Hitler Youth exist today in the United States? How are they similar or different?

Three Dictators: Mussolini, Stalin, and Hitler

	Benito Mussolini (1883–1945)	Joseph Stalin (1879–1953)	Adolf Hitler (1889–1945)
Country	Italy	USSR	Germany
Political Title	Prime Minister	General Secretary	Chancellor
Date in Power	1922	1929	1933
Political Party	Fascist Party	Communist Party	National Socialist German Workers' Party (NSDAP, or Nazi)
Type of Government	Fascist	Communist	Fascist
Source(s) of Support	Middle-class industrialists and large land owners	Party officials	Industrial leaders, landed aristocrats, military, and bureaucracy
Methods of Controlling Opposition	Secret police (OVRA), imprisonment, outlawing other parties, propaganda, censorship of the press	Purges, prison camps, secret police, state-run press, forced labor camps, executions	*Schutzstaffeln* (SS) police force, propaganda, state-run press, terror, repression, racial laws, concentration and death camps
Policies	Support for Catholic Church, nationalism, antisocialism, anticommunism	Five-Year Plans for rapid industrialization, collectivization of farms	Rearmament, public projects to put people to work, anti-Semitism, racism, Social Darwinism, extreme nationalism

Chart *Skills*

Mussolini, Stalin, and Hitler all came to power after World War I.

1. **Making Comparisons** Compare the governments of Mussolini, Stalin, and Hitler. How were they similar?
2. **Identifying** What methods do people in a democracy use to express their opposition to government policies? Why would these methods not have worked under these dictators?

The SS was based on two principles: terror and ideology. Terror included the instruments of repression and murder—secret police, criminal police, concentration camps, and later, execution squads and death camps (concentration camps where prisoners are killed). For Himmler, the chief goal of the SS was to further the Aryan master race.

Economic Policies In the economic sphere, Hitler used public works projects and grants to private construction firms to put people back to work and end the depression. A massive rearmament program, however, was the key to solving the unemployment problem.

Unemployment, which had reached 6 million people in 1932, dropped to 2.6 million in 1934 and less than 500,000 in 1937. The regime claimed full credit for solving Germany's economic woes. The new regime's part in bringing an end to the depression was an important factor in leading many Germans to accept Hitler and the Nazis.

Spectacles and Organizations Mass demonstrations and spectacles were also used to make the German people an instrument of Hitler's policies. These meetings, especially the **Nuremberg** party rallies that were held every September, had great appeal. They usually evoked mass enthusiasm and excitement.

Institutions, such as the Catholic and Protestant churches, primary and secondary schools, and universities, were also brought under the control of the Nazi totalitarian state. Nazi professional organizations and leagues were formed for civil servants, teachers, women, farmers, doctors, and lawyers. In addition, youth organizations taught Nazi ideals.

Women and Nazism Women played a crucial role in the Aryan state as bearers of the children who, it was believed, would bring about the triumph of the Aryan race. The Nazis believed men were destined to be warriors and political leaders, while women were meant to be wives and mothers. By preserving this clear distinction, each could best serve to "maintain the whole community."

Nazi ideas determined employment opportunities for women. Jobs in heavy industry, it was thought, might hinder women from bearing healthy children. Certain professions, including university teaching, medicine, and law, were also considered unsuitable for women, especially married women. The Nazis instead encouraged women to pursue other occupations, such as social work and nursing. The Nazi regime pushed its campaign against working women with poster slogans such as "Get ahold of pots and pans and broom and you'll sooner find a groom!"

Anti-Semitic Policies From its beginning, the Nazi Party reflected the strong anti-Semitic beliefs of Adolf Hitler. Once in power, the Nazis translated anti-Semitic ideas into anti-Semitic policies.

In September 1935, the Nazis announced new racial laws at the annual party rally in Nuremberg. These **Nuremberg laws** excluded Jews from German citizenship and forbade marriages between Jews and German citizens. In 1941, German Jews were also required to wear yellow Stars of David and to carry identification cards saying they were Jewish.

A more violent phase of anti-Jewish activity began on the night of November 9, 1938—the *Kristallnacht*, or "night of shattered glass." In a destructive rampage against the Jews, Nazis burned synagogues and

"The broad mass of a nation . . . will more easily fall victim to a big lie than to a small one."
—*Adolf Hitler*

destroyed some seven thousand Jewish businesses. At least a hundred Jews were killed. Thirty thousand Jewish males were rounded up and sent to concentration camps.

Kristallnacht led to further drastic steps. Jews were barred from all public transportation and all public buildings including schools and hospitals. They were prohibited from owning, managing, or working in any retail store. The Jews were forced to clean up all the debris and damage due to Kristallnacht. Finally, under the direction of the SS, Jews were encouraged to "emigrate from Germany."

Reading Check **Summarizing** What steps did Hitler take to establish a Nazi totalitarian state in Germany?

🔺**TAKS Practice**

SECTION 3 ASSESSMENT

Checking for Understanding

1. **Define** Reichstag, concentration camp.

2. **Identify** Adolf Hitler, National Socialist German Workers' Party, *Mein Kampf*, lebensraum, Enabling Act, Aryan, Heinrich Himmler, Nuremberg laws, *Kristallnacht.*

3. **Locate** Munich, Nuremberg.

4. **Summarize** the steps that Hitler took to become the sole ruler of Germany.

5. **List** the rights taken from the Jews by the Nazi government.

Critical Thinking

6. **Analyze** How did mass demonstrations and meetings contribute to the success of the Nazi Party?

7. **Organizing Information** Use a table to describe the policies and programs used by the Nazis to create a Third Reich. Identify the goals for each policy or program.

Policy/Program	Goals

Analyzing Visuals

8. **Examine** any two photos from this section. Compare and contrast the two photos. How do you think they relate to Hitler's vision of Nazi Germany?

Writing About History

9. **Expository Writing** Find a library book by a German who lived under Nazism. Read several chapters that tell about the author's life. In a report, give your opinion about whether that person could have resisted the government and why.

Cultural and Intellectual Trends

Guide to Reading

Main Ideas
- Radios and movies were popular forms of entertainment that were used to spread political messages.
- New artistic and intellectual trends reflected the despair created by World War I and the Great Depression.

Key Terms
photomontage, surrealism, uncertainty principle

People to Identify
Salvador Dalí, James Joyce, Hermann Hesse

Places to Locate
Berlin, Dublin

Preview Questions
1. What trends dominated the arts and popular culture after 1918?
2. How did the new movements in arts and literature reflect the changes after World War I?

Reading Strategy
Categorizing Information Use a table like the one below to list literary works by Hesse and Joyce. Describe the techniques used in each work.

Literary Works	Techniques

Preview of Events

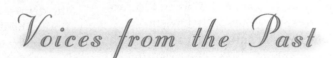

✦1915	✦1920	✦1925	✦1930

1920
First Dada show in Berlin

1922
James Joyce's *Ulysses* is published

1927
Werner Heisenberg explains the uncertainty principle

Voices from the Past

Tristan Tzara

In 1922, Tristan Tzara, a Romanian-French poet, gave a lecture on the new artistic movement called dadaism:

❝I know that you have come here today to hear explanations. Well, don't expect to hear any explanations about Dada. You explain to me why you exist. You haven't the faintest idea. . . . Dada is a state of mind. Dada applies itself to everything, and yet it is nothing, it is the point where the yes and the no and all the opposites meet, not solemnly in the castles of human philosophies, but very simply at street corners, like dogs and grasshoppers. Like everything in life, Dada is useless. Dada is without pretension, as life should be.❞
— **Tristan Tzara, *The Dada Painters and Poets*, Robert Motherwell, ed., 1922**

Influenced by the insanity of World War I, dadaists attempted to give expression to what they saw as the absurdity of life.

Mass Culture: Radio and Movies

A series of inventions in the late nineteenth century had led the way for a revolution in mass communications. Especially important was Marconi's discovery of wireless radio waves. A musical concert transmitted in June of 1920 had a major impact on radio broadcasting. Broadcasting facilities were built in the United States, Europe, and Japan during 1921 and 1922. At the same time, the mass

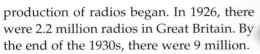

production of radios began. In 1926, there were 2.2 million radios in Great Britain. By the end of the 1930s, there were 9 million.

Although motion pictures had first emerged in the 1890s, full-length features did not appear until shortly before World War I. The Italian film *Quo Vadis* and the American film *Birth of a Nation* made it apparent that cinema was an important new form of mass entertainment. By 1939, about 40 percent of adults in the more industrialized countries were attending a movie once a week. That figure had increased to 60 percent by the end of World War II.

Of course, radio and the movies could be used for political purposes. Hitler said, "Without motor-cars, sound films, and wireless, [there would be] no victory of Nazism." Radio offered great opportunities for reaching the masses. This became obvious when it was discovered that Adolf Hitler's fiery speeches made just as great an impact on people when heard over the radio as they did in person. The Nazi regime encouraged radio listening by urging manufacturers to produce inexpensive radios that could be bought on an installment plan.

Film, too, had propaganda potential, a fact not lost on Joseph Goebbels (GUH[R]•buhlz), the propaganda minister of Nazi Germany. Believing that film was one of the "most modern and scientific means of influencing the masses," Goebbels created a special film division in his Propaganda Ministry.

The Propaganda Ministry supported the making of both documentaries—nonfiction films—and popular feature films that carried the Nazi message. *The Triumph of the Will,* for example, was a documentary of the 1934 Nuremberg party rally. This movie was filmed by Leni Riefenstahl, an actress turned director. It forcefully conveyed to viewers the power of National Socialism.

Reading Check **Explaining** Why was the radio an important propaganda tool for the Nazis?

Mass Leisure

After World War I, new work patterns provided people with more free time to take advantage of the leisure activities that had developed at the turn of the century. By 1920, the eight-hour day had become the norm for many office and factory workers in northern and western Europe.

Professional sporting events aimed at large audiences were an important aspect of mass leisure. Travel was another favorite activity. Trains, buses, and cars made trips to beaches or holiday resorts increasingly popular and affordable. Beaches, such as the one at Brighton in Great Britain, were mobbed by crowds of people from all social classes.

Mass leisure offered new ways for totalitarian states to control the people. The Nazi regime, for example, adopted a program called *Kraft durch Freude* ("Strength through Joy"). The program offered a variety of leisure activities to fill the free time of the working class. These activities included concerts, operas, films, guided tours, and sporting events. Especially popular were the program's inexpensive vacations, which were similar to modern package tours. A vacation could be a cruise to Scandinavia or the Mediterranean. More likely for workers, it was a shorter trip within Germany.

Reading Check **Examining** How did the "Strength through Joy" program help to support the Nazi regime?

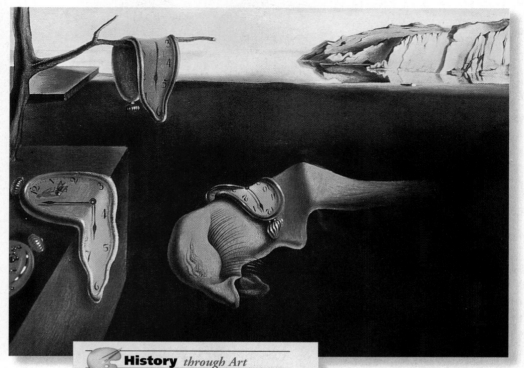

Artistic and Literary Trends

Four years of devastating war had left many Europeans with a profound sense of despair. To many people, the horrors of World War I meant that something was dreadfully wrong with Western values, that human beings were violent animals who were incapable of creating a sane and rational world. The Great Depression and the growth of violent fascist movements only added to the despair created by the war.

With political, economic, and social uncertainties came intellectual uncertainties. These were evident in the artistic and intellectual achievements of the years following World War I.

Art: Nightmares and New Visions After 1918, artistic trends mainly reflected developments made before the war. Abstract art, for example, became ever more popular. In addition, a prewar fascination with the absurd and the unconscious content of the mind seemed even more appropriate in light of the nightmare landscapes of the World War I battlefronts. "The world does not make sense, so why should

art?" was a common remark. This sentiment gave rise to both the Dada movement and surrealism.

The dadaists were artists who were obsessed with the idea that life has no purpose. They were revolted by what they saw as the insanity of life and tried to express that feeling in their art. Dada artist Hannah Höch, for example, used photomontage (a picture made of a combination of photographs) to comment on women's roles in the new mass culture. Her work was part of the first Dada show in **Berlin** in 1920.

A more important artistic movement than dadaism was surrealism. This movement sought a reality beyond the material world and found it in the world of the unconscious. By portraying fantasies, dreams, and even nightmares, the surrealists sought to show the greater reality that exists beyond the world of physical appearances.

The Spaniard **Salvador Dalí** was the high priest of surrealism. Dalí painted everyday objects but separated them from their normal contexts. By placing recognizable objects in unrecognizable relationships, Dalí created a strange world in which the irrational became visible.

Not everybody accepted modern art forms. Many people denounced what they saw as decay in the arts. Nowhere was this more evident than in Nazi Germany. In the 1920s, Weimar Germany was one of the chief European centers for modern arts and sciences. Hitler and the Nazis, however, rejected modern art as "degenerate." In a speech in July 1937, Hitler proclaimed:

> ❝The people regarded this art [modern art] as the outcome of an impudent and shameless arrogance or of a simply shocking lack of skill; it felt that . . . these achievements which might have been produced by untalented children of from eight to ten years old—could never be valued as an expression of our own times or of the German future.❞

Hitler and the Nazis believed that they could create a new and genuine German art. It would glorify the strong, the healthy, and the heroic—the qualities valued by the Aryan race. The new German art developed by the Nazis, however, was actually derived from nineteenth-century folk art and emphasized realistic scenes of everyday life.

Literature: The Search for the Unconscious The interest in the unconscious that was evident in art was also found in new literary techniques. For example, "stream of consciousness" was a technique used by writers to report the innermost thoughts of each character. The most famous example of this approach is the novel *Ulysses,* published by the Irish writer **James Joyce** in 1922. *Ulysses* tells the story of one day in the life of ordinary people in **Dublin** by following the flow of their inner thoughts.

The German writer **Hermann Hesse** dealt with the unconscious in a quite different fashion. His novels reflect the influence of both Freud's psychology and Asian religions. The works focus on, among other things, the spiritual loneliness of modern human beings in a mechanized urban society. In both *Siddhartha* and *Steppenwolf,* Hesse uses Buddhist ideas to show the psychological confusion of modern existence. Hesse's novels had a great impact on German youth in the 1920s. He won the Nobel Prize for literature in 1946.

✓**Reading Check** **Examining** Why were artists and writers after World War I attracted to Freud's theory of the unconscious?

The Heroic Age of Physics

The prewar revolution in physics begun by Albert Einstein continued in the years between the wars. In fact, Ernest Rutherford, one of the physicists who showed that the atom could be split, called the 1920s the "heroic age of physics."

The new picture of the universe that was unfolding in physics undermined the old certainties of the classical physics of Newton. Newtonian physics had made people believe that all phenomena could be completely defined and predicted. In 1927, this belief was shaken when the German physicist Werner Heisenberg explained an observation he called the uncertainty principle.

Physicists knew that atoms were made up of smaller parts (subatomic particles). The fact that the behavior of these subatomic particles is unpredictable provides the foundation for the uncertainty principle. Heisenberg's theory essentially suggests that all physical laws are based on uncertainty. The theory's emphasis on randomness challenges Newtonian physics and thus, in a way, represents a new worldview. It is unlikely that many nonscientists understood the implications of Heisenberg's work. Nevertheless, the principle of uncertainty fit in well with the other uncertainties of the interwar years.

✓**Reading Check** **Explaining** How did Heisenberg's uncertainty principle challenge the Newtonian world view?

🌟**TAKS Practice**

SECTION 4 ASSESSMENT

Checking for Understanding

1. **Define** photomontage, surrealism, uncertainty principle.

2. **Identify** *The Triumph of the Will,* Salvador Dalí, James Joyce, Hermann Hesse.

3. **Locate** Berlin, Dublin.

4. **Explain** how dadaism and surrealism reflected economic and political developments after World War I. Also explain how the painting on page 774, Dalí's *The Persistence of Memory,* supports your explanation.

5. **List** the qualities that the Nazis wanted German art to glorify. Why do you think Hitler was concerned with issues such as the content and style of art?

Critical Thinking

6. **Evaluate** What impact did technological advances in transportation and communication have on Western culture between the wars?

7. **Compare and Contrast** Use a Venn diagram like the one below to compare the Dada movement and surrealism.

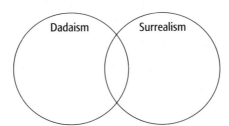
Dadaism Surrealism

Analyzing Visuals

8. **Examine** the photographs on page 773. Describe how our culture has been influenced by radio and movies. What communication technology is most influential today?

Writing About History

9. **Informative Writing** Prepare a poster that shows the development of mass communication from the radio to modern technological advances in computers. Include photos and illustrations in your poster. Write a brief paragraph that summarizes twentieth-century innovations.

Using Key Terms

1. A _____ is a picture made of a combination of photographs.

2. A _____ is a period of low economic activity and rising unemployment.

3. The Soviet government followed a policy of _____ when it took private property after World War I without payments to the former owners.

4. A _____ exists when almost all power in a nation is held by the central government.

5. Lenin abandoned war communism in 1921 in favor of his _____, a modified version of the old capitalist system.

6. The government policy of going into debt to pay for public works projects, such as building highways, is called _____.

7. According to the _____, no one could determine the path of subatomic particles, meaning all physical laws had elements of unpredictability.

8. The German parliament is known as the _____.

9. The _____ was the leading policy maker of the Communist Party.

10. _____ is the right of unions to negotiate with employers.

Reviewing Key Facts

11. **History** What did President Roosevelt call the program designed to fight the depression in the United States?

12. **Economics** Why were the Germans unable to pay all of the reparations assessed by the Treaty of Versailles?

13. **History** Why did Germany choose to become involved in the Spanish Civil War?

14. **Culture** Why did Hitler label modern art as degenerate?

15. **Economics** What did Germany do to cause high rates of inflation after World War I?

16. **Government** Describe how Stalin defeated Trotsky.

17. **Culture** What was the significance of the Italian Fascist slogan "Woman into the Home"?

18. **Economics** Describe Lenin's New Economic Policy.

19. **History** What was the basic purpose of the Nuremberg laws?

20. **Government** Why did Trotsky and his followers want to spread communism to other nations?

Critical Thinking

21. **Cause and Effect** Why did the depression help extremist leaders gain power in many nations during the 1930s?

22. **Compare and Contrast** How was Roosevelt's New Deal both similar to and different from Stalin's Five-Year Plan?

Writing About History

23. **Expository Writing** Write an essay in which you relate one of the following to the uncertainties and disillusionment of the interwar years: mass entertainment, mass leisure, professional sports, dadaism, surrealism, or the "stream of consciousness" technique in literature. Research your topic and provide references and a bibliography to accompany your essay.

Chapter Summary

Between 1919 and 1939, the West experienced great economic and political challenges.

Political and Economic Changes

- In Britain, the Conservative Party implements traditional economic policies.
- In the United States, President Roosevelt develops the New Deal, a policy of active government intervention in the economy.
- In France, the Popular Front establishes the French New Deal, which promotes workers' rights.

Rise of Totalitarianism

- In Italy, Mussolini leads the Fascists to power.
- Stalin becomes dictator of the Soviet Union and purges the Communist Party of Old Bolsheviks.
- In Germany, Hitler establishes a totalitarian Nazi regime and starts the large-scale persecution of Jews.

Innovations and Ideas

- The artistic movements of dadaism and surrealism reflect the uncertainty of life created by World War I.
- Radio and film transform communications.
- Literary techniques reflect an interest in the unconscious.
- Heisenberg's uncertainty principle suggests that physical laws are based on uncertainty.

Analyzing Sources

The crisis of confidence in Western civilization ran deep. It was well captured in the words of the French poet Paul Valéry in the early 1920s:

> 66 The storm has died away, and we are still restless, Uneasy, as if the storm were about to break. Almost all the affairs of men remain in a terrible uncertainty. We think of what has disappeared, and we are almost destroyed by what has been destroyed; we do not know what will be born, and we fear the future. . . . Doubt and disorder are in us and with us. There is no thinking man, however shrewd or learned he may be, who can hope to dominate this anxiety, to escape from this impression of darkness. 99

24. Pretend you do not know when Valéry wrote this poem. What might you be able to conclude about the time in which Valéry lived from this passage?

25. What do the first two lines of this poem convey?

Applying Technology Skills

26. **Creating a Multimedia Presentation** Search the Internet for sources on the Great Depression. Based on your research, create a multimedia presentation about the causes leading up to the depression and the effect the depression had on Europe and the United States. Use images from the Internet in your presentation. Include a plan describing the type of presentation you would like to develop and the steps you will take to ensure a successful presentation.

Making Decisions

27. Imagine that you are living in 1928. Pretend that you know everything that is going to occur because of the Great Depression and that you have the ability to move to any major country in the world. Where would you go and why? Would being part of a particular social class influence your decision?

28. Imagine that you are a young person living in Germany during 1935. Write a letter to your cousin who lives in the United States describing the influence of the increasingly powerful Nazi regime upon your life. Do you support Hitler's rise to power, or are you concerned about his policies?

NATIONAL GEOGRAPHIC | **Spanish Civil War, 1936–1939**

Nationalist-controlled area, February 1939
Republican-controlled area, February 1939
Area of intense fighting

Analyzing Maps and Charts

Study the map above to answer the following questions.

29. What advantage would the Nationalists seem to have had over the Republicans in February 1939?

30. How would the geographic location of the Republicans in 1939 have affected their supply routes?

31. Where was the most intense fighting concentrated?

TAKS Test Practice

Directions: Choose the best answer to the following question.

The *General Theory of Employment, Interest, and Money* by John Maynard Keynes was published in 1936. The book argued for

A mercantilism.

B disarmament.

C deficit spending.

D isolationism.

Test-Taking Tip: If you do not know the right answer to this question, use common sense to eliminate answer choices that do not make sense. Recall the context in which Keynes has been discussed in class or in your textbook. Think about the title of his book. These clues may help you eliminate incorrect answer choices.

CHAPTER 25
Nationalism Around the World
1919–1939

Key Events

As you read this chapter, look for the key events in the history of nationalism around the world.
- The Balfour Declaration issued by the British foreign secretary in 1917 turned Palestine, a country with an 80 percent Muslim population, into a homeland for the Jews.
- Chiang Kai-shek positioned his Nationalist forces against Mao Zedong's Communists.
- Key oil fields were discovered in the Persian Gulf area in 1938.

The Impact Today

The events that occurred during this time period still impact our lives today.
- The conflict over Palestine continues to bring violence and unrest to the region.
- Today China remains a communist state, and Mao Zedong is remembered as one of the country's most influential leaders.
- The Western world is very dependent upon oil from the Middle East.

World History Video *The Chapter 25 video, "Gandhi and Passive Resistance," chronicles India's fight for independence between the two World Wars.*

British enter Jerusalem, January 1918

1917
Britain issues
Balfour Declaration

1923
Turkish Republic is
formed, ending the
Ottoman Empire

1910　　　1915　　　1920　　　1925

1928
Chiang Kai-shek
founds a new
Chinese republic

Chiang Kai-shek

The Destruction of the Old Order by José Clemente Orozco, c. 1922

1930
Gandhi's Salt March protests British laws in India

Aramco oil refinery in Ras Tanura, Saudi Arabia

1938
Oil is discovered in Saudi Arabia

1930   *1935*   *1940*   *1945*

1931
Japanese forces invade Manchuria

1933
Franklin D. Roosevelt announces the Good Neighbor policy

Franklin D. Roosevelt

HISTORY
Online
Chapter Overview
Visit the *Glencoe World History* Web site at tx.wh.glencoe.com and click on **Chapter 25–Chapter Overview** to preview chapter information.

A Story That Matters

Gandhi leading the Salt March to Dandi to protest the British monopoly on salt production

Gandhi's March to the Sea

*I*n 1930, Mohandas Gandhi, the 61-year-old leader of the Indian movement for independence from British rule, began a march to the sea with 78 followers. Their destination was Dandi, a little coastal town some 240 miles (386 km) away. The group covered about 12 miles (19 km) a day.

As they went, Gandhi preached his doctrine of nonviolent resistance to British rule in every village through which he passed: "Civil disobedience is the inherent right of a citizen. He dare not give it up without ceasing to be a man." By the time Gandhi reached Dandi, 24 days later, his small group had become a nonviolent army of thousands.

When Gandhi and his followers arrived at Dandi, Gandhi picked up a pinch of crystallized sea salt from the sand. Thousands of people all along the coast did likewise. In so doing, they were openly breaking British laws that prohibited Indians from making their own salt. The British had long profited from their monopoly on the making and selling of salt, an item much in demand in India. They used coastal saltflats to collect crystallized sea salt to sell.

By their simple acts of disobedience, Gandhi and the Indian people had taken yet another step on their long march to independence from the British. The Salt March was one of many nonviolent activities that Gandhi undertook to win India's national independence between World War I and World War II.

Why It Matters

With Europe in disorder after World War I, people living in colonies controlled by European countries began to think that the independence they desired might now be achieved. In Africa and Asia, movements for national independence began to take shape. In the Middle East, World War I ended the rule of the Ottoman Empire and created new states. For some Latin American countries, the fascist dictatorships of Italy and Germany provided models for change.

History and You You have read about many religious conflicts. In this chapter, you will learn about the conflict between the Muslims and the Hindus in India. Make a chart listing the differences between the groups. Explain how religious differences expand into other areas of conflict. How did this rivalry affect the development of India?

Nationalism in the Middle East

Main Ideas
- Nationalism led to the creation of the modern states of Turkey, Iran, and Saudi Arabia.
- The Balfour Declaration made Palestine a national Jewish homeland.

Key Terms
genocide, ethnic cleansing

People to Identify
Abdulhamid II, T. E. Lawrence, Atatürk, Reza Shah Pahlavi, Ibn Saud

Places to Locate
Tehran, Iran, Saudi Arabia, Palestine

Preview Questions
1. What important force led to the fall of the Ottoman Empire?
2. What was the relationship between Arab nationalism and the mandate system?

Reading Strategy
Compare and Contrast Make a Venn diagram like the one below comparing and contrasting Atatürk's and Reza Shah Pahlavi's national policies.

Atatürk — Reza Shah Pahlavi

Preview of Events

♦1910	♦1915	♦1920	♦1925	♦1930	♦1935	♦1940

1915
Turkish government massacres Armenians

1916
The local governor of Makkah declares Arabia independent

1924
Caliphate formally abolished in Turkey

1932
Saudi Arabia is established

Voices from the Past

In 1925, Hayyim Bialik, a Ukrainian Jew who had settled in Palestine the year before, spoke at the opening of the Hebrew University of Palestine:

❝Through cruel and bitter trials and tribulations, through blasted hopes and despair of the soul, through innumerable humiliations, we have slowly arrived at the realization that without a tangible homeland, without private national premises that are entirely ours, we can have no sort of a life, either material or spiritual. . . . We have not come here to seek wealth, or dominion, or greatness. How much of these can this poor little country give us? We wish to find here only a domain of our own for our physical and intellectual labor.❞

—The Human Record: Sources of Global History,
Alfred J. Andrea and James H. Overfield, eds., 1998

Committee discussing plans for a Jewish university in Palestine

Bialik was a believer in Zionism, a movement that supported the establishment of Palestine as a homeland for Jews.

Decline and Fall of the Ottoman Empire

The empire of the Ottoman Turks—which once had included parts of eastern Europe, the Middle East, and North Africa—had been growing steadily weaker since the end of the eighteenth century. Indeed, European nations called it "the sick man of Europe."

The empire's size had decreased dramatically. Much of its European territory had been lost. In North Africa, Ottoman rule had ended in the nineteenth century when France seized Algeria and Tunisia and Great Britain took control of Egypt. Greece also declared its independence in the nineteenth century.

In 1876, Ottoman reformers seized control of the empire's government and adopted a constitution aimed at forming a legislative assembly. However, the sultan they placed on the throne, **Abdulhamid II,** suspended the new constitution and ruled by authoritarian means.

Abdulhamid paid a high price for his actions—he lived in constant fear of assassination. He kept a thousand loaded revolvers hidden throughout his guarded estate and insisted that his pets taste his food before he ate it.

The suspended constitution became a symbol of change to a group of reformers named the Young Turks. This group was able to force the restoration of the constitution in 1908 and to depose the sultan the following year. However, the Young Turks lacked strong support for their government. The stability of the empire was also challenged by many ethnic Turks who had begun to envision a Turkish state that would encompass all people of Turkish nationality.

Impact of World War I
The final blow to the old empire came from World War I. After the Ottoman government allied with Germany, the British sought to undermine Ottoman rule in the Arabian Peninsula by supporting Arab nationalist activities there. The nationalists were aided by the efforts of the dashing British adventurer **T. E. Lawrence,** popularly known as "Lawrence of Arabia."

T. E. Lawrence

In 1916, the local governor of Makkah, encouraged by Great Britain, declared Arabia independent from Ottoman rule. British troops, advancing from Egypt, seized Palestine. After suffering more than three hundred thousand deaths during the war, the Ottoman Empire made peace with the Allies in October 1918.

Massacre of the Armenians
During the war, the Ottoman Turks had alienated the Allies with their policies toward minority subjects, especially the Armenians. The Christian Armenian minority had

Armenian children who have been orphaned wait to board a ship that will take them from Turkey to Greece. The Turks killed approximately 1 million Armenians and deported half a million.

been pressing the Ottoman government for its independence for years. In 1915, the government violently reacted to an Armenian uprising by killing Armenian men and expelling women and children from the empire.

Within seven months, six hundred thousand Armenians had been killed, and five hundred thousand had been deported (sent out of the country). Of those deported, four hundred thousand died while marching through the deserts and swamps of Syria and Mesopotamia.

By September 1915, an estimated 1 million Armenians were dead. They were victims of genocide, the deliberate mass murder of a particular racial, political, or cultural group. (A similar practice would be called ethnic cleansing in the Bosnian War of 1993 to 1996.) One eyewitness to the 1915 Armenian deportation wrote:

❝[She] saw vultures hovering over children who had fallen dead by the roadside. She saw beings crawling along, maimed, starving and begging for bread. From time to time she passed soldiers driving before them with whips and rifle-butts whole families, men, women and children, shrieking, pleading, wailing. These were the Armenian people setting out for exile into the desert from which there was no return.❞

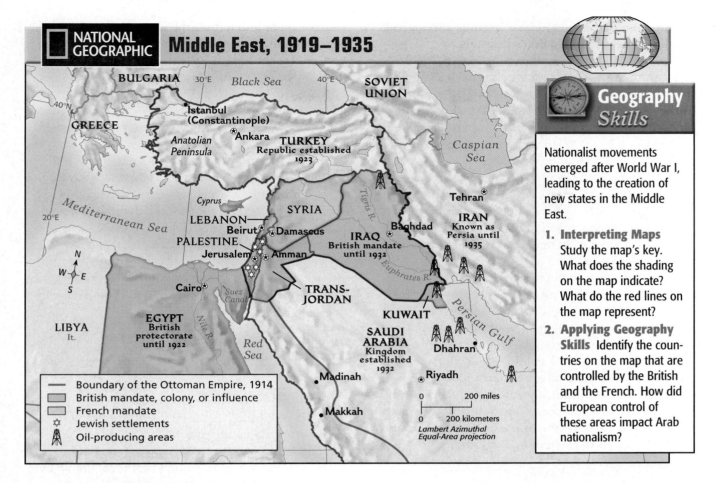

Middle East, 1919–1935

NATIONAL GEOGRAPHIC

BULGARIA
Black Sea
SOVIET UNION
GREECE
Istanbul (Constantinople)
Ankara
Anatolian Peninsula
TURKEY
Republic established 1923
Caspian Sea
Cyprus
Mediterranean Sea
SYRIA
Tigris R.
Tehran
LEBANON
Beirut
Damascus
IRAN
Known as Persia until 1935
PALESTINE
Jerusalem
Amman
IRAQ
British mandate until 1932
Baghdad
Euphrates R.
Cairo
Suez Canal
TRANS-JORDAN
KUWAIT
Persian Gulf
EGYPT
British protectorate until 1922
Nile R.
SAUDI ARABIA
Kingdom established 1932
Dhahran
LIBYA
It.
Red Sea
Madinah
Riyadh
Makkah

— Boundary of the Ottoman Empire, 1914
☐ British mandate, colony, or influence
☐ French mandate
✡ Jewish settlements
⛏ Oil-producing areas

0   200 miles
0   200 kilometers
Lambert Azimuthal Equal-Area projection

Geography Skills

Nationalist movements emerged after World War I, leading to the creation of new states in the Middle East.

1. **Interpreting Maps** Study the map's key. What does the shading on the map indicate? What do the red lines on the map represent?

2. **Applying Geography Skills** Identify the countries on the map that are controlled by the British and the French. How did European control of these areas impact Arab nationalism?

By 1918, another four hundred thousand Armenians had been massacred. Russia, France, and Britain denounced the Turkish killing of the Armenians as "against humanity and civilization." Because of the war, however, the killings went on.

Emergence of the Turkish Republic At the end of World War I, the tottering Ottoman Empire collapsed. Great Britain and France made plans to divide up Ottoman territories in the Middle East. Only the area of present-day Turkey remained under Ottoman control. Then, Greece invaded Turkey and seized the western parts of the Anatolian Peninsula.

The invasion alarmed key elements in Turkey, who were organized under the leadership of the war hero Colonel Mustafa Kemal. Kemal resigned from the army and summoned a national congress calling for the creation of an elected government and a new Republic of Turkey. His forces drove the Greeks from the Anatolian Peninsula. In 1923, the last of the Ottoman sultans fled the country,

Kemal Atatürk

which was now declared to be the Turkish Republic. The Ottoman Empire had finally come to an end.

☑ **Reading Check** **Evaluating** How did the Ottoman Empire finally end?

The Modernization of Turkey

President Kemal was now popularly known as **Atatürk** (AT•uh•TUHRK), or "father Turk." Over the next several years, he tried to transform Turkey into a modern state. A democratic system was put in place, but the president did not tolerate opposition and harshly suppressed his critics.

Atatürk's changes went beyond politics. Many Arabic elements were eliminated from the Turkish language, which was now written in the Roman alphabet. Popular education was introduced. All Turkish citizens were forced to adopt family (last) names, in the European style.

Atatürk also took steps to modernize Turkey's economy. Factories were established, and a five-year plan provided for state direction over the economy.

Atatürk also tried to modernize farming, although he had little effect on the nation's peasants.

Perhaps the most significant aspect of Atatürk's reform program was his attempt to break the power of the Islamic religion. He wanted to transform Turkey into a secular state—a state that rejects religious influence on its policies. Atatürk said, "Religion is like a heavy blanket that keeps the people of Turkey asleep."

The caliphate was formally abolished in 1924. Men were forbidden to wear the fez, the brimless cap worn by Turkish Muslims. When Atatürk began wearing a Western panama hat, one of his critics remarked, "You cannot make a Turk into a Westerner by giving him a hat."

Women were forbidden to wear the veil, a traditional Islamic custom. New laws gave women marriage and inheritance rights equal to men's. In 1934, women received the right to vote. All citizens were also given the right to convert to other religions.

The legacy of Kemal Atatürk was enormous. In practice, not all of his reforms were widely accepted, especially by devout Muslims. However, most of the changes that he introduced were kept after his death in 1938. By and large, the Turkish Republic was the product of Atatürk's determined efforts.

✓ **Reading Check** **Identifying** What radical step did Atatürk take to modernize Turkey?

The Beginnings of Modern Iran

A similar process of modernization was underway in Persia. Under the Qajar dynasty (1794–1925), the country had not been very successful in resolving its domestic problems. Increasingly, the dynasty had turned to Russia and Great Britain to protect itself from its own people, which led to a growing foreign presence in Persia. The discovery of oil in the southern part of the country in 1908 attracted more foreign interest. Oil exports increased rapidly, and most of the profits went to British investors.

The growing foreign presence led to the rise of a native Persian nationalist movement. In 1921, Reza Khan, an officer in the Persian army, led a military mutiny that seized control of **Tehran,** the capital city. In 1925, Reza Khan established himself as shah, or king, and was called **Reza Shah Pahlavi.** The name of the new dynasty he created, Pahlavi, was the name of the ancient Persian language.

During the next few years, Reza Shah Pahlavi tried to follow the example of Kemal Atatürk in Turkey. He introduced a number of reforms to strengthen and modernize the government, the military, and the economic system. Persia became the modern state of **Iran** in 1935.

Unlike Kemal Atatürk, Reza Shah Pahlavi did not try to destroy the power of Islamic beliefs. However, he did encourage the creation of a Western-style educational system and forbade women to wear the veil in public.

Foreign powers continued to harass Iran. To free himself from Great Britain and the Soviet Union, Reza Shah Pahlavi drew closer to Nazi Germany. During World War II, the shah rejected the demands of Great Britain and the Soviet Union to expel a large number of Germans from Iran. In response, the Soviet Union and Great Britain sent troops into the country. Reza Shah Pahlavi resigned in protest and was replaced by his son, Mohammad Reza Pahlavi.

✓ **Reading Check** **Comparing** How was Reza Shah Pahlavi's modernization of Persia different from Atatürk's transformation of Turkey?

Arab Nationalism

World War I offered the Arabs an opportunity to escape from Ottoman rule. However, there was a question as to what would replace that rule. The Arabs were not a nation, though they were united by their language and their Islamic cultural and religious heritage.

Because Britain had supported the efforts of Arab nationalists in 1916, the nationalists hoped this support would continue after the war ended. Instead, Britain made an agreement with France to create a number of mandates in the area. These mandates were former Ottoman territories that were now supervised by the new League of Nations. The league, in

Sultan Ibn Saud, who established the kingdom of Saudi Arabia

turn, granted league members the right to govern particular mandates. Iraq, Palestine, and Jordan were assigned to Great Britain; Syria and Lebanon to France.

For the most part, Europeans created these Middle Eastern states. The Europeans determined the nations' borders and divided the peoples. In general, the people in these states had no strong identification with their designated country. However, a sense of Arab nationalism remained.

In the early 1920s, a reform leader, **Ibn Saud,** united Arabs in the northern part of the Arabian Peninsula. Devout and gifted, Ibn Saud (from whom came the name *Saudi Arabia*) won broad support. He established the kingdom of Saudi Arabia in 1932.

At first, the new kingdom, which consisted mostly of the vast desert of central Arabia, was desperately poor. Its main source of income came from the Muslim pilgrims who visited Makkah and Madinah.

During the 1930s, however, U.S. prospectors began to explore for oil. Standard Oil made a successful strike at Dhahran, on the Persian Gulf, in 1938. Soon, an Arabian-American oil company, popularly called Aramco, was created. The isolated kingdom was suddenly flooded with Western oil industries that brought the promise of wealth.

 **Reading Check** **Examining** How were many Middle Eastern states created after World War I?

The Problem of Palestine

The situation in **Palestine** made matters even more complicated in the Middle East. While Palestine had been the home of the Jews in antiquity, few had lived there for almost two thousand years. While some Christians and Jews did live in Palestine, it was inhabited primarily by Muslim Palestinians. Britain, however, stated its intention to support a national home for the Jews in the 1917 Balfour Declaration: "His Majesty's Government views with favor the establishment in Palestine of a national home for the Jewish people."

The British promised that the Balfour Declaration would not undermine the rights of the non-Jewish peoples living in the area. Still, Arab nationalists were angered. They questioned how a national home for the Jewish people could be established in a territory that was 80 percent Muslim.

In the meantime, the promises of the Balfour Declaration drew Jewish settlers to Palestine. The Zionist movement (see Chapter 20) had advocated the return of Jews to Palestine since the late 1890s. During the 1930s, tensions increased between the new arrivals and the existing Muslim residents. At the same time, the rising persecution of Jews in Nazi Germany caused many European Jews to flee to Palestine. By 1939, there were about 450,000 Jews in Palestine.

The British, fearing aroused Arab nationalism, tried to restrict Jewish immigration into the territory. In 1939, the British declared that only 75,000 Jewish immigrants would be allowed into Palestine over the next five years. After that, no more Jews could enter the country. This decision would eventually produce severe conflicts in the region.

Reading Check **Explaining** Why did the Balfour Declaration produce problems in Palestine?

TAKS Practice

SECTION 1 ASSESSMENT

Checking for Understanding

1. **Define** genocide, ethnic cleansing.

2. **Identify** Abdulhamid II, T. E. Lawrence, Atatürk, Reza Shah Pahlavi, Ibn Saud.

3. **Locate** Tehran, Iran, Saudi Arabia, Palestine.

4. **Explain** why the British supported Arab nationalist activities in 1916.

5. **List** the mandates assigned to Great Britain and France.

Critical Thinking

6. **Evaluate** Why was it difficult for the Arab peoples to form one nation?

7. **Summarizing Information** Make a diagram like the one below showing eight aspects of the modernization of Turkey.

Modernization of Turkey

Analyzing Visuals

8. **Examine** the photo on page 782 showing Armenian children who lost their parents. Why were hundreds of thousands of Armenians killed or driven from their homes by the Turks?

Writing About History

9. **Expository Writing** Locate information regarding the current political policies of Iran. Write two paragraphs comparing this information with the policies of Reza Shah Pahlavi. Document your sources.

Nationalism in Africa and Asia

Guide to Reading

Main Ideas
- Peoples in Africa and Asia began to agitate for independence.
- Japan became an aggressive military state.
- Soviet agents worked to spread communism around the world.

Key Terms
Pan-Africanism, Mahatma, civil disobedience, *zaibatsu*

People to Identify
W.E.B. Du Bois, Marcus Garvey, Mohandas Gandhi, Jawaharlal Nehru, Ho Chi Minh

Places to Locate
Kenya, Manchuria

Preview of Events
1. What different forms did protest against Western rule take?
2. How was communism received in Asia?

Reading Strategy
Contrasting Information Using a table like the one below, contrast the backgrounds and values of Gandhi and the younger Nehru.

Mahatma Gandhi	Jawaharlal Nehru

Preview of Events

♦1915	♦1920	♦1925	♦1930	♦1935	♦1940	♦1945

1920
Marcus Garvey issues *Declaration of the Rights of the Negro Peoples of the World*

1935
Government of India Act is passed

1938
Japan passes military draft law

Voices from the Past

Jomo Kenyatta, an advocate of independence in Kenya, wrote:

❝By driving the African off his ancestral lands, the Europeans have reduced him to a state of serfdom incompatible with human happiness. The African is conditioned, by the cultural and social institutions of centuries, to a freedom of which Europe has little conception, and it is not in his nature to accept serfdom forever. He realizes that he must fight unceasingly for his own complete emancipation [freedom]; for without this he is doomed to remain the prey of rival imperialisms, which in every successive year will drive their fangs more deeply into his vitality and strength.❞
— *Facing Mount Kenya,* Jomo Kenyatta, 1959

Jomo Kenyatta

Between 1919 and 1939, leaders emerged in Africa and Asia who sought to free their people from the power of the West. While none of these nationalist movements were successful before World War II, they did begin the journey toward independence.

Movements toward Independence in Africa

Black Africans had fought in World War I in British and French armies. Many Africans hoped they would be rewarded with independence after the war. As one newspaper in the Gold Coast argued, if African volunteers who fought on European battlefields were "good enough to fight and die in the Empire's cause, they were good enough to have a share in the government of their countries."

The peace settlement after World War I was a great disappointment. Germany was stripped of its African colonies, but these colonies were awarded to Great Britain and France to be administered as mandates for the League of Nations. Britain and France now governed a vast portion of Africa.

African Protests After World War I, Africans became more active politically. Africans who had fought in World War I had learned new ideas about freedom and nationalism in the West. In Africa itself, missionary schools taught their pupils about liberty and equality. As more Africans became aware of the enormous gulf between Western ideals and practices, they decided to seek reform.

Reform movements took different forms. In **Kenya** in 1921, the Young Kikuyu Association, organized by Harry Thuku, a telephone operator, protested the high taxes levied by the British rulers. His message was simple: "Hearken, every day you pay . . . tax to the Europeans of Government. Where is it sent? It is their task to steal the property of the Kikuyu people." Thuku was arrested. When an angry crowd stormed the jail and demanded his release, government authorities fired into the crowd and killed at least 20 people. Thuku was sent into exile.

A struggle against Italian rule in Libya also occurred in the 1920s. Forces led by Omar Mukhtar used guerrilla warfare against the Italians and defeated them a number of times. The Italians reacted ferociously. They established concentration camps and used all available modern weapons to crush the revolt. Mukhtar's death ended the movement.

Although colonial powers typically responded to such movements with force, they also began to make some reforms. They made these reforms in the hope of satisfying African peoples. Reforms, however, were too few and too late. By the 1930s, an increasing number of African leaders were calling for independence, not reform.

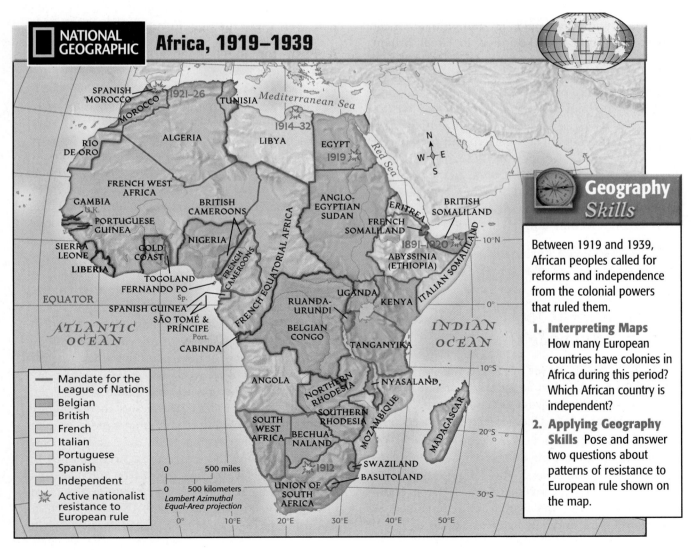

NATIONAL GEOGRAPHIC
Africa, 1919–1939

Legend:
— Mandate for the League of Nations
Belgian
British
French
Italian
Portuguese
Spanish
Independent
✳ Active nationalist resistance to European rule

0   500 miles
0   500 kilometers
Lambert Azimuthal Equal-Area projection

Geography Skills

Between 1919 and 1939, African peoples called for reforms and independence from the colonial powers that ruled them.

1. **Interpreting Maps** How many European countries have colonies in Africa during this period? Which African country is independent?

2. **Applying Geography Skills** Pose and answer two questions about patterns of resistance to European rule shown on the map.

New Leaders Calls for independence came from a new generation of young African leaders. Many had been educated abroad, in Europe and the United States. Those who had studied in the United States were especially influenced by the ideas of **W.E.B. Du Bois** and **Marcus Garvey.**

Du Bois, an African American educated at Harvard University, was the leader of a movement that tried to make all Africans aware of their own cultural heritage. Garvey, a Jamaican who lived in Harlem in New York City, stressed the need for the unity of all Africans, a movement known as Pan-Africanism. His *Declaration of the Rights of the Negro Peoples of the World,* issued in 1920, had a strong impact on later African leaders.

Leaders and movements in individual African nations also appeared. Educated in Great Britain, Jomo Kenyatta of Kenya argued in his book *Facing Mount Kenya* that British rule was destroying the traditional culture of the peoples of Africa. Léopold Senghor, who had studied in France and written poetry about African culture, organized an independence movement in Senegal. Nnamdi Azikiwe, of Nigeria, began a newspaper, *The West African Pilot,* in 1937 and urged nonviolence as a method to gain independence. These are but three of the leaders who worked to end colonial rule in Africa. Success, however, would not come until after World War II.

✓ **Reading Check** **Analyzing** Why did many Africans become more politically active after World War I?

The Movement for Indian Independence

←TURNING POINT→ **As you read, you will learn how Mohandas Gandhi called on Indians to protest British laws by using the technique of civil disobedience. Gandhi was one leader in India's independence movement.**

Mohandas Gandhi had become active in the movement for Indian self-rule before World War I. By the time of World War I, the Indian people had already begun to refer to him as India's "Great Soul," or Mahatma. After the war, Gandhi remained an important figure, and new leaders also arose.

HISTORY Online

Web Activity Visit the *Glencoe World History* Web site at tx.wh.glencoe.com and click on **Chapter 25–Student Web Activity** to learn more about nationalist movements.

Protest and Reform Gandhi left South Africa in 1914. When he returned to India, he began to organize mass protests to achieve his aims. A believer in nonviolence, Gandhi protested British laws by using the methods of civil disobedience—refusal to obey laws considered to be unjust.

In 1919, the protests led to violence and a strong British reaction. British troops killed hundreds of unarmed protesters in the city of Amritsar, in northwestern India. Horrified at the violence, Gandhi briefly retreated from active politics. He was later arrested for his role in protests against British rule and spent several years in prison.

In 1935, Great Britain passed the Government of India Act. This act expanded the role of Indians in the governing process. Before, the Legislative Council had only given advice to the British governor. Now, it became a two-house parliament. Two-thirds of its Indian members were to be elected. Similar bodies were created at the provincial level. Five million Indians (still only a small percentage of the total population) were given the right to vote.

A Push for Independence The Indian National Congress (INC) was founded in 1885 to seek reforms in Britain's government of India (see Chapter 21). Reforms, however, were no longer enough for many members of the INC. Under its new leader, Motilal Nehru, the INC wanted to push for full independence.

Gandhi, now released from prison, returned to his earlier policy of civil disobedience. He worked hard to inform ordinary Indians of his beliefs and methods. It was wrong, he said, to harm any living being. Hate could only be overcome by love, and love, rather than force, could win people over to one's position.

Nonviolence was central to Gandhi's campaign of noncooperation and civil disobedience. To protest unjust British laws, Gandhi told his people: "Don't pay your taxes or send your children to an English-supported school. . . . Make your own cotton cloth by spinning the thread at home, and don't buy English-made goods. Provide yourselves with home-made salt, and do not buy government-made salt."

Britain had introduced measures increasing the salt tax and prohibiting the Indian people from manufacturing or harvesting their own salt. In 1930, Gandhi protested these measures. Accompanied by supporters, he walked to the sea on what became known as the Salt March. On reaching the coast, Gandhi picked up a pinch of salt. Thousands of Indians followed his act of civil disobedience. Gandhi

and many other members of the INC were arrested.
📖 *(See page 999 to read excerpts from* Gandhi Takes the Path of Civil Disobedience *in the Primary Sources Library.)*

New Leaders and New Problems In the 1930s, a new figure entered the movement. **Jawaharlal Nehru,** the son of Motilal Nehru, studied law in Great Britain. The younger Nehru was an example of a new kind of Indian politician. He was upper class and intellectual.

The independence movement split into two paths. The one identified with Gandhi was religious, Indian, and traditional. The other, identified with Nehru, was secular, Western, and modern. The existence of two approaches created uncertainty about India's future path.

In the meantime, another problem had arisen in the independence movement. Hostility between Hindus and Muslims had existed for centuries. Muslims were dissatisfied with the Hindu dominance of the INC and raised the cry "Islam is in danger."

By the 1930s, the Muslim League, under the leadership of Muhammad Ali Jinnah, was beginning to believe in the creation of a separate Muslim state of Pakistan (meaning "the land of the pure") in the northwest.

✔ **Reading Check** **Identifying** What three non-British conflicts affected the Indian independence movements in the 1930s?

The Rise of a Militarist Japan

During the first two decades of the twentieth century, Japanese society developed along a Western model. The economic and social reforms launched during the Meiji Era led to increasing prosperity and the development of a modern industrial and commercial sector.

A *Zaibatsu* Economy In the Japanese economy, various manufacturing processes were concentrated within a single enterprise called the *zaibatsu,* a large financial and industrial corporation. These firms gradually developed, often with government help, into vast companies that controlled major segments of the Japanese industrial sector. By 1937, the four largest *zaibatsu* (Mitsui, Mitsubishi, Sumitomo, and Yasuda) controlled 21 percent of the banking

CONNECTIONS Around The World

Paths to Modernization

After World War I, new states in the Middle East and Asia sought to modernize their countries. To many people, modernization meant Westernization, the adoption of political and economic reforms based on Western models. These models included government based on democratic principles and a free-market, or capitalist, economic system based on industrialization.

After the success of the Communist revolution in Russia, however, a second model for modernization appeared. To some people, a Marxist system seemed to offer a better and quicker way to transform an agricultural state into a modern industrial state. The new system would be a socialist model in which an authoritarian state, not private industry, would own and control the economy.

◄ *Dubai, United Arab Emirates, a thriving, modern port city*

Between World War I and World War II, some new republics combined features of both systems. In Turkey, Kemal Atatürk, creator of the new Turkish republic, set up a national assembly but ruled with an iron fist. His economic modernization combined private industries with state direction of the economy.

In China, the Nanjing Republic under Chiang Kai-shek supported the idea of democracy but maintained the need for dictatorial government as a first stage to prepare the Chinese people for democracy. Economic modernization in the new Chinese republic combined a modern industrial state with the traditional Chinese values of hard work and obedience.

Comparing Cultures

Using outside sources, research the current government of Turkey. How has the government developed since the rule of Kemal Atatürk? Does the current government reflect the influence of Western principles or has it evolved according to a Marxist model?

industry, 26 percent of mining, 35 percent of ship-building, and over 60 percent of paper manufacturing and insurance.

The concentration of wealth led to growing economic inequalities. City workers were poorly paid and housed. Economic crises added to this problem shortly after World War I when inflation in food prices led to food riots. A rapid increase in population led to food shortages. (The population of the Japanese islands increased from 43 million in 1900 to 73 million in 1940.) Later, when the Great Depression struck, workers and farmers suffered the most.

With hardships came calls for a return to traditional Japanese values. Traditionalists especially objected to the growing influence of Western ideas and values on Japanese educational and political systems. At the same time, many citizens denounced Japan's attempt to find security through cooperation with the Western powers. Instead, they demanded that Japan use its own strength to dominate Asia and meet its needs.

Japan and the West In the early twentieth century, Japanese leaders began to have difficulty finding sources of raw materials and foreign markets for the nation's manufactured goods. Until World War I, Japan had dealt with the problem by seizing territories—such as Formosa, Korea, and southern Manchuria—and making them part of the growing Japanese Empire. That policy succeeded but aroused the concern of the Western nations.

The United States was especially worried about Japanese expansion. The United States wanted to keep Asia open for U.S. trading activities. In 1922, the United States held a major conference of nations with interests in the Pacific. The major achievement of this conference was a nine-power treaty that recognized the territorial integrity of China and the maintenance of the Open Door policy. Japan accepted the provisions in return for recognition of its control of southern Manchuria.

During the remainder of the 1920s, the Japanese government tried to follow the rules established by the Washington Conference. This meant using diplomatic and economic means to realize Japanese interests in Asia. However, this approach did not prove popular.

Japanese industrialists began to expand into new areas, such as heavy industry, mining, chemicals, and the manufacturing of appliances and automobiles. These industries desperately needed resources not found in abundance in Japan. The Japanese government came under increasing pressure to find new sources for raw materials abroad.

The Rise of Militarism During the first two decades of the twentieth century, Japan moved toward a more democratic government. The parliament and political parties grew stronger. The influence of the old ruling oligarchy, however, remained strong. At the end of the 1920s, new problems led to the emergence of militant forces that encouraged Japan to become a militaristic state.

The rise of militant forces in Japan resulted when a group within the ruling party was able to gain control of the political system. Some of the militants were civilians convinced that the parliamentary system had been corrupted by Western ideas. Others were members of the military who were angered by the cuts in military spending and the government's pacifist policies during the early 1920s.

Japanese Expansion, 1910–1933

NATIONAL GEOGRAPHIC

Japanese territory, 1910
Japanese acquisitions to 1933

Geography *Skills*

The Japanese Empire expanded during the early twentieth century.

1. **Interpreting Maps** How did Japan's territory change between 1910 and 1933?

2. **Applying Geography Skills** Describe Japan's geographical features. How was geography a factor in Japanese expansion?

During the early 1930s, civilians formed extremist patriotic organizations, such as the Black Dragon Society. Members of the army and navy created similar societies. One group of middle-level army officers invaded **Manchuria** without government approval in the autumn of 1931. Within a short time, all of Manchuria had been conquered.

The Japanese government opposed the conquest of Manchuria but the Japanese people supported it. Unable to act, the government was soon dominated by the military and other supporters of Japanese expansionism.

Japanese society was put on wartime status. A military draft law was passed in 1938. Economic resources were placed under strict government control. All political parties were merged into the Imperial Rule Assistance Association, which called for Japanese expansion abroad. Labor unions were disbanded. Education and culture were purged of most Western ideas. Militant leaders insisted on the need for stressing traditional Japanese values instead.

✓ Reading Check **Examining** How did the Japanese government change from the 1920s to the 1930s?

Nationalism and Revolution in Asia

Before World War I, the Marxist doctrine of social revolution had no appeal for Asian intellectuals. After all, most Asian societies were still agricultural and were hardly ready for revolution.

That situation began to change after the revolution in Russia in 1917. The rise to power of Lenin and the Bolsheviks showed that a revolutionary Marxist party could overturn an outdated system—even one that was not fully industrialized—and begin a new one.

The Spread of Communism In 1920, Lenin adopted a new revolutionary strategy aimed at societies outside the Western world. The chief means of spreading the word of Karl Marx was the Communist International, or Comintern for short. Formed in 1919, the Comintern was a worldwide organization of Communist parties dedicated to the advancement of world revolution.

At the Comintern's headquarters in Moscow, agents were trained and then returned to their own countries to form Marxist parties and promote the cause of social revolution. By the end of the 1920s, practically every colonial society in Asia had a Communist party.

Communist Parties in Asia How successful were these new parties? In some countries, the local Communists were briefly able to establish a cooperative relationship with existing nationalist parties in a common struggle against Western imperialism. This was true in French Indochina, where Vietnamese Communists were organized by the Moscow-trained revolutionary **Ho Chi Minh** in the 1920s. The strongest Communist-nationalist alliance was formed in China (see Section 3). In most colonial societies, though, Communist parties had little success in the 1930s. They failed to build a secure base of support among the mass of the population.

✓ Reading Check **Evaluating** What was the relationship between communism and imperialism?

🔻TAKS Practice

SECTION 2 ASSESSMENT

Checking for Understanding

1. **Define** Pan-Africanism, Mahatma, civil disobedience, *zaibatsu.*

2. **Identify** W.E.B. Du Bois, Marcus Garvey, Mohandas Gandhi, Jawaharlal Nehru, Ho Chi Minh.

3. **Locate** Kenya, Manchuria.

4. **Explain** the goals of the Comintern and how it pursued these goals.

5. **List** at least three leaders who worked to end colonial rule in Africa.

Critical Thinking

6. **Compare** What did young African leaders who wanted independence for their countries have in common?

7. **Sequencing Information** On a sequence chain like the one below, show five events that contributed to Japan's becoming a military state in the 1930s.

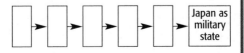

Japan as military state

Analyzing Visuals

8. **Examine** the photo of Dubai in the feature on page 789. What do you see in the picture that tells you this is a modern port city?

Writing About History

9. **Expository Writing** Japanese conglomerates today are called *keiretsu.* Research one of them, such as Mitsui or Mitsubishi, and write two paragraphs comparing their operations to American industry.

The Path to Liberation

THE VIETNAMESE REVOLUTIONARY Ho Chi Minh learned about the revolution in Bolshevik Russia in 1919 while living in France. He became a dedicated follower of Lenin and eventually became a leader of the Vietnamese Communist movement. In the following passage, Ho Chi Minh talks about his reasons for becoming a Communist.

▲ *Communist Party meeting in Hanoi, April 2001*

❝After World War I, I made my living in Paris, now as a retoucher at a photographer's, now as a painter of 'Chinese antiquities' (made in France!). I would distribute leaflets denouncing the crimes committed by the French colonialists in Vietnam.

At that time, I supported the Russian Revolution only instinctively, not yet grasping all its historic importance. I loved and admired Lenin because he was a great patriot who liberated his compatriots; until then, I had read none of his books.

The reason for my joining the French Socialist Party was that these 'ladies and gentlemen'—as I called my comrades at that moment—had shown their sympathy toward me, toward the struggle of the oppressed peoples. But I understood neither what was a party, a trade-union, nor what was Socialism nor Communism. . . . A comrade gave me Lenin's 'Thesis on the National and Colonial Questions' to read.

There were political terms difficult to understand in this thesis. But by dint of reading it again and again, finally I could grasp the main part of it. What emotion, enthusiasm, clear-sightedness, and confidence it instilled in me! I was overjoyed to tears. Though sitting alone in my room, I shouted aloud

Ho Chi Minh, leader ▶ *of the Vietnamese Communist movement*

as if addressing large crowds. 'Dear martyrs, compatriots! This is what we need, this is the path to our liberation!'

After that, I had entire confidence in Lenin.**❞**

—Ho Chi Minh,
The Path which Led Me to Leninism

Analyzing Primary Sources

1. Why was Ho Chi Minh living in France?
2. What were Ho Chi Minh's feelings toward Lenin?
3. Why did Ho Chi Minh join the French Socialist Party?

Revolutionary Chaos in China

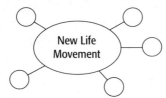
Voices from the Past

Mao Zedong (at left)

In the fall of 1926, the young Communist Mao Zedong submitted a report to the Chinese Communist Party Central Committee calling for a massive peasant revolt against the ruling order:

❝In a very short time, in China's Central, Southern, and Northern provinces, several hundred million peasants will rise like a mighty storm, like a hurricane, a force so swift and violent that no power, however great, will be able to hold it back. They will smash all the restraints that bind them and rush forward along the road to liberation. They will sweep all the imperialists, warlords, corrupt officials, local tyrants, and evil gentry into their graves. . . . In force and momentum the attack is tempestuous; those who bow before it survive and those who resist perish.❞

—*Selected Works of Mao Tse-Tung, 1954*

The report shows Mao's confidence that peasants could play an active role in a Chinese revolution.

Nationalists and Communists

Revolutionary Marxism had its greatest impact in China. By 1920, central authority had almost ceased to exist in China. Two political forces began to emerge as competitors for the right to rule China: Sun Yat-sen's Nationalist Party, which had been driven from the political arena several years earlier, and the Chinese Communist Party.

In 1921, a group of young radicals, including several faculty and staff members from Beijing University, founded the Chinese Communist Party (CCP) in the commercial and industrial city of **Shanghai.** Comintern agents soon advised the new party to join with the more experienced Nationalist Party.

Sun Yat-sen, leader of the Nationalists (see Chapter 22), welcomed the cooperation. He needed the expertise that the Soviet Union could provide. His anti-imperialist words had alienated many Western powers. One English-language newspaper in Shanghai wrote, "All his life, all his influence, are devoted to ideas that keep China in turmoil, and it is utterly undesirable that he should be allowed to prosecute those aims here." In 1923, the two parties—Nationalists and Communists—formed an alliance to oppose the warlords and drive the imperialist powers out of China.

For over three years, the two parties overlooked their mutual suspicions and worked together. They mobilized and trained a revolutionary army to march north and seize control over China. This Northern Expedition began in the summer of 1926. By the following spring, revolutionary forces had taken control of all of China south of the **Chang Jiang** (Yangtze), including the major river ports of Wuhan and Shanghai.

Tensions between the two parties eventually rose to the surface. Sun Yat-sen died in 1925 and was succeeded as head of the Nationalist Party by the general **Chiang Kai-shek** (JEE•AHNG KY•SHEHK).

Chiang pretended to support the alliance with the Communists. In April 1927, however, he struck against the Communists and their supporters in Shanghai, killing thousands in what is called the **Shanghai Massacre.** The Communist-Nationalist alliance ceased to exist.

In 1928, Chiang Kai-shek founded a new Chinese republic at **Nanjing.** During the next three years, he worked to reunify China. Although Chiang saw Japan as a serious threat to the Chinese nation, he believed that Japan was less dangerous than his other enemy, the Communists. He once remarked that "the Communists are a disease of the heart."

✓**Reading Check** **Explaining** How did Chiang Kai-shek change the Communist-Nationalist alliance?

The Communists in Hiding

After the Shanghai Massacre, most of the Communist leaders went into hiding in the city. There, they tried to revive the Communist movement among the working class. Shanghai was a rich recruiting ground for the party. People were discontented and looking for leadership.

Some party members fled to the mountainous Jiangxi (jee•AHNG•SHEE) Province south of the Chiang Jiang. They were led by the young Communist organizer **Mao Zedong** (MOW DZUH•DOONG). Unlike most other leading members of the Communist Party, Mao was convinced that a Chinese revolution would be driven by the poverty-stricken peasants in the countryside rather than by the urban working class.

Picturing **History**

Members of the Communist forces prepare to evacuate Shanghai during the Nationalists' takeover in 1927. Why did Chiang Kai-shek initiate this military action against the Communists?

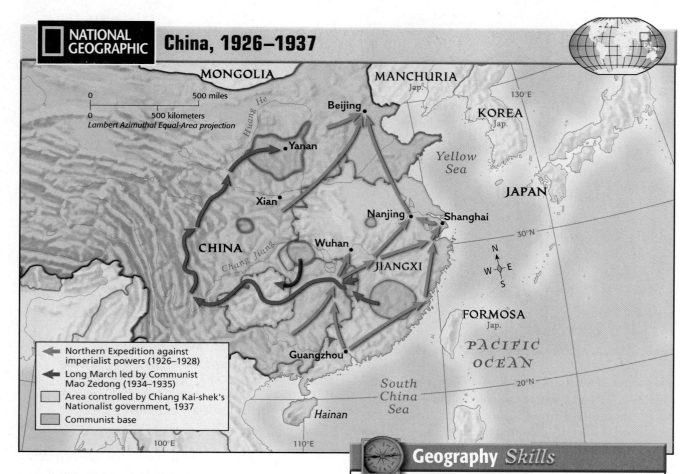

MONGOLIA

MANCHURIA
Jap.

0   500 miles

0   500 kilometers
Lambert Azimuthal Equal-Area projection

Huang He

Beijing

KOREA
Jap.

130°E

•Yanan

*Yellow
Sea*

Xian•

JAPAN

Nanjing• •Shanghai

CHINA

Chang Jiang

Wuhan•

30°N

JIANGXI

N
W   E
S

FORMOSA
Jap.

*PACIFIC
OCEAN*

← Northern Expedition against
    imperialist powers (1926–1928)
← Long March led by Communist
    Mao Zedong (1934–1935)
☐ Area controlled by Chiang Kai-shek's
    Nationalist government, 1937
▨ Communist base

Guangzhou•

*South
China
Sea*

20°N

Hainan

100°E   110°E

Geography *Skills*

Communists and Nationalists fought imperialist powers and each other for control of China in the 1920s and 1930s.

1. **Interpreting Maps** What major cities were the destination of the Northern Expedition? Why do you think the Northern Expedition headed toward these cities?

2. **Applying Geography Skills** Use this map and others of China in this text to identify the mountains, rivers, and deserts Mao's army crossed during the Long March.

Chiang Kai-shek now tried to root the Communists out of their urban base in Shanghai and their rural base in Jiangxi Province. He succeeded in the first task in 1931. Most party leaders in Shanghai were forced to flee to Mao's base in South China.

Chiang Kai-shek then turned his forces against Mao's stronghold in Jiangxi Province. Chiang's forces far outnumbered Mao's, but Mao made effective use of guerrilla tactics, using unexpected maneuvers like sabotage and subterfuge to fight the enemy. Four slogans describe his methods: "When the enemy advances, we retreat! When the enemy halts and camps, we trouble them! When the enemy tries to avoid battle, we attack! When the enemy retreats, we pursue!"

✓Reading Check **Identifying** Which group did Mao believe would start the Communist revolution in China?

The Long March

In 1934, Chiang's troops, using their superior military strength, surrounded the Communist base in Jiangxi. However, Mao's army, the People's Liberation Army **(PLA),** broke through the Nationalist lines and began its famous Long March.

Moving on foot through mountains, marshes, and deserts, Mao's army traveled almost 6,000 miles (9,600 km) to reach the last surviving Communist base in the northwest of China. His troops had to fight all the way. Many froze or starved. One survivor remembered, "As the days went by, there was less and less to eat. After our grain was finished, we ate the horses, and then we lived on wild vegetables. When even the wild vegetables were finished, we ate our leather belts. After that we had to march on empty stomachs."

One year later, Mao's troops reached safety in the dusty hills of North China. Of the ninety thousand troops who had embarked on the journey, only nine

Picturing **History**

Chinese Communists gather in North China following the year-long, 6,000-mile (9,600-km) Long March. Describe the difficulties Mao Zedong's forces had to overcome to reach safety in North China.

thousand remained. In the course of the Long March, Mao Zedong had become the sole leader of the Chinese Communist Party. To people who lived at the time, it must have seemed that the Communist threat to the Nanjing regime was over. To the Communists, however, there remained hope for the future.

Reading Check **Explaining** Why did it seem that communism was no longer a threat to China after the Long March?

The New China of Chiang Kai-shek

In the meantime, Chiang Kai-shek had been trying to build a new nation. Chiang had publicly declared his commitment to the plans of Sun Yat-sen, which called for a republican government. First, however, there would be a transitional period. In Sun's words:

66China . . . needs a republican government just as a boy needs school. As a schoolboy must have good teachers and helpful friends, so the Chinese people, being for the first time under republican rule, must have a farsighted revolutionary government for their training. This calls for the period of political tutelage, which is a necessary transitional stage from monarchy to republicanism. Without this, disorder will be unavoidable.99

In keeping with Sun's program, Chiang announced a period of political tutelage (training) to prepare the Chinese people for a final stage of constitutional government. In the meantime, the Nationalists would use their dictatorial power to carry out a land-reform program and to modernize industry.

It would take more than plans on paper to create a new China, however. Years of neglect and civil war had severely weakened the political, economic, and social fabric of the nation. Most of the people who lived in the countryside were drained by warfare and civil strife. The peasants there were still very poor and overwhelmingly illiterate, and they made up 80 percent of China's population.

A westernized middle class had begun to form in the cities. It was there that the new Nanjing government found much of its support. However, the new westernized elite pursued the middle-class values of individual advancement and material accumulation. They had few links with the peasants in the countryside.

Chiang Kai-shek was aware of the problem of introducing foreign ideas into a population that was still culturally conservative. Thus, while attempting to build a modern industrial state, he tried to bring together modern Western innovations with traditional Confucian values of hard work, obedience, and integrity. With his U.S.-educated wife Mei-ling Soong, Chiang set up a **"New Life Movement."** Its goal was to promote traditional Confucian social ethics, such as integrity, propriety, and righteousness.

People In History

Mao Zedong
1893–1976—Chinese leader

Mao Zedong was the creator of the People's Republic of China. The son of a prosperous peasant, he insisted that the Communist Party support peasant demands for land reform. In 1949, Communist forces under Mao drove out Chiang Kai-shek's Nationalists and assumed complete control of China. Mao's sayings were collected in *Quotations from Chairman Mao Zedong,* which came to be known simply as *The Little Red Book.*

Chiang Kai-shek
1887–1975—Chinese general

Chiang Kai-shek became the leader of the Chinese Nationalist Party in 1925 and established a Nationalist government over China three years later. After the defeat of Japan in 1945, Chiang became president of China, but his forces lost to the Communists in a civil war in 1949. Chiang fled with his forces to Taiwan, where he established a dictatorship, claiming all the while to be the only legitimate ruler of China.

At the same time, it rejected what was viewed as the excessive individualism and material greed of Western capitalist values.

Chiang Kai-shek faced a host of other problems as well. The Nanjing government had total control over only a handful of provinces in the Chang Jiang Valley. As we shall see in the next chapter, the Japanese threatened to gain control of northern China. The Great Depression was also having an ill effect on China's economy.

In spite of all of these problems, Chiang did have some success. He undertook a massive road-building project and repaired and extended much of the country's railroad system as well. He also established a national bank and improved the education system.

In other areas, Chiang was less successful and progress was limited. For example, a land-reform program was enacted in 1930, but it had little effect. Because Chiang's support came from the rural landed gentry, as well as the urban middle class, he did not press for programs that would lead to a redistribution of wealth, the shifting of wealth from a rich minority to a poor majority.

The government was also repressive. Fearing Communist influence, Chiang suppressed all opposition and censored free expression. In so doing, he alienated many intellectuals and political moderates.

✓ Reading Check **Identifying** What was the intended final stage of Chiang Kai-shek's reform program?

TAKS Practice

SECTION 3 ASSESSMENT

Checking for Understanding

1. **Define** guerrilla tactics, redistribution of wealth.

2. **Identify** Sun Yat-sen, Chiang Kai-shek, Shanghai Massacre, Mao Zedong, PLA, New Life Movement.

3. **Locate** Shanghai, Chang Jiang, Nanjing.

4. **Explain** why the Communist Party aligned with the Nationalist Party.

5. **List** the external problems that threatened Chiang Kai-shek's regime.

Critical Thinking

6. **Analyze** What did Mao's Long March accomplish? Why was it successful?

7. **Summarizing Information** Use a diagram like the one below to show Chiang Kai-shek's successes during the 1930s.

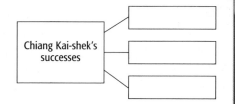

Analyzing Visuals

8. **Describe** the action taking place in the photo on page 794. What clues in the photo indicate the different kinds of warfare undertaken by soldiers during this time?

Writing About History

9. **Persuasive Writing** Conduct research to learn how the United States supported Chiang Kai-shek and why. Write an editorial for or against United States intervention in China.

TECHNOLOGY
SKILLBUILDER

Using an Electronic Spreadsheet

Why Learn This Skill?

Electronic spreadsheets can help people manage data quickly and easily. For example, if you want to know your grade average throughout the year, you could create a spreadsheet in which you enter your latest test and homework scores.

Learning the Skill

A spreadsheet is an electronic worksheet. All spreadsheets follow a basic design of columns and rows.

- Each *column* (vertical) is assigned a letter or number.

- Each *row* (horizontal) is assigned a number.

- A *cell* is where a column and row intersect.

- A cell's position on the spreadsheet is labeled according to its corresponding column and row— Column A, Row 1 (A1); Column B, Row 2 (B2); and so on (see diagram).

	A	B	C	D
1	A1	B1	C1	D1
2	A2	B2	C2	D2
3	A3	B3	C3	D3

Spreadsheets use standard formulas to calculate the numbers. You create a simple mathematical equation that uses these standard formulas and the computer does the calculations for you.

You can make changes in the spreadsheet by using the mouse or cursor to move to the appropriate cell. If you change any number in the cell, the computer will automatically recompute the totals. The computer will even copy a formula from one cell to another.

Practicing the Skill

Suppose you want to know the population densities (populations per square mile or square kilometer) of the countries in South Asia. Use these steps to create a spreadsheet.

① In cell A1 type Country, in cell B1 type Population, in cell C1 type Land Area, and in cell D1 type Population Density.

② In cells A2–A5 type India, Pakistan, Bangladesh, and Sri Lanka. In cell A6, type Total for South Asia.

③ In cells B2–B5, enter the population of each country shown in cells A2–A5.

④ In cells C2–C5, enter the land area (square miles or square kilometers) of each country.

⑤ In cell D2, use the mathematical formula (B1÷C1) to calculate the population density of each country. Copy this formula into cells D3–D5, changing the cell numbers in the formula as you enter each row.

⑥ In cell B6, create a formula to calculate the total population of South Asia (B2+B3+B4+B5).

⑦ In cell C6, create a formula to calculate the total land area of South Asia (C2+C3+C4+C5).

⑧ For cell D6, create a formula to calculate the total population density of South Asia (B6÷C6).

Applying the Skill

Use a spreadsheet to enter your test scores and your homework grades for each of your classes. Calculate your average grade in each class, and then calculate your average grade in all your classes.

Nationalism in Latin America

Main Ideas
- Before the Great Depression, the United States was the foremost investor in Latin America.
- The Great Depression created instability in Latin America, which led to military coups and the creation of military dictatorships.

Key Terms
oligarchy

People to Identify
Juan Vicente Gómez, Hipólito Irigoyen, Getúlio Vargas, Lázaro Cárdenas

Places to Locate
Argentina, Chile, Brazil, Peru, Mexico

Preview Questions
1. What was the Good Neighbor policy?
2. How did the Great Depression affect the economies of Latin America?

Reading Strategy
Summarizing Information Make a chart like the one below listing the main exports of Latin America.

Country	Exports
Argentina	
Chile	
Brazil	
Peru	

Preview of Events

♦1915	♦1920	♦1925	♦1930	♦1935	♦1940

1920
United States becomes the main investor in Latin America

1930
Latin American exports decrease by 50 percent

1938
Getúlio Vargas establishes his New State in Brazil

Getúlio Vargas

Voices from the Past

In July 1938, Getúlio Vargas spoke to the Brazilian nation to explain his dictatorial regime, which he called the New State:

❝If you would ask me what is the program of the New State, I would tell you that its program is to crisscross the nation with railroads, highways, and airlines; to increase production; to provide for the workers and to encourage agriculture; to expand exports; to prepare the armed forces; to organize public opinion so that there is, body and soul, one Brazilian thought . . . finally [that] the preparation of internal and external defense by the rearmament of our brave armed forces and the simultaneous education of the new generations [is] inculcating [implanting] in them the spirit and love of the fatherland.❞

—*A Documentary History of Brazil,* Bradford E. Burns, 1966

Vargas's New State drew much of its inspiration from the Fascist regimes of Mussolini and Hitler.

The Latin American Economy

At the beginning of the twentieth century, the Latin American economy was based largely on the export of foodstuffs and raw materials. Some countries relied on only one or two products for sale abroad. **Argentina,** for example, sent beef and wheat; **Chile,** nitrates and copper; **Brazil** and Caribbean nations, sugar; and

Central America, bananas. A few reaped large profits from these exports. For the majority of the population, however, the returns were small.

Role of the United States Beginning in the 1920s, the United States began to replace Great Britain as the foremost investor in Latin America. British investors had put money into stocks and other forms of investment that did not give them direct control of Latin American companies. Unlike British investors, U.S. investors put their funds directly into production enterprises and ran companies themselves. In this way, large segments of Latin America's export industries fell into the United States's hands. A number of smaller Central American countries became independent republics, but their economies were often dependent on large, wealthy nations. The U.S.-owned United Fruit Company, for example, owned land, packing plants, and railroads in Central America. American firms also gained control of the copper-mining industry in Chile and **Peru,** as well as of the oil industry in **Mexico,** Peru, and Bolivia.

The fact that investors in the United States controlled many Latin American industries angered Latin Americans. A growing nationalist consciousness led many of them to view the United States as an imperialist power. It was not difficult for Latin American nationalists to show that profits from U.S. businesses were sometimes used to keep ruthless dictators in power. In Venezuela, for example, U.S. oil companies had a close relationship with the dictator **Juan Vicente Gómez.**

The United States had always cast a large shadow over Latin America. It had intervened militarily in Latin American affairs for years. This was especially true in Central America and the Caribbean. Many Americans considered both regions vital to the security of the United States.

The United States made some attempts to change its relationship with Latin America, however. In 1933, President Franklin D. Roosevelt announced the **Good Neighbor policy.** This policy rejected the use of U.S. military force in Latin America. Adhering to his word, the president withdrew the last United States Marines from Haiti in 1934. For the first time in 30 years, there were no U.S. troops in Latin American countries.

Impact of the Great Depression The Great Depression was a disaster for Latin America's economy. The weakening of the economies in the United States and Europe led to a decreased demand for Latin

NATIONAL GEOGRAPHIC **Latin America, 1939**

Geography Skills

The economic and political stability of Latin America was strongly affected by World War I and the Great Depression.

1. **Interpreting Maps** How many countries made up Latin America in 1939?
2. **Applying Geography Skills** What evidence of the European occupation of Latin America can you find on this map? What inferences can you draw about this occupation by looking at northern South America?

American foodstuffs and raw materials, especially coffee, sugar, metals, and meat. The total value of Latin American exports in 1930 was almost 50 percent below the figures for the years between 1925 and 1929. The countries that depended on the export of only one product, rather than multiple products, were especially damaged.

The Great Depression had one positive effect on the Latin American economy. With a decline in exports, Latin American countries no longer had the revenues to buy manufactured goods. Many Latin American governments encouraged the development of new industries that would produce goods that were formerly imported. This process of industrial development was supposed to achieve greater economic independence for Latin America.

Often, however, the new industries were not started by individual capitalists. Because of a shortage of capital in the private sector, governments frequently invested in the new industries. This led to government-run steel industries in Chile and Brazil, along with government-run oil industries in Argentina and Mexico.

✓ **Reading Check** **Comparing** How did the United States's method of investing in Latin America differ from that of Britain?

The Move to Authoritarianism

Most Latin American countries had republican forms of government. In reality, however, a relatively small group of church officials, military leaders, and large landowners dominated each country. This elite group controlled the masses of people, who were mostly poverty-stricken peasants. Military forces were crucial in keeping these special-interest groups in power. Indeed, military leaders often took control of the government.

This trend toward authoritarianism increased during the 1930s, largely because of the impact of the Great Depression. Domestic instability caused by economic crises led to the creation of many military dictatorships at the beginning of the 1930s. This trend was especially evident in Argentina, Brazil, and Mexico. Together, these nations possessed over half of the land and wealth of Latin America.

Argentina Argentina was controlled by an oligarchy, a government where a select group of people exercises control. This oligarchy of large landowners who had grown wealthy from the export of beef and wheat failed to realize the growing importance of industry and cities in their country. It also ignored the growing middle class, which reacted by forming the Radical Party in 1890.

In 1916, **Hipólito Irigoyen** (ee•PAW•lee•TOH IHR•ih•GOH•YEHN), leader of the Radical Party, was elected president of Argentina. The Radical Party, however, feared the industrial workers, who were using strikes to improve their conditions. The party thus drew closer to the large landowners and became more corrupt.

The military was also concerned with the rising power of the industrial workers. In 1930, the Argentine army overthrew President Irigoyen and reestablished the power of the large landowners. Through this action, the military hoped to continue the old export economy and thus stop the growth of working-class power that would come with more industrialization.

During World War II, restless military officers formed a new organization, known as the Group of United Officers (GOU). They were unhappy with the government and overthrew it in June 1943. Three years later, one GOU member, Juan Perón, was elected president of Argentina (see Chapter 29).

Brazil In 1889, the army had overthrown the Brazilian monarchy and established a republic. The republic was controlled chiefly by the landed elites, who had become wealthy by growing coffee on large plantations.

By 1900, three-quarters of the world's coffee was grown in Brazil. As long as coffee prices remained high, the ruling oligarchy was able to maintain its power. The oligarchy largely ignored the growth of urban industry and the working class that came with it.

The Great Depression devastated the coffee industry. By the end of 1929, coffee prices had hit a record low. In 1930, a military coup made **Getúlio Vargas**, a wealthy rancher, president of Brazil. Vargas ruled Brazil from 1930 to 1945. Early in his rule, he appealed to workers by instituting an eight-hour day and a minimum wage.

Faced with strong opposition in 1937, Vargas made himself dictator. Beginning in 1938, he established his New State. It was basically an authoritarian state with some Fascist-like features. Political parties were outlawed and civil rights restricted. A secret police used torture to silence Vargas's opponents.

The price of coffee has had a major impact on almost every aspect of life in Brazil.

Selected Nationalist Movements in the Early Twentieth Century

	Latin America			Africa and Asia			Middle East		
Country	Argentina	Brazil	Mexico	Kenya	Libya	India	Turkey	Persia	Northern Arabian Peninsula
Leader	Argentine army; Group of United Officers	Getúlio Vargas	Lázaro Cárdenas	Harry Thuku (Young Kikuyu Association); Jomo Kenyatta	Omar Mukhtar	Mohandas Gandhi	Mustafa Kemal (Atatürk)	Reza Khan (Reza Shah Pahlavi)	Ibn Saud
Driving Force	Fear of workers; dissatisfaction with government	Bad economy	Foreign control of oil industry	High taxes; British rule	Italian rule	British rule	Greek seizure of Anatolian Peninsula	British and Soviet presence	European creation of states
Outcome	New governments (1930, 1943)	Vargas's New State (1938)	Seizure of oil and property (1938); PEMEX	Exile of Thuku (1922)	Revolt crushed (1920s)	Government of India Act (1935)	Turkish Republic (1923)	Iran (1935)	Saudi Arabia (1932)

Chart Skills

Between World War I and World War II, many countries around the world struggled to achieve independence and national identity.

1. **Analyzing** What was the most frequent motivation for revolt in the countries identified above?

2. **Summarizing** How successful were those who sought to create a new nation or a new form of government? Using the information above and in this chapter, write a paragraph that summarizes the attempts at independence and nationalism made by the above countries.

Vargas also pursued a policy of stimulating new industries. The government established the Brazilian steel industry and set up a company to explore for oil. By the end of World War II, Brazil had become Latin America's chief industrial power. In 1945, the army, fearing that Vargas might prolong his power illegally after calling for new elections, forced him to resign.

Mexico Mexico was not an authoritarian state, but neither was it truly democratic. The Mexican Revolution of the early twentieth century had been the first significant effort in Latin America to overturn the system of large landed estates and raise the living standards of the masses (see Chapter 21). Out of the revolution had emerged a relatively stable political order.

The government was democratic in form. However, the official political party of the Mexican Revolution, known as the Institutional Revolutionary Party, or PRI, controlled the major groups within Mexican society. Every six years, party bosses of the PRI chose the party's presidential candidate. That candidate was then dutifully elected by the people.

A new wave of change began with **Lázaro Cárdenas** (KAHR•duhn•AHS), president of Mexico from 1934 to 1940. He moved to fulfill some of the original goals of the revolution. His major step was to distribute 44 million acres (17.8 million ha) of land to landless Mexican peasants, an action that made him enormously popular with the peasants.

Cárdenas also took a strong stand with the United States, especially over oil. By 1900, Mexico was known to have enormous oil reserves. Over the next 30 years, foreign oil companies from Britain and, in particular, the United States, made large investments in Mexico. After a dispute with the foreign-owned oil companies over workers' wages, the Cárdenas government seized control of the oil fields and the property of the oil companies.

The U.S. oil companies were furious and asked President Franklin D. Roosevelt to intervene. He refused, reminding them of his promise in the Good Neighbor policy not to send U.S. troops into Latin America. Mexicans cheered Cárdenas as the president who had stood up to the United States.

Eventually, the Mexican government did pay the oil companies for their property. It then set up **PEMEX,** a national oil company, to run the oil industry.

☑ **Reading Check** **Examining** How was the Mexican government democratic in form but not in practice?

Culture in Latin America

During the early twentieth century, European artistic and literary movements began to penetrate Latin America. In major cities, such as Buenos Aires in Argentina and São Paulo in Brazil, wealthy elites expressed great interest in the work of modern artists.

Latin American artists went abroad and brought back modern techniques, which they often adapted to their own native roots. Many artists and writers used their work to promote the emergence of a new national spirit. An example was the Mexican artist Diego Rivera.

Rivera had studied in Europe, where he was especially influenced by fresco painting in Italy. After his return to Mexico, he developed a monumental style that filled wall after wall with murals. Rivera's wall paintings can be found in such diverse places as the Ministry of Education, the Chapel of the Agriculture School at Chapingo, and the Social Security Hospi-

🎨 **History** *through Art*

The Arrival of Cortez at Veracruz (detail) by Diego Rivera, 1929–1935
In this mural, what is Rivera saying about the impact of Europeans on Mexico's past?

tal. His works were aimed at the masses of people, many of whom could not read.

Rivera sought to create a national art that would portray Mexico's past, especially its Aztec legends, as well as Mexican festivals and folk customs. His work also carried a political and social message. Rivera did not want people to forget the Mexican Revolution, which had overthrown the large landowners and the foreign interests that supported them.

☑ **Reading Check** **Examining** How did Diego Rivera use his artistic talent as a political tool?

🌟 **TAKS Practice**

SECTION 4 ASSESSMENT

Checking for Understanding

1. **Define** oligarchy.

2. **Identify** Juan Vicente Gómez, Good Neighbor policy, Hipólito Irigoyen, Getúlio Vargas, Lázaro Cárdenas, PEMEX.

3. **Locate** Argentina, Chile, Brazil, Peru, Mexico.

4. **Explain** how Vargas's dictatorship ended.

5. **List** some of the industries the United States owned in Latin America.

Critical Thinking

6. **Examine** Why did the Great Depression cause many Latin American countries to improve their economic systems and gain more independence from foreign economic dominance?

7. **Compare and Contrast** Make a chart like the one below comparing and contrasting political struggles in Argentina and Brazil.

Argentina	Brazil

Analyzing Visuals

8. **Analyze** the photo on page 801. What does this photo reveal about what working conditions were like on Brazilian coffee plantations?

Writing About History

9. **Descriptive Writing** Using outside sources, find one or two examples of Diego Rivera's murals. In an essay, compare Rivera's paintings to the frescoes of medieval Italian painters like Giotto. How do Rivera's murals reflect the influence of Italian frescoes? How are they different?

Using Key Terms

1. The name given by his followers to Mohandas Gandhi was _____, which means "great soul."

2. Serbian forces in the recent war in Bosnia followed a policy called _____ when they tried to eliminate Muslims from their land.

3. A policy of killing people of a particular ethnic or racial group is called _____.

4. An advocate of nonviolence, Gandhi urged _____ as a powerful method to achieve justice and bring an end to oppressive British rule in India.

5. When Mao Zedong's forces were outnumbered at their rural base in Jiangxi Province, they used _____ such as sabotage and subterfuge to fight Chiang Kai-shek's Nationalist troops.

6. Argentina, Brazil, and Mexico were controlled by _____, or governments where only a select group of people exercises control.

7. Chinese peasants did not support Chiang Kai-shek because he did not favor _____.

8. The concentration of various manufacturing processes within a single Japanese industry is called a _____, or large financial and industrial corporation.

9. _____ was a movement stressing unity of all Africans.

Reviewing Key Facts

10. **Citizenship** Why were many Arabs opposed to the Balfour Declaration?

11. **Government** Identify the Comintern and explain why it was formed.

12. **Government** What reforms did Atatürk implement to transform the Turkish Republic into a modern and secular state?

13. **History** What happened to cause Chinese Communists to undertake the Long March in 1933?

14. **History** What did the United States hope to accomplish through its Good Neighbor policy toward Latin America?

15. **History** Why did the Nationalists and Communists in China form an alliance in 1928?

16. **Economics** Explain an import-export economy.

17. **Government** What did the British do to make Indian people less opposed to their colonial government in 1935?

18. **Citizenship** Why do people in some apparently democratic Latin American nations have little voice in their country's government?

19. **Economics** Explain how the entrenched system of *zaibatsu* contributed to increased nationalism and a move toward militarism in Japan.

20. **Citizenship** What message did Jomo Kenyatta use as the basic theme of his book *Facing Mount Kenya?*

Critical Thinking

21. **Cause and Effect** How did harsh treatment of Jewish people in Europe create problems for Arab people in the Middle East?

22. **Evaluating** How did Chiang Kai-shek's fear of communism cause him to alienate many intellectuals and political moderates?

23. **Making Generalizations** What was the cultural impact of World War I on Africans? How did the political status of Africa change after the war?

Chapter Summary

Between the two World Wars, a growing sense of nationalism inspired many countries to seek their independence from foreign rulers, as shown in the chart below.

Middle East	Africa and Asia	China	Latin America
The decline of the Ottoman Empire results in the emergence of many new Arab states.	Black Africans who fought in World War I become more politically active. They organize reform movements then call for independence.	In 1923, the Nationalists and the Communists form an alliance to oppose the warlords and drive the imperialist powers out of China.	After the Great Depression, Latin American countries work to become economically independent by creating new industries to produce goods that were formerly imported.

Writing about History

24. **Expository Writing** Nationalism first became a significant political force in the movement against Napoleon. Write an essay comparing the early nationalist movements to the later battles against imperialism discussed in this chapter.

Analyzing Sources

Chiang Kai-shek declared his commitment to Sun Yat-sen's plans for building a new nation. Chiang announced a period of political training, as described by Sun in the following quote.

> ❝China . . . needs a republican government just as a boy needs school. As a schoolboy must have good teachers and helpful friends, so the Chinese people, being for the first time under republican rule, must have a farsighted revolutionary government for their training. This calls for the period of political tutelage, which is a necessary transitional stage from monarchy to republicanism. Without this, disorder will be unavoidable.❞

25. What did Chiang Kai-shek mean when he compared China to a boy in school?

26. What does the quote seem to say, compared to what you think it really means? Is there a self-serving bias in Sun's statement? If so, explain.

Applying Technology Skills

27. **Using the Internet** Use the Internet to determine how the contemporary governments of Argentina and Brazil compare with the dictatorships that ruled these countries in the 1930s.

28. **Using the Internet** Use the Internet to learn more about Jomo Kenyatta, Léopold Senghor, Nnamdi Azikiwe, or other nationalist leaders who worked to end colonial rule in Africa. What methods did they use and how successful were they?

Making Decisions

29. Imagine that you are a female American foreign exchange student. Which Middle Eastern country would you choose to live in for a year? Discuss the reasons for your choice and also the concessions that would be required of you.

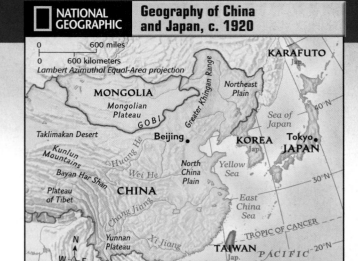

NATIONAL GEOGRAPHIC Geography of China and Japan, c. 1920

Analyzing Maps and Charts

Use the map above to answer the following questions.

30. Near what latitudes are the cities of Beijing and Tokyo located?

31. Name the bodies of water that separate Japan from Korea, and Japan from China.

32. List three geographical features of China.

33. Compare this map to the map shown on page 790. What major territory did Japan acquire between the date indicated on the above map and 1933?

The Princeton Review **TAKS** Test Practice

Directions: Choose the best answer to the question below.

Which of the following is a true statement about the relationship between World War I and nationalism?

A World War I brought nationalist movements to a standstill.

B Most nationalist movements had reached their goals by the conclusion of World War I.

C The weakening of European countries fostered national independence movements.

D World War I helped the European economy, which fueled nationalist movements.

Test-Taking Tip: Read each answer choice carefully and eliminate any statements that you know are false. Getting rid of these wrong answer choices will help you find the correct answer.

CHAPTER 26

World War II
1939–1945

Key Events

As you read this chapter, look for the key events in the history of World War II.
- Adolf Hitler's philosophy of Aryan superiority led to World War II in Europe and was also the source of the Holocaust.
- Two separate and opposing alliances, the Allies and the Axis Powers, waged a world-wide war.
- World War II left lasting impressions on civilian populations.

The Impact Today

The events that occurred during this time period still impact our lives today.
- By the end of World War II, the balance of power had shifted away from Europe.
- Germany and Japan's search for expanded "living space" is comparable to nations fighting over borders today.
- Atomic weapons pose a threat to all nations.

 World History Video The Chapter 26 video, "The Holocaust," illustrates the horrors of Hitler's Final Solution.

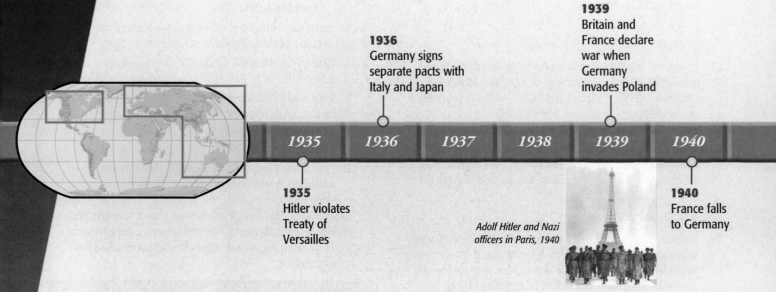

1936
Germany signs separate pacts with Italy and Japan

1939
Britain and France declare war when Germany invades Poland

1935   1936   1937   1938   1939   1940

1935
Hitler violates Treaty of Versailles

Adolf Hitler and Nazi officers in Paris, 1940

1940
France falls to Germany

The Marine Corps War Memorial in Arlington County, Virginia, depicts marines raising the American flag on Iwo Jima in February 1945.

Self-Portrait with a Jewish Identity Card *by Felix Nussbaum, 1943*

1942
Nazi death camps in full operation

Atomic bomb dropped on Hiroshima

1945
Japanese surrender after United States drops atomic bombs on Japan

1941   1942   1943   1944   1945   1946

1941
United States enters war after Japan attacks Pearl Harbor

Soldiers and civilians celebrate V-E Day, Paris

1945
Germany surrenders

1946
Churchill proclaims existence of "iron curtain" in Europe

HISTORY Online
Chapter Overview
Visit the *Glencoe World History* Web site at tx.wh.glencoe.com and click on **Chapter 26–Chapter Overview** to preview chapter information.

A Story That Matters

Poster, c. 1938, which proclaims "One People, one State, one Leader!"

After becoming dictator in 1933, Hitler often held large rallies to inspire the loyalty of Germans.

Hitler's Vision

On February 3, 1933, Adolf Hitler met secretly with Germany's leading generals. He had been appointed chancellor of Germany only four days before and was by no means assured that he would remain in office for long. Nevertheless, he spoke with confidence.

Hitler told the generals about his desire to remove the "cancer of democracy," create "the highest authoritarian state leadership," and forge a new domestic unity. All Germans would need to realize that "only a struggle can save us and that everything else must be subordinated to this idea." The youth especially would have to be trained and their wills strengthened "to fight with all means."

Hitler went on to say that Germany must rearm by instituting a military draft. Leaders must ensure that the men who were going to be drafted were not "poisoned by pacifism, Marxism, or Bolshevism." Once Germany had regained its military strength, how should this strength be used? Hitler had an answer. Because Germany's living space was too small for its people, it must prepare for "the conquest of new living space in the east and its ruthless Germanization."

Even before he had consolidated his power, Hitler had a clear vision of his goals. Reaching those goals meant another European war. Although World War I has been described as a total war, World War II was even more so. It was fought on a scale unprecedented in history and led to the most widespread human-made destruction that the world had ever seen.

Why It Matters

World War II in Europe was clearly Hitler's war. Other countries may have helped make the war possible by not resisting Germany earlier, before it grew strong, but it was Nazi Germany's actions that made the war inevitable. Globally, World War II was more than just Hitler's war. It consisted of two conflicts. One arose, as mentioned above, from the ambitions of Germany in Europe. The other arose from the ambitions of Japan in Asia. By 1941, with the involvement of the United States in both conflicts, these two conflicts merged into one global world war.

History and You The decision by the United States to use atomic bombs against Japan led to the end of World War II. Find two contrasting views on the potential of nuclear warfare today and analyze the perspectives.

Paths to War

Main Ideas
- Adolf Hitler's theory of Aryan racial domination laid the foundation for aggressive expansion outside of Germany.
- The actions and ambitions of Japan and Germany paved the way for the outbreak of World War II.

Key Terms
demilitarized, appeasement, sanction

People to Identify
Adolf Hitler, Benito Mussolini, Joseph Stalin, Chiang Kai-shek

Places to Locate
Rhineland, Sudetenland, Manchukuo

Preview Questions
1. What agreement was reached at the Munich Conference?
2. Why did Germany believe it needed more land?

Reading Strategy
Categorizing Information Create a chart listing examples of Japanese aggression and German aggression prior to the outbreak of World War II.

Japanese Aggression	German Aggression

Preview of Events

◆1931	◆1932	◆1933	◆1934	◆1935	◆1936	◆1937	◆1938	◆1939

1931
Japanese forces invade Manchuria

1936
Hitler and Mussolini create Rome-Berlin Axis

1937
Japanese seize Chinese capital

1938
Hitler annexes Austria

1939
World War II begins

Voices from the Past

After the leaders of France and Great Britain gave in to Hitler's demands on Czechoslovakia in 1938, Winston Churchill spoke to the British House of Commons:

❝I will begin by saying what everybody would like to ignore or forget but which must nevertheless be stated, namely, that we have sustained a total and unmitigated defeat. . . . And I will say this, that I believe the Czechs, left to themselves and told they were going to get no help from the Western Powers, would have been able to make better terms than they have got. . . . We are in the presence of a disaster of the first magnitude which has befallen Great Britain and France. . . . And do not suppose that this is the end. This is only the beginning of the reckoning.❞
—*Parliamentary Debates,* London, 1938

Winston Churchill

Churchill believed that Hitler's actions would lead to another war. He proved to be right.

The German Path to War

World War II in Europe had its beginnings in the ideas of **Adolf Hitler.** He believed that Germans belonged to a so-called Aryan race that was superior to all other races and nationalities. Consequently, Hitler believed that Germany was capable of building a great civilization. To be a great power, however, Germany needed more land to support a larger population.

Already in the 1920s, Hitler had indicated that a Nazi regime would find this land to the east—in the Soviet Union. Germany therefore must prepare for war with the Soviet Union. Once the Soviet Union had been conquered, according to Hitler, its land would be resettled by German peasants. The Slavic peoples could be used as slave labor to build the Third Reich, an Aryan racial state that Hitler thought would dominate Europe for a thousand years.

The First Steps

After World War I, the Treaty of Versailles had limited Germany's military power. As chancellor, Hitler, posing as a man of peace, stressed that Germany wished to revise the unfair provisions of the treaty by peaceful means. Germany, he said, only wanted its rightful place among the European states.

On March 9, 1935, however, Hitler announced the creation of a new air force. One week later, he began a military draft that would expand Germany's army from 100,000 to 550,000 troops. These steps were in direct violation of the Treaty of Versailles.

France, Great Britain, and Italy condemned Germany's actions and warned against future aggressive steps. In the midst of the Great Depression, however, these nations were distracted by their own internal problems and did nothing further.

Hitler was convinced that the Western states had no intention of using force to maintain the Treaty of Versailles. Hence, on March 7, 1936, he sent German troops into the **Rhineland.** The Rhineland was part of Germany, but, according to the Treaty of Versailles, it was a demilitarized area. That is, Germany was not permitted to have weapons or fortifications there. France had the right to use force against any violation of the

demilitarized Rhineland but would not act without British support.

Great Britain did not support the use of force against Germany, however. The British government viewed the occupation of German territory by German troops as a reasonable action by a dissatisfied power. The London *Times* noted that the Germans were only "going into their own back garden." Great Britain thus began to practice a policy of appeasement. This policy was based on the belief that if European states satisfied the reasonable demands of dissatisfied powers, the dissatisfied powers would be content, and stability and peace would be achieved in Europe.

New Alliances

Meanwhile, Hitler gained new allies. **Benito Mussolini** had long dreamed of creating a new Roman Empire in the Mediterranean, and, in October 1935, Fascist Italy invaded Ethiopia. Angered by French and British opposition to his invasion, Mussolini welcomed Hitler's support. He began to draw closer to the German dictator.

In 1936, both Germany and Italy sent troops to Spain to help General Francisco Franco in the Spanish Civil War. In October 1936, Mussolini and Hitler made an agreement recognizing their common political and economic interests. One month later, Mussolini spoke of the new alliance between Italy and Germany, called the Rome-Berlin Axis. Also in November, Germany and Japan signed the Anti-Comintern Pact, promising a common front against communism.

Union with Austria

By 1937, Germany was once more a "world power," as Hitler proclaimed. He was convinced that neither France nor Great Britain would provide much opposition to his plans. In 1938, he decided to pursue one of his goals: *Anschluss* (ANSH•luhs), or union, with Austria, his native land.

By threatening Austria with invasion, Hitler forced the Austrian chancellor to put Austrian Nazis in charge of the government. The new government promptly invited German troops to enter Austria and "help" in maintaining law and order. One day later, on March 13, 1938, after his triumphal return to his native land, Hitler annexed Austria to Germany.

LA TRIBUNA ILLUSTRATA

LA STORICA VISITA DEL DUCE AL FÜHRER

Picturing **History**

This 1937 Italian illustration depicts Hitler and Mussolini. **What ideology brought Hitler and Mussolini together?**

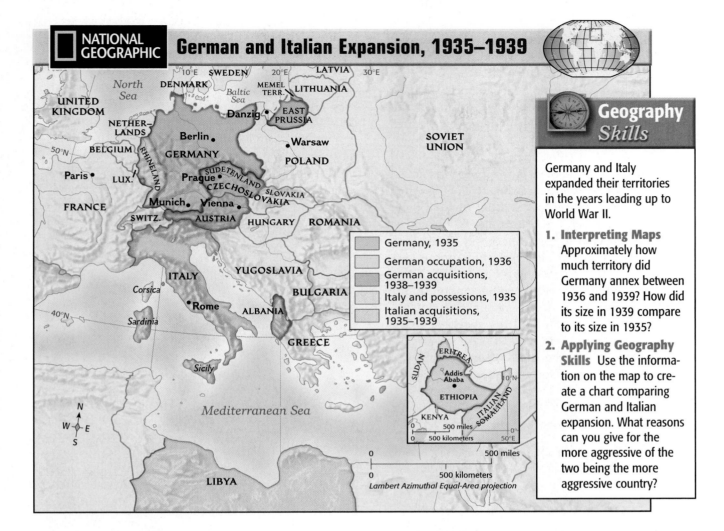

German and Italian Expansion, 1935–1939

NATIONAL GEOGRAPHIC

Legend:
- Germany, 1935
- German occupation, 1936
- German acquisitions, 1938–1939
- Italy and possessions, 1935
- Italian acquisitions, 1935–1939

Lambert Azimuthal Equal-Area projection

Geography Skills

Germany and Italy expanded their territories in the years leading up to World War II.

1. **Interpreting Maps** Approximately how much territory did Germany annex between 1936 and 1939? How did its size in 1939 compare to its size in 1935?

2. **Applying Geography Skills** Use the information on the map to create a chart comparing German and Italian expansion. What reasons can you give for the more aggressive of the two being the more aggressive country?

Demands and Appeasement Hitler's next objective was the destruction of Czechoslovakia. On September 15, 1938, he demanded that Germany be given the **Sudetenland,** an area in northwestern Czechoslovakia that was inhabited largely by Germans. He expressed his willingness to risk "world war" to achieve his objective.

At a hastily arranged conference in Munich, British, French, German, and Italian representatives did not object to Hitler's plans but instead reached an agreement that met virtually all of Hitler's demands. German troops were allowed to occupy the Sudetenland. The Czechs, abandoned by their Western allies, stood by helplessly.

The Munich Conference was the high point of Western appeasement of Hitler. When Neville Chamberlain, the British prime minister, returned to England from Munich, he boasted that the agreement meant "peace for our time." Hitler had promised Chamberlain that he would make no more demands. Like many others, Chamberlain believed Hitler's promises.

Great Britain and France React In fact, Hitler was more convinced than ever that the Western democracies were weak and would not fight. Increasingly, Hitler was sure that he could not make a mistake, and he had by no means been satisfied at Munich.

In March 1939, Hitler invaded and took control of Bohemia and Moravia in western Czechoslovakia. In the eastern part of the country, Slovakia became a puppet state controlled by Nazi Germany. On the evening of March 15, 1939, Hitler triumphantly declared in Prague that he would be known as the greatest German of them all.

At last, the Western states reacted to the Nazi threat. Hitler's aggression had made clear that his promises were worthless. When Hitler began to demand the Polish port of Danzig, Great Britain saw the danger and offered to protect Poland in the event of war. At the same time, both France and Britain realized that only the Soviet Union was powerful enough to help contain Nazi aggression. They began political and military negotiations with **Joseph Stalin,** the Soviet dictator.

Hitler and the Soviets Meanwhile, Hitler pressed on in the belief that the West would not fight over Poland. He now feared, however, that the West and the Soviet Union might make an alliance. Such an alliance could mean a two-front war for Germany. To prevent this possibility, Hitler made his own agreement with Joseph Stalin.

On August 23, 1939, Germany and the Soviet Union signed the Nazi-Soviet Nonaggression Pact. In it, the two nations promised not to attack each other. To get the nonaggression pact, Hitler offered Stalin control of eastern Poland and the Baltic states. Because he expected to fight the Soviet Union anyway, it did not matter to Hitler what he promised—he was accustomed to breaking promises.

Hitler shocked the world when he announced the nonaggression pact. The treaty gave Hitler the freedom to attack Poland. He told his generals, "Now Poland is in the position in which I wanted her. . . . I am only afraid that at the last moment some swine will submit to me a plan for mediation."

Hitler need not have worried. On September 1, German forces invaded Poland. Two days later, Britain and France declared war on Germany.

✓ Reading Check **Identifying** Where did Hitler believe he could find more "living space" to expand Germany?

The Japanese Path to War

In September 1931, Japanese soldiers had seized Manchuria, which had natural resources Japan needed. Japan used as an excuse a Chinese attack on a Japanese railway near the city of Mukden. In fact, the "Mukden incident" had been carried out by Japanese soldiers disguised as Chinese.

Worldwide protests against the Japanese led the League of Nations to send investigators to Manchuria. When the investigators issued a report condemning the seizure, Japan withdrew from the league. Over the next several years, Japan strengthened its hold on Manchuria, which was renamed **Manchukuo.** Japan now began to expand into North China.

By the mid-1930s, militants connected to the government and the armed forces had gained control of Japanese politics. The United States refused to recognize the Japanese takeover of Manchuria but was unwilling to threaten force.

War with China **Chiang Kai-shek** tried to avoid a conflict with Japan so that he could deal with what he considered the greater threat from the Communists. When clashes between Chinese and

Japanese troops broke out, he sought to appease Japan by allowing it to govern areas in North China.

As Japan moved steadily southward, protests against Japanese aggression grew stronger in Chinese cities. In December 1936, Chiang ended his military efforts against the Communists and formed a new united front against the Japanese. In July 1937, Chinese and Japanese forces clashed south of Beijing and hostilities spread.

Japan had not planned to declare war on China. However, the 1937 incident eventually turned into a major conflict. The Japanese seized the Chinese capital of Nanjing in December. Chiang Kai-shek refused to surrender and moved his government upriver, first to Hankou, then to Chongqing.

NATIONAL GEOGRAPHIC

Japanese Expansion, 1933–1941

Japanese territory, 1933
Japanese acquisitions to November 1941

0   1,000 miles
0   1,000 kilometers
Two-Point Equidistant projection

Geography *Skills*

Like Germany, Japan attempted to expand its territories prior to the beginning of the war.

1. **Applying Geography Skills** Pose and answer your own question about the territories Japan did *not* acquire but wanted to acquire.

The New Asian Order Japanese military leaders had hoped to force Chiang to agree to join a New Order in East Asia, comprising Japan, Manchuria, and China. Japan would attempt to establish a new system of control in Asia with Japan guiding its Asian neighbors to prosperity. After all, who could better teach Asian societies how to modernize than the one Asian country that had already done it?

Part of Japan's plan was to seize Soviet Siberia, with its rich resources. During the late 1930s, Japan began to cooperate with Nazi Germany. Japan assumed that the two countries would ultimately launch a joint attack on the Soviet Union and divide Soviet resources between them.

When Germany signed the nonaggression pact with the Soviets in August 1939, Japanese leaders had to rethink their goals. Japan did not have the resources to defeat the Soviet Union without help. Thus, the Japanese became interested in the raw materials that could be found in Southeast Asia to fuel its military machine.

A move southward, however, would risk war with the European colonial powers and the United States. Japan's attack on China in the summer of 1937 had already aroused strong criticism, especially in the United States. Nevertheless, in the summer of 1940, Japan demanded the right to exploit economic resources in French Indochina.

The United States objected. It warned Japan that it would apply economic sanctions—restrictions intended to enforce international law—unless Japan

Cabinet of Japanese prime minister Tojo (front center), 1941

withdrew from the area and returned to its borders of 1931. Japan badly needed the oil and scrap iron it was getting from the United States. Should these resources be cut off, Japan would have to find them elsewhere. Japan viewed the possibility of economic sanctions as a threat to its long-term objectives.

Japan was now caught in a dilemma. To guarantee access to the raw materials it wanted in Southeast Asia, Japan had to risk losing raw materials from the United States. After much debate, Japan decided to launch a surprise attack on U.S. and European colonies in Southeast Asia.

Reading Check **Explaining** Why did Japan want to establish a New Order in East Asia?

TAKS Practice

SECTION 1 ASSESSMENT

Checking for Understanding

1. **Define** appeasement, demilitarized, sanction.

2. **Identify** Adolf Hitler, Benito Mussolini, Joseph Stalin, Chiang Kai-shek.

3. **Locate** Rhineland, Sudetenland, Manchukuo.

4. **Explain** why Japan felt the need to control other nations. Also explain the dilemma facing Japan as it sought to acquire access to needed resources.

5. **List** the reasons why Hitler's pact with Stalin was a key factor in forcing Britain and France to declare war on Germany.

Critical Thinking

6. **Explain** In what sense was World War II a product of World War I?

7. **Sequencing Information** Create a chart like the one below listing in chronological order the agreements that emboldened Hitler in his aggressive expansion policies.

Agreements Encouraging Hitler's Aggression Leading to World War II

Analyzing Visuals

8. **Analyze** the illustration on page 810 to determine what opinion the artist had about Italy's alliance with Germany. What aspects of the illustration indicate that its creator and its publisher either did or did not support Hitler's relationship with Mussolini and Italy?

Writing About History

9. **Persuasive Writing** Imagine you are the editor of a British newspaper in 1938. Write an editorial that captures the essence of your viewpoint. Use a headline that offers suggestions on how war can be avoided.

The Course of World War II

Main Ideas
- The bombing of Pearl Harbor created a global war between the Allied and the Axis forces.
- Allied perseverance and effective military operations, as well as Axis miscalculations, brought an end to the war.

Key Terms
blitzkrieg, partisan

People to Identify
Franklin D. Roosevelt, Douglas MacArthur, Winston Churchill, Harry S Truman

Places to Locate
Stalingrad, Midway Island, Normandy, Hiroshima

Preview Questions
1. Why did the United States not enter the war until 1941?
2. What major events helped to end the war in Europe and Asia?

Reading Strategy
Cause and Effect Create a chart listing key events during World War II and their effect on the outcome of the war.

Event	Effect

Preview of Events

♦1939	♦1940	♦1941	♦1942	♦1943	♦1944	♦1945

1940
Germans bomb British cities

1942
Japanese defeated at the Battle of Midway Island

1943
Germans defeated at Stalingrad

1944
Allied forces invade France on D-Day

Voices from the Past

On September 1, 1939, after beginning his attack on Poland, Hitler addressed the German Reichstag:

❝I do not want to be anything other than the first soldier of the German Reich. I have once more put on the uniform which was once most holy and precious to me. I shall only take it off after victory or I shall not live to see the end. . . . As a National Socialist and as a German soldier, I am going into this struggle strong in heart. My whole life has been nothing but a struggle for my people, for their revival, for Germany . . . Just as I myself am ready to risk my life any time for my people and for Germany, so I demand the same of everyone else. But anyone who thinks that he can oppose this national commandment, whether directly or indirectly, will die! Traitors can expect death.❞

—*Nazism 1919–1945, A Documentary Reader*, J. Noakes and G. Pridham, 1995

Hitler addresses the Reichstag on September 1, 1939.

Hitler had committed Germany to a life-or-death struggle.

Europe at War

Hitler stunned Europe with the speed and efficiency of the German attack on Poland. His blitzkrieg, or "lightning war," used armored columns, called panzer divisions, supported by airplanes. Each panzer division was a strike force of about three hundred tanks with accompanying forces and supplies.

The forces of the blitzkrieg broke quickly through Polish lines and encircled the bewildered Polish troops. Regular infantry units then moved in to hold the newly conquered territory. Within four weeks, Poland had surrendered. On September 28, 1939, Germany and the Soviet Union divided Poland.

Hitler's Early Victories

After a winter of waiting (called the "phony war"), Hitler resumed the attack on April 9, 1940, with another blitzkrieg against Denmark and Norway. One month later, on May 10, Germany launched an attack on the Netherlands, Belgium, and France. The main assault was through Luxembourg and the Ardennes (ahr•DEHN) Forest. German panzer divisions broke through weak French defensive positions there and raced across northern France. French and British forces were taken by surprise when the Germans went around, instead of across, the Maginot Line (a series of concrete and steel fortifications armed with heavy artillery along France's border with Germany). The Germans' action split the Allied armies, trapping French troops and the entire British army on the beaches of Dunkirk. Only by the heroic efforts of the Royal Navy and civilians in private boats did the British manage to evacuate 338,000 Allied (mostly British) troops.

The French signed an armistice on June 22. German armies now occupied about three-fifths of France. An authoritarian regime under German control was set up over the remainder of the country. It was known as Vichy France and was led by an aged French hero of World War I, Marshal Henri Pétain. Germany was now in control of western and central Europe, but Britain had still not been defeated. After Dunkirk, the British appealed to the United States for help.

President **Franklin D. Roosevelt** denounced the aggressors, but the United States followed a strict policy of isolationism. A series of neutrality acts, passed in the 1930s, prevented the United States from taking sides or becoming involved in any European wars. Many Americans felt that the United States had been drawn into World War I due to economic involvement in Europe and they wanted to prevent a recurrence. Roosevelt was convinced that the neutrality acts actually encouraged Axis aggression and wanted the acts repealed. They were gradually relaxed as the United States supplied food, ships, planes, and weapons to Britain.

The Battle of Britain

Hitler realized that an amphibious (land-sea) invasion of Britain could succeed only if Germany gained control of the air. At the beginning of August 1940, the Luftwaffe (LOOFT•vah•fuh)—the German air force—launched a major offensive. German planes bombed British air and naval bases, harbors, communication centers, and war industries.

The British fought back with determination. They were supported by an effective radar system that gave them early warning of German attacks. Nevertheless, by the end of August, the British air force had suffered critical losses.

In September, in retaliation for a British attack on Berlin, Hitler ordered a shift in strategy. Instead of bombing military targets, the Luftwaffe began massive bombing of British cities. Hitler hoped in this way to break British morale. Instead, because military targets were not being hit, the British were able to rebuild their air strength quickly. Soon, the British air force was inflicting major losses on Luftwaffe bombers. At the end of September, Hitler postponed the invasion of Britain indefinitely.

London buildings collapse as a result of nightly German bombing.

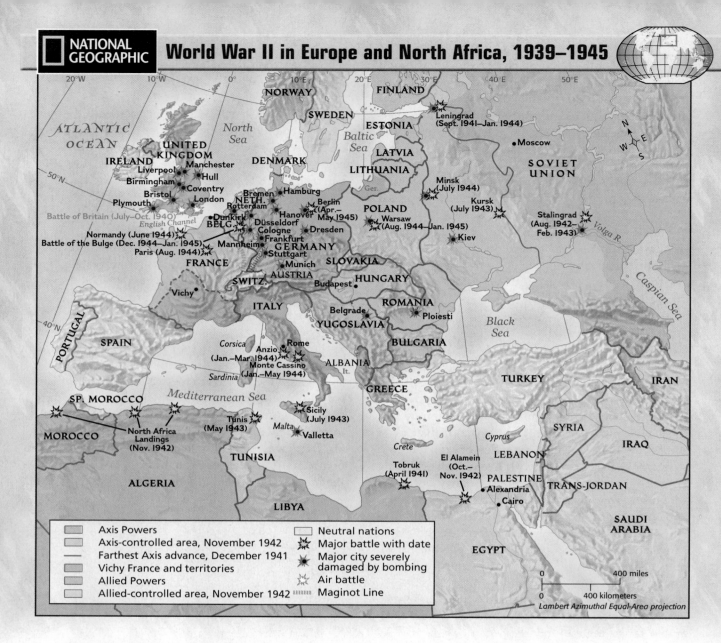

Map labels:

20°W · 10°W · 0° · 10°E · 20°E · 30°E · 40°E · 50°E

NORWAY · FINLAND · SWEDEN · ESTONIA · Leningrad (Sept. 1941–Jan. 1944) · Moscow

ATLANTIC OCEAN · North Sea · Baltic Sea · LATVIA · SOVIET UNION

UNITED KINGDOM · IRELAND · Manchester · Liverpool · Hull · DENMARK · LITHUANIA · Minsk (July 1944)

Birmingham · Coventry · Bristol · London · Plymouth · Bremen · Hamburg · POLAND · Kursk (July 1943) · Stalingrad (Aug. 1942–Feb. 1943)

Battle of Britain (July–Oct. 1940) · English Channel · NETH. · Rotterdam · Berlin (Apr.–May 1945) · Hanover · Warsaw (Aug. 1944–Jan. 1945) · Volga R.

Dunkirk · BELG. · Düsseldorf · Cologne · Dresden · Kiev · Ger.

Normandy (June 1944) · Frankfurt · GERMANY

Battle of the Bulge (Dec. 1944–Jan. 1945) · Mannheim · Paris (Aug. 1944) · FRANCE · Stuttgart · Munich · SLOVAKIA

Vichy · SWITZ. · AUSTRIA · HUNGARY · Budapest · Caspian Sea

PORTUGAL · ITALY · Belgrade · ROMANIA · Ploiesti · Black Sea

SPAIN · Corsica · Rome · YUGOSLAVIA · BULGARIA

Anzio (Jan.–Mar. 1944) · Monte Cassino (Jan.–May 1944) · ALBANIA It. · TURKEY · IRAN

Sardinia · GREECE · SYRIA · IRAQ

SP. MOROCCO · Mediterranean Sea · Sicily (July 1943) · Tunis (May 1943) · Malta · Valletta · Cyprus

MOROCCO · North Africa Landings (Nov. 1942) · Crete · El Alamein (Oct.–Nov. 1942) · LEBANON · PALESTINE · TRANS-JORDAN

TUNISIA · Tobruk (April 1941) · Alexandria · Cairo

ALGERIA · LIBYA · EGYPT · SAUDI ARABIA

Legend:
- Axis Powers
- Axis-controlled area, November 1942
- Farthest Axis advance, December 1941
- Vichy France and territories
- Allied Powers
- Allied-controlled area, November 1942
- Neutral nations
- Major battle with date
- Major city severely damaged by bombing
- Air battle
- Maginot Line

0 — 400 miles
0 — 400 kilometers
Lambert Azimuthal Equal-Area projection

Attack on the Soviet Union Although he had no desire for a two-front war, Hitler became convinced that Britain was remaining in the war only because it expected Soviet support. If the Soviet Union was smashed, Britain's last hope would be eliminated. Moreover, Hitler had convinced himself that the Soviet Union had a pitiful army and could be defeated quickly.

Hitler's invasion of the Soviet Union was scheduled for the spring of 1941, but the attack was delayed because of problems in the Balkans. Hitler had already gained the political cooperation of Hungary, Bulgaria, and Romania. However, the failure of Mussolini's invasion of Greece in 1940 had exposed Hitler's southern flank to British air bases in Greece. To secure his Balkan flank, Hitler therefore seized both Greece and Yugoslavia in April.

Reassured, Hitler invaded the Soviet Union on June 22, 1941. He believed that the Russians could still be decisively defeated before the brutal winter weather set in.

The massive attack stretched out along a front some 1,800 miles (about 2,900 km) long. German troops advanced rapidly, capturing two million Russian soldiers. By November, one German army group had swept through Ukraine. A second army was besieging the city of Leningrad, while a third approached within 25 miles (about 40 km) of Moscow, the Soviet capital.

An early winter and fierce Soviet resistance, however, halted the German advance. Because of the planned spring date for the invasion, the Germans had no winter uniforms. For the first time in the war, German armies had been stopped. A counterattack in

Axis Offensives, 1939–1941

← Axis offensives, 1939
← Axis offensives, 1940
← Axis offensives, 1941

Allied Offensives, 1942–1945

← Allied offensives, 1942–1943
← Allied offensives, 1944–1945

Battle Deaths in World War II	
Country	**Battle Deaths**
USSR	7,500,000
Germany	3,500,000
Yugoslavia	410,000
Poland	320,000
Romania	300,000
United States	292,000
United Kingdom	245,000
France	210,000
Hungary	140,000
Finland	82,000
Italy	77,000
Greece	74,000
Canada	37,000

Geography *Skills*

Heavy fighting took place in Europe and North Africa.

1. **Interpreting Maps** Name at least six major land battles of the war in Europe. Which side, the Allies or the Axis Powers, was more aggressive at the beginning of the war? Summarize the changes in direction of this side's offensives during the first three years of the war.

2. **Applying Geography Skills** Using information from all of the maps on pages 816 and 817, create an imaginary model of the war's outcome had Hitler chosen not to invade the Soviet Union. Your model could take the form of a map, a chart, or a database and include such items as battles, offensives, and casualties.

December 1941 by a Soviet army came as an ominous ending to the year for the Germans.

✔ **Reading Check** **Evaluating** In the spring of 1941, what caused Hitler to delay his invasion of the Soviet Union? What halted the German advance once it had begun?

Japan at War

⎯TURNING **POINT**⎯ **As you will learn, the Japanese attack on Pearl Harbor outraged Americans and led to the entry of the United States into the war.**

On December 7, 1941, Japanese aircraft attacked the U.S. naval base at Pearl Harbor in the Hawaiian Islands. The same day, other Japanese units launched additional assaults on the Philippines and began advancing toward the British colony of Malaya. Soon after, Japanese forces invaded the Dutch East Indies and occupied a number of islands in the Pacific Ocean. In some cases, as on the Bataan Peninsula and the island of Corregidor in the Philippines, resistance was fierce. By the spring of 1942, however, almost all of Southeast Asia and much of the western Pacific had fallen into Japanese hands.

A triumphant Japan now declared the creation of a community of nations. The name given to this new "community" was the Greater East-Asia Co-prosperity Sphere. The entire region would now be under Japanese direction. Japan also announced its intention to liberate the colonial areas of Southeast Asia from Western colonial rule. For the moment, however, Japan needed the resources of the region for its war machine, and it treated the countries under its rule as conquered lands.

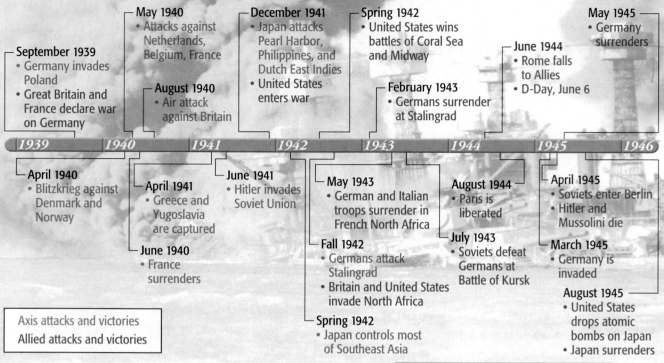

World War II: Attack and Counterattack

September 1939
• Germany invades Poland
• Great Britain and France declare war on Germany

May 1940
• Attacks against Netherlands, Belgium, France

August 1940
• Air attack against Britain

December 1941
• Japan attacks Pearl Harbor, Philippines, and Dutch East Indies
• United States enters war

Spring 1942
• United States wins battles of Coral Sea and Midway

February 1943
• Germans surrender at Stalingrad

June 1944
• Rome falls to Allies
• D-Day, June 6

May 1945
• Germany surrenders

1939 — 1940 — 1941 — 1942 — 1943 — 1944 — 1945 — 1946

April 1940
• Blitzkrieg against Denmark and Norway

April 1941
• Greece and Yugoslavia are captured

June 1940
• France surrenders

June 1941
• Hitler invades Soviet Union

May 1943
• German and Italian troops surrender in French North Africa

Fall 1942
• Germans attack Stalingrad
• Britain and United States invade North Africa

Spring 1942
• Japan controls most of Southeast Asia

August 1944
• Paris is liberated

July 1943
• Soviets defeat Germans at Battle of Kursk

April 1945
• Soviets enter Berlin
• Hitler and Mussolini die

March 1945
• Germany is invaded

August 1945
• United States drops atomic bombs on Japan
• Japan surrenders

Axis attacks and victories
Allied attacks and victories

Japanese leaders had hoped that their lightning strike at American bases would destroy the U.S. fleet in the Pacific. The Roosevelt administration, they thought, would now accept Japanese domination of the Pacific. The American people, in the eyes of Japanese leaders, had been made soft by material indulgence.

The Japanese miscalculated, however. The attack on Pearl Harbor unified American opinion about becoming involved in the war. The United States now joined with European nations and Nationalist China in a combined effort to defeat Japan. Believing the American involvement in the Pacific would make the United States ineffective in the European theater of war, Hitler declared war on the United States four days after Pearl Harbor. Another European conflict had turned into a global war.

✓**Reading Check** **Describing** By the spring of 1942, which territories did Japan control?

The Allies Advance

The entry of the United States into the war created a new coalition, the Grand Alliance. To overcome mutual suspicions, the three major Allies—Great Britain, the United States, and the Soviet Union—

Graphic Organizer ➜ Skills

The time line above traces the major events of the war, from September 1939 to Japan's surrender in August 1945.

1. **Identifying** How much time elapsed from the beginning of the war until France's surrender? From France's surrender until Germany's surrender?

2. **Compare and Contrast** Use the time line and your knowledge of world history to compare the Soviet Union's involvement in World War II to Russia's involvement in World War I. How do you explain the successes and failures of the Soviet Union and Russia in these two wars?

agreed to stress military operations and ignore political differences. At the beginning of 1943, the Allies agreed to fight until the Axis Powers—Germany, Italy, and Japan—surrendered unconditionally. The unconditional surrender principle, which required the Axis nations to surrender without any favorable condition, cemented the Grand Alliance by making it nearly impossible for Hitler to divide his foes.

The European Theater Defeat was far from Hitler's mind at the beginning of 1942. As Japanese forces advanced into Southeast Asia and the Pacific,

Hitler and his European allies continued fighting the war in Europe against the armies of Britain and the Soviet Union.

Until late 1942, it appeared that the Germans might still prevail on the battlefield. In North Africa, the Afrika Korps, German forces under General Erwin Rommel, broke through the British defenses in Egypt and advanced toward Alexandria. A renewed German offensive in the Soviet Union led to the capture of the entire Crimea in the spring of 1942. In August, Hitler boasted:

❝As the next step, we are going to advance south of the Caucasus and then help the rebels in Iran and Iraq against the English. Another thrust will be directed along the Caspian Sea toward Afghanistan and India. Then the English will run out of oil. In two years we'll be on the borders of India. Twenty to thirty elite German divisions will do. Then the British Empire will collapse.❞

This would be Hitler's last optimistic outburst. By the fall of 1942, the war had turned against the Germans.

In North Africa, British forces had stopped Rommel's troops at El Alamein (EL A•luh•MAYN) in the summer of 1942. The Germans then retreated back across the desert. In November 1942, British and American forces invaded French North Africa. They forced the German and Italian troops there to surrender in May 1943.

On the Eastern Front, after the capture of the Crimea, Hitler's generals wanted him to concentrate on the Caucasus and its oil fields. Hitler, however, decided that **Stalingrad,** a major industrial center on the Volga, should be taken first.

In perhaps the most terrible battle of the war, between November 1942 and February 2, 1943, the Soviets launched a counterattack. German troops were stopped, then encircled, and supply lines were cut off, all in frigid winter conditions. The Germans

CONNECTIONS Around The World

Women as Spies in World War II

For thousands of years, governments have relied on spies to gather information about their enemies. Until the twentieth century, most spies were men. During World War II, however, many women became active in the world of espionage.

Yoshiko Kawashima was born in China but raised in Japan. In 1932, she was sent to China by Japanese authorities to gather information for the invasion of China. Disguised as a young man, Kawashima was an active and effective spy until her arrest by the Chinese in 1945. The Chinese news agency announced that "a long-sought-for beauty in male costume was arrested today in Beijing." She was executed soon after her arrest.

Hekmath Fathmy was an Egyptian dancer. Her hatred of the British, who had occupied Egypt, caused her to become a spy for the Germans. Fathmy sang and danced for British troops in the Kit Kat Club, a nightclub in Cairo. After shows, she took British officers to her houseboat on the banks of the Nile. Any information she was able to obtain from her guests was passed on to John Eppler, a German spy in Cairo. Eventually, she was caught, but she served only a year in prison for her spying activities.

Violette Szabo of French/English background became a spy after her husband died fighting the Germans in North Africa. She joined Special Operations Executive, an arm of British Intelligence, and was sent to France several times. In August 1944, she parachuted into France to spy on the Germans. Caught by Gestapo forces at Salon La Tour, she was tortured and then shipped to Ravensbruck, a women's concentration camp near Berlin. She was executed there in April 1945.

▲ *Violette Szabo spied for the Allies to avenge her husband's death.*

Comparing Cultures

People have different motives for becoming spies. List several motives that might draw someone to espionage. Do you think the motives are different in peacetime? Investigate current espionage activities using the Internet or library. What various methods do governments use today to gather intelligence?

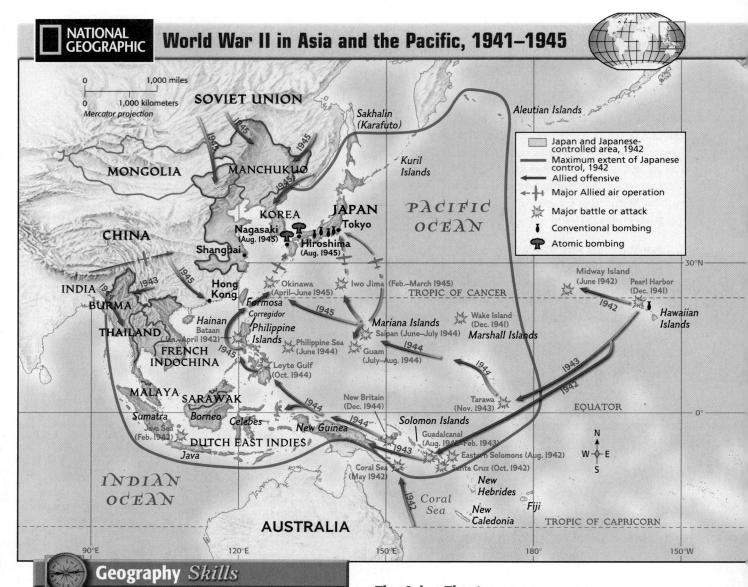

0 | 1,000 miles
0 | 1,000 kilometers
Mercator projection

SOVIET UNION

MONGOLIA

MANCHUKUO

CHINA

KOREA

JAPAN
Tokyo

Nagasaki (Aug. 1945)
Hiroshima (Aug. 1945)

Shanghai

INDIA

BURMA

Hong Kong

THAILAND

FRENCH INDOCHINA

Hainan
Bataan (Jan.–April 1942)

Formosa
Corregidor
Philippine Islands

MALAYA SARAWAK

Sumatra
Borneo
Celebes

Java Sea (Feb. 1942)

DUTCH EAST INDIES
Java

New Guinea

Coral Sea (May 1942)

AUSTRALIA

Sakhalin (Karafuto)

Kuril Islands

PACIFIC OCEAN

Aleutian Islands

Okinawa (April–June 1945)
Iwo Jima (Feb.–March 1945)
TROPIC OF CANCER

Midway Island (June 1942)
Pearl Harbor (Dec. 1941)

Hawaiian Islands

Mariana Islands
Wake Island (Dec. 1941)
Saipan (June–July 1944)
Marshall Islands
Guam (July–Aug. 1944)
Philippine Sea (June 1944)
Leyte Gulf (Oct. 1944)

New Britain (Dec. 1944)

Tarawa (Nov. 1943)
EQUATOR

Solomon Islands
Guadalcanal (Aug. 1942–Feb. 1943)
Eastern Solomons (Aug. 1942)
Santa Cruz (Oct. 1942)

New Hebrides

Coral Sea

New Caledonia
Fiji
TROPIC OF CAPRICORN

INDIAN OCEAN

N
W E
S

90°E | 120°E | 150°E | 180° | 150°W
30°N
0°

Legend:
- Japan and Japanese-controlled area, 1942
- Maximum extent of Japanese control, 1942
- Allied offensive
- Major Allied air operation
- Major battle or attack
- Conventional bombing
- Atomic bombing

Geography Skills

"Island hopping," the Allied strategy in Asia and the Pacific, focused more on the islands in the Pacific than on the mainland of Asia.

1. **Interpreting Maps** What was the approximate distance from Japan, in miles and kilometers, to its farthest point of control?

2. **Applying Geography Skills** Compare this map to the earlier maps in the chapter dealing with the war in Europe. Then analyze the effects of geographic factors on the major events in the two different theatres of war.

were forced to surrender at Stalingrad. The entire German Sixth Army, considered the best of the German troops, was lost.

By February 1943, German forces in Russia were back to their positions of June 1942. By the spring of 1943, even Hitler knew that the Germans would not defeat the Soviet Union.

The Asian Theater In 1942, the tide of battle in the East also changed dramatically. In the Battle of the Coral Sea on May 7 and 8, 1942, American naval forces stopped the Japanese advance and saved Australia from the threat of invasion.

The turning point of the war in Asia came on June 4, at the Battle of **Midway Island.** U.S. planes destroyed four attacking Japanese aircraft carriers. The United States defeated the Japanese navy and established naval superiority in the Pacific.

By the fall of 1942, Allied forces in Asia were gathering for two operations. One, commanded by U.S. general **Douglas MacArthur,** would move into the Philippines through New Guinea and the South Pacific Islands. The other would move across the Pacific with a combination of U.S. Army, Marine, and Navy attacks on Japanese-held islands. The policy was to capture some Japanese-held islands and bypass others, "island hopping" up to Japan. After a series of bitter engagements in the waters off the Solomon

Islands from August to November 1942, Japanese fortunes were fading.

Reading Check **Summarizing** Why was the German assault on Stalingrad a crushing defeat for the Germans?

Last Years of the War

By the beginning of 1943, the tide of battle had turned against Germany, Italy, and Japan. Axis forces in Tunisia surrendered on May 13, 1943. The Allies then crossed the Mediterranean and carried the war to Italy, an area that **Winston Churchill** had called the "soft underbelly" of Europe. After taking Sicily, Allied troops began an invasion of mainland Italy in September.

The European Theater After the fall of Sicily, Mussolini was removed from office and placed under arrest by Victor Emmanuel III, king of Italy. A new Italian government offered to surrender to the Allied forces. However, Mussolini was liberated by the Germans in a daring raid and then set up as the head of a puppet German state in northern Italy. At the same time, German troops moved in and occupied much of Italy.

The Germans set up effective new defensive lines in the hills south of Rome. The Allied advance up the Italian Peninsula turned into a painstaking affair with very heavy casualties. Rome did not fall to the

People In History

Winston Churchill
1874–1965
British prime minister

Winston Churchill was Great Britain's wartime leader. At the beginning of the war, Churchill had already had a long political career. He had advocated a hard-line policy toward Nazi Germany in the 1930s. On May 10, 1940, he became British prime minister.

Churchill was confident that he could guide Britain to ultimate victory. "I thought I knew a great deal about it all," he later wrote, "and I was sure I should not fail." Churchill proved to be an inspiring leader who rallied the British people with stirring speeches: "We shall fight on the beaches, we shall fight on the landing grounds, in the fields, in the streets, and in the hills. We shall never surrender." *Time* magazine designated Churchill the Man of the Year in 1940 and named him the Man of the Half Century in 1950.

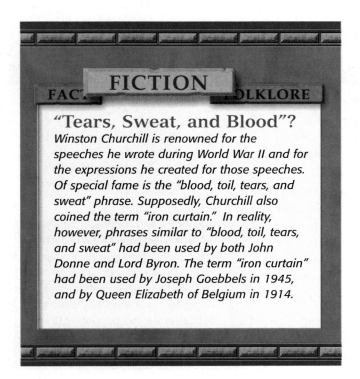

FICTION

FACT FOLKLORE

"Tears, Sweat, and Blood"?

Winston Churchill is renowned for the speeches he wrote during World War II and for the expressions he created for those speeches. Of special fame is the "blood, toil, tears, and sweat" phrase. Supposedly, Churchill also coined the term "iron curtain." In reality, however, phrases similar to "blood, toil, tears, and sweat" had been used by both John Donne and Lord Byron. The term "iron curtain" had been used by Joseph Goebbels in 1945, and by Queen Elizabeth of Belgium in 1914.

Allies until June 4, 1944. By that time, the Italian war had assumed a secondary role as the Allied forces opened their long-awaited "second front" in western Europe.

Since the autumn of 1943, the Allies had been planning an invasion of France from Great Britain, across the English Channel. Finally, on June 6, 1944 (D-Day), Allied forces under U.S. general Dwight D. Eisenhower landed on the **Normandy** beaches in history's greatest naval invasion. The Allies fought their way past underwater mines, barbed wire, and horrible machine gun fire. There was heavy German resistance even though the Germans thought the battle was a diversion and the real invasion would occur elsewhere. Their slow response enabled the Allied forces to set up a beachhead. Within three months, the Allies had landed two million men and a half-million vehicles. Allied forces then pushed inland and broke through German defensive lines.

After the breakout, Allied troops moved south and east. In Paris, resistance fighters rose up against the occupying Germans. The Allies liberated Paris by the end of August. In March 1945, they crossed the Rhine River and advanced into Germany. At the end of April 1945, Allied armies in northern Germany moved toward the Elbe River, where they linked up with the Soviets.

The Soviets had come a long way since the Battle of Stalingrad in 1943. In the summer of 1943, Hitler gambled on taking the offensive using newly developed heavy tanks. German forces were soundly defeated by the Soviets at the Battle of Kursk (July 5 to 12), the greatest tank battle of World War II.

Soviet forces now began a steady advance westward. They had reoccupied Ukraine by the end of 1943 and moved into the Baltic states by the beginning of 1944. Advancing along a northern front, Soviet troops occupied Warsaw in January 1945 and entered Berlin in April. Meanwhile, Soviet troops, along a southern front, swept through Hungary, Romania, and Bulgaria.

By January 1945, Adolf Hitler had moved into a bunker 55 feet (almost 17 m) under the city of Berlin to direct the final stages of the war. In his final political testament, Hitler, consistent to the end in his anti-Semitism, blamed the Jews for the war. He wrote, "Above all I charge the leaders of the nation and those under them to scrupulous observance of the laws of race and to merciless opposition to the universal poisoner of all peoples, international Jewry."

Hitler committed suicide on April 30, two days after Mussolini had been shot by Italian partisans, or resistance fighters. On May 7, 1945, German commanders surrendered. The war in Europe was finally over.

The Asian Theater The war in Asia continued. Beginning in 1943, U.S. forces had gone on the offensive and advanced, slowly at times, across the Pacific. As Allied military power drew closer to the main Japanese islands in the first months of 1945, **Harry S Truman,** who had become president after the death of Roosevelt in April, had a difficult decision to make. Should he use newly developed atomic weapons to bring the war to an end or find another way to defeat the Japanese forces?

Using atomic weapons would, Truman hoped, enable the United States to avoid an invasion of Japan. The Japanese had made extensive preparations to defend their homeland. Truman and his advisers had become convinced that American troops would suffer heavy casualties if they invaded Japan. At the time, however, only two bombs were available, and no one knew how effective they would be.

Truman decided to use the bombs. The first bomb was dropped on the Japanese city of **Hiroshima** on August 6. Three days later, a second bomb was dropped on Nagasaki. Both cities were leveled. Thousands of people died immediately after the bombs were dropped. Thousands more died in later months from radiation. Japan surrendered on August 14.

World War II was finally over. Seventeen million had died in battle. Perhaps twenty million civilians had perished as well. Some estimates place total losses at fifty million.

✔ **Reading Check** **Identifying** What was the "second front" that the Allies opened in Western Europe?

🔺**TAKS Practice**

SECTION 2 ASSESSMENT

Checking for Understanding

1. **Define** blitzkrieg, partisan.

2. **Identify** Franklin D. Roosevelt, Douglas MacArthur, Winston Churchill, Harry S Truman.

3. **Locate** Stalingrad, Midway Island, Normandy, Hiroshima.

4. **Explain** Hitler's strategy of attacking the Soviet Union. Why did his delay in launching the attack ultimately contribute to the Soviet victory over the Germans?

5. **List** events leading to U.S. entry into the war.

Critical Thinking

6. **Evaluate** How might the Allied demand for unconditional surrender have helped Hitler to maintain his control over Germany?

7. **Sequencing Information** Using a chart like the one below, place the events of World War II in chronological order.

Year	Country	Event
1939		

Analyzing Visuals

8. **Examine** the photo on page 815 showing the destruction caused by the Luftwaffe's bombing raids on London. Explain how this strategy of Hitler's hurt, rather than helped, Germany's efforts.

Writing About History

9. **Descriptive Writing** Imagine you lived in California during World War II. Write an essay about your expectations of a Japanese invasion of California. You can choose to believe that an invasion was possible or impossible.

A German Soldier at Stalingrad

THE SOVIET VICTORY AT STALINGRAD WAS A major turning point in World War II. These words come from the diary of a German soldier who fought and died there.

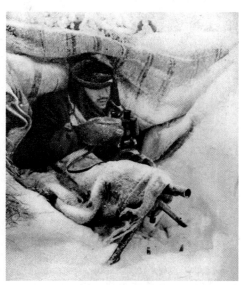

A German machine gunner endures the freezing Stalingrad winter in January 1943.

❝Today, after we'd had a bath, the company commander told us that if our future operations are as successful, we'll soon reach the Volga, take Stalingrad and then the war will inevitably soon be over. Perhaps we'll be home by Christmas.

July 29. The company commander says the Russian troops are completely broken, and cannot hold out any longer. To reach the Volga and take Stalingrad is not so difficult for us. The Führer knows where the Russians' [Soviets'] weak point is. Victory is not far away. . . .

September 4. We are being sent northward along the front towards Stalingrad. . . . It's a happy thought that the end of the war is getting nearer.

September 8. Two days of non-stop fighting. The Russians [Soviets] are defending themselves with insane stubbornness.

October 10. The Russians [Soviets] are so close to us that our planes cannot bomb them. We are preparing for a decisive attack. The Führer has ordered the whole of Stalingrad to be taken as rapidly as possible. . . .

October 22. Our regiment has failed to break into the factory. We have lost many men; every time you move you have to jump over bodies. . . .

November 10. A letter from Elsa today. Everyone expects us home for Christmas. In Germany everyone believes we already hold Stalingrad. How wrong they are. If they could only see what Stalingrad has done to our army. . . .

November 21. The Russians [Soviets] have gone over to the offensive along the whole front. Fierce fighting is going on. So, there it is—the Volga, victory and soon home to our families! We shall obviously be seeing them next in the other world.

November 29. We are encircled. It was announced this morning that the Führer has said:

"The army can trust me to do everything necessary to rapidly break the encirclement."

December 3. We are on hunger rations and waiting for the rescue that the Führer promised. . . .

December 26. The horses have already been eaten. I would eat a cat; they say its meat is also tasty. The soldiers look like corpses or lunatics, looking for something to put in their mouths. They no longer take cover from Russian [Soviet] shells; they haven't the strength to walk, run away and hide. A curse on this war!❞

—A German Soldier, On the Battle of Stalingrad

Analyzing Primary Sources

1. What city was the German army trying to take?
2. How accurate was the information received by the German soldiers prior to the attack?
3. What evidence is there of both the effectiveness of Nazi propaganda, and of the soldiers' disenchantment?

The New Order and the Holocaust

Guide to Reading

Main Ideas
- Adolf Hitler's philosophy of Aryan superiority led to the Holocaust.
- The Japanese conquest of Southeast Asia forced millions of native peoples to labor for the Japanese war machine.

Key Terms
genocide, collaborator

People to Identify
Heinrich Himmler, Reinhard Heydrich

Places to Locate
Poland, Auschwitz

Preview Questions
1. How did the Nazis carry out their Final Solution?
2. How did the Japanese create a dilemma for nationalists in the lands they occupied?

Reading Strategy
Compare and Contrast Using a Venn diagram like the one below, compare and contrast the New Order of Germany with the New Order of Japan.

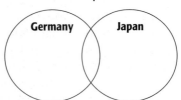
Germany   Japan

Preview of Events

♦ 1940	♦ 1941	♦ 1942	♦ 1943	♦ 1944	♦ 1945

1941
Einsatzgruppen active in Poland

1942
Two million ethnic Germans resettled in Poland

1943
Japan uses forced labor to build Burma-Thailand railroad

1944
Nazis continue Final Solution even as they start losing the war

Voices from the Past

Rudolf Höss

Rudolf Höss, commanding officer at the Auschwitz death camp, described the experience awaiting the Jews when they arrived there:

❝We had two SS doctors on duty at Auschwitz to examine the incoming transports of prisoners. The prisoners would be marched by one of the doctors who would make spot decisions as they walked by. Those who were fit for work were sent into the camp. Others were sent immediately to the extermination plants. Children of tender years were invariably exterminated since by reason of their youth they were unable to work. . . . At Auschwitz we fooled the victims into thinking that they were to go through a delousing process. Frequently they realized our true intentions and we sometimes had riots and difficulties due to that fact.❞

— *Nazi Conspiracy and Aggression*, vol. 6, 1946

Millions of Jews died in the Nazi death camps.

The New Order in Europe

In 1942, the Nazi regime stretched across continental Europe from the English Channel in the west to the outskirts of Moscow in the east. Nazi-occupied Europe was largely organized in one of two ways. Some areas, such as western Poland, were directly annexed by Nazi Germany and made into German provinces. Most of occupied Europe, however, was run by German military or civilian officials with help from local people who were willing to collaborate with the Nazis.

Resettlement in the East Nazi administration in the conquered lands to the east was especially ruthless. These lands were seen as the living space for German expansion. They were populated, Nazis thought, by racially inferior Slavic peoples. Hitler's plans for an Aryan racial empire were so important to him that he and the Nazis began to put their racial program into effect soon after the conquest of **Poland.**

Heinrich Himmler, the leader of the SS, was put in charge of German resettlement plans in the east. Himmler's task was to move the Slavic peoples out and replace them with Germans. Slavic peoples included Czech, Polish, Serbo-Croatian, Slovene, and Ukrainian. This policy was first applied to the new German provinces created from the lands of western Poland.

One million Poles were uprooted and moved to southern Poland. Hundreds of thousands of ethnic Germans (descendants of Germans who had migrated years ago from Germany to different parts of southern and eastern Europe) were brought in to colonize the German provinces in Poland. By 1942, two million ethnic Germans had been settled in Poland.

The invasion of the Soviet Union made the Nazis even more excited about German colonization in the east. Hitler spoke to his intimate circle of a colossal project of social engineering after the war. Poles, Ukrainians, and Russians would be removed from their lands and become slave labor. German peasants would settle on the abandoned lands and "germanize" them.

Himmler told a gathering of SS officers that 30 million Slavs might die in order to achieve German plans in the east. He continued, "Whether nations live in prosperity or starve to death interests me only insofar as we need them as slaves for our culture. Otherwise it is of no interest."

Slave Labor in Germany Labor shortages in Germany led to a policy of rounding up foreign workers for Germany. In 1942, a special office was set up to recruit labor for German farms and industries. By the summer of 1944, seven million European workers were laboring in Germany. They made up 20 percent of Germany's labor force. Another seven million workers were forced to labor for the Nazis in their own countries on farms, in industries, and even in military camps.

The use of forced labor often caused problems, however. Sending so many workers to Germany disrupted industrial production in the occupied countries that could have helped Germany. Then, too, the

brutal way in which Germany recruited foreign workers led more and more people to resist the Nazi occupation forces.

Reading Check **Describing** What was Hitler's vision for the residents of eastern Europe?

The Holocaust

No aspect of the Nazi New Order was more terrifying than the deliberate attempt to exterminate the Jews. Racial struggle was a key element in Hitler's world of ideas. To him, racial struggle was a clearly defined conflict of opposites. On one side were the Aryans, creators of human cultural development. On the other side were the Jews, parasites, in Hitler's view, who were trying to destroy the Aryans.

Himmler and the SS closely shared Hitler's racial ideas. The SS was given responsibility for what the Nazis called their Final Solution to the Jewish problem. The Final Solution was genocide (physical extermination) of the Jewish people.

The *Einsatzgruppen* **Reinhard Heydrich,** head of the SS's Security Service, was given the task of administering the Final Solution. Heydrich created special strike forces, called *Einsatzgruppen,* to carry out Nazi plans. After the defeat of Poland, he ordered these forces to round up all Polish Jews and put them in ghettos set up in a number of Polish cities. Conditions in the ghettos were horrible. Families were crowded together in unsanitary housing. The Nazis attempted to starve residents by allowing only minimal amounts of food. Despite suffering, residents tried to carry on and some ghettos organized resistance against the Nazis.

In June 1941, the *Einsatzgruppen* were given the new job of acting as mobile killing units. These SS death squads followed the regular army's advance into the Soviet Union. Their job was to round up Jews in their villages, execute them, and bury them in mass graves. The graves were often giant pits dug by the victims themselves before they were shot.

The leader of one of these death squads described the mode of operation:

❝The unit selected for this task would enter a village or city and order the prominent Jewish citizens to call together all Jews for the purpose of resettlement. They were requested to hand over their valuables to the leaders of the unit, and shortly before the execution to surrender their outer clothing. The men, women, and children were led to a place of execution which in most cases was located next to a more deeply excavated anti-tank ditch. Then they were shot, kneeling or standing, and the corpses thrown into the ditch.❞

The Death Camps Probably one million Jews were killed by the *Einsatzgruppen.* As appalling as that sounds, it was too slow by Nazi standards. They

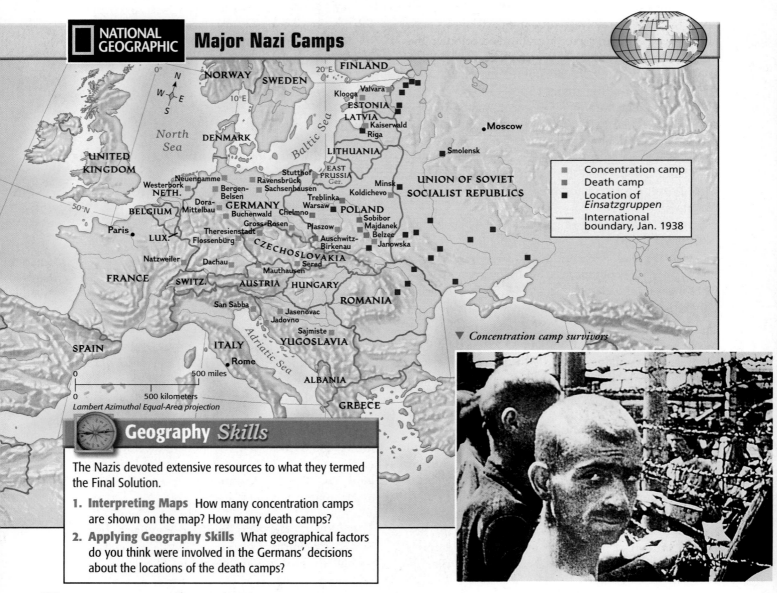

NATIONAL GEOGRAPHIC Major Nazi Camps

Legend:
- ■ Concentration camp
- ■ Death camp
- ■ Location of *Einsatzgruppen*
- — International boundary, Jan. 1938

Lambert Azimuthal Equal-Area projection

▼ *Concentration camp survivors*

Geography *Skills*

The Nazis devoted extensive resources to what they termed the Final Solution.

1. **Interpreting Maps** How many concentration camps are shown on the map? How many death camps?

2. **Applying Geography Skills** What geographical factors do you think were involved in the Germans' decisions about the locations of the death camps?

decided to kill the European Jewish population in specially built death camps.

Beginning in 1942, Jews from countries occupied by Germany (or sympathetic to Germany) were rounded up, packed like cattle into freight trains, and shipped to Poland. Six extermination centers were built in Poland for this purpose. The largest was **Auschwitz** (AUSH•VIHTS).

About 30 percent of the arrivals at Auschwitz were sent to a labor camp, where many were starved or worked to death. The remainder went to the gas chambers. Some inmates were subjected to cruel and painful "medical" experiments.

By the spring of 1942, the death camps were in full operation. First priority was given to the elimination of the ghettos in Poland. By the summer of 1942, however, Jews were also being shipped from France, Belgium, and Holland. Even as the Allies were winning the war in 1944, Jews were being shipped from Greece and Hungary. Despite desperate military needs, even late in the war when Germany faced utter defeat, the Final Solution had priority in using railroad cars to ship Jews to death camps.

Jewish men, women, and children being taken by the Nazis

The Death Toll The Germans killed between five and six million Jews, over three million of them in the death camps. Virtually 90 percent of the Jewish populations of Poland, the Baltic countries, and Germany were killed. Overall, the Holocaust was responsible for the death of nearly two out of every three European Jews.

The Nazis were also responsible for the deliberate death by shooting, starvation, or overwork of at least another nine to ten million non-Jewish people. The Nazis considered the Roma (sometimes known as Gypsies), like the Jews, to be an alien race. The Roma were rounded up for mass killing. About 40 percent of Europe's one million Roma were killed in the death camps.

The leading citizens of the Slavic peoples—the clergy, intellectuals, civil leaders, judges, and lawyers—were arrested and killed. Probably an additional four million Poles, Ukrainians, and Belorussians lost their lives as slave laborers for Nazi Germany. Finally, probably at least three million to four million Soviet prisoners of war were killed in captivity.

This mass slaughter of European civilians, particularly European Jews, is known as the Holocaust. Jews in and out of the camps attempted to resist the Nazis. Some were aided by friends and even strangers, hidden in villages or smuggled into safe areas. Foreign diplomats would try to save Jews by issuing exit visas. The nation of Denmark saved almost its entire Jewish population.

Some people did not believe the accounts of death camps because, during World War I, allies had greatly exaggerated German atrocities to arouse enthusiasm for the war. Most often, people pretended not to notice what was happening. Even worse, **collaborators** (people who assisted the enemy) helped the Nazis hunt down Jews. The Allies were aware of the concentration camps and death camps but chose to concentrate on ending the war. Not until after the war did they learn the full extent of the horror and inhumanity of the Holocaust. 📖 *(See page 999 to read excerpts from* The Holocaust—The Camp Victims *in the Primary Sources Library.)*

Children in the War Young people of all ages were also victims of World War II. Because they were unable to work, Jewish children, along with their mothers, were the first ones selected for gas chambers upon their arrival in the death camps of Poland. Young Jewish males soon learned to look as adult as possible in order to survive. Altogether, 1.2 million Jewish children died in the Holocaust.

HISTORY Online

Web Activity Visit the *Glencoe World History* Web site at tx.wh.glencoe.com and click on **Chapter 26– Student Web Activity** to learn more about concentration camps.

Many children were evacuated from cities during the war in order to avoid the bombing. The Germans created about 9,000 camps for children in the countryside. In Japan, 15,000 children were evacuated from Hiroshima before its destruction. The British moved about 6 million children and their mothers in 1939.

Some British parents even sent their children to Canada and the United States. This, too, could be dangerous. When the ocean liner *Arandora Star* was hit by a German torpedo, it had 77 British children on board. They never made it to Canada.

Children evacuated to the countryside did not always see their parents again. Some of them, along with many other children, became orphaned when their parents were killed. In 1945, there were perhaps 13 million orphaned children in Europe.

In Eastern Europe, children especially suffered under harsh German occupation policies. All secondary schools in German-occupied Eastern Europe were closed. Their facilities and equipment were destroyed.

Heinrich Himmler, head of the SS, said of these Slavic children that their education should consist only "in teaching simple arithmetic up to 500, the writing of one's name, and that God has ordered obedience to the Germans, honesty, diligence, and politeness. I do not consider an ability to read as necessary."

At times, young people were expected to carry the burden of fighting the war. In the last year of the war,

Hitler Youth members, often only 14 or 15 years old, could be found in the front lines. In the Soviet Union, children as young as 13 or 14 spied on German positions and worked with the resistance movement. Some were even given decorations for killing the enemy.

Reading Check **Summarizing** What was the job of the *Einsatzgruppen?*

The New Order in Asia

Japanese war policy in the areas in Asia occupied by Japan was basically defensive. Japan hoped to use its new possessions to meet its growing need for raw materials, such as tin, oil, and rubber. The new possessions also would be an outlet for Japanese manufactured goods. To organize these possessions, Japanese leaders included them in the Greater East-Asia Co-prosperity Sphere. This was the economic community supposedly designed to provide mutual benefits to the occupied areas and the home country.

Japanese Policies The Japanese had conquered Southeast Asia under the slogan "Asia for the Asiatics." Japanese officials in occupied territories quickly made contact with anticolonialists. They promised the people that local governments would be established under Japanese control. Such governments were eventually set up in Burma, the Dutch East Indies, Vietnam, and the Philippines.

Picturing **History**

American and Filipino prisoners of war were held in the Philippines. What role did prisoners of war play in the Japanese war effort?

In fact, real power rested with Japanese military authorities in each territory. In turn, the local Japanese military command was directly subordinated to the Army General Staff in Tokyo. The economic resources of the colonies were used for the benefit of the Japanese war machine. The native peoples in occupied lands were recruited to serve in local military units or were forced to work on public works projects.

In some cases, these policies brought severe hardships to peoples living in the occupied areas. In Vietnam, for example, local Japanese authorities forcibly took rice and shipped it abroad. This led directly to a food shortage that caused over a million Vietnamese to starve to death in 1944 and 1945.

Japanese Behavior At first, many Southeast Asian nationalists took Japanese promises at face value and agreed to cooperate with their new masters. In Burma, for example, an independent government was set up in 1943 and declared war on the Allies. Eventually, the nature of Japanese occupation policies became clear, and sentiment turned against Japan.

Japanese officials provoked such attitudes by their arrogance and contempt for local customs. In the Dutch East Indies, for example, Indonesians were required to bow in the direction of Tokyo and to recognize the divinity of the Japanese emperor. In Burma, Buddhist pagodas were used as military latrines.

Like German soldiers in occupied Europe, Japanese military forces often had little respect for the lives of their subject peoples. After their conquest of Nanjing, China, in 1937, Japanese soldiers spent several days killing, raping, and looting. After the conquest

of Korea, almost eight hundred thousand Korean people were sent to Japan, most of them as forced laborers.

In construction projects to help their war effort, the Japanese made extensive use of labor forces composed of both prisoners of war and local peoples. In building the Burma-Thailand railway in 1943, for example, the Japanese used 61,000 Australian, British, and Dutch prisoners of war and almost 300,000 workers from Burma, Malaya, Thailand, and the Dutch East Indies. An inadequate diet and appalling work conditions in an unhealthy climate led to the death of 12,000 Allied prisoners of war and 90,000 workers by the time the railway was completed.

Such Japanese behavior created a dilemma for many nationalists in the occupied lands. They had no desire to see the return of the colonial powers, but they did not like what the Japanese were doing. Some turned against the Japanese. Others simply did nothing.

Indonesian patriots tried to have it both ways. They pretended to support Japan while actually sabotaging the Japanese administration. In French Indochina, Ho Chi Minh's Communist Party made contact with U.S. military units in South China. The Communists agreed to provide information on Japanese troop movements and to rescue downed American fliers in the area. By the end of the war, little support remained in the region for the Japanese "liberators."

✓ **Reading Check** **Examining** How did the Japanese treat the native peoples in occupied lands?

TAKS Practice

SECTION 3 ASSESSMENT

Checking for Understanding

1. **Define** genocide, collaborator.

2. **Identify** Heinrich Himmler, Reinhard Heydrich.

3. **Locate** Poland, Auschwitz.

4. **Explain** what the Nazis meant by the Final Solution. How did Hitler's commitment to the Final Solution hinder Germany's war effort?

5. **List** examples of objectionable Japanese occupation policies in Asia.

Critical Thinking

6. **Evaluate** What was the impact of the Holocaust on history? What lessons does the Holocaust have for us today?

7. **Cause and Effect** Create a chart giving examples of Hitler's actions to create a New World Order in Europe and the outcome of his efforts.

Hitler's Actions	Outcome

Analyzing Visuals

8. **Examine** the scene pictured on page 827. Describe, based on your reading, the series of events that will most likely follow.

Writing About History

9. **Persuasive Writing** Imagine you are a member of Hitler's inner circle in 1941 and are alarmed about Hitler's Final Solution. Compose a letter to Hitler, outlining the reasons why he should abandon plans to send Jews to the death camps.

The Home Front and the Aftermath of the War

Guide to Reading

Main Ideas
- World War II left a lasting impression on civilian populations.
- The end of the war created a new set of problems for the Allies as the West came into conflict with the Soviet Union.

Key Terms
mobilization, kamikaze, Cold War

People to Identify
Albert Speer, General Hideki Tojo

Places to Locate
London, Dresden, Hiroshima

Preview Questions
1. Why were the Japanese encouraged to serve as kamikaze pilots?
2. What was the outcome of the Yalta Conference in 1945?

Reading Strategy
Compare and Contrast Create a chart comparing and contrasting the impact of World War II on the lives of civilians.

Country	Impact on Lives of Civilians
Soviet Union	
United States	
Japan	
Germany	

Preview of Events

◆1942	◆1943	◆1944	◆1945	◆1946	◆1947

1943
Stalin, Roosevelt, and Churchill meet in Tehran to determine future course of war

1945
Allies bomb Dresden

1946
Churchill proclaims existence of "iron curtain" in Europe

Voices from the Past

A German civilian described an Allied bombing raid on Hamburg in 1943:

66As the many fires broke through the roofs of the burning buildings, a column of heated air rose more than two and a half miles high and one and a half miles in diameter. . . . This column was fed from its base by in-rushing cooler ground-surface air. One and one half miles from the fires this draft increased the wind velocity from eleven to thirty-three miles per hour. At the edge of the area the velocities must have been much greater, as trees three feet in diameter were uprooted. In a short time the temperature reached ignition point for all combustibles, and the entire area was ablaze. In such fires, complete burnout occurred, that is, no trace of combustible material remained.99

— *The Bombing of Germany*, **Hans Rumpf, 1963**

The bombing of civilians in World War II made the home front dangerous.

A B-26 drops bombs on Germany.

The Mobilization of Peoples: Four Examples

Even more than World War I, World War II was a total war. Fighting was much more widespread and covered most of the world. Economic mobilization (the act of assembling and preparing for war) was more extensive; so, too, was the mobilization of women. The number of civilians killed—almost twenty million—was far higher. Many of these victims were children.

World War II had an enormous impact on civilian life in the Soviet Union, the United States, Germany, and Japan. We consider the home fronts of those four nations next.

The Soviet Union

The initial defeats of the Soviet Union led to drastic emergency measures that affected the lives of the civilian population. Leningrad, for example, experienced nine hundred days of siege. Its inhabitants became so desperate for food that they ate dogs, cats, and mice. Probably 1.5 million people died in the city.

As the German army made its rapid advance into Soviet territory, Soviet workers dismantled and shipped the factories in the western part of the Soviet Union to the interior—to the Urals, western Siberia, and the Volga regions. Machines were placed on the bare ground. As laborers began their work, walls went up around them.

Stalin called the widespread military and industrial mobilization of the nation a "battle of machines." The Soviets won, producing 78,000 tanks and 98,000 artillery pieces. In 1943, 55 percent of the Soviet national income went for war materials, compared with 15 percent in 1940. As a result of the emphasis on military goods, Soviet citizens experienced severe shortages of both food and housing.

Soviet women played a major role in the war effort. Women and girls worked in industries, mines, and railroads. Overall, the number of women working in industry increased almost 60 percent. Soviet women were also expected to dig antitank ditches and work as air raid wardens. In addition, the Soviet Union was the only country in World War II to use women in battle. Soviet women served as snipers and also in aircrews of bomber squadrons.

The United States

The home front in the United States was quite different from that of the other major powers. The United States was not fighting the war in its own territory. Eventually, the United States became the arsenal of the Allied Powers; it produced much of the military equipment the Allies needed. At the height of war production in November 1943, the country was building six ships a day and ninety-six thousand planes per year.

The mobilization of the American economy resulted in some social turmoil, however. The construction of new factories created boomtowns. Thousands came there to work but then faced a shortage of houses and schools. Widespread movements of people took place. Sixteen million men and women were enrolled in the military and moved frequently. Another sixteen million, mostly wives and girlfriends of servicemen or workers looking for jobs, also moved around the country.

Over a million African Americans moved from the rural South to the cities of the North and West, looking for jobs in industry. The presence of African Americans in areas where they had not lived before led to racial tensions and sometimes even racial riots. In Detroit in June 1943, for example, white mobs roamed the streets attacking African Americans.

One million African Americans enrolled in the military. There they were segregated in their own battle units. Angered by the way they were treated, some became militant and prepared to fight for their civil rights.

Picturing **History**

Many Japanese American families in southern California were transported to internment camps. Would you have supported the internment policy for Japanese Americans during the war? Explain.

Japanese Americans faced even more serious difficulties. On the West Coast, 110,000 Japanese Americans, 65 percent of whom had been born in the United States, were removed to camps surrounded by barbed wire and required to take loyalty oaths. Public officials claimed this policy was necessary for security reasons.

The racism in the treatment of Japanese Americans was evident when the California governor, Culbert Olson, said, "You know, when I look out at a group of Americans of German or Italian descent, I can tell whether they're loyal or not. I can tell how they think and even perhaps what they are thinking. But it is impossible for me to do this with inscrutable Orientals, and particularly the Japanese."

Germany In August 1914, Germans had enthusiastically cheered their soldiers marching off to war. In September 1939, the streets were quiet. Many Germans did not care. Even worse for the Nazi regime, many feared disaster.

Hitler was well aware of the importance of the home front. He believed that the collapse of the home front in World War I had caused Germany's defeat. In his determination to avoid a repetition of that experience, he adopted economic policies that may have cost Germany the war.

To maintain the morale of the home front during the first two years of the war, Hitler refused to cut consumer goods production or to increase the production of armaments. After German defeats on the Russian front and the American entry into the war, however, the economic situation in Germany changed.

Early in 1942, Hitler finally ordered a massive increase in armaments production and in the size of the army. Hitler's architect, **Albert Speer,** was made minister for armaments and munitions in 1942. Speer was able to triple the production of armaments between 1942 and 1943, despite Allied air raids.

A total mobilization of the economy was put into effect in July 1944. Schools, theaters, and cafes were closed. By that time, though, total war mobilization was too late to save Germany from defeat.

Nazi attitudes toward women changed over the course of the war. Before the war, the Nazis had worked to keep women out of the job market. As the war progressed and more and more men were called up for military service, this position no longer made sense. Nazi magazines now proclaimed, "We see the woman as the eternal mother of our people, but also as the working and fighting comrade of the man."

Kamikaze attacker being shot down in the Pacific, 1945

In spite of this change, the number of women working in industry, agriculture, commerce, and domestic service increased only slightly. The total number of employed women in September 1944 was 14.9 million, compared with 14.6 million in May 1939. Many women, especially those of the middle class, did not want jobs, particularly in factories.

Japan Wartime Japan was a highly mobilized society. To guarantee its control over all national resources, the government created a planning board to control prices, wages, labor, and resources. Traditional habits of obedience and hierarchy were used to encourage citizens to sacrifice their resources, and sometimes their lives, for the national cause.

The calls for sacrifice reached a high point in the final years of the war. Young Japanese were encouraged to volunteer to serve as pilots in suicide missions against U.S. fighting ships at sea. These pilots were known as kamikaze, or "divine wind."

Japan was extremely reluctant to mobilize women on behalf of Japan's war effort. **General Hideki Tojo,** prime minister from 1941 to 1944, opposed female employment. He argued that "the weakening of the family system would be the weakening of the nation . . . we are able to do our duties only because we have wives and mothers at home."

Female employment increased during the war, but only in such areas as the textile industry and farming, where women had traditionally worked. Instead of using women to meet labor shortages, the Japanese government brought in Korean and Chinese laborers.

✓ **Reading Check** **Evaluating** How did World War II contribute to racial tensions in the United States?

Frontline Civilians: The Bombing of Cities

Bombing was used in World War II against a variety of targets, including military targets, enemy troops, and civilian populations. The bombing of civilians in World War II made the home front a dangerous place.

A few bombing raids had been conducted in the last year of World War I. The bombing of civilian populations had led to a public outcry. The bombings and the reaction to them had given rise to the argument that bombing civilian populations would be an effective way to force governments to make peace. As a result, European air forces began to develop long-range bombers in the 1930s.

Britain The first sustained use of civilian bombing began in early September 1940. Londoners took the first heavy blows. For months, the German air force bombed **London** nightly. Thousands of civilians were killed or injured, and enormous damage was done. Nevertheless, Londoners' morale remained high.

The blitz, as the British called the German air raids, soon became a national experience. The blitz was carried to many other British cities and towns. The ability of Londoners to maintain their morale set the standard for the rest of the British population. The theory that the bombing of civilian targets would force peace was proved wrong.

Germany The British failed to learn from their own experience, however. Churchill and his advisers believed that destroying German communities would break civilian morale and bring victory. Major bombing raids on German cities began in 1942. On May 31, 1942, Cologne became the first German city to be attacked by a thousand bombers.

Bombing raids added an element of terror to circumstances already made difficult by growing shortages of food, clothing, and fuel. Germans especially feared the incendiary bombs, which created firestorms that swept through cities. The ferocious bombing of **Dresden** from February 13 to 15, 1945, created a firestorm that may have killed as many as a hundred thousand inhabitants and refugees.

Germany suffered enormously from the Allied bombing raids. Millions of buildings were destroyed, and possibly half a million civilians died. Nevertheless, it is highly unlikely that Allied bombing sapped the morale of the German people. Instead, Germans, whether pro-Nazi or anti-Nazi, fought on stubbornly, often driven simply by a desire to live.

Nor did the bombing destroy Germany's industrial capacity. Production of war materials actually increased between 1942 and 1944, despite the bombing. Nevertheless, the widespread destruction of transportation systems and fuel supplies made it extremely difficult for the new materials to reach the German military.

Then *and* Now

In 1945, as the war ended, the people of Dresden were faced with the daunting task of rebuilding a city. List all the obstacles you can think of that confronted Dresden's city leaders as they planned their rebuilding efforts in 1945.

Dresden in the year 2000 ▶

▼ *Dresden after the bombing in 1945*

The Atomic Bomb

Scientists at the beginning of the twentieth century discovered that atoms contained an enormous amount of energy. The discovery gave rise to the idea that releasing this energy by splitting the atom might create a devastating weapon.

The idea was not taken seriously until World War II. Then, the fear that the Germans might make an atomic bomb convinced the U.S. government to try to develop one first. In 1942, the United States set in motion the Manhattan Project.

The Manhattan Project was a code name for the enormous industrial and technical enterprise that produced the first atomic bomb. It cost 2 billion dollars and employed the efforts of 600,000 people. U.S. Army Brigadier General Leslie Groves had overall supervision. The physicist J. Robert Oppenheimer was director of the Los Alamos, New Mexico, center where the bomb was actually built.

A successful test explosion on July 16, 1945, near Alamogordo, New Mexico, meant that the bomb was ready. The war in Europe had ended, but the bomb could be used against the Japanese. A committee had already chosen the city of Hiroshima as the first target.

The bomb was dropped on August 6, 1945, by a U.S. B-29 bomber nicknamed *Enola Gay.* The destruction was incredible. An area of about 5 square miles (13 sq km) was turned to ashes. Of the 76,000 buildings in Hiroshima, 70,000 were flattened. Of the city's 350,000 inhabitants, 140,000 had died by the end of 1945. By the end of 1950, another 50,000 had died from the effects of radiation. A second bomb was dropped on Nagasaki on August 9. The world had entered the Nuclear Age.

Evaluating *Was the decision to use the atomic bomb in Japan any different from Allied decisions to bomb civilian population centers in Europe? Why or why not?*

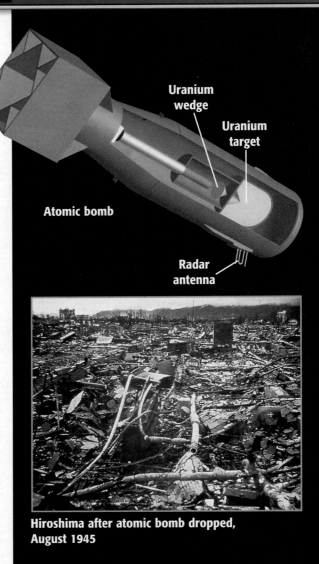

Uranium wedge

Uranium target

Atomic bomb

Radar antenna

Hiroshima after atomic bomb dropped, August 1945

Japan In Japan, the bombing of civilians reached a new level with the use of the first atomic bomb. Japan was open to air raids toward the end of the war because its air force had almost been destroyed. Moreover, its crowded cities were built of flimsy materials that were especially vulnerable to fire.

Attacks on Japanese cities by the new U.S. B-29 Superfortresses, the biggest bombers of the war, had begun on November 24, 1944. By the summer of 1945, many of Japan's industries had been destroyed, along with one-fourth of its dwellings.

The Japanese government decreed the mobilization of all people between the ages of 13 and 60 into a People's Volunteer Corps. Fearing high U.S. casualties in a land invasion of Japan, President Truman and his advisers decided to drop the atomic bomb on **Hiroshima** and Nagasaki in August of 1945.

✔ **Reading Check** **Explaining** Why were civilian populations targeted in bombing raids?

Peace and a New War

The total victory of the Allies in World War II was followed not by a real peace but by a period of political tensions, known as the Cold War. Primarily an ideological conflict between the United States and the Soviet Union, the Cold War was to dominate world affairs until the end of the 1980s.

Europe after World War II

Area of Soviet influence
Area of Western influence

0 — 500 miles
0 — 500 kilometers
Lambert Azimuthal Equal-Area projection

Geography Skills

The political map of Europe changed dramatically as a result of World War II.

1. **Interpreting Maps** Compare the map on page 753 to this map and identify the political changes in Europe from the 1920s to 1945.

2. **Applying Geography Skills** Create a chart that shows how Europe was divided according to Soviet and Western influence.

The Tehran Conference

Stalin, Roosevelt, and Churchill were the leaders of what was called the Big Three (the Soviet Union, the United States, and Great Britain) of the Grand Alliance. They met at Tehran in November 1943 to decide the future course of the war. Their major tactical decision had concerned the final assault on Germany. Stalin and Roosevelt had argued successfully for an American-British invasion through France. This was scheduled for the spring of 1944.

The acceptance of this plan had important consequences. It meant that Soviet and British-American forces would meet in defeated Germany along a north-south dividing line. Most likely, Eastern Europe would be liberated by Soviet forces. The Allies also agreed to a partition of postwar Germany.

The Yalta Conference

The Big Three powers met again at Yalta in southern Russia in February 1945. By then, the defeat of Germany was obvious. The Western powers, which had once believed that the Soviets were in a weak position, were now faced with the reality of eleven million Soviet soldiers taking possession of Eastern and much of Central Europe.

Stalin was deeply suspicious of the Western powers. He wanted a buffer to protect the Soviet Union from possible future Western aggression. This would mean establishing pro-Soviet governments along the border of the Soviet Union.

Roosevelt, however, favored the idea of self-determination for Europe. This involved a pledge to

help liberated Europe in the creation of "democratic institutions of their own choice." Liberated countries would hold free elections to determine their political systems.

At Yalta, Roosevelt sought Soviet military help against Japan. (At that time, the atomic bomb was not yet a certainty.) Roosevelt therefore agreed to Stalin's price for military aid against Japan: possession of Sakhalin and the Kuril Islands, which were ruled by Japan, as well as two warm-water ports and railroad rights in Manchuria.

The creation of the United Nations was a major American concern at Yalta. Roosevelt wanted the Big Three powers to pledge to be part of such an international organization before difficult issues divided them into hostile camps. Both Churchill and Stalin accepted Roosevelt's plans for the establishment of a United Nations organization and set the first meeting for San Francisco in April 1945.

The issues of Germany and Eastern Europe were treated less decisively. The Big Three reaffirmed that Germany must surrender unconditionally. It would be divided into four zones, which would be occupied and governed by the military forces of the United States, Great Britain, France, and the Soviet Union. A compromise was also worked out in regard to Poland. Stalin agreed to free elections in the future to determine a new government in that country.

The issue of free elections in Eastern Europe caused a serious split between the Soviets and the

Churchill, Roosevelt, and Stalin at Yalta

Europe. Stalin responded, "A freely elected government in any of these East European countries would be anti-Soviet, and that we cannot allow."

After a bitter and devastating war in which the Soviets had lost more people than any other country, Stalin sought absolute military security. To him, this security could be gained only by the presence of Communist states in Eastern Europe. Free elections might result in governments hostile to the Soviets.

By the middle of 1945, only an invasion by Western forces would have been able to undo the developments in Eastern Europe. At the end of the world's most destructive conflict, few people favored such a policy.

A New Struggle As the war slowly receded into the past, a new struggle was already beginning. Many in the West thought Soviet policy was part of a worldwide Communist conspiracy. The Soviets viewed Western, and especially American, policy as nothing less than global capitalist expansionism.

In March 1946, in a speech to an American audience, the former British prime minister Winston Churchill declared that "an iron curtain" had "descended across the continent," dividing Europe into two hostile camps. Stalin branded Churchill's speech a "call to war with the Soviet Union." Only months after the world's most devastating conflict had ended, the world seemed to be bitterly divided once again.

✓**Reading Check** **Identifying** Why did Stalin want to control Eastern Europe after World War II?

Americans. Eastern European governments were to be freely elected, but it was clear that Stalin might not honor this provision. This attempt to reconcile two irreconcilable goals was doomed, as soon became evident at the next conference of the Big Three at Potsdam, Germany.

The Potsdam Conference The Potsdam conference of July 1945 began under a cloud of mistrust. Roosevelt had died on April 12 and had been succeeded as president by Harry Truman. At Potsdam, Truman demanded free elections throughout Eastern

---

SECTION 4 ASSESSMENT

Checking for Understanding

1. **Define** mobilization, kamikaze.

2. **Identify** Albert Speer, General Hideki Tojo, Cold War.

3. **Locate** London, Dresden, Hiroshima.

4. **Explain** how Hitler's bombing of civilians in England backfired. What strategy do you think Hitler should have pursued instead?

5. **List** examples of Japan's vulnerability to Allied air attack in late 1944. What type of U.S. aircraft was used for the heaviest bombing of Japanese targets?

Critical Thinking

6. **Explain** Why did General Hideki Tojo oppose female employment in Japan?

7. **Organizing Information** Create a chart listing countries where bombing of heavily populated cities took place.

Country	City

Analyzing Visuals

8. **Analyze** the photo at the top of this page. How might the seating arrangement for the three leaders be significant? Which of the three leaders do you think came away from the meeting most pleased with the results?

Writing About History

9. **Persuasive Writing** President Truman concluded that dropping the atomic bomb on Japan was a justifiable way to end the war. Write an essay either condemning or agreeing with Truman's decision.

CRITICAL THINKING
SKILLBUILDER

Synthesizing Information

Why Learn This Skill?

Consider what it would be like to get funding for a new after-school club. In order to present your case, you would need to talk to other students and to school administrators, and to read reports and articles. Once you had gathered all the information you needed, you would synthesize—or put together—the most important points that could help you achieve your objective.

Synthesizing information involves combining information from two or more sources. The ability to synthesize information is important because information gained from one source often sheds new light upon other information. It is like putting the pieces of a puzzle together to form a complete picture. Being able to synthesize information will help you read and write more effectively.

Learning the Skill

To write a research report, you study several sources—encyclopedias, books, and articles. Once you have gathered information, you synthesize it into a report.

Before synthesizing information, analyze each source separately. Determine the value and reliability of each source. Then, look for connections and relationships among the different sources.

Practicing the Skill

Study the passage and the photo on this page.

> Bombing was used in World War II against a variety of targets, including military targets, enemy troops, and civilian populations. The bombing of civilians in World War II made the home front a dangerous place. A few bombing raids had been conducted in the last year of World War I. The bombings and the reaction to them had given rise to the argument that bombing civilian populations would be an effective way to force governments to make peace.

> Beginning in early September 1940, the German air force bombed London and many other British cities

Scottish city bombed in 1941

and towns nightly. The Blitz, as the British called the German air raids, became a national experience. Londoners took the first heavy blows. Their ability to maintain their morale set the standard for the rest of the British population.

❶ What is the main idea of the passage?

❷ What does the photo tell you about this topic?

❸ By synthesizing the two sources, what information do you have about the bombing of Britain?

Applying the Skill

Find two sources of information about a current event and write a short report. For your report, try to use a primary and a secondary source, if possible. Answer these questions: What are the main ideas from these sources? How does each source add to your understanding of the topic? Do the sources support or contradict each other? If there are contradictions, how would you include the conflicting information in your report?

Glencoe's **Skillbuilder Interactive Workbook, Level 2,** provides instruction and practice in key social studies skills.

Using Key Terms

1. The policy of giving in to Hitler's demands before World War II has been called _____.

2. The German style of attack that called for rapidly overrunning the positions of opposing forces was called a _____.

3. Because the Rhineland was _____, Germany was not permitted to have weapons or fortifications there.

4. The United States threatened economic _____ unless Japan returned to its borders of 1931.

5. Civilians in occupied countries who joined resistance movements were often called _____.

6. What the Nazis called the Final Solution was actually _____ of the Jewish people.

7. Japanese pilots who volunteered for suicide missions were known as _____.

8. People who assisted the Nazis in carrying out atrocities against Jewish people were known as _____.

Reviewing Key Facts

9. **Geography** Where was the Sudetenland located? Why was it important to Hitler?

10. **Science and Technology** What did the British develop to prepare for German air attack?

11. **History** What significant military action occurred at Midway Island in 1942?

12. **Government** Why did the Allied agreement to fight until the Axis Powers surrendered unconditionally possibly prolong the war?

13. **Citizenship** In what way were Japanese Americans treated differently than German Americans and Italian Americans?

14. **Citizenship** What percentage of the Jewish populations of Poland, the Baltic countries, and Germany were killed during the Holocaust?

15. **Government** What event triggered the entry of the United States into the war?

Chapter Summary

World War II was the most devastating total war in human history. Events engaged four continents, involved countless people and resources, and changed subsequent history. The chart below summarizes some of the themes and developments.

Country	Movement	Cooperation	Conflict
United States	• Retakes Japanese positions in Southeast Asia	• Relaxes neutrality acts • Meets with Allies at Tehran, Yalta, and Potsdam	• Leads war effort • Conducts island-hopping counterattacks • Drops atomic bombs on Japan
Great Britain	• Makes huge troop movements at Dunkirk and Normandy	• Meets with Allies at Tehran, Yalta, and Potsdam	• Stops Rommel at El Alamein • Withstands heavy German bombing
Soviet Union	• Occupies Kuril and Sakhalin Islands • Takes control of much of Eastern Europe	• Meets with Allies at Tehran, Yalta, and Potsdam	• Defeats Germany at Stalingrad • Forces Germany to fight war on two fronts
Germany	• Takes over Austria, Poland, and Sudetenland	• Forms Rome-Berlin Axis • Signs Anti-Comintern Pact	• Uses blitzkrieg tactics • Conducts genocide of Jews and others • Besieges Leningrad
Italy	• Invades Ethiopia	• Forms Rome-Berlin Axis	• Becomes German puppet state (northern Italy)
Japan	• Seizes Manchuria and renames it Manchukuo • Invades China	• Signs Anti-Comintern Pact	• Attacks Pearl Harbor • Conquers Southeast Asia from Indochina to Philippines

Critical Thinking

16. **Cause and Effect** What factors caused President Truman to order the dropping of atomic bombs in Japan?

17. **Drawing Conclusions** How did World War II affect the world balance of power? What nations emerged from the conflict as world powers?

Writing About History

18. **Informative Writing** Write an essay that examines the different approaches to colonial governing in Asia taken by the Japanese during World War II and by Europeans before the war. Be sure to include information about key people, places, and events from each of the two periods in history.

Analyzing Sources

Heinrich Himmler, head of the German SS, argued:

❝Whether nations live in prosperity or starve to death interests me only insofar as we need them as slaves for our culture. Otherwise it is of no interest.❞

19. Describe Heinrich Himmler's opinion of the people that Germany conquered.

20. Compare the Nazi philosophy of creating a New Order with the Japanese philosophy of Asia for the Asiatics.

Applying Technology Skills

21. **Using the Internet** Use the Internet to research the daily life of a Japanese American citizen in a U.S. internment camp. Compare and contrast the treatment of Japanese Americans to that of German Americans and Italian Americans during this time.

Making Decisions

22. Some historians believe that President Truman dropped atomic weapons on Japan not to end the war in the Pacific, but to impress the Soviet Union with U.S. military power. Write a position paper evaluating this hypothesis in light of what you have learned about Stalin and the United States. What were Truman's other options? Do you think a leader today would make the same decision?

Analyzing Maps and Charts

Refer to the map on page 820 to answer the following questions.

23. Why did the Allies not retake every Japanese-held island?

24. How far is it from Pearl Harbor to Japan?

TAKS
Test Practice

Directions: Use the map *and* your knowledge of world history to answer the following question.

German-Controlled Territory, 1943

What geographic factors influenced German military advances?

F German troops had to cover long distances.

G Colder climates created problems that the German military could not overcome.

H The blitzkrieg relied on tanks that were most effective on flatter terrain.

J All of the above.

Test-Taking Tip: To answer this question about how geography affected history, look at the map carefully. Notice which areas the German military did not occupy. Use these clues to make an inference about how geography affected the German army.

WORLD LITERATURE

from A Room of One's Own

Virginia Woolf

Virginia Woolf, who was born in 1882 in London, is considered one of the most significant modernist writers of our time. Her work changed the ways the novel was perceived and written. She developed a technique known as stream of consciousness in which the writer portrays the inner lives and thoughts of multiple characters. Additionally, she is known for her feminist writings. One of the most famous of these is *A Room of One's Own.* The title of this work is based on her assertion that a woman "must have money and a room of her own" in order to write.

Read to Discover
How does Virginia Woolf express her belief that gender influences the development of talent? Do you think Woolf is being fair in her assessment? Does her analysis of the differences between treatment of men and women apply today?

Reader's Dictionary
agog: full of intense interest or excitement

moon: to dream

. . . Let me imagine, since facts are so hard to come by, what would have happened had Shakespeare had a wonderfully gifted sister, called Judith, let us say. Shakespeare himself went, very probably—his mother was an heiress—to the grammar school, where he may have learnt Latin—Ovid, Virgil and Horace—and the elements of grammar and logic. He was, it is well known, a wild boy who poached rabbits, perhaps shot a deer, and had, rather sooner than he should have done, to marry a woman in the neighbourhood, who bore him a child rather quicker than was right. That escapade sent him to seek his fortune in London. He had, it seemed, a taste for the theatre; he began by holding horses at the stage door. Very soon he got work in the theatre, became a successful actor, and lived at the hub of the universe, meeting everybody, knowing everybody, practising his art on the boards, exercising his wits in the street, and even getting access

◀ *Many of William Shakespeare's plays were performed at the Globe theater in London, shown left.*

to the palace of the queen. Meanwhile his extraordinarily gifted sister, let us suppose, remained at home. She was as adventurous, as imaginative, as agog to see the world as he was. But she was not sent to school. She had no chance of learning grammar and logic, let alone of reading Horace and Virgil. She picked up a book now and then, one of her brother's perhaps, and read a few pages. But then her parents came in and told her to mend the stockings or mind the stew and not moon about with books and papers. They would have spoken sharply but kindly, for they were substantial people who knew the conditions of life for a woman and loved their daughter—indeed, more likely than not she was the apple of her father's eye. Perhaps she scribbled some pages up in an apple loft on the sly, but was careful to hide them or set fire to them. Soon, however, before she was out of her teens, she was to be betrothed to the son of a neighbouring wool-stapler. She cried out that marriage was hateful to her, and for that she was severely beaten by her father. Then he ceased to scold her. He begged her instead not to hurt him, not to shame him in this matter of her marriage. He would give her a chain of beads or a fine petticoat, he said; and there were tears in his eyes. How could she disobey him? How could she break his heart? The force of her own gift alone drove her to it. She made up a small parcel of her belongings, let herself down by a rope one summer's night and took the road to London. She was not seventeen. The birds that sang in the hedge were not more musical than she was. She had the quickest fancy, a gift like her brother's, for the tune of words. Like him, she had a taste for the theatre. She stood at the stage door; she wanted to act, she said. Men laughed in her face. The manager—a fat, loose-lipped man—guffawed. He bellowed something about poodles dancing and women acting—no woman, he said could possibly be an actress. He hinted—you can imagine what. She could get no training in her craft. Could she even seek her dinner in a tavern or roam the streets at midnight? Yet her genius was for fiction . . . At

▲ *William Shakespeare*

last—for she was very young, oddly like Shakespeare the poet in her face, with the same grey eyes and rounded brows—at last Nick Greene the actor-manager took pity on her; [but] she . . . killed herself one winter's night and lies buried at some cross-roads where the omnibuses now stop outside the Elephant and Castle. That, more or less, is how the story would run, I think, if a woman in Shakespeare's day had had Shakespeare's genius.

Interpreting World Literature

1. What were "the conditions of life for a woman" that made Judith's parents scold her for attempting to read and write?

2. Why does Judith's father beat her?

3. What is Woolf's conclusion about the possibility of a woman becoming Shakespeare?

4. **CRITICAL THINKING** Why does Virginia Woolf have Shakespeare marry, but Shakespeare's sister run away from marriage?

Applications Activity

What does a person today need to succeed as a writer or artist? Write a descriptive account to illustrate your argument.

UNIT 6

Toward a Global Civilization

1945–Present

The Period in Perspective

World War II can be seen as the end of an era of European domination of the world. After the war, Europe quickly divided into hostile camps as the Cold War rivalry between the United States and the Soviet Union forced nations to take sides. In the late 1980s, however, the Soviet Empire began to come apart, and the Cold War quickly ended.

World War II severely undermined the stability of the colonial order in Asia and Africa. By the end of the 1940s, most colonies in Asia had gained their independence. Later, African colonies, too, would become independent nations.

Primary Sources Library

See pages 1000–1001 for primary source readings to accompany Unit 6.

Use The World History **Primary Source Document Library CD-ROM** to find additional primary sources about Global Civilization.

▲ Contemporary African art featuring Nelson Mandela

▶ African National Congress campaign rally

". . . there is no easy walk to freedom anywhere . . ."

—Nelson Mandela

Communication

The invention of writing and printing reshaped history. Today, electronic technology is moving communications forward at a startling rate. People can now be instantaneously linked around the world by satellites and the Internet.

1901
Guglielmo Marconi sends first radio waves across Atlantic

1930s
Television developed

1948
First electronic computer with stored memory is developed

1957
Soviet Union launches *Sputnik I*

❶ *The United States*

Satellite Communication

The first telephone developed by Alexander Graham Bell in 1876 was nothing more than a wooden stand with a funnel, some wires, and a cup of acid, but the telephone was soon to revolutionize communication worldwide.

Similarly, when the Soviet Union launched a tiny communications satellite named *Sputnik I* in 1957, the device could do little more than transmit radio signal beeps. However, this satellite also represented a major step in communication technology.

Three years later, the United States launched its first satellites, which could relay telephone calls between Europe and the United States. In 1962, the United States satellite *Telstar* was the first to relay live television programs to distant locations.

By the 1980s, people around the world with satellite dish antennas could tune in to hundreds of television programs. The effect was revolutionary. Repressive governments in Eastern Europe and elsewhere could not legislate against free speech beamed down from the skies.

Telstar

to See Ahead

Cybercafe

❷ *Africa*

The Internet

In Africa, UNESCO is helping the Pan-African News Agency and others to link to the Internet. Project leaders see the Internet as one of the keys to unlocking Africa's economic potential. Currently, there is one Internet access site for every 200 Africans, compared to a world average of one site for every 30 people. Internet access will improve, and as it does, African communications, education, business, and government endeavors will be profoundly impacted.

1960
United States launches its first satellites

1971
Microprocessor is invented

1977
Apple II computer introduced

1990
African agencies link to the Internet

1993
Chinese government bans satellite dishes

---

❸ *China*

Satellite Dishes

Satellite dishes made it possible for people across the People's Republic of China to listen to Mandarin-speaking rappers out of Hong Kong, English broadcasts of CNN News, and movies from Japan. The uncensored broadcasts enraged government officials, who tried to ban satellite dishes in 1993. However, even as officials dismantled thousands of large dishes, kits for smaller dishes were being smuggled into the country.

Other countries with repressive policies, such as Iran and Myanmar, tried and failed to ban satellite reception. Even free governments, like India's, were concerned about the "cultural invasion," but satellite television was here to stay.

Satellite dish, Tibet

Why It Matters

While it used to take months to send a letter from the United States to Africa, today it can take only seconds. How has instantaneous communication made the world smaller? What are the good and bad results of this phenomenon?

845

CHAPTER 27

Cold War and Postwar Changes

1945–1970

Key Events

As you read this chapter, look for the key events of the Cold War.
- At the end of World War II, the United States and the Soviet Union competed for political domination of the world.
- The United States fought in Korea and Vietnam to prevent the spread of communism.
- The Soviet Union used armies to maintain Soviet regimes in Eastern Europe.
- The creation of NATO and the European Economic Community helped Western Europe move toward political and economic unity during the Cold War.

The Impact Today

The events that occurred during this time period still impact our lives today.
- NATO continues to flourish. Representatives of its 19 member nations form the North Atlantic Council, which is headquartered in Brussels, Belgium.
- Nuclear weapons remain a threat to the peace and stability of the world.
- The civil rights struggle brought greater equality to African Americans and altered American attitudes toward race, discrimination, and poverty.

 World History Video *The Chapter 27 video, "The Berlin Airlift," shows how American and British planes circumvented the Soviet blockade.*

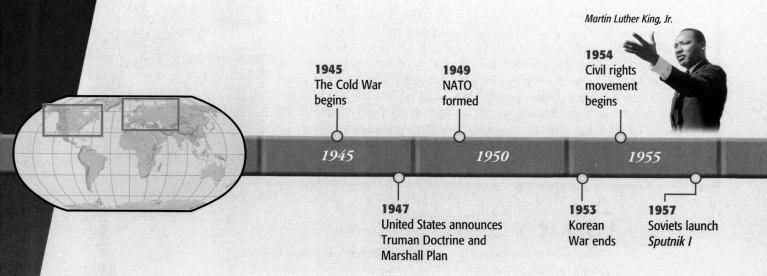

Martin Luther King, Jr.

1945
The Cold War begins

1949
NATO formed

1954
Civil rights movement begins

1945

1950

1955

1947
United States announces Truman Doctrine and Marshall Plan

1953
Korean War ends

1957
Soviets launch *Sputnik I*

The Soviet government displays its military strength in Moscow's annual May Day parade.

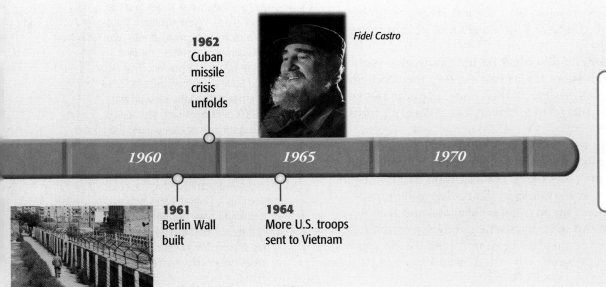

1962
Cuban
missile
crisis
unfolds

Fidel Castro

1960 1965 1970

1961
Berlin Wall
built

1964
More U.S. troops
sent to Vietnam

Berlin Wall

HISTORY
Online
Chapter Overview
Visit the *Glencoe World History* Web site at
tx.wh.glencoe.com and click
on **Chapter 27–Chapter
Overview** to preview
chapter information.

A Story That Matters

Cleaning up after the London Blitz

A Sober Victory

*T*he end of World War II in Europe had been met with great joy. One visitor in Moscow reported, "I looked out of the window [at 2 A.M.], almost everywhere there were lights in the windows—people were staying awake. Everyone embraced everyone else, someone sobbed aloud."

After the victory parades and celebrations, however, Europeans awoke to a devastating realization: their civilization was in ruins. As many as fifty million people (both soldiers and civilians) had been killed over the last six years. Massive air raids had reduced many of the great cities of Europe to heaps of rubble.

An American general described Berlin: "Wherever we looked we saw desolation. It was like a city of the dead. Suffering and shock were visible in every face. Dead bodies still remained in canals and lakes and were being dug out from under bomb debris."

Millions of Europeans faced starvation. Grain harvests were only half of what they had been in 1939. Millions were also homeless. In the parts of the Soviet Union that had been occupied by the Germans, almost twenty-five million people were without homes. Fifteen million Germans and East Europeans were driven out of countries where they were no longer wanted. Millions of people had been uprooted by the war and became "displaced persons" who tried to find food and a way home.

Why It Matters

Despite the chaos, Europe was soon on the road to a remarkable recovery. However, World War II had destroyed European supremacy in world affairs, and from this, Europe did not recover. As the Cold War between the world's two superpowers—the United States and the Soviet Union—grew stronger, European nations were divided into two armed camps dependent on one of these two major powers. The United States and the Soviet Union, whose rivalry brought the world to the brink of nuclear war, seemed to hold the survival of Europe and the world in their hands.

History and You Create a world map. As you read the chapter, color the map as a United States policy maker might have during the Cold War. Indicate the Soviet and United States spheres of influence as well as areas under contention.

Development of the Cold War

Guide to Reading

Main Ideas
- A period of conflict called the Cold War developed between the United States and the Soviet Union after 1945.
- As the Cold War developed, European nations were forced to support one of the two major powers.

Key Terms
satellite state, policy of containment, arms race, domino theory

People to Identify
Dean Acheson, Nikita Khrushchev

Places to Locate
Berlin, Federal Republic of Germany, German Democratic Republic

Preview Questions
1. What were the major turning points in the development of the Cold War?
2. What was the Cuban missile crisis?

Reading Strategy
Summarizing Information Use a table like the one below to list the American presidents who held office during the Cold War and major events related to the Cold War that took place during their administrations.

President	Major Event

Preview of Events

♦1945	♦1950	♦1955	♦1960	♦1965

1948 Berlin Air Lift begins

1949 Chinese Communists take control of China

1950 Korean War begins

1961 Soviets and East Germans build the Berlin Wall

1964 Lyndon B. Johnson increases number of troops sent to Vietnam

Voices from the Past

On March 5, 1946, Winston Churchill said in a speech in Fulton, Missouri:

❝From Stettin in the Baltic to Trieste in the Adriatic, an iron curtain has descended across the continent. Behind that line lie all the capitals of the ancient states of central and eastern Europe, Warsaw, Berlin, Prague, Vienna, Budapest, Belgrade, Bucharest, and Sofia; all these famous cities and the populations around them lie in the Soviet sphere and all are subject, in one form or another, not only to Soviet influence but to a very high and increasing measure of control from Moscow.❞

— *The Congressional Record,* 79th Congress, 1946

In 1946, Stalin replied: "In substance, Mr. Churchill now stands in the position of a firebrand of war." The division between Western Europe and Soviet-controlled Eastern Europe marked the beginning of the Cold War.

Winston Churchill

Confrontation of the Superpowers

Once the Axis Powers were defeated, the differences between the United States and the Soviet Union became clear. Stalin still feared the capitalist West, and U.S. (and other Western) leaders continued to fear communism. Who, then, was responsible for beginning the Cold War between the United States and the Soviet Union? Both took steps that were unwise and might have been avoided. It should not surprise us that two such different systems would come into conflict.

Because of its need to feel secure on its western border, the Soviet government was not prepared to give up its control of Eastern Europe after Germany's defeat. American leaders were not willing to give up the power and prestige the United States had gained throughout the world. Suspicious of each other's motives, the United States and the Soviet Union soon became rivals. Between 1945 and 1949, a number of events led the two superpowers (countries whose military power is combined with political influence) to oppose each other.

Rivalry in Europe

Eastern Europe was the first area of disagreement. The United States and Great Britain believed that the liberated nations of Eastern Europe should freely determine their own governments. Stalin, fearful that the Eastern European nations would be anti-Soviet if they were permitted free elections, opposed the West's plans. Having freed Eastern Europe from the Nazis, the Soviet army stayed in the conquered areas.

A civil war in Greece created another area of conflict between the superpowers. The Communist People's Liberation Army and anticommunist forces supported by Great Britain were fighting each other for control of Greece in 1946. However, Britain had its own economic problems, which caused it to withdraw its aid from Greece.

The Truman Doctrine

President Harry S Truman of the United States, alarmed by the British withdrawal and the possibility of Soviet expansion into the eastern Mediterranean, responded in early 1947 with the **Truman Doctrine.** The Truman Doctrine stated that the United States would provide money to countries (in this case, Greece) threatened by Communist expansion. If the Soviets were not stopped in Greece, the

President Truman asked Congress for money to aid European recovery.

Truman argument ran, then the United States would have to face the spread of communism throughout the free world.

As **Dean Acheson,** the U.S. secretary of state, explained, "Like apples in a barrel infected by disease, the corruption of Greece would infect Iran and all the East . . . likewise Africa, Italy, France. . . . Not since Rome and Carthage had there been such a polarization of power on this earth."

The Marshall Plan

The Truman Doctrine was followed in June 1947 by the European Recovery Program. Proposed by General George C. Marshall, U.S. secretary of state, it is better known as the **Marshall Plan.** The program was designed to rebuild the prosperity and stability of war-torn Europe. It included $13 billion in aid for Europe's economic recovery. Underlying the Marshall Plan was the belief that Communist aggression was successful in countries where there were economic problems.

The Marshall Plan was not meant to shut out the Soviet Union or its economically and politically dependent Eastern European satellite states. They refused to participate, however. According to the Soviet view, the Marshall Plan guaranteed "American loans in return for the relinquishing by the European states of their economic and later also their political independence." The Soviets saw the Marshall Plan as an attempt to buy the support of countries.

In 1949, the Soviet Union responded to the Marshall Plan by founding the Council for Mutual Economic Assistance (COMECON) for the economic cooperation of the Eastern European states. COMECON largely failed, however, because the Soviet Union was unable to provide much financial aid.

By 1947, the split in Europe between the United States and the Soviet Union had become a fact of life. In July 1947, George Kennan, a well-known U.S. diplomat with much knowledge of Soviet affairs, argued for a policy of containment to keep communism within its existing boundaries and prevent further Soviet aggressive moves. Containment became U.S. policy.

The Division of Germany

The fate of Germany also became a source of heated contention between the Soviets and the West. At the end of the war, the Allied Powers had divided Germany into four zones, each occupied by one of the Allies—the United States, the Soviet Union, Great Britain, and France. **Berlin,** located deep inside the Soviet zone, was also divided into four zones.

The foreign ministers of the four occupying powers met repeatedly in an attempt to arrive at a final peace treaty with Germany but had little success. By February 1948, Great Britain, France, and the United States were making plans to unify the three Western sections of Germany (and Berlin) and create a West German government.

The Soviets opposed the creation of a separate West German state. They attempted to prevent it by mounting a blockade of West Berlin. Soviet forces allowed neither trucks, trains, nor barges to enter the city's three Western zones. Food and supplies could no longer get through to the 2.5 million people in these zones.

The Western powers faced a dilemma. No one wanted World War III, but how could the people in the Western zones of Berlin be kept alive, when the whole city was inside the Soviet zone? The solution was the Berlin Air Lift—supplies would be flown in by American and British airplanes. For more than 10 months, more than 200,000 flights carried 2.3 million tons (1.4 million t) of supplies. The Soviets, who wanted to avoid war as much as the Western powers, finally gave in and lifted the blockade in May 1949.

In September 1949, the **Federal Republic of Germany,** or West Germany, was formally created. Its capital was Bonn. Less than a month later, a separate East German state, the **German Democratic Republic,** was set up by the Soviets. East Berlin became its capital. Berlin was now divided into two parts, a reminder of the division of West and East.

✓**Reading Check** **Describing** What was the intention of the Marshall Plan?

The Spread of the Cold War

⌐TURNING POINT ¬ **As you will learn, the spread of the Cold War led to the creation of military alliances that influenced the development of the postwar world.**

In 1949, Chinese Communists took control of the government in China, strengthening U.S. fears about the spread of communism. The Soviet Union also exploded its first atomic bomb in 1949. All too soon, the United States and the Soviet Union were involved in a growing arms race, in which both countries built up their armies and weapons. Nuclear weapons became increasingly destructive.

Both sides came to believe that an arsenal of nuclear weapons would prevent war. They believed that if one nation attacked with nuclear weapons, the other nation would still be able to respond and devastate the attacker. According to this policy, neither side could risk using their massive supplies of weapons.

New Military Alliances The search for security during the Cold War led to the formation of new military alliances. The North Atlantic Treaty Organization **(NATO)** was formed in April 1949 when Belgium, Luxembourg, France, the Netherlands, Great Britain, Italy, Denmark, Norway, Portugal, and

NATIONAL GEOGRAPHIC **Divided Germany and the Berlin Air Lift**

- ☐ Allied occupation zone
- ☐ Soviet occupation zone
- ←✛→ Routes of the Berlin Airlift, 1948–1949
- — Iron Curtain
- -- Division of Allied zone

Chamberlin Trimetric projection

Geography *Skills*

During the Berlin Air Lift, Western planes delivered food and supplies to the people of West Berlin.

1. **Interpreting Maps** Approximately how much German land was occupied by the Allies? How much was occupied by the Soviets?

2. **Applying Geography Skills** Why could the Allies not deliver food to West Berlin by land?

Balance of Power after World War II

North Atlantic Treaty Organization
(NATO) member nations, 1949

Nations joining NATO as of 1955

Warsaw Pact members as of 1955

Nonmember nations as of 1955

PACIFIC OCEAN

UNITED STATES

CANADA

ARCTIC OCEAN

NORTH POLE

SOVIET UNION

GREENLAND
Den.

ICELAND

NORWAY

UNITED KINGDOM

NETHERLANDS

BELGIUM
LUX.
FRANCE

PORTUGAL

Mediterranean Sea

Dates indicate when
countries came under
Communist control.

DENMARK
Copenhagen

Berlin POLAND
EAST   1947
GERMANY   Warsaw
1949   Prague
WEST
GERMANY CZECH. 1948
Vienna   SOVIET
SWITZ AUSTRIA   UNION
HUNGARY Budapest
1947   ROMANIA
Belgrade   1947
ITALY YUGOSLAVIA   Bucharest
1945   BULGARIA
Rome   1946
Tirana Sofia
Yugoslavia left   ALBANIA
the Communist   1946
Bloc in 1948. GREECE TURKEY

0   200 mi.
0   200 km
*Lambert Azimuthal
Equal-Area projection*

0   1,000 miles
0   1,000 kilometers
Orthographic projection

Iceland signed a treaty with the United States and Canada. All the powers agreed to provide mutual help if any one of them was attacked. A few years later, West Germany, Turkey, and Greece also joined.

In 1955, the Soviet Union joined with Albania, Bulgaria, Czechoslovakia, East Germany, Hungary, Poland, and Romania in a formal military alliance known as the **Warsaw Pact.** Now, Europe was once again divided into hostile alliance systems, just as it had been before World War I.

New military alliances spread to the rest of the world after the United States became involved in the Korean War (discussed in Chapter 31). The war began in 1950 as an attempt by the Communist government of North Korea, which was allied with the Soviet Union, to take over South Korea. The Korean War confirmed American fears of Communist expansion. More determined than ever to contain Soviet power, the United States extended its military alliances around the world.

Geography *Skills*

After World War II, the spread of the Cold War created new military alliances.

1. **Interpreting Maps** Are there any geographic factors that could have determined whether a country became a member of NATO or of the Warsaw Pact?

2. **Applying Geography Skills** Use the map to create a chart listing all of the countries in NATO and all the members of the Warsaw Pact. Which European countries did not join either alliance?

To stem Soviet aggression in the East, the United States, Great Britain, France, Pakistan, Thailand, the Philippines, Australia, and New Zealand formed the Southeast Asia Treaty Organization **(SEATO).** The Central Treaty Organization **(CENTO),** which included Turkey, Iraq, Iran, Pakistan, Great Britain, and the United States, was meant to prevent the Soviet Union from expanding to the south. By the mid-1950s, the United States found itself allied militarily with 42 states around the world.

The Arms Race The Soviet Union had set off its first atomic bomb in 1949. In the early 1950s, the Soviet Union and the United States developed the even more deadly hydrogen bomb. By the mid-1950s, both had intercontinental ballistic missiles (ICBMs) capable of sending bombs anywhere.

Both the United States and the Soviet Union now worked to build up huge arsenals of nuclear weapons. They believed that having these arsenals would prevent war. Neither side would launch a nuclear attack, because both knew that the other side would be able to strike back with devastating power.

In 1957, the Soviets sent *Sputnik I*, the first human-made space satellite, to orbit the earth. New fears seized the American public. Did the Soviet Union have a massive lead in building missiles? Was there a "missile gap" between the United States and the Soviet Union?

A Wall in Berlin Nikita Khrushchev (kroosh● CHAWF), who emerged as the new leader of the Soviet Union in 1955, tried to take advantage of the American concern over missiles to solve the problem of West Berlin. West Berlin remained a "Western island" of prosperity in the midst of the relatively poverty-stricken East Germany. Many East Germans, tired of Communist repression, managed to escape East Germany by fleeing through West Berlin.

Khrushchev realized the need to stop the flow of refugees from East Germany through West Berlin. In August 1961, the East German government began to build a wall separat-

ing West Berlin from East Berlin. Eventually it became a massive barrier guarded by barbed wire, floodlights, machine-gun towers, minefields, and vicious dog patrols. The Berlin Wall became a striking symbol of the division between the two superpowers.

✓ **Reading Check** **Identifying** Name the military alliances formed during the Cold War.

The Cuban Missile Crisis

During the administration of John F. Kennedy, the Cold War confrontation between the United States and the Soviet Union reached frightening levels. In 1959, a left-wing revolutionary named Fidel Castro overthrew the Cuban dictator Fulgencio Batista and set up a Soviet-supported totalitarian regime in Cuba (see Chapter 29). President Kennedy approved a secret plan for Cuban exiles to invade Cuba in the hope of causing a revolt against Castro. The invasion was a disaster. Many of the exiles were killed or captured when they attempted a landing at the Bay of Pigs.

After the Bay of Pigs, the Soviet Union sent arms and military advisers to Cuba. Then, in 1962, Khrushchev began to place nuclear missiles in Cuba. The missiles were meant to counteract U.S. nuclear weapons placed in Turkey within easy range of the Soviet Union. Khrushchev was quick to point out, "Your rockets are in Turkey. You are worried by Cuba . . . because it is 90 miles from the American coast. But Turkey is next to us."

The United States was not willing to allow nuclear weapons within such close striking distance of its mainland. In October 1962, Kennedy found out that Soviet ships carrying missiles were heading to Cuba. He decided to blockade Cuba and prevent the fleet from reaching its destination. This approach gave each side time to find a peaceful solution. Khrushchev agreed to turn back the fleet and remove Soviet missiles from Cuba if Kennedy pledged not to invade Cuba. Kennedy quickly agreed.

The Cuban missile crisis seemed to bring the world frighteningly close to nuclear war. Indeed, in 1992 a high-ranking Soviet officer revealed that short-range rockets armed with nuclear devices would have been used against U.S. troops if the United States had invaded Cuba, an option that Kennedy fortunately had rejected. The realization that the world might have been destroyed in a few days had a profound influence on both sides. A hot-line communications system between Moscow and Washington, D.C., was installed in 1963. The two superpowers could now communicate quickly in times of crisis.

✓ **Reading Check** **Explaining** How was the Cuban missile crisis resolved?

Vietnam and the Domino Theory

By that time, the United States had been drawn into a new struggle that had an important impact on the Cold War—the Vietnam War (see Chapter 31). In 1964, under President Lyndon B. Johnson, increasing numbers of U.S. troops were sent to Vietnam. Their purpose was to keep the Communist regime of North Vietnam from gaining control of South Vietnam.

U.S. policy makers saw the conflict in terms of a domino theory. If the Communists succeeded

Picturing History

Many young Americans were proud to serve their country in Vietnam, but increasingly the mood on college campuses was antiwar. **Why?**

in South Vietnam, the argument went, other countries in Asia would also fall (like dominoes) to communism.

Despite the massive superiority in equipment and firepower of the American forces, the United States failed to defeat the determined North Vietnamese. The growing number of American troops sent to Vietnam soon produced an antiwar movement in the United States, especially among college students of draft age. The mounting destruction of the conflict, brought into American homes every evening on television, also turned American public opinion against the war.

President Johnson, condemned for his handling of the costly and indecisive war, decided not to run for reelection. Former Vice President Richard M. Nixon won the election with his pledge to stop the war and bring the American people together. Ending the war was difficult, and Nixon's administration was besieged by antiwar forces.

Finally, in 1973, President Nixon reached an agreement with North Vietnam that allowed the United States to withdraw its forces. Within two years after the American withdrawal, Vietnam had been forcibly reunited by Communist armies from the North.

Despite the success of the North Vietnamese Communists, the domino theory proved unfounded. A split between Communist China and the Soviet Union, including border clashes and different implementations of communism, put an end to the Western idea that there was a single form of communism directed by Moscow. Under President Nixon, American relations with China were resumed. New nations in Southeast Asia managed to avoid Communist governments.

Above all, Vietnam helped show the limitations of American power. By the end of the Vietnam War, a new era in American-Soviet relations had begun to emerge.

✓ **Reading Check** **Examining** What did the Vietnam War prove about the state of global communism?

🇹🇽**TAKS Practice**

SECTION 1 ASSESSMENT

Checking for Understanding

1. **Define** satellite state, policy of containment, arms race, domino theory.

2. **Identify** Truman Doctrine, Dean Acheson, Marshall Plan, NATO, Warsaw Pact, SEATO, CENTO, Nikita Khrushchev.

3. **Locate** Berlin, Federal Republic of Germany, German Democratic Republic.

4. **Explain** why the Berlin Wall was built. What did the wall symbolize?

5. **List** the four powers that divided and occupied Germany.

Critical Thinking

6. **Evaluate** In your opinion, why did the United States assume global responsibility for containing communism?

7. **Organizing Information** Use a table like the one below to list the military alliances formed during the Cold War. In the next column list the countries belonging to the alliance.

Alliance	Countries

Analyzing Visuals

8. **Examine** the photo of a campus sit-in shown on this page. Students often used sit-ins to protest government policy in the 1960s and 1970s. What methods of protest do people use today?

Writing About History

9. **Informative Writing** Imagine that you are a resident of Berlin in 1948. Write a letter to a friend living in another part of Germany explaining what is happening in Berlin and your reaction to the actions of the foreign governments involved.

SECTION 2 — The Soviet Union and Eastern Europe

Guide to Reading

Main Ideas
- As Soviet leader, Khrushchev initiated policies of de-Stalinization.
- The Soviet Union faced revolts and protests in its attempt to gain and maintain control over Eastern Europe.

Key Terms
heavy industry, de-Stalinization

People to Identify
Alexander Solzhenitsyn, Tito, Imre Nagy, Alexander Dubček

Places to Locate
Soviet Union, Albania, Yugoslavia, Poland, Hungary, Czechoslovakia

Preview Questions
1. What were Khrushchev's policies of de-Stalinization?
2. How did the Soviet Union exert its power over Eastern Europe?

Reading Strategy
Categorizing Information Use a diagram like the one below to identify how the Soviet Union carried out Communist policies.

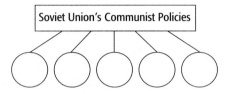

Soviet Union's Communist Policies

Preview of Events

◆1950	◆1955	◆1960	◆1965	◆1970

1953 Khrushchev named general secretary

1962 Solzhenitsyn's *A Day in the Life of Ivan Denisovich* is published

1964 Khrushchev is voted out of office

1968 The Soviet Army invades Czechoslovakia

Voices from the Past

Soviet tanks in Hungary

In 1956, Hungary revolted against Soviet control. The Soviet Union sent in troops and announced:

❝Forces of reaction and counterrevolution . . . are trying to take advantage of the discontent of part of the working people to undermine the foundations of the people's democratic order in Hungary and to restore the old landlord and capitalist order. The Soviet government and all the people deeply regret that the development of events in Hungary has led to bloodshed. On the request of the Hungarian People's Government the Soviet government consented to the entry into Budapest of the Soviet Army units to assist the Hungarian authorities to establish order in the town.❞

—*Department of State Bulletin*, **November 12, 1956**

After World War II, Stalin and the Soviet forces kept a tight hold on Eastern Europe—a hold that many countries struggled against.

The Reign of Stalin

World War II devastated the **Soviet Union.** To create a new industrial base, Stalin returned to the method that he had used in the 1930s. Soviet workers were expected to produce goods for export with little in return for themselves. The incoming capital from abroad could then be used to buy machinery and Western technology.

Economic recovery in the Soviet Union was spectacular in some respects. By 1950, Russian industrial production had surpassed prewar levels by 40 percent. New power plants, canals, and giant factories were built. Heavy industry (the manufacture of machines and equipment for factories and mines) increased, chiefly for the benefit of the military. The testing of hydrogen bombs in 1953 and the first space satellite, *Sputnik I*, in 1957 enhanced the Soviet state's reputation as a world power abroad.

The Soviet people, however, were shortchanged. The growth rate for heavy industry was three times that for consumer goods. Moreover, the housing shortage was severe. An average Russian family lived in a one-room apartment. A British official in Moscow reported that "every room is both a living room by day and a bedroom by night."

Stalin remained the undisputed master of the Soviet Union. He distrusted competitors, exercised sole power, and had little respect for other Communist Party leaders. He is reported to have said to members of his inner circle in 1952, "You are as blind as kittens. What would you do without me?"

Stalin's suspicions added to the increasing repression of the regime. In 1946, the government decreed that all literary and scientific work must conform to the political needs of the state. Along with this anti-intellectual campaign came political terror. A new series of purges seemed likely in 1953, but Stalin's death on March 5 prevented more bloodletting.

✓ Reading Check **Summarizing** What costs did Stalin's economic policy impose on the Russian people?

The Khrushchev Era

A group of leaders succeeded Stalin, but the new general secretary of the Communist Party, Nikita Khrushchev, soon emerged as the chief Soviet policy maker. Once in power, Khrushchev took steps to undo some of the worst features of Stalin's regime.

At the Twentieth Congress of the Communist Party in 1956, Khrushchev condemned Stalin for his "administrative violence, mass repression, and terror." The process of eliminating the more ruthless policies of Stalin became known as de-Stalinization.

Khrushchev loosened government controls on literary works. In 1962, for example, he allowed the publication of *A Day in the Life of Ivan Denisovich,* a grim portrayal of life in a Siberian forced-labor camp written by **Alexander Solzhenitsyn** (SOHL•zhuh•NEET•suhn). Each day, as Solzhenitsyn related, prisoners were marched from the prison camp to a work project through subzero temperatures: "There were escort guards all over the place, . . . their machine guns sticking out and pointed right at your face. And there were guards with gray dogs." Many Soviets identified with Ivan as a symbol of the suffering they had endured under Stalin.

Khrushchev tried to place more emphasis on producing consumer goods. He also attempted to increase agricultural output by growing corn and cultivating vast lands east of the Ural Mountains. The attempt to increase agricultural output was not successful and damaged his reputation within the party. This failure, combined with increased military spending, hurt the Soviet economy. The industrial

Picturing **History**

A Soviet scientist is shown working on *Sputnik I.* The launch of *Sputnik I,* which orbited the earth for 57 days, stunned the United States and enhanced the prestige of the Soviet Union. Today, many space endeavors are international efforts. Why?

Nikita Khrushchev
1894–1971—Soviet leader

First secretary of the Communist Party after Stalin's death, Khrushchev eventually came to be the sole Soviet ruler. In 1956, he denounced the rule of Stalin, arguing that "Stalin showed in a whole series of cases his intolerance, his brutality and his abuse of power. . . . He was a very distrustful man, sickly suspicious. Everywhere and in everything he saw enemies, two-facers, and spies."

Khrushchev alienated other Soviet leaders by his policy in Cuba. He had other problems with the higher Soviet officials as well. They frowned on his tendency to crack jokes and play the clown. They also were displeased when he tried to curb their privileges.

growth rate, which had soared in the early 1950s, now declined dramatically from 13 percent in 1953 to 7.5 percent in 1964.

Foreign policy failures also damaged Khrushchev's reputation among his colleagues. His rash plan to place missiles in Cuba was the final straw. While he was away on vacation in 1964, a special meeting of the Soviet leaders voted him out of office (because of "deteriorating health") and forced him into retirement.

Reading Check Explaining Why did the Soviet leaders vote Khrushchev out of power?

Eastern Europe: Behind the Iron Curtain

At the end of World War II, Soviet military forces occupied all of Eastern Europe and the Balkans (except for Greece, Albania, and Yugoslavia). All of the occupied states came under Soviet control.

Communist Patterns of Control The timetable of the Soviet takeover varied from country to country. Between 1945 and 1947, Soviet-controlled Communist governments became firmly entrenched in East Germany, Bulgaria, Romania, Poland, and Hungary. In Czechoslovakia, where there was a strong tradition of democracy and a multi-party system, the Soviets did not seize control of the government until 1948. At that time they dissolved all but the Communist Party.

Albania and Yugoslavia were exceptions to this pattern of Soviet dominance. During the war, both countries had had strong Communist movements that resisted the Nazis. After the war, local Communist parties took control. Communists in **Albania** set up a Stalinist-type regime that grew more and more independent of the Soviet Union.

In **Yugoslavia,** Josip Broz, known as **Tito,** had been the leader of the Communist resistance movement. After the war, he moved toward the creation of an independent Communist state in Yugoslavia. Stalin hoped to take control of Yugoslavia, just as he had done in other Eastern European countries. Tito, however, refused to give in to Stalin's demands. He gained the support of the people by portraying the struggle as one of Yugoslav national freedom. Tito ruled Yugoslavia until his death in 1980. Although Yugoslavia had a Communist government, it was not a Soviet satellite state.

Between 1948 and Stalin's death in 1953, the Eastern European satellite states, directed by the Soviet Union, followed Stalin's example. They instituted Soviet-type five-year plans with emphasis on heavy industry rather than consumer goods. They began to collectivize agriculture. They eliminated all noncommunist parties and set up the institutions of repression—secret police and military forces.

Revolts Against Communism Communism did not develop deep roots among the peoples of Eastern Europe. Moreover, the Soviets exploited Eastern Europe economically for their own benefit and made living conditions harsh for most people.

After Stalin's death, many Eastern European states began to pursue a new course. In the late 1950s and 1960s, however, the Soviet Union made it clear—especially in **Poland, Hungary,** and **Czechoslovakia**—that it would not allow its Eastern European satellites to become independent of Soviet control.

In 1956, protests erupted in Poland. In response, the Polish Communist Party adopted a series of reforms in October 1956 and elected Wladyslaw Gomulka as first secretary. Gomulka declared that Poland had the right to follow its own socialist path. Fearful of Soviet armed response, however, the Poles compromised. Poland pledged to remain loyal to the Warsaw Pact.

The Soviet army invaded Czechoslovakia in 1968.

Developments in Poland in 1956 led Hungarian Communists to seek the same kinds of reforms. Unrest in Hungary, combined with economic difficulties, led to calls for revolt. To quell the rising rebellion, **Imre Nagy,** the Hungarian leader, declared Hungary a free nation on November 1, 1956, and promised free elections. It soon became clear that this could mean the end of Communist rule in Hungary.

Khrushchev was in no position at home to allow a member of the Communist group of nations to leave, however. Three days after Nagy's declaration, the Soviet Army attacked Budapest. The Soviets reestablished control over the country. Nagy was seized by the Soviet military and executed two years later.

The situation in Czechoslovakia in the 1950s was different. There, the "Little Stalin," Antonin Novotny, had been placed in power in 1953 by Stalin himself and remained firmly in control. By the late 1960s, however, Novotny had alienated many members of his own party. He was especially disliked by Czechoslovakia's writers. A writers' rebellion, which encouraged the people to take control of their own lives, led to Novotny's resignation, in 1968.

In January 1968, **Alexander Dubček** (DOOB•chehk) was elected first secretary of the Communist Party. He introduced a number of reforms, including freedom of speech and press and freedom to travel abroad. He relaxed censorship, began to pursue an independent foreign policy, and promised a gradual democratization of the Czechoslovakian political system. Dubček hoped to create "socialism with a human face." A period of euphoria broke out that came to be known as the "Prague Spring."

The euphoria proved to be short-lived, however. To forestall the spreading of this "spring fever," the Soviet Army invaded Czechoslovakia in August 1968 and crushed the reform movement. Gustav Husák replaced Dubček, did away with his reforms, and reestablished the old order.

✔**Reading Check** **Evaluating** What caused the battles between the Eastern European states and the Soviet Union?

TAKS Practice

SECTION 2 ASSESSMENT

Checking for Understanding

1. **Define** heavy industry, de-Stalinization.

2. **Identify** Alexander Solzhenitsyn, Tito, Imre Nagy, Alexander Dubček.

3. **Locate** Soviet Union, Albania, Yugoslavia, Poland, Hungary, Czechoslovakia.

4. **Explain** Khrushchev's relationship to Stalinism.

5. **List** two countries in Eastern Europe that resisted Soviet dominance.

Critical Thinking

6. **Explain** Why did Yugoslavia and Albania not come under the direct control of the Soviet Union?

7. **Organizing Information** Use a table like the one below to identify the policies of Stalin and the policies of Khrushchev.

Stalin	Khrushchev

Analyzing Visuals

8. **Compare** the photograph on page 856 with the one shown above. How does each photograph symbolize a different aspect of the Cold War?

Writing About History

9. **Informative Writing** You are a Western journalist in Hungary in 1956. Write an article for an American newspaper that describes the events leading to the Soviet attack on Budapest and what effect the attack will have on the Cold War.

SOCIAL STUDIES
SKILLBUILDER

TAKS Practice

Understanding World Time Zones

Why Learn This Skill?

Imagine that you work in Boston and call a client in London at 2:00 P.M. No one answers, because when it is 2:00 P.M. in Boston, it is already 7:00 P.M. in London.

Learning the Skill

In 1884, an international conference divided the world into 24 time zones.

The Prime Meridian (0° longitude), which runs through Greenwich, England, became the reference point. Traveling east from Greenwich, the time is one hour later in each time zone. Traveling west from Greenwich, the time is one hour earlier per zone.

The International Date Line is at 180° longitude. When crossing this line from west to east, you lose one day; when crossing in the opposite direction, you gain a day.

Using the map on this page:
- Locate Los Angeles and note its time.
- Locate Mumbai, India.
- Determine whether Mumbai lies east or west of Los Angeles.
- Count the number of time zones between the two cities. Each time zone is an hour difference.
- Add or subtract the number of hours difference between Mumbai and Los Angeles.
- Is the International Date Line between the two points? If so, add or subtract a day.
- Check the time above Mumbai to see if you are correct.

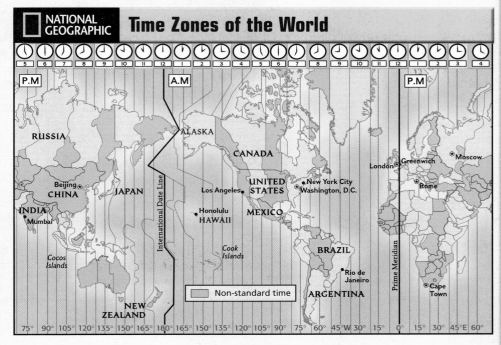

NATIONAL GEOGRAPHIC — Time Zones of the World

Practicing the Skill

Use the map to calculate these times.

1. If it is 3:00 P.M. in Greenwich, what time is it in Moscow?
2. If it is 9:00 A.M. in Cape Town, what time is it in Washington, D.C.?
3. It is 5:00 P.M. on Tuesday in Beijing. What day and time is it in Honolulu?

Applying the Skill

Create four time zone problems. Be sure at least one problem involves the International Date Line. Exchange problems with a classmate and check the accuracy of each other's computation.

 GO TO

Glencoe's **Skillbuilder Interactive Workbook, Level 2,** provides instruction and practice in key social studies skills.

Western Europe and North America

Main Ideas
- Postwar Western societies rebuilt their economies and communities.
- Shifting social structures in the West led to upheaval and change.

Key Terms
welfare state, bloc, real wages

People to Identify
Charles de Gaulle, John F. Kennedy, Martin Luther King, Jr., Simone de Beauvoir

Places to Locate
France, West Germany

Preview Questions
1. How did the EEC benefit the member nations?
2. What were the major social changes in Western society after 1945?

Reading Strategy
Categorizing Information Use a table like the one below to list programs instituted by Great Britain, the United States, and Canada to promote social welfare.

Great Britain	United States	Canada

Preview of Events

◆1945	◆1950	◆1955	◆1960	◆1965	◆1970	◆1975

1949
Simone de Beauvoir publishes *The Second Sex*

1957
The Rome Treaty establishes the EEC

1964
The Civil Rights Act is passed

1968
Student revolts peak

Voices from the Past

Student protestor in Paris

In 1968, student protestors scribbled the following on the walls of the University of Paris:

❝May 1968. World revolution is the order of the day.
To be free in 1968 is to take part.
Make love, not war.
The mind travels farther than the heart but it doesn't go as far.
Exam = servility, social promotion, hierarchic society.
Love each other.
Are you consumers or participants?
Revolution, I love you.❞
— *The Western Tradition from the Renaissance to the Present*, **Eugen Weber, 1972**

Student revolts in the United States and Europe were a part of larger problems that faced Western society after 1945.

Western Europe: Recovery

With the economic aid of the Marshall Plan, the countries of Western Europe recovered relatively rapidly from the devastation of World War II. Between 1947 and 1950, European countries received $9.4 billion for new equipment and raw materials. By 1950, industrial output in Europe was 30 percent above prewar levels.

This economic recovery continued well into the 1950s and 1960s. The decades of the 1950s and 1960s were periods of dramatic economic growth and prosperity in Western Europe. Indeed, Western Europe had virtually full employment during these decades.

France and de Gaulle The history of **France** for nearly a quarter of a century after the war was dominated by one man—the war hero **Charles de Gaulle.** In 1946, de Gaulle helped establish a new government called the Fourth Republic. It featured a strong parliament and a weak presidency. No party was strong enough to dominate, and the government was largely ineffective.

Unhappy with the Fourth Republic, de Gaulle withdrew from politics. Then, in 1958, he returned. Leaders of the Fourth Republic, frightened by bitter divisions caused by a crisis in the French colony of Algeria (discussed in Chapter 30), asked de Gaulle to form a new government and revise the constitution.

In 1958, de Gaulle drafted a new constitution for the Fifth Republic that greatly enhanced the power of the president. The president would now have the right to choose the prime minister, dissolve parliament, and supervise both defense and foreign policy. The constitution was overwhelmingly approved by French voters, and de Gaulle became the first president of the Fifth Republic.

People In History

Charles de Gaulle
1890–1970—French president

Charles de Gaulle had an unshakable faith in his mission to restore the greatness of the French nation. De Gaulle followed a military career and, before World War II, he argued for a new type of mobile tank warfare. After France fell to the Nazis, he fled to Britain and became leader of the French Resistance.

As president of France, de Gaulle realized that France was wasting its economic strength by maintaining its colonial empire. By 1962, he had granted independence to France's black African colonies and to Algeria. At the same time, he believed that playing an important role in the Cold War would enhance France's stature. For that reason, he pulled France out of NATO, saying that France did not want to be an American "vassal state."

As the new president, de Gaulle sought to return France to a position of great power. To achieve the status of a world power, de Gaulle invested heavily in nuclear arms. France exploded its first nuclear bomb in 1960.

During de Gaulle's presidency, the French economy grew at an annual rate of 5.5 percent, faster than that of the United States. France became a major industrial producer and exporter, especially of automobiles and weapons.

Nevertheless, problems remained. Large government deficits and a rise in the cost of living led to unrest. In May 1968, a series of student protests was followed by a general labor strike. Tired and discouraged, de Gaulle resigned from office in April 1969 and died within a year.

The Economic Miracle of West Germany The three Western zones of Germany were unified as the Federal Republic of Germany in 1949. From 1949 to 1963, Konrad Adenauer (A•duhn•OWR), the leader of the **Christian Democratic Union** (CDU), served as chancellor (head of state). Adenauer sought respect for **West Germany.** He cooperated with the United States and other Western European nations and especially wanted to work with France—Germany's longtime enemy.

Konrad Adenauer

Under Adenauer, West Germany experienced an "economic miracle." This revival of the West German economy was largely guided by the minister of finance, Ludwig Erhard. Unemployment fell from 8 percent in 1950 to 0.4 percent in 1965. To maintain its economic expansion, West Germany even brought in hundreds of thousands of "guest" workers on visas from Italy, Spain, Greece, Turkey, and Yugoslavia.

Adenauer resigned in 1963, after 14 years of guiding West Germany through its postwar recovery. Ludwig Erhard succeeded Adenauer as chancellor and largely continued his policies.

An economic downturn in the mid-1960s opened the door to the Social Democratic Party, which became the leading party in 1969. The Social Democrats, a moderate socialist party, were led by Willy Brandt, mayor of West Berlin.

The Decline of Great Britain The end of World War II left Great Britain with massive economic

CONNECTIONS Around The World

Economic Miracles: Germany and Japan

Both Germany and Japan were devastated by World War II. Their economies were in shambles. Their cities lay in ruins. At the end of the twentieth century, though, Germany and Japan were two of the world's greatest economic powers. What explains their economic miracles?

Because of the destruction of the war, both countries were forced to build new industrial plants. For many years, neither country spent much on defense. Their governments focused instead on rebuilding the infrastructure (roads, bridges, canals, and buildings) that had been destroyed during the war. Both German and Japanese workers had a long tradition of hard work and basic skills.

In both countries, U.S. occupation policy was committed to economic recovery, a goal that was made easier by American foreign aid.

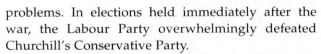

◀ *German bridge*

Today, Germany and Japan share many similarities in economic structure. Both rely on imports of raw materials for their industries. Both depend for their prosperity on exports of manufactured goods, including machinery, automobiles, steel, textiles, electrical and electronic equipment, and ships. Both nations must import food to feed their populations.

▲ *Japanese railroad station*

Comparing Cultures

The United States has never experienced the kind of destruction experienced by Germany and Japan during World War II. How might your life be different if the United States was in the process of rebuilding after a war? What cultural, political, and economic factors might influence the process of rebuilding in the United States?

---

problems. In elections held immediately after the war, the Labour Party overwhelmingly defeated Churchill's Conservative Party.

The Labour Party had promised far-reaching reforms, especially in the area of social welfare. Under Clement Attlee, the new prime minister, the Labour government set out to create a modern **welfare state**—a state in which the government takes responsibility for providing citizens with services and a minimal standard of living.

In 1946, the new government passed the National Insurance Act and the National Health Service Act. The insurance act provided government funds to help the unemployed, the sick, and the aged. The health act created a system of socialized medicine that ensured medical care for everyone. The British welfare state became the norm for most European states after the war.

The cost of building a welfare state at home forced Britain to reduce expenses abroad. This meant the dismantling of the British Empire. Economic necessity forced Britain to give in to the demands of its many colonies for national independence. Britain was no longer able to play the role of a world power.

Continuing economic problems brought the Conservatives back into power from 1951 to 1964. Although they favored private enterprise, the Conservatives accepted the welfare state and even extended it by financing an ambitious building program to improve British housing.

✔ **Reading Check** **Explaining** Why did de Gaulle invest heavily in nuclear arms?

Western Europe: The Move toward Unity

As we have seen, the divisions created by the Cold War led the nations of Western Europe to form the North Atlantic Treaty Organization in 1949. The destructiveness of two world wars caused many thoughtful Europeans to consider the need for some additional form of European unity. National feeling was still too powerful, however, for European nations to give up their political sovereignty. As a result, the desire for unity focused chiefly on the economic arena, not the political one.

In 1957, France, West Germany, the Benelux countries (Belgium, the Netherlands, and Luxembourg), and Italy signed the Rome Treaty. This treaty created the **European Economic Community** (EEC), also known as the Common Market.

The EEC was a free-trade area made up of the six member nations. These six nations would impose no tariffs, or import charges, on each other's goods. However, as a group, they would be protected by a tariff imposed on goods from non-EEC nations. In this way, the EEC encouraged cooperation among the member nations' economies. All the member nations benefited economically.

By the 1960s, the EEC had become an important trading bloc (a group of nations with a common purpose). With a total population of 165 million, the EEC was the world's largest exporter and purchaser of raw materials.

Reading Check **Evaluating** Why did European unity come in the form of an economic alliance?

The United States in the 1950s

Between 1945 and 1970, the ideals of Franklin Delano Roosevelt's New Deal largely determined the patterns of American domestic politics. The New Deal had brought basic changes to American society. They included a dramatic increase in the role and power of the federal government, the rise of organized labor as a significant force in the economy and politics, the beginning of a welfare state, and a realization of the need to deal fairly with the concerns of minorities, especially African Americans.

The New Deal tradition in American politics was reinforced by the election of Democratic presidents—Harry S Truman in 1948, John F. Kennedy in 1960, and Lyndon B. Johnson in 1964. Even the election of a Republican president, Dwight D. Eisenhower, in 1952 and 1956 did not change the basic direction of the New Deal. Eisenhower said, "Should any political party attempt to abolish Social Security and eliminate labor laws, you would not hear of that party again in our political history."

An economic boom followed World War II. A shortage of consumer goods during the war had left Americans with both extra income and the desire to buy goods after the war. In addition, the growth of labor unions brought higher wages and gave more workers the ability to buy consumer goods. Between

European Economic Community, 1957

Original European Economic Community (EEC) members, 1957

Geography Skills

The signing of the Rome Treaty in 1957 established the European Economic Community (EEC).

1. **Interpreting Maps** What countries were members of the EEC in 1957?

2. **Applying Geography Skills** What geographical factors could help to explain why some European countries joined the EEC in 1957 but others did not?

1945 and 1973, **real wages** (the actual purchasing power of income) grew an average of 3 percent a year, the most prolonged advance in American history.

Prosperity was not the only characteristic of the early 1950s, however. Cold War struggles abroad led to the widespread fear that Communists had infiltrated the United States. President Truman's attorney general warned that Communists were "everywhere—in factories, offices, butcher stores, on street corners, in private businesses." For many Americans, proof of this threat became more evident when thousands of American soldiers were sent to Korea to fight and die in a war against Communist aggression.

This climate of fear produced a dangerous political agitator, Senator Joseph R. McCarthy of Wisconsin. His charges that hundreds of supposed communists were in high government positions helped create a massive "Red Scare"—fear of communist subversion. Under McCarthy, several individuals, including intellectuals and movie stars, were questioned about Communist activities. When McCarthy attacked alleged "Communist conspirators" in the U.S. Army, he was condemned by the Senate in 1954. Very quickly, his anticommunist crusade came to an end.

✓ **Reading Check** **Describing** What effect did the Cold War have on many Americans?

The United States in the 1960s

The 1960s began on a youthful and optimistic note. At age 43, **John F. Kennedy** became the youngest elected president in the history of the United States. His administration was cut short when the president was killed by an assassin on November 22, 1963. Vice President Lyndon B. Johnson then became president. Johnson won a new term as president in a landslide victory in 1964.

The Johnson Administration President Johnson used his stunning victory to pursue the growth of the welfare state, begun in the New Deal. Johnson's programs included health care for the elderly, vari-

Lyndon B. Johnson taking the oath of office

ous measures to combat poverty, and federal assistance for education.

Johnson's other domestic passion was the civil rights movement, or equal rights for African Americans. The civil rights movement had its beginnings in 1954, when the United States Supreme Court ruled that the practice of racial segregation (separation) in public schools was illegal. According to Chief Justice Earl Warren, "separate educational facilities

THE WAY IT WAS

FOCUS ON EVERYDAY LIFE

Youth Protest in the 1960s

The decade of the 1960s witnessed a dramatic change in traditional manners and morals. The new standards were evident in the breakdown of the traditional family as divorce rates increased dramatically. Movies, plays, and books broke new ground in the treatment of once-hidden subjects.

A new youth movement also emerged in the 1960s. New attitudes toward sex and the use of drugs were two of its features. Young people also questioned authority and rebelled against the older generation. Spurred on by the Vietnam War, the youth rebellion in the United States had become

a youth protest movement by the second half of the 1960s. Active participants in the movement were often called "hippies."

In the 1960s, the lyrics of rock music reflected the rebellious mood of many young people. Bob Dylan, a well-known recording artist, expressed the feelings of the younger generation. His song "The Times They Are A-Changin'," released in 1964, has been called an "anthem for the protest movement." Some of its words, which follow, tell us why.

"The Times They Are A-Changin'"
    Come gather round people
    Wherever you roam
    And admit that the waters

are inherently unequal." African Americans also boy-cotted segregated buses and other public places.

In August 1963, The Reverend **Martin Luther King, Jr.,** leader of a growing movement for racial equality, led a march on Washington, D.C., to drama-tize the African American desire for equality. King advocated the principle of passive disobedience practiced by Mohandas Gandhi. King's march and his impassioned plea for racial equality had an elec-trifying effect on the American people. By the end of 1963, a majority of the American people called civil rights the most significant national issue.

President Johnson took up the cause of civil rights. The Civil Rights Act in 1964 created the machinery to end segregation and discrimination in the workplace and all public places. The Voting Rights Act the following year made it easier for African Americans to vote in southern states.

Laws alone, however, could not guarantee the Great Society that Johnson talked about creating. He soon faced bitter social unrest.

Social Upheaval In the North and West, blacks had had voting rights for many years. However, local pat-terns of segregation led to higher unemployment rates for blacks than for whites. In the summer of 1965, race riots broke out in the Watts district of Los Angeles. Thirty-four people died, and over a thou-sand buildings were destroyed. In 1968, Martin Luther King, Jr., was assassinated. Riots hit over a hundred cities, including Washington, D.C. The riots led to a "white backlash" (whites became less sym-pathetic to the cause of racial equality) and continued the racial division of the United States.

Antiwar protests also divided the American people after President Johnson sent American troops to war in Vietnam (see Chapter 31). As the war progressed through the second half of the 1960s, the protests grew. Then, in 1970, four students at Kent State University were killed and nine others were wounded by the Ohio National Guard during a student demonstration. The tragedy startled the nation. By this time Ameri-cans were less willing to continue the war.

The combination of antiwar demonstrations and riots in the cities caused many people to call for "law and order." This was the appeal used by Richard Nixon, the Republican presidential candidate in 1968. With Nixon's election in 1968, a shift to the political right in American politics began.

✓ **Reading Check** **Identifying** Name President Johnson's two most important domestic policy goals.

Around you have grown
And accept it that soon
You'll be drenched to the bone
If your time to you
Is worth savin'
Then you better start swimmin'
Or you'll sink like a stone
For the times they are a-changin' . . .

Come mothers and fathers
Throughout the land
And don't criticize
What you can't understand
Your sons and your daughters
Are beyond your command
Your old road
Is rapidly agin'
Please get out of the new one
If you can't lend your hand
For the times they are a-changin'

Young people expressed their rebellion through clothing, music, and government protests.

CONNECTING TO THE PAST

1. **Identifying** What does Bob Dylan say is the conse-quence of not changing?

2. **Comparing** Are there songs or artists today who have the same cultural outlook as Bob Dylan?

3. **Writing about History** What social or political issues are being expressed in music, literature, tele-vision, or movies today? Write a brief essay high-lighting one or two cultural examples, including lyrics or other relevant materials.

865

Gunfire breaks up an antiwar protest at Kent State University, Ohio, in 1970. Today, a memorial inscribed "Inquire, Learn, Reflect" marks the site where four student protestors were killed by the National Guard. What message or lesson is conveyed to you by the events at Kent State?

The Development of Canada

For 25 years after World War II, a prosperous Canada set out on a new path of industrial development. Canada had always had a strong export economy based on its abundant natural resources. Now it developed electronic, aircraft, nuclear, and chemical engineering industries on a large scale. Much of the Canadian growth, however, was financed by capital from the United States, which led to U.S. ownership of Canadian businesses. Some Canadians feared American economic domination of Canada.

Canadians also worried about playing a secondary role politically and militarily to the United States. They sought to establish their own identity in world politics. Canada was a founding member of the United Nations in 1945 and joined the North Atlantic Treaty Organization in 1949.

The Liberal Party dominated Canadian politics throughout most of this period. Under Lester Pearson, the Liberal government created Canada's welfare state by enacting a national social security system (the Canada Pension Plan) and a national health insurance program.

Reading Check **Explaining** Why did some Canadians fear U.S. economic domination of Canada?

The Emergence of a New Society

After World War II, Western society witnessed rapid change. Such new inventions as computers, televisions, and jet planes altered the pace and nature of human life. The rapid changes in postwar society led many to view it as a new society.

A Changing Social Structure Postwar Western society was marked by a changing social structure.

Especially noticeable were changes in the middle class. Traditional middle-class groups were made up of businesspeople, lawyers, doctors, and teachers. A new group of managers and technicians, hired by large companies and government agencies, now joined the ranks of the middle class.

Changes also occurred among the lower classes. The shift of people from rural to urban areas continued. The number of people in farming declined drastically. By the 1950s, the number of farmers in most parts of

▼ *Early 1950s television*

▼ *1959 De Soto*

Europe had dropped by 50 percent. The number of industrial workers also began to decline as the amount of white-collar workers increased.

At the same time, a noticeable increase in the real wages of workers made it possible for them to imitate the buying patterns of the middle class. This led to what some observers have called the **consumer society**—a society preoccupied with buying goods.

Buying on credit became widespread in the 1950s. Workers could now buy such products as televisions, washing machines, refrigerators, vacuum cleaners, and stereos. The automobile was the most visible symbol of the new consumerism. In 1948, there were 5 million cars in all of Europe. By the 1960s, there were almost 45 million.

Women in the Postwar World

Women's participation in the world wars had resulted in several gains. They had achieved one of the major aims of the nineteenth-century feminist movement—the right to vote. After World War I, many governments had expressed thanks to women by granting them voting rights. Sweden, Great Britain, Germany, Poland, Hungary, Austria, and Czechoslovakia did so in 1918, followed by the United States in 1920. French women only gained the vote in 1944, while Italian women did so in 1945.

During World War II, women had entered the workforce in huge numbers. At the war's end, however, they were removed to provide jobs for soldiers returning home. For a time, women fell back into traditional roles. Birthrates rose, creating a "baby boom" in the late 1940s and the 1950s.

By the end of the 1950s, however, the birthrate had begun to fall, and with it, the size of families. The structure of the workplace changed once again as the number of married women in the workforce increased in both Europe and the United States.

These women, especially working-class women, faced an old problem. They still earned less than men for equal work. For example, in the 1960s, women earned 60 percent of men's wages in Britain, 50 percent in France, and 63 percent in West Germany.

In addition, women still tended to enter traditionally female jobs. Many faced the double burden of earning income on the one hand and raising a family on the other. Such inequalities led increasing numbers of women to rebel.

By the late 1960s, women had begun to assert their rights again. In the late 1960s came renewed interest in feminism, or the **women's liberation movement,** as it was now called.

Of great importance to the emergence of the postwar women's liberation movement was the work of **Simone de Beauvoir** (duh•boh•VWAHR). In 1949, she published her highly influential work, *The Second Sex.* As a result of male-dominated societies, she argued, women had been defined by their differences from men and consequently received second-class status. De Beauvoir's book influenced both the American and European women's movements.

Student Revolt As we have seen, students in U.S. universities in the mid- to late 1960s launched an antiwar protest movement. At the same time, European students were engaging in protests of their own.

Before World War II, it was mostly members of Europe's wealthier classes who went to universities. After the war, European states began to encourage more people to gain higher education by eliminating fees. As a result, universities saw an influx of students from the middle and lower classes. Enrollments grew dramatically. In France, 4.5 percent of young people went to universities in 1950. By 1965, the figure had increased to 14.5 percent.

There were problems, however. Many European university classrooms were overcrowded, and many professors paid little attention to their students.

People In History

Simone de Beauvoir
1908–1986—French author

A prominent French intellectual, Simone de Beauvoir became a major voice in the European feminist movement. Born into a Catholic middle-class family and educated at the Sorbonne in Paris, she supported herself as a teacher and later as a novelist and writer.

De Beauvoir believed that she lived a "liberated" life for a twentieth-century European woman. Despite all her freedom, she still came to perceive that, as a woman, she faced limits that men did not: "What particularly signalizes the situation of woman is that she—a free autonomous being like all human creatures—nevertheless finds herself in a world where men compel her to assume the status of the Other."

Growing discontent led to an outburst of student revolts in the late 1960s.

This student radicalism had several causes. Many of these protests were an extension of the revolts in U.S. universities, which were often sparked by student opposition to the Vietnam War. Some students, particularly in Europe, wished to reform the university system. They did not believe that universities responded to their needs or to the realities of the modern world. Others expressed concerns about becoming small cogs in the large and impersonal bureaucratic wheels of the modern world. Student protest movements in both Europe and the United States reached a high point in 1968. By the early 1970s, the movements had largely disappeared.

The student protests of the late 1960s caused many people to rethink some of their basic assumptions. Looking back, however, we can see that the student upheavals were not a turning point in the history of postwar Europe, as some people thought at the time. In the 1970s and 1980s, student rebels would become middle-class professionals. The vision of revolutionary politics would remain mostly a memory.

Reading Check **Identifying** What was the women's liberation movement trying to accomplish?

TAKS Practice

SECTION 3 ASSESSMENT

Checking for Understanding

1. **Define** welfare state, bloc, real wages.

2. **Identify** Charles de Gaulle, Christian Democratic Union, European Economic Community, John F. Kennedy, Martin Luther King, Jr., consumer society, women's liberation movement, Simone de Beauvoir.

3. **Locate** France, West Germany.

4. **Explain** why many British colonies gained their independence after World War II.

5. **List** the original members of the Common Market.

Critical Thinking

6. **Analyze** Do you think the student revolts of this period contributed positively or negatively to society? Why?

7. **Cause and Effect** Use a diagram like the one below to identify factors leading to the emergence of the postwar women's liberation movement.

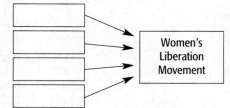

Analyzing Visuals

8. **Compare** the Kent State photo on page 866 with the photo above. What do these two scenes have in common? In your opinion, were the costs of these protests justified? What causes today could motivate this type of passion and sacrifice?

Writing About History

9. **Persuasive Writing** Demonstrations, marches, and riots were used in the 1960s and 1970s to communicate popular opinion. Write an essay that argues for or against the effectiveness of these methods for changing public opinion and policy.

"I Have a Dream"

ON AUGUST 28, 1963, MARTIN LUTHER KING, Jr., led a civil rights march on Washington, D.C., and gave an inspired speech that energized the movement.

❝I am happy to join with you today in what will go down in history as the greatest demonstration for freedom in the history of our nation . . . .

I say to you today, my friends, so even though we face the difficulties of today and tomorrow, I still have a dream. It is a dream deeply rooted in the American dream. I have a dream that one day this nation will rise up and live out the true meaning of its creed, 'We hold these truths to be self-evident, that all men are created equal.' I have a dream that one day on the red hills of Georgia, sons of former slaves and the sons of former slave owners will be able to sit down together at the table of brotherhood. . . . I have a dream that my four little children will one day live in a nation where they will not be judged by the color of their skin, but by the content of their character . . . .

This is our hope. This is the faith that I go back to the South with. With this faith we will be able to hew out of the mountain of despair a stone of hope. With this faith we will be able to transform the jangling discords of our nation into a beautiful symphony of brotherhood. With this faith we will be able to work together, to pray together, to struggle together, to go to jail together, to stand up for freedom together, knowing that we will be free one day. And this will be the day. This will be the day when all of God's children will be able to sing with new meaning, 'My country 'tis of thee, sweet land of liberty, of thee I sing. Land where my father died, land of the pilgrims' pride, from every mountainside, let freedom ring.' And if America is to be a great nation, this must become true . . . .

And when this happens, and when we allow freedom to ring, when we let it ring from every village and every hamlet, from every state and every

Martin Luther King, Jr., was an inspiring speaker.

city, we will be able to speed up that day when all of God's children, black men and white men, Jews and Gentiles, Protestants and Catholics, will be able to join hands and sing in the words of the old Negro spiritual: 'Free at last, Free at last. Thank God Almighty, we are free at last.'**❞**

—Martin Luther King, Jr., Speech Delivered August 28, 1963, in Washington, D.C.

Analyzing Primary Sources

1. Why do you think this speech has become so famous? Has King's dream been realized? Why or why not?
2. Describe King's dream in your own words.
3. Based on your earlier reading, how do you think Adolf Hitler would have reacted to King's speech? Explain.

Using Key Terms

1. The actual purchasing power of income is called _____.

2. The idea that allowing communist aggressors to take over one country will encourage them to take over other nations has been called the_____.

3. The process of removing Stalin's influence from the Soviet government, economy, and social system was called _____.

4. A nation that is preoccupied with the desire to provide its people with material goods may be said to be a _____.

5. Nations with governments that intervene in the economy to assure a minimal standard of living for all people are said to be _____.

6. The attempt of non-communist world powers to prevent a further spread of communism to other states was called a _____.

7. The _____ is a force that is working for greater equality and rights for women.

8. A country that was economically and politically dependent on the Soviet Union was called a _____.

9. The United States and the Soviet Union were involved in a growing _____ in which both countries built up their armies and weapons.

Reviewing Key Facts

10. **Economics** What was COMECON and why was it formed?

11. **Economics** What changes were made in the British government's role in its economic system after World War II?

12. **History** What caused the Soviet Union to invade Hungary in 1956?

13. **History** Describe what happened when satellite states tried to become independent of the Soviet Union.

14. **Culture** What book influenced the women's movement in America and Europe? What was its significance to the movement?

15. **Science and Technology** Name some inventions that altered the pace and nature of life in postwar Western society.

16. **History** What happened during the Cuban missile crisis in 1962?

17. **Culture** Name the social movements that altered American society after World War II.

18. **Government** What prevented even greater repression and terror from taking place in the Soviet Union during the early 1950s?

19. **History** What were some of the political and economic "weapons" of the Cold War?

Chapter Summary

Following World War II, two new superpowers, the United States and the Soviet Union, engaged in a Cold War that was fought around the globe.

	Conflict/Crisis	Significant Event(s)	Result(s)
Greece (1944–1949)	Civil war erupts.	Great Britain aids government forces against communism.	United States creates Truman Doctrine.
Berlin (1949)	Soviets and Western powers divide Germany.	Western powers airlift supplies to Soviet-blockaded West Berlin.	Blockade is lifted.
Korea (1950–1953)	Civil war begins when North Korea invades South Korea.	United Nations forces fight to save South Korea from communism.	United States extends military alliances around the world.
Berlin (1961)	Refugees escape from East to West Berlin.	Soviets build Berlin Wall.	Berlin Wall becomes symbol of divided Germany.
Cuba (1962)	Soviets support Castro's totalitarian regime in Cuba.	United States invades Bay of Pigs; Soviets place nuclear missiles in Cuba; United States blockades Cuba.	Soviets withdraw missiles; hotline is established between Moscow and Washington, D.C.
Vietnam (1964–1973)	Civil war erupts between North and South Vietnam.	United States intervenes to prevent North Vietnam from taking over South Vietnam.	United States withdraws from Vietnam; Vietnam is reunited by Communists.

Self-Check Quiz

Visit the *Glencoe World History* Web site at tx.wh.glencoe.com and click on **Chapter 27–Self-Check Quiz** to prepare for the Chapter Test.

Cuban Missile Crisis, 1962

NATIONAL GEOGRAPHIC

Soviet missile site
U.S. blockade zone
U.S. naval base

500 miles
500 kilometers
Albers Conic Equal-Area projection

Critical Thinking

20. **Analyzing** How did de-Stalinization help Khrushchev gain control of the Soviet government?

21. **Explaining** Is containment an important or pressing issue in American foreign policy today? Explain your reasoning.

Writing about History

22. **Expository Writing** In an essay, identify and explain possible reasons for the comparatively slow growth of social benefits provided to Americans, compared to the rapid growth of these programs in Europe, after World War II.

Analyzing Sources

Read the following excerpt from Solzhenitsyn's *A Day in the Life of Ivan Denisovich* in which prisoners march from the prison camp to a work project through temperatures of seventeen degrees below zero:

> 66There were escort guards all over the place, . . . their machine guns sticking out and pointed right at your face. And there were guards with gray dogs.99

23. Why might Soviets identify with this story?

24. Why did Khrushchev allow this book to be published?

Applying Technology Skills

25. **Using the Internet** Search the Internet for information about technological inventions since World War II that have greatly affected our lives. Use a search engine to focus your search. Create a time line including pictures and illustrations of the inventions you researched.

Making Decisions

26. The Cuban missile crisis developed out of a tense power struggle between two nuclear powers. What decisions created the crisis? What else might have been done?

Analyzing Maps and Charts

Using the map above, answer the following questions.

27. How many miles did the blockade zone of Cuba extend from west to east?

28. Why was the United States so concerned that the Soviets were placing missiles in Cuba? What other islands fall within the blockade zone?

The Princeton Review

TAKS
Test Practice

Directions: Use the quote *and* your knowledge of world history to answer the following question.

66And even today woman is heavily handicapped, though her situation is beginning to change. Almost nowhere is her legal status the same as man's, and frequently it is much to her disadvantage. Even when her rights are legally recognized in the abstract, long-standing custom prevents their full expression 99

—*The Second Sex,* Simone de Beauvoir

Simone de Beauvoir's book, *The Second Sex,* was published in 1949. Her book was influential because it

A helped women gain the right to vote.

B contributed to a women's movement in the 1950s and 1960s.

C greatly increased the number of married women in the labor force.

D influenced and shaped the student protest movement.

Test-Taking Tip: A date can be an important clue. When a question contains a date, think about major events that occurred during or around that time. Then eliminate answer choices that do not reflect that history.

The Contemporary Western World

1970–Present

Key Events

As you read this chapter, look for the key events in the development of the contemporary Western world.

- *Political and social changes led to the end of the Cold War and the fall of communism in Eastern Europe and the Soviet Union.*
- *Economic challenges helped bring about and accompanied these sweeping political and social changes.*
- *Society and culture reflected these changes with the advent of the women's movement, the growth of technology, and a rise in terrorism.*

The Impact Today

The events that occurred during this time period still impact our lives today.

- *Energy prices continue to climb as world oil supplies diminish, causing economic challenges for oil-dependent nations.*
- *The computer and the Internet contribute to the creation of a global society.*
- *Film, television, music, and advertising spread the American way of life throughout the world.*

World History Video *The Chapter 28 video, "Solidarity," chronicles the history of the movement for democracy in Poland.*

1980
Lech Walesa organizes trade union Solidarity in Poland

1987
Soviet Union and United States sign INF Treaty

1970　　1974　　1978　　1982　　1986

1972
Equal Pay Act passed in United States

Women's liberation march

Advances in space exploration have been made possible by new technology.

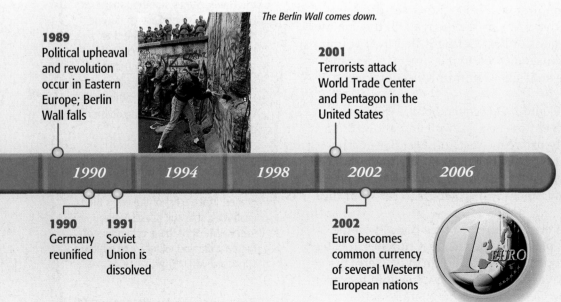

The Berlin Wall comes down.

1989
Political upheaval and revolution occur in Eastern Europe; Berlin Wall falls

2001
Terrorists attack World Trade Center and Pentagon in the United States

1990   1994   1998   2002   2006

1990
Germany reunified

1991
Soviet Union is dissolved

2002
Euro becomes common currency of several Western European nations

Euro coin

HISTORY *Online*

Chapter Overview
Visit the *Glencoe World History* Web site at tx.wh.glencoe.com and click on **Chapter 28–Chapter Overview** to preview chapter information.

A Story That Matters

Near Berlin's Brandenburg Gate in 1990, crowds of people celebrate the reunification of Germany.

"Tear Down This Wall"

*I*n 1988, the American president, Ronald Reagan, traveled to West Berlin. Facing the Berlin Wall, he challenged Mikhail Gorbachev, leader of the Soviet bloc, to "tear down this wall." During his own visit to West Germany a year later, Gorbachev responded, "The wall could disappear once the conditions that generated the need for it disappear. I do not see much of a problem here."

East Germany's Communist leaders, however, did see a problem, and they refused to remove the wall. In the summer of 1989, tens of thousands of East Germans fled their country while hundreds of thousands took to the streets to demand the resignation of the hard-line Communist leader, Erich Honecker.

Honecker finally relented. On November 9, 1989, a new East German government opened the wall and allowed its citizens to travel freely between West and East Berlin. The next day, government workers began to knock down the wall. They were soon joined by thousands of West and East Berliners who used sledgehammers and crowbars to rip apart the Cold War symbol.

Germans were overcome with joy. Many danced on the wall while orchestras played in the streets. Churches, theaters, and shops remained open day and night in West Germany as East Germans took advantage of their new freedom to travel. In 1990, West and East Germany became a single nation, and Berlin was once again the capital of Germany.

Why It Matters

In 1970, after more than two decades of the Cold War, the division of Europe between West and East seemed well established to most Europeans. A prosperous Western Europe that was allied to the United States stood opposed to a still-struggling Eastern Europe that remained largely subject to the Soviet Union. However, within 20 years, a revolutionary upheaval in the Soviet Union and Eastern Europe brought an end to the Cold War and the long-standing division of postwar Europe.

History and You Research contemporary Berlin. Use sources ranging from academic histories to travel guides. Make a list of the ways the East/West split still affects Berlin today. Which of these reminders of the past did you expect, and which surprised you? Why?

Decline of the Soviet Union

Guide to Reading

Main Ideas
- The Cold War ended after leadership changed in the Soviet Union.
- Gorbachev's policies contributed to the disintegration of the Soviet Union.
- Conversion from a socialist to a free-market economy has created many problems in the former Soviet states.

Key Terms
détente, dissident, perestroika

People To Identify
Ronald Reagan, Mikhail Gorbachev, Leonid Brezhnev, Boris Yeltsin, Vladimir Putin

Places To Locate
Afghanistan, Ukraine, Belarus

Preview Questions
1. How and why did the Cold War end?
2. What problems arose when the Soviet Union disintegrated?

Reading Strategy
Compare and Contrast Create a chart like the one below comparing the policies of Brezhnev and Gorbachev.

	Leonid Brezhnev	Mikhail Gorbachev
Foreign Policy		
Economic Policy		
Military Policy		
Personal Policy		

Preview of Events

◆1985	◆1988	◆1991	◆1994	◆1997	◆2000

1985
Mikhail Gorbachev assumes leadership of Soviet Union

1988
Communist Party conference initiates political reforms

1991
Boris Yeltsin becomes president of Russia

2000
Ex-KGB agent Vladimir Putin becomes president of Russia

Voices from the Past

In his book *Perestroika,* Soviet leader Mikhail Gorbachev wrote:

❝There is a great thirst for mutual understanding and mutual communication in the world. It is felt among politicians, it is gaining momentum among the intelligentsia, representatives of culture, and the public at large. And if the Russian word 'perestroika' has easily entered the international lexicon [vocabulary], this is due to more than just interest in what is going on in the Soviet Union. Now the whole world needs restructuring, i.e., progressive development, a fundamental change . . . I believe that more and more people will come to realize that through RESTRUCTURING in the broad sense of the word, the integrity of the world will be enhanced.❞

Mikhail Gorbachev

—*Perestroika,* 1987

After Mikhail Gorbachev came to power in 1985, the Soviet Union began to make changes in its foreign policy, and the Cold War rapidly came to an end.

From Cold War to Post-Cold War

By the 1970s, American-Soviet relations had entered a new phase, known as détente, which was marked by a relaxation of tensions and improved relations between the two superpowers. Grain and consumer goods were sold to the Soviet Union. Beginning in 1979, however, the apparent collapse of détente began a new period of East-West confrontation.

The Cold War Intensifies Détente received a major setback in 1979, when the Soviet Union invaded **Afghanistan.** The Soviet Union wanted to restore a pro-Soviet regime there, which the United States viewed as an act of expansion. President Jimmy Carter canceled American participation in the 1980 Olympic Games to be held in Moscow and placed an embargo on the shipment of American grain to the Soviets.

The Cold War further intensified when **Ronald Reagan** was elected president in 1980. Calling the Soviet Union an "evil empire," Reagan began a military buildup and a new arms race. Reagan also gave military aid to the Afghan rebels, in order to maintain a war in Afghanistan that the Soviet Union could not win.

End of the Cold War The accession of **Mikhail Gorbachev** (GAWR•buh•CHAWF) to power in the Soviet Union in 1985 eventually brought a dramatic end to the Cold War. Gorbachev's "New Thinking"— his willingness to rethink Soviet foreign policy—led to stunning changes.

Gorbachev made an agreement with the United States in 1987 (the Intermediate-range Nuclear Force [INF] Treaty) to eliminate intermediate-range nuclear weapons. Both sides had reasons to slow down the expensive arms race. Gorbachev hoped to make far-reaching economic and internal reforms. As its national debt tripled, the United States had moved from being a creditor nation (a country that exports more than it imports), to being the world's biggest debtor nation. By 1990, both countries knew that their large military budgets would make it difficult for them to solve their domestic problems.

In another policy change, Gorbachev stopped giving Soviet military support to Communist governments in Eastern Europe. This opened the door to the overthrow of Communist regimes in these countries. A mostly peaceful revolutionary movement swept through Eastern Europe in 1989. The reunification of Germany on October 3, 1990, was a powerful symbol of the end of the Cold War. In 1991, the Soviet Union was dissolved. Renewal of the rivalry between the two superpowers was now almost impossible.

✓ **Reading Check** **Summarizing** What events immediately preceded the end of the Cold War?

Upheaval in the Soviet Union

⌐TURNING POINT¬ **You will learn how movements for independence caused the breakup of the Soviet Union.**

Between 1964 and 1982, drastic change in the Soviet Union had seemed highly unlikely. What happened to create such a dramatic turnaround in such a short time?

The Brezhnev Era When Nikita Khrushchev was removed from office in 1964, two men, Alexei Kosygin and **Leonid Brezhnev** (BREHZH•NEFF), replaced him. Brezhnev emerged as the dominant leader in the 1970s. He was determined to keep Eastern Europe in Communist hands and was uninterested in reform. Brezhnev insisted on the right of the Soviet Union to intervene if communism was threatened in another Communist state (known as the **Brezhnev Doctrine**).

At the same time, Brezhnev benefited from the more relaxed atmosphere associated with détente. The Soviet Union was roughly equal to the United States in nuclear arms. Its leaders thus felt secure and were willing to relax their authoritarian rule. Under Brezhnev, the regime allowed more access to Western styles of music, dress, and art. However, dissidents— those who spoke out against the regime—were still punished.

In his economic policies, Brezhnev continued to emphasize heavy industry. Two problems, however, weakened the Soviet economy. The government's central planning led to a huge, complex bureaucracy that discouraged efficiency and led to indifference. Moreover, collective farmers had no incentive to work hard. Many preferred working their own small private plots to laboring in the collective work brigades.

By the 1970s, the Communist ruling class in the Soviet Union had become complacent and corrupt. Party and state leaders—as well as leaders of the army and secret police (KGB)— enjoyed a high standard of living. Brezhnev was unwilling to tamper with the party leadership and state bureaucracy, regardless of the inefficiency and corruption that the system encouraged.

By 1980, the Soviet Union was seriously ailing, with a declining economy, a rise in infant mortality rates, a dramatic surge in alcoholism, and poor working conditions. Many felt the system was in trouble. Within the Communist Party, a small group of reformers emerged. One of these was Mikhail Gorbachev. A new era began in March 1985 when party leaders chose him to lead the Soviet Union.

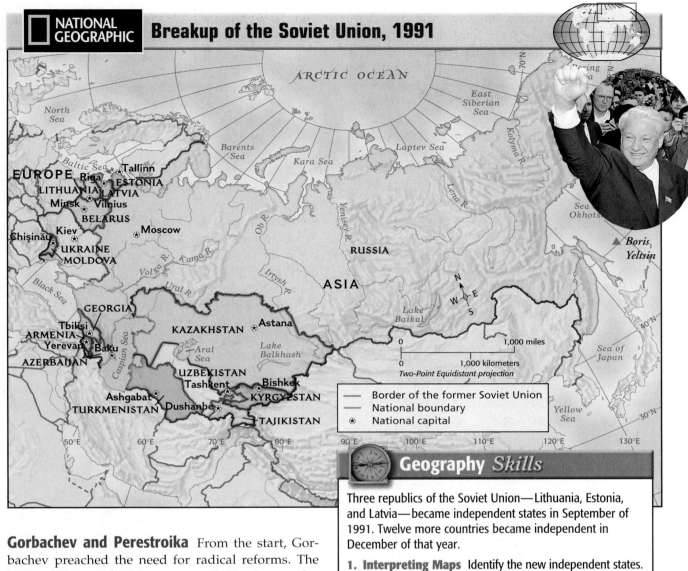

NATIONAL GEOGRAPHIC

Breakup of the Soviet Union, 1991

Boris Yeltsin

Map legend:
— Border of the former Soviet Union
— National boundary
⊛ National capital

1,000 miles
1,000 kilometers
Two-Point Equidistant projection

Geography Skills

Three republics of the Soviet Union—Lithuania, Estonia, and Latvia—became independent states in September of 1991. Twelve more countries became independent in December of that year.

1. **Interpreting Maps** Identify the new independent states.
2. **Applying Geography Skills** Why would trade become more difficult for Russia after the breakup?

Gorbachev and Perestroika From the start, Gorbachev preached the need for radical reforms. The basis of these reforms was perestroika (PEHR•uh•STROY•kuh), or restructuring. At first, this meant restructuring economic policy. Gorbachev wanted to start a market economy, where consumers influence what is produced. This economy would have limited free enterprise (based on private ownership of businesses) and some private property. Soon, however, Gorbachev realized that an attempt to reform the economy without political reform would be doomed to failure.

At the Communist Party conference in 1988, Gorbachev established a new Soviet parliament, the Congress of People's Deputies, whose members were to be elected. This parliament met in 1989—the first such meeting in Russia since 1918. Early in 1990, Gorbachev decreed that non-Communist political parties could organize. He also did away with a constitutional provision that guaranteed the Communist Party a "leading role" in government.

At the same time, Gorbachev strengthened his power by creating a new state presidency. The position of first secretary of the party (Gorbachev's position) had been the most important post in the Soviet Union. However, as the Communist Party became less closely tied to the state, the position of first secretary carried less power. In March 1990, Gorbachev became the Soviet Union's first (and last) president.

The End of the Soviet Union One of Gorbachev's most serious problems was the multiethnic nature of the Soviet Union. It included 92 nationalities and 112 different languages. The iron hand of the Communist Party, centered in Moscow, had kept centuries-old ethnic tensions contained.

As Gorbachev released this iron grip, these tensions again came to the forefront. Nationalist movements emerged throughout the republics of the Soviet Union. In 1989 and 1990, there were calls for independence first in Soviet Georgia and then in Latvia, Estonia, Moldavia, Uzbekistan, Azerbaijan, and Lithuania.

During 1990 and 1991, Gorbachev struggled to deal with the problems unleashed by his reforms. By 1991, the conservative leaders of the traditional Soviet institutions—the army, government, KGB, and military industries—were worried. The possible breakup of the Soviet Union would mean an end to their privileges.

On August 19, 1991, a group of these conservative leaders arrested Gorbachev and tried to seize power. The attempt failed, however, when **Boris Yeltsin,** president of the Russian Republic, and thousands of Russians bravely resisted the rebel forces in Moscow.

The Soviet republics now moved for complete independence. Ukraine voted for independence on December 1, 1991. A week later, the leaders of Russia, **Ukraine,** and **Belarus** announced that the Soviet Union had "ceased to exist."

Gorbachev resigned on December 25, 1991, and turned over his responsibilities as commander in chief to Boris Yeltsin, the new president of Russia. By the end of 1991, one of the largest empires in world history had come to an end. A new era had begun in its now-independent states.

The New Russia Boris Yeltsin was committed to introducing a free market economy as quickly as possible, but the transition was not easy. Economic hardships and social disarray were made worse by a dramatic rise in the activities of organized crime. Yeltsin's brutal use of force against the Chechens (CHET• chunz), who wanted to secede from Russia and create their own independent republic, also undermined his support. Despite the odds against him, however, Yeltsin won reelection in 1996.

At the end of 1999, Yeltsin resigned and was replaced by **Vladimir Putin,** who was elected president in 2000. Putin vowed to return the breakaway state of Chechnya to Russian authority and to adopt a more assertive role in international affairs. Fighting in Chechnya continued throughout 2000, nearly reducing the republic's capital city of Grozny to ruins.

In July 2001, Putin launched reforms aimed at boosting growth and budget revenues and keeping Russia on a strong economic track. The reforms included free sale and purchase of land, tax cuts, and efforts to join the international World Trade Organization. Since then, Russia has experienced a budget surplus and a growing economy.

✓ **Reading Check** **Cause and Effect** How did Gorbachev's reforms cause the breakup of the Soviet Union?

🤠 TAKS Practice

SECTION 1 ASSESSMENT

Checking for Understanding

1. **Define** détente, dissident, perestroika.

2. **Identify** Ronald Reagan, Mikhail Gorbachev, Leonid Brezhnev, Brezhnev Doctrine, Boris Yeltsin, Vladimir Putin.

3. **Locate** Afghanistan, Ukraine, Belarus.

4. **Explain** why the conservative leaders of the traditional Soviet institutions opposed the breakup of the Soviet Union. Name the institutions these leaders represented.

5. **List** the problems that weakened the Soviet economy during the 1960s and 1970s.

Critical Thinking

6. **Drawing Inferences** Why did the former Soviet Union have problems adapting to a free-market society?

7. **Organizing Information** Create a diagram like the one below showing the problems the Soviet Union faced under communism and the problems the former Soviet republics face today.

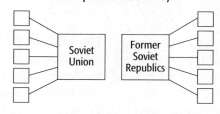

Analyzing Visuals

8. **Examine** the photograph on page 873 of a man tearing down the Berlin Wall. How would you describe the reaction of the Soviet soldiers?

Writing About History

9. **Expository Writing** Locate biographical information on Leonid Brezhnev, Mikhail Gorbachev, Boris Yeltsin, and Vladimir Putin. In an essay, analyze each leader's strengths and weaknesses. How did each man come to power?

Eastern Europe

Guide to Reading

Main Ideas
- Gorbachev's policy of not giving military support to Communist governments created the opportunity for revolution.
- Massive demonstrations peacefully ended some Communist regimes, while violence ended others.

Key Terms
ethnic cleansing, autonomous

People To Identify
Lech Walesa, Václav Havel, Slobodan Milošević

Places To Locate
Bosnia-Herzegovina, Kosovo

Preview Questions
1. What caused the East German government to open its border in 1989?
2. What effect did the 1990 collapse of communism have on Yugoslavia?

Reading Strategy
Categorizing Information Create a chart listing one or two reasons for, and the results of, revolution.

Country	Reasons for Revolution	Results of Revolution
Poland		
Czechoslovakia		
Romania		
East Germany		
Yugoslavia		

Preview of Events

♦1987	♦1988	♦1989	♦1990	♦1991	♦1992

1989
Poland holds the first free elections in Eastern Europe in forty years

1989
Berlin Wall opens; communism falls in Czechoslovakia and Romania

1991
Slovenia and Croatia declare independence

1992
Serbs pursue policy of ethnic cleansing in Bosnia-Herzegovina

Voices from the Past

War-damaged Bosnia

Roy Gutman, a journalist for *Newsday,* wrote from Bosnia in July 1992:

❝Visegrad, with a population of about 30,000, is one of a number of towns where Serb forces carried out 'ethnic cleansing' of Muslims in the past two weeks, according to the Bosnian government. 'There was chaos in Visegrad. Everything was burned, looted and destroyed,' said [one man], 43, who spoke of the terrible events but would give neither his name nor his profession. He escaped only because he was an invalid with a gangrenous [diseased] leg. The survivors of the massacre are the old, the infirm, the women and the children. They are traumatized by what they witnessed, barely able to speak or to control their emotions.❞

—*The Mammoth Book of Eyewitness History,* Jon E. Lewis, 2000

Ethnic cleansing was one aspect of an upheaval in Eastern Europe that began in 1989.

Revolutions in Eastern Europe

People in Eastern Europe had not always been happy with their Soviet-style Communist regimes. After Gorbachev made it clear that the Soviet Union would not intervene militarily in their states, revolutions broke out throughout Eastern Europe. By looking at four Eastern European states, we can see how the process worked.

Poland Workers' protests led to demands for change in Poland. In 1980, a worker named **Lech Walesa** (lehk vah•LEHN•suh) organized a national trade union known as Solidarity. Solidarity gained the support of the workers and of the

Solidarity organizer Lech Walesa became president of Poland in 1990.

Roman Catholic Church, which was under the leadership of Pope John Paul II, the first Polish pope. During a period of military rule in the 1980s, Walesa was arrested, but the movement continued.

Finally, after a new wave of demonstrations in 1988, the Polish regime agreed to free parliamentary elections—the first free elections in Eastern Europe in 40 years. A new government was elected, ending 45 years of Communist rule in Poland.

In December 1990, Walesa was chosen as president. Poland's new path, however, was not an easy one. Rapid free-market reforms led to severe unemployment and popular discontent.

At the end of 1995, Aleksander Kwasniewski, a former Communist, defeated Walesa and became the new president. He has continued Poland's move toward an increasingly prosperous free market economy.

Czechoslovakia

After Soviet troops crushed the reform movement in Czechoslovakia in 1968, Communists used massive repression to maintain their power. Writers and other intellectuals continued to oppose the government, but they initially had little success.

Then, in 1988 and 1989, mass demonstrations took place throughout Czechoslovakia. By November 1989, crowds as large as five hundred thousand were forming in Prague. In December 1989, the Communist government collapsed.

At the end of December, **Václav Havel** (VAHT•SLAHF HAH•vel), a writer who had played an important role in bringing down the Communist government, became the new president. Havel became an eloquent spokesperson for Czech democracy and a new order in Europe.

Within Czechoslovakia, the new government soon faced old ethnic conflicts. The two national groups, Czechs and Slovaks, agreed to a peaceful division of the country. On January 1, 1993, Czechoslovakia split into the Czech Republic and Slovakia. Václav Havel was elected the first president of the new Czech Republic. Michal Kovác was elected president of Slovakia.

Romania

In 1965, the Communist leader Nicolae Ceauşescu, (NEE•koh•lay chow•SHEHS•koo) and his wife, Elena, set up a rigid and dictatorial regime in Romania. Ceauşescu ruled Romania with an iron grip, using secret police to crush all dissent. Nonetheless, opposition to his regime grew.

Ceauşescu's economic policies led to a sharp drop in living standards, including food shortages and the rationing of bread, flour, and sugar. His plan for rapid urbanization, especially a program that called for the bulldozing of entire villages, further angered the Romanian people.

One incident ignited the flames of revolution. In December 1989, the secret police murdered thousands of men, women, and children who were peacefully demonstrating. Finally, the army refused to support any more repression. Ceauşescu and his wife were captured on December 22 and executed on Christmas Day. A new government was quickly formed.

German Reunification

In 1971, Erich Honecker became head of the Communist Party in East Germany. He used the Stasi, the secret police, to rule for the next 18 years. In 1989, however, popular unrest, fueled by Honecker's harsh regime, led many East Germans to flee their country. Mass demonstrations against the regime broke out in the fall of 1989.

On November 9, the Communist government

HISTORY Online

Web Activity Visit the *Glencoe World History* Web site at tx.wh.glencoe.com and click on **Chapter 28– Student Web Activity** to learn more about the fall of the Berlin Wall.

surrendered to popular pressure by opening its entire border with the West. Hundreds of thousands of East Germans swarmed across the border. Families and friends who had not seen each other in decades were reunited. People on both sides of the wall began tearing it down. The government, helpless before this popular uprising, ordered the rest of the wall torn down. The Berlin Wall, long a symbol of the Cold War, was no more.

During East Germany's first free elections in March 1990, the Christian Democrats won almost 50 percent

of the vote. The Christian Democrats supported political union with West Germany. The reunification of East and West took place on October 3, 1990. What had seemed almost impossible at the beginning of 1989 had become a reality by the end of 1990—the countries of West and East Germany had reunited to form one Germany.

Reading Check **Describing** How did the inhabitants of Eastern Europe respond to the repression of their totalitarian leaders?

The Disintegration of Yugoslavia

Although Yugoslavia had a Communist government, it had never been a Soviet satellite state. After World War II, its dictatorial leader, Josip Broz Tito, worked to keep the six republics and two provinces that made up Yugoslavia together. After Tito died in 1980, a collective federal government composed of representatives from the separate republics and provinces kept Yugoslavia under Communist rule. At the end of the 1980s, Yugoslavia was caught up in the reform movements sweeping Eastern Europe. By 1990, new parties had emerged, and the authority of the Communist Party had collapsed.

Calls for Independence The Yugoslav political scene was complex. In 1990, the Yugoslav republics of Slovenia, Croatia, **Bosnia-Herzegovina,** and Macedonia began to lobby for independence. **Slobodan Milošević** (SLOH•buh•DAHN muh•LOH•suh•VIHCH), who became leader of the Yugoslav republic of Serbia in 1987, rejected these efforts. The populations of these republics included Serb minorities. In Milošević's view, the republics could only be

independent if their borders were re-drawn to include the Serb minorities in a new Greater Serbian state.

After negotiations failed, Slovenia and Croatia declared their independence in June 1991. In September 1991, the Yugoslavian army began a full assault against Croatia. Increasingly, the Yugoslavian army was dominated by Serbia, and it was aided by Serbian minorities in Croatia. Before a cease-fire was arranged, the Serbian forces had captured one-third of Croatia's territory in brutal fighting.

The War in Bosnia Early in 1992, the Serbs turned their guns on Bosnia-Herzegovina. By mid-1993, Serbian forces had acquired 70 percent of Bosnian territory.

Many Bosnians were Muslims. Toward them, the Serbs followed a policy they called ethnic cleansing—killing them or forcibly removing them from their lands. Ethnic cleansing revived memories of Nazi atrocities in World War II. By 1995, 250,000 Bosnians (mostly civilians) had been killed. Two million others were left homeless.

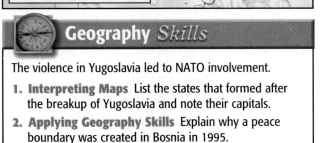

Geography *Skills*

The violence in Yugoslavia led to NATO involvement.

1. **Interpreting Maps** List the states that formed after the breakup of Yugoslavia and note their capitals.
2. **Applying Geography Skills** Explain why a peace boundary was created in Bosnia in 1995.

In 1995, new offensives by Bosnian government army forces and by the Croatian army regained considerable territory that had been lost to Serbian forces. Air strikes by NATO bombers, strongly advocated by U.S. President Bill Clinton, were launched in retaliation for Serb attacks on civilians.

These attacks forced the Serbs to sign a formal peace treaty on December 14. The agreement split Bosnia into a loose union of a Serb republic and a Muslim-Croat federation. NATO sent a force of sixty thousand troops to monitor the frontier between the new political entities.

The War in Kosovo Peace in Bosnia did not bring peace to the region. A new war erupted in 1998 over **Kosovo.** In 1974, Tito had made Kosovo an autonomous (self-governing) province within Yugoslavia. Kosovo's inhabitants were mainly ethnic Albanians who had kept their own language and customs.

In 1989, Slobodan Milošević stripped Kosovo of its autonomous status. Some groups of ethnic Albanians founded the Kosovo Liberation Army (KLA) in the mid-1990s and began a campaign against Serbian rule in Kosovo. In an effort to crush the KLA, Serb forces began to massacre ethnic Albanians. The United States and its NATO allies then sought to arrange a settlement.

Picturing **History**

In 1999, Serbs forced hundreds of thousands of ethnic Albanians from their homes in Kosovo, creating a massive refugee crisis. What issues led to conflict in Kosovo?

In 1999, Albanians in Kosovo gained autonomy within Serbia. When Milošević objected, a NATO bombing campaign forced Yugoslav cooperation. Elections held in 2000 ended Milošević's rule, and he was brought to trial for his role in the Balkans' bloodshed. In 2002, Serbia and Montenegro formed a looser union, dropping the name "Yugoslavia."

✓ **Reading Check** **Identifying** What events resulted from the disintegration of Yugoslavia?

🐾 **TAKS Practice**

SECTION 2 ASSESSMENT

Checking for Understanding

1. **Define** ethnic cleansing, autonomous.

2. **Identify** Lech Walesa, Václav Havel, Slobodan Milošević.

3. **Locate** Bosnia-Herzegovina, Kosovo.

4. **Explain** why the Communist government ordered the Berlin Wall to be torn down.

5. **List** four Eastern European states discussed in this section that had been Soviet satellites. What events occurred in each state after the withdrawal of Soviet influence?

Critical Thinking

6. **Explain** Why did the inhabitants of Communist countries in Eastern Europe feel it was safe to rebel in 1989?

7. **Summarizing Information** Create a chart like the one below listing the Yugoslav republics that wanted independence after 1990, the inhabitants of these republics (if listed), and the reasons the republics fought each other.

Republics	Inhabitants	Causes of Fighting

Analyzing Visuals

8. **Study** the photo of ethnic Albanians shown on this page. What do they have in common with other victims of oppression throughout history? If you and your family were forced to leave your home, what would be your greatest concerns?

Writing About History

9. **Informative Writing** Research and write an essay about the Polish Solidarity movement begun by Lech Walesa in 1980. Why was it successful? Be sure to discuss Walesa's supporters, his adversaries, and the status of the movement today.

Václav Havel—
The Call for a New Politics

IN THEIR ATTEMPTS TO DEAL WITH THE WORLD'S problems, some European leaders have pointed to the need for a new perspective. This excerpt is taken from a speech that Václav Havel delivered to the United States Congress on February 21, 1990, two months after he had become president of Czechoslovakia.

After addressing the United States Congress, Václav Havel gives a victory sign.

❝For this reason, the salvation of this human world lies nowhere else than in the human heart, in the human power to reflect, in human meekness and in human responsibility.

Without a global revolution in the sphere of human consciousness, nothing will change for the better in the sphere of our being as humans, and the catastrophe toward which this world is headed—be it ecological, social, demographic or a general breakdown of civilization—will be unavoidable. . . .

We are still a long way from that "family of man." In fact, we seem to be receding from the ideal rather than growing closer to it. Interests of all kinds—personal, selfish, state, nation, group, and if you like, company interests—still considerably outweigh genuinely common and global interests. We are still under the sway of the destructive and vain belief that man is the pinnacle of creation and not just a part of it and that therefore everything is permitted. . . .

In other words, we still don't know how to put morality ahead of politics, science and economics. We are still incapable of understanding that the only genuine backbone of all our actions, if they are to be moral, is responsibility.

Responsibility to something higher than my family, my country, my company, my success—responsibility to the order of being where all our actions are indelibly recorded and where and only where they will be properly judged.

The interpreter or mediator between us and this higher authority is what is traditionally referred to as human conscience.❞

—Václav Havel, Speech to the U.S. Congress

Analyzing Primary Sources

1. What is the difference between the way Václav Havel views politics and the way that most politicians have traditionally viewed politics?
2. Political ideas are of little value unless they can be implemented. What is your opinion—do you think that Havel's ideas could be turned into political reality? Why or why not?

Europe and North America

Guide to Reading

Main Ideas
- Western European nations moved to unite their economies after 1970.
- Domestic problems arose in the United States, Great Britain, France, Germany, and Canada.

Key Terms
Thatcherism, budget deficit

People To Identify
Willy Brandt, Margaret Thatcher, Richard Nixon, Pierre Trudeau

Places To Locate
France, Northern Ireland

Preview Questions
1. What problems faced Western Europe after 1980?
2. What was the focus of U.S. domestic politics in the 1970s?

Reading Strategy
Compare and Contrast Draw a Venn diagram comparing and contrasting economic policies of Thatcherism with those of the Reagan Revolution.

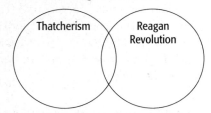

Preview of Events

♦1970   ♦1975   ♦1980   ♦1985   ♦1990   ♦1995   ♦2000

1971
West German chancellor Willy Brandt wins Nobel Peace Prize

1974
Richard Nixon resigns the presidency of the United States

1995
Canadian voters reject independence for Quebec

Voices from the Past

A German reporter described violence against foreigners in Germany in 1991:

German neo-Nazis

❝The municipality in northern Saxony has a population of just under 70,000, including 70 people from Mozambique and Vietnam who live in a hostel [inn] at the other end of town. The 'political situation' was triggered by an attack by a neo-Nazi gang on Vietnamese traders selling their goods on the market square on 17 September. After being dispersed by the police the Faschos [neo-Nazis] carried out their first attack on the hostel for foreigners. The attacks then turned into a regular evening hunt by a growing group of right-wing radicals, some of them minors, who presented their idea of a clean Germany by roaming the streets armed with truncheons, stones, steel balls, bottles and Molotov cocktails.❞

— *The German Tribune*, October 6, 1991

Attacks against foreigners by neo-Nazis became a problem in Germany during the 1990s.

Winds of Change in Western Europe

Between the early 1950s and late 1970s, Western Europe experienced virtually full employment. An economic downturn, however, occurred in the mid-1970s and early 1980s. Both inflation and unemployment rose dramatically. Undoubtedly, a dramatic increase in the price of oil following the Arab-Israeli conflict in 1973 (see Chapter 30) was a major cause for the downturn. Western European economies recovered in the course of the 1980s, but problems remained.

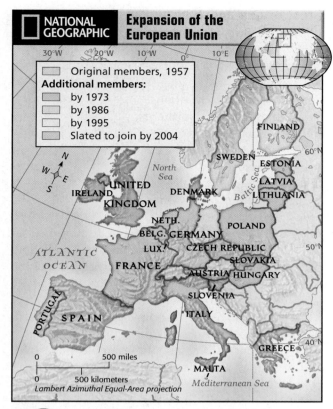

Expansion of the European Union

NATIONAL GEOGRAPHIC

Original members, 1957
Additional members:
by 1973
by 1986
by 1995
Slated to join by 2004

Geography *Skills*

The European Union (EU) allows members to work together to increase trade and develop favorable economic policies.

1. **Interpreting Maps** How long have the original members been part of the EU?

2. **Applying Geography Skills** What does the EU's growth suggest about its value to European states?

The Western European nations moved toward a greater union of their economies after 1970. The European Economic Community (EEC) expanded in 1973 to include Great Britain, Ireland, and Denmark. By 1986, Spain, Portugal, and Greece had become members. Austria, Finland, and Sweden joined in 1995.

The EEC or European Community (EC) was chiefly an economic union. By 1992, it comprised 344 million people and made up the world's largest single trading bloc. The Treaty on European Union, which went into effect on January 1, 1994, turned the EC into the principal organization within the even more solidified European Union (EU). One of the EU's first goals was to establish a common European currency, the euro. Twelve of the fifteen EU nations abandoned their currency in favor of the euro on January 1, 2002.

Uncertainties in France France's deteriorating economic situation in the 1970s caused a shift to the left politically. By 1981, the Socialists had become the chief party in the National Assembly. The Socialist leader, François Mitterrand, was elected president.

Mitterrand initiated a number of measures to aid workers: an increased minimum wage, a 39-hour work week, and higher taxes for the rich. The Socialist government also nationalized, or took over, major banks, the steel industry, the space and electronics industries, and insurance firms.

Socialist policies, however, largely failed to work, and France's economic decline continued. In 1993, French unemployment stood at 10.6 percent. In the elections in March of that year, the Socialists won only 28 percent of the vote. A coalition of conservative parties gained 80 percent of the seats in the National Assembly. The move to the right in France was strengthened when the conservative mayor of Paris, Jacques Chirac, was elected president in May 1995.

From West Germany to Germany In 1969, the Social Democrats, a moderate Socialist party, replaced the Christian Democrats as the leading party in West Germany. The first Social Democratic chancellor of West Germany was **Willy Brandt.** In December 1972, Brandt signed a treaty with East Germany that led to greater cultural, personal, and economic contacts between West and East Germany. For this, he received the Nobel Peace Prize for 1971.

In 1982, the Christian Democratic Union of Helmut Kohl formed a new, more conservative government. Kohl was a smart politician who benefited greatly from an economic boom in the mid-1980s. Then events in East Germany led to the unexpected reunification of the two Germanies in 1990. With a population of 79 million people, the new Germany became the leading power in Europe.

The joy over reunification soon faded as new problems arose. It became clear that the rebuilding of eastern Germany would take far more money than had originally been thought.

Willy Brandt

Kohl's government was soon forced to face the politically undesirable task of raising taxes. In addition, the virtual collapse of the economy in eastern Germany had led to extremely high levels of unemployment and severe discontent. One result was a return to power for the Social Democrats, who were victorious in the 1998 elections.

The collapse of the economy also led to increasing attacks on foreigners. For years, illegal immigrants and foreigners seeking refuge had found haven in Germany because of its very liberal immigration laws. In 1992, over 440,000 immigrants came to Germany seeking refuge; 123,000 came from former Yugoslavia alone. Increased unemployment and economic problems, however, caused tensions to grow between some Germans and immigrant groups. Attacks against foreigners by right-wing extremists—especially young neo-Nazis who believed in Hitler's idea of a pure Aryan race—became part of German life.

Economic Spectrum

Left	Right
• The economy is controlled by the state.	• The economy is based on free enterprise.
• Industries are owned by the national government.	• Industries are privately owned.
• The government determines allowable profit.	• Owners set prices and work for profit.
• Workers' rights are valued over owners' privileges.	• Workers and owners negotiate.
• The state supplies social services.	• Consumers pay for social services.

Chart Skills

The chart above represents a simplified view of two opposite economic models.

1. **Identifying** Select a minimum of five countries from this chapter. On which side of the economic spectrum would their economies belong?

2. **Describing** Look up the following words and phrases in a dictionary: *laissez-faire, command economy, capitalism, invisible hand, communism, socialism.* Decide if the definition describes a term on the left or the right of the economic spectrum.

Great Britain and Thatcherism Between 1964 and 1979, Great Britain's Conservative Party and Labour Party alternated being in power. One problem both parties had to face was the intense fighting between Catholics and Protestants in **Northern Ireland.** An ailing economy and frequent labor strikes were two other issues that the government struggled to solve.

In 1979, the Conservatives came to power under **Margaret Thatcher.** Thatcher pledged to limit social welfare, restrict union power, and end inflation. Although she did not eliminate the basic parts of the social welfare system, she did break the power of the labor unions and control inflation.

Thatcherism, as her economic policy was termed, improved the British economic situation, but at a price. The south of England, for example, prospered. Old industrial areas elsewhere, however, were beset by high unemployment, poverty, and even violence.

Thatcher dominated British politics in the 1980s. Only in 1990 did Labour's fortunes seem to revive. At that time, Thatcher's government tried to replace local property taxes with a flat-rate tax payable by every adult. In 1990, antitax riots broke out. Thatcher's popularity fell to an all-time low, and she resigned as prime minister.

The Conservative Party, now led by John Major, continued to hold a narrow majority. His government, however, failed to capture the imagination of most Britons. In new elections in 1997, the Labour Party won a landslide victory. Tony Blair, a moderate, became prime minister.

✓ Reading Check **Explaining** What were the policies of Thatcherism?

The U.S. Domestic Scene

With the election of **Richard Nixon** as president in 1968, politics in the United States shifted to the right. Economic issues became the focus of domestic politics by the mid-1970s.

Nixon and Watergate In his campaign for the presidency, Nixon believed that "law and order" issues and a slowdown in racial desegregation would appeal to southern whites. The South, which had once been a stronghold for the Democrats, began to form a new allegiance to the Republican Party.

As president, Nixon began to use illegal methods to gain political information about his opponents. Nixon's zeal led to the Watergate scandal. A group of men working for Nixon's reelection campaign broke into the Democratic National Headquarters, located in the Watergate Hotel in Washington, D.C. They were caught there trying to install electronic listening devices.

Nixon repeatedly lied to the American public about his involvement in the affair. Secret tapes of his own conversations in the White House, however, revealed the truth. On August 9, 1974, Nixon resigned the presidency rather than face possible impeachment.

The Carter Administration

Vice President Gerald Ford became president when Nixon resigned, only to lose in the 1976 election to the former governor of Georgia, Jimmy Carter. By 1980, the Carter administration was faced with two devastating problems. First, high rates of inflation and a noticeable decline in average weekly earnings were causing a drop in American living standards.

At the same time, a crisis abroad erupted when 52 Americans were held hostage by the Iranian government of the Ayatollah Ruhollah Khomeini (koh•MAY•nee) (see Chapter 30). Carter's inability to gain the release of the American hostages contributed to his overwhelming loss to Ronald Reagan in the election of 1980.

The Reagan Revolution

The Reagan Revolution, as it has been called, sent U.S. policy in new directions. Reversing decades of policy, Reagan cut back on the welfare state by decreasing spending on food stamps, school lunch programs, and job programs. At the same time, his administration oversaw the largest peacetime military buildup in U.S. history.

Total federal spending rose from $631 billion in 1981 to over a trillion dollars by 1987. The spending policies of the Reagan administration produced record government budget deficits. A budget deficit exists when the government spends more than it collects in revenues. In the 1970s, the total deficit was $420 billion. Between 1981 and 1987, budget deficits were three times that amount.

The Clinton Years

George Bush, Reagan's vice president, succeeded him as president. Bush's inability to deal with the deficit problem, as well as an economic downturn, enabled a Democrat, Bill Clinton, to be elected president in 1992.

The new president was a southern Democrat who claimed to be a new Democrat—one who favored a number of the Republican policies of the 1980s. This was a clear indication that the rightward drift in American politics was by no means ended by this Democratic victory.

President Clinton's political fortunes were aided considerably by a lengthy economic revival. Much of Clinton's second term, however, was overshadowed by charges of presidential misconduct. Clinton was threatened with removal from office when the House of Representatives voted two articles of impeachment—formal charges of misconduct—against him. He was tried in the Senate and acquitted after a bitter partisan struggle. Clinton's problems, however, helped the Republican candidate, George W. Bush, to win the presidential election in 2000.

✔ **Reading Check** **Summarizing** What changes in U.S. policy were part of the Reagan Revolution?

Canada

During a major economic recession in Canada in the early 1960s, the Liberals came into power. The most prominent Liberal government of the time was that of **Pierre Trudeau** (TROO•DOH), who became prime minister in 1968. Although he came from a French-Canadian background, Trudeau was dedicated to preserving a united Canada, while at the same time acknowledging the rights of French-speaking Canadians. His government passed the Official Languages Act, which allowed both English and French to be used in the federal civil service. Trudeau's government also supported a vigorous program of industrialization.

An economic recession in the early 1980s brought Brian Mulroney to power in 1984. Mulroney's government sought to return some of Canada's state-run corporations to private owners. In 1993, Canada approved the North American Free Trade Agreement (NAFTA) along with the United States and Mexico. The purpose of NAFTA was to make trade easier and more profitable by establishing guidelines for cooperation between the countries. The agreement, bitterly attacked by many Canadians as being too favorable to the United States, cost Mulroney much of his popularity. In 1993, the Liberal Party came to power with Jean Chrétien as prime minister. Chrétien was reelected in both 1997 and 2000.

Neither Trudeau's nor Mulroney's government was able to settle an ongoing crisis over the French-speaking province of Quebec. In the late 1960s, the Parti Québecois (KAY•buh•KWAH), headed by René Lévesque, had begun to advocate that Quebec secede from the Canadian union. In 1980, the party called for a vote that would grant Quebec's independence from the rest of Canada. In 1995, voters in Quebec narrowly rejected the plan. Debate over Quebec's status continues to divide Canada.

What If...

Quebec had seceded from Canada?

Only about 50,000 votes kept Quebec a part of Canada in 1995. Although the separatists are still fighting to secede, the 1995 vote reflects how close they are to winning. Quebec's secession from Canada would make it an entirely independent country.

Consider the Consequences Consider what would be different if the separatists had won the 1995 referendum. Identify at least two changes that would have occurred if Quebec had become a separate country at that time.

✓ **Reading Check** **Summarizing** What was the purpose of the Official Languages Act?

▶ TAKS Practice

SECTION 3 ASSESSMENT

Checking for Understanding

1. **Define** Thatcherism, budget deficit.

2. **Identify** Willy Brandt, Margaret Thatcher, Richard Nixon, Pierre Trudeau.

3. **Locate** France, Northern Ireland.

4. **Explain** the ongoing debate in Canada over the status of Quebec. Why do some people want Quebec to become independent?

5. **List** some of the changes initiated by François Mitterrand's government in France. How successful were Mitterrand's socialist policies?

Critical Thinking

6. **Cause and Effect** What factors led to the economic downturn of the 1970s? How did European nations respond?

7. **Organizing Information** Create a chart like the one below listing the problems faced by Germany when it was unified in 1990.

Problems Created by German Unification

Analyzing Visuals

8. **Compare** the photo on page 884 with the Nazi photos on pages 749 and 768. What similarities and differences do you see among the photos?

Writing About History

9. **Expository Writing** When a country faces economic problems, its inhabitants often blame a person or a group. Look up the word *scapegoating.* Do you think that the way some Germans treated foreigners in the 1990s is an example of scapegoating? Write an essay about the use of scapegoating, including two or three examples from history.

Western Society and Culture

Guide to Reading

Main Ideas
- Technological and scientific advances have created a global society.
- Artistic trends reflect how the emerging global society has led to a blending of cultural forms and ideas.

Key Terms
pop art, postmodernism

People To Identify
Jackson Pollock, Andy Warhol, Elvis Presley, Beatles

Places To Locate
Northern Ireland, Afghanistan

Preview Questions
1. What have been the major social developments since 1970?
2. What have been the major cultural, scientific, and technological developments in the postwar world?

Reading Strategy
Categorizing Information Complete a cluster chart like the one below illustrating how women have been involved with causes related solely to women's issues and to broader, more universal causes.

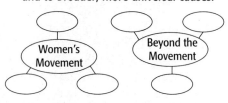

Women's Movement

Beyond the Movement

Preview of Events

♦1970   ♦1975   ♦1980   ♦1985   ♦1990   ♦1995   ♦2000

1972
Fighting escalates in Northern Ireland

1981
Women protest presence of American nuclear missiles in Britain

2001
Global opposition to terrorism forms

Voices from the Past

In his 1975 book *Small Is Beautiful,* the British economist E. F. Schumacher wrote:

❝We must begin to see the possibility of evolving a new lifestyle, with new methods of production and new patterns of consumption: a lifestyle designed for permanence. To give only two examples: in agriculture, we can interest ourselves in the perfection of production methods which are biologically sound and produce health, beauty and permanence. In industry, we can interest ourselves in small-scale technology, 'technology with a human face,' so that people have a chance to enjoy themselves while they are working, instead of working solely for their pay packet and hoping for enjoyment solely during their leisure time.❞
— *Small Is Beautiful,* E. F. Schumacher, 1973

E. F. Schumacher

Schumacher was a major critic of the sometimes destructive aspects of the new science and technology of the postwar world.

Changes in Women's Lives

Since 1970, the number of women in the work force has continued to rise. In Britain, for example, the number of women in the labor force went from 32 percent to 44 percent between 1970 and 1990. Greater access to universities enabled more women to pursue careers in such fields as law, medicine, and government. However, women continued to receive lower wages than men for the same work and to have fewer chances to advance to top positions.

In the 1960s and 1970s, some women in the women's liberation movement came to believe that women themselves must transform the fundamental conditions of their lives. Women formed "consciousness-raising" groups to make people aware of women's issues. Gender stereotyping, contraception, and social and economic equality were a few of the issues that became politicized. During this time in the United States, for example, the Equal Pay Act was passed, giving legal support to equal pay for equal work for women.

As more women became activists in the 1980s and 1990s, they became involved in other issues. To affect the political environment, some women joined the antinuclear movement. In 1981, for example, a group of women protested American nuclear missiles in Britain by chaining themselves to the fence of an American military base. Other feminists focused on changing cultural attitudes through university programs in women's studies or worked for environmental causes.

In the 1990s, there was a backlash to the women's movement as some women advocated a return to traditional values and gender roles. Other women either rejected or attempted to redefine the term "feminism" as the struggle to balance career, family, and personal goals continued for both men and women.

✓ **Reading Check** **Summarizing** What reforms did women want when they started the women's movement?

The Growth of Terrorism

Acts of terror have become a regular aspect of modern Western society. Bands of terrorists use the killing of civilians (especially by bombing), the taking of hostages, and the hijacking of airplanes to draw attention to their demands or to achieve their political goals.

Some terrorists are militant nationalists who wish to create separatist states. One such group is the Irish Republican Army (IRA), whose goal is to unite **Northern Ireland,** governed by Great Britain, with the Irish Republic. The IRA has resorted to attacks against government and civilian targets. Since the early 1970s, IRA terrorists have been responsible for the deaths of thousands of people.

State-sponsored terrorism has often been an important part of international terrorism. Some militant governments, such as those in Iraq, Syria, Cuba, and North Korea, have provided sanctuary and support to numerous terrorist organizations.

One of the most destructive acts of terrorism occurred on September 11, 2001, in the United States. Four groups of terrorists hijacked four commercial jet airplanes in Boston, Newark, and Washington, D.C. The hijackers flew two of the airplanes directly into the World Trade Center towers in New York City, destroying both buildings and causing a number of surrounding buildings to collapse. A third hijacked plane slammed into the Pentagon in Washington, D.C. The fourth plane crashed into an isolated area of Pennsylvania, diverted from its apparent objective in Washington, D.C., by heroic passengers. Thousands of people were killed, including all persons aboard the airliners.

The U.S. government accumulated evidence indicating that these acts had been carried out by al-Qaeda, the terrorist organization of Osama bin Laden. Bin Laden had used his inherited fortune to train

CONNECTIONS Around The World

Global Terrorism

Terrorist acts became more frequent in the second half of the twentieth century. A growing number of groups have used terrorism to achieve their political goals. By March 2002, the U.S. State Department, for example, had designated 33 such groups around the world as Foreign Terrorist Organizations. These groups include urban guerrilla groups in Latin America; militants dedicated to the liberation of Palestine; Islamic militants fighting Western influence in the Middle East; and separatists seeking independent states, such as the Basques in Spain and the Tamils in Sri Lanka.

International terrorists have not limited their targets to their own countries. In 1972, three members of the neo-Marxist Japanese Red Army, who had been hired by the Popular Front for the Liberation of Palestine, opened fire at Tel Aviv's airport in Israel, killing 24 people, chiefly Christian pilgrims from Puerto Rico. The goal of the terrorists was to hurt Israel by discouraging people from visiting there.

Worldwide television newscasts have contributed to the expansion of global terrorism. International terrorists know that these news broadcasts create instant publicity for their causes. Televised images of American commercial jetliners flying into the twin towers of the World Trade Center in New York in 2001, for example, provided vivid evidence of the war that some militant groups have long threatened to wage against the United States.

Comparing Cultures

Using outside sources, locate recent acts of terrorism that occurred in two separate countries. Compare how these acts were similar and how they were different. Do you think the terrorists will achieve their goals by performing these acts?

---

terrorists in **Afghanistan,** which was controlled at the time by a militant Islamic group, the Taliban. Bin Laden was also suspected of directing earlier terrorist attacks against the United States, including the bombing of two U.S. embassies in Africa in 1998 and the attack on the USS *Cole* in 2000.

Following the World Trade Center and Pentagon attacks, United States president George W. Bush vowed to wage war on terrorism. The United States developed a global coalition of nations to rid the world of terrorist groups, a process that began with military action against Afghanistan in October 2001.

United States and NATO air strikes targeted Taliban-controlled command centers, airfields, and al-Qaeda hiding places. At the same time, food and supplies were dropped to aid the starving Afghan people. On the ground, opposition forces in Afghanistan pushed the Taliban out of the capital at Kabul and claimed control of more than half of the country by mid-November. Weeks later, representatives of rival Afghan factions met in Germany for UN-sponsored talks about Afghanistan's future.

At home, President Bush established a new cabinet department—the Department of Homeland Security —to protect the United States from terrorism and respond to any future attacks. Bush also signed an air security bill that made baggage screeners federal employees and required the inspection of all luggage checked on U.S. domestic flights. Across the nation, Americans flew flags, gave blood, and donated millions of dollars to charities to aid the families of victims of the September 11 attacks.

During 2002, as the war on global terrorism progressed, the Bush administration focused on the dangers from **weapons of mass destruction.** These are nuclear, chemical, and biological weapons that can kill tens of thousands of people all at once. In the early 1990s, UN Security Council resolutions had called for Iraq to disarm such weapons programs. Iraq repeatedly violated these resolutions.

On September 12, 2002, President Bush asked the UN to pass a new resolution against Iraq. If Iraqi leader Saddam Hussein wanted peace, he had to give up the nation's weapons of mass destruction, readmit the UN weapons inspectors he had expelled in 1998, stop supporting terrorism, and stop oppressing his people. On November 8, the UN Security Council unanimously approved a resolution imposing tough new arms inspections on Iraq. The resolution pledged that Iraq would face "serious consequences" if it did not cooperate. Throughout the rest of 2002 and into 2003, the Bush administration worked with international leaders to ensure that the Iraqi regime met the dictates of the UN resolution. In March 2003, the United States, with support from a coalition of nations, declared that Iraq had failed to meet those requirements. On March 20, war began in Iraq.

✔ Reading Check **Explaining** What methods do terrorists use to achieve their goals?

Science and Technology

Scientific and technological achievements since World War II have revolutionized people's lives. During the war, many scientists were recruited by governments to develop new weapons and other instruments of war. Perhaps the most famous product of wartime scientific research was the atomic bomb, created by a team of scientists.

By sponsoring projects, governments and the military created a new model for scientific research during World War II. Wartime projects were complex and required large teams of scientists, huge laboratories, and sophisticated equipment. Such facilities were so expensive that they could only be provided by governments and large corporations.

A stunning example of how the new scientific establishment operated is the space race. In 1961, four years after the Soviet Union sent *Sputnik I* into orbit, President Kennedy predicted that the United States would land astronauts on the Moon within a decade. Massive government funding enabled the United States to do so in 1969. 📖 (*See page 1000 to read excerpts from John Glenn's* Progress Never Stops *in the Primary Sources Library.*)

The postwar alliance of science and technology led to a fast rate of change that became a fact of life in Western society. Underlying this alliance was the assumption that scientific knowledge gave human beings the ability and the right to manipulate the environment for their benefit.

Critics in the 1960s and 1970s noted that some technological advances had far-reaching side effects that were damaging to the environment. Chemical fertilizers, for example, were used for growing more abundant crops, but these fertilizers also destroyed the ecological balance of streams, rivers, and woodlands. In 2000, debates over organic farming and genetically enhanced food intensified as people continued to disagree over the role science should play in food production.

✔ Reading Check **Summarizing** How did governmental projects help to create a new model for scientific research?

Religious Revival

Many people perceived a collapse in values during the twentieth century. The revival of religion was one response to that collapse. Ever since the Enlightenment of the eighteenth century, Christianity, as well as religion in general, had been on the defensive. A number of religious thinkers and leaders tried to bring new life to Christianity in the twentieth century. Despite the attempts of the Communist world to build an atheistic society and the attempts of the West to build a secular society, religion continued to play an important role in the lives of many people.

One expression of the religious revival was the attempt by Christian thinkers, such as the Protestant Karl Barth (BART), to breathe new life into traditional Christian teachings. In his numerous writings, Barth tried to show how the religious insights of the Reformation were still relevant for the modern world. To Barth the imperfect nature of human beings meant that humans could know religious truth not through reason but only through the grace of God.

In the Catholic Church, attempts at religious renewal came from two popes—John XXIII and John Paul II. Pope John XXIII reigned as pope for only a short time (1958 to 1963). Nevertheless, he sparked a dramatic revival of Catholicism when he summoned the twenty-first ecumenical council of the Catholic Church. Known as Vatican Council II, it liberalized a number of Catholic practices. For example, the mass could now be celebrated in the vernacular languages as well as Latin.

John Paul II, who had been the archbishop of Cracow in Poland before he became pope in 1978, was the first non-Italian pope since the sixteenth century. Pope John Paul's numerous travels around the world helped strengthen the Catholic Church throughout the non-Western world. Although he alienated a number of people by reasserting traditional Catholic teaching on such issues as birth control and a ban on women in the priesthood, John Paul II has been a powerful figure in reminding Catholics of the need to temper the pursuit of materialism with spiritual concerns.

✔ Reading Check **Describing** What are two ways that the revival of religion was expressed in the twentieth century?

Trends in Art

For the most part, the United States has dominated the art world since the end of World War II. American art, often vibrantly colored and filled with activity, reflected the energy of the postwar United States. After 1945, New York City became the artistic center of the Western world.

Abstractionism, especially abstract expressionism, was the most popular form of modern art after World War II. Such artists as **Jackson Pollock** conveyed emotion and feeling and were less concerned about representing subject matter.

The early 1960s saw the emergence of pop art, which took images of popular culture and transformed them into works of fine art. **Andy Warhol** took his subject matter from commercial art, such as Campbell soup cans, and photographs of celebrities such as Marilyn Monroe.

In the 1980s, styles emerged that some have referred to as postmodern. Postmodernism is marked by a revival of traditional elements and techniques, including not only traditional painting styles but also traditional crafts.

During the 1980s and 1990s, many artists experimented with emerging technologies such as digital cameras and computer programs to create new art forms. These new art forms are often interactive, and they give the viewer the opportunity to influence the production of the art work itself.

✔ **Reading Check** **Describing** What are the characteristics of pop art?

Popular Culture

The United States has been a powerful force in shaping popular culture. Through movies, television, and music, the United States has spread its ideals and values of material prosperity—the American Dream—to millions around the world. Other countries object to the influence of American culture. It has often been called "cultural imperialism." Some nations, notably France, have taken active measures to resist the Americanization of their culture.

Already in 1923, the New York *Morning Post* noted that "the film is to America what the flag was once to Britain. By its means Uncle Sam may hope some day . . . to Americanize the world." That day has come. Movies were important vehicles for the spread of American popular culture in the years immediately after World War II. In the following decades, American movies have continued to dominate both

Jackson Pollock
1912–1956—American painter

Jackson Pollock became well known for his abstract expressionist paintings. Born in Wyoming, he was a child of the American West and was influenced by the sand paintings of Native Americans.

Pollock moved to New York in the early 1930s. Self-destructive and alcoholic, he saw painting as a way to deal with his problems. In such works as his *Lavender Mist* (1950), paint seems to explode, assaulting the viewer with emotion and movement.

In the 1940s, Pollock began to produce drip paintings. These he created by dropping paint with sticks and brushes on large canvases on the floor of his studio. He said: "On the floor I am more at ease. This way I can literally be in the painting. When I am in the painting I am not aware of what I am doing. There is pure harmony."

European and American markets. In the 1960s, as television spread around the world, U.S. programs became popular in both European and non-Western nations.

The United States has also dominated popular music since the end of World War II. Jazz, blues, rhythm and blues, rock, and rap have been by far the most popular music forms in the Western world.

When American popular music spread to the rest of the world, it inspired artists who transformed the music in their own way. For example, in the 1950s, American figures such as Chuck Berry and **Elvis Presley** inspired the **Beatles** and other British performers.

The establishment of the video music channel MTV in the early 1980s changed the music scene by making image as important as sound to the selling of records. In the late 1990s, teen and preteen consumers made performers such as 'N Sync and Britney Spears into multimillion-dollar musical acts.

Between music videos and computer technology, consumer access to a variety of artists and musical genres has grown tremendously. An increasing number of performers are moving beyond regional boundaries to develop international audiences. For example, in the late 1990s, Latin American artists became popular in non-Latin markets. In this way, musical styles and markets continue to diversify.

✔ **Reading Check** **Identifying** Through what different media has American culture spread throughout the world?

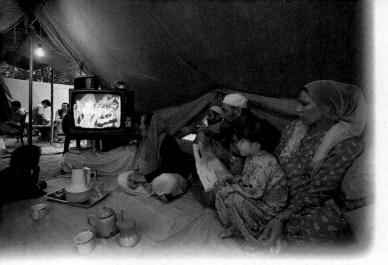
Television dominates popular culture around the world.

Sports, Television, Politics

In the postwar years, sports became a major product of both popular culture and the leisure industry. Through television, sports were transformed into a worldwide experience. The Olympic Games, for example, could now be broadcast across the globe from any location.

Televised sports were an inexpensive form of entertainment from consumers' point of view. Fans could now enjoy sporting events without buying tickets. In fact, some sports organizations at first resisted televising events because they feared that it would hurt ticket sales. Enormous revenues from television contracts helped change their minds.

Many sports organizations came to receive most of their yearly revenues from television contracts. The Olympics, for example, are now funded chiefly by American television. These funds come from advertising sponsors.

Sports have become big politics as well as big business. Indeed, politicization has been one of the most important recent trends in sports. Soccer, for example, is a vehicle for national feeling. Although the sport has been a positive outlet for national pride, all too often it has also been marked by violence.

The most telling example of the mix of politics and sport is the Olympic Games. When the Soviets entered Olympic competition in 1952, the Olympics became part of the Cold War. They were known as the "war without weapons." The Soviets used the Olympics to promote the Communist system as the best path for social progress.

The political nature of the games found expression in other ways as well. In 1972, at the Munich Games, a Palestinian terrorist group seized 11 Israeli athletes as hostages. Two hostages were killed immediately and the other 9 died in a shootout at the airport. The Soviets refused to participate in the Los Angeles Games in 1984 after the United States boycotted the 1980 Moscow Olympics.

✓ Reading Check **Explaining** How have sports become big politics?

🤠 **TAKS Practice**

SECTION 4 ASSESSMENT

Checking for Understanding

1. **Define** pop art, postmodernism.

2. **Identify** Jackson Pollock, Andy Warhol, Elvis Presley, Beatles.

3. **Locate** Northern Ireland, Afghanistan.

4. **Explain** why some critics began to question the value of technological progress in postwar society. Give an example of a scientific or technological achievement that was criticized and explain why.

5. **List** the reasons why terrorists choose to pursue terrorism. What are some of the political goals of terrorists? In what ways are some terrorists associated with governments?

Critical Thinking

6. **Summarize** What are the components of the new scientific establishment? Explain the benefits and shortcomings of these components.

7. **Organizing Information** Create a chart like the one below listing the main goals of terrorists, the methods they use to achieve these goals, and how governments have responded.

Terrorism		
Goals	Methods	Government Responses

Analyzing Visuals

8. **Examine** the photograph of the destruction of the World Trade Center, shown on page 890. Describe the different roles citizens play during times of national or international crisis.

Writing About History

9. **Descriptive Writing** Abstractionism, abstract expressionism, and pop art became popular art forms after World War II. Research these art forms and make a list of two or three artists who followed each form. Find examples of these artists' works and describe in an essay how these works represent the innovations of the new art forms.

TAKS Practice

Preparing A Bibliography

Why Learn This Skill?

In Chapter 22 you learned how to write a report. At the end of any report that you write, you need to list all the sources you used. A bibliography is a list of the books and articles used to research the material in your report.

Learning the Skill

A bibliography must follow a specific format:

- Entries should be arranged alphabetically by the author's last name. If there is no author, as in an encyclopedia reference, use the words in the title of the article to put it into alphabetical order.

- Different types of sources have different formats:

Books Author's last name, first name. *Full Title.* Place of publication: publisher, copyright date.
Reich, Charles. *The Greening of America.* New York: Random House, 1970.

Articles from magazines Author's last name, first name. "Title of Article." *Periodical* in which article appears, Volume number (issue date): page numbers.
Watson, Bruce. "The New Peace Corps in the New Kazakhstan." *Smithsonian,* Vol. 25 (August 1994): pp. 26–35.

Articles from newspapers Author's last name, first name (if given). "Title of Article." *Newspaper* in which article appears, date, section and page numbers. (If the newspaper has more than one edition, the edition should be cited rather than the page number, since the page number might be different in each edition.)
Finnonian, Albert. "The Iron Curtain Rises." *Wilberton Journal,* February 7, 1990, final edition.

Different types of sources require different formats in the bibliography.

Articles from encyclopedias "Title of article." *Encyclopedia's Name.* Edition (if not the first).
"Cold War." *Encyclopedia Britannica.* 11th Edition.

Web sites Title of referenced source. Web site's name (if given).
www.Internet address.com.
A Concrete Curtain: The Life and Death of the Berlin Wall.
www.wall-berlin.org.

Practicing the Skill

Review the sample bibliography, then answer the questions that follow.

Bibliography

Winkler, Allan M. *The Cold War: a history in documents.* Oxford, New York: Oxford University Press, 2000.

Hazen, Walter A. Post-Cold War Europe. Grand Rapids, Mich: Instructional Fair/TS Denison, 2000.

Havel, Václav. "The Call for New Politics." *The Washington Post.* February 22, 1990, p. A28.

The European Union: A Guide for Americans.
www.eurunion.org.

❶ Are the bibliography entries in the correct order? Why or why not?

❷ What is incorrect in the second book listing?

❸ What is incorrect in the article listing?

Applying the Skill

Compile a bibliography for the research report you completed in Chapter 22. Include at least five sources.

Glencoe's **Skillbuilder Interactive Workbook, Level 2,** provides instruction and practice in key social studies skills.

Chapter Summary

The end of the Cold War brought dramatic economic, political, and social changes to Europe and North America. Many of these changes can be understood through the themes of conflict, change, regionalism, and cooperation. Below, some of the major events in postwar society are categorized according to these themes.

Conflict

- Serb forces carry out "ethnic cleansing" of Muslims.
- Terrorism becomes a regular aspect of modern society.
- Soviet troops crush a reform movement in Czechoslovakia.
- Nicolae Ceauşescu is arrested and executed.

Change

- The Soviet Union adopts a policy of perestroika under Gorbachev.
- Lech Walesa becomes the first freely elected president of an Eastern European nation in 40 years.
- The national debt triples in the United States during Ronald Reagan's presidency.
- Television, movies, and music spread American culture throughout the world.

Regionalism

- Ethnic Albanians declare Kosovo an independent province.
- Bosnian Serbs fight Bosnian Muslims and Croats.
- Bands of German youths attack immigrants.
- Intense fighting breaks out between Protestants and Catholics in Northern Ireland.

Cooperation

- British women hold an antinuclear protest.
- American culture spreads through popular media.
- East Germany and West Germany are reunited into one nation.
- The Soviet Union and the United States sign the INF Treaty.

Using Key Terms

1. _____ was a phase in American/Soviet relations that was marked by decreased tension.
2. Serbian forces engaged in _____ to forcibly remove Bosnian Muslims from their lands.
3. The conservative British economic policy that limited social welfare, restricted union power, and ended inflation was known as _____.
4. _____ spoke out against the repressive Soviet regime.
5. Mikhail Gorbachev introduced _____ to restructure Soviet economic policy.

Reviewing Key Facts

6. **Government** What doctrine gave the Soviet Union the right to intervene if communism in another Communist state was threatened?
7. **Economics** What problems arose in Russia after the Soviet Union dissolved?
8. **Society** How did religion contribute to changes in Bosnia and Poland?
9. **Government** List the three Eastern European countries that made peaceful transitions from Communist to free-market societies.
10. **Government** Which countries' transitions to free-market societies were filled with violence and bloodshed?
11. **Economics** What caused the economic downturn in Western Europe from the mid-1970s to the early 1980s?
12. **Society** What problems surfaced in Germany as a result of reunification?
13. **Culture** Why was the Official Languages Act passed in Canada in 1968?
14. **Society** What goal did women in the United States and Europe work toward when the women's movement began?
15. **Society** List the methods terrorists use to draw attention to their causes or achieve their political goals.
16. **Science and Technology** Name the World War II invention that has become a fixture in homes, schools, and businesses in the United States and other developed countries.

Critical Thinking

17. **Evaluating** What were the results of the Reagan administration's military buildup?
18. **Analyzing** Explain why the United States, Great Britain, France, and Canada alternated between liberal and conservative government leaders from 1970 through 2000.

19. Analyzing The United States has been accused of "cultural
imperialism." What positive and negative effects does the
spread of American popular culture have? How has American popular culture been influenced in return?

Writing about History

20. Persuasive Writing In the latter part of the twentieth century, Communist governments ceased to exist in the Soviet
Union and Eastern Europe. Countries instantly converted
their economic systems from socialist to free-market societies. These conversions created many problems for the new
societies. Write a paper listing the problems created by the
fall of communism and describe solutions that would have
made the transition easier.

Analyzing Sources

In his book *Perestroika*, Mikhail Gorbachev wrote:

❝There is a great thirst for mutual understanding and
mutual communication in the world. It is felt among politicians, it is gaining momentum among the intelligentsia, representatives of culture, and the public at large. . . . Now the
whole world needs restructuring, i.e., progressive development, a fundamental change . . . I believe that more and
more people will come to realize that through restructuring
in the broad sense of the word, the integrity of the world
will be enhanced.❞

21. What does Gorbachev think is gaining momentum among
the public at large?

22. How does Gorbachev's quote apply to today's world?

Making Decisions

23. Imagine that it is 1991 and you are in Ukraine, casting a vote
for or against independence. What are the reasons you might
choose to sever Ukraine from the Soviet Union? Why might
you want to remain part of the Soviet Union? What factors do
you consider most important? What is your final decision?

24. As the editor of a history textbook, you plan to include a feature on the popular culture of the 2000s. Who would you
include as influential musicians, artists, and entertainers?
What values do these individuals model? Who are the heroes
and who are the superstars? Is there a difference?

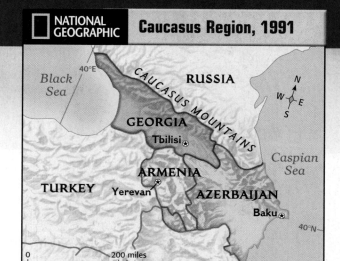

NATIONAL GEOGRAPHIC **Caucasus Region, 1991**

Analyzing Maps and Charts

Study the map above to answer the following questions.

25. Which of these states is completely landlocked?

26. Which state's territory is separated by Armenia? What
problems might that present?

Applying Technology Skills

27. Using the Internet Using the information in your text and
outside sources, develop a PowerPoint presentation on the
history of communism. Use specific examples.

The Princeton Review

TAKS
Test Practice

**Directions: Choose the best answer to the
question below.**

What happened after the Communist Party collapsed in
Czechoslovakia?

F Rival ethnic states could not agree on national borders.

G East Germany remained loyal to the Soviets.

H Conservative movements came to power in America and
Great Britain.

J Mikhail Gorbachev invaded Czechoslovakia to regain
control.

Test-Taking Tip: If you do not know the correct answer to
this question, read the answer choices carefully. Eliminate
any statement that is historically incorrect. This will help
you focus on the remaining answer choices and increase
your chances of choosing the correct answer.

CHAPTER 29

Latin America

1945–Present

Key Events

As you read this chapter, look for the key events in the history of Latin American nations.

- *Many Latin American nations have experienced severe economic problems, and their governments have been led by military dictators.*
- *Successful Marxist revolutions in Cuba and Nicaragua fed fears in the United States about the spread of communism in the Americas.*

The Impact Today

The events that occurred during this time period still impact our lives today.

- *Latin American influence in the United States can be seen in art, music, literature, and foods.*
- *Rapid and unplanned industrial development in some Latin American countries has led to heightened concern about the environment.*

 World History Video *The Chapter 29 video, "The Cuban Revolution," chronicles the causes and effects of Castro's revolution in Cuba.*

Juan Perón

1951
Juan Perón elected to second term as president of Argentina

1961
Bay of Pigs invasion fails

1962
Cuban missile crisis resolved

1940   1950   1960

1946
Juan Perón establishes authoritarian regime in Argentina

1948
Organization of American States formed

1959
Fidel Castro seizes power in Cuba

Sugarloaf Mountain overlooks Rio de Janeiro, one of Brazil's most populous cities.

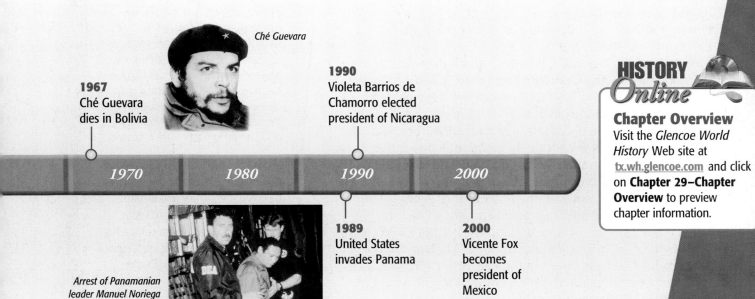

Ché Guevara

1967
Ché Guevara dies in Bolivia

1990
Violeta Barrios de Chamorro elected president of Nicaragua

1970   1980   1990   2000

1989
United States invades Panama

2000
Vicente Fox becomes president of Mexico

Arrest of Panamanian leader Manuel Noriega

HISTORY
Online

Chapter Overview
Visit the *Glencoe World History* Web site at tx.wh.glencoe.com and click on **Chapter 29–Chapter Overview** to preview chapter information.

A Story That Matters

A victorious Fidel Castro rides through the streets of Havana in 1959.

The Castro Brothers

On July 26, 1953, two brothers, Fidel and Raúl Castro, led a band of 165 young people in an attack on the Moncada army camp at Santiago de Cuba. While a law student at the University of Havana, Fidel Castro had become a revolutionary. He was determined to overthrow the government of Fulgencio Batista, the dictator of Cuba.

The attack on Moncada, however, was a disaster. Many of the troops led by the Castro brothers were killed, wounded, or arrested. Fidel and Raúl Castro escaped but were later captured and sentenced to prison for 15 years.

The Castro brothers could easily have died in prison, where political prisoners were routinely tortured. Instead, they were released after 11 months. By freeing political prisoners, Batista hoped to win the favor of the Cuban people.

He certainly did not gain the favor of the Castros. After his release, Fidel Castro fled to Mexico and built a new revolutionary army. Six years later, on January 1, 1959, Fidel Castro and his forces finally seized control of Cuba. Hundreds of thousands of Cubans swept into the streets, overcome with joy. One person remarked, "We were walking on a cloud." To the many Latin Americans who wanted major social and economic changes, Castro soon became a source of hope.

Why It Matters

Since 1945, the nations of Latin America have followed different paths of change. In some countries military dictators have maintained political stability and initiated economic changes. A few nations, like Cuba, have used Marxist revolutions to create a new political, economic, and social order. Many Latin American nations have struggled to build democratic systems, especially since the late 1980s. The Cold War has also had an impact on Latin America.

History and You As you read this chapter, document the struggle between democracy and dictatorship in the Latin American states. Make a chart or diagram comparing the different states, their leadership, and reasons why the regimes were able to gain power.

General Trends in Latin America

Guide to Reading

Main Ideas
• Exporting raw materials and importing manufactured goods has led to economic and political troubles for Latin American nations.
• Many Latin American nations began to build democratic systems in the late 1980s.

Key Terms
multinational corporation, magic realism

People to Identify
Gabriel García Márquez, Oscar Niemeyer

Places to Locate
Chile, Brazil, Bolivia, Peru, Colombia

Preview Questions
1. What factors undermined the stability of Latin American countries?
2. How did the roles of women change in Latin America after 1945?

Reading Strategy
Categorizing Information Use a chart like the one below to identify social and political challenges in Latin America since 1945.

Social Challenges — Political Challenges

Preview of Events

♦1940	♦1950	♦1960	♦1970	♦1980	♦1990

1948
The Organization of American States is formed

1980
A movement toward democracy takes place in Latin America

1982
Gabriel García Márquez wins the Nobel Prize for literature

1990
Twenty-nine Latin American cities have over a million people

Voices from the Past

U.S. soldiers in Panama

One Latin American observer discussed the United States's invasion of Panama in 1989 in the following words:

❝The first official [U.S.] reason for the invasion of Panama was 'to protect American lives there.' This pretext was not credible, for the cry of 'wolf! wolf!' has been used before in Latin America. . . . The danger to American lives is a hundred times greater every day and night in Washington, D.C., 'the murder capital of the United States,' and in other American cities to which President Bush has hardly applied his policy of protecting North American lives and waging war against drugs (he prefers to wage that war on foreign battlefields).❞
—*Latin American Civilization: History and Society, 1492 to the Present,*
Benjamin Keen, 1996

U.S. intervention in Latin American affairs has been a general trend in Latin American history since 1945.

Economic and Political Developments

Since the nineteenth century, Latin Americans had exported raw materials while buying manufactured goods from industrialized countries. As a result of the Great Depression, however, exports fell, and the revenues that had been used to buy manufactured goods declined. In response, many Latin American countries developed industries to produce goods that were formerly imported.

① MEXICO
1994: U.S., Mexico, and Canada enter into North American Free Trade Agreement (NAFTA).

⑬ HONDURAS
1981–1990: U.S. supports contra rebels in Nicaragua from bases in Honduras.

⑫ CUBA
1959: Castro overthrows Batista.
1960: U.S. declares trade embargo upon Cuba.
1961: U.S. supports attempted overthrow of Castro's government (Bay of Pigs invasion).
1962: U.S. blockades Cuba during Cuban Missile Crisis.
1980: Thousands of Cuban refugees enter U.S.

② GUATEMALA
1954: U.S. supports overthrow of Socialist government.

⑪ DOMINICAN REPUBLIC
1965: U.S. military forces intervene to suppress possible communist influence.

③ EL SALVADOR
Late 1970s and 1980s: U.S. supports Salvadoran army against Marxist-led guerrillas in civil war.
1992: Peace settlement ends civil war.

⑩ GRENADA
1979: U.S. ends aid as Marxist government assumes power.
1983: Extremists overthrow government; U.S. invades to restore stable government.

④ NICARAGUA
1979: U.S. withdraws support for corrupt Somoza family; Somozas are overthrown by Sandinistas (Marxist guerrilla forces).
1981–1990: U.S. secretly aids contra rebel efforts to overthrow Sandinista government.

⑨ PANAMA
1989: U.S. invades Panama and arrests and imprisons General Noriega on charges of drug trafficking.
1999: U.S relinquishes rights to Panama Canal Zone.

⑤ PERU
1958: Riots against U.S.

⑧ VENEZUELA
1958: Riots against U.S.

⑥ CHILE
1970: U.S. tries and fails to prevent election of Socialist President Allende.

⑦ ARGENTINA
1946: U.S. tries and fails to prevent election of President Perón.

0   1,000 miles
0   1,000 kilometers
Lambert Azimuthal Equal-Area projection

By the 1960s, however, Latin American countries were still experiencing economic problems. They were dependent on the United States, Europe, and Japan, especially for the advanced technology needed for modern industries. Also, many Latin American countries had failed to find markets abroad to sell their manufactured products.

These economic failures led to instability and reliance on military regimes. In the 1960s, repressive military regimes in **Chile, Brazil,** and Argentina abolished political parties and returned to export-import economies financed by foreigners. These regimes also encouraged multinational corporations (companies with divisions in more than two countries) to come to Latin America. This made these Latin American countries even more dependent on industrialized nations.

In the 1970s, Latin American nations grew more dependent as they attempted to maintain their weak economies by borrowing money. Between 1970 and 1982, debt to foreigners grew from $27 billion to $315.3 billion. By 1982, a number of Latin American economies had begun to crumble. Wages fell, and unemployment and inflation skyrocketed.

To get new loans, Latin American governments were now forced to make basic reforms. During this process, however, many people came to believe that

Per Capita Income, 1960s

Average annual per capita income, late 1960s:
- Below $200
- $200–$350
- $351–$500
- Above $500
- Information not available

1,000 miles
1,000 kilometers
Lambert Azimuthal Equal-Area projection

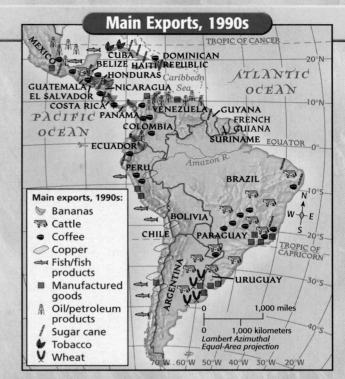

Main Exports, 1990s

Main exports, 1990s:
- Bananas
- Cattle
- Coffee
- Copper
- Fish/fish products
- Manufactured goods
- Oil/petroleum products
- Sugar cane
- Tobacco
- Wheat

1,000 miles
1,000 kilometers
Lambert Azimuthal Equal-Area projection

Geography *Skills*

Over the past 50 to 60 years, the United States has been actively involved in Latin American affairs.

1. **Interpreting Maps** What information can you find in the map on page 902 that supports the view that the people of Latin America would prefer that the United States *not* interfere in Latin American affairs?

2. **Applying Geography Skills** Create a thematic time line based on the data presented in the map on the left page. Then, pose and answer a question about the patterns in world history shown on your time line.

3. **Applying Geography Skills** Create a database for Latin America that includes elements from each of the maps and the graph on pages 902 and 903. Analyze your data, then write one paragraph stating which Latin American country you think will have the greatest population increase over the next 20 years.

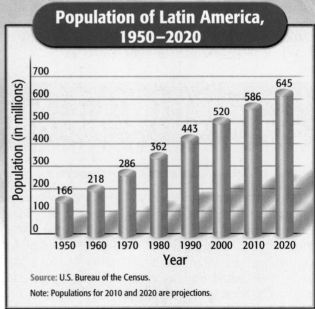

Population of Latin America, 1950–2020

Source: U.S. Bureau of the Census.

Note: Populations for 2010 and 2020 are projections.

government had taken control of too many industries. Trying to industrialize too quickly had led to the decline of the economy in the countryside as well.

Many hoped that encouraging peasants to grow food for home consumption rather than export would stop the flow of people from the countryside to the cities. At the same time, they believed that more people would now be able to buy the products from Latin American industries.

With the debt crisis in the 1980s came a movement toward democracy. Some military leaders were unwilling to deal with the monstrous debt problems.

At the same time, many people realized that military power without popular consent could not maintain a strong state. By the mid-1990s, several democratic regimes had been established.

The movement toward democracy was the most noticeable trend of the 1980s and the early 1990s in Latin America. This revival of democracy was fragile. In 1992, President Alberto Fujimori returned Peru to an authoritarian system.

✔**Reading Check** **Explaining** Why did the debt crisis of the 1980s create a movement toward democracy?

Latin American Society

Latin America's economic problems were made worse by dramatic growth in population. By the mid-1980s, the population in Latin America had grown from about 165 million people in 1950 to 400 million.

With the increase in population came a rapid rise in the size of cities. By 1990, 29 Latin American cities had over a million people. Slums, or shantytowns, became part of many of these cities.

The gap between the poor and the rich remained enormous in Latin America. Landholding and urban elites owned huge estates and businesses, while peasants and the urban poor struggled just to survive.

The traditional role of homemaker continues for women, who have also moved into new jobs. In addition to farm labor, women have found jobs in industry and as teachers, professors, doctors, and lawyers.

The international drug trade brought crime and corruption to some Latin American countries, undermining their stability. **Bolivia, Peru,** and **Colombia** were especially big producers of cocaine and marijuana.

✓**Reading Check** **Evaluating** Describe the effect(s) of Latin America's dramatic increase in population.

The United States and Latin America

The United States has always played a large role in Latin America. For years, the United States had sent troops into Latin American countries to protect U.S. interests and bolster friendly dictators.

In 1948, the states of the Western Hemisphere formed the **Organization of American States** (OAS), which called for an end to military action by one state in the affairs of any other state. The formation of the OAS, however, did not end U.S. involvement in Latin American affairs.

As the Cold War developed, so, too, did the anxiety of American policy makers about the possibility of Communist regimes in Latin America. As a result, the United States returned to a policy of taking action when it believed that Soviet agents were trying to establish Communist governments or governments hostile to United States interests. The United States also provided massive amounts of military aid to anti-Communist regimes.

✓**Reading Check** **Examining** How did the Cold War impact United States policy in Latin America?

CONNECTIONS Around The World

International Women's Conferences

As women around the world organized movements to change the conditions of their lives, an international women's movement emerged. Especially in the 1970s, much attention was paid to a series of international conferences on women's issues. Between 1975 and 1985, the United Nations celebrated the Decade for Women by holding conferences in such cities as Mexico City, Copenhagen, and Nairobi.

The conferences made clear how women in both industrialized and developing nations were organizing to make people aware of women's issues. They also made clear the differences between women from Western and non-Western countries.

Women from Western countries spoke about political, economic, cultural, and sexual rights. In contrast, women from developing countries in Latin America, Africa, and Asia focused on bringing an end to the violence, hunger, and disease that haunt their lives.

At the International Women's Year Tribunal in Mexico in 1974, sponsored by the United Nations, Dimitila Barrios de Chungara, a miner's wife from Bolivia, expressed her lack of patience with professional women at the conference. She said, "So, I went up and spoke. I made them see that they don't live in our world. I made them see that in Bolivia human rights aren't respected. . . . Women like us, housewives, who get organized to better our people well, they [the Bolivian police] beat us up and persecute us."

◀ *Latin American mother with children*

Comparing Cultures

Women from industrialized and developing nations focus on very different issues.

1. Which concerns of women are most important?
2. Do you think women's conferences are needed? What purposes might conferences serve other than raising issues?

Latin American Culture

Writers and artists have played important roles in Latin American society. They have been given a public status granted to very few writers and artists in other countries. In Latin America, writers and artists are seen as people who can express the hopes of the people. One celebrated Latin American writer is the Chilean poet Gabriela Mistral.

In literature, Latin Americans developed a unique form of expression called magic realism. Magic realism brings together realistic events with dreamlike or fantastic backgrounds.

Perhaps the foremost example of magic realism is *One Hundred Years of Solitude,* a novel by **Gabriel García Márquez.** In this story of the fictional town of Macondo, the point of view slips back and forth between fact and fantasy. Villagers are not surprised when a local priest rises into the air and floats. However, when these villagers are introduced to magnets, telescopes, and magnifying glasses, they are dumbfounded by what they see as magic. According to García Márquez, fantasy and fact depend on one's point of view.

García Márquez, a Colombian, was the most famous of the Latin American novelists. He was a former journalist who took up writing when he became angered by the negative reviews Latin American authors were receiving. He was awarded the Nobel Prize for literature in 1982.

People In History

Gabriela Mistral
1889–1957—Chilean poet

Gabriela Mistral, whose real name was Lucila Godoy Alcayaga, was a poet and educator. She was trained to be a teacher and became the director of a school for girls in Santiago, Chile. In 1922, she was invited by the Mexican government to introduce educational programs for the poor in that country. Later, she took up residence in the United States and taught at Middlebury and Barnard Colleges.

In 1945, she became the first Latin American author to win the Nobel Prize for literature. Her poems explored the many dimensions of love, tinged with an element of sadness.

Latin American art and architecture were strongly influenced by international styles after World War II. In painting, abstract styles were especially important. Perhaps the most notable example of modern architecture can be seen in Brasília, the capital city of Brazil, built in the 1950s and 1960s. Latin America's greatest modern architect, **Oscar Niemeyer,** designed some of the major buildings in Brasília.

✓ **Reading Check** **Identifying** What novel is the foremost example of magic realism?

🟥 TAKS Practice

SECTION 1 ASSESSMENT

Checking for Understanding

1. **Define** multinational corporation, magic realism.

2. **Identify** Organization of American States (OAS), Gabriel García Márquez, Oscar Niemeyer.

3. **Locate** Chile, Brazil, Bolivia, Peru, Colombia.

4. **Explain** how the Great Depression hurt Latin American economies. Have these economies recovered from the problems caused by the Great Depression?

5. **List** two well-known Latin American writers. Why are writers and artists held in such high regard in Latin America?

Critical Thinking

6. **Analyze** Why did the rapid rate of population growth in many Latin American countries cause problems for their political and economic systems?

7. **Organizing Information** Draw a chart like the one below to list economic challenges in Latin America since 1945. On your chart, use dates and names of countries from the text to make each entry as specific as possible.

Analyzing Visuals

8. **Examine** the photograph of a Latin American mother with her children shown on page 904 of the text. How does this photograph reflect the concerns faced by many Latin American women?

Writing About History

9. **Descriptive Writing** A uniquely Latin American literary form is magic realism, which combines realistic events with elements of magic and fantasy. Research further the elements of magic realism and then write a short story about a real or imagined event, using that style.

Mexico, Cuba, and Central America

Guide to Reading

Main Ideas
- Mexico and Central America faced political and economic crises after World War II.
- The United States feared the spread of communism in Central American countries, which led to active American involvement in the region.

Key Terms
privatization, trade embargo, contra

People to Identify
Vicente Fox, Fidel Castro, Manuel Noriega

Places to Locate
Havana, El Salvador, Nicaragua, Panama

Preview Questions
1. What problems did Mexico and the nations of Central America face after 1945?
2. What were the chief features and impact of the Cuban Revolution?

Reading Strategy
Categorizing Information Use a table like the one below to identify the political and economic challenges faced by El Salvador, Nicaragua, and Panama after 1945.

El Salvador	Nicaragua	Panama

Preview of Events

◆1950	◆1960	◆1970	◆1980	◆1990	◆2000
1959 Castro's revolutionaries seize Havana	**1961** United States breaks diplomatic relations with Cuba	**1979** The Sandinistas overthrow Somoza rule in Nicaragua	**1983** Noriega takes control of Panama	**2000** Vicente Fox defeats the PRI candidate for the presidency of Mexico	

Voices from the Past

Contra soldiers

Nancy Donovan, a Catholic missionary in Nicaragua, described her encounter with the military forces known as the contras:

❝It is not easy to live in a war zone. The least of it was my being kidnapped by contras early this year. The hard part is seeing people die and consoling families. . . . In those eight hours I was held, as I walked in a column of 60 or so men and a few women—all in uniform—I could hear shooting and realized that people I knew were being killed. Earlier I had seen bodies brought back to town, some burned, some cut to pieces.❞

—*Latin American Civilization: History and Society, 1492 to the Present*,
Benjamin Keen, 1996

Financed by the United States, the contras were trying to overthrow the Sandinista rulers of Nicaragua in one of several bloody wars fought in Central America.

The Mexican Way

The Mexican Revolution at the beginning of the twentieth century created a political order that remained stable for many years. The official political party of the Mexican Revolution—the Institutional Revolutionary Party, or PRI—came to dominate Mexico. Every six years, leaders of the PRI chose the party's presidential candidate, who was then elected by the people.

During the 1950s and 1960s, steady economic growth led to real gains in wages for more and more people in Mexico. At the end of the 1960s, however, students began to protest Mexico's one-party government system. On October 2, 1968, university students gathered in Mexico City to protest government policies. Police forces opened fire and killed hundreds. Leaders of the PRI grew concerned about the need for change in the system.

The next two presidents, Luís Echeverría and José López Portillo, made political reforms and opened the door to the emergence of new political parties. Greater freedom of debate in the press and universities was allowed. Economic problems, however, would soon reappear.

In the late 1970s, vast new reserves of oil were discovered in Mexico. The sale of oil abroad increased dramatically, and the government became more dependent on oil revenues. When world oil prices dropped in the mid-1980s, Mexico was no longer able to make payments on its foreign debt. The government was forced to adopt new economic policies. One of these policies was privatization, the sale of government-owned companies to private firms.

The debt crisis and rising unemployment increased dissatisfaction with the government. Support for the PRI dropped, and in 2000, **Vicente Fox** defeated the PRI candidate for the presidency.

✓**Reading Check** Evaluating How was Mexico's economy affected by its oil industry?

The Cuban Revolution

⌐TURNING POINT¬ **As you will learn, the Bay of Pigs invasion was an attempt by the United States to move forcefully against Fidel Castro and the threat of communism that he represented.**

In the 1950s, a strong opposition movement arose in Cuba. Led by **Fidel Castro,** the movement aimed to overthrow the government of the dictator Fulgencio Batista, who had controlled Cuba since 1934. Castro's army used guerrilla warfare against Batista's regime. As the rebels gained more support, the regime collapsed. Castro's revolutionaries seized **Havana** on January 3, 1959. Many Cubans who disagreed with Castro fled to the United States.

Relations between Cuba and the United States quickly deteriorated when the Castro regime began to receive aid from the Soviet Union. Arms from Eastern Europe also began to arrive in Cuba. In October 1960, the United States declared a trade embargo,

prohibiting trade with Cuba, and just three months later, on January 3, 1961, broke all diplomatic relations with Cuba.

Soon after that, in April 1961, the American president, John F. Kennedy, supported an attempt to overthrow Castro's government. When the invasion at the Bay of Pigs failed, the Soviets were encouraged to make an even greater commitment to Cuba. In December 1961, Castro declared himself a Marxist, drawing ever closer to the Soviet Union. The Soviets began placing nuclear missiles in Cuba in 1962, an act that led to a showdown with the United States (see Chapter 27).

The Cuban missile crisis caused Castro to realize that the Soviet Union had been unreliable. If the revolutionary movement in Cuba was to survive, the Cubans would have to start a social revolution in the rest of Latin America. They would do this by starting guerrilla wars and encouraging peasants to overthrow the old regimes. Ernesto Ché Guevara, an Argentinian and an ally of Castro, led such a war in

HISTORY Online

Web Activity Visit the *Glencoe World History* Web site at **tx.wh.glencoe.com** and click on **Chapter 29– Student Web Activity** to learn more about Fidel Castro.

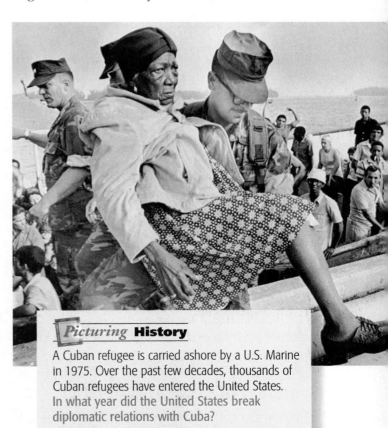

Picturing **History**

A Cuban refugee is carried ashore by a U.S. Marine in 1975. Over the past few decades, thousands of Cuban refugees have entered the United States. In what year did the United States break diplomatic relations with Cuba?

Government Reforms in Latin America

	Argentina	Brazil	Chile	El Salvador	Nicaragua	Panama	Peru
Military Regime	**1955:** Military overthrows Perón. **1973:** Perón is reelected. **1976:** Military takes over again.	**1964:** Military seizes control. **1982:** Severe recession undermines military control.	**1973:** Military, under Pinochet, overthrows Marxist Allende and establishes regime.	**1972:** Military prevents free elections. **1979:** Military takes over.	**1979:** Sandinistas (Marxist guerrilla forces) bring down dictatorship of Somoza family.	**1983:** National Guard, under Noriega, seizes control. **1989:** Noriega nullifies election results.	**1968:** Military, under Alvarado, takes over. **1975:** Military removes Alvarado.
Civilian Rule	**1983:** Civilian rule returns; Alfonsín is elected. **1994:** Constitution is reformed.	**1985:** Free elections held. **1989:** 80 million Brazilians vote. **1999:** Military put under civilian control.	**1989:** Pinochet is defeated in free elections. **2000:** Socialist Ricardo Lagos Escobar elected president.	**1984:** Moderate Duarte is elected but civil war continues. **1992:** Peace settlement ends civil war.	**1990:** Sandinistas lose free elections but remain strongest party. **1996:** Elections result in peaceful transfer of power.	**1989:** U.S. troops arrest Noriega; democracy returns. **1999:** Female, Mireya Moscoso de Gruber, elected president.	**1980:** Civilian rule returns. **1990–2000:** Fujimori is dictatorial president. **2001:** Toledo wins free elections.

Chart *Skills*

Many Latin American countries have had problems maintaining stable governments.

1. **Problem Solving** Use a problem-solving process and the information in this chapter to list options and choose possible solutions to suggest how these countries might avoid takeovers by military regimes in the future.

Bolivia but was killed by the Bolivian army in the fall of 1967. The Cuban strategy failed.

Nevertheless, in Cuba, Castro's Marxist regime continued, but with mixed results. The Cuban people did secure some social gains. The regime provided free medical services for all citizens, and illiteracy was nearly eliminated.

The Cuban economy continued to rely on the production and sale of sugar. Economic problems forced the Castro regime to depend on Soviet aid and the purchase of Cuban sugar by Soviet bloc countries. After the collapse of these Communist regimes in 1989, Cuba lost their support. Economic conditions in Cuba have steadily declined. Nevertheless, Castro has managed to remain in power.

✓**Reading Check** **Describing** How was Castro's Cuba affected by the collapse of Communist governments in Eastern Europe?

Upheaval in Central America

Central America includes seven countries: Costa Rica, Nicaragua, Honduras, El Salvador, Panama, Belize, and Guatemala. Economically, Central America has depended on the export of bananas, coffee, and cotton. Prices for these products have varied over time, however, creating economic crises. In addition, an enormous gulf between a wealthy elite and poor peasants has created a climate of instability.

Fear in the United States of the spread of communism often led to American support for repressive regimes in the area. American involvement was especially evident in El Salvador, Nicaragua, and Panama.

El Salvador After World War II, the wealthy elite and the military controlled the government in **El Salvador.** The rise of an urban middle class led to some hopes for a more democratic government. The army, however, refused to accept the results of free elections that were held in 1972.

In the late 1970s and the 1980s, El Salvador was rocked by a bitter civil war. Marxist-led, leftist guerrillas and right-wing groups battled one another. During the presidency of Ronald Reagan, the United States provided weapons and training to the Salvadoran army to defeat the guerrillas.

In 1984, a moderate, José Duarte, was elected president. However, the elections failed to stop the savage killing. By the early 1990s, the civil war had led to the deaths of at least 75,000 people. Finally, in 1992, a peace settlement brought the war to an end.

Nicaragua In **Nicaragua,** the Somoza family seized control of the government in 1937 and kept control for the next 42 years. Over most of this period, the Somoza regime had the support of the United States. The Somozas enriched themselves at the nation's expense and used murder and torture to silence opposition.

By 1979, the United States, under President Jimmy Carter, had grown unwilling to support the corrupt regime. In that same year, Marxist guerrilla forces known as the Sandinista National Liberation Front won a number of military victories against government forces and gained virtual control of the country.

The Sandinistas inherited a poverty-stricken nation. Soon, a group opposed to the Sandinistas' policies, called the contras, began to try to overthrow the new government. The Reagan and Bush administrations in the United States, worried by the Sandinistas' alignment with the Soviet Union, supported the contras.

The war waged by the contras undermined support for the Sandinistas. In 1990, the Sandinistas agreed to free elections, and they lost to a coalition headed by Violeta Barrios de Chamorro. They lost again in 2001 but remained one of the strongest parties in Nicaragua.

Panama Panama became a nation in 1903, when it broke away from Colombia with help from the United States. In return for this aid, the United States was able to build the Panama Canal and gained influence over the government and economy of Panama. A wealthy oligarchy ruled, with American support.

After 1968, power in Panama came into the hands of the military leaders of Panama's National Guard. One such leader was **Manuel Noriega,** who took control of Panama in 1983.

People In History

Rigoberta Menchú
1959– Guatemalan activist

Rigoberta Menchú is a reformer who worked to save her fellow Quiché Indians from the murder squads of the Guatemalan government. She grew up in a poor family. Her father helped organize a peasant movement, but he and other family members were killed by government troops.

Rigoberta Menchú then began to play an active role in her father's movement. Condemned by the Guatemalan government, she fled to Mexico. Her autobiography, *I . . . Rigoberta Menchú,* brought world attention to the fact that 150,000 Native Americans had been killed by the Guatemalan authorities. In 1992, she received the Nobel Peace Prize and used the money from the award to set up a foundation to help Native Americans.

At first, Noriega was supported by the United States. His brutality and involvement with the drug trade, however, turned American leaders against him. In 1989, President George Bush sent U.S. troops to Panama. Noriega was arrested and sent to prison in the United States on charges of drug trafficking.

✓ **Reading Check** **Summarizing** What factors led to conflicts in Central America from the 1970s to the 1990s?

🔺**TAKS Practice**

SECTION 2 ASSESSMENT

Checking for Understanding

1. **Define** privatization, trade embargo, contra.

2. **Identify** Vicente Fox, Fidel Castro, Manuel Noriega.

3. **Locate** Havana, Nicaragua, Panama, El Salvador.

4. **Explain** why the Cubans attempted to spur revolution in the rest of Latin America.

5. **List** the political reforms enacted by Mexican presidents Luís Echeverría and José López Portillo.

Critical Thinking

6. **Evaluate** Why did relations between the Soviet Union and Cuba become more difficult after 1962?

7. **Cause and Effect** Use a chart like the one below to show how Mexico has reacted to political and economic crises since World War II.

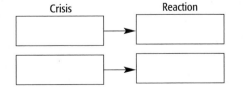

Crisis		Reaction
	→	
	→	

Analyzing Visuals

8. **Examine** the photo of Castro on page 900 and the photo of a Cuban refugee on page 907. What inferences can you draw about Castro's reign in Cuba from looking at these photos?

Writing About History

9. **Persuasive Writing** The United States has increasingly tried to negotiate conflicts using economic tools rather than military force. Research the trade embargo imposed upon Cuba. Write a persuasive argument for or against this embargo.

Student Revolt in Mexico

A GROWING CONFLICT BETWEEN THE government and university students in Mexico came to a violent climax on October 2, 1968, just before the Olympic Games were to begin in Mexico City. The official government report said that Mexican authorities were fired upon, and they returned the gunfire. This excerpt is taken from an account of the events by the student National Strike Council.

Student demonstrators in Mexico City

66 After an hour and a half of a peaceful meeting attended by 10,000 people and witnessed by scores of domestic and foreign reporters, a helicopter gave the army the signal to attack by dropping flares into the crowd. Simultaneously, the plaza was surrounded and attacked by members of the army and police forces.

The local papers have given the following information, confirmed by firsthand witnesses, about the attack:

1. Numerous secret policemen had infiltrated the meeting in order to attack it from within, with orders to kill. They were known to each other by the use of a white handkerchief tied around their right hands. . . .

2. High-caliber weapons and expansion bullets were used. Seven hours after the massacre began, tanks cleaned up the residential buildings of Nonoalco-Tlatelolco with short cannon blasts and machine-gun fire.

3. On the morning of October 3, the apartments of supposedly guilty individuals were still being searched, without a search warrant.

4. Doctors in the emergency wards of the city hospitals were under extreme pressure, being forced to forego attention to the victims until they had been interrogated and placed under guard. . . .

5. The results of this brutal military operation include hundreds of dead (including women and children), thousands of wounded, an unwarranted search of all the apartments in the area, and thousands of violent arrests. . . . It should be added that members of the National Strike Council who were captured were stripped and herded into a small archaeological excavation at Tlatelolco, converted for the moment into a dungeon. Some of them were put up against a wall and shot.

All this has occurred only ten days before the start of the Olympics. The repression is expected to become even greater after the Games. . . .

We are not against the Olympic Games. Welcome to Mexico. 99

—Account of the Clash Between the Government and Students in Mexico, October 2, 1968

Analyzing Primary Sources

1. What was the reason for the military attack on the students?
2. Why do you think the government reacted with such violence?
3. Do you think the government handled the situation well? Why or why not?

The Nations of South America

Guide to Reading

Main Ideas
- South American nations have experienced economic, social, and political problems.
- Democracy has advanced in South America since the late 1980s.

Key Terms
cooperative, Shining Path

People to Identify
Juan Perón, Salvador Allende, Augusto Pinochet, Juan Velasco Alvarado

Places to Locate
Argentina, Falkland Islands

Preview Questions
1. What obstacles does the new democratic government in Brazil face?
2. What factors have been the greatest causes of South American instability?

Reading Strategy
Categorizing Information Use a table like the one below to describe the factors leading to the change from military rule to civilian rule in Argentina, Brazil, and Chile.

Argentina	Brazil	Chile

Preview of Events

♦1945	♦1955	♦1965	♦1975	♦1985	♦1995	♦2005

1946
Juan Perón is elected president of Argentina

1973
Military forces overthrow Allende presidency in Chile

1982
Argentina sends troops to the Falkland Islands

2001
Alejandro Toledo is elected president of Peru

Voices from the Past

Brazilian city, 1971

In 1974, a group of Brazilian Catholic priests talked about an economic miracle that had taken place in Brazil:

❝Beginning in 1968, Brazil's gross domestic product grew at an annual rate of about 10 [percent]. . . . The consequences of this 'miracle' were the impoverishment of the Brazilian people. Between 1960 and 1970 the 20 [percent] of the population with the highest income increased its share of the national income from 54.5 [percent] to 64.1 [percent], while the remaining 80 [percent] saw its share reduced from 45.5 [percent] to 36.8 [percent]. . . . In the same period the 1 [percent] of the population that represents the richest group increased its share of the national income from 11.7 [percent] to 17 [percent].❞

—*Latin American Civilization: History and Society, 1492 to the Present,*
Benjamin Keen, 1996

The countries of South America shared in the economic, political, and social problems that plagued Latin America after 1945. Argentina, Brazil, Chile, Colombia, and Peru provide examples of these problems.

Argentina

Argentina is Latin America's second largest country. For years, it had been ruled by a powerful oligarchy whose wealth was based on growing wheat and raising cattle. Support from the army was crucial to the continuing power of the oligarchy.

In 1943, in the midst of World War II, a group of army officers overthrew the oligarchy. The new military regime was unsure of how to deal with the working classes until one of its members, **Juan Perón,** devised a new strategy.

Using his position as labor secretary in the military government, Perón sought to win over the workers, known as the descamisados (the shirtless ones). He encouraged them to join labor unions. He also increased job benefits, as well as the number of paid holidays and vacations.

In 1944, Perón became vice president of the military government and made sure that people knew he was responsible for the better conditions for workers. As Perón grew more popular, however, other army officers began to fear his power, and they arrested him. An uprising by workers forced the officers to back down.

Perón was elected president of Argentina in 1946. His chief support came from labor and the urban middle class, and to please them, he followed a policy of increased industrialization. At the same time, he sought to free Argentina from foreign investors. The government bought the railways and took over the banking, insurance, shipping, and communications industries.

People In History

Eva Perón
1919–1952—Argentine first lady

Eva Perón, known as Evita to her followers, was the first lady of Argentina from 1946 to 1952. Raised in poverty, Eva dreamed of being an actress. At 15, she moved to Buenos Aires, Argentina's largest city, where she eventually gained fame as a radio performer.

Eva met Juan Perón in 1944 and became his wife a year later. She was an important force in her husband's rise to power. Together, they courted the working-class poor with promises of higher wages and better working conditions. As first lady, Eva Perón formed a charitable organization that built hospitals, schools, and orphanages. She campaigned for women's rights. The masses adored her. To this day, monuments and street names in Argentina keep her memory alive. The American musical and movie *Evita* are based on her life.

Perón's regime was authoritarian. He created Fascist gangs modeled after Hitler's Brownshirts. The gangs used violent means to terrify Perón's opponents.

Fearing Perón's power, the military overthrew the Argentinian leader in September 1955. Perón went into exile in Spain. Overwhelmed by problems, however, military leaders later allowed Perón to return. He was reelected as president in 1973 but died a year later.

In 1976, the military once again took over power. The new regime tolerated no opposition. Perhaps 36,000 people were killed.

At the same time, economic problems plagued the nation. To divert people's attention, the military regime invaded the **Falkland Islands,** off the coast of Argentina, in April 1982. Great Britain, which had controlled the islands since the nineteenth century, sent ships and troops and took the islands back. The loss discredited the military and opened the door to civilian rule in Argentina.

In 1983, Raúl Alfonsín was elected president and worked to restore democratic practices. The Perónist Carlos Saúl Menem won the presidential elections of 1989. This peaceful transfer of power gave rise to the hope that Argentina was moving on a democratic path.

✔ Reading Check **Explaining** How did Juan Perón free Argentina from foreign investors?

Brazil

Like other Latin American countries, Brazil experienced severe economic problems following World War II. When democratically elected governments proved unable to solve these problems, the military stepped in and seized control in 1964.

The armed forces remained in direct control of the country for the next 20 years. The military set a new economic direction, reducing government interference in the economy and stressing free-market forces. Beginning in 1968, the new policies seemed to be working. Brazil experienced an "economic miracle" as its economy grew spectacularly.

Ordinary Brazilians benefited little from this economic growth, however. The gulf between rich and poor, which had always been wide, grew even wider.

Furthermore, rapid development led to an inflation rate of 100 percent a year. Overwhelmed, the generals retreated and opened the door for a return to democracy in 1985.

The new democratic government faced enormous obstacles—a massive foreign debt, increasingly severe inflation (it was 800 percent in 1987), and a lack of social unity. In the 1990s, however, a series of democratically elected presidents managed to restore some stability to Brazil's economy.

✓ **Reading Check** **Evaluating** What factors led to the return to democracy in Brazil in 1985?

Chile

In elections held in 1970, **Salvador Allende** (ah•YEHN•day), a Marxist, became president of Chile. Allende tried to create a socialist society by constitutional means. He increased the wages of industrial workers and nationalized the largest domestic and foreign-owned corporations.

Allende's policies were not popular with everyone. Nationalization of the copper industry, Chile's major source of export income, angered the copper companies' American owners, as well as the American government. Wealthy landholders were angry when radical workers began to take control of their estates and the government did nothing to stop these takeovers.

In March 1973, new elections increased the number of Allende's supporters in the Chilean congress. Afraid of Allende's growing strength, the Chilean army, under the direction of General **Augusto Pinochet** (PEE•noh•CHEHT), moved to overthrow the government. In September 1973, military forces seized the presidential palace, resulting in Allende's death. The military then set up a dictatorship.

The Pinochet regime was one of the most brutal in Chile's history. Thousands of opponents were imprisoned. Thousands more were tortured and murdered. The regime also outlawed all political parties and did away with the congress. While some estates and industries were returned to their owners, the copper industries remained in government hands.

The regime's horrible abuses of human rights led to growing unrest in the mid-1980s. In 1989, free presidential elections led to the defeat of Pinochet, and Chile moved toward a more democratic system.

✓ **Reading Check** **Explaining** Why did the armed forces of Chile overthrow the government of Salvador Allende in 1973?

What If...

Salvador Allende had lost the Chilean election?

In 1970, Salvador Allende beat Jorge Alessandri, former president of Chile, by 40,000 votes out of almost 3 million cast in the general election. Since Allende won by a plurality rather than a majority (over 50 percent of the vote), the election was referred to the Chilean National Congress for a final decision. The Congress chose Allende, bringing the Western world its first democratically elected Marxist president.

Consider the Consequences What if Alessandri had been reelected to continue his regime? Explain why the United States would not have had the same incentives to oppose Alessandri as it had to oppose Allende.

Peru

The history of Peru has been marked by instability. Peru's dependence on the sale abroad of its products has led to extreme ups and downs in the economy. With these ups and downs have come many government changes. A large, poor, and landless peasant population has created an additional source of unrest.

A military takeover in 1968 led to some change. General **Juan Velasco Alvarado** sought to help the peasants. His government seized almost 75 percent of the nation's large landed estates and put ownership of the land into the hands of peasant cooperatives (farm organizations owned by and operated for the peasants' benefit). The government also nationalized many foreign-owned companies and held food prices at low levels to help urban workers.

Economic problems continued, however, and Peruvian military leaders removed General Alvarado from power in 1975. Five years later, unable to cope with Peru's economic problems, the military returned Peru to civilian rule.

New problems made the task of the civilian government even more difficult. A radical Communist guerrilla group based in rural areas, known as Shining Path, killed mayors, missionaries, priests, and peasants. The goal of Shining Path was to smash all authority and create a classless society.

In 1990, Peruvians chose Alberto Fujimori as president. Fujimori, the son of Japanese immigrants, promised reforms. Two years later, he suspended the constitution and congress, became a dictator, and began a campaign against Shining Path guerrillas. Corruption led to his ouster from power in 2000. In June 2001, Alejandro Toledo became Peru's first freely elected president of Native American descent.

✓**Reading Check** **Identifying** How did General Juan Velasco Alvarado earn the support of many Peruvian peasants?

Colombia

Colombia has long had a democratic political system, but a conservative elite led by the owners of coffee plantations has dominated the government.

After World War II, Marxist guerrilla groups began to organize Colombian peasants. The government responded violently. More than two hundred thousand peasants had been killed by the mid-1960s. Violence remained a constant feature of Colombian life in the 1980s and 1990s.

Peasants who lived in poverty turned to a new cash crop—coca leaves, used to make cocaine. The drug trade increased, and so, too, did the number of drug lords. Drug lords formed cartels (groups of drug businesses) that used bribes and violence to force government cooperation in the drug traffic and

Drug lords often use terrorism to threaten those people who try to stop the flow of illegal drugs.

eliminate competitors. Attempts to stop the traffic in drugs had little success, and drug traffickers thrived. Currently, Colombia supplies the majority of cocaine to the international drug market. The government has begun an aerial eradication program.

High unemployment (around 20 percent in 2000) continues to hamper Colombia's economic growth. Colombia's leading exports, coffee and oil, are subject to price fluctuations. However, President Andres Pastrana has a well-respected economic team working to keep the economy on track.

✓**Reading Check** **Explaining** Why have some Colombian peasants turned to the production of coca leaves?

🟥**TAKS Practice**

SECTION 3 ASSESSMENT

Checking for Understanding

1. **Define** cooperative, Shining Path.

2. **Identify** Juan Perón, Salvador Allende, Augusto Pinochet, Juan Velasco Alvarado.

3. **Locate** Argentina, Falkland Islands.

4. **Explain** why the Argentine military invaded the Falkland Islands. What was the impact of this invasion on the government of Argentina?

5. **List** the obstacles Brazil's new democratic government faced in 1985. How did economic conditions help this democratic government come to power?

Critical Thinking

6. **Analyze** Why is it often easier for the military to seize power in a nation than it is for the military to rule that nation effectively? Which countries discussed in this chapter seem to support this theory?

7. **Organizing Information** Use a chart like the one below to show how democracy has advanced in South America since the late 1980s.

How Democracy Advanced

Analyzing Visuals

8. **Examine** the photograph of a Brazilian city shown on page 911 of your text. How does this photograph reflect the problems created by the Brazilian "economic miracle"?

Writing About History

9. **Informative Writing** Pretend you are an American journalist sent to Argentina to cover Perón's presidency. Write an article based on your interviews with the workers and government officials. Include the pros and cons of living under the Perón regime.

TECHNOLOGY
SKILLBUILDER

Developing a Database

Why Learn This Skill?

Do you have an address book with your friends' names; addresses; and phone, fax, pager, and cell numbers? Do you have to cross out information when numbers change? When you have a party, do you address all the invitations by hand? If your address book were stored in a computer, you could find a name instantly. You could update your address book easily and use the computer to print out invitations and envelopes.

When you collect information in a computer file, the file is called an electronic database. The database can contain any kind of information: lists detailing your CD collection; notes for a research paper; your daily expenses. Using an electronic database can help you locate information quickly and organize and manage it, no matter how large the file.

Learning the Skill

An electronic database is a collection of facts that is stored in a file on the computer. Although you can build your own database, there is special software—called a database management system (DBMS)—that makes it easy to add, delete, change, or update information. Some popular commercial DBMS programs allow you to create address books, note cards, financial reports, family trees, and many other types of records.

A database can be organized and reorganized in any way that is useful to you.

- The DBMS software program will usually give clear instructions about entering and arranging your information.

- The information in a database is organized into different fields. For example, in an address book, one field might be your friends' names and another could be their addresses.

- When you retrieve information, the computer will search through the files and display the information on the screen. Often it can be organized and displayed in a variety of ways, depending on what you want.

Fidel Castro with farmers

Practicing the Skill

Fidel Castro is one of the Latin American leaders discussed in this chapter. Follow these steps to build a database of the political events that have taken place during his years as Cuba's leader.

1. Determine what facts you want to include in your database.

2. Follow the instructions in the DBMS that you are using to set up fields.

3. Determine how you want to organize the facts in the database—chronologically by the date of the event, or alphabetically by the name of the event.

4. Follow the instructions in your computer program to place the information in order of importance.

Applying the Skill

Research and build a database that organizes information about current political events in Latin American countries. Explain to a partner why the database is organized the way it is and how it might be used in this class.

CHAPTER 29 ASSESSMENT and ACTIVITIES

Using Key Terms

1. Corporations with headquarters in several countries are called _____.
2. The anti-Communist forces that fought the Sandinistas in Nicaragua were called _____.
3. A style of literature that combines elements of the real world with imaginary events is called _____.
4. Selling government-owned companies to individuals or to corporations is called _____.
5. The refusal to import or export goods to or from another country is a _____.
6. The Communist guerrilla movement in Peru is called the _____.
7. Farms owned and operated by groups of peasants are called _____.

Reviewing Key Facts

8. **History** What is the purpose of the Organization of American States?
9. **Economics** What did Fidel Castro do in 1960 that probably contributed to the decision of the United States to sponsor an invasion of Cuba at the Bay of Pigs in 1961?
10. **Culture** Who is considered the most famous of the Latin American novelists?

11. **History** How was the U.S. involved in El Salvador?
12. **History** What happened that ended Manuel Noriega's control of Panama in 1989?
13. **Government** Why was President Carter unwilling to continue support of the Somoza family?
14. **Government** What was the goal of the guerrilla group known as Shining Path?
15. **Economics** What effect does the wide gap between the rich and the poor have in Latin American countries?
16. **Government** Why was Castro able to maintain control of Cuba even after he lost his foreign support?

Critical Thinking

17. **Compare and Contrast** Compare the policies of the United States toward Latin American countries to those of the Soviet Union toward countries in Eastern Europe.
18. **Drawing Inferences** Analyze why the United States used its military power to arrest Manuel Noriega after ignoring many other dishonest and corrupt leaders in Latin America.

Writing about History

19. **Expository Writing** Analyze how Cuba's revolution affected the United States and the Soviet Union. Explain the background and context of the revolution. How were these events particular to the time period?

Chapter Summary

Several Latin American countries have moved from conflict to cooperation.

Country	Conflict	Revolution	Change	Cooperation
Cuba	Corruption and canceled elections create unrest.	Castro ousts Batista.	Castro improves social welfare system but suspends elections.	Castro allows limited foreign investment, improving relations with Canada and other countries.
Nicaragua	Repressive Somoza regime owns a quarter of the country's land.	Social movement led by Sandinistas overthrows Somoza in 1979.	Sandinistas initiate social reforms but are hampered by contras.	Sandinista regime agrees to hold free elections in 1990; Chamorro is elected president.
Mexico	PRI dominates.	University students protest government policies.	PRI allows new political parties and more freedoms.	Mexico elects non-PRI candidate as president.
Argentina	Economy is poor.	Argentine military overthrows Perón.	Economy recovers; many citizens lose lives to death squads.	Democracy is gradually restored after Falkland Islands disaster.
El Salvador	Elites control most wealth and land.	Leftist guerrillas and right-wing groups battle.	U.N.-sponsored peace agreement ends civil war in 1992.	Economy grows; ties with neighbors are renewed.

HISTORY Online

Self-Check Quiz

Visit the *Glencoe World History* Web site at tx.wh.glencoe.com and click on **Chapter 29 Self-Check Quiz** to prepare for the Chapter Test.

Analyzing Sources

Read the following excerpt from Nancy Donovan, a Catholic missionary in Nicaragua:

> ❝It is not easy to live in a war zone. The least of it was my being kidnapped by contras early this year. The hardest part is seeing people die and consoling families. . . . In those eight hours I was held, as I walked in a column of 60 or so men and a few women—all in uniform—I could hear shooting and realized that people I knew were being killed. Earlier I had seen bodies brought back to town, some burned, some cut to pieces.❞

20. Why did the United States finance the contras?

21. What role do you think the United States should play in Central America? Should the United States have supported rebels capable of the type of warfare described in this passage?

Applying Technology Skills

22. **Create a Database** Research the major political events in South America since 1945. Include the following information in your database:
    - Year
    - Country
    - Event

Making Decisions

23. Identify one of the challenges faced by the countries of Latin America today. Create a poster that illustrates the issue you have selected. Include a clear statement of the issue, information you have gathered about the background of the challenge, and key individuals or countries involved with the issue. Identify options, predict consequences, and offer possible solutions.

Analyzing Maps and Charts

Using the map above, answer the following questions:

24. Which South American country has the largest geographic area? Which countries have the largest populations?

NATIONAL GEOGRAPHIC

Population of Latin America, 2000

Population:
- Under 15 million
- 15–30 million
- 30–100 million
- Over 100 million

25. How do the populations of Central American countries compare to the populations of other Latin American countries?

26. Which South American countries are landlocked? Between what degrees of latitude and longitude are they located?

The Princeton Review

TAKS Test Practice

Directions: Choose the best answer to the following question.

Why are Latin American countries economically important to the United States?

A American banks need countries such as Brazil and Mexico to default on their loans.

B Latin American countries are popular destinations for American tourists.

C Latin American countries are colonies of European nations.

D America imports raw goods such as oil, coffee, and copper from Mexico, El Salvador, Colombia, and Chile.

Test-Taking Tip: Read test questions carefully because every word is important. This question asks why Latin America is *economically* important. Therefore, you can eliminate any answer choices that do not offer explanations about their economic importance.

Africa and the Middle East

1945–Present

Key Events

As you read this chapter, look for the key events in the development of Africa and the Middle East.
* *From the 1950s to the 1970s, most African nations gained independence from colonial powers.*
* *Israel declared statehood on May 14, 1948, creating conflict and struggle between the new state and its neighbors.*

The Impact Today

The events that occurred during this time period still impact our lives today.
* *Many African nations struggle with political and economic instability.*
* *The United States continues to work with the Israelis and Palestinians to find a peaceful solution to their territorial disputes.*

 World History Video *The Chapter 30 video, "Apartheid," chronicles segregation and its demise in South Africa.*

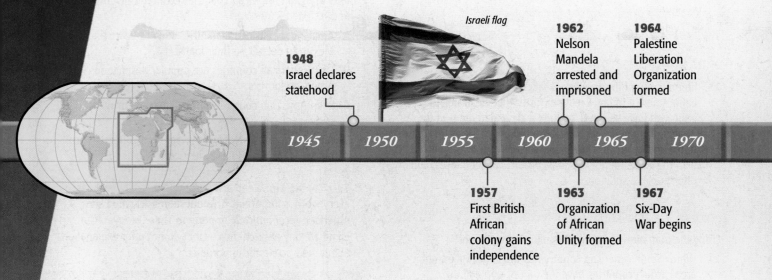

Israeli flag

1948 Israel declares statehood

1962 Nelson Mandela arrested and imprisoned

1964 Palestine Liberation Organization formed

1945   1950   1955   1960   1965   1970

1957 First British African colony gains independence

1963 Organization of African Unity formed

1967 Six-Day War begins

Kwame Nkrumah celebrates independence. Ghana gained its independence from Great Britain in 1957.

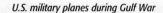

U.S. military planes during Gulf War

1990
Iraqi attack on
Kuwait leads to
Persian Gulf crisis

| 1975 | 1980 | 1985 | 1990 | 1995 | 2000 |

1979
Israel and Egypt
sign the Camp
David Accords

1984
Desmond Tutu
wins Nobel
Peace Prize

1994
Nelson Mandela
becomes South
Africa's first black
president

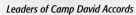

Leaders of Camp David Accords

*Inauguration of
Nelson Mandela*

HISTORY
Online

Chapter Overview
Visit the *Glencoe World
History* Web site at
tx.wh.glencoe.com and click
on **Chapter 30–Chapter
Overview** to preview
chapter information.

A Story That Matters

Mohammad Reza Pahlavi

Anti-American protesters in Iran

Revolution in Iran

*I*n the 1970s, many Iranians began to grow dissatisfied with their ruler, Mohammad Reza Pahlavi, the shah of Iran. An opposition movement, led by the Muslim clergy under the guidance of the Ayatollah Ruhollah Khomeini, grew in strength. (An ayatollah is a major religious leader. The word means "the sign of God.")

One observer described a political rally in the capital city of Tehran in 1978: "On Sunday, December 11, hundreds of thousands of people held a procession in the center of Tehran. . . . Slogans against the shah rippled in the wind—'Death to the Shah!' 'Death to the Americans!' 'Khomeini is our leader,' and so on. People from all walks of life could be found in the crowd."

In January 1979, the shah left Iran, officially for a "period of rest and holiday." Three weeks later, the Ayatollah Khomeini returned to Iran from exile in Paris. On April 1, his forces seized control and proclaimed Iran to be an Islamic republic. Included in the new government's program was an attack on the United States, viewed by Khomeini as the "Great Satan."

On November 4, after the shah had gone to the United States for medical treatment, Iranian revolutionaries seized the United States Embassy in Tehran, taking 52 Americans hostage. Not until the inauguration of a new American president, Ronald Reagan, in January 1981 did the Iranians free their American captives.

Why It Matters

These revolutionary events in Iran are examples of the upheavals that changed both Africa and the Middle East after 1945. In both these areas of the world, Europeans were forced to give up their control and allow independent states to emerge. The change from colony to free nation was not easy. In Africa, the legacy of colonialism left arbitrary boundaries, political inexperience, and continued European economic domination. In the Middle East, ethnic and religious disputes persist.

History and You The Arab-Israeli war is not one war but a continual series of struggles. Using your textbook and outside resources, make a time line of the conflict. Choose three points on your time line to highlight, then describe the events that led to those specific episodes.

Independence in Africa

Guide to Reading

Main Ideas
- People hoped that independence would bring democratic governments, but many African nations fell victim to military regimes and one-party states.
- Culturally and economically, African nations struggled to resolve the tension between the modern and the traditional.

Key Terms
apartheid, Pan-Africanism

People to Identify
Kwame Nkrumah, Nelson Mandela, Julius Nyerere, Desmond Tutu, Chinua Achebe

Places to Locate
South Africa, Kenya, Liberia, Nigeria

Preview Questions
1. What economic problems did independent African nations face?
2. How have social tensions impacted African culture?

Reading Strategy
Categorizing Information As you read this section, complete a chart like the one below identifying the problems in Africa during its first stages of independence.

Africa	
Economic	
Social	
Political	

Preview of Events

♦1960   ♦1962   ♦1964   ♦1966   ♦1968   ♦1970   ♦1972

1960
Blacks massacred in Sharpeville

1962
Arrest of ANC leader Nelson Mandela

1963
Organization of African Unity forms

1967
Civil war in Nigeria

1971
Idi Amin seizes control of Uganda

Voices from the Past

Demonstration against white rule

On March 21, 1960, Humphrey Taylor, a reporter, described a peaceful march by black South Africans against white rule:

❝We went into Sharpeville the back way, around lunch time last Monday, driving along behind a big grey police car and three armoured cars. As we went through the fringes of the township many people were shouting the Pan-Africanist slogan 'Our Land.' They were grinning and cheerful. . . . Then the shooting started. We heard the chatter of a machine gun, then another, then another. . . . One woman was hit about ten yards from our car. . . . Hundreds of kids were running, too. Some of the children, hardly as tall as the grass, were leaping like rabbits. Some of them were shot, too.❞
— *The Mammoth Book of Eyewitness History 2000*, Jon E. Lewis, 2000

The Sharpeville massacre was a stunning example of the white government's oppression of the black majority in South Africa.

The Transition to Independence

European rule had been imposed on nearly all of Africa by 1900. However, after World War II, Europeans realized that colonial rule in Africa would have to end. When both Great Britain and France decided to let go of their colonial empires in the late 1950s and 1960s, most black African nations achieved their independence.

In 1957, the Gold Coast, renamed Ghana and under the guidance of **Kwame Nkrumah,** was the first former British colony to gain independence. Nigeria, the Belgian Congo (renamed Zaire, now the Democratic Republic of Congo), Kenya, and others soon followed. Seventeen new African nations emerged in 1960.

Another 11 nations followed between 1961 and 1965. After a series of brutal guerrilla wars, the Portuguese finally surrendered their colonies of Mozambique and Angola in the 1970s.

In North Africa, the French granted full independence to Morocco and Tunisia in 1956. Because Algeria was home to one million French settlers, France chose to keep control there. Meanwhile, however, Algerian nationalists had organized the National Liberation Front (FLN) and in 1954 initiated a guerrilla war to liberate their homeland. The French leader, Charles de Gaulle, granted Algeria its independence in 1962.

In **South Africa,** where the political system was dominated by whites, the process was more complicated. Political activity on the part of blacks had begun with the formation of the African National Congress (ANC) in 1912. Its goal was economic and political reform. The ANC's efforts, however, met with little success.

At the same time, by the 1950s, South African whites (descendants of the Dutch, known as Afrikaners) had strengthened the laws separating whites and blacks. The result was a system of racial segregation known as apartheid ("apartness").

Blacks demonstrated against the apartheid laws, but the white government brutally repressed the demonstrators. In 1960, police opened fire on people who were leading a peaceful march in Sharpeville, killing 69, two-thirds of whom were shot in the back. After the arrest of ANC leader **Nelson Mandela** in 1962, members of the ANC called for armed resistance to the white government.

✓**Reading Check** **Describing** How did Algeria gain independence from France?

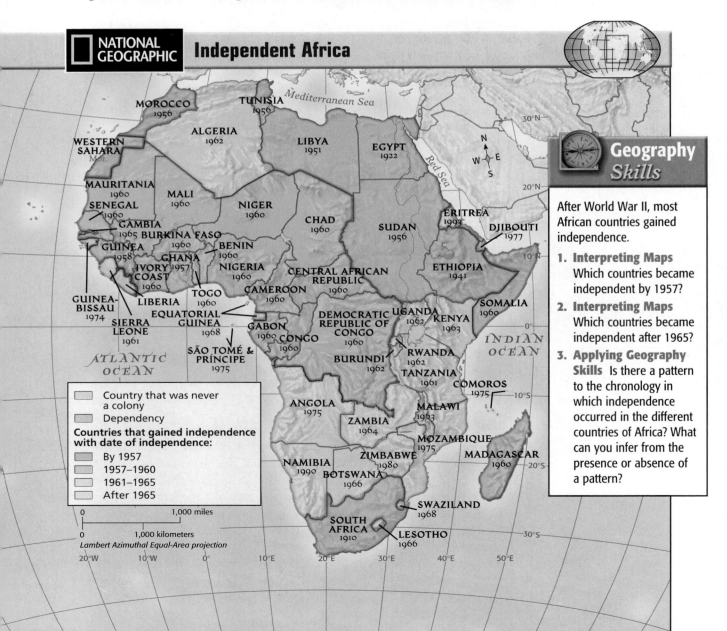

NATIONAL GEOGRAPHIC Independent Africa

Country that was never a colony
Dependency

Countries that gained independence with date of independence:
By 1957
1957–1960
1961–1965
After 1965

0   1,000 miles
0   1,000 kilometers
Lambert Azimuthal Equal-Area projection

Geography Skills

After World War II, most African countries gained independence.

1. **Interpreting Maps** Which countries became independent by 1957?

2. **Interpreting Maps** Which countries became independent after 1965?

3. **Applying Geography Skills** Is there a pattern to the chronology in which independence occurred in the different countries of Africa? What can you infer from the presence or absence of a pattern?

The New Nations

The African states that achieved independence in the 1950s, 1960s, and 1970s still faced many problems. The leaders of these states, as well as their citizens, dreamed of stable governments and economic prosperity. Many of these dreams have yet to be realized.

New African Leaders Most of the leaders of the newly independent African states came from the urban middle class and had studied in either Europe or the United States. They spoke and read European languages and believed in using the Western democratic model in Africa.

The views of these African leaders on economics were somewhat more diverse. Some, such as Jomo Kenyatta of **Kenya** and General Mobutu Sese Seko of the present-day Democratic Republic of Congo, believed in Western-style capitalism. Others, such as **Julius Nyerere** of Tanzania, Kwame Nkrumah of Ghana, and Sékou Touré of Guinea, preferred an "African form of socialism."

The African form of socialism was not like that practiced in the Soviet Union or Eastern Europe. Instead, it was based on African traditions of community in which ownership of the country's wealth would be put into the hands of the people. As Nyerere declared in 1967, "The basis of socialism is a belief in the oneness of man and the common historical destiny of mankind. Its basis . . . is human equality."

Some African leaders believed in the dream of Pan-Africanism—the unity of all black Africans, regardless of national boundaries. In the view of Pan-Africanists, all black African peoples shared a common identity. Pan-Africanism was supported by several of the new African leaders, including Léopold Senghor of Senegal, Kwame Nkrumah, and Jomo Kenyatta.

Nkrumah in particular hoped that a Pan-African union would join all of the new countries of the continent in a broader community. Although his dream never became a reality, the Organization of African Unity (OAU), founded by the leaders of 32 African states in 1963, was a concrete result of the belief in Pan-Africanism. In 2002 the African Union (AU) replaced the OAU. The new 53-nation group aims to promote democracy and economic growth in the region.

Economic Problems Independence did not bring economic prosperity to the new African nations. Most still relied on the export of a single crop or natural resource. **Liberia,** for example, depended on the

---

People In History

Nelson Mandela
1918–
South African leader

Nelson Mandela was the first black president of South Africa. Mandela was trained to be a leader of the Thembu people, and, later, he received a Western education.

In 1952, Mandela became one of the leaders of the African National Congress (ANC). The ANC at first advocated a policy of passive resistance to white rule in South Africa. Later, it supported more violent methods. The result was a sentence of life imprisonment for Mandela.

During his stay in prison, Mandela's reputation grew throughout Africa and the world. Finally, the South African government released Mandela and agreed to hold free elections. In 1994, he became president.

Desmond Tutu
1931–
South African activist

Head of the Anglican Church in South Africa, Archbishop Desmond Tutu became a leader of the nonviolent movement against apartheid. Raised in Johannesburg, he studied theology and was ordained an Anglican priest in 1961. He rose quickly through the ranks and became an archbishop and head of the Anglican Church in South Africa in 1986. As a passionate believer in nonviolence, he supported a policy of economic sanctions against his own country in order to break the system of apartheid peacefully. He wrote: "If we cannot consider all peaceful means then people are in effect saying that there are no peaceful means." For his efforts, he was awarded the Nobel Peace Prize in 1984.

export of rubber; **Nigeria,** on oil. When prices dropped, their economies suffered. To make matters worse, most African states had to import technology and manufactured goods from the West.

The new states also sometimes created their own problems. Scarce national resources were spent on military equipment or expensive consumer goods rather than on building the foundations for an industrial economy. In addition, corruption and bribery became common.

Population growth also crippled efforts to create modern economies. By the 1980s, population growth averaged nearly 3 percent throughout Africa, the highest rate of any continent.

Drought conditions led to widespread hunger and starvation, first in West African countries such as Niger and Mali and then in Ethiopia, Somalia, and the Sudan. Millions fled to neighboring countries in search of food.

In recent years, the spread of acquired immunodeficiency syndrome (AIDS) in Africa has reached epidemic proportions. According to one estimate, about eight percent of the adult population of sub-Saharan Africa is infected with the AIDS virus.

As a result of all these problems, poverty is widespread in Africa, especially among the three-quarters of the population still living off the land. Cities have grown tremendously and are often surrounded by massive slums populated by rural people who came to the cities looking for employment. The growth of the cities has overwhelmed sanitation and transportation systems. Pollution and perpetual traffic jams are the result.

Millions live without water and electricity in their homes. In the meantime, the fortunate few enjoy lavish lifestyles. The rich in many East African countries are known as the *wabenzi,* or Mercedes-Benz people.

Political Challenges Many people had hoped that independence would lead to stable political order based on "one person, one vote." They were soon disappointed as democratic governments gave way to military regimes and one-party states. Between 1957 and 1982, over 70 leaders of African countries were overthrown by violence. In 1984, 34 of the 41 major African states were under single-party regimes or were ruled by the military.

Within many African nations, the concept of nationhood was undermined by warring ethnic groups. This is not surprising, since the boundaries of African nations had generally been arbitrarily drawn by colonial powers. Virtually all of these states included widely different ethnic, linguistic, and territorial groups.

During the late 1960s, civil war tore Nigeria apart. When northerners began to kill the Ibo people, thousands of Ibo fled to their home region in the eastern part of Nigeria. There, Lieutenant Colonel Odumegu Ojukwu organized the Ibo in a rebellion and declared the eastern region of Nigeria an independent state

Picturing **History**

This shantytown is in Cape Town, South Africa. Tremendous urban growth has led to the rise of slums outside many African cities. What factors contribute to the spread of poverty in Africa?

called Biafra. After two and a half years of bloody civil war, Biafra finally surrendered and accepted the authority of the central government of Nigeria.

Conflicts also broke out among ethnic groups in Zimbabwe. In central Africa, fighting between the Hutu and Tutsi created unstable governments in both Burundi and Rwanda. In 1994, a Hutu rampage left some five hundred thousand Tutsi dead in Rwanda.

✓ **Reading Check** **Explaining** Why was the Organization of African Unity formed?

New Hopes

TURNING POINT **As you will learn, worldwide pressure on the South African government led to the end of apartheid and the election of that country's first black president in 1994.**

Not all the news in Africa has been bad. In recent years, popular demonstrations have led to the collapse of one-party regimes and the emergence of democracies in several countries. One case was that of Idi Amin of Uganda. After ruling by terror and brutal repression throughout the 1970s, Amin was deposed in 1979. Dictatorships also came to an end in Ethiopia, Liberia, and Somalia. In these cases, however, the fall of the regime was later followed by bloody civil war.

One of the most remarkable events of recent African history was the election of Nelson Mandela to the presidency of the Republic of South Africa.

Mandela had been sentenced to life imprisonment in 1962 for his activities with the African National Congress. He spent almost 26 years of his life in maximum-security prisons in South Africa. For all those years, Mandela never wavered from his determination to secure the liberation of his country. In January 1985, he was offered his freedom, given certain conditions, from then President Botha. At this point, Mandela had served over 20 years of a life sentence and had passed his 66th birthday. Yet, he refused to accept a conditional freedom: "Only free men can negotiate; prisoners cannot enter into contracts. Your freedom and mine cannot be separated." Over the years, Nobel Peace prize winner (1984) Bishop **Desmond Tutu** and others worked to free him and to end apartheid in South Africa. Worldwide pressure on the white South African government led to reforms and the gradual dismantling of apartheid laws. In 1990, Mandela was finally released from prison.

In 1993, the government of President F. W. de Klerk agreed to hold democratic national elections—the first in South Africa's history. In 1994, Nelson Mandela became South Africa's first black president. In his presidential inaugural address, he expressed his hopes for unity: "We shall build a

society in which all South Africans, both black and white, will be able to walk tall, without any fear in their hearts, assured of their inalienable right to human dignity—a rainbow nation at peace with itself and the world." 📖 *(See page 1001 to read excerpts from Nelson Mandela's* An Ideal for Which I am Prepared to Die *in The Primary Sources Library.)*

✔️ **Reading Check** **Identifying** Which African countries overthrew dictatorships?

Society and Culture in Modern Africa

Africa is a study in contrasts. Old and new, native and foreign live side by side. One result is a constant tension between traditional ways and Western culture.

City and Countryside
In general, the impact of the West has been greater in the cities than in the countryside. After all, the colonial presence was first and most firmly established in the cities. Many cities, including Dakar, Lagos, Cape Town, Brazzaville, and Nairobi, are direct products of colonial rule. Most African cities today look like cities elsewhere in the world. They have high-rise apartments, wide boulevards, neon lights, movie theaters, and, of course, traffic jams.

Outside the major cities, where about three-quarters of the inhabitants of Africa live, modern influence has had less of an impact. Millions of people throughout Africa live much as their ancestors did, in thatched dwellings without modern plumbing and electricity. They farm, hunt, or raise livestock by traditional methods, wear traditional clothing, and practice traditional beliefs. Conditions such as drought or flooding affect the ability of rural Africans to grow crops or tend herds. Migration to the cities for work is one solution. This can be very disruptive to families and villages. Many urban people view rural people as backward. Rural dwellers view the cities as corrupting and destructive to traditional African values and customs.

Women's Roles
Independence from colonial powers had a significant impact on women's roles in African society. Almost without exception women were allowed to vote and run for political office. Few women hold political offices. Although women dominate some professions, such as teaching, child care, and clerical work, they do not have the range of career opportunities available to men. Most African women are employed in low-paid positions such as farm laborers, factory workers, and servants. Furthermore, in many rural areas, traditional attitudes toward women, including arranged marriages, still prevail.

▲ *Modern office buildings and contemporary art in Pretoria, South Africa, demonstrate the Westernization of Africa's cities.*

Picturing **History**

The contrast between modern and traditional lifestyles often creates tension in African society. About what percentage of the African people live in cities?

▲ *Tea pickers on a plantation in Kenya*

African Culture The tension between traditional and modern and between native and foreign also affects African culture. Africans have kept their native artistic traditions while adapting them to foreign influences. A dilemma for many contemporary African artists is the need to find a balance between Western techniques and training on the one hand, and the rich heritage of traditional African art forms on the other.

In some countries, governments make the artists' decisions for them. Artists are told to depict scenes of traditional African life. These works are designed to serve the tourist industry.

African writers have often addressed the tensions and dilemmas that modern Africans face. The conflicting demands of town versus country and native versus foreign were the themes of most of the best-known works of the 1960s and 1970s.

These themes certainly characterize the work of **Chinua Achebe,** a Nigerian novelist who has won international acclaim. Achebe's four novels show the problems of Africans caught up in the conflict between traditional and Western values. Most famous of Achebe's four novels is *Things Fall Apart,* in which the author portrays the simple dignity of traditional African village life.

✓ **Reading Check** **Summarizing** What themes are characterized in the work of Chinua Achebe?

Picturing **History**

A Nigerian craftsman is in the process of carving a wooden drum. How do you think tourism has affected traditional African art forms?

🌟 **TAKS Practice**

SECTION 1 ASSESSMENT

Checking for Understanding

1. **Define** apartheid, Pan-Africanism.

2. **Identify** Kwame Nkrumah, Nelson Mandela, Julius Nyerere, Desmond Tutu, Chinua Achebe.

3. **Locate** South Africa, Kenya, Liberia, Nigeria.

4. **Explain** how population growth has crippled the efforts of African nations to create stable, modern economies. Identify at least two other recent obstacles to an improved economy.

5. **Describe** the relationship between the Hutu and the Tutsi. Identify other nations in the news today with ethnic or religious conflict.

Critical Thinking

6. **Explain** Why was the idea of Pan-Africanism never realized?

7. **Organizing Information** Create a chart comparing the characteristics of the modern African city and rural areas.

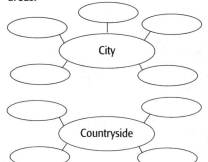

Analyzing Visuals

8. **Examine** the photograph of Kwame Nkrumah shown on page 919 of your text. How does this photograph reflect the pride that Kwame Nkrumah and his companions feel about Ghana's newly won independence? Use specific visual evidence from the photograph to support your answer.

Writing About History

9. **Persuasive Writing** Assume the role of an African leader of a newly independent nation. Write a speech to your citizens in which you explain Pan-Africanism and convince them that Pan-Africanism will benefit both the nation and the people.

SOCIAL STUDIES
SKILLBUILDER

Interpreting Statistics

Why Learn This Skill?

A news report comes out that statistical evidence from a recent scientific study proves that chocolate can prevent cancer. The next day, a doctor is interviewed saying that the statistics are misleading. What are you to believe?

Statistics are used to support a claim or an opinion. They can be used to support opposing sides of an issue. To avoid being misled, it is important to understand how to interpret statistics.

Learning the Skill

Statistics are sets of tabulated information that may be gathered through surveys and other sources. When studying statistics, consider each of the following:

- **Biased sample** The sample may affect the results. A sample that does not represent the entire population is called a biased sample. An unbiased sample is called a representative sample.

- **Correlation** Two sets of data may be related or unrelated. If they are related, we say that there is a correlation between them. For example, there is a positive correlation between academic achievement and wages. There is a negative correlation, however, between smoking and life expectancy.

- **Statistical Significance** Researchers determine whether the data support a generalization or whether the results are due to chance. If the probability that the results were due to chance is less than 5 percent, researchers say that the result is statistically significant.

Practicing the Skill

The table at the top of the next column rates countries according to economic freedom, that is the fewest restrictions on trade, property rights, and monetary policies. The scores are on a scale from 1 to 5, with 1 being the greatest economic freedom. Study the table. Then answer the questions that follow.

2001 Index of Economic Freedom

Nation (rank)	Trade	Gov't Intervention	Wages/Prices	Overall Score
Hong Kong (1)	1.0	2.0	2.0	1.30
United States (5)	2.0	2.0	2.0	1.75
United Arab Emirates (14)	2.0	3.0	3.0	2.05
Israel (54)	2.0	3.5	2.0	2.75
Lebanon (59)	3.0	3.0	2.0	2.85
Botswana (68)	3.0	4.0	2.0	2.95
Cameroon (90)	4.0	2.0	3.0	3.20
Syria (141)	5.0	3.0	4.0	4.00
Zimbabwe (146)	5.0	2.5	4.0	4.25

Source: The Heritage Foundation.

❶ Which category or categories show a positive correlation with economic freedom?

❷ Which category or categories show a negative correlation with economic freedom?

Applying the Skill

Create a two-question survey that will generate answers that can be correlated. For example, ask: "How many hours of television do you watch per day?" and "How many hours of homework do you do per day?" Gather responses, then develop a correlation between the topics addressed by the two questions.

GO TO

Glencoe's **Skillbuilder Interactive Workbook, Level 2,** provides instruction and practice in key social studies skills.

SECTION 2 Conflict in the Middle East

Guide to Reading

Main Ideas
- Instability in various parts of the Middle East has led to armed conflict and mediation attempts from countries outside the region.
- In many Middle Eastern countries, an Islamic revival has influenced political and social life.

Key Terms
Pan-Arabism, *intifada*

People to Identify
Gamal Abdel Nasser, Anwar el-Sadat, Yasir Arafat, Ayatollah Ruhollah Khomeini, Saddam Hussein, Naguib Mahfouz

Places to Locate
Israel, Egypt, Sinai Peninsula, West Bank, Iran, Iraq, Kuwait, Persian Gulf

Preview Questions
1. How was the state of Israel created?
2. How did the Islamic revival affect Middle Eastern Society?

Reading Strategy
Categorizing Information As you read this section, fill in the important events in the history of Arab-Israeli conflicts.

YEAR	EVENT

Preview of Events

♦1955	♦1960	♦1965	♦1970	♦1975	♦1980	♦1985

1956
Suez War begins

1964
PLO is founded

1979
Khomeini seizes control of Iran

1981
Iran frees American hostages

Voices from the Past

David Ben-Gurion

On May 14, 1948, David Ben-Gurion stood in Museum Hall in Tel Aviv and announced to the people assembled there:

❝The land of Israel was the birthplace of the Jewish people. Here their spiritual, religious and national identity was formed. In their exile from the land of Israel the Jews remained faithful to it in all the countries of their dispersal, never ceasing to hope and pray for the restoration of their national freedom. Therefore by virtue of the natural and historic right of the Jewish people to be a nation as other nations, and of the Resolution of the General Assembly of the United Nations, we hereby proclaim the establishment of the Jewish nation in Palestine, to be called the State of Israel.❞

—Jon E. Lewis, *The Mammoth Book of Eyewitness History,* 2000

The creation of the state of Israel made Arab-Israeli conflict a certainty.

The Question of Palestine

⌐TURNING POINT┐ **As you will learn, in 1948, Palestine was divided into two states: an Arab state and a Jewish state.**

In the Middle East, as in other areas of Asia, World War II led to the emergence of new independent states. Syria and Lebanon gained their independence near the end of World War II. Jordan achieved complete self-rule soon after the war. These new states were predominantly Muslim.

In the years between the two world wars, many Jews had immigrated to Palestine, believing this area to be their promised land. Tensions between Jews and Arabs had intensified during the 1930s. Great Britain, which governed Palestine under a United Nations (UN) mandate, had limited Jewish immigration into the area and had rejected proposals for an independent Jewish state in Palestine. The Muslim states agreed with this position.

The **Zionists** who wanted Palestine as a home for Jews were not to be denied, however. Many people had been shocked at the end of World War II when they learned about the Holocaust, the deliberate killing of six million European Jews in Nazi death camps. As a result, sympathy for the Jewish cause grew. In 1948, a United Nations resolution divided Palestine into a Jewish state and an Arab state. The Jews in Palestine proclaimed the state of **Israel** on May 14, 1948.

Its Arab neighbors saw the new state as a betrayal of the Palestinian people, most of whom were Muslim. Outraged, several Arab countries invaded the new Jewish state. The invasion failed, but the Arab states still refused to recognize Israel's right to exist.

As a result of the division of Palestine, hundreds of thousands of Palestinians fled to neighboring Arab countries, where they lived in refugee camps. Other Palestinians came under Israeli rule. The issue of a homeland and self-governance for the Palestinians remains a problem today.

✔**Reading Check** **Identifying** Why was there international support for Palestine to serve as a home for Jews?

Nasser and Pan-Arabism

In **Egypt,** a new leader arose who would play an important role in the Arab world. Colonel **Gamal Abdel Nasser** took control of the Egyptian government in the early 1950s. On July 26, 1956, Nasser seized the Suez Canal Company, which had been under British and French administration.

Concerned over this threat to their route to the Indian Ocean, Great Britain and France decided to strike back. They were quickly joined by Israel. The forces of the three nations launched a joint attack on Egypt, starting the Suez War of 1956. The United States and the Soviet Union supported Nasser and forced Britain, France, and Israel to withdraw their troops

CONNECTIONS Around The World

Global Migrations

Since 1945, tens of millions of people have migrated from one part of the world to another. There are many reasons for these migrations. Persecution for political reasons caused many people from Pakistan, Bangladesh, Sri Lanka, Eastern Europe, and East Germany to seek refuge in Western European countries. Brutal civil wars in Asia, Africa, the Middle East, and Europe led millions of refugees to seek safety in neighboring countries. A devastating famine in Africa in 1984–1985 drove hundreds of thousands of Africans to relief camps throughout the continent to find food.

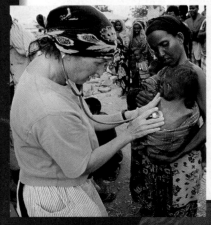

◀ *Mobile clinic in Somalia, Africa*

Most people who have migrated, however, have done so to find jobs. Latin Americans seeking a better life have migrated to the United States. Guest workers from Turkey, southern and Eastern Europe, North Africa, and South Asia have entered more prosperous Western European lands. In the 1980s, about fifteen million guest workers worked and lived in Europe.

Many host countries allowed guest workers to stay for several years. In the 1980s and 1990s, however, foreign workers often became scapegoats when countries faced economic problems. Political parties in France and Norway, for example, called for the removal of blacks and Arabs.

Comparing Cultures

Are there immigrant populations where you live? Describe some of the attitudes your friends and families have toward foreign workers. Think of several reasons why foreign populations have migrated to the United States.

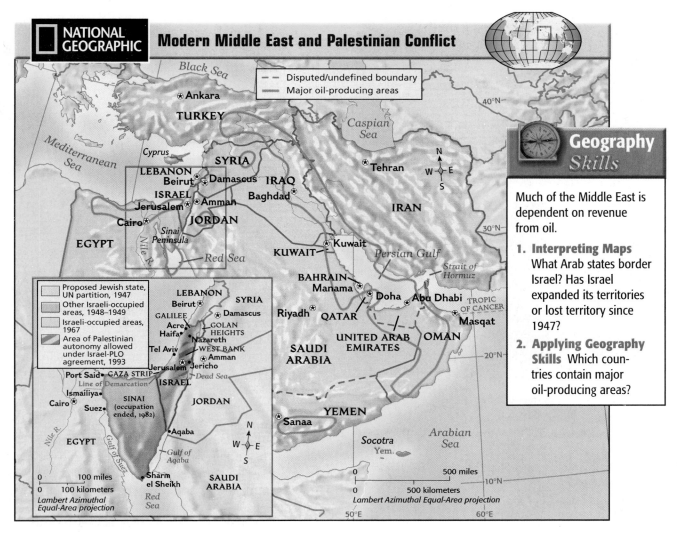

NATIONAL GEOGRAPHIC Modern Middle East and Palestinian Conflict

Disputed/undefined boundary
Major oil-producing areas

Geography Skills

Much of the Middle East is dependent on revenue from oil.

1. **Interpreting Maps** What Arab states border Israel? Has Israel expanded its territories or lost territory since 1947?

2. **Applying Geography Skills** Which countries contain major oil-producing areas?

Proposed Jewish state, UN partition, 1947
Other Israeli-occupied areas, 1948–1949
Israeli-occupied areas, 1967
Area of Palestinian autonomy allowed under Israel-PLO agreement, 1993

Lambert Azimuthal Equal-Area projection

---

from Egypt. These Cold War enemies were opposed to French and British influence in the Middle East.

Nasser emerged from the conflict as a powerful leader. He now began to promote Pan-Arabism, or Arab unity. In February 1958, Egypt formally united with Syria in the United Arab Republic (UAR). Nasser was named the first president of the new state. Egypt and Syria hoped that the union would eventually include all the Arab states. Many other Arab leaders were suspicious of Pan-Arabism, however. Oil-rich Arab states were concerned they would have to share revenues with poorer states in the Middle East. Indeed, in Nasser's view, Arab unity meant that wealth derived from oil, which currently flowed into a few Arab states or to foreign interests, could be used to improve the standard of living throughout the Middle East.

In 1961, military leaders took over Syria and withdrew the country from its union with Egypt. Nasser continued to work on behalf of Arab interests.

✓ **Reading Check** **Evaluating** Why were France and Great Britain threatened when Nasser seized the Suez Canal?

The Arab-Israeli Dispute

During the late 1950s and 1960s, the dispute between Israel and other states in the Middle East became more heated. In 1967, Nasser imposed a blockade against Israeli shipping through the Gulf of Aqaba. He declared: "Now we are ready to confront Israel. We are ready to deal with the entire Palestine question."

Fearing attack, on June 5, 1967, Israel launched air strikes against Egypt and several of its Arab neighbors. Israeli warplanes wiped out most of the Egyptian air force. Israeli armies broke the blockade and occupied the **Sinai Peninsula.** Israel seized territory on the **West Bank** of the Jordan River, occupied Jerusalem, and took control of the Golan Heights. During this Six-Day War, Israel tripled the size of its territory. Another million Palestinians now lived inside Israel's new borders, most of them on the West Bank.

Over the next few years, Arab states continued to demand the return of the occupied territories. Nasser died in 1970 and was succeeded in office by

Palestinians clash with Israeli soldiers.

Anwar el-Sadat. In 1973, Arab forces led by Sadat launched a new attack against Israel. This conflict was ended in 1974 by a cease-fire agreement negotiated by the UN.

Meanwhile, however, the war was having indirect results in Western nations. A number of Arab oil-producing states had formed the Organization of Petroleum Exporting Countries **(OPEC)** in 1960 to gain control over oil prices. During the 1973 war, some OPEC nations announced large increases in the price of oil to foreign countries. The price hikes, coupled with cuts in oil production, led to oil shortages and serious economic problems in the United States and Europe.

In 1977, U.S. president Jimmy Carter began to press for a compromise peace between Arabs and Israelis. In September 1978, Carter met with President Sadat of Egypt and Israeli Prime Minister Menachem Begin (BAY•gihn) at Camp David in the United States. The result was the Camp David Accords, an agreement to sign an Israeli-Egyptian peace treaty. The treaty, signed by Sadat and Begin in March 1979, ended the state of war between Egypt and Israel. Many Arab countries continued to refuse to recognize Israel, however.

Reading Check **Identifying** What are the Camp David Accords?

The PLO and the *Intifada*

In 1964, the Egyptians took the lead in forming the Palestine Liberation Organization (PLO) to represent the interests of the Palestinians. The PLO believed that only the Palestinian peoples had the right to create a state in Palestine. At the same time, a guerrilla movement called al-Fatah, headed by the PLO political leader **Yasir Arafat,** began to launch terrorist attacks on Israeli territory. Terrorist actions against Israel continued for decades.

Yasir Arafat

During the early 1980s, Palestinian Arabs, frustrated by their failure to achieve self-rule, became even more militant. This militancy led to a movement called the *intifada* ("uprising") among PLO supporters living inside Israel. The *intifada* was marked by protests throughout the nation. A second *intifada* began in September 2000 and continued for over a year.

As the 1990s began, U.S.-sponsored peace talks to address the Palestinian issue opened between Israel and a number of its Arab neighbors. Finally, in 1993, Israel and the PLO reached an agreement calling for Palestinian autonomy in certain areas of Israel. In return, the PLO recognized the Israeli state. Yasir Arafat became the head of the semi-independent area known as the Palestinian Authority. Progress in making this agreement work, however, has been slow.

Reading Check **Summarizing** What were the terms of the agreement reached in 1993?

Revolution in Iran

The leadership of Shah Mohammad Reza Pahlavi and revenue from oil helped **Iran** to become a rich country. Iran was also the chief ally of the United States in the Middle East in the 1950s and 1960s.

However, there was much opposition to the shah in Iran. Millions of devout Muslims looked with distaste at the new Iranian civilization. In their eyes, it was based on greed and materialism, which they identified with American influence.

Leading the opposition to the shah was the **Ayatollah Ruhollah Khomeini** (ko•MAY•nee), a member of the Muslim clergy. By the late 1970s, large numbers of Iranians had begun to respond to

Ayatollah Khomeini

Khomeini's words. In 1979, the shah's government collapsed and was replaced by an Islamic republic.

The new government, led by the Ayatollah Khomeini, moved to restore Islamic law. Supporters of the shah were executed or fled the country. Anti-American sentiments erupted when militants seized 52 Americans in the United States embassy in Tehran and held them hostage for over a year.

After the death of Khomeini in 1989, a new government, under President Hashemi Rafsanjani, began to loosen control over personal expression and social activities. Rising criticism of official corruption and a high rate of inflation, however, sparked a new wave of government repression in the mid-1990s.

✓ **Reading Check** **Summarizing** List the reasons that the shah's government collapsed.

Iraq's Aggression

To the west of Iran was a militant and hostile **Iraq,** under the leadership of **Saddam Hussein** since 1979. Iraq and Iran have long had an uneasy relationship, fueled by religious differences. Both are Muslim nations. The Iranians, however, are largely Shiites, whereas most Iraqi leaders are Sunnis. Iran and Iraq have engaged for years in disputes over territory, especially the Strait of Hormuz, which connects the Persian Gulf and the Gulf of Oman.

In 1980, President Saddam Hussein launched an attack on Iran. Poison gas was used against civilians,

In 1990, Saddam Hussein's troops set many of Kuwait's oil fields on fire as they retreated from the country.

and children were used to clear minefields. A cease-fire was finally arranged in 1988.

In 1990, Iraqi troops moved across the border and occupied the small neighboring country of **Kuwait,** at the head of the **Persian Gulf.** The invasion sparked an international outcry. The United States led an international force that freed Kuwait and destroyed a large part of Iraq's armed forces. The allies hoped that an internal revolt would overthrow Hussein, but he remained in power.

✓ **Reading Check** **Describing** Describe why Iran and Iraq have been in conflict for many years.

Afghanistan and the Taliban

After World War II, the king of Afghanistan, in search of economic assistance for his country, developed close ties with the Soviet Union. In 1973, the king was overthrown by his cousin, who himself was removed during a pro-Soviet coup in 1978. The new leaders attempted to create a Communist government but were opposed by groups who wanted an Islamic state. The Soviets then launched a full-scale invasion of Afghanistan in 1979, installing Babrak Karmal as prime minister.

The Soviets occupied Afghanistan for 10 years but were forced to withdraw by anti-Communist forces supported by the United States and Pakistan. Though a pro-Soviet government was left in the capital at Kabul, various Islamic rebel groups began to fight for control. One of these, the Taliban, seized Kabul in 1996. By the fall of 1998, the Taliban controlled more than two-thirds of the country. Opposing factions controlled northern Afghanistan.

Condemned for its human rights abuses and imposition of harsh social policies, the Taliban was also suspected of sheltering Osama bin Laden and his al-Qaeda organization. In 1999 and 2000, the United Nations Security Council demanded the Taliban hand over bin Laden for trial, but it refused. In 2001, the Taliban was driven out of Kabul by rebel forces and American bombers.

✓ **Reading Check** **Explaining** What was the political situation in Afghanistan in 1996?

Society and Culture

In recent years, conservative religious forces have tried to replace foreign culture and values with Islamic forms of belief and behavior. This movement is called Islamic revivalism or Islamic activism. For most Muslims, the Islamic revival is a reassertion of cultural identity, formal religious observance, family values, and morality.

Islamic Militants Actions of militants have often been fueled by hostility to the culture of the West. In the eyes of some Islamic leaders, Western values and culture are based on materialism, greed, and immorality. The goal of extremists is to remove all Western influence in Muslim countries.

The movement to return to the pure ideals of Islam began in Iran under the Ayatollah Khomeini. In revolutionary Iran, traditional Muslim beliefs reached into clothing styles, social practices, and the legal system. These ideas and practices spread to other Muslim countries. In Egypt, for example, militant Muslims assassinated President Sadat in 1981. Unfortunately for Islam, the extreme and militant movements received much media exposure, giving many people an unfavorable impression of Islam.

Women's Roles At the beginning of the twentieth century, women's place in Middle Eastern society had changed little for hundreds of years. Early Muslim women had participated in the political life of society and had extensive legal, political, and social rights. Cultural practices in many countries had overshadowed those rights, however.

In the nineteenth and twentieth centuries, Muslim scholars debated issues surrounding women's roles in society. Many argued for the need to rethink outdated interpretations and cultural practices that prevented women from realizing their potential. This had an impact on a number of societies, including Turkey and Iran.

Until the 1970s, the general trend in urban areas was toward a greater role for women. Beginning in the 1970s, however, there was a shift toward more traditional roles for women. This trend was especially noticeable in Iran.

Middle Eastern Culture The literature of the Middle East since 1945 has reflected a rise in national awareness, which encouraged interest in historical traditions. Writers also began to deal more with secular themes. Literature is no longer the preserve of the elite but is increasingly written for broader audiences.

The most famous contemporary Egyptian writer is **Naguib Mahfouz.** He was the first writer in Arabic to win the Nobel Prize for literature (in 1988). His *Cairo Trilogy,* published in 1957, is considered the finest writing in Arabic since World War II. The story follows a merchant family in Egypt in the 1920s. The changes in the family parallel the changes in Egypt.

The artists of the Middle East at first tended to imitate Western models. Later, however, they began to experiment with national styles and returned to earlier forms for inspiration.

✓ **Reading Check** **Identifying** Which Arabic writer won the Nobel Prize for literature?

🔺 **TAKS Practice**

SECTION 2 ASSESSMENT

Checking for Understanding

1. **Define** Pan-Arabism, *intifada.*

2. **Identify** Zionists, Gamal Abdel Nasser, Anwar el-Sadat, Yasir Arafat, Ayatollah Ruhollah Khomeini, OPEC, Saddam Hussein, Naguib Mahfouz.

3. **Locate** Israel, Egypt, Sinai Peninsula, West Bank, Iran, Iraq, Kuwait, Persian Gulf.

4. **Explain** the meaning and purpose of OPEC. What control does it have?

5. **Summarize** the events that led to the Six-Day War. What gains and losses resulted from the war?

Critical Thinking

6. **Explain** Why do some people believe it was a mistake for the UN and the United States not to occupy Iraq after the Persian Gulf crisis? What did the Allies hope would happen in Iraq after the Iraqi forces were defeated?

7. **Taking Notes** Organize the information presented in this section in outline form, following the model below.

   I. Palestine
      A. Great Britain limits Jewish immigration.
      B. Zionists want Jewish homeland.
   II. Nasser takes control of Egypt

Analyzing Visuals

8. **Examine** the photograph of Kuwait shown on page 933. Why do you think the Iraqi troops decided to set fire to the oil fields as they retreated from Kuwait? Do you think that they set the fires for military, political, or economic reasons, or for all three?

Writing About History

9. **Persuasive Writing** Choose the role of either an Arab Palestinian or a Jewish settler. Write a letter to the United Nations General Assembly arguing your position on the Palestine issue. What do you think should be done in Palestine and why?

The Suez Canal Belongs to Egypt

THE SUEZ CANAL WAS built between 1859 and 1869, using mainly French money and Egyptian labor. It was managed by a Paris-based corporation called the Suez Canal Company. In this excerpt from a speech, Egyptian president Gamal Abdel Nasser declared that it was time for the canal to be owned and managed by Egyptians.

Freighters in the Suez Canal

66The Suez Canal is an Egyptian canal built as a result of great sacrifices. The Suez Canal Company is an Egyptian company that was expropriated [taken away] from Egypt by the British who, since the canal was dug, have been obtaining the profits of the Company. . . . And yet the Suez Canal Company is an Egyptian limited liability company. The annual Canal revenue is 35 million Egyptian pounds. From this sum Egypt—which lost 120,000 workers in digging the Canal—takes one million pounds from the Company.

It is a shame when the blood of people is sucked, and it is no shame that we should borrow for construction. We will not allow the past to be repeated again, but we will cancel the past by restoring our rights in the Suez Canal. . . .

The Suez Canal Company was a state within a state, depending on the conspiracies of imperialism and its supporters. The Canal was built for the sake of Egypt, but it was a source of exploitation. There is no shame in being poor, but it is a shame to suck blood. Today we restore these rights, and I declare in the name of the Egyptian people that we will protect these rights with our blood and soul. . . .

The people will stand united as one man to resist imperialist acts of treachery. We shall do whatever we like. When we restore all our rights, we shall become stronger and our production will increase. At this moment, some of your brethren, the sons of Egypt, are now taking over the Egyptian Suez Canal and directing it. We have taken this decision to restore part of the glories of the past and to safeguard our national dignity and pride. May God bless you and guide you in the path of righteousness.99

—Nasser's Speech Nationalizing the Suez Canal Company

Analyzing Primary Sources

1. What problem was President Nasser addressing?
2. According to Nasser, why does the Suez Canal rightfully belong to Egypt?

Using Key Terms

1. The former South African policy of separating the races was called _____.

2. The belief in Arab unity has been called _____.

3. The uprising to protest Israeli domination of Palestine was called the _____.

4. The Organization of African Unity was a result of the belief in _____.

Reviewing Key Facts

5. **Government** Why did France grant independence to Morocco and Tunisia in 1956, but not to Algeria?

6. **Government** What was the philosophy behind African socialism?

7. **History** Why was Nelson Mandela imprisoned by the white South African government?

8. **Citizenship** What did Nelson Mandela achieve in 1994?

9. **Government** Why is Desmond Tutu an important international leader?

10. **Economy** Why has Israel allocated a large part of its national production to maintaining highly trained and well-equipped military forces?

11. **Government** Why did Shah Mohammad Reza Pahlavi of Iran lose the support of his people despite rapid growth in Iran's economy and standard of living?

12. **Culture** What problems resulted from the migration of Africans from rural areas into cities?

13. **Culture** How has the literature of the Middle East dealt with traditional versus modern values?

14. **History** How was Israel created and which factors contributed to its founding?

15. **History** What effect did the Six-Day War have on the relationship between Arabs and Israelis?

16. **Government** Name some major accomplishments of Egyptian leader Gamal Abdel Nasser that elevated his status as a leader in the Arab world.

17. **History** How was the concept of nationhood undermined in many African countries?

18. **Economy** How did price increases and production cuts by OPEC nations in 1973 affect the United States and Europe?

19. **History** Give two reasons for the war that broke out in 1980 between Iran and Iraq.

Critical Thinking

20. **Evaluating** Why have English and French been used as official languages of government in many African nations?

21. **Analyzing** Could a lasting peace have been established between Iraq and its neighbors even if UN forces had captured Saddam Hussein? Explain your answer.

22. **Evaluating** Compare the legacy of European colonialism in Africa and the Middle East. Discuss the consequences of colonialism still being felt in these areas.

23. **Analyzing** Why do you think Israel was able to seize so much territory during the Six-Day War?

Writing About History

24. **Expository Writing** Compare and contrast the role of women and their positions and rights in the Middle East and Africa.

Chapter Summary

In the postwar period, Africa and the Middle East faced many challenges that threatened their stability.

	Government	Economy	Society
Africa	• Many new nations are undermined by civil war. • Democracy is threatened by military regimes. • Democratic national elections are held in South Africa.	• Most new nations rely on the export of a single crop or resource. • Population growth cripples efforts to create modern economies. • Poverty is widespread.	• Tension between traditional ways and Western culture continues.
Middle East	• Palestine is divided into two states. • Arab-Israeli dispute results in war and peace treaties. • Israel and PLO reach agreement about autonomy.	• Much of the Middle East is dependent on oil revenue. • OPEC is formed to gain control over oil prices.	• Islamic revival reasserts cultural identity and values over foreign, Western influences.

Self-Check Quiz

Visit the *Glencoe World History* Web site at tx.wh.glencoe.com and click on **Chapter 30–Self-Check Quiz** to prepare for the Chapter Test.

Analyzing Sources

Read the following quote describing a political rally in Tehran in 1978.

> 66On Sunday, December 11, hundreds of thousands of people held a procession in the center of Tehran . . . . Slogans against the shah rippled in the wind—'Death to the Shah!' 'Death to the Americans!' 'Khomeini is our leader,' and so on. People from all walks of life could be found in the crowd.99

25. What is meant by the phrase "people from all walks of life?"

26. Why were the people protesting the shah? Why were anti-American slogans included in the protest? What resulted when the shah left Iran and the Ayatollah Khomeini became the leader? Who are the leaders of Iran today? Does the quote above reflect current sentiments?

Making Decisions

27. Create a new peace accord for Israel and the Palestinians. Why do the Israelis and the Palestinians need a peace accord? What do you need to consider in creating the terms of the agreement? What country would both parties agree to accept as an intermediary to help them settle their problems? What resistance to your accord might you face from either party? How do you get both Israelis and Palestinians to accept the accord? Once it is accepted, how would you enforce this agreement?

28. You have been elected South Africa's first president after the end of apartheid. What challenges will you face now that apartheid is over? How will you try to solve these problems? What are your hopes for South Africa?

Analyzing Maps and Charts

Refer to the map on page 931 of your textbook to answer the following questions.

29. What do you think Iraq hoped to gain by invading the country of Kuwait?

30. How far is Tehran from Baghdad?

31. How important is access to the Persian Gulf and the Strait of Hormuz for oil-producing countries?

Applying Technology Skills

32. Using the Internet Use the Internet to create a bibliography of resource materials about Nelson Mandela and Desmond Tutu. Design a Web page to organize the links.

Directions: Use the time line and your knowledge of world history to answer the following question.

Selected Events in Middle Eastern Politics

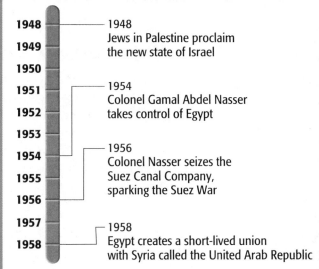

1948	1948 Jews in Palestine proclaim the new state of Israel
1949	
1950	
1951	1954 Colonel Gamal Abdel Nasser takes control of Egypt
1952	
1953	
1954	1956 Colonel Nasser seizes the Suez Canal Company, sparking the Suez War
1955	
1956	
1957	1958 Egypt creates a short-lived union with Syria called the United Arab Republic
1958	

Which of the following events resulted from the events on this time line?

F Shock over the Holocaust helped Jews realize their goals for a homeland.

G Nasser imposed a blockade against Israeli shipping.

H Iraq launched an attack on its enemy, Iran.

J The Balfour Declaration gave support to Zionist Jews.

Test-Taking Tip: Time lines show chronology, or the order in which events happened. You can use your knowledge of chronology to get rid of incorrect answer choices. Think about what events happened *before* this time line begins. Those answer choices must be wrong.

CHAPTER 31

Asia and the Pacific

1945–Present

Key Events

As you read, look for the key events in the history of postwar Asia.
- Communists in China introduced socialist measures and drastic reforms under the leadership of Mao Zedong.
- After World War II, India gained its independence from Britain and divided into two separate countries — India and Pakistan.
- Japan modernized its economy and society after 1945 and became one of the world's economic giants.

The Impact Today

The events that occurred during this time period still impact our lives today.
- Today China and Japan play significant roles in world affairs: China for political and military reasons, Japan for economic reasons.
- India and Pakistan remain rivals. In 1998, India carried out nuclear tests and Pakistan responded by testing its own nuclear weapons.
- Although the people of Taiwan favor independence, China remains committed to eventual unification.

World History Video *The Chapter 31 video, "Vietnam," chronicles the history and impact of the Vietnam War.*

Mao Zedong

1949
Communist Party takes over China

1953
Korean War ends

1965
Lyndon Johnson sends U.S. troops to South Vietnam

1935   *1945*   *1955*   *1965*

1947
India and Pakistan become independent nations

Indira Gandhi

1966
Indira Gandhi elected prime minister of India

Singapore's architecture is a mixture of modern and colonial buildings.

Nixon in China

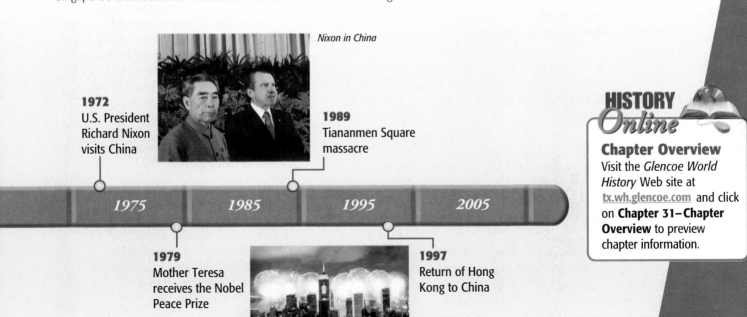

1972
U.S. President Richard Nixon visits China

1989
Tiananmen Square massacre

1975   1985   1995   2005

1979
Mother Teresa receives the Nobel Peace Prize

1997
Return of Hong Kong to China

Fireworks celebrate the handover of Hong Kong to China.

HISTORY *Online*

Chapter Overview
Visit the *Glencoe World History* Web site at tx.wh.glencoe.com and click on **Chapter 31–Chapter Overview** to preview chapter information.

A Story That Matters

The events in Tiananmen Square ended tragically for pro-democracy protesters.

A Movement for Democracy

*I*n the spring of 1989, China began to experience a remarkable series of events. Crowds of students, joined by workers and journalists, filled Tiananmen Square in Beijing day after day to demonstrate in favor of a democratic government for China. Some students waged a hunger strike, and others carried posters calling for democracy.

To China's elderly rulers, calls for democracy were a threat to the dominant role that the Communist Party had played in China since 1949. Some leaders interested in reform advised restraint in handling the protesters. Most of the Communist leaders, however, wanted to repress the movement. When students erected a 30-foot (9-m)-high statue called "The Goddess of Democracy" that looked similar to the American Statue of Liberty, party leaders became especially incensed.

On June 3, 1989, the Chinese army moved into the square. Soldiers carrying automatic rifles fired into the unarmed crowds. Tanks and troops moved in and surrounded the remaining students. At 5:30 in the morning on June 4, the mayor of Beijing announced that Tiananmen Square had been "handed back to the people." Even then, the killing of unarmed citizens continued. At least 500 civilians were killed—perhaps as many as 2,000. The movement for democracy in China had ended.

Why It Matters

The movement for democracy in China in the 1980s was only one of many tumultuous events in Asia after World War II. In China, a civil war gave way to a new China under Communist control. Japan recovered from the devastation of World War II and went on to build an economic powerhouse. In South Asia and Southeast Asia, nations that had been dominated by Western colonial powers struggled to gain their freedom. Throughout Asia, nations worked to develop modern industrialized states.

History and You Find online or in the library a commentary on the Tiananmen Square incident written from the perspective of the Chinese government. Analyze the work to determine whether or not it displays bias. Support your opinion.

Communist China

Guide to Reading

Main Ideas
- Mao Zedong established a socialist society in China.
- After Mao's death, modified capitalist techniques were used to encourage growth in industry and farming.

Key Terms
commune, permanent revolution, per capita

People to Identify
Deng Xiaoping, Richard Nixon

Places to Locate
Taiwan, South Korea, North Korea

Preview Questions
1. How did the Great Leap Forward and the Great Proletarian Cultural Revolution affect China?
2. What were the major economic, social, and political developments in China after the death of Mao Zedong?

Reading Strategy
Cause and Effect Use a chart like the one below to list communism's effects on China's international affairs.

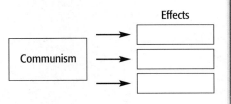

Preview of Events

♦1950	♦1960	♦1970	♦1980

1950
A marriage law guarantees women equal rights with men in China

1958
Mao Zedong institutes the Great Leap Forward

1972
President Nixon visits China

1979
China establishes diplomatic ties with the United States

Voices from the Past

Students in support of Mao Zedong

Nien Cheng, the widow of an official of Chiang Kai-shek's regime, described a visit by Red Guards to her home:

66Mounting the stairs, I was astonished to see several Red Guards taking pieces of my porcelain collection out of their padded boxes. One young man . . . was stepping on them. . . . Impulsively I leapt forward and caught his leg just as he raised his foot to crush the next cup. He toppled. We fell in a heap together. . . . The young man whose revolutionary work of destruction I had interrupted said angrily, 'You shut up! These things belong to the old culture. . . . Our Great Leader Chairman Mao taught us, "If we do not destroy, we cannot establish." The old culture must be destroyed to make way for the new socialist culture.'99

—*Life and Death in Shanghai,* Nien Cheng, 1986

The Red Guards were established to create a new order in China.

Civil War and the Great Leap Forward

By 1945, there were two Chinese governments. The Nationalist government of Chiang Kai-shek, based in southern and central China, was supported by the United States. The Communist government, under the leadership of Mao Zedong, had its base in North China.

In 1945, full-scale war between the Nationalists and the Communists broke out. In the countryside, millions of peasants were attracted to the Communists by promises of land. Many joined Mao's People's Liberation Army.

By the spring of 1949, the People's Liberation Army had defeated the Nationalists. Chiang and two million followers fled to the island of **Taiwan.**

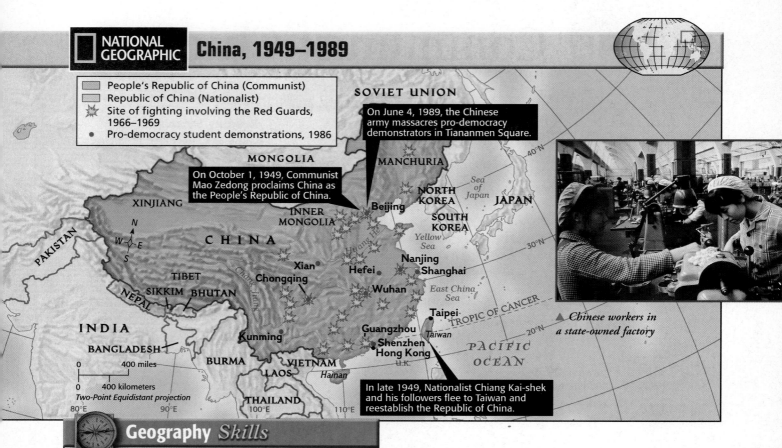

People's Republic of China (Communist)
Republic of China (Nationalist)
Site of fighting involving the Red Guards, 1966–1969
Pro-democracy student demonstrations, 1986

SOVIET UNION

On June 4, 1989, the Chinese army massacres pro-democracy demonstrators in Tiananmen Square.

MONGOLIA

MANCHURIA

On October 1, 1949, Communist Mao Zedong proclaims China as the People's Republic of China.

XINJIANG

INNER MONGOLIA

Beijing

NORTH KOREA
Sea of Japan
JAPAN
SOUTH KOREA
Yellow Sea

CHINA

Xian
Chongqing
Hefei
Nanjing
Shanghai
Wuhan

TIBET

Chang Jiang
Huang He

East China Sea

NEPAL
SIKKIM
BHUTAN

PAKISTAN

INDIA

Kunming

BANGLADESH

0   400 miles
0   400 kilometers
Two-Point Equidistant projection
80°E   90°E   100°E   110°E

BURMA

VIETNAM
LAOS
THAILAND

Hainan

Taipei
Guangzhou
Shenzhen
Hong Kong
Taiwan

TROPIC OF CANCER

PACIFIC OCEAN

In late 1949, Nationalist Chiang Kai-shek and his followers flee to Taiwan and reestablish the Republic of China.

▲ *Chinese workers in a state-owned factory*

Geography *Skills*

The People's Republic of China originated in 1949.

1. **Interpreting Maps** Identify the places where pro-democracy student demonstrations took place in 1986. Which of these cities had also been sites of fighting involving the Red Guards 20 years earlier?

2. **Applying Geography Skills** Use the map's scale to determine the approximate distance from Taiwan to mainland China. Use an atlas to help you name two U.S. cities that are about this same distance apart.

The Communist Party, under the leadership of its chairman, Mao Zedong, now ruled China. In 1955, the Chinese government launched a program to build a socialist society. To win the support of the peasants, lands were taken from wealthy landlords and given to poor peasants. About two-thirds of the peasant households in China received land under the new program. Most private farmland was collectivized, and most industry and commerce was nationalized.

Chinese leaders hoped that collective farms would increase food production, allowing more people to work in industry. Food production, however, did not grow.

To speed up economic growth, Mao began a more radical program, known as the Great Leap Forward, in 1958. Existing collective farms, normally the size of a village, were combined into vast communes. Each commune contained more than thirty thousand people who lived and worked together. Mao hoped this program would enable China to reach the final stage of communism—the classless society—before the end of the twentieth century. The government official slogan promised the following: "Hard work for a few years, happiness for a thousand."

The Great Leap Forward was a disaster. Bad weather and the peasants' hatred of the new system drove food production down. As a result, almost fifteen million people died of starvation. In 1960, the government began to break up the communes and return to collective farms and some private plots.

✓ **Reading Check** **Explaining** Why was the Great Leap Forward an economic disaster for China?

The Great Proletarian Cultural Revolution

Mao now faced opposition within the Communist Party. Despite this opposition and the commune failure, he still dreamed of a classless society. In Mao's eyes, only permanent revolution, an atmosphere of constant revolutionary fervor, could enable the

Chinese to overcome the past and achieve the final stage of communism.

In 1966, Mao launched the **Great Proletarian Cultural Revolution.** The Chinese name literally meant "great revolution to create a proletarian (working class) culture." A collection of Mao's thoughts, called the *Little Red Book,* was hailed as the most important source of knowledge in all areas.

Web Activity Visit the *Glencoe World History* Web site at tx.wh.glencoe.com and click on **Chapter 31– Student Web Activity** to learn more about the Cultural Revolution.

To further the Cultural Revolution, the Red Guards were formed. These were revolutionary groups composed largely of young people. Red Guards set out across the nation to eliminate the "Four Olds"—old ideas, old culture, old customs, and old habits. The Red Guard destroyed temples, books written by foreigners, and foreign music. They tore down street signs and replaced them with ones carrying revolutionary names. The city of Shanghai even ordered that red (the revolutionary color) traffic lights would indicate that traffic could move, not stop.

Vicious attacks were made on individuals who had supposedly deviated from Mao's plan. Intellectuals and artists accused of being pro-Western were especially open to attack. Key groups, however, including Communist Party members, urban professionals, and many military officers, did not share Mao's desire for permanent revolution. People, disgusted by the actions of the Red Guards, began to turn against the movement.

✔ **Reading Check** **Identifying** What were the "Four Olds" and how did the Red Guards try to eliminate them?

China After Mao

In September 1976, Mao Zedong died at the age of 82. A group of practical-minded reformers, led by **Deng Xiaoping** (DUNG SHOW•PIHNG), seized power and brought the Cultural Revolution to an end.

Policies of Deng Xiaoping Under Deng Xiaoping, the government followed a policy called the Four Modernizations, which focused on four areas—industry, agriculture, technology, and national defense. For over 20 years, China had been isolated from the technological advances taking place elsewhere in the world. To make up for lost time, the government invited foreign investors to China.

Thousands of students were sent abroad to study science, technology, and modern business techniques.

A new agricultural policy was begun. Collective farms could now lease land to peasant families who paid rent to the collective. Anything produced on the land above the amount of that payment could be sold on the private market. Peasants were also allowed to make goods they could sell to others.

Overall, modernization worked. Industrial output skyrocketed. **Per capita** (per person) income, including farm income, doubled during the 1980s. The standard of living rose for most people. The average Chinese citizen in the early 1980s had barely earned enough to buy a bicycle, radio, or watch. By the 1990s, many were buying refrigerators and color television sets.

Movement for Democracy Despite these achievements, many people complained that Deng Xiaoping's program had failed to achieve a fifth modernization—democracy. The new leaders did not allow direct criticism of the Communist Party. Those who called for democracy were often sentenced to long terms in prison.

The problem began to intensify in the late 1980s. More Chinese began to study abroad. More information about Western society reached educated people

People In History

Deng Xiaoping
1904–1997—Chinese leader

Deng Xiaoping was one of China's major leaders after the death of Mao Zedong. Deng studied in France, where he joined the Chinese Communist Party. Back in China, he helped organize the Communist army. At the end of World War II, Deng became a member of the Central Committee of the Communist Party. An opponent of Mao's Cultural Revolution, he was labeled a "renegade, scab, and traitor" and sent to work in a tractor factory.

In 1978, after the failure of the Cultural Revolution, Deng became the leader of China's modernization and economic reform. Deng took a practical approach to change. He said, "I do not care whether a cat is black or white, the important thing is whether it catches mice." Between 1982 and 1989, Deng was the chief leader of China.

inside the country. The economic improvements of the early 1980s led to pressure from students and other city residents for better living conditions and more freedom to choose jobs after graduation.

In the late 1980s, rising inflation led to growing discontent among salaried workers, especially in the cities. Corruption and special treatment for officials and party members led to increasing criticism as well. In May 1989, student protesters called for an end to the corruption and demanded the resignation of China's aging Communist Party leaders. These demands received widespread support from people in the cities and led to massive demonstrations in **Tiananmen Square** in Beijing.

Some Communist leaders were divided over how to respond. However, Deng Xiaoping saw the student desire for democracy as a demand for an end to the Communist Party. He ordered tanks and troops into Tiananmen Square to crush the demonstrators. Democracy remained a dream.

Throughout the 1990s, China's human rights violations and its determination to unify with Taiwan strained its relationship with the West. China's increasing military power has also created international concern. However, China still maintains diplomatic relations with the West.

✔**Reading Check** Explaining What was the fifth modernization, and why was it not achieved?

What If...

Mao Zedong had died on the Long March?

Chairman Mao was the dominant figure of Chinese communism. During his regime, he was close to a cult figure; schoolchildren would trade Mao cards, pins, and photographs like they were baseball cards or marbles. He rose to power during the Long March of 1934 to 1935 and quickly became the People's Republic of China's greatest leader.

Consider the Consequences The Communists lost over half of their forces during the 6,000-mile (9,660-km) trek of the Long March. Consider the consequences for Chinese communism if Mao had been one of the casualties. How might recent Chinese history have been altered if Mao had not survived this ordeal?

Chinese Society Under Communism

From the start, the Chinese Communist Party wanted to create a new kind of citizen. These new citizens would be expected to contribute their utmost for the good of all. In the words of Mao Zedong, the people "should be resolute, fear no sacrifice, and surmount every difficulty to win victory."

During the 1950s, the Communist government in China took steps to end the old system. One change involved the role of women. Women were now allowed to take part in politics. At the local level, an increasing number of women became active in the Communist Party. In 1950, a new marriage law guaranteed women equal rights with men.

The new regime also tried to destroy the influence of the traditional family system. To the Communists, loyalty to the family, an important element in the Confucian social order, undercut loyalty to the state. For Communist leaders, family loyalty was against the basic principle of Marxism—dedication to society at large.

During the Great Leap Forward, children were encouraged for the first time to report to the authorities any comments by their parents that criticized the system. These practices continued during the Cultural Revolution. Red Guards expected children to report on their parents, students on their teachers, and employees on their superiors.

At the time, many foreign observers feared that the Cultural Revolution would transform the Chinese people into robots spouting the slogans fed to them by their leaders. This did not happen, however. After the death of Mao Zedong there was a noticeable shift away from revolutionary fervor and a return to family traditions.

For most people, this shift meant better living conditions. Married couples who had been given patriotic names such as "Protect Mao Zedong" and "Build the Country" by their parents chose more elegant names for their own children.

The new attitudes were also reflected in people's clothing choices. For a generation after the civil war, clothing had been restricted to a baggy "Mao suit" in olive drab or dark blue. Today, young Chinese people wear jeans, sneakers, and sweat suits. 📖 *(See page 1001 to read excerpts from Xiao-huang Yin's China's Gilded Age in the Primary Sources Library.)*

✔**Reading Check** Evaluating What was the impact of Communist rule on women, marriage, and family in China?

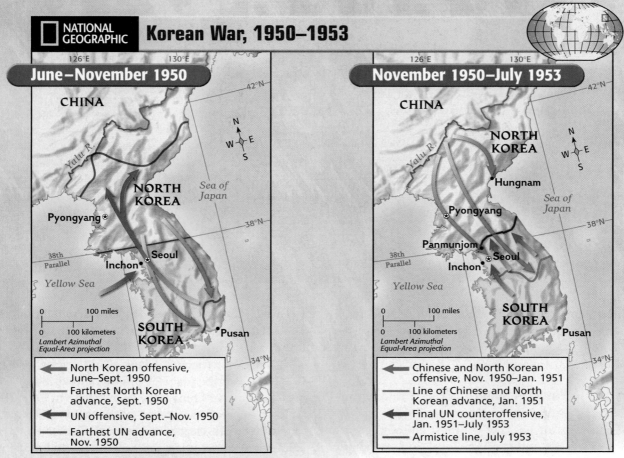

June–November 1950

CHINA

NORTH KOREA

Sea of Japan

Pyongyang

38th Parallel

Inchon

Seoul

Yellow Sea

0   100 miles
0   100 kilometers
Lambert Azimuthal Equal-Area projection

SOUTH KOREA

Pusan

← North Korean offensive, June–Sept. 1950
— Farthest North Korean advance, Sept. 1950
← UN offensive, Sept.–Nov. 1950
— Farthest UN advance, Nov. 1950

November 1950–July 1953

CHINA

NORTH KOREA

Yalu R.

Hungnam

Pyongyang

Sea of Japan

Panmunjom

38th Parallel

Inchon

Seoul

Yellow Sea

0   100 miles
0   100 kilometers
Lambert Azimuthal Equal-Area projection

SOUTH KOREA

Pusan

← Chinese and North Korean offensive, Nov. 1950–Jan. 1951
— Line of Chinese and North Korean advance, Jan. 1951
← Final UN counteroffensive, Jan. 1951–July 1953
— Armistice line, July 1953

Geography *Skills*

Three years of fighting resulted in no change to the boundary between North and South Korea.

1. **Interpreting Maps** Identify the offensive shown in the map on the left that caused the Chinese to enter the war.

2. **Applying Geography Skills** How would you compare the UN offensives in the two maps? What reasons can you suggest for the differences?

China and the World: The Cold War in Asia

When Chinese Communists came to power, American fears about the spread of communism intensified. In 1950, China signed a pact of friendship and cooperation with the Soviet Union, and some Americans began to worry about a Communist desire for world domination. With the outbreak of war in Korea, the Cold War had clearly arrived in Asia.

The Korean War Korea was a part of the Japanese Empire from 1905 until 1945. In August 1945, the Soviet Union and the United States agreed to divide Korea into two zones at the 38th parallel. The plan was to hold elections after the war (World War II) to reunify Korea. As American-Soviet relations grew worse, however, two separate governments emerged in Korea—a Communist one in the north and an anti-Communist one in the south.

There was great tension between the two governments. With the approval of Joseph Stalin, North Korean troops invaded **South Korea** on June 25, 1950. President Harry Truman, with the support of the United Nations, sent U.S. troops to repel the invaders.

In October 1950, UN forces—mostly Americans—marched northward across the 38th parallel with the aim of unifying Korea. The Chinese, greatly alarmed, sent hundreds of thousands of Chinese troops into **North Korea** and pushed UN forces back across the 38th parallel.

Harry Truman

Picturing History

The Korean War was the first war to utilize a United Nations coalition, the first to see integrated U.S. forces, and the first time that African American women enlisted in the Marines. Research other first time events of the Korean War.

Three more years of fighting produced no final victory. An armistice was finally signed in 1953. The 38th parallel remained, and remains today, the boundary line between North and South Korea.

The Shifting Power Balance in Asia Western fears led to China's isolation from the major Western powers. China was forced to rely almost entirely on the Soviet Union for both technological and economic aid. In the late 1950s, however, relations between China and the Soviet Union began to deteriorate. Matters grew worse in the 1960s, when military units on both sides of the frontier between the two countries often clashed.

Faced with a serious security threat from the Soviet Union, along with internal problems, Chinese leaders decided to improve relations with the United States. In 1972, President **Richard Nixon** made a state visit to China. He was the first U.S. president to visit the People's Republic of China since its inception in 1949. The two sides agreed to improve relations. In 1979, diplomatic ties were established with the United States. Chinese relations with the Soviet Union gradually improved throughout the 1980s. By the 1990s, China was playing an increasingly active role in Asian affairs.

✓**Reading Check** **Examining** Why did China decide to improve relations with the United States?

▼ TAKS Practice

SECTION 1 ASSESSMENT

Checking for Understanding

1. **Define** commune, permanent revolution, per capita.

2. **Identify** Great Proletarian Cultural Revolution, *Little Red Book,* Deng Xiaoping,Tiananmen Square, Richard Nixon.

3. **Locate** Taiwan, South Korea, North Korea.

4. **Explain** the original plan developed by the United States and the Soviet Union for the future of Korea.

5. **List** the actions the Chinese government took to promote technological development.

Critical Thinking

6. **Compare and Contrast** Identify the changes the Communist takeover brought to China during the 1950s. Then, compare and contrast how policies have changed in China since the 1970s.

7. **Contrasting Information** Use a table like the one below to contrast the policies of the two Chinese leaders Mao Zedong and Deng Xiaoping.

Mao Zedong	Deng Xiaoping

Analyzing Visuals

8. **Compare** the photographs on pages 940 and 941. Imagine you are in each photo. What are you expressing? Is more than one point of view being expressed in each photo? What are some of the things that might happen to you after the event shown in each photo? How will you be remembered by historians?

Writing About History

9. **Descriptive Writing** Pretend that you are a visitor to China during the Cultural Revolution. Write a letter to a friend at home describing the purpose of the Red Guards.

CRITICAL THINKING
SKILLBUILDER

Reading a Cartogram

Why Learn This Skill?

Most maps show countries in proportion to their amount of land area. For example, Japan is much smaller than China and is usually depicted that way on a map. Japan, however, has a greater gross national product than China. If we wanted to depict that on a map, how would it look?

Cartograms are maps that show countries according to a value other than land area. They might portray features such as populations or economies. To visually compare these features, cartograms distort countries' sizes and shapes. This makes it possible to see at a glance how each country or region compares with another in a particular value. Therefore, on a cartogram showing gross national products, Japan looks larger than China.

Learning the Skill

To use a cartogram:

- Read the title and key to identify what value the cartogram illustrates.

- Examine the cartogram to see which countries or regions appear.

- Find the largest and smallest countries.

- Compare the cartogram with a conventional land-area map to determine the degree of distortion of particular countries.

- Draw conclusions about the countries and the feature you are comparing.

Practicing the Skill

Study the cartogram on this page and answer these questions.

❶ What is the subject of the cartogram?

❷ What countries are represented?

❸ Which country appears largest on the cartogram? Which appears smallest?

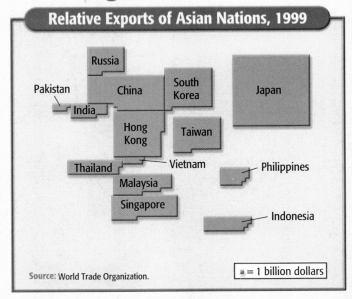

Relative Exports of Asian Nations, 1999

Russia
Pakistan
China
South Korea
Japan
India
Hong Kong
Taiwan
Thailand
Vietnam
Philippines
Malaysia
Singapore
Indonesia

Source: World Trade Organization.

■ = 1 billion dollars

❹ Compare the cartogram to the map of Asia found in the Atlas. Which countries are most distorted in size compared to a land-area map?

❺ What accounts for these distortions?

Applying the Skill

At the library, find statistics that compare some value for different countries. For example, you might compare the amount of oil consumption of countries in North America.

Convert these statistics into a simple cartogram. Determine the relative size of each country according to the chosen value. If the United States consumes five times more oil than Mexico, then the United States should appear five times larger than Mexico on the cartogram.

GO TO

Glencoe's **Skillbuilder Interactive Workbook, Level 2,** provides instruction and practice in key social studies skills.

TRANSFORMING
BeijinG

1

In 1979, after decades of watching China's economy stagnate, Communist Party leader Deng Xiaoping took a gamble. He began relaxing the state's tight economic controls while trying to keep a firm grip on political power. In the Chinese capital of Beijing, the result of Deng's "second revolution" has been a big construction boom, new foreign investment—and the kind of Western cultural influence that China has resisted for centuries.

Geographically, Beijing's location in Asia is roughly similar to New York's in North America. Both lie near the 40th parallel, and in both places the most comfortable seasons are autumn and spring. But the similarities end there. The city now known as Beijing began as a frontier outpost nearly 3,000 years ago. It was built to guard the North China Plain against marauding groups who attacked through mountain passes in the north.

Without access to the sea or a significant river to link it to the outside world, Beijing might have remained a dusty outpost. But in the seventh century A.D., a 1,000-mile (1,609-km) canal was dug to link the city with the fertile Chang Jiang Valley in the south. Three centuries later the city became the capital of the Liao dynasty. Then came the Mongols under Genghis Khan, who sacked and burned the capital in 1215.

About 50 years later, however, Genghis's grandson, Kublai Khan, rebuilt the city so gloriously that the Venetian traveler Marco Polo marveled at its streets "so straight and wide that you can see right along from end to end and from one gate to another." Kublai Khan's Dadu (meaning "Great Capital"), Marco Polo wrote, "is arranged like a chessboard."

Indeed, Beijing is laid out on a precise north-south axis, in harmony with the ancient practice of *feng shui* ("wind and water"). According to this tradition, buildings (and the furnishings inside them) must be properly aligned to take advantage of the natural energy (qi) that flows through all things. The proper placement of a house or temple will thus attract positive qi and good luck; the wrong placement invites disaster.

The north-south axis passes directly through Qian Men (Front Gate), proceeds through the red walls of Tian An Men (Gate of Heavenly Peace), and then on to Wu Men (Meridian Gate), beyond which lies the Forbidden City.

An area once barred to everyone except the emperor, his family, and his most favored concubines, guards, and

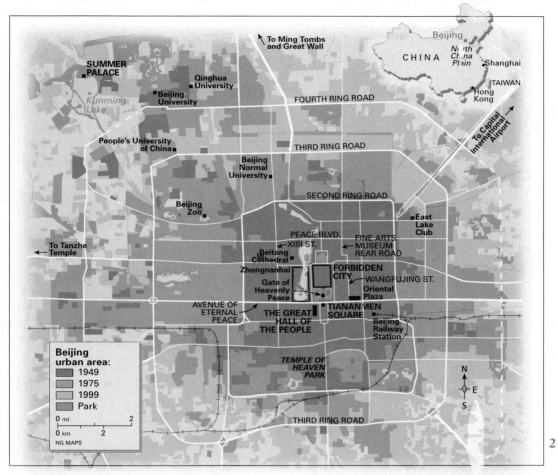

Beijing

CHINA
North China Plain
Shanghai
TAIWAN
Hong Kong

To Ming Tombs and Great Wall

SUMMER PALACE

Qinghua University
Beijing University

Kunming Lake

FOURTH RING ROAD

To Capital International Airport

People's University of China

THIRD RING ROAD

Beijing Normal University

SECOND RING ROAD

Beijing Zoo

East Lake Club

To Tanzhe Temple

PEACE BLVD.
XISI ST.
FINE ARTS MUSEUM REAR ROAD

Beitang Cathedral
Zhongnanhai
FORBIDDEN CITY

WANGFUJING ST.

Gate of Heavenly Peace
Oriental Plaza

AVENUE OF ETERNAL PEACE

THE GREAT HALL OF THE PEOPLE
TIANANMEN SQUARE

Beijing Railway Station

Beijing urban area:
- 1949
- 1975
- 1999
- Park

TEMPLE OF HEAVEN PARK

N
W — E
S

0 mi 2
0 km 2
NG MAPS

THIRD RING ROAD

2

officials, the Forbidden City lay at the very center of a series of cities-within-cities, concentric rectangles defined by their high walls. Today the walls are largely gone and the Forbidden City is a museum overflowing with tourists.

The Gate of Heavenly Peace, on the north side of nearby Tiananmen Square, is the spiritual heart of all China. Centuries ago, orders from the emperor were sent down from the top of the gate to officials waiting below.

1 A migrant worker balances on his cart as he stacks bricks at the construction site of a large apartment complex.

2 The Forbidden City (above map) was once considered the stable core of the empire. In spite of its growth, urban Beijing accounts for only a fraction of the territory the city includes. By an administrative decision of 1959, Beijing's boundaries now cover a 6,600 square-mile (17,094 square-km) municipality that includes satellite towns and agricultural communes as well as such tourist attractions as the Ming Tombs and the Great Wall.

3 Mao Zedong's mausoleum and the Monument to the People's Heroes dominate Tiananmen Square.

3

4
5

From that same high place, on the afternoon of October 1, 1949, Mao Zedong formally proclaimed the establishment of the People's Republic of China. His portrait now hangs on the wall of the gate, staring out at the square and providing a backdrop for tourist photographs.

In the late 1950s, during the Great Leap Forward, homes around Tiananmen Square were torn down to expand the square from 27 acres (10.9 ha) to 98 acres (39.7 ha)—large enough to hold a million people. In the center stands the 124-foot (37.8-m) high Monument to the People's Heroes. On the west side is the many-columned Great Hall of the People, where the government meets and visiting dignitaries are entertained. Across the square on the east side is the Historical Museum. To the south, opposite his portrait on Tian An Men, is the huge mausoleum where Mao Zedong's body is on display.

◼

In the 20-some years since Deng Xiaoping's experiment in free enterprise began, the blocky Soviet-style monuments built by Mao have been overtaken by the bright lights of McDonald's, Kentucky Fried Chicken, and thousands of private restaurants and nightclubs catering to foreign visitors and investors.

The building boom has swept away much of what was once a major characteristic of the old city: the low, walled alleyways called *hutong*. Some of the family compounds were hundreds of years old and housed three generations. The government is moving more than 2 million of the city's 11 million residents out to the suburbs to make room for new tourism centers, department stores, and expensive apartment compounds.

As one long-time Beijing resident put it, "The old city is gone. Old things like the Forbidden City or a temple are scattered between skyscrapers like toys thrown here and there. Old Beijing is dismembered."

Along with all the tearing down

德先生,你好
HELLO, Mr. DEMOCRACY

and building up that has occurred in the last two decades, China's production has climbed steadily. Per capita annual income for city dwellers has almost doubled since 1990 to more than $600. Foreign businesses hoping for a share of the vast Chinese market have rushed in.

Not all of these entrepreneurs have been welcomed by Beijing's residents, however. A mammoth complex called the Oriental Plaza, for example, has been the focus of controversy. Built by a Hong Kong business partnership, the complex contains eight office towers, two apartment towers, and a five-star international hotel. It also includes more than a million square feet (93,000 square m) of retail mall and a parking structure for 2,000 cars and 10,000 bicycles.

Even for a city of large monuments, the Oriental Plaza is beyond big. Residents complain that the project destroys the character of the old city, dwarfing as it does The Gate of Heavenly Peace.

As the site of countless demonstrations over the years, Tiananmen Square has become familiar to television viewers around the world. The most vivid scenes in recent memory are from early June 1989, when the Chinese Army attacked unarmed demonstrators who had been protesting government corruption. Perhaps as many as 2,000 people were killed. Although the government would prefer the event be forgotten, the anniversary of the June 4th attack has been marked repeatedly with some form of protest.

Yet even as the government clamps down on highly visible political demonstrations, activists have found a more subtle way to make their points—the Internet. More and more young Chinese are making their way online. Their access to an open market of ideas and uncensored information brings with it a new sense of individualism. Undoubtedly this will have a lasting impact on the future of their city and their nation.

4 Demolition of the old makes way for the new as downtown Beijing undergoes a massive face-lift.

5 Residents of old family compounds haul out their belongings as they load a truck to move to housing projects in the suburbs.

6 Students protest in Tiananmen Square in 1989. The peaceful protests turned violent when the army attacked.

INTERPRETING THE PAST

1. Why was Beijing established?

2. How is the capital city laid out ?

3. How has Beijing changed during the last twenty years?

4. Do you think the lives of the residents of Beijing have improved or deteriorated during the last two decades?

Independent States in South and Southeast Asia

Guide to Reading

Main Ideas
- British India was divided into two states: India, mostly Hindu, and Pakistan, mostly Muslim.
- Many of the newly independent states of Southeast Asia attempted to form democratic governments but often fell subject to military regimes.

Key Terms
stalemate, discrimination

People to Identify
Pol Pot, Ferdinand Marcos

Places to Locate
Punjab, Bangladesh

Preview Questions
1. What policies did Jawaharlal Nehru put into effect in India?
2. What internal and external problems did the Southeast Asian nations face after 1945?

Reading Strategy
Categorizing Information Use a web diagram like the one below to identify challenges India faced after independence.

Challenges in India

Preview of Events

| ♦1945 | ♦1950 | ♦1955 | ♦1960 | ♦1965 | ♦1970 | ♦1975 |

1948
A Hindu militant assassinates Mohandas Gandhi

1949
The independent Republic of Indonesia is established

1966
Indira Gandhi becomes prime minister of India

1971
East Pakistan becomes the independent nation of Bangladesh

Voices from the Past

An example of Western influence in India

In 1989, Maneka Gandhi, former minister of the environment for India, wrote an article entitled "Why India Doesn't Need Fast Food" in the *Hindustan Times:*

❝India's decision to allow Pepsi Foods Ltd. to open 60 restaurants in India—30 each of Pizza Hut and Kentucky Fried Chicken—marks the first entry of multinational, meat-based junk-food chains into India. . . . The implications of allowing junk-food chains into India are quite stark. As the name denotes, the foods served at Kentucky Fried Chicken are chicken-based and fried. This is the worst combination possible for the body and can create a host of health problems, including obesity, high cholesterol, heart ailments, and many kinds of cancer. . . . Can our health systems take care of the fallout from these chicken restaurants?❞

—*World Press Review,* September 1995

Many Indians continue to reject Western influence.

India Divided

At the end of World War II, British India's Muslims and Hindus were bitterly divided. The leaders in India realized that British India would have to be divided into two countries, one Hindu (India) and one Muslim (Pakistan). Pakistan consisted of two regions separated by India. One part, West Pakistan, was to the northwest of India. The other, East Pakistan, was to the northeast.

On August 15, 1947, India and Pakistan became independent. Millions of Hindus and Muslims fled across the new borders, Hindus toward India and Muslims toward Pakistan. Violence resulted from these mass migrations, and more than a million people were killed.

One of the dead was well known. On January 30, 1948, a Hindu militant assassinated Mohandas Gandhi as he was going to morning prayer. India's new beginning had not been easy.

Reading Check **Summarizing** Why was British India divided into two new nations after World War II? What was the immediate result?

The New India

With independence, the Indian National Congress, renamed the Congress Party, began to rule India. Jawaharlal Nehru (jah•wah•HAR•lahl NAY•roo), the new prime minister, was a popular figure with strong ideas about the future of Indian society. He admired Great Britain's political institutions and the socialist ideals of the British Labour Party. Nehru's vision of the new India combined a parliamentary form of government led by a prime minister. In his view the new India would have a moderate socialist economic structure.

Accordingly, the state took over the ownership of major industries, utilities, and transportation. Private enterprise was permitted at the local level. Farmland remained in private hands. India developed a large industrial sector, and industrial production almost tripled between 1950 and 1965.

Nehru died in 1964. In 1966, the leaders of the Congress Party selected Nehru's daughter, Indira Gandhi (who was not related to Mohandas Gandhi), as the new prime minister. Except for a brief 22-month interval in the late 1970s, she retained that office until 1984.

India faced many problems during this period. Its growing population was one of the most serious. Even in 1948, the country had been unable to support its population. In the 1950s and 1960s, India's population grew at a rate of more than 2 percent per year. In spite of government efforts, India was unable to control this growth.

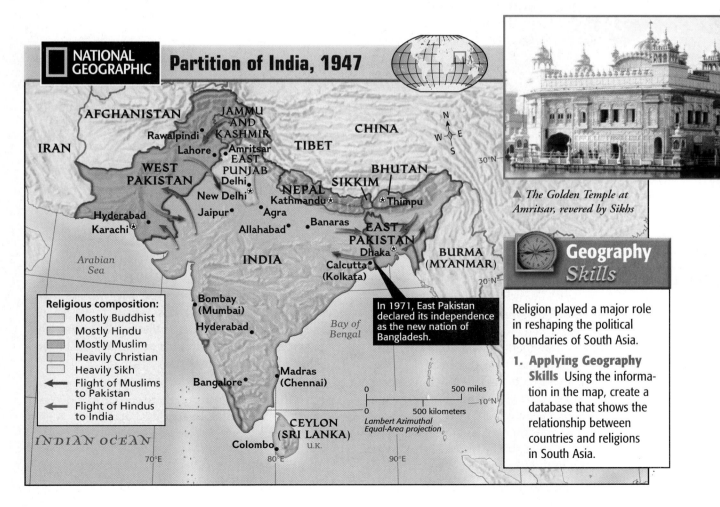

NATIONAL GEOGRAPHIC

Partition of India, 1947

AFGHANISTAN
IRAN
Rawalpindi
Lahore
WEST PAKISTAN
Delhi
New Delhi
Jaipur
Hyderabad
Karachi
Arabian Sea
JAMMU AND KASHMIR
Amritsar
EAST PUNJAB
Agra
Allahabad
Banaras
NEPAL
Kathmandu
CHINA
TIBET
BHUTAN
SIKKIM
Thimpu
EAST PAKISTAN
Dhaka
Calcutta (Kolkata)
BURMA (MYANMAR)
INDIA
Bombay (Mumbai)
Hyderabad
Bay of Bengal
Bangalore
Madras (Chennai)
CEYLON (SRI LANKA) U.K.
Colombo
INDIAN OCEAN

In 1971, East Pakistan declared its independence as the new nation of Bangladesh.

30°N
20°N
10°N
70°E 80°E 90°E

0 ———— 500 miles
0 ———— 500 kilometers
Lambert Azimuthal Equal-Area projection

Religious composition:
- Mostly Buddhist
- Mostly Hindu
- Mostly Muslim
- Heavily Christian
- Heavily Sikh
← Flight of Muslims to Pakistan
← Flight of Hindus to India

▲ *The Golden Temple at Amritsar, revered by Sikhs*

Geography *Skills*

Religion played a major role in reshaping the political boundaries of South Asia.

1. **Applying Geography Skills** Using the information in the map, create a database that shows the relationship between countries and religions in South Asia.

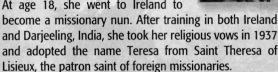

Mother Teresa of Calcutta
1910–1997
Roman Catholic nun

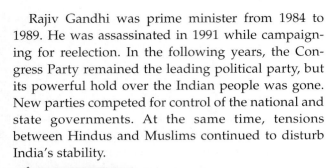

Mother Teresa was born Agnes Gonxha Bojaxhiu to Albanian parents. At age 18, she went to Ireland to become a missionary nun. After training in both Ireland and Darjeeling, India, she took her religious vows in 1937 and adopted the name Teresa from Saint Theresa of Lisieux, the patron saint of foreign missionaries.

When she was sent to Calcutta, Teresa was amazed at the large numbers of suffering people she saw on the streets. She believed it was her destiny to help these people and, in 1948, the Vatican gave her permission to follow her calling. In 1950, she and her followers established the Missionaries of Charity to help the poor and the sick.

Over the years, Mother Teresa and her followers established numerous centers throughout the world to aid the hungry, the sick, and the poor. When she won the Nobel Peace Prize in 1979 for her humanitarian efforts, Mother Teresa asked that the money for the celebration banquet be donated to the poor. When Mother Teresa died in 1997, she left behind a legacy that continues to inspire people around the world.

One result was worsening poverty for many people. Millions lived in vast city slums. It was in the slums of Calcutta, India, that Mother Teresa helped the poor, sick, and dying Indian people.

Growing ethnic and religious strife presented another problem in India. This conflict involved the **Sikhs,** followers of a religion based on both Hindu and Muslim ideas. Many Sikhs lived in a northern province called the **Punjab.** Militant Sikhs demanded that this province be independent from India. Gandhi refused and, in 1984, she used military force against Sikh rebels taking refuge in the Golden Temple, one of the Sikhs' most important shrines. More than 450 Sikhs were killed. Seeking revenge for these killings, two Sikh members of Gandhi's personal bodyguard assassinated her later that year.

Indira Gandhi's son Rajiv replaced his mother as prime minister and began to move the government in new directions. Private enterprise was encouraged, as well as foreign investment. His successors have continued to transfer state-run industries into private hands and to rely on the free market. This has led to a noticeable growth in India's middle class.

Rajiv Gandhi was prime minister from 1984 to 1989. He was assassinated in 1991 while campaigning for reelection. In the following years, the Congress Party remained the leading political party, but its powerful hold over the Indian people was gone. New parties competed for control of the national and state governments. At the same time, tensions between Hindus and Muslims continued to disturb India's stability.

Reading Check **Examining** What are the underlying causes of political strife in India?

Pakistan

Unlike its neighbor India, Pakistan was a completely new nation when it attained independence in 1947. Its early years were marked by intense internal conflicts. Most dangerous was the growing division between East and West Pakistan. These two separate regions are very different in nature. West Pakistan, for example, is a dry and mountainous area, while East Pakistan has marshy land densely populated with rice farmers.

Many people in East Pakistan felt that the government, based in West Pakistan, ignored their needs. In 1971, East Pakistan declared its independence. After a brief civil war, it became the new nation of **Bangladesh.**

Both Bangladesh and Pakistan (as West Pakistan is now known) have had difficulty in establishing stable governments. In both nations, military officials have often seized control of the civilian government. Both nations also remain very poor.

Reading Check **Describing** What problems did Pakistan face after it achieved independence?

Southeast Asia

TURNING POINT **After World War II, most of the states of Southeast Asia received independence from their colonial rulers. France's refusal to let go of Indochina led to a long war in Vietnam that ultimately involved other Southeast Asian nations and the United States in a widening conflict.**

Colonies in Southeast Asia, like colonies elsewhere, gained their independence at the end of World War II. The process varied considerably across the region, however.

Independence In July 1946, the United States granted total independence to the Philippines. Great

Britain was also willing to end its colonial rule in Southeast Asia. In 1948, Burma became independent. Malaya's turn came in 1957.

The Netherlands and France were less willing to abandon their colonial empires in Southeast Asia. The Dutch tried to suppress a new Indonesian republic that had been set up by Achmed Sukarno. When the Indonesian Communist Party attempted to seize power, however, the United States pressured the Netherlands to grant independence to Sukarno and his non-Communist Nationalist Party. In 1949, the Netherlands recognized the new Republic of Indonesia.

The situation was very different in Vietnam. The leading force in the movement against colonial French rule there was the local Communist Party, led by Ho Chi Minh. In August 1945, the **Vietminh,** an alliance of forces under Communist leadership, seized power throughout most of Vietnam. Ho Chi Minh was elected president of a new provisional republic in Hanoi. France, however, refused to accept the new government and seized the southern part of the country.

The Vietnam War Over the following years, France fought Ho Chi Minh's Vietminh for control of Vietnam without success. In 1954, France finally agreed to a peace settlement. Vietnam was divided into two parts. In the north, the Communists were based in Hanoi, and in the south, the non-Communists were based in Saigon.

Both sides agreed to hold elections in two years to create a single government. Instead, however, the conflict continued. The United States, opposed to any

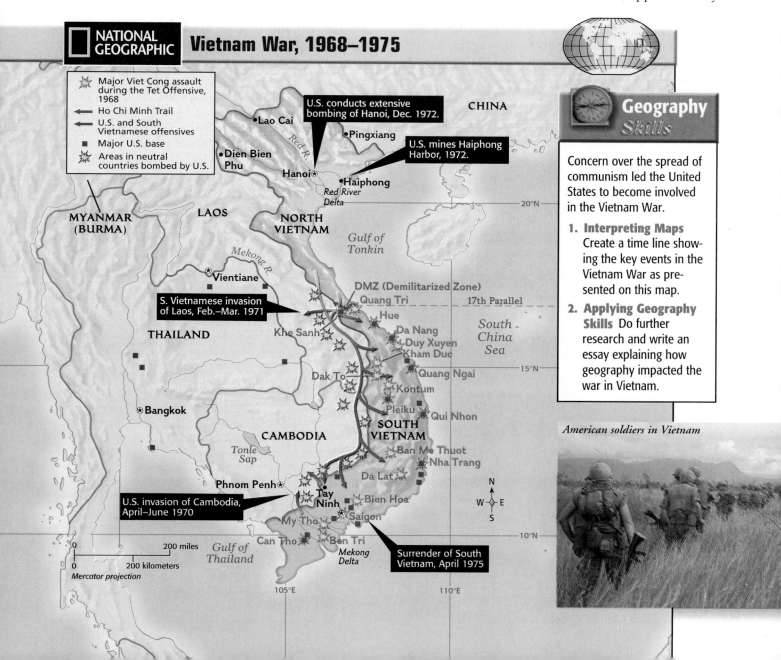

American soldiers in Vietnam

further spread of communism, began to provide aid to South Vietnam. In spite of this aid, South Vietnamese Communist guerrillas known as Viet Cong, supported by military units from North Vietnam, were on the verge of seizing control of the entire country by early 1965.

In March 1965, President Lyndon Johnson decided to send U.S. troops to South Vietnam to prevent a total victory for the Communists. The Communist government in North Vietnam responded by sending more of its forces into the south.

By the end of the 1960s, the war had reached a stalemate—neither side was able to make significant gains. With American public opinion sharply divided, President Richard Nixon reached an agreement with North Vietnam in 1973 that allowed the United States to withdraw its forces. Within two years, Communist armies had forcibly reunited Vietnam.

The reunification of Vietnam under Communist rule had an immediate impact on the region. By the end of 1975, both Laos and Cambodia had Communist governments. In Cambodia, a brutal revolutionary regime under the dictator **Pol Pot,** leader of the **Khmer Rouge** (kuh•MEHR ROOZH), massacred more than a million Cambodians. However, the Communist triumph in Indochina did not lead to the "falling dominoes" that many U.S. policy makers had feared (see Chapter 27).

Government in the Independent States
In the beginning, many of the leaders of the newly independent states in Southeast Asia admired Western political and economic practices. They hoped to form democratic, capitalist states like those in the West.

By the end of the 1950s, however, hopes for rapid economic growth had failed. Internal disputes within the new countries weakened democratic governments, opening the door to both military and one-party autocratic regimes.

In more recent years, some Southeast Asian societies have shown signs of moving again toward more democratic governments. One example is the Philippines. There, President **Ferdinand Marcos** came to power in 1965. Fraud and corruption became widespread in the Marcos regime. In the early 1980s, Marcos was accused of involvement in the killing of Benigno Aquino, a leader of the political opposition. A massive public uprising forced Marcos to flee the country. In 1986, Corazon Aquino, wife of the murdered opposition leader, became president and worked for democratic reforms.

Women in South and Southeast Asia
Across South and Southeast Asia, women's roles have changed considerably. After independence, India's leaders sought to extend women's rights. The constitution of 1950 forbade discrimination (prejudicial treatment) based on gender and called for equal pay for equal work. Child marriage was outlawed. Women were encouraged to attend school and to enter the labor market. In Southeast Asia, virtually all of the newly independent states granted women full legal and political rights. Women have become more active in politics and occasionally hold senior political or corporate positions.

Reading Check **Identifying** Give the reasons for the United States's entry into and withdrawal from the Vietnam War.

TAKS Practice

SECTION 2 ASSESSMENT

Checking for Understanding
1. **Define** stalemate, discrimination.

2. **Identify** Sikhs, Vietminh, Pol Pot, Khmer Rouge, Ferdinand Marcos.

3. **Locate** Punjab, Bangladesh.

4. **Explain** how the reunification of Vietnam under Communist rule affected the region.

5. **Summarize** Nehru's vision of the new India.

Critical Thinking
6. **Evaluate** Has the division of British India into two countries been beneficial? Explain your answer.

7. **Organizing Information** Use a table like the one below to list the political status or type of government of the Southeast Asian countries discussed in this section.

Country			
Government			

Analyzing Visuals
8. **Examine** the photograph on page 953, then locate Amritsar on the map. How does Amritsar's location support the statement that Sikhism has been influenced by both Hinduism and Islam?

Writing About History

9. **Expository Writing** Write an essay comparing political, economic, and cultural developments in India and Pakistan from World War II to the present.

SECTION 3 | Japan and the Pacific

Guide to Reading

Main Ideas
- Japan and the "Asian tigers" have created successful industrial societies.
- Although Australia and New Zealand have identified themselves culturally and politically with Europe, in recent years they have been drawing closer to their Asian neighbors.

Key Terms
occupied, state capitalism

People to Identify
Douglas MacArthur, Kim Il Sung, Syngman Rhee

Places to Locate
Singapore, Hong Kong

Preview Questions
1. What important political, economic, and social changes have occurred in Japan since 1945?
2. What did the "Asian tigers" accomplish in Asia?

Reading Strategy
Categorizing Information Use a table like the one below to list the key areas of industrial development in South Korea, Taiwan, and Singapore.

South Korea	Taiwan	Singapore

Preview of Events

♦1940	♦1950	♦1960	♦1970	♦1980	♦1990	♦2000

1947
Japan adopts new constitution

1951
A peace treaty restores Japanese independence

1963
General Chung Hee Park is elected president of South Korea

1997
Great Britain returns control of Hong Kong to mainland China

Voices from the Past

In an introduction to the book *Japanese Women,* published in 1995, Kumiko Fujimura-Fanselow wrote:

❝A quick glance at educational statistics reveals a higher percentage of female as compared to male high school graduates entering colleges and universities. The overwhelming majority of female college and university graduates, over 80 percent, are taking up employment and doing so in a wider range of fields than in the past. Better education and the availability of more job opportunites have increasingly made it possible for women to look upon marriage as an option rather than a prescribed lifestyle. . . . A dramatic development has been the advancement by married women, including those with children, into the labor force.❞

— *Japanese Women: New Feminist Perspectives on the Past, Present, and Future,*
Kumiko Fujimura-Fanselow et al., eds., 1995

Japanese woman at work in a Toyota factory

After World War II, many Japanese women began to abandon their old roles to pursue new opportunities.

The Allied Occupation

From 1945 to 1952, Japan was an occupied country—its lands held and controlled by Allied military forces. An Allied administration under the command of United States general **Douglas MacArthur** governed Japan. As commander of the occupation administration, MacArthur was responsible for destroying the Japanese war machine, trying Japanese civilian and military officials charged with war crimes, and laying the foundations of postwar Japanese society.

Under MacArthur's firm direction, Japanese society was remodeled along Western lines. A new constitution renounced war as a national policy. Japan agreed to maintain armed forces at levels that were only sufficient for self-defense. The constitution also established a parliamentary system, reduced the power of the emperor (who was forced to announce that he was not a god), guaranteed basic civil and political rights, and gave women the right to vote.

General Douglas MacArthur

On September 8, 1951, the United States and other former World War II allies (but not the Soviet Union) signed a peace treaty restoring Japanese independence. On the same day, Japan and the United States signed a defensive alliance in which the Japanese agreed that the United States could maintain military bases in Japan.

✓ **Reading Check** **Identifying** What reforms were instituted in Japan under the command of U.S. general Douglas MacArthur?

The Japanese Miracle

In August 1945, Japan was in ruins and its land occupied by a foreign army. Half a century later, Japan was the second greatest industrial power in the world.

Japan's rapid emergence as an economic giant has often been described as the "Japanese miracle." Japan has made a dramatic recovery from the war. To understand this phenomenon fully, we must examine not just the economy but also the changes that have occurred in Japanese society.

Politics and Government Japan's new constitution embodied the principles of universal suffrage and a balance of power among the executive, legislative, and judicial branches of government. These principles have held firm. Japan today is a stable democratic society.

At the same time, the current Japanese political system retains some of Japan's nineteenth-century political system under the Meiji. An example involves the distribution of political power. Japan has a multiparty system with two major parties—the Liberal Democrats and the Socialists. In practice, however, the Liberal Democrats have dominated the government. At one point, they remained in office for 30 years. During this period decisions on key issues, such as who should become prime minister, were decided by a small group within the party. A dramatic change, however, did occur in 1993, when the Liberal Democrats were defeated on charges of government corruption. Mirohiro Hosokawa was elected prime minister and promised to clean up the political system.

Today, the central government plays an active role in the economy. It establishes price and wage policies and subsidizes vital industries. This government role in the economy is widely accepted in Japan. Indeed, it is often cited as a key reason for the efficiency of Japanese industry and the emergence of the country as an industrial giant. Japan's economic system has been described as "state capitalism."

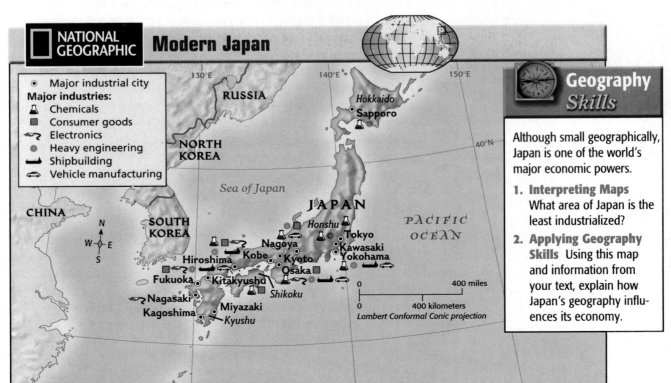

NATIONAL GEOGRAPHIC **Modern Japan**

• Major industrial city
Major industries:
♨ Chemicals
■ Consumer goods
⌇ Electronics
◉ Heavy engineering
⊨ Shipbuilding
⇔ Vehicle manufacturing

RUSSIA
NORTH KOREA
CHINA
SOUTH KOREA
Sea of Japan
Hokkaido
Sapporo
JAPAN
Honshu
Nagoya
Kobe
Hiroshima
Kyoto
Osaka
Fukuoka
Kitakyushu
Shikoku
Nagasaki
Kagoshima
Miyazaki
Kyushu
Tokyo
Kawasaki
Yokohama
PACIFIC OCEAN
130°E 140°E 150°E
40°N

0   400 miles
0   400 kilometers
Lambert Conformal Conic projection

Geography Skills

Although small geographically, Japan is one of the world's major economic powers.

1. **Interpreting Maps** What area of Japan is the least industrialized?

2. **Applying Geography Skills** Using this map and information from your text, explain how Japan's geography influences its economy.

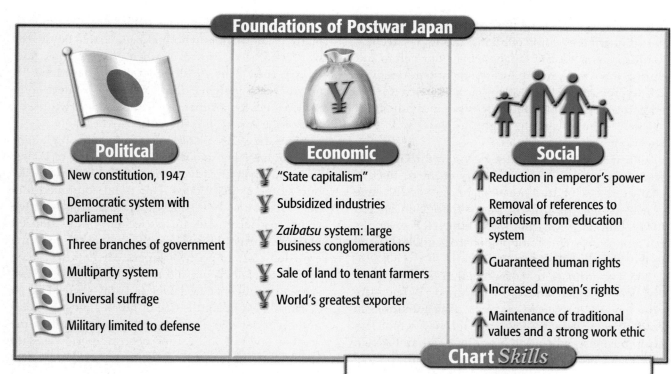

Foundations of Postwar Japan

Political
- New constitution, 1947
- Democratic system with parliament
- Three branches of government
- Multiparty system
- Universal suffrage
- Military limited to defense

Economic
- "State capitalism"
- Subsidized industries
- *Zaibatsu* system: large business conglomerations
- Sale of land to tenant farmers
- World's greatest exporter

Social
- Reduction in emperor's power
- Removal of references to patriotism from education system
- Guaranteed human rights
- Increased women's rights
- Maintenance of traditional values and a strong work ethic

Some problems remain, however. Two recent prime ministers have been forced to resign over improper financial dealings with business associates. Critics at home and abroad have charged that, owing to government policies, the textbooks used in Japanese schools do not adequately discuss the crimes committed by the Japanese government and armed forces during World War II.

The Economy During their occupation of Japan, Allied officials had planned to dismantle the large business conglomerations known as the *zaibatsu*. With the rise of the Cold War, however, the policy was scaled back. Only the 19 largest companies were affected. In addition, the new policy did not keep Japanese companies from forming loose ties with each other, which basically gave rise to another *zaibatsu* system.

The occupation administration had more success with its land-reform program. Half of the population lived on farms, and half of all farmers were tenants of large landowners. Under the reform program, lands were sold on easy credit terms to the tenants. The reform program created a strong class of independent farmers.

At the end of the Allied occupation in 1952, the Japanese gross national product was one-third that of Great Britain or France. Today, it is larger than both put together and well over half that of the United States. Japan is the greatest exporting nation in the world. Its per capita income equals or surpasses that of most Western states.

What explains the Japanese success? Some analysts point to cultural factors. The Japanese are group oriented and find it easy to cooperate with one another. Hardworking and frugal, they are more inclined to save than to buy. This boosts the savings rate and labor productivity. The labor force is highly skilled. In addition, Japanese people share common values and respond in similar ways to the challenges of the modern world.

Other analysts have cited more practical reasons for the Japanese economic success. For example, because its industries were destroyed in World War II, Japan was forced to build entirely new, modern factories. Japanese workers spend a substantially longer period of time at their jobs than do workers in other advanced societies. Corporations reward innovation and maintain good management-labor relations. Finally, some experts contend that Japan uses unfair trade practices—that it dumps goods at prices below cost to break into a foreign market and restricts imports from other countries.

Social Changes During the occupation, Allied planners thought they could eliminate the aggressiveness that had characterized Japanese behavior before and during the war. A new educational system removed all references to patriotism and loyalty to the emperor. At the same time, it stressed individualism. Women were given the right to vote and were encouraged to enter politics.

Efforts to remake Japanese behavior through laws were only partly successful. Many of the distinctive characteristics of traditional Japanese society have persisted into the present day, although in altered form. Emphasis on the work ethic, for example, remains strong. The tradition of hard work is stressed in the educational system.

The subordinate role of women in Japanese society has not been entirely eliminated. Women are now legally protected against discrimination in employment, yet very few have reached senior levels in business, education, or politics. Japan has had no female prime ministers and few female cabinet ministers.

Women now make up more than 40 percent of the workforce, but most are in retail or service occupations. Their average salary is only about 60 percent that of males.

Culture After the Japanese defeat in World War II, many of the writers who had been active before the war resurfaced. However, their writing was now more sober. This "lost generation" described its anguish and piercing despair. Several writers committed suicide. For them, defeat was made worse by fear of the Americanization of postwar Japan.

Since the 1970s, increasing wealth and a high literacy rate have led to a massive outpouring of books. In 1975, Japan already produced twice as much fiction as the United States. This trend continued into the 1990s. Much of this new literature deals with the common concerns of all the wealthy industrialized nations. Current Japanese authors were raised in the crowded cities of postwar Japan, where they soaked up movies, television, and rock music. These writers speak the universal language of today's world.

Haruki Murakami is one of Japan's most popular authors today. He was one of the first to discard the somber style of the earlier postwar period and to speak the contemporary language. *A Wild Sheep Chase,* published in 1982, is an excellent example of his gripping, yet humorous, writing.

✓ **Reading Check** **Explaining** How is the Japanese government involved in Japan's economy?

CONNECTIONS Around The World

Cities and Cars

Since the beginning of the Industrial Revolution in the nineteenth century, the growth of industrialization has been accompanied by the growth of cities. In both industrialized and developing countries, congested and polluted cities have become a way of life. In recent years, as more people have been able to buy cars, traffic jams have also become a regular feature.

In São Paulo, Brazil, for example, traffic jams in which nobody moves last for hours. There are 4.5 million cars in São Paulo, twice the number in New York City, although the cities have about the same population (16 million people). Workers in auto factories in Brazil work around the clock to meet the demand for cars.

The same situation is evident in other cities around the world. In Cairo, a city of 10.6 million people, pollution from stalled traffic erodes the surface of the Sphinx outside the city. In Bangkok, the capital city of Thailand, it can take six hours to reach the airport.

A major cause of traffic congestion is lack of roads. As more and more poor people have fled the countryside for the city, many cities have tripled in population in just 20 years. At the same time, few new roads have been built.

Comparing Cultures

Using outside sources, research traffic problems in three cities in different parts of the world (for example, Los Angeles, Hong Kong, and Paris). How are the traffic problems in these cities similar, and how are they different? What solutions are people developing to solve traffic problems in these particular cities?

Traffic in Thailand

The "Asian Tigers"

A number of Asian nations have imitated Japan in creating successful industrial societies. Sometimes called the "Asian tigers," they are South Korea, Taiwan, Singapore, and Hong Kong. Along with Japan, they have become economic power-houses.

South Korea

South Korea In 1953, the Korean Peninsula was exhausted from three years of bitter war. Two heavily armed countries now faced each other across the 38th parallel. North of this line was the People's Republic of Korea (North Korea), under the dictatorial rule of the Communist leader **Kim Il Sung.** To the south was the Republic of Korea (South Korea), under the dictatorial president **Syngman Rhee.**

After several years of harsh rule and government corruption in South Korea, demonstrations broke out in the capital city of Seoul in the spring of 1960. Rhee was forced to retire. A coup d'etat in 1961 put General Chung Hee Park in power. Two years later, Park was elected president and began to strengthen the South Korean economy. Land reform provided land for peasants, and new industries were promoted.

South Korea gradually emerged as a major industrial power in East Asia. The key areas for industrial development were chemicals, textiles, and shipbuilding. By the 1980s, South Korea was moving into automobile production. The largest Korean corporations are Samsung, Daewoo, and Hyundai.

Like many other countries in the region, South Korea was slow to develop democratic principles. Park ruled by autocratic means and suppressed protest. However, opposition to military rule began to develop. Students, as well as many people in the cities, demonstrated against government policies. Democracy finally came in the 1990s. Elections held during an economic crisis in 1997 brought the reformer Kim Tae-jung to the presidency.

Taiwan: The Other China

Taiwan: The Other China After they were defeated by the Communists and forced to retreat to Taiwan, Chiang Kai-shek and his followers established a capital at Taipei. The government continued to call itself the Republic of China.

Chiang Kai-shek's government maintained that it was the legitimate government of all the Chinese people and would eventually return in triumph to the mainland. At the same time, however, the Communist government on the mainland claimed to rule all of China, including Taiwan.

Protection by American military forces enabled the new regime to concentrate on economic growth without worrying about a Communist invasion. Making good use of foreign aid and the efforts of its own energetic people, the Republic of China built a modern industrialized society.

A land-reform program, which put farmland in the hands of peasants, doubled food production in Taiwan. With government help, local manufacturing and commerce expanded. During the 1960s and 1970s, industrial growth averaged well over 10 percent a year. By 2000, over three-quarters of the population lived in urban areas.

Prosperity, however, did not at first lead to democracy. Under Chiang Kai-shek, the government ruled by emergency decree and refused to allow the formation of new political parties. After the death of Chiang in 1975, the Republic of China slowly began to evolve toward a more representative form of government. By 2002, free elections had enabled opposition parties to win control of the presidency and the legislature.

A major issue for Taiwan is whether it will become an independent state or will be united with mainland China. The United States supports self-determination for the people of Taiwan and believes that any final decision on Taiwan's future must be made by peaceful means. Meanwhile, the People's

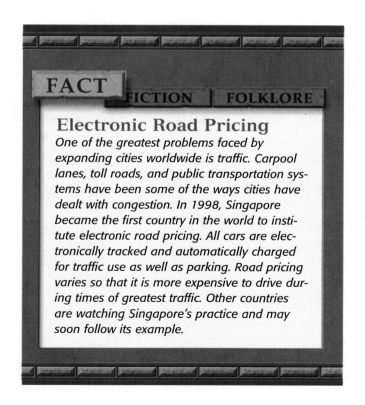

FACT FICTION FOLKLORE

Electronic Road Pricing

One of the greatest problems faced by expanding cities worldwide is traffic. Carpool lanes, toll roads, and public transportation systems have been some of the ways cities have dealt with congestion. In 1998, Singapore became the first country in the world to institute electronic road pricing. All cars are electronically tracked and automatically charged for traffic use as well as parking. Road pricing varies so that it is more expensive to drive during times of greatest traffic. Other countries are watching Singapore's practice and may soon follow its example.

Republic of China on the mainland remains committed to eventual unification.

Singapore and Hong Kong Singapore, once a British colony and briefly a part of the state of Malaysia, is now an independent state. Under the leadership of Prime Minister Lee Kuan Yew (kwahn yoo), Singapore developed an industrial economy based on shipbuilding, oil refineries, and electronics. Singapore has also become the banking center of the region.

In Singapore, an authoritarian political system has created a stable environment for economic growth. The prime minister once stated that the Western model of democracy was not appropriate for Singapore. Its citizens, however, are beginning to demand more political freedoms.

Like Singapore, **Hong Kong** became an industrial powerhouse with standards of living well above the levels of its neighbors. For over 150 years, Hong Kong was under British rule. In 1997, however, Great Britain returned control of Hong Kong to mainland China. China, in turn, promised that, for the next 50 years, Hong Kong would enjoy a high degree of economic freedom under a capitalist system. The shape of Hong Kong's future, however, remains uncertain.

✓ **Reading Check** Evaluating What is the relationship between Taiwan and China?

Australia and New Zealand

Both Australia and the country of New Zealand, located to the south and east of Australia, have iden-

tified themselves culturally and politically with Europe rather than with their Asian neighbors. Their political institutions and values are derived from European models, and their economies resemble those of the industrialized countries of the world. Both are members of the British Commonwealth. Both are also part of the United States-led ANZUS defensive alliance (Australia, New Zealand, and the United States).

In recent years, however, trends have been drawing both states closer to Asia. First, immigration from East and Southeast Asia has increased rapidly. More than one-half of current immigrants into Australia come from East Asia.

Second, trade relations with Asia are increasing rapidly. About 60 percent of Australia's export markets today are in East Asia. Asian trade with New Zealand is also on the increase.

Whether Australia and New Zealand will ever become an integral part of the Asia-Pacific region is uncertain. Since the majority of the population in both Australia and New Zealand has European origins, cultural differences often hinder mutual understanding between the two countries and their Asian neighbors.

✓ **Reading Check** Examining How have Australia and New Zealand been drawn closer to their Asian neighbors? How are they linked to Europe?

▶ **TAKS Practice**

SECTION 3 ASSESSMENT

Checking for Understanding

1. **Define** occupied, state capitalism.

2. **Identify** Douglas MacArthur, Kim Il Sung, Syngman Rhee.

3. **Locate** Singapore, Hong Kong.

4. **Explain** the impact of Japan's land-reform program. What other programs or policies did the occupation administration implement in Japan?

5. **List** the ways in which Australia and New Zealand are similar to European nations.

Critical Thinking

6. **Predict Consequences** What further impact do you think the return of Hong Kong to China will have on either country?

7. **Organizing Information** Use a diagram like the one below to show factors contributing to Japan's economic success.

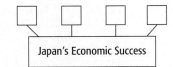

Analyzing Visuals

8. **Locate** the photo of Douglas MacArthur on page 958. What military rank did he hold? Why did the Allies choose a military leader instead of a politician or diplomat to command postwar Japan? What were some of MacArthur's responsibilities in Japan?

Writing About History

9. **Informative Writing** Do additional research on Japan and the "Asian tigers" and analyze their sources of growth. Explain in an essay why these states have been so successful.

School Regulations, Japanese Style

JAPANESE CHILDREN ARE exposed to a school environment much more regimented than that of U.S. public school children. The following regulations are examples of rules adopted by middle school systems in various parts of Japan.

Japanese school children in their uniforms

"1. Boys' hair should not touch the eyebrows, the ears, or the top of the collar.

2. No one should have a permanent wave, or dye his or her hair. Girls should not wear ribbons or accessories in their hair. Hair dryers should not be used. . . .

3. Keep your uniform clean and pressed at all times. Girls' middy blouses should have two buttons on the back collar. Boys' pant cuffs should be of the prescribed width. No more than 12 eyelets should be on shoes.

4. Wear your school badge at all times. It should be positioned exactly.

5. Going to school in the morning, wear your book bag strap on the right shoulder; in the afternoon on the way home, wear it on the left shoulder.

6. When you raise your hand to be called on, your arm should extend forward and up at the angle prescribed in your handbook.

7. Your own route to and from school is marked in your student rule handbook; carefully observe which side of each street you are to use on the way to and from school.

8. After school you are to go directly home, unless your parent has written a note permitting you to go to another location. Permission will not be granted by the school unless this other location is a suitable one. You must not go to coffee shops.

9. Before and after school, no matter where you are, you represent our school, so you should behave in ways we can all be proud of."

—Japanese School Regulations

Analyzing Primary Sources

1. In your own words, describe the Japanese system of education for young people.
2. Compare the Japanese system of education to the American system with which you are familiar. How are they similar? How are they different?

Chapter Summary

Since 1945, Asia and the Pacific region have seen many changes, as shown below.

Change

Out of defeat comes a new political and economic system.
- After gaining independence, Japan becomes an economic powerhouse.
- Imitating Japan, other Asian nations also develop strong economies.

Revolution

Communists assume power and introduce socialist methods.
- In China, Mao Zedong initiates programs like the Great Leap Forward and the Great Proletarian Cultural Revolution. After Mao, Deng Xiaoping institutes the Four Modernizations.

Regionalism

Decades of rivalry and suspicion cause divisions.
- Tensions between Communist North Korea and non-Communist South Korea lead to war.
- China resists Taiwanese independence.

Conflict

Nationalism and Cold War competition lead to war.
- The United States enters the war in Vietnam.
- The Khmer Rouge devastates Cambodia.

Diversity

Religious and ethnic rivalries hinder unity and lead to violence.
- Religious and ethnic differences produce conflict between Hindus and Muslims in India and Pakistan.

Cultural Diffusion

Political and economic changes link Asian countries to the world.
- Democracy develops in the Philippines.
- Chinese students demand democratic reforms.
- Increased immigration and trade draw Australia and New Zealand closer to their Asian neighbors.

Using Key Terms

1. _____ is an economic system in which the central government plays an active role in the country's economy.
2. An idea supported by Mao, that a constant state of revolution could create perfect communism, was called _____.
3. A country is _____ when its lands are held and controlled by a foreign military force.
4. The amount of income earned by each person in a country is called _____ income.
5. A _____ is reached when neither side in a conflict is able to achieve significant gains.
6. Massive collective farms created in China's Great Leap Forward were called _____.
7. Many governments now have laws that forbid acts of prejudice or _____ from being committed against people in their countries.

Reviewing Key Facts

8. **Geography** What nations are called the "Asian tigers" and why?
9. **Economics** How did promises of military protection from the United States help Taiwan develop its economy?
10. **History** What were the consequences of Great Britain's withdrawal from India?
11. **History** What nation fought for control of Vietnam before the United States became involved?
12. **Government** What policy did the Khmer Rouge follow toward the people they regarded as enemies after they gained control of Cambodia?
13. **Economics** What help did China require to improve its economy after the Cultural Revolution?
14. **History** What happened to Hong Kong in 1997?
15. **History** What events took place in Tiananmen Square in 1989?
16. **Government** Who was Indira Gandhi?

Critical Thinking

17. **Making Predictions** Analyze what conditions in India contributed to the assassinations of political leaders. Do you believe it is possible for India to maintain a stable democratic government?
18. **Drawing Conclusions** Evaluate the impact Japan's recovery has had on global affairs since World War II.

Writing About History

19. Expository Writing Compare North and South Korea. In what ways are they similar? In what ways are they different? Do supplementary research online or at the library to learn about their cultures and histories.

Analyzing Sources

Read the following excerpt from the book *Japanese Women,* published in 1955:

> ❝A quick glance at educational statistics reveals a higher percentage of female as compared to male high school graduates entering colleges and universities. The overwhelming majority of female college and university graduates, over 80 percent, are taking up employment and doing so in a wider range of fields than in the past. Better education and the availability of more job opportunities have increasingly made it possible for women to look upon marriage as an option rather than a prescribed lifestyle. . . .❞

20. What does this passage reveal about the role of women in Japan after World War II?

21. Do you think it was difficult for Japanese women to break from their old roles in society?

Applying Technology Skills

22. Developing Multimedia Presentations Locate sources about present-day North Korea and South Korea. Organize your findings by creating a fact sheet comparing the two countries. Use a word processor to create a chart. Headings to include are population, type of economy, type of government, currency, infant mortality rate, literacy rate, and official religion. Provide a map of each country that shows political boundaries, major cities, and natural resources.

Making Decisions

23. What is the conflict regarding Taiwan's independence? Research the reasons for the tension between China and Taiwan. How do you think this conflict would be best resolved? Create a compromise solution that would satisfy the demands of those who want a self-determined Taiwan, as well as those who want Taiwan reunified with China.

Indochina, 1946–1954

Extent of Communist control, 1946–1954
Boundary of Indochina, 1954

Analyzing Maps and Charts

24. Approximately how much of Vietnam was controlled by the Communists between 1946 and 1954?

25. Which countries separate North and South Vietnam from Thailand?

26. What river runs from China to the Gulf of Tonkin?

Test Practice

Directions: Choose the best answer to the question below.

Between 1966 and 1976, the destruction of many temples, the seizure of many books, and the imprisonment of some artists and intellectuals were closely related to which movement?

A China's Cultural Revolution

B Conservatism

C Women's rights movement

D Humanism

Test-Taking Tip: Even if you know the correct answer immediately, read all of the answer choices and eliminate those you know are wrong. Doing so will help you confirm that the answer choice you think is correct is indeed correct.

32 Challenges and Hopes for the Future

Key Events

As you read this chapter, look for key issues that challenge the contemporary world.
* *Today's world faces the challenges of protecting and preserving the environment, addressing economic and social changes, implementing new technologies, resolving political conflicts, and eliminating international terrorism.*
* *The world's inhabitants must adopt a cooperative global vision to address the problems that confront all humankind.*

The Impact Today

The events that occurred during this time period still impact our lives today.
* *The debate over nuclear weapons continues as European leaders question the United States government's desire to deploy a nuclear missile defense system in outer space.*
* *Peacekeeping forces remain in the Balkan Peninsula.*
* *Automakers, fuel companies, and other manufacturers are developing methods to reduce harmful emissions.*

 World History Video *The Chapter 32 video, "In the Twenty-first Century," explores various issues that the world is facing today.*

1962
Publication of *Silent Spring* begins environmental protection movement

1969
Two American astronauts land on the moon

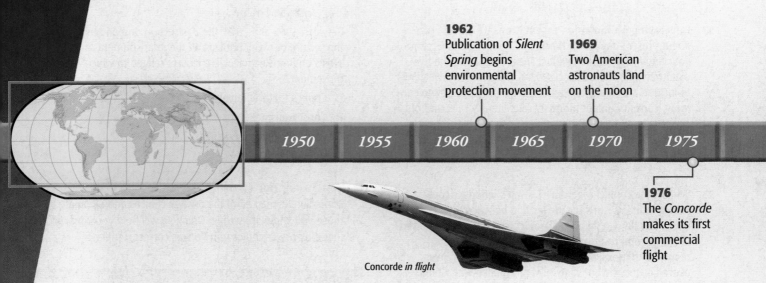

1950   1955   1960   1965   1970   1975

1976
The *Concorde* makes its first commercial flight

Concorde *in flight*

The International Space Station, shown here in 2000, combines the scientific and technological resources of 16 nations.

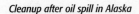
Cleanup after oil spill in Alaska

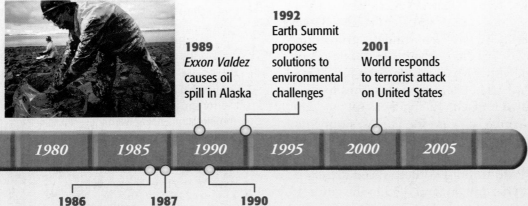

1989
Exxon Valdez causes oil spill in Alaska

1992
Earth Summit proposes solutions to environmental challenges

2001
World responds to terrorist attack on United States

1980   1985   1990   1995   2000   2005

1986
Explosion at nuclear plant in Chernobyl releases deadly radiation

1987
Montreal meeting creates first world environmental pact

1990
World Wide Web created

HISTORY Online
Chapter Overview
Visit the *Glencoe World History* Web site at tx.wh.glencoe.com and click on **Chapter 32–Chapter Overview** to preview chapter information.

A Story That Matters

Rescue workers search for survivors in the ruins of the World Trade Center.

A Time for Heroes

On September 11, 2001, international terrorists hijacked four commercial airplanes, two of which were used to destroy the twin towers of the World Trade Center in New York City. Thousands of people died in the attack when first one tower, and then the other, collapsed. Many of those who died were firefighters, police officers, and other rescue workers who rushed into the buildings to help people to safety.

In the days following the attack, countless tales of unimaginable bravery emerged. Two office workers carried a disabled woman down 68 floors to safety. Peter Ganci, a 33-year veteran of the New York City Fire Department, survived the collapse of the first tower but died trying to evacuate people from the second tower. Father Mychal Judge, the Fire Department chaplain, removed his helmet to give last rites to a dying firefighter but died himself when he was hit by debris. One firefighter, as he climbed toward the flames, stopped to give a fleeing woman a bottle of water. She escaped, but he did not.

George Howard, a Port Authority officer, raced to help people, even though it was his day off, and died in the effort. In an address to the American nation, President George W. Bush said that he would carry Howard's badge as a reminder of the horrors of terrorism, for "Freedom and fear are at war. The advance of human freedom, the great achievement of our time and the great hope of every time, now depends on us. . . . We will not falter and we will not fail."

Why It Matters

The destruction of the World Trade Center was not an attack on the United States alone. People from over 80 countries were killed in what the United Nations condemned as a "crime against humanity." More and more, people are coming to understand that destructive forces unleashed in one part of the world soon affect the entire world. As British prime minister Tony Blair said, "We are realizing how fragile are our frontiers in the face of the world's new challenges. Today, conflicts rarely stay within national boundaries." Terrorism, worldwide hunger, nuclear proliferation, global warming—these issues make us aware of the global nature of contemporary problems. Increasingly, the world's nations must unite to create lasting solutions.

History and You What contemporary global problem concerns you the most? Write an essay explaining what the world's nations should do, together, to solve this problem.

The Challenges of Our World

Main Ideas
- The world faces environmental, social, economic, and political challenges.
- The benefits of the technological revolution must be balanced against its costs.

Key Terms
ecology, deforestation, ozone layer, greenhouse effect, acid rain, biowarfare, bioterrorism, global economy

People to Identify
Rachel Carson, Neil Armstrong, Buzz Aldrin

Places to Locate
Bhopal, Chernobyl, Sudan

Preview Questions
1. What challenges face the world in the twenty-first century?
2. What are the promises and perils of the technological revolution?

Reading Strategy
Cause and Effect Complete the table below as you read the chapter.

Concern	Cause	Effect
Deforestation		
Loss of ozone layer		
Greenhouse effect		
Acid rain		
Weapons		
Hunger		

Preview of Events

♦1984	♦1985	♦1986	♦1987	♦1988	♦1989	♦1990

1984
Toxic fumes kill 3,800 people in Bhopal, India

1989
Oil spill from tanker in Alaska devastates environment

Voices from the Past

Biologist and author, Rachel Carson

In 1962, Rachel Carson wrote:

❝It is not my contention that chemical pesticides must never be used. I do contend that we have put poisons and biologically potent chemicals into the hands of persons largely or wholly ignorant of their potentials for harm. We have subjected enormous numbers of people to contact with these poisons, without their consent and often without their knowledge. . . . I contend, furthermore, that we have allowed these chemicals to be used with little or no advance investigation of their effect on soil, water, wildlife, and man himself. Future generations are unlikely to condone our lack of prudent concern for the integrity of the natural world that supports all life.❞
—*Silent Spring*, Rachel Carson, 1962

The modern movement to protect the environment began with Rachel Carson's *Silent Spring*.

The Environmental Crisis

In 1962, American scientist **Rachel Carson** argued that the use of pesticides—chemicals sprayed on crops to kill insects—was having deadly, unforeseen results. Besides insects, birds, fish, and other wild animals were being killed by the buildup of these pesticides in the environment. Also, the pesticide residue on food was harmful to human beings.

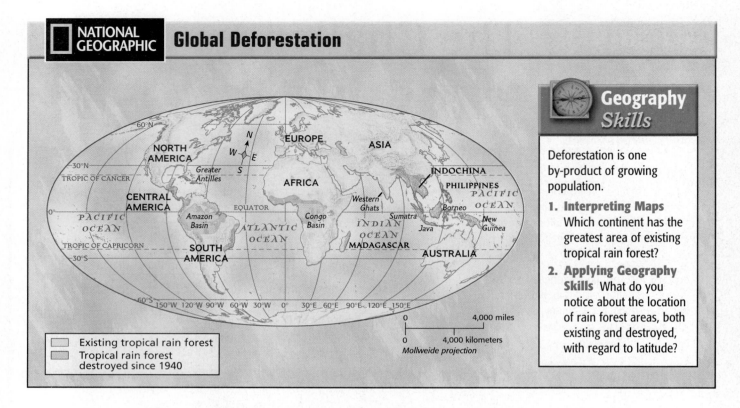

NATIONAL GEOGRAPHIC — Global Deforestation

Existing tropical rain forest
Tropical rain forest destroyed since 1940

0   4,000 miles
0   4,000 kilometers
Mollweide projection

Geography Skills

Deforestation is one by-product of growing population.

1. **Interpreting Maps** Which continent has the greatest area of existing tropical rain forest?

2. **Applying Geography Skills** What do you notice about the location of rain forest areas, both existing and destroyed, with regard to latitude?

Carson's warnings alarmed many scientists and gave rise to a new field of science called ecology, the study of the relationship between living things and their environment. Many people became more aware of the dangers to the environment on which they depended for their survival.

Impact of Population Growth Dangers to the environment have many sources. A rapid increase in world population has led to fears that Earth's resources simply cannot support the growing number of human beings. Deforestation—the clearing of forests—is one by-product of the growing population. More and more forests and jungles have been cut down to provide farmland and firewood for the people on Earth. As forests are cut down, natural dwelling places for plants and animals are destroyed.

Especially worrisome is the rapid destruction of tropical rain forests near Earth's equator. Although the tropical rain forests cover only 6 percent of Earth's surface, they support 50 percent of the world's species of plants and animals. The tropical rain forests are also crucial to human survival. They remove carbon dioxide from the air and return oxygen to it.

Chemical Wastes and Disasters Another danger to the environment is chemical waste. One concern involves chlorofluorocarbons, which are gases used in aerosol cans, refrigerators, and automobile air conditioners. Many scientists warn that the release of chlorofluorocarbons is destroying the ozone layer, a thin layer of gas in the upper atmosphere that shields Earth from the Sun's ultraviolet rays.

Other scientists have proposed the existence of a greenhouse effect, global warming caused by the buildup of carbon dioxide in the atmosphere. Global warming could create various problems. Sea levels could rise because of melting polar ice, for example, and cause flooding of coastal areas.

Yet another problem is acid rain, the rainfall that results when sulfur produced by factories mixes with moisture in the air. Acid rain has been held responsible for killing forests in both North America and Europe.

Major ecological disasters have also occurred during the last 20 years. In 1984, a chemical plant at **Bhopal**, India, released toxic fumes into the air,

killing 3,800 people and injuring another 100,000. A nuclear explosion at **Chernobyl** in 1986 released radiation that killed hundreds. In 1989, the oil tanker *Exxon Valdez* ran aground in Alaska. Thousands of birds were killed, fishing grounds were polluted, and the local environment was devastated.

These ecological disasters made people more aware of the need to deal with environmental problems. In 1987, representatives of 43 nations meeting in Montreal agreed to protect Earth's ozone layer by reducing the use of chlorofluorocarbons. In 1992, an Earth Summit in Rio de Janeiro examined the challenges to the environment and proposed new solutions.

Individual nations have reacted to environmental problems by enacting recycling programs, curbing the dumping of toxic materials, and instituting water conservation measures.

✔ **Reading Check** **Summarizing** What global concerns have arisen since the 1960s?

The Technological Revolution

┌TURNING**POINT**┐ **In this section, you will learn how two American astronauts landed on the moon in 1969. This landing opened the new frontier of space to world exploration.**

Since World War II, a stunning array of changes has created a technological revolution.

Transportation, Communications, and Space

Modern transportation and communication systems are transforming the world community. Since the 1970s, jumbo jet airlines have moved millions of people around the world each year. The Internet—the world's largest computer network—provides quick access to enormous quantities of information. The development of the World Wide Web in the 1990s made the Internet even more accessible to people everywhere. Satellites, cable television, facsimile (fax) machines, and cellular telephones allow people to communicate with each other practically everywhere on Earth.

The exploration of space is another world-changing development. In 1969, the American astronauts **Neil Armstrong** and **Buzz Aldrin** landed on the moon. Space probes and shuttle flights have increased scientific knowledge, but not without human costs. In 1986, space shuttle *Challenger* exploded a minute or so after liftoff, killing all onboard. In 2003, seven astronauts died when the shuttle *Columbia* abruptly disintegrated over Texas in the last minutes of a 16-day mission. In both cases, Americans responded with a profound sense of grief.

Health Care and Agriculture In the field of health, new medicines enable doctors to treat both physical and mental illnesses. New technologies, including computer-aided imaging, have enabled doctors to perform "miracle" operations. Mechanical valves and pumps for the heart as well as organ transplants have allowed people to live longer and more productive lives.

Technological changes in the field of health have raised new concerns, however. For example, genetic engineering is a new scientific field that alters the genetic information of cells to produce new variations. Some scientists have questioned whether genetic engineering might accidentally create new strains of deadly bacteria that could not be controlled. Already, the overuse of antibiotics has created "supergerms" that do not respond to treatment with available antibiotics. The issues of stem-cell research and human cloning have also generated intense debate.

In agriculture, the Green Revolution has promised immense returns. The Green Revolution refers to the development of new strains of rice, corn, and other grains that have greater yields. It was promoted as the technological solution to feeding the world's ever-growing population. However, immense quantities of chemical fertilizers are needed to grow the new strains, and many farmers cannot afford them.

Astronaut Buzz Aldrin on the moon with the Apollo 11 *lunar module*

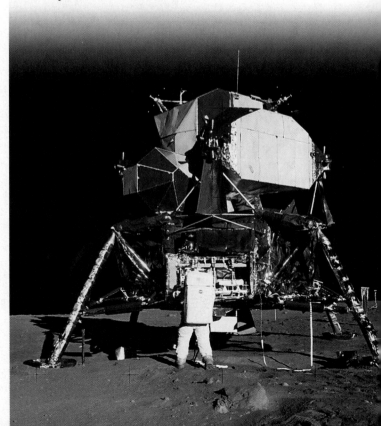

In addition, the new crops have been subject to insects. The pesticides used to control the insects create environmental problems.

Weapons The technological revolution has also led to the development of more advanced methods of destruction. Most frightening are nuclear, biological, and chemical weapons.

The end of the Cold War in the late 1980s reduced the chances of a major nuclear war. However, nuclear weapons continue to spread, making a regional nuclear war possible. Another concern is whether nuclear materials—bombs or radioactive matter—will be obtained and used by terrorists.

After anthrax-filled letters were used to kill U.S. citizens in 2001, people around the world became more aware of the increased availability and the potential threat of biological and chemical weapons. Biowarfare, the use of disease and poison against civilians and soldiers in wartime, is not new, however. The first incident occurred in Europe in the 1300s when, during a siege, plague-infested corpses were launched over city walls to infect the populace. Chemical weapons were used extensively in World War I and during the Iran-Iraq war in the 1980s. The Japanese used biological weapons on China and Manchuria in the 1930s and 1940s.

Governments have made agreements to limit the research, production, and use of biological and chemical weapons. The 1925 Geneva Protocol, for example, prohibits the use, though not the research or production, of biological and chemical weapons. In 1972, the United States and the Soviet Union agreed only to permit work on defensive biological weapons.

These measures have not prevented terrorists and terrorist-supporting governments from practicing bioterrorism, the use of biological and chemical weapons in terrorist attacks. For example, in 1995 members of a Japanese religious sect named Aum Shinrikyo released a chemical agent, sarin gas, in a Tokyo subway, killing 12 people and injuring thousands.

Reading Check **Identifying** List the industries that the technological revolution has affected since World War II.

Economic and Social Challenges

Since World War II, the nations of the world have developed a global economy—an economy in which the production, distribution, and sale of goods take place on a worldwide scale. In 1995, the **World Trade Organization** (WTO) was established. Trade agree-ments are negotiated, signed, and upheld by its member nations, which number over 140. The WTO has been criticized for placing commercial interests over environmental and health concerns and leaving out small and developing countries. Still, the WTO is the only global international organization dealing with rules of trade between nations.

The Gap between Rich and Poor Nations One of the features of the global economy is the wide gap between rich and poor nations. The rich, industrialized nations are mainly in the Northern Hemisphere. They include countries such as the United States, Canada, and Japan, as well as countries in western Europe. These nations have well-organized industrial and agricultural systems, make use of advanced technologies, and have strong educational systems.

The poor nations, sometimes called developing countries, are located mainly in the Southern Hemisphere and include many nations in Africa, Asia, and Latin America. Developing countries are primarily farming nations with little technology.

A serious problem in developing countries is explosive population growth. The world's population today is 6.2 billion. The United Nations projects that by 2050, the world's population could reach 9 billion. Much of that rapid growth is taking place in developing countries, which can least afford it.

Rapidly growing populations have caused many people to move to cities to find jobs. In developing countries, the size of some cities has grown dramatically as a result of this shift. São Paulo, Brazil, for example, had 8.1 million people in 1970. Today, it has over 17 million. Millions of people in such cities live in terrible conditions in slums or shantytowns.

Hunger has also become a staggering problem. Every year, over 8 million people die of hunger, many of them children under five years of age. Besides rapid population growth, poor soil, natural catastrophes, and economic and political factors contribute to widespread hunger. In Afghanistan, for example, most of the population is hungry. Over the last two decades, the country has experienced a major earthquake, severe drought, and political and military upheaval.

Civil wars have been especially devastating in creating food shortages. In **Sudan,** civil war broke out in the 1980s. Both sides refused to allow food to

be sent to their enemies. By the early 1990s, 1.3 million people had died in Sudan from starvation.

To improve their economic situations, developing nations have sought to establish industrial economies. This goal has not been easy to reach, however. Rapidly growing populations place enormous burdens on the economies of developing nations and make it extremely difficult to create a new industrial order.

The Gender Gap The gap between rich and poor nations is also reflected in the status of women. In the Western world, the gap between men and women has been steadily narrowing. The number of women in the workforce continues to increase, along with the number of women university graduates. Many countries have passed laws that require equal pay for women and men who are doing the same work. A number of Western countries also have laws that prohibit discrimination based on gender.

Women in developing countries, by contrast, often remain bound to their homes and families and subordinate to their fathers and husbands. They continue to face difficulties in obtaining education, property rights, or decent jobs.

✓**Reading Check** **Comparing** What are the differences between developing and industrialized nations?

Political Challenges

After World War II, African and Asian leaders identified democracy as the defining theme of their new political cultures. Within a decade, however, democratic systems in many developing countries had been replaced by military dictatorships or one-party governments. Many leaders underestimated the difficulties of building democratic political institutions.

In recent years, there have been signs of renewed interest in democracy in various parts of the world, particularly in Asia, Africa, and Latin America. Examples are the free elections held in South Korea, Taiwan, and the Philippines. Similar developments have taken place in a number of African countries and throughout Latin America.

Unfortunately, regional, ethnic, and religious differences continue to create conflict around the world. In Europe, Yugoslavia has been torn apart by ethnic divisions. In the Middle East, the conflict between Israelis and Palestinians continues to produce acts of terror. Conflicts among hostile ethnic groups in Africa have led to massacres of hundreds of thousands. It remains to be seen how such conflicts can be resolved.

✓**Reading Check** **Explaining** Name the areas of the world where conflict exists. Describe the nature of the conflicts.

⬥ TAKS Practice

SECTION 1 ASSESSMENT

Checking for Understanding

1. **Define** ecology, deforestation, ozone layer, greenhouse effect, acid rain, biowarfare, bioterrorism, global economy.

2. **Identify** Rachel Carson, Neil Armstrong, Buzz Aldrin, World Trade Organization.

3. **Locate** Bhopal, Chernobyl, Sudan.

4. **Explain** why it is difficult for developing nations to establish industrial economies. What specific problems are many developing nations attempting to solve?

5. **List** three countries in which free elections have demonstrated great progress toward democracy. Also list three types of political challenges that remain unsolved and give an example of each.

Critical Thinking

6. **Analyze** What are the individual and global consequences of overpopulation?

7. **Summarizing Information** Create a chart like the one below listing technological advances in transportation, communications, space exploration, health care, agriculture, and weaponry. List the drawback or cost of each technological advance.

Technological Advances	Drawback or Cost
Transportation	
Communications	
Space Exploration	
Health Care	
Agriculture	
Weaponry	

Analyzing Visuals

8. **Compare** the photo on page 971 to the photo of the International Space Station on page 967. Describe the advances and changes in space technology that are reflected in these two photos. How many years have elapsed between the two photos?

Writing About History

9. **Expository Writing** By now, most leaders of major nations have recognized that environmental damage is a significant issue. For this reason, these leaders frequently hold meetings and summits to negotiate solutions. In an essay, discuss why negotiations are needed. What concerns can cause nations or individuals to ignore the environment?

Global Visions

Guide to Reading

Main Ideas
- Organizations have been established to respond to global challenges.
- Citizens' groups and nongovernmental organizations have also formed to address global concerns.

Key Terms
peacekeeping force, disarmament

People To Identify
Franklin Delano Roosevelt, Hazel Henderson, Elise Boulding

Places To Locate
China, Canada

Preview Questions
1. What international organization arose at the end of World War II to help maintain the peace?
2. How have ordinary citizens worked to address the world's problems?

Reading Strategy
Organizing Information Create a pyramid like the one below that depicts the structure of the United Nations. The Security Council is at the top of the pyramid.

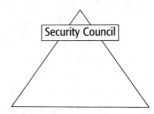

Security Council

Preview of Events

♦1945	♦1946	♦1947	♦1948	♦1949

1945
United Nations becomes world organization

1946
United Nations International Children's Emergency Fund (UNICEF) founded

1948
United Nations General Assembly adopts Universal Declaration of Human Rights

Voices from the Past

Eleanor Roosevelt holds the Universal Declaration of Human Rights.

On December 10, 1948, the General Assembly of the United Nations adopted the Universal Declaration of Human Rights:

❝All human beings are born free and equal in dignity and rights. . . . Everyone is entitled to all the rights and freedoms set forth in this Declaration, without distinction of any kind, such as race, color, sex, language, religion, political or other opinion, national or social origin, property, birth or other status. . . . Everyone has the right to life, liberty, and security of person. . . . Everyone has the right to freedom of movement. . . . Everyone has the right to freedom of opinion and expression.❞
— *The Universal Declaration of Human Rights,* 1948

The United Nations took the lead in affirming the basic human rights of all peoples.

The United Nations

As people have become aware that many problems humans face are global—not national—they have responded to this realization in different ways. The United Nations (UN) has been one of the most visible symbols of the new globalism.

The United Nations was founded in 1945 in San Francisco, when representatives of the Allied forces worked out a plan for a new international organization. U.S. president **Franklin Delano Roosevelt** was especially eager to create such an organization to help maintain the peace after the war. At the Yalta Conference in February 1945, Joseph Stalin of the Soviet Union agreed to join the new organization.

In the original charter, the members pledged "to save succeeding generations from the scourge of war, which twice in our lifetime . . . brought untold sorrow to mankind, and to reaffirm faith in fundamental human rights, in the dignity and worth of the human person, in the equal rights of men and women and of nations large and small, and to promote social progress and better standards of life in larger freedom." The United Nations, then, has two chief goals: peace and human dignity.

The General Assembly of the United Nations is comprised of representatives of all member nations. It has the power to discuss any question of importance to the organization and to recommend the action to be taken. The day-to-day administrative business of the United Nations is supervised by the secretary-general, whose offices are located in New York City.

The most important advisory group of the United Nations is the Security Council. It is composed of 5 permanent members—the United States, Russia, Great Britain, France, and **China**—and 10 members chosen by the General Assembly to serve limited terms. The Security Council decides what actions the United Nations should take to settle international disputes. Because each of the permanent members can veto the council's decision, a stalemate has frequently resulted from Security Council deliberations.

A number of specialized agencies function under the direction of the United Nations. These include the United Nations Educational, Scientific, and Cultural Organization (UNESCO), the World Health Organization (WHO), and the United Nations International Children's Emergency Fund (UNICEF).

All these agencies have been successful in providing aid to address economic and social problems. The United Nations has also performed a valuable service in organizing international conferences on important issues such as population growth and the environment.

The United Nations has on various occasions provided peacekeeping forces, which are military forces drawn from neutral member states to settle conflicts and supervise truces. Missions in Somalia and Bosnia, however, raised questions about the effectiveness of the United Nations in peacekeeping operations.

Until recently, the basic weakness of the United Nations was that, throughout its history, it had been subject to the whims of the two superpowers. The rivalry of the United States and the Soviet Union during the Cold War was often

HISTORY Online

Web Activity Visit the *Glencoe World History* Web site at **tx.wh.glencoe.com** and click on **Chapter 32– Student Web Activity** to learn more about the United Nations.

United Nations troops give food to starving Bosnian Muslims.

played out at the expense of the United Nations. The United Nations had little success, for example, in reducing the arms race between the two superpowers. With the end of the Cold War, the United Nations has played a more active role in keeping alive a vision of international order.

✔ **Reading Check** **Describing** Outline the history of the United Nations, name its three main divisions, list its specialized agencies, and explain how each unit functions.

New Global Visions

One approach to the global problems we face has been the development of social movements led by ordinary citizens. These movements have addressed issues including environmental problems, women's and men's liberation, human potential, appropriate technology, and nonviolence. "Think globally, act locally" is frequently the slogan of such grassroots groups.

Hazel Henderson, a British-born economist, has been especially active in founding public interest groups. She believes that citizen groups can be an important force for greater global unity and justice.

In *Creating Alternative Futures,* Henderson explained: "These aroused citizens are by no means all mindless young radicals. Well-dressed, clean-shaven, middle-class businessmen and their suburban wives comprise the major forces in California fighting against nuclear power. Hundreds of thousands of middle-class mothers are bringing massive

Peace march

pressure to ban commercials and violent programs from children's television."

Related to the emergence of social movements is the growth of nongovernmental organizations (NGOs). NGOs include professional, business, and cooperative organizations; foundations; religious, peace, and disarmament groups, which work to limit or reduce armed forces and weapons; youth and women's organizations; environmental and human rights groups; and research institutes.

According to the American educator **Elise Boulding,** who has been active in encouraging the existence of these groups, NGOs are an important instrument in the cultivation of global perspectives. Boulding states: "Since NGOs by definition are identified with interests that transcend national boundaries, we expect all NGOs to define problems in global terms, to take account of human interests and needs as they are found in all parts of the planet." The number of international NGOs increased from 176 in 1910 to nearly 29,000 in 1995.

Global approaches to global problems, however, have been hindered by political, ethnic, and religious disputes. The Palestinian-Israeli conflict keeps much of the Middle East in constant turmoil. Religious differences between Hindus and Muslims help to inflame relations between India and Pakistan. The United States and **Canada** have argued about the effects of acid rain on Canadian forests.

The collapse of the Soviet Union has led to the emergence of new nations in conflict and a general atmosphere of friction and tension throughout much of Eastern Europe. The bloody conflict in the lands of the former Yugoslavia clearly indicates the dangers in the rise of nationalist sentiment among various ethnic and religious groups in that region. Even as the world becomes more global in culture and as the nations of the world become more interdependent, disruptive forces still exist that can work against efforts to enhance our human destiny.

Many lessons can be learned from the study of world history. One of them is especially clear: a lack of involvement in the affairs of society can easily lead to a sense of powerlessness. An understanding of our world heritage and its lessons might well give us the opportunity to make wise choices in an age that is often crisis laden and chaotic. We are all creators of history. The choices we make in our everyday lives will affect the future of world civilization.

✔**Reading Check** **Examining** List two ways people have attempted to resolve global problems and describe the obstacles to solving these problems.

TAKS Practice

SECTION 2 ASSESSMENT

Checking for Understanding

1. **Define** peacekeeping force, disarmament.

2. **Identify** Franklin Delano Roosevelt, Hazel Henderson, Elise Boulding.

3. **Locate** China, Canada.

4. **Explain** why global approaches to global problems are sometimes difficult to coordinate.

5. **List** the permanent members of the United Nations Security Council. How many members serve limited terms at any one time?

Critical Thinking

6. **Analyze** Why was an international peacekeeping organization created after World War II?

7. **Categorizing Information** Create a chart like the one below listing areas of the world that have political, ethnic, and religious disputes. Place each country in the correct category.

Nature of Dispute	Country
Political	
Ethnic	
Religious	

Analyzing Visuals

8. **Describe** the photo on page 975 in your own words. Then explain why peacekeepers wear military clothing.

Writing About History

9. **Descriptive Writing** Thousands of nongovernmental organizations (NGOs) represent citizens' interests throughout the world. Choose one NGO to examine in detail. Write an essay about the organization's mission, its goals, its accomplishments, and its failures. How has it impacted the world?

TECHNOLOGY
SKILLBUILDER

Developing Multimedia Presentations

Why Learn This Skill?

You have been assigned a research project about Brazil's rain forest. To vividly present the important issues to your classmates, you would like to show them slides of the endangered animals and plants in the rain forest, along with videos of the region and recordings of native music. This type of presentation is called a multimedia presentation because it uses a variety of media, such as photographs, music, and video, to convey information to others.

Learning the Skill

At its most basic, a multimedia presentation can be as simple as using equipment such as a slide projector, a VCR, a TV, and a portable stereo. You can use pre-recorded materials or make your own videotapes or sound recordings.

With the right tools, you can also develop a multimedia presentation on a computer. Computer presentations can combine text, graphics, audio, animation, and video in an interactive program. To create this kind of presentation, you might use traditional graphic tools and draw programs, animation programs that make still images move, and authoring systems that tie everything together. Your computer manual will tell you which tools your computer can support.

Practicing the Skill

Suppose you want to give a report about the importance of the Brazilian rain forest. Ask yourself the following questions to develop an effective multimedia presentation.

- Which forms of media do I want to include? Video? Sound? Photographs? Graphics? Animation? Anything else?

- What equipment would I need to present the media I want to use?

- If I want to make a computer presentation, which of these media forms does my computer support?

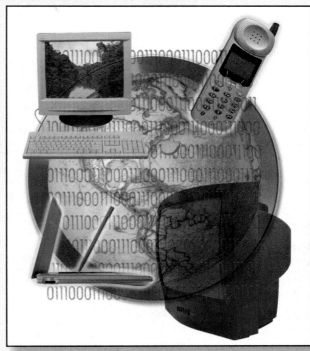

Multimedia equipment

- What kind of software programs or systems do I need? A graphics program? An animation program? A program that allows users to interact with the on-screen presentation? An authoring system that will allow me to change images, sound, and motion?

- Is there a "do-it-all" program I can use to develop the kind of presentation I want?

Applying the Skill

Think of a topic that would be suitable for a multimedia presentation. Keeping in mind the guidelines given above, create a plan that describes the presentation you would like to develop. Indicate what tools you will need and what steps you must take to make the presentation an exciting reality.

Using Key Terms

1. The destruction of large forests and jungles that affects the world's climate, animals, and plants is called _____.

2. A _____ is based on the interdependency of nations' economic systems.

3. The science of _____ studies the relationship between living things and their environment.

4. Organizations that seek to limit or reduce armed forces and weapons are called _____ groups.

5. When the sulfur produced by factories mixes with moisture in the air the result is _____.

Reviewing Key Facts

6. **History** What environmental message was the theme of *Silent Spring?*

7. **Science and Technology** What chemical is suspected of harming the Earth's ozone layer?

8. **Science and Technology** Explain the greenhouse effect and the problems it could create.

9. **History** When and where did the world's nations meet to discuss environmental issues?

10. **Government** What problems do developing nations face?

11. **Science and Technology** What contributes to the hunger problem in developing nations? What are some of the possible solutions to the hunger problem?

12. **Citizenship** Why are nongovernmental organizations taking greater responsibility for protecting the world's environment?

13. **Culture** How have the introduction of Western ideas and customs had a destabilizing effect in many areas of the world?

14. **Government** What is the United Nations Security Council? Why is it difficult for this council to make decisions?

15. **Citizenship** What is the slogan of grassroots public interest groups? What kind of issues do these groups address, and what kind of members do these groups usually attract?

Critical Thinking

16. **Evaluating** Analyze the interdependency of developing and industrialized nations.

17. **Cause and Effect** Explain the increased potential for regional nuclear wars since the Soviet Union disintegrated.

Chapter Summary

At the beginning of the twenty-first century, the world has become a global society. Nations are politically and economically dependent on each other, and the world's problems are of a global nature, as shown in the chart below.

Cultural Diffusion

- Jumbo jetliners transport passengers around the world.
- Corporations have offices in more than one country.
- Advances in communication, such as the Internet, connect people around the globe.

Technological Innovation

- The science of ecology is born.
- American astronauts land on the moon.
- Super strains of corn, rice, and other grains produce greater crop yields.
- Health care advances prolong lives.
- Developments in transportation and communication transform the world community.

Cooperation

- The Earth Summit meets in Rio de Janeiro.
- Nations enact recycling programs and curb the dumping of toxic materials.
- The United Nations forms to promote world peace.
- Nongovernmental organizations advocate social and environmental change.

Conflict

- Massive growth in world population causes overcrowding and hunger in many countries.
- Regional, ethnic, and religious differences continue to produce violence around the world.
- International terrorists remain a threat to peace and security.

Writing About History

18. **Expository Writing** Write an essay comparing the nuclear
disaster at Chernobyl with the chemical plant accident in
Bhopal and the grounding of the *Exxon Valdez* in Alaska.
Which disaster was the most devastating to the environment
in your opinion? Why do you have this opinion, and how
would you prevent a future disaster?

Analyzing Sources

Rachel Carson cautioned about the dangers of harmful chemicals
in her book, *Silent Spring:*

> ❝It is not my contention that chemical pesticides
> must never be used. I do contend that we have put poi-
> sons and biologically potent chemicals into the hands
> of persons largely or wholly ignorant of their potentials
> for harm. . . . Future generations are unlikely to con-
> done our lack of prudent concern for the integrity of
> the natural world that supports all life.❞

19. Summarize the argument that Carson is presenting in this
quotation.

20. Who will question the lack of concern shown for the natural
world, in Carson's opinion?

21. Why was *Silent Spring* a groundbreaking book? How has it
influenced the ways in which people view the relationship
between humans and the natural world?

Applying Technology Skills

22. **Using the Internet** The science of ecology has led to a new
form of travel known as ecotourism. Use the Internet to
research an area of the world where ecotours take place.
Select an area to visit as an ecotourist, explain why you have
selected this area, and describe what you will see on your
travels in your journal.

Making Decisions

23. Grassroots politics have moved the burden of decision making from the politicians to the individual citizen. Having read
this chapter, what global issues concern you? What have you
done or what would you like to do to help resolve these
issues?

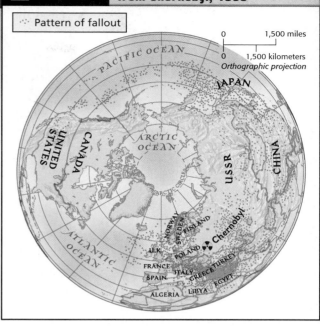

NATIONAL GEOGRAPHIC **Radioactive Fallout from Chernobyl, 1986**

Pattern of fallout

Analyzing Maps and Charts

Use the above map and the text to answer the following
questions.

24. Where is the radioactive fallout most concentrated?

25. Where are the furthest traces of radioactive fallout found
(using Chernobyl as the point of origin)?

26. What global effects did the explosion at Chernobyl have?

WORLD LITERATURE

Civil Peace *from* Girls and War and Other Stories

Chinua Achebe

Chinua Achebe was born in Nigeria and was christened Albert Chinualamogu. He rejected his British name while studying at the University College of Ibadan. Many of his works deal with the impact of Western values and culture on African society. He has done more than almost any other author to spread the understanding and influence of African literature worldwide. "Civil Peace" is one of the stories from *Girls and War and Other Stories* in which Achebe responds to the Nigerian civil war.

Read to Discover

How does Chinua Achebe describe the conditions of the civil war? Do you think this story accurately reflects conditions for African families following civil war?

Reader's Dictionary

commandeer: to seize for military purposes

Biro: a British term for a ballpoint pen

raffia: fiber of a type of palm tree

Jonathan Iwegbu counted himself extraordinarily lucky. "Happy survival!" meant so much more to him than just a current fashion of greeting old friends in the first hazy days of peace. It went deep to his heart. He had come out of the war with five inestimable blessings—his head, his wife Maria's head and the heads of three out of their four children. As a bonus he also had his old bicycle—a miracle too but naturally not to be compared to the safety of five human heads.

The bicycle had a little history of its own. One day at the height of the war it was commandeered "for urgent military action." Hard as its loss would have been to him he would still have let it go without a thought had he not had some doubts about the genuineness of the officer. It wasn't his disreputable rags, nor the toes peeping out of one blue and one brown canvas shoes, nor yet the two stars of his rank done obviously in a hurry in Biro, that troubled Jonathan; many good and heroic soldiers looked the same or worse. It was rather a certain lack of grip and firmness in his manner. So Jonathan, suspecting he might be

amenable to influence, rummaged in his raffia bag and produced the two pounds with which he had been going to buy firewood which his wife, Maria, retailed to camp officials for extra stock-fish and corn meal, and got his bicycle back. That night he buried it in the little clearing in the bush where the dead of the camp, including his own youngest son, were buried. When he dug it up again a year later after the surrender all it needed was a little palm-oil greasing. "Nothing puzzles God," he said in wonder.

He put it to immediate use as a taxi and accumulated a small pile of Biafran money ferrying camp officials and their families across the four-mile stretch to the nearest tarred road. His standard charge per trip was six pounds and those who had the money were only glad to be rid of some of it in this way. At the end of a fortnight he had made a small fortune of one hundred and fifteen pounds.

Then he made the journey to Enugu and found another miracle waiting for him. It was unbelievable. He rubbed his eyes and looked again and it was still standing there before him. But, needless to say, even that monumental blessing must be accounted also totally inferior to the five heads in the family. This newest miracle was his little house in Ogui Overside. Indeed nothing puzzles God! Only two houses away a huge concrete edifice some wealthy contractor had put up just before the war was a mountain of rubble. And here was Jonathan's little zinc house of no regrets built with mud blocks quite intact! Of course the doors and windows were missing and five sheets off the roof. But what was that? And anyhow he had returned to Enugu early enough to pick up bits of old zinc and wood and soggy sheets of cardboard lying around the neighborhood before thousands more came out of their forest holes looking for the same things. He got a

▲ **Children Dancing, c. 1948, by Robert Gwathmey**

destitute carpenter with one old hammer, a blunt plane and a few bent and rusty nails in his tool bag to turn this assortment of wood, paper and metal into door and window shutters for five Nigerian shillings or fifty Biafran pounds. He paid the pounds, and moved in with his overjoyed family carrying five heads on their shoulders.

Interpreting World Literature

1. What does Jonathan's encounter with the false officer reveal about the conditions of the war?

2. Biafra lost the civil war. What clues in the text indicate this outcome?

3. Why was having a bicycle a "miracle"?

4. **CRITICAL THINKING** Do you think it is effective for Achebe to discuss the war through an individual account rather than as a direct discussion of the devastation created? Why or why not?

Applications Activity
Choose a contemporary problem and describe it through the effect it has on an individual or family.

Appendix

Contents

TAKS
Preparation Handbook

The Texas Assessment of Knowledge and Skills, or TAKS, test is one way educators in Texas measure what you have learned. This handbook is designed to help you prepare for the TAKS tests in Social Studies at Grades 10 and 11. On the pages that follow, you will find a review of major Social Studies concepts encompassed in the Texas Essential Knowledge and Skills (TEKS) that are tested on the TAKS at Grades 10 and 11.

TAKS Objectives

Grade 10 Social Studies and
Grade 11 Exit Level Social Studies

There are five objectives for the Social Studies TAKS. These objectives are listed below.

For the test the student will be expected to:

1. Demonstrate an understanding of issues and events in United States history.

2. Demonstrate an understanding of geographic influences on historical issues and events.

3. Demonstrate an understanding of economic and social influences on historical issues and events.

4. Demonstrate an understanding of political influences on historical issues and events.

5. Use critical thinking skills to analyze social studies information.

Contributing Writer
Carey Boswell, M.Ed.
Humble I.S.D.
Humble, Texas

Reviewed by

TEKS Covered:
Obj. 2 – 8.10B (10), WH12BC (10), WG1AB (10, 11), WH23A (10, 11), US8B (11)
Obj. 3 – WG18A (10)
Obj. 5 – WH25C (10), WG8B (10, 11), WG21C (10, 11), WH26C (10, 11), US24B (11)

TAKS Practice Lesson 1

Era of Exploration

*By completing and understanding the activities on this page, you will practice for **TAKS Objectives 2, 3,** and **5,** and review Chapter 13 of this textbook.*

Skills Practice: Making Inferences

After the Crusades, Europeans used spices from Asian lands to flavor food, preserve meat, and make perfumes, cosmetics, and medicines. Arab and Venetian merchants controlled the spice trade between Asia and Europe. The weakening of the Mongol Empire had reduced the safety of overland trade, so Europeans sought sea routes to China and India. Innovations in technology, such as the magnetic compass, astrolabe, and triangular-shaped sail, set the stage for new journeys of exploration. These journeys expanded Europeans' knowledge of the world.

By comparing maps of different time periods, you can make inferences. Study the maps and

DIRECTIONS: Use the maps and your knowledge of social studies to answer the following questions.

1. European efforts to reach China and India by sea had occurred by
   A A.D. 1400.   **C** A.D. 1600.
   B A.D. 1500.   **D** A.D. 1700.

2. Europeans discovered the Pacific Ocean by
   F 1450.   **H** 1550.
   G 1500.   **J** 1600.

answer the following questions on a separate sheet of paper.

1. What is being compared on the maps?

2. According to the maps, by what year did Europeans have knowledge of North America?

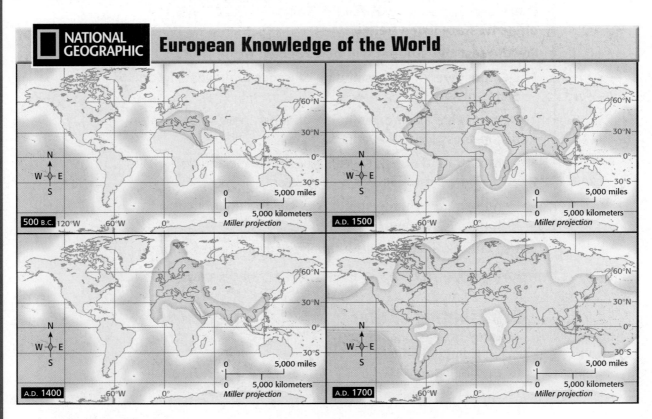

NATIONAL GEOGRAPHIC **European Knowledge of the World**

500 B.C.   A.D. 1500   A.D. 1400   A.D. 1700

TAKS Practice Lesson 2

Technology and Exploration

TEKS Covered:
Obj. 2 – 8.10B (10), WH12BC (10), WG1AB (10, 11), WH23A (10, 11), US8B (11)
Obj. 3 – WG18A (10)
Obj. 5 – WH25C (10), WG8B (10, 11), WG21C (10, 11), WH26C (10, 11), US24B (11)

By completing and understanding the activities on this page, you will practice for **TAKS** *Objectives* **2, 3,** *and* **5,** *and review Chapter 13 of this textbook.*

Skills Practice: Drawing Conclusions

In 1500, Christopher Columbus and other explorers combined their knowledge of sophisticated naval technologies with bravery and determination to explore lands that, to them, were new. Voyages by Columbus in 1492, Vasco da Gama in 1497, Ferdinand Magellan in 1519, and others linked Europe with the rest of the world. European voyages of exploration brought about many developments, such as colonization of the Americas and expansion of the slave trade.

A conclusion is a reasoned judgment you draw from the facts you have. Study the map below and answer the following questions on a separate sheet of paper.

1. How many voyages did Columbus make to the Americas? When did these trips occur?

2. In 1492, what island group did Columbus reach before sailing on to Cuba?

DIRECTIONS: Use the map and your knowledge of social studies to answer the following questions.

1. Which of the statements below is an accurate conclusion?
  A Columbus's arrival in the Americas was a step forward for humankind.
  B All European explorers wanted to colonize the Americas.
  C Vasco da Gama's preferred ship was the caravel.
  D Advances in technology made European voyages of exploration possible.

2. Between 1492 and 1502, Columbus
  F explored the eastern coasts of North and South America.
  G explored Central America and the West Indies.
  H sailed as far as the Pacific Ocean.
  J reached only the islands of the Caribbean Sea.

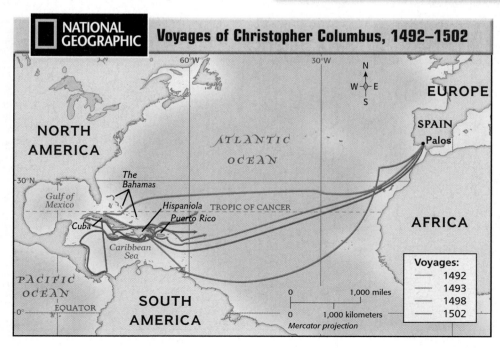

Voyages of Christopher Columbus, 1492–1502

TAKS Practice Lesson 3

Nations and Colonies

*By completing and understanding the activities on this page, you will practice for **TAKS Objectives 1, 2, 4,** and **5,** and review Chapters 17 and 18 of this textbook.*

Skills Practice: Interpreting a Map

Several European countries established colonies in the Americas by 1700. Spain founded the first permanent colonies. Great Britain, France, Portugal, and Russia followed suit. While Great Britain had evolved into a constitutional monarchy, the French, Spanish, and Russian monarchs struggled to maintain absolute power. Due to lack of representation in the British Parliament, the 13 British colonies revolted and established a new nation in North America. The United States of America became a constitutional republic based on democratic principles.

Examine and compare the maps on this page, then answer the following questions on a separate sheet of paper.

1. Which nation held the most territory in North America in 1763?

2. What parts of North America did Great Britain control after 1783?

3. In 1783, what geographic feature constituted the western border of the United States?

The Princeton Review

TAKS Test Practice

DIRECTIONS: Use the maps and your knowledge of social studies to answer the following questions.

1. In 1783, which monarchy held the most territory in North America?
   A Russia   **C** England
   B Spain   **D** France

2. How did landholdings change from 1763 to 1783?
   F France gained territory and the United States was formed.
   G Great Britain lost territory and the United States was formed.
   H Russia gained territory.
   J The United States formed while Great Britain gained territory.

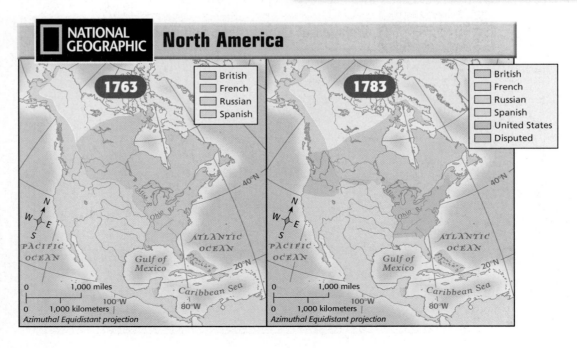

NATIONAL GEOGRAPHIC **North America**

Political Change in Latin America

TEKS Covered:
Obj. 1 – 8.1C (10, 11)
Obj. 2 – 8.10B (10), WH12B (10), WG1A (10, 11), US8B (11)
Obj. 4 – 8.16A (10, 11)
Obj. 5 – WH25C (10), WH26C (10, 11), WG21C (10, 11), US24AB (11)

*By completing and understanding the activities on this page, you will practice for **TAKS Objectives 1, 2, 4,** and **5,** and review Chapters 17, 18, 19, and 21 of this textbook.*

Skills Practice: Synthesizing Information

On July 4, 1776, thirteen American colonies issued the Declaration of Independence and broke away from Great Britain as the United States of America. Their struggle became a war for independence. In 1781, the Americans, aided by the French, forced the British to surrender. Two years later, the Treaty of Paris officially ended the war. The American Revolution influenced France. In 1789, French citizens issued the Declaration of the Rights of Man and the Citizen and revolted against the monarchy, eventually forming a republic.

Inspired by the examples of the American and French Revolutions, Latin Americans began their own struggles for independence. Although the Spanish and Portuguese colonies had been loyal to their European parent countries for 300 years, they resented the rigid colonial social structure. By the early 1800s, many nations in Latin America had gained their independence from European rulers.

To synthesize information means to combine information from separate sources. For example, when you write a research report, you may use facts obtained from various sources, such as encyclopedias, books, the Internet, and magazines. Before you synthesize information, analyze the information from each source. Then look for connections among the facts in the different sources. Study the map on this page and answer the following questions on a separate sheet of paper.

1. In what year did Chile achieve independence?

2. Which Latin American country is landlocked?

3. Why did Latin Americans desire independence in the 1800s?

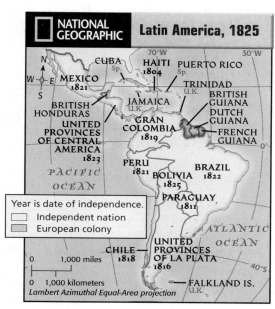

NATIONAL GEOGRAPHIC — Latin America, 1825

Year is date of independence.
☐ Independent nation
☐ European colony

The Princeton Review

TAKS Test Practice

DIRECTIONS: Use the map and your knowledge of social studies to answer the following questions on a separate sheet of paper.

1. In what year was the Declaration of Independence for the United States issued?

A 1763   C 1804
B 1776   D 1821

2. Based on the map, one could conclude that nationalism

F was an advantage for European nations.
G can lead to revolution.
H was a disadvantage for Latin American countries.
J will always lead to democratic republics.

3. Which was the first Latin American nation to gain independence?

A Mexico   C Chile
B Peru   D Haiti

TAKS Practice Lesson 5

Early Representative Governments

*By completing and understanding the activities on this page, you will practice for **TAKS Objectives 1, 3, 4,** and **5,** and review Chapters 11 and 17 of this textbook.*

Skills Practice: Determining Cause and Effect

In North America, before the arrival of Europeans, Native Americans lived and prospered in the Eastern Woodlands. Although fighting took place between their many villages, these Native Americans were united by a common language and many customs. The Iroquois became the most powerful group.

Legend holds that during the 1500s, the warring groups were on the verge of being torn apart when among them arose a leader named Hiawatha, who preached the need for peace. Hiawatha motivated the Native Americans to form an alliance of five groups—the Mohawk, Oneida, Onondaga, Cayuga, and Seneca. Europeans would later call this alliance the Iroquois League.

According to the League, a council of representatives known as the Grand Council met regularly to settle disputes peacefully. Each group of the alliance was made up of clans, and each clan selected a representative to the Grand Council.

Later, in the 1600s, as Europeans arrived in the New England area, they encountered the Iroquois. In 1754, Benjamin Franklin used the example of the Iroquois League as a model for the Albany Plan of Union, a proposed government for the American colonies.

To understand history you must figure out which actions or events caused other actions or events. As you read about historical chains of events, identify causes that led to other actions, or effects. To better understand cause-and-effect relationships, it is helpful to create a diagram like the one on this page. On a separate sheet of paper, create a diagram summarizing a cause-and-effect relationship from the information presented on this page.

Title: _____

Cause	Effect (Cause)	Effect (Cause)	Effect
→	→	→	

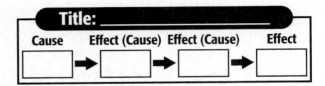

DIRECTIONS: Use the information on this page and your knowledge of social studies to answer the following questions on a separate sheet of paper.

1. The Iroquois League was important because it
   A protected the Aztec from the Spanish.
   B was created by Hiawatha.
   C was an early American form of democratic assembly.
   D was copied by the Maya.

2. The Albany Plan of Union called for a single elected legislature to govern all the colonies. It would have the power to collect taxes, raise troops, and regulate trade. All of the colonial assemblies voted against it because they were not willing to give up power. In the previous sentence, what is the *cause?*
   F Colonial assemblies were not willing to give up power.
   G A single legislature would govern all of the colonies.
   H All of the colonial assemblies voted against the plan.
   J The legislature would have the power to collect taxes, raise troops, and regulate trade.

An American Revolt

TEKS Covered:
Obj. 1 – 8.4C (10, 11), 8.16C (10, 11),
    US1AB (11)
Obj. 3 – WG18A (10), WG5B (10,11)
Obj. 4 – 8.3A (10, 11)
Obj. 5 – 8.30ADF (10), WH25C (10),
    US24ABCF (11)

*By completing and understanding the activities on this page, you will practice for **TAKS Objectives 1, 3, 4,** and **5,** and review Chapters 14 and 17 of this textbook.*

Skills Practice: Analyzing Primary and Secondary Sources

During the 1600s, Great Britain struggled through civil war and a changing government while its colonies in North America grew. British leaders generally let the colonists rule themselves, only stepping in to regulate trade. British leaders held the mercantilist view that the colonies were valuable only in that they benefited British trade. When the American colonies began to prosper, though, the British Parliament passed a series of navigation acts to protect its profitable trade. As the colonies grew economically and politically they struggled against tightening British controls.

To learn about events such as these, historians examine primary and secondary sources. A primary source is produced by an eyewitness to an event. Secondary sources use information gathered from other sources. When you use primary and secondary sources, you need to evaluate the reliability of the sources.

Read the following passages and determine whether they are primary or secondary sources, then answer the following questions on a separate sheet of paper.

❝Friends! Brethren! Country-men! That worst of plagues, the detested tea, shipped for this port by the East India Company, is now arrived in this harbor; the hour of destruction or manly opposition to the machinations [schemes] of tyranny stares you in the face; every friend . . . is now called upon . . . to make a united and successful resistance.❞

❝In 1772 the law was changed to permit the British East India Company to export tea directly to America and sell it in wholesale markets. Although this law

meant much cheaper prices for tea, colonists reacted against the 3-cents-per-pound tax. Some American ports turned tea ships away. At Boston, colonists disguised as Native Americans boarded the ships and dumped the chests of tea into the harbor.❞

1. What is the general topic of the two sources?

2. Which of these passages seems to have been written when events happened, or very near the time they happened? Explain your answer.

3. List any differences in the material or the way the events are described.

DIRECTIONS: Use the passage below and your knowledge of social studies to answer the following questions on a separate sheet of paper.

"With malice toward none, with charity for all . . . let us strive to finish the work we are in, to bind up the nation's wounds . . . to do all which may achieve and cherish a just and lasting peace among ourselves and with all nations."

1. This passage is most likely
   A a paragraph from a textbook.
   B a quotation by Abraham Lincoln.
   C a quotation by King George during the American Revolution.
   D a letter to the editor of a current newspaper.

2. This passage indicates that the author feels
   F a desire to get along with an enemy after a war.
   G a deep hatred for the enemy.
   H that the war must come to an end immediately.
   J that in hindsight, the war was a mistake.

TEKS Covered:
Obj. 2 – 8.10B (10), WG1A (10, 11), WG6A (10, 11), US8B (11)
Obj. 3 – WG18A (10)
Obj. 5 – 8.30A (10), WH25C (10), WH26C (10, 11), US24ABC (11)

TAKS Practice Lesson 7

Colonizing the Americas

*By completing and understanding the activities on this page, you will practice for **TAKS Objectives 2, 3,** and **5,** and review Chapters 13 and 21 of this textbook.*

Skills Practice: Comparing Graphs

Soon after Christopher Columbus reached the Americas, European settlements arose on American lands. Within a century, citizens of Spain, Portugal, England, France, and the Netherlands built American colonies.

Competing European nations laid down territorial claims. Portugal came to dominate Brazil, while Spain established an enormous colonial empire that included Mexico, Central America, most of South America, and part of North America. The Dutch established a colony in what is now New York, while the English colonized the rest of the eastern coast of North America. France claimed lands north of the English colonies and along the St. Lawrence waterway. Later the French would claim, explore, and settle the mouth of the Mississippi River, too. As a result of all these national claims, the languages, religions, and cultures of the Americas varied widely.

The graphs on this page show present-day ethnic groups in Canada and Latin America. Study the graphs and answer the following questions on a separate sheet of paper.

1. What are the two largest ethnic groups in Canada?

2. Which Latin American country shown has the smallest percentage of Europeans?

3. What is the largest ethnic group in Brazil today?

NATIONAL GEOGRAPHIC | **Ethnic Origins in Canada**

Multiple Origin or Other 40%
British Isles 28%
French 23%
Asian 7%
Native American (including Inuit) 2.0%

Source: Statistics Canada, 1996

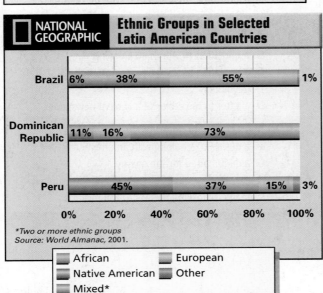

NATIONAL GEOGRAPHIC | **Ethnic Groups in Selected Latin American Countries**

Brazil: 6% | 38% | 55% | 1%
Dominican Republic: 11% | 16% | 73%
Peru: 45% | 37% | 15% | 3%

0% 20% 40% 60% 80% 100%

*Two or more ethnic groups
Source: World Almanac, 2001.*

African | European
Native American | Other
Mixed*

The Princeton Review

★TAKS
Test Practice

DIRECTIONS: Use the graphs and your knowledge of social studies to answer the following questions on a separate sheet of paper.

1. Which country has the largest percentage of Native Americans?
  A Peru
  B Canada
  C Brazil
  D Dominican Republic

2. Why does Canada have a large French population?
  F because of recent French immigration to Canada
  G because of its colonial history
  H because the French are its native inhabitants
  J because of the French and Indian War

Settlements in the Americas

By completing and understanding the activities on this page, you will practice for TAKS Objectives 1, 2, and 5, and review Chapters 13 and 17 of this textbook.

Skills Practice: Interpreting Elevation Profiles and Time Lines

Soon after Europeans arrived in the Americas, they founded settlements. Europeans traveled over the Atlantic Ocean to the eastern coast of the Americas. After a time, European explorers traveled to the interior of the continents and gradually built settlements there. The terrain, the location of navigable rivers, the climate, and the behaviors of Native American groups all determined where Europeans settled. Study the time line and elevation profile on this page. Use the information presented to answer the following questions on a separate sheet of paper.

1. What European nation founded settlements in Brazil? When?

2. Use an atlas to estimate, roughly, the line of latitude across which the elevation profile is taken.

3. To reach the Great Plains from the Pacific Ocean, what mountain range would you have to cross?

4. Approximately how high above sea level do the Appalachians rise?

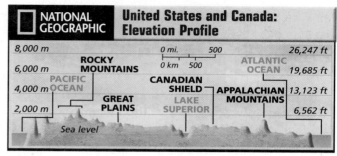

NATIONAL GEOGRAPHIC
United States and Canada: Elevation Profile

The Princeton Review
TAKS Test Practice

DIRECTIONS: Use the time line, elevation profile, and your knowledge of social studies to answer the following questions on a separate sheet of paper.

1. What major barrier did the Dutch face when colonizing Fort Orange (later Albany)?
   A Rocky Mountains
   B Appalachian Mountains
   C Canadian Shield
   D Andes

2. What was one reason cities like Jamestown, New Orleans, and Quebec were founded relatively early?
   F These cities are located west of the Appalachian Mountains.
   G These cities are located on the Great Plains.
   H These cities are located on the coasts of the Americas.
   J All of the above.

1607
• English establish Jamestown, Virginia

1610
• Spanish found Santa Fe in present-day New Mexico

1718
• French establish New Orleans

early 1700s
• Spanish establish San Antonio

1500 — **1600** — **1700** — **1800**

1500s
• Spanish establish settlements in Central America and Portuguese take control of Brazil

1608
• French found Quebec

early 1600s
• Dutch found present-day Albany and New York City

1769
• Spanish missionaries found San Diego

TEKS Covered:
Obj. 1 – US1ABC (11), US3A (11)
Obj. 2 – 8.10B (10), WH12BC (10), WG1A
(10, 11), US8B (11)
Obj. 5 – 8.30AD (10), WH25C (10), WG21C
(10, 11), WH26C (10, 11), US24ABC (11)

TAKS Practice Lesson 9

The Spanish-American War

By completing and understanding the activities on this page, you will practice for TAKS Objectives 1, 2, and 5, and review Chapter 21 of this textbook.

Skills Practice: Making Generalizations

The nineteenth century was an age of imperialism, during which strong nations exercised political and economic control over weaker nations. Viewing Asia and Africa as sources of raw materials and markets for Western manufactured goods, European nations scrambled to grab territories. The United States also became a colonial power, practicing many of the imperialist policies of European nations.

In January 1898, the USS *Maine* was sent to Havana, Cuba, to protect U.S. lives and property there during a time of local insurrection against Spanish rule. On February 15, the battleship was sunk by a massive explosion of unknown origin, killing 266 officers and crew members. Americans blamed Spain and cried for revenge. On

April 25, 1898, Congress declared war on Spain, starting the Spanish-American War. During the war, American forces seized the former Spanish colonies of Cuba, Puerto Rico, Guam, and the Philippines. Meanwhile, the United States also acquired formerly independent Hawaii.

When you make generalizations, you form general ideas about a subject. Examine the map on this page and answer the following questions on a separate sheet of paper.

1. What is the subject of the map?
2. How does the map reflect events of the Spanish-American War?

U.S. Possessions in the Pacific, 1899

NATIONAL GEOGRAPHIC

RUSSIA

Alaska (1867)

ASIA

NORTH AMERICA

PACIFIC OCEAN

JAPAN

Midway Islands (1867)

CHINA

Wake I. (1899)

TROPIC OF CANCER — 30°N

Philippines (1898)

Guam (1898)

Johnston Atoll (1858)

Hawaiian Islands (1898)

Howland I. (1857)

Kingman Reef (1858)
Palmyra Atoll (1898)

EQUATOR

Baker I. (1857)

Jarvis I. (1857)

American Samoa (1899)

0   1,000 miles   TROPIC OF CAPRICORN

AUSTRALIA

0   1,000 kilometers
Mercator projection

DIRECTIONS: Use the map and your knowledge of social studies to answer the following questions on a separate sheet of paper.

1. Which of the following statements is a valid generalization?
   A The United States gained control of the Philippines in 1898.
   B From 1857 to 1899, the United States acquired much land in the Pacific as a result of its policy of imperialism.
   C Because of the Spanish-American War, the United States gained control of Alaska.
   D The United States should not have taken over territories in the Pacific.

2. This map shows American imperialism because
   F it portrays effects of the Spanish-American War.
   G it shows regions in the Pacific Ocean.
   H it shows American expansion into one region of the world.
   J it illustrates how far the United States is from its possessions in the Pacific.

TEKS Covered:
Obj. 1 – US1ABC (11), US3B (11)
Obj. 2 – WH23A (10, 11)
Obj. 3 – WG18A (10)
Obj. 5 – 8.30DF (10), WG8B (10), WH25C
  (10), WH26C (10, 11), US24BCF (11)

TAKS Practice Lesson 10

World War I

By completing and understanding the activities on this page, you will practice for **TAKS Objectives 1, 2, 3,** and **5,** and review Chapter 23 of this textbook.

Skills Practice: Analyzing Visuals

By 1914, Europe's great powers had formed alliances. Nationalism and militarism were growing forces. The assassination of Archduke Francis Ferdinand (heir to the throne of Austria-Hungary) on June 28, 1914, drew the great powers of Europe into war. Although the United States tried to stay neutral, it entered the war in 1917.

Imperial War Museum

During World War I, both sides (Allies and Central Powers) used a combination of old-fashioned strategies and new technologies to fight the enemy. For example, Germans introduced poisonous gas to battlefields, while British soldiers drove tanks. Soldiers in muddy trenches fought with fixed bayonets, but they often had to scramble to avoid grenades and the small bombs dropped by planes. Soldiers also used automatic machine guns that fired hundreds of rounds in rapid succession. The result was a greater loss of life and property than the world had seen in any previous war.

Visual images, such as paintings, illustrations, and photographs, present information in ways that can have a greater impact than text alone. Such images, however, may not portray information objectively, since painters and artists make choices about what to include and how to show it. To analyze an image, ask yourself: Is anything missing? What is the complete picture? Study the details to draw conclusions.

Examine the photograph above and describe it in a brief summary on a separate sheet of paper.

DIRECTIONS: Use the image and your knowledge of social studies to answer the following questions on a separate sheet of paper.

1. Which type of warfare used in World War I does the photograph depict?
   A "no-man's-land"   **C** limited
   B guerrilla   **D** trench

2. One of the causes of U.S. involvement in World War I was
   F unrestricted submarine warfare.
   G use of poisonous gas.
   H bombing of naval bases.
   J flights of spy planes over U.S. territory.

TAKS Preparation Handbook

Nationalist Movements

TEKS Covered:
Obj. 1 – US1A (11)
Obj. 2 – WG1B (10, 11)
Obj. 3 – WG18A (10)
Obj. 5 – 8.30A (10), WH25C (10), WH26C (10, 11), US24ABC (11)

*By completing and understanding the activities on this page, you will practice for **TAKS Objectives 1, 2, 3,** and **5,** and review Chapter 25 of this textbook.*

Skills Practice: Categorizing Information

The world experienced a period of nationalism in the early twentieth century. Before this time, people had generally expressed loyalty to their individual rulers. As the concept of nationalism spread, though, people took pride in their heritage, or those things handed down to them from their ancestors. They began to desire self-determination, the right of national groups to set up independent nations.

The chart on this page categorizes a large amount of information. This organization makes comparing facts easier. Read the chart and answer the following questions on a separate sheet of paper.

1. What was the most common driving force behind the nationalist movements of the countries on the chart?

2. What was the general result of these nationalist movements?

The Princeton Review

TAKS
Test Practice

DIRECTIONS: Use the chart and your knowledge of social studies to answer the following questions on a separate sheet of paper.

1. The country where a nationalist movement of the early twentieth century was crushed is
A Persia.
B Turkey.
C Argentina.
D Libya.

2. If you had to add the American Revolution to this chart, how would you describe its driving force?
F bad economy
G tax protest; struggle to protect American rights
H revolt against borders defined by Europeans
J revolt against seizure of American land

Selected Nationalist Movements in the Early Twentieth Century

	Latin America			Africa and Asia			Middle East		
Country	Argentina	Brazil	Mexico	Kenya	Libya	India	Turkey	Persia	Northern Arabian Peninsula
Driving Force	Fear of workers; dissatisfaction with government	Bad economy	Foreign control of oil industry	High taxes; British rule	Italian rule	British rule	Greek seizure of Anatolian Peninsula	British and Soviet presence	European creation of states
Outcome	New governments (1930, 1943)	Vargas's New State (1938)	Seizure of oil and property (1938); PEMEX	Exile of Thuku (1922)	Revolt crushed (1920s)	Government of India Act (1935)	Turkish Republic (1923)	Iran (1935)	Saudi Arabia (1932)

TAKS Preparation Handbook

The People of World War II

*By completing and understanding the activities on this page, you will practice for **TAKS Objectives 1** and **5,** and review Chapter 26 of this textbook.*

Skills Practice: Comparing and Contrasting

On September 1, 1939, the forces of German Nazi leader Adolf Hitler invaded Poland. Two days later, Great Britain and France declared war on Germany, beginning World War II. The United States did not declare war at that time. On December 7, 1941, Japanese warplanes attacked the American military base at Pearl Harbor, Hawaii. The next day, President Franklin D. Roosevelt asked Congress to declare war on Japan. On December 11, 1941, Germany and Italy declared war on the United States.

Historians piece together facts from primary and secondary sources to learn about the lives of people involved in World War II. They draw conclusions about these facts by comparing and contrasting them. Read the excerpts below and answer the following questions on a separate sheet of paper.

66Yesterday, December 7, 1941—a date which will live in infamy—the United States of America was suddenly and deliberately attacked by naval and air forces of the Empire of Japan. . . . I believe I interpret the will of the Congress and of the people when I assert that we will not only defend ourselves to the uttermost, but we will make very certain that this form of treachery shall never endanger us again. . . . No matter how long it may take us . . . the American people in their righteous might will win through to absolute victory.99

—**President Franklin D. Roosevelt, 1941**

66I do not want to be anything other than the first soldier of the German Reich. I have once more put on the uniform which was once most holy and precious to me. I shall only take it off after victory or I shall not live to see the end. . . . As a National Socialist and as a German soldier, I am going into this struggle strong in heart. My whole life has been nothing but a struggle for my people, for their revival, for Germany . . . Just as I myself am ready to risk my life any time for my people and for Germany, so I demand the same of everyone else.99

— **Adolf Hitler as quoted in**
Nazism 1919–1945, A Documentary Reader,
J. Noakes and G. Pridham, 1995

1. Who is speaking in each passage? To whom is each person speaking?

2. What is the situation in each instance?

3. In what ways are the excerpts similar?

4. What does the first speaker mean by the word *infamy*?

TAKS *Test Practice*

DIRECTIONS: Use the passages and your knowledge of social studies to answer the following questions on a separate sheet of paper.

1. In the first quotation, President Franklin Roosevelt used certain phrases to characterize the Japanese attack, such as
A *absolute victory.*
B *the will of the Congress.*
C *form of treachery.*
D *defend ourselves to the uttermost.*

2. In the second quotation, the phrase that best describes Adolf Hitler's central idea is
F the German people can rely on their brave army.
G all male civilians should join the army immediately.
H all Germans should be as devoted to their country as he has always been.
J the German cause is a just one.

TAKS Practice Lesson 13

The Cold War

TEKS Covered:
Obj. 1 – US1ABC (11), US6DE (11)
Obj. 2 – WG1B (10, 11)
Obj. 5 – 8.30D (10), WH25C (10), WH26C (10, 11), US24B (11)

By completing and understanding the activities on this page, you will practice for **TAKS Objectives 1, 2,** *and* **5,** *and review Chapter 27 of this textbook.*

Skills Practice: Reading a Time Line

World War II left the United States and the Soviet Union the world's dominant powers. Although they had been allies during the global struggle, these nations emerged from the war suspicious of each other. A bitter rivalry developed. This rivalry, called the Cold War, affected much of the world, as each side sought to gain allies.

The mission of the United States was to build and lead a world founded on democracy and free enterprise, whereas the Soviet Union's goal was to spread communism. When Soviet forces brought communism to Eastern Europe, the United States reacted with a policy of "containment"—containing Soviet expansion through both military and nonmilitary means in strategic areas of the world. For example, American soldiers implemented the policy of containment during the Korean War. The time line below presents events of the Cold War. To read the time line, determine its time span and the relationships among events. Then answer the following questions on a separate sheet of paper.

1. What is the time span of the time line?
2. What is the first Cold War event identified on the time line?
3. How long did the Korean War last?
4. When was *Sputnik* launched?

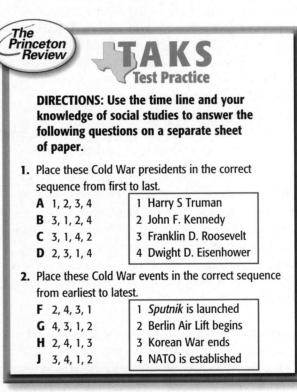

The Princeton Review

TAKS Test Practice

DIRECTIONS: Use the time line and your knowledge of social studies to answer the following questions on a separate sheet of paper.

1. Place these Cold War presidents in the correct sequence from first to last.

   A 1, 2, 3, 4
   B 3, 1, 2, 4
   C 3, 1, 4, 2
   D 2, 3, 1, 4

   | 1 Harry S Truman |
   | 2 John F. Kennedy |
   | 3 Franklin D. Roosevelt |
   | 4 Dwight D. Eisenhower |

2. Place these Cold War events in the correct sequence from earliest to latest.

   F 2, 4, 3, 1
   G 4, 3, 1, 2
   H 2, 4, 1, 3
   J 3, 4, 1, 2

   | 1 *Sputnik* is launched |
   | 2 Berlin Air Lift begins |
   | 3 Korean War ends |
   | 4 NATO is established |

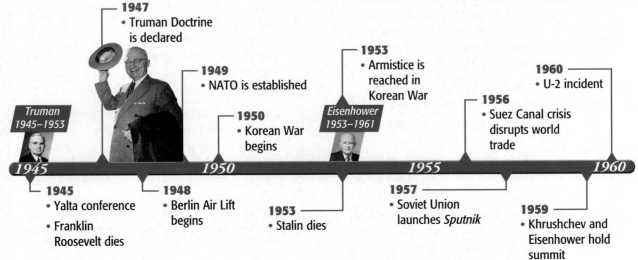

1947
• Truman Doctrine is declared

1949
• NATO is established

1953
• Armistice is reached in Korean War

1960
• U-2 incident

Truman 1945–1953

1950
• Korean War begins

Eisenhower 1953–1961

1956
• Suez Canal crisis disrupts world trade

1945

1950

1955

1960

1945
• Yalta conference
• Franklin Roosevelt dies

1948
• Berlin Air Lift begins

1953
• Stalin dies

1957
• Soviet Union launches *Sputnik*

1959
• Khrushchev and Eisenhower hold summit

TAKS Practice Lesson 14

World Economic Systems

*By completing and understanding the activities on this page, you will practice for **TAKS Objectives** 3 and 5, and review Chapters 2, 17, 27, and 31 of this textbook.*

Skills Practice: Interpreting a Chart

Economic systems describe the ways in which societies produce and distribute goods and services. Early societies, such as Mesopotamia, used bartering as their system of trade. In the seventeenth and eighteenth centuries, European countries practiced mercantilism, in which colonies provided wealth to the parent country.

In a command economy, decisions are made by the upper levels of government. A command economy is called either socialism or communism, depending on how much the government is involved. The economy of the United States is a mixed system based on the principle of free enterprise. American citizens have the freedom to own businesses with limited government interference. This freedom has helped our country become the world's economic leader.

Grouping information into categories on a chart is one way of making large amounts of information easier to understand. Study the chart on this page and answer the following questions on a separate sheet of paper.

1. Under which economic system does the government have the most control?

2. Under which system would people be most likely to have the same job as their parents?

3. Which economic system does the United States have?

DIRECTIONS: Use the chart and your knowledge of social studies to answer the following questions on a separate sheet of paper.

1. Which economic system provides individuals with the most economic freedom?
   A traditional
   B command
   C market
   D mixed

2. In China, government officials decide what crops are grown, what products are made, and what prices are charged. China has a
   F traditional economic system.
   G command economic system.
   H market economic system.
   J mixed economic system.

3. In Myanmar, most businesses are owned and run by the government's military leaders. What type of economic system does Myanmar have?
   A traditional
   B command
   C market
   D mixed

World Economic Systems

Traditional	Command	Market	Mixed
Based on customs	Government controls production, prices, and wages	Individuals control production, prices, and wages	Individuals control some aspects of economy
Trades are passed down through generations	Communism; government owns businesses	Free enterprise; individuals own businesses	Government regulates selected industries and restricts others

The Importance of Geography

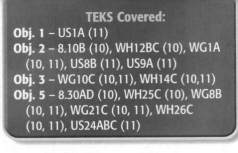

TEKS Covered:

Obj. 1 – US1A (11)
Obj. 2 – 8.10B (10), WH12BC (10), WG1A (10, 11), US8B (11), US9A (11)
Obj. 3 – WG10C (10,11), WH14C (10,11)
Obj. 5 – 8.30AD (10), WH25C (10), WG8B (10, 11), WG21C (10, 11), WH26C (10, 11), US24ABC (11)

By completing and understanding the activities on this page, you will practice for **TAKS Objectives 1, 2, 3,** *and* **5,** *and review Chapters 30 and 32 of this textbook.*

Skills Practice: Analyzing Information

Geography has a profound impact on the way we live. The climate, the food we eat, and our culture are affected by our location on the earth's surface and its relation to resources and other places. A place's physical features can determine whether that place is easy to defend or is vulnerable to attack. The Strait of Hormuz, for example, is considered a transportation "choke point" because of its strategic location.

Most of the crude oil produced in the Middle East must pass through the strait to reach worldwide markets. The waterway is only about 40 miles (64 km) across at its widest point. It is possible for a country or group to block the passage of ships through the strait. It was this fear that prompted the United States to escort oil tankers through the strait to protect them from Iranian attacks in the 1980s.

The text, the map, and the graph on this page present you with information about world oil production and the geography of the Middle East. To analyze the information presented, you must identify the topic, examine how the information is organized, and summarize the information. Study the information and answer the following questions on a separate sheet of paper.

1. What are the subjects of the map and the graph?

2. Define *strait*.

3. What region of the world is the second largest producer of oil?

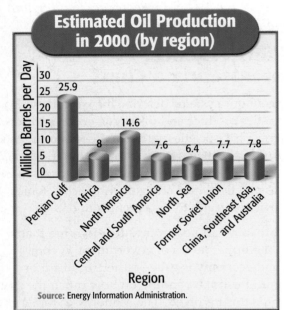

Estimated Oil Production in 2000 (by region)

Source: Energy Information Administration.

The Princeton Review

TAKS
Test Practice

DIRECTIONS: Use the map, graph, and your knowledge of social studies to answer the following questions on a separate sheet of paper.

1. The Strait of Hormuz connects the Arabian Sea and the
  A Mediterranean Sea.
  B Persian Gulf.
  C Red Sea.
  D Caspian Sea.

2. Why is the United States interested in traffic through the Strait of Hormuz?
  F It separates the countries of the United Arab Emirates and Iran.
  G It is located in the Middle East.
  H It is crucial to the domestic security of the United States.
  J It is a crucial shipping lane for oil from the Persian Gulf states.

Mini Almanac

An almanac is a book or table that contains a variety of statistical, tabular, or general information. The most common almanacs in history have been those that kept astronomical data or that gave weather predictions and related advice to farmers. In agricultural societies it was important to keep accounts of natural phenomena so that farmers would have an idea of when to plant and harvest their crops. Ancient Egyptians carved their almanacs on sticks of wood and called them "fingers of the sun." The first printed almanac was prepared in Europe in 1457. The *Old Farmer's Almanac* has been published continuously since 1792. Because almanacs are compact and concise, they are a popular way of presenting a wide variety of information.

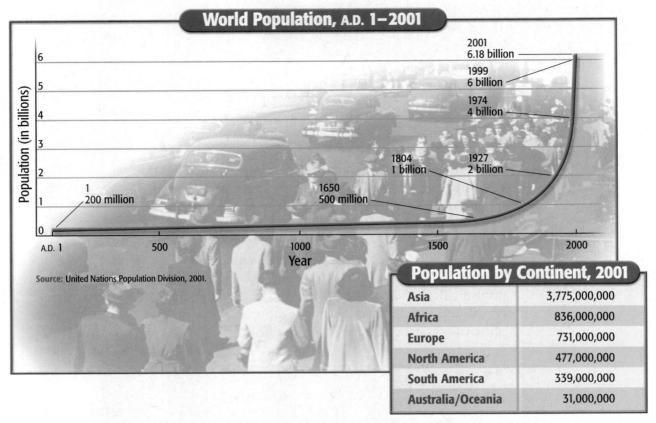

World Population, A.D. 1–2001

2001
6.18 billion

1999
6 billion

1974
4 billion

1927
2 billion

1804
1 billion

1650
500 million

1
200 million

Population (in billions)

A.D. 1   500   1000   1500   2000

Year

Source: United Nations Population Division, 2001.

Population by Continent, 2001

Asia	3,775,000,000
Africa	836,000,000
Europe	731,000,000
North America	477,000,000
South America	339,000,000
Australia/Oceania	31,000,000

Sources: *World Atlas* and *World Gazeteer*.
Note: Populations are estimates.

Life Expectancy

Country	Years
Andorra	83.47
Japan	80.80
France	78.90
Israel	78.71
New Zealand	77.99
United Kingdom	77.82
United States	77.26
Chile	75.94
China	71.62
Russia	67.34
Egypt	63.69
Brazil	63.24
India	62.86
South Africa	48.09
Mozambique	36.45

Source: U.S. Bureau of the Census, 2001.

Infant Mortality

Country	Infant Deaths per 1,000 Live Births
India	70
South Africa	54
Egypt	41
Brazil	34
China	33
Russia	18
Chile	11
United States	7
Canada	6
United Kingdom	6
France	5
Germany	5
South Korea	5
Japan	4

Source: United Nations, UNICEF, 2001.

Most Populous Countries

Country	Population
China	1,273,111,290
India	1,029,991,145
United States	278,058,881
Indonesia	228,437,870
Brazil	174,468,575
Russia	145,470,197
Pakistan	144,616,639
Bangladesh	131,269,860
Japan	126,771,662
Nigeria	126,635,626

Source: U.S. Bureau of the Census, 2001.

World's Richest Countries

Country	Gross National Product, per Capita (in U.S. dollars)
Luxembourg	45,360
Switzerland	44,355
Japan	41,010
Liechtenstein	40,000
Norway	34,515

Source: World Development Indicators 2000, World Bank.

World's Poorest Countries

Country	Gross National Product, per Capita (in U.S. dollars)
Mozambique	80
Congo, DNC	100
Eritrea	100
Ethiopia	100
Somalia	100

Source: World Development Indicators 2000, World Bank.

Highest Inflation Rates

Country	Rate of Inflation (percent)
Congo, DNC	540
Angola	325
Belarus	200
Iraq	100
Somalia	100
Ecuador	96
Suriname	78
Zimbabwe	60
Cyprus (Turkish)	58
Romania	46

Source: *The World Factbook, 2001.*
Note: Estimates are for 1999 and 2000.

Lowest Inflation Rates

Country	Rate of Inflation (percent)
Argentina	−0.9
Oman	−0.8
Japan	−0.7
Vietnam	−0.6
Fiji	0.0
Lebanon	0.0
Israel	0.1
Cuba	0.3
China	0.4
Saudi Arabia	0.5

Source: *The World Factbook, 2001.*
Note: Estimates are for 1999 and 2000.

World's Ten Largest Companies, 2000

Rank	Company	Revenue (in millions of U.S. dollars)
1.	ExxonMobil (United States)	210,392.0
2.	Wal-Mart Stores (United States)	193,295.0
3.	General Motors (United States)	184,632.0
4.	Ford Motor (United States)	180,598.0
5.	DaimlerChrysler (Germany)	150,069.7
6.	Royal Dutch/Shell Group (Netherlands)	149,146.0
7.	BP (United Kingdom)	148,062.0
8.	General Electric (United States)	129,853.0
9.	Mitsubishi (Japan)	126,579.4
10.	Toyota Motor (Japan)	121,416.2

Source: Fortune 500, 2001.

Most Livable Countries

Rank	Country	Rank	Country	Rank	Country
1.	Norway	10.	Finland	19.	New Zealand
2.	Australia	11.	Switzerland	20.	Italy
3.	Canada	12.	Luxembourg	21.	Spain
4.	Sweden	13.	France	22.	Israel
5.	Belgium	14.	United Kingdom	23.	Greece
6.	United States	15.	Denmark	24.	Cyprus
7.	Iceland	16.	Austria	25.	Singapore
8.	Netherlands	17.	Germany		
9.	Japan	18.	Ireland		

Source: United Nations Human Development Index, 2001.
Note: The criteria include life expectancy, adult literacy, school enrollment, educational attainment, and per capita gross domestic product (GDP).

Highest Adult Literacy Rates

Country	Rate of Literacy (percent)
Andorra	100
Australia	100
Denmark	100
Estonia	100
Finland	100
Latvia	100
Liechtenstein	100
Luxembourg	100
Norway	100
Czech Republic	99.9

Source: *The World Factbook, 2001.*
Note: Literacy is defined by each country.

Lowest Adult Literacy Rates

Country	Rate of Literacy (percent)
Niger	14
Burkina Faso	19
Somalia	24
Eritrea	25
Nepal	28
Mali	31
Sierra Leone	31
Afghanistan	32
Senegal	33
Cambodia	35

Source: *The World Factbook, 2001.*
Note: Literacy is defined by each country.

World Adult Illiteracy by Gender

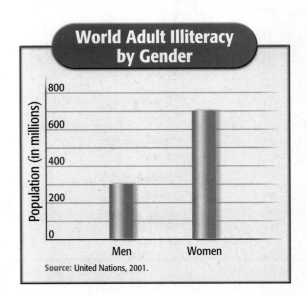

Source: United Nations, 2001.

Years, by Country, in Which Women Gained the Right to Vote

Year	Country	Year	Country
1893	New Zealand	1945	Italy
1902	Australia	1945	Japan
1913	Norway	1947	Argentina
1918	United Kingdom	1947	Mexico
1918	Canada	1950	India
1919	Germany	1952	Greece
1920	United States	1956	Egypt
1930	South Africa	1963	Kenya
1934	Brazil	1971	Switzerland
1944	France	1980	Iraq

Highest Military Expenditures

	Billions of U.S. Dollars per Year	Percentage of Gross Domestic Product (GDP)
United States	276.7	3.2
Japan	43.0	1.0
France	39.8	2.5
United Kingdom	36.9	2.7
Germany	32.8	1.5
Italy	20.7	1.7
Saudi Arabia	18.3	13.0
Brazil	13.4	1.9
India	13.0	2.5
China	12.6	1.2

Source: *The World Factbook, 2001.*

Nuclear Weapons Capability

Country	Date of First Test
United States	1945
Russia (Soviet Union)	1949
United Kingdom	1952
France	1960
China	1964
India	1998
Pakistan	1998

Sources: U.S. Department of State and *Time* magazine.

Communication around the World

	Daily newspaper circulation per 1,000 persons	Radios per 1,000 persons	Televisions per 1,000 persons	Telephone main lines per 1,000 persons	Cellular phone subscribers per 1,000 persons	Estimated personal computers per 1,000 persons
Canada	158	1,067	710	677	285	39
China	n/a	335	321	111	66	2
Cuba	118	352	239	44	1	1
France	218	946	595	580	494	30
Germany	311	948	567	601	586	34
Italy	104	880	528	474	737	21
Japan	578	956	686	653	526	32
Mexico	97	329	272	125	142	5
Russia	105	417	410	218	22	4
South Africa	34	355	134	114	12	6
United Kingdom	331	1,443	521	557	670	34
United States	212	2,116	806	700	365	59

Sources: United Nations and International Telecommunications Union, 2001.

Primary Sources Library

CONTENTS

What Is It and How Do I Use It?

The primary sources as defined here are written testimony or documents from a particular era in history or about an important development. The source may be the writings of a noted historian or political leader, or it may be from the diary of someone who lived at the time and recorded the events of the day.

Reading primary sources is an excellent way to understand how and why people believed and acted as they did in the past. While many people might have written down their stories or beliefs, the sources chosen here are from witnesses who were close to events or especially sensitive to them.

Checking Your Sources

When you read primary or secondary sources, you should analyze them to determine if they are dependable or reliable. Historians usually prefer primary sources to secondary sources, but both can be reliable or unreliable, depending on the following factors.

Time Span

With primary sources, it is important to consider how much time passed from the date the event occurred to the date that the primary source was written. Generally, the longer the time span between the event and the account, the less reliable the account is. As time passes, people often forget details and fill in gaps with events that never took place. Although we like to think we remember things exactly as they happened, the fact is, we often remember them very differently than they occurred.

Reliability

Another factor to consider when evaluating a primary source is the writer's background and reliability. When reading a historical document, try to determine if the statements and information can be proved. If the information can be verified as true by independent sources, then it probably is fact.

Opinions

When evaluating a primary source, you should also decide whether or not the account has been influenced by emotion, opinion, or exaggeration. Writers sometimes distort the truth to suit their personal purposes. Ask yourself: Why did the person write the account? Do any words or expressions reveal the author's emotions or opinions? Again, you may wish to compare the account with another primary source document about the same event. If the two accounts differ, ask yourself why they differ and then conduct your own outside research to determine which account can be verified by other authoritative sources.

Interpreting Primary Sources

To help you analyze a primary source, use the following steps:

- **Examine the origins of the document.**
  You need to determine if it is indeed a primary source.

- **Find the main ideas.**
  Read the document and summarize the main ideas in your own words.

- **Reread the document.**
  Difficult ideas and historical documents are not always easily understood on the first reading.

- **Use a variety of resources.**
  Use a dictionary, an encyclopedia, and maps to further your understanding of the topic. These resources are tools to help you discover new ideas and knowledge and check the validity of sources.

Classifying Primary Sources

Primary sources fall into different categories. While the documents presented here are primarily printed publications, there are other types of primary sources.

Printed publications include books such as autobiographies. Printed publications also include newspapers and magazines.

Visual materials include a wide range of forms: original paintings, drawings, and sculpture, photographs, film, videos, and maps.

Oral history collects spoken memories and personal observations through recorded interviews. In contrast, oral tradition involves stories that people have passed along by word of mouth from generation to generation.

Personal records are accounts of events kept by an individual who is a participant in or witness to these events. Personal records include diaries, journals, and letters.

Artifacts are objects such as tools or ornaments. Artifacts provide archaeologists and historians with information about a particular culture or a stage of technological development.

The First Civilizations and Empires

For thousands of years, prehistoric humans were migratory hunters and gatherers. With the development of agriculture, people began to live in settled communities. Throughout the world, these communities emerged into great civilizations with cultures, customs, governments, laws, and written histories.

Reader's Dictionary

fraud: deception

imperial: relating to the empire or the emperor

archives: official documents that are preserved for historical or public use

discourse: discussion

decree: an order that has the force of law

calamity: distress or misery

This rendition of an Egyptian father teaching his son is on the wall of the Tomb of Sennedjem.

An Egyptian Father's Advice to His Son

 **Personal Records**

Upper-class Egyptians enjoyed compiling collections of wise sayings to provide guidance for leading an upright and successful life. This excerpt from *The Instruction of the Vizier Ptah-hotep dates from around 2450 B.C.*

Then he said to his son:

If you are a leader commanding the affairs of the many, seek out for yourself every good deed, until it may be that your own affairs are without wrong. Justice is great, and it is lasting; it has been disturbed since the time of him who made it, whereas there is punishment for him who passes over its laws. Wrongdoing has never brought its undertaking into port. It may be that it is fraud that gains riches, but the strength of justice is that it lasts. . . .

If you are a man of standing and found a household and produce a son who is pleasing to god, if he is correct and inclines toward your ways and listens to your instruction, while his manners in your house are fitting, and if he takes care of your property as it should be, seek out for him every useful action. He is your son, . . . you should not cut your heart off from him.

If he [the son] goes astray and does not carry out your instruction, so that his manners in your household are wretched, and he rebels against all that you say, while his mouth runs on in the most wretched talk, quite apart from his experience, while he possesses nothing, you should cast him off: he is not your son at all. He was not really born to you. . . . He is one whom god has condemned in the very womb.

The Burning of Books

Li Su was a chief minister of the First Qin Emperor. A follower of Legalism, he hoped to eliminate all rival theories of government.

Your servant suggests that all books in the imperial archives, save the memoirs of Qin, be burned. All persons in the empire, except members of the Academy of Learned Scholars, in possession of the Book of Odes, the Book of History, and discourses of the hundred philosophers [including Confucius] should take them to the local governors and have them burned. Those who dare to talk to each other about the Book of Ideas and the Book of History should be executed and their bodies exposed in the market place. Anyone referring to the past to criticize the present should, together with all members of his family, be put to death. Officials who fail to report cases that have come under their attention are equally guilty. After thirty days from the time of issuing the decree, those who have not destroyed their books are to be branded and sent to build the Great Wall. Books not to be destroyed will be those on medicine and pharmacy, agriculture and arboriculture [the cultivation of trees and shrubs]. People wishing to pursue learning should take the officials as their teachers.

Chinese scroll

Plague in Athens

Printed Publications

Thucydides (471–c. 400 B.C.) is regarded as the first scientific historian. In his account of the plague that broke out in Athens in 430 B.C., Thucydides simply presents the facts, describing the disease's symptoms and impact on the city itself.

. . . Externally, the body was not so very warm to the touch; it was not pale, but reddish, livid, and breaking out in small blisters and ulcers. But internally it was consumed by such a heat that the patients could not bear to have on them the lightest coverings or linen sheets. . . .

The Athenians suffered further hardship owing to the crowding into the city of the people from the country districts; and this affected the new arrivals especially. For since no houses were available for them and they had to live in huts that were stifling in the hot season, they perished in wild disorder. Bodies of dying men lay one upon another, and half-dead people rolled about in the streets and, in their longing for water, near all the fountains. . . . The calamity which weighed upon them was so overpowering that men became careless of all law, sacred as well as profane. And the customs which they had hitherto observed regarding burial were all thrown into confusion, and they buried their dead each one as he could. . . .

Analyzing Primary Sources

1. Does any part of the Egyptian father's advice have value today for sons or daughters? Be specific and support your answer.
2. Why did Li Su think that burning books would eliminate all rival theories of government?
3. Explain why it was dangerous to have a new idea during the reign of the First Qin Emperor.
4. What hardships did newcomers to Athens face during the time of the plague?

New Patterns of Civilization

As civilizations and empires emerged in different parts of the world, new political systems, religions, arts, and sciences developed. These new systems and these new ways of life continue to influence the societies of the modern world.

Reader's Dictionary

cobble: repair shoes

accrue: to happen as a direct result of some other action

remonstrate: to scold or reproach

err: make mistakes

lamentation: an expression of mourning

Woman playing a lute

Muhammad's Wife Remembers the Prophet

Printed Publications

What kind of man was Muhammad that he could achieve such profound changes in Arab civilization? This description comes from his wife, Ayesha, the daughter of Abu Bakr.

When Ayesha was questioned about Muhammad she used to say:

He was a man just such as yourselves. He laughed often and smiled much. He would mend his clothes and cobble his shoes. He used to help me in my household duties; but what he did oftenest was to sew. If he had the choice between two matters, he would choose the easiest, so long as no sin could accrue therefrom. He never took revenge excepting where the honor of God was concerned. When angry with anyone, he would say, "What hath taken such a one that he should soil his forehead in the mud."

His humility was shown by his accepting the invitation even of slaves. . . . He would say: "I sit at meals as a servant does and I eat like a servant. For I really am a servant."

Muhammad hated nothing more than lying. Whenever he knew that any of his followers had erred in this respect, he would hold himself aloof from them until he was assured of their repentance.

He did not speak rapidly, running the words into one another, but enunciated each syllable distinctly, so that what he said was imprinted in the memory of everyone who heard him.

He used to stand for such a long time at his prayers that his legs would swell. When remonstrated, he said: "What! Shall I not behave as a thankful servant should?"

He refused to accept presents that had been offered as alms. Neither would he allow anyone in his family to use what had been brought as alms. "For," said he, "alms are the impurity of mankind."

A Woman May Need to Have the Heart of a Man

Christine de Pizan was widowed at age 25. She supported her three children by copying manuscripts, compiling a manual of instructions for knights, and writing books. The following is from her 1405 publication, The Treasure of the City of Ladies.

It is the responsibility of every baron to spend the least possible time at his manors and his own estate, for his duties are to bear arms, to attend the court of his prince and to travel. Now, his lady stays behind and must take his place. . . . Her men should be able to rely on her for all kinds of protection in the absence of their lord. . . . She ought to have the heart of a man, that is, she ought to know how to use weapons and be familiar with everything that pertains to them, so that she may be ready to command her men if the need arises. She should know how to launch an attack or to defend against one.

In addition she will do well to be a very good manager of the estate. . . . She should often take time to visit the fields to see how the men are getting on with the work. . . . She will busy herself around the house; she will find plenty of orders to give. She will have the animals brought in at the right time [and] take care how the shepherd looks after them. . . .

In the winter-time, she will have her men cut her willow groves and make vine props to sell in the season. She will never let them be idle. . . . She will employ her women . . . to attend to the livestock, . . . [and] to weed the courtyards. . . . There is a great need to run an estate well, and the one who is most diligent and careful about it is more than wise and ought to be highly praised for it.

A wandering Buddhist sage

The Buddha's Sermon

Siddhartha Gautama, the Buddha, gave sermons in India, which were written down after 250 B.C. An excerpt from one of these follows.

1. Now this, O monks, is the noble truth of pain: birth is painful, old age is painful, sickness is painful, death is painful, sorrow, lamentation, dejection, and despair are painful. Contact with unpleasant things is painful, not getting what one wishes is painful. In short the five khandhas of grasping are painful.

2. Now this, O monks, is the noble truth of the cause of pain: that craving which leads to rebirth, combined with pleasure and lust, finding pleasure here and there, namely, the craving for passion, the craving for existence, the craving for non-existence.

3. Now this, O monks, is the noble truth of the cessation of pain: the cessation without a remainder of that craving, abandonment, forsaking, release, non-attachment.

4. Now this, O monks, is the noble truth of the way that leads to the cessation of pain: this is the noble Eightfold Path. . . .

Analyzing Primary Sources

1. According to Ayesha, what kind of man was Muhammad? Did he behave like a ruler?
2. What are some of the duties and responsibilities of the medieval gentlewoman, according to Christine de Pizan's account?
3. What does de Pizan mean when she says a woman "ought to have the heart of a man"?
4. According to the Buddha, what is the cause of pain?

The Early Modern World

Beginning with the 1400s, European and Asian nations began exploring the world, learning about new cultures, new peoples, and new technologies. Then, between 1600 and the early 1800s, Western civilization was transformed by scientific discoveries and new philosophies. The growing desire for democracy paved the way for political revolution in France and in America.

Reader's Dictionary

Scripture: passage from the Bible

revered: honored or respected

contention: point made in an argument

hemp: a fiber from the mulberry bush

imprescriptible: cannot be taken away by law

▲ *Martin Luther*

Ulrich Zwingli ▶

A Reformation Debate

Printed Publications

In 1529, Martin Luther and Ulrich Zwingli debated over the sacrament of the Lord's Supper, or Communion.

LUTHER: Although I have no intention of changing my mind, which is firmly made up, I will nevertheless present the grounds of my belief and show where the others are in error. . . . Your basic contentions are these: In the last analysis you wish to prove that a body cannot be in two places at once, and you produce arguments about the unlimited body which are based on natural reason. I do not question how Christ can be God and man and how the two natures can be joined. For God is more powerful than all our ideas, and we must submit to his word.

Prove that Christ's body is not there where the Scripture says, "This is my body!" God is beyond all mathematics and the words of God are to be revered and carried out in awe. It is God who commands, "Take, eat, this is my body." I request, therefore, valid scriptural proof to the contrary.

ZWINGLI: I insist that the words of the Lord's Supper must be figurative. This is ever apparent, and even required by the article of faith; "taken up into heaven, seated at the right hand of the Father." Otherwise, it would be absurd to look for him in the Lord's Supper at the same time that Christ is telling us that he is in heaven. One and the same body cannot possibly be in different places. . . .

LUTHER: I call upon you as before: your basic contentions are shaky. Give way, and give glory to God!

ZWINGLI: And we call upon you to give glory to God and to quit begging the question! The issue at stake is this: Where is the proof of your position?

LUTHER: It is your point that must be proved, not mine. But let us stop this sort of thing. It serves no purpose.

ZWINGLI: It certainly does! It is for you to prove that the passage in John 6 speaks of a physical meal.

LUTHER: You express yourself poorly. . . . You're going nowhere.

The Silk Industry in China

During the 1600s Sung Ying-Hsing wrote a book on Chinese industry called the T'ien-kung K'ai-wu (Chinese Technology in the Seventeenth Century), *which included sections on the production of silk.*

. . . Members of the aristocracy are clothed in flowing robes decorated with patterns of magnificent mountain dragons, and they are the rulers of the country. Those of lowly stations would be dressed in hempen jackets and cotton garments to protect themselves from the cold in winter and cover their nakedness in summer, in order to distinguish themselves from the birds and beasts. Therefore Nature has provided the materials for clothing. Of these, the vegetable [plant] ones are cotton, hemp, *meng* hemp, and creeper hemp; those derived from birds, animals, and insects are furs, woolens, silk, and spun silk. . . .

But, although silk looms are to be found in all parts of the country, how many persons have actually seen the remarkable functioning of the draw-loom: Such words as "orderly government" [*chih*, i.e. the word used in silk reeling], "chaos" [*luan*, i.e. when the fibers are entangled], "knowledge or good policy" [*ching-lun*, i.e. the warp thread and the woven pattern] are known by every schoolboy, but is it not regrettable that he should never see the actual things that gave rise to these words? . . .

Emperor's robe, Qing dynasty

Declaration of the Rights of Woman and the Female Citizen

Olympe de Gouges composed her own Declaration of the Rights of Woman and the Female Citizen *in 1791. Following are excerpts.*

1. Woman is born free and lives equal to man in her rights. Social distinctions can be based only on the common utility.
2. The purpose of any political association is the conservation of the natural and imprescriptible rights of woman and man; these rights are liberty, property, security, and especially resistance to oppression. . . .
4. Liberty and justice consist of restoring all that belongs to others; thus, the only limits on the exercise of the natural rights of woman are perpetual male tyranny; these limits are to be reformed by the laws of nature and reason. . . .
6. The law must be . . . the same for all: male and female citizens. . . .
7. No woman is an exception; she is accused, arrested, and detained in cases determined by law. Women, like men, obey this rigorous law. . . .
11. The free communication of thoughts and opinions is one of the most precious rights of woman, since that liberty assured the recognition of children by their fathers. . . .

Analyzing Primary Sources

1. Was a conclusion reached in the debate presented between Luther and Zwingli?
2. According to Sung Ying-Hsing, from what two sources was all clothing made?
3. What are the rights of women as listed in the excerpts from *Declaration of the Rights of Woman and the Female Citizen*?
4. Olympe de Gouges states that free communication of thoughts is one of the most precious rights of women. Do you agree or disagree?

An Era of European Imperialism

During the late 1700s and throughout the 1800s, the nations of Europe and North America began an Industrial Revolution that had far-reaching effects, including the demand for social and political reforms. At the same time, Western nations extended their hold on new lands and on foreign markets.

Reader's Dictionary

autocrat: a monarch who rules with unlimited authority

close: an enclosed area of land

enumerated: counted

abject: existing in a low state or condition

infanticide: killing an infant

resuscitation: restoration or renewal

Czar Alexander II

Imperial Decree to Free the Serfs

In 1861, the Russian czar Alexander II issued the Emancipation Manifesto, an imperial decree to free his country's serfs.

By the grace of God, we, Alexander II, Emperor and Autocrat of all the Russias, King of Poland, Grand Duke of Finland, etc., to all our faithful subjects, make known:

Examining the condition of classes and professions comprising the state, we became convinced that the present state legislation favors the upper and middle classes, . . . but does not equally favor the serfs. . . . These facts had already attracted the attention of our predecessors, and they had adopted measures aimed at improving the conditions of the peasants. But decrees on free farmers and serfs have been carried out on a limited scale only.

We thus came to the conviction that the work of a serious improvement of the condition of the peasants was a sacred inheritance bequeathed to us by our ancestors, a mission which, in the course of events Divine Providence called upon us to fulfill. . . .

In virtue of the new dispositions above mentioned, the peasants attached to the soil will be invested within a term fixed by the law with all the rights of free cultivators. . . .

At the same time, they are granted the right of purchasing their close, and, with the consent of the proprietors, they may acquire in full property the arable lands and other appurtenances [rights of way] which are allotted to them as a permanent holding. By the acquisition in full property of the quantity of land fixed, the peasants are free from their obligations towards the proprietors for land thus purchased, and they enter definitely into the condition of free peasants-landholders.

The Unfortunate Situation of Working Women

This article was published in L'Atelier, *a Parisian workingman's newspaper, in 1842.*

Although women's work is less productive for society than that of men, it does, nevertheless, have a certain value, and, moreover, there are professions that only women can practice. For these, women are indispensable. . . . It is these very workers in all these necessary trades who earn the least and who are subject to the longest layoffs. Since for so much work they earn only barely enough to live from day to day, it happens that during times of unemployment they sink into abject poverty.

Who has not heard of the women silkworkers' dirty, unhealthy, and badly paid work; of the women in the spinning and weaving factories working fourteen to sixteen hours (except for one hour for both meals); always standing, without a single minute for repose, putting forth an enormous amount of effort. And many of them have to walk a league or more, morning and evening, to get home. Nor should we neglect to mention the danger that exists merely from working in these large factories, surrounded by wheels, gears, enormous leather belts that always threaten to seize you and pound you to pieces.

The existence of women who work as day laborers, and are obliged to abandon . . . the care of their children to indifferent neighbors is no better. . . . We believe that the condition of women will never really improve until workingmen can earn enough to support their families, which is only fair. Woman is so closely linked to man that the position of the one cannot be improved without reference to the position of the other.

The Impact of British Rule in India

In 1871, Dadabhai Naroji commented on the benefits and the problems of British rule in India.

Benefits of British Rule:

In the Cause of Humanity: Abolition of suttee and infanticide. *Civilization:* Education, both male and female. . . . Resuscitation of India's own noble literature. *Politically:* Peace and order. Freedom of speech and liberty of the press. . . . Improvement of government in the native states. Security of life and property. Freedom from oppression. . . . *Materially:* Loans for railways and irrigation. Development of a few valuable products, such as indigo, tea, coffee, silk, etc. Increase of exports. Telegraphs.

The Detriments of British Rule:

In the Cause of Humanity: Nothing. *Civilization:* [T]here has been a failure to do as much as might have been done. *Politically:* Repeated breach of pledges to give the natives a fair and reasonable share in the higher administration of their own country, . . . an utter disregard of the feelings and views of the natives. *Financially:* [N]ew modes of taxation, without any adequate effort to increase the means of the people to pay.

Summary: British rule has been: morally, a great blessing; politically, peace and order on one hand, blunders on the other; materially, impoverishment. . . . Our great misfortune is that you do not know our wants. When you will know our real wishes, I have not the least doubt that you would do justice. The genius and spirit of the British people is fair play and justice.

Analyzing Primary Sources

1. What reason does Czar Alexander II give for freeing the serfs?
2. What physical and economic problems of women workers are described in the Parisian newspaper article? What solution(s) does the author offer?
3. What is the attitude of the *L'Atelier* writer toward women and women's work? Is the author of the article more likely to be a woman or a man? What makes you think so?
4. Summarize the benefits and problems of British rule in India.

The Twentieth-Century Crisis

During the first half of the 1900s, two destructive wars raged throughout the world and brought tremendous political and social change. World War I destroyed the power of European monarchies, while Nazi aggression in Germany eventually led to World War II and the Holocaust.

Reader's Dictionary

parapet: wall of earth piled on top of a trench

snipers: people who shoot at exposed individuals from a concealed location

civil disobedience: refusal to obey governmental demands

exploitation: unfair use for one's own advantage

disarmament: reducing or eliminating weapons

Battle of the Somme

Over the Top—World War I

Personal Records

Arthur Guy Empey reflects upon his experiences during World War I in the trenches in France.

Suddenly, the earth seemed to shake and a thunderclap burst in my ears. I opened my eyes,—I was splashed all over with sticky mud, and men were picking themselves up from the bottom of the trench. The parapet on my left had toppled into the trench, completely blocking it with a wall of tossed-up earth. The man on my left lay still. . . . A German "Minnie" (trench mortar) had exploded in the [trench]. . . . Stretcher-bearers came up the trench on the double. After a few minutes of digging, three still, muddy forms on stretchers were carried down the communication trench to the rear. Soon they would be resting "somewhere in France," with a little wooden cross over their heads. They had done their bit for King and Country, had died without firing a shot. . . . I was dazed and motionless. Suddenly a shovel was pushed into my hands, and a rough but kindly voice said: "Here, my lad, lend a hand clearing the trench, but keep your head down, and look out for snipers. . . ."

Lying on my belly on the bottom of the trench, I filled sandbags with the sticky mud. . . . The harder I worked, the better I felt.

Occasionally a bullet would crack overhead, and a machine gun would kick up the mud on the bashed-in parapet. At each crack I would duck and shield my face with my arm. One of the older men noticed this action of mine, and whispered: "Don't duck at the crack of a bullet, Yank; the danger has passed,—you never hear the one that wings you. Always remember that if you are going to get it, you'll get it, so never worry." . . . [Days later] we received the cheerful news that at four in the morning we were to go over the top and take the German frontline trench. My heart turned to lead.

Gandhi Takes the Path of Civil Disobedience

 Printed Publications

Mohandas Gandhi explains why British rule in India must end.

Before embarking on civil disobedience and taking the risk I have dreaded to take all these years, I would fain approach you and find a way out.

My personal faith is absolutely clear. I cannot intentionally hurt anything that lives, much less  fellow human beings, even though they may do the greatest wrong to me and mine. Whilst, therefore, I hold the British rule to be a curse, I do not intend harm to a single Englishman or to any legitimate interest he may have in India.

I must not be misunderstood. Though I hold the British rule in India to be a curse, I do not, therefore, consider Englishmen in general to be worse than any other people on earth. I have the privilege of claiming many Englishmen as dearest friends. Indeed much that I have learned of the evil of British rule is due to the writings of frank and courageous Englishmen who have not hesitated to tell the truth about that rule.

And why do I regard British rule as a curse? It has impoverished the ignorant millions by a system of progressive exploitation and by a ruinously expensive military and civil administration which the country can never afford.

It has reduced us politically to serfdom. It has sapped the foundations of our culture. And, by the policy of cruel disarmament, it has degraded us spiritually. Lacking the inward strength, we have been reduced . . . to a state bordering on cowardly helplessness. . . .

The Holocaust—The Camp Victims

 Printed Publications

A French doctor describes the victims of one of the crematoriums at Auschwitz-Birkenau during the Holocaust.

It is mid-day, when a long line of women, children, and old people enter the yard. The senior official in charge . . . climbs on a bench to tell them that they are going to have a bath and that afterwards they will get a drink of hot coffee. They all undress in the yard. . . . The doors are opened and an indescribable jostling begins. The first people to enter the gas chamber begin to draw back. They sense the death which awaits them. The SS men put an end to the pushing and shoving with blows from their rifle butts beating the heads of the horrified women who are desperately  hugging their children. The massive oak double doors are shut. For two endless minutes one can hear banging on the walls and screams which are no longer human. And then—not a sound. Five minutes later the doors are opened. The corpses, squashed together and distorted, fall out like a waterfall. The bodies which are still warm pass through the hands of the hairdresser who cuts their hair and the dentist who pulls out their gold teeth . . . One more transport has just been processed through No. IV crematorium.

Analyzing Primary Sources

1. How did Arthur Empey feel and act during his time in the trenches of World War I?
2. According to Gandhi, what had British rule done to India?
3. Why do you think Gandhi believed that nonviolent civil disobedience would encourage the British to free India?
4. What is the French doctor's point of view about the events he describes at the Auschwitz-Birkenau death camp?

Toward a Global Civilization

Following World War II, the balance of power in the world shifted dramatically. Many nations and peoples came under the political and ideological influence of the United States, which promoted capitalism and individual rights and liberties.

Reader's Dictionary

reserve: a reservation; land set aside for use by a particular group

squatters: those who settle on public land without rights or permission

perturbation: major change or disturbance

John Glenn

Progress Never Stops

Printed Publications

In 1962, John J. Glenn, Jr. was commander of the first U.S. crewed spacecraft to orbit the earth. Glenn spoke to a joint meeting of Congress six days after he returned from orbit.

What did we learn from the flight? . . . The Mercury spacecraft and systems design concepts are sound and have now been verified during manned flight. We also proved that man can operate intelligently in space and can adapt rapidly to this new environment.

Zero G or weightlessness appears to be no problem. As a matter of act, lack of gravity is a rather fascinating thing. Objects within the cockpit can be parked in midair. For example, at one time during the flight, I was using a hand-held camera. Another system needed attention; so it seemed quite natural to let go of the camera, take care of the other chore, then reach out, grasp the camera, and go back about my business.

There seemed to be little sensation of speed although the craft was traveling at about five miles per second—a speed that I too find difficult to comprehend.

The view from that altitude defies description. The horizon colors are brilliant and sunsets are spectacular. It is hard to beat a day in which you are permitted the luxury of seeing four sunsets. . . .

Our efforts today and what we have done so far are but small building blocks in a huge pyramid to come.

But questions are sometimes raised regarding the immediate payoffs from our efforts. Explorations and the pursuit of knowledge have always paid dividends in the long run—usually far greater than anything expected at the outset. Experimenters with common, green mold, little dreamed what effect their discovery of penicillin would have.

We are just probing the surface of the greatest advancements in man's knowledge of his surroundings that has ever been made. . . . Knowledge begets knowledge. Progress never stops.

An Ideal for Which I Am Prepared to Die

*N*elson Mandela gave this speech during his trial in South Africa in 1964. Following the trial, he was sentenced to life in prison.

The whites enjoy what may well be the highest standard of living in the world, whilst Africans live in poverty and misery. Forty percent of the Africans live in hopelessly overcrowded and, in some cases, drought-stricken reserves, where soil erosion and the overworking of the soil make it impossible for them to live properly off the land. Thirty percent are labourers, labour tenants, and squatters on white farms. The other thirty percent live in towns where they have developed economic and social habits which bring them closer, in many respects, to white standards. Yet forty-six percent of all African families in Johannesburg do not earn enough to keep them going.

The complaint of Africans, however, is not only that they are poor and whites are rich, but that the laws which are made by the whites are designed to preserve this situation. . . .

During my lifetime I have dedicated my life to this struggle of the African people. I have fought against white domination, and I have fought against black domination. I have cherished the ideal of a democratic and free society in which all persons live together in harmony with equal opportunities. It is an ideal which I hope to live for, and to see realized. But my lord, if needs be, it is an ideal for which I am prepared to die.

China's Gilded Age

*X*iao-huang Yin recounts his trip through China in 1994.

Recently I took a six-week journey across China. It was my first trip back since . . . 1985. In the course of my visit I saw—I felt—the perturbations of profound and chaotic social change. China's stunning hurtle from a centrally planned economy to a free market has set off an economic explosion and generated tremendous prosperity. Its economic growth was 13 percent in 1993, and average personal income in urban areas had doubled since 1985. With the state-owned sector accounting for less than 30 percent of total economic output, the socialist system is becoming an empty shell. Across China the lines between the state and private economies are blurring. At the largest national department store in Shanghai, a symbol of Chinese socialist business, customers now bargain for better prices. The counters within the store have been contracted out to shop clerks, who decide the prices. Dual ownership has in essence turned this state enterprise into a private business. . . .

Not everyone gets rich quick, but the economic boom has brought most urban Chinese a huge improvement in their standard of living. Color TV sets, refrigerators, and VCRs, considered luxuries when I lived in China, can be found in almost every working-class urban household— at least in the prosperous coastal cities.

Analyzing Primary Sources

1. What are the immediate and long-term "payoffs" of John Glenn's 1962 space mission, according to his report to Congress?
2. Summarize the demographics of the African population discussed by Nelson Mandela.
3. What ideal does Nelson Mandela discuss?
4. Why does Xiao-huang Yin believe that socialism is becoming an "empty shell" in China?

Honoring America

For Americans, the flag has always had a special meaning. It is a symbol of our nation's freedom and democracy.

Flag Etiquette

Over the years, Americans have developed rules and customs concerning the use and display of the flag. One of the most important things every American should remember is to treat the flag with respect.

- The flag should be raised and lowered by hand and displayed only from sunrise to sunset. On special occasions, the flag may be displayed at night, but it should be illuminated.

- The flag may be displayed on all days, weather permitting, particularly on national and state holidays and on historic and special occasions.

- No flag may be flown above the American flag or to the right of it at the same height.

- The flag should never touch the ground or floor beneath it.

- The flag may be flown at half-staff by order of the president, usually to mourn the death of a public official.

- The flag may be flown upside down only to signal distress.

- When the flag becomes old and tattered, it should be destroyed by burning. According to an approved custom, the Union (stars on blue field) is first cut from the flag; then the two pieces, which no longer form a flag, are burned.

★ ★ ★ ★ ★ ★ ★ ★

The Star-Spangled Banner

O! say can you see, by the dawn's early light,
What so proudly we hail'd at the twilight's last gleaming,
Whose broad stripes and bright stars through the perilous fight,
O'er the ramparts we watched, were so gallantly streaming?
And the Rockets' red glare, the Bombs bursting in air,
Gave proof through the night that our Flag was still there;
O! say, does that star-spangled banner yet wave
O'er the Land of the free and the home of the brave!

The Pledge of Allegiance

I pledge allegiance to the Flag of the United States of America and to the Republic for which it stands, one Nation under God, indivisible, with liberty and justice for all.

Glossary

A

abbess the head of a convent (p. 288)

abolitionism a movement to end slavery (p. 602)

absolutism a political system in which a ruler holds total power (p. 441)

acid rain the rainfall that results when sulfur produced by factories mixes with moisture in the air (p. 970)

acropolis in early Greek city-states, a fortified gathering place at the top of a hill which was sometimes the site of temples and public buildings (p. 115)

adobe sun-dried brick (p. 350)

Age of Pericles the period between 461 and 429 B.C. when Pericles dominated Athenian politics and Athens reached the height of its power (p. 123)

agora in early Greek city-states, an open area that served as a gathering place and as a market (p. 115)

agricultural society a group of people whose economy is largely based on farming (p. 277)

anarchy political disorder; lawlessness (p. 470)

annex incorporate territory into an existing political unit, such as a city or country (p. 655)

annul declare invalid (p. 397)

anthropology the study of human life and culture based on artifacts and human fossils (p. 20)

anti-Semitism hostility toward or discrimination against Jews (p. 336)

apartheid "apartness," the system of racial segregation in South Africa from the 1950s until 1991 (p. 922)

appeasement satisfying demands of dissatisfied powers in an effort to maintain peace and stability (p. 810)

arabesque geometric patterns repeated over and over to completely cover a surface with decoration (p. 210)

archaeology the study of past societies through an analysis of the items people left behind them (p. 19)

archipelago a chain of islands (p. 273)

arete in early Greece, the qualities of excellence that a hero strives to win in a struggle or contest (p. 113)

aristocracy an upper class whose wealth is based on land and whose power is passed on from one generation to another (p. 89)

armada a fleet of warships (p. 432)

armistice a truce or agreement to end fighting (p. 740)

arms race building up armies and stores of weapons to keep up with an enemy (p. 851)

artifact tools, pottery, paintings, weapons, buildings, and household items left behind by early people (p. 20)

artisan a skilled craftsperson who makes products such as weapons and jewelry (p. 29)

ascetic a person who practices self-denial to achieve an understanding of ultimate reality (p. 78)

astrolabe an instrument used by sailors to determine their location by observing the positions of stars (p. 208)

australopithecine "southern apes," the earliest humanlike creatures that flourished in eastern and southern Africa three to four million years ago (p. 21)

autonomous self-governing (p. 882)

B

balance of trade the difference in value between what a nation imports and what it exports over time (p. 413)

banana republic a small country that is economically dependent on a single product that it markets to large, wealthy nations (p. 800)

banner in Qing China, a separate military unit made up of Manchus; the empire's chief fighting force (p. 489)

Bantu a family of languages spoken in central and southern Africa; a member of any group of the African peoples who speak that language (p. 232)

baroque an artistic style of the seventeenth century characterized by complex forms, bold ornamentation, and contrasting elements (p. 449)

bazaar a covered market in Islamic cities (p. 204)

bioterrorism the use of biological and chemical weapons in terrorist attacks (p. 972)

biowarfare the use of disease or poison against civilians and soldiers in wartime (p. 972)

bishopric a group of Christian communities, or parishes, under the authority of a bishop (p. 287)

Black Death a form of bubonic plague, spread by fleas carried by rats (p. 335)

blitzkrieg German for "lightning war," a swift and sudden military attack; used by the Germans during World War II (p. 814)

bloc a group of nations with a common purpose (p. 863)

bourgeoisie the middle class, including merchants, industrialists, and professional people (pp. 548, 619)

boyar a Russian noble (p. 446)

Bronze Age the period from around 3000 to 1200 B.C. characterized by the widespread use of bronze for tools and weapons (p. 30)

Buddhism a religious doctrine introduced in northern India in the sixth century B.C. by Siddhartha Gautama, known as the Buddha, or "Enlightened One" (p. 78)

budget deficit the state that exists when a government spends more than it collects in revenues (p. 887)

bureaucracy an administrative organization that relies on nonelective officials and regular procedures (pp. 48, 422)

Bushido "the way of the warrior," the strict code by which Japanese samurai were supposed to live (p. 265)

C

caliph a successor of Muhammad as spiritual and temporal leader of the Muslims (p. 197)

capital money available for investment (p. 582)

caste one of the five major divisions of Indian classes in ancient times: Brahmans, Kshatriyas, Vaisyas, Sudras, and Untouchables (p. 75)

caste system a set of rigid categories in ancient India that determined a person's occupation and economic potential as well as his or her position in society, based partly on skin color (p. 75)

caudillo in postrevolutionary Latin America, a strong leader who ruled chiefly by military force, usually with the support of the landed elite (p. 674)

censorate part of the Chinese bureaucracy that made sure government officials were doing their jobs (p. 99)

centuriate assembly in the Roman Republic, the most important of the people's assemblies; it elected the chief officials, such as the consuls and praetors, and passed laws (p. 152)

chivalry in the Middle Ages, the ideal of civilized behavior that developed among the nobility; it was a code of ethics that knights were supposed to uphold (p. 295)

Christian humanism a movement that developed in northern Europe during the Renaissance combining classical learning (humanism) with the goal of reforming the Catholic Church (p. 390)

Christianity monotheistic religion that emerged during the first century A.D. (p. 171)

city-state a city with political and economic control over the surrounding countryside (p. 39)

civil disobedience refusal to obey laws that are considered to be unjust (p. 788)

civilization a complex culture in which large numbers of people share a number of common elements such as social structure, religion, and art (p. 30)

clan a group of related families (pp. 349, 493)

clergy church leaders (p. 173)

Cold War the period of political tension following World War II and ending with the fall of Communism in the Soviet Union at the end of the 1980s (p. 834)

collaborator a person who assists the enemy (p. 827)

collective bargaining the right of unions to negotiate with employers over wages and hours (p. 755)

collectivization a system in which private farms are eliminated and peasants work land owned by the government (p. 763)

colony a settlement of people living in a new territory, linked with the parent country by trade and direct government control (p. 413)

commercial capitalism economic system in which people invest in trade or goods to make profits (pp. 320, 492)

commodity a marketable product (p. 694)

common law a uniform system of law that developed in England based on court decisions and on customs and usage rather than on written law codes; replaced law codes that varied from place to place (p. 298)

commonwealth a republic (p. 438)

commune in China during the 1950s, a group of collective farms, each of which contained more than 30,000 people who lived and worked together (p. 942)

concentration camp a camp where prisoners of war, political prisoners, or members of minority groups are confined, typically under harsh conditions (p. 768)

concession political compromise (p. 698)

Confucianism the system of political and ethical ideas formulated by the Chinese philosopher Confucius toward the end of the Zhou dynasty; it was intended to help restore order to a society that was in a state of confusion (p. 95)

conquistador a Spanish conqueror of the Americas (p. 412)

conscription military draft (p. 718)

conservatism a political philosophy based on tradition and social stability, favoring obedience to political authority and organized religion (p. 590)

consul a chief executive officer of the Roman Republic; two were elected each year, one to run the government and one to lead the army into battle (p. 152)

consulate government established in France after the overthrow of the Directory in 1799, with Napoleon as first consul in control of the entire government (p. 564)

consumer society a society preoccupied with buying goods (p. 867)

contras rebels financed by the United States who began a guerrilla war against the Sandinista government in Nicaragua (p. 909)

cooperative a farm organization owned by and operated for the benefit of the farmers (p. 913)

cottage industry a method of production in which tasks are done by individuals in their rural homes (p. 582)

coup d'état a sudden overthrow of the government (p. 561)

creole a person of European descent born in the New World and living there permanently (p. 672)

Crusade military expedition carried out by European Christians in the Middle Ages to regain the Holy Land from the Muslims (p. 306)

culture the way of life a people follows (p. 30)

cuneiform "wedge-shaped," a system of writing developed by the Sumerians using a reed stylus to create wedge-shaped impressions on a clay tablet (p. 42)

czar Russian for "caesar," the title used by Russian emperors (p. 445)

daimyo "great names," heads of noble families in Japan who controlled vast landed estates and relied on samurai for protection (pp. 265, 496)

Dao "Way," the key to proper behavior under Confucianism (p. 92)

Daoism a system of ideas based on the teachings of Laozi; teaches that the will of Heaven is best followed through inaction so that nature is allowed to take its course (p. 96)

deficit spending when a government pays out more money than it takes in through taxation and other revenues, thus going into debt (p. 756)

deforestation the clearing of forests (p. 970)

deism an eighteenth-century religious philosophy based on reason and natural law (p. 520)

demilitarize eliminate or prohibit weapons, fortifications, and other military installations (p. 810)

democracy "the rule of the many," government by the people, either directly or through their elected representatives (p. 118)

depression a period of low economic activity and rising unemployment (p. 754)

de-Stalinization the process of eliminating Stalin's more ruthless policies (p. 856)

détente a phase of relaxed tensions and improved relations between two adversaries (p. 875)

dharma in Hinduism, the divine law that rules karma; it requires all people to do their duty based on their status in society (p. 77)

dictator an absolute ruler (p. 158)

dictatorship a form of government in which a person or small group has absolute power (p. 619)

direct democracy a system of government in which the people participate directly in government decision making through mass meetings (p. 123)

direct rule colonial government in which local elites are removed from power and replaced by a new set of officials brought from the mother country (p. 651)

disarmament a limit or reduction of armed forces and weapons (p. 976)

discrimination prejudice, usually based on race, religion, class, sex, or age (p. 956)

dissident a person who speaks out against the regime in power (p. 876)

divine right of kings the belief that kings receive their power from God and are responsible only to God (p. 437)

diviner a person who is believed to have the power to foretell events (p. 238)

domestication adaptation for human use (p. 28)

domino theory idea that, if one country falls to communism, neighboring countries will also fall (p. 853)

dowry a gift of money or property paid at the time of marriage, either by the bride's parents to her husband or, in Islamic societies, by a husband to his wife (pp. 206, 252, 381)

Duma the Russian legislative assembly (p. 632)

dynasty a family of rulers whose right to rule is passed on within the family (p. 47)

E

ecology the study of the relationships between living things and their environment (p. 970)

elector an individual qualified to vote in an election (p. 561)

emancipation the act of setting free (p. 601)

empire a large political unit, usually under a single leader, that controls many peoples or territories (p. 40)

enlightened absolutism a system in which rulers tried to govern by Enlightenment principles while maintaining their full royal powers (p. 529)

entrepreneur a person interested in finding new business opportunities and new ways to make profits (p. 582)

ephor one of the five men elected each year in ancient Sparta who were responsible for the education of youth and the conduct of all citizens (p. 119)

epic poem a long poem that tells the deeds of a great hero, such as the *Iliad* and the *Odyssey* of Homer (p. 112)

Epicureanism school of thought developed by the philosopher Epicurus in Hellenistic Athens; it held that happiness is the chief goal in life, and the means to achieve happiness was the pursuit of pleasure (p. 143)

estate one of the three classes into which French society was divided before the revolution: the clergy (first estate), the nobles (second estate), and the townspeople (third estate) (pp. 299, 548)

eta Japan's outcast class, whose way of life was strictly regulated by the Tokugawa (p. 499)

ethnic cleansing a policy of killing or forcibly removing an ethnic group from its lands; used by the Serbs against the Muslim minority in Bosnia (pp. 782, 881)

extraterritoriality living in a section of a country set aside for foreigners but not subject to the host country's laws (p. 685)

F

faction a dissenting group (p. 556)

fascism a political philosophy that glorifies the state above the individual by emphasizing the need for a strong central government led by a dictatorial ruler (p. 759)

federal system a form of government in which power is shared between the national government and state governments (p. 540)

feminism the movement for women's rights (p. 625)

feudal contract under feudalism, the unwritten rules that determined the relationship between a lord and his vassal (p. 294)

feudalism political and social system that developed during the Middle Ages, when royal governments were no longer able to defend their subjects; nobles offered protection and land in return for service (p. 293)

fief under feudalism, a grant of land made to a vassal; the vassal held political authority within his fief (p. 294)

filial piety the duty of family members to subordinate their needs and desires to those of the male head of the family, a concept important in Confucianism (p. 93)

fossil a remnant or impression of an organism from a past geologic age that has been preserved in the earth's crust (p. 20)

fresco a painting done on fresh, wet plaster with water-based paints (p. 384)

G

genocide the deliberate mass murder of a particular racial, political, or cultural group (pp. 782, 825)

geocentric literally, earth-centered; a system of planetary motion that places Earth at the center of the universe, with the sun, moon, and other planets revolving around it (p. 513)

global economy an economy in which the production, distribution, and sale of goods take place on a worldwide scale, as in a multinational corporation (p. 972)

grand vizier the Ottoman sultan's chief minister, who led the meetings of the imperial council (p. 461)

Great Schism a split in the Catholic Church that lasted from 1378 to 1418, during which time there were rival popes in Rome and in the French city of Avignon; France and its allies supported the pope in Avignon, while France's enemy England and its allies supported the pope in Rome (p. 337)

greenhouse effect global warming caused by the buildup of carbon dioxide in the atmosphere (p. 970)

griot a special class of African storytellers who help keep alive a people's history (p. 241)

guerrilla tactics the use of unexpected maneuvers like sabotage and subterfuge to fight an enemy (p. 795)

guild a business association associated with a particular trade or craft; guilds evolved in the twelfth century and came to play a leading role in the economic life of medieval cities (p. 322)

gunpowder empire an empire formed by outside conquerors who unified the regions that they conquered through their mastery of firearms (p. 460)

H

hajj a pilgrimage to Makkah, one of the requirements of the Five Pillars of Islam (p. 193)

han one of the approximately 250 domains into which Japan was divided under the Tokugawa (p. 497)

harem "sacred place," the private domain of an Ottoman sultan, where he and his wives resided (p. 461)

heavy industry the manufacture of machines and equipment for factories and mines (p. 856)

heliocentric literally, sun-centered; the system of the universe proposed in 1543 by Nicholas Copernicus, who argued that the earth and planets revolve around the sun (p. 513)

Hellenistic Era the age of Alexander the Great; period when the Greek language and ideas were carried to the non-Greek world (p. 141)

helot in ancient Sparta, captive peoples who were forced to work for their conquerors (p. 118)

heresy the denial of basic church doctrines (p. 326)

hieratic script simplified version of hieroglyphics used in ancient Egypt for business transactions, record keeping, and the general needs of daily life (p. 52)

hieroglyph a picture or symbol used in a hieroglyphic system of writing (p. 354)

hieroglyphics "priest-carvings" or "sacred writings," a complex system of writing that used both pictures and more abstract forms; used by the ancient Egyptians and Mayans (p. 52)

Hijrah the journey of Muhammad and his followers to Madinah in 622, which became year 1 of the official calendar of Islam (p. 193)

Hinduism the major Indian religious system, which had its origins in the religious beliefs of the Aryans who settled India after 1500 B.C. (p. 77)

hominid humans and other humanlike creatures that walk upright (p. 21)

Homo erectus "upright human being," a species that emerged around 1.5 million years ago and marked a second stage of early human development (p. 21)

Homo sapiens "wise human being," a species that emerged around 250,000 years ago and marked a third stage in human development (p. 21)

Homo sapiens sapiens "wise, wise human being," a species that appeared in Africa between 150,000 and 200,000 years ago; they were the first anatomically modern humans (p. 22)

hoplite in the early Greek military system, heavily armed foot soldiers (p. 116)

hostage system a system used by the shogunate to control the daimyo in Tokugawa Japan; the family of a daimyo lord was forced to stay at their residence in the capital whenever the lord was absent from it (p. 498)

humanism an intellectual movement of the Renaissance based on the study of the humanities, which included grammar, rhetoric, poetry, moral philosophy, and history (p. 382)

I

imperator commander in chief; the Latin origin of the word *emperor* (p. 159)

imperialism the extension of a nation's power over other lands (p. 648)

indemnity payment for damages (p. 689)

indigenous native to a region (p. 658)

indirect rule colonial government in which local rulers are allowed to maintain their positions of authority and status (p. 651)

Glossary

inductive reasoning the doctrine that scientists should proceed from the particular to the general by making systematic observations and carefully organized experiments to test hypotheses or theories, a process that will lead to correct general principles (p. 517)

indulgence a release from all or part of punishment for sin by the Catholic Church, reducing time in purgatory after death (p. 391)

industrial capitalism an economic system based on industrial production or manufacturing (p. 586)

infidel an unbeliever, a term applied to the Muslims during the Crusades (p. 306)

inflation a rapid increase in prices (pp. 177, 434)

Inquisition a court established by the Catholic Church in 1232 to discover and try heretics; also called the Holy Office (p. 326)

insulae Roman apartment blocks constructed of concrete (p. 167)

interdict a decree by the pope that forbade priests to give the sacraments of the church to the people (p. 325)

intifada "uprising," militant movement that arose during the 1980s among supporters of the Palestine Liberation Organization living in Israel (p. 932)

Islam monotheistic religion that emerged in the Arabian Peninsula during the seventh century A.D. (p. 193)

janissary a soldier in the elite guard of the Ottoman Turks (p. 458)

jihad "struggle in the way of God" (p. 197)

Judaism monotheistic religion developed among the Israelites (p. 56)

kaiser German for "caesar," the title of the emperors of the Second German Empire (p. 599)

kamikaze Japanese for "divine wind," a suicide mission in which young Japanese pilots intentionally flew their airplanes into U.S. fighting ships at sea (p. 832)

karma in Hinduism, the force generated by a person's actions that determines how the person will be reborn in the next life (p. 77)

khanate one of the several separate territories into which Genghis Khan's empire was split, each under the rule of one of his sons (p. 254)

knight under feudalism, a member of the heavily armored cavalry (p. 293)

laissez-faire literally, "let [people] do [what they want]," the concept that the state should not impose government regulations but should leave the economy alone (p. 521)

laity regular church members (p. 173)

lay investiture the practice by which secular rulers both chose nominees to church offices and gave them the symbols of their office (p. 324)

Legalism a popular philosophy developed in China toward the end of the Zhou dynasty, it proposes that human beings are evil by nature and can only be brought to the correct path by harsh laws (p. 97)

liberalism a political philosophy originally based largely on Enlightenment principles, holding that people should be as free as possible from government restraint and that civil liberties—the basic rights of all people—should be protected (p. 591)

lineage group an extended family unit that has combined into a larger community (p. 237)

literacy the ability to read (p. 627)

longhouse Iroquois house about 150 to 200 feet (46 to 61 m) long built of wooden poles covered with sheets of bark and housing about a dozen families (p. 348)

magic realism a form of expression unique to Latin American literature; it combines realistic events with dreamlike or fantastic backgrounds (p. 905)

Magna Carta the "Great Charter" of rights, which King John was forced to sign by the English nobles at Runnymeade in 1215 (p. 299)

Mahatma "Great Soul," title given to Mohandas Gandhi by the Indian people (p. 788)

Mahayana a school of Buddhism that developed in northwest India, stressing the view that nirvana can be achieved through devotion to the Buddha; its followers consider Buddhism a religion, not a philosophy, and the Buddha is a divine figure (p. 268)

mainland states part of a continent, as distinguished from peninsulas or offshore islands (p. 421)

maize corn (p. 360)

mandate a nation governed by another nation on behalf of the League of Nations (p. 744)

Mandate of Heaven claim by Chinese kings of the Zhou dynasty that they had direct authority from heaven to rule and to keep order in the universe (p. 91)

Mannerism an artistic movement that emerged in Italy in the 1520s and 1530s; it marked the end of the Renaissance by breaking down the principles of balance, harmony, and moderation (p. 448)

manor in medieval Europe, an agricultural estate run by a lord and worked by peasants (p. 317)

masterpiece piece created by a journeyman who aspires to be a master craftsperson; it allowed the members of a guild to judge whether the journeyman was qualified to become a master and join the guild (p. 322)

matrilineal tracing lineage through the mother rather than the father (p. 237)

mercantilism a set of principles that dominated economic thought in the seventeenth century; it held that the prosperity of a nation depended on a large supply of gold and silver (p. 413)

mercenary a soldier who sells his services to the highest bidder (p. 377)

Mesoamerica the name used for areas of Mexico and Central America that were civilized before the arrival of the Spanish (p. 352)

mestizo a person of mixed European and native American Indian descent (pp. 537, 672)

Middle Passage the journey of slaves from Africa to the Americas, so called because it was the middle portion of the triangular trade route (p. 416)

militant combative (p. 429)

militarism reliance on military strength (p. 598)

minaret the tower of a mosque from which the muezzin calls the faithful to prayer five times a day (p. 209)

ministerial responsibility the idea that the prime minister is responsible to the popularly elected executive body and not to the executive officer (p. 631)

missionary a person sent out to carry a religious message (p. 288)

mobilization the process of assembling troops and supplies and making them ready for war (pp. 720, 830)

modernism a movement in which writers and artists between 1870 and 1914 rebelled against the traditional literary and artistic styles that had dominated European cultural life since the Renaissance (p. 639)

monarch a king or queen who rules a kingdom (p. 30)

monarchy government by a sovereign ruler such as a king or queen (p. 64)

monasticism practice of living the life of a monk (p. 288)

money economy an economic system based on money rather than barter (p. 320)

monk a man who separates himself from ordinary human society in order to dedicate himself to God; monks live in monasteries headed by abbots (p. 288)

monotheistic having one god (p. 59)

Monroe Doctrine the United States policy guaranteeing the independence of Latin American nations and warning against European intervention in the Americas, made by President James Monroe in 1823 (p. 673)

monsoon a seasonal wind pattern in southern Asia that blows warm, moist air from the southwest during the summer, bringing heavy rains, and cold, dry air from the northeast during the winter (p. 72)

mosque a Muslim house of worship (p. 202)

muezzin the crier who calls the Muslim faithful to prayer from the minaret of a mosque (p. 209)

mulatto a person of mixed African and European descent (p. 537)

multinational corporation a company with divisions in more than two countries (p. 902)

mummification a process of slowly drying a dead body to prevent it from decaying (p. 48)

nationalism the unique cultural identity of a people based on common language, religion, and national symbols (p. 568)

natural rights rights with which all humans are supposedly born, including the rights to life, liberty, and property (p. 451)

natural selection the principle set forth by Darwin that some organisms are more adaptable to the environment than others; in popular terms, "survival of the fittest" (p. 608)

Neanderthal type of *Homo sapiens* that lived in Europe and the Middle East between 100,000 and 30,000 B.C. (p. 21)

neo-Confucianism a revised form of Confucianism that evolved as a response to Buddhism and held sway in China from the late Tang dynasty to the end of the dynastic system in the twentieth century (p. 256)

Neolithic Revolution the shift from hunting of animals and gathering of food to the keeping of animals and the growing of food on a regular basis that occurred around 8000 B.C. (p. 27)

New Economic Policy (NEP) a modified version of the old capitalist system adopted by Lenin in 1921 to replace war communism in Russia; peasants were allowed to sell their produce, and retail stores and small industries could be privately owned, but heavy industry, banking, and mines remained in the hands of the government (p. 761)

new monarchy in the fifteenth century, government in which power had been centralized under a king or queen, i.e., France, England, and Spain (p. 339)

New Testament the second part of the Christian Bible, it provides a record of Jesus' life and teachings (p. 172)

nirvana in Buddhism, ultimate reality, the end of the self and a reunion with the Great World Soul (p. 78)

nomad a person who moves from place to place (p. 23)

nun a woman who separates herself from ordinary human society in order to dedicate herself to God; nuns live in convents headed by abbesses (p. 288)

occupied held by a foreign power (p. 957)

oligarchy "the rule of the few," a form of government in which a small group of people exercises controls (pp. 118, 801)

oracle in ancient Greece, a sacred shrine where a god or goddess was said to reveal the future through a priest or priestess (p. 128)

ordeal a means of determining guilt in Germanic law, based on the idea of divine intervention: if the accused person was unharmed after a physical trial, he or she was presumed innocent (p. 287)

organic evolution the principle set forth by Darwin that every plant or animal has evolved, or changed, over a long period of time from earlier, simpler forms of life to more complex forms (p. 608)

orthodoxy traditional beliefs, especially in religion (p. 469)

ostracism in ancient Athens, the process for temporarily banning ambitious politicians from the city by popular vote (p. 123)

ozone layer a thin layer of gas in the upper atmosphere that shields Earth from the sun's ultraviolet rays (p. 970)

P

Paleolithic Age from the Greek for "Old Stone," the early period of human history, from approximately 2,500,000 to 10,000 B.C., during which humans used simple stone tools; sometimes called the Old Stone Age (p. 22)

Pan-Africanism the unity of all black Africans, regardless of national boundaries (pp. 788, 923)

Pan-Arabism Arab unity, regardless of national boundaries (p. 931)

partisan a resistance fighter in World War II (p. 822)

pasha an appointed official in the Ottoman Empire who collected taxes, maintained law and order, and was directly responsible to the sultan's court (p. 459)

pastoral nomad a person who domesticates animals for food and clothing and moves along regular migratory routes to provide a steady source of nourishment for those animals (p. 55)

paterfamilias in the Roman social structure, the dominant male head of the household, which also included his wife, sons and their wives and children, unmarried daughters, and slaves (p. 165)

patriarch the head of the Eastern Orthodox Church, originally appointed by the Byzantine emperor (p. 305)

patriarchal dominated by men (p. 41)

patrician great landowners, they formed the ruling class in the Roman Republic (p. 152)

patrilineal tracing lineage through the father (p. 237)

peacekeeping force a military force drawn from neutral members of the United Nations to settle conflicts and supervise truces (p. 975)

peninsular a person born on the Iberian Peninsula; typically, a Spanish or Portuguese official who resided temporarily in Latin America for political and economic gain and then returned to Europe (p. 672)

per capita per person (p. 943)

perestroika Mikhail Gorbachev's plan to reform the Soviet Union by restructuring its economy (p. 877)

permanent revolution an atmosphere of constant revolutionary fervor favored by Mao Zedong to enable China to overcome the past and achieve the final stage of communism (p. 942)

phalanx a wall of shields created by foot soldiers marching close together in a rectangular formation (p. 116)

pharaoh the most common of the various titles for ancient Egyptian monarchs; the term originally meant "great house" or "palace" (p. 47)

philosophe French for "philosopher"; applied to all intellectuals—i.e., writers, journalists, economists, and social reformers—during the Enlightenment (p. 519)

philosophy an organized system of thought, from the Greek for "love of wisdom" (p. 130)

photomontage a picture made of a combination of photographs (p. 774)

pilgrim a person who travels to a shrine or other holy place (p. 85)

plague an epidemic disease (p. 176)

planned economy an economic system directed by government agencies (p. 726)

plantation a large agricultural estate (p. 416)

plateau a relatively high, flat land area (p. 225)

plebeian in the Roman Republic, a social class made up of minor landholders, craftspeople, merchants, and small farmers (p. 152)

plebiscite a popular vote (p. 600)

pogrom organized persecution or massacre of a minority group, especially Jews (p. 639)

policy of containment a plan to keep something, such as communism, within its existing geographical boundaries and prevent further aggressive moves (p. 850)

polis the early Greek city-state, consisting of a city or town and its surrounding territory (p. 115)

Politburo a seven-member committee that became the leading policy-making body of the Communist Party in Russia (p. 761)

polytheistic having many gods (p. 42)

pop art an artistic movement that emerged in the early 1960s; pop artists took images from popular culture and transformed them into works of fine art (p. 892)

pope the bishop of Rome and head of the Roman Catholic Church (p. 287)

porcelain a ceramic made of fine clay baked at very high temperatures (pp. 257, 494)

postmodernism an artistic movement that emerged in the 1980s; its artists do not expect rationality in the world and are comfortable with many "truths." (p. 893)

praetor an official of the Roman Republic in charge of enforcing civil law (p. 152)

predestination the belief that God has determined in advance who will be saved (the elect) and who will be damned (the reprobate) (p. 396)

prefecture in the Japanese Meiji Restoration, a territory governed by its former daimyo lord (p. 699)

prehistory the period before writing was developed (p. 19)

Glossary

principle of intervention idea that great powers have the right to send armies into countries where there are revolutions to restore legitimate governments (p. 591)

privatization the sale of government-owned companies to private firms (p. 907)

procurator in the Roman Empire, an official in charge of a province (p. 170)

proletariat the working class (p. 619)

propaganda ideas spread to influence public opinion for or against a cause (p. 721)

protectorate a political unit that depends on another government for its protection (p. 649)

provincial local; of or relating to a province (p. 691)

psychoanalysis a method by which a therapist and patient probe deeply into the patient's memory; by making the patient's conscious mind aware of repressed thoughts, healing can take place (p. 637)

Ptolemaic system the geocentric model of the universe that prevailed in the Middle Ages; named after the astronomer Ptolemy, who lived in Alexandria during the second century A.D. (p. 513)

puddling process in which coke derived from coal is used to burn away impurities in crude iron to produce high quality iron (p. 583)

pueblo a multistoried structure of the Anasazi that could house up to 250 people (p. 350)

queue the braided pigtail that was traditionally worn by Chinese males (p. 488)

quipu a system of knotted strings used by the Inca people for keeping records (p. 362)

Quran the holy scriptures of the religion of Islam (p. 193)

raja an Aryan leader or prince (p. 74)

rationalism a system of thought expounded by René Descartes based on the belief that reason is the chief source of knowledge (p. 517)

real wages the actual purchasing power of income (p. 863)

realism mid-nineteenth century movement that rejected romanticism and sought to portray lower- and middle-class life as it actually was (p. 608)

redistribution of wealth the shifting of wealth from a rich minority to a poor majority (p. 797)

regime the government in power (p. 99)

Reichstag the German parliament (p. 767)

reincarnation the rebirth of an individual's soul in a different form after death (p. 77)

relic bones or other objects connected with saints; considered worthy of worship by the faithful (p. 328)

relics of feudalism obligations of peasants to noble landlords that survived into the modern era (p. 548)

reparation payment made to the victors by the vanquished to cover the costs of a war (p. 742)

republic a form of government in which the leader is not a king and certain citizens have the right to vote (p. 151)

revisionist a Marxist who rejected the revolutionary approach, believing instead in evolution by democratic means to achieve the goal of socialism (p. 619)

ritual a ceremony or rite (p. 128)

rococo an artistic style that replaced baroque in the 1730s; it was highly secular, emphasizing grace, charm, and gentle action (p. 527)

romanticism an intellectual movement that emerged at the end of the eighteenth century in reaction to the ideas of the Enlightenment; it stressed feelings, emotion, and imagination as sources of knowing (p. 605)

sacrament Christian rites (p. 325)

salon the elegant drawing rooms of great urban houses where, in the eighteenth century, writers, artists, aristocrats, government officials, and wealthy middle-class people gathered to discuss the ideas of the philosophes, helping to spread the ideas of the Enlightenment (p. 524)

salvation the state of being saved (that is, going to heaven) through faith alone or through faith and good works (p. 390)

samurai "those who serve," Japanese warriors similar to the knights of medieval Europe (p. 265)

sanction a restriction intended to enforce international law (p. 813)

sans-culottes "without breeches," members of the Paris Commune who considered themselves ordinary patriots (in other words, they wore long trousers instead of fine knee-length breeches) (p. 553)

Sanskrit the first writing system of the Aryans, developed around 1000 B.C. (p. 74)

satellite state a country that is economically and politically dependent on another country (p. 850)

satrap "protector of the Kingdom," the governor of a province (satrapy) of the Persian Empire under Darius (p. 63)

satrapy one of the 20 provinces into which Darius divided the Persian Empire (p. 63)

savanna broad grassland dotted with small trees and shrubs (p. 225)

schism the separation between the two great branches of Christianity that occurred when the Roman Pope Leo IX and the Byzantine patriarch Michael Cerularius excommunicated each other in 1054 (p. 305)

scholar-gentry in China, a group of people who controlled much of the land and produced most of the candidates for the civil service (p. 252)

Glossary

scholasticism a medieval philosophical and theological system that tried to reconcile faith and reason (p. 330)

scientific method a systematic procedure for collecting and analyzing evidence that was crucial to the evolution of science in the modern world (p. 517)

secede withdraw (p. 603)

secular worldly (p. 375)

secularization indifference to or rejection of religion or religious consideration (p. 607)

self-strengthening a policy promoted by reformers toward the end of the Qing dynasty under which China would adopt Western technology while keeping its Confucian values and institutions (p. 686)

Senate in the Roman Republic, a select group of about 300 patricians who served for life; originally formed to advise government officials, it came to have the force of law by the third century B.C. (p. 152)

separation of powers a form of government in which the executive, legislative, and judicial branches limit and control each other through a system of checks and balances (p. 520)

sepoy an Indian soldier hired by the British East India Company to protect the company's interests in the region (p. 666)

serf in medieval Europe, a peasant legally bound to the land who had to provide labor services, pay rents, and be subject to the lord's control (p. 317)

shah king (used in Persia and Iran) (p. 469)

shari'ah a law code drawn up by Muslim scholars after Muhammad's death; it provided believers with a set of practical laws to regulate their daily lives (p. 194)

sheikh the ruler of an Arabic tribe, chosen from one of the leading families by a council of elders (p. 191)

Shiite a Muslim group that accepts only the descendants of Muhammad's son-in-law Ali as the true rulers of Islam (p. 199)

Shining Path a radical guerrilla group in Peru with ties to Communist China (p. 913)

Shinto "the Sacred Way" or "the Way of the Gods," the Japanese state religion; among its doctrines are the divinity of the emperor and the sacredness of the Japanese nation (p. 266)

shogun "general," a powerful military leader in Japan (p. 265)

shogunate the Japanese system of centralized government under a shogun, who exercised actual power while the emperor was reduced to a figurehead (p. 265)

Silk Road a route between the Roman Empire and China, so called because silk was China's most valuable product (p. 83)

social contract the concept proposed by Rousseau that an entire society agrees to be governed by its general will, and all individuals should be forced to abide by the general will since it represents what is best for the entire community (p. 522)

socialism a system in which society, usually in the form of the government, owns and controls the means of production (p. 588)

Socratic method the method of teaching used by the Greek philosopher Socrates, it employs a question-and-answer format to lead pupils to see things for themselves by using their own reason (p. 130)

soviet a Russian council composed of representatives from the workers and soldiers (p. 734)

sphere of influence an area in which a foreign power has been granted exclusive rights and privileges, such as trading rights and mining privileges (p. 687)

stalemate the condition that exists when neither of two opposing sides is able to make significant gains (p. 956)

state capitalism an economic system in which the central government plays an active role in the economy, establishing price and wage policies and subsidizing vital industries (p. 958)

stateless society a group of independent villages organized into clans and led by a local ruler or clan head without any central government (p. 234)

Stoicism a school of thought developed by the teacher Zeno in Hellenistic Athens; it says that happiness can be achieved only when people gain inner peace by living in harmony with the will of God, and that people should bear whatever life offers (p. 143)

subsistence farming the practice of growing just enough crops for personal use, not for sale (p. 232)

sultan "holder of power," the military and political head of state under the Seljuk Turks and the Ottomans (pp. 201, 460)

Sunni a Muslim group that accepts only the descendants of the Umayyads as the true rulers of Islam (p. 199)

surrealism artistic movement that seeks to depict the world of the unconscious (p. 774)

suttee the Hindu custom of cremating a widow on her husband's funeral pyre (p. 475)

Swahili a mixed African-Arabic culture that developed along the east coast of Africa; also, the major language used in that area, combining Bantu with Arabic words and phrases (p. 233)

systematic agriculture the keeping of animals and the growing of food on a regular basis (p. 28)

taille an annual direct tax, usually on land or property, that provided a regular source of income for the French monarchy (p. 339)

tepee a circular tent made by stretching buffalo skins over wooden poles (p. 349)

Thatcherism the economic policy of British Prime Minister Margaret Thatcher, which limited social welfare and restricted union power (p. 886)

theocracy government by divine authority (p. 39)

theology the study of religion and God (p. 330)

Theravada "the teachings of the elders," a school of Buddhism that developed in India; its followers view Buddhism as a way of life, not a religion centered on individual salvation (p. 268)

total war a war that involves the complete mobilization of resources and people, affecting the lives of all citizens in the warring countries, even those remote from the battlefields (p. 726)

totalitarian state a government that aims to control the political, economic, social, intellectual, and cultural lives of its citizens (p. 759)

tournament under feudalism, a series of martial activities such as jousts designed to keep knights busy during peacetime and help them prepare for war (p. 295)

trade embargo a policy prohibiting trade with a particular country (p. 907)

trading society a group of people who depend primarily on trade for income (p. 277)

tragedy a form of drama that portrays a conflict between the protagonist and a superior force and having a protagonist who is brought to ruin or extreme sorrow, especially as a result of a fatal flaw (p. 129)

trench warfare fighting from ditches protected by barbed wire, as in World War I (p. 722)

triangular trade a pattern of trade that connected Europe, Africa and Asia, and the American continents; typically, manufactured goods from Europe were sent to Africa, where they were exchanged for slaves, who were sent to the Americas, where they were exchanged for raw materials that were then sent to Europe (p. 416)

tribute goods or money paid by conquered peoples to their conquerors (p. 356)

triumvirate a government by three people with equal power (p. 157)

ulema a group of religious advisers to the Ottoman sultan; this group administered the legal system and schools for educating Muslims (p. 461)

uncertainty principle the idea put forth by Heisenberg in 1927 that the behavior of subatomic particles is uncertain, suggesting that all of the physical laws governing the universe are based in uncertainty (p. 775)

universal law of gravitation one of the three rules of motion governing the planetary bodies set forth by Sir Isaac Newton in his *Principia;* it explains that planetary bodies do not go off in straight lines but instead continue in elliptical orbits about the sun because every object in the universe is attracted to every other object by a force called gravity (p. 514)

universal male suffrage the right of all males to vote in elections (p. 592)

urban society a system in which cities are the center of political, economic, and social life (p. 375)

vassal under feudalism, a man who served a lord in a military capacity (p. 293)

vernacular the language of everyday speech in a particular region (p. 331)

viceroy a governor who ruled as a representative of a monarch (p. 667)

vizier a high government official in ancient Egypt or in Muslim countries (p. 48, 200)

war communism in World War I Russia, government control of banks and most industries, the seizing of grain from peasants, and the centralization of state administration under Communist control (p. 737)

war of attrition a war based on wearing the other side down by constant attacks and heavy losses, such as World War I (p. 724)

welfare state a state in which the government takes responsibility for providing citizens with services such as health care (p. 862)

wergild "money for a man," the value of a person in money, depending on social status; in Germanic society, a fine paid by a wrongdoer to the family of the person he or she had injured or killed (p. 287)

witchcraft the practice of magic by people supposedly in league with the devil (p. 435)

women's liberation movement the renewed feminist movement of the late 1960s, which demanded political and economic equality with men (p. 867)

yoga a method of training developed by the Hindus that is supposed to lead to oneness with God (p. 77)

zaibatsu in the Japanese economy, a large financial and industrial corporation (p. 789)

zamindar a local official in Mogul India who received a plot of farmland for temporary use in return for collecting taxes for the central government (p. 474)

Zen a sect of Buddhism that became popular with Japanese aristocrats and became part of the samurai's code of behavior; under Zen Buddhism, there are different paths to enlightenment (p. 266)

ziggurat a massive stepped tower on which was built a temple dedicated to the chief god or goddess of a Sumerian city (p. 39)

Glossary

Spanish Glossary

A

abbess/*abadesa* la líder de un convento (pág. 288)

abolitionism/*abolicionismo* un movimiento para poner fin a la esclavitud (pág. 602)

absolutism/*absolutismo* un sistema político en el cual la autoridad tiene el poder total o absoluto (pág. 441)

acid rain/*lluvia ácida* la lluvia que resulta cuando azufre producido por industrias se mezcla con la humedad en el aire (pág. 970)

acropolis/*acrópolis* en las antiguas ciudades-estados griegas, un lugar de reunión fortificado ubicado en la cima de una colina que a veces era el lugar de templos y edificios públicos (pág. 115)

adobe/*adobe* ladrillo secado al sol (pág. 350)

Age of Pericles/*Era de Pericles* el período durante el cual Pericles dominó la política en Atenas, entre los años 461 y 429 antes de Cristo, durante el cual Atenas alcanzó la cúspide de su poder (pág. 123)

agora/*ágora* en las antiguas ciudades-estado griegas, un espacio abierto que fue utilizado como lugar de asamblea para el pueblo y para un mercado (pág. 115)

agricultural society/*sociedad agrícola* un grupo de personas cuya economía se basa en gran medida en la agricultura (pág. 277)

anarchy/*anarquía* ausencia de autoridad política (pág. 470)

annul/*anular* declarar inválida una cosa (pág. 397)

anthropology/*antropología* el estudio de la vida humana y la cultura basado en artículos y fósiles humanos (pág. 20)

anti-Semitism/*antisemitismo* hostilidad hacia los judíos o discriminación hacia los judíos (pág. 336)

apartheid/*segregación racial* "separación," el sistema de segregación racial aplicado en Sudáfrica desde la década de 1950 hasta 1991 (pág. 922)

appeasement/*apaciguamiento* satisfacción de las demandas razonables de poderes insatisfechos en un esfuerzo por mantener la paz y la estabilidad (pág. 810)

arabesque/*arabescos* patrones geométricos que se repiten una y otra vez hasta cubrir por completo una superficie con decoración (pág. 210)

archaeology/*arqueología* el estudio de sociedades pasadas a través de un análisis de los artículos que la gente ha dejado (pág. 19)

archipelago/*archipiélago* una cadena de islas (pág. 273)

arete/virtud en la antigua Grecia, las cualidades de excelencia que un héroe se esfuerza por alcanzar en una lucha o competencia (pág. 113)

aristocracy/*aristocracia* una clase alta cuya riqueza está basada en tierras y cuyo poder pasa de una generación a otra (pág. 89)

armada/*armada* una flota de buques de guerra (pág. 432)

armistice/*armisticio* una tregua o acuerdo para dar fin a una guerra (pág. 740)

arms race/*carrera armamentista* constitución de ejércitos y acopio de armas mantenerse a la par con un enemigo (pág. 851)

artifact/*artefacto* herramientas, artículos de alfarería, pinturas, armas, edificaciones, y artículos para el hogar dejados por pueblos antiguos (pág. 20)

artisan/*artesano* un trabajador diestro o persona con habilidades manuales, que elabora productos tales como armas y joyas (pág. 29)

ascetic/*asceta* una persona que practica la abnegación para alcanzar un entendimiento de la realidad última (pág. 78)

astrolabe/*astrolabio* un instrumento utilizado por los navegantes para determinar su ubicación mediante la observación de las estrellas y los planetas (pág. 208)

australopithecine/*australopitecino* "simios del sur," las primera criatura humanoide que floreció en el este y sur de África hace tres o cuatro millones de años (pág. 21)

autonomous/*autónomo* de gobierno propio (pág. 882)

B

balance of trade/*balanza comercial* la diferencia en valor entre lo que una nación importa y lo que exporta en un período de tiempo (pág. 413)

banana republic/*república banana* país pequeño dependiente de una nación grande y rica (pág. 800)

banner/*estandarte* en la China Qing, una unidad militar independiente constituida por Manchúes, y la principal fuerza de combate del imperio (pág. 489)

Bantu/*bantú* una familia de idiomas hablados en el centro y sur de África; un miembro de cualquier grupo de los pueblos africanos que hablan dicho idioma (pág. 232)

baroque/*barroco* un estilo artístico de el siglo XVII y caracterizado por formas complejas, ornamentación audaz, y elementos contrastantes (pág. 449)

bazaar/*bazar* un mercado cubierto en las ciudades y pueblos islámicos (pág. 204)

bioterrorism/*terrorismo biológico* el uso de armas biológicas y químicas en ataques terroristas (pág. 972)

biowarfare/*guerra biológica* el uso de enfermedades comunicables y agentes tóxicos contra el público y el ejército en tiempo de guerra (pág. 972)

bishopric/*obispado* un grupo de comunidades o parroquias cristianas, bajo la autoridad de un obispo (pág. 287)

blitzkrieg/*guerra relámpago* término alemán para "guerra relámpago," una táctica utilizada por los alemanes durante la Segunda Guerra Mundial (pág. 814)

bloc/*bloque* un grupo de naciones con un objetivo común (pág. 863)

bourgeois/*burgués* una persona de clase media, incluyendo personas involucradas en la industria y la banca, así como también profesionales, tales como abogados, maestros, doctores, y oficiales del gobierno (pág. 548, 619)

bourgeoisie/*burguesía* la clase media (pág. 548, 619)

boyar/*boyar* un noble ruso (pág. 446)

Bronze Age/*Edad de Bronce* el período desde alrededor del año 3000 al 1200 A.C. caracterizado por el uso generalizado del bronce para herramientas y armas (pág. 30)

Buddhism/*budismo* una doctrina religiosa introducida en el norte de la India en el siglo sexto A.C. por Siddhartha Gautama, conocido como Buda (o "el Iluminado") (pág. 78)

budget deficit/*déficit presupuestario* el estado que existe cuando un gobierno gasta más de lo que cobra en la forma de ingresos (pág. 887)

bureaucracy/*burocracia* una organización administrativa con funcionarios y procedimientos habituales (pág. 48, 422)

Bushido/*bushido* "el código del guerrero," el estricto código según el cual debían vivir los samurai japoneses (pág. 265)

caliph/*califa* un sucesor de Mahoma como líder espiritual y temporal de los musulmanes (pág. 197)

caliphate/*califato* el oficio del califa, que se hizo hereditario con el establecimiento de la dinastía Umayyad en Damasco (pág. 197)

capital/*capital* dinero disponible para inversiones (pág. 582)

caste/*casta* una de las cinco grandes divisiones de las clases en la India en tiempos antiguos: Brahmanes, Kshatriyas, Vaisyas, Sudras, e Intocables (pág. 75)

caste system/*sistema de castas* un conjunto de categorías rígidas en la antigua India que determinaba la ocupación de una persona y su potencial económico, así como también su posición en la sociedad, parcialmente sobre la base de del color de la piel (pág. 75)

caudillo/*caudillo* en Latinoamérica post revolucionaria, un líder poderoso que gobernaba principalmente mediante la fuerza militar, a menudo con el respaldo de la elite hacendada (pág. 674)

censorate/*censorate* una rama de la burocracia central de la dinastía Qin de China que fue hecha de inspectores que miraron a los oficiales gubernamentales (pág. 99)

centuriate assembly/*asamblea centurión* la más importante asamblea del pueblo de la República de Roma; elegía a los principales oficiales, tales como los cónsules y pretores, y promulgaba leyes (pág. 152)

chivalry/*caballerosidad* en la Edad Media, el ideal de conducta civilizada que se desarrolló entre la nobleza; fue el código de ética que los caballeros debían mantener (pág. 295)

Christian humanism/*humanismo cristiano* un movimiento que se desarrolló en el norte de Europa durante el Renacimiento que combinaba el aprendizaje clásico (humanismo) con el objetivo de reformar la Iglesia Católica (pág. 390)

Christianity/*cristianismo* religión monoteísta que surgió en el siglo primero D.C. (pág. 171)

city-state/*ciudad-estado* una ciudad con control político y económico sobre el campo alrededor (pág. 39)

civil disobedience/*desobediencia civil* rechazo a obedecer leyes que son consideradas injustas (pág. 788)

civilization/*civilización* una compleja cultura en la que grandes números de personas comparten un gran número de elementos tales como la estructura social, la religión, y el arte (pág. 30)

clan/*clan* un grupo de familias relacionadas (pág. 349, 493)

clergy/*clero* líderes de la iglesia (pág. 173)

Cold War/*Guerra fría* el período de tensión política que siguió a la Segunda Guerra Mundial y que culminó con la caída del comunismo en la Unión Soviética a fines de la década de 1980 (pág. 834)

collaborator/*colaborador* una persona que ayuda al enemigo (pág. 827)

collective bargaining/*convenio colectivo* el derecho de los sindicatos a negociar con los empleadores acerca de remuneraciones y horarios (pág. 755)

collectivization/*colectivización* un sistema en el cual se eliminan las fincas privadas y los campesinos trabajan la tierra de propiedad del gobierno (pág. 763)

colony/*colonia* un asentamiento de personas que están viviendo en un nuevo territorio, enlazado a la madre patria por el comercio y el control directo del gobierno (pág. 413)

commercial capitalism/*capitalismo comercial* un sistema económico en el cual la gente invertía en comercio y bienes con el fin de obtener ganancias (pág. 320, 492)

common law/*derecho consuetudinario* sistema de leyes desarrollado en Inglaterra y que era uniforme en todo el país; reemplazó los códigos legales que variaban de lugar en lugar (pág. 298)

commonwealth/*mancomunidad* nación o estado gobernando por el pueblo o representantes del mismo (pág. 438)

commune/*comuna* en China durante la década de los 1950s, un grupo de granjas colectivas cada una de las cuales contenía más de 30.000 personas que vivían y trabajaban juntas (pág. 942)

concentration camp/*campo de concentración* un campo donde se confina a prisioneros de guerra, prisioneros políticos, o miembros de grupos minoritarios, típicamente bajo condiciones duras (pág. 768)

Confucianism/*confucianismo* el sistema de ideas políticas y éticas formuladas por el filósofo chino Confucio hacia fines de la dinastía Zhou; fue concebido para restaurar el orden en una sociedad que estaba en estado de confusión (pág. 95)

conquistador/*conquistador* uno de los conquistadores españoles de las Américas (pág. 412)

conscription/*conscripción* llamado obligatorio al servicio militar (pág. 718)

conservatism/*conservatismo* una filosofía política basada en la tradición y estabilidad social sobre la base de la obediencia a la autoridad política y la religión organizada (pág. 590)

consul/*cónsul* uno de los dos oficiales electos cada año para gobernar la República de Roma y liderar al ejército en la batalla (pág. 152)

consulate/*consulado* el nuevo gobierno establecido en Francia después del derrocamiento del Directorio en 1799, siendo Napoleón el primer cónsul en control de todo el gobierno (pág. 564)

consumer society/*sociedad de consumo* una sociedad preocupada de comprar bienes (pág. 867)

contras/*contras* rebeldes financiados por los Estados Unidos que empezaron una guerra guerrillera contra el gobierno sandinista en Nicaragua (pág. 909)

cooperative/*cooperativa* una sociedad agrícola perteneciente a, y a menudo administrada para beneficio de los agricultores (pág. 913)

cottage industry/*industria de casa de campo* un método de producción en el que las tareas las realizan las personas en sus hogares (pág. 582)

coup d'état/*golpe de estado* un súbito derrocamiento del gobierno (pág. 561)

creole/*criollo* descendiente de europeos nacido en el Nuevo Mundo (pág. 672)

Crusade/*Cruzada* expediciones militares llevadas a cabo por cristianos europeos para conquistar la Tierra Santa de manos de los musulmanes (pág. 306)

culture/*cultura* forma de vida de las personas (pág. 30)

cuneiform/*cuneiforme* "forma de cuña," sistema de escritura desarrollado por los sumerios utilizando un punzón de lengüeta para crear impresiones con forma de cuña en una tableta de arcilla (pág. 42)

czar/*zar* (de "caesar") título adoptado por los gobernantes de Rusia desde finales del siglo XV (pág. 445)

daimyo/*daimyo* "grandes nombres," líderes de familias nobles en Japón, quienes controlaban vastas propiedades y confiaban su protección a los samurai (pág. 265, 496)

Dao/*Dao* "Camino," la clave para la conducta apropiada bajo el confucianismo (pág. 92)

Daoism/*Daoísmo* sistema de ideas basado en la doctrina de Laozi; enseña que la verdadera manera de seguir la voluntad del Cielo es inacción—permiter que la naturaleza tome su curso (pág. 96)

deficit spending/*gastos deficitarios* los gastos gubernamentales que exceden a lo que se recibe a través de los impuestos y otros ingresos, por ende entrando en deuda (pág. 756)

deforestation/*deforestación* la tala de bosques (pág. 970)

deism/*deísmo* una filosofía religiosa del siglo XVIII basada en la razón y en la ley natural (pág. 520)

demilitarize/*desmilitarizar* eliminar o prohibir las armas, fortificaciones, y oras instalaciones militares (pág. 810)

democracy/*democracia* literalmente, el gobierno de muchos, bajo el cual los ciudadanos eligen quién los gobernará (pág. 118)

depression/*depresión* un período de baja actividad económica y aumento del desempleo (pág. 754)

de-Stalinization/*de-Stalinización* el proceso de eliminar las políticas más crueles de Stalin (pág. 856)

détente/*disminución* una fase de relajamiento de relaciones o tensiones entre dos adversarios (pág. 875)

dharma/*ley divina* en el Hinduismo, la ley divina que gobierna el karma; exige que toda la gente cumpla con su deber sobre la base de su estatus en la sociedad (pág. 77)

dictator/*dictador* un líder que goza de poder absoluto (pág. 158)

dictatorship/*dictadura* una forma de gobierno en la cual una persona o pequeño grupo tiene el poder absoluto (pág. 619)

direct democracy/*democracia directa* un sistema de gobierno en que las personas participan directamente en la toma de decisiones del gobierno a través de asambleas (pág. 123)

direct rule/*dominio directo* gobierno colonial en el que las elites locales son removidos del poder y reemplazadas por un nuevo grupo de oficiales traídos desde la madre patria (pág. 651)

disarmament/*desarme* un límite o reducción de las fuerzas armadas y del armamento (pág. 976)

discrimination/*discriminación* prejuicio, habitualmente sobre la base de la raza, la religión, clase, sexo, o edad (pág. 956)

dissident/*disidente* una persona que critica abiertamente al régimen que tiene el poder (pág. 876)

divine right of kings/*derecho divino de reyes* la creencia de que los reyes reciben su poder de parte de Dios y de que son responsables sólo ante Dios (pág. 437)

diviner/*adivino* una persona de quien se cree tiene el poder de predecir eventos (pág. 238)

domestication/*domesticar* adiestrar animales o adaptar plantas para satisfacer necesidades humanas (pág. 28)

domino theory/*teoría dominó* la idea de que, si un país cae ante el comunismo, los países colindantes también lo harán (pág. 853)

dowry/*dote* dinero o bienes pagados por los padres de una novia a su esposo al casarse ella (pág. 206, 252, 381)

Duma/*Duma* la asamblea legislativa rusa (pág. 632)

dynasty/*dinastía* una familia de gobernantes cuyo derecho a gobernar se transmite dentro de la familia (pág. 47)

ecology/*ecología* el estudio de las relaciones entre cosas vivas y su ambiente (pág. 970)

elector/*elector* una persona calificada para votar en una elección (pág. 561)

emancipation/*emancipación* liberación (pág. 601)

empire/*imperio* una grande unidad política, comúnmente bajo un solo líder, y que controla a muchos pueblos o territorios (pág. 40)

enlightened absolutism/*absolutimo ilustrado* un sistema en el cual los gobernantes trataban de gobernar por medio de principios de Ilustración mientras mantenían sus poderes reales totales (pág. 529)

entrepreneur/*empresario* una persona interesada en hallar nuevas oportunidades de negocios y nuevas formas de obtener ganancias (pág. 582)

ephor/*éforo* uno de los cinco hombres elegidos cada año en la antigua Esparta, quienes eran responsables de la educación de los jóvenes y de la conducta de todos los ciudadanos (pág. 119)

epic poem/*poema épico* un extenso poema que cuenta las hazañas de un gran héroe, tales como la *Ilíada* y la *Odisea* de Homero (pág. 112)

Epicureanism/*Epicureanismo* escuela del pensamiento desarrollada por el filósofo Epicuro en la Atenas Helena; sostenía que la felicidad es la principal meta en la vida, y que el medio para lograr la felicidad era la búsqueda del placer (pág. 143)

estate/*estado* una de las tres clases en las que se dividía la sociedad francesa medieval: el clero (primer estado), los nobles (segundo estado), y la plebe (tercer estado) (pág. 299, 548)

eta/*eta* la clase más baja de la sociedad japonesa, cuya forma de vida era estrictamente regulada por el Tokugawa (pág. 499)

ethnic cleansing/*purificación étnica* una política de matar o remover por la fuerza a un grupo étnico desde sus territorios (pág. 782, 881)

extraterritoriality/*extraterritorialidad* vivir en una sección de un país apartada para extranjeros pero no sujeta a las leyes del país anfitrión (pág. 685)

F

faction/*facción* un grupo de personas disidentes (pág. 556)

fascism/*fascismo* filosofia politica basada en el nacionalismo y en un estado todopoderoso (pág. 759)

federal system/*sistema federal* una forma de gobierno en la cual el poder es compartido entre el gobierno nacional y los gobiernos estatales (pág. 540)

feminism/*feminismo* el movimiento para promover los derechos e intereses de las mujeres (pág. 625)

feudal contract/*contrato feudal* bajo el feudalismo, las reglas no escritas que determinaban la relación entre un señor y su vasallo (pág. 294)

feudalism/*feudalismo* sistema político y social que se desarrolló durante la Edad Media cuando gobiernos reales ya no podían defender a su pueblo; los nobles ofrecían protección y tierras a cambio de servicio (pág. 293)

fief/*feudo* bajo el feudalismo, una concesión de tierras hecha a un vasallo; el vasallo tenía autoridad política dentro de su feudo (pág. 294)

filial piety/*piedad filial* el deber de los miembros de la familia de subordinar sus necesidades y deseos a aquellos del líder de la familia, un concepto importante en el Confucianismo (pág. 93)

fossil/*fósil* un residuo o impresión de un organismo de una era geológica pasada que se ha preservado en la corteza terrestre (pág. 20)

fresco/*fresco* una pintura hecha en yeso fresco y húmedo con pinturas a base de agua (pág. 384)

G

genocide/*genocidio* la matanza masiva de un grupo racial, político o cultural en particular (pág. 782, 825)

geocentric/*geocéntrico* literalmente, centrado en la tierra; un sistema de movimiento planetario que ubica a la Tierra como el centro del universo, con el sol, la luna y otros planetas girando en torno a ella (pág. 513)

global economy/*economía global* una economía en la cual la producción, distribución, y venta de bienes se realiza a escala mundial, tipificada por la empresa multinacional (pág. 972)

grand vizier/*gran visir* el ministro jefe del sultán Otomán, quien encabezaba las reuniones del consejo imperial (pág. 461)

Great Schism/*Gran Cisma* una división en la Iglesia Católica que duró desde 1378 hasta 1418, durante la cual hubo papas rivales en Roma y en la ciudad francesa de Aviñón; Francia y sus aliados respaldaban al papa de Aviñón, mientras que el enemigo de Francia, Inglaterra y sus aliados respaldaban al papa de Roma (pág. 337)

greenhouse effect/*efecto invernadero* calentamiento global causado por la acumulación de dióxido de carbono en la atmósfera (pág. 970)

griot/*griot* un tipo especial de narradores de historias africanos que contribuían a mantener viva la historia de un pueblo (pág. 241)

guerrilla tactics/*táctica de guerrillas* el uso de maniobras inesperadas tales como el sabotaje y subterfugio para luchar contra un enemigo (pág. 795)

guild/*gremio* una asociación comercial relacionada con un oficio o artesanía en particular; los gremios evolucionaron en el siglo XII y pasaron a tener un papel importante en la vida económica de las ciudades medievales (pág. 322)

H

hajj/*hajj* una peregrinación a La Meca; uno de los requisitos de los Cinco Pilares del Islam (pág. 193)

han/*han* uno de los aproximadamente 250 dominios independientes en los que se dividió Japón bajo Tokugawa (pág. 497)

harem/*harén* "lugar sagrado," el dominio privado de un sultán, en donde residía él y sus esposas (pág. 461)

heavy industry/*industria pesada* la manufactura de máquinas y equipo para fábricas y minas (pág. 856)

heliocentric/*heliocéntrico* literalmente, centrado en el sol; el sistema del universo propuesto en 1543 por Nicolás Copérnico, quien sostuvo que la tierra y los planetas giraban en torno al sol (pág. 513)

Hellenistic Era/*Era Helenística* la era de Alejandro el Grande de Grecia, durante la cual el idioma griego y las ideas griegas fueron llevados al mundo no-griego (pág. 141)

helot/*ilota* en la antigua Esparta, los pueblos cautivos eran esclavizados y forzados a trabajar para sus conquistadores (pág. 118)

heresy/*herejía* desacuerdo con las enseñanzas básicas de la iglesia (pág. 326)

hieratic script/*escritura hierática* una versión altamente simplificada de los jeroglíficos utilizados en el antiguo Egipto principalmente para transacciones de negocios, mantenimiento de registros y las necesidades generales de la vida diaria (pág. 52)

hieroglyphics/*jeroglíficos* "grabados sacerdotales" o "escrituras sagradas", un complejo sistema de escritura del antiguo Egipto que utilizaba tanto imágenes como formas más abstractas (pág. 52)

Hijrah/*Hijrah* el viaje de Mahoma y sus seguidores a Medina en el año 622, que pasó a ser el año 1 del calendario oficial del Islam (pág. 193)

Hinduism/*hinduismo* el mayor sistema religioso de la India, que tuvo sus orígenes en las creencias religiosas de los arios que se establecieron en la India después del año 1500 A.C. (pág. 77)

hominid/*homínido* humanos y otras criaturas humanoides que caminan erectos (pág. 21)

Homo erectus/Homo erectus "ser humano erecto," una especie que emergió hace 1,5 millones de años y marcó una segunda etapa del desarrollo humano temprano (pág. 21)

Homo sapiens/Homo sapiens "ser humano sabio," una especie que emergió hace unos 250.000 años y marcó una tercera etapa en el desarrollo humano (pág. 21)

Homo sapiens sapiens/Homo sapiens sapiens "ser humano sabio, sabio," una especie que apareció en África entre 150.000 y 200.000 años atrás; fueron los primeros humanos anatómicamente modernos (pág. 22)

hoplite/*hoplita* en el sistema militar de la antigua Grecia, soldados de infantería fuertemente armados (pág. 116)

hostage system/*sistema de rehén* un sistema utilizado por el shogunado para controlar el daimyo en Tokugawa Japón; cada daimyo debía mantener dos residencias, una en sus propias tierras y una en Edo, donde se encontraba la corte del shogun; la familia del daimyo era obligada a permanecer en la residencia de Edo cuando él estaba ausente (pág. 498)

humanism/*humanismo* un movimiento intelectual del Renacimiento basado en el estudio de las humanidades, que incluía gramática, retórica, poesía, moral filosofía, e historia (pág. 382)

I

imperator/*imperator* comandante en jefe; el origen latino de la palabra "emperador" (pág. 159)

imperialism/*imperialismo* la extensión del poder de una nación hacia otras tierras (pág. 648)

indemnity/*indemnización* un pago por daños (pág. 689)

indirect rule/*dominio indirecto* gobierno colonial en el que los gobernantes locales pueden mantener sus posiciones de autoridad y estatus (pág. 651)

inductive reasoning/*razonamiento inductivo* la noción de que los científicos debían proceder desde lo particular a lo general efectuando observaciones sistemáticas y experimentos cuidadosamente organizados para probar hipótesis o teorías, que a su vez conducirían a principios generales correctos (pág. 517)

indulgence/*indulgencia* perdón de todo o parte de un castigo por pecados otorgado por la Iglesia Católica, reduciendo el tiempo en el purgatorio tras la muerte (pág. 391)

industrial capitalism/*capitalismo industrial* un sistema económico basado en la producción industrial o la fabricación (pág. 586)

infidel/*infiel* un no-creyente, un término aplicado a los musulmanes durante las Cruzadas (pág. 306)

inflation/*inflación* una situación en la cual los precios suben rápidamente mientras que el valor del dinero disminuye (pág. 177, 434)

Inquisition/*Inquisición* un tribunal establecido por la Iglesia Católica en 1232 para descubrir y someter a juicio a los herejes; llamado además el Santo Oficio (pág. 326)

insulae/insulae bloques de apartamentos hasta seis pisos de altura, pobremente construidos de concreto, donde la gente pobre de Roma Imperial residió (pág. 167)

interdict/*interdicción* un decreto papal que prohibía a los sacerdotes impartieran los sacramentos de la iglesia a la gente (pág. 325)

intifada/intifada "levantamiento," un movimiento que surgió durante la década de 1980 entre quienes respaldaban a la Organización Para la Liberación de Palestina radicada dentro de Israel (pág. 932)

Islam/*Islam* religión monoteísta que surgió en la Península Arábiga en el siglo séptimo D.C. (pág. 193)

J

janissary/*jenízaro* un soldado de la guardia de elite del imperio turco otomano (pág. 458)

jihad/*jihad* "lucha en el camino de Dios" (pág. 197)

Judaism/*judaísmo* religión monoteísta desarrollada por los israelitas (pág. 56)

K

kaiser/*káiser* término alemán para "césar," el título de los emperadores del Segundo Imperio Alemán (pág. 599)

kamikaze/*kamikaze* término japonés para "viento divino," una misión suicida en la que jóvenes pilotos japoneses intencionalmente estrellaban sus aviones contra buques de guerra de los EE.UU. (pág. 832)

karma/*karma* en el Hinduismo, la fuerza generada por las acciones de una persona, lo que determina cómo renacerá esta persona en la próxima vida (pág. 77)

khanate/*kanato* uno de los diversos territorios independientes en los que se dividió el imperio de Genghis Khan, cada uno bajo el gobierno de uno de sus hijos (pág. 254)

knight/*caballero* bajo el feudalismo, un miembro de la caballería fuertemente blindada (pág. 293)

L

laissez-faire/*laissez-faire* literalmente, "dejar [a las personas] hacer [lo que quieran]," el concepto de que el estado no debe imponer regulaciones gubernamentales si no que debe dejar la economía sola (pág. 521)

laity/*laicado* miembros no clericales de la iglesia cristiana (pág. 173)

lay investiture/*investidura secular* la práctica mediante la cual los líderes seculares elegían nominados a cargos en la iglesia y los investían con los símbolos de su oficio (pág. 324)

Legalism/*Legalismo* una filosofía popular desarrollada en China hacia fines de la dinastía Zhou, postula que los seres humanos son malvados por naturaleza y sólo pueden ser llevados a la senda correcta mediante leyes fuertes y castigos rígidos (pág. 97)

liberalism/*liberalismo* una filosofía política originalmente basada principalmente en principios de Ilustración, que sostenía que las personas deberían ser lo más libres dentro de lo posible de las restricciones gubernamentales y que las libertades civiles—los derechos básicos de las personas—deberían ser protegidos (pág. 591)

lineage group/*grupo de linaje* una unidad extendida de una familia que se ha combinado en una comunidad mayor (pág. 237)

literacy/*alfabetización* la capacidad de leer y escribir (pág. 627)

longhouse/*vivienda comunal de los indios iroqueses* una vivienda iroquesa de aproximadamente 150 a 200 pies de longitud construida sobre pilares de madera cubiertos con láminas de corteza y que alberga a aproximadamente una docena de familias (pág. 348)

M

magic realism/*realismo mágico* una singular forma de expresión de la literatura latinoamericana; combina eventos realistas con fondos como sueños o fantásticos (pág. 905)

Magna Carta/*Carta Magna* la Gran Cédula de derechos, que el Rey Juan Sin Tierra fue obligado a firmar por los nobles ingleses en Runnymede en 1215 (pág. 299)

Mahatma/*Mahatma* "Gran Alma," un título que los indios utilizaron para referirse a Mohandas Gandhi (pág. 788)

Mahayana/*Mahayana* una escuela de budismo que se desarrolló en el noroeste de la India y que enfatiza la visión de que se puede alcanzar el nirvana a través de la devoción al Buda; sus seguidores consideran al Budismo una religión, no una filosofía, y a Buda como una figura divina (pág. 268)

maize/*maíz* el maíz nativo de la América (pag. 360)

mandate/*mandato* una nación gobernada por otra nación en nombre de la Liga de Naciones (pág. 744)

Mandate of Heaven/*Mandato del Cielo* la reclamación por parte de los reyes de la dinastía Zhou de China en el sentido de que ellos tenían la autoridad para gobernar y mantener el universo en orden directamente por derecho celestial (pág. 91)

manor/*palacete* en la Europa medieval, una propiedad agrícola administrada por un señor y trabajada por campesinos (pág. 317)

masterpiece/*obra maestra* una obra terminada creada por un aprendiz que aspira a ser maestro artesano; permitía a los miembros de un gremio juzgar si un aprendiz estaba calificado para convertirse en maestro y formar parte del gremio (pág. 322)

matrilineal/*línea materna* que traza el linaje por medio de la madre y sus ancestros, no a través del padre (pág. 237)

mercantilism/*mercantilismo* un conjunto de principios que dominaban el pensamiento económico en el siglo XVII; sostenía que la prosperidad de una nación dependía de tener grandes cantidades de oro y plata (pág. 413)

mercenary/*mercenario* soldado que sirve a un país extranjero por dinero (pág. 377)

mestizo/*mestizo* la progenie de europeos e indígenas americanos (pág. 537, 672)

Middle Passage/*paso central* sección intermedia del comercio triangular, en el cual los africanos esclavizados eran traídos a la América por barco (pág. 416)

militant/*militante* persona que respalda activa y agresivamente una causa (pág. 429)

militarism/*militarismo* política nacional basada en la fuerza militar y la glorificación de la guerra (pág. 598)

minaret/*minarete* la torre de una mezquita desde la cual el muecín llama a los fieles a orar cinco veces al día (pág. 209)

ministerial responsibility/*responsabilidad ministerial* la idea de que el primer ministro es responsable ante el ejecutivo popularmente electo y no ante el oficial ejecutivo (pág. 631)

missionary/*misionero* persona que viaja para llevar las principios de una religión a otras personas (pág. 288)

mobilization/*movilización* el proceso de agrupar tropas y suministros y prepararlos para la guerra (pág. 720, 830)

modernism/*modernismo* un movimiento resultante de la rebelión por parte de escritores y artistas entre 1870 y 1914 en contra de los estilos literarios y artísticos tradicionales que habían dominado la vida cultural europea desde el Renacimiento (pág. 639)

monarch/*monarca* un rey o una reina (pág. 30)

monarchy/*monarquía* gobierno de un gobernante soberano como un rey o reina (pág. 64)

monasticism/*monacato* la práctica de vivir la vida de un monje (pág. 288)

money economy/*economía monetaria* un sistema económico basado en el dinero y no en el trueque (pág. 320)

monk/*monje* un hombre que se auto separa de la sociedad humana con el fin de dedicarse a Dios; los monjes vivían en monasterios liderados por abades (pág. 288)

monotheistic/*monoteísta* con un solo dios (pág. 59)

monsoon/*monzón* un patrón estacionario de viento en el sur de Asia que sopla aire cálido y húmedo desde el suroeste durante el verano, trayendo fuertes lluvias, y aire frío y seco desde el noreste durante el invierno (pág. 72)

mosque/*mezquita* un templo musulmán de adoración (pág. 202)

muezzin/*muecín* el pregonero que llama a los fieles a orar desde el minarete de una mezquita (pág. 209)

mulatto/*mulato* la progenie de europeos y africanos (pág. 537)

multinational corporation/*compañía multinacional* una compañía con divisiones en más de dos países (pág. 902)

mummification/*momificación* proceso consistente en secar lentamente un cadáver para prevenir su descomposición (pág. 48)

N

nationalism/*nacionalismo* la singular identidad cultural de un pueblo basada en un idioma, religión, y símbolos nacionales en común (pág. 568)

natural rights/*derechos naturales* derechos con los que todos los humanos supuestamente nacen, incluyendo el derecho a la vida, la libertad y la propiedad (pág. 451)

natural selection/*selección natural* el principio establecido por Darwin en el sentido de que algunos organismos son más adaptables al medio que otros; en términos populares, "supervivencia de los aptos" (pág. 608)

Neanderthal/*Neanderthal* un tipo de *Homo sapiens* que vivió en Europa y el Oriente Medio entre 100.000 y 30.000 A.C. (pág. 21)

neo-Confucianism/*neo-confucianismo* una forma modificada de confucianismo que evolucionó como respuesta al Budismo y mantuvo su dominio en China desde el fin de la dinastía Tang hasta fines del sistema de dinastías en el siglo XX (pág. 256)

Neolithic Revolution/*Revolución Neolítica* el cambio desde la caza de animales y recolección de alimentos hasta el mantenimiento de animales y el cultivo de alimentos de manera habitual que ocurrió alrededor del 8000 A.C. (pág. 27)

New Economic Policy (NEP)/*Nueva Política Económica* una versión modificada del antiguo sistema capitalista adoptado por Lenin en 1921 para reemplazar el comunismo de guerra en Rusia; se permitió a los campesinos vender sus producto, las tiendas y pequeñas industrias podían ser privadas, pero la gran industria, la banca y las minas permanecieron en manos del gobierno (pág. 761)

new monarchy/*nueva monarquía* en el siglo XV, uno de los gobiernos en los que el poder se había centralizado bajo un rey o reina, particularmente en Francia, Inglaterra y España (pág. 339)

New Testament/*Nuevo Testamento* la segunda parte de la Biblia Cristiana, entrega un registro de la vida y enseñanzas de Jesucristo (pág. 172)

nirvana/*nirvana* en el Budismo, la realidad última, el fin del yo y una reunión con el Gran Alma Mundial (pág. 78)

nomad/*nómada* una persona sin residencia fija, que se desplaza de un lugar a otro (pág. 23)

nun/*monja* mujer que se aparta de la sociedad humana común para dedicarse a Dios; las monjas vivían en conventos liderados por abadesas (pág. 288)

O

occupied/*ocupado* país cuyas tierras son poseídas por un poder extranjero (pág. 957)

oligarchy/*oligarquía* literalmente, el gobierno de unos pocos, en el cual un pequeño grupo de personas controla el gobierno (pág. 118, 801)

oracle/*oráculo* en la antigua Grecia, un templo sagrado donde se decía que un dios o una diosa revelaba el futuro a través de un sacerdote o una sacerdotisa (pág. 128)

ordeal/*ordalía* medio para determinar culpa en la ley germánica, basándose en la idea de una intervención divina: si el acusado no resultaba dañado luego de una prueba física, se presumía que era inocente (pág. 287)

organic evolution/*evolución orgánica* el principio establecido por Darwin de que cada planta o animal ha evolucionado, o cambiado, durante un largo periodo desde formas más primitivas y simples de vida hasta formas más complejas (pág. 608)

ostracism/*ostracismo* en la antigua Atenas, proceso para prohibir temporalmente el acceso a políticos ambiciosos a la ciudad por voto popular (pág. 123)

ozone layer/*capa de ozono* delgada capa de gas en la atmósfera superior que protege a la Tierra de los rayos ultravioleta provenientes del sol (pág. 970)

P

Paleolithic Age/*Era Paleolítica* del griego "Piedra Antigua", el antiguo periodo de la historia humana, desde aproximadamente el 2.500.000 al 10.000 A.C., durante el cual, los humanos utilizaban simples herramientas de piedra; algunas veces se le conoce como Edad de Piedra (pág. 22)

Pan-Africanism/*Panafricanismo* movimiento que promociona la unidad de todos los africanos por todo el mundo (pág. 788, 923)

Pan-Arabism/*Panarabismo* política que promueve la unidad árabe internacional (pág. 931)

partisan/*partisano* guerreo de resistencia en la Segunda Guerra Mundial (pág. 822)

pasha/*pachá* oficial designado en el Imperio Otomano que cobraba impuestos, mantenía la ley y el orden y era directamente responsable ante la corte del sultán (pág. 459)

pastoral nomad/*nómade pastoril* persona que domestica animales para alimentarse y vestirse y se traslada a lo largo de rutas migratorias regulares para proporcionar una fuente estable de comida para aquellos animales (pág. 55)

paterfamilias/*jefes de familia* en la antigua estructura social romana, el cabeza de familia del hogar, que también incluía su mujer, sus hijos y las mujeres de sus ellos con sus niños, hijas que no estuvieran casadas y esclavos (pág. 165)

patriarch/*patriarca* el líder de la Iglesia Ortodoxa Oriental, originalmente designado por el emperador bizantino (pág. 305)

patriarchal/*patriarcal* dominado por los hombres (pág. 41)

patrician/*patricio* grandes terratenientes, formaban la clase dominante en la República Romana (pág. 152)

patrilineal/*patrilineal* que viene de la línea paterna (pág. 237)

peacekeeping force/*fuerza para mantener la paz* fuerza militar traída de miembros neutrales de las Naciones Unidas para resolver conflictos y supervisar treguas (pág. 975)

peninsular/*peninsular* persona nacida en la Península Ibérica; comúnmente, un oficial español o portugués que residía temporalmente en Latinoamérica para obtener ganancia política y económica y luego regresaba a Europa (pág. 672)

per capita/*per cápita* por persona (pág. 943)

perestroika/*perestroika* plan de Mikhail Gorbachev para reformar la URSS, reestructurando su economía (pág. 877)

permanent revolution/*revolución permanente* una atmósfera constante de fervor revolucionario apoyado por Mao Zedong para permitir que China venza a su pasado y logre la etapa final del comunismo (pág. 942)

phalanx/*falange* muralla de escudos creada por hoplitas que marchan hombro con hombro en formación rectangular (pág. 116)

pharaoh/*faraón* el más común de los diversos títulos que existían para los monarcas del antiguo Egipto; el término originalmente significaba "gran casa" o "palacio" (pág. 47)

philosophe/*filósofo* término francés para "filósofo", se aplica a todos los intelectuales—escritores, periodistas, economistas y reformadores sociales—durante la Ilustración (pág. 519)

philosophy/*filosofía* sistema organizado del pensamiento, del griego "amor a la sabiduría" (pág. 130)

photomontage/*fotomontaje* una imagen compuesta de una combinación de fotografías (pág. 774)

pilgrim/*peregrino* persona que viaja a un santuario u otro lugar sagrado (pág. 85)

plague/*peste* una enfermedad epidémica; también se llama *plaga* (pág. 176)

planned economy/*economía planificada* sistema económico dirigido por agencias gubernamentales (pág. 726)

plantation/*plantación* una propiedad agrícola grande (pág. 416)

plateau/*altiplanicie* región relativamente llana más elevada que el área circundante (pág. 225)

plebeian/*plebeyo* en la República de Roma, una clase social compuesta de terratenientes menores, artesanos, mercaderes y pequeños granjeros (pág. 152)

plebiscite/*plebiscito* voto popular (pág. 600)

pogrom/*pogrom* persecución organizada de un grupo minoritario, usualmente judíos, en la Rusia de los zares (pág. 639)

policy of containment/*política de contención* plan para mantener algo, como por ejemplo el comunismo, dentro de sus fronteras geográficas existentes e impedir posteriores movimientos agresivos (pág. 850)

polis/*polis* la ciudad-estado de la antigua Grecia, que constaba de una ciudad o pueblo y el territorio de sus alrededores que existe como entidad política (pág. 115)

Politburo/*Politburó* comité de siete miembros que se convirtió en el organismo dominante de determinación de normas del partido comunista en Rusia (pág. 761)

polytheistic/*politeísta* que posee muchos dioses (pág. 42)

pop art/*arte pop* movimiento artístico que surgió a comienzos de la década del 1960; los artistas de este movimiento tomaban imágenes de la cultura popular y las transformaban en obras de bellas artes (pág. 892)

pope/*papa* el obispo de Roma y líder de la Iglesia Católica Romana (pág. 287)

porcelain/*porcelana* cerámica hecha de arcilla fina horneada a temperaturas muy altas (pág. 257, 494)

postmodernism/*posmodernismo* un movimiento artístico que surgió en los años 1980; los artistas no esperan que el mundo sea razonable y aceptan muchas "verdades" (pág. 893)

praetor/*pretor* oficial de la República de Roma a cargo de hacer que se cumpla la ley civil (pág. 152)

predestination/*predestinación* la creencia de que Dios ha determinado anticipadamente quién se salvará (el elegido) y quien se condenará (el réprobo) (pág. 396)

prefecture/*prefectura* en la Restauración Meiji japonesa, un territorio gobernado por su anterior señor daimyo (pág. 699)

prehistory/*prehistoria* el periodo anterior a que se creara la escritura (pág. 19)

principle of intervention/*principio de intervención* la idea de que las grandes potencias tienen el derecho de enviar ejércitos a países donde existen revoluciones a fin de restaurar los gobiernos legítimos (pág. 591)

privatization/*privatización* la venta de compañías del Estado a firmas privadas (pág. 907)

procurator/*procurador* en el Imperio romano, un oficial a cargo de una provincia (pág. 170)

proletariat/*proletariado* la clase trabajadora (pág. 619)

propaganda/*propaganda* ideas que se difunden para influir en la opinión pública a favor de una causa o en contra de ella (pág. 721)

protectorate/*protectorado* unidad política que depende de otro gobierno para su protección (pág. 649)

psychoanalysis/*psicoanálisis* método mediante el cual un terapeuta y un paciente indagan profundamente en la memoria del paciente; haciendo que la mente consciente del paciente tenga consciencia pensamientos reprimidos, podrá ocurrir una cura (pág. 637)

Ptolemaic system/*sistema ptolemaico* el modelo geocéntrico del universo que prevaleció en la Edad Media; nombrado en honor a astrónomo Ptolomeo, que vivió en Alejandría durante el siglo segundo d.C. (pág. 513)

puddling/*pudelación* procesos en el cual se utiliza coque derivado del carbón para extraer impurezas por medio del fuego en hierro bruto y producir un hierro de alta calidad (pág. 583)

pueblo/*pueblo* estructuras de múltiples pisos de Anasazi que podían albergar hasta 250 personas (pág. 350)

Spanish Glossary

Q

queue/*coleta* trenza de pelo única en las parte posterior de la cabeza (pág. 488)

quipu*/*quipu un sistema de cuerdas con nudos usado para por los incas mantener registros (pág. 362)

Quran/*Corán* las escrituras sagradas de la religión del Islam (pág. 193)

R

raja/*rajá* líder ario (príncipe) (pág. 74)

rationalism/*racionalismo* sistema del pensamiento expuesto por René Descartes basado en la creencia de que la razón es la fuente principal del conocimiento (pág. 517)

real wages/*salario efectivo* el poder adquisitivo de los ingresos (pág. 863)

realism/*realismo* estilo y literatura de mediados del Siglo XIX, que reflejaba las realidades de la vida cotidiana (pág. 608)

redistribution of wealth/*redistribución de la riqueza* el cambio de la riqueza de una minoría rica a una mayoría pobre (pág. 797)

Reichstag/*Reichstag* el parlamento alemán (pág. 767)

reincarnation/*reencarnación* el renacimiento del alma de una persona en una forma diferente después de la muerte (pág. 77)

relic/*reliquia* huesos u otros objetos relacionados con santos que se consideraban dignos de adoración por la fe (pág. 328)

relics of feudalism/*reliquias del feudalismo* obligaciones de los campesinos hacia sus patrones aristocráticos que sobrevivieron en la época moderna (pág. 548)

reparation/*reparación* pago hecho a los victoriosos por los derrotados para cubrir los costos de una guerra (pág. 742)

republic/*república* forma de gobierno en la cual el líder no es un rey y ciertos ciudadanos tienen derecho a votar (pág. 151)

revisionist/*revisionista* un marxista que rechazó el enfoque revolucionario, creyendo en cambio en una evolución por medio de una democracia para lograr el objetivo del socialismo (pág. 619)

ritual/*ritual* ceremonia o rito (pág. 128)

romanticism/*romanticismo* un movimiento intelectual que surgió e finales del siglo XVIII en reacción a las ideas de la Ilustración, daba énfasis a los sentimientos, la emoción y la imaginación como fuentes del conocimiento (pág. 605)

S

sacrament/*sacramento* ritos cristianos (pág. 325)

salon/*salón* las elegantes salas de las grandes casas urbanas donde, en el siglo VIII, escritores, artistas, aristócratas, funcionarios de gobierno y gente de la clase media se reunían y hablaban de las ideas de los filósofos y ayudaban a difundir las ideas de la Ilustración (pág. 524)

salvation/*salvación* el estado de ser salvado (es decir, ir al cielo) a través de la fe sola o a través de la fe y buenas obras (pág. 390)

samurai/*samurai* "aquellos que sirven," guerreros japoneses similares a los caballeros de la Europa medieval (pág. 265)

sanction/*sanción* restricción para hacer cumplir la ley internacional (pág. 813)

sans-culottes*/*revolucionarios "sin pantalones," miembros de la Comuna de París, que se consideraban patriotas ordinarios (en otras palabras, usaban pantalones largos en vez de pantalones hasta la rodilla) (pág. 553)

Sanskrit/*sánscrito* el primer sistema de escritura de los arios, creado alrededor del año 1000 A.C. (pág. 74)

satellite state/*estado satélite* país que depende económica y políticamente de otro país (pág. 850)

satrap/*sátrapa* "protector del Reino", el gobernador de una provincia (satrapía) del Imperio Persa bajo el régimen de Darío (pág. 63)

satrapy/*satrapía* una de las 20 provincias en las que Darío dividió el Imperio Persa (pág. 63)

savanna/*sabana* amplias tierras de pastoreo dotadas de pequeños árboles y arbustos (pág. 225)

schism/*cisma* la separación entre dos grandes divisiones de la cristianidad que tuvo lugar cuando el papa romano León IX y el patriarca bizantino Miguel Cerularius se excomulgaron mutuamente en el año 1054 (pág. 305)

scholar-gentry/*erudito* en China, un grupo de personas que controlaba gran parte de la tierra y entregaba la mayoría de los candidatos para el servicio civil (pág. 252)

scholasticism/*escolástica* sistema filosófico y teológico medieval que trataba de conciliar la fe y la razón (pág. 330)

scientific method/*método científico* procedimiento sistemático para recolectar y analizar evidencia que fue crucial para la evolución de la ciencia en el mundo moderno (pág. 517)

secede/*separar* separarse (pág. 603)

secular/*secular* mundano; que no es abiertamente religioso (pág. 375)

secularization/*secularización* viendo el mundo en términos materiales, no espirituales (pág. 607)

self-strengthening/*autofortalecimiento* política promovida por reformadores hacia fines de la dinastía Qing en China bajo la cual China adoptaría la tecnología occidental aunque manteniendo sus valores e instituciones confucianos (pág. 686)

Senate/*Senado* en la República de Roma, un grupo selecto de alrededor de 300 patricios que trabajaban de por vida; formado originalmente para aconsejar a los oficiales de gobierno, llegó a tener el vigor de la ley durante el siglo III A.C. (pág. 152)

separation of powers/*separación de los poderes* forma de gobierno en la cual las divisiones ejecutiva, legislativa y judicial se limitan y controlan entre sí a través de un sistema de revisiones y balances (pág. 520)

sepoy/*cipayo* soldado indio contratado por la British East India Company para proteger los intereses de la compañía en la región (pág. 666)

serf/*siervo* en la Europa medieval, un campesino confinado legalmente a la tierra que tenía que proporcionar servicios de manos de obra, pagar rentas y estar sujeto al control del señor (pág. 317)

shah/*sha* rey (se usa en Persia e Irán) (pág. 469)

shari'ah/*shari'ah* código legal formulado por eruditos musulmanes después de la muerte de Mahoma; le entregó a los creyentes un conjunto de leyes prácticas para regular sus vidas diarias (pág. 194)

sheikh/*jeque* el soberano de una tribu arábica, elegido de una de las familias dominantes por un consejo de ancianos (pág. 191)

Shiite/*chiíta* un grupo musulmán que sólo acepta a los descendientes de Ali, yerno de Mahoma, como los verdaderos gobernantes del islam (pág. 199)

Shining Path/*Sendero Luminoso* grupo de guerrilla radical en Perú con lazos con la China comunista (pág. 913)

Shinto/*sintoísmo* "el Camino Sagrado" o "el Camino de los Dioses," un tipo de religión del estado que se practica en Japón; entre sus doctrinas están la divinidad del emperador y la santidad de la nación japonesa (pág. 266)

shogun/*shogún* "general," líder militar con poder en Japón (pág. 265)

shogunate/*shogunado* el sistema japonés de gobierno centralizado bajo un shogún, que ejercía un poder real mientras el emperador era meramente nominativo (pág. 265)

Silk Road/*Ruta de la Seda* ruta entre el Imperio romano y China, se llamaba así porque la seda era el producto más valioso de China (pág. 83)

social contract/*contrato social* el concepto propuesto por Rousseau de que una sociedad completa accede a ser gobernada por su voluntad general y que todos los individuos deben ser forzados a soportar por el deseo general, lo que representa qué es lo mejor para la comunidad completa (pág. 522)

socialism/*socialismo* sistema en el cual la sociedad, por lo general en la forma del gobierno, posee y controla el medio de producción (pág. 588)

Socratic method/*método socrático* el método de enseñanza utilizado por el filósofo griego Sócrates, emplea un formato de pregunta y respuesta para llevar a los alumnos a ver las cosas por sí mismos, usando su propia razón (pág. 130)

soviet/*soviet* consejo ruso compuesto de representantes de los trabajadores y los soldados (pág. 734)

sphere of influence/*esfera de influencia* área en la que a un poder extranjero se le ha garantizado derechos y privilegios exclusivos, tales como derechos de comercio y privilegios de minería (pág. 687)

stalemate/*estancamiento* la condición que existe cuando ninguno de los dos lados puede obtener ganancias significativas (pág. 956)

state capitalism/*capitalismo del estado* sistema económico en el cual el gobierno central tiene una función activa en la economía, estableciendo políticas de precios y sueldos y subsidiando industrias vitales (pág. 958)

stateless society/*sociedad apátrida* grupo de aldeas independientes organizadas por clanes y lideradas por un soberano local o líder de un clan sin un gobierno central (pág. 234)

Stoicism/*estoicismo* escuela de pensamiento creada por el profesor Zenón en la Atenas helenística; sostenía que podría lograrse la felicidad sólo cuando las personas consigan paz interior, viviendo en armonía con el deseo de Dios y que las personas deban soportar todo lo que la vida les depare (pág. 143)

subsistence farming/*agricultura de subsistencia* la práctica de sembrar sólo las cosechas suficientes para uso personal, no para la venta (pág. 232)

sultan/*sultán* "poseedor del poder," el líder militar y político del estado bajo los turcos Seljuk y otomanos (pág. 201, 460)

Sunni/*sunnita* un grupo musulmán que sólo acepta a los descendientes de los Omeya como los verdaderos gobernantes del islam (pág. 199)

surrealism/*surrealismo* movimiento artístico que trata de representar la vida del inconsciente (pág. 774)

Swahili/*Swahili* cultura mixta africana y arábica que se creó a lo largo de la costa oriental de África; la lengua principal que se emplea en esa área, combinando Bantu con palabras y frases arábicas (pág. 233)

systematic agriculture/*agricultura sistemática* el mantenimiento de animales y la siembra de alimento regularmente (pág. 28)

taille/*taille* impuesto directo anual, por lo general sobre la tierra o propiedad, que entregaba una fuente regular de ingresos para la monarquía francesa (pág. 339)

tepee/*tepee* tienda circular hecha de pieles de búfalo estiradas sobre postes de madera (pág. 349)

Thatcherism/*thatcherismo* la política económica de la Primera Ministra británica Margaret Thatcher, que limitaba el bienestar social y restringía el poder de sindicatos (pág. 886)

theocracy/*teocracia* gobierno por autoridad divina (pág. 39)

theology/*teología* el estudio de la religión y Dios (pág. 330)

Theravada/*Theravada* "las enseñanzas de los ancianos," escuela del budismo que se creo en la India; sus seguidores consideran al budismo como un estilo de vida, no una religión centrada en la salvación del individuo (pág. 268)

total war/*guerra total* guerra que implica la movilización completa recursos y personas, afecta las vidas de todos los ciudadanos en los países en guerra, incluso aquellos alejados de los campos de batalla (pág. 726)

totalitarian state/*estado totalitario* gobierno que se centra en controlar no sólo el lado político de la vida, sino también la vida económica, social, intelectual y cultural de sus ciudadanos (pág. 759)

tournament/*torneo* bajo el feudalismo, una serie de actividades marciales, tales como justas diseñadas para mantener a los caballeros ocupados durante los tiempos de paz y ayudarlos a prepararse para la guerra (pág. 295)

trade embargo/*embargo comercial* política que prohibe el comercio con un país en particular (pág. 907)

trading society/*sociedad comercial* grupo de personas que dependen principalmente del comercio para sus ingresos (pág. 277)

tragedy/*tragedia* forma de drama que representa un conflicto entre el protagonista y una fuerza superior y que tiene un protagonista que es llevado a la ruina o un dolor extremo, en especial como resultado de una racha fatal (pág. 129)

trench warfare/*guerra de trincheras* pelea desde trincheras protegidas por alambres de púa, como en la Primera Guerra Mundial (pág. 722)

triangular trade/*comercio triangular* ruta de tres direcciones entre Europa, África y América en el Siglo XVII (pág. 416)

tribute/*tributo* bienes o dinero pagado por pueblos conquistados a sus conquistadores (pág. 356)

triumvirate/*triunvirato* gobierno de tres personas con igual poder (pág. 157)

ulema/*ulema* grupo de consejeros religiosos para el sultán Otomano; este grupo administraba el sistema legal y las escuelas para educar a los musulmanes (pág. 461)

uncertainty principle/*principio de incertidumbre* la idea establecida por Heiseneberg en 1927 de que el comportamiento de las partículas subatómicas no es certero, lo que sugiere que en el fondo de todas las leyes físicas que rigen el universo está la incertidumbre (pág. 775)

universal law of gravitation/*ley universal de gravitación* una de las tres reglas de movimiento que rigen los cuerpos planetarios establecida por Sir Isaac Newton en su *Principia*; explica que los cuerpos planetarios no se mueven en línea recta, más bien continúan en órbitas elípticas alrededor del sol porque cada objeto en el universo se atrae a otro objeto por una fuerza llamada gravedad (pág. 514)

universal male suffrage/*sufragio masculino universal* el derecho de todos los hombres a votar en elecciones (pág. 592)

urban society/*sociedad urbana* sistema social en el cual las ciudades son el centro de la política económica y la vida social (pág. 375)

vassal/*vasallo* bajo el feudalismo, un hombre que servía a un señor en calidad de militar (pág. 293)

vernacular/*vernacular* la lengua de habla diaria en una región particular (pág. 331)

viceroy/*virrey* gobernanate que representa a un monarca (pag. 667)

vizier/*visir* el ministro de gobierno principal responsable directamente ante un faraón o un califa (pág. 48, 200)

war communism/*comunismo de guerra* en la Rusia de la Primera Guerra Mundial, el control del gobierno de bancos y la mayoría de las industrias, la confiscación de granos de los campesinos y la centralización de la administración estatal bajo el control comunista (pág. 737)

war of attrition/*guerra de desgaste* guerra que se basa en desgastar al otro bando con constantes ataques y grandes pérdidas, tal como en la Primera Guerra Mundial (pág. 724)

welfare state/*estado benefactor* estado en el cual el gobierno tiene responsabilidad de entregarle a los ciudadanos servicios tales como la atención de salud (pág. 862)

wergild/*indemnización* "dinero para un hombre," el valor de una persona, dependiendo del estatus social; en la sociedad alemana, una multa pagada por un malhechor a la familia de la persona que dañó o mató (pág. 287)

witchcraft/*brujería* la práctica de magia por parte de personas que supuestamente están implicadas con el diablo (pág. 435)

women's liberation movement/*movimiento de liberación de la mujer* el movimiento feminista renovado de finales de la década de 1960, que exigía igualdad política y económica con los hombres (pág. 867)

yoga/*yoga* método de ejercitación creado por los hindúes que se supone conduce a la unicidad con Dios (pág. 77)

zaibatsu/*zaibatsu* en la economía japonesa, una gran sociedad financiera e industrial (pág. 789)

zamindar/*zamindar* un oficial a local en la India Mogol que recibía un lote de terreno agrícola para uso temporal a cambio de cobrar impuestos para el gobierno central (pág. 474)

Zen/*Zen* secta del budismo que se hizo popular entre los aristócratas japoneses y se volvió parte del código de conducta de los samurai; según el budismo Zen, existen diferentes vías para llegar a la ilustración (pág. 266)

ziggurat/*ziggurat* una torre escalonada en la cual se construyó un templo dedicado al dios o diosa principal de una ciudad sumeria (pág. 39)

Spanish Glossary

Italicized page numbers refer to illustrations. The following abbreviations are used in the index:
m = map, c = chart, p = photograph or picture, g = graph, crt = cartoon, ptg = painting, q = quote

Index

Index

Index

Index

Index

Index

Index

Index

Index

Index

Index

Index

Index

Index

Acknowledgements and Photo Credits

Acknowledgements

366 "Taking Leave of a Friend" by Li Po, translated by Ezra Pound, from *Personae*, copyright (c) 1926 by Ezra Pound. Reprinted by permission of New Directions Publishing Corp.
367 "Hard Is the Journey" from Li Po and Tu Fu: *Poems*, translation copyright (c) 1973 by Arthur Cooper. Reprinted by permission of Penguin Books Ltd.
572 Excerpt from *Candide* by Voltaire, translated by Robert M. Adams. Reprinted by permission of W.W. Norton and Company.
708 Excerpt from "Shooting an Elephant" in *Shooting an Elephant and Other Essays* by George Orwell, copyright 1950 by Sonia Brownell Orwell and renewed 1978 by Sonia Pitt-Rivers, reprinted by permission of Harcourt, Inc.
840 Excerpt from Chapter 3 in *A Room of One's Own* by Virginia Woolf, copyright (c) 1929 by Harcourt, Inc. and renewed 1957 by Leonard Woolf, reprinted by permission of the publisher.
864 "The Times They Are A-Changin" by Bob Dylan. Copyright (c) 1963, 1964 by Warner Bros. Inc. Copyright renewed 1991 by Special Rider Music. All rights reserved. International copyright secured. Reprinted by permission.
980 "Civil Peace" from *Girls at War and Other Stories* by Chinua Achebe. Copyright (c) 1972, 1973 by Chinua Achebe. Reprinted by permission of Doubleday, a division of Random House, Inc.
990 Excerpt from *Ancient Near Eastern Texts: Relating to the Old Testament*, edited by James B. Pritchard. Copyright (c) 1950, 1955, 1969, renewed 1978 by Princeton University Press. Reprinted by permission of Princeton University Press.
991 Excerpt from *Sources of Chinese Tradition* by William Theodore de Bary. Copyright (c) 1960 by Columbia University Press. Reprinted by permission of Columbia University Press.
992 Excerpt from *The Arabs: Their Heritage and Their Way of Life* by Rhonda Hoff Deterra. Copyright (c) 1979 by Rhonda Hoff Deterra. Reprinted by permission of Random House, Inc.
993 Excerpt from *The Treasure of the City of Ladies* by Christine de Pizan, translated by Sarah Lawson. Copyright (c) 1985 by Sarah Lawson. Reprinted by permission of Penguin Books Ltd.
999 Excerpt from *Ghandi in India: In His Own Words*. Copyright (c) 1987 Navajivan Trust. Reprinted by permission of the University Press of New England.
999 Excerpt from *Nazism: A History in Documents and Eyewitness Accounts, Volume 2* by J. Noakes and G. Pridham. Copyright (c) 1968, Department of Archaeology, University of Exeter. Reprinted by permission.
1001 Excerpt from "China's Gilded Age" by Xiao-huang Yin. *The Atlantic Monthly*, April 1994. Reprinted by permission.

Glencoe would like to acknowledge the artists and agencies who participated in illustrating this program: Morgan Cain & Associates; Ortelius Design, Inc.; QA Digital.

Photo Credits

v (b)SuperStock, Inc.; **v** (t)Erich Lessing/Art Resource, NY; **vi** (t)AKG London; **vi–vii** The Metropolitan Museum of Art, Gift of Lincoln Kirstein, 1959 (JP 3276), photograph by Otto E. Nelson; **viii** Morris, Christopher/Black Star; **xii** United Nations Photo Library; **xiii** The Bodleian Library, Oxford, Ms. Bodl. 264, fol.219R; **xv** Snark/Art Resource, NY; **xx** (l)Boltin Picture Library; **xx** (c)Museo Archeologico, Chusi, Italy/Canali PhotoBank, Milan/SuperStock, Inc.; **xx** (r)Michael Holford; **xxi** Bettmann/Corbis; **xxi** (book) Matt Meadows; **xxii** (t Beatles)AP/Wide World Photos; (bl earth)PhotoDisc; (bc shuttle)PhotoDisc; (br circuit board)PhotoDisc; **xxiii** Digital Stock; **xxvi** PhotoDisc; **xxvii** PhotoDisc; **1** (t)Dallas and John Heaton/Corbis; (c)Papilio/Corbis; (b)Owen Franken/Corbis; **9** AFP/Corbis; **12** Réunion des Musées Nationaux/Art Resource, NY; **12–13** SuperStock, Inc.; **13** Hulton Archive/Getty Images; **14** Bodleian Library, University of Oxford; **15** (l)Joseph Sohm; Visions of America/Corbis; (r)Giraudon/Art Resource, NY; **16** (l)Michael Holford; (r)AP/Wide World Photos; **16–17** AFP Worldwide; **17** (l)The Art Archive/Museo di Antropologia ed Etnografia Turin/Dagli Orti; (r)file photo; **18** (l)Bettmann/Corbis; (r)Jonathan Blair/Corbis; **19** Michael Holford; **20** Photo Researchers, Inc.; **21** Bettmann/Corbis; **23** Erich Lessing/Art Resource, NY.; **24** Corbis/Sygma; **25** Lascaux Caves II, France/Explorer, Paris/SuperStock, Inc.; **27** file photo; **29** Paolo Koch/Photo Researchers; **30** Michael Jenner/Robert Harding; **34** (l)Boltin Picture Library; (r)Musée de Louvre, Paris/E.T. Archives/SuperStock, Inc.; **34–35** SuperStock, Inc.; **35** (l)Erich Lessing/Art Resource, NY; (r)AKG London; **36** Nik Wheeler/Corbis; **37** Robert Harding Picture Library; **39** Ancient Art & Architecture Collection , Ltd.; **40** Michael Holford; **41** Louvre Museum, Paris/Bridgeman Art Library; **42** Aleppo Museum, Syria/E.T. Archives/SuperStock, Inc.; **44** Babylonian, Stele of Hammurabi, Musée du Louvre, ©Photo R.M.N.; **45** Erich Lessing/Art Resource, NY; **47** (l)Musée du Louvre, Paris/Explorer/SuperStock, Inc.; (r)Musée du Louvre, Paris/Explorer/SuperStock, Inc.; **48** (l)Michael Holford; (r)Vanni Archive/Corbis; **49** (l)O. Louis Mazzatenta; (r)O. Louis Mazzatenta; **50** E. Rooney/Robert Harding Picture Library; **51** (t)Bettmann/Corbis; (b)SuperStock, Inc.; **52** (l)Erich Lessing/Art Resource, NY; (tr)Gianni Dagli Orti/Corbis; (br)Pilkington Glass Museum, St. Helens, Merseyside, UK/Bridgeman Art Library; **54** SuperStock, Inc.; **57** (t)Stock Montage/SuperStock, Inc.; (b)Matthews/Network/SABA; **58** The Israel Museum, Jerusalem; **59** SuperStock, Inc.; **61** Dagli Orti/Art Archive; **63** H. Linke/SuperStock, Inc.; **68** (l)Paul Almasy/Corbis; (r)Archivo Iconografico/Corbis; **68–69** Keren Su/Corbis; **69** (tl)National Geographic Image Collection; (bl)Erich Lessing/Art Resource, NY; **69** (r)Asian Art & Archaeology, Inc/Corbis; **70** (l)Christies, London/Bridgeman Art Library/SuperStock, Inc.; (r)Vanni/Art Resource, NY; **71** British Museum, London/Bridgeman Art Library, London/SuperStock, Inc.; **73** (l)Robert Harding Picture Library; (r)Borromeo/Art Resource, NY; **75** (l)Hulton Archive/Getty Images; (r)Sion Touhig/Newsmakers/Getty/Liaison Agency; **76** (l)©Carl Purcell/The Purcell Team; (r)AFP Worldwide; **77** Victoria & Albert Museum, London/Art Resource, NY; **78** (l)Hugh Sitton/Stone; (r)Robert Harding Picture Library; **81** Hulton Archive/Getty Images; **84** B. Kapbor/SuperStock, Inc.; **85** British Library/Bridgeman Art Library; **86** (l)Ancient Art & Architecture Collection , Ltd.; (r)Viren Desai/Dinodia Picture Agency; **87** (t)Courtesy of William J. Duiker; (b)Charles & Josette Lenars/Corbis; **88** Robert Frerck/Odyssey Productions; **90** (t)Bridgeman Art Library/Art Resource, NY; (b)Freer Gallery of Art, Washington, DC; **92** Jean-Marc Truchet/Stone; **93** Hulton Archive/Getty Images; **94** Bettmann/Corbis; **95** Giraudon/Art Resource, NY; **96** ChinaStock; **98** Louis O. Mazzatenta/National Geographic Image Collection; **99** (t)British Library/Art Archive; (b)E.T. Archive/Bibliotheque Nationale, Paris; **102** (l)Ontario Science Centre; (r)Wolfgang Kaehler/Corbis; **103** Robert Harding Picture Library; **106** (l)Nimatallah/Art Resource, NY; **106–107** Scala/Art Resource, NY; **107** (l)Art Resource, NY; (c)SuperStock, Inc.; **7** (r)Lee Boltin/Boltin Picture Library; **108** Stock Montage; **109** Museo Capitolino, Rome/E.T. Archives/SuperStock, Inc.; **110** SuperStock, Inc.; **111** Alberto Incrocci/The Image Bank; **112** The Brooklyn Museum, Charles Wilbour Fund; **113** Nimatallah/Art Resource, NY; **114** Archivo Iconografico, S.A./Corbis; **115** Erich Lessing/Art Resource, NY; **116** Bill Bachmann/Photo Researchers, Inc.; **118** Michael Holford; **121** Erich Lessing/Art Resource, NY; **123** Ronald Sheridan/Ancient Art & Architecture Collection, Ltd.; **126** Erich Lessing/Art Resource, NY; **127** Réunion des Musées Nationaux/Art Resource, NY; **128** Staatliche Museen, Berlin, Germany/Bridgeman Art Library; **129** SuperStock, Inc.; **131** Museo Delle Terme, Rome/E.T. Archives/SuperStock, Inc.; **132** Scala/Art Resource, NY; **133** Bettmann/Corbis; **134** Kunsthistoriches Museum, Vienna; **136** Robert Frerck/Woodfin Camp & Associates; **137** (t)James L. Stanfield; (b)Mykonos Archaeological Museum, Mykonos, courtesy of the Hellenic Republic Ministry of Culture; **138** Erich Lessing/Art Resource, NY; **139** Musée de Louvre, Paris/E.T. Archives/SuperStock, Inc.; **141** Yann Arthus-Bertrand/Corbis; **142** Giraudon/Art Resource, NY; **143** North Wind Picture Archives; **146** (l)David Lee/Corbis; (r)Scala, Art Resource, NY; **146–147** Ric Ergenbright/Stone; **147** (l)Nimatallah, Art Resource, NY; (r)Hulton Archive/Getty Images; **148** Archive Photos; **149** Giraudon/Art Resource, NY; **151** Scala/Art Resource, NY; **152** Art Resource, NY; **154** North Wind Picture Archive; **155** North Wind Picture Archives; **156** Scala/Art Resource, NY; **157** Christie's Images/SuperStock, Inc.; **158** North Wind Picture Archive; **161** (l)Roma,Museo, Nazion/Art Resource, NY; (cl)Archive Iconografico, S.A./Corbis; (c)Archive Iconografico, S.A./Corbis; (cr)Staaliche Glypothek, Munich, Germany/ET Archive, London/SuperStock, Inc.; (r)Archive Iconografico, S.A./Corbis; **162** ©Villa of the Mysteries, Pompeii/Euramax/SuperStock, Inc.; **163** Frances Schroeder/SuperStock, Inc.; **164** (l)Sean Sexton Collection/Corbis; (r)Rob Crandall/Stock Boston; **165** Scala/Art Resource, NY; **166** Pictor; **167** Pierre Belzeaux/Photo Researchers, Inc.; **168** Scala/Art Resource, NY; **169** Bridgeman Art Library/Art Resource, NY; **170** Réunion des Musées/Art Resource, NY; **171** Bridgeman Art Library; **172** (t)Scala/Art Resource, NY; (b)Mary Evans Picture Library; **174** Scala/Art Resource, NY; **175** Art Resource, NY; **177** Erich Lessing/Art Resource, NY; **179** Robert Emmett Bright/Photo Researchers, Inc.; **182** (t)Erich Lessing/Art Resource NY; (b)Alinari/Art Resource, NY; **183** Réunion des Musées Nationaux/Art Resource, NY; **184** Gianni Dagli Orti/Corbis; **184–185** Danny Lehman/Corbis; **185** Gianni Dagli Orti/Corbis; **186** Erich Lessing/Art Resource, NY; **187** (t)Glencoe file; (b)Gianni Dagli Orti/Corbis; **188** (l)Ronald Sheridan/Ancient Art & Architecture Collection, Ltd.; (r)Lynn Abercrombie; **188–189** George Chan/Photo Researchers; 189 David & Peter Turnley/Corbis; **190** Chris Hellier/Ancient Art & Architecture Collection; **191** R. Sheridan/Ancient Art & Architecture Collection; **192** SuperStock, Inc.; **193** Giraudon/Art Resource, NY; **195** AFP/Corbis; **196** Ancient Art & Architecture Collection , Ltd.; **198** Francoise de Mulder/Corbis; **203** Nik Wheeler; **204** Kevin Fleming/Corbis; **205** Richard Bickel/Corbis; **206** Corbis; **207** Scala/Art Resource, NY; Scala/Art Resource, NY; **208** (l)R&S Michaud/Woodfin Camp & Associates; (r)Paul Dupuy Museum, Toulouse, France/Lauros-Giraudon, Paris/SuperStock, Inc.; **209** Lynn Abercrombie; **210** SuperStock, Inc.; **211** AKG Berlin/SuperStock, Inc.; **215** (t)Paul Chesley/Stone; (tc)Edward Parker/Hutchison Library; (b)L. Clarke/Corbis; (bc)Michael Freeman/Corbis; **216** (t)The Newark Museum/Art Resource, NY; (c)Victoria & Albert Museum/Art Resource, NY; (b)Bibliotheque Nationale/Bridgeman Art Library; **217** (t)Historical Picture Archive/Corbis; (c)Corbis; (b)The Jewish Museum/Art Resource, NY; **218** (t)Bettmann/Corbis; (c)Phil Schermeister/Corbis; (b)PictureQuest; **219** (t)Small Planet Photography/FPG International; (c)Peter Sanders/HAGA/The Image Works/The Image Works, Inc.; (b)Bill Aron/Stone; **220** Dave Bartruff/Corbis; **220–221** Sandro Vannini/Corbis; **221** (tl)British Museum/Bridgeman Art Library; (bl)Aldona Sabalis/Photo Researchers, Inc.; (r)Burstein Collection/Corbis; **222** M. P. Kahl/Photo Researchers, Inc.; **223** Werner Forman/Art Resource, NY; **224** (tl)Jason Lauré/Lauré Communications; (tr)Barbara Maurer/Stone; (bl)P Joynson-Hicks/Art Directors & TRIP Photo Library; **224** (br)James Sugar/Black Star; **226** Merilyn Thorold/Bridgeman Art Library; **227** National Commission for Museums and Monuments/Heini Schneebeli/Bridgeman Art Library; **228** Werner Forman/Art Resource, NY; **229** Giraudon/Art Resource, NY; **231** file photo; **233** Bruce Dale/National Geographic Image Collection; **235** (l)James L. Stanfield/National Geographic Image Collection; (r)Volkmar Kurt Wentzel/National Geographic Image Collection; **236** The British Museum, London/Bridgeman Art Library/SuperStock, Inc.;

237 Jason Lauré/Lauré Communications; 239 Jason Lauré/Lauré Communications; 240 (l)Papilio/Corbis; (r)Dat's Jazz/Corbis; 241 (l)Courtesy, Detroit Institute of Arts; 241 (c)Bettmann/Corbis; (r)Werner Forman Archive, British Museum/Art Resource, NY; 244 (l)Réunion des Musées Nationaux/Art Resource, NY; (r)ChinaStock; 244–245 Werner Forman Archive/Art Resource, NY; 245 (l)AKG London; (r)British Library, London, UK/Bridgeman Art Library; 246 (l)Ancient Art & Architecture Collection, Ltd. for Kadokawa; (r)Ancient Art & Architecture Collection , Ltd.; 247 Bibliotheque National, Paris/Bridgeman Art Library, London/SuperStock, Inc.; 249 Bridgeman Art Library/Art Resource, NY; 250 Private Collection/Bridgeman Art Library; 251 Giraudon/Art Resource, NY; 252 Private Collection/Bridgeman Art Library; 253 National Palace Museum, Taipei, Taiwan, Republic of China; 254 Werner-Forman Archive/Art Resource, NY; 256 Stock Boston; 257 Zhang Shui Cheng/Bridgeman Art Library; 258 William H. bond; 259 (t)James L. Stanfield; (b)James L. Stanfield; 259 (inset)James L. Stanfield; 260 (t)Koji Nakamura; (b)William H. Bond; 262 (l)Hulton Archive/Getty Images; (r)The Bodleian Library, Oxford, Ms. Bodl. 264, fol.219R; 263 Art Resource, NY; 265 (l)R. Sheridan/Ancient Art & Arcitecture Collection, Ltd.; (r)Sakamoto Photo Research Library/Corbis; 266 Chester Beatty Library, Dublin/Bridgeman Art Library; 267 SuperStock, Inc.; 268 M. Bryan Ginsberg; 270 Bettmann/Corbis; 271 AP/Wide World Photos; 272 (l)Scala/Art Resource, NY; (r)SuperStock, Inc.; 273 Boltin Picture Library; 275 (l)Roman Sounmar/Corbis; (r)Courtesy of William J. Duiker; 277 Hidekazu Nishibata/SuperStock, Inc.; (inset)A. Barrington/Ancient Art & Architecture, Ltd.; 278 Charles Marden Fitch/SuperStock, Inc.; 279 Bettmann Archive; 282 (l)Scala/Art Resource, NY; (r)Erich Lessing/Art Resource, NY; 282–283 Mark C. Burnett/Stock Boston; 283 (l)Bridgeman Art Library; (r)Erich Lessing/Art Resource, NY; 284 Scala/Art Resource, NY; 285 North Wind Picture Archives; 287 Hulton Archive/Getty Images; 288 Scala/Art Resource, NY; 289 Ali Meyer/Corbis; 291 Stock Montage; 292 Werner Forman Archive; 293 Sakamoto Photo Research Laboratory/Corbis; 294 Susan McCartney/Photo Researchers, Inc.; 296 SuperStock, Inc.; 297 Giraudon/Art Resource, NY; 299 Réunion des Musées Nationaux/Art Resource, NY; 302 Giraudon/Art Resource, NY; 303 Scala/Art Resource, NY; 306 Scala/Art Resource, NY; 309 Michael Holford; 312 (t)Notre Dame, Paris, France/Peter Willi/Bridgeman Art Library; (b)AKG London; 312–313 Adam Woolfitt; 313 (l)Giraudon/Art Resource, NY; (r)AKG London; 314 (l)SuperStock, Inc./British Library, London; (r)R. Sheridan/Ancient Art & Architecture; 315 Ancient Art & Architecture Collection , Ltd.; 316 Elly Beintema/Ancient Art & Architecture Collection Ltd.; 319 Giraudon/Art Resource, NY; 321 Bibliotheque Nationale, Paris; 323 Mary Evans Picture Library; 324 Scala/Art Resource, NY; 325 Archivo Oconographico, S.A./Corbis; 326 (t)AKG London/Michael Teller; (b)San Francesco, Assisi/Canali PhotoBank, Milan/SuperStock, Inc.; 327 AKG London; 328 AKG London/Jean-Paul Dumontier; 329 Leonard de Salva/Corbis; 330 Staatliche Museen, Berlin, Photo ©Bildarchiv Preussischer Kulturbesitz; 331 Stock Montage; 332 (tl)Scala/Art Resource, NY; (tr)Lauros Giraudon/Art Resource, NY.; (cl)Ancient Art & Architecture Collection , Ltd.; (cr)AKG London; (bl)Scala/Art Resource, NY; (br)SuperStock, Inc.; 335 Museo del Prado, Madrid, Spain/A.K.G., Berlin/SuperStock, Inc.; 338 Mary Evans Picture Library; 341 ©Bibliotheque Royale Albert Ier, Brussels (Ms. 13076-77, f. 12v); 344 Museum of Mankind/E.T. Archives, London/SuperStock, Inc.; 344–345 Enrico Ferorelli; 345 (l)Richard A. Cooke/Corbis; (r)Franke Keating/Photo Researchers, Inc.; 346 Charles & Josette Lenars/Corbis; 347 Christie's Images/Corbis; 350 Charles & Josette Lenars/Corbis; 352 Boltin Picture Library; 354 Gianni Dagli Orti/Corbis; 355 Amwell/Stone; 356 ©2003 Banco de México Diego Rivera & Frida Kahlo Museums Trust. Av. Cinco de Mayo No.2, Col. Centro, Del. Cuauhtémoc 06059, México, D.F./Schalkwijk/Art Resource, NY; 357 ©1997 Suzanne-Murphy-Larronde; 358 North Wind Picture Archives; 359 Robert Frerck/Woodfin Camp & Associates; 360 Gianni Dagli Orti/Corbis; 361 (t)Stock Montage; (b)Robert Harding Picture Library; 362 Gianni Dagli Orti/Corbis; 363 Museum fuer Voelkerkunde, Staaliche Museen/Art Resource, NY; 366 (t)Mary Evans Picture Library; (b)The Metropolitan Museum of Art, Edward Elliott Family Collection. Purchase, The Dillon Fund Gift, 1982. !982.2.2; 367 Bettmann Archive; 368 Bettmann/Corbis; 368–369 Bettmann/Corbis; 369 Bridgeman Art Library; 370 Architect of the Capitol, Washington, D.C.; 371 (t)Gianni Dagli Orti/Corbis; (b)Bettmann Archive; 372 (l)AKG London/Rabatti - Dominigie; (r)AKG London; 372–373 AKG London/S. Domingie; 373 Stock Montage; 374 Sistine Chapel, Vatican, Rome/SuperStock, Inc.; 375 Scala/Art Resource, NY; 376 Art Resource, NY; 377 (l)Scala/Art Resource, NY; (r)Galleria Degli, Uffizi, Florence/SuperStock, Inc.; 378 AKG London; 379 (t)Archive/Photo Researchers, Inc.; (b)Musée du Louvre, Paris/SuperStock, Inc.; 380 Mary Evans Picture Library; 381 Scala/Art Resource, NY; 382 Scala/Art Resource, NY; 383 (l)Nicolo Orsi Battaglini/Art Resource, NY; (r)Art Resource, NY; 384 Scala/Art Resource, NY; 385 Vatican Museums & Galleries, Rome/Fratelli Alinari/SuperStock, Inc.; 386 (l)AKG London; (r)Vatican Museums & Galleries, Rome/Fratelli Alinari/SuperStock, Inc.; 387 (l)Erich Lessing/Art Resource, NY; (r)Scala/Art Resource, NY; 388 Victor R. Boswell, Jr.; (t)Mary Evans Picture Library; 389 ARCHIV/Photo Researchers, Inc.; 390 Ted Spiegel/Corbis; 391 (t)AKG London; (b)Erich Lessing/Art Resource, NY; 394 Art Resource, NY; 395 Mary Evans Picture Library; 396 Hulton Archive/Getty Images; 397 Scala/Art Resource, NY; 398 SuperStock, Inc.; 400 Giraudon/Art Resource, NY; 401 Scala/Art Resource, NY; 404 (br)Archiv/Photo Researchers, Inc.; (tr)North Wind Picture Archives; (l)Scala/Art Resource, NY; 404–405 Réunion des Musées Nationaux/Art Resource, NY; 405 Bluestone Production/SuperStock, Inc.; 406 (l)North Wind Picture Archives; (r)AKG Berlin/SuperStock, Inc.; 407 The Metropolitan Museum of Art, Gift of J. Pierpont Morgan, 1900(00.18.2); 409 (t)Peabody Essex Museum, Salem, MA; (b)AKG London; 412 AKG London/Ulrich Zillmann; 414 Bettmann/Corbis; 415 North Wind Picture Archives; 417 Art Resource, NY; 418 Corbis; 419 Réunion des Musées Nationaux/Art Resource, NY; 420 (l)North Wind Picture Archives; (r)Gunshots/Art Archive; 421 AFP/Corbis; 422 Bettmann/Corbis; 423 Adam Woolfit/Corbis; 426 (l)AKG London/Joseph Martin; (r)National Portrait Gallery/SuperStock, Inc.; 426–427 Giraudon/Art Resource, NY; 427 (l)AKG London; (r)Stock Montage/SuperStock, Inc.; 428 (l)Scala/Art Resource, NY; (r)AKG London; 429 Francois Dubois D'Amiens, "The St. Barthlomew's Day Massacre," Musée Cantonal des Beaux-Arts, Lausanne; 430 Giraudon/Art Resource, NY.; 431 Archiv/Photo Researchers Inc.; 432 Bettmann/Corbis; 433 AKG London; 434 AKG London; 436 (pistol) Armee Museum, Ingolstadt, Germany/Bridgeman Art Library; (soldier) AKG London; 438 North Wind Pictures; 439 (l)Ronald Sheridan/Ancient Art & Architecture; (r)Peter Hoadley, William III and Mary Stuart, Rijksmuseum, Amersterdam; 440 (l)Museo Correr, Venice, Italy/Bridgeman Art Library; (r)Brian Wilson/Ancient Art & Architecture; 441 National Museum of American Art, Washington/Art Resource, NY; Réunion des Musées Nationaux/Art Resource, NY; 442 Giraudon/Art Resource, NY; 443 Giraudon/Art Resource, NY; 444 Hyacinthe Rigaud, "Louis XIV," Musée du Louvre, Photo R.M.N.; 445 AKG London; 447 Michael Holford; 448 John Taylor, "William Shakespeare", by courtesy of the National Portrait Gallery, London; 449 Scala/Art Resource, NY; 450 Musée des Beaux-Arts, Pau, France/Bridgeman Art Library; 454 (l)Historical Picture Archive/Corbis; (r)Arte & Immagini srl/Corbis; 454–455 Adam Woolfitt/Corbis; 455 (l)Otis Imboden; (r)Seattle Art Museum/Corbis; 456 Historical Picture Archive/Corbis; 457 Archivo Iconografico, S.A./Corbis; 458 AFP/Corbis; 461 Bettmann/Corbis; 462 Robert Frerck/Stone; 464 James L. Stanfield; 466 (l)James L. Stanfield; (r)James L. Stanfield; 467 (t b)James L. Stanfield; 468 Roger Wood/Corbis; 471 George Holton/Photo Researchers, Inc.; 472 SuperStock, Inc.; 473 Victoria and Albert Museum/Art Resource, NY; 476 Bettmann/Corbis; 478 Stone; 479 North Wind Picture Archives; 482 (l)ChinaStock; (r)Art Trade, Bonhams, London/Bridgeman Art Library; 482–483 Todd Gipstein/Corbis; 483 Fitzwilliam Museum, University of Cambridge, UK/Bridgeman Art Library; 484 (l)Reproduced by courtesy of the Trustees of the British Museum; (r)The Palace Museum, Beijing; 485 The Metropolitan Museum of Art, Rogers Fund, 1942 (42.121.2); 487 Christie's Images/Corbis; 488 Victoria & Albert Museum, London. UK/Bridgeman Art Library; 489 Wolfgang Kaehler/Corbis; 490 Mary Evans Picture Library; 491 2001 North Wind Pictures; 492 Bridgeman Art Library; 493 (l)Philadelphia Free Library/AKG, Berlin/SuperStock, Inc.; (r)Ronald Sheridan/Ancient Art & Architecture; 494 G. Hunter/SuperStock, Inc.; 495 AFP/Corbis; 496 Michale Maslan Historic Photographs/Corbis; 497 Werner Forman Archive/Art Institute of Chicago/Art Resource, NY; 499 Tenri University, Japan; 500 Reuters NewMedia Inc./Corbis; 501 Michael Holford; 505 (tr)PhotoDisc; (l)Bettmann/Corbis; (br)The Huntington Library, Art Collections and Botanical Gardens/SuperStock, Inc.; 507 (t)Hulton Archive/Getty Images; (b)Robert Holmes/Corbis; 508 (l)Hulton Archive/Getty Images; (r)Archivo Iconografica, S.A./Corbis; 508–509 Giraudon/Art Resource, NY; 509 (t)Erich Lessing/Art Resource, NY; (b)Reproduction of a watercolour by JSC Schaak/Mary Evans Picture Library; 510 Private collection/Bridgeman Art Library; 511 North Wind Picture Archives; 512 Louvre, Paris, France/Bridgeman Art Library; 513 Bettmann/Corbis; 514 (t)Jean-Leon Huens; (b)North Wind Picture Archives; 515 (t)Library of Congress; (b)Hulton Archive/Getty Images; 516 Dumesnil, Queen Christina of Sweden with Descartes, Musée du Louvre, Photo ©R.M.N.; 517 Giraudon/Art Resource, NY; 518 Giraudon/Art Resource, NY; 519 (l)Bettmann/Corbis; (r)Bettmann/Corbis; 520 Erich Lessing/Art Resource, NY; 521 SuperStock, Inc.; 522 (l)Tate Gallery/Art Resource, NY; (r)Giraudon/Art Resource, NY; 523 Pablo Corral V/Corbis; 525 Nathaniel Hone, John Wesley, ca. 1766, courtesy of the National Portrait Gallery, London; 526 Christel Gerstenberg/Corbis; 527 Francis G. Mayer/Corbis; 528 (l)Giraudon/Art Resource, NY; (r)Bettmann/Corbis; 529 Giraudon/Art Resource, NY; 530 (tr)Scala/Art Resource, NY; (l)Hermitage/Bridgeman Art Library; (br)Giraudon/Art Resource, NY; 532 Archivo Iconografico, S.A./Corbis; 533 North Wind Picture Archives; 535 Stock Montage; 536 Giraudon/Art Resource, NY; 538 Mexican, unknown artist, Portrait of Sister Juana Ines de la Cruz [Detail], Philadelphia Museum of Art: The Robert H Lamborn Collection/Philadelphia Museum of Art; 539 Yale University Art Gallery; 541 Corbis; 544 (l)Musée de la Ville de Paris, Musée Carnavalet, Paris, France/Bridgeman Art Library; (r)Réunion des Musées Nationaux/Art Resource, NY; 544–545 Erich Lessing/Art Resource, NY; 545 (l)Chateau de Versailles, France/Bridgeman Giraudon; (r)Bonhams, London, UK/Bridgeman Art Library; 546 AKG London; 547 Giraudon/Art Resource, NY; 549 Musée Carnavalet, Paris, France/Bridgeman Giraudon; 550 AKG London; 551 Rueters NewMedia Inc./Corbis; 552 (t)Stock Montage; (b)Giraudon/Art Resource, NY; 553 Giraudon/Art Resource, NY; 554 Erich Lessing/Art Resource, NY; 555 AKG London/Jerome da Cunha; 556 (l)Giraudon/Art Resource, NY; (r)Mary Evans Picture Library; 557 (l)Hulton-Deutsch Collection/Corbis; (c)Stock Montage; (r)Giraudon/Art Resource, NY; 558 Musée Carnavalet, Paris, France/Roger-Viollet, Paris/Bridgeman Art Library; 559 Dupelessis-Bertaux, engraved by Malapeau/Mary Evans Picture Library; 561 Réunion des Musées Nationaux/Art Resource, NY; 563 Museum of Art History, Vienna/AKG, Berlin/SuperStock, Inc.; 564 Giraudon/Art Resource, NY; 565 Gianni Dagli Orti/Corbis; 566 Giraudon/Art Resource, NY; 568 AKG London; 572 (l)Giraudon/Art Resource, NY; (r)Christel Gerstenberg/Corbis; 573 Réunion des Musées Nationaux/Art Archive; 574 SuperStock, Inc.; 574–575 Hulton-Deutsch Collection/Corbis; 575 Rhodes Memorial Museum, USA/Bridgeman Art Library; 576 Stock Montage; 577 (t)Library of Congress; (b)Laurie Platt Winfrey; 578 Bettmann/Corbis; 578–579 Science Museum/Science & Society Picture Library; 579 (l)Mary Evans Picture Library; (c)Archivo Iconografico, S.A./Corbis; (r)Mary Evans Picture Library; 580 (l)Stock Montage/SuperStock, Inc.; (r)Bettmann/Corbis; 581 National Trust/Art Resource, NY; 582 Bettmann/Corbis; 583 Gianni Dagli Orti/Corbis; 586 Library of Congress, Prints and Photographs Division, Detroit Publishing Co. Collection; 587 Culver Pictures, Inc.; 588 Mary Evans Picture Library; 589 Woldemar Friedrich in Die Deutschen Befreiungskriege/Mary Evans Picture Library; 591 Austrian Information Service; 592 (l)Lecomte, Battle in the rue de Rohan, 1830, Giraudon/Art Resource, NY; (r)Giraudon/Art Resource, NY; 593 Hulton-Deutsch Collection/Corbis; 595 (l)Bettmann/Corbis; (r)Mary Evans Picture Library; 596